MW01056397

CODE OF , ___ _. _ _
REGULATIONS

Title 29
Labor

Part 1926

Revised as of July 1, 2015

Containing a codification of documents
of general applicability and future effect

As of July 1, 2015

This was initially published by the Office of the
Federal Register National Archives and Records
Administration as a Special Edition of the
Federal Register. It has been republished in its
entirety and without modification by Regulations
Press.

Table of Contents

Cite this Code: **CFR**

To cite the regulations in this volume use title, part and section number. Thus, **29 CFR 1926.1** *refers to title 29, part 1926, section 1.*

Explanation

The Code of Federal Regulations is a codification of the general and permanent rules published in the Federal Register by the Executive departments and agencies of the Federal Government. The Code is divided into 50 titles which represent broad areas subject to Federal regulation. Each title is divided into chapters which usually bear the name of the issuing agency. Each chapter is further subdivided into parts covering specific regulatory areas.

Each volume of the Code is revised at least once each calendar year and issued on a quarterly basis approximately as follows:

Title 1 through Title 16...as of January 1
Title 17 through Title 27 ....as of April 1
Title 28 through Title 41 ....as of July 1
Title 42 through Title 50...as of October 1

The appropriate revision date is printed on the cover of each volume.

LEGAL STATUS

The contents of the Federal Register are required to be judicially noticed (44 U.S.C. 1507). The Code of Federal Regulations is prima facie evidence of the text of the original documents (44 U.S.C. 1510).

HOW TO USE THE CODE OF FEDERAL REGULATIONS

The Code of Federal Regulations is kept up to date by the individual issues of the Federal Register. These two publications must be used together to determine the latest version of any given rule.

To determine whether a Code volume has been amended since its revision date (in this case, July 1, 2015), consult the "List of CFR Sections Affected (LSA)," which is issued monthly, and the "Cumulative List of Parts Affected," which appears in the Reader Aids section of the daily Federal Register. These two lists will identify the Federal Register page number of the latest amendment of any given rule.

EFFECTIVE AND EXPIRATION DATES

Each volume of the Code contains amendments published in the Federal Register since the last revision of that volume of the Code. Source citations for the regulations are referred to by volume number and page number of the Federal Register and date of publication. Publication dates and effective dates are usually not the same and care must be exercised by the user in determining the actual effective date. In instances where the effective date is beyond the cut-off date for the Code a note has been inserted to reflect the future effective date. In those instances where a regulation published in the Federal Register states a date certain for expiration, an appropriate note will be inserted following the text.

OMB CONTROL NUMBERS

The Paperwork Reduction Act of 1980 (Pub. L. 96–511) requires Federal agencies to display an OMB control number with their information collection request.

Many agencies have begun publishing numerous OMB control numbers as amendments to existing regulations in the CFR. These OMB numbers are placed as close as possible to the applicable recordkeeping or reporting requirements.

PAST PROVISIONS OF THE CODE

Provisions of the Code that are no longer in force and effect as of the revision date stated on the cover of each volume are not carried. Code users may find the text of provisions in effect on any given date in the past by using the appropriate List of CFR Sections Affected (LSA). For the convenience of the reader, a "List of CFR Sections Affected" is published at the end of each CFR volume. For changes to the Code prior to the LSA listings at the end of the volume, consult previous annual editions of the LSA. For changes to the Code prior to 2001, consult the List of CFR Sections Affected compilations, published for 1949-1963, 1964-1972, 1973-1985, and 1986-2000.

"[RESERVED]" TERMINOLOGY

The term "[Reserved]" is used as a place holder within the Code of Federal Regulations. An agency may add regulatory information at a "[Reserved]" location at any time. Occasionally "[Reserved]" is used editorially to indicate that a portion of the CFR was left vacant and not accidentally dropped due to a printing or computer error.

INCORPORATION BY REFERENCE

What is incorporation by reference? Incorporation by reference was established by statute and allows Federal agencies to meet the requirement to publish regulations in the Federal Register by referring to materials already published elsewhere. For an incorporation to be valid, the Director of the Federal Register must approve it. The legal effect of incorporation by reference is that the material is treated as if it were published in full in the Federal Register (5 U.S.C. 552(a)). This material, like any other properly issued regulation, has the force of law.

What is a proper incorporation by reference? The Director of the Federal Register will approve an incorporation by reference only when the requirements of 1 CFR part 51 are met. Some of the elements on which approval is based are:

(a) The incorporation will substantially reduce the volume of material published in the Federal Register.

(b) The matter incorporated is in fact available to the extent necessary to afford fairness and uniformity in the administrative process.

(c) The incorporating document is drafted and submitted for publication in accordance with 1 CFR part 51.

What if the material incorporated by reference cannot be found? If you have any problem locating or obtaining a copy of material listed as an approved incorporation by reference, please contact the agency that issued the regulation containing that incorporation. If, after contacting the agency, you find the material is not available, please notify the Director of the Federal Register, National Archives and Records Administration, 8601 Adelphi Road, College Park, MD 20740-6001, or call 202-741-6010.

CFR INDEXES AND TABULAR GUIDES

A subject index to the Code of Federal Regulations is contained in a separate volume, revised annually as of January 1, entitled CFR INDEX AND FINDING AIDS. This volume contains the Parallel Table of Authorities and Rules. A list of CFR titles, chapters, subchapters, and parts and an alphabetical list of agencies publishing in the CFR are also included in this volume.

An index to the text of "Title 3—The President" is carried within that volume.

The Federal Register Index is issued monthly in cumulative form. This index is based on a consolidation of the "Contents" entries in the daily Federal Register.

A List of CFR Sections Affected (LSA) is published monthly, keyed to the revision dates of the 50 CFR titles.

REPUBLICATION OF MATERIAL

There are no restrictions on the republication of material appearing in the Code of Federal Regulations.

INQUIRIES

For a legal interpretation or explanation of any regulation in this volume, contact the issuing agency. The issuing agency's name appears at the top of odd-numbered pages.

For inquiries concerning CFR reference assistance, call 202–741–6000 or write to the Director, Office of the Federal Register, National Archives and Records Administration, 8601 Adelphi Road, College Park, MD 20740-6001 or e-mail *fedreg.info@nara.gov.*

SALES

The Government Publishing Office (GPO) processes all sales and distribution of the CFR. For payment by credit card, call toll-free, 866-512-1800, or DC area, 202-512-1800, M-F 8 a.m. to 4 p.m. e.s.t. or fax your order to 202-512-2104, 24 hours a day. For payment by check, write to: US Government Publishing Office – New Orders, P.O. Box 979050, St. Louis, MO 63197-9000.

ELECTRONIC SERVICES

The full text of the Code of Federal Regulations, the LSA (List of CFR Sections Affected), The United States Government Manual, the Federal Register, Public Laws, Public Papers of the Presidents of the United States, Compilation of Presidential Documents and the Privacy Act Compilation are available in electronic format via *www.ofr.gov.* For more information, contact the GPO Customer Contact Center, U.S. Government Publishing Office. Phone 202-512-1800, or 866-512-1800 (toll-free). E-mail, *ContactCenter@gpo.gov.*

The Office of the Federal Register also offers a free service on the National Archives and Records Administration's (NARA) World Wide Web site for public law numbers, Federal Register finding aids, and related information. Connect to NARA's web site at *www.archives.gov/federal-register.*

The e-CFR is a regularly updated, unofficial editorial compilation of CFR material and Federal Register amendments, produced by the Office of the Federal Register and the Government Publishing Office. It is available at *www.ecfr.gov.*

JOHN HYRUM MARTINEZ,
Acting Director,
Office of the Federal Register.
July 1, 2015.

THIS TITLE

Title 29—LABOR is composed of nine volumes. The parts in these volumes are arranged in the following order: Parts 0–99, parts 100–499, parts 500–899, parts 900–1899, part 1900–§1910.999, part 1910.1000–end of part 1910, parts 1911–1925, part 1926, and part 1927 to end. The contents of these volumes represent all current regulations codified under this title as of July 1, 2015.

The OMB control numbers for title 29 CFR part 1910 appear in §1910.8. For the convenience of the user, §1910.8 appears in the Finding Aids section of the volume containing §1910.1000 to the end.

For this volume, Ann Worley was Chief Editor. The Code of Federal Regulations publication program is under the direction of John Hyrum Martinez, assisted by Stephen J. Frattini.

Title 29—Labor

(This book contains part 1926)

1

Subtitle B—Regulations Relating to Labor (Continued)

CHAPTER XVII—OCCUPATIONAL SAFETY AND HEALTH ADMINISTRATION, DEPARTMENT OF LABOR (CONTINUED)

PART 1926—SAFETY AND HEALTH REGULATIONS FOR CONSTRUCTION

Subpart A—General

Subpart B—General Interpretations

Subpart C—General Safety and Health Provisions

Subpart D—Occupational Health and Environmental Controls

Subpart E—Personal Protective and Life Saving Equipment

Subpart F—Fire Protection and Prevention

Subpart G—Signs, Signals, and Barricades

Subpart H—Materials Handling, Storage, Use, and Disposal

Subpart I—Tools—Hand and Power

SOURCE: 44 FR 8577, Feb. 9, 1979; 44 FR 20940, Apr. 6, 1979, unless otherwise noted.

EDITORIAL NOTE: At 44 FR 8577, Feb. 9, 1979, and corrected at 44 FR 20940, Apr. 6, 1979, OSHA reprinted without change the entire text of 29 CFR part 1926 together with certain General Industry Occupational Safety and Health Standards contained in 29 CFR part 1910, which have been identified as also applicable to construction work. This republication developed a single set of OSHA regulations for both labor and management forces within the construction industry.

Subpart A—General

AUTHORITY: 40 U.S.C. 3701 *et seq.*; 29 U.S.C. 653, 655, 657; Secretary of Labor's Order No. 12–71 (36 FR 8754), 8–76 (41 FR 25059), 9–83 (48 FR 35736), 1–90 (55 FR 9033), 6–96 (62 FR 111), 3–2000 (65 FR 50017), 5–2002 (67 FR 65008), or 5–2007 (72 FR 31160), 5–2007 (72 FR 31160), 4–2010 (75 FR 55355), or 1–2012 (77 FR 3912), as applicable; and 29 CFR Part 1911.

§ 1926.1 Purpose and scope.

(a) This part sets forth the safety and health standards promulgated by the Secretary of Labor under section 107 of the Contract Work Hours and Safety Standards Act. The standards are published in subpart C of this part and following subparts.

(b) Subpart B of this part contains statements of general policy and interpretations of section 107 of the Contract Work Hours and Safety Standards Act having general applicability.

§ 1926.2 Variances from safety and health standards.

(a) Variances from standards which are, or may be, published in this part may be granted under the same circumstances whereunder variances may be granted under section 6(b)(A) or 6(d) of the Williams-Steiger Occupational Safety and Health Act of 1970 (29 U.S.C. 65). The procedures for the granting of variances and for related relief under this part are those published in part 1905 of this title.

(b) Any requests for variances under this section shall also be considered requests for variances under the Williams-Steiger Occupational Safety and Health Act of 1970, and any requests for variances under Williams-Steiger Occupational Safety and Health Act with respect to construction safety or health standards shall be considered to be also variances under the Construction Safety Act. Any variance from a construction safety or health standard which is contained in this part and which is incorporated by reference in part 1910 of this title shall be deemed a variance from the standard under both the Construction Safety Act and the Williams-Steiger Occupational Safety and Health Act of 1970.

§ 1926.3 Inspections—right of entry.

(a) It shall be a condition of each contract which is subject to section 107 of the Contract Work Hours and Safety Standards Act that the Secretary of Labor or any authorized representative shall have a right of entry to any site of contract performance for the following purposes:

(1) To inspect or investigate the matter of compliance with the safety and health standards contained in subpart C of this part and following subparts; and

(2) To carry out the duties of the Secretary under section 107(b) of the Act.

(b) For the purpose of carrying out his investigative duties under the Act, the Secretary of Labor may, by agreement, use with or without reimbursement the services, personnel, and facilities of any State or Federal agency. Any agreements with States under this section shall be similar to those provided for under the Walsh-Healey Public Contracts Act under 41 CFR part 50–205.

§ 1926.4 Rules of practice for administrative adjudications for enforcement of safety and health standards.

(a) The rules of practice for administrative adjudications for the enforcement of the safety and health standards contained in subpart C of this part and the following subparts shall be the same as those published in part 6 of this title with respect to safety and health violations of the Service Contract Act of 1965 (69 Stat. 1035), except as provided in paragraph (b) of this section.

(b) In the case of debarment, the findings required by section 107(d) of the Act shall be made by the hearing examiner or the Assistant Secretary of Labor for Occupational Safety and Health, as the case may be. Whenever, as provided in section 107(d)(2), a contractor requests termination of debarment before the end of the 3-year period prescribed in that section, the request shall be filed in writing with the Assistant Secretary of Labor for Occupational Safety and Health who shall publish a notice in the FEDERAL REGISTER that the request has been received and afford interested persons an opportunity to be heard upon the request, and thereafter the provisions of part 6 of this title shall apply with respect to prehearing conferences, hearings and related matters, and decisions and orders.

§ 1926.5 OMB control numbers under the Paperwork Reduction Act.

The following sections or paragraphs each contain a collection of information requirement which has been approved by the Office of Management and Budget under the control number listed.

29 CFR citation	OMB control No.
1926.33	1218–0065
1926.50	1218–0093
1926.52	1218–0048
1926.53	1218–0103
1926.59	1218–0072
1926.60	1218–0183
1926.62	1218–0189
1926.64	1218–0200
1926.65	1218–0202
1926.103	1218–0099
1926.200	1218–0132
1926.250	1218–0093
1926.251	1218–0233
1926.403	1218–0130
1926.404	1218–0130
1926.405	1218–0130
1926.407	1218–0130
1926.408	1218–0130
1926.453(a)(2)	1218–0216
1926.502	1218–0197
1926.503	1218–0197
1926.550(a)(1)	1218–0115
1926.550(a)(2)	1218–0115
1926.550(a)(4)	1218–0115
1926.550(a)(6)	1218–0113
1926.550(a)(11)	1218–0054
1926.550(a)(16)	1218–0115
1926.550(b)(2)	1218–0232
1926.550(g)	1218–0151
1926.552	1218–0231
1926.652	1218–0137
1926.703	1218–0095
1926.800	1218–0067
1926.803	1218–0067
1926.900	1218–0217
1926.903	1218–0227
1926.1080	1218–0069
1926.1081	1218–0069
1926.1083	1218–0069
1926.1090	1218–0069
1926.1091	1218–0069
1926.1101	1218–0134
1926.1103	1218–0085
1926.1104	1218–0084
1926.1106	1218–0086
1926.1107	1218–0083
1926.1108	1218–0087
1926.1109	1218–0089
1926.1110	1218–0082
1926.1111	1218–0090
1926.1112	1218–0080
1926.1113	1218–0079
1926.1114	1218–0088

29 CFR citation	OMB control No.
1926.1115	1218–0044
1926.1116	1218–0081
1926.1117	1218–0010
1926.1118	1218–0104
1926.1126	1218–0252
1926.1127	1218–0186
1926.1128	1218–0129
1926.1129	1218–0128
1926.1144	1218–0101
1926.1145	1218–0126
1926.1147	1218–0108
1926.1148	1218–0145
1926.1402	1218–0261
1926.1403	1218–0261
1926.1404	1218–0261
1926.1406	1218–0261
1926.1407	1218–0261
1926.1408	1218–0261
1926.1409	1218–0261
1926.1410	1218–0261
1926.1411	1218–0261
1926.1412	1218–0261
1926.1413	1218–0261
1926.1414	1218–0261
1926.1417	1218–0261
1926.1423	1218–0261
1926.1424	1218–0261
1926.1427	1218–0261
1926.1428	1218–0261
1926.1431	1218–0261
1926.1433	1218–0261
1926.1434	1218–0261
1926.1435	1218–0261
1926.1436	1218–0261
1926.1437	1218–0261
1926.1441	1218–0261

[61 FR 5509, Feb. 13, 1996, as amended at 63 FR 3814, Jan. 27, 1998; 63 FR 13340, Mar. 19, 1998; 63 FR 17094, Apr. 8, 1998; 64 FR 18810, Apr. 16, 1999; 71 FR 38086, July 5, 2006; 75 FR 68430, Nov. 8, 2010]

§ 1926.6 Incorporation by reference.

(a) The standards of agencies of the U.S. Government, and organizations which are not agencies of the U.S. Government which are incorporated by reference in this part, have the same force and effect as other standards in this part. Only the mandatory provisions (*i.e.*, provisions containing the word "shall" or other mandatory language) of standards incorporated by reference are adopted as standards under the Occupational Safety and Health Act. The locations where these standards may be examined are as follows:

(1) Offices of the Occupational Safety and Health Administration, U.S. Department of Labor, Frances Perkins Building, Washington, DC 20210.

(2) The Regional and Field Offices of the Occupational Safety and Health

Administration, which are listed in the U.S. Government Manual.

(b) The materials listed in paragraphs (g) through (ff) of this section are incorporated by reference in the corresponding sections noted as they exist on the date of the approval, and a notice of any change in these materials will be published in the FEDERAL REGISTER. These incorporations by reference were approved by the Director of the Federal Register in accordance with 5 U.S.C. 552(a) and 1 CFR part 51.

(c) Copies of standards listed in this section and issued by private standards organizations are available for purchase from the issuing organizations at the addresses or through the other contact information listed below for these private standards organizations. In addition, these standards are available for inspection at the National Archives and Records Administration (NARA). For information on the availability of these standards at NARA, telephone: 202–741–6030, or go to *http://www.archives.gov/federal_register/code_of_federal_regulations/ibr_locations.html*. Also, the standards are available for inspection at any Regional Office of the Occupational Safety and Health Administration (OSHA), or at the OSHA Docket Office, U.S. Department of Labor, 200 Constitution Avenue, NW., Room N–2625, Washington, DC 20210; telephone: 202–693–2350 (TTY number: 877–889–5627).

(d)–(f) [Reserved]

(g) The following material is available for purchase from the American Conference of Governmental Industrial Hygienists (ACGIH), 1330 Kemper Meadow Drive, Cincinnati, OH 45240; telephone: 513–742–6163; fax: 513–742–3355; e-mail: *mail@acgih.org*; Web site: *http://www.acgih.org*:

(1) Threshold Limit Values of Airborne Contaminants for 1970, 1970, IBR approved for § 1926.55(a) and appendix A of § 1926.55.

(h) The following material is available for purchase from the American National Standards Institute (ANSI), 25 West 43rd Street, Fourth Floor, New York, NY 10036; telephone: 212–642–4900; fax: 212–302–1286; e-mail: *info@ansi.org*; Web site: *http://www.ansi.org/*.

(1) ANSI A10.3–1970, Safety Requirements for Explosive-Actuated Fastening Tools, IBR approved for § 1926.302(e).

(2) ANSI A10.4–1963, Safety Requirements for Workmen's Hoists, IBR approved for § 1926.552(c).

(3) ANSI A10.5–1969, Safety Requirements for Material Hoists, IBR approved for § 1926.552(b).

(4) ANSI A11.1–1965 (R1970), Practice for Industrial Lighting, IBR approved for § 1926.56(b).

(5) ANSI A17.1–1965, Elevators, Dumbwaiters, Escalators, and Moving Walks, IBR approved for § 1926.552(d).

(6) ANSI A17.1a–1967, Elevators, Dumbwaiters, Escalators, and Moving Walks Supplement, IBR approved for § 1926.552(d).

(7) ANSI A17.1b–1968, Elevators, Dumbwaiters, Escalators, and Moving Walks Supplement, IBR approved for § 1926.552(d).

(8) ANSI A17.1c–1969, Elevators, Dumbwaiters, Escalators, and Moving Walks Supplement, IBR approved for § 1926.552(d).

(9) ANSI A17.1d–1970, Elevators, Dumbwaiters, Escalators, and Moving Walks Supplement, IBR approved for § 1926.552(d).

(10) ANSI A17.2–1960, Practice for the Inspection of Elevators (Inspector's Manual), IBR approved for § 1926.552(d).

(11) ANSI A17.2a–1965, Practice for the Inspection of Elevators (Inspector's Manual) Supplement, IBR approved for § 1926.552(d).

(12) ANSI A17.2b–1967, Practice for the Inspection of Elevators (Inspector's Manual) Supplement, IBR approved for § 1926.552(d).

(13) ANSI A92.2–1969, Vehicle Mounted Elevating and Rotating Work Platforms, IBR approved for §§ 1926.453(a) and 1926.453(b).

(14) ANSI B7.1–1970, Safety Code for the Use, Care, and Protection of Abrasive Wheels, IBR approved for §§ 1926.57(g), 1926.303(b), 1926.303(c), and 1926.303(d).

(15) ANSI B20.1–1957, Safety Code for Conveyors, Cableways, and Related Equipment, IBR approved for § 1926.555(a).

(16) ANSI B56.1–1969, Safety Standards for Powered Industrial Trucks, IBR approved for § 1926.602(c).

(17)—(22) [Reserved]

14

(23) ANSI O1.1–1961, Safety Code for Woodworking Machinery, IBR approved for §1926.304(f).

(24) ANSI Z35.1–1968, Specifications for Accident Prevention Signs; IBR approved for §1926.200(b), (c), and 1 (i). Copies available for purchase from the IHS Standards Store, 15 Inverness Way East, Englewood, CO 80112; telephone: 1–877–413–5184; Web site: *www.global.ihs.com*.

(25) ANSI Z35.2–1968, Specifications for Accident Prevention Tags, IBR approved for §1926.200(i).

(26) ANSI Z49.1–1967, Safety in Welding and Cutting, IBR approved for §1926.350(j).

(27) USA Z53.1–1967 (also referred to as ANSI Z53.1–1967), Safety Color Code for Marking Physical Hazards, ANSI approved October 9, 1967; IBR approved for §1926.200(c). Copies available for purchase from the IHS Standards Store, 15 Inverness Way East, Englewood, CO 80112; telephone: 1–877–413–5184; Web site: *www.global.ihs.com*.

(28) ANSI Z535.1–2006 (R2011), Safety Colors, reaffirmed July 19, 2011; IBR approved for §1926.200(c). Copies available for purchase from the:

(i) American National Standards Institute's e-Standards Store, 25 W 43rd Street, 4th Floor, New York, NY 10036; telephone: 212–642–4980; Web site: *http://webstore.ansi.org/;*

(ii) IHS Standards Store, 15 Inverness Way East, Englewood, CO 80112; telephone: 877–413–5184; Web site: *www.global.ihs.com;* or

(iii) TechStreet Store, 3916 Ranchero Dr., Ann Arbor, MI 48108; telephone: 877–699–9277; Web site: *www.techstreet.com*.

(29) ANSI Z535.2–2011, Environmental and Facility Safety Signs, published September 15, 2011; IBR approved for §1926.200(b), (c), and (i). Copies available for purchase from the:

(i) American National Standards Institute's e-Standards Store, 25 W 43rd Street, 4th Floor, New York, NY 10036; telephone: 212–642–4980; Web site: *http://webstore.ansi.org/;*

(ii) IHS Standards Store, 15 Inverness Way East, Englewood, CO 80112; telephone: 877–413–5184; Web site: *www.global.ihs.com;* or

(iii) TechStreet Store, 3916 Ranchero Dr., Ann Arbor, MI 48108; telephone: 877–699–9277; Web site: *www.techstreet.com*.

(30) ANSI Z535.5–2011, Safety Tags and Barricade Tapes (for Temporary Hazards), published September 15, 2011, including Errata, November 14, 2011; IBR approved for §1926.200(h) and (i). Copies available for purchase from the:

(i) American National Standards Institute's e-Standards Store, 25 W 43rd Street, 4th Floor, New York, NY 10036; telephone: 212–642–4980; Web site: *http://webstore.ansi.org/;*

(ii) IHS Standards Store, 15 Inverness Way East, Englewood, CO 80112; telephone: 877–413–5184; Web site: *www.global.ihs.com;* or

(iii) TechStreet Store, 3916 Ranchero Dr., Ann Arbor, MI 48108; telephone: 877–699–9277; Web site: *www.techstreet.com*.

(31) ANSI Z87.1–1968, Practice for Occupational and Educational Eye and Face Protection, IBR approved for §1926.102(a).

(32) American National Standards Institute (ANSI) Z89.1–2009, American National Standard for Industrial Head Protection, approved January 26, 2009; IBR approved for §1926.100(b)(1)(i). Copies of ANSI Z89.1–2009 are available for purchase only from the International Safety Equipment Association, 1901 North Moore Street, Arlington, VA 22209–1762; telephone: 703–525–1695; fax: 703–528–2148; Web site: *www.safetyequipment.org*.

(33) American National Standards Institute (ANSI) Z89.1–2003, American National Standard for Industrial Head Protection; IBR approved for §1926.100(b)(1)(ii). Copies of ANSI Z89.1–2003 are available for purchase only from the International Safety Equipment Association, 1901 North Moore Street, Arlington, VA 22209–1762; telephone: 703–525–1695; fax: 703–528–2148; Web site: *www.safetyequipment.org*.

(34) American National Standards Institute (ANSI) Z89.1–1997, American National Standard for Personnel Protection—Protective Headwear for Industrial Workers—Requirements; IBR approved for §1926.100(b)(1)(iii). Copies of ANSI Z89.1–1997 are available for purchase only from the International Safety Equipment Association, 1901 North Moore Street, Arlington, VA 22209–1762;

telephone: 703–525–1695; fax: 703–528–2148; Web site: *www.safetyequipment.org.*

(i) [Reserved]

(j) The following material is available for purchase from the American Society for Testing and Materials (ASTM), ASTM International, 100 Barr Harbor Drive, PO Box C700, West Conshohocken, PA, 19428–2959; telephone: 610–832–9585; fax: 610–832–9555; e-mail: *service@astm.org;* Web site: *http://www.astm.org/:*

(1) ASTM A370–1968, Methods and Definitions for Mechanical Testing and Steel Products, IBR approved for § 1926.1001(f).

(2) [Reserved]

(3) ASTM D56–1969, Standard Method of Test for Flash Point by the Tag Closed Tester, IBR approved for § 1926.155(i).

(4) ASTM D93–1969, Standard Method of Test for Flash Point by the Pensky Martens Closed Tester, IBR approved for § 1926.155(i).

(5) ASTM D323–1958 (R1968), Standard Method of Test for Vapor Pressure of Petroleum Products (Reid Method), IBR approved for § 1926.155(m).

(k) The following material is available for purchase from the American Society of Agricultural and Biological Engineers (ASABE), 2950 Niles Road, St. Joseph, MI 49085; telephone: 269–429–0300; fax: 269–429–3852; e-mail: *hq@asabe.org;* Web site: *http://www.asabe.org/:*

(1) ASAE R313.1–1971, Soil Cone Penetrometer, reaffirmed 1975, IBR approved for § 1926.1002(e).

(l) The following material is available for purchase from the American Society of Mechanical Engineers (ASME), Three Park Avenue, New York, NY 10016; telephone: 1–800–843–2763; fax: 973–882–1717; e-mail: *infocentral@asme.org;* Web site: *http://www.asme.org/:*

(1) ASME B30.2–2005, Overhead and Gantry Cranes (Top Running Bridge, Single or Multiple Girder, Top Running Trolley Hoist), issued Dec. 30, 2005 ("ASME B30.2–2005"), IBR approved for § 1926.1438(b).

(2) ASME B30.5–2004, Mobile and Locomotive Cranes, issued Sept. 27, 2004 ("ASME B30.5–2004"), IBR approved for §§ 1926.1414(b); 1926.1414(e); 1926.1433(b).

(3) ASME B30.7–2001, Base-Mounted Drum Hoists, issued Jan. 21, 2002 ("ASME B30.7–2001"), IBR approved for § 1926.1436(e).

(4) ASME B30.14–2004, Side Boom Tractors, issued Sept. 20, 2004 ("ASME B30.14–2004"), IBR approved for § 1926.1440(c).

(5) ASME Boiler and Pressure Vessel Code, Section VIII, 1968, IBR approved for §§ 1926.152(i), 1926.306(a), and 1926.603(a).

(6) ASME Power Boilers, Section I, 1968, IBR approved for § 1926.603(a).

(m) The following material is available for purchase from the American Welding Society (AWS), 550 N.W. LeJeune Road, Miami, Florida 33126; telephone: 1–800–443–9353; Web site: *http://www.aws.org/:*

(1) AWS D1.1/D1.1M:2002, Structural Welding Code—Steel, 18th ed., ANSI approved Aug. 31, 2001 ("AWS D1.1/D1.1M:2002"), IBR approved for § 1926.1436(c).

(2) ANSI/AWS D14.3–94, Specification for Welding Earthmoving and Construction Equipment, ANSI approved Jun. 11, 1993 ("ANSI/AWS D14.3–94"), IBR approved for § 1926.1436(c).

(n) The following material is available for purchase from the British Standards Institution (BSI), 389 Chiswick High Road, London, W4 4AL, United Kingdom; telephone: +44 20 8996 9001; fax: +44 20 8996 7001; e-mail: *cservices@bsigroup.com;* Web site: *http://www.bsigroup.com/:*

(1) BS EN 13000:2004, Cranes—Mobile Cranes, published Jan. 4, 2006 ("BS EN 13000:2004"), IBR approved for § 1926.1433(c).

(2) BS EN 14439:2006, Cranes—Safety—Tower Cranes, published Jan. 31, 2007 ("BS EN 14439:2006"), IBR approved for § 1926.1433(c).

(o) The following material is available for purchase from the Bureau of Reclamation, United States Department of the Interior, 1849 C Street, NW., Washington DC 20240; telephone: 202–208–4501; Web site: *http://www.usbr.gov/:*

(1) Safety and Health Regulations for Construction, Part II, Sept. 1971, IBR approved for § 1926.1000(f).

(p) The following material is available for purchase from the California Department of Industrial Relations, 455

Golden Gate Avenue, San Francisco CA 94102; telephone: (415) 703–5070; e-mail: *info@dir.ca.gov;* Web site: *http://www.dir.ca.gov/:*

(1) Construction Safety Orders, IBR approved for §1926.1000(f).

(q)–(t) [Reserved]

(u) The following material is available for purchase from the Federal Highway Administration, United States Department of Transportation, 1200 New Jersey Ave., SE., Washington, DC 20590; telephone: 202–366–4000; Web site: *http://www.fhwa.dot.gov/:*

(1) Manual on Uniform Traffic Control Devices (MUTCD), Part VI, Standards and Guides for Traffic Controls for Street and Highway Construction, Maintenance, Utility, and Incident Management Operation, 1988 Edition, Revision 3, September 3, 1993; IBR approved for §§1926.200(g), 1926.201(a), and 1926.202. Electronic copies of the MUTCD, 1988 Edition, Revision 3, are available for downloading at *http://www.osha.gov/doc/highway_workzones/mutcd/index.html.*

(2) Manual on Uniform Traffic Control Devices (MUTCD), Millennium Edition, Dec. 2000; IBR approved for §§1926.200(g)), 1926.201(a), and 1926.202. Electronic copies of the MUTCD 2000 are available for downloading at *http://mutcd.fhwa.dot.gov/kno-millennium_12.18.00.htm.*

(v) The following material is available for purchase from the General Services Administration (GSA), 1800 F Street, NW., Washington, DC 20405; telephone: (202) 501–0800; Web site: *http://www.gsa.gov/:*

(1) QQ–P–416, Federal Specification Plating Cadmium (Electrodeposited), IBR approved for §1926.104(e).

(w) The following material is available for purchase from the Institute of Makers of Explosives (IME), 1120 19th Street, NW., Suite 310, Washington, DC 20036; telephone: 202–429–9280; fax: 202–429–9280; e-mail: *info@ime.org;* Web site: *http://www.ime.org/:*

(1) IME Pub. No. 2, American Table of Distances for Storage of Explosives, Jun. 5, 1964, IBR approved for §1926.914(a).

(2) IME Pub. No. 20, Radio Frequency Energy—A Potential Hazard in the Use of Electric Blasting Caps, Mar. 1968, IBR approved for §1926.900(k).

(x) The following material is available for purchase from the International Organization for Standardization (ISO), 1, ch. de la Voie-Creuse, Case postale 56, CH–1211 Geneva 20, Switzerland; telephone: +41 22 749 01 11; fax: +41 22 733 34 30; Web site: *http://www.iso.org/:*

(1) ISO 11660–1:2008(E), Cranes—Access, guards and restraints—Part 1: General, 2d ed., Feb. 15, 2008 ("ISO 11660–1:2008(E)"), IBR approved for §1926.1423(c).

(2) ISO 11660–2:1994(E), Cranes—Access, guards and restraints—Part 2: Mobile cranes, 1994 ("ISO 11660–2:1994(E)"), IBR approved for §1926.1423(c).

(3) ISO 11660–3:2008(E), Cranes—Access, guards and restraints—Part 3: Tower cranes, 2d ed., Feb. 15, 2008 ("ISO 11660–3:2008(E)"), IBR approved for §1926.1423(c).

(y) The following material is available for purchase from the National Fire Protection Association (NFPA), 1 Batterymarch Park, Quincy, MA 02169; telephone: 617–770–3000; fax: 617–770–0700; Web site: *http://www.nfpa.org/:*

(1) NFPA 10A–1970, Maintenance and Use of Portable Fire Extinguishers, IBR approved for §1926.150(c).

(2) NFPA 13–1969, Standard for the Installation of Sprinkler Systems, IBR approved for §1926.152(d).

(3) NFPA 30–1969, The Flammable and Combustible Liquids Code, IBR approved for §1926.152(c).

(4) NFPA 80–1970, Standard for Fire Doors and Windows, Class E or F Openings, IBR approved for §1926.152(b).

(5) NFPA 251–1969, Standard Methods of Fire Test of Building Construction and Material, IBR approved for §§1926.152(b) and 1926.155(f).

(6) NFPA 385–1966, Standard for Tank Vehicles for Flammable and Combustible Liquids, IBR approved for §1926.152(g).

(z) [Reserved]

(aa) The following material is available for purchase from the Power Crane and Shovel Association (PCSA), 6737 W. Washington Street, Suite 2400, Milwaukee, WI 53214; telephone: 1–800–369–2310; fax: 414–272–1170; Web site: *http://www.aem.org/CBC/ProdSpec/PCSA/:*

(1) PCSA Std. No. 1, Mobile Crane and Excavator Standards, 1968, IBR approved for §1926.602(b).

(2) PCSA Std. No. 2, Mobile Hydraulic Crane Standards, 1968 ("PCSA Std. No. 2 (1968)"), IBR approved for §§ 1926.602(b), 1926.1433(a), and 1926.1501(a).

(3) PCSA Std. No. 3, Mobile Hydraulic Excavator Standards, 1969, IBR approved for § 1926.602(b).

(bb)–(cc) [Reserved]

(dd) The following material is available for purchase from the Society of Automotive Engineers (SAE), 400 Commonwealth Drive, Warrendale, PA 15096; telephone: 1-877-606-7323; fax: 724-776-0790; Web site: *http://www.sae.org/*:

(1) SAE 1970 Handbook, IBR approved for § 1926.602(b).

(2) SAE 1971 Handbook, IBR approved for § 1926.1001(h).

(3) SAE J166-1971, Trucks and Wagons, IBR approved for § 1926.602(a).

(4) SAE J168-1970, Protective Enclosures—Test Procedures and Performance Requirements, IBR approved for § 1926.1002(a).

(5) SAE J185 (reaf. May 2003), Access Systems for Off-Road Machines, reaffirmed May 2003 ("SAE J185 (May 1993)"), IBR approved for § 1926.1423(c).

(6) SAE J236-1971, Self-Propelled Graders, IBR approved for § 1926.602(a).

(7) SAE J237-1971, Front End Loaders and Dozers, IBR approved for § 126.602(a).

(8) SAE J319b-1971, Self-Propelled Scrapers, IBR approved for § 1926.602(a).

(9) SAE J320a-1971, Minimum Performance Criteria for Roll-Over Protective Structure for Rubber-Tired, Self-Propelled Scrapers, IBR approved for § 1926.1001(h).

(10) SAE J321a-1970, Fenders for Pneumatic-Tired Earthmoving Haulage Equipment, IBR approved for § 1926.602(a).

(11) SAE J333a-1970, Operator Protection for Agricultural and Light Industrial Tractors, IBR approved for § 1926.602(a).

(11) SAE J386-1969, Seat Belts for Construction Equipment, IBR approved for § 1926.602(a).

(12) SAE J394-1971, Minimum Performance Criteria for Roll-Over Protective Structure for Rubber-Tired Front End Loaders and Robber-Tired Dozers, IBR approved for § 1926.1001(h).

(13) SAE J395-1971, Minimum Performance Criteria for Roll-Over Protec-

tive Structure for Crawler Tractors and Crawler-Type Loaders, IBR approved for § 1926.1001(h).

(14) SAE J396-1971, Minimum Performance Criteria for Roll-Over Protective Structure for Motor Graders, IBR approved for § 1926.1001(h).

(15) SAE J397-1969, Critical Zone Characteristics and Dimensions for Operators of Construction and Industrial Machinery, IBR approved for § 1926.1001(f).

(16) SAE J743a-1964, Tractor Mounted Side Boom, 1964 ("SAE J743a-1964"), IBR approved for § 1926.1501(a).

(17) SAE J959-1966, Lifting Crane Wire-Rope Strength Factors, 1966 ("SAE J959-1966"), IBR approved for § 1926.1501(a).

(18) SAE J987 (rev. Jun. 2003), Lattice Boom Cranes—Method of Test, revised Jun. 2003 ("SAE J987 (Jun. 2003)"), IBR approved for § 1926.1433(c).

(19) SAE J1063 (rev. Nov. 1993), Cantilevered Boom Crane Structures—Method of Test, revised Nov. 1993 ("SAE J1063 (Nov. 1993)"), IBR approved for § 1926.1433(c).

(ee) The following material is available for purchase from the United States Army Corps of Engineers, 441 G Street, NW., Washington, DC 20314; telephone: 202-761-0011; e-mail: *hqpublicaffairs@usace.army.mil;* Web site: *http://www.usace.army.mil/*:

(1) EM-385-1-1, General Safety Requirements, Mar. 1967, IBR approved for § 1926.1000(f).

(ff) The following material is available for purchase from standards resellers such as the Document Center Inc., 111 Industrial Road, Suite 9, Belmont, CA 94002; telephone: 650-591-7600; fax: 650-591-7617; e-mail: *info@document-center.com;* Web site: *http://www.document-center.com/*:

(1) ANSI B15.1-1953 (R1958), Safety Code for Mechanical Power-Transmission Apparatus, revised 1958, IBR approved for §§ 1926.300(b)(2) and 1926.1501(a).

(2) ANSI B30.2.0-1967, Safety Code for Overhead and Gantry Cranes, approved May 4, 1967, IBR approved for § 1926.1501(d).

(3) ANSI B30.5-1968, Crawler, Locomotive, and Truck Cranes, approved Dec. 16, 1968, IBR approved for

§§1926.1433(a), 1926.1501(a), and 1926.1501(b).

(4) ANSI B30.6–1969, Safety Code for Derricks, approved Dec. 18, 1967, IBR approved for §1926.1501(e).

[75 FR 48130, Aug. 9, 2010, as amended at 77 FR 37600, June 22, 2012; 78 FR 35566, June 13, 2013; 78 FR 66641, Nov. 6, 2013; 79 FR 20692, Apr. 11, 2014]

Subpart B—General Interpretations

AUTHORITY: Sec. 107, Contract Work Hours and Safety Standards Act (Construction Safety Act) (40 U.S.C. 333).

§1926.10 Scope of subpart.

(a) This subpart contains the general rules of the Secretary of Labor interpreting and applying the construction safety and health provisions of section 107 of the Contract Work Hours and Safety Standards Act (83 Stat. 96). Section 107 requires as a condition of each contract which is entered into under legislation subject to Reorganization Plan Number 14 of 1950 (64 Stat. 1267), and which is for construction, alteration, and/or repair, including painting and decorating, that no contractor or subcontractor contracting for any part of the contract work shall require any laborer or mechanic employed in the performance of the contract to work in surroundings or under working conditions which are unsanitary, hazardous, or dangerous to his health or safety, as determined under construction safety and health standards promulgated by the Secretary by regulation.

§1926.11 Coverage under section 103 of the act distinguished.

(a) *Coverage under section 103.* It is important to note that the coverage of section 107 differs from that for the overtime requirements of the Contract Work Hours and Safety Standards Act. The application of the overtime requirements is governed by section 103, which subject to specific exemptions, includes: (1) Federal contracts requiring or involving the employment of laborers or mechanics (thus including, but not limited to, contracts for construction), and (2) contracts assisted in whole or in part by Federal loans, grants, or guarantees under any stat-

ute "providing wage standards for such work." The statutes "providing wage standards for such work" include statutes for construction which require the payment of minimum wages in accordance with prevailing wage findings by the Secretary of Labor in accordance with the Davis-Bacon Act. A provision to section 103 excludes from the overtime requirements work where the Federal assistance is only in the form of a loan guarantee or insurance.

(b) *Coverage under section 107.* To be covered by section 107 of the Contract Work Hours and Safety Standards Act, a contract must be one which (1) is entered into under a statute that is subject to Reorganization Plan No. 14 of 1950 (64 Stat. 1267); and (2) is for "construction, alteration, and/or repair, including painting and decorating."SECTION≤ §1926.12 Reorganization Plan No. 14 of 1950.

(a) *General provisions.* Reorganization Plan No. 14 of 1950 relates to the prescribing by the Secretary of Labor of "appropriate standards, regulations, and procedures" with respect to the enforcement of labor standards under Federal and federally assisted contracts which are subject to various statutes subject to the Plan. The rules of the Secretary of Labor implementing the Plan are published in part 5 of this title. Briefly, the statutes subject to the Plan include the Davis-Bacon Act, including its extension to Federal-aid highway legislation subject to 23 U.S.C. 113, and other statutes subject to the Plan by its original terms, statutes by which the Plan is expressly applied, such as the Contract Work Hours Standards Act by virtue of section 104(d) thereof.

(b) *The Plan.* (1) The statutes subject to Reorganization Plan No. 14 of 1950 are cited and briefly described in the remaining paragraphs of this section. These descriptions are general in nature and not intended to convey the full scope of the work to be performed under each statute. The individual statutes should be resorted to for a more detailed scope of the work.

(2) *Federal-Aid Highway Acts.* The provisions codified in 23 U.S.C. 113 apply to the initial construction, reconstruction, or improvement work performed by contractors or subcontractors on

highway projects on the Federal-aid systems, the primary and secondary, as well as their extensions in urban areas, and the Interstate System, authorized under the highway laws providing for the expenditure of Federal funds upon the Federal-aid system. As cited in 41 Op. A.G. 488, 496, the Attorney General ruled that the Federal-Aid Highway Acts are subject to Reorganization Plan No. 14 of 1950.

(3) *National Housing Act (12 U.S.C. 1713, 1715a, 1715e, 1715k, 1715l(d)(3) and (4), 1715v, 1715w, 1715x, 1743, 1747, 1748, 1748h–2, 1750g, 1715l(h)(1), 1715z(j)(1), 1715z–1, 1715y(d), Subchapter 1x-A and 1x-B, 1715z–7).* This act covers construction which is financed with assistance by the Federal Government through programs of loan and mortgage insurance for the following purposes:

(i) Rental Housing—Section 1713 provides mortgage and insurance on rental housing of eight or more units and on mobile-home courts.

(ii) Section 1715a—Repealed.

(iii) Cooperative Housing—Section 1715e authorizes mortgage insurance on cooperative housing of five or more units as well as supplementary loans for improvement of repair or resale of memberships.

(iv) Urban Renewal Housing—Section 1715k provides mortgage insurance on single family or multifamily housing in approved urban renewal areas.

(v) Low or Moderate Income Housing—Section 1715L(d) (3) and (4) insures mortgages on low-cost single family or multifamily housing.

(vi) Housing for Elderly—Section 1715v provides mortgage insurance on rental housing for elderly or handicapped persons.

(vii) Nursing Homes—Section 1715w authorizes mortgage insurance on nursing home facilities and major equipment.

(viii) Experimental Housing—Section 1715x provides mortgage insurance on single family or multifamily housing with experimental design of materials.

(ix) War Housing Insurance—Section 1743 not active.

(x) Yield Insurance—Section 1747 insures investment returns on multifamily housing.

(xi) Armed Services Housing—Section 1748b to assist in relieving acute shortage and urgent need for family housing at or in areas adjacent to military installations.

(xii) Defense Housing for Impacted Areas—Section 1748h–2 provides mortgage insurance on single family or multifamily housing for sale or rent primarily to military or civilian personnel of the Armed Services, National Aeronautics and Space Administration, or Atomic Energy Commission.

(xiii) Defense Rental Housing—Section 1750g provides for mortgage insurance in critical defense housing areas.

(xiv) Rehabilitation—Section 1715L (h)(1) provides mortgage insurance for nonprofit organizations to finance the purchase and rehabilitation of deteriorating or substandard housing for subsequent resale to low-income home purchasers. There must be located on the property five or more single family dwellings of detached, semidetached, or row construction.

(xv) Homeowner Assistance—Section 1715Z(j)(1) authorizes mortgage insurance to nonprofit organizations or public bodies or agencies executed to finance sale of individual dwellings to lower income individuals or families. Also includes the rehabilitation of such housing if it is deteriorating or substandard for subsequent resale to lower income home purchasers.

(xvi) Rental Housing Assistance—Section 1715Z–1 authorizes mortgage insurance and interest reduction payments on behalf of owners of rental housing projects designed for occupancy by lower income families. Payments are also authorized for certain State or locally aided projects.

(xvii) Condominium Housing—Section 1715y(d) provides mortgage insurance on property purchased for the development of building sites. This includes waterlines and water supply installations, sewer lines and sewage disposal installations, steam, gas, and electrical lines and installations, roads, streets, curbs, gutters, sidewalks, storm drainage facilities, and other installations or work.

(xviii) Group Medical Practice Facilities—Subchapter LX-B authorizes mortgage insurance for the financing of construction and equipment, of facilities for group practice of medicine, optometry, or dentistry.

(xix) Nonprofit Hospitals—1715z–7 authorizes mortgage insurance to cover new and rehabilitated hospitals, including initial equipment.

(4) *Hospital Survey and Construction Act, as amended by the Hospital and Medical Facilities Amendments of 1964 (42 U.S.C. 291e).*The provisions of this Act cover construction contracts made by State or local authorities or private institutions under Federal grant-in-aid programs for the construction of hospitals and other medical facilities.

(5) *Federal Airport Act (49 U.S.C. 1114(b)).* The act provides grant-in-aid funds for airport construction limited to general site preparation runways, taxiways, aprons, lighting appurtenant thereto, and fire, rescue, and maintenance buildings. The act excludes construction intended for use as a public parking facility for passenger automobiles and the cost of construction of any part of an airport building except such of those buildings or parts of buildings to house facilities or activities directly related to the safety of persons at the airport.

(6) *Housing Act of 1949 (42 U.S.C. 1459).* Construction contracts awarded by local authorities financed with the assistance of loans and grants from the Federal Government. The construction programs are for slum clearance and urban renewal which includes rehabilitation grants, neighborhood development programs, neighborhood renewal plans, community renewal, demolition projects, and assistance for blighted areas. See the Housing Act of 1964, paragraph (b)(21) of this section, concerning financial assistance for low-rent housing for domestic farm labor.

(7) *School Survey and Construction Act of 1950 (20 U.S.C. 636).* This act provides for a Federal grant-in-aid program to assist in the construction of schools in federally affected areas.

(8) *Defense Housing & Community Facilities & Services Act of 1951 (42 U.S.C. 1592i).* Inactive Program.

(9) *United States Housing Act of 1937 (42 U.S.C. 1416).* This statute covers the construction of low-rent public housing and slum clearance projects awarded by local authorities. These projects are financed with the assistance of loans and grants from the Federal Government. The slum clearance is the demolition and removal of buildings from any slum area to be used for a low-rent housing project.

(10) *Federal Civil Defense Act of 1950 (50 U.S.C. App. 2281).* This act provides for Federal assistance to the several States and their political subdivisions in the field of civil defense which includes procurement, construction, leasing, or renovating of materials and facilities.

(11) *Delaware River Basin Compact (sec. 15.1, 75 Stat. 714).* This joint resolution creates, by intergovernmental compact between the United States, Delaware, New Jersey, New York, and Pennsylvania, a regional agency for planning, conservation, utilization, development, management and control of the water and related sources of the Delaware River.

(12) *Cooperative Research Act (20 U.S.C. 332a(c)).* This act provides Federal grants to a university, college, or other appropriate public or nonprofit private agency or institution for part or all of the cost of constructing a facility for research or for research and related purposes. Research and related purposes means research, research training, surveys, or demonstrations in the field of education, or the dissemination of information derived therefrom, or all of such activities, including (but without limitation) experimental schools, except that such term does not include research, research training, surveys, or demonstrations in the field of sectarian instruction or the dissemination of information derived therefrom. Construction includes new buildings, and the acquisition, expansion, remodeling, replacement, and alteration of existing buildings and the equipping of new buildings and existing buildings.

(13) *Health Professions Educational Assistance Act of 1963 (42 U.S.C. 292d (c)(4), 293a(c)(5)).* The provisions of this act provide for grants to assist public and nonprofit medical, dental, and similar schools for the construction, expansion, or renovation of teaching facilities.

(14) *Mental Retardation Facilities Construction Act (42 U.S.C. 295(a)(2)(D), 2662(5), 2675(a)(5)).* This act authorizes Federal financial assistance in the construction of centers for research on

mental retardation and related aspects of human development, of university-affiliated facilities for the mentally retarded and of facilities for the mentally retarded.

(15) *Community Mental Health Centers Act (42 U.S.C. 2685(a)(5))*. This act authorizes Federal grants for the construction of public and other nonprofit community mental health centers.

(16) *Higher Education Facilities Act of 1963 (20 U.S.C. 753)*. This act authorizes the grant or loan of Federal funds to assist public and other nonprofit institutions of higher education in financing the construction, rehabilitation, or improvement of academic and related facilities in undergraduate and graduate schools.

(17) *Vocational Educational Act of 1963 (20 U.S.C. 35f)*. This act provides for Federal grants to the various States for construction of area vocational education school facilities.

(18) *Library Services and Construction Act (20 U.S.C. 355e(a)(4))*. This act provides for Federal assistance to the various States for the construction of public libraries.

(19) *Urban Mass Transportation Act of 1954 (49 U.S.C. 1609)*. This act provides for grants and loans to assist States and local public bodies and agencies thereof in financing the acquisition, construction, reconstruction, and improvement of facilities and equipment for use, by operation or lease or otherwise, in mass transportation service in urban areas and in coordinating such service with highway and other transportation in such areas.

(20) *Economic Opportunity Act of 1964 (42 U.S.C. 2947)*. This act covers construction which is financed with assistance of the Federal Government for the following purposes:

(i) Authorizes Federal assistance for construction of projects, buildings and works which will provide young men and women in rural and urban residential centers with education, vocational training, and useful work experience (Title I).

(ii) Authorizes financial assistance for construction work planned and carried out at the community level for antipoverty programs (Title II):

(*a*) Authorizes loans to low income rural families by assisting them to acquire or improve real estate or reduce encumbrances or erect improvements thereon, and to participate in cooperative associations and/or to finance non-agricultural enterprises which will enable such families to supplement their income (Title III);

(*b*) Authorizes loans to local cooperative associations furnishing essential processing, purchasing, or marketing services, supplies, or facilities predominantly to low-income rural families (Title III);

(*c*) Authorizes financial assistance to States, political subdivisions of States, public and nonprofit agencies, institutions, organizations, farm associations, or individuals in establishing housing, sanitation, education, and child day-care programs for migrants and other seasonally employed agricultural employees and their families (Title III).

(iii) Authorizes loans or guarantees loans to small businesses for construction work (Title IV).

(iv) Authorizes the payment of the cost of experimental, pilot, or demonstration projects to foster State programs providing construction work experience or training for unemployed fathers and needy people (Title V).

(21) *Housing Act of 1964 (42 U.S.C. 1486(f); 42 U.S.C. 1452b(e))*. Provides financial assistance for low-rent housing for domestic farm labor. The Act further provides for loans, through public or private agencies, where feasible, to owners or tenants of property in urban renewal areas to finance rehabilitation required to conform the property to applicable code requirements or carry out the objectives of the urban renewal plan for the area.

(22) *The Commercial Fisheries Research and Development Act of 1964 (16 U.S.C. 779e(b))*. This Act authorizes financial assistance to State agencies for construction projects designed for the research and development of the commercial fisheries resources of the Nation.

(23) *The Nurse Training Act of 1964 (42 U.S.C. 296a(b)(5))*. This act provides for grants to assist in the construction of new facilities for collegiate, associate degree, and diploma schools of nursing, or replacement or rehabilitation of existing facilities of such schools.

(24) *Elementary and Secondary Education Act of 1965 (20 U.S.C. 241i, 848).* The purpose of the act is to provide financial assistance to local educational agencies serving areas with concentrations of children from low-income families for construction in connection with the expansion or improvement of their educational programs.

(25) *Federal Water Pollution Control Act, as amended by the Water Quality Act of 1965 (3 U.S.C. 466e(g)).* Provides for financial assistance to States or municipalities for construction of facilities in connection with the prevention and control of water pollution. This includes projects that will control the discharge into any waters of untreated or inadequately treated sewage.

(26) *Appalachian Regional Development Act of 1965 (40 U.S.C. App. 402).* Authorizes Federal assistance in the construction of an Appalachian development highway system; construction of multi-county demonstration health facilities, hospitals, regional health, diagnostic and treatment centers, and other facilities for health; seal and fill voids in abandoned mines and to rehabilitate strip mine areas; construction of school facilities for vocational education; and to assist in construction of sewage treatment works.

(27) *National Technical Institute for the Deaf Act (20 U.S.C. 684(b)(5)).* Provides for financial assistance for institutions of higher education for the establishment, construction, including equipment and operation, of a National Institution for the Deaf.

(28) *Housing Act of 1959 (12 U.S.C. 1701(q)(c)(3)).* This act authorizes loans to nonprofit corporations to be used for the construction of housing and related facilities for elderly families. Also, the provisions of the act provide for rehabilitation, alteration, conversion or improvement of existing structures which are otherwise inadequate for proposed dwellings used by such families.

(29) *College Housing Act of 1950, as amended (12 U.S.C. 1749a(f)).* This act provides for Federal loans to assist educational institutions in providing housing and other educational facilities for students and faculties.

(30) *Housing and Urban Development Act of 1965 (42 U.S.C. 1500c–3, 3107).* This act provides for Federal assistance for the following purposes:

(i) Grants to States and local public bodies to assist in any construction work to be carried out under the open-space land and urban beautification provisions contained therein. It provides for parks and recreation areas, conservation of land and other natural resources, and historical and scenic purposes.

(ii) Grants to local public bodies and agencies to finance specific projects for basic public water facilities (including works for the storage, treatment, purification, and distribution of water), and for basic public sewer facilities (other than "treatment works" as defined in the Federal Water Pollution Control Act).

(iii) Grants to any local public body or agency to assist in financing neighborhood facilities. These facilities must be necessary for carrying out a program of health, recreational, social, or similar community service and located so as to be available for the use of the area's low or moderate income residents.

(31) *National Foundation on the Arts and the Humanities Act of 1965 (20 U.S.C. 954(k)).* The act establishes the "National Foundation on the Arts and the Humanities" which may provide matching grants to groups (nonprofit organizations and State and other public organizations) and to individuals engaged in creative and performing arts for the entire range of artistic activity, including construction of necessary facilities.

(32) *Public Works and Economic Development Act of 1965 (42 U.S.C. 3222).* This act provides for Federal assistance for the following purposes:

(i) Grants for the acquisition or development of land or improvements for public works or development facility usage in redevelopment areas. It authorizes loans to assist in financing the purchase or development of land for public works which will assist in the creation of long-term employment opportunities in the area.

(ii) Loans for the purchase or development of land and facilities (including machinery and equipment) for industrial or commercial usage within redevelopment areas; guarantee of loans for working capital made to private borrowers by private lending institutions in connection with direct loan projects; and to contract to pay to, or on behalf of, business entities locating in redevelopment areas, a portion of the interest costs which they incur in financing their expansions from private sources.

(iii) Loans and grants to create economic development centers within designated county economic development districts.

(33) *High-Speed Ground Transportation Study (40 U.S.C. 1636(b))*. This act provides for financial assistance for construction activities in connection with research and development of different forms of high-speed ground transportation and demonstration projects relating to intercity rail passenger service.

(34) *Heart Disease, Cancer and Stroke Amendments of 1965 (42 U.S.C. 299(b)(4))*. This act provides for grants to public or nonprofit private universities, medical schools, research, institutions, hospitals, and other public and nonprofit agencies and institutions, or associations thereof to assist in construction and equipment of facilities in connection with research, training, demonstration of patient care, diagnostic and treatment related to heart disease, cancer, stroke, and other major diseases.

(35) *Mental Retardation Facilities and Community Mental Health Centers Construction Act Amendments of 1965 (20 U.S.C. 618(g))*. These provisions provide for grants to institutions of higher education for construction of facilities for research or for research and related purposes relating to education for mentally retarded, hard of hearing, deaf, speech impaired, visually handicapped, seriously emotionally disturbed, crippled, or other health impaired children who by reason thereof require special education.

(36) *Vocational Rehabilitation Act Amendments of 1965 (29 U.S.C. 41a(b)(4))*. This act authorizes grants to assist in meeting the costs of construction of public or other nonprofit workshops and rehabilitation facilities.

(37) *Clean Air and Solid Waste Disposal Acts (42 U.S.C. 3256)*. This act provides for financial assistance to public (Federal, State, interstate, or local) authorities, agencies, and institutions, private agencies and institutions, and individuals in the construction of facilities for solid-waste disposal. The term construction includes the installation of initial equipment.

(38) *Medical Library Assistance Act of 1965 (42 U.S.C. 280b–3(b)(3))*. This act provides for grants to public or private non-profit agencies or institutions for the cost of construction of medical library facilities.

(39) *Veterans Nursing Home Care Act (38 U.S.C. 5035(a)(8))*. The construction industry health and safety standards do not apply to this act since it is not subject to Reorganization Plan No. 14 of 1950.

(40) *National Capital Transportation Act of 1965 (40 U.S.C. 682(b)(4))*. This act provides for Federal assistance to the National Capital Transportation Agency for construction of a rail rapid transit system and related facilities for the Nation's Capital.

(41) *Alaska Centennial—1967 (80 Stat. 82)*. The program under this legislation has expired.

(42) *Model Secondary School for the Deaf Act (80 Stat. 1028)*. This act provides for funds to establish and operate, including construction and initial equipment of new buildings, expansion, remodeling, and alteration of existing buildings and equipment thereof, a model secondary school for the deaf to serve the residents of the District of Columbia and nearby States.

(43) *Allied Health Professions Personnel Training Act of 1966 (42 U.S.C. 295h(b)(2)(E))*. This act provides for grants to assist in the construction of new facilities for training centers for allied health professions, or replacement or rehabilitation of existing facilities for such centers.

(44) *Demonstration Cities and Metropolitan Development Act of 1966 (42 U.S.C. 3310; 12 U.S.C. 1715c; 42 U.S.C. 1416)*. This act provides for Federal assistance for the following purposes:

(i) Grants to assist in the construction, rehabilitation, alteration, or repair of residential property only if such residential property is designed for residential use for eight or more families to enable city demonstration agencies to carry out comprehensive city demonstration programs (42 U.S.C. 3310).

(ii) Amends the National Housing Act (12 U.S.C. 1715c) and the Housing Act of 1937 (42 U.S.C. 1416). See these acts for coverage.

(45) *Air Quality Act of 1967 (42 U.S.C. 1857j–3)*. This act provides for Federal assistance to public or nonprofit agencies, institutions, and organizations and to individuals, and contracts with public or private agencies, institutions, or persons for construction of research and development facilities and demonstration plants relating to the application of preventing or controlling discharges into the air of various types of pollutants.

(46) *Elementary and Secondary Education Amendments of 1967 (Title VII—Bilingual Education Act) (20 U.S.C. 880b–6)*. This act provides for Federal assistance to local educational agencies or to an institution of higher education applying jointly with a local educational agency for minor remodeling projects in connection with bilingual education programs to meet the special needs of children with limited English-speaking ability in the United States.

(47) *Vocational Rehabilitation Amendments of 1967 (29 U.S.C. 42a(c)(3))*. This act authorizes Federal assistance to any public or nonprofit private agency or organization for the construction of a center for vocational rehabilitation of handicapped individuals who are both deaf and blind which shall be known as the National Center for Deaf-Blind Youths and Adults. Construction includes new buildings and expansion, remodeling, alteration and renovation of existing buildings, and initial equipment of such new, newly acquired, expanded, remodeled, altered, or renovated buildings.

(48) *National Visitor Center Facilities Act of 1968 (40 U.S.C. 808)*. This act authorizes agreements and leases with the owner of property in the District of Columbia known as Union Station for the use of all or a part of such property for a national visitor center to be known as the National Visitor Center. The agreements and leases shall provide for such alterations of the Union Station Building as necessary to provide adequate facilities for visitors. They also provide for the construction of a parking facility, including necessary approaches and ramps.

(49) *Juvenile Delinquency Prevention and Control Act of 1968 (42 U.S.C. 3843)*. This act provides for Federal grants to State, county, municipal, or other public agency or combination thereof for the construction of facilities to be used in connection with rehabilitation services for the diagnosis, treatment, and rehabilitation of delinquent youths and youths in danger of becoming delinquent.

(50) *Housing and Urban Development Act of 1968 (including New Communities Act of 1968) (42 U.S.C. 3909)*. This act provides for Federal assistance for the following purposes:

(i) Guarantees, and commitments to guarantee, the bonds, debentures, notes, and other obligations issued by new community developers to help finance new community development projects.

(ii) Amends section 212(a) of the National Housing Act, adding section 236 for "Rental Housing for Lower Income Families" and section 242 "Mortgage Insurance for Nonprofit Hospitals" thereto.

(51) *Public Health Service Act Amendment (Alcoholic and Narcotic Addict Rehabilitation Amendments of 1968) (42 U.S.C. 2681, et seq.)*. This act provides for grants to a public and nonprofit private agency or organization for construction projects consisting of any facilities (including post-hospitalization treatment facilities for the prevention and treatment of alcoholism or treatment of narcotic addicts.)

(52) *Vocational Education Amendments of 1968 (20 U.S.C. 1246)*. This act provides for grants to States for the construction of area vocational education school facilities. The act further provides grants to public educational agencies, organizations, or institutions for construction of residential schools to provide vocational education for the purpose of demonstrating the feasibility and desirability of such schools. The act still further provides grants to State boards, to colleges and universities, to public educational agencies, organizations or institutions to reduce the cost of borrowing funds for the construction of residential schools and dormitories.

(53) *Postal Reorganization Act (39 U.S.C. 410(d)(2))*. This Act provides for

construction, modification, alteration, repair, and other improvements of postal facilities located in leased buildings.

(54) *Airport and Airway Development Act of 1970 (Pub. L. 91–258, section 52(b)(7)).* This Act provides for Federal financial assistance to States and localities for the construction, improvement, or repair of public airports.

(55) (i) *Public Law 91–230.* This Act provides for federal financial assistance to institutions of higher learning for the construction of a National Center on Educational Media and Materials for the Handicapped. The program under this statute expires on July 1, 1971. Public Law 91–230, section 662(1).

(ii) *Education of the Handicapped Act (20 U.S.C. 12326, 1404(a)).* This Act provides for financial assistance to States for construction, expansion, remodeling, or alteration of facilities for the education of handicapped children at the preschool, elementary school, and secondary school levels.

(56) *Housing and Urban Development Act of 1970 (Pub. L. 91–609, section 707(b)).* This Act provides for grants to States and local public agencies to help finance the development of open-space or other land in urban areas for open-space uses. This Act becomes effective on July 1, 1971.

(57) *Developmental Disabilities Services and Facilities Construction Amendments of 1970 (Pub. L. 91–517, section 135(a)(5)).* This Act authorizes grants to States for construction of facilities for the provision of services to persons with developmental disabilities who are unable to pay for such services.

(58) *Rail Passenger Service Act of 1970 (Pub. L. 91–518, section 405(d)).* This statute provides that the National Railroad Passenger Corporation may construct physical facilities necessary to intercity rail passenger operations within the basic national rail passenger system designated by the Secretary of Transportation.

(c) *VA and FHA housing.* In the course of the legislative development of section 107, it was recognized that section 107 would not apply to housing construction for which insurance was issued by the Federal Housing Authority and Veterans' Administration for individual home ownership. Concerning construction under the National Housing Act, Reorganization Plan No. 14 of 1950 applies to construction which is subject to the minimum wage requirements of section 212(a) thereof (12 U.S.C. 1715c).

§ 1926.13 Interpretation of statutory terms.

(a) The terms *construction, alteration,* and *repair* used in section 107 of the Act are also used in section 1 of the Davis-Bacon Act (40 U.S.C. 276a), providing minimum wage protection on Federal construction contracts, and section 1 of the Miller Act (40 U.S.C. 270a), providing performance and payment bond protection on Federal construction contracts. Similarly, the terms *contractor* and *subcontractor* are used in those statutes, as well as in Copeland (Anti-Kickback) Act (40 U.S.C. 276c) and the Contract Work Hours and Safety Standards Act itself, which apply concurrently with the Miller Act and the Davis-Bacon Act on Federal construction contracts and also apply to most federally assisted construction contracts. The use of the same or identical terms in these statutes which apply concurrently with section 107 of the Act have considerable precedential value in ascertaining the coverage of section 107.

(b) It should be noted that section 1 of the Davis-Bacon Act limits minimum wage protection to laborers and mechanics "employed directly" upon the "site of the work." There is no comparable limitation in section 107 of the Act. Section 107 expressly requires as a self-executing condition of each covered contract that no contractor or subcontractor shall require "any laborer or mechanic employed in the performance of the contract to work in surroundings or under working conditions which are unsanitary, hazardous, or dangerous to his health or safety" as these health and safety standards are applied in the rules of the Secretary of Labor.

(c) The term *subcontractor* under section 107 is considered to mean a person who agrees to perform any part of the labor or material requirements of a contract for construction, alteration or repair. Cf. MacEvoy Co. v. United

States, 322 U.S. 102, 108–9 (1944). A person who undertakes to perform a portion of a contract involving the furnishing of supplies or materials will be considered a "subcontractor" under this part and section 107 if the work in question involves the performance of construction work and is to be performed: (1) Directly on or near the construction site, or (2) by the employer for the specific project on a customized basis. Thus, a supplier of materials which will become an integral part of the construction is a "subcontractor" if the supplier fabricates or assembles the goods or materials in question specifically for the construction project and the work involved may be said to be construction activity. If the goods or materials in question are ordinarily sold to other customers from regular inventory, the supplier is not a "subcontractor." Generally, the furnishing of prestressed concrete beams and prestressed structural steel would be considered manufacturing; therefore a supplier of such materials would not be considered a "subcontractor." An example of material supplied "for the specific project on a customized basis" as that phrase is used in this section would be ventilating ducts, fabricated in a shop away from the construction job site and specifically cut for the project according to design specifications. On the other hand, if a contractor buys standard size nails from a foundry, the foundry would not be a covered "subcontractor." Ordinarily a contract for the supplying of construction equipment to a contractor would not, in and of itself, be considered a "subcontractor" for purposes of this part.

§1926.14 **Federal contract for "mixed" types of performance.**

(a) It is the intent of the Congress to provide safety and health protection of Federal, federally financed, or federally assisted construction. See, for example, H. Report No. 91–241, 91st Cong., first session, p. 1 (1969). Thus, it is clear that when a Federal contract calls for mixed types of performance, such as both manufacturing and construction, section 107 would apply to the construction. By its express terms, section 107 applies to a contract which is "for

construction, alteration, and/or repair." Such a contract is not required to be exclusively for such services. The application of the section is not limited to contracts which permit an overall characterization as "construction contracts." The text of section 107 is not so limited.

(b) When the mixed types of performances include both construction and manufacturing, see also §1926.15(b) concerning the relationship between the Walsh-Healey Public Contracts Act and section 107.

§1926.15 **Relationship to the Service Contract Act; Walsh-Healey Public Contracts Act.**

(a) A contract for "construction" is one for nonpersonal service. See, e.g., 41 CFR 1–1.208. Section 2(e) of the Service Contract Act of 1965 requires as a condition of every Federal contract (and bid specification therefor) exceeding $2,500, the "principal purpose" of which is to furnish services to the United States through the use of "service employees," that certain safety and health standards be met. See 29 CFR part 1925, which contains the Department rules concerning these standards. Section 7 of the Service Contract Act provides that the Act shall not apply to "any contract of the United States or District of Columbia for construction, alteration, and/or repair, including painting and decorating of public buildings or public works." It is clear from the legislative history of section 107 that no gaps in coverage between the two statutes are intended.

(b) The Walsh-Healey Public Contracts Act requires that contracts entered into by any Federal agency for the manufacture or furnishing of materials, supplies, articles, and equipment in any amount exceeding $10,000 must contain, among other provisions, a requirement that "no part of such contract will be performed nor will any of the materials, supplies, articles or equipment to be manufactured or furnished under said contract be manufactured or fabricated in any plants, factories, buildings, or surroundings or under working conditions which are unsanitary or hazardous or dangerous to the health and safety of employees engaged in the performance of said contract.'' The rules of the Secretary concerning these standards are published in 41 CFR part 50–204, and express the Secretary of Labor's interpretation and application of section 1(e) of the Walsh-Healey Public Contracts Act to certain particular working conditions. None of the described working conditions are intended to deal with construction activities, although such activities may conceivably be a part of a contract which is subject to the Walsh-Healey Public Contracts Act. Nevertheless, such activities remain subject to the general statutory duty prescribed by section 1(e). Section 103(b) of the Contract Work Hours and Safety Standards Act provides, among other things, that the Act shall not apply to any work required to be done in accordance with the provisions of the Walsh-Healey Public Contracts Act.

§ 1926.16 Rules of construction.

(a) The prime contractor and any subcontractors may make their own arrangements with respect to obligations which might be more appropriately treated on a jobsite basis rather than individually. Thus, for example, the prime contractor and his subcontractors may wish to make an express agreement that the prime contractor or one of the subcontractors will provide all required first-aid or toilet facilities, thus relieving the subcontractors from the actual, but not any legal, responsibility (or, as the case may be, relieving the other subcontractors from this responsibility). In no case shall the prime contractor be relieved of overall responsibility for compliance with the requirements of this part for all work to be performed under the contract.

(b) By contracting for full performance of a contract subject to section 107 of the Act, the prime contractor assumes all obligations prescribed as employer obligations under the standards contained in this part, whether or not he subcontracts any part of the work.

(c) To the extent that a subcontractor of any tier agrees to perform any part of the contract, he also assumes responsibility for complying with the standards in this part with respect to that part. Thus, the prime contractor assumes the entire responsibility under the contract and the subcontractor assumes responsibility with respect to his portion of the work. With respect to subcontracted work, the prime contractor and any subcontractor or subcontractors shall be deemed to have joint responsibility.

(d) Where joint responsibility exists, both the prime contractor and his subcontractor or subcontractors, regardless of tier, shall be considered subject to the enforcement provisions of the Act.

Subpart C—General Safety and Health Provisions

AUTHORITY: Sec. 3704, Contract Work Hours and Safety Standards Act (40 U.S.C. 333); secs. 4, 6, and 8, Occupational Safety and Health Act of 1970 (29 U.S.C. 653, 655, 657); Secretary of Labor's Order No. 12–71 (36 FR 8754), 8–76 (41 FR 25059), 9–83 (48 FR 35736), 6–96 (62 FR 111), or 5–2007 (72 FR 31160) as applicable; and 29 CFR part 1911.

EFFECTIVE DATE NOTE: At 80 FR 25518, May 4, 2015, the authority citation for subpart C to part 1926 was revised, effective Aug. 3, 2015. For the convenience of the user, the revised text is set forth as follows:

AUTHORITY: 40 U.S.C. 3701 et seq.; 29 U.S.C. 653, 655, 657; Secretary of Labor's Order No. 12–71 (36 FR 8754), 8–76 (41 FR 25059), 9–83 (48 FR 35736), 6–96 (62 FR 111), 5–2007 (72 FR 31160), or 1–2012 (77 FR 3912) as applicable; and 29 CFR part 1911.

§ 1926.20 General safety and health provisions.

(a) *Contractor requirements.* (1) Section 107 of the Act requires that it shall be a condition of each contract which is entered into under legislation subject to Reorganization Plan Number 14 of 1950 (64 Stat. 1267), as defined in § 1926.12, and is for construction, alteration, and/or repair, including painting and decorating, that no contractor or subcontractor for any part of the contract work shall require any laborer or mechanic employed in the performance of the contract to work in surroundings or under working conditions which are unsanitary, hazardous, or dangerous to his health or safety.

(b) *Accident prevention responsibilities.* (1) It shall be the responsibility of the employer to initiate and maintain such programs as may be necessary to comply with this part.

(2) Such programs shall provide for frequent and regular inspections of the job sites, materials, and equipment to be made by competent persons designated by the employers.

(3) The use of any machinery, tool, material, or equipment which is not in compliance with any applicable requirement of this part is prohibited. Such machine, tool, material, or equipment shall either be identified as unsafe by tagging or locking the controls to render them inoperable or shall be physically removed from its place of operation.

(4) The employer shall permit only those employees qualified by training or experience to operate equipment and machinery.

(c) The standards contained in this part shall apply with respect to employments performed in a workplace in a State, the District of Columbia, the Commonwealth of Puerto Rico, the Virgin Islands, American Samoa, Guam, Trust Territory of the Pacific Islands, Wake Island, Outer Continental Shelf lands defined in the Outer Continental Shelf Lands Act, Johnston Island, and the Canal Zone.

(d) (1) If a particular standard is specifically applicable to a condition, practice, means, method, operation, or process, it shall prevail over any different general standard which might otherwise be applicable to the same condition, practice, means, method, operation, or process.

(2) On the other hand, any standard shall apply according to its terms to any employment and place of employment in any industry, even though particular standards are also prescribed for the industry to the extent that none of such particular standards applies.

(e) In the event a standard protects on its face a class of persons larger than employees, the standard shall be applicable under this part only to employees and their employment and places of employment.

(f) *Compliance duties owed to each employee*—(1) *Personal protective equipment.* Standards in this part requiring the employer to provide personal protective equipment (PPE), including respirators and other types of PPE, because of hazards to employees impose a separate compliance duty with respect to each employee covered by the requirement. The employer must provide PPE to each employee required to use the PPE, and each failure to provide PPE to an employee may be considered a separate violation.

(2) *Training.* Standards in this part requiring training on hazards and related matters, such as standards requiring that employees receive training or that the employer train employees, provide training to employees, or institute or implement a training program, impose a separate compliance duty with respect to each employee covered by the requirement. The employer must train each affected employee in the manner required by the standard, and each failure to train an employee may be considered a separate violation.

[44 FR 8577, Feb. 9, 1979; 44 FR 20940, Apr. 6, 1979, as amended at 58 FR 35078, June 30, 1993; 73 FR 75588, Dec. 12, 2008]

§1926.21 Safety training and education.

(a) *General requirements.* The Secretary shall, pursuant to section 107(f) of the Act, establish and supervise programs for the education and training of employers and employees in the recognition, avoidance and prevention of unsafe conditions in employments covered by the act.

(b) *Employer responsibility.* (1) The employer should avail himself of the safety and health training programs the Secretary provides.

(2) The employer shall instruct each employee in the recognition and avoidance of unsafe conditions and the regulations applicable to his work environment to control or eliminate any hazards or other exposure to illness or injury.

(3) Employees required to handle or use poisons, caustics, and other harmful substances shall be instructed regarding the safe handling and use, and be made aware of the potential hazards, personal hygiene, and personal protective measures required.

(4) In job site areas where harmful plants or animals are present, employees who may be exposed shall be instructed regarding the potential hazards, and how to avoid injury, and the first aid procedures to be used in the event of injury.

(5) Employees required to handle or use flammable liquids, gases, or toxic materials shall be instructed in the safe handling and use of these materials and made aware of the specific requirements contained in subparts D, F, and other applicable subparts of this part.

(6)(i) All employees required to enter into confined or enclosed spaces shall be instructed as to the nature of the hazards involved, the necessary precautions to be taken, and in the use of protective and emergency equipment required. The employer shall comply with any specific regulations that apply to work in dangerous or potentially dangerous areas.

(ii) For purposes of paragraph (b)(6)(i) of this section, *confined or enclosed space* means any space having a limited means of egress, which is subject to the accumulation of toxic or flammable contaminants or has an oxygen deficient atmosphere. Confined or enclosed spaces include, but are not limited to, storage tanks, process vessels, bins, boilers, ventilation or exhaust ducts, sewers, underground utility vaults, tunnels, pipelines, and open top spaces more than 4 feet in depth such as pits, tubs, vaults, and vessels.

EFFECTIVE DATE NOTE: At 80 FR 25518, May 4, 2015, § 1926.21 was amended by removing paragraph (b)(6), effective Aug. 3, 2015.

§ 1926.22   Recording and reporting of injuries. [Reserved]

§ 1926.23   First aid and medical attention.

First aid services and provisions for medical care shall be made available by the employer for every employee covered by these regulations. Regulations prescribing specific requirements for first aid, medical attention, and emergency facilities are contained in subpart D of this part.

§ 1926.24   Fire protection and prevention.

The employer shall be responsible for the development and maintenance of an effective fire protection and prevention program at the job site throughout all phases of the construction, repair, alteration, or demolition work. The employer shall ensure the availability of the fire protection and suppression equipment required by subpart F of this part.

§ 1926.25   Housekeeping.

(a) During the course of construction, alteration, or repairs, form and scrap lumber with protruding nails, and all other debris, shall be kept cleared from work areas, passageways, and stairs, in and around buildings or other structures.

(b) Combustible scrap and debris shall be removed at regular intervals during the course of construction. Safe means shall be provided to facilitate such removal.

(c) Containers shall be provided for the collection and separation of waste, trash, oily and used rags, and other refuse. Containers used for garbage and other oily, flammable, or hazardous wastes, such as caustics, acids, harmful dusts, etc. shall be equipped with covers. Garbage and other waste shall be disposed of at frequent and regular intervals.

§ 1926.26   Illumination.

Construction areas, aisles, stairs, ramps, runways, corridors, offices, shops, and storage areas where work is in progress shall be lighted with either natural or artificial illumination. The minimum illumination requirements for work areas are contained in subpart D of this part.

§ 1926.27   Sanitation.

Health and sanitation requirements for drinking water are contained in subpart D of this part.

§ 1926.28   Personal protective equipment.

(a) The employer is responsible for requiring the wearing of appropriate personal protective equipment in all operations where there is an exposure to hazardous conditions or where this part indicates the need for using such equipment to reduce the hazards to the employees.

(b) Regulations governing the use, selection, and maintenance of personal protective and lifesaving equipment are described under subpart E of this part.

§1926.29   Acceptable certifications.

(a) *Pressure vessels.* Current and valid certification by an insurance company or regulatory authority shall be deemed as acceptable evidence of safe installation, inspection, and testing of pressure vessels provided by the employer.

(b) *Boilers.* Boilers provided by the employer shall be deemed to be in compliance with the requirements of this part when evidence of current and valid certification by an insurance company or regulatory authority attesting to the safe installation, inspection, and testing is presented.

(c) *Other requirements.* Regulations prescribing specific requirements for other types of pressure vessels and similar equipment are contained in subparts F and O of this part.

§1926.30   Shipbuilding and ship repairing.

(a) *General.* Shipbuilding, ship repairing, alterations, and maintenance performed on ships under Government contract, except naval ship construction, is work subject to the Act.

(b) *Applicable safety and health standards.* For the purpose of work carried out under this section, the safety and health regulations in part 1915 of this title, Shipyard Employment, shall apply.

[44 FR 8577, Feb. 9, 1979; 44 FR 20940, Apr. 6, 1979, as amended at 61 FR 9249, Mar. 7, 1996]

§1926.32   Definitions.

The following definitions shall apply in the application of the regulations in this part:

(a) *Act* means section 107 of the Contract Work Hours and Safety Standards Act, commonly known as the Construction Safety Act (86 Stat. 96; 40 U.S.C. 333).

(b) *ANSI* means American National Standards Institute.

(c) *Approved* means sanctioned, endorsed, accredited, certified, or accepted as satisfactory by a duly constituted and nationally recognized authority or agency.

(d) *Authorized person* means a person approved or assigned by the employer to perform a specific type of duty or duties or to be at a specific location or locations at the jobsite.

(e) *Administration* means the Occupational Safety and Health Administration.

(f) *Competent person* means one who is capable of identifying existing and predictable hazards in the surroundings or working conditions which are unsanitary, hazardous, or dangerous to employees, and who has authorization to take prompt corrective measures to eliminate them.

(g) *Construction work.* For purposes of this section, *Construction work* means work for construction, alteration, and/or repair, including painting and decorating.

(h) *Defect* means any characteristic or condition which tends to weaken or reduce the strength of the tool, object, or structure of which it is a part.

(i) *Designated person* means "authorized person" as defined in paragraph (d) of this section.

(j) *Employee* means every laborer or mechanic under the Act regardless of the contractual relationship which may be alleged to exist between the laborer and mechanic and the contractor or subcontractor who engaged him. "Laborer and mechanic" are not defined in the Act, but the identical terms are used in the Davis-Bacon Act (40 U.S.C. 276a), which provides for minimum wage protection on Federal and federally assisted construction contracts. The use of the same term in a statute which often applies concurrently with section 107 of the Act has considerable precedential value in ascertaining the meaning of "laborer and mechanic" as used in the Act. *Laborer* generally means one who performs manual labor or who labors at an occupation requiring physical strength; *mechanic* generally means a worker skilled with tools. See 18 Comp. Gen. 341.

(k) *Employer* means contractor or subcontractor within the meaning of the Act and of this part.

(l) *Hazardous substance* means a substance which, by reason of being explosive, flammable, poisonous, corrosive, oxidizing, irritating, or otherwise harmful, is likely to cause death or injury.

(m) *Qualified* means one who, by possession of a recognized degree, certificate, or professional standing, or who by extensive knowledge, training, and experience, has successfully demonstrated his ability to solve or resolve problems relating to the subject matter, the work, or the project.

(n) *Safety factor* means the ratio of the ultimate breaking strength of a member or piece of material or equipment to the actual working stress or safe load when in use.

(o) *Secretary* means the Secretary of Labor.

(p) *SAE* means Society of Automotive Engineers.

(q) *Shall* means mandatory.

(r) *Should* means recommended.

(s) *Suitable* means that which fits, and has the qualities or qualifications to meet a given purpose, occasion, condition, function, or circumstance.

[44 FR 8577, Feb. 9, 1979; 44 FR 20940, Apr. 6, 1979, as amended at 58 FR 35078, June 30, 1993]

§ 1926.33 Access to employee exposure and medical records.

NOTE: The requirements applicable to construction work under this section are identical to those set forth at § 1910.1020 of this chapter.

[61 FR 31431, June 20, 1996]

§ 1926.34 Means of egress.

(a) *General.* In every building or structure exits shall be so arranged and maintained as to provide free and unobstructed egress from all parts of the building or structure at all times when it is occupied. No lock or fastening to prevent free escape from the inside of any building shall be installed except in mental, penal, or corrective institutions where supervisory personnel is continually on duty and effective provisions are made to remove occupants in case of fire or other emergency.

(b) *Exit marking.* Exits shall be marked by a readily visible sign. Access to exits shall be marked by readily visible signs in all cases where the exit or way to reach it is not immediately visible to the occupants.

(c) *Maintenance and workmanship.* Means of egress shall be continually maintained free of all obstructions or impediments to full instant use in the case of fire or other emergency.

[58 FR 35083, June 30, 1993]

§ 1926.35 Employee emergency action plans.

(a) *Scope and application.* This section applies to all emergency action plans required by a particular OSHA standard. The emergency action plan shall be in writing (except as provided in the last sentence of paragraph (e)(3) of this section) and shall cover those designated actions employers and employees must take to ensure employee safety from fire and other emergencies.

(b) *Elements.* The following elements, at a minimum, shall be included in the plan:

(1) Emergency escape procedures and emergency escape route assignments;

(2) Procedures to be followed by employees who remain to operate critical plant operations before they evacuate;

(3) Procedures to account for all employees after emergency evacuation has been completed;

(4) Rescue and medical duties for those employees who are to perform them;

(5) The preferred means of reporting fires and other emergencies; and

(6) Names or regular job titles of persons or departments who can be contacted for further information or explanation of duties under the plan.

(c) *Alarm system.* (1) The employer shall establish an employee alarm system which complies with § 1926.159.

(2) If the employee alarm system is used for alerting fire brigade members, or for other purposes, a distinctive signal for each purpose shall be used.

(d) *Evacuation.* The employer shall establish in the emergency action plan the types of evacuation to be used in emergency circumstances.

(e) *Training.* (1) Before implementing the emergency action plan, the employer shall designate and train a sufficient number of persons to assist in the safe and orderly emergency evacuation of employees.

(2) The employer shall review the plan with each employee covered by the plan at the following times:

(i) Initially when the plan is developed,

(ii) Whenever the employee's responsibilities or designated actions under the plan change, and

(iii) Whenever the plan is changed.

(3) The employer shall review with each employee upon initial assignment those parts of the plan which the employee must know to protect the employee in the event of an emergency. The written plan shall be kept at the workplace and made available for employee review. For those employers with 10 or fewer employees the plan may be communicated orally to employees and the employer need not maintain a written plan.

[58 FR 35083, June 30, 1993]

Subpart D—Occupational Health and Environmental Controls

AUTHORITY: Section 107 of the Contract Work Hours and Safety Standards Act (40 U.S.C. 3704); Sections 4, 6, and 8 of the Occupational Safety and Health Act of 1970 (29 U.S.C. 653, 655, and 657); and Secretary of Labor's Order No. 12–71 (36 FR 8754), 8–76 (41 FR 25059), 9–83 (48 FR 35736), 1–90 (55 FR 9033), 6–96 (62 FR 111), 3–2000 (65 FR 50017), 5–2002 (67 FR 65008), 5–2007 (72 FR 31159), 4–2010 (75 FR 55355), or 1–2012 (77 FR 3912) as applicable; and 29 CFR part 1911.

Sections 1926.58, 1926.59, 1926.60, and 1926.65 also issued under 5 U.S.C. 553 and 29 CFR part 1911.

Section 1926.61 also issued under 49 U.S.C. 1801–1819 and 6 U.S.C. 553.

Section 1926.62 also issued under section 1031 of the Housing and Community Development Act of 1992 (42 U.S.C. 4853).

Section 1926.65 also issued under section 126 of the Superfund Amendments and Reauthorization Act of 1986, as amended (reprinted at 29 U.S.C.A. 655 Note), and 5 U.S.C. 553.

§1926.50 Medical services and first aid.

(a) The employer shall insure the availability of medical personnel for advice and consultation on matters of occupational health.

(b) Provisions shall be made prior to commencement of the project for prompt medical attention in case of serious injury.

(c) In the absence of an infirmary, clinic, hospital, or physician, that is reasonably accessible in terms of time and distance to the worksite, which is available for the treatment of injured employees, a person who has a valid certificate in first-aid training from the U.S. Bureau of Mines, the American Red Cross, or equivalent training that can be verified by documentary evidence, shall be available at the worksite to render first aid.

(d)(1) First aid supplies shall be easily accessible when required.

(2) The contents of the first aid kit shall be placed in a weatherproof container with individual sealed packages for each type of item, and shall be checked by the employer before being sent out on each job and at least weekly on each job to ensure that the expended items are replaced.

(e) Proper equipment for prompt transportation of the injured person to a physician or hospital, or a communication system for contacting necessary ambulance service, shall be provided.

(f) In areas where 911 is not available, the telephone numbers of the physicians, hospitals, or ambulances shall be conspicuously posted.

(g) Where the eyes or body of any person may be exposed to injurious corrosive materials, suitable facilities for quick drenching or flushing of the eyes and body shall be provided within the work area for immediate emergency use.

APPENDIX A TO §1926.50—FIRST AID KITS (NON-MANDATORY)

First aid supplies are required to be easily accessible under paragraph §1926.50(d)(1). An example of the minimal contents of a generic first aid kit is described in American National Standard (ANSI) Z308.1–1978 "Minimum Requirements for Industrial Unit-Type First-aid Kits". The contents of the kit listed in the ANSI standard should be adequate for small work sites. When larger operations or multiple operations are being conducted at the same location, employers should determine the need for additional first aid kits at the worksite, additional types of first aid equipment and supplies and additional quantities and types of supplies and equipment in the first aid kits.

In a similar fashion, employers who have unique or changing first-aid needs in their workplace may need to enhance their first-aid kits. The employer can use the OSHA 300 log, OSHA 301 log, or other reports to identify these unique problems. Consultation from the local fire/rescue department, appropriate medical professional, or local emergency room may be helpful to employers in these circumstances. By assessing the specific needs of their workplace, employers can ensure that reasonably anticipated supplies are available. Employers should assess the specific needs of their worksite periodically and augment the first aid kit appropriately. If it is reasonably anticipated employees will be exposed to blood or other potentially infectious materials while using first-aid supplies, employers should provide personal protective equipment (PPE). Appropriate PPE includes gloves, gowns, face shields, masks and eye protection (see "Occupational Exposure to Blood borne Pathogens", 29 CFR 1910.1030(d)(3)) (56 FR 64175).

[44 FR 8577, Feb. 9, 1979; 44 FR 20940, Apr. 6, 1979, as amended at 49 FR 18295, Apr. 30, 1984; 58 FR 35084, June 30, 1993; 61 FR 5510, Feb. 13, 1996; 63 FR 33469, June 18, 1998; 76 FR 80740, Dec. 27, 2011]

§ 1926.51   Sanitation.

(a) *Potable water.* (1) An adequate supply of potable water shall be provided in all places of employment.

(2) Portable containers used to dispense drinking water shall be capable of being tightly closed, and equipped with a tap. Water shall not be dipped from containers.

(3) Any container used to distribute drinking water shall be clearly marked as to the nature of its contents and not used for any other purpose.

(4) The common drinking cup is prohibited.

(5) Where single service cups (to be used but once) are supplied, both a sanitary container for the unused cups and a receptacle for disposing of the used cups shall be provided.

(6) *Potable water* means water that meets the standards for drinking purposes of the State or local authority having jurisdiction, or water that meets the quality standards prescribed by the U.S. Environmental Protection Agency's National Primary Drinking Water Regulations (40 CFR part 141).

(b) *Nonpotable water.* (1) Outlets for nonpotable water, such as water for industrial or firefighting purposes only, shall be identified by signs meeting the requirements of subpart G of this part, to indicate clearly that the water is unsafe and is not to be used for drinking, washing, or cooking purposes.

(2) There shall be no cross-connection, open or potential, between a system furnishing potable water and a system furnishing nonpotable water.

(c) *Toilets at construction jobsites.* (1) Toilets shall be provided for employees according to the following table:

TABLE D–1

Number of employees	Minimum number of facilities
20 or less	1.
20 or more	1 toilet seat and 1 urinal per 40 workers.
200 or more	1 toilet seat and 1 urinal per 50 workers.

(2) Under temporary field conditions, provisions shall be made to assure not less than one toilet facility is available.

(3) Job sites, not provided with a sanitary sewer, shall be provided with one of the following toilet facilities unless prohibited by local codes:

(i) Privies (where their use will not contaminate ground or surface water);

(ii) Chemical toilets;

(iii) Recirculating toilets;

(iv) Combustion toilets.

(4) The requirements of this paragraph (c) for sanitation facilities shall not apply to mobile crews having transportation readily available to nearby toilet facilities.

(d) *Food handling.* (1) All employees' food service facilities and operations shall meet the applicable laws, ordinances, and regulations of the jurisdictions in which they are located.

(2) All employee food service facilities and operations shall be carried out in accordance with sound hygienic principles. In all places of employment where all or part of the food service is provided, the food dispensed shall be wholesome, free from spoilage, and shall be processed, prepared, handled, and stored in such a manner as to be protected against contamination.

(e) *Temporary sleeping quarters.* When temporary sleeping quarters are provided, they shall be heated, ventilated, and lighted.

(f) *Washing facilities.* (1) The employer shall provide adequate washing facilities for employees engaged in the application of paints, coating, herbicides, or insecticides, or in other operations where contaminants may be harmful to the employees. Such facilities shall be in near proximity to the worksite and shall be so equipped as to enable employees to remove such substances.

(2) *General.* Washing facilities shall be maintained in a sanitary condition.

(3) *Lavatories.* (i) Lavatories shall be made available in all places of employment. The requirements of this subdivision do not apply to mobile crews or to normally unattended work locations if employees working at these locations have transportation readily available to nearby washing facilities which meet the other requirements of this paragraph.

(ii) Each lavatory shall be provided with hot and cold running water, or tepid running water.

(iii) Hand soap or similar cleansing agents shall be provided.

(iv) Individual hand towels or sections thereof, of cloth or paper, air blowers or clean individual sections of continuous cloth toweling, convenient to the lavatories, shall be provided.

(4) *Showers.* (i) Whenever showers are required by a particular standard, the showers shall be provided in accordance with paragraphs (f)(4) (ii) through (v) of this section.

(ii) One shower shall be provided for each 10 employees of each sex, or numerical fraction thereof, who are required to shower during the same shift.

(iii) Body soap or other appropriate cleansing agents convenient to the showers shall be provided as specified in paragraph (f)(3)(iii) of this section.

(iv) Showers shall be provided with hot and cold water feeding a common discharge line.

(v) Employees who use showers shall be provided with individual clean towels.

(g) *Eating and drinking areas.* No employee shall be allowed to consume food or beverages in a toilet room nor in any area exposed to a toxic material.

(h) *Vermin control.* Every enclosed workplace shall be so constructed, equipped, and maintained, so far as reasonably practicable, as to prevent the entrance or harborage of rodents, insects, and other vermin. A continuing and effective extermination program shall be instituted where their presence is detected.

(i) *Change rooms.* Whenever employees are required by a particular standard to wear protective clothing because of the possibility of contamination with toxic materials, change rooms equipped with storage facilities for street clothes and separate storage facilities for the protective clothing shall be provided.

[44 FR 8577, Feb. 9, 1979; 44 FR 20940, Apr. 6, 1979, as amended at 58 FR 35084, June 30, 1993; 76 FR 33611, June 8, 2011]

§1926.52 Occupational noise exposure.

(a) Protection against the effects of noise exposure shall be provided when the sound levels exceed those shown in Table D–2 of this section when measured on the A-scale of a standard sound level meter at slow response.

(b) When employees are subjected to sound levels exceeding those listed in Table D–2 of this section, feasible administrative or engineering controls shall be utilized. If such controls fail to reduce sound levels within the levels of the table, personal protective equipment as required in subpart E, shall be provided and used to reduce sound levels within the levels of the table.

(c) If the variations in noise level involve maxima at intervals of 1 second or less, it is to be considered continuous.

(d)(1) In all cases where the sound levels exceed the values shown herein, a continuing, effective hearing conservation program shall be administered.

TABLE D–2—PERMISSIBLE NOISE EXPOSURES

Duration per day, hours	Sound level dBA slow response
8	90
6	92
4	95
3	97
2	100
1½	102
1	105
½	110
¼ or less	115

(2)(i) When the daily noise exposure is composed of two or more periods of noise exposure of different levels, their combined effect should be considered, rather than the individual effect of each. Exposure to different levels for various periods of time shall be computed according to the formula set forth in paragraph (d)(2)(ii) of this section.

(ii) $F_e = (T_1/L_1)+(T_2/L_2)+\cdots+(T_n/L_n)$

Where:

F_e = The equivalent noise exposure factor.
T = The period of noise exposure at any essentially constant level.
L = The duration of the permissible noise exposure at the constant level (from Table D–2).

If the value of F_e exceeds unity (1) the exposure exceeds permissible levels.

(iii) A sample computation showing an application of the formula in paragraph (d)(2)(ii) of this section is as follows. An employee is exposed at these levels for these periods:

110 db A ¼ hour.
100 db A ½ hour.
90 db A 1½ hours.

$F_e = (¼/½)+(½/2)+(1½/8)$
$F_e = 0.500+0.25+0.188$
$F_e = 0.938$

Since the value of F_e does not exceed unity, the exposure is within permissible limits.

(e) Exposure to impulsive or impact noise should not exceed 140 dB peak sound pressure level.

§ 1926.53 Ionizing radiation.

(a) In construction and related activities involving the use of sources of ionizing radiation, the pertinent provisions of the Nuclear Regulatory Commission's Standards for Protection Against Radiation (10 CFR part 20), relating to protection against occupational radiation exposure, shall apply.

(b) Any activity which involves the use of radioactive materials or X-rays, whether or not under license from the Nuclear Regulatory Commission, shall be performed by competent persons specially trained in the proper and safe operation of such equipment. In the case of materials used under Commission license, only persons actually licensed, or competent persons under di-

rection and supervision of the licensee, shall perform such work.

(c)–(r) [Reserved]

NOTE: The requirements applicable to construction work under paragraphs (c) through (r) of this section are identical to those set forth at paragraphs (a) through (p) of § 1910.1096 of this chapter.

[44 FR 8577, Feb. 9, 1979; 44 FR 20940, Apr. 6, 1979, as amended at 61 FR 5510, Feb. 13, 1996; 61 FR 31431, June 20, 1996]

§ 1926.54 Nonionizing radiation.

(a) Only qualified and trained employees shall be assigned to install, adjust, and operate laser equipment.

(b) Proof of qualification of the laser equipment operator shall be available and in possession of the operator at all times.

(c) Employees, when working in areas in which a potential exposure to direct or reflected laser light greater than 0.005 watts (5 milliwatts) exists, shall be provided with antilaser eye protection devices as specified in subpart E of this part.

(d) Areas in which lasers are used shall be posted with standard laser warning placards.

(e) Beam shutters or caps shall be utilized, or the laser turned off, when laser transmission is not actually required. When the laser is left unattended for a substantial period of time, such as during lunch hour, overnight, or at change of shifts, the laser shall be turned off.

(f) Only mechanical or electronic means shall be used as a detector for guiding the internal alignment of the laser.

(g) The laser beam shall not be directed at employees.

(h) When it is raining or snowing, or when there is dust or fog in the air, the operation of laser systems shall be prohibited where practicable; in any event, employees shall be kept out of range of the area of source and target during such weather conditions.

(i) Laser equipment shall bear a label to indicate maximum output.

(j) Employees shall not be exposed to light intensities above:

(1) Direct staring: 1 micro-watt per square centimeter;

(2) Incidental observing: 1 milliwatt per square centimeter;

(3) Diffused reflected light: 2½ watts per square centimeter.

(k) Laser unit in operation should be set up above the heads of the employees, when possible.

(l) Employees shall not be exposed to microwave power densities in excess of 10 milliwatts per square centimeter.

§1926.55 Gases, vapors, fumes, dusts, and mists.

(a) Exposure of employees to inhalation, ingestion, skin absorption, or contact with any material or substance at a concentration above those specified in the "Threshold Limit Values of Airborne Contaminants for 1970" of the American Conference of Governmental Industrial Hygienists, shall be avoided. See appendix A to this section.

(b) To achieve compliance with paragraph (a) of this section, administrative or engineering controls must first be implemented whenever feasible. When such controls are not feasible to achieve full compliance, protective equipment or other protective measures shall be used to keep the exposure of employees to air contaminants within the limits prescribed in this section. Any equipment and technical measures used for this purpose must first be approved for each particular use by a competent industrial hygienist or other technically qualified person. Whenever respirators are used, their use shall comply with §1926.103.

(c) Paragraphs (a) and (b) of this section do not apply to the exposure of employees to airborne asbestos, tremolite, anthophyllite, or actinolite dust. Whenever any employee is exposed to airborne asbestos, tremolite, anthophyllite, or actinolite dust, the requirements of §1910.1101 or §1926.58 of this title shall apply.

(d) Paragraphs (a) and (b) of this section do not apply to the exposure of employees to formaldehyde. Whenever any employee is exposed to formaldehyde, the requirements of §1910.1048 of this title shall apply.

APPENDIX A TO §1926.55—1970 AMERICAN CONFERENCE OF GOVERNMENTAL INDUSTRIAL HYGIENISTS' THRESHOLD LIMIT VALUES OF AIRBORNE CONTAMINANTS

THRESHOLD LIMIT VALUES OF AIRBORNE CONTAMINANTS FOR CONSTRUCTION

Substance	CAS No. [d]	ppm [a]	mg/m³ [b]	Skin Designation
Abate; see Temephos.				
Acetaldehyde	75–07–0	200	360	—
Acetic acid	64–19–7	10	25	—
Acetic anhydride	108–24–7	5	20	—
Acetone	67–64–1	1000	2400	—
Acetonitrile	75–05–8	40	70	—
2-Acetylaminofluorine; see §1926.1114	53–96–3			
Acetylene	74–86–2	E		
Acetylene dichloride; see 1,2-Dichloroethylene.				
Acetylene tetrabromide	79–27–6	1	14	—
Acrolein	107–02–8	0.1	0.25	—
Acrylamide	79–06–1	—	0.3	X
Acrylonitrile; see §1926.1145	107–13–1			
Aldrin	309–00–2	—	0.25	X
Allyl alcohol	107–18–6	2	5	X
Allyl chloride	107–05–1	1	3	—
Allyl glycidyl ether (AGE)	106–92–3	(C)10	(C)45	—
Allyl propyl disulfide	2179–59–1	2	12	—
alpha-Alumina	1344–28–1			
Total dust		—		—
Respirable fraction		—		—
Alundum; see alpha-Alumina.				
4-Aminodiphenyl; see §1926.1111	92–67–1			
2-Aminoethanol; see Ethanolamine.				
2-Aminopyridine	504–29–0	0.5	2	—
Ammonia	7664–41–7	50	35	—

37

THRESHOLD LIMIT VALUES OF AIRBORNE CONTAMINANTS FOR CONSTRUCTION—Continued

Substance	CAS No.[d]	ppm[a]	mg/m[3][b]	Skin Designation
Ammonium sulfamate	7773–06–0			
Total dust		—	15	—
Respirable fraction		—	5	—
n-Amyl acetate	628–63–7	100	525	—
sec-Amyl acetate	626–38–0	125	650	—
Aniline and homologs	62–53–3	5	19	X
Anisidine (o-, p-isomers)	29191–52–4	—	0.5	X
Antimony and compounds (as Sb)	7440–36–0	—	0.5	—
ANTU (alpha Naphthylthiourea)	86–88–4	—	0.3	—
Argon	7440–37–1	E		
Arsenic, inorganic compounds (as As); see § 1926.1118	7440–38–2	—	—	—
Arsenic, organic compounds (as As)	7440–38–2	—	0.5	—
Arsine	7784–42–1	0.05	0.2	—
Asbestos; see 1926.58.				
Azinphos-methyl	86–50–0	—	0.2	X
Barium, soluble compounds (as Ba)	7440–39–3	—	0.5	—
Benzene[g]; see § 1926.1128	71–43–2			
Benzidine; see § 1926.1110	92–87–5			
p-Benzoquinone; see Quinone.				
Benzo(a)pyrene; see Coal tar pitch volatiles.				
Benzoyl peroxide	94–36–0	—	5	—
Benzyl chloride	100–44–7	1	5	—
Beryllium and beryllium compounds (as Be)	7440–41–7	—	0.002	—
Biphenyl; see Diphenyl.				
Bisphenol A; see Diglycidyl ether.				
Boron oxide	1303–86–2			
Total dust		—	15	—
Boron tribromide	10294–33–4	1	10	—
Boron trifluoride	7637–07–2	(C)1	(C)3	—
Bromine	7726–95–6	0.1	0.7	—
Bromine pentafluoride	7789–30–2	0.1	0.7	—
Bromoform	75–25–2	0.5	5	X
Butadiene (1,3-Butadiene); see 29 CFR 1910.1051; 29 CFR 1910.19(l)	106–99–0	STEL 1 ppm/5 ppm		—
Butanethiol; see Butyl mercaptan.				
2-Butanone (Methyl ethyl ketone)	78–93–3	200	590	—
2-Butoxyethanol	111–76–2	50	240	X
n-Butyl-acetate	123–86–4	150	710	—
sec-Butyl acetate	105–46–4	200	950	—
tert-Butyl acetate	540–88–5	200	950	—
n-Butyl alcohol	71–36–3	100	300	—
sec-Butyl alcohol	78–92–2	150	450	—
tert-Butyl alcohol	75–65–0	100	300	—
Butylamine	109–73–9	(C)5	(C)15	X
tert-Butyl chromate (as CrO3); see 1926.1126[n]	1189–85–1			
n-Butyl glycidyl ether (BGE)	2426–08–6	50	270	—
Butyl mercaptan	109–79–5	0.5	1.5	—
p-tert-Butyltoluene	98–51–1	10	60	—
Cadmium (as Cd); see 1926.1127	7440–43–9			
Calcium carbonate	1317–65–3			
Total dust		—		—
Respirable fraction		—		—
Calcium oxide	1305–78–8	—	5	—
Calcium sulfate	7778–18–9			
Total dust		—	15	—
Respirable fraction		—	5	—
Camphor, synthetic	76–22–2	—	2	—

THRESHOLD LIMIT VALUES OF AIRBORNE CONTAMINANTS FOR CONSTRUCTION—Continued

Substance	CAS No. [d]	ppm [a]	mg/m^3 [b]	Skin Designation
Carbaryl (Sevin)	63–25–2	—	5	—
Carbon black	1333–86–4	—	3.5	—
Carbon dioxide	124–38–9	5000	9000	—
Carbon disulfide	75–15–0	20	60	X
Carbon monoxide	630–08–0	50	55	—
Carbon tetrachloride	56–23–5	10	65	X
Cellulose	9004–34–6			
Total dust		—		—
Respirable fraction		—		—
Chlordane	57–74–9	—	0.5	X
Chlorinated camphene	8001–35–2	—	0.5	X
Chlorinated diphenyl oxide	55720–99–5	—	0.5	—
Chlorine	7782–50–5	1	3	—
Chlorine dioxide	10049–04–4	0.1	0.3	—
Chlorine trifluoride	7790–91–2	(C)0.1	(C)0.4	—
Chloroacetaldehyde	107–20–0	(C)1	(C)3	—
a-Chloroacetophenone (Phenacyl chloride)	532–27–4	0.05	0.3	—
Chlorobenzene	108–90–7	75	350	—
o-Chlorobenzylidene malononitrile	2698–41–1	0.05	0.4	—
Chlorobromomethane	74–97–5	200	1050	—
2-Chloro-1,3-butadiene; see beta-Chloroprene.				
Chlorodiphenyl (42% Chlorine) (PCB)	53469–21–9	—	1	X
Chlorodiphenyl (54% Chlorine) (PCB)	11097–69–1	—	0.5	X
1-Chloro,2,3-epoxypropane; see Epichlorohydrin.				
2-Chloroethanol; see Ethylene chlorohydrin.				
Chloroethylene; see Vinyl chloride.				
Chloroform (Trichloromethane)	67–66–3	(C)50	(C)240	—
bis(Chloromethyl) ether; see §1926.1108	542–88–1			
Chloromethyl methyl ether; see §1926.1106	107–30–2			
1-Chloro-1-nitropropane	600–25–9	20	100	—
Chloropicrin	76–06–2	0.1	0.7	—
beta-Chloroprene	126–99–8	25	90	X
Chromium (II) compounds.				
(as Cr)	7440–47–3	—	0.5	—
Chromium (III) compounds.				
(as Cr)	7440–47–3	—	0.5	—
Chromium (VI) compounds; See 1926.1126 °.				
Chromium metal and insol. salts (as Cr)	7440–47–3	—	1	—
Chrysene; see Coal tar pitch volatiles.				
Coal tar pitch volatiles (benzene soluble fraction), anthracene, BaP, phenanthrene, acridine, chrysene, pyrene	65996–93–2	—	0.2	—
Cobalt metal, dust, and fume (as Co)	7440–48–4	—	0.1	—
Coke oven emissions; see §1926.1129.				
Copper	7440–50–8			
Fume (as Cu)		—	0.1	—
Dusts and mists (as Cu)		—	1	—
Corundum; see Emery.				
Cotton dust (raw)		—	1	
Crag herbicide (Sesone)	136–78–7			
Total dust		—		—
Respirable fraction		—		—
Cresol, all isomers	1319–77–3	5	22	X
Crotonaldehyde	123–73–9;	2	6	

39

THRESHOLD LIMIT VALUES OF AIRBORNE CONTAMINANTS FOR CONSTRUCTION—Continued

Substance	CAS No. [d]	ppm [a]	mg/m³ [b]	Skin Designation
	4170–30–3			
Cumene	98–82–8	50	245	X
Cyanides (as CN)	Varies with Compound	—	5	X
Cyanogen	460–19–5	10	—	—
Cyclohexane	110–82–7	300	1050	—
Cyclohexanol	108–93–0	50	200	—
Cyclohexanone	108–94–1	50	200	—
Cyclohexene	110–83–8	300	1015	—
Cyclonite	121–82–4	—	1.5	X
Cyclopentadiene	542–92–7	75	200	—
DDT, see Dichlorodiphenyltrichloroethane.				
DDVP, see Dichlorvos.				
2,4-D (Dichlorophenoxyacetic acid)	94–75–7	—	10	—
Decaborane	17702–41–9	0.05	0.3	X
Demeton (Systox)	8065–48–3	—	0.1	X
Diacetone alcohol (4-Hydroxy-4-methyl-2-pentanone)	123–42–2	50	240	—
1,2-Diaminoethane; see Ethylenediamine.				
Diazomethane	334–88–3	0.2	0.4	—
Diborane	19287–45–7	0.1	0.1	—
1,2-Dibromo-3-chloropropane (DBCP); see § 1926.1144	96–12–8			
1,2-Dibromoethane; see Ethylene dibromide.				
Dibutyl phosphate	107–66–4	1	5	—
Dibutyl phthalate	84–74–2	—	5	—
Dichloroacetylene	7572–29–4	(C)0.1	(C)0.4	—
o-Dichlorobenzene	95–50–1	(C)50	(C)300	—
p-Dichlorobenzene	106–46–7	75	450	—
3,3′-Dichlorobenzidine; see § 1926.1107	91–94–1			
Dichlorodifluoromethane	75–71–8	1000	4950	—
1,3-Dichloro-5,5-dimethyl hydantoin	118–52–5	—	0.2	—
Dichlorodiphenyltrichloroethane (DDT)	50–29–3	—	1	X
1,1-Dichloroethane	75–34–3	100	400	—
1,2-Dichloroethane; see Ethylene dichloride.				
1,2-Dichloroethylene	540–59–0	200	790	—
Dichloroethyl ether	111–44–4	(C)15	(C)90	X
Dichloromethane; see Methylene chloride.				
Dichloromonofluoromethane	75–43–4	1000	4200	—
1,1-Dichloro-1-nitroethane	594–72–9	(C)10	(C)60	—
1,2-Dichloropropane; see Propylene dichloride.				
Dichlorotetrafluoroethane	76–14–2	1000	7000	—
Dichlorvos (DDVP)	62–73–7	—	1	X
Dieldrin	60–57–1	—	0.25	X
Diethylamine	109–89–7	25	75	—
2-Diethylaminoethanol	100–37–8	10	50	X
Diethylene triamine	111–40–0	(C)10	(C)42	X
Diethyl ether; see Ethyl ether.				
Difluorodibromomethane	75–61–6	100	860	—
Diglycidyl ether (DGE)	2238–07–5	(C)0.5	(C)2.8	—
Dihydroxybenzene; see Hydroquinone.				
Diisobutyl ketone	108–83–8	50	290	—
Diisopropylamine	108–18–9	5	20	X
4-Dimethylaminoazobenzene; see § 1926.1115	60–11–7			

40

THRESHOLD LIMIT VALUES OF AIRBORNE CONTAMINANTS FOR CONSTRUCTION—Continued

Substance	CAS No. [d]	ppm [a]	mg/m³ [b]	Skin Designation
Dimethoxymethane; see Methylal.				
Dimethyl acetamide	127–19–5	10	35	X
Dimethylamine	124–40–3	10	18	—
Dimethylaminobenzene; see Xylidine.				
Dimethylaniline (N,N-Dimethylaniline)	121–69–7	5	25	X
Dimethylbenzene; see Xylene.				
Dimethyl-1,2-dibromo- 2,2-dichloroethyl phosphate	300–76–5	—	3	—
Dimethylformamide	68–12–2	10	30	X
2,6-Dimethyl-4-heptanone; see Diisobutyl ketone.				
1,1-Dimethylhydrazine	57–14–7	0.5	1	X
Dimethylphthalate	131–11–3	—	5	—
Dimethyl sulfate	77–78–3	1	5	X
Dinitrobenzene (all isomers)			1	X
(ortho)	528–29–0			
(meta)	99–65–0			
(para)	100–25–4			
Dinitro-o-cresol	534–52–1	—	0.2	X
Dinitrotoluene	25321–14–6	—	1.5	X
Dioxane (Diethylene dioxide)	123–91–1	100	360	X
Diphenyl (Biphenyl)	92–52–4	0.2	1	—
Diphenylamine	122–39–4	—	10	—
Diphenylmethane diisocyanate; see Methylene bisphenyl isocyanate.				
Dipropylene glycol methyl ether	34590–94–8	100	600	X
Di-sec octyl phthalate (Di-(2-ethylhexyl) phthalate)	117–81–7	—	5	—
Emery	12415–34–8			
Total dust		—		—
Respirable fraction		—		—
Endosulfan	115–29–7	—	0.1	X
Endrin	72–20–8	—	0.1	X
Epichlorohydrin	106–89–8	5	19	X
EPN	2104–64–5	—	0.5	X
1,2-Epoxypropane; see Propylene oxide.				
2,3-Epoxy-1-propanol; see Glycidol.				
Ethane	74–84–0	E		
Ethanethiol; see Ethyl mercaptan.				
Ethanolamine	141–43–5	3	6	—
2-Ethoxyethanol (Cellosolve)	110–80–5	200	740	X
2-Ethoxyethyl acetate (Cellosolve acetate)	111–15–9	100	540	X
Ethyl acetate	141–78–6	400	1400	—
Ethyl acrylate	140–88–5	25	100	X
Ethyl alcohol (Ethanol)	64–17–5	1000	1900	—
Ethylamine	75–04–7	10	18	—
Ethyl amyl ketone (5-Methyl-3-heptanone)	541–85–5	25	130	—
Ethyl benzene	100–41–4	100	435	—
Ethyl bromide	74–96–4	200	890	—
Ethyl butyl ketone (3-Heptanone)	106–35–4	50	230	—
Ethyl chloride	75–00–3	1000	2600	—
Ethyl ether	60–29–7	400	1200	—
Ethyl formate	109–94–4	100	300	—
Ethyl mercaptan	75–08–1	0.5	1	—
Ethyl silicate	78–10–4	100	850	—
Ethylene	74–85–1	E		
Ethylene chlorohydrin	107–07–3	5	16	X
Ethylenediamine	107–15–3	10	25	—
Ethylene dibromide	106–93–4	(C)25	(C)190	X

THRESHOLD LIMIT VALUES OF AIRBORNE CONTAMINANTS FOR CONSTRUCTION—Continued

Substance	CAS No. [d]	ppm [a]	mg/m³ [b]	Skin Designation
Ethylene dichloride (1,2-Dichloroethane)	107–06–2	50	200	—
Ethylene glycol dinitrate	628–96–6	(C)0.2	(C)1	X
Ethylene glycol methyl acetate; see Methyl cellosolve acetate.				
Ethyleneimine; see § 1926.1112	151–56–4			
Ethylene oxide; see § 1926.1147	75–21–8			
Ethylidene chloride; see 1,1-Dichloroethane.				
N-Ethylmorpholine	100–74–3	20	94	X
Ferbam	14484–64–1			
Total dust		—	15	—
Ferrovanadium dust	12604–58–9	—	1	
Fibrous Glass.				
Total dust				—
Respirable fraction				—
Fluorides (as F)	Varies with compound	—	2.5	—
Fluorine	7782–41–4	0.1	0.2	—
Fluorotrichloromethane (Trichlorofluoromethane)	75–69–4	1000	5600	
Formaldehyde; see § 1926.1148	50–00–0			
Formic acid	64–18–6	5	9	—
Furfural	98–01–1	5	20	X
Furfuryl alcohol	98–00–0	50	200	—
Gasoline	8006–61–9		A³	—
Glycerin (mist)	56–81–5			
Total dust		—		—
Respirable fraction		—		—
Glycidol	556–52–5	50	150	—
Glycol monoethyl ether; see 2-Ethoxyethanol.				
Graphite, natural, respirable dust	7782–42–5	(2)	(2)	(2)
Graphite, synthetic.				
Total dust		—		—
Respirable fraction		—		—
Guthion; see Azinphos methyl.				
Gypsum	13397–24–5			
Total dust		—		—
Respirable fraction		—		—
Hafnium	7440–58–6	—	0.5	—
Helium	7440–59–7	E		
Heptachlor	76–44–8	—	0.5	X
Heptane (n-Heptane)	142–82–5	500	2000	—
Hexachloroethane	67–72–1	1	10	X
Hexachloronaphthalene	1335–87–1	—	0.2	X
n-Hexane	110–54–3	500	1800	—
2-Hexanone (Methyl n-butyl ketone)	591–78–6	100	410	—
Hexone (Methyl isobutyl ketone)	108–10–1	100	410	—
sec-Hexyl acetate	108–84–9	50	300	—
Hydrazine	302–01–2	1	1.3	X
Hydrogen	1333–74–0	E		
Hydrogen bromide	10035–10–6	3	10	—
Hydrogen chloride	7647–01–0	(C)5	(C)7	—
Hydrogen cyanide	74–90–8	10	11	X
Hydrogen fluoride (as F)	7664–39–3	3	2	—
Hydrogen peroxide	7722–84–1	1	1.4	—
Hydrogen selenide (as Se)	7783–07–5	0.05	.02	—
Hydrogen sulfide	7783–06–4	10	15	—
Hydroquinone	123–31–9	—	2	—
Indene	95–13–6	10	45	—
Indium and compounds (as In)	7440–74–6	—	0.1	—

THRESHOLD LIMIT VALUES OF AIRBORNE CONTAMINANTS FOR CONSTRUCTION—Continued

Substance	CAS No.[d]	ppm[a]	mg/m$^{3\,b}$	Skin Designation
Iodine	7553–56–2	(C)0.1	(C)1	—
Iron oxide fume	1309–37–1	—	10	—
Iron salts (soluble) (as Fe)	Varies with compound	—	1	—
Isoamyl acetate	123–92–2	100	525	—
Isoamyl alcohol (primary and secondary)	123–51–3	100	360	—
Isobutyl acetate	110–19–0	150	700	—
Isobutyl alcohol	78–83–1	100	300	—
Isophorone	78–59–1	25	140	—
Isopropyl acetate	108–21–4	250	950	—
Isopropyl alcohol	67–63–0	400	980	—
Isopropylamine	75–31–0	5	12	—
Isopropyl ether	108–20–3	500	2100	—
Isopropyl glycidyl ether (IGE)	4016–14–2	50	240	—
Kaolin	1332–58–7			
Total dust		—		—
Respirable fraction		—		—
Ketene	463–51–4	0.5	0.9	—
Lead, inorganic (as Pb); see 1926.62 ..	7439–92–1			
Limestone	1317–65–3			
Total dust		—		—
Respirable fraction		—		—
Lindane	58–89–9	—	0.5	X
Lithium hydride	7580–67–8	—	0.025	—
L.P.G. (Liquefied petroleum gas)	68476–85–7	1000	1800	—
Magnesite	546–93–0			
Total dust		—		—
Respirable fraction		—		—
Magnesium oxide fume	1309–48–4			
Total particulate		15	—	
Malathion	121–75–5			
Total dust		—	15	X
Maleic anhydride	108–31–6	0.25		
Manganese compounds (as Mn)	7439–96–5	—	(C)5	—
Manganese fume (as Mn)	7439–96–5	—	(C)5	—
Marble	1317–65–3			
Total dust		—		—
Respirable fraction		—		—
Mercury (aryl and inorganic)(as Hg)	7439–97–6		0.1	X
Mercury (organo) alkyl compounds (as Hg)	7439–97–6	—	0.01	X
Mercury (vapor) (as Hg)	7439–97–6	—	0.1	X
Mesityl oxide	141–79–7	25	100	—
Methane	74–82–8	E		
Methanethiol; see Methyl mercaptan.				
Methoxychlor	72–43–5			
Total dust		—	15	—
2-Methoxyethanol (Methyl cellosolve) ...	109–86–4	25	80	X
2-Methoxyethyl acetate (Methyl cellosolve acetate)	110–49–6	25	120	X
Methyl acetate	79–20–9	200	610	—
Methyl acetylene (Propyne)	74–99–7	1000	1650	—
Methyl acetylene-propadiene mixture (MAPP)		1000	1800	—
Methyl acrylate	96–33–3	10	35	X
Methylal (Dimethoxy-methane)	109–87–5	1000	3100	—
Methyl alcohol	67–56–1	200	260	—
Methylamine	74–89–5	10	12	—
Methyl amyl alcohol; see Methyl isobutyl carbinol.				
Methyl n-amyl ketone	110–43–0	100	465	—

43

THRESHOLD LIMIT VALUES OF AIRBORNE CONTAMINANTS FOR CONSTRUCTION—Continued

Substance	CAS No. [d]	ppm [a]	mg/m³ [b]	Skin Designation
Methyl bromide	74–83–9	(C)20	(C)80	X
Methyl butyl ketone; see 2-Hexanone.				
Methyl cellosolve; see 2-Methoxyethanol.				
Methyl cellosolve acetate; see 2-Methoxyethyl acetate.				
Methylene chloride; see § 1910.1052.				
Methyl chloroform (1,1,1-Trichloroethane)	71–55–6	350	1900	—
Methylcyclohexane	108–87–2	500	2000	—
Methylcyclohexanol	25639–42–3	100	470	—
o-Methylcyclohexanone	583–60–8	100	460	X
Methylene chloride	75–09–2	500	1740	—
Methylenedianiline (MDA)	101–77–9			
Methyl ethyl ketone (MEK); see 2-Butanone.				
Methyl formate	107–31–3	100	250	—
Methyl hydrazine (Monomethyl hydrazine)	60–34–4	(C)0.2	(C)0.35	X
Methyl iodide	74–88–4	5	28	X
Methyl isoamyl ketone	110–12–3	100	475	—
Methyl isobutyl carbinol	108–11–2	25	100	X
Methyl isobutyl ketone; see Hexone.				
Methyl isocyanate	624–83–9	0.02	0.05	X
Methyl mercaptan	74–93–1	0.5	1	—
Methyl methacrylate	80–62–6	100	410	—
Methyl propyl ketone; see 2-Pentanone.				
Methyl silicate	681–84–5	(C)5	(C)30	—
alpha-Methyl styrene	98–83–9	(C)100	(C)480	—
Methylene bisphenyl isocyanate (MDI)	101–68–8	(C)0.02	(C)0.2	—
Mica; see Silicates.				
Molybdenum (as Mo)	7439–98–7			
Soluble compounds		—	5	
Insoluble compounds.				
Total dust		—	15	—
Monomethyl aniline	100–61–8	2	9	X
Monomethyl hydrazine; see Methyl hydrazine.				
Morpholine	110–91–8	20	70	X
Naphtha (Coal tar)	8030–30–6	100	400	—
Naphthalene	91–20–3	10	50	—
alpha-Naphthylamine; see § 1926.1104	134–32–7			
beta-Naphthylamine; see § 1926.1109	91–59–8			—
Neon	7440–01–9	E		
Nickel carbonyl (as Ni)	13463–39–3	0.001	0.007	—
Nickel, metal and insoluble compounds (as Ni)	7440–02–0	—	1	—
Nickel, soluble compounds (as Ni)	7440–02–0	—	1	—
Nicotine	54–11–5	—	0.5	X
Nitric acid	7697–37–2	2	5	—
Nitric oxide	10102–43–9	25	30	—
p-Nitroaniline	100–01–6	1	6	X
Nitrobenzene	98–95–3	1	5	X
p-Nitrochlorobenzene	100–00–5	—	1	X
4-Nitrodiphenyl; see § 1926.1103	92–93–3			
Nitroethane	79–24–3	100	310	—
Nitrogen	7727–37–9	E		
Nitrogen dioxide	10102–44–0	(C)5	(C)9	—
Nitrogen trifluoride	7783–54–2	10	29	—
Nitroglycerin	55–63–0	(C)0.2	(C)2	X
Nitromethane	75–52–5	100	250	—
1-Nitropropane	108–03–2	25	90	—

44

THRESHOLD LIMIT VALUES OF AIRBORNE CONTAMINANTS FOR CONSTRUCTION—Continued

Substance	CAS No. [d]	ppm [a]	mg/m³ [b]	Skin Designation
2-Nitropropane	79-46-9	25	90	—
N-Nitrosodimethylamine; see § 1926.1116	62-79-9			—
Nitrotoluene (all isomers)		5	30	X
o-isomer	88-72-2;			
m-isomer	99-08-1;			
p-isomer	99-99-0			
Nitrotrichloromethane; see Chloropicrin.				
Nitrous oxide	10024-97-2	E		
Octachloronaphthalene	2234-13-1	—	0.1	X
Octane	111-65-9	400	1900	—
Oil mist, mineral	8012-95-1	—	5	—
Osmium tetroxide (as Os)	20816-12-0	—	0.002	—
Oxalic acid	144-62-7	—	1	—
Oxygen difluoride	7783-41-7	0.05	0.1	—
Ozone	10028-15-6	0.1	0.2	—
Paraquat, respirable dust	4685-14-7; 1910-42-5; 2074-50-2	—	0.5	X
Parathion	56-38-2	—	0.1	X
Particulates not otherwise regulated.				
Total dust organic and inorganic		—	15	—
PCB; see Chlorodiphenyl (42% and 54% chlorine).				
Pentaborane	19624-22-7	0.005	0.01	—
Pentachloronaphthalene	1321-64-8	—	0.5	X
Pentachlorophenol	87-86-5	—	0.5	X
Pentaerythritol	115-77-5			
Total dust		—		—
Respirable fraction		—		—
Pentane	109-66-0	500	1500	—
2-Pentanone (Methyl propyl ketone)	107-87-9	200	700	—
Perchloroethylene (Tetrachloroethylene)	127-18-4	100	670	—
Perchloromethyl mercaptan	594-42-3	0.1	0.8	—
Perchloryl fluoride	7616-94-6	3	13.5	—
Petroleum distillates (Naphtha)(Rubber Solvent)			A³	—
Phenol	108-95-2	5	19	X
p-Phenylene diamine	106-50-3	—	0.1	X
Phenyl ether, vapor	101-84-8	1	7	—
Phenyl ether-biphenyl mixture, vapor		1	7	—
Phenylethylene; see Styrene.				
Phenyl glycidyl ether (PGE)	122-60-1	10	60	—
Phenylhydrazine	100-63-0	5	22	X
Phosdrin (Mevinphos)	7786-34-7	—	0.1	X
Phosgene (Carbonyl chloride)	75-44-5	0.1	0.4	—
Phosphine	7803-51-2	0.3	0.4	—
Phosphoric acid	7664-38-2	—	1	—
Phosphorus (yellow)	7723-14-0	—	0.1	—
Phosphorus pentachloride	10026-13-8	—	1	—
Phosphorus pentasulfide	1314-80-3	—	1	—
Phosphorus trichloride	7719-12-2	0.5	3	—
Phthalic anhydride	85-44-9	2	12	—
Picric acid	88-89-1	—	0.1	X
Pindone (2-Pivalyl-1,3-indandione)	83-26-1	—	0.1	—
Plaster of Paris	26499-65-0			
Total dust		—		—
Respirable fraction		—		—
Platinum (as Pt)	7440-06-4			
Metal		—	—	—
Soluble salts		—	0.002	—

THRESHOLD LIMIT VALUES OF AIRBORNE CONTAMINANTS FOR CONSTRUCTION—Continued

Substance	CAS No. [d]	ppm [a]	mg/m^3 [b]	Skin Designation
Polytetrafluoroethylene decomposition products			A [2]	
Portland cement	65997-15-1			
Total dust		—	15	—
Respirable fraction		5		—
Propane	74-98-6	E		
Propargyl alcohol	107-19-7	1	—	X
beta-Propriolactone; see § 1926.1113	57-57-8			
n-Propyl acetate	109-60-4	200	840	—
n-Propyl alcohol	71-23-8	200	500	—
n-Propyl nitrate	627-13-4	25	110	—
Propylene dichloride	78-87-5	75	350	—
Propylene imine	75-55-8	2	5	X
Propylene oxide	75-56-9	100	240	—
Propyne; see Methyl acetylene.				
Pyrethrum	8003-34-7	—	5	—
Pyridine	110-86-1	5	15	—
Quinone	106-51-4	0.1	0.4	—
RDX; see Cyclonite.				
Rhodium (as Rh), metal fume and insoluble compounds	7440-16-6	—	0.1	—
Rhodium (as Rh), soluble compounds	7440-16-6	—	0.001	—
Ronnel	299-84-3	—	10	—
Rotenone	83-79-4	—	5	—
Rouge.				
Total dust		—		—
Respirable fraction		—		—
Selenium compounds (as Se)	7782-49-2	—	0.2	—
Selenium hexafluoride (as Se)	7783-79-1	0.05	0.4	—
Silica, amorphous, precipitated and gel	112926-00-8	(2)	(2)	(2)
Silica, amorphous, diatomaceous earth, containing less than 1% crystalline silica	61790-53-2	(2)	(2)	(2)
Silica, crystalline cristobalite, respirable dust	14464-46-1	(2)	(2)	(2)
Silica, crystalline quartz, respirable dust	14808-60-7	(2)	(2)	(2)
Silica, crystalline tripoli (as quartz), respirable dust	1317-95-9	(2)	(2)	(2)
Silica, crystalline tridymite, respirable dust	15468-32-3	(2)	(2)	(2)
Silica, fused, respirable dust	60676-86-0	(2)	(2)	(2)
Silicates (less than 1% crystalline silica).				
Mica (respirable dust)	12001-26-2	(2)	(2)	(2)
Soapstone, total dust		(2)	(2)	(2)
Soapstone, respirable dust		(2)	(2)	(2)
Talc (containing asbestos); use asbestos limit; see 1926.58.				
Talc (containing no asbestos), respirable dust	14807-96-6	(2)	(2)	(2)
Tremolite, asbestiform; see 1926.58.				
Silicon carbide	409-21-2			
Total dust		—		—
Respirable fraction		—		—
Silver, metal and soluble compounds (as Ag)	7440-22-4	—	0.01	—
Soapstone; see Silicates.				
Sodium fluoroacetate	62-74-8	—	0.05	X
Sodium hydroxide	1310-73-2	—	2	—
Starch	9005-25-8			
Total dust		—		—

THRESHOLD LIMIT VALUES OF AIRBORNE CONTAMINANTS FOR CONSTRUCTION—Continued

Substance	CAS No.[d]	ppm[a]	mg/m³[b]	Skin Designation
Respirable fraction		—		—
Stibine	7803–52–3	0.1	0.5	—
Stoddard solvent	8052–41–3	200	1150	—
Strychnine	57–24–9	—	0.15	—
Styrene	100–42–5	(C)100	(C)420	—
Sucrose	57–50–1			
Total dust		—		—
Respirable fraction		—		—
Sulfur dioxide	7446–09–5	5	13	—
Sulfur hexafluoride	2551–62–4	1000	6000	—
Sulfuric acid	7664–93–9	—	1	—
Sulfur monochloride	10025–67–9	1	6	—
Sulfur pentafluoride	5714–22–7	0.025	0.25	—
Sulfuryl fluoride	2699–79–8	5	20	—
Systox, see Demeton.				
2,4,5-T (2,4,5-trichlorophenoxyacetic acid)	93–76–5	—	10	—
Talc; see Silicates—.				
Tantalum, metal and oxide dust	7440–25–7	—	5	—
TEDP (Sulfotep)	3689–24–5	—	0.2	X
Teflon decomposition products			A2	
Tellurium and compounds (as Te)	13494–80–9	—	0.1	—
Tellurium hexafluoride (as Te)	7783–80–4	0.02	0.2	—
Temephos	3383–96–8			
Total dust		—		—
Respirable fraction		—		—
TEPP (Tetraethyl pyrophosphate)	107–49–3	—	0.05	X
Terphenyls	26140–60–3	(C)1	(C)9	—
1,1,1,2-Tetrachloro-2,2-difluoroethane ..	76–11–9	500	4170	—
1,1,2,2-Tetrachloro-1,2-difluoroethane ..	76–12–0	500	4170	—
1,1,2,2-Tetrachloroethane	79–34–5	5	35	X
Tetrachloroethylene; see Perchloroethylene.				
Tetrachloromethane; see Carbon tetrachloride.				
Tetrachloronaphthalene	1335–88–2	—	2	X
Tetraethyl lead (as Pb)	78–00–2	—	0.1	X
Tetrahydrofuran	109–99–9	200	590	—
Tetramethyl lead, (as Pb)	75–74–1	—	0.15	X
Tetramethyl succinonitrile	3333–52–6	0.5	3	X
Tetranitromethane	509–14–8	1	8	—
Tetryl (2,4,6-Trinitrophenylmethylnitramine)	479–45–8	—	1.5	X
Thallium, soluble compounds (as Tl)	7440–28–0	—	0.1	X
Thiram	137–26–8	—	5	—
Tin, inorganic compounds (except oxides) (as Sn)	7440–31–5	—	2	—
Tin, organic compounds (as Sn)	7440–31–5	—	0.1	—
Tin oxide (as Sn)	21651–19–4	—	—	—
Total dust		—		—
Respirable fraction		—		—
Titanium dioxide	13463–67–7			
Total dust		—		—
Toluene	108–88–3	200	750	—
Toluene-2,4-diisocyanate (TDI)	584–84–9	(C)0.02	(C)0.14	—
o-Toluidine	95–53–4	5	22	X
Toxaphene; see Chlorinated camphene.				
Tremolite; see Silicates.				
Tributyl phosphate	126–73–8	—	5	—
1,1,1-Trichloroethane; see Methyl chloroform.				
1,1,2-Trichloroethane	79–00–5	10	45	X

47

THRESHOLD LIMIT VALUES OF AIRBORNE CONTAMINANTS FOR CONSTRUCTION—Continued

Substance	CAS No. [d]	ppm [a]	mg/m³ [b]	Skin Designation
Trichloroethylene	79–01–6	100	535	—
Trichloromethane; see Chloroform.				
Trichloronaphthalene	1321–65–9	—	5	X
1,2,3-Trichloropropane	96–18–4	50	300	—
1,1,2-Trichloro-1,2,2-trifluoroethane	76–13–1	1000	7600	—
Triethylamine	121–44–8	25	100	—
Trifluorobromomethane	75–63–8	1000	6100	—
Trimethyl benzene	25551–13–7	25	120	—
2,4,6-Trinitrophenol; see Picric acid.				
2,4,6-Trinitrophenylmethylnitramine; see Tetryl.				
2,4,6-Trinitrotoluene (TNT)	118–96–7	—	1.5	X
Triorthocresyl phosphate	78–30–8	—	0.1	—
Triphenyl phosphate	115–86–6	—	3	—
Tungsten (as W)	7440–33–7			
Insoluble compounds		—	5	—
Soluble compounds		—	1	—
Turpentine	8006–64–2	100	560	—
Uranium (as U)	7440–61–1			
Soluble compounds		—	0.2	—
Insoluble compounds		—	0.2	—
Vanadium	1314–62–1			
Respirable dust (as V_2O_5)		—	(C)0.5	—
Fume (as V_2O_5)		—	(C)0.1	—
Vegetable oil mist.				
Total dust		—		—
Respirable fraction		—		—
Vinyl benzene; see Styrene.				
Vinyl chloride; see § 1926.1117	75–01–4			
Vinyl cyanide; see Acrylonitrile.				
Vinyl toluene	25013–15–4	100	480	—
Warfarin	81–81–2	—	0.1	—
Xylenes (o-, m-, p-isomers)	1330–20–7	100	435	—
Xylidine	1300–73–8	5	25	X
Yttrium	7440–65–5	—	1	—
Zinc chloride fume	7646–85–7	—	1	—
Zinc oxide fume	1314–13–2	—	5	—
Zinc oxide	1314–13–2			
Total dust		—	15	—
Respirable fraction		—	5	—
Zirconium compounds (as Zr)	7440–67–7	—	5	

MINERAL DUSTS

SILICA:
  Crystalline
Quartz. Threshold Limit calculated from the formula .... 250 [k]

	%SiO₂+5

Cristobalite.
  Amorphous, including natural diatomaceous earth 20
SILICATES (less than 1% crystalline silica)
  Mica ... 20
  Portland cement ... 50
  Soapstone ... 20
  Talc (non-asbestiform) ... 20
  Talc (fibrous), use asbestos limit ... --
Graphite (natural) ... 15

MINERAL DUSTS—Continued

Inert or Nuisance Particulates: (m)	50 (or 15 mg/m^3 whichever is the smaller) of total dust <1% SiO$_2$

[Inert or Nuisance Dusts includes all mineral, inorganic, and organic dusts as indicated by examples in TLV's appendix D]

Conversion factors.
mppcf × 35.3 = million particles per cubic meter = particles per c.c.

Footnotes
1 [Reserved]
2 See Mineral Dusts Table.
3 Use Asbestos Limit §1926.58.
4 See 1926.58.
* The PELs are 8-hour TWAs unless otherwise noted; a (C) designation denotes a ceiling limit.
** As determined from breathing-zone air samples.
a Parts of vapor or gas per million parts of contaminated air by volume at 25 °C and 760 torr.
b Milligrams of substance per cubic meter of air. When entry is in this column only, the value is exact; when listed with a ppm entry, it is approximate.
c [Reserved]
d The CAS number is for information only. Enforcement is based on the substance name. For an entry covering more than one metal compound, measured as the metal, the CAS number for the metal is given—not CAS numbers for the individual compounds.
e f [Reserved]
g For sectors excluded from §1926.1128 the limit is 10 ppm TWA.
h i [Reserved]
j Millions of particles per cubic foot of air, based on impinger samples counted by light-field techniques.
k The percentage of crystalline silica in the formula is the amount determined from airborne samples, except in those instances in which other methods have been shown to be applicable.
l [Reserved]
m Covers all organic and inorganic particulates not otherwise regulated. Same as Particulates Not Otherwise Regulated.
n If the exposure limit in §1926.1126 is stayed or is otherwise not in effect, the exposure limit is a ceiling of 0.1 mg/m^3.
o If the exposure limit in §1926.1126 is stayed or is otherwise not in effect, the exposure limit is 0.1 mg/m^3 (as CrO$_3$) as an 8-hour TWA.
The 1970 TLV uses letter designations instead of a numerical value as follows:
A 1 [Reserved]
A 2 Polytetrafluoroethylene decomposition products. Because these products decompose in part by hydrolysis in alkaline solution, they can be quantitatively determined in air as fluoride to provide an index of exposure. No TLV is recommended pending determination of the toxicity of the products, but air concentrations should be minimal.
A 3 Gasoline and/or Petroleum Distillates. The composition of these materials varies greatly and thus a single TLV for all types of these materials is no longer applicable. The content of benzene, other aromatics and additives should be determined to arrive at the appropriate TLV.
E Simple asphyxiants. The limiting factor is the available oxygen which shall be at least 19.5% and be within the requirements addressing explosion in part 1926.

[39 FR 22801, June 24, 1974, as amended at 51 FR 37007, Oct. 17, 1986; 52 FR 46312, Dec. 4, 1987; 58 FR 35089, June 30, 1993; 61 FR 9249, 9250, Mar. 7, 1996; 61 FR 56856, Nov. 4, 1996; 62 FR 1619, Jan. 10, 1997; 71 FR 10381, Feb. 28, 2006; 71 FR 36009, June 23, 2006]

§1926.56 Illumination.

(a) *General.* Construction areas, ramps, runways, corridors, offices, shops, and storage areas shall be lighted to not less than the minimum illumination intensities listed in Table D–3 while any work is in progress:

TABLE D–3—MINIMUM ILLUMINATION INTENSITIES IN FOOT-CANDLES

Foot-candles	Area or operation
5	General construction area lighting.
3	General construction areas, concrete placement, excavation and waste areas, accessways, active storage areas, loading platforms, refueling, and field maintenance areas.
5	Indoors: warehouses, corridors, hallways, and exitways.

TABLE D–3—MINIMUM ILLUMINATION INTENSITIES IN FOOT-CANDLES—Continued

Foot-candles	Area or operation
5	Tunnels, shafts, and general underground work areas: (Exception: minimum of 10 foot-candles is required at tunnel and shaft heading during drilling, mucking, and scaling. Bureau of Mines approved cap lights shall be acceptable for use in the tunnel heading.)
10	General construction plant and shops (e.g., batch plants, screening plants, mechanical and electrical equipment rooms, carpenter shops, rigging lofts and active storerooms, barracks or living quarters, locker or dressing rooms, mess halls, and indoor toilets and workrooms).
30	First aid stations, infirmaries, and offices.

(b) *Other areas.* For areas or operations not covered above, refer to the

American National Standard A11.1–1965, R1970, Practice for Industrial Lighting, for recommended values of illumination.

§ 1926.57 Ventilation.

(a) *General.* Whenever hazardous substances such as dusts, fumes, mists, vapors, or gases exist or are produced in the course of construction work, their concentrations shall not exceed the limits specified in § 1926.55(a). When ventilation is used as an engineering control method, the system shall be installed and operated according to the requirements of this section.

(b) *Local exhaust ventilation.* Local exhaust ventilation when used as described in (a) shall be designed to prevent dispersion into the air of dusts, fumes, mists, vapors, and gases in concentrations causing harmful exposure. Such exhaust systems shall be so designed that dusts, fumes, mists, vapors, or gases are not drawn through the work area of employees.

(c) *Design and operation.* Exhaust fans, jets, ducts, hoods, separators, and all necessary appurtenances, including refuse receptacles, shall be so designed, constructed, maintained and operated as to ensure the required protection by maintaining a volume and velocity of exhaust air sufficient to gather dusts, fumes, vapors, or gases from said equipment or process, and to convey them to suitable points of safe disposal, thereby preventing their dispersion in harmful quantities into the atmosphere where employees work.

(d) *Duration of operations.* (1) The exhaust system shall be in operation continually during all operations which it is designed to serve. If the employee remains in the contaminated zone, the system shall continue to operate after the cessation of said operations, the length of time to depend upon the individual circumstances and effectiveness of the general ventilation system.

(2) Since dust capable of causing disability is, according to the best medical opinion, of microscopic size, tending to remain for hours in suspension in still air, it is essential that the exhaust system be continued in operation for a time after the work process or equipment served by the same shall have ceased, in order to ensure the removal of the harmful elements to the required extent. For the same reason, employees wearing respiratory equipment should not remove same immediately until the atmosphere seems clear.

(e) *Disposal of exhaust materials.* The air outlet from every dust separator, and the dusts, fumes, mists, vapors, or gases collected by an exhaust or ventilating system shall discharge to the outside atmosphere. Collecting systems which return air to work area may be used if concentrations which accumulate in the work area air do not result in harmful exposure to employees. Dust and refuse discharged from an exhaust system shall be disposed of in such a manner that it will not result in harmful exposure to employees.

(f) *Abrasive blasting*—(1) *Definitions applicable to this paragraph*—(i) *Abrasive.* A solid substance used in an abrasive blasting operation.

(ii) *Abrasive-blasting respirator.* A respirator constructed so that it covers the wearer's head, neck, and shoulders to protect the wearer from rebounding abrasive.

(iii) *Blast cleaning barrel.* A complete enclosure which rotates on an axis, or which has an internal moving tread to tumble the parts, in order to expose various surfaces of the parts to the action of an automatic blast spray.

(iv) *Blast cleaning room.* A complete enclosure in which blasting operations are performed and where the operator works inside of the room to operate the blasting nozzle and direct the flow of the abrasive material.

(v) *Blasting cabinet.* An enclosure where the operator stands outside and operates the blasting nozzle through an opening or openings in the enclosure.

(vi) *Clean air.* Air of such purity that it will not cause harm or discomfort to an individual if it is inhaled for extended periods of time.

(vii) *Dust collector.* A device or combination of devices for separating dust from the air handled by an exhaust ventilation system.

(viii) *Exhaust ventilation system.* A system for removing contaminated air from a space, comprising two or more of the following elements (A) enclosure or hood, (B) duct work, (C) dust collecting equipment, (D) exhauster, and (E) discharge stack.

(ix) *Particulate-filter respirator.* An air purifying respirator, commonly referred to as a dust or a fume respirator, which removes most of the dust or fume from the air passing through the device.

(x) *Respirable dust.* Airborne dust in sizes capable of passing through the upper respiratory system to reach the lower lung passages.

(xi) *Rotary blast cleaning table.* An enclosure where the pieces to be cleaned are positioned on a rotating table and are passed automatically through a series of blast sprays.

(xii) *Abrasive blasting.* The forcible application of an abrasive to a surface by pneumatic pressure, hydraulic pressure, or centrifugal force.

(2) *Dust hazards from abrasive blasting.* (i) Abrasives and the surface coatings on the materials blasted are shattered and pulverized during blasting operations and the dust formed will contain particles of respirable size. The composition and toxicity of the dust from these sources shall be considered in making an evaluation of the potential health hazards.

(ii) The concentration of respirable dust or fume in the breathing zone of the abrasive-blasting operator or any other worker shall be kept below the levels specified in §1926.55 or other pertinent sections of this part.

(iii) Organic abrasives which are combustible shall be used only in automatic systems. Where flammable or explosive dust mixtures may be present, the construction of the equipment, including the exhaust system and all electric wiring, shall conform to the requirements of American National Standard Installation of Blower and Exhaust Systems for Dust, Stock, and Vapor Removal or Conveying, Z33.1–1961 (NFPA 91–1961), and subpart S of this part. The blast nozzle shall be bonded and grounded to prevent the build up of static charges. Where flammable or explosive dust mixtures may be present, the abrasive blasting enclosure, the ducts, and the dust collector shall be constructed with loose panels or explosion venting areas, located on sides away from any occupied area, to provide for pressure relief in case of explosion, following the principles set forth in the National Fire Protection Association Explosion Venting Guide. NFPA 68–1954.

(3) *Blast-cleaning enclosures.* (i) Blast-cleaning enclosures shall be exhaust ventilated in such a way that a continuous inward flow of air will be maintained at all openings in the enclosure during the blasting operation.

(A) All air inlets and access openings shall be baffled or so arranged that by the combination of inward air flow and baffling the escape of abrasive or dust particles into an adjacent work area will be minimized and visible spurts of dust will not be observed.

(B) The rate of exhaust shall be sufficient to provide prompt clearance of the dust-laden air within the enclosure after the cessation of blasting.

(C) Before the enclosure is opened, the blast shall be turned off and the exhaust system shall be run for a sufficient period of time to remove the dusty air within the enclosure.

(D) Safety glass protected by screening shall be used in observation windows, where hard deep-cutting abrasives are used.

(E) Slit abrasive-resistant baffles shall be installed in multiple sets at all small access openings where dust might escape, and shall be inspected regularly and replaced when needed.

(*1*) Doors shall be flanged and tight when closed.

(*2*) Doors on blast-cleaning rooms shall be operable from both inside and outside, except that where there is a small operator access door, the large work access door may be closed or opened from the outside only.

(4) *Exhaust ventilation systems.* (i) The construction, installation, inspection, and maintenance of exhaust systems shall conform to the principles and requirements set forth in American National Standard Fundamentals Governing the Design and Operation of Local Exhaust Systems, Z9.2–1960, and ANSI Z33.1–1961.

(*a*) When dust leaks are noted, repairs shall be made as soon as possible.

(*b*) The static pressure drop at the exhaust ducts leading from the equipment shall be checked when the installation is completed and periodically

51

thereafter to assure continued satisfactory operation. Whenever an appreciable change in the pressure drop indicates a partial blockage, the system shall be cleaned and returned to normal operating condition.

(ii) In installations where the abrasive is recirculated, the exhaust ventilation system for the blasting enclosure shall not be relied upon for the removal of fines from the spent abrasive instead of an abrasive separator. An abrasive separator shall be provided for the purpose.

(iii) The air exhausted from blast-cleaning equipment shall be discharged through dust collecting equipment. Dust collectors shall be set up so that the accumulated dust can be emptied and removed without contaminating other working areas.

(5) *Personal protective equipment.* (i) Employers must use only respirators approved by NIOSH under 42 CFR part 84 for protecting employees from dusts produced during abrasive-blasting operations.

(ii) Abrasive-blasting respirators shall be worn by all abrasive-blasting operators:

(A) When working inside of blast-cleaning rooms, or

(B) When using silica sand in manual blasting operations where the nozzle and blast are not physically separated from the operator in an exhaust ventilated enclosure, or

(C) Where concentrations of toxic dust dispersed by the abrasive blasting may exceed the limits set in § 1926.55 or other pertinent sections of this part and the nozzle and blast are not physically separated from the operator in an exhaust-ventilated enclosure.

(iii) Properly fitted particulate-filter respirators, commonly referred to as dust-filter respirators, may be used for short, intermittent, or occasional dust exposures such as cleanup, dumping of dust collectors, or unloading shipments of sand at a receiving point when it is not feasible to control the dust by enclosure, exhaust ventilation, or other means. The respirators used must be approved by NIOSH under 42 CFR part 84 for protection against the specific type of dust encountered.

(iv) A respiratory protection program as defined and described in § 1926.103,

shall be established wherever it is necessary to use respiratory protective equipment.

(v) Operators shall be equipped with heavy canvas or leather gloves and aprons or equivalent protection to protect them from the impact of abrasives. Safety shoes shall be worn to protect against foot injury where heavy pieces of work are handled.

(A) Safety shoes shall conform to the requirements of American National Standard for Men's Safety-Toe Footwear, Z41.1-1967.

(B) Equipment for protection of the eyes and face shall be supplied to the operator when the respirator design does not provide such protection and to any other personnel working in the vicinity of abrasive blasting operations. This equipment shall conform to the requirements of § 1926.102.

(6) *Air supply and air compressors.* Air for abrasive-blasting respirators must be free of harmful quantities of dusts, mists, or noxious gases, and must meet the requirements for supplied-air quality and use specified in 29 CFR 1910.134(i).

(7) *Operational procedures and general safety.* Dust shall not be permitted to accumulate on the floor or on ledges outside of an abrasive-blasting enclosure, and dust spills shall be cleaned up promptly. Aisles and walkways shall be kept clear of steel shot or similar abrasive which may create a slipping hazard.

(8) *Scope.* This paragraph applies to all operations where an abrasive is forcibly applied to a surface by pneumatic or hydraulic pressure, or by centrifugal force. It does not apply to steam blasting, or steam cleaning, or hydraulic cleaning methods where work is done without the aid of abrasives.

(g) *Grinding, polishing, and buffing operations*—(1) Definitions applicable to this paragraph—

(i) *Abrasive cutting-off wheels.* Organic-bonded wheels, the thickness of which is not more than one forty-eighth of their diameter for those up to, and including, 20 inches (50.8 cm) in diameter, and not more than one-sixtieth of their diameter for those larger than 20 inches (50.8 cm) in diameter, used for a multitude of operations variously known as cutting, cutting off, grooving, slotting, coping, and jointing, and the like. The wheels may be "solid" consisting of organic-bonded abrasive material throughout, "steel centered" consisting of a steel disc with a rim of organic-bonded material moulded around the periphery, or of the "inserted tooth" type consisting of a steel disc with organic-bonded abrasive teeth or inserts mechanically secured around the periphery.

(ii) *Belts.* All power-driven, flexible, coated bands used for grinding, polishing, or buffing purposes.

(iii) *Branch pipe.* The part of an exhaust system piping that is connected directly to the hood or enclosure.

(iv) *Cradle.* A movable fixture, upon which the part to be ground or polished is placed.

(v) *Disc wheels.* All power-driven rotatable discs faced with abrasive materials, artificial or natural, and used for grinding or polishing on the side of the assembled disc.

(vi) *Entry loss.* The loss in static pressure caused by air flowing into a duct or hood. It is usually expressed in inches of water gauge.

(vii) *Exhaust system.* A system consisting of branch pipes connected to hoods or enclosures, one or more header pipes, an exhaust fan, means for separating solid contaminants from the air flowing in the system, and a discharge stack to outside.

(viii) *Grinding wheels.* All power-driven rotatable grinding or abrasive wheels, except disc wheels as defined in this standard, consisting of abrasive particles held together by artificial or natural bonds and used for peripheral grinding.

(ix) *Header pipe (main pipe).* A pipe into which one or more branch pipes enter and which connects such branch pipes to the remainder of the exhaust system.

(x) *Hoods and enclosures.* The partial or complete enclosure around the wheel or disc through which air enters an exhaust system during operation.

(xi) *Horizontal double-spindle disc grinder.* A grinding machine carrying two power-driven, rotatable, coaxial, horizontal spindles upon the inside ends of which are mounted abrasive disc wheels used for grinding two surfaces simultaneously.

(xii) *Horizontal single-spindle disc grinder.* A grinding machine carrying an abrasive disc wheel upon one or both ends of a power-driven, rotatable single horizontal spindle.

(xiii) *Polishing and buffing wheels.* All power-driven rotatable wheels composed all or in part of textile fabrics, wood, felt, leather, paper, and may be coated with abrasives on the periphery of the wheel for purposes of polishing, buffing, and light grinding.

(xiv) *Portable grinder.* Any power-driven rotatable grinding, polishing, or buffing wheel mounted in such manner that it may be manually manipulated.

(xv) *Scratch brush wheels.* All power-driven rotatable wheels made from wire or bristles, and used for scratch cleaning and brushing purposes.

(xvi) *Swing-frame grinder.* Any power-driven rotatable grinding, polishing, or buffing wheel mounted in such a manner that the wheel with its supporting framework can be manipulated over stationary objects.

(xvii) *Velocity pressure (vp).* The kinetic pressure in the direction of flow necessary to cause a fluid at rest to flow at a given velocity. It is usually expressed in inches of water gauge.

(xviii) *Vertical spindle disc grinder.* A grinding machine having a vertical, rotatable power-driven spindle carrying a horizontal abrasive disc wheel.

(2) *Application.* Wherever dry grinding, dry polishing or buffing is performed, and employee exposure, without regard to the use of respirators, exceeds the permissible exposure limits prescribed in § 1926.55 or other pertinent sections of this part, a local exhaust ventilation system shall be provided and used to maintain employee exposures within the prescribed limits.

(3) *Hood and branch pipe requirements.* (i) Hoods connected to exhaust systems shall be used, and such hoods shall be designed, located, and placed so that the dust or dirt particles shall fall or be projected into the hoods in the direction of the air flow. No wheels, discs, straps, or belts shall be operated in such manner and in such direction as to cause the dust and dirt particles to be thrown into the operator's breathing zone.

(ii) Grinding wheels on floor stands, pedestals, benches, and special-purpose grinding machines and abrasive cutting-off wheels shall have not less than the minimum exhaust volumes shown in Table D–57.1 with a recommended minimum duct velocity of 4,500 feet per minute in the branch and 3,500 feet per minute in the main. The entry losses from all hoods except the vertical-spindle disc grinder hood, shall equal 0.65 velocity pressure for a straight takeoff and 0.45 velocity pressure for a tapered takeoff. The entry loss for the vertical-spindle disc grinder hood is shown in figure D–57.1 (following paragraph (g) of this section).

TABLE D–57.1—GRINDING AND ABRASIVE CUTTING-OFF WHEELS

Wheel diameter, inches (cm)	Wheel width, inches (cm)	Minimum exhaust volume (feet³/min.)
To 9 (22.86)	1½ (3.81)	220
Over 9 to 16 (22.86 to 40.64)	2 (5.08)	390
Over 16 to 19 (40.64 to 48.26)	3 (7.62)	500
Over 19 to 24 (48.26 to 60.96)	4 (10.16)	610
Over 24 to 30 (60.96 to 76.2)	5 (12.7)	880
Over 30 to 36 (76.2 to 91.44)	6 (15.24)	1,200

For any wheel wider than wheel diameters shown in Table D–57.1, increase the exhaust volume by the ratio of the new width to the width shown.

Example: If wheel width = 4½ inches (11.43 cm),

then 4.5 ÷ 4 × 610 = 686 (rounded to 690).

(iii) Scratch-brush wheels and all buffing and polishing wheels mounted on floor stands, pedestals, benches, or special-purpose machines shall have not less than the minimum exhaust volume shown in Table D–57.2.

TABLE D–57.2—BUFFING AND POLISHING WHEELS

Wheel diameter, inches (cm)	Wheel width, inches cm)	Minimum exhaust volume (feet³/min.)
To 9 (22.86)	2 (5.08)	300
Over 9 to 16 (22.86 to 40.64)	3 (7.62)	500
Over 16 to 19 (40.64 to 48.26)	4 (10.16)	610
Over 19 to 24 (48.26 to 60.96)	5 (12.7)	740
Over 24 to 30 (60.96 to 76.2)	6 (15.24)	1,040
Over 30 to 36 (76.2 to 91.44)	6 (15.24)	1,200

(iv) Grinding wheels or discs for horizontal single-spindle disc grinders shall be hooded to collect the dust or dirt generated by the grinding operation and the hoods shall be connected to branch pipes having exhaust volumes as shown in Table D–57.3.

TABLE D–57.3—HORIZONTAL SINGLE-SPINDLE DISC GRINDER

Disc diameter, inches (cm)	Exhaust volume (ft.³/min.)
Up to 12 (30.48)	220
Over 12 to 19 (30.48 to 48.26)	390
Over 19 to 30 (48.26 to 76.2)	610
Over 30 to 36 (76.2 to 91.44)	880

(v) Grinding wheels or discs for horizontal double-spindle disc grinders shall have a hood enclosing the grinding chamber and the hood shall be connected to one or more branch pipes having exhaust volumes as shown in Table D–57.4.

TABLE D–57.4—HORIZONTAL DOUBLE-SPINDLE DISC GRINDER

Disc diameter, inches (cm)	Exhaust volume (ft.³/min.)
Up to 19 (48.26)	610
Over 19 to 25 (48.26 to 63.5)	880
Over 25 to 30 (63.5 to 76.2)	1,200
Over 30 to 53 (76.2 to 134.62)	1,770
Over 53 to 72 (134.62 to 182.88)	6,280

(vi) Grinding wheels or discs for vertical single-spindle disc grinders shall be encircled with hoods to remove the dust generated in the operation. The hoods shall be connected to one or more branch pipes having exhaust volumes as shown in Table D–57.5.

TABLE D–57.5—VERTICAL SPINDLE DISC GRINDER

Disc diameter, inches (cm)	One-half or more of disc covered		Disc not covered	
	Number[1]	Exhaust foot³/min.	Number[1]	Exhaust foot³/min.
Up to 20 (50.8)	1	500	2	780
Over 20 to 30 (50.8 to 76.2)	2	780	2	1,480
Over 30 to 53 (76.2 to 134.62)	2	1,770	4	3,530
Over 53 to 72 (134.62 to 182.88)	2	3,140	5	6,010

[1] Number of exhaust outlets around periphery of hood, or equal distribution provided by other means.

(vii) Grinding and polishing belts shall be provided with hoods to remove

54

dust and dirt generated in the operations and the hoods shall be connected to branch pipes having exhaust volumes as shown in Table D–57.6.

TABLE D–57.6—GRINDING AND POLISHING BELTS

Belts width, inches (cm)	Exhaust volume (ft.^{3}/min.)
Up to 3 (7.62)	220
Over 3 to 5 (7.62 to 12.7)	300
Over 5 to 7 (12.7 to 17.78)	390
Over 7 to 9 (17.78 to 22.86)	500
Over 9 to 11 (22.86 to 27.94)	610
Over 11 to 13 (27.94 to 33.02)	740

(viii) Cradles and swing-frame grinders. Where cradles are used for handling the parts to be ground, polished, or buffed, requiring large partial enclosures to house the complete operation, a minimum average air velocity of 150 feet per minute shall be maintained over the entire opening of the enclosure. Swing-frame grinders shall also be exhausted in the same manner as provided for cradles. (See fig. D–57.3)

(ix) Where the work is outside the hood, air volumes must be increased as shown in American Standard Fundamentals Governing the Design and Operation of Local Exhaust Systems, Z9.2–1960 (section 4, exhaust hoods).

(4) *Exhaust systems.* (i) Exhaust systems for grinding, polishing, and buffing operations should be designed in accordance with American Standard Fundamentals Governing the Design and Operation of Local Exhaust Systems, Z9.2–1960.

(ii) Exhaust systems for grinding, polishing, and buffing operations shall be tested in the manner described in American Standard Fundamentals Governing the Design and Operation of Local Exhaust Systems, Z9.2–1960.

(iii) All exhaust systems shall be provided with suitable dust collectors.

(5) *Hood and enclosure design.* (i) (A) It is the dual function of grinding and abrasive cutting-off wheel hoods to protect the operator from the hazards of bursting wheels as well as to provide a means for the removal of dust and dirt generated. All hoods shall be not less in structural strength than specified in the American National Standard Safety Code for the Use, Care, and Protection of Abrasive Wheels, B7.1–1970.

(B) Due to the variety of work and types of grinding machines employed, it is necessary to develop hoods adaptable to the particular machine in question, and such hoods shall be located as close as possible to the operation.

(ii) Exhaust hoods for floor stands, pedestals, and bench grinders shall be designed in accordance with figure D–57.2. The adjustable tongue shown in the figure shall be kept in working order and shall be adjusted within one-fourth inch (0.635 cm) of the wheel periphery at all times.

(iii) Swing-frame grinders shall be provided with exhaust booths as indicated in figure D–57.3.

(iv) Portable grinding operations, whenever the nature of the work permits, shall be conducted within a partial enclosure. The opening in the enclosure shall be no larger than is actually required in the operation and an average face air velocity of not less than 200 feet per minute shall be maintained.

(v) Hoods for polishing and buffing and scratch-brush wheels shall be constructed to conform as closely to figure D–57.4 as the nature of the work will permit.

(vi) Cradle grinding and polishing operations shall be performed within a partial enclosure similar to figure D–57.5. The operator shall be positioned outside the working face of the opening of the enclosure. The face opening of the enclosure should not be any greater in area than that actually required for the performance of the operation and the average air velocity into the working face of the enclosure shall not be less than 150 feet per minute.

(vii) Hoods for horizontal single-spindle disc grinders shall be constructed to conform as closely as possible to the hood shown in figure D–57.6. It is essential that there be a space between the back of the wheel and the hood, and a space around the periphery of the wheel of at least 1 inch (2.54 cm) in order to permit the suction to act around the wheel periphery. The opening on the side of the disc shall be no larger than is required for the grinding operation, but must never be less than twice the area of the branch outlet.

(viii) Horizontal double-spindle disc grinders shall have a hood encircling

55

the wheels and grinding chamber similar to that illustrated in figure D–57.7. The openings for passing the work into the grinding chamber should be kept as small as possible, but must never be less than twice the area of the branch outlets.

(ix) Vertical-spindle disc grinders shall be encircled with a hood so constructed that the heavy dust is drawn off a surface of the disc and the lighter dust exhausted through a continuous slot at the top of the hood as shown in figure D–57.1.

(x) Grinding and polishing belt hoods shall be constructed as close to the operation as possible. The hood should extend almost to the belt, and 1-inch (2.54 cm) wide openings should be provided on either side. Figure D–57.8 shows a typical hood for a belt operation.

Dia. D inches (cm)		Exhaust E		Volume Exhausted at 4,500 ft/min ft³/min	Note
Min.	Max.	No Pipes	Dia.		
....	20 (50.8)	1	4¼ (10.795)	500	When one-half or more of the disc can be hooded, use exhaust ducts as shown at the left.
Over 20 (50.8)	30 (76.2)	2	4 (10.16)	780	

Dia. *D* inches (cm)		Exhaust *E*		Volume Exhausted at 4,500 ft/min ft³/min	Note
Min.	Max.	No Pipes	Dia.		
Over 30 (76.2)	72 (182.88)	2	6 (15.24)	1,770	
Over 53 (134.62)	72 (182.88)	2	8 (20.32)	3,140	
....	20 (50.8)	2	4 (10.16)	780	When no hood can be used over disc, use exhaust ducts as shown at left.
Over 20 (50.8)	20 (50.8)	2	4 (10.16)	780	
Over 30 (76.2)	30 (76.2)	2	5½ (13.97)	1,480	
Over 53 (134.62)	53 (134.62)	4	6 (15.24)	3,530	
	72 (182.88)	5	7 (17.78)	6,010	

Entry loss=1.0 slot velocity pressure + 0.5 branch velocity pressure.
Minimum slot velocity=2,000 ft/min—½-inch (1.27 cm) slot width.

Wheel dimension, inches (centimeters)			Exhaust outlet, inches (centimeters) *E*	Volume of air at 4,500 ft/min
Diameter		Width, Max		
Min= *d*	Max= *D*			
	9 (22.86)	1½ (3.81)	3	220
Over 9 (22.86)	16 (40.64)	2 (5.08)	4	390
Over 16 (40.64)	19 (48.26)	3 (7.62)	4½	500
Over 19 (48.26)	24 (60.96)	4 (10.16)	5	610
Over 24 (60.96)	30 (76.2)	5 (12.7)	6	880
Over 30 (76.2)	36 (91.44)	6 (15.24)	7	1,200

Entry loss = 0.45 velocity pressure for tapered takeoff 0.65 velocity pressure for straight takeoff.

FIGURE D–57.3—A METHOD OF APPLYING AN EXHAUST ENCLOSURE TO SWING-FRAME GRINDERS

NOTE: Baffle to reduce front opening as much as possible

STANDARD BUFFING AND POLISHING HOOD

Wheel dimension, inches (centimeters)			Exhaust outlet, inches *E*	Volume of air at 4,500 ft/min
Diameter		Width, Max		
Min= *d*	Max= *D*			
	9 (22.86)	2 (5.08)	3½ (3.81)	300
Over 9 (22.86)	16 (40.64)	3 (5.08)	4	500
Over 16 (40.64)	19 (48.26)	4 (11.43)	5	610
Over 19 (48.26)	24 (60.96)	5 (12.7)	5½	740
Over 24 (60.96)	30 (76.2)	6 (15.24)	6½	1.040
Over 30 (76.2)	36 (91.44)	6 (15.24)	7	1.200

Entry loss = 0.15 velocity pressure for tapered takeoff; 0.65 velocity pressure for straight takeoff.

FIGURE D–57.5—CRADLE POLISHING OR GRINDING ENCLOSURE

Entry loss = 0.45 velocity pressure for
        tapered takeoff

Dia D, inches (centimeters)		Exhaust E, dia. inches (cm)	Volume exhausted at 4,500 ft/min ft³/min
Min.	Max.		
	12 (30.48)	3 (7.6)	220
Over 12 (30.48)	19 (48.26)	4 (10.16)	390
Over 19 (48.26)	30 (76.2)	5 (12.7)	610
Over 30 (76.2)	36 (91.44)	6 (15.24)	880

NOTE: If grinding wheels are used for disc grinding purposes, hoods must conform to structural strength and materials as described in 9.1.

Entry loss = 0.45 velocity pressure for tapered takeoff.

Disc dia. inches (centimeters)		Exhaust E		Volume exhaust at 4,500 ft/ min. ft³/ min	Note
Min.	Max.	No Pipes	Dia.		
	19 (48.26)	1	5	610	
Over 19 (48.26)	25 (63.5)	1	6	880	When width "W" permits, exhaust ducts should be as near heaviest grinding as possible.
Over 25 (63.5)	30 (76.2)	1	7	1,200	
Over 30 (76.2)	53 (134.62)	2	6	1,770	
Over 53 (134.62)	72 (182.88)	4	8	6,280	

Entry loss = 0.45 velocity pressure for tapered takeoff.

FIGURE D–57.8—A TYPICAL HOOD FOR A BELT OPERATION

Entry loss = 0.45 velocity pressure for tapered takeoff

Belt width W. inches (centimeters)	Exhaust volume. ft.¹/min
Up to 3 (7.62)	220
3 to 5 (7.62 to 12.7)	300
5 to 7 (12.7 to 17.78)	390
7 to 9 (17.78 to 22.86)	500
9 to 11 (22.86 to 27.94)	610
11 to 13 (27.94 to 33.02)	740

Minimum duct velocity = 4,500 ft/min branch, 3,500 ft/min main.

Entry loss = 0.45 velocity pressure for tapered takeoff; 0.65 velocity pressure for straight takeoff.

(6) *Scope.* This paragraph (g), prescribes the use of exhaust hood enclosures and systems in removing dust, dirt, fumes, and gases generated through the grinding, polishing, or buffing of ferrous and nonferrous metals.

(h) *Spray finishing operations—(1) Definitions applicable to this paragraph—(i) Spray-finishing operations.* Spray-finishing operations are employment of methods wherein organic or inorganic materials are utilized in dispersed form for deposit on surfaces to be coated, treated, or cleaned. Such methods of deposit may involve either automatic, manual, or electrostatic deposition but do not include metal spraying or metallizing, dipping, flow coating, roller coating, tumbling, centrifuging, or spray washing and degreasing as conducted in self-contained washing and degreasing machines or systems.

(ii) *Spray booth.* Spray booths are defined and described in § 1926.66(a). (See sections 103, 104, and 105 of the Standard for Spray Finishing Using Flammable and Combustible Materials, NFPA No. 33–1969).

(iii) *Spray room.* A spray room is a room in which spray-finishing operations not conducted in a spray booth are performed separately from other areas.

(iv) *Minimum maintained velocity.* Minimum maintained velocity is the velocity of air movement which must be maintained in order to meet minimum specified requirements for health and safety.

(2) *Location and application.* Spray booths or spray rooms are to be used to enclose or confine all operations. Spray-finishing operations shall be located as provided in sections 201 through 206 of the Standard for Spray Finishing Using Flammable and Combustible Materials, NFPA No. 33–1969.

(3) *Design and construction of spray booths.* (i) Spray booths shall be designed and constructed in accordance with § 1926.66(b) (1) through (4) and (6) through (10) (see sections 301–304 and 306–310 of the Standard for Spray Finishing Using Flammable and Combustible Materials, NFPA No. 33–1969), for general construction specifications. For a more detailed discussion of fundamentals relating to this subject, see ANSI Z9.2–1960

(A) Lights, motors, electrical equipment, and other sources of ignition shall conform to the requirements of § 1926.66(b)(10) and (c). (See section 310 and chapter 4 of the Standard for Spray Finishing Using Flammable and Combustible Materials NFPA No. 33–1969.)

(B) In no case shall combustible material be used in the construction of a spray booth and supply or exhaust duct connected to it.

(ii) Unobstructed walkways shall not be less than 6½ feet (1.976 m) high and shall be maintained clear of obstruction from any work location in the booth to a booth exit or open booth front. In booths where the open front is the only exit, such exits shall be not less than 3 feet (0.912 m) wide. In booths having multiple exits, such exits shall not be less than 2 feet (0.608 m) wide, provided that the maximum distance from the work location to the exit is 25 feet (7.6 m) or less. Where booth exits are provided with doors, such doors shall open outward from the booth.

(iii) Baffles, distribution plates, and dry-type overspray collectors shall conform to the requirements of § 1926.66(b) (4) and (5). (See sections 304 and 305 of the Standard for Spray Finishing Using Flammable and Combustible Materials, NFPA No. 33–1969.)

(A) Overspray filters shall be installed and maintained in accordance with the requirements of § 1926.66(b)(5), (see section 305 of the Standard for Spray Finishing Using Flammable and Combustible Materials, NFPA No. 33–1969), and shall only be in a location easily accessible for inspection, cleaning, or replacement.

(B) Where effective means, independent of the overspray filters, are installed which will result in design air distribution across the booth cross section, it is permissible to operate the booth without the filters in place.

(iv) (A) For wet or water-wash spray booths, the water-chamber enclosure, within which intimate contact of contaminated air and cleaning water or other cleaning medium is maintained, if made of steel, shall be 18 gage or heavier and adequately protected against corrosion.

(B) Chambers may include scrubber spray nozzles, headers, troughs, or other devices. Chambers shall be provided with adequate means for creating and maintaining scrubbing action for removal of particulate matter from the exhaust air stream.

(v) Collecting tanks shall be of welded steel construction or other suitable non-combustible material. If pits are used as collecting tanks, they shall be concrete, masonry, or other material having similar properties.

(A) Tanks shall be provided with weirs, skimmer plates, or screens to prevent sludge and floating paint from entering the pump suction box. Means for automatically maintaining the proper water level shall also be provided. Fresh water inlets shall not be submerged. They shall terminate at least one pipe diameter above the safety overflow level of the tank.

(B) Tanks shall be so constructed as to discourage accumulation of hazardous deposits.

(vi) Pump manifolds, risers, and headers shall be adequately sized to insure sufficient water flow to provide efficient operation of the water chamber.

(4) *Design and construction of spray rooms.* (i) Spray rooms, including floors, shall be constructed of masonry, concrete, or other noncombustible material.

(ii) Spray rooms shall have noncombustible fire doors and shutters.

(iii) Spray rooms shall be adequately ventilated so that the atmosphere in the breathing zone of the operator shall be maintained in accordance with the requirements of paragraph (h)(6)(ii) of this section.

(iv) Spray rooms used for production spray-finishing operations shall conform to the requirements for spray booths.

(5) *Ventilation.* (i) Ventilation shall be provided in accordance with provisions of § 1926.66(d) (see chapter 5 of the Standard for Spray Finishing Using Flammable or Combustible Materials, NFPA No. 33–1969), and in accordance with the following:

(A) Where a fan plenum is used to equalize or control the distribution of exhaust air movement through the booth, it shall be of sufficient strength or rigidity to withstand the differential air pressure or other superficially imposed loads for which the equipment is designed and also to facilitate cleaning. Construction specifications shall be at least equivalent to those of paragraph (h)(5)(iii) of this section.

(B) [Reserved]

(ii) Inlet or supply ductwork used to transport makeup air to spray booths or surrounding areas shall be constructed of noncombustible materials.

(A) If negative pressure exists within inlet ductwork, all seams and joints shall be sealed if there is a possibility of infiltration of harmful quantities of noxious gases, fumes, or mists from areas through which ductwork passes.

(B) Inlet ductwork shall be sized in accordance with volume flow requirements and provide design air requirements at the spray booth.

(C) Inlet ductwork shall be adequately supported throughout its length to sustain at least its own weight plus any negative pressure which is exerted upon it under normal operating conditions.

(iii) [Reserved]

(A) Exhaust ductwork shall be adequately supported throughout its length to sustain its weight plus any normal accumulation in interior during normal operating conditions and any negative pressure exerted upon it.

(B) Exhaust ductwork shall be sized in accordance with good design practice which shall include consideration of fan capacity, length of duct, number of turns and elbows, variation in size, volume, and character of materials being exhausted. See American National Standard Z9.2–1960 for further details and explanation concerning elements of design.

(C) Longitudinal joints in sheet steel ductwork shall be either lock-seamed, riveted, or welded. For other than steel construction, equivalent securing of joints shall be provided.

(D) Circumferential joints in ductwork shall be substantially fastened together and lapped in the direction of airflow. At least every fourth joint shall be provided with connecting flanges, bolted together, or of equivalent fastening security.

(E) Inspection or clean-out doors shall be provided for every 9 to 12 feet (2.736 to 3.648 m) of running length for ducts up to 12 inches (0.304 m) in diameter, but the distance between cleanout doors may be greater for larger pipes. (See 8.3.21 of American National Standard Z9.1–1951.) A clean-out door or doors shall be provided for servicing the fan, and where necessary, a drain shall be provided.

(F) Where ductwork passes through a combustible roof or wall, the roof or wall shall be protected at the point of penetration by open space or fire-resistive material between the duct and the roof or wall. When ducts pass through firewalls, they shall be provided with automatic fire dampers on both sides of the wall, except that three-eighth-inch steel plates may be used in lieu of automatic fire dampers for ducts not exceeding 18 inches (45.72 cm) in diameter.

(G) Ductwork used for ventilating any process covered in this standard shall not be connected to ducts ventilating any other process or any chimney or flue used for conveying any products of combustion.

(6) *Velocity and air flow requirements.* (i) Except where a spray booth has an adequate air replacement system, the velocity of air into all openings of a spray booth shall be not less than that specified in Table D–57.7 for the operating conditions specified. An adequate air replacement system is one which introduces replacement air upstream or above the object being sprayed and is so designed that the velocity of air in the booth cross section is not less than that specified in Table D–57.7 when measured upstream or above the object being sprayed.

TABLE D–57.7—MINIMUM MAINTAINED VELOCITIES INTO SPRAY BOOTHS

Operating conditions for objects completely inside booth	Crossdraft, f.p.m.	Airflow velocities, f.p.m.	
		Design	Range
Electrostatic and automatic airless operation contained in booth without operator.	Negligible	50 large booth	50–75
Air-operated guns, manual or automatic	....	100 small booth	75–125
	Up to 50	100 large booth	75–125
Air-operated guns, manual or automatic	....	150 small booth	125–175
	Up to 100	150 large booth	125–175
	....	200 small booth	150–250

NOTES:

65

(1) Attention is invited to the fact that the effectiveness of the spray booth is dependent upon the relationship of the depth of the booth to its height and width.

(2) Crossdrafts can be eliminated through proper design and such design should be sought. Crossdrafts in excess of 100fpm (feet per minute) should not be permitted.

(3) Excessive air pressures result in loss of both efficiency and material waste in addition to creating a backlash that may carry overspray and fumes into adjacent work areas.

(4) Booths should be designed with velocities shown in the column headed "Design." However, booths operating with velocities shown in the column headed "Range" are in compliance with this standard.

(ii) In addition to the requirements in paragraph (h)(6)(i) of this section the total air volume exhausted through a spray booth shall be such as to dilute solvent vapor to at least 25 percent of the lower explosive limit of the solvent being sprayed. An example of the method of calculating this volume is given below.

Example: To determine the lower explosive limits of the most common solvents used in spray finishing, see Table D–57.8. Column 1 gives the number of cubic feet of vapor per gallon of solvent and column 2 gives the lower explosive limit (LEL) in percentage by volume of air. Note that the quantity of solvent will be diminished by the quantity of solids and nonflammables contained in the finish.

To determine the volume of air in cubic feet necessary to dilute the vapor from 1 gallon of solvent to 25 percent of the lower explosive limit, apply the following formula:

Dilution volume required per gallon of solvent=4 (100–LEL) (cubic feet of vapor per gallon)÷ LEL

Using toluene as the solvent.

(1) LEL of toluene from Table D–57.8, column 2, is 1.4 percent.

(2) Cubic feet of vapor per gallon from Table D–57.8, column 1, is 30.4 cubic feet per gallon.

(3) Dilution volume required = 4 (100–1.4) 30.4÷1.4=8,564 cubic feet.

(4) To convert to cubic feet per minute of required ventilation, multiply the dilution volume required per gallon of solvent by the number of gallons of solvent evaporated per minute.

TABLE D–57.8—LOWER EXPLOSIVE LIMIT OF SOME COMMONLY USED SOLVENTS

Solvent	Cubic feet per gallon of vapor of liquid at 70 °F (21.11 °C).	Lower explosive limit in percent by volume of air at 70 °F (21.11 °C)
	Column 1	Column 2
Acetone	44.0	2.6
Amyl Acetate (iso)	21.6	[1] 1.0
Amyl Alcohol (n)	29.6	1.2
Amyl Alcohol (iso)	29.6	1.2
Benzene	36.8	[1] 1.4
Butyl Acetate (n)	24.8	1.7

TABLE D–57.8—LOWER EXPLOSIVE LIMIT OF SOME COMMONLY USED SOLVENTS—Continued

Solvent	Cubic feet per gallon of vapor of liquid at 70 °F (21.11 °C).	Lower explosive limit in percent by volume of air at 70 °F (21.11 °C)
Butyl Alcohol (n)	35.2	1.4
Butyl Cellosolve	24.8	1.1
Cellosolve	33.6	1.8
Cellosolve Acetate	23.2	1.7
Cyclohexanone	31.2	[1] 1.1
1,1 Dichloroethylene	42.4	5.9
1,2 Dichloroethylene	42.4	9.7
Ethyl Acetate	32.8	2.5
Ethyl Alcohol	55.2	4.3
Ethyl Lactate	28.0	[1] 1.5
Methyl Acetate	40.0	3.1
Methyl Alcohol	80.8	7.3
Methyl Cellosolve	40.8	2.5
Methyl Ethyl Ketone	36.0	1.8
Methyl n-Propyl Ketone	30.4	1.5
Naphtha (VM&P) (76°Naphtha)	22.4	0.9
Naphtha (100°Flash) Safety Solvent—Stoddard Solvent	23.2	1.0
Propyl Acetate (n)	27.2	2.8
Propyl Acetate (iso)	28.0	1.1
Propyl Alcohol (n)	44.8	2.1
Propyl Alcohol (iso)	44.0	2.0
Toluene	30.4	1.4
Turpentine	20.8	0.8
Xylene (o)	26.4	1.0

[1] At 212 °F (100 °C).

(iii)(A) When an operator is in a booth downstream of the object being sprayed, an air-supplied respirator or other type of respirator approved by NIOSH under 42 CFR part 84 for the material being sprayed should be used by the operator.

(B) Where downdraft booths are provided with doors, such doors shall be closed when spray painting.

(7) *Make-up air.* (i) Clean fresh air, free of contamination from adjacent industrial exhaust systems, chimneys, stacks, or vents, shall be supplied to a spray booth or room in quantities equal to the volume of air exhausted through the spray booth.

(ii) Where a spray booth or room receives make-up air through self-closing doors, dampers, or louvers, they shall be fully open at all times when the booth or room is in use for spraying. The velocity of air through such doors,

66

dampers, or louvers shall not exceed 200 feet per minute. If the fan characteristics are such that the required air flow through the booth will be provided, higher velocities through the doors, dampers, or louvers may be used.

(iii) (A) Where the air supply to a spray booth or room is filtered, the fan static pressure shall be calculated on the assumption that the filters are dirty to the extent that they require cleaning or replacement.

(B) The rating of filters shall be governed by test data supplied by the manufacturer of the filter. A pressure gage shall be installed to show the pressure drop across the filters. This gage shall be marked to show the pressure drop at which the filters require cleaning or replacement. Filters shall be replaced or cleaned whenever the pressure drop across them becomes excessive or whenever the air flow through the face of the booth falls below that specified in Table D–57.7.

(iv) (A) Means for heating make-up air to any spray booth or room, before or at the time spraying is normally performed, shall be provided in all places where the outdoor temperature may be expected to remain below 55 °F. (12.77 °C.) for appreciable periods of time during the operation of the booth except where adequate and safe means of radiant heating for all operating personnel affected is provided. The replacement air during the heating seasons shall be maintained at not less than 65 °F. (18.33 °C.) at the point of entry into the spray booth or spray room. When otherwise unheated make-up air would be at a temperature of more than 10 °F. below room temperature, its temperature shall be regulated as provided in section 3.6.3 of ANSI Z9.2–1960.

(B) As an alternative to an air replacement system complying with the preceding section, general heating of the building in which the spray room or booth is located may be employed provided that all occupied parts of the building are maintained at not less than 65 °F. (18.33 °C.) when the exhaust system is in operation or the general heating system supplemented by other sources of heat may be employed to meet this requirement.

(C) No means of heating make-up air shall be located in a spray booth.

(D) Where make-up air is heated by coal or oil, the products of combustion shall not be allowed to mix with the make-up air, and the products of combustion shall be conducted outside the building through a flue terminating at a point remote from all points where make-up air enters the building.

(E) Where make-up air is heated by gas, and the products of combustion are not mixed with the make-up air but are conducted through an independent flue to a point outside the building remote from all points where make-up air enters the building, it is not necessary to comply with paragraph (h)(7)(iv)(F) of this section.

(F) Where make-up air to any manually operated spray booth or room is heated by gas and the products of combustion are allowed to mix with the supply air, the following precautions must be taken:

(1) The gas must have a distinctive and strong enough odor to warn workmen in a spray booth or room of its presence if in an unburned state in the make-up air.

(2) The maximum rate of gas supply to the make-up air heater burners must not exceed that which would yield in excess of 200 p.p.m. (parts per million) of carbon monoxide or 2,000 p.p.m. of total combustible gases in the mixture if the unburned gas upon the occurrence of flame failure were mixed with all of the make-up air supplied.

(3) A fan must be provided to deliver the mixture of heated air and products of combustion from the plenum chamber housing the gas burners to the spray booth or room.

(8) *Scope.* Spray booths or spray rooms are to be used to enclose or confine all spray finishing operations covered by this paragraph (h). This paragraph does not apply to the spraying of the exteriors of buildings, fixed tanks, or similar structures, nor to small portable spraying apparatus not used repeatedly in the same location.

(i) *Open surface tanks*—(1) *General.* (i) This paragraph applies to all operations involving the immersion of materials in liquids, or in the vapors of such liquids, for the purpose of cleaning or altering the surface or adding to

67

or imparting a finish thereto or changing the character of the materials, and their subsequent removal from the liquid or vapor, draining, and drying. These operations include washing, electroplating, anodizing, pickling, quenching, dying, dipping, tanning, dressing, bleaching, degreasing, alkaline cleaning, stripping, rinsing, digesting, and other similar operations.

(ii) Except where specific construction specifications are prescribed in this section, hoods, ducts, elbows, fans, blowers, and all other exhaust system parts, components, and supports thereof shall be so constructed as to meet conditions of service and to facilitate maintenance and shall conform in construction to the specifications contained in American National Standard Fundamentals Governing the Design and Operation of Local Exhaust Systems, Z9.2–1960.

(2) *Classification of open-surface tank operations.* (i) Open-surface tank operations shall be classified into 16 classes, numbered A–1 to D–4, inclusive.

(ii) *Determination of class.* Class is determined by two factors, hazard potential designated by a letter from A to D, inclusive, and rate of gas, vapor, or mist evolution designated by a number from 1 to 4, inclusive (for example, B.3).

(iii) Hazard potential is an index, on a scale of from A to D, inclusive, of the severity of the hazard associated with the substance contained in the tank because of the toxic, flammable, or explosive nature of the vapor, gas, or mist produced therefrom. The toxic hazard is determined from the concentration, measured in parts by volume of a gas or vapor, per million parts by volume of contaminated air (p.p.m.), or in milligrams of mist per cubic meter of air (mg./m.^{3}), below which ill effects are unlikely to occur to the exposed worker. The concentrations shall be those in § 1926.55 or other pertinent sections of this part.

(iv) The relative fire or explosion hazard is measured in degrees Fahrenheit in terms of the closed-cup flash point of the substance in the tank. Detailed information on the prevention of fire hazards in dip tanks may be found in Dip Tanks Containing Flammable or Combustible Liquids, NFPA No. 34–1966, National Fire Protection Associa-

tion. Where the tank contains a mixture of liquids, other than organic solvents, whose effects are additive, the hygienic standard of the most toxic component (for example, the one having the lowest p.p.m. or mg./m.^{3}) shall be used, except where such substance constitutes an insignificantly small fraction of the mixture. For mixtures of organic solvents, their combined effect, rather than that of either individually, shall determine the hazard potential. In the absence of information to the contrary, the effects shall be considered as additive. If the sum of the ratios of the airborne concentration of each contaminant to the toxic concentration of that contaminant exceeds unity, the toxic concentration shall be considered to have been exceeded. (See Note A to paragraph (i)(2)(v) of this section.)

(v) Hazard potential shall be determined from Table D–57.9, with the value indicating greater hazard being used. When the hazardous material may be either a vapor with a threshold limit value (*TLV*) in p.p.m. or a mist with a *TLV* in mg./m.$_3$, the *TLV* indicating the greater hazard shall be used (for example, A takes precedence over B or C; B over C; C over D).

NOTE A:

$$(c_1 \div TLV_1) + (c_2 \div TLV_2) + (c_3 \div TLV_3) + ; \ldots (c_N \div TLV_N)1$$

Where:

c = Concentration measured at the operation in p.p.m.

TABLE D–57.9—DETERMINATION OF HAZARD POTENTIAL

Hazard potential	Toxicity group		
	Gas or vapor (p.p.m.)	Mist (mg./m^3)	Flash point in degrees F. (C.)
A	0–10	0–0.1	
B	11–100	0.11–1.0	Under 100 (37.77)
C	101–500	1.1–10	100 200 (37.77–93.33)
D	Over 500	Over 10	Over 200 (93.33)

(vi) Rate of gas, vapor, or mist evolution is a numerical index, on a scale of from 1 to 4, inclusive, both of the relative capacity of the tank to produce gas, vapor, or mist and of the relative energy with which it is projected or carried upwards from the tank. Rate is evaluated in terms of

(A) The temperature of the liquid in the tank in degrees Fahrenheit;

(B) The number of degrees Fahrenheit that this temperature is below the boiling point of the liquid in degrees Fahrenheit;

(C) The relative evaporation of the liquid in still air at room temperature in an arbitrary scale—fast, medium, slow, or nil; and

(D) The extent that the tank gases or produces mist in an arbitrary scale—high, medium, low, and nil. (See Table D–57.10, Note 2.) Gassing depends upon electrochemical or mechanical processes, the effects of which have to be individually evaluated for each installation (see Table D–57.10, Note 3).

(vii) Rate of evolution shall be determined from Table D–57.10. When evaporation and gassing yield different rates, the lowest numerical value shall be used.

TABLE D–57.10—DETERMINATION OF RATE OF GAS, VAPOR, OR MIST EVOLUTION [1]

Rate	Liquid temperature, °F. (C.)	Degrees below boiling point	Relative evaporation [2]	Gassing [3]
1	Over 200 (93.33)	0–20	Fast	High.
2	150–200 (65.55–93.33)	21–50	Medium	Medium.
3	94–149 (34.44–65)	51–100	Slow	Low.
4	Under 94 (34.44)	Over 100	Nil	Nil.

[1] In certain classes of equipment, specifically vapor degreasers, an internal condenser or vapor level thermostat is used to prevent the vapor from leaving the tank during normal operation. In such cases, rate of vapor evolution from the tank into the workroom is not dependent upon the factors listed in the table, but rather upon abnormalities of operating procedure, such as carry-out of vapors from excessively fast action, dragout of liquid by entrainment in parts, contamination of solvent by water and other materials, or improper heat balance. When operating procedure is excellent, effective rate of evolution may be taken as 4. When operating procedure is average, the effective rate of evolution may be taken as 3. When operation is poor, a rate of 2 or 1 is indicated, depending upon observed conditions.

[2] Relative evaporation rate is determined according to the methods described by A. K. Doolittle in Industrial and Engineering Chemistry, vol. 27, p. 1169, (3) where time for 100-percent evaporation is as follows: Fast: 0–3 hours; Medium: 3–12 hours; Slow: 12–50 hours; Nil: more than 50 hours.

[3] Gassing means the formation by chemical or electrochemical action of minute bubbles of gas under the surface of the liquid in the tank and is generally limited to aqueous solutions.

(3) *Ventilation.* Where ventilation is used to control potential exposures to workers as defined in paragraph (i)(2)(iii) of this section, it shall be adequate to reduce the concentration of the air contaminant to the degree that a hazard to the worker does not exist. Methods of ventilation are discussed in American National Standard Fundamentals Governing the Design and Operation of Local Exhaust Systems, Z9.2–1960.

(4) *Control requirements.* (i) Control velocities shall conform to Table D–57.11 in all cases where the flow of air past the breathing or working zone of the operator and into the hoods is undisturbed by local environmental conditions, such as open windows, wall fans, unit heaters, or moving machinery.

(ii) All tanks exhausted by means of hoods which

(A) Project over the entire tank;

(B) Are fixed in position in such a location that the head of the workman, in all his normal operating positions while working at the tank, is in front of all hood openings; and

(C) Are completely enclosed on at least two sides, shall be considered to be exhausted through an enclosing hood.

(D) The quantity of air in cubic feet per minute necessary to be exhausted through an enclosing hood shall be not less than the product of the control velocity times the net area of all openings in the enclosure through which air can flow into the hood.

TABLE D–57.11—CONTROL VELOCITIES IN FEET PER MINUTE (F.P.M.) FOR UNDISTURBED LOCATIONS

Class	Enclosing hood		Lateral exhaust [1]	Canopy hood [2]	
	One open side	Two open sides		Three open sides	Four open sides
B–1 and A–2	100	150	150	Do not use	Do not use
A–3 [2], B–1, B–2, and C–1	75	100	100	125	175
A–3, C–2, and D–1 [3]	65	90	75	100	150
B–4 [2], C–3, and D–2 [3]	50	75	50	75	125
A–4, C–4, D–3 [3], and D–4 [4]	....	....	....	....	....

[1] See Table D–57.12 for computation of ventilation rate.
[2] Do not use canopy hood for Hazard Potential A processes.
[3] Where complete control of hot water is desired, design as next highest class.
[4] General room ventilation required.

(iii) All tanks exhausted by means of hoods which do not project over the entire tank, and in which the direction of air movement into the hood or hoods is substantially horizontal, shall be considered to be laterally exhausted. The quantity of air in cubic feet per minute necessary to be laterally exhausted per square foot of tank area in order to maintain the required control velocity shall be determined from Table D–57.12 for all variations in ratio of tank width (W) to tank length (L). The total quantity of air in cubic feet per minute required to be exhausted per tank shall be not less than the product of the area of tank surface times the cubic feet per minute per square foot of tank area, determined from Table D–57.12.

(A) For lateral exhaust hoods over 42 inches (1.06 m) wide, or where it is desirable to reduce the amount of air removed from the workroom, air supply slots or orifices shall be provided along the side or the center of the tank opposite from the exhaust slots. The design of such systems shall meet the following criteria:

(1) The supply air volume plus the entrained air shall not exceed 50 percent of the exhaust volume.

(2) The velocity of the supply airstream as it reaches the effective control area of the exhaust slot shall be less than the effective velocity over the exhaust slot area.

TABLE D–57.12—MINIMUM VENTILATION RATE IN CUBIC FEET OF AIR PER MINUTE PER SQUARE FOOT OF TANK AREA FOR LATERAL EXHAUST

Required minimum control velocity, f.p.m. (from Table D–57.11)	C.f.m. per sq. ft. to maintain required minimum velocities at following ratios (tank width (W)/tank length (L)). [1][2]				
	0.0–0.09	0.1–0.24	0.25–0.49	0.5–0.99	1.0–2.0
Hood along one side or two parallel sides of tank when one hood is against a wall or baffle. [2] Also for a manifold along tank centerline. [3]					
50	50	60	75	90	100
75	75	90	110	130	150
100	100	125	150	175	200
150	150	190	225	260	300
Hood along one side or two parallel sides of free standing tank not against wall or baffle.					
50	75	90	100	110	125
75	110	130	150	170	190
100	150	175	200	225	250
150	225	260	300	340	375

[1] It is not practicable to ventilate across the long dimension of a tank whose ratio W/L exceeds 2.0.
It is undesirable to do so when W/L exceeds 1.0. For circular tanks with lateral exhaust along up to ½ the circumference, use W/L=1.0; for over one-half the circumference use W/L=0.5.
[2] Baffle is a vertical plate the same length as the tank, and with the top of the plate as high as the tank is wide. If the exhaust hood is on the side of a tank against a building wall or close to it, it is perfectly baffled.
[3] Use $W/2$ as tank width in computing when manifold is along centerline, or when hoods are used on two parallel sides of a tank.
Tank Width (W) means the effective width over which the hood must pull air to operate (for example, where the hood face is set back from the edge of the tank, this set back must be added in measuring tank width). The surface area of tanks can frequently be reduced and better control obtained (particularly on conveyorized systems) by using covers extending from the upper edges of the slots toward the center of the tank.

(3) The vertical height of the receiving exhaust hood, including any baffle, shall not be less than one-quarter the width of the tank.

(4) The supply airstream shall not be allowed to impinge on obstructions between it and the exhaust slot in such a manner as to significantly interfere with the performance of the exhaust hood.

(5) Since most failure of push-pull systems result from excessive supply air volumes and pressures, methods of measuring and adjusting the supply air shall be provided. When satisfactory control has been achieved, the adjustable features of the hood shall be fixed so that they will not be altered.

(iv) All tanks exhausted by means of hoods which project over the entire tank, and which do not conform to the definition of enclosing hoods, shall be considered to be overhead canopy hoods. The quantity of air in cubic feet per minute necessary to be exhausted through a canopy hood shall be not less than the product of the control velocity times the net area of all openings between the bottom edges of the hood and the top edges of the tank.

(v) The rate of vapor evolution (including steam or products of combustion) from the process shall be estimated. If the rate of vapor evolution is equal to or greater than 10 percent of the calculated exhaust volume required, the exhaust volume shall be increased in equal amount.

(5) *Spray cleaning and degreasing.* Wherever spraying or other mechanical means are used to disperse a liquid above an open-surface tank, control must be provided for the airborne spray. Such operations shall be enclosed as completely as possible. The inward air velocity into the enclosure shall be sufficient to prevent the discharge of spray into the workroom. Mechanical baffles may be used to help prevent the discharge of spray. Spray painting operations are covered by paragraph (h) of this section.

(6) *Control means other than ventilation.* Tank covers, foams, beads, chips, or other materials floating on the tank surface so as to confine gases, mists, or vapors to the area under the cover or to the foam, bead, or chip layer; or surface tension depressive agents added to the liquid in the tank to minimize mist formation, or any combination thereof, may all be used as gas, mist, or vapor control means for open-surface tank operations, provided that they effectively reduce the concentrations of hazardous materials in the vicinity of the worker below the limits set in accordance with paragraph (i)(2) of this section.

(7) *System design.* (i) The equipment for exhausting air shall have sufficient capacity to produce the flow of air required in each of the hoods and openings of the system.

(ii) The capacity required in paragraph (i)(7)(i) of this section shall be obtained when the airflow producing equipment is operating against the following pressure losses, the sum of which is the static pressure:

(A) Entrance losses into the hood.

(B) Resistance to airflow in branch pipe including bends and transformations.

(C) Entrance loss into the main pipe.

(D) Resistance to airflow in main pipe including bends and transformations.

(E) Resistance of mechanical equipment; that is, filters, washers, condensers, absorbers, etc., plus their entrance and exit losses.

(F) Resistance in outlet duct and discharge stack.

(iii) Two or more operations shall not be connected to the same exhaust system where either one or the combination of the substances removed may constitute a fire, explosion, or chemical reaction hazard in the duct system. Traps or other devices shall be provided to insure that condensate in ducts does not drain back into any tank.

(iv) The exhaust system, consisting of hoods, ducts, air mover, and discharge outlet, shall be designed in accordance with American National Standard Fundamentals Governing the Design and Operation of Local Exhaust Systems, Z9.2–1960, or the manual, Industrial Ventilation, published by the American Conference of Governmental Industrial Hygienists 1970. Airflow and pressure loss data provided by the manufacturer of any air cleaning device shall be included in the design calculations.

(8) *Operation*. (i) The required airflow shall be maintained at all times during which gas, mist, or vapor is emitted from the tank, and at all times the tank, the draining, or the drying area is in operation or use. When the system is first installed, the airflow from each hood shall be measured by means of a pitot traverse in the exhaust duct and corrective action taken if the flow is less than that required. When the proper flow is obtained, the hood static pressure shall be measured and recorded. At intervals of not more than 3 months operation, or after a prolonged shutdown period, the hoods and duct system shall be inspected for evidence of corrosion or damage. In any case where the airflow is found to be less than required, it shall be increased to the required value. (Information on airflow and static pressure measurement and calculations may be found in American National Standard Fundamental Governing the Design and Operation of Local Exhaust Systems, Z9.2–1960, or in the manual, Industrial Ventilation, published by the American Conference of Governmental Industrial Hygienists.)

(ii) The exhaust system shall discharge to the outer air in such a manner that the possibility of its effluent entering any building is at a minimum. Recirculation shall only be through a device for contaminant removal which will prevent the creation of a health hazard in the room or area to which the air is recirculated.

(iii) A volume of outside air in the range of 90 percent to 110 percent of the exhaust volume shall be provided to each room having exhaust hoods. The outside air supply shall enter the workroom in such a manner as not to be detrimental to any exhaust hood. The airflow of the makeup air system shall be measured on installation. Corrective action shall be taken when the airflow is below that required. The makeup air shall be uncontaminated.

(9) *Personal protection*. (i) All employees working in and around open-surface tank operations must be instructed as to the hazards of their respective jobs, and in the personal protection and first aid procedures applicable to these hazards.

(ii) All persons required to work in such a manner that their feet may become wet shall be provided with rubber or other impervious boots or shoes, rubbers, or wooden-soled shoes sufficient to keep feet dry.

(iii) All persons required to handle work wet with a liquid other than water shall be provided with gloves impervious to such a liquid and of a length sufficient to prevent entrance of liquid into the tops of the gloves. The interior of gloves shall be kept free from corrosive or irritating contaminants.

(iv) All persons required to work in such a manner that their clothing may become wet shall be provided with such aprons, coats, jackets, sleeves, or other garments made of rubber, or of other materials impervious to liquids other than water, as are required to keep their clothing dry. Aprons shall extend well below the top of boots to prevent liquid splashing into the boots. Provision of dry, clean, cotton clothing along with rubber shoes or short boots and an apron impervious to liquids other than water shall be considered a satisfactory substitute where small parts are cleaned, plated, or acid dipped in open tanks and rapid work is required.

(v) Whenever there is a danger of splashing, for example, when additions are made manually to the tanks, or when acids and chemicals are removed from the tanks, the employees so engaged shall be required to wear either tight-fitting chemical goggles or an effective face shield. See § 1926.102.

(vi) When, during the emergencies specified in paragraph (i)(11)(v) of this section, employees must be in areas where concentrations of air contaminants are greater than the limits set by paragraph (i)(2)(iii) of this section or oxygen concentrations are less than 19.5 percent, they must use respirators that reduce their exposure to a level below these limits or that provide adequate oxygen. Such respirators must also be provided in marked, quickly-accessible storage compartments built for this purpose when the possibility exists of accidental release of hazardous concentrations of air contaminants. Respirators must be approved by NIOSH under 42 CFR part 84, selected by a competent industrial hygienist or other technically-qualified source, and used in accordance with 29 CFR 1926.103.

(vii) Near each tank containing a liquid which may burn, irritate, or otherwise be harmful to the skin if splashed upon the worker's body, there shall be a supply of clean cold water. The water pipe (carrying a pressure not exceeding 25 pounds (11.325 kg)) shall be provided with a quick opening valve and at least 48 inches (1.216 m) of hose not smaller than three-fourths inch, so that no time may be lost in washing off liquids from the skin or clothing. Alternatively, deluge showers and eye flushes shall be provided in cases where harmful chemicals may be splashed on parts of the body.

(viii) Operators with sores, burns, or other skin lesions requiring medical treatment shall not be allowed to work at their regular operations until so authorized by a physician. Any small skin abrasions, cuts, rash, or open sores which are found or reported shall be treated by a properly designated person so that chances of exposures to the chemicals are removed. Workers exposed to chromic acids shall have a periodic examination made of the nostrils and other parts of the body, to detect incipient ulceration.

(ix) Sufficient washing facilities, including soap, individual towels, and hot water, shall be provided for all persons required to use or handle any liquids which may burn, irritate, or otherwise be harmful to the skin, on the basis of at least one basin (or its equivalent) with a hot water faucet for every 10 employees. See § 1926.51(f).

(x) Locker space or equivalent clothing storage facilities shall be provided to prevent contamination of street clothing.

(xi) First aid facilities specific to the hazards of the operations conducted shall be readily available.

(10) *Special precautions for cyanide.* Dikes or other arrangements shall be provided to prevent the possibility of intermixing of cyanide and acid in the event of tank rupture.

(11) *Inspection, maintenance, and installation.* (i) Floors and platforms around tanks shall be prevented from becoming slippery both by original type of construction and by frequent flushing. They shall be firm, sound, and of the design and construction to minimize the possibility of tripping.

(ii) Before cleaning the interior of any tank, the contents shall be drained off, and the cleanout doors shall be opened where provided. All pockets in tanks or pits, where it is possible for hazardous vapors to collect, shall be ventilated and cleared of such vapors.

(iii) Tanks which have been drained to permit employees to enter for the purposes of cleaning, inspection, or maintenance may contain atmospheres which are hazardous to life or health, through the presence of flammable or toxic air contaminants, or through the absence of sufficient oxygen. Before employees shall be permitted to enter any such tank, appropriate tests of the atmosphere shall be made to determine if the limits set by paragraph (i)(2)(iii) of this section are exceeded, or if the oxygen concentration is less than 19.5 percent.

(iv) If the tests made in accordance with paragraph (i)(11)(iii) of this section indicate that the atmosphere in the tank is unsafe, before any employee is permitted to enter the tank, the tank shall be ventilated until the hazardous atmosphere is removed, and ventilation shall be continued so as to prevent the occurrence of a hazardous atmosphere as long as an employee is in the tank.

(v) If, in emergencies, such as rescue work, it is necessary to enter a tank which may contain a hazardous atmosphere, suitable respirators, such as self-contained breathing apparatus; hose mask with blower, if there is a possibility of oxygen deficiency; or a gas mask, selected and operated in accordance with paragraph (i)(9)(vi) of this section, shall be used. If a contaminant in the tank can cause dermatitis, or be absorbed through the skin, the employee entering the tank shall also wear protective clothing. At least one trained standby employee, with suitable respirator, shall be present in the nearest uncontaminated area. The standby employee must be able to communicate with the employee in the tank and be able to haul him out of the tank with a lifeline if necessary.

(vi) Maintenance work requiring welding or open flame, where toxic metal fumes such as cadmium, chromium, or lead may be evolved, shall be done only with sufficient local exhaust ventilation to prevent the creation of a health hazard, or be done with respirators selected and used in accordance with paragraph (i)(9)(vi) of this section. Welding, or the use of open flames near any solvent cleaning equipment shall be permitted only after such equipment has first been thoroughly cleared of solvents and vapors.

(12) *Vapor degreasing tanks.* (i) In any vapor degreasing tank equipped with a condenser or vapor level thermostat, the condenser or thermostat shall keep the level of vapors below the top edge of the tank by a distance at least equal to one-half the tank width, or at least 36 inches (0.912 m), whichever is shorter.

(ii) Where gas is used as a fuel for heating vapor degreasing tanks, the combustion chamber shall be of tight construction, except for such openings as the exhaust flue, and those that are necessary for supplying air for combustion. Flues shall be of corrosion-resistant construction and shall extend to the outer air. If mechanical exhaust is used on this flue, a draft diverter shall be used. Special precautions must be taken to prevent solvent fumes from entering the combustion air of this or any other heater when chlorinated or fluorinated hydrocarbon solvents (for example, trichloroethylene, Freon) are used.

(iii) Heating elements shall be so designed and maintained that their surface temperature will not cause the solvent or mixture to decompose, break down, or be converted into an excessive quantity of vapor.

(iv) Tanks or machines of more than 4 square feet (0.368 m²) of vapor area, used for solvent cleaning or vapor degreasing, shall be equipped with suitable cleanout or sludge doors located near the bottom of each tank or still. These doors shall be so designed and gasketed that there will be no leakage of solvent when they are closed.

(13) *Scope.* (i) This paragraph (i) applies to all operations involving the immersion of materials in liquids, or in the vapors of such liquids, for the purpose of cleaning or altering their surfaces, or adding or imparting a finish thereto, or changing the character of the materials, and their subsequent removal from the liquids or vapors, draining, and drying. Such operations include washing, electroplating, anodizing, pickling, quenching, dyeing, dipping, tanning, dressing, bleaching, degreasing, alkaline cleaning, stripping, rinsing, digesting, and other similar operations, but do not include molten materials handling operations, or surface coating operations.

(ii) *Molten materials handling operations* means all operations, other than welding, burning, and soldering operations, involving the use, melting, smelting, or pouring of metals, alloys, salts, or other similar substances in the molten state. Such operations also include heat treating baths, descaling baths, die casting stereotyping, galvanizing, tinning, and similar operations.

(iii) *Surface coating operations* means all operations involving the application of protective, decorative, adhesive, or strengthening coating or impregnation to one or more surfaces, or into the interstices of any object or material, by means of spraying, spreading, flowing, brushing, roll coating, pouring, cementing, or similar means; and any subsequent draining or drying operations, excluding open-tank operations.

[44 FR 8577, Feb. 9, 1979; 44 FR 20940, Apr. 6, 1979, as amended at 58 FR 35099, June 30, 1993; 61 FR 9250, Mar. 3, 1996; 63 FR 1295, Jan. 8, 1998]

§ 1926.58 [Reserved]

§ 1926.59 Hazard communication.

NOTE: The requirements applicable to construction work under this section are identical to those set forth at § 1910.1200 of this chapter.

[61 FR 31431, June 20, 1996]

§ 1926.60 Methylenedianiline.

(a) *Scope and application.* (1) This section applies to all construction work as defined in 29 CFR 1910.12(b), in which there is exposure to MDA, including but not limited to the following:

(i) Construction, alteration, repair, maintenance, or renovation of structures, substrates, or portions thereof, that contain MDA;

(ii) Installation or the finishing of surfaces with products containing MDA;

(iii) MDA spill/emergency cleanup at construction sites; and

(iv) Transportation, disposal, storage, or containment of MDA or products containing MDA on the site or location at which construction activities are performed.

(2) Except as provided in paragraphs (a)(7) and (f)(5) of this section, this section does not apply to the processing, use, and handling of products containing MDA where initial monitoring indicates that the product is not capable of releasing MDA in excess of the action level under the expected conditions of processing, use, and handling which will cause the greatest possible release; and where no "dermal exposure to MDA" can occur.

(3) Except as provided in paragraph (a)(7) of this section, this section does not apply to the processing, use, and handling of products containing MDA where objective data are reasonably relied upon which demonstrate the product is not capable of releasing MDA under the expected conditions of processing, use, and handling which will cause the greatest possible release; and where no "dermal exposure to MDA" can occur.

(4) Except as provided in paragraph (a)(7) of this section, this section does not apply to the storage, transportation, distribution or sale of MDA in intact containers sealed in such a manner as to contain the MDA dusts, vapors, or liquids, except for the provisions of 29 CFR 1910.1200 and paragraph (e) of this section.

(5) Except as provided in paragraph (a)(7) of this section, this section does not apply to materials in any form which contain less than 0.1% MDA by weight or volume.

(6) Except as provided in paragraph (a)(7) of this section, this section does not apply to "finished articles containing MDA."

(7) Where products containing MDA are exempted under paragraphs (a)(2) through (a)(6) of this section, the em-

ployer shall maintain records of the initial monitoring results or objective data supporting that exemption and the basis for the employer's reliance on the data, as provided in the record-keeping provision of paragraph (o) of this section.

(b) *Definitions.* For the purpose of this section, the following definitions shall apply:

Action level means a concentration of airborne MDA of 5 ppb as an eight (8)-hour time-weighted average.

Assistant Secretary means the Assistant Secretary of Labor for Occupational Safety and Health, U.S. Department of Labor, or designee.

Authorized person means any person specifically authorized by the employer whose duties require the person to enter a regulated area, or any person entering such an area as a designated representative of employees for the purpose of exercising the right to observe monitoring and measuring procedures under paragraph (p) of this section, or any other person authorized by the Act or regulations issued under the Act.

Container means any barrel, bottle, can, cylinder, drum, reaction vessel, storage tank, commercial packaging or the like, but does not include piping systems.

Decontamination area means an area outside of but as near as practical to the regulated area, consisting of an equipment storage area, wash area, and clean change area, which is used for the decontamination of workers, materials, and equipment contaminated with MDA.

Dermal exposure to MDA occurs where employees are engaged in the handling, application or use of mixtures or materials containing MDA, with any of the following non-airborne forms of MDA:

(i) Liquid, powdered, granular, or flaked mixtures containing MDA in concentrations greater than 0.1% by weight or volume; and

(ii) Materials other than "finished articles" containing MDA in concentrations greater than 0.1% by weight or volume.

Director means the Director of the National Institute for Occupational Safety and Health, U.S. Department of

Health and Human Services, or designee.

Emergency means any occurrence such as, but not limited to, equipment failure, rupture of containers, or failure of control equipment which results in an unexpected and potentially hazardous release of MDA.

Employee exposure means exposure to MDA which would occur if the employee were not using respirators or protective work clothing and equipment.

Finished article containing MDA is defined as a manufactured item:

(i) Which is formed to a specific shape or design during manufacture;

(ii) Which has end use function(s) dependent in whole or part upon its shape or design during end use; and

(iii) Where applicable, is an item which is fully cured by virtue of having been subjected to the conditions (temperature, time) necessary to complete the desired chemical reaction.

Historical monitoring data means monitoring data for construction jobs that meet the following conditions:

(i) The data upon which judgments are based are scientifically sound and were collected using methods that are sufficiently accurate and precise;

(ii) The processes and work practices that were in use when the historical monitoring data were obtained are essentially the same as those to be used during the job for which initial monitoring will not be performed;

(iii) The characteristics of the MDA-containing material being handled when the historical monitoring data were obtained are the same as those on the job for which initial monitoring will not be performed;

(iv) Environmental conditions prevailing when the historical monitoring data were obtained are the same as those on the job for which initial monitoring will not be performed; and

(v) Other data relevant to the operations, materials, processing, or employee exposures covered by the exception are substantially similar. The data must be scientifically sound, the characteristics of the MDA containing material must be similar and the environmental conditions comparable.

4,4′Methylenedianiline or MDA means the chemical; 4,4′-diaminodiphenylmethane, Chemical Abstract Service Registry number 101–77–9, in the form of a vapor, liquid, or solid. The definition also includes the salts of MDA.

Regulated Areas means areas where airborne concentrations of MDA exceed or can reasonably be expected to exceed, the permissible exposure limits, or where "dermal exposure to MDA" can occur.

STEL means short term exposure limit as determined by any 15-minute sample period.

(c) *Permissible exposure limits.* The employer shall assure that no employee is exposed to an airborne concentration of MDA in excess of ten parts per billion (10 ppb) as an 8-hour time-weighted average and a STEL of one hundred parts per billion (100 ppb).

(d) *Communication among employers.* On multi-employer worksites, an employer performing work involving the application of MDA or materials containing MDA for which establishment of one or more regulated areas is required shall inform other employers on the site of the nature of the employer's work with MDA and of the existence of, and requirements pertaining to, regulated areas.

(e) *Emergency situations—(1) Written plan.* (i) A written plan for emergency situations shall be developed for each construction operation where there is a possibility of an emergency. The plan shall include procedures where the employer identifies emergency escape routes for his employees at each construction site before the construction operation begins. Appropriate portions of the plan shall be implemented in the event of an emergency.

(ii) The plan shall specifically provide that employees engaged in correcting emergency conditions shall be equipped with the appropriate personal protective equipment and clothing as required in paragraphs (i) and (j) of this section until the emergency is abated.

(iii) The plan shall specifically include provisions for alerting and evacuating affected employees as well as the applicable elements prescribed in 29 CFR 1910.38 and 29 CFR 1910.39, "Emergency action plans" and "Fire prevention plans," respectively.

(2) *Alerting employees.* Where there is the possibility of employee exposure to MDA due to an emergency, means shall be developed to promptly alert employees who have the potential to be directly exposed. Affected employees not engaged in correcting emergency conditions shall be evacuated immediately in the event that an emergency occurs. Means shall also be developed for alerting other employees who may be exposed as a result of the emergency.

(f) *Exposure monitoring—(1) General.* (i) Determinations of employee exposure shall be made from breathing zone air samples that are representative of each employee's exposure to airborne MDA over an eight (8) hour period. Determination of employee exposure to the STEL shall be made from breathing zone air samples collected over a 15 minute sampling period.

(ii) Representative employee exposure shall be determined on the basis of one or more samples representing full shift exposure for each shift for each job classification in each work area where exposure to MDA may occur.

(iii) Where the employer can document that exposure levels are equivalent for similar operations in different work shifts, the employer shall only be required to determine representative employee exposure for that operation during one shift.

(2) *Initial monitoring.* Each employer who has a workplace or work operation covered by this standard shall perform initial monitoring to determine accurately the airborne concentrations of MDA to which employees may be exposed unless:

(i) The employer can demonstrate, on the basis of objective data, that the MDA-containing product or material being handled cannot cause exposures above the standard's action level, even under worst-case release conditions; or

(ii) The employer has historical monitoring or other data demonstrating that exposures on a particular job will be below the action level.

(3) *Periodic monitoring and monitoring frequency.* (i) If the monitoring required by paragraph (f)(2) of this section reveals employee exposure at or above the action level, but at or below the PELs, the employer shall repeat such monitoring for each such employee at least every six (6) months.

(ii) If the monitoring required by paragraph (f)(2) of this section reveals employee exposure above the PELs, the employer shall repeat such monitoring for each such employee at least every three (3) months.

(iii) Employers who are conducting MDA operations within a regulated area can forego periodic monitoring if the employees are all wearing supplied-air respirators while working in the regulated area.

(iv) The employer may alter the monitoring schedule from every three months to every six months for any employee for whom two consecutive measurements taken at least 7 days apart indicate that the employee exposure has decreased to below the PELs but above the action level.

(4) *Termination of monitoring.* (i) If the initial monitoring required by paragraph (f)(2) of this section reveals employee exposure to be below the action level, the employer may discontinue the monitoring for that employee, except as otherwise required by paragraph (f)(5) of this section.

(ii) If the periodic monitoring required by paragraph (f)(3) of this section reveals that employee exposures, as indicated by at least two consecutive measurements taken at least 7 days apart, are below the action level the employer may discontinue the monitoring for that employee, except as otherwise required by paragraph (f)(5) of this section.

(5) *Additional monitoring.* The employer shall institute the exposure monitoring required under paragraphs (f)(2) and (f)(3) of this section when there has been a change in production process, chemicals present, control equipment, personnel, or work practices which may result in new or additional exposures to MDA, or when the employer has any reason to suspect a change which may result in new or additional exposures.

(6) *Accuracy of monitoring.* Monitoring shall be accurate, to a confidence level of 95 percent, to within plus or minus 25 percent for airborne concentrations of MDA.

(7) *Employee notification of monitoring results.* (i) The employer must, as soon

as possible but no later than 5 working days after the receipt of the results of any monitoring performed under this section, notify each affected employee of these results either individually in writing or by posting the results in an appropriate location that is accessible to employees.

(ii) The written notification required by paragraph (f)(7)(i) of this section shall contain the corrective action being taken by the employer or any other protective measures which have been implemented to reduce the employee exposure to or below the PELs, wherever the PELs are exceeded.

(8) *Visual monitoring.* The employer shall make routine inspections of employee hands, face and forearms potentially exposed to MDA. Other potential dermal exposures reported by the employee must be referred to the appropriate medical personnel for observation. If the employer determines that the employee has been exposed to MDA the employer shall:

(i) Determine the source of exposure;

(ii) Implement protective measures to correct the hazard; and

(iii) Maintain records of the corrective actions in accordance with paragraph (o) of this section.

(g) *Regulated areas*—(1) *Establishment*—(i) *Airborne exposures.* The employer shall establish regulated areas where airborne concentrations of MDA exceed or can reasonably be expected to exceed, the permissible exposure limits.

(ii) *Dermal exposures.* Where employees are subject to "dermal exposure to MDA" the employer shall establish those work areas as regulated areas.

(2) *Demarcation.* Regulated areas shall be demarcated from the rest of the workplace in a manner that minimizes the number of persons potentially exposed.

(3) *Access.* Access to regulated areas shall be limited to authorized persons.

(4) *Personal protective equipment and clothing.* Each person entering a regulated area shall be supplied with, and required to use, the appropriate personal protective clothing and equipment in accordance with paragraphs (i) and (j) of this section.

(5) *Prohibited activities.* The employer shall ensure that employees do not eat, drink, smoke, chew tobacco or gum, or apply cosmetics in regulated areas.

(h) *Methods of compliance*—(1) *Engineering controls and work practices and respirators.* (i) The employer shall use one or any combination of the following control methods to achieve compliance with the permissible exposure limits prescribed by paragraph (c) of this section:

(A) Local exhaust ventilation equipped with HEPA filter dust collection systems;

(B) General ventilation systems;

(C) Use of workpractices; or

(D) Other engineering controls such as isolation and enclosure that the Assistant Secretary can show to be feasible.

(ii) Wherever the feasible engineering controls and work practices "which can be instituted are not sufficient to reduce employee exposure to or below the PELs, the employer shall use them to reduce employee exposure to the lowest levels achievable by these controls and shall supplement them by the use of respiratory protective devices which comply with the requirements of paragraph (i) of this section.

(2) *Special Provisions.* For workers engaged in spray application methods, respiratory protection must be used in addition to feasible engineering controls and work practices to reduce employee exposure to or below the PELs.

(3) *Prohibitions.* Compressed air shall not be used to remove MDA, unless the compressed air is used in conjunction with an enclosed ventilation system designed to capture the dust cloud created by the compressed air.

(4) *Employee rotation.* The employer shall not use employee rotation as a means of compliance with the exposure limits prescribed in paragraph (c) of this section.

(5) *Compliance program.* (i) The employer shall establish and implement a written program to reduce employee exposure to or below the PELs by means of engineering and work practice controls, as required by paragraph (h)(1) of this section, and by use of respiratory protection where permitted under this section.

(ii) Upon request this written program shall be furnished for examination and copying to the Assistant Secretary, the Director, affected employees and designated employee representatives. The employer shall review and, as necessary, update such plans at least once every 12 months to make certain they reflect the current status of the program.

(i) *Respiratory protection*—(1) *General.* For employees who use respirators required by this section, the employer must provide each employee an appropriate respirator that complies with the requirements of this paragraph. Respirators must be used during:

(i) Periods necessary to install or implement feasible engineering and work-practice controls.

(ii) Work operations, such as maintenance and repair activities and spray-application processes, for which engineering and work-practice controls are not feasible.

(iii) Work operations for which feasible engineering and work-practice controls are not yet sufficient to reduce employee exposure to or below the PELs.

(iv) Emergencies.

(2) *Respirator program.* The employer must implement a respiratory protection program in accordance with § 1910.134 (b) through (d) (except (d)(1)(iii)), and (f) through (m), which covers each employee required by this section to use a respirator.

(3) *Respirator selection.* (i) Employers must:

(A) Select, and provide to employees, the appropriate respirators specified in paragraph (d)(3)(i)(A) of 29 CFR 1910.134.

(B) Provide HEPA filters for powered and non-powered air-purifying respirators.

(C) For escape, provide employees with one of the following respirator options: Any self-contained breathing apparatus with a full facepiece or hood operated in the positive-pressure or continuous-flow mode; or a full facepiece air-purifying respirator.

(D) Provide a combination HEPA filter and organic vapor canister or cartridge with air-purifying respirators when MDA is in liquid form or used as part of a process requiring heat.

(ii) An employee who cannot use a negative-pressure respirator must be given the option of using a positive-pressure respirator, or a supplied-air respirator operated in the continuous-flow or pressure-demand mode.

(j) *Protective work clothing and equipment*—(1) *Provision and use.* Where employees are subject to dermal exposure to MDA, where liquids containing MDA can be splashed into the eyes, or where airborne concentrations of MDA are in excess of the PEL, the employer shall provide, at no cost to the employee, and ensure that the employee uses, appropriate protective work clothing and equipment which prevent contact with MDA such as, but not limited to:

(i) Aprons, coveralls or other full-body work clothing;

(ii) Gloves, head coverings, and foot coverings; and

(iii) Face shields, chemical goggles; or

(iv) Other appropriate protective equipment which comply with 29 CFR 1910.133.

(2) *Removal and storage.* (i) The employer shall ensure that, at the end of their work shift, employees remove MDA-contaminated protective work clothing and equipment that is not routinely removed throughout the day in change areas provided in accordance with the provisions in paragraph (k) of this section.

(ii) The employer shall ensure that, during their work shift, employees remove all other MDA-contaminated protective work clothing or equipment before leaving a regulated area.

(iii) The employer shall ensure that no employee takes MDA-contaminated work clothing or equipment out of the decontamination areas, except those employees authorized to do so for the purpose of laundering, maintenance, or disposal.

(iv) MDA-contaminated work clothing or equipment shall be placed and stored and transported in sealed, impermeable bags, or other closed impermeable containers.

(v) Containers of MDA-contaminated protective work clothing or equipment which are to be taken out of decontamination areas or the workplace for cleaning, maintenance, or disposal, shall bear labels warning of the hazards of MDA.

(3) *Cleaning and replacement.* (i) The employer shall provide the employee with clean protective clothing and equipment. The employer shall ensure that protective work clothing or equipment required by this paragraph is cleaned, laundered, repaired, or replaced at intervals appropriate to maintain its effectiveness.

(ii) The employer shall prohibit the removal of MDA from protective work clothing or equipment by blowing, shaking, or any methods which allow MDA to re-enter the workplace.

(iii) The employer shall ensure that laundering of MDA-contaminated clothing shall be done so as to prevent the release of MDA in the workplace.

(iv) Any employer who gives MDA-contaminated clothing to another person for laundering shall inform such person of the requirement to prevent the release of MDA.

(v) The employer shall inform any person who launders or cleans protective clothing or equipment contaminated with MDA of the potentially harmful effects of exposure.

(4) *Visual Examination.* (i) The employer shall ensure that employees' work clothing is examined periodically for rips or tears that may occur during performance of work.

(ii) When rips or tears are detected, the protective equipment or clothing shall be repaired and replaced immediately.

(k) *Hygiene facilities and practices*—(1) *General.* (i) The employer shall provide decontamination areas for employees required to work in regulated areas or required by paragraph (j)(1) of this section to wear protective clothing. *Exception:* In lieu of the decontamination area requirement specified in paragraph (k)(1)(i) of this section, the employer may permit employees engaged in small scale, short duration operations, to clean their protective clothing or dispose of the protective clothing before such employees leave the area where the work was performed.

(ii) *Change areas.* The employer shall ensure that change areas are equipped with separate storage facilities for protective clothing and street clothing, in accordance with 29 CFR 1910.141(e).

(iii) *Equipment area.* The equipment area shall be supplied with impermeable, labeled bags and containers for the containment and disposal of contaminated protective clothing and equipment.

(2) *Shower area.* (i) Where feasible, shower facilities shall be provided which comply with 29 CFR 1910.141(d)(3) wherever the possibility of employee exposure to airborne levels of MDA in excess of the permissible exposure limit exists.

(ii) Where dermal exposure to MDA occurs, the employer shall ensure that materials spilled or deposited on the skin are removed as soon as possible by methods which do not facilitate the dermal absorption of MDA.

(3) *Lunch Areas.* (i) Whenever food or beverages are consumed at the worksite and employees are exposed to MDA the employer shall provide clean lunch areas were MDA levels are below the action level and where no dermal exposure to MDA can occur.

(ii) The employer shall ensure that employees wash their hands and faces with soap and water prior to eating, drinking, smoking, or applying cosmetics.

(iii) The employer shall ensure that employees do not enter lunch facilities with contaminated protective work clothing or equipment.

(l) *Communication of hazards to employees*—(1) *Hazard communication.* The employer shall include Methylenedianiline (MDA) in the program established to comply with the Hazard Communication Standard (HCS) (§ 1910.1200). The employer shall ensure that each employee has access to labels on containers of MDA and safety data sheets, and is trained in accordance with the provisions of HCS and paragraph (l)(3) of this section. The employer shall ensure that at least the following hazards are addressed: Cancer; liver effects; and skin sensitization.

(2) *Signs and labels*—(i) *Signs.* (A) The employer shall post and maintain legible signs demarcating regulated areas and entrances or access-ways to regulated areas that bear the following legend:

DANGER
MDA

MAY CAUSE CANCER
CAUSES DAMAGE TO THE LIVER
RESPIRATORY PROTECTION AND PRO-
TECTIVE CLOTHING MAY BE REQUIRED
IN THIS AREA
AUTHORIZED PERSONNEL ONLY

(B) Prior to June 1, 2016, employers may use the following legend in lieu of that specified in paragraph (l)(2)(i)(A) of this section:

DANGER
MDA
MAY CAUSE CANCER
LIVER TOXIN
AUTHORIZED PERSONNEL ONLY
RESPIRATORS AND PROTECTIVE CLOTH-
ING MAY BE REQUIRED TO BE WORN IN
THIS AREA

(ii) *Labels.* (A) The employer shall ensure that labels or other appropriate forms of warning are provided for containers of MDA within the workplace. The labels shall comply with the requirements of § 1910.1200(f) and shall include at least the following information for pure MDA and mixtures containing MDA:

DANGER
CONTAINS MDA
MAY CAUSE CANCER
CAUSES DAMAGE TO THE LIVER

(B) Prior to June 1, 2015, employers may include the following information workplace labels in lieu of the labeling requirements in paragraph (l)(2)(ii)(A) of this section:

(*1*) For Pure MDA:

DANGER
CONTAINS MDA
MAY CAUSE CANCER
LIVER TOXIN

(*2*) For mixtures containing MDA:

DANGER
CONTAINS MDA
CONTAINS MATERIALS WHICH MAY
CAUSE CANCER
LIVER TOXIN

(3) *Information and training.* (i) The employer shall provide employees with information and training on MDA, in accordance with 29 CFR 1910.1200(h), at the time of initial assignment and at least annually thereafter.

(ii) In addition to the information required under 29 CFR 1910.1200, the employer shall:

(A) Provide an explanation of the contents of this section, including appendices A and B of this section, and indicate to employees where a copy of the standard is available;

(B) Describe the medical surveillance program required under paragraph (n) of this section, and explain the information contained in appendix C of this section; and

(C) Describe the medical removal provision required under paragraph (n) of this section.

(4) *Access to training materials.* (i) The employer shall make readily available to all affected employees, without cost, all written materials relating to the employee training program, including a copy of this regulation.

(ii) The employer shall provide to the Assistant Secretary and the Director, upon request, all information and training materials relating to the employee information and training program.

(m) *Housekeeping.* (1) All surfaces shall be maintained as free as practicable of visible accumulations of MDA.

(2) The employer shall institute a program for detecting MDA leaks, spills, and discharges, including regular visual inspections of operations involving liquid or solid MDA.

(3) All leaks shall be repaired and liquid or dust spills cleaned up promptly.

(4) Surfaces contaminated with MDA may not be cleaned by the use of compressed air.

(5) Shoveling, dry sweeping, and other methods of dry clean-up of MDA may be used where HEPA filtered vacuuming and/or wet cleaning are not feasible or practical.

(6) Waste, scrap, debris, bags, containers, equipment, and clothing contaminated with MDA shall be collected and disposed of in a manner to prevent the re-entry of MDA into the workplace.

(n) *Medical surveillance—*(1) *General.* (i) The employer shall make available a medical surveillance program for employees exposed to MDA under the following circumstances:

(A) Employees exposed at or above the action level for 30 or more days per year;

(B) Employees who are subject to dermal exposure to MDA for 15 or more days per year;

(C) Employees who have been exposed in an emergency situation;

(D) Employees whom the employer, based on results from compliance with paragraph (f)(8) of this section, has reason to believe are being dermally exposed; and

(E) Employees who show signs or symptoms of MDA exposure.

(ii) The employer shall ensure that all medical examinations and procedures are performed by or under the supervision of a licensed physician at a reasonable time and place, and provided without cost to the employee.

(2) *Initial examinations.* (i) Within 150 days of the effective date of this standard, or before the time of initial assignment, the employer shall provide each employee covered by paragraph (n)(1)(i) of this section with a medical examination including the following elements:

(A) A detailed history which includes:

(*1*) Past work exposure to MDA or any other toxic substances;

(*2*) A history of drugs, alcohol, tobacco, and medication routinely taken (duration and quantity); and

(*3*) A history of dermatitis, chemical skin sensitization, or previous hepatic disease.

(B) A physical examination which includes all routine physical examination parameters, skin examination, and examination for signs of liver disease.

(C) Laboratory tests including:

(*1*) Liver function tests and (*2*) Urinalysis.

(D) Additional tests as necessary in the opinion of the physician.

(ii) No initial medical examination is required if adequate records show that the employee has been examined in accordance with the requirements of this section within the previous six months prior to the effective date of this standard or prior to the date of initial assignment.

(3) *Periodic examinations.* (i) The employer shall provide each employee covered by this section with a medical examination at least annually following the initial examination. These periodic examinations shall include at least the following elements:

(A) A brief history regarding any new exposure to potential liver toxins, changes in drug, tobacco, and alcohol intake, and the appearance of physical signs relating to the liver, and the skin;

(B) The appropriate tests and examinations including liver function tests and skin examinations; and

(C) Appropriate additional tests or examinations as deemed necessary by the physician.

(ii) If in the physician's opinion the results of liver function tests indicate an abnormality, the employee shall be removed from further MDA exposure in accordance with paragraph (n)(9) of this section. Repeat liver function tests shall be conducted on advice of the physician.

(4) *Emergency examinations.* If the employer determines that the employee has been exposed to a potentially hazardous amount of MDA in an emergency situation under paragraph (e) of this section, the employer shall provide medical examinations in accordance with paragraphs (n)(3) (i) and (ii) of this section. If the results of liver function testing indicate an abnormality, the employee shall be removed in accordance with paragraph (n)(9) of this section. Repeat liver function tests shall be conducted on the advice of the physician. If the results of the tests are normal, tests must be repeated two to three weeks from the initial testing. If the results of the second set of tests are normal and on the advice of the physician, no additional testing is required.

(5) *Additional examinations.* Where the employee develops signs and symptoms associated with exposure to MDA, the employer shall provide the employee with an additional medical examination including liver function tests. Repeat liver function tests shall be conducted on the advice of the physician. If the results of the tests are normal, tests must be repeated two to three weeks from the initial testing. If the results of the second set of tests are normal and on the advice of the physician, no additional testing is required.

(6) *Multiple physician review mechanism.* (i) If the employer selects the initial physician who conducts any medical examination or consultation provided to an employee under this section, and the employee has signs or symptoms of occupational exposure to

MDA (which could include an abnormal liver function test), and the employee disagrees with the opinion of the examining physician, and this opinion could affect the employee's job status, the employee may designate an appropriate and mutually acceptable second physician:

(A) To review any findings, determinations or recommendations of the initial physician; and

(B) To conduct such examinations, consultations, and laboratory tests as the second physician deems necessary to facilitate this review.

(ii) The employer shall promptly notify an employee of the right to seek a second medical opinion after each occasion that an initial physician conducts a medical examination or consultation pursuant to this section. The employer may condition its participation in, and payment for, the multiple physician review mechanism upon the employee doing the following within fifteen (15) days after receipt of the foregoing notification, or receipt of the initial physician's written opinion, whichever is later:

(A) The employee informing the employer that he or she intends to seek a second medical opinion, and

(B) The employee initiating steps to make an appointment with a second physician.

(iii) If the findings, determinations, or recommendations of the second physician differ from those of the initial physician, then the employer and the employee shall assure that efforts are made for the two physicians to resolve any disagreement.

(iv) If the two physicians have been unable to quickly resolve their disagreement, then the employer and the employee through their respective physicians shall designate a third physician:

(A) To review any findings, determinations, or recommendations of the prior physicians; and

(B) To conduct such examinations, consultations, laboratory tests, and discussions with the prior physicians as the third physician deems necessary to resolve the disagreement of the prior physicians.

(v) The employer shall act consistent with the findings, determinations, and recommendations of the second physician, unless the employer and the employee reach a mutually acceptable agreement.

(7) *Information provided to the examining physician.* (i) The employer shall provide the following information to the examining physician:

(A) A copy of this regulation and its appendices;

(B) A description of the affected employee's duties as they relate to the employee's potential exposure to MDA;

(C) The employee's current actual or representative MDA exposure level;

(D) A description of any personal protective equipment used or to be used; and

(E) Information from previous employment related medical examinations of the affected employee.

(ii) The employer shall provide the foregoing information to a second physician under this section upon request either by the second physician, or by the employee.

(8) *Physician's written opinion.* (i) For each examination under this section, the employer shall obtain, and provide the employee with a copy of, the examining physician's written opinion within 15 days of its receipt. The written opinion shall include the following:

(A) The occupationally pertinent results of the medical examination and tests;

(B) The physician's opinion concerning whether the employee has any detected medical conditions which would place the employee at increased risk of material impairment of health from exposure to MDA;

(C) The physician's recommended limitations upon the employee's exposure to MDA or upon the employee's use of protective clothing or equipment and respirators; and

(D) A statement that the employee has been informed by the physician of the results of the medical examination and any medical conditions resulting from MDA exposure which require further explanation or treatment.

(ii) The written opinion obtained by the employer shall not reveal specific findings or diagnoses unrelated to occupational exposures.

(9) *Medical removal—*(i) *Temporary medical removal of an employee—*(A)

83

Temporary removal resulting from occupational exposure. The employee shall be removed from work environments in which exposure to MDA is at or above the action level or where dermal exposure to MDA may occur, following an initial examination (paragraph (n)(2) of this section), periodic examinations (paragraph (n)(3) of this section), an emergency situation (paragraph (n)(4) of this section), or an additional examination (paragraph (n)(5) of this section) in the following circumstances:

(*1*) When the employee exhibits signs and/or symptoms indicative of acute exposure to MDA; or

(*2*) When the examining physician determines that an employee's abnormal liver function tests are not associated with MDA exposure but that the abnormalities may be exacerbated as a result of occupational exposure to MDA.

(B) *Temporary removal due to a final medical determination.* (*1*) The employer shall remove an employee from work having an exposure to MDA at or above the action level or where the potential for dermal exposure exists on each occasion that a final medical determination results in a medical finding, determination, or opinion that the employee has a detected medical condition which places the employee at increased risk of material impairment to health from exposure to MDA.

(*2*) For the purposes of this section, the phrase "final medical determination" shall mean the outcome of the physician review mechanism used pursuant to the medical surveillance provisions of this section.

(*3*) Where a final medical determination results in any recommended special protective measures for an employee, or limitations on an employee's exposure to MDA, the employer shall implement and act consistent with the recommendation.

(ii) *Return of the employee to former job status.* (A) The employer shall return an employee to his or her former job status:

(*1*) When the employee no longer shows signs or symptoms of exposure to MDA, or upon the advice of the physician.

(*2*) When a subsequent final medical determination results in a medical finding, determination, or opinion that the employee no longer has a detected medical condition which places the employee at increased risk of material impairment to health from exposure to MDA.

(B) For the purposes of this section, the requirement that an employer return an employee to his or her former job status is not intended to expand upon or restrict any rights an employee has or would have had, absent temporary medical removal, to a specific job classification or position under the terms of a collective bargaining agreement.

(iii) *Removal of other employee special protective measure or limitations.* The employer shall remove any limitations placed on an employee or end any special protective measures provided to an employee pursuant to a final medical determination when a subsequent final medical determination indicates that the limitations or special protective measures are no longer necessary.

(iv) *Employer options pending a final medical determination.* Where the physician review mechanism used pursuant to the medical surveillance provisions of this section, has not yet resulted in a final medical determination with respect to an employee, the employer shall act as follows:

(A) *Removal.* The employer may remove the employee from exposure to MDA, provide special protective measures to the employee, or place limitations upon the employee, consistent with the medical findings, determinations, or recommendations of the physician who has reviewed the employee's health status.

(B) *Return.* The employer may return the employee to his or her former job status, and end any special protective measures provided to the employee, consistent with the medical findings, determinations, or recommendations of any of the physicians who have reviewed the employee's health status, with two exceptions:

(*1*) If the initial removal, special protection, or limitation of the employee resulted from a final medical determination which differed from the findings, determinations, or recommendations of the initial physician; or

(*2*) The employee has been on removal status for the preceding six months as a result of exposure to MDA, then the employer shall await a final medical determination.

(v) *Medical removal protection benefits*—(A) *Provisions of medical removal protection benefits.* The employer shall provide to an employee up to six (6) months of medical removal protection benefits on each occasion that an employee is removed from exposure to MDA or otherwise limited pursuant to this section.

(B) *Definition of medical removal protection benefits.* For the purposes of this section, the requirement that an employer provide medical removal protection benefits means that the employer shall maintain the earnings, seniority, and other employment rights and benefits of an employee as though the employee had not been removed from normal exposure to MDA or otherwise limited.

(C) *Follow-up medical surveillance during the period of employee removal or limitations.* During the period of time that an employee is removed from normal exposure to MDA or otherwise limited, the employer may condition the provision of medical removal protection benefits upon the employee's participation in follow-up medical surveillance made available pursuant to this section.

(D) *Workers' compensation claims.* If a removed employee files a claim for workers' compensation payments for a MDA-related disability, then the employer shall continue to provide medical removal protection benefits pending disposition of the claim. To the extent that an award is made to the employee for earnings lost during the period of removal, the employer's medical removal protection obligation shall be reduced by such amount. The employer shall receive no credit for workers' compensation payments received by the employee for treatment-related expenses.

(E) *Other credits.* The employer's obligation to provide medical removal protection benefits to a removed employee shall be reduced to the extent that the employee receives compensation for earnings lost during the period of removal either from a publicly or employer-funded compensation program, or receives income from employment with any employer made possible by virtue of the employee's removal.

(F) *Employees who do not recover within the 6 months of removal.* The employer shall take the following measures with respect to any employee removed from exposure to MDA:

(1) The employer shall make available to the employee a medical examination pursuant to this section to obtain a final medical determination with respect to the employee;

(2) The employer shall assure that the final medical determination obtained indicates whether or not the employee may be returned to his or her former job status, and, if not, what steps should be taken to protect the employee's health;

(3) Where the final medical determination has not yet been obtained, or once obtained indicates that the employee may not yet be returned to his or her former job status, the employer shall continue to provide medical removal protection benefits to the employee until either the employee is returned to former job status, or a final medical determination is made that the employee is incapable of ever safely returning to his or her former job status; and

(4) Where the employer acts pursuant to a final medical determination which permits the return of the employee to his or her former job status despite what would otherwise be an unacceptable liver function test, later questions concerning removing the employee again shall be decided by a final medical determination. The employer need not automatically remove such an employee pursuant to the MDA removal criteria provided by this section.

(vi) *Voluntary removal or restriction of an employee.* Where an employer, although not required by this section to do so, removes an employee from exposure to MDA or otherwise places limitations on an employee due to the effects of MDA exposure on the employee's medical condition, the employer shall provide medical removal protection benefits to the employee equal to that required by paragraph (n)(9)(v) of this section.

(o) *Recordkeeping*—(1) *Objective data for exempted operations.* (i) Where the employer has relied on objective data that demonstrate that products made from or containing MDA are not capable of releasing MDA or do not present a dermal exposure problem under the expected conditions of processing, use, or handling to exempt such operations from the initial monitoring requirements under paragraph (f)(2) of this section, the employer shall establish and maintain an accurate record of objective data reasonably relied upon in support of the exemption.

(ii) The record shall include at least the following information:

(A) The product qualifying for exemption;

(B) The source of the objective data;

(C) The testing protocol, results of testing, and/or analysis of the material for the release of MDA;

(D) A description of the operation exempted and how the data support the exemption; and

(E) Other data relevant to the operations, materials, processing, or employee exposures covered by the exemption.

(iii) The employer shall maintain this record for the duration of the employer's reliance upon such objective data.

(2) *Historical monitoring data.* (i) Where the employer has relied on historical monitoring data that demonstrate that exposures on a particular job will be below the action level to exempt such operations from the initial monitoring requirements under paragraph (f)(2) of this section, the employer shall establish and maintain an accurate record of historical monitoring data reasonably relied upon in support of the exception.

(ii) The record shall include information that reflect the following conditions:

(A) The data upon which judgments are based are scientifically sound and were collected using methods that are sufficiently accurate and precise;

(B) The processes and work practices that were in use when the historical monitoring data were obtained are essentially the same as those to be used during the job for which initial monitoring will not be performed;

(C) The characteristics of the MDA-containing material being handled when the historical monitoring data were obtained are the same as those on the job for which initial monitoring will not be performed;

(D) Environmental conditions prevailing when the historical monitoring data were obtained are the same as those on the job for which initial monitoring will not be performed; and

(E) Other data relevant to the operations, materials, processing, or employee exposures covered by the exception.

(iii) The employer shall maintain this record for the duration of the employer's reliance upon such historical monitoring data.

(3) The employer may utilize the services of competent organizations such as industry trade associations and employee associations to maintain the records required by this section.

(4) *Exposure measurements.* (i) The employer shall keep an accurate record of all measurements taken to monitor employee exposure to MDA.

(ii) This record shall include at least the following information:

(A) The date of measurement;

(B) The operation involving exposure to MDA;

(C) Sampling and analytical methods used and evidence of their accuracy;

(D) Number, duration, and results of samples taken;

(E) Type of protective devices worn, if any; and

(F) Name, social security number, and exposure of the employees whose exposures are represented.

(iii) The employer shall maintain this record for at least thirty (30) years, in accordance with 29 CFR 1910.33.

(5) *Medical surveillance.* (i) The employer shall establish and maintain an accurate record for each employee subject to medical surveillance by paragraph (n) of this section, in accordance with 29 CFR 1910.33.

(ii) The record shall include at least the following information:

(A) The name and social security number of the employee;

(B) A copy of the employee's medical examination results, including the medical history, questionnaire responses, results of any tests, and physician's recommendations.

(C) Physician's written opinions;

(D) Any employee medical complaints related to exposure to MDA; and

(E) A copy of the information provided to the physician as required by paragraph (n) of this section.

(iii) The employer shall ensure that this record is maintained for the duration of employment plus thirty (30) years, in accordance with 29 CFR 1910.33.

(iv) A copy of the employee's medical removal and return to work status.

(6) *Training records.* The employer shall maintain all employee training records for one (1) year beyond the last date of employment.

(7) *Availability.* (i) The employer, upon written request, shall make all records required to be maintained by this section available to the Assistant Secretary and the Director for examination and copying.

(ii) The employer, upon request, shall make any exposure records required by paragraphs (f) and (n) of this section available for examination and copying to affected employees, former employees, designated representatives, and the Assistant Secretary, in accordance with 29 CFR 1910.33(a)–(e) and (g)–(i).

(iii) The employer, upon request, shall make employee medical records required by paragraphs (n) and (o) of this section available for examination and copying to the subject employee, anyone having the specific written consent of the subject employee, and the Assistant Secretary, in accordance with 29 CFR 1910.33.

(8) *Transfer of records.* The employer shall comply with the requirements concerning transfer of records set forth in 29 CFR 1910.1020(h).

(ii) Whenever the employer ceases to do business and there is no successor employer to receive and retain the records for the prescribed period, the employer shall notify the Director at least 90 days prior to disposal and, upon request, transmit them to the Director.

(p) *Observation of monitoring—(1) Employee observation.* The employer shall provide affected employees, or their designated representatives, an opportunity to observe the measuring or monitoring of employee exposure to MDA conducted pursuant to paragraph (f) of this section.

(2) *Observation procedures.* When observation of the measuring or monitoring of employee exposure to MDA requires entry into areas where the use of protective clothing and equipment or respirators is required, the employer shall provide the observer with personal protective clothing and equipment or respirators required to be worn by employees working in the area, assure the use of such clothing and equipment or respirators, and require the observer to comply with all other applicable safety and health procedures.

(q) *Appendices.* The information contained in appendices A, B, C, and D of this section is not intended, by itself, to create any additional obligations not otherwise imposed by this standard nor detract from any existing obligation.

APPENDIX A TO §1926.60—SUBSTANCE DATA SHEET, FOR 4–4′ METHYLENEDIANILINE

NOTE: The requirements applicable to construction work under this appendix A are identical to those set forth in appendix A to §1910.1050 of this chapter.

APPENDIX B TO §1926.60—SUBSTANCE TECHNICAL GUIDELINES, MDA

NOTE: The requirements applicable to construction work under this appendix B are identical to those set forth in appendix B to §1910.1050 of this chapter.

APPENDIX C TO §1926.60—MEDICAL SURVEILLANCE GUIDELINES FOR MDA

NOTE: The requirements applicable to construction work under this appendix C are identical to those set forth in appendix C to §1910.1050 of this chapter.

APPENDIX D TO §1926.60—SAMPLING AND ANALYTICAL METHODS FOR MDA MONITORING AND MEASUREMENT PROCEDURES

NOTE: The requirements applicable to construction work under this appendix D are identical to those set forth in appendix D to §1910.1050 of this chapter.

[57 FR 35681, Aug. 10, 1992, as amended at 57 FR 49649, Nov. 3, 1992; 61 FR 5510, Feb. 13, 1996; 61 FR 31431, June 20, 1996; 63 FR 1296, Jan. 8, 1998; 69 FR 70373, Dec. 6, 2004; 70 FR 1143, Jan. 5, 2005; 71 FR 16674, Apr. 3, 2006; 71 FR 50191, Aug. 24, 2006; 73 FR 75588, Dec. 12, 2008; 76 FR 33611, June 8, 2011; 77 FR 17889, Mar. 26, 2012]

§ 1926.61 Retention of DOT markings, placards and labels.

NOTE: The requirements applicable to construction work under this section are identical to those set forth at § 1910.1201 of this chapter.

[61 FR 31432, June 20, 1996]

§ 1926.62 Lead.

(a) *Scope.* This section applies to all construction work where an employee may be occupationally exposed to lead. All construction work excluded from coverage in the general industry standard for lead by 29 CFR 1910.1025(a)(2) is covered by this standard. Construction work is defined as work for construction, alteration and/or repair, including painting and decorating. It includes but is not limited to the following:

(1) Demolition or salvage of structures where lead or materials containing lead are present;

(2) Removal or encapsulation of materials containing lead;

(3) New construction, alteration, repair, or renovation of structures, substrates, or portions thereof, that contain lead, or materials containing lead;

(4) Installation of products containing lead;

(5) Lead contamination/emergency cleanup;

(6) Transportation, disposal, storage, or containment of lead or materials containing lead on the site or location at which construction activities are performed, and

(7) Maintenance operations associated with the construction activities described in this paragraph.

(b) *Definitions.*

Action level means employee exposure, without regard to the use of respirators, to an airborne concentration of lead of 30 micrograms per cubic meter of air (30 µg/m³) calculated as an 8-hour time-weighted average (TWA).

Assistant Secretary means the Assistant Secretary of Labor for Occupational Safety and Health, U.S. Department of Labor, or designee.

Competent person means one who is capable of identifying existing and predictable lead hazards in the surroundings or working conditions and who has authorization to take prompt corrective measures to eliminate them.

Director means the Director, National Institute for Occupational Safety and Health (NIOSH), U.S. Department of Health and Human Services, or designee.

Lead means metallic lead, all inorganic lead compounds, and organic lead soaps. Excluded from this definition are all other organic lead compounds.

This section means this standard.

(c) *Permissible exposure limit.* (1) The employer shall assure that no employee is exposed to lead at concentrations greater than fifty micrograms per cubic meter of air (50 µg/m³) averaged over an 8-hour period.

(2) If an employee is exposed to lead for more than 8 hours in any work day the employees' allowable exposure, as a time weighted average (TWA) for that day, shall be reduced according to the following formula:

Allowable employee exposure (in µg/m³) = 400 divided by hours worked in the day.

(3) When respirators are used to limit employee exposure as required under paragraph (c) of this section and all the requirements of paragraphs (e)(1) and (f) of this section have been met, employee exposure may be considered to be at the level provided by the protection factor of the respirator for those periods the respirator is worn. Those periods may be averaged with exposure levels during periods when respirators are not worn to determine the employee's daily TWA exposure.

(d) *Exposure assessment*—(1) *General.* (i) Each employer who has a workplace or operation covered by this standard shall initially determine if any employee may be exposed to lead at or above the action level.

(ii) For the purposes of paragraph (d) of this section, employee exposure is that exposure which would occur if the employee were not using a respirator.

(iii) With the exception of monitoring under paragraph (d)(3), where monitoring is required under this section, the employer shall collect personal samples representative of a full shift including at least one sample for each job classification in each work area either for each shift or for the shift with the highest exposure level.

(iv) Full shift personal samples shall be representative of the monitored employee's regular, daily exposure to lead.

(2) *Protection of employees during assessment of exposure.* (i) With respect to the lead related tasks listed in paragraph (d)(2)(i) of this section, where lead is present, until the employer performs an employee exposure assessment as required in paragraph (d) of this section and documents that the employee performing any of the listed tasks is not exposed above the PEL, the employer shall treat the employee as if the employee were exposed above the PEL, and not in excess of ten (10) times the PEL, and shall implement employee protective measures prescribed in paragraph (d)(2)(v) of this section. The tasks covered by this requirement are:

(A) Where lead containing coatings or paint are present: Manual demolition of structures (e.g, dry wall), manual scraping, manual sanding, heat gun applications, and power tool cleaning with dust collection systems;

(B) Spray painting with lead paint.

(ii) In addition, with regard to tasks not listed in paragraph (d)(2)(i), where the employee has any reason to believe that an employee performing the task may be exposed to lead in excess of the PEL, until the employer performs an employee exposure assessment as required by paragraph (d) of this section and documents that the employee's lead exposure is not above the PEL the employer shall treat the employee as if the employee were exposed above the PEL and shall implememt employee protective measures as prescribed in paragraph (d)(2)(v) of this section.

(iii) With respect to the tasks listed in paragraph (d)(2)(iii) of this section, where lead is present, until the employer performs an employee exposure assessment as required in paragraph (d) of this section, and documents that the employee performing any of the listed tasks is not exposed in excess of 500 µg/m³, the employer shall treat the employee as if the employee were exposed to lead in excess of 500 µg/m³ and shall implement employee protective measures as prescribed in paragraph (d)(2)(v) of this section. Where the employer does establish that the employee is exposed to levels of lead below 500 µg/m³, the employer may provide the exposed employee with the appropriate respirator prescribed for such use at such lower exposures, in accordance with Table 1 of this section. The tasks covered by this requirement are:

(A) Using lead containing mortar; lead burning

(B) Where lead containing coatings or paint are present: rivet busting; power tool cleaning without dust collection systems; cleanup activities where dry expendable abrasives are used; and abrasive blasting enclosure movement and removal.

(iv) With respect to the tasks listed in paragraph (d)(2)(iv) of this section, where lead is present, until the employer performs an employee exposure assessment as required in paragraph (d) of this section and documents that the employee performing any of the listed tasks is not exposed to lead in excess of 2,500 µg/m³ (50×PEL), the employer shall treat the employee as if the employee were exposed to lead in excess of 2,500 µg/m³ and shall implement employee protective measures as prescribed in paragraph (d)(2)(v) of this section. Where the employer does establish that the employee is exposed to levels of lead below 2,500 µg/m3, the employer may provide the exposed employee with the appropriate respirator prescribed for use at such lower exposures, in accordance with Table I of this section. Interim protection as described in this paragaraph is required where lead containing coatings or paint are present on structures when performing:

(A) Abrasive blasting,

(B) Welding,

(C) Cutting, and

(D) Torch burning.

(v) Until the employer performs an employee exposure assessment as required under paragraph (d) of this section and determines actual employee exposure, the employer shall provide to employees performing the tasks described in paragraphs (d)(2)(i), (d)(2)(ii), (d)(2)(iii), and (d)(2)(iv) of this section with interim protection as follows:

(A) Appropriate respiratory protection in accordance with paragraph (f) of this section.

(B) Appropriate personal protective clothing and equipment in accordance with paragraph (g) of this section.

(C) Change areas in accordance with paragraph (i)(2) of this section.

(D) Hand washing facilities in accordance with paragraph (i)(5) of this section.

(E) Biological monitoring in accordance with paragraph (j)(1)(i) of this section, to consist of blood sampling and analysis for lead and zinc protoporphyrin levels, and

(F) Training as required under paragraph (l)(1)(i) of this section regarding 29 CFR 1926.59, Hazard Communication; training as required under paragraph (l)(2)(iii) of this section, regarding use of respirators; and training in accordance with 29 CFR 1926.21, Safety training and education.

(3) *Basis of initial determination.* (i) Except as provided under paragraphs (d)(3)(iii) and (d)(3)(iv) of this section the employer shall monitor employee exposures and shall base initial determinations on the employee exposure monitoring results and any of the following, relevant considerations:

(A) Any information, observations, or calculations which would indicate employee exposure to lead;

(B) Any previous measurements of airborne lead; and

(C) Any employee complaints of symptoms which may be attributable to exposure to lead.

(ii) Monitoring for the initial determination where performed may be limited to a representative sample of the exposed employees who the employer reasonably believes are exposed to the greatest airborne concentrations of lead in the workplace.

(iii) Where the employer has previously monitored for lead exposures, and the data were obtained within the past 12 months during work operations conducted under workplace conditions closely resembling the processes, type of material, control methods, work practices, and environmental conditions used and prevailing in the employer's current operations, the employer may rely on such earlier monitoring results to satisfy the requirements of paragraphs (d)(3)(i) and (d)(6) of this section if the sampling and analytical methods meet the accuracy and

confidence levels of paragraph (d)(10) of this section.

(iv) Where the employer has objective data, demonstrating that a particular product or material containing lead or a specific process, operation or activity involving lead cannot result in employee exposure to lead at or above the action level during processing, use, or handling, the employer may rely upon such data instead of implementing initial monitoring.

(A) The employer shall establish and maintain an accurate record documenting the nature and relevancy of objective data as specified in paragraph (n)(4) of this section, where used in assessing employee exposure in lieu of exposure monitoring.

(B) Objective data, as described in paragraph (d)(3)(iv) of this section, is not permitted to be used for exposure assessment in connection with paragraph (d)(2) of this section.

(4) *Positive initial determination and initial monitoring.* (i) Where a determination conducted under paragraphs (d) (1), (2) and (3) of this section shows the possibility of any employee exposure at or above the action level the employer shall conduct monitoring which is representative of the exposure for each employee in the workplace who is exposed to lead.

(ii) Where the employer has previously monitored for lead exposure, and the data were obtained within the past 12 months during work operations conducted under workplace conditions closely resembling the processes, type of material, control methods, work practices, and environmental conditions used and prevailing in the employer's current operations, the employer may rely on such earlier monitoring results to satisfy the requirements of paragraph (d)(4)(i) of this section if the sampling and analytical methods meet the accuracy and confidence levels of paragraph (d)(10) of this section.

(5) *Negative initial determination.* Where a determination, conducted under paragraphs (d) (1), (2), and (3) of this section is made that no employee is exposed to airborne concentrations of lead at or above the action level the employer shall make a written record of such determination. The record shall

include at least the information specified in paragraph (d)(3)(i) of this section and shall also include the date of determination, location within the worksite, and the name and social security number of each employee monitored.

(6) *Frequency.* (i) If the initial determination reveals employee exposure to be below the action level further exposure determination need not be repeated except as otherwise provided in paragraph (d)(7) of this section.

(ii) If the initial determination or subsequent determination reveals employee exposure to be at or above the action level but at or below the PEL the employer shall perform monitoring in accordance with this paragraph at least every 6 months. The employer shall continue monitoring at the required frequency until at least two consecutive measurements, taken at least 7 days apart, are below the action level at which time the employer may discontinue monitoring for that employee except as otherwise provided in paragraph (d)(7) of this section.

(iii) If the initial determination reveals that employee exposure is above the PEL the employer shall perform monitoring quarterly. The employer shall continue monitoring at the required frequency until at least two consecutive measurements, taken at least 7 days apart, are at or below the PEL but at or above the action level at which time the employer shall repeat monitoring for that employee at the frequency specified in paragraph (d)(6)(ii) of this section, except as otherwise provided in paragraph (d)(7) of this section. The employer shall continue monitoring at the required frequency until at least two consecutive measurements, taken at least 7 days apart, are below the action level at which time the employer may discontinue monitoring for that employee except as otherwise provided in paragraph (d)(7) of this section.

(7) *Additional exposure assessments.* Whenever there has been a change of equipment, process, control, personnel or a new task has been initiated that may result in additional employees being exposed to lead at or above the action level or may result in employees already exposed at or above the action

level being exposed above the PEL, the employer shall conduct additional monitoring in accordance with this paragraph.

(8) *Employee notification.* (i) The employer must, as soon as possible but no later than 5 working days after the receipt of the results of any monitoring performed under this section, notify each affected employee of these results either individually in writing or by posting the results in an appropriate location that is accessible to employees.

(ii) Whenever the results indicate that the representative employee exposure, without regard to respirators, is at or above the PEL the employer shall include in the written notice a statement that the employees exposure was at or above that level and a description of the corrective action taken or to be taken to reduce exposure to below that level.

(9) *Accuracy of measurement.* The employer shall use a method of monitoring and analysis which has an accuracy (to a confidence level of 95%) of not less than plus or minus 25 percent for airborne concentrations of lead equal to or greater than 30 µg/m^3.

(e) *Methods of compliance*—(1) *Engineering and work practice controls.* The employer shall implement engineering and work practice controls, including administrative controls, to reduce and maintain employee exposure to lead to or below the permissible exposure limit to the extent that such controls are feasible. Wherever all feasible engineering and work practices controls that can be instituted are not sufficient to reduce employee exposure to or below the permissible exposure limit prescribed in paragraph (c) of this section, the employer shall nonetheless use them to reduce employee exposure to the lowest feasible level and shall supplement them by the use of respiratory protection that complies with the requirements of paragraph (f) of this section.

(2) *Compliance program.* (i) Prior to commencement of the job each employer shall establish and implement a written compliance program to achieve compliance with paragraph (c) of this section.

(ii) Written plans for these compliance programs shall include at least the following:

(A) A description of each activity in which lead is emitted; e.g. equipment used, material involved, controls in place, crew size, employee job responsibilities, operating procedures and maintenance practices;

(B) A description of the specific means that will be employed to achieve compliance and, where engineering controls are required engineering plans and studies used to determine methods selected for controlling exposure to lead;

(C) A report of the technology considered in meeting the PEL;

(D) Air monitoring data which documents the source of lead emissions;

(E) A detailed schedule for implementation of the program, including documentation such as copies of purchase orders for equipment, construction contracts, etc.;

(F) A work practice program which includes items required under paragraphs (g), (h) and (i) of this section and incorporates other relevant work practices such as those specified in paragraph (e)(5) of this section;

(G) An administrative control schedule required by paragraph (e)(4) of this section, if applicable;

(H) A description of arrangements made among contractors on multi-contractor sites with respect to informing affected employees of potential exposure to lead and with respect to responsibility for compliance with this section as set-forth in § 1926.16.

(I) Other relevant information.

(iii) The compliance program shall provide for frequent and regular inspections of job sites, materials, and equipment to be made by a competent person.

(iv) Written programs shall be submitted upon request to any affected employee or authorized employee representatives, to the Assistant Secretary and the Director, and shall be available at the worksite for examination and copying by the Assistant Secretary and the Director.

(v) Written programs must be revised and updated at least annually to reflect the current status of the program.

(3) *Mechanical ventilation.* When ventilation is used to control lead exposure, the employer shall evaluate the mechanical performance of the system in controlling exposure as necessary to maintain its effectiveness.

(4) *Administrative controls.* If administrative controls are used as a means of reducing employees TWA exposure to lead, the employer shall establish and implement a job rotation schedule which includes:

(i) Name or identification number of each affected employee;

(ii) Duration and exposure levels at each job or work station where each affected employee is located; and

(iii) Any other information which may be useful in assessing the reliability of administrative controls to reduce exposure to lead.

(5) The employer shall ensure that, to the extent relevant, employees follow good work practices such as described in appendix B of this section.

(f) *Respiratory protection—(1) General.* For employees who use respirators required by this section, the employer must provide each employee an appropriate respirator that complies with the requirements of this paragraph. Respirators must be used during:

(i) Periods when an employee's exposure to lead exceeds the PEL.

(ii) Work operations for which engineering and work-practice controls are not sufficient to reduce employee exposures to or below the PEL.

(iii) Periods when an employee requests a respirator.

(iv) Periods when respirators are required to provide interim protection of employees while they perform the operations specified in paragraph (d)(2) of this section.

(2) *Respirator program.* (i) The employer must implement a respiratory protection program in accordance with § 1910.134(b) through (d) (except (d)(1)(iii)), and (f) through (m), which covers each employee required by this section to use a respirator.

(ii) If an employee has breathing difficulty during fit testing or respirator use, the employer must provide the employee with a medical examination in accordance with paragraph (j)(3)(i)(B) of this section to determine whether or not the employee can use a respirator while performing the required duty.

(3) *Respirator selection.* (i) Employers must:

(A) Select, and provide to employees, the appropriate respirators specified in paragraph (d)(3)(i)(A) of 29 CFR 1910.134.

(B) Provide employees with a full facepiece respirator instead of a half mask respirator for protection against lead aerosols that may cause eye or skin irritation at the use concentrations.

(C) Provide HEPA filters for powered and non-powered air-purifying respirators.

(ii) The employer must provide a powered air-purifying respirator when an employee chooses to use such a respirator and it will provide adequate protection to the employee.

(g) *Protective work clothing and equipment*—(1) *Provision and use.* Where an employee is exposed to lead above the PEL without regard to the use of respirators, where employees are exposed to lead compounds which may cause skin or eye irritation (e.g. lead arsenate, lead azide), and as interim protection for employees performing tasks as specified in paragraph (d)(2) of this section, the employer shall provide at no cost to the employee and assure that the employee uses appropriate protective work clothing and equipment that prevents contamination of the employee and the employee's garments such as, but not limited to:

(i) Coveralls or similar full-body work clothing;

(ii) Gloves, hats, and shoes or disposable shoe coverlets; and

(iii) Face shields, vented goggles, or other appropriate protective equipment which complies with §1910.133 of this chapter.

(2) *Cleaning and replacement.* (i) The employer shall provide the protective clothing required in paragraph (g)(1) of this section in a clean and dry condition at least weekly, and daily to employees whose exposure levels without regard to a respirator are over 200 µg/ m^3 of lead as an 8-hour TWA.

(ii) The employer shall provide for the cleaning, laundering, and disposal of protective clothing and equipment

required by paragraph (g)(1) of this section.

(iii) The employer shall repair or replace required protective clothing and equipment as needed to maintain their effectiveness.

(iv) The employer shall assure that all protective clothing is removed at the completion of a work shift only in change areas provided for that purpose as prescribed in paragraph (i)(2) of this section.

(v) The employer shall assure that contaminated protective clothing which is to be cleaned, laundered, or disposed of, is placed in a closed container in the change area which prevents dispersion of lead outside the container.

(vi) The employer shall inform in writing any person who cleans or launders protective clothing or equipment of the potentially harmful effects of exposure to lead.

(vii)(A) The employer shall ensure that the containers of contaminated protective clothing and equipment required by paragraph (g)(2)(v) of this section are labeled as follows:

DANGER: CLOTHING AND EQUIPMENT CONTAMINATED WITH LEAD. MAY DAMAGE FERTILITY OR THE UNBORN CHILD. CAUSES DAMAGE TO THE CENTRAL NERVOUS SYSTEM. DO NOT EAT, DRINK OR SMOKE WHEN HANDLING. DO NOT REMOVE DUST BY BLOWING OR SHAKING. DISPOSE OF LEAD CONTAMINATED WASH WATER IN ACCORDANCE WITH APPLICABLE LOCAL, STATE, OR FEDERAL REGULATIONS.

(B) Prior to June 1, 2015, employers may include the following information on bags or containers of contaminated protective clothing and equipment required by paragraph (g)(2)(v) in lieu of the labeling requirements in paragraph (g)(2)(vii)(A) of this section:

Caution: Clothing contaminated with lead. Do not remove dust by blowing or shaking. Dispose of lead contaminated wash water in accordance with applicable local, state, or federal regulations.

(viii) The employer shall prohibit the removal of lead from protective clothing or equipment by blowing, shaking, or any other means which disperses lead into the air.

(h) *Housekeeping*—(1) All surfaces shall be maintained as free as practicable of accumulations of lead.

(2) Clean-up of floors and other surfaces where lead accumulates shall wherever possible, be cleaned by vacuuming or other methods that minimize the likelihood of lead becoming airborne.

(3) Shoveling, dry or wet sweeping, and brushing may be used only where vacuuming or other equally effective methods have been tried and found not to be effective.

(4) Where vacuuming methods are selected, the vacuums shall be equipped with HEPA filters and used and emptied in a manner which minimizes the reentry of lead into the workplace.

(5) Compressed air shall not be used to remove lead from any surface unless the compressed air is used in conjunction with a ventilation system designed to capture the airborne dust created by the compressed air.

(i) *Hygiene facilities and practices.* (1) The employer shall assure that in areas where employees are exposed to lead above the PEL without regard to the use of respirators, food or beverage is not present or consumed, tobacco products are not present or used, and cosmetics are not applied.

(2) *Change areas.* (i) The employer shall provide clean change areas for employees whose airborne exposure to lead is above the PEL, and as interim protection for employees performing tasks as specified in paragraph (d)(2) of this section, without regard to the use of respirators.

(ii) The employer shall assure that change areas are equipped with separate storage facilities for protective work clothing and equipment and for street clothes which prevent cross-contamination.

(iii) The employer shall assure that employees do not leave the workplace wearing any protective clothing or equipment that is required to be worn during the work shift.

(3) *Showers.* (i) The employer shall provide shower facilities, where feasible, for use by employees whose airborne exposure to lead is above the PEL.

(ii) The employer shall assure, where shower facilities are available, that employees shower at the end of the work shift and shall provide an adequate supply of cleansing agents and towels for use by affected employees.

(4) *Eating facilities.* (i) The employer shall provide lunchroom facilities or eating areas for employees whose airborne exposure to lead is above the PEL, without regard to the use of respirators.

(ii) The employer shall assure that lunchroom facilities or eating areas are as free as practicable from lead contamination and are readily accessible to employees.

(iii) The employer shall assure that employees whose airborne exposure to lead is above the PEL, without regard to the use of a respirator, wash their hands and face prior to eating, drinking, smoking or applying cosmetics.

(iv) The employer shall assure that employees do not enter lunchroom facilities or eating areas with protective work clothing or equipment unless surface lead dust has been removed by vacuuming, downdraft booth, or other cleaning method that limits dispersion of lead dust.

(5) *Hand washing facilities.* (i) The employer shall provide adequate handwashing facilities for use by employees exposed to lead in accordance with 29 CFR 1926.51(f).

(ii) Where showers are not provided the employer shall assure that employees wash their hands and face at the end of the work-shift.

(j) *Medical surveillance*—(1) *General.* (i) The employer shall make available initial medical surveillance to employees occupationally exposed on any day to lead at or above the action level. Initial medical surveillance consists of biological monitoring in the form of blood sampling and analysis for lead and zinc protoporphyrin levels.

(ii) The employer shall institute a medical surveillance program in accordance with paragraphs (j)(2) and (j)(3) of this section for all employees who are or may be exposed by the employer at or above the action level for more than 30 days in any consecutive 12 months;

(iii) The employer shall assure that all medical examinations and procedures are performed by or under the supervision of a licensed physician.

(iv) The employer shall make available the required medical surveillance including multiple physician review under paragraph (j)(3)(iii) without cost to employees and at a reasonable time and place.

(2) *Biological monitoring*—(i) *Blood lead and ZPP level sampling and analysis.* The employer shall make available biological monitoring in the form of blood sampling and analysis for lead and zinc protoporphyrin levels to each employee covered under paragraphs (j)(1)(i) and (ii) of this section on the following schedule:

(A) For each employee covered under paragraph (j)(1)(ii) of this section, at least every 2 months for the first 6 months and every 6 months thereafter;

(B) For each employee covered under paragraphs (j)(1) (i) or (ii) of this section whose last blood sampling and analysis indicated a blood lead level at or above 40 µg/dl, at least every two months. This frequency shall continue until two consecutive blood samples and analyses indicate a blood lead level below 40 µg/dl; and

(C) For each employee who is removed from exposure to lead due to an elevated blood lead level at least monthly during the removal period.

(ii) *Follow-up blood sampling tests.* Whenever the results of a blood lead level test indicate that an employee's blood lead level is at or above the numerical criterion for medical removal under paragraph (k)(1)(i) of this section, the employer shall provide a second (follow-up) blood sampling test within two weeks after the employer receives the results of the first blood sampling test.

(iii) *Accuracy of blood lead level sampling and analysis.* Blood lead level sampling and analysis provided pursuant to this section shall have an accuracy (to a confidence level of 95 percent) within plus or minus 15 percent or 6 µg/dl, whichever is greater, and shall be conducted by a laboratory approved by OSHA.

(iv) *Employee notification.* (A) Within five working days after the receipt of biological monitoring results, the employer shall notify each employee in writing of his or her blood lead level; and

(B) The employer shall notify each employee whose blood lead level is at or above 40 µg/dl that the standard requires temporary medical removal with Medical Removal Protection benefits when an employee's blood lead level is at or above the numerical criterion for medical removal under paragraph (k)(1)(i) of this section.

(3) *Medical examinations and consultations*—(i) *Frequency.* The employer shall make available medical examinations and consultations to each employee covered under paragraph (j)(1)(ii) of this section on the following schedule:

(A) At least annually for each employee for whom a blood sampling test conducted at any time during the preceding 12 months indicated a blood lead level at or above 40 µg/dl;

(B) As soon as possible, upon notification by an employee either that the employee has developed signs or symptoms commonly associated with lead intoxication, that the employee desires medical advice concerning the effects of current or past exposure to lead on the employee's ability to procreate a healthy child, that the employee is pregnant, or that the employee has demonstrated difficulty in breathing during a respirator fitting test or during use; and

(C) As medically appropriate for each employee either removed from exposure to lead due to a risk of sustaining material impairment to health, or otherwise limited pursuant to a final medical determination.

(ii) *Content.* The content of medical examinations made available pursuant to paragraph (j)(3)(i)(B)–(C) of this section shall be determined by an examining physician and, if requested by an employee, shall include pregnancy testing or laboratory evaluation of male fertility. Medical examinations made available pursuant to paragraph (j)(3)(i)(A) of this section shall include the following elements:

(A) A detailed work history and a medical history, with particular attention to past lead exposure (occupational and non-occupational), personal habits (smoking, hygiene), and past gastrointestinal, hematologic, renal, cardiovascular, reproductive and neurological problems;

(B) A thorough physical examination, with particular attention to teeth, gums, hematologic, gastrointestinal, renal, cardiovascular, and neurological systems. Pulmonary status should be evaluated if respiratory protection will be used;

(C) A blood pressure measurement;

(D) A blood sample and analysis which determines:

(1) Blood lead level;

(2) Hemoglobin and hematocrit determinations, red cell indices, and examination of peripheral smear morphology;

(3) Zinc protoporphyrin;

(4) Blood urea nitrogen; and,

(5) Serum creatinine;

(E) A routine urinalysis with microscopic examination; and

(F) Any laboratory or other test relevant to lead exposure which the examining physician deems necessary by sound medical practice.

(iii) *Multiple physician review mechanism.* (A) If the employer selects the initial physician who conducts any medical examination or consultation provided to an employee under this section, the employee may designate a second physician:

(1) To review any findings, determinations or recommendations of the initial physician; and

(2) To conduct such examinations, consultations, and laboratory tests as the second physician deems necessary to facilitate this review.

(B) The employer shall promptly notify an employee of the right to seek a second medical opinion after each occasion that an initial physician conducts a medical examination or consultation pursuant to this section. The employer may condition its participation in, and payment for, the multiple physician review mechanism upon the employee doing the following within fifteen (15) days after receipt of the foregoing notification, or receipt of the initial physician's written opinion, whichever is later:

(1) The employee informing the employer that he or she intends to seek a second medical opinion, and

(2) The employee initiating steps to make an appointment with a second physician.

(C) If the findings, determinations or recommendations of the second physician differ from those of the initial physician, then the employer and the employee shall assure that efforts are made for the two physicians to resolve any disagreement.

(D) If the two physicians have been unable to quickly resolve their disagreement, then the employer and the employee through their respective physicians shall designate a third physician:

(1) To review any findings, determinations or recommendations of the prior physicians; and

(2) To conduct such examinations, consultations, laboratory tests and discussions with the prior physicians as the third physician deems necessary to resolve the disagreement of the prior physicians.

(E) The employer shall act consistent with the findings, determinations and recommendations of the third physician, unless the employer and the employee reach an agreement which is otherwise consistent with the recommendations of at least one of the three physicians.

(iv) *Information provided to examining and consulting physicians.* (A) The employer shall provide an initial physician conducting a medical examination or consultation under this section with the following information:

(1) A copy of this regulation for lead including all Appendices;

(2) A description of the affected employee's duties as they relate to the employee's exposure;

(3) The employee's exposure level or anticipated exposure level to lead and to any other toxic substance (if applicable);

(4) A description of any personal protective equipment used or to be used;

(5) Prior blood lead determinations; and

(6) All prior written medical opinions concerning the employee in the employer's possession or control.

(B) The employer shall provide the foregoing information to a second or third physician conducting a medical examination or consultation under this section upon request either by the second or third physician, or by the employee.

(v) *Written medical opinions.* (A) The employer shall obtain and furnish the employee with a copy of a written medical opinion from each examining or consulting physician which contains only the following information:

(*1*) The physician's opinion as to whether the employee has any detected medical condition which would place the employee at increased risk of material impairment of the employee's health from exposure to lead;

(*2*) Any recommended special protective measures to be provided to the employee, or limitations to be placed upon the employee's exposure to lead;

(*3*) Any recommended limitation upon the employee's use of respirators, including a determination of whether the employee can wear a powered air purifying respirator if a physician determines that the employee cannot wear a negative pressure respirator; and

(*4*) The results of the blood lead determinations.

(B) The employer shall instruct each examining and consulting physician to:

(*1*) Not reveal either in the written opinion or orally, or in any other means of communication with the employer, findings, including laboratory results, or diagnoses unrelated to an employee's occupational exposure to lead; and

(*2*) Advise the employee of any medical condition, occupational or non-occupational, which dictates further medical examination or treatment.

(vi) *Alternate physician determination mechanisms.* The employer and an employee or authorized employee representative may agree upon the use of any alternate physician determination mechanism in lieu of the multiple physician review mechanism provided by paragraph (j)(3)(iii) of this section so long as the alternate mechanism is as expeditious and protective as the requirements contained in this paragraph.

(4) *Chelation.* (i) The employer shall assure that any person whom he retains, employs, supervises or controls does not engage in prophylactic chelation of any employee at any time.

(ii) If therapeutic or diagnostic chelation is to be performed by any person in paragraph (j)(4)(i) of this section,

the employer shall assure that it be done under the supervision of a licensed physician in a clinical setting with thorough and appropriate medical monitoring and that the employee is notified in writing prior to its occurrence.

(k) *Medical removal protection*—(1) *Temporary medical removal and return of an employee*—(i) *Temporary removal due to elevated blood lead level.* The employer shall remove an employee from work having an exposure to lead at or above the action level on each occasion that a periodic and a follow-up blood sampling test conducted pursuant to this section indicate that the employee's blood lead level is at or above 50 µg/dl; and,

(ii) *Temporary removal due to a final medical determination.* (A) The employer shall remove an employee from work having an exposure to lead at or above the action level on each occasion that a final medical determination results in a medical finding, determination, or opinion that the employee has a detected medical condition which places the employee at increased risk of material impairment to health from exposure to lead.

(B) For the purposes of this section, the phrase *final medical determination* means the written medical opinion on the employees' health status by the examining physician or, where relevant, the outcome of the multiple physician review mechanism or alternate medical determination mechanism used pursuant to the medical surveillance provisions of this section.

(C) Where a final medical determination results in any recommended special protective measures for an employee, or limitations on an employee's exposure to lead, the employer shall implement and act consistent with the recommendation.

(iii) *Return of the employee to former job status.* (A) The employer shall return an employee to his or her former job status:

(*1*) For an employee removed due to a blood lead level at or above 50 µg/dl when two consecutive blood sampling tests indicate that the employee's blood lead level is below 40 µg/dl;

(*2*) For an employee removed due to a final medical determination, when a subsequent final medical determination results in a medical finding, determination, or opinion that the employee no longer has a detected medical condition which places the employee at increased risk of material impairment to health from exposure to lead.

(B) For the purposes of this section, the requirement that an employer return an employee to his or her former job status is not intended to expand upon or restrict any rights an employee has or would have had, absent temporary medical removal, to a specific job classification or position under the terms of a collective bargaining agreement.

(iv) *Removal of other employee special protective measure or limitations.* The employer shall remove any limitations placed on an employee or end any special protective measures provided to an employee pursuant to a final medical determination when a subsequent final medical determination indicates that the limitations or special protective measures are no longer necessary.

(v) *Employer options pending a final medical determination.* Where the multiple physician review mechanism, or alternate medical determination mechanism used pursuant to the medical surveillance provisions of this section, has not yet resulted in a final medical determination with respect to an employee, the employer shall act as follows:

(A) *Removal.* The employer may remove the employee from exposure to lead, provide special protective measures to the employee, or place limitations upon the employee, consistent with the medical findings, determinations, or recommendations of any of the physicians who have reviewed the employee's health status.

(B) *Return.* The employer may return the employee to his or her former job status, end any special protective measures provided to the employee, and remove any limitations placed upon the employee, consistent with the medical findings, determinations, or recommendations of any of the physicians who have reviewed the employee's health status, with two exceptions.

(*1*) If the initial removal, special protection, or limitation of the employee resulted from a final medical determination which differed from the findings, determinations, or recommendations of the initial physician or;

(*2*) If the employee has been on removal status for the preceding eighteen months due to an elevated blood lead level, then the employer shall await a final medical determination.

(2) *Medical removal protection benefits*—(i) *Provision of medical removal protection benefits.* The employer shall provide an employee up to eighteen (18) months of medical removal protection benefits on each occasion that an employee is removed from exposure to lead or otherwise limited pursuant to this section.

(ii) *Definition of medical removal protection benefits.* For the purposes of this section, the requirement that an employer provide medical removal protection benefits means that, as long as the job the employee was removed from continues, the employer shall maintain the total normal earnings, seniority and other employment rights and benefits of an employee, including the employee's right to his or her former job status as though the employee had not been medically removed from the employee's job or otherwise medically limited.

(iii) *Follow-up medical surveillance during the period of employee removal or limitation.* During the period of time that an employee is medically removed from his or her job or otherwise medically limited, the employer may condition the provision of medical removal protection benefits upon the employee's participation in follow-up medical surveillance made available pursuant to this section.

(iv) *Workers' compensation claims.* If a removed employee files a claim for workers' compensation payments for a lead-related disability, then the employer shall continue to provide medical removal protection benefits pending disposition of the claim. To the extent that an award is made to the employee for earnings lost during the period of removal, the employer's medical removal protection obligation shall be reduced by such amount. The employer shall receive no credit for workers' compensation payments received by the employee for treatment-related expenses.

(v) *Other credits.* The employer's obligation to provide medical removal protection benefits to a removed employee shall be reduced to the extent that the employee receives compensation for earnings lost during the period of removal either from a publicly or employer-funded compensation program, or receives income from employment with another employer made possible by virtue of the employee's removal.

(vi) *Voluntary removal or restriction of an employee.* Where an employer, although not required by this section to do so, removes an employee from exposure to lead or otherwise places limitations on an employee due to the effects of lead exposure on the employee's medical condition, the employer shall provide medical removal protection benefits to the employee equal to that required by paragraph (k)(2) (i) and (ii) of this section.

(l) *Communication of hazards—(1) General—(i) Hazard communication.* The employer shall include lead in the program established to comply with the Hazard Communication Standard (HCS) (§1910.1200). The employer shall ensure that each employee has access to labels on containers of lead and safety data sheets, and is trained in accordance with the provisions of HCS and paragraph (l) of this section. The employer shall ensure that at least the following hazards are addressed:

(A) Reproductive/developmental toxicity;

(B) Central nervous system effects;

(C) Kidney effects;

(D) Blood effects; and

(E) Acute toxicity effects.

(ii) The employer shall train each employee who is subject to exposure to lead at or above the action level on any day, or who is subject to exposure to lead compounds which may cause skin or eye irritation (*e.g.*, lead arsenate, lead azide), in accordance with the requirements of this section. The employer shall institute a training program and ensure employee participation in the program.

(iii) The employer shall provide the training program as initial training prior to the time of job assignment or prior to the start up date for this requirement, whichever comes last.

(iv) The employer shall also provide the training program at least annually for each employee who is subject to lead exposure at or above the action level on any day.

(2) *Training program.* The employer shall assure that each employee is trained in the following:

(i) The content of this standard and its appendices;

(ii) The specific nature of the operations which could result in exposure to lead above the action level;

(iii) The purpose, proper selection, fitting, use, and limitations of respirators;

(iv) The purpose and a description of the medical surveillance program, and the medical removal protection program including information concerning the adverse health effects associated with excessive exposure to lead (with particular attention to the adverse reproductive effects on both males and females and hazards to the fetus and additional precautions for employees who are pregnant);

(v) The engineering controls and work practices associated with the employee's job assignment including training of employees to follow relevant good work practices described in appendix B of this section;

(vi) The contents of any compliance plan in effect;

(vii) Instructions to employees that chelating agents should not routinely be used to remove lead from their bodies and should not be used at all except under the direction of a licensed physician; and

(viii) The employee's right of access to records under 29 CFR 1910.20.

(3) *Access to information and training materials.* (i) The employer shall make readily available to all affected employees a copy of this standard and its appendices.

(ii) The employer shall provide, upon request, all materials relating to the employee information and training program to affected employees and their designated representatives, and to the Assistant Secretary and the Director.

(m) *Signs—(1) General.* (i) The employer shall post the following warning signs in each work area where an employee's exposure to lead is above the PEL.

DANGER
LEAD WORK AREA
MAY DAMAGE FERTILITY OR THE UN-
BORN CHILD
CAUSES DAMAGE TO THE CENTRAL
NERVOUS SYSTEM
DO NOT EAT, DRINK OR SMOKE IN THIS
AREA

(ii) The employer shall ensure that no statement appears on or near any sign required by this paragraph (m) that contradicts or detracts from the meaning of the required sign.

(iii) The employer shall ensure that signs required by this paragraph (m) are illuminated and cleaned as necessary so that the legend is readily visible.

(iv) The employer may use signs required by other statutes, regulations or ordinances in addition to, or in combination with, signs required by this paragraph (m).

(v) Prior to June 1, 2016, employers may use the following legend in lieu of that specified in paragraph (m)(1)(i) of this section:

WARNING
LEAD WORK AREA
POISON
NO SMOKING OR EATING

(n) *Recordkeeping*—(1) *Exposure assessment.* (i) The employer shall establish and maintain an accurate record of all monitoring and other data used in conducting employee exposure assessments as required in paragraph (d) of this section.

(ii) Exposure monitoring records shall include:

(A) The date(s), number, duration, location and results of each of the samples taken if any, including a description of the sampling procedure used to determine representative employee exposure where applicable;

(B) A description of the sampling and analytical methods used and evidence of their accuracy;

(C) The type of respiratory protective devices worn, if any;

(D) Name, social security number, and job classification of the employee monitored and of all other employees whose exposure the measurement is intended to represent; and

(E) The environmental variables that could affect the measurement of employee exposure.

(iii) The employer shall maintain monitoring and other exposure assessment records in accordance with the provisions of 29 CFR 1910.33.

(2) *Medical surveillance.* (i) The employer shall establish and maintain an accurate record for each employee subject to medical surveillance as required by paragraph (j) of this section.

(ii) This record shall include:

(A) The name, social security number, and description of the duties of the employee;

(B) A copy of the physician's written opinions;

(C) Results of any airborne exposure monitoring done on or for that employee and provided to the physician; and

(D) Any employee medical complaints related to exposure to lead.

(iii) The employer shall keep, or assure that the examining physician keeps, the following medical records:

(A) A copy of the medical examination results including medical and work history required under paragraph (j) of this section;

(B) A description of the laboratory procedures and a copy of any standards or guidelines used to interpret the test results or references to that information;

(C) A copy of the results of biological monitoring.

(iv) The employer shall maintain or assure that the physician maintains medical records in accordance with the provisions of 29 CFR 1910.33.

(3) *Medical removals.* (i) The employer shall establish and maintain an accurate record for each employee removed from current exposure to lead pursuant to paragraph (k) of this section.

(ii) Each record shall include:

(A) The name and social security number of the employee;

(B) The date of each occasion that the employee was removed from current exposure to lead as well as the corresponding date on which the employee was returned to his or her former job status;

(C) A brief explanation of how each removal was or is being accomplished; and

(D) A statement with respect to each removal indicating whether or not the reason for the removal was an elevated blood lead level.

(iii) The employer shall maintain each medical removal record for at least the duration of an employee's employment.

(4) *Objective data for exemption from requirement for initial monitoring.* (i) For purposes of this section, objective data are information demonstrating that a particular product or material containing lead or a specific process, operation, or activity involving lead cannot release dust or fumes in concentrations at or above the action level under any expected conditions of use. Objective data can be obtained from an industry-wide study or from laboratory product test results from manufacturers of lead containing products or materials. The data the employer uses from an industry-wide survey must be obtained under workplace conditions closely resembling the processes, types of material, control methods, work practices and environmental conditions in the employer's current operations.

(ii) The employer shall maintain the record of the objective data relied upon for at least 30 years.

(5) *Availability.* The employer shall make available upon request all records required to be maintained by paragraph (n) of this section to affected employees, former employees, and their designated representatives, and to the Assistant Secretary and the Director for examination and copying.

(6) *Transfer of records.* (i) Whenever the employer ceases to do business, the successor employer shall receive and retain all records required to be maintained by paragraph (n) of this section.

(ii) The employer shall also comply with any additional requirements involving the transfer of records set forth in 29 CFR 1910.1020(h).

(o) *Observation of monitoring*—(1) *Employee observation.* The employer shall provide affected employees or their designated representatives an opportunity to observe any monitoring of employee exposure to lead conducted pursuant to paragraph (d) of this section.

(2) *Observation procedures.* (i) Whenever observation of the monitoring of employee exposure to lead requires entry into an area where the use of respirators, protective clothing or equipment is required, the employer shall provide the observer with and assure the use of such respirators, clothing and equipment, and shall require the observer to comply with all other applicable safety and health procedures.

(ii) Without interfering with the monitoring, observers shall be entitled to:

(A) Receive an explanation of the measurement procedures;

(B) Observe all steps related to the monitoring of lead performed at the place of exposure; and

(C) Record the results obtained or receive copies of the results when returned by the laboratory.

(p) *Appendices.* The information contained in the appendices to this section is not intended by itself, to create any additional obligations not otherwise imposed by this standard nor detract from any existing obligation.

APPENDIX A TO §1926.62—SUBSTANCE DATA SHEET FOR OCCUPATIONAL EXPOSURE TO LEAD

I. Substance Identification

A. *Substance:* Pure lead (Pb) is a heavy metal at room temperature and pressure and is a basic chemical element. It can combine with various other substances to form numerous lead compounds.

B. *Compounds covered by the standard:* The word *lead* when used in this interim final standard means elemental lead, all inorganic lead compounds and a class of organic lead compounds called lead soaps. This standard does not apply to other organic lead compounds.

C. *Uses:* Exposure to lead occurs in several different occupations in the construction industry, including demolition or salvage of structures where lead or lead-containing materials are present; removal or encapsulation of lead-containing materials, new construction, alteration, repair, or renovation of structures that contain lead or materials containing lead; installation of products containing lead. In addition, there are construction related activities where exposure to lead may occur, including transportation, disposal, storage, or containment of lead or materials containing lead on construction sites, and maintenance operations associated with construction activities.

D. *Permissible exposure:* The permissible exposure limit (PEL) set by the standard is 50 micrograms of lead per cubic meter of air (50 µg/m³), averaged over an 8-hour workday.

E. *Action level:* The interim final standard establishes an action level of 30 micrograms of lead per cubic meter of air (30 μg/m³), averaged over an 8-hour workday. The action level triggers several ancillary provisions of the standard such as exposure monitoring, medical surveillance, and training.

II. Health Hazard Data

A. *Ways in which lead enters your body.* When absorbed into your body in certain doses, lead is a toxic substance. The object of the lead standard is to prevent absorption of harmful quantities of lead. The standard is intended to protect you not only from the immediate toxic effects of lead, but also from the serious toxic effects that may not become apparent until years of exposure have passed. Lead can be absorbed into your body by inhalation (breathing) and ingestion (eating). Lead (except for certain organic lead compounds not covered by the standard, such as tetraethyl lead) is not absorbed through your skin. When lead is scattered in the air as a dust, fume respiratory tract. Inhalation of airborne lead is generally the most important source of occupational lead absorption. You can also absorb lead through your digestive system if lead gets into your mouth and is swallowed. If you handle food, cigarettes, chewing tobacco, or make-up which have lead on them or handle them with hands contaminated with lead, this will contribute to ingestion. A significant portion of the lead that you inhale or ingest gets into your blood stream. Once in your blood stream, lead is circulated throughout your body and stored in various organs and body tissues. Some of this lead is quickly filtered out of your body and excreted, but some remains in the blood and other tissues. As exposure to lead continues, the amount stored in your body will increase if you are absorbing more lead than your body is excreting. Even though you may not be aware of any immediate symptoms of disease, this lead stored in your tissues can be slowly causing irreversible damage, first to individual cells, then to your organs and whole body systems.

B. *Effects of overexposure to lead—(1) Short term (acute) overexposure.* Lead is a potent, systemic poison that serves no known useful function once absorbed by your body. Taken in large enough doses, lead can kill you in a matter of days. A condition affecting the brain called acute encephalopathy may arise which develops quickly to seizures, coma, and death from cardiorespiratory arrest. A short term dose of lead can lead to acute encephalopathy. Short term occupational exposures of this magnitude are highly unusual, but not impossible. Similar forms of encephalopathy may, however, arise from extended, chronic exposure to lower doses of lead. There is no sharp dividing line between rapidly developing acute effects of lead, and chronic effects which take longer to acquire. Lead adversely affects numerous body systems, and causes forms of health impairment and disease which arise after periods of exposure as short as days or as long as several years.

(2) *Long-term (chronic) overexposure.* Chronic overexposure to lead may result in severe damage to your blood-forming, nervous, urinary and reproductive systems. Some common symptoms of chronic overexposure include loss of appetite, metallic taste in the mouth, anxiety, constipation, nausea, pallor, excessive tiredness, weakness, insomnia, headache, nervous irritability, muscle and joint pain or soreness, fine tremors, numbness, dizziness, hyperactivity and colic. In lead colic there may be severe abdominal pain. Damage to the central nervous system in general and the brain (encephalopathy) in particular is one of the most severe forms of lead poisoning. The most severe, often fatal, form of encephalopathy may be preceded by vomiting, a feeling of dullness progressing to drowsiness and stupor, poor memory, restlessness, irritability, tremor, and convulsions. It may arise suddenly with the onset of seizures, followed by coma, and death. There is a tendency for muscular weakness to develop at the same time. This weakness may progress to paralysis often observed as a characteristic "wrist drop" or "foot drop" and is a manifestation of a disease to the nervous system called peripheral neuropathy. Chronic overexposure to lead also results in kidney disease with few, if any, symptoms appearing until extensive and most likely permanent kidney damage has occurred. Routine laboratory tests reveal the presence of this kidney disease only after about two-thirds of kidney function is lost. When overt symptoms of urinary dysfunction arise, it is often too late to correct or prevent worsening conditions, and progression to kidney dialysis or death is possible. Chronic overexposure to lead impairs the reproductive systems of both men and women. Overexposure to lead may result in decreased sex drive, impotence and sterility in men. Lead can alter the structure of sperm cells raising the risk of birth defects. There is evidence of miscarriage and stillbirth in women whose husbands were exposed to lead or who were exposed to lead themselves. Lead exposure also may result in decreased fertility, and abnormal menstrual cycles in women. The course of pregnancy may be adversely affected by exposure to lead since lead crosses the placental barrier and poses risks to developing fetuses. Children born of parents either one of whom were exposed to excess lead levels are more likely to have birth defects, mental retardation, behavioral disorders or die during the first year of childhood. Overexposure to lead also disrupts the blood-forming system resulting in decreased

hemoglobin (the substance in the blood that carries oxygen to the cells) and ultimately anemia. Anemia is characterized by weakness, pallor and fatigability as a result of decreased oxygen carrying capacity in the blood.

(3) *Health protection goals of the standard.* Prevention of adverse health effects for most workers from exposure to lead throughout a working lifetime requires that a worker's blood lead level (BLL, also expressed as PbB) be maintained at or below forty micrograms per deciliter of whole blood (40 µg/dl). The blood lead levels of workers (both male and female workers) who intend to have children should be maintained below 30 µg/dl to minimize adverse reproductive health effects to the parents and to the developing fetus. The measurement of your blood lead level (BLL) is the most useful indicator of the amount of lead being absorbed by your body. Blood lead levels are most often reported in units of milligrams (mg) or micrograms (µg) of lead (1 mg=1000 µg) per 100 grams (100g), 100 milliliters (100 ml) or deciliter (dl) of blood. These three units are essentially the same. Sometime BLLs are expressed in the form of mg% or µg%. This is a shorthand notation for 100g, 100 ml, or dl. (References to BLL measurements in this standard are expressed in the form of µg/dl.)

BLL measurements show the amount of lead circulating in your blood stream, but do not give any information about the amount of lead stored in your various tissues. BLL measurements merely show current absorption of lead, not the effect that lead is having on your body or the effects that past lead exposure may have already caused. Past research into lead-related diseases, however, has focused heavily on associations between BLLs and various diseases. As a result, your BLL is an important indicator of the likelihood that you will gradually acquire a lead-related health impairment or disease.

Once your blood lead level climbs above 40 µg/dl, your risk of disease increases. There is a wide variability of individual response to lead, thus it is difficult to say that a particular BLL in a given person will cause a particular effect. Studies have associated fatal encephalopathy with BLLs as low as 150 µg/dl. Other studies have shown other forms of diseases in some workers with BLLs well below 80 µg/dl. Your BLL is a crucial indicator of the risks to your health, but one other factor is also extremely important. This factor is the length of time you have had elevated BLLs. The longer you have an elevated BLL, the greater the risk that large quantities of lead are being gradually stored in your organs and tissues (body burden). The greater your overall body burden, the greater the chances of substantial permanent damage. The best way to prevent all forms of lead-related impairments and diseases—both short term and long term—is to maintain your BLL below 40 µg/dl. The provisions of the standard are designed with this end in mind.

Your employer has prime responsibility to assure that the provisions of the standard are complied with both by the company and by individual workers. You, as a worker, however, also have a responsibility to assist your employer in complying with the standard. You can play a key role in protecting your own health by learning about the lead hazards and their control, learning what the standard requires, following the standard where it governs your own actions, and seeing that your employer complies with provisions governing his or her actions.

(4) *Reporting signs and symptoms of health problems.* You should immediately notify your employer if you develop signs or symptoms associated with lead poisoning or if you desire medical advice concerning the effects of current or past exposure to lead or your ability to have a healthy child. You should also notify your employer if you have difficulty breathing during a respirator fit test or while wearing a respirator. In each of these cases, your employer must make available to you appropriate medical examinations or consultations. These must be provided at no cost to you and at a reasonable time and place. The standard contains a procedure whereby you can obtain a second opinion by a physician of your choice if your employer selected the initial physician.

APPENDIX B TO §1926.62—EMPLOYEE STANDARD SUMMARY

This appendix summarizes key provisions of the interim final standard for lead in construction that you as a worker should become familiar with.

I. Permissible Exposure Limit (PEL)— Paragraph (C)

The standard sets a permissible exposure limit (PEL) of 50 micrograms of lead per cubic meter of air (50 µg/m³), averaged over an 8-hour workday which is referred to as a time-weighted average (TWA). This is the highest level of lead in air to which you may be permissibly exposed over an 8-hour workday. However, since this is an 8-hour average, short exposures above the PEL are permitted so long as for each 8-hour work day your average exposure does not exceed this level. This interim final standard, however, takes into account the fact that your daily exposure to lead can extend beyond a typical 8-hour workday as the result of overtime or other alterations in your work schedule. To deal with this situation, the standard contains a formula which reduces your permissible exposure when you are exposed more than 8 hours. For example, if you are exposed to lead for 10 hours a day, the maximum permitted average exposure would be 40 µg/m³.

II. Exposure Assessment—Paragraph (D)

If lead is present in your workplace in any quantity, your employer is required to make an initial determination of whether any employee's exposure to lead exceeds the action level (30 µg/m³ averaged over an 8-hour day). Employee exposure is that exposure which would occur if the employee were not using a respirator. This initial determination requires your employer to monitor workers' exposures unless he or she has objective data which can demonstrate conclusively that no employee will be exposed to lead in excess of the action level. Where objective data is used in lieu of actual monitoring the employer must establish and maintain an accurate record, documenting its relevancy in assessing exposure levels for current job conditions. If such objective data is available, the employer need proceed no further on employee exposure assessment until such time that conditions have changed and the determination is no longer valid.

Objective data may be compiled from various sources, e.g., insurance companies and trade associations and information from suppliers or exposure data collected from similar operations. Objective data may also comprise previously-collected sampling data including area monitoring. If it cannot be determined through using objective data that worker exposure is less than the action level, your employer must conduct monitoring or must rely on relevant previous personal sampling, if available. Where monitoring is required for the initial determination, it may be limited to a representative number of employees who are reasonably expected to have the highest exposure levels. If your employer has conducted appropriate air sampling for lead in the past 12 months, he or she may use these results, provided they are applicable to the same employee tasks and exposure conditions and meet the requirements for accuracy as specified in the standard. As with objective data, if such results are relied upon for the initial determination, your employer must establish and maintain a record as to the relevancy of such data to current job conditions.

If there have been any employee complaints of symptoms which may be attributable to exposure to lead or if there is any other information or observations which would indicate employee exposure to lead, this must also be considered as part of the initial determination.

If this initial determination shows that a reasonable possibility exists that any employee may be exposed, without regard to respirators, over the action level, your employer must set up an air monitoring program to determine the exposure level representative of each employee exposed to lead at your workplace. In carrying out this air monitoring program, your employer is not required to monitor the exposure of every employee, but he or she must monitor a representative number of employees and job types. Enough sampling must be done to enable each employee's exposure level to be reasonably represent full shift exposure. In addition, these air samples must be taken under conditions which represent each employee's regular, daily exposure to lead. Sampling performed in the past 12 months may be used to determine exposures above the action level if such sampling was conducted during work activities essentially similar to present work conditions.

The standard lists certain tasks which may likely result in exposures to lead in excess of the PEL and, in some cases, exposures in excess of 50 times the PEL. If you are performing any of these tasks, your employer must provide you with appropriate respiratory protection, protective clothing and equipment, change areas, hand washing facilities, biological monitoring, and training until such time that an exposure assessment is conducted which demonstrates that your exposure level is below the PEL.

If you are exposed to lead and air sampling is performed, your employer is required to notify you in writing within 5 working days of the air monitoring results which represent your exposure. If the results indicate that your exposure exceeds the PEL (without regard to your use of a respirator), then your employer must also notify you of this in writing, and provide you with a description of the corrective action that has been taken or will be taken to reduce your exposure.

Your exposure must be rechecked by monitoring, at least every six months if your exposure is at or over the action level but below the PEL. Your employer may discontinue monitoring for you if 2 consecutive measurements, taken at least 7 days apart, are at or below the action level. Air monitoring must be repeated every 3 months if you are exposed over the PEL. Your employer must continue monitoring for you at this frequency until 2 consecutive measurements, taken at least 7 days apart, are below the PEL but above the action level, at which time your employer must repeat monitoring of your exposure every six months and may discontinue monitoring only after your exposure drops to or below the action level. However, whenever there is a change of equipment, process, control, or personnel or a new type of job is added at your workplace which may result in new or additional exposure to lead, your employer must perform additional monitoring.

III. Methods of Compliance—Paragraph (E)

Your employer is required to assure that no employee is exposed to lead in excess of the PEL as an 8-hour TWA. The interim final standard for lead in construction requires employers to institute engineering and work practice controls including administrative controls to the extent feasible to reduce employee exposure to lead. Where such controls are feasible but not adequate to reduce exposures below the PEL they must be used nonetheless to reduce exposures to the lowest level that can be accomplished by these means and then supplemented with appropriate respiratory protection.

Your employer is required to develop and implement a written compliance program prior to the commencement of any job where employee exposures may reach the PEL as an 8-hour TWA. The interim final standard identifies the various elements that must be included in the plan. For example, employers are required to include a description of operations in which lead is emitted, detailing other relevant information about the operation such as the type of equipment used, the type of material involved, employee job responsibilities, operating procedures and maintenance practices. In addition, your employer's compliance plan must specify the means that will be used to achieve compliance and, where engineering controls are required, include any engineering plans or studies that have been used to select the control methods. If administrative controls involving job rotation are used to reduce employee exposure to lead, the job rotation schedule must be included in the compliance plan. The plan must also detail the type of protective clothing and equipment, including respirators, housekeeping and hygiene practices that will be used to protect you from the adverse effects of exposure to lead.

The written compliance program must be made available, upon request, to affected employees and their designated representatives, the Assistant Secretary and the Director.

Finally, the plan must be reviewed and updated at least every 6 months to assure it reflects the current status in exposure control.

IV. Respiratory Protection—Paragraph (F)

Your employer is required to provide and assure your use of respirators when your exposure to lead is not controlled below the PEL by other means. The employer must pay the cost of the respirator. Whenever you request one, your employer is also required to provide you a respirator even if your air exposure level is not above the PEL. You might desire a respirator when, for example, you have received medical advice that your lead absorption should be decreased. Or, you may intend to have children in the near future, and want to reduce the level of lead in your body to minimize adverse reproductive effects. While respirators are the least satisfactory means of controlling your exposure, they are capable of providing significant protection if properly chosen, fitted, worn, cleaned, maintained, and replaced when they stop providing adequate protection.

Your employer is required to select respirators from the types listed in Table I of the Respiratory Protection section of the standard (§ 1926.62 (f)). Any respirator chosen must be approved by the National Institute for Occupational Safety and Health (NIOSH) under the provisions of 42 CFR part 84. This respirator selection table will enable your employer to choose a type of respirator that will give you a proper amount of protection based on your airborne lead exposure. Your employer may select a type of respirator that provides greater protection than that required by the standard; that is, one recommended for a higher concentration of lead than is present in your workplace. For example, a powered air-purifying respirator (PAPR) is much more protective than a typical negative pressure respirator, and may also be more comfortable to wear. A PAPR has a filter, cartridge, or canister to clean the air, and a power source that continuously blows filtered air into your breathing zone. Your employer might make a PAPR available to you to ease the burden of having to wear a respirator for long periods of time. The standard provides that you can obtain a PAPR upon request.

Your employer must also start a Respiratory Protection Program. This program must include written procedures for the proper selection, use, cleaning, storage, and maintenance of respirators.

Your employer must ensure that your respirator facepiece fits properly. Proper fit of a respirator facepiece is critical to your protection from airborne lead. Obtaining a proper fit on each employee may require your employer to make available several different types of respirator masks. To ensure that your respirator fits properly and that facepiece leakage is minimal, your employer must give you either a qualitative or quantitative fit test as specified in appendix A of the Respiratory Protection standard located at 29 CFR 1910.134.

You must also receive from your employer proper training in the use of respirators. Your employer is required to teach you how to wear a respirator, to know why it is needed, and to understand its limitations.

The standard provides that if your respirator uses filter elements, you must be given an opportunity to change the filter elements whenever an increase in breathing resistance is detected. You also must be permitted to periodically leave your work area to wash your face and respirator facepiece whenever necessary to prevent skin irritation. If you ever have difficulty in breathing during a fit test or while using a respirator, your employer must make a medical examination available to you to determine whether you can safely wear a respirator. The result of this examination may be to give you a positive pressure respirator (which reduces breathing resistance) or to provide alternative means of protection.

V. Protective Work Clothing and Equipment— Paragraph (G)

If you are exposed to lead above the PEL as an 8-hour TWA, without regard to your use of a respirator, or if you are exposed to lead compounds such as lead arsenate or lead azide which can cause skin and eye irritation, your employer must provide you with protective work clothing and equipment appropriate for the hazard. If work clothing is provided, it must be provided in a clean and dry condition at least weekly, and daily if your airborne exposure to lead is greater than 200 µg/m³. Appropriate protective work clothing and equipment can include coveralls or similar full-body work clothing, gloves, hats, shoes or disposable shoe coverlets, and face shields or vented goggles. Your employer is required to provide all such equipment at no cost to you. In addition, your employer is responsible for providing repairs and replacement as necessary, and also is responsible for the cleaning, laundering or disposal of protective clothing and equipment.

The interim final standard requires that your employer assure that you follow good work practices when you are working in areas where your exposure to lead may exceed the PEL. With respect to protective clothing and equipment, where appropriate, the following procedures should be observed prior to beginning work:

1. Change into work clothing and shoe covers in the clean section of the designated changing areas;

2. Use work garments of appropriate protective gear, including respirators before entering the work area; and

3. Store any clothing not worn under protective clothing in the designated changing area.

Workers should follow these procedures upon leaving the work area:

1. HEPA vacuum heavily contaminated protective work clothing while it is still being worn. At no time may lead be removed from protective clothing by any means which result in uncontrolled dispersal of lead into the air;

2. Remove shoe covers and leave them in the work area;

3. Remove protective clothing and gear in the dirty area of the designated changing area. Remove protective coveralls by carefully rolling down the garment to reduce exposure to dust.

4. Remove respirators last; and

5. Wash hands and face.

Workers should follow these procedures upon finishing work for the day (in addition to procedures described above):

1. Where applicable, place disposal coveralls and shoe covers with the abatement waste;

2. Contaminated clothing which is to be cleaned, laundered or disposed of must be placed in closed containers in the change room.

3. Clean protective gear, including respirators, according to standard procedures;

4. Wash hands and face again. If showers are available, take a shower and wash hair. If shower facilities are not available at the work site, shower immediately at home and wash hair.

VI. Housekeeping—Paragraph (H)

Your employer must establish a housekeeping program sufficient to maintain all surfaces as free as practicable of accumulations of lead dust. Vacuuming is the preferred method of meeting this requirement, and the use of compressed air to clean floors and other surfaces is generally prohibited unless removal with compressed air is done in conjunction with ventilation systems designed to contain dispersal of the lead dust. Dry or wet sweeping, shoveling, or brushing may not be used except where vacuuming or other equally effective methods have been tried and do not work. Vacuums must be used equipped with a special filter called a high-efficiency particulate air (HEPA) filter and emptied in a manner which minimizes the reentry of lead into the workplace.

VII. Hygiene Facilities and Practices— Paragraph (I)

The standard requires that hand washing facilities be provided where occupational exposure to lead occurs. In addition, change areas, showers (where feasible), and lunchrooms or eating areas are to be made available to workers exposed to lead above the PEL. Your employer must assure that except in these facilities, food and beverage is not present or consumed, tobacco products are not present or used, and cosmetics are not applied, where airborne exposures are above the PEL. Change rooms provided by your employer must be equipped with separate storage facilities for your protective clothing and equipment and street clothes to avoid cross-contamination. After showering, no required protective clothing or equipment worn during the shift may be worn home. It is important that contaminated clothing or equipment be removed in change areas and not be worn home or you will extend your exposure and expose your family since lead from your clothing can accumulate in your house, car, etc.

Lunchrooms or eating areas may not be entered with protective clothing or equipment unless surface dust has been removed by vacuuming, downdraft booth, or other cleaning method. Finally, workers exposed above the PEL must wash both their hands and faces prior to eating, drinking, smoking or applying cosmetics.

All of the facilities and hygiene practices just discussed are essential to minimize additional sources of lead absorption from inhalation or ingestion of lead that may accumulate on you, your clothes, or your possessions. Strict compliance with these provisions can virtually eliminate several sources of lead exposure which significantly contribute to excessive lead absorption.

VIII. Medical Surveillance—Paragraph (J)

The medical surveillance program is part of the standard's comprehensive approach to the prevention of lead-related disease. Its purpose is to supplement the main thrust of the standard which is aimed at minimizing airborne concentrations of lead and sources of ingestion. Only medical surveillance can determine if the other provisions of the standard have affectively protected you as an individual. Compliance with the standard's provision will protect most workers from the adverse effects of lead exposure, but may not be satisfactory to protect individual workers (1) who have high body burdens of lead acquired over past years, (2) who have additional uncontrolled sources of non-occupational lead exposure, (3) who exhibit unusual variations in lead absorption rates, or (4) who have specific non-work related medical conditions which could be aggravated by lead exposure (e.g., renal disease, anemia). In addition, control systems may fail, or hygiene and respirator programs may be inadequate. Periodic medical surveillance of individual workers will help detect those failures. Medical surveillance will also be important to protect your reproductive ability-regardless of whether you are a man or woman.

All medical surveillance required by the interim final standard must be performed by or under the supervision of a licensed physician. The employer must provide required medical surveillance without cost to employees and at a reasonable time and place. The standard's medical surveillance program has two parts—periodic biological monitoring and medical examinations. Your employer's obligation to offer you medical surveillance is triggered by the results of the air monitoring program. Full medical surveillance must be made available to all employees who are or may be exposed to lead in excess of the action level for more than 30 days a year and whose blood lead level exceeds 40 µg/dl. Initial medical surveillance consisting of blood sampling and analysis for lead and zinc protoporphyrin must be provided to all employees exposed at any time (1 day) above the action level.

Biological monitoring under the standard must be provided at least every 2 months for the first 6 months and every 6 months thereafter until your blood lead level is below 40

µg/dl. A zinc protoporphyrin (ZPP) test is a very useful blood test which measures an adverse metabolic effect of lead on your body and is therefore an indicator of lead toxicity.

If your BLL exceeds 40 µg/dl the monitoring frequency must be increased from every 6 months to at least every 2 months and not reduced until two consecutive BLLs indicate a blood lead level below 40 µg/dl. Each time your BLL is determined to be over 40 µg/dl, your employer must notify you of this in writing within five working days of his or her receipt of the test results. The employer must also inform you that the standard requires temporary medical removal with economic protection when your BLL exceeds 50 µg/dl. (See Discussion of Medical Removal Protection-Paragraph (k).) Anytime your BLL exceeds 50 µg/dl your employer must make available to you within two weeks of receipt of these test results a second follow-up BLL test to confirm your BLL. If the two tests both exceed 50 µg/dl, and you are temporarily removed, then your employer must make successive BLL tests available to you on a monthly basis during the period of your removal.

Medical examinations beyond the initial one must be made available on an annual basis if your blood lead level exceeds 40 µg/dl at any time during the preceding year and you are being exposed above the airborne action level of 30 µg/m³ for 30 or more days per year. The initial examination will provide information to establish a baseline to which subsequent data can be compared.

An initial medical examination to consist of blood sampling and analysis for lead and zinc protoporphyrin must also be made available (prior to assignment) for each employee being assigned for the first time to an area where the airborne concentration of lead equals or exceeds the action level at any time. In addition, a medical examination or consultation must be made available as soon as possible if you notify your employer that you are experiencing signs or symptoms commonly associated with lead poisoning or that you have difficulty breathing while wearing a respirator or during a respirator fit test. You must also be provided a medical examination or consultation if you notify your employer that you desire medical advice concerning the effects of current or past exposure to lead on your ability to procreate a healthy child.

Finally, appropriate follow-up medical examinations or consultations may also be provided for employees who have been temporarily removed from exposure under the medical removal protection provisions of the standard. (See Part IX, below.)

The standard specifies the minimum content of pre-assignment and annual medical examinations. The content of other types of medical examinations and consultations is left up to the sound discretion of the examining physician. Pre-assignment and annual medical examinations must include (1) a detailed work history and medical history; (2) a thorough physical examination, including an evaluation of your pulmonary status if you will be required to use a respirator; (3) a blood pressure measurement; and (4) a series of laboratory tests designed to check your blood chemistry and your kidney function. In addition, at any time upon your request, a laboratory evaluation of male fertility will be made (microscopic examination of a sperm sample), or a pregnancy test will be given.

The standard does not require that you participate in any of the medical procedures, tests, etc. which your employer is required to make available to you. Medical surveillance can, however, play a very important role in protecting your health. You are strongly encouraged, therefore, to participate in a meaningful fashion. The standard contains a multiple physician review mechanism which will give you a chance to have a physician of your choice directly participate in the medical surveillance program. If you are dissatisfied with an examination by a physician chosen by your employer, you can select a second physician to conduct an independent analysis. The two doctors would attempt to resolve any differences of opinion, and select a third physician to resolve any firm dispute. Generally your employer will choose the physician who conducts medical surveillance under the lead standard-unless you and your employer can agree on the choice of a physician or physicians. Some companies and unions have agreed in advance, for example, to use certain independent medical laboratories or panels of physicians. Any of these arrangements are acceptable so long as required medical surveillance is made available to workers.

The standard requires your employer to provide certain information to a physician to aid in his or her examination of you. This information includes (1) the standard and its appendices, (2) a description of your duties as they relate to occupational lead exposure, (3) your exposure level or anticipated exposure level, (4) a description of any personal protective equipment you wear, (5) prior blood lead level results, and (6) prior written medical opinions concerning you that the employer has. After a medical examination or consultation the physician must prepare a written report which must contain (1) the physician's opinion as to whether you have any medical condition which places you at increased risk of material impairment to health from exposure to lead, (2) any recommended special protective measures to be provided to you, (3) any blood lead level determinations, and (4) any recommended limitation on your use of respirators. This last element must include a determination of whether you can wear a powered air purifying respirator (PAPR) if you are found unable to wear a negative pressure respirator.

The medical surveillance program of the interim lead standard may at some point in time serve to notify certain workers that they have acquired a disease or other adverse medical condition as a result of occupational lead exposure. If this is true, these workers might have legal rights to compensation from public agencies, their employers, firms that supply hazardous products to their employers, or other persons. Some states have laws, including worker compensation laws, that disallow a worker who learns of a job-related health impairment to sue, unless the worker sues within a short period of time after learning of the impairment. (This period of time may be a matter of months or years.) An attorney can be consulted about these possibilities. It should be stressed that OSHA is in no way trying to either encourage or discourage claims or lawsuits. However, since results of the standard's medical surveillance program can significantly affect the legal remedies of a worker who has acquired a job-related disease or impairment, it is proper for OSHA to make you aware of this.

The medical surveillance section of the standard also contains provisions dealing with chelation. Chelation is the use of certain drugs (administered in pill form or injected into the body) to reduce the amount of lead absorbed in body tissues. Experience accumulated by the medical and scientific communities has largely confirmed the effectiveness of this type of therapy for the treatment of very severe lead poisoning. On the other hand, it has also been established that there can be a long list of extremely harmful side effects associated with the use of chelating agents. The medical community has balanced the advantages and disadvantages resulting from the use of chelating agents in various circumstances and has established when the use of these agents is acceptable. The standard includes these accepted limitations due to a history of abuse of chelation therapy by some lead companies. The most widely used chelating agents are calcium disodium EDTA, (Ca Na2 EDTA), Calcium Disodium Versenate (Versenate), and d-penicillamine (pencillamine or Cupramine).

The standard prohibits "prophylactic chelation" of any employee by any person the employer retains, supervises or controls. *Prophylactic chelation* is the routine use of chelating or similarly acting drugs to prevent elevated blood levels in workers who are occupationally exposed to lead, or the use of these drugs to routinely lower blood lead levels to predesignated concentrations believed to be "safe". It should be emphasized that where an employer takes a worker who has no symptoms of lead poisoning and has chelation carried out by a physician (either inside or outside of a hospital) solely to reduce the worker's blood lead level, that will generally be considered prophylactic chelation. The use of a hospital and a physician does not mean that prophylactic chelation is not being performed. Routine chelation to prevent increased or reduce current blood lead levels is unacceptable whatever the setting.

The standard allows the use of "therapeutic" or "diagnostic" chelation if administered under the supervision of a licensed physician in a clinical setting with thorough and appropriate medical monitoring. Therapeutic chelation responds to severe lead poisoning where there are marked symptoms. Diagnostic chelation involved giving a patient a dose of the drug then collecting all urine excreted for some period of time as an aid to the diagnosis of lead poisoning.

In cases where the examining physician determines that chelation is appropriate, you must be notified in writing of this fact before such treatment. This will inform you of a potentially harmful treatment, and allow you to obtain a second opinion.

IX. Medical Removal Protection—Paragraph (K)

Excessive lead absorption subjects you to increased risk of disease. Medical removal protection (MRP) is a means of protecting you when, for whatever reasons, other methods, such as engineering controls, work practices, and respirators, have failed to provide the protection you need. MRP involves the temporary removal of a worker from his or her regular job to a place of significantly lower exposure without any loss of earnings, seniority, or other employment rights or benefits. The purpose of this program is to cease further lead absorption and allow your body to naturally excrete lead which has previously been absorbed. Temporary medical removal can result from an elevated blood lead level, or a medical opinion. For up to 18 months, or for as long as the job the employee was removed from lasts, protection is provided as a result of either form of removal. The vast majority of removed workers, however, will return to their former jobs long before this eighteen month period expires.

You may also be removed from exposure even if your blood lead level is below 50 μg/dl if a final medical determination indicates that you temporarily need reduced lead exposure for medical reasons. If the physician who is implementing your employers medical program makes a final written opinion recommending your removal or other special protective measures, your employer must implement the physician's recommendation. If you are removed in this manner, you may only be returned when the doctor indicates that it is safe for you to do so.

The standard does not give specific instructions dealing with what an employer must do with a removed worker. Your job assignment upon removal is a matter for you, your employer and your union (if any) to work out consistent with existing procedures for job assignments. Each removal must be accomplished in a manner consistent with existing collective bargaining relationships. Your employer is given broad discretion to implement temporary removals so long as no attempt is made to override existing agreements. Similarly, a removed worker is provided no right to veto an employer's choice which satisfies the standard.

In most cases, employers will likely transfer removed employees to other jobs with sufficiently low lead exposure. Alternatively, a worker's hours may be reduced so that the time weighted average exposure is reduced, or he or she may be temporarily laid off if no other alternative is feasible.

In all of these situation, MRP benefits must be provided during the period of removal—i.e., you continue to receive the same earnings, seniority, and other rights and benefits you would have had if you had not been removed. Earnings includes more than just your base wage; it includes overtime, shift differentials, incentives, and other compensation you would have earned if you had not been removed. During the period of removal you must also be provided with appropriate follow-up medical surveillance. If you were removed because your blood lead level was too high, you must be provided with a monthly blood test. If a medical opinion caused your removal, you must be provided medical tests or examinations that the doctor believes to be appropriate. If you do not participate in this follow up medical surveillance, you may lose your eligibility for MRP benefits.

When you are medically eligible to return to your former job, your employer must return you to your "former job status." This means that you are entitled to the position, wages, benefits, etc., you would have had if you had not been removed. If you would still be in your old job if no removal had occurred that is where you go back. If not, you are returned consistent with whatever job assignment discretion your employer would have had if no removal had occurred. MRP only seeks to maintain your rights, not expand them or diminish them.

If you are removed under MRP and you are also eligible for worker compensation or other compensation for lost wages, your employer's MRP benefits obligation is reduced by the amount that you actually receive from these other sources. This is also true if you obtain other employment during the time you are laid off with MRP benefits.

The standard also covers situations where an employer voluntarily removes a worker from exposure to lead due to the effects of lead on the employee's medical condition, even though the standard does not require removal. In these situations MRP benefits must still be provided as though the standard required removal. Finally, it is important to note that in all cases where removal is required, respirators cannot be used as a substitute. Respirators may be used before removal becomes necessary, but not as an alternative to a transfer to a low exposure job, or to a lay-off with MRP benefits.

*X. Employee Information and Training—
Paragraph (L)*

Your employer is required to provide an information and training program for all employees exposed to lead above the action level or who may suffer skin or eye irritation from lead compounds such as lead arsenate or lead azide. The program must train these employees regarding the specific hazards associated with their work environment, protective measures which can be taken, including the contents of any compliance plan in effect, the danger of lead to their bodies (including their reproductive systems), and their rights under the standard. All employees must be trained prior to initial assignment to areas where there is a possibility of exposure over the action level.

This training program must also be provided at least annually thereafter unless further exposure above the action level will not occur.

XI. Signs—Paragraph (M)

The standard requires that the following warning sign be posted in work areas when the exposure to lead is above the PEL:

DANGER
LEAD WORK AREA
MAY DAMAGE FERTILITY OR THE UN-
  BORN CHILD
CAUSES DAMAGE TO THE CENTRAL
  NERVOUS SYSTEM
DO NOT EAT, DRINK OR SMOKE IN THIS
  AREA

Prior to June 1, 2016, employers may use the following legend in lieu of that specified above:

WARNING
LEAD WORK AREA
POISON
NO SMOKING OR EATING

XII. Recordkeeping—Paragraph (N)

Your employer is required to keep all records of exposure monitoring for airborne lead. These records must include the name and job classification of employees measured, details of the sampling and analytical techniques, the results of this sampling, and the type of respiratory protection being worn by the person sampled. Such records are to be retained for at least 30 years. Your employer is also required to keep all records of biological monitoring and medical examination results. These records must include the names of the employees, the physician's written opinion, and a copy of the results of the examination. Medical records must be preserved and maintained for the duration of employment plus 30 years. However, if the employee's duration of employment is less than one year, the employer need not retain that employee's medical records beyond the period of employment if they are provided to the employee upon termination of employment.

Recordkeeping is also required if you are temporarily removed from your job under the medical removal protection program. This record must include your name and social security number, the date of your removal and return, how the removal was or is being accomplished, and whether or not the reason for the removal was an elevated blood lead level. Your employer is required to keep each medical removal record only for as long as the duration of an employee's employment.

The standard requires that if you request to see or copy environmental monitoring, blood lead level monitoring, or medical removal records, they must be made available to you or to a representative that you authorize. Your union also has access to these records. Medical records other than BLL's must also be provided upon request to you, to your physician or to any other person whom you may specifically designate. Your union does not have access to your personal medical records unless you authorize their access.

*XIII. Observation of Monitoring—Paragraph
(O)*

When air monitoring for lead is performed at your workplace as required by this standard, your employer must allow you or someone you designate to act as an observer of the monitoring. Observers are entitled to an explanation of the measurement procedure, and to record the results obtained. Since results will not normally be available at the time of the monitoring, observers are entitled to record or receive the results of the monitoring when returned by the laboratory. Your employer is required to provide the observer with any personal protective devices required to be worn by employees working in the area that is being monitored. The employer must require the observer to wear all such equipment and to comply with all other applicable safety and health procedures.

XIV. For Additional Information

A. A copy of the interim standard for lead in construction can be obtained free of charge by calling or writing the OSHA Office of Publications, room N-3101, United States

Department of Labor, Washington, DC 20210: Telephone (202) 219–4667.

B. Additional information about the standard, its enforcement, and your employer's compliance can be obtained from the nearest OSHA Area Office listed in your telephone directory under United States Government/ Department of Labor.

APPENDIX C TO § 1926.62—MEDICAL
SURVEILLANCE GUIDELINES

Introduction

The primary purpose of the Occupational Safety and Health Act of 1970 is to assure, so far as possible, safe and healthful working conditions for every working man and woman. The interim final occupational health standard for lead in construction is designed to protect workers exposed to inorganic lead including metallic lead, all inorganic lead compounds and organic lead soaps.

Under this interim final standard occupational exposure to inorganic lead is to be limited to 50 µg/m³ (micrograms per cubic meter) based on an 8 hour time-weighted average (TWA). This permissible exposure limit (PEL) must be achieved through a combination of engineering, work practice and administrative controls to the extent feasible. Where these controls are in place but are found not to reduce employee exposures to or below the PEL, they must be used nonetheless, and supplemented with respirators to meet the 50 µg/m³ exposure limit.

The standard also provides for a program of biological monitoring for employees exposed to lead above the action level at any time, and additional medical surveillance for all employees exposed to levels of inorganic lead above 30 µg/m³ (TWA) for more than 30 days per year and whose BLL exceeds 40 µg/ dl.

The purpose of this document is to outline the medical surveillance provisions of the interim standard for inorganic lead in construction, and to provide further information to the physician regarding the examination and evaluation of workers exposed to inorganic lead.

Section 1 provides a detailed description of the monitoring procedure including the required frequency of blood testing for exposed workers, provisions for medical removal protection (MRP), the recommended right of the employee to a second medical opinion, and notification and recordkeeping requirements of the employer. A discussion of the requirements for respirator use and respirator monitoring and OSHA's position on prophylactic chelation therapy are also included in this section.

Section 2 discusses the toxic effects and clinical manifestations of lead poisoning and effects of lead intoxication on enzymatic pathways in heme synthesis. The adverse effects on both male and female reproductive capacity and on the fetus are also discussed.

Section 3 outlines the recommended medical evaluation of the worker exposed to inorganic lead, including details of the medical history, physical examination, and recommended laboratory tests, which are based on the toxic effects of lead as discussed in Section 2.

Section 4 provides detailed information concerning the laboratory tests available for the monitoring of exposed workers. Included also is a discussion of the relative value of each test and the limitations and precautions which are necessary in the interpretation of the laboratory results.

I. Medical Surveillance and Monitoring Requirements for Workers Exposed to Inorganic Lead

Under the interim final standard for inorganic lead in the construction industry, initial medical surveillance consisting of biological monitoring to include blood lead and ZPP level determination shall be provided to employees exposed to lead at or above the action level on any one day. In addition, a program of biological monitoring is to be made available to all employees exposed above the action level at any time and additional medical surveillance is to be made available to all employees exposed to lead above 30 µg/m³ TWA for more than 30 days each year and whose BLL exceeds 40 µg/dl. This program consists of periodic blood sampling and medical evaluation to be performed on a schedule which is defined by previous laboratory results, worker complaints or concerns, and the clinical assessment of the examining physician.

Under this program, the blood lead level (BLL) of all employees who are exposed to lead above 30 µg/m³ for more than 30 days per year or whose blood lead is above 40 µg/dl but exposed for no more than 30 days per year is to be determined at least every two months for the first six months of exposure and every six months thereafter. The frequency is increased to every two months for employees whose last blood lead level was 40 µg/dl or above. For employees who are removed from exposure to lead due to an elevated blood lead, a new blood lead level must be measured monthly. A zinc protoporphyrin (ZPP) measurement is strongly recommended on each occasion that a blood lead level measurement is made.

An annual medical examination and consultation performed under the guidelines discussed in Section 3 is to be made available to each employee exposed above 30 µg/m³ for more than 30 days per year for whom a blood test conducted at any time during the preceding 12 months indicated a blood lead level at or above 40 µg/dl. Also, an examination is to be given to all employees prior to their assignment to an area in which airborne lead concentrations reach or exceed the 30 µg/m³ for more than 30 days per year. In addition, a medical examination must be provided as soon as possible after notification by an employee that the employee has developed signs or symptoms commonly associated with lead intoxication, that the employee desires medical advice regarding lead exposure and the ability to procreate a healthy child, or that the employee has demonstrated difficulty in breathing during a respirator fitting test or during respirator use. An examination is also to be made available to each employee removed from exposure to lead due to a risk of sustaining material impairment to health, or otherwise limited or specially protected pursuant to medical recommendations.

Results of biological monitoring or the recommendations of an examining physician may necessitate removal of an employee from further lead exposure pursuant to the standard's medical removal protection (MRP) program. The object of the MRP program is to provide temporary medical removal to workers either with substantially elevated blood lead levels or otherwise at risk of sustaining material health impairment from continued substantial exposure to lead.

Under the standard's ultimate worker removal criteria, a worker is to be removed from any work having an eight hour TWA exposure to lead of 30 µg/m³ when his or her blood lead level reaches 50 µg/dl and is confirmed by a second follow-up blood lead level performed within two weeks after the employer receives the results of the first blood sampling test. Return of the employee to his or her job status depends on a worker's blood lead level declining to 40 µg/dl.

As part of the interim standard, the employer is required to notify in writing each employee whose blood lead level exceeds 40 µg/dl. In addition each such employee is to be informed that the standard requires medical removal with MRP benefits, discussed below, when an employee's blood lead level exceeds the above defined limit.

In addition to the above blood lead level criterion, temporary worker removal may also take place as a result of medical determinations and recommendations. Written medical opinions must be prepared after each examination pursuant to the standard. If the examining physician includes a medical finding, determination or opinion that the employee has a medical condition which places the employee at increased risk of material health impairment from exposure to lead, then the employee must be removed from exposure to lead at or above 30 µg/m³. Alternatively, if the examining physician recommends special protective measures for an employee (e.g., use of a powered air purifying respirator) or recommends limitations on an employee's exposure to lead, then the employer must implement these recommendations.

Recommendations may be more stringent than the specific provisions of the standard. The examining physician, therefore, is given broad flexibility to tailor special protective procedures to the needs of individual employees. This flexibility extends to the evaluation and management of pregnant workers and male and female workers who are planning to raise children. Based on the history, physical examination, and laboratory studies, the physician might recommend special protective measures or medical removal for an employee who is pregnant or who is planning to conceive a child when, in the physician's judgment, continued exposure to lead at the current job would pose a significant risk. The return of the employee to his or her former job status, or the removal of special protections or limitations, depends upon the examining physician determining that the employee is no longer at increased risk of material impairment or that special measures are no longer needed.

During the period of any form of special protection or removal, the employer must maintain the worker's earnings, seniority, and other employment rights and benefits (as though the worker had not been removed) for a period of up to 18 months or for as long as the job the employee was removed from lasts if less than 18 months. This economic protection will maximize meaningful worker participation in the medical surveillance program, and is appropriate as part of the employer's overall obligation to provide a safe and healthful workplace. The provisions of MRP benefits during the employee's removal period may, however, be conditioned upon participation in medical surveillance.

The lead standard provides for a multiple physician review in cases where the employee wishes a second opinion concerning potential lead poisoning or toxicity. If an employee wishes a second opinion, he or she can make an appointment with a physician of his or her choice. This second physician will review the findings, recommendations or determinations of the first physician and conduct any examinations, consultations or tests deemed necessary in an attempt to make a final medical determination. If the first and second physicians do not agree in their assessment they must try to resolve their differences. If they cannot reach an agreement then they must designate a third physician to resolve the dispute.

The employer must provide examining and consulting physicians with the following specific information: A copy of the lead regulations and all appendices, a description of the employee's duties as related to exposure, the exposure level or anticipated level to lead and any other toxic substances (if applicable), a description of personal protective equipment used, blood lead levels, and all prior written medical opinions regarding the employee in the employer's possession or control. The employer must also obtain from the physician and provide the employee with a written medical opinion containing blood lead levels, the physicians's opinion as to whether the employee is at risk of material impairment to health, any recommended protective measures for the employee if further exposure is permitted, as well as any recommended limitations upon an employee's use of respirators.

Employers must instruct each physician not to reveal to the employer in writing or in any other way his or her findings, laboratory results, or diagnoses which are felt to be unrelated to occupational lead exposure. They must also instruct each physician to advise the employee of any occupationally or non-occupationally related medical condition requiring further treatment or evaluation.

The standard provides for the use of respirators where engineering and other primary controls are not effective. However, the use of respirator protection shall not be used in lieu of temporary medical removal due to elevated blood lead levels or findings that an employee is at risk of material health impairment. This is based on the numerous inadequacies of respirators including skin rash where the facepiece makes contact with the skin, unacceptable stress to breathing in some workers with underlying cardiopulmonary impairment, difficulty in providing adequate fit, the tendency for respirators to create additional hazards by interfering with vision, hearing, and mobility, and the difficulties of assuring the maximum effectiveness of a complicated work practice program involving respirators. Respirators do, however, serve a useful function where engineering and work practice controls are inadequate by providing supplementary, interim, or short-term protection, provided they are properly selected for the environment in which the employee will be working, properly fitted to the employee, maintained and cleaned periodically, and worn by the employee when required.

In its interim final standard on occupational exposure to inorganic lead in the construction industry, OSHA has prohibited prophylactic chelation. Diagnostic and therapeutic chelation are permitted only under the supervision of a licensed physician with appropriate medical monitoring in an acceptable clinical setting. The decision to initiate chelation therapy must be made on an individual basis and take into account the severity of symptoms felt to be a result of lead toxicity along with blood lead levels, ZPP levels, and other laboratory tests as appropriate. EDTA and penicillamine which are the primary chelating agents used in the therapy of occupational lead poisoning have significant potential side effects and their

use must be justified on the basis of expected benefits to the worker. Unless frank and severe symptoms are present, therapeutic chelation is not recommended, given the opportunity to remove a worker from exposure and allow the body to naturally excrete accumulated lead. As a diagnostic aid, the chelation mobilization test using CA-EDTA has limited applicability. According to some investigators, the test can differentiate between lead-induced and other nephropathies. The test may also provide an estimation of the mobile fraction of the total body lead burden.

Employers are required to assure that accurate records are maintained on exposure assessment, including environmental monitoring, medical surveillance, and medical removal for each employee. Exposure assessment records must be kept for at least 30 years. Medical surveillance records must be kept for the duration of employment plus 30 years except in cases where the employment was less than one year. If duration of employment is less than one year, the employer need not retain this record beyond the term of employment if the record is provided to the employee upon termination of employment. Medical removal records also must be maintained for the duration of employment. All records required under the standard must be made available upon request to the Assistant Secretary of Labor for Occupational Safety and Health and the Director of the National Institute for Occupational Safety and Health. Employers must also make environmental and biological monitoring and medical removal records available to affected employees and to former employees or their authorized employee representatives. Employees or their specifically designated representatives have access to their entire medical surveillance records.

In addition, the standard requires that the employer inform all workers exposed to lead at or above 30 µg/m³ of the provisions of the standard and all its appendices, the purpose and description of medical surveillance and provisions for medical removal protection if temporary removal is required. An understanding of the potential health effects of lead exposure by all exposed employees along with full understanding of their rights under the lead standard is essential for an effective monitoring program.

II. Adverse Health Effects of Inorganic Lead

Although the toxicity of lead has been known for 2,000 years, the knowledge of the complex relationship between lead exposure and human response is still being refined. Significant research into the toxic properties of lead continues throughout the world, and it should be anticipated that our understanding of thresholds of effects and margins of safety will be improved in future years. The provisions of the lead standard are founded on two prime medical judgments: First, the prevention of adverse health effects from exposure to lead throughout a working lifetime requires that worker blood lead levels be maintained at or below 40 µg/dl and second, the blood lead levels of workers, male or female, who intend to parent in the near future should be maintained below 30 µg/dl to minimize adverse reproductive health effects to the parents and developing fetus. The adverse effects of lead on reproduction are being actively researched and OSHA encourages the physician to remain abreast of recent developments in the area to best advise pregnant workers or workers planning to conceive children.

The spectrum of health effects caused by lead exposure can be subdivided into five developmental stages: Normal, physiological changes of uncertain significance, pathophysiological changes, overt symptoms (morbidity), and mortality. Within this process there are no sharp distinctions, but rather a continuum of effects. Boundaries between categories overlap due to the wide variation of individual responses and exposures in the working population. OSHA's development of the lead standard focused on pathophysiological changes as well as later stages of disease.

1. Heme Synthesis Inhibition. The earliest demonstrated effect of lead involves its ability to inhibit at least two enzymes of the heme synthesis pathway at very low blood levels. Inhibition of delta aminolevulinic acid dehydrase (ALA-D) which catalyzes the conversion of delta-aminolevulinic acid (ALA) to protoporphyrin is observed at a blood lead level below 20 µg/dl. At a blood lead level of 40 µg/dl, more than 20% of the population would have 70% inhibition of ALA-D. There is an exponential increase in ALA excretion at blood lead levels greater than 40 µg/dl.

Another enzyme, ferrochelatase, is also inhibited at low blood levels. Inhibition of ferrochelatase leads to increased free erythrocyte protoporphyrin (FEP) in the blood which can then bind to zinc to yield zinc protoporphyrin. At a blood lead level of 50 µg/dl or greater, nearly 100% of the population will have an increase in FEP. There is also an exponential relationship between blood lead levels greater than 40 µg/dl and the associated ZPP level, which has led to the development of the ZPP screening test for lead exposure.

While the significance of these effects is subject to debate, it is OSHA's position that these enzyme disturbances are early stages of a disease process which may eventually result in the clinical symptoms of lead poisoning. Whether or not the effects do progress to the later stages of clinical disease, disruption of these enzyme processes

over a working lifetime is considered to be a material impairment of health.

One of the eventual results of lead-induced inhibition of enzymes in the heme synthesis pathway is anemia which can be asymptomatic if mild but associated with a wide array of symptoms including dizziness, fatigue, and tachycardia when more severe. Studies have indicated that lead levels as low as 50 µg/dl can be associated with a definite decreased hemoglobin, although most cases of lead-induced anemia, as well as shortened red-cell survival times, occur at lead levels exceeding 80 µg/dl. Inhibited hemoglobin synthesis is more common in chronic cases whereas shortened erythrocyte life span is more common in acute cases.

In lead-induced anemias, there is usually a reticulocytosis along with the presence of basophilic stippling, and ringed sideroblasts, although none of the above are pathognomonic for lead-induced anemia.

2. Neurological Effects. Inorganic lead has been found to have toxic effects on both the central and peripheral nervous systems. The earliest stages of lead-induced central nervous system effects first manifest themselves in the form of behavioral disturbances and central nervous system symptoms including irritability, restlessness, insomnia and other sleep disturbances, fatigue, vertigo, headache, poor memory, tremor, depression, and apathy. With more severe exposure, symptoms can progress to drowsiness, stupor, hallucinations, delirium, convulsions and coma.

The most severe and acute form of lead poisoning which usually follows ingestion or inhalation of large amounts of lead is acute encephalopathy which may arise precipitously with the onset of intractable seizures, coma, cardiorespiratory arrest, and death within 48 hours.

While there is disagreement about what exposure levels are needed to produce the earliest symptoms, most experts agree that symptoms definitely can occur at blood lead levels of 60 µg/dl whole blood and therefore recommend a 40 µg/dl maximum. The central nervous system effects frequently are not reversible following discontinued exposure or chelation therapy and when improvement does occur, it is almost always only partial.

The peripheral neuropathy resulting from lead exposure characteristically involves only motor function with minimal sensory damage and has a marked predilection for the extensor muscles of the most active extremity. The peripheral neuropathy can occur with varying degrees of severity. The earliest and mildest form which can be detected in workers with blood lead levels as low as 50 µg/dl is manifested by slowing of motor nerve conduction velocity often without clinical symptoms. With progression of the neuropathy there is development of painless extensor muscle weakness usually involving the extensor muscles of the fingers and hand in the most active upper extremity, followed in severe cases by wrist drop or, much less commonly, foot drop.

In addition to slowing of nerve conduction, electromyographical studies in patients with blood lead levels greater than 50 µg/dl have demonstrated a decrease in the number of acting motor unit potentials, an increase in the duration of motor unit potentials, and spontaneous pathological activity including fibrillations and fasciculations. Whether these effects occur at levels of 40 µg/dl is undetermined.

While the peripheral neuropathies can occasionally be reversed with therapy, again such recovery is not assured particularly in the more severe neuropathies and often improvement is only partial. The lack of reversibility is felt to be due in part to segmental demyelination.

3. Gastrointestinal. Lead may also affect the gastrointestinal system producing abdominal colic or diffuse abdominal pain, constipation, obstipation, diarrhea, anorexia, nausea and vomiting. Lead colic rarely develops at blood lead levels below 80 µg/dl.

4. Renal. Renal toxicity represents one of the most serious health effects of lead poisoning. In the early stages of disease nuclear inclusion bodies can frequently be identified in proximal renal tubular cells. Renal function remains normal and the changes in this stage are probably reversible. With more advanced disease there is progressive interstitial fibrosis and impaired renal function. Eventually extensive interstitial fibrosis ensues with sclerotic glomeruli and dilated and atrophied proximal tubules; all represent end stage kidney disease. Azotemia can be progressive, eventually resulting in frank uremia necessitating dialysis. There is occasionally associated hypertension and hyperuricemia with or without gout.

Early kidney disease is difficult to detect. The urinalysis is normal in early lead nephropathy and the blood urea nitrogen and serum creatinine increase only when two-thirds of kidney function is lost. Measurement of creatinine clearance can often detect earlier disease as can other methods of measurement of glomerular filtration rate. An abnormal Ca-EDTA mobilization test has been used to differentiate between lead-induced and other nephropathies, but this procedure is not widely accepted. A form of Fanconi syndrome with aminoaciduria, glycosuria, and hyperphosphaturia indicating severe injury to the proximal renal tubules is occasionally seen in children.

5. Reproductive effects. Exposure to lead can have serious effects on reproductive function in both males and females. In male workers exposed to lead there can be a decrease in sexual drive, impotence, decreased ability to produce healthy sperm, and sterility. Malformed sperm (teratospermia), decreased number of sperm (hypospermia), and sperm with decreased motility (asthenospermia) can all occur. Teratospermia has been noted at mean blood lead levels of 53 µg/dl and hypospermia and asthenospermia at 41 µg/dl. Furthermore, there appears to be a dose-response relationship for teratospermia in lead exposed workers.

Women exposed to lead may experience menstrual disturbances including dysmenorrhea, menorrhagia and amenorrhea. Following exposure to lead, women have a higher frequency of sterility, premature births, spontaneous miscarriages, and stillbirths.

Germ cells can be affected by lead and cause genetic damage in the egg or sperm cells before conception and result in failure to implant, miscarriage, stillbirth, or birth defects.

Infants of mothers with lead poisoning have a higher mortality during the first year and suffer from lowered birth weights, slower growth, and nervous system disorders.

Lead can pass through the placental barrier and lead levels in the mother's blood are comparable to concentrations of lead in the umbilical cord at birth. Transplacental passage becomes detectable at 12–14 weeks of gestation and increases until birth.

There is little direct data on damage to the fetus from exposure to lead but it is generally assumed that the fetus and newborn would be at least as susceptible to neurological damage as young children. Blood lead levels of 50–60 µg/dl in children can cause significant neurobehavioral impairments and there is evidence of hyperactivity at blood levels as low as 25 µg/dl. Given the overall body of literature concerning the adverse health effects of lead in children, OSHA feels that the blood lead level in children should be maintained below 30 µg/dl with a population mean of 15 µg/dl. Blood lead levels in the fetus and newborn likewise should not exceed 30 µg/dl.

Because of lead's ability to pass through the placental barrier and also because of the demonstrated adverse effects of lead on reproductive function in both the male and female as well as the risk of genetic damage of lead on both the ovum and sperm, OSHA recommends a 30 µg/dl maximum permissible blood lead level in both males and females who wish to bear children.

6. Other toxic effects. Debate and research continue on the effects of lead on the human body. Hypertension has frequently been noted in occupationally exposed individuals although it is difficult to assess whether this is due to lead's adverse effects on the kidney or if some other mechanism is involved. Vascular and electrocardiographic changes have been detected but have not been well characterized. Lead is thought to impair thyroid

115

function and interfere with the pituitary-adrenal axis, but again these effects have not been well defined.

III. Medical Evaluation

The most important principle in evaluating a worker for any occupational disease including lead poisoning is a high index of suspicion on the part of the examining physician. As discussed in Section 2, lead can affect numerous organ systems and produce a wide array of signs and symptoms, most of which are non-specific and subtle in nature at least in the early stages of disease. Unless serious concern for lead toxicity is present, many of the early clues to diagnosis may easily be overlooked.

The crucial initial step in the medical evaluation is recognizing that a worker's employment can result in exposure to lead. The worker will frequently be able to define exposures to lead and lead containing materials but often will not volunteer this information unless specifically asked. In other situations the worker may not know of any exposures to lead but the suspicion might be raised on the part of the physician because of the industry or occupation of the worker. Potential occupational exposure to lead and its compounds occur in many occupations in the construction industry, including demolition and salvaging operations, removal or encapsulation of materials containing lead, construction, alteration, repair or renovation of structures containing lead, transportation, disposal, storage or containment of lead or lead-containing materials on construction sites, and maintenance operations associated with construction activities.

Once the possibility for lead exposure is raised, the focus can then be directed toward eliciting information from the medical history, physical exam, and finally from laboratory data to evaluate the worker for potential lead toxicity.

A complete and detailed work history is important in the initial evaluation. A listing of all previous employment with information on job description, exposure to fumes or dust, known exposures to lead or other toxic substances, a description of any personal protective equipment used, and previous medical surveillance should all be included in the worker's record. Where exposure to lead is suspected, information concerning on-the-job personal hygiene, smoking or eating habits in work areas, laundry procedures, and use of any protective clothing or respiratory protection equipment should be noted. A complete work history is essential in the medical evaluation of a worker with suspected lead toxicity, especially when long term effects such as neurotoxicity and nephrotoxicity are considered.

The medical history is also of fundamental importance and should include a listing of all past and current medical conditions, current medications including proprietary drug intake, previous surgeries and hospitalizations, allergies, smoking history, alcohol consumption, and also non-occupational lead exposures such as hobbies (hunting, riflery). Also known childhood exposures should be elicited. Any previous history of hematological, neurological, gastrointestinal, renal, psychological, gynecological, genetic, or reproductive problems should be specifically noted.

A careful and complete review of systems must be performed to assess both recognized complaints and subtle or slowly acquired symptoms which the worker might not appreciate as being significant. The review of symptoms should include the following:

1. General—weight loss, fatigue, decreased appetite.

2. Head, Eyes, Ears, Nose, Throat (HEENT)—headaches, visual disturbances or decreased visual acuity, hearing deficits or tinnitus, pigmentation of the oral mucosa, or metallic taste in mouth.

3. Cardio-pulmonary—shortness of breath, cough, chest pains, palpitations, or orthopnea.

4. Gastrointestinal—nausea, vomiting, heartburn, abdominal pain, constipation or diarrhea.

5. Neurologic—irritability, insomnia, weakness (fatigue), dizziness, loss of memory, confusion, hallucinations, incoordination, ataxia, decreased strength in hands or feet, disturbances in gait, difficulty in climbing stairs, or seizures.

6. Hematologic—pallor, easy fatigability, abnormal blood loss, melena.

7. Reproductive (male and female and spouse where relevant)—history of infertility, impotence, loss of libido, abnormal menstrual periods, history of miscarriages, stillbirths, or children with birth defects.

8. Musculo-skeletal—muscle and joint pains.

The physical examination should emphasize the neurological, gastrointestinal, and cardiovascular systems. The worker's weight and blood pressure should be recorded and the oral mucosa checked for pigmentation characteristic of a possible Burtonian or lead line on the gingiva. It should be noted, however, that the lead line may not be present even in severe lead poisoning if good oral hygiene is practiced.

The presence of pallor on skin examination may indicate an anemia which, if severe, might also be associated with a tachycardia. If an anemia is suspected, an active search for blood loss should be undertaken including potential blood loss through the gastrointestinal tract.

A complete neurological examination should include an adequate mental status evaluation including a search for behavioral and psychological disturbances, memory testing, evaluation for irritability, insomnia, hallucinations, and mental clouding. Gait and coordination should be examined along with close observation for tremor. A detailed evaluation of peripheral nerve function including careful sensory and motor function testing is warranted. Strength testing particularly of extensor muscle groups of all extremities is of fundamental importance.

Cranial nerve evaluation should also be included in the routine examination.

The abdominal examination should include auscultation for bowel sounds and abdominal bruits and palpation for organomegaly, masses, and diffuse abdominal tenderness.

Cardiovascular examination should evaluate possible early signs of congestive heart failure. Pulmonary status should be addressed particularly if respirator protection is contemplated.

As part of the medical evaluation, the interim lead standard requires the following laboratory studies:

1. Blood lead level
2. Hemoglobin and hematocrit determinations, red cell indices, and examination of the peripheral blood smear to evaluate red blood cell morphology
3. Blood urea nitrogen
4. Serum creatinine
5. Routine urinalysis with microscopic examination.
6. A zinc protoporphyrin level.

In addition to the above, the physician is authorized to order any further laboratory or other tests which he or she deems necessary in accordance with sound medical practice. The evaluation must also include pregnancy testing or laboratory evaluation of male fertility if requested by the employee. Additional tests which are probably not warranted on a routine basis but may be appropriate when blood lead and ZPP levels are equivocal include delta aminolevulinic acid and coproporphyrin concentrations in the urine, and dark-field illumination for detection of basophilic stippling in red blood cells.

If an anemia is detected further studies including a careful examination of the peripheral smear, reticulocyte count, stool for occult blood, serum iron, total iron binding capacity, bilirubin, and, if appropriate, vitamin B12 and folate may be of value in attempting to identify the cause of the anemia.

If a peripheral neuropathy is suspected, nerve conduction studies are warranted both for diagnosis and as a basis to monitor any therapy.

If renal disease is questioned, a 24 hour urine collection for creatinine clearance, protein, and electrolytes may be indicated. Elevated uric acid levels may result from lead-induced renal disease and a serum uric acid level might be performed.

An electrocardiogram and chest x-ray may be obtained as deemed appropriate.

Sophisticated and highly specialized testing should not be done routinely and where indicated should be under the direction of a specialist.

IV. Laboratory Evaluation

The blood lead level at present remains the single most important test to monitor lead exposure and is the test used in the medical surveillance program under the lead standard to guide employee medical removal. The ZPP has several advantages over the blood lead level. Because of its relatively recent development and the lack of extensive data concerning its interpretation, the ZPP currently remains an ancillary test.

This section will discuss the blood lead level and ZPP in detail and will outline their relative advantages and disadvantages. Other blood tests currently available to evaluate lead exposure will also be reviewed.

The blood lead level is a good index of current or recent lead absorption when there is no anemia present and when the worker has not taken any chelating agents. However, blood lead levels along with urinary lead levels do not necessarily indicate the total body burden of lead and are not adequate measures of past exposure. One reason for this is that lead has a high affinity for bone and up to 90% of the body's total lead is deposited there. A very important component of the total lead body burden is lead in soft tissue (liver, kidney, and brain). This fraction of the lead body burden, the biologically active lead, is not entirely reflected by blood lead levels since it is a function of the dynamics of lead absorption, distribution, deposition in bone and excretion. Following discontinuation of exposure to lead, the excess body burden is only slowly mobilized from bone and other relatively stable body stores and excreted. Consequently, a high blood lead level may only represent recent heavy exposure to lead without a significant total body excess and likewise a low blood lead level does not exclude an elevated total body burden of lead.

Also due to its correlation with recent exposures, the blood lead level may vary considerably over short time intervals.

To minimize laboratory error and erroneous results due to contamination, blood specimens must be carefully collected after thorough cleaning of the skin with appropriate methods using lead-free blood containers and analyzed by a reliable laboratory. Under the standard, samples must be analyzed in laboratories which are approved by OSHA. Analysis is to be made using atomic absorption spectrophotometry, anodic stripping voltammetry or any method which meets the accuracy requirements set forth by the standard.

The determination of lead in urine is generally considered a less reliable monitoring technique than analysis of whole blood primarily due to individual variability in urinary excretion capacity as well as the technical difficulty of obtaining accurate 24 hour urine collections. In addition, workers with renal insufficiency, whether due to lead or some other cause, may have decreased lead clearance and consequently urine lead levels may underestimate the true lead burden. Therefore, urine lead levels should not be used as a routine test.

The zinc protoporphyrin test, unlike the blood lead determination, measures an adverse metabolic effect of lead and as such is a better indicator of lead toxicity than the level of blood lead itself. The level of ZPP reflects lead absorption over the preceding 3 to 4 months, and therefore is a better indicator of lead body burden. The ZPP requires more time than the blood lead to read significantly elevated levels; the return to normal after discontinuing lead exposure is also slower. Furthermore, the ZPP test is simpler, faster, and less expensive to perform and no contamination is possible. Many investigators believe it is the most reliable means of monitoring chronic lead absorption.

Zinc protoporphyrin results from the inhibition of the enzyme ferrochelatase which catalyzes the insertion of an iron molecule into the protoporphyrin molecule, which then becomes heme. If iron is not inserted into the molecule then zinc, having a greater affinity for protoporphyrin, takes the place of the iron, forming ZPP.

An elevation in the level of circulating ZPP may occur at blood lead levels as low as 20-30 µg/dl in some workers. Once the blood lead level has reached 40 µg/dl there is more marked rise in the ZPP value from its normal range of less than 100 µg/dl100 ml. Increases in blood lead levels beyond 40 µg/100 g are associated with exponential increases in ZPP.

Whereas blood lead levels fluctuate over short time spans, ZPP levels remain relatively stable. ZPP is measured directly in red blood cells and is present for the cell's entire 120 day life-span. Therefore, the ZPP level in blood reflects the average ZPP production over the previous 3-4 months and consequently the average lead exposure during that time interval.

It is recommended that a hematocrit be determined whenever a confirmed ZPP of 50 µg/100 ml whole blood is obtained to rule out a significant underlying anemia. If the ZPP is in excess of 100 µg/100 ml and not associated with abnormal elevations in blood lead levels, the laboratory should be checked to be sure that blood leads were determined using atomic absorption spectrophotometry anodic stripping voltammetry, or any method which meets the accuracy requirements set forth

by the standard by an OSHA approved laboratory which is experienced in lead level determinations. Repeat periodic blood lead studies should be obtained in all individuals with elevated ZPP levels to be certain that an associated elevated blood lead level has not been missed due to transient fluctuations in blood leads.

ZPP has a characteristic fluorescence spectrum with a peak at 594 nm which is detectable with a hematofluorimeter. The hematofluorimeter is accurate and portable and can provide on-site, instantaneous results for workers who can be frequently tested via a finger prick.

However, careful attention must be given to calibration and quality control procedures. Limited data on blood lead-ZPP correlations and the ZPP levels which are associated with the adverse health effects discussed in Section 2 are the major limitations of the test. Also it is difficult to correlate ZPP levels with environmental exposure and there is some variation of response with age and sex. Nevertheless, the ZPP promises to be an important diagnostic test for the early detection of lead toxicity and its value will increase as more data is collected regarding its relationship to other manifestations of lead poisoning.

Levels of delta-aminolevulinic acid (ALA) in the urine are also used as a measure of lead exposure. Increasing concentrations of ALA are believed to result from the inhibition of the enzyme delta-aminolevulinic acid dehydrase (ALA-D). Although the test is relatively easy to perform, inexpensive, and rapid, the disadvantages include variability in results, the necessity to collect a complete 24 hour urine sample which has a specific gravity greater than 1.010, and also the fact that ALA decomposes in the presence of light.

The pattern of porphyrin excretion in the urine can also be helpful in identifying lead intoxication. With lead poisoning, the urine concentrations of coproporphyrins I and II, porphobilinogen and uroporphyrin I rise. The most important increase, however, is that of coproporphyrin III; levels may exceed 5,000 µg/l in the urine in lead poisoned individuals, but its correlation with blood lead levels and ZPP are not as good as those of ALA. Increases in urinary porphyrins are not diagnostic of lead toxicity and may be seen in porphyria, some liver diseases, and in patients with high reticulocyte counts.

Summary. The Occupational Safety and Health Administration's interim standard for inorganic lead in the construction industry places significant emphasis on the medical surveillance of all workers exposed to levels of inorganic lead above 30 µg/m³ TWA. The physician has a fundamental role in this surveillance program, and in the operation of the medical removal protection program.

Even with adequate worker education on the adverse health effects of lead and appropriate training in work practices, personal hygiene and other control measures, the physician has a primary responsibility for evaluating potential lead toxicity in the worker. It is only through a careful and detailed medical and work history, a complete physical examination and appropriate laboratory testing that an accurate assessment can be made. Many of the adverse health effects of lead toxicity are either irreversible or only partially reversible and therefore early detection of disease is very important.

This document outlines the medical monitoring program as defined by the occupational safety and health standard for inorganic lead. It reviews the adverse health effects of lead poisoning and describes the important elements of the history and physical examinations as they relate to these adverse effects. Finally, the appropriate laboratory testing for evaluating lead exposure and toxicity is presented.

It is hoped that this review and discussion will give the physician a better understanding of the OSHA standard with the ultimate goal of protecting the health and well-being of the worker exposed to lead under his or her care.

[58 FR 26627, May 4, 1993, as amended at 58 FR 34218, June 24, 1993; 61 FR 5510, Feb. 13, 1996; 63 FR 1296, Jan. 8, 1998; 70 FR 1143, Jan. 5, 2005; 71 FR 16674, Apr. 3, 2006; 71 FR 50191, Aug. 24, 2006; 73 FR 75588, Dec. 12, 2008; 76 FR 33611, June 8, 2011; 76 FR 80741, Dec. 27, 2011; 77 FR 17890, Mar. 26, 2012]

§1926.64 Process safety management of highly hazardous chemicals.

Purpose. This section contains requirements for preventing or minimizing the consequences of catastrophic releases of toxic, reactive, flammable, or explosive chemicals. These releases may result in toxic, fire or explosion hazards.

(a) *Application.* (1) This section applies to the following:

(i) A process which involves a chemical at or above the specified threshold quantities listed in appendix A to this section;

(ii) A process which involves a Category 1 flammable gas (as defined in §1910.1200(c)) or flammable liquid with a flashpoint below 100 °F (37.8 °C) on site in one location, in a quantity of 10,000 pounds (4535.9 kg) or more except for:

(A) Hydrocarbon fuels used solely for workplace consumption as a fuel (e.g., propane used for comfort heating, gaso-

line for vehicle refueling), if such fuels are not a part of a process containing another highly hazardous chemical covered by this standard;

(B) Flammable liquids with a flashpoint below 100 °F (37.8 °C) stored in atmospheric tanks or transferred that are kept below their normal boiling point without benefit of chilling or refrigeration.

(2) This section does not apply to:

(i) Retail facilities;

(ii) Oil or gas well drilling or servicing operations; or,

(iii) Normally unoccupied remote facilities.

(b) *Definitions. Atmospheric tank* means a storage tank which has been designed to operate at pressures from atmospheric through 0.5 p.s.i.g. (pounds per square inch gauge, 3.45 Kpa).

Boiling point means the boiling point of a liquid at a pressure of 14.7 pounds per square inch absolute (p.s.i.a.) (760 mm.). For the purposes of this section, where an accurate boiling point is unavailable for the material in question, or for mixtures which do not have a constant boiling point, the 10 percent point of a distillation performed in accordance with the Standard Method of Test for Distillation of Petroleum Products, ASTM D-86-62, may be used as the boiling point of the liquid.

Catastrophic release means a major uncontrolled emission, fire, or explosion, involving one or more highly hazardous chemicals, that presents serious danger to employees in the workplace.

Facility means the buildings, containers or equipment which contain a process.

Highly hazardous chemical means a substance possessing toxic, reactive, flammable, or explosive properties and specified by paragraph (a)(1) of this section.

Hot work means work involving electric or gas welding, cutting, brazing, or similar flame or spark-producing operations.

Normally unoccupied remote facility means a facility which is operated, maintained or serviced by employees who visit the facility only periodically to check its operation and to perform necessary operating or maintenance tasks. No employees are permanently stationed at the facility. Facilities meeting this definition are not contiguous with, and must be geographically remote from all other buildings, processes or persons.

Process means any activity involving a highly hazardous chemical including any use, storage, manufacturing, handling, or the on-site movement of such chemicals, or combination of these activities. For purposes of this definition, any group of vessels which are interconnected and separate vessels which are located such that a highly hazardous chemical could be involved in a potential release shall be considered a single process.

Replacement in kind means a replacement which satisfies the design specification.

Trade secret means any confidential formula, pattern, process, device, information or compilation of information that is used in an employer's business, and that gives the employer an opportunity to obtain an advantage over competitors who do not know or use it. Appendix D contained in § 1926.59 sets out the criteria to be used in evaluating trade secrets.

(c) *Employee participation.* (1) Employers shall develop a written plan of action regarding the implementation of the employee participation required by this paragraph.

(2) Employers shall consult with employees and their representatives on the conduct and development of process hazards analyses and on the development of the other elements of process safety management in this standard.

(3) Employers shall provide to employees and their representatives access to process hazard analyses and to all other information required to be developed under this standard.

(d) *Process safety information.* In accordance with the schedule set forth in paragraph (e)(1) of this section, the employer shall complete a compilation of written process safety information before conducting any process hazard analysis required by the standard. The compilation of written process safety information is to enable the employer and the employees involved in operating the process to identify and understand the hazards posed by those processes involving highly hazardous

chemicals. This process safety information shall include information pertaining to the hazards of the highly hazardous chemicals used or produced by the process, information pertaining to the technology of the process, and information pertaining to the equipment in the process.

(1) *Information pertaining to the hazards of the highly hazardous chemicals in the process.* This information shall consist of at least the following:

(i) Toxicity information;

(ii) Permissible exposure limits;

(iii) Physical data;

(iv) Reactivity data:

(v) Corrosivity data;

(vi) Thermal and chemical stability data; and

(vii) Hazardous effects of inadvertent mixing of different materials that could foreseeably occur.

NOTE TO PARAGRAPH (d)(1): Safety data sheets meeting the requirements of § 1910.1200(g) may be used to comply with this requirement to the extent they contain the information required by this paragraph (d)(1).

(2) *Information pertaining to the technology of the process.* (i) Information concerning the technology of the process shall include at least the following:

(A) A block flow diagram or simplified process flow diagram (see appendix B to this section);

(B) Process chemistry;

(C) Maximum intended inventory;

(D) Safe upper and lower limits for such items as temperatures, pressures, flows or compositions; and,

(E) An evaluation of the consequences of deviations, including those affecting the safety and health of employees.

(ii) Where the original technical information no longer exists, such information may be developed in conjunction with the process hazard analysis in sufficient detail to support the analysis.

(3) *Information pertaining to the equipment in the process.* (i) Information pertaining to the equipment in the process shall include:

(A) Materials of construction;

(B) Piping and instrument diagrams (P&ID's);

(C) Electrical classification;

(D) Relief system design and design basis;

(E) Ventilation system design;

(F) Design codes and standards employed;

(G) Material and energy balances for processes built after May 26, 1992; and,

(H) Safety systems (e.g. interlocks, detection or suppression systems).

(ii) The employer shall document that equipment complies with recognized and generally accepted good engineering practices.

(iii) For existing equipment designed and constructed in accordance with codes, standards, or practices that are no longer in general use, the employer shall determine and document that the equipment is designed, maintained, inspected, tested, and operating in a safe manner.

(e) *Process hazard analysis.* (1) The employer shall perform an initial process hazard analysis (hazard evaluation) on processes covered by this standard. The process hazard analysis shall be appropriate to the complexity of the process and shall identify, evaluate, and control the hazards involved in the process. Employers shall determine and document the priority order for conducting process hazard analyses based on a rationale which includes such considerations as extent of the process hazards, number of potentially affected employees, age of the process, and operating history of the process. The process hazard analysis shall be conducted as soon as possible, but not later than the following schedule:

(i) No less than 25 percent of the initial process hazards analyses shall be completed by May 26, 1994;

(ii) No less than 50 percent of the initial process hazards analyses shall be completed by May 26, 1995;

(iii) No less than 75 percent of the initial process hazards analyses shall be completed by May 26, 1996;

(iv) All initial process hazards analyses shall be completed by May 26, 1997.

(v) Process hazards analyses completed after May 26, 1987 which meet the requirements of this paragraph are acceptable as initial process hazards analyses. These process hazard analyses shall be updated and revalidated, based on their completion date, in accordance with paragraph (e)(6) of this standard.

(2) The employer shall use one or more of the following methodologies that are appropriate to determine and evaluate the hazards of the process being analyzed.

(i) What-If;

(ii) Checklist;

(iii) What-If/Checklist;

(iv) Hazard and Operability Study (HAZOP);

(v) Failure Mode and Effects Analysis (FMEA);

(vi) Fault-Tree Analysis; or

(vii) An appropriate equivalent methodology.

(3) The process hazard analysis shall address:

(i) The hazards of the process;

(ii) The identification of any previous incident which had a likely potential for catastrophic consequences in the workplace;

(iii) Engineering and administrative controls applicable to the hazards and their interrelationships such as appropriate application of detection methodologies to provide early warning of releases. (Acceptable detection methods might include process monitoring and control instrumentation with alarms, and detection hardware such as hydrocarbon sensors.);

(iv) Consequences of failure of engineering and administrative controls;

(v) Facility siting;

(vi) Human factors; and

(vii) A qualitative evaluation of a range of the possible safety and health effects of failure of controls on employees in the workplace.

(4) The process hazard analysis shall be performed by a team with expertise in engineering and process operations, and the team shall include at least one employee who has experience and knowledge specific to the process being evaluated. Also, one member of the team must be knowledgeable in the specific process hazard analysis methodology being used.

(5) The employer shall establish a system to promptly address the team's findings and recommendations; assure that the recommendations are resolved in a timely manner and that the resolution is documented; document what

121

actions are to be taken; complete actions as soon as possible; develop a written schedule of when these actions are to be completed; communicate the actions to operating, maintenance and other employees whose work assignments are in the process and who may be affected by the recommendations or actions.

(6) At least every five (5) years after the completion of the initial process hazard analysis, the process hazard analysis shall be updated and revalidated by a team meeting the requirements in paragraph (e)(4) of this section, to assure that the process hazard analysis is consistent with the current process.

(7) Employers shall retain process hazards analyses and updates or revalidations for each process covered by this section, as well as the documented resolution of recommendations described in paragraph (e)(5) of this section for the life of the process.

(f) *Operating procedures.* (1) The employer shall develop and implement written operating procedures that provide clear instructions for safely conducting activities involved in each covered process consistent with the process safety information and shall address at least the following elements.

(i) Steps for each operating phase:

(A) Initial startup;

(B) Normal operations;

(C) Temporary operations;

(D) Emergency shutdown including the conditions under which emergency shutdown is required, and the assignment of shutdown responsibility to qualified operators to ensure that emergency shutdown is executed in a safe and timely manner.

(E) Emergency operations;

(F) Normal shutdown; and,

(G) Startup following a turnaround, or after an emergency shutdown.

(ii) Operating limits:

(A) Consequences of deviation; and

(B) Steps required to correct or avoid deviation.

(iii) Safety and health considerations:

(A) Properties of, and hazards presented by, the chemicals used in the process;

(B) Precautions necessary to prevent exposure, including engineering controls, administrative controls, and personal protective equipment;

(C) Control measures to be taken if physical contact or airborne exposure occurs;

(D) Quality control for raw materials and control of hazardous chemical inventory levels; and,

(E) Any special or unique hazards.

(iv) Safety systems and their functions.

(2) Operating procedures shall be readily accessible to employees who work in or maintain a process.

(3) The operating procedures shall be reviewed as often as necessary to assure that they reflect current operating practice, including changes that result from changes in process chemicals, technology, and equipment, and changes to facilities. The employer shall certify annually that these operating procedures are current and accurate.

(4) The employer shall develop and implement safe work practices to provide for the control of hazards during operations such as lockout/tagout; confined space entry; opening process equipment or piping; and control over entrance into a facility by maintenance, contractor, laboratory, or other support personnel. These safe work practices shall apply to employees and contractor employees.

(g) *Training—(1) Initial training.* (i) Each employee presently involved in operating a process, and each employee before being involved in operating a newly assigned process, shall be trained in an overview of the process and in the operating procedures as specified in paragraph (f) of this section. The training shall include emphasis on the specific safety and health hazards, emergency operations including shutdown, and safe work practices applicable to the employee's job tasks.

(ii) In lieu of initial training for those employees already involved in operating a process on May 26, 1992, an employer may certify in writing that the employee has the required knowledge, skills, and abilities to safely carry out the duties and responsibilities as specified in the operating procedures.

(2) *Refresher training.* Refresher training shall be provided at least every

three years, and more often if necessary, to each employee involved in operating a process to assure that the employee understands and adheres to the current operating procedures of the process. The employer, in consultation with the employees involved in operating the process, shall determine the appropriate frequency of refresher training.

(3) *Training documentation.* The employer shall ascertain that each employee involved in operating a process has received and understood the training required by this paragraph. The employer shall prepare a record which contains the identity of the employee, the date of training, and the means used to verify that the employee understood the training.

(h) *Contractors*—(1) *Application.* This paragraph applies to contractors performing maintenance or repair, turnaround, major renovation, or specialty work on or adjacent to a covered process. It does not apply to contractors providing incidental services which do not influence process safety, such as janitorial work, food and drink services, laundry, delivery or other supply services.

(2) *Employer responsibilities.* (i) The employer, when selecting a contractor, shall obtain and evaluate information regarding the contract employer's safety performance and programs.

(ii) The employer shall inform contract employers of the known potential fire, explosion, or toxic release hazards related to the contractor's work and the process.

(iii) The employer shall explain to contract employers the applicable provisions of the emergency action plan required by paragraph (n) of this section.

(iv) The employer shall develop and implement safe work practices consistent with paragraph (f)(4) of this section, to control the entrance, presence and exit of contract employers and contract employees in covered process areas.

(v) The employer shall periodically evaluate the performance of contract employers in fulfilling their obligations as specified in paragraph (h)(3) of this section.

(vi) The employer shall maintain a contract employee injury and illness log related to the contractor's work in process areas.

(3) *Contract employer responsibilities.* (i) The contract employer shall assure that each contract employee is trained in the work practices necessary to safely perform his/her job.

(ii) The contract employer shall assure that each contract employee is instructed in the known potential fire, explosion, or toxic release hazards related to his/her job and the process, and the applicable provisions of the emergency action plan.

(iii) The contract employer shall document that each contract employee has received and understood the training required by this paragraph. The contract employer shall prepare a record which contains the identity of the contract employee, the date of training, and the means used to verify that the employee understood the training.

(iv) The contract employer shall assure that each contract employee follows the safety rules of the facility including the safe work practices required by paragraph (f)(4) of this section.

(v) The contract employer shall advise the employer of any unique hazards presented by the contract employer's work, or of any hazards found by the contract employer's work.

(i) *Pre-startup safety review.* (1) The employer shall perform a pre-startup safety review for new facilities and for modified facilities when the modification is significant enough to require a change in the process safety information.

(2) The pre-startup safety review shall confirm that prior to the introduction of highly hazardous chemicals to a process:

(i) Construction and equipment is in accordance with design specifications;

(ii) Safety, operating, maintenance, and emergency procedures are in place and are adequate;

(iii) For new facilities, a process hazard analysis has been performed and recommendations have been resolved or implemented before startup; and modified facilities meet the requirements contained in management of change, paragraph (l).

(iv) Training of each employee involved in operating a process has been completed.

(j) *Mechanical integrity*—(1) *Application.* Paragraphs (j)(2) through (j)(6) of this section apply to the following process equipment:

(i) Pressure vessels and storage tanks;

(ii) Piping systems (including piping components such as valves);

(iii) Relief and vent systems and devices;

(iv) Emergency shutdown systems;

(v) Controls (including monitoring devices and sensors, alarms, and interlocks) and,

(vi) Pumps.

(2) *Written procedures.* The employer shall establish and implement written procedures to maintain the on-going integrity of process equipment.

(3) *Training for process maintenance activities.* The employer shall train each employee involved in maintaining the on-going integrity of process equipment in an overview of that process and its hazards and in the procedures applicable to the employee's job tasks to assure that the employee can perform the job tasks in a safe manner.

(4) *Inspection and testing.* (i) Inspections and tests shall be performed on process equipment.

(ii) Inspection and testing procedures shall follow recognized and generally accepted good engineering practices.

(iii) The frequency of inspections and tests of process equipment shall be consistent with applicable manufacturers' recommendations and good engineering practices, and more frequently if determined to be necessary by prior operating experience.

(iv) The employer shall document each inspection and test that has been performed on process equipment. The documentation shall identify the date of the inspection or test, the name of the person who performed the inspection or test, the serial number or other identifier of the equipment on which the inspection or test was performed, a description of the inspection or test performed, and the results of the inspection or test.

(5) *Equipment deficiencies.* The employer shall correct deficiencies in equipment that are outside acceptable limits (defined by the process safety information in paragraph (d) of this section) before further use or in a safe and timely manner when necessary means are taken to assure safe operation.

(6) *Quality assurance.* (i) In the construction of new plants and equipment, the employer shall assure that equipment as it is fabricated is suitable for the process application for which they will be used.

(ii) Appropriate checks and inspections shall be performed to assure that equipment is installed properly and consistent with design specifications and the manufacturer's instructions.

(iii) The employer shall assure that maintenance materials, spare parts and equipment are suitable for the process application for which they will be used.

(k) *Hot work permit.* (1) The employer shall issue a hot work permit for hot work operations conducted on or near a covered process.

(2) The permit shall document that the fire prevention and protection requirements in 29 CFR 1926.352 have been implemented prior to beginning the hot work operations; it shall indicate the date(s) authorized for hot work; and identify the object on which hot work is to be performed. The permit shall be kept on file until completion of the hot work operations.

(l) *Management of change.* (1) The employer shall establish and implement written procedures to manage changes (except for "replacements in kind") to process chemicals, technology, equipment, and procedures; and, changes to facilities that affect a covered process.

(2) The procedures shall assure that the following considerations are addressed prior to any change:

(i) The technical basis for the proposed change;

(ii) Impact of change on safety and health;

(iii) Modifications to operating procedures;

(iv) Necessary time period for the change; and,

(v) Authorization requirements for the proposed change.

(3) Employees involved in operating a process and maintenance and contract

employees whose job tasks will be affected by a change in the process shall be informed of, and trained in, the change prior to start-up of the process or affected part of the process.

(4) If a change covered by this paragraph results in a change in the process safety information required by paragraph (d) of this section, such information shall be updated accordingly.

(5) If a change covered by this paragraph results in a change in the operating procedures or practices required by paragraph (f) of this section, such procedures or practices shall be updated accordingly.

(m) *Incident investigation.* (1) The employer shall investigate each incident which resulted in, or could reasonably have resulted in a catastrophic release of highly hazardous chemical in the workplace.

(2) An incident investigation shall be initiated as promptly as possible, but not later than 48 hours following the incident.

(3) An incident investigation team shall be established and consist of at least one person knowledgeable in the process involved, including a contract employee if the incident involved work of the contractor, and other persons with appropriate knowledge and experience to thoroughly investigate and analyze the incident.

(4) A report shall be prepared at the conclusion of the investigation which includes at a minimum:

(i) Date of incident;

(ii) Date investigation began;

(iii) A description of the incident;

(iv) The factors that contributed to the incident; and,

(v) Any recommendations resulting from the investigation.

(5) The employer shall establish a system to promptly address and resolve the incident report findings and recommendations. Resolutions and corrective actions shall be documented.

(6) The report shall be reviewed with all affected personnel whose job tasks are relevant to the incident findings including contract employees where applicable.

(7) Incident investigation reports shall be retained for five years.

(n) Emergency planning and response. The employer shall establish and implement an emergency action plan for the entire plant in accordance with the provisions of 29 CFR 1926.35(a). In addition, the emergency action plan shall include procedures for handling small releases. Employers covered under this standard may also be subject to the hazardous waste and emergency response provisions contained in 29 CFR 1926.65(a), (p) and (q).

(o) *Compliance audits.* (1) Employers shall certify that they have evaluated compliance with the provisions of this section at least every three years to verify that the procedures and practices developed under the standard are adequate and are being followed.

(2) The compliance audit shall be conducted by at least one person knowledgeable in the process.

(3) A report of the findings of the audit shall be developed.

(4) The employer shall promptly determine and document an appropriate response to each of the findings of the compliance audit, and document that deficiencies have been corrected.

(5) Employers shall retain the two (2) most recent compliance audit reports.

(p) *Trade secrets.* (1) Employers shall make all information necessary to comply with the section available to those persons responsible for compiling the process safety information (required by paragraph (d) of this section), those assisting in the development of the process hazard analysis (required by paragraph (e) of this section), those responsible for developing the operating procedures (required by paragraph (f) of this section), and those involved in incident investigations (required by paragraph (m) of this section), emergency planning and response (paragraph (n) of this section) and compliance audits (paragraph (o) of this section) without regard to possible trade secret status of such information.

(2) Nothing in this paragraph shall preclude the employer from requiring the persons to whom the information is made available under paragraph (p)(1) of this section to enter into confidentiality agreements not to disclose the information as set forth in 29 CFR 1926.59.

(3) Subject to the rules and procedures set forth in 29 CFR 1926.59(i) (1)

through (12), employees and their designated representatives shall have access to trade secret information contained within the process hazard analysis and other documents required to be developed by this standard.

APPENDIX A TO § 1926.64—LIST OF HIGHLY HAZARDOUS CHEMICALS, TOXICS AND REACTIVES (MANDATORY)

This appendix contains a listing of toxic and reactive highly hazardous chemicals which present a potential for a catastrophic event at or above the threshold quantity.

Chemical Name	CAS*	TQ**
Acetaldehyde	75-07-0	2500
Acrolein (2-Propenal)	107-02-8	150
Acrylyl Chloride	814-68-6	250
Allyl Chloride	107-05-1	1000
Allylamine	107-11-9	1000
Alkylaluminums	Varies	5000
Ammonia, Anhydrous	7664-41-7	10000
Ammonia solutions (greater than 44% ammonia by weight)	7664-41-7	15000
Ammonium Perchlorate	7790-98-9	500
Ammonium Permanganate	7787-36-2	7500
Arsine (also called Arsenic Hydride)	7784-42-1	100
Bis(Chloromethyl) Ether	542-88-1	100
Boron Trichloride	10294-34-5	2500
Boron Trifluoride	7637-07-2	250
Bromine	7726-95-6	1500
Bromine Chloride	13863-41-7	1500
Bromine Pentafluoride	7789-30-2	2500
Bromine Trifluoride	7787-71-5	15000
3-Bromopropyne (also called Propargyl Bromide)	106-96-7	100
Butyl Hydroperoxide (Tertiary)	75-91-2	5000
Butyl Perbenzoate (Tertiary)	614-45-9	7500
Carbonyl Chloride (see Phosgene)	75-44-5	100
* Carbonyl Fluoride	353-50-4	2500
Cellulose Nitrate (concentration greater than 12.6% nitrogen)	9004-70-0	2500
Chlorine	7782-50-5	1500
Chlorine Dioxide	10049-04-4	1000
Chlorine Pentafluoride	13637-63-3	1000
Chlorine Trifluoride	7790-91-2	1000
Chlorodiethylaluminum (also called Diethylaluminum Chloride)	96-10-6	5000
1-Chloro-2,4-Dinitrobenzene	97-00-7	5000
Chloromethyl Methyl Ether	107-30-2	500
Chloropicrin	76-06-2	500
Chloropicrin and Methyl Bromide mixture	None	1500
Chloropicrin and Methyl Chloride mixture	None	1500
Cumene Hydroperoxide	80-15-9	5000
Cyanogen	460-19-5	2500
Cyanogen Chloride	506-77-4	500

Chemical Name	CAS*	TQ**
Cyanuric Fluoride	675-14-9	100
Diacetyl Peroxide (concentration greater than 70%)	110-22-5	5000
Diazomethane	334-88-3	500
Dibenzoyl Peroxide	94-36-0	7500
Diborane	19287-45-7	100
Dibutyl Peroxide (Tertiary)	110-05-4	5000
Dichloro Acetylene	7572-29-4	250
Dichlorosilane	4109-96-0	2500
Diethylzinc	557-20-0	10000
Diisopropyl Peroxydicarbonate	105-64-6	7500
Dilauroyl Peroxide	105-74-8	7500
Dimethyldichlorosilane	75-78-5	1000
Dimethylhydrazine, 1,1-	57-14-7	1000
Dimethylamine, Anhydrous	124-40-3	2500
2,4-Dinitroaniline	97-02-9	5000
Ethyl Methyl Ketone Peroxide (also Methyl Ethyl Ketone Peroxide; concentration greater than 60%)	1338-23-4	5000
Ethyl Nitrite	109-95-5	5000
Ethylamine	75-04-7	7500
Ethylene Fluorohydrin	371-62-0	100
Ethylene Oxide	75-21-8	5000
Ethyleneimine	151-56-4	1000
Fluorine	7782-41-4	1000
Formaldehyde (Formalin)	50-00-0	1000
Furan	110-00-9	500
Hexafluoroacetone	684-16-2	5000
Hydrochloric Acid, Anhydrous	7647-01-0	5000
Hydrofluoric Acid, Anhydrous	7664-39-3	1000
Hydrogen Bromide	10035-10-6	5000
Hydrogen Chloride	7647-01-0	5000
Hydrogen Cyanide, Anhydrous	74-90-8	1000
Hydrogen Fluoride	7664-39-3	1000
Hydrogen Peroxide (52% by weight or greater)	7722-84-1	7500
Hydrogen Selenide	7783-07-5	150
Hydrogen Sulfide	7783-06-4	1500
Hydroxylamine	7803-49-8	2500
Iron, Pentacarbonyl	13463-40-6	250
Isopropylamine	75-31-0	5000
Ketene	463-51-4	100
Methacrylaldehyde	78-85-3	1000
Methacryloyl Chloride	920-46-7	150
Methacryloyloxyethyl Isocyanate	30674-80-7	100
Methyl Acrylonitrile	126-98-7	250
Methylamine, Anhydrous	74-89-5	1000
Methyl Bromide	74-83-9	2500
Methyl Chloride	74-87-3	15000
Methyl Chloroformate	79-22-1	500
Methyl Ethyl Ketone Peroxide (concentration greater than 60%)	1338-23-4	5000
Methyl Fluoroacetate	453-18-9	100
Methyl Fluorosulfate	421-20-5	100
Methyl Hydrazine	60-34-4	100
Methyl Iodide	74-88-4	7500
Methyl Isocyanate	624-83-9	250
Methyl Mercaptan	74-93-1	5000
Methyl Vinyl Ketone	79-84-4	100

Chemical Name	CAS*	TQ**	Chemical Name	CAS*	TQ**
Methyltrichlorosilane	75-79-6	500	Phosphine (Hydrogen Phosphide)	7803-51-2	100
Nickel Carbonly (Nickel Tetracarbonyl)	13463-39-3	150	Phosphorus Oxychloride (also called Phosphoryl Chloride)	10025-87-3	1000
Nitric Acid (94.5% by weight or greater)	7697-37-2	500	Phosphorus Trichloride	7719-12-2	1000
Nitric Oxide	10102-43-9	250	Phosphoryl Chloride (also called Phosphorus Oxychloride)	10025-87-3	1000
Nitroaniline (para Nitroaniline	100-01-6	5000			
Nitromethane	75-52-5	2500	Propargyl Bromide	106-96-7	100
Nitrogen Dioxide	10102-44-0	250	Propyl Nitrate	627-3-4	2500
Nitrogen Oxides (NO; NO(2); N2O4; N2O3)	10102-44-0	250	Sarin	107-44-8	100
Nitrogen Tetroxide (also called Nitrogen Peroxide)	10544-72-6	250	Selenium Hexafluoride	7783-79-1	1000
			Stibine (Antimony Hydride)	7803-52-3	500
Nitrogen Trifluoride	7783-54-2	5000	Sulfur Dioxide (liquid)	7446-09-5	1000
Nitrogen Trioxide	10544-73-7	250	Sulfur Pentafluoride	5714-22-7	250
Oleum (65% to 80% by weight; also called Fuming Sulfuric Acid)	8014-94-7	1000	Sulfur Tetrafluoride	7783-60-0	250
			Sulfur Trioxide (also called Sulfuric Anhydride)	7446-11-9	1000
Osmium Tetroxide	20816-12-0	100	Sulfuric Anhydride (also called Sulfur Trioxide)	7446-11-9	1000
Oxygen Difluoride (Fluorine Monoxide)	7783-41-7	100	Tellurium Hexafluoride	7783-80-4	250
Ozone	10028-15-6	100	Tetrafluoroethylene	116-14-3	5000
Pentaborane	19624-22-7	100	Tetrafluorohydrazine	10036-47-2	5000
Peracetic Acid (concentration greater 60% Acetic Acid; also called Peroxyacetic Acid)	79-21-0	1000	Tetramethyl Lead	75-74-1	1000
			Thionyl Chloride	7719-09-7	250
			Trichloro (chloromethyl) Silane	1558-25-4	100
Perchloric Acid (concentration greater than 60% by weight)	7601-90-3	5000	Trichloro (dichlorophenyl) Silane	27137-85-5	2500
Perchloromethyl Mercaptan	594-42-3	150	Trichlorosilane	10025-78-2	5000
Perchloryl Fluoride	7616-94-6	5000	Trifluorochloroethylene	79-38-9	10000
Peroxyacetic Acid (concentration greater than 60% Acetic Acid; also called Peracetic Acid)	79-21-0	1000	Trimethyoxysilane	2487-90-3	1500
Phosgene (also called Carbonyl Chloride)	75-44-5	100			

*Chemical Abstract Service Number
**Threshold Quantity in Pounds (Amount necessary to be covered by this standard.)

APPENDIX B TO § 1926.64—BLOCK FLOW DIAGRAM AND SIMPLIFIED PROCESS
FLOW DIAGRAM (NONMANDATORY)

Example of a Block Flow Diagram

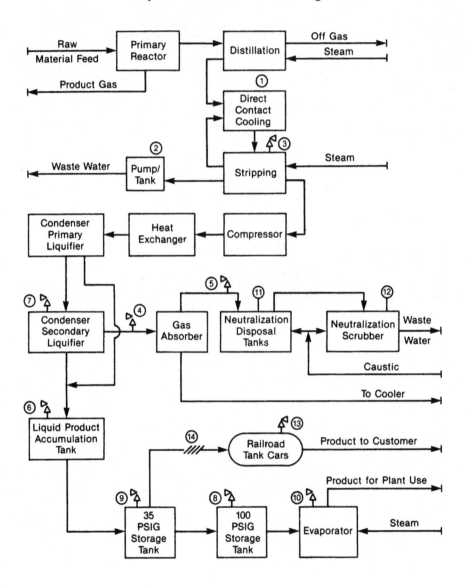

Example of a Process Flow Diagram

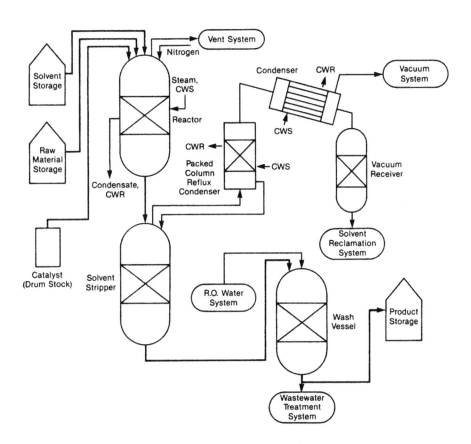

APPENDIX C TO §1926.64—COMPLIANCE GUIDE-
LINES AND RECOMMENDATIONS FOR PROCESS
SAFETY MANAGEMENT (NONMANDATORY)

This appendix serves as a nonmandatory guideline to assist employers and employees in complying with the requirements of this section, as well as provides other helpful recommendations and information. Examples presented in this appendix are not the only means of achieving the performance goals in the standard. This appendix neither adds nor detracts from the requirements of the standard.

1. *Introduction to Process Safety Management.* The major objective of process safety management of highly hazardous chemicals is to prevent unwanted releases of hazardous chemicals especially into locations which could expose employees and others to serious hazards. An effective process safety management program requires a systematic approach to evaluating the whole process. Using this approach the process design, process technology, operational and maintenance activities and procedures, nonroutine activities and procedures, emergency preparedness plans and procedures, training programs, and other elements which impact the process are all considered in the evaluation. The various lines of defense that have been incorporated into the design and operation of the process to prevent or mitigate the release of hazardous chemicals need to be evaluated and strengthened to assure their effectiveness at each level. Process safety management is the proactive identification, evaluation and mitigation or prevention of chemical releases that could occur as a result of failures in process, procedures or equipment.

The process safety management standard targets highly hazardous chemicals that have the potential to cause a catastrophic incident. This standard as a whole is to aid employers in their efforts to prevent or mitigate episodic chemical releases that could lead to a catastrophe in the workplace and possibly to the surrounding community. To control these types of hazards, employers need to develop the necessary expertise, experiences, judgement and proactive initiative within their workforce to properly implement and maintain an effective process safety management program as envisioned in the OSHA standard. This OSHA standard is required by the Clean Air Act Amendments as is the Environmental Protection Agency's Risk Management Plan. Employers, who merge the two sets of requirements into their process safety management program, will better assure full compliance with each as well as enhancing their relationship with the local community.

While OSHA believes process safety management will have a positive effect on the safety of employees in workplaces and also offers other potential benefits to employers (increased productivity), smaller businesses which may have limited resources available to them at this time, might consider alternative avenues of decreasing the risks associated with highly hazardous chemicals at their workplaces. One method which might be considered is the reduction in the inventory of the highly hazardous chemical. This reduction in inventory will result in a reduction of the risk or potential for a catastrophic incident. Also, employers including small employers may be able to establish more efficient inventory control by reducing the quantities of highly hazardous chemicals on site below the established threshold quantities. This reduction can be accomplished by ordering smaller shipments and maintaining the minimum inventory necessary for efficient and safe operation. When reduced inventory is not feasible, then the employer might consider dispersing inventory to several locations on site. Dispersing storage into locations where a release in one location will not cause a release in another location is a practical method to also reduce the risk or potential for catastrophic incidents.

2. *Employee Involvement in Process Safety Management.* Section 304 of the Clean Air Act Amendments states that employers are to consult with their employees and their representatives regarding the employers efforts in the development and implementation of the process safety management program elements and hazard assessments. Section 304 also requires employers to train and educate their employees and to inform affected employees of the findings from incident investigations required by the process safety management program. Many employers, under their safety and health programs, have already established means and methods to keep employees and their representatives informed about relevant safety and health issues and employers may be able to adapt these practices and procedures to meet their obligations under this standard. Employers who have not implemented an occupational safety and health program may wish to form a safety and health committee of employees and management representatives to help the employer meet the obligations specified by this standard. These committees can become a significant ally in helping the employer to implement and maintain an effective process safety management program for all employees.

3. *Process Safety Information.* Complete and accurate written information concerning process chemicals, process technology, and process equipment is essential to an effective process safety management program and to a process hazards analysis. The compiled information will be a necessary resource to a variety of users including the team that will perform the process hazards analysis as required under paragraph (e); those developing the training programs and the operating procedures; contractors whose employees will be working with the process; those conducting the pre-startup reviews; local emergency preparedness planners; and insurance and enforcement officials.

The information to be compiled about the chemicals, including process intermediates, needs to be comprehensive enough for an accurate assessment of the fire and explosion characteristics, reactivity hazards, the safety and health hazards to workers, and the corrosion and erosion effects on the process equipment and monitoring tools. Current safety data sheet (SDS) information can be used to help meet this requirement which must be supplemented with process chemistry information including runaway reaction and over pressure hazards if applicable.

Process technology information will be a part of the process safety information package and it is expected that it will include diagrams of the type shown in appendix B of this section as well as employer established criteria for maximum inventory levels for process chemicals; limits beyond which would be considered upset conditions; and a qualitative estimate of the consequences or results of deviation that could occur if operating beyond the established process limits. Employers are encouraged to use diagrams which will help users understand the process.

A block flow diagram is used to show the major process equipment and interconnecting process flow lines and show flow rates, stream composition, temperatures, and pressures when necessary for clarity. The block flow diagram is a simplified diagram.

130

Process flow diagrams are more complex and will show all main flow streams including valves to enhance the understanding of the process, as well as pressures and temperatures on all feed and product lines within all major vessels, in and out of headers and heat exchangers, and points of pressure and temperature control. Also, materials of construction information, pump capacities and pressure heads, compressor horsepower and vessel design pressures and temperatures are shown when necessary for clarity. In addition, major components of control loops are usually shown along with key utilities on process flow diagrams.

Piping and instrument diagrams (P&Ids) may be the more appropriate type of diagrams to show some of the above details and to display the information for the piping designer and engineering staff. The P&IDs are to be used to describe the relationships between equipment and instrumentation as well as other relevant information that will enhance clarity. Computer software programs which do P&Ids or other diagrams useful to the information package, may be used to help meet this requirement.

The information pertaining to process equipment design must be documented. In other words, what were the codes and standards relied on to establish good engineering practice. These codes and standards are published by such organizations as the American Society of Mechanical Engineers, American Petroleum Institute, American National Standards Institute, National Fire Protection Association, American Society for Testing and Materials, National Board of Boiler and Pressure Vessel Inspectors, National Association of Corrosion Engineers, American Society of Exchange Manufacturers Association, and model building code groups.

In addition, various engineering societies issue technical reports which impact process design. For example, the American Institute of Chemical Engineers has published technical reports on topics such as two phase flow for venting devices. This type of technically recognized report would constitute good engineering practice.

For existing equipment designed and constructed many years ago in accordance with the codes and standards available at that time and no longer in general use today, the employer must document which codes and standards were used and that the design and construction along with the testing, inspection and operation are still suitable for the intended use. Where the process technology requires a design which departs from the applicable codes and standards, the employer must document that the design and construction is suitable for the intended purpose.

4. *Process Hazard Analysis.* A process hazard analysis (PHA), sometimes called a process hazard evaluation, is one of the most important elements of the process safety management program. A PHA is an organized and systematic effort to identify and analyze the significance of potential hazards associated with the processing or handling of highly hazardous chemicals. A PHA provides information which will assist employers and employees in making decisions for improving safety and reducing the consequences of unwanted or unplanned releases of hazardous chemicals. A PHA is directed toward analyzing potential causes and consequences of fires, explosions, releases of toxic or flammable chemicals and major spills of hazardous chemicals. The PHA focuses on equipment, instrumentation, utilities, human actions (routine and nonroutine), and external factors that might impact the process. These considerations assist in determining the hazards and potential failure points or failure modes in a process.

The selection of a PHA methodology or technique will be influenced by many factors including the amount of existing knowledge about the process. Is it a process that has been operated for a long period of time with little or no innovation and extensive experience has been generated with its use? Or, is it a new process or one which has been changed frequently by the inclusion of innovative features? Also, the size and complexity of the process will influence the decision as to the appropriate PHA methodology to use. All PHA methodologies are subject to certain limitations. For example, the checklist methodology works well when the process is very stable and no changes are made, but it is not as effective when the process has undergone extensive change. The checklist may miss the most recent changes and consequently the changes would not be evaluated. Another limitation to be considered concerns the assumptions made by the team or analyst. The PHA is dependent on good judgement and the assumptions made during the study need to be documented and understood by the team and reviewer and kept for a future PHA.

The team conducting the PHA need to understand the methodology that is going to be used. A PHA team can vary in size from two people to a number of people with varied operational and technical backgrounds. Some team members may only be a part of the team for a limited time. The team leader needs to be fully knowledgeable in the proper implementation of the PHA methodology that is to be used and should be impartial in the evaluation. The other full or part time team members need to provide the team with expertise in areas such as process technology, process design, operating procedures and practices, including how the work is actually performed, alarms, emergency procedures, instrumentation, maintenance procedures, both routine and nonroutine tasks, including how the tasks are authorized, procurement of parts and supplies, safety and health, and any other relevant subject as the need dictates. At least one team member must be familiar with the process.

The ideal team will have an intimate knowledge of the standards, codes, specifications and regulations applicable to the process being studied. The selected team members need to be compatible and the team leader needs to be able to manage the team and the PHA study. The team needs to be able to work together while benefiting from the expertise of others on the team or outside the team, to resolve issues, and to forge a consensus on the findings of the study and the recommendations.

The application of a PHA to a process may involve the use of different methodologies for various parts of the process. For example, a process involving a series of unit operations of varying sizes, complexities, and ages may use different methodologies and team members for each operation. Then the conclusions can be integrated into one final study and evaluation. A more specific example is the use of a checklist PHA for a standard boiler or heat exchanger and the use of a Hazard and Operability PHA for the overall process. Also, for batch type processes like custom batch operations, a generic PHA of a representative batch may be used where there are only small changes of monomer or other ingredient ratios and the chemistry is documented for the full range and ratio of batch ingredients. Another process that might consider using a generic type of PHA is a gas plant. Often these plants are simply moved from site to site and therefore, a generic PHA may be used for these movable plants. Also, when an employer has several similar size gas plants and no sour gas is being processed at the site, then a generic PHA is feasible as long as the variations of the individual sites are accounted for in the PHA. Finally, when an employer has a large continuous process which has several control rooms for different portions of the process such as for a distillation tower and a blending operation, the employer may wish to do each segment separately and then integrate the final results.

Additionally, small businesses which are covered by this rule, will often have processes that have less storage volume, less capacity, and less complicated than processes at a large facility. Therefore, OSHA would anticipate that the less complex methodologies would be used to meet the process hazard analysis criteria in the standard. These process hazard analyses can be done in less time and with a few people being involved. A less complex process generally means that less data, P&IDs, and process information is needed to perform a process hazard analysis.

Many small businesses have processes that are not unique, such as cold storage lockers or water treatment facilities. Where employer associations have a number of members with such facilities, a generic PHA, evolved from a checklist or what-if questions, could be developed and used by each employer effectively to reflect his/her particular process; this would simplify compliance for them.

When the employer has a number of processes which require a PHA, the employer must set up a priority system of which PHAs to conduct first. A preliminary or gross hazard analysis may be useful in prioritizing the processes that the employer has determined are subject to coverage by the process safety management standard. Consideration should first be given to those processes with the potential of adversely affecting the largest number of employees. This prioritizing should consider the potential severity of a chemical release, the number of potentially affected employees, the operating history of the process such as the frequency of chemical releases, the age of the process and any other relevant factors. These factors would suggest a ranking order and would suggest either using a weighing factor system or a systematic ranking method. The use of a preliminary hazard analysis would assist an employer in determining which process should be of the highest priority and thereby the employer would obtain the greatest improvement in safety at the facility.

Detailed guidance on the content and application of process hazard analysis methodologies is available from the American Institute of Chemical Engineers' Center for Chemical Process Safety (see appendix D).

5. *Operating Procedures and Practices.* Operating procedures describe tasks to be performed, data to be recorded, operating conditions to be maintained, samples to be collected, and safety and health precautions to be taken. The procedures need to be technically accurate, understandable to employees, and revised periodically to ensure that they reflect current operations. The process safety information package is to be used as a resource to better assure that the operating procedures and practices are consistent with the known hazards of the chemicals in the process and that the operating parameters are accurate. Operating procedures should be reviewed by engineering staff and operating personnel to ensure that they are accurate and provide practical instructions on how to actually carry out job duties safely.

Operating procedures will include specific instructions or details on what steps are to be taken or followed in carrying out the stated procedures. These operating instructions for each procedure should include the applicable safety precautions and should contain appropriate information on safety implications. For example, the operating procedures addressing operating parameters will contain operating instructions about pressure limits, temperature ranges, flow rates, what to do when an upset condition occurs, what alarms and instruments are pertinent if an upset condition occurs, and other subjects. Another example of using operating instructions to properly implement operating procedures is in starting up or shutting down the process. In these cases, different parameters will be required from those of normal operation. These operating instructions need to clearly indicate the distinctions between startup and normal operations such as the appropriate allowances for heating up a unit to reach the normal operating parameters. Also the operating instructions need to describe the proper method for increasing the temperature of the unit until the normal operating temperature parameters are achieved.

Computerized process control systems add complexity to operating instructions. These operating instructions need to describe the logic of the software as well as the relationship between the equipment and the control system; otherwise, it may not be apparent to the operator.

Operating procedures and instructions are important for training operating personnel. The operating procedures are often viewed as the standard operating practices (SOPs) for operations. Control room personnel and operating staff, in general, need to have a full understanding of operating procedures. If workers are not fluent in English then procedures and instructions need to be prepared in a second language understood by the workers. In addition, operating procedures need to be changed when there is a change in the process as a result of the management of change procedures. The consequences of operating procedure changes need to be fully evaluated and the information conveyed to the personnel. For example, mechanical changes to the process made by the maintenance department (like changing a valve from steel to brass or other subtle changes) need to be evaluated to determine if operating procedures and practices also need to be changed. All management of change actions must be coordinated and integrated with current operating procedures and operating personnel must be oriented to the changes in procedures before the change is made. When the process is shutdown in order to make a change, then the operating procedures must be updated before startup of the process.

Training in how to handle upset conditions must be accomplished as well as what operating personnel are to do in emergencies such as when a pump seal fails or a pipeline ruptures. Communication between operating personnel and workers performing work within the process area, such as nonroutine tasks, also must be maintained. The hazards of the tasks are to be conveyed to operating personnel in accordance with established procedures and to those performing the actual tasks. When the work is completed, operating personnel should be informed to provide closure on the job.

6. *Employee Training.* All employees, including maintenance and contractor employees, involved with highly hazardous chemicals need to fully understand the safety and health hazards of the chemicals and processes they work with for the protection of themselves, their fellow employees and the citizens of nearby communities. Training conducted in compliance with 1926.59, the Hazard Communication standard, will help employees to be more knowledgeable about the chemicals they work with as well as familiarize them with reading and understanding SDS. However, additional training in subjects such as operating procedures and safety work practices, emergency evacuation and response, safety procedures, routine and nonroutine work authorization activities, and other areas pertinent to process safety and health will need to be covered by an employer's training program.

In establishing their training programs, employers must clearly define the employees to be trained and what subjects are to be covered in their training. Employers in setting up their training program will need to clearly establish the goals and objectives they wish to achieve with the training that they provide to their employees. The learning goals or objectives should be written in clear measurable terms before the training begins. These goals and objectives need to be tailored to each of the specific training modules or segments. Employers should describe the important actions and conditions under which the employee will demonstrate competence or knowledge as well as what is acceptable performance.

Hands-on-training where employees are able to use their senses beyond listening, will enhance learning. For example, operating personnel, who will work in a control room or at control panels, would benefit by being trained at a simulated control panel or panels. Upset conditions of various types could be displayed on the simulator, and then the employee could go through the proper operating procedures to bring the simulator panel back to the normal operating parameters. A training environment could be created to help the trainee feel the full reality of the situation but, of course, under controlled conditions. This realistic type of training can be very effective in teaching employees correct procedures while allowing them to also see the consequences of what might happens if they do not follow established operating procedures. Other training techniques using videos or on-the-job training can also be very effective for teaching other job tasks, duties, or other important information. An effective training program will allow the employee to fully participate in the training process and to practice their skill or knowledge.

Employers need to periodically evaluate their training programs to see if the necessary skills, knowledge, and routines are being properly understood and implemented by their trained employees. The means or methods for evaluating the training should be developed along with the training program goals and objectives. Training program evaluation will help employers to determine the amount of training their employees understood, and whether the desired results were obtained. If, after the evaluation, it appears that the trained employees are not at the level of knowledge and skill that was expected, the employer will need to revise the training program, provide retraining, or provide more frequent refresher training sessions until the deficiency is resolved. Those who conducted the training and those who received the training should also be consulted as to how best to improve the training process. If there is a language barrier, the language known to the trainees should be used to reinforce the training messages and information.

Careful consideration must be given to assure that employees including maintenance and contract employees receive current and updated training. For example, if changes are made to a process, impacted employees must be trained in the changes and understand the effects of the changes on their job tasks (e.g., any new operating procedures pertinent to their tasks). Additionally, as already discussed the evaluation of the employee's absorption of training will certainly influence the need for training.

7. *Contractors.* Employers who use contractors to perform work in and around processes that involve highly hazardous chemicals, will need to establish a screening process so that they hire and use contractors who accomplish the desired job tasks without compromising the safety and health of employees at a facility. For contractors, whose safety performance on the job is not known to the hiring employer, the employer will need to obtain information on injury and illness rates and experience and should obtain contractor references. Additionally, the employer must assure that the contractor has the appropriate job skills, knowledge and certifications (such as for pressure vessel welders). Contractor work methods and experiences should be evaluated. For example, does the contractor conducting demolition work swing loads over operating processes or does the contractor avoid such hazards?

Maintaining a site injury and illness log for contractors is another method employers must use to track and maintain current knowledge of work activities involving contract employees working on or adjacent to covered processes. Injury and illness logs of both the employer's employees and contract employees allow an employer to have full knowledge of process injury and illness experience. This log will also contain information which will be of use to those auditing process safety management compliance and those involved in incident investigations.

Contract employees must perform their work safely. Considering that contractors often perform very specialized and potentially hazardous tasks such as confined space entry activities and nonroutine repair activities it is quite important that their activities be controlled while they are working on or near a covered process. A permit system or work authorization system for these activities would also be helpful to all affected employers. The use of a work authorization system keeps an employer informed of contract employee activities, and as a benefit the employer will have better coordination and more management control over the work being performed in the process area. A well run and well maintained process where employee safety is fully recognized will benefit all of those who work in the facility whether they be contract employees or employees of the owner.

8. *Pre-Startup Safety.* For new processes, the employer will find a PHA helpful in improving the design and construction of the process from a reliability and quality point of view. The safe operation of the new process will be enhanced by making use of the PHA recommendations before final installations are completed. P&IDs are to be completed along with having the operating procedures in place and the operating staff trained to run the process before startup. The initial startup procedures and normal operating procedures need to be fully evaluated as part of the pre-startup review to assure a safe transfer into the normal operating mode for meeting the process parameters.

For existing processes that have been shutdown for turnaround, or modification, etc., the employer must assure that any changes other than "replacement in kind" made to the process during shutdown go through the management of change procedures. P&IDs will need to be updated as necessary, as well as operating procedures and instructions. If the changes made to the process during shutdown are significant and impact the training program, then operating personnel as well as employees engaged in routine and nonroutine work in the process area may need some refresher or additional training in light of the changes. Any incident investigation recommendations, compliance audits or PHA recommendations need to be reviewed as well to see what impacts they may have on the process before beginning the startup.

9. *Mechanical Integrity.* Employers will need to review their maintenance programs and schedules to see if there are areas where "breakdown" maintenance is used rather than an on-going mechanical integrity program. Equipment used to process, store, or handle highly hazardous chemicals needs to be designed, constructed, installed and maintained to minimize the risk of releases of such chemicals. This requires that a mechanical integrity program be in place to assure the continued integrity of process equipment. Elements of a mechanical integrity program include the identification and categorization of equipment and instrumentation, inspections and tests, testing and inspection frequencies, development of maintenance procedures, training of maintenance personnel, the establishment of criteria for acceptable test results, documentation of test and inspection results, and documentation of manufacturer recommendations as to meantime to failure for equipment and instrumentation.

The first line of defense an employer has available is to operate and maintain the process as designed, and to keep the chemicals contained. This line of defense is backed up by the next line of defense which is the controlled release of chemicals through venting to scrubbers or flares, or to surge or overflow tanks which are designed to receive such chemicals, etc. These lines of defense are the primary lines of defense or means to prevent unwanted releases. The secondary lines of defense would include fixed fire protection systems like sprinklers, water spray, or deluge systems, monitor guns, etc., dikes, designed drainage systems, and other systems which would control or mitigate hazardous chemicals once an unwanted release occurs. These primary and secondary lines of defense are what the mechanical integrity program needs to protect and strengthen these primary and secondary lines of defenses where appropriate.

The first step of an effective mechanical integrity program is to compile and categorize a list of process equipment and instrumentation for inclusion in the program. This list would include pressure vessels, storage tanks, process piping, relief and vent systems, fire protection system components, emergency shutdown systems and alarms and interlocks and pumps. For the categorization of instrumentation and the listed equipment the employer would prioritize which pieces of equipment require closer scrutiny than others. Meantime to failure of various instrumentation and equipment parts would be known from the manufacturers data or the employer's experience with the parts, which would then influence the inspection and testing frequency and associated procedures. Also, applicable codes and standards such as the National Board Inspection Code, or those from the American Society for Testing and Material, American Petroleum Institute, National Fire Protection Association, American National Standards Institute, American Society of Mechanical Engineers, and other groups, provide information to help establish an effective testing and inspection frequency, as well as appropriate methodologies.

The applicable codes and standards provide criteria for external inspections for such items as foundation and supports, anchor bolts, concrete or steel supports, guy wires, nozzles and sprinklers, pipe hangers, grounding connections, protective coatings and insulation, and external metal surfaces of piping and vessels, etc. These codes and standards also provide information on methodologies for internal inspection, and a frequency formula based on the corrosion rate of the materials of construction. Also, erosion both internal and external needs to be considered along with corrosion effects for piping and valves. Where the corrosion rate is not known, a maximum inspection frequency is recommended, and methods of developing the corrosion rate are available in the codes. Internal inspections need to cover items such as vessel shell, bottom and head; metallic linings; nonmetallic linings; thickness measurements for vessels and piping; inspection for erosion, corrosion, cracking and bulges; internal equipment like trays, baffles, sensors and screens for erosion, corrosion or cracking and other deficiencies. Some of these inspections may be performed by state or local government inspectors under state and local statutes. However, each employer needs to develop procedures to ensure that tests and inspections are conducted properly and that consistency is maintained even where different employees may be involved. Appropriate training is to be provided to maintenance personnel to ensure that they understand the preventive maintenance program procedures, safe practices, and the proper use and application of special equipment or unique tools that may be required. This training is part of the overall training program called for in the standard.

A quality assurance system is needed to help ensure that the proper materials of construction are used, that fabrication and inspection procedures are proper, and that installation procedures recognize field installation concerns. The quality assurance program is an essential part of the mechanical integrity program and will help to maintain the primary and secondary lines of defense that have been designed into the process to prevent unwanted chemical releases or those which control or mitigate a release. "As built" drawings, together with certifications of coded vessels and other equipment, and materials of construction need to be verified and retained in the quality assurance documentation. Equipment installation jobs need to be properly inspected in the field for use of proper materials and procedures and to assure that qualified craftsmen are used to do the job. The use of appropriate gaskets, packing, bolts, valves, lubricants and welding rods need to be verified in the field. Also, procedures for installation of safety devices need to be verified, such as the torque on the bolts on ruptured disc installations, uniform torque on flange bolts, proper installation of pump seals, etc. If the quality of parts is a problem, it may be appropriate to conduct audits of the equipment supplier's facilities to better assure proper purchases of required equipment which is suitable for its intended service. Any changes in equipment that may become necessary will need to go through the management of change procedures.

10. *Nonroutine Work Authorizations.* Nonroutine work which is conducted in process areas needs to be controlled by the employer in a consistent manner. The hazards identified involving the work that is to be accomplished must be communicated to those doing the work, but also to those operating personnel whose work could affect the safety of the process. A work authorization notice or permit must have a procedure that describes the steps the maintenance supervisor, contractor representative or other person needs to follow to obtain the necessary clearance to get the job started. The work authorization procedures need to reference and coordinate, as applicable, lockout/tagout procedures, line breaking procedures, confined space entry procedures and hot work authorizations. This procedure also needs to provide clear steps to follow once the job is completed in order to provide closure for those that need to know the job is now completed and equipment can be returned to normal.

11. *Managing Change.* To properly manage changes to process chemicals, technology, equipment and facilities, one must define what is meant by change. In this process safety management standard, change includes all modifications to equipment, procedures, raw materials and processing conditions other than "replacement in kind." These changes need to be properly managed by identifying and reviewing them prior to implementation of the change. For example, the operating procedures contain the operating parameters (pressure limits, temperature ranges, flow rates, etc.) and the importance of operating within these limits. While the operator must have the flexibility to maintain safe operation within the established parameters, any operation outside of these parameters requires review and approval by a written management of change procedure.

Management of change covers such as changes in process technology and changes to equipment and instrumentation. Changes in process technology can result from changes in production rates, raw materials, experimentation, equipment unavailability, new equipment, new product development, change in catalyst and changes in operating conditions to improve yield or quality. Equipment changes include among others change in materials of construction, equipment specifications, piping pre-arrangements, experimental equipment, computer program revisions and changes in alarms and interlocks. Employers need to establish means and methods to detect both technical changes and mechanical changes.

Temporary changes have caused a number of catastrophes over the years, and employers need to establish ways to detect temporary changes as well as those that are permanent. It is important that a time limit for temporary changes be established and monitored since, without control, these changes may tend to become permanent. Temporary changes are subject to the management of change provisions. In addition, the management of change procedures are used to insure that the equipment and procedures are returned to their original or designed conditions at the end of the temporary change. Proper documentation and review of these changes is invaluable in assuring that the safety and health considerations are being incorporated into the operating procedures and the process.

Employers may wish to develop a form or clearance sheet to facilitate the processing of changes through the management of change procedures. A typical change form may include a description and the purpose of the change, the technical basis for the change, safety and health considerations, documentation of changes for the operating procedures, maintenance procedures, inspection and testing, P&IDs, electrical classification, training and communications, pre-startup inspection, duration if a temporary change, approvals and authorization. Where the impact of the change is minor and well understood, a check list reviewed by an authorized person with proper communication to others who are affected may be sufficient. However, for a more complex or significant design change, a hazard evaluation procedure with approvals by operations, maintenance, and safety departments may be appropriate. Changes in documents such as P&IDs, raw materials, operating procedures, mechanical integrity programs, electrical classifications, etc., need to be noted so that these revisions can be made permanent when the drawings and procedure manuals are updated. Copies of process changes need to be kept in an accessible location to ensure that design changes are available to operating personnel as well as to PHA team members when a PHA is being done or one is being updated.

12. *Investigation of Incidents.* Incident investigation is the process of identifying the underlying causes of incidents and implementing steps to prevent similar events from occurring. The intent of an incident investigation is for employers to learn from past experiences and thus avoid repeating past mistakes. The incidents for which OSHA expects employers to become aware and to investigate are the types of events which result in or could reasonably have resulted in a catastrophic release. Some of the events are sometimes referred to as "near misses," meaning that a serious consequence did not occur, but could have.

Employers need to develop in-house capability to investigate incidents that occur in their facilities. A team needs to be assembled by the employer and trained in the techniques of investigation including how to conduct interviews of witnesses, needed documentation and report writing. A multi-disciplinary team is better able to gather the facts of the event and to analyze them and develop plausible scenarios as to what happened, and why. Team members should be selected on the basis of their training, knowledge and ability to contribute to a team effort to fully investigate the incident. Employees in the process area where the incident occurred should be consulted, interviewed or made a member of the team. Their knowledge of the events form a significant set of facts about the incident which occurred. The report, its findings and recommendations are to be shared with those who can benefit from the information. The cooperation of employees is essential to an effective incident investigation. The focus of the investigation should be to obtain facts, and not to place blame. The team and the investigation process should clearly deal with all involved individuals in a fair, open and consistent manner.

13. *Emergency Preparedness.* Each employer must address what actions employees are to take when there is an unwanted release of highly hazardous chemicals. Emergency preparedness or the employer's tertiary (third) lines of defense are those that will be relied on along with the secondary lines of defense when the primary lines of defense which are used to prevent an unwanted release fail to stop the release. Employers will need to decide if they want employees to handle and stop small or minor incidental releases. Whether they wish to mobilize the available resources at the plant and have them brought to bear on a more significant release. Or whether employers want their employees to evacuate the danger area and promptly escape to a preplanned safe zone area, and allow the local community emergency response organizations to handle the release. Or whether the employer wants to use some combination of these actions. Employers will need to select how many different emergency preparedness or tertiary lines of defense they plan to have and then develop the necessary plans and procedures, and appropriately train employees in their emergency duties and responsibilities and then implement these lines of defense.

Employers at a minimum must have an emergency action plan which will facilitate the prompt evacuation of employees when an unwanted release of highly hazardous chemical. This means that the employer will have a plan that will be activated by an alarm system to alert employees when to evacuate and, that employees who are physically impaired, will have the necessary support and assistance to get them to the safe zone as well. The intent of these requirements is to alert and move employees to a safe zone quickly. Delaying alarms or confusing alarms are to be avoided. The use of process control centers or similar process buildings in the process area as safe areas is discouraged. Recent catastrophes have shown that a large life loss has occurred in these structures because of where they have been sited and because they are not necessarily designed to withstand over-pressures from shockwaves resulting from explosions in the process area.

Unwanted incidental releases of highly hazardous chemicals in the process area must be addressed by the employer as to what actions employees are to take. If the employer wants employees to evacuate the area, then the emergency action plan will be activated. For outdoor processes where wind direction is important for selecting the safe route to a refuge area, the employer should place a wind direction indicator such as a wind sock or pennant at the highest point that can be seen throughout the process area. Employees can move in the direction of cross wind to upwind to gain safe access to the refuge area by knowing the wind direction.

If the employer wants specific employees in the release area to control or stop the minor emergency or incidental release, these actions must be planned for in advance and procedures developed and implemented. Preplanning for handling incidental releases for minor emergencies in the process area needs to be done, appropriate equipment for the hazards must be provided, and training conducted for those employees who will perform the emergency work before they respond to handle an actual release. The employer's training program, including the Hazard Communication standard training is to address the training needs for employees who are expected to handle incidental or minor releases.

Preplanning for releases that are more serious than incidental releases is another important line of defense to be used by the employer. When a serious release of a highly hazardous chemical occurs, the employer through preplanning will have determined in advance what actions employees are to take. The evacuation of the immediate release area and other areas as necessary would be accomplished under the emergency action plan. If the employer wishes to use plant personnel such as a fire brigade, spill control team, a hazardous materials team, or use employees to render aid to those in the immediate release area and control or mitigate the incident, these actions are covered by 1926.65, the Hazardous Waste Operations and Emergency Response (HAZWOPER) standard. If outside assistance is necessary, such as through mutual aid agreements between employers or local government emergency response organizations, these emergency responders are also covered by HAZWOPER. The safety and health protections required for emergency responders are the responsibility of their employers and of the on-scene incident commander.

Responders may be working under very hazardous conditions and therefore the objective is to have them competently led by an on-scene incident commander and the commander's staff, properly equipped to do their assigned work safely, and fully trained to carry out their duties safely before they respond to an emergency. Drills, training exercises, or simulations with the local community emergency response planners and responder organizations is one means to obtain better preparedness. This close cooperation and coordination between plant and local community emergency preparedness managers will also aid the employer in complying with the Environmental Protection Agency's Risk Management Plan criteria.

One effective way for medium to large facilities to enhance coordination and communication during emergencies for on plant operations and with local community organizations is for employers to establish and equip an emergency control center. The emergency control center would be sited in a safe zone area so that it could be occupied throughout the duration of an emergency. The center would serve as the major communication link between the on-scene incident commander and plant or corporate management as well as with the local community officials. The communication equipment in the emergency control center should include a network to receive and transmit information by telephone, radio or other means. It is important to have a backup communication network in case of power failure or one communication means fails. The center should also be equipped with the plant layout and community maps, utility drawings including fire water, emergency lighting, appropriate reference materials such as a government agency notification list, company personnel phone list, SARA Title III reports and safety data sheets, emergency plans and procedures manual, a listing with the location of emer-

gency response equipment, mutual aid information, and access to meteorological or weather condition data and any dispersion modeling data.

14. *Compliance Audits.* Employers need to select a trained individual or assemble a trained team of people to audit the process safety management system and program. A small process or plant may need only one knowledgeable person to conduct an audit. The audit is to include an evaluation of the design and effectiveness of the process safety management system and a field inspection of the safety and health conditions and practices to verify that the employer's systems are effectively implemented. The audit should be conducted or lead by a person knowledgeable in audit techniques and who is impartial towards the facility or area being audited. The essential elements of an audit program include planning, staffing, conducting the audit, evaluation and corrective action, follow-up and documentation.

Planning in advance is essential to the success of the auditing process. Each employer needs to establish the format, staffing, scheduling and verification methods prior to conducting the audit. The format should be designed to provide the lead auditor with a procedure or checklist which details the requirements of each section of the standard. The names of the audit team members should be listed as part of the format as well. The checklist, if properly designed, could serve as the verification sheet which provides the auditor with the necessary information to expedite the review and assure that no requirements of the standard are omitted. This verification sheet format could also identify those elements that will require evaluation or a response to correct deficiencies. This sheet could also be used for developing the follow-up and documentation requirements.

The selection of effective audit team members is critical to the success of the program. Team members should be chosen for their experience, knowledge, and training and should be familiar with the processes and with auditing techniques, practices and procedures. The size of the team will vary depending on the size and complexity of the process under consideration. For a large, complex, highly instrumented plant, it may be desirable to have team members with expertise in process engineering and design, process chemistry, instrumentation and computer controls, electrical hazards and classifications, safety and health disciplines, maintenance, emergency preparedness, warehousing or shipping, and process safety auditing. The team may use part-time members to provide for the depth of expertise required as well as for what is actually done or followed, compared to what is written.

An effective audit includes a review of the relevant documentation and process safety information, inspection of the physical facilities, and interviews with all levels of plant personnel. Utilizing the audit procedure and checklist developed in the preplanning stage, the audit team can systematically analyze compliance with the provisions of the standard and any other corporate policies that are relevant. For example, the audit team will review all aspects of the training program as part of the overall audit. The team will review the written training program for adequacy of content, frequency of training, effectiveness of training in terms of its goals and objectives as well as to how it fits into meeting the standard's requirements, documentation, etc. Through interviews, the team can determine the employee's knowledge and awareness of the safety procedures, duties, rules, emergency response assignments, etc. During the inspection, the team can observe actual practices such as safety and health policies, procedures, and work authorization practices. This approach enables the team to identify deficiencies and determine where corrective actions or improvements are necessary.

An audit is a technique used to gather sufficient facts and information, including statistical information, to verify compliance with standards. Auditors should select as part of their preplanning a sample size sufficient to give a degree of confidence that the audit reflects the level of compliance with the standard. The audit team, through this systematic analysis, should document areas which require corrective action as well as those areas where the process safety management system is effective and working in an effective manner. This provides a record of the audit procedures and findings, and serves as a baseline of operation data for future audits. It will assist future auditors in determining changes or trends from previous audits.

Corrective action is one of the most important parts of the audit. It includes not only addressing the identified deficiencies, but also planning, followup, and documentation. The corrective action process normally begins with a management review of the audit findings. The purpose of this review is to determine what actions are appropriate, and to establish priorities, timetables, resource allocations and requirements and responsibilities. In some cases, corrective action may involve a simple change in procedure or minor maintenance effort to remedy the concern. Management of change procedures need to be used, as appropriate, even for what may seem to be a minor change. Many of the deficiencies can be acted on promptly, while some may require engineering studies or indepth review of actual procedures and practices. There may be instances where no action is necessary and this is a valid response to an audit finding. All actions taken, in-

cluding an explanation where no action is taken on a finding, needs to be documented as to what was done and why.

It is important to assure that each deficiency identified is addressed, the corrective action to be taken noted, and the audit person or team responsible be properly documented by the employer. To control the corrective action process, the employer should consider the use of a tracking system. This tracking system might include periodic status reports shared with affected levels of management, specific reports such as completion of an engineering study, and a final implementation report to provide closure for audit findings that have been through management of change, if appropriate, and then shared with affected employees and management. This type of tracking system provides the employer with the status of the corrective action. It also provides the documentation required to verify that appropriate corrective actions were taken on deficiencies identified in the audit.

APPENDIX D TO §1926.64—SOURCES OF FURTHER INFORMATION (NONMANDATORY)

1. Center for Chemical Process Safety, American Institute of Chemical Engineers, 345 East 47th Street, New York, NY 10017, (212) 705-7319.

2. "Guidelines for Hazard Evaluation Procedures," American Institute of Chemical Engineers; 345 East 47th Street, New York, NY 10017.

3. "Guidelines for Technical Management of Chemical Process Safety," Center for Chemical Process Safety of the American Institute of Chemical Engineers; 345 East 47th Street, New York, NY 10017.

4. "Evaluating Process Safety in the Chemical Industry," Chemical Manufacturers Association; 2501 M Street NW, Washington, DC 20037.

5. "Safe Warehousing of Chemicals," Chemical Manufacturers Association; 2501 M Street NW, Washington, DC 20037.

6. "Management of Process Hazards," American Petroleum Institute (API Recommended Practice 750); 1220 L Street, N.W., Washington, DC 20005.

7. "Improving Owner and Contractor Safety Performance," American Petroleum Institute (API Recommended Practice 2220); API, 1220 L Street N.W., Washington, DC 20005.

8. Chemical Manufacturers Association (CMA's Manager Guide), First Edition, September 1991; CMA, 2501 M Street, N.W., Washington, DC 20037.

9. "Improving Construction Safety Performance," Report A-3, The Business Roundtable; The Business Roundtable, 200 Park Avenue, New York, NY 10166. (Report includes criteria to evaluate contractor safety performance and criteria to enhance contractor safety performance).

10. "Recommended Guidelines for Contractor Safety and Health," Texas Chemical Council; Texas Chemical Council, 1402 Nueces Street, Austin, TX 78701-1534.

11. "Loss Prevention in the Process Industries," Volumes I and II; Frank P. Lees, Butterworth; London 1983.

12. "Safety and Health Program Management Guidelines," 1989; U.S. Department of Labor, Occupational Safety and Health Administration.

13. "Safety and Health Guide for the Chemical Industry," 1986, (OSHA 3091); U.S. Department of Labor, Occupational Safety and Health Administration; 200 Constitution Avenue, N.W., Washington, DC 20210.

14. "Review of Emergency Systems," June 1988; U.S. Environmental Protection Agency (EPA), Office of Solid Waste and Emergency Response, Washington, DC 20460.

15. "Technical Guidance for Hazards Analysis, Emergency Planning for Extremely Hazardous Substances," December 1987; U.S. Environmental Protection Agency (EPA), Federal Emergency Management Administration (FEMA) and U.S. Department of Transportation (DOT), Washington, DC 20460.

16. "Accident Investigation...A New Approach," 1983, National Safety Council; 444 North Michigan Avenue, Chicago, IL 60611-3991.

17. "Fire & Explosion Index Hazard Classification Guide," 6th Edition, May 1987, Dow Chemical Company; Midland, Michigan 48674.

18. "Chemical Exposure Index," May 1988, Dow Chemical Company; Midland, Michigan 48674.

[58 FR 35115, June 30, 1993, as amended at 77 FR 17890, Mar. 26, 2012; 78 FR 9315, Feb. 8, 2013]

§ 1926.65 Hazardous waste operations and emergency response.

(a) *Scope, application, and definitions*— (1) *Scope.* This section covers the following operations, unless the employer can demonstrate that the operation does not involve employee exposure or the reasonable possibility for employee exposure to safety or health hazards:

(i) Clean-up operations required by a governmental body, whether Federal, state, local or other involving hazardous substances that are conducted at uncontrolled hazardous waste sites (including, but not limited to, the EPA's National Priority Site List (NPL), state priority site lists, sites recommended for the EPA NPL, and initial investigations of government identified sites which are conducted before the presence or absence of haz-

ardous substances has been ascertained);

(ii) Corrective actions involving clean-up operations at sites covered by the Resource Conservation and Recovery Act of 1976 (RCRA) as amended (42 U.S.C. 6901 *et seq.*);

(iii) Voluntary clean-up operations at sites recognized by Federal, state, local or other governmental bodies as uncontrolled hazardous waste sites;

(iv) Operations involving hazardous wastes that are conducted at treatment, storage, and disposal (TSD) facilities regulated by 40 CFR parts 264 and 265 pursuant to RCRA; or by agencies under agreement with U.S.E.P.A. to implement RCRA regulations; and

(v) Emergency response operations for releases of, or substantial threats of releases of, hazardous substances without regard to the location of the hazard.

(2) *Application.* (i) All requirements of part 1910 and part 1926 of title 29 of the Code of Federal Regulations apply pursuant to their terms to hazardous waste and emergency response operations whether covered by this section or not. If there is a conflict or overlap, the provision more protective of employee safety and health shall apply without regard to 29 CFR 1926.20(e)(1).

(ii) Hazardous substance clean-up operations within the scope of paragraphs (a)(1)(i) through (a)(1)(iii) of this section must comply with all paragraphs of this section except paragraphs (p) and (q).

(iii) Operations within the scope of paragraph (a)(1)(iv) of this section must comply only with the requirements of paragraph (p) of this section.

NOTES AND EXCEPTIONS: (A) All provisions of paragraph (p) of this section cover any treatment, storage or disposal (TSD) operation regulated by 40 CFR parts 264 and 265 or by state law authorized under RCRA, and required to have a permit or interim status from EPA pursuant to 40 CFR 270.1 or from a state agency pursuant to RCRA.

(B) Employers who are not required to have a permit or interim status because they are conditionally exempt small quantity generators under 40 CFR 261.5 or are generators who qualify under 40 CFR 262.34 for exemptions from regulation under 40 CFR parts 264, 265 and 270 ("excepted employers") are not covered by paragraphs (p)(1) through (p)(7) of this section. Excepted employers who are required by the EPA or state agency to have their employees engage in emergency response or who direct their employees to engage in emergency response are covered by paragraph (p)(8) of this section, and cannot be exempted by (p)(8)(i) of this section. Excepted employers who are not required to have employees engage in emergency response, who direct their employees to evacuate in the case of such emergencies and who meet the requirements of paragraph (p)(8)(i) of this section are exempt from the balance of paragraph (p)(8) of this section.

(C) If an area is used primarily for treatment, storage or disposal, any emergency response operations in that area shall comply with paragraph (p)(8) of this section. In other areas not used primarily for treatment, storage, or disposal, any emergency response operations shall comply with paragraph (q) of this section. Compliance with the requirements of paragraph (q) of this section shall be deemed to be in compliance with the requirements of paragraph (p)(8) of this section.

(iv) Emergency response operations for releases of, or substantial threats of releases of, hazardous substances which are not covered by paragraphs (a)(1)(i) through (a)(1)(iv) of this section must only comply with the requirements of paragraph (q) of this section.

(3) *Definitions—Buddy system* means a system of organizing employees into work groups in such a manner that each employee of the work group is designated to be observed by at least one other employee in the work group. The purpose of the buddy system is to provide rapid assistance to employees in the event of an emergency.

Clean-up operation means an operation where hazardous substances are removed, contained, incinerated, neutralized, stabilized, cleared-up, or in any other manner processed or handled with the ultimate goal of making the site safer for people or the environment.

Decontamination means the removal of hazardous substances from employees and their equipment to the extent necessary to preclude the occurrence of foreseeable adverse health affects.

Emergency response or *responding to emergencies* means a response effort by employees from outside the immediate release area or by other designated responders (i.e., mutual-aid groups, local fire departments, etc.) to an occurrence which results, or is likely to result, in an uncontrolled release of a hazardous substance. Responses to incidental releases of hazardous substances where the substance can be absorbed, neutralized, or otherwise controlled at the time of release by employees in the immediate release area, or by maintenance personnel are not considered to be emergency responses within the scope of this standard. Responses to releases of hazardous substances where there is no potential safety or health hazard (i.e., fire, explosion, or chemical exposure) are not considered to be emergency responses.

Facility means (A) any building, structure, installation, equipment, pipe or pipeline (including any pipe into a sewer or publicly owned treatment works), well, pit, pond, lagoon, impoundment, ditch, storage container, motor vehicle, rolling stock, or aircraft, or (B) any site or area where a hazardous substance has been deposited, stored, disposed of, or placed, or otherwise come to be located; but does not include any consumer product in consumer use or any water-borne vessel.

Hazardous materials response (HAZMAT) team means an organized group of employees, designated by the employer, who are expected to perform work to handle and control actual or potential leaks or spills of hazardous substances requiring possible close approach to the substance. The team members perform responses to releases or potential releases of hazardous substances for the purpose of control or stabilization of the incident. A HAZMAT team is not a fire brigade nor is a typical fire brigade a HAZMAT team. A HAZMAT team, however, may be a separate component of a fire brigade or fire department.

Hazardous substance means any substance designated or listed under paragraphs (A) through (D) of this definition, exposure to which results or may result in adverse affects on the health or safety of employees:

(A) Any substance defined under section 101(14) of CERCLA;

(B) Any biological agent and other disease-causing agent which after release into the environment and upon

141

exposure, ingestion, inhalation, or assimilation into any person, either directly from the environment or indirectly by ingestion through food chains, will or may reasonably be anticipated to cause death, disease, behavioral abnormalities, cancer, genetic mutation, physiological malfunctions (including malfunctions in reproduction) or physical deformations in such persons or their offspring;

(C) Any substance listed by the U.S. Department of Transportation as hazardous materials under 49 CFR 172.101 and appendices; and

(D) Hazardous waste as herein defined.

Hazardous waste means—(A) A waste or combination of wastes as defined in 40 CFR 261.3, or

(B) Those substances defined as hazardous wastes in 49 CFR 171.8.

Hazardous waste operation means any operation conducted within the scope of this standard.

Hazardous waste site or *Site* means any facility or location within the scope of this standard at which hazardous waste operations take place.

Health hazard means a chemical or a pathogen where acute or chronic health effects may occur in exposed employees. It also includes stress due to temperature extremes. The term *health hazard* includes chemicals that are classified in accordance with the Hazard Communication Standard, § 1910.1200, as posing one of the following hazardous effects: acute toxicity (any route of exposure); skin corrosion or irritation; serious eye damage or eye irritation; respiratory or skin sensitization; germ cell mutagenicity; carcinogenicity; reproductive toxicity; specific target organ toxicity (single or repeated exposure); aspiration toxicity or simple asphyxiant. (*See* Appendix A to § 1910.1200—Health Hazard Criteria (Mandatory) for the criteria for determining whether a chemical is classified as a health hazard.)

IDLH or *Immediately dangerous to life or health* means an atmospheric concentration of any toxic, corrosive or asphyxiant substance that poses an immediate threat to life or would cause irreversible or delayed adverse health effects or would interfere with an individual's ability to escape from a dangerous atmosphere.

Oxygen deficiency means that concentration of oxygen by volume below which atmosphere supplying respiratory protection must be provided. It exists in atmospheres where the percentage of oxygen by volume is less than 19.5 percent oxygen.

Permissible exposure limit means the exposure, inhalation or dermal permissible exposure limit specified either in § 1926.55, elsewhere in subpart D, or in other pertinent sections of this part.

Published exposure level means the exposure limits published in "NIOSH Recommendations for Occupational Health Standards" dated 1986 incorporated by reference, or if none is specified, the exposure limits published in the standards specified by the American Conference of Governmental Industrial Hygienists in their publication "Threshold Limit Values and Biological Exposure Indices for 1987-88" dated 1987 incorporated by reference.

Post emergency response means that portion of an emergency response performed after the immediate threat of a release has been stabilized or eliminated and clean-up of the site has begun. If post emergency response is performed by an employer's own employees who were part of the initial emergency response, it is considered to be part of the initial response and not post emergency response. However, if a group of an employer's own employees, separate from the group providing initial response, performs the clean-up operation, then the separate group of employees would be considered to be performing post-emergency response and subject to paragraph (q)(11) of this section.

Qualified person means a person with specific training, knowledge and experience in the area for which the person has the responsibility and the authority to control.

Site safety and health supervisor (or official) means the individual located on a hazardous waste site who is responsible to the employer and has the authority and knowledge necessary to implement the site safety and health plan and verify compliance with applicable safety and health requirements.

142

Small quantity generator means a generator of hazardous wastes who in any calendar month generates no more than 1,000 kilograms (2,205 pounds) of hazardous waste in that month.

Uncontrolled hazardous waste site, means an area identified as an uncontrolled hazardous waste site by a governmental body, whether Federal, state, local or other where an accumulation of hazardous substances creates a threat to the health and safety of individuals or the environment or both. Some sites are found on public lands such as those created by former municipal, county or state landfills where illegal or poorly managed waste disposal has taken place. Other sites are found on private property, often belonging to generators or former generators of hazardous substance wastes. Examples of such sites include, but are not limited to, surface impoundments, landfills, dumps, and tank or drum farms. Normal operations at TSD sites are not covered by this definition.

(b) *Safety and health program.*

NOTE TO (b): Safety and health programs developed and implemented to meet other Federal, state, or local regulations are considered acceptable in meeting this requirement if they cover or are modified to cover the topics required in this paragraph. An additional or separate safety and health program is not required by this paragraph.

(1) *General.* (i) Employers shall develop and implement a written safety and health program for their employees involved in hazardous waste operations. The program shall be designed to identify, evaluate, and control safety and health hazards, and provide for emergency response for hazardous waste operations.

(ii) The written safety and health program shall incorporate the following:

(A) An organizational structure;

(B) A comprehensive workplan;

(C) A site-specific safety and health plan which need not repeat the employer's standard operating procedures required in paragraph (b)(1)(ii)(F) of this section;

(D) The safety and health training program;

(E) The medical surveillance program;

(F) The employer's standard operating procedures for safety and health; and

(G) Any necessary interface between general program and site specific activities.

(iii) *Site excavation.* Site excavations created during initial site preparation or during hazardous waste operations shall be shored or sloped as appropriate to prevent accidental collapse in accordance with subpart P of 29 CFR part 1926.

(iv) *Contractors and sub-contractors.* An employer who retains contractor or sub-contractor services for work in hazardous waste operations shall inform those contractors, sub-contractors, or their representatives of the site emergency response procedures and any potential fire, explosion, health, safety or other hazards of the hazardous waste operation that have been identified by the employer, including those identified in the employer's information program.

(v) *Program availability.* The written safety and health program shall be made available to any contractor or subcontractor or their representative who will be involved with the hazardous waste operation; to employees; to employee designated representatives; to OSHA personnel, and to personnel of other Federal, state, or local agencies with regulatory authority over the site.

(2) *Organizational structure part of the site program*—(i) The organizational structure part of the program shall establish the specific chain of command and specify the overall responsibilities of supervisors and employees. It shall include, at a minimum, the following elements:

(A) A general supervisor who has the responsibility and authority to direct all hazardous waste operations.

(B) A site safety and health supervisor who has the responsibility and authority to develop and implement the site safety and health plan and verify compliance.

(C) All other personnel needed for hazardous waste site operations and emergency response and their general functions and responsibilities.

(D) The lines of authority, responsibility, and communication.

143

(ii) The organizational structure shall be reviewed and updated as necessary to reflect the current status of waste site operations.

(3) *Comprehensive workplan part of the site program.* The comprehensive workplan part of the program shall address the tasks and objectives of the site operations and the logistics and resources required to reach those tasks and objectives.

(i) The comprehensive workplan shall address anticipated clean-up activities as well as normal operating procedures which need not repeat the employer's procedures available elsewhere.

(ii) The comprehensive workplan shall define work tasks and objectives and identify the methods for accomplishing those tasks and objectives.

(iii) The comprehensive workplan shall establish personnel requirements for implementing the plan.

(iv) The comprehensive workplan shall provide for the implementation of the training required in paragraph (e) of this section.

(v) The comprehensive workplan shall provide for the implementation of the required informational programs required in paragraph (i) of this section.

(vi) The comprehensive workplan shall provide for the implementation of the medical surveillance program described in paragraph (f) of this section.

(4) *Site-specific safety and health plan part of the program*—(i) *General.* The site safety and health plan, which must be kept on site, shall address the safety and health hazards of each phase of site operation and include the requirements and procedures for employee protection.

(ii) *Elements.* The site safety and health plan, as a minimum, shall address the following:

(A) A safety and health risk or hazard analysis for each site task and operation found in the workplan.

(B) Employee training assignments to assure compliance with paragraph (e) of this section.

(C) Personal protective equipment to be used by employees for each of the site tasks and operations being conducted as required by the personal protective equipment program in paragraph (g)(5) of this section.

(D) Medical surveillance requirements in accordance with the program in paragraph (f) of this section.

(E) Frequency and types of air monitoring, personnel monitoring, and environmental sampling techniques and instrumentation to be used, including methods of maintenance and calibration of monitoring and sampling equipment to be used.

(F) Site control measures in accordance with the site control program required in paragraph (d) of this section.

(G) Decontamination procedures in accordance with paragraph (k) of this section.

(H) An emergency response plan meeting the requirements of paragraph (l) of this section for safe and effective responses to emergencies, including the necessary PPE and other equipment.

(I) Confined space entry procedures.

(J) A spill containment program meeting the requirements of paragraph (j) of this section.

(iii) *Pre-entry briefing.* The site specific safety and health plan shall provide for pre-entry briefings to be held prior to initiating any site activity, and at such other times as necessary to ensure that employees are apprised of the site safety and health plan and that this plan is being followed. The information and data obtained from site characterization and analysis work required in paragraph (c) of this section shall be used to prepare and update the site safety and health plan.

(iv) *Effectiveness of site safety and health plan.* Inspections shall be conducted by the site safety and health supervisor or, in the absence of that individual, another individual who is knowledgeable in occupational safety and health, acting on behalf of the employer as necessary to determine the effectiveness of the site safety and health plan. Any deficiencies in the effectiveness of the site safety and health plan shall be corrected by the employer.

(c) *Site characterization and analysis*— (1) *General.* Hazardous waste sites shall be evaluated in accordance with this paragraph to identify specific site hazards and to determine the appropriate safety and health control procedures needed to protect employees from the identified hazards.

(2) *Preliminary evaluation.* A preliminary evaluation of a site's characteristics shall be performed prior to site entry by a qualified person in order to aid in the selection of appropriate employee protection methods prior to site entry. Immediately after initial site entry, a more detailed evaluation of the site's specific characteristics shall be performed by a qualified person in order to further identify existing site hazards and to further aid in the selection of the appropriate engineering controls and personal protective equipment for the tasks to be performed.

(3) *Hazard identification.* All suspected conditions that may pose inhalation or skin absorption hazards that are immediately dangerous to life or health (IDLH), or other conditions that may cause death or serious harm, shall be identified during the preliminary survey and evaluated during the detailed survey. Examples of such hazards include, but are not limited to, confined space entry, potentially explosive or flammable situations, visible vapor clouds, or areas where biological indicators such as dead animals or vegetation are located.

(4) *Required information.* The following information to the extent available shall be obtained by the employer prior to allowing employees to enter a site:

(i) Location and approximate size of the site.

(ii) Description of the response activity and/or the job task to be performed.

(iii) Duration of the planned employee activity.

(iv) Site topography and accessibility by air and roads.

(v) Safety and health hazards expected at the site.

(vi) Pathways for hazardous substance dispersion.

(vii) Present status and capabilities of emergency response teams that would provide assistance to hazardous waste clean-up site employees at the time of an emergency.

(viii) Hazardous substances and health hazards involved or expected at the site, and their chemical and physical properties.

(5) *Personal protective equipment.* Personal protective equipment (PPE) shall be provided and used during initial site entry in accordance with the following requirements:

(i) Based upon the results of the preliminary site evaluation, an ensemble of PPE shall be selected and used during initial site entry which will provide protection to a level of exposure below permissible exposure limits and published exposure levels for known or suspected hazardous substances and health hazards, and which will provide protection against other known and suspected hazards identified during the preliminary site evaluation. If there is no permissible exposure limit or published exposure level, the employer may use other published studies and information as a guide to appropriate personal protective equipment.

(ii) If positive-pressure self-contained breathing apparatus is not used as part of the entry ensemble, and if respiratory protection is warranted by the potential hazards identified during the preliminary site evaluation, an escape self-contained breathing apparatus of at least five minute's duration shall be carried by employees during initial site entry.

(iii) If the preliminary site evaluation does not produce sufficient information to identify the hazards or suspected hazards of the site, an ensemble providing protection equivalent to Level B PPE shall be provided as minimum protection, and direct reading instruments shall be used as appropriate for identifying IDLH conditions. (See appendix B for a description of Level B hazards and the recommendations for Level B protective equipment.)

(iv) Once the hazards of the site have been identified, the appropriate PPE shall be selected and used in accordance with paragraph (g) of this section.

(6) *Monitoring.* The following monitoring shall be conducted during initial site entry when the site evaluation produces information that shows the potential for ionizing radiation or IDLH conditions, or when the site information is not sufficient reasonably to eliminate these possible conditions:

(i) Monitoring with direct reading instruments for hazardous levels of ionizing radiation.

(ii) Monitoring the air with appropriate direct reading test equipment (i.e., combustible gas meters, detector tubes) for IDLH and other conditions that may cause death or serious harm (combustible or explosive atmospheres, oxygen deficiency, toxic substances).

(iii) Visually observing for signs of actual or potential IDLH or other dangerous conditions.

(iv) An ongoing air monitoring program in accordance with paragraph (h) of this section shall be implemented after site characterization has determined the site is safe for the start-up of operations.

(7) *Risk identification.* Once the presence and concentrations of specific hazardous substances and health hazards have been established, the risks associated with these substances shall be identified. Employees who will be working on the site shall be informed of any risks that have been identified. In situations covered by the Hazard Communication Standard, 29 CFR 1926.59, training required by that standard need not be duplicated.

NOTE TO (c)(7). Risks to consider include, but are not limited to:

(a) Exposures exceeding the permissible exposure limits and published exposure levels.

(b) IDLH concentrations.

(c) Potential skin absorption and irritation sources.

(d) Potential eye irritation sources.

(e) Explosion sensitivity and flammability ranges.

(f) Oxygen deficiency.

(8) *Employee notification.* Any information concerning the chemical, physical, and toxicologic properties of each substance known or expected to be present on site that is available to the employer and relevant to the duties an employee is expected to perform shall be made available to the affected employees prior to the commencement of their work activities. The employer may utilize information developed for the hazard communication standard for this purpose.

(d) *Site control*—(1) *General.* Appropriate site control procedures shall be implemented to control employee exposure to hazardous substances before clean-up work begins.

(2) *Site control program.* A site control program for protecting employees which is part of the employer's site safety and health program required in paragraph (b) of this section shall be developed during the planning stages of a hazardous waste clean-up operation and modified as necessary as new information becomes available.

(3) *Elements of the site control program.* The site control program shall, as a minimum, include: A site map; site work zones; the use of a "buddy system"; site communications including alerting means for emergencies; the standard operating procedures or safe work practices; and, identification of the nearest medical assistance. Where these requirements are covered elsewhere they need not be repeated.

(e) *Training*—(1) *General.* (i) All employees working on site (such as but not limited to equipment operators, general laborers and others) exposed to hazardous substances, health hazards, or safety hazards and their supervisors and management responsible for the site shall receive training meeting the requirements of this paragraph before they are permitted to engage in hazardous waste operations that could expose them to hazardous substances, safety, or health hazards, and they shall receive review training as specified in this paragraph.

(ii) Employees shall not be permitted to participate in or supervise field activities until they have been trained to a level required by their job function and responsibility.

(2) *Elements to be covered.* The training shall thoroughly cover the following:

(i) Names of personnel and alternates responsible for site safety and health;

(ii) Safety, health and other hazards present on the site;

(iii) Use of personal protective equipment;

(iv) Work practices by which the employee can minimize risks from hazards;

(v) Safe use of engineering controls and equipment on the site;

(vi) Medical surveillance requirements, including recognition of symptoms and signs which might indicate overexposure to hazards; and

(vii) The contents of paragraphs (G) through (J) of the site safety and health plan set forth in paragraph (b)(4)(ii) of this section.

(3) *Initial training.* (i) General site workers (such as equipment operators, general laborers and supervisory personnel) engaged in hazardous substance removal or other activities which expose or potentially expose workers to hazardous substances and health hazards shall receive a minimum of 40 hours of instruction off the site, and a minimum of three days actual field experience under the direct supervision of a trained, experienced supervisor.

(ii) Workers on site only occasionally for a specific limited task (such as, but not limited to, ground water monitoring, land surveying, or geo-physical surveying) and who are unlikely to be exposed over permissible exposure limits and published exposure limits shall receive a minimum of 24 hours of instruction off the site, and the minimum of one day actual field experience under the direct supervision of a trained, experienced supervisor.

(iii) Workers regularly on site who work in areas which have been monitored and fully characterized indicating that exposures are under permissible exposure limits and published exposure limits where respirators are not necessary, and the characterization indicates that there are no health hazards or the possibility of an emergency developing, shall receive a minimum of 24 hours of instruction off the site and the minimum of one day actual field experience under the direct supervision of a trained, experienced supervisor.

(iv) Workers with 24 hours of training who are covered by paragraphs (e)(3)(ii) and (e)(3)(iii) of this section, and who become general site workers or who are required to wear respirators, shall have the additional 16 hours and two days of training necessary to total the training specified in paragraph (e)(3)(i).

(4) *Management and supervisor training.* On-site management and supervisors directly responsible for, or who supervise employees engaged in, hazardous waste operations shall receive 40 hours initial training, and three days of supervised field experience (the training may be reduced to 24 hours and one day if the only area of their responsibility is employees covered by paragraphs (e)(3)(ii) and (e)(3)(iii)) and at least eight additional hours of specialized training at the time of job assignment on such topics as, but not limited to, the employer's safety and health program and the associated employee training program, personal protective equipment program, spill containment program, and health hazard monitoring procedure and techniques.

(5) *Qualifications for trainers.* Trainers shall be qualified to instruct employees about the subject matter that is being presented in training. Such trainers shall have satisfactorily completed a training program for teaching the subjects they are expected to teach, or they shall have the academic credentials and instructional experience necessary for teaching the subjects. Instructors shall demonstrate competent instructional skills and knowledge of the applicable subject matter.

(6) *Training certification.* Employees and supervisors that have received and successfully completed the training and field experience specified in paragraphs (e)(1) through (e)(4) of this section shall be certified by their instructor or the head instructor and trained supervisor as having successfully completed the necessary training. A written certificate shall be given to each person so certified. Any person who has not been so certified or who does not meet the requirements of paragraph (e)(9) of this section shall be prohibited from engaging in hazardous waste operations.

(7) *Emergency response.* Employees who are engaged in responding to hazardous emergency situations at hazardous waste clean-up sites that may expose them to hazardous substances shall be trained in how to respond to such expected emergencies.

(8) *Refresher training.* Employees specified in paragraph (e)(1) of this section, and managers and supervisors specified in paragraph (e)(4) of this section, shall receive eight hours of refresher training annually on the items specified in paragraph (e)(2) and/or (e)(4) of this section, any critique of incidents that have occurred in the past year that can serve as training examples of related work, and other relevant topics.

(9) *Equivalent training.* Employers who can show by documentation or certification that an employee's work experience and/or training has resulted in training equivalent to that training required in paragraphs (e)(1) through (e)(4) of this section shall not be required to provide the initial training requirements of those paragraphs to such employees and shall provide a copy of the certification or documentation to the employee upon request. However, certified employees or employees with equivalent training new to a site shall receive appropriate, site specific training before site entry and have appropriate supervised field experience at the new site. Equivalent training includes any academic training or the training that existing employees might have already received from actual hazardous waste site work experience.

(f) *Medical surveillance—*(1) *General.* Employers engaged in operations specified in paragraphs (a)(1)(i) through (a)(1)(iv) of this section and not covered by (a)(2)(iii) exceptions and employers of employees specified in paragraph (q)(9) shall institute a medical surveillance program in accordance with this paragraph.

(2) *Employees covered.* The medical surveillance program shall be instituted by the employer for the following employees:

(i) All employees who are or may be exposed to hazardous substances or health hazards at or above the permissible exposure limits or, if there is no permissible exposure limit, above the published exposure levels for these substances, without regard to the use of respirators, for 30 days or more a year;

(ii) All employees who wear a respirator for 30 days or more a year or as required by § 1926.103;

(iii) All employees who are injured, become ill or develop signs or symptoms due to possible overexposure involving hazardous substances or health hazards from an emergency response or hazardous waste operation; and

(iv) Members of HAZMAT teams.

(3) *Frequency of medical examinations and consultations.* Medical examinations and consultations shall be made available by the employer to each em-

ployee covered under paragraph (f)(2) of this section on the following schedules:

(i) For employees covered under paragraphs (f)(2)(i), (f)(2)(ii), and (f)(2)(iv):

(A) Prior to assignment;

(B) At least once every twelve months for each employee covered unless the attending physician believes a longer interval (not greater than biennially) is appropriate;

(C) At termination of employment or reassignment to an area where the employee would not be covered if the employee has not had an examination within the last six months;

(D) As soon as possible upon notification by an employee that the employee has developed signs or symptoms indicating possible overexposure to hazardous substances or health hazards, or that the employee has been injured or exposed above the permissible exposure limits or published exposure levels in an emergency situation;

(E) At more frequent times, if the examining physician determines that an increased frequency of examination is medically necessary.

(ii) For employees covered under paragraph (f)(2)(iii) and for all employees including those of employers covered by paragraph (a)(1)(v) who may have been injured, received a health impairment, developed signs or symptoms which may have resulted from exposure to hazardous substances resulting from an emergency incident, or exposed during an emergency incident to hazardous substances at concentrations above the permissible exposure limits or the published exposure levels without the necessary personal protective equipment being used:

(A) As soon as possible following the emergency incident or development of signs or symptoms;

(B) At additional times, if the examining physician determines that follow-up examinations or consultations are medically necessary.

(4) *Content of medical examinations and consultations.* (i) Medical examinations required by paragraph (f)(3) of this section shall include a medical and work history (or updated history if one is in the employee's file) with special emphasis on symptoms related to the handling of hazardous substances and

health hazards, and to fitness for duty including the ability to wear any required PPE under conditions (i.e., temperature extremes) that may be expected at the work site.

(ii) The content of medical examinations or consultations made available to employees pursuant to paragraph (f) shall be determined by the attending physician. The guidelines in the *Occupational Safety and Health Guidance Manual for Hazardous Waste Site Activities* (See appendix D, Reference #10) should be consulted.

(5) *Examination bv a physician and costs.* All medical examinations and procedures shall be performed by or under the supervision of a licensed physician, preferably one knowledgeable in occupational medicine, and shall be provided without cost to the employee, without loss of pay, and at a reasonable time and place.

(6) *Information provided to the physician.* The employer shall provide one copy of this standard and its appendices to the attending physician, and in addition the following for each employee:

(i) A description of the employee's duties as they relate to the employee's exposures.

(ii) The employee's exposure levels or anticipated exposure levels.

(iii) A description of any personal protective equipment used or to be used.

(iv) Information from previous medical examinations of the employee which is not readily available to the examining physician.

(v) Information required by § 1926.103.

(7) *Physician's written opinion.* (i) The employer shall obtain and furnish the employee with a copy of a written opinion from the attending physician containing the following:

(A) The physician's opinion as to whether the employee has any detected medical conditions which would place the employee at increased risk of material impairment of the employee's health from work in hazardous waste operations or emergency response, or from respirator use.

(B) The physician's recommended limitations upon the employee's assigned work.

(C) The results of the medical examination and tests if requested by the employee.

(D) A statement that the employee has been informed by the physician of the results of the medical examination and any medical conditions which require further examination or treatment.

(ii) The written opinion obtained by the employer shall not reveal specific findings or diagnoses unrelated to occupational exposures.

(8) *Recordkeeping.* (i) An accurate record of the medical surveillance required by paragraph (f) of this section shall be retained. This record shall be retained for the period specified and meet the criteria of 29 CFR 1926.33.

(ii) The record required in paragraph (f)(8)(i) of this section shall include at least the following information:

(A) The name and social security number of the employee;

(B) Physician's written opinions, recommended limitations, and results of examinations and tests;

(C) Any employee medical complaints related to exposure to hazardous substances;

(D) A copy of the information provided to the examining physician by the employer, with the exception of the standard and its appendices.

(g) *Engineering controls, work practices, and personal protective equipment for employee protection.* Engineering controls, work practices, personal protective equipment, or a combination of these shall be implemented in accordance with this paragraph to protect employees from exposure to hazardous substances and safety and health hazards.

(1) *Engineering controls, work practices and PPE for substances regulated either in § 1926.55, elsewhere in subpart D, or in other pertinent sections of this part.* (i) Engineering controls and work practices shall be instituted to reduce and maintain employee exposure to or below the permissible exposure limits for substances regulated either in § 1926.55 or other pertinent sections of this part, except to the extent that such controls and practices are not feasible.

NOTE TO (g)(1)(i): Engineering controls which may be feasible include the use of pressurized cabs or control booths on equipment, and/or the use of remotely operated material handling equipment. Work practices which may be feasible are removing all non-essential employees from potential exposure during opening of drums, wetting down dusty operations and locating employees upwind of possible hazards.

(ii) Whenever engineering controls and work practices are not feasible or not required, any reasonable combination of engineering controls, work practices and PPE shall be used to reduce and maintain employee exposures to or below the permissible exposure limits or dose limits for substances regulated either in § 1926.55 or other pertinent sections of this part.

(iii) The employer shall not implement a schedule of employee rotation as a means of compliance with permissible exposure limits or dose limits except when there is no other feasible way of complying with the airborne or dermal dose limits for ionizing radiation.

(iv) The provisions of subpart D shall be followed.

(2) *Engineering controls, work practices, and PPE for substances not regulated either in § 1926.55, elsewhere in subpart D, or in other pertinent sections of this part.* An appropriate combination of engineering controls, work practices and personal protective equipment shall be used to reduce and maintain employee exposure to or below published exposure levels for hazardous substances and health hazards not regulated either in § 1926.55, elsewhere in subpart D, or in other pertinent sections of this part. The employer may use the published literature and MSDS as a guide in making the employer's determination as to what level of protection the employer believes is appropriate for hazardous substances and health hazards for which there is no permissible exposure limit or published exposure limit.

(3) *Personal protective equipment selection.* (i) Personal protective equipment (PPE) shall be selected and used which will protect employees from the hazards and potential hazards they are likely to encounter as identified during the site characterization and analysis.

(ii) Personal protective equipment selection shall be based on an evaluation of the performance characteristics of the PPE relative to the requirements and limitations of the site, the task-specific conditions and duration, and the hazards and potential hazards identified at the site.

(iii) Positive pressure self-contained breathing apparatus, or positive pressure air-line respirators equipped with an escape air supply, shall be used when chemical exposure levels present will create a substantial possibility of immediate death, immediate serious illness or injury, or impair the ability to escape.

(iv) Totally-encapsulating chemical protective suits (protection equivalent to Level A protection as recommended in appendix B) shall be used in conditions where skin absorption of a hazardous substance may result in a substantial possibility of immediate death, immediate serious illness or injury, or impair the ability to escape.

(v) The level of protection provided by PPE selection shall be increased when additional information on site conditions indicates that increased protection is necessary to reduce employee exposures below permissible exposure limits and published exposure levels for hazardous substances and health hazards. (See appendix B for guidance on selecting PPE ensembles.)

NOTE TO (g)(3): The level of employee protection provided may be decreased when additional information or site conditions show that decreased protection will not result in hazardous exposures to employees.

(vi) Personal protective equipment shall be selected and used to meet the requirements of subpart E of this part and additional requirements specified in this section.

(4) *Totally-encapsulating chemical protective suits.* (i) Totally-encapsulating suits shall protect employees from the particular hazards which are identified during site characterization and analysis.

(ii) Totally-encapsulating suits shall be capable of maintaining positive air pressure. (See appendix A for a test method which may be used to evaluate this requirement.)

(iii) Totally-encapsulating suits shall be capable of preventing inward test gas leakage of more than 0.5 percent. (See appendix A for a test method which may be used to evaluate this requirement.)

(5) *Personal protective equipment (PPE) program.* A written personal protective equipment program, which is part of

the employer's safety and health program required in paragraph (b) of this section or required in paragraph (p)(1) of this section and which is also a part of the site-specific safety and health plan shall be established. The PPE program shall address the elements listed below. When elements, such as donning and doffing procedures, are provided by the manufacturer of a piece of equipment and are attached to the plan, they need not be rewritten into the plan as long as they adequately address the procedure or element.

(i) PPE selection based upon site hazards,

(ii) PPE use and limitations of the equipment,

(iii) Work mission duration,

(iv) PPE maintenance and storage,

(v) PPE decontamination and disposal,

(vi) PPE training and proper fitting,

(vii) PPE donning and doffing procedures,

(viii) PPE inspection procedures prior to, during, and after use,

(ix) Evaluation of the effectiveness of the PPE program, and

(x) Limitations during temperature extremes, heat stress, and other appropriate medical considerations.

(h) *Monitoring*—(1) *General.* (i) Monitoring shall be performed in accordance with this paragraph where there may be a question of employee exposure to hazardous concentrations of hazardous substances in order to assure proper selection of engineering controls, work practices and personal protective equipment so that employees are not exposed to levels which exceed permissible exposure limits, or published exposure levels if there are no permissible exposure limits, for hazardous substances.

(ii) Air monitoring shall be used to identify and quantify airborne levels of hazardous substances and safety and health hazards in order to determine the appropriate level of employee protection needed on site.

(2) *Initial entry.* Upon initial entry, representative air monitoring shall be conducted to identify any IDLH condition, exposure over permissible exposure limits or published exposure levels, exposure over a radioactive material's dose limits or other dangerous condition such as the presence of flammable atmospheres or oxygen-deficient environments.

(3) *Periodic monitoring.* Periodic monitoring shall be conducted when the possibility of an IDLH condition or flammable atmosphere has developed or when there is indication that exposures may have risen over permissible exposure limits or published exposure levels since prior monitoring. Situations where it shall be considered whether the possibility that exposures have risen are as follows:

(i) When work begins on a different portion of the site.

(ii) When contaminants other than those previously identified are being handled.

(iii) When a different type of operation is initiated (e.g., drum opening as opposed to exploratory well drilling).

(iv) When employees are handling leaking drums or containers or working in areas with obvious liquid contamination (e.g., a spill or lagoon).

(4) *Monitoring of high-risk employees.* After the actual clean-up phase of any hazardous waste operation commences; for example, when soil, surface water or containers are moved or disturbed; the employer shall monitor those employees likely to have the highest exposures to hazardous substances and health hazards likely to be present above permissible exposure limits or published exposure levels by using personal sampling frequently enough to characterize employee exposures. If the employees likely to have the highest exposure are over permissible exposure limits or published exposure limits, then monitoring shall continue to determine all employees likely to be above those limits. The employer may utilize a representative sampling approach by documenting that the employees and chemicals chosen for monitoring are based on the criteria stated above.

NOTE TO (h): It is not required to monitor employees engaged in site characterization operations covered by paragraph (c) of this section.

(i) *Informational programs.* Employers shall develop and implement a program, which is part of the employer's safety and health program required in paragraph (b) of this section, to inform

151

employees, contractors, and sub-contractors (or their representative) actually engaged in hazardous waste operations of the nature, level and degree of exposure likely as a result of participation in such hazardous waste operations. Employees, contractors and subcontractors working outside of the operations part of a site are not covered by this standard.

(j) *Handling drums and containers*—(1) *General.* (i) Hazardous substances and contaminated soils, liquids, and other residues shall be handled, transported, labeled, and disposed of in accordance with this paragraph.

(ii) Drums and containers used during the clean-up shall meet the appropriate DOT, OSHA, and EPA regulations for the wastes that they contain.

(iii) When practical, drums and containers shall be inspected and their integrity shall be assured prior to being moved. Drums or containers that cannot be inspected before being moved because of storage conditions (i.e., buried beneath the earth, stacked behind other drums, stacked several tiers high in a pile, etc.) shall be moved to an accessible location and inspected prior to further handling.

(iv) Unlabelled drums and containers shall be considered to contain hazardous substances and handled accordingly until the contents are positively identified and labeled.

(v) Site operations shall be organized to minimize the amount of drum or container movement.

(vi) Prior to movement of drums or containers, all employees exposed to the transfer operation shall be warned of the potential hazards associated with the contents of the drums or containers.

(vii) U.S. Department of Transportation specified salvage drums or containers and suitable quantities of proper absorbent shall be kept available and used in areas where spills, leaks, or ruptures may occur.

(viii) Where major spills may occur, a spill containment program, which is part of the employer's safety and health program required in paragraph (b) of this section, shall be implemented to contain and isolate the entire volume of the hazardous substance being transferred.

(ix) Drums and containers that cannot be moved without rupture, leakage, or spillage shall be emptied into a sound container using a device classified for the material being transferred.

(x) A ground-penetrating system or other type of detection system or device shall be used to estimate the location and depth of buried drums or containers.

(xi) Soil or covering material shall be removed with caution to prevent drum or container rupture.

(xii) Fire extinguishing equipment meeting the requirements of subpart F of this part shall be on hand and ready for use to control incipient fires.

(2) *Opening drums and containers.* The following procedures shall be followed in areas where drums or containers are being opened:

(i) Where an airline respirator system is used, connections to the source of air supply shall be protected from contamination and the entire system shall be protected from physical damage.

(ii) Employees not actually involved in opening drums or containers shall be kept a safe distance from the drums or containers being opened.

(iii) If employees must work near or adjacent to drums or containers being opened, a suitable shield that does not interfere with the work operation shall be placed between the employee and the drums or containers being opened to protect the employee in case of accidental explosion.

(iv) Controls for drum or container opening equipment, monitoring equipment, and fire suppression equipment shall be located behind the explosion-resistant barrier.

(v) When there is a reasonable possibility of flammable atmospheres being present, material handling equipment and hand tools shall be of the type to prevent sources of ignition.

(vi) Drums and containers shall be opened in such a manner that excess interior pressure will be safely relieved. If pressure can not be relieved from a remote location, appropriate shielding shall be placed between the employee and the drums or containers to reduce the risk of employee injury.

(vii) Employees shall not stand upon or work from drums or containers.

(3) *Material handling equipment.* Material handling equipment used to transfer drums and containers shall be selected, positioned and operated to minimize sources of ignition related to the equipment from igniting vapors released from ruptured drums or containers.

(4) *Radioactive wastes.* Drums and containers containing radioactive wastes shall not be handled until such time as their hazard to employees is properly assessed.

(5) *Shock sensitive wastes.* As a minimum, the following special precautions shall be taken when drums and containers containing or suspected of containing shock-sensitive wastes are handled:

(i) All non-essential employees shall be evacuated from the area of transfer.

(ii) Material handling equipment shall be provided with explosive containment devices or protective shields to protect equipment operators from exploding containers.

(iii) An employee alarm system capable of being perceived above surrounding light and noise conditions shall be used to signal the commencement and completion of explosive waste handling activities.

(iv) Continuous communications (i.e., portable radios, hand signals, telephones, as appropriate) shall be maintained between the employee-in-charge of the immediate handling area and both the site safety and health supervisor and the command post until such time as the handling operation is completed. Communication equipment or methods that could cause shock sensitive materials to explode shall not be used.

(v) Drums and containers under pressure, as evidenced by bulging or swelling, shall not be moved until such time as the cause for excess pressure is determined and appropriate containment procedures have been implemented to protect employees from explosive relief of the drum.

(vi) Drums and containers containing packaged laboratory wastes shall be considered to contain shock-sensitive or explosive materials until they have been characterized.

CAUTION: Shipping of shock sensitive wastes may be prohibited under U.S. Department of Transportation regulations. Employers and their shippers should refer to 49 CFR 173.21 and 173.50.

(6) *Laboratory waste packs.* In addition to the requirements of paragraph (j)(5) of this section, the following precautions shall be taken, as a minimum, in handling laboratory waste packs (lab packs):

(i) Lab packs shall be opened only when necessary and then only by an individual knowledgeable in the inspection, classification, and segregation of the containers within the pack according to the hazards of the wastes.

(ii) If crystalline material is noted on any container, the contents shall be handled as a shock-sensitive waste until the contents are identified.

(7) *Sampling of drum and container contents.* Sampling of containers and drums shall be done in accordance with a sampling procedure which is part of the site safety and health plan developed for and available to employees and others at the specific worksite.

(8) *Shipping and transport.* (i) Drums and containers shall be identified and classified prior to packaging for shipment.

(ii) Drum or container staging areas shall be kept to the minimum number necessary to identify and classify materials safely and prepare them for transport.

(iii) Staging areas shall be provided with adequate access and egress routes.

(iv) Bulking of hazardous wastes shall be permitted only after a thorough characterization of the materials has been completed.

(9) *Tank and vault procedures.* (i) Tanks and vaults containing hazardous substances shall be handled in a manner similar to that for drums and containers, taking into consideration the size of the tank or vault.

(ii) Appropriate tank or vault entry procedures as described in the employer's safety and health plan shall be followed whenever employees must enter a tank or vault.

(k) *Decontamination*—(1) *General.* Procedures for all phases of decontamination shall be developed and implemented in accordance with this paragraph.

(2) *Decontamination procedures.* (i) A decontamination procedure shall be developed, communicated to employees and implemented before any employees or equipment may enter areas on site where potential for exposure to hazardous substances exists.

(ii) Standard operating procedures shall be developed to minimize employee contact with hazardous substances or with equipment that has contacted hazardous substances.

(iii) All employees leaving a contaminated area shall be appropriately decontaminated; all contaminated clothing and equipment leaving a contaminated area shall be appropriately disposed of or decontaminated.

(iv) Decontamination procedures shall be monitored by the site safety and health supervisor to determine their effectiveness. When such procedures are found to be ineffective, appropriate steps shall be taken to correct any deficiencies.

(3) *Location.* Decontamination shall be performed in geographical areas that will minimize the exposure of uncontaminated employees or equipment to contaminated employees or equipment.

(4) *Equipment and solvents.* All equipment and solvents used for decontamination shall be decontaminated or disposed of properly.

(5) *Personal protective clothing and equipment.* (i) Protective clothing and equipment shall be decontaminated, cleaned, laundered, maintained or replaced as needed to maintain their effectiveness.

(ii) Employees whose non-impermeable clothing becomes wetted with hazardous substances shall immediately remove that clothing and proceed to shower. The clothing shall be disposed of or decontaminated before it is removed from the work zone.

(6) *Unauthorized employees.* Unauthorized employees shall not remove protective clothing or equipment from change rooms.

(7) *Commercial laundries or cleaning establishments.* Commercial laundries or cleaning establishments that decontaminate protective clothing or equipment shall be informed of the potentially harmful effects of exposures to hazardous substances.

(8) *Showers and change rooms.* Where the decontamination procedure indicates a need for regular showers and change rooms outside of a contaminated area, they shall be provided and meet the requirements of 29 CFR 1910.141. If temperature conditions prevent the effective use of water, then other effective means for cleansing shall be provided and used.

(l) *Emergency response by employees at uncontrolled hazardous waste sites*—(1) *Emergency response plan.* (i) An emergency response plan shall be developed and implemented by all employers within the scope of paragraphs (a)(1)(i)–(ii) of this section to handle anticipated emergencies prior to the commencement of hazardous waste operations. The plan shall be in writing and available for inspection and copying by employees, their representatives, OSHA personnel and other governmental agencies with relevant responsibilities.

(ii) Employers who will evacuate their employees from the danger area when an emergency occurs, and who do not permit any of their employees to assist in handling the emergency, are exempt from the requirements of this paragraph if they provide an emergency action plan complying with § 1926.35 of this part.

(2) *Elements of an emergency response plan.* The employer shall develop an emergency response plan for emergencies which shall address, as a minimum, the following:

(i) Pre-emergency planning.

(ii) Personnel roles, lines of authority, and communication.

(iii) Emergency recognition and prevention.

(iv) Safe distances and places of refuge.

(v) Site security and control.

(vi) Evacuation routes and procedures.

(vii) Decontamination procedures which are not covered by the site safety and health plan.

(viii) Emergency medical treatment and first aid.

(ix) Emergency alerting and response procedures.

(x) Critique of response and follow-up.

(xi) PPE and emergency equipment.

(3) *Procedures for handling emergency incidents.* (i) In addition to the elements for the emergency response plan required in paragraph (1)(2) of this section, the following elements shall be included for emergency response plans:

(A) Site topography, layout, and prevailing weather conditions.

(B) Procedures for reporting incidents to local, state, and federal governmental agencies.

(ii) The emergency response plan shall be a separate section of the Site Safety and Health Plan.

(iii) The emergency response plan shall be compatible and integrated with the disaster, fire and/or emergency response plans of local, state, and federal agencies.

(iv) The emergency response plan shall be rehearsed regularly as part of the overall training program for site operations.

(v) The site emergency response plan shall be reviewed periodically and, as necessary, be amended to keep it current with new or changing site conditions or information.

(vi) An employee alarm system shall be installed in accordance with 29 CFR 1926.159 to notify employees of an emergency situation; to stop work activities if necessary; to lower background noise in order to speed communication; and to begin emergency procedures.

(vii) Based upon the information available at time of the emergency, the employer shall evaluate the incident and the site response capabilities and proceed with the appropriate steps to implement the site emergency response plan.

(m) *Illumination.* Areas accessible to employees shall be lighted to not less than the minimum illumination intensities listed in the following Table D–65.1 while any work is in progress:

TABLE D–65.1—MINIMUM ILLUMINATION INTENSITIES IN FOOT-CANDLES

Foot-can-dles	Area or operations
5	General site areas.
3	Excavation and waste areas, accessways, active storage areas, loading platforms, refueling, and field maintenance areas.
5	Indoors: Warehouses, corridors, hallways, and exitways.

TABLE D–65.1—MINIMUM ILLUMINATION INTENSITIES IN FOOT-CANDLES—Continued

Foot-can-dles	Area or operations
5	Tunnels, shafts, and general underground work areas. (Exception: Minimum of 10 foot-candles is required at tunnel and shaft heading during drilling mucking, and scaling. Mine Safety and Health Administration approved cap lights shall be acceptable for use in the tunnel heading.)
10	General shops (e.g., mechanical and electrical equipment rooms, active storerooms, barracks or living quarters, locker or dressing rooms, dining areas, and indoor toilets and workrooms.)
30	First aid stations, infirmaries, and offices.

(n) *Sanitation at temporary workplaces*—(1) *Potable water.* (i) An adequate supply of potable water shall be provided on the site.

(ii) Portable containers used to dispense drinking water shall be capable of being tightly closed, and equipped with a tap. Water shall not be dipped from containers.

(iii) Any container used to distribute drinking water shall be clearly marked as to the nature of its contents and not used for any other purpose.

(iv) Where single service cups (to be used but once) are supplied, both a sanitary container for the unused cups and a receptacle for disposing of the used cups shall be provided.

(2) *Nonpotable water.* (i) Outlets for nonpotable water, such as water for firefighting purposes, shall be identified to indicate clearly that the water is unsafe and is not to be used for drinking, washing, or cooking purposes.

(ii) There shall be no cross-connection, open or potential, between a system furnishing potable water and a system furnishing nonpotable water.

(3) *Toilet facilities.* (i) Toilets shall be provided for employees according to the following Table D–65.2.

TABLE D–65.2—TOILET FACILITIES

Number of employees	Minimum number of facilities
20 or fewer	One.
More than 20, fewer than 200	One toilet seat and one urinal per 40 employees.
More than 200	One toilet seat and one urinal per 50 employees.

(ii) Under temporary field conditions, provisions shall be made to assure that at least one toilet facility is available.

(iii) Hazardous waste sites not provided with a sanitary sewer shall be provided with the following toilet facilities unless prohibited by local codes:

(A) Chemical toilets;

(B) Recirculating toilets;

(C) Combustion toilets; or

(D) Flush toilets.

(iv) The requirements of this paragraph for sanitation facilities shall not apply to mobile crews having transportation readily available to nearby toilet facilities.

(v) Doors entering toilet facilities shall be provided with entrance locks controlled from inside the facility.

(4) *Food handling.* All food service facilities and operations for employees shall meet the applicable laws, ordinances, and regulations of the jurisdictions in which they are located.

(5) *Temporary sleeping quarters.* When temporary sleeping quarters are provided, they shall be heated, ventilated, and lighted.

(6) *Washing facilities.* The employer shall provide adequate washing facilities for employees engaged in operations where hazardous substances may be harmful to employees. Such facilities shall be in near proximity to the worksite; in areas where exposures are below permissible exposure limits and published exposure levels and which are under the controls of the employer; and shall be so equipped as to enable employees to remove hazardous substances from themselves.

(7) *Showers and change rooms.* When hazardous waste clean-up or removal operations commence on a site and the duration of the work will require six months or greater time to complete, the employer shall provide showers and change rooms for all employees exposed to hazardous substances and health hazards involved in hazardous waste clean-up or removal operations.

(i) Showers shall be provided and shall meet the requirements of 29 CFR 1926.51(f)(4).

(ii) Change rooms shall be provided and shall meet the requirements of 29 CFR 1926.51(i). Change rooms shall consist of two separate change areas separated by the shower area required in paragraph (n)(7)(i) of this section. One change area, with an exit leading off the worksite, shall provide employees with a clean area where they can remove, store, and put on street clothing. The second area, with an exit to the worksite, shall provide employees with an area where they can put on, remove and store work clothing and personal protective equipment.

(iii) Showers and change rooms shall be located in areas where exposures are below the permissible exposure limits and published exposure levels. If this cannot be accomplished, then a ventilation system shall be provided that will supply air that is below the permissible exposure limits and published exposure levels.

(iv) Employers shall assure that employees shower at the end of their work shift and when leaving the hazardous waste site.

(o) *New technology programs.* (1) The employer shall develop and implement procedures for the introduction of effective new technologies and equipment developed for the improved protection of employees working with hazardous waste clean-up operations, and the same shall be implemented as part of the site safety and health program to assure that employee protection is being maintained.

(2) New technologies, equipment or control measures available to the industry, such as the use of foams, absorbents, adsorbents, neutralizers, or other means to suppress the level of air contaminates while excavating the site or for spill control, shall be evaluated by employers or their representatives. Such an evaluation shall be done to determine the effectiveness of the new methods, materials, or equipment before implementing their use on a large scale for enhancing employee protection. Information and data from manufacturers or suppliers may be used as part of the employer's evaluation effort. Such evaluations shall be made available to OSHA upon request.

(p) *Certain operations conducted under the Resource Conservation and Recovery Act of 1976 (RCRA).* Employers conducting operations at treatment, storage and disposal (TSD) facilities specified in paragraph (a)(1)(iv) of this section shall provide and implement the programs specified in this paragraph. See the "Notes and Exceptions" to paragraph (a)(2)(iii) of this section for employers not covered.)''.

(1) *Safety and health program.* The employer shall develop and implement a written safety and health program for employees involved in hazardous waste operations that shall be available for inspection by employees, their representatives and OSHA personnel. The program shall be designed to identify, evaluate and control safety and health hazards in their facilities for the purpose of employee protection, to provide for emergency response meeting the requirements of paragraph (p)(8) of this section and to address as appropriate site analysis, engineering controls, maximum exposure limits, hazardous waste handling procedures and uses of new technologies.

(2) *Hazard communication program.* The employer shall implement a hazard communication program meeting the requirements of 29 CFR 1926.59 as part of the employer's safety and program.

NOTE TO 1926.65: The exemption for hazardous waste provided in §1926.59 is applicable to this section.

(3) *Medical surveillance program.* The employer shall develop and implement a medical surveillance program meeting the requirements of paragraph (f) of this section.

(4) *Decontamination program.* The employer shall develop and implement a decontamination procedure meeting the requirements of paragraph (k) of this section.

(5) *New technology program.* The employer shall develop and implement procedures meeting the requirements of paragraph (o) of this section for introducing new and innovative equipment into the workplace.

(6) *Material handling program.* Where employees will be handling drums or containers, the employer shall develop and implement procedures meeting the requirements of paragraphs (j)(1) (ii) through (viii) and (xi) of this section, as well as (j)(3) and (j)(8) of this section prior to starting such work.

(7) *Training program—*(i) *New employees.* The employer shall develop and implement a training program, which is part of the employer's safety and health program, for employees exposed to health hazards or hazardous substances at TSD operations to enable the employees to perform their assigned duties and functions in a safe and healthful manner so as not to endanger themselves or other employees. The initial training shall be for 24 hours and refresher training shall be for eight hours annually. Employees who have received the initial training required by this paragraph shall be given a written certificate attesting that they have successfully completed the necessary training.

(ii) *Current employees.* Employers who can show by an employee's previous work experience and/or training that the employee has had training equivalent to the initial training required by this paragraph, shall be considered as meeting the initial training requirements of this paragraph as to that employee. Equivalent training includes the training that existing employees might have already received from actual site work experience. Current employees shall receive eight hours of refresher training annually.

(iii) *Trainers.* Trainers who teach initial training shall have satisfactorily completed a training course for teaching the subjects they are expected to teach or they shall have the academic credentials and instruction experience necessary to demonstrate a good command of the subject matter of the courses and competent instructional skills.

(8) *Emergency response program—*(i) *Emergency response plan.* An emergency response plan shall be developed and implemented by all employers. Such plans need not duplicate any of the subjects fully addressed in the employer's contingency planning required by permits, such as those issued by the U.S. Environmental Protection Agency, provided that the contingency plan is made part of the emergency response plan. The emergency response plan shall be a written portion of the employers safety and health program required in paragraph (p)(1) of this section. Employers who will evacuate their employees from the worksite location when an emergency occurs and who do not permit any of their employees to assist in handling the emergency are exempt from the requirements of paragraph (p)(8) if they provide an

emergency action plan complying with § 1926.35 of this part.

(ii) *Elements of an emergency response plan.* The employer shall develop an emergency response plan for emergencies which shall address, as a minimum, the following areas to the extent that they are not addressed in any specific program required in this paragraph:

(A) Pre-emergency planning and coordination with outside parties.

(B) Personnel roles, lines of authority, and communication.

(C) Emergency recognition and prevention.

(D) Safe distances and places of refuge.

(E) Site security and control.

(F) Evacuation routes and procedures.

(G) Decontamination procedures.

(H) Emergency medical treatment and first aid.

(I) Emergency alerting and response procedures.

(J) Critique of response and follow-up.

(K) PPE and emergency equipment.

(iii) *Training.* (A) Training for emergency response employees shall be completed before they are called upon to perform in real emergencies. Such training shall include the elements of the emergency response plan, standard operating procedures the employer has established for the job, the personal protective equipment to be worn and procedures for handling emergency incidents.

Exception #1: An employer need not train all employees to the degree specified if the employer divides the work force in a manner such that a sufficient number of employees who have responsibility to control emergencies have the training specified, and all other employees, who may first respond to an emergency incident, have sufficient awareness training to recognize that an emergency response situation exists and that they are instructed in that case to summon the fully trained employees and not attempt control activities for which they are not trained.

Exception #2: An employer need not train all employees to the degree specified if arrangements have been made in advance for an outside fully-trained emergency response team to respond in a reasonable period and all employees, who may come to the incident first, have sufficient aware-

ness training to recognize that an emergency response situation exists and they have been instructed to call the designated outside fully-trained emergency response team for assistance.

(B) Employee members of TSD facility emergency response organizations shall be trained to a level of competence in the recognition of health and safety hazards to protect themselves and other employees. This would include training in the methods used to minimize the risk from safety and health hazards; in the safe use of control equipment; in the selection and use of appropriate personal protective equipment; in the safe operating procedures to be used at the incident scene; in the techniques of coordination with other employees to minimize risks; in the appropriate response to over exposure from health hazards or injury to themselves and other employees; and in the recognition of subsequent symptoms which may result from over exposures.

(C) The employer shall certify that each covered employee has attended and successfully completed the training required in paragraph (p)(8)(iii) of this section, or shall certify the employee's competency at least yearly. The method used to demonstrate competency for certification of training shall be recorded and maintained by the employer.

(iv) *Procedures for handling emergency incidents.* (A) In addition to the elements for the emergency response plan required in paragraph (p)(8)(ii) of this section, the following elements shall be included for emergency response plans to the extent that they do not repeat any information already contained in the emergency response plan:

(*1*) Site topography, layout, and prevailing weather conditions.

(*2*) Procedures for reporting incidents to local, state, and federal governmental agencies.

(B) The emergency response plan shall be compatible and integrated with the disaster, fire and/or emergency response plans of local, state, and federal agencies.

(C) The emergency response plan shall be rehearsed regularly as part of the overall training program for site operations.

158

(D) The site emergency response plan shall be reviewed periodically and, as necessary, be amended to keep it current with new or changing site conditions or information.

(E) An employee alarm system shall be installed in accordance with 29 CFR 1926.159 to notify employees of an emergency situation; to stop work activities if necessary; to lower background noise in order to speed communication; and to begin emergency procedures.

(F) Based upon the information available at time of the emergency, the employer shall evaluate the incident and the site response capabilities and proceed with the appropriate steps to implement the site emergency response plan.

(q) *Emergency response to hazardous substance releases.* This paragraph covers employers whose employees are engaged in emergency response no matter where it occurs except that it does not cover employees engaged in operations specified in paragraphs (a)(1)(i) through (a)(1)(iv) of this section. Those emergency response organizations who have developed and implemented programs equivalent to this paragraph for handling releases of hazardous substances pursuant to section 303 of the Superfund Amendments and Reauthorization Act of 1986 (Emergency Planning and Community Right-to-Know Act of 1986, 42 U.S.C. 11003) shall be deemed to have met the requirements of this paragraph.

(1) *Emergency response plan.* An emergency response plan shall be developed and implemented to handle anticipated emergencies prior to the commencement of emergency response operations. The plan shall be in writing and available for inspection and copying by employees, their representatives and OSHA personnel. Employers who will evacuate their employees from the danger area when an emergency occurs, and who do not permit any of their employees to assist in handling the emergency, are exempt from the requirements of this paragraph if they provide an emergency action plan in accordance with § 1926.35 of this part.

(2) *Elements of an emergency response plan.* The employer shall develop an emergency response plan for emergencies which shall address, as a minimum, the following to the extent that they are not addressed elsewhere:

(i) Pre-emergency planning and coordination with outside parties.

(ii) Personnel roles, lines of authority, training, and communication.

(iii) Emergency recognition and prevention.

(iv) Safe distances and places of refuge.

(v) Site security and control.

(vi) Evacuation routes and procedures.

(vii) Decontamination.

(viii) Emergency medical treatment and first aid.

(ix) Emergency alerting and response procedures.

(x) Critique of response and follow-up.

(xi) PPE and emergency equipment.

(xii) Emergency response organizations may use the local emergency response plan or the state emergency response plan or both, as part of their emergency response plan to avoid duplication. Those items of the emergency response plan that are being properly addressed by the SARA Title III plans may be substituted into their emergency plan or otherwise kept together for the employer and employee's use.

(3) *Procedures for handling emergency response.* (i) The senior emergency response official responding to an emergency shall become the individual in charge of a site-specific Incident Command System (ICS). All emergency responders and their communications shall be coordinated and controlled through the individual in charge of the ICS assisted by the senior official present for each employer.

NOTE TO (g)(3)(i): The *senior official* at an emergency response is the most senior official on the site who has the responsibility for controlling the operations at the site. Initially it is the senior officer on the first-due piece of responding emergency apparatus to arrive on the incident scene. As more senior officers arrive (i.e., battalion chief, fire chief, state law enforcement official, site coordinator, etc.) the position is passed up the line of authority which has been previously established.

(ii) The individual in charge of the ICS shall identify, to the extent possible, all hazardous substances or conditions present and shall address as appropriate site analysis, use of engineering controls, maximum exposure limits, hazardous substance handling procedures, and use of any new technologies.

(iii) Based on the hazardous substances and/or conditions present, the individual in charge of the ICS shall implement appropriate emergency operations, and assure that the personal protective equipment worn is appropriate for the hazards to be encountered. However, personal protective equipment shall meet, at a minimum, the criteria contained in 29 CFR 1926.97 when worn while performing fire fighting operations beyond the incipient stage for any incident.

(iv) Employees engaged in emergency response and exposed to hazardous substances presenting an inhalation hazard or potential inhalation hazard shall wear positive pressure self-contained breathing apparatus while engaged in emergency response, until such time that the individual in charge of the ICS determines through the use of air monitoring that a decreased level of respiratory protection will not result in hazardous exposures to employees.

(v) The individual in charge of the ICS shall limit the number of emergency response personnel at the emergency site, in those areas of potential or actual exposure to incident or site hazards, to those who are actively performing emergency operations. However, operations in hazardous areas shall be performed using the buddy system in groups of two or more.

(vi) Back-up personnel shall stand by with equipment ready to provide assistance or rescue. Advance first aid support personnel, as a minimum, shall also stand by with medical equipment and transportation capability.

(vii) The individual in charge of the ICS shall designate a safety official, who is knowledgable in the operations being implemented at the emergency response site, with specific responsibility to identify and evaluate hazards and to provide direction with respect to the safety of operations for the emergency at hand.

(viii) When activities are judged by the safety official to be an IDLH condition and/or to involve an imminent danger condition, the safety official shall have the authority to alter, suspend, or terminate those activities. The safety official shall immediately inform the individual in charge of the ICS of any actions needed to be taken to correct these hazards at the emergency scene.

(ix) After emergency operations have terminated, the individual in charge of the ICS shall implement appropriate decontamination procedures.

(x) When deemed necessary for meeting the tasks at hand, approved self-contained compressed air breathing apparatus may be used with approved cylinders from other approved self-contained compressed air breathing apparatus provided that such cylinders are of the same capacity and pressure rating. All compressed air cylinders used with self-contained breathing apparatus shall meet U.S. Department of Transportation and National Institute for Occupational Safety and Health criteria.

(4) *Skilled support personnel.* Personnel, not necessarily an employer's own employees, who are skilled in the operation of certain equipment, such as mechanized earth moving or digging equipment or crane and hoisting equipment, and who are needed temporarily to perform immediate emergency support work that cannot reasonably be performed in a timely fashion by an employer's own employees, and who will be or may be exposed to the hazards at an emergency response scene, are not required to meet the training required in this paragraph for the employer's regular employees. However, these personnel shall be given an initial briefing at the site prior to their participation in any emergency response. The initial briefing shall include instruction in the wearing of appropriate personal protective equipment, what chemical hazards are involved, and what duties are to be performed. All other appropriate safety and health precautions provided to the employer's own employees shall be used to assure the safety and health of these personnel.

(5) *Specialist employees.* Employees who, in the course of their regular job duties, work with and are trained in the hazards of specific hazardous substances, and who will be called upon to provide technical advice or assistance at a hazardous substance release incident to the individual in charge, shall receive training or demonstrate competency in the area of their specialization annually.

(6) *Training.* Training shall be based on the duties and function to be performed by each responder of an emergency response organization. The skill and knowledge levels required for all new responders, those hired after the effective date of this standard, shall be conveyed to them through training before they are permitted to take part in actual emergency operations on an incident. Employees who participate, or are expected to participate, in emergency response, shall be given training in accordance with the following paragraphs:

(i) *First responder awareness level.* First responders at the awareness level are individuals who are likely to witness or discover a hazardous substance release and who have been trained to initiate an emergency response sequence by notifying the proper authorities of the release. They would take no further action beyond notifying the authorities of the release. First responders at the awareness level shall have sufficient training or have had sufficient experience to objectively demonstrate competency in the following areas:

(A) An understanding of what hazardous substances are, and the risks associated with them in an incident.

(B) An understanding of the potential outcomes associated with an emergency created when hazardous substances are present.

(C) The ability to recognize the presence of hazardous substances in an emergency.

(D) The ability to identify the hazardous substances, if possible.

(E) An understanding of the role of the first responder awareness individual in the employer's emergency response plan including site security and control and the U.S. Department of

Transportation's Emergency Response Guidebook.

(F) The ability to realize the need for additional resources, and to make appropriate notifications to the communication center.

(ii) *First responder operations level.* First responders at the operations level are individuals who respond to releases or potential releases of hazardous substances as part of the initial response to the site for the purpose of protecting nearby persons, property, or the environment from the effects of the release. They are trained to respond in a defensive fashion without actually trying to stop the release. Their function is to contain the release from a safe distance, keep it from spreading, and prevent exposures. First responders at the operational level shall have received at least eight hours of training or have had sufficient experience to objectively demonstrate competency in the following areas in addition to those listed for the awareness level and the employer shall so certify:

(A) Knowledge of the basic hazard and risk assessment techniques.

(B) Know how to select and use proper personal protective equipment provided to the first responder operational level.

(C) An understanding of basic hazardous materials terms.

(D) Know how to perform basic control, containment and/or confinement operations within the capabilities of the resources and personal protective equipment available with their unit.

(E) Know how to implement basic decontamination procedures.

(F) An understanding of the relevant standard operating procedures and termination procedures.

(iii) *Hazardous materials technician.* Hazardous materials technicians are individuals who respond to releases or potential releases for the purpose of stopping the release. They assume a more aggressive role than a first responder at the operations level in that they will approach the point of release in order to plug, patch or otherwise stop the release of a hazardous substance. Hazardous materials technicians shall have received at least 24 hours of training equal to the first responder operations level and in addition have competency in the following areas and the employer shall so certify:

(A) Know how to implement the employer's emergency response plan.

(B) Know the classification, identification and verification of known and unknown materials by using field survey instruments and equipment.

(C) Be able to function within an assigned role in the Incident Command System.

(D) Know how to select and use proper specialized chemical personal protective equipment provided to the hazardous materials technician.

(E) Understand hazard and risk assessment techniques.

(F) Be able to perform advance control, containment, and/or confinement operations within the capabilities of the resources and personal protective equipment available with the unit.

(G) Understand and implement decontamination procedures.

(H) Understand termination procedures.

(I) Understand basic chemical and toxicological terminology and behavior.

(iv) *Hazardous materials specialist.* Hazardous materials specialists are individuals who respond with and provide support to hazardous materials technicians. Their duties parallel those of the hazardous materials technician, however, those duties require a more directed or specific knowledge of the various substances they may be called upon to contain. The hazardous materials specialist would also act as the site liaison with Federal, state, local and other government authorities in regards to site activities. Hazardous materials specialists shall have received at least 24 hours of training equal to the technician level and in addition have competency in the following areas and the employer shall so certify:

(A) Know how to implement the local emergency response plan.

(B) Understand classification, identification and verification of known and unknown materials by using advanced survey instruments and equipment.

(C) Know of the state emergency response plan.

(D) Be able to select and use proper specialized chemical personal protective equipment provided to the hazardous materials specialist.

(E) Understand in-depth hazard and risk techniques.

(F) Be able to perform specialized control, containment, and/or confinement operations within the capabilities of the resources and personal protective equipment available.

(G) Be able to determine and implement decontamination procedures.

(H) Have the ability to develop a site safety and control plan.

(I) Understand chemical, radiological and toxicological terminology and behavior.

(v) *On scene incident commander.* Incident commanders, who will assume control of the incident scene beyond the first responder awareness level, shall receive at least 24 hours of training equal to the first responder operations level and in addition have competency in the following areas and the employer shall so certify:

(A) Know and be able to implement the employer's incident command system.

(B) Know how to implement the employer's emergency response plan.

(C) Know and understand the hazards and risks associated with employees working in chemical protective clothing.

(D) Know how to implement the local emergency response plan.

(E) Know of the state emergency response plan and of the Federal Regional Response Team.

(F) Know and understand the importance of decontamination procedures.

(7) *Trainers.* Trainers who teach any of the above training subjects shall have satisfactorily completed a training course for teaching the subjects they are expected to teach, such as the courses offered by the U.S. National Fire Academy, or they shall have the training and/or academic credentials and instructional experience necessary to demonstrate competent instructional skills and a good command of the subject matter of the courses they are to teach.

(8) *Refresher training.* (i) Those employees who are trained in accordance with paragraph (q)(6) of this section

shall receive annual refresher training of sufficient content and duration to maintain their competencies, or shall demonstrate competency in those areas at least yearly.

(ii) A statement shall be made of the training or competency, and if a statement of competency is made, the employer shall keep a record of the methodology used to demonstrate competency.

(9) *Medical surveillance and consultation.* (i) Members of an organized and designated HAZMAT team and hazardous materials specialists shall receive a baseline physical examination and be provided with medical surveillance as required in paragraph (f) of this section.

(ii) Any emergency response employees who exhibits signs or symptoms which may have resulted from exposure to hazardous substances during the course of an emergency incident, either immediately or subsequently, shall be provided with medical consultation as required in paragraph (f)(3)(ii) of this section.

(10) *Chemical protective clothing.* Chemical protective clothing and equipment to be used by organized and designated HAZMAT team members, or to be used by hazardous materials specialists, shall meet the requirements of paragraphs (g) (3) through (5) of this section.

(11) *Post-emergency response operations.* Upon completion of the emergency response, if it is determined that it is necessary to remove hazardous substances, health hazards, and materials contaminated with them (such as contaminated soil or other elements of the natural environment) from the site of the incident, the employer conducting the clean-up shall comply with one of the following:

(i) Meet all of the requirements of paragraphs (b) through (o) of this section; or

(ii) Where the clean-up is done on plant property using plant or workplace employees, such employees shall have completed the training requirements of the following: 29 CFR 1926.35, 1926.59, and 1926.103, and other appropriate safety and health training made necessary by the tasks that they are expected to be performed such as personal protective equipment and decontamination procedures. All equipment to be used in the performance of the clean-up work shall be in serviceable condition and shall have been inspected prior to use.

APPENDICES TO §1926.65—HAZARDOUS WASTE OPERATIONS AND EMERGENCY RESPONSE

NOTE: The following appendices serve as non-mandatory guidelines to assist employees and employers in complying with the appropriate requirements of this section. However §1926.65(g) makes mandatory in certain circumstances the use of Level A and Level B PPE protection.

APPENDIX A TO §1926.65—PERSONAL PROTECTIVE EQUIPMENT TEST METHODS

This appendix sets forth the non-mandatory examples of tests which may be used to evaluate compliance with §1926.65(g)(4) (ii) and (iii). Other tests and other challenge agents may be used to evaluate compliance.

A. Totally-encapsulating chemical protective suit pressure test

1.0—Scope

1.1 This practice measures the ability of a gas tight totally-encapsulating chemical protective suit material, seams, and closures to maintain a fixed positive pressure. The results of this practice allow the gas tight integrity of a totally-encapsulating chemical protective suit to be evaluated.

1.2 Resistance of the suit materials to permeation, penetration, and degradation by specific hazardous substances is not determined by this test method.

2.0—Definition of terms

2.1 *Totally-encapsulated chemical protective suit (TECP suit)* means a full body garment which is constructed of protective clothing materials; covers the wearer's torso, head, arms, legs and respirator; may cover the wearer's hands and feet with tightly attached gloves and boots; completely encloses the wearer and respirator by itself or in combination with the wearer's gloves and boots.

2.2 *Protective clothing material* means any material or combination of materials used in an item of clothing for the purpose of isolating parts of the body from direct contact with a potentially hazardous liquid or gaseous chemicals.

2.3 *Gas tight* means, for the purpose of this test method, the limited flow of a gas under pressure from the inside of a TECP suit to atmosphere at a prescribed pressure and time interval.

3.0—Summary of test method

3.1 The TECP suit is visually inspected and modified for the test. The test apparatus is attached to the suit to permit inflation to the pre-test suit expansion pressure for removal of suit wrinkles and creases. The pressure is lowered to the test pressure and monitored for three minutes. If the pressure drop is excessive, the TECP suit fails the test and is removed from service. The test is repeated after leak location and repair.

4.0—Required Supplies

4.1 Source of compressed air.

4.2 Test apparatus for suit testing, including a pressure measurement device with a sensitivity of at least ¼ inch water gauge.

4.3 Vent valve closure plugs or sealing tape.

4.4 Soapy water solution and soft brush.

4.5 Stop watch or appropriate timing device.

5.0—Safety Precautions

5.1 Care shall be taken to provide the correct pressure safety devices required for the source of compressed air used.

6.0—Test Procedure

6.1 Prior to each test, the tester shall perform a visual inspection of the suit. Check the suit for seam integrity by visually examining the seams and gently pulling on the seams. Ensure that all air supply lines, fittings, visor, zippers, and valves are secure and show no signs of deterioration.

6.1.1 Seal off the vent valves along with any other normal inlet or exhaust points (such as umbilical air line fittings or face piece opening) with tape or other appropriate means (caps, plugs, fixture, etc.). Care should be exercised in the sealing process not to damage any of the suit components.

6.1.2 Close all closure assemblies.

6.1.3 Prepare the suit for inflation by providing an improvised connection point on the suit for connecting an airline. Attach the pressure test apparatus to the suit to permit suit inflation from a compressed air source equipped with a pressure indicating regulator. The leak tightness of the pressure test apparatus should be tested before and after each test by closing off the end of the tubing attached to the suit and assuring a pressure of three inches water gauge for three minutes can be maintained. If a component is removed for the test, that component shall be replaced and a second test conducted with another component removed to permit a complete test of the ensemble.

6.1.4 The pre-test expansion pressure (A) and the suit test pressure (B) shall be supplied by the suit manufacturer, but in no case shall they be less than: (A)=three inches water gauge; and (B)=two inches water gauge. The ending suit pressure (C) shall be no less than 80 percent of the test pressure (B); i.e., the pressure drop shall not exceed 20 percent of the test pressure (B).

6.1.5 Inflate the suit until the pressure inside is equal to pressure (A), the pre-test expansion suit pressure. Allow at least one minute to fill out the wrinkles in the suit. Release sufficient air to reduce the suit pressure to pressure (B), the suit test pressure. Begin timing. At the end of three minutes, record the suit pressure as pressure (C), the ending suit pressure. The difference between the suit test pressure and the ending suit test pressure (B-C) shall be defined as the suit pressure drop.

6.1.6 If the suit pressure drop is more than 20 percent of the suit test pressure (B) during the three-minute test period, the suit fails the test and shall be removed from service.

7.0—Retest Procedure

7.1 If the suit fails the test check for leaks by inflating the suit to pressure (A) and brushing or wiping the entire suit (including seams, closures, lens gaskets, glove-to-sleeve joints, etc.) with a mild soap and water solution. Observe the suit for the formation of soap bubbles, which is an indication of a leak. Repair all identified leaks.

7.2 Retest the TECP suit as outlined in Test procedure 6.0.

8.0—Report

8.1 Each TECP suit tested by this practice shall have the following information recorded:

8.1.1 Unique identification number, identifying brand name, date of purchase, material of construction, and unique fit features, e.g., special breathing apparatus.

8.1.2 The actual values for test pressures (A), (B), and (C) shall be recorded along with the specific observation times. If the ending pressure (C) is less than 80 percent of the test pressure (B), the suit shall be identified as failing the test. When possible, the specific leak location shall be identified in the test records. Retest pressure data shall be recorded as an additional test.

8.1.3 The source of the test apparatus used shall be identified and the sensitivity of the pressure gauge shall be recorded.

8.1.4 Records shall be kept for each pressure test even if repairs are being made at the test location.

CAUTION

Visually inspect all parts of the suit to be sure they are positioned correctly and secured tightly before putting the suit back into service. Special care should be taken to examine each exhaust valve to make sure it is not blocked.

Care should also be exercised to assure that the inside and outside of the suit is completely dry before it is put into storage.

B. Totally-encapsulating chemical protective suit qualitative leak test

1.0—Scope

1.1 This practice semi-qualitatively tests gas tight totally-encapsulating chemical protective suit integrity by detecting inward leakage of ammonia vapor. Since no modifications are made to the suit to carry out this test, the results from this practice provide a realistic test for the integrity of the entire suit.

1.2 Resistance of the suit materials to permeation, penetration, and degradation is not determined by this test method. ASTM test methods are available to test suit materials for these characteristics and the tests are usually conducted by the manufacturers of the suits.

2.0—Definition of terms

2.1 *Totally-encapsulated chemical protective suit (TECP suit)* means a full body garment which is constructed of protective clothing materials; covers the wearer's torso, head, arms, legs and respirator; may cover the wearer's hands and feet with tightly attached gloves and boots; completely encloses the wearer and respirator by itself or in combination with the wearer's gloves, and boots.

2.2 *Protective clothing material* means any material or combination of materials used in an item of clothing for the purpose of isolating parts of the body from direct contact with a potentially hazardous liquid or gaseous chemicals.

2.3 *Gas tight* means, for the purpose of this test method, the limited flow of a gas under pressure from the inside of a TECP suit to atmosphere at a prescribed pressure and time interval.

2.4 *Intrusion Coefficient* means a number expressing the level of protection provided by a gas tight totally-encapsulating chemical protective suit. The intrusion coefficient is calculated by dividing the test room challenge agent concentration by the concentration of challenge agent found inside the suit. The accuracy of the intrusion coefficient is dependent on the challenge agent monitoring methods. The larger the intrusion coefficient the greater the protection provided by the TECP suit.

3.0—Summary of recommended practice

3.1 The volume of concentrated aqueous ammonia solution (ammonia hydroxide NH_4OH) required to generate the test atmosphere is determined using the directions outlined in 6.1. The suit is donned by a person wearing the appropriate respiratory equipment (either a positive pressure self-contained breathing apparatus or a positive pressure supplied air respirator) and worn inside the enclosed test room. The concentrated aqueous ammonia solution is taken by the suited individual into the test room and poured into an open plastic pan. A two-minute evaporation period is observed before the test room concentration is measured, using a high range ammonia length of stain detector tube. When the ammonia vapor reaches a concentration of between 1000 and 1200 ppm, the suited individual starts a standardized exercise protocol to stress and flex the suit. After this protocol is completed, the test room concentration is measured again. The suited individual exits

the test room and his stand-by person measures the ammonia concentration inside the suit using a low range ammonia length of stain detector tube or other more sensitive ammonia detector. A stand-by person is required to observe the test individual during the test procedure; aid the person in donning and doffing the TECP suit; and monitor the suit interior. The intrusion coefficient of the suit can be calculated by dividing the average test area concentration by the interior suit concentration. A colorimetric ammonia indicator strip of bromophenol blue or equivalent is placed on the inside of the suit face piece lens so that the suited individual is able to detect a color change and know if the suit has a significant leak. If a color change is observed the individual shall leave the test room immediately.

4.0—Required supplies

4.1 A supply of concentrated aqueous ammonium hydroxide (58% by weight).

4.2 A supply of bromophenol/blue indicating paper or equivalent, sensitive to 5–10 ppm ammonia or greater over a two-minute period of exposure. [pH 3.0 (yellow) to pH 4.6 (blue)]

4.3 A supply of high range (0.5–10 volume percent) and low range (5–700 ppm) detector tubes for ammonia and the corresponding sampling pump. More sensitive ammonia detectors can be substituted for the low range detector tubes to improve the sensitivity of this practice.

4.4 A shallow plastic pan (PVC) at least 12″:14″:1″ and a half pint plastic container (PVC) with tightly closing lid.

4.5 A graduated cylinder or other volumetric measuring device of at least 50 milliliters in volume with an accuracy of at least ±1 milliliters.

5.0—SAFETY PRECAUTIONS

5.1 Concentrated aqueous ammonium hydroxide, NH_4OH, is a corrosive volatile liquid requiring eye, skin, and respiratory protection. The person conducting the test shall review the MSDS for aqueous ammonia.

5.2 Since the established permissible exposure limit for ammonia is 35 ppm as a 15 minute STEL, only persons wearing a positive pressure self-contained breathing apparatus or a positive pressure supplied air respirator shall be in the chamber. Normally only the person wearing the totally-encapsulating suit will be inside the chamber. A stand-by person shall have a positive pressure self-contained breathing apparatus, or a positive pressure supplied air respirator available to enter the test area should the suited individual need assistance.

5.3 A method to monitor the suited individual must be used during this test. Visual contact is the simplest but other methods using communication devices are acceptable.

5.4 The test room shall be large enough to allow the exercise protocol to be carried out and then to be ventilated to allow for easy exhaust of the ammonia test atmosphere after the test(s) are completed.

5.5 Individuals shall be medically screened for the use of respiratory protection and checked for allergies to ammonia before participating in this test procedure.

6.0—TEST PROCEDURE

6.1.1 Measure the test area to the nearest foot and calculate its volume in cubic feet. Multiply the test area volume by 0.2 milliliters of concentrated aqueous ammonia solution per cubic foot of test area volume to determine the approximate volume of concentrated aqueous ammonia required to generate 1000 ppm in the test area.

6.1.2 Measure this volume from the supply of concentrated aqueous ammonia and place it into a closed plastic container.

6.1.3 Place the container, several high range ammonia detector tubes, and the pump in the clean test pan and locate it near the test area entry door so that the suited individual has easy access to these supplies.

6.2.1 In a non-contaminated atmosphere, open a pre-sealed ammonia indicator strip and fasten one end of the strip to the inside of the suit face shield lens where it can be seen by the wearer. Moisten the indicator strip with distilled water. Care shall be taken not to contaminate the detector part of the indicator paper by touching it. A small piece of masking tape or equivalent should be used to attach the indicator strip to the interior of the suit face shield.

6.2.2 If problems are encountered with this method of attachment, the indicator strip can be attached to the outside of the respirator face piece lens being used during the test.

6.3 Don the respiratory protective device normally used with the suit, and then don the TECP suit to be tested. Check to be sure all openings which are intended to be sealed (zippers, gloves, etc.) are completely sealed. DO NOT, however, plug off any venting valves.

6.4 Step into the enclosed test room such as a closet, bathroom, or test booth, equipped with an exhaust fan. No air should be exhausted from the chamber during the test because this will dilute the ammonia challenge concentrations.

6.5 Open the container with the pre-measured volume of concentrated aqueous ammonia within the enclosed test room, and pour the liquid into the empty plastic test pan. Wait two minutes to allow for adequate volatilization of the concentrated aqueous ammonia. A small mixing fan can be used near the evaporation pan to increase the evaporation rate of the ammonia solution.

6.6 After two minutes a determination of the ammonia concentration within the chamber should be made using the high range colorimetric detector tube. A concentration of 1000 ppm ammonia or greater shall be generated before the exercises are started.

6.7 To test the integrity of the suit the following four minute exercise protocol should be followed:

6.7.1 Raising the arms above the head with at least 15 raising motions completed in one minute.

6.7.2 Walking in place for one minute with at least 15 raising motions of each leg in a one-minute period.

6.7.3 Touching the toes with a least 10 complete motions of the arms from above the head to touching of the toes in a one-minute period.

6.7.4 Knee bends with at least 10 complete standing and squatting motions in a one-minute period.

6.8 If at any time during the test the colorimetric indicating paper should change colors, the test should be stopped and section 6.10 and 6.12 initiated (See ¶ 4.2).

6.9 After completion of the test exercise, the test area concentration should be measured again using the high range colorimetric detector tube.

6.10 Exit the test area.

6.11 The opening created by the suit zipper or other appropriate suit penetration should be used to determine the ammonia concentration in the suit with the low range length of stain detector tube or other ammonia monitor. The internal TECP suit air should be sampled far enough from the enclosed test area to prevent a false ammonia reading.

6.12 After completion of the measurement of the suit interior ammonia concentration the test is concluded and the suit is doffed and the respirator removed.

6.13 The ventilating fan for the test room should be turned on and allowed to run for enough time to remove the ammonia gas. The fan shall be vented to the outside of the building.

6.14 Any detectable ammonia in the suit interior (five ppm ammonia (NH_3) or more for the length of stain detector tube) indicates that the suit has failed the test. When other ammonia detectors are used a lower level of detection is possible, and it should be specified as the pass/fail criteria.

6.15 By following this test method, an intrusion coefficient of approximately 200 or more can be measured with the suit in a completely operational condition. If the intrusion coefficient is 200 or more, then the suit is suitable for emergency response and field use.

7.0—Retest procedures

7.1 If the suit fails this test, check for leaks by following the pressure test in test A above.

7.2 Retest the TECP suit as outlined in the test procedure 6.0.

8.0—Report

8.1 Each gas tight totally-encapsulating chemical protective suit tested by this practice shall have the following information recorded.

8.1.1 Unique identification number, identifying brand name, date of purchase, material of construction, and unique suit features; e.g., special breathing apparatus.

8.1.2 General description of test room used for test.

8.1.3 Brand name and purchase date of ammonia detector strips and color change data.

8.1.4 Brand name, sampling range, and expiration date of the length of stain ammonia detector tubes. The brand name and model of the sampling pump should also be recorded. If another type of ammonia detector is used, it should be identified along with its minimum detection limit for ammonia.

8.1.5 Actual test results shall list the two test area concentrations, their average, the interior suit concentration, and the calculated intrusion coefficient. Retest data shall be recorded as an additional test.

8.2 The evaluation of the data shall be specified as "suit passed" or "suit failed," and the date of the test. Any detectable ammonia (five ppm or greater for the length of stain detector tube) in the suit interior indicates the suit has failed this test. When other ammonia detectors are used, a lower level of detection is possible and it should be specified as the pass fail criteria.

CAUTION

Visually inspect all parts of the suit to be sure they are positioned correctly and secured tightly before putting the suit back into service. Special care should be taken to examine each exhaust valve to make sure it is not blocked.

Care should also be exercised to assure that the inside and outside of the suit is completely dry before it is put into storage.

APPENDIX B TO § 1926.65—GENERAL DESCRIPTION AND DISCUSSION OF THE LEVELS OF PROTECTION AND PROTECTIVE GEAR

This appendix sets forth information about personal protective equipment (PPE) protection levels which may be used to assist employers in complying with the PPE requirements of this section.

As required by the standard, PPE must be selected which will protect employees from the specific hazards which they are likely to encounter during their work on-site.

Selection of the appropriate PPE is a complex process which should take into consideration a variety of factors. Key factors involved in this process are identification of the hazards, or suspected hazards; their routes of potential hazard to employees (inhalation, skin absorption, ingestion, and eye or skin contact); and the performance of the PPE *materials* (and seams) in providing a barrier to these hazards. The amount of protection provided by PPE is material-hazard specific. That is, protective equipment materials will protect well against some hazardous substances and poorly, or not at all, against others. In many instances, protective equipment materials cannot be found which will provide continuous protection from the particular hazardous substance. In these cases the breakthrough time of the protective material should exceed the work durations.

Other factors in this selection process to be considered are matching the PPE to the employee's work requirements and task-specific conditions. The durability of PPE materials, such as tear strength and seam strength, should be considered in relation to the employee's tasks. The effects of PPE in relation to heat stress and task duration are a factor in selecting and using PPE. In some cases layers of PPE may be necessary to provide sufficient protection, or to protect expensive PPE inner garments, suits or equipment.

The more that is known about the hazards at the site, the easier the job of PPE selection becomes. As more information about the hazards and conditions at the site becomes available, the site supervisor can make decisions to up-grade or down-grade the level of PPE protection to match the tasks at hand.

The following are guidelines which an employer can use to begin the selection of the appropriate PPE. As noted above, the site information may suggest the use of combinations of PPE selected from the different protection levels (i.e., A, B, C, or D) as being more suitable to the hazards of the work. It should be cautioned that the listing below does not fully address the performance of the specific PPE material in relation to the specific hazards at the job site, and that PPE selection, evaluation and re-selection is an ongoing process until sufficient information about the hazards and PPE performance is obtained.

Part A. Personal protective equipment is divided into four categories based on the degree of protection afforded. (See part B of this appendix for further explanation of Levels A, B, C, and D hazards.)

I. *Level A—* To be selected when the greatest level of skin, respiratory, and eye protection is required.

The following constitute Level A equipment; it may be used as appropriate;

1. Positive pressure, full face-piece self-contained breathing apparatus (SCBA), or positive pressure supplied air respirator with escape SCBA, approved by the National Institute for Occupational Safety and Health (NIOSH).

167

2. Totally-encapsulating chemical-protective suit.
3. Coveralls. [1]
4. Long underwear. [1]
5. Gloves, outer, chemical-resistant.
6. Gloves, inner, chemical-resistant.
7. Boots, chemical-resistant, steel toe and shank.
8. Hard hat (under suit). [1]
9. Disposable protective suit, gloves and boots (depending on suit construction, may be worn over totally-encapsulating suit).

II. *Level B*—The highest level of respiratory protection is necessary but a lesser level of skin protection is needed.

The following constitute Level B equipment; it may be used as appropriate.
1. Positive pressure, full-facepiece self-contained breathing apparatus (SCBA), or positive pressure supplied air respirator with escape SCBA (NIOSH approved).
2. Hooded chemical-resistant clothing (overalls and long-sleeved jacket; coveralls; one or two-piece chemical-splash suit; disposable chemical-resistant overalls).
3. Coveralls. [1]
4. Gloves, outer, chemical-resistant.
5. Gloves, inner, chemical-resistant.
6. Boots, outer, chemical-resistant steel toe and shank.
7. Boot-covers, outer, chemical-resistant (disposable). [1]
8. Hard hat. [1]
9. [Reserved]
10. Face shield. [1]

III. *Level C*—The concentration(s) and type(s) of airborne substance(s) is known and the criteria for using air purifying respirators are met.

The following constitute Level C equipment; it may be used as appropriate.
1. Full-face or half-mask, air purifying respirators (NIOSH approved).
2. Hooded chemical-resistant clothing (overalls; two-piece chemical-splash suit; disposable chemical-resistant overalls).
3. Coveralls. [1]
4. Gloves, outer, chemical-resistant.
5. Gloves, inner, chemical-resistant.
6. Boots (outer), chemical-resistant steel toe and shank. [1]
7. Boot-covers, outer, chemical-resistant (disposable) [1].
8. Hard hat. [1]
9. Escape mask. [1]
10. Face shield. [1]

IV. *Level D*—A work uniform affording minimal protection, used for nuisance contamination only.

The following constitute Level D equipment; it may be used as appropriate:
1. Coveralls.
2. Gloves. [1]
3. Boots/shoes, chemical-resistant steel toe and shank.

_____
[1] Optional, as applicable.

4. Boots, outer, chemical-resistant (disposable). [1]
5. Safety glasses or chemical splash goggles*.
6. Hard hat. [1]
7. Escape mask. [1]
8. Face shield. [1]

Part B. The types of hazards for which levels A, B, C, and D protection are appropriate are described below:

I. *Level A*—Level A protection should be used when:
1. The hazardous substance has been identified and requires the highest level of protection for skin, eyes, and the respiratory system based on either the measured (or potential for) high concentration of atmospheric vapors, gases, or particulates; or the site operations and work functions involve a high potential for splash, immersion, or exposure to unexpected vapors, gases, or particulates of materials that are harmful to skin or capable of being absorbed through the skin;
2. Substances with a high degree of hazard to the skin are known or suspected to be present, and skin contact is possible; or
3. Operations are being conducted in confined, poorly ventilated areas, and the absence of conditions requiring Level A have not yet been determined.

II. *Level B*—Level B protection should be used when:
1. The type and atmospheric concentration of substances have been identified and require a high level of respiratory protection, but less skin protection;
2. The atmosphere contains less than 19.5 percent oxygen; or
3. The presence of incompletely identified vapors or gases is indicated by a direct-reading organic vapor detection instrument, but vapors and gases are not suspected of containing high levels of chemicals harmful to skin or capable of being absorbed through the skin.

NOTE: This involves atmospheres with IDLH concentrations of specific substances that present severe inhalation hazards and that do not represent a severe skin hazard; or that do not meet the criteria for use of air-purifying respirators.

III. *Level C*—Level C protection should be used when:
1. The atmospheric contaminants, liquid splashes, or other direct contact will not adversely affect or be absorbed through any exposed skin;
2. The types of air contaminants have been identified, concentrations measured, and an air-purifying respirator is available that can remove the contaminants; and
3. All criteria for the use of air-purifying respirators are met.

IV. *Level D*—Level D protection should be used when:

1. The atmosphere contains no known hazard; and

2. Work functions preclude splashes, immersion, or the potential for unexpected inhalation of or contact with hazardous levels of any chemicals.

NOTE: As stated before, combinations of personal protective equipment other than those described for Levels A, B, C, and D protection may be more appropriate and may be used to provide the proper level of protection.

As an aid in selecting suitable chemical protective clothing, it should be noted that the National Fire Protection Association (NFPA) has developed standards on chemical protective clothing. The standards that have been adopted by include:

NFPA 1991—Standard on Vapor-Protective Suits for Hazardous Chemical Emergencies (EPA Level A Protective Clothing).

NFPA 1992—Standard on Liquid Splash-Protective Suits for Hazardous Chemical Emergencies (EPA Level B Protective Clothing).

NFPA 1993—Standard on Liquid Splash-Protective Suits for Non-emergency, Non-flammable Hazardous Chemical Situations (EPA Level B Protective Clothing).

These standards apply documentation and performance requirements to the manufacture of chemical protective suits. Chemical protective suits meeting these requirements are labelled as compliant with the appropriate standard. It is recommended that chemical protective suits that meet these standards be used.

APPENDIX C TO § 1926.65—COMPLIANCE GUIDELINES

1. *Occupational Safety and Health Program.* Each hazardous waste site clean-up effort will require an occupational safety and health program headed by the site coordinator or the employer's representative. The purpose of the program will be the protection of employees at the site and will be an extension of the employer's overall safety and health program. The program will need to be developed before work begins on the site and implemented as work proceeds as stated in paragraph (b). The program is to facilitate coordination and communication of safety and health issues among personnel responsible for the various activities which will take place at the site. It will provide the overall means for planning and implementing the needed safety and health training and job orientation of employees who will be working at the site. The program will provide the means for identifying and controlling worksite hazards and the means for monitoring program effectiveness. The program will need to cover the responsibilities and authority of the site coordinator or the employer's manager on the site for the safety and health of employees at the site, and the relationships with contractors or support services as to what each employer's safety and health responsibilities are for their employees on the site. Each contractor on the site needs to have its own safety and health program so structured that it will smoothly interface with the program of the site coordinator or principal contractor.

Also those employers involved with treating, storing or disposal of hazardous waste as covered in paragraph (p) must have implemented a safety and health program for their employees. This program is to include the hazard communication program required in paragraph (p)(1) and the training required in paragraphs (p)(7) and (p)(8) as parts of the employers comprehensive overall safety and health program. This program is to be in writing.

Each site or workplace safety and health program will need to include the following: (1) Policy statements of the line of authority and accountability for implementing the program, the objectives of the program and the role of the site safety and health supervisor or manager and staff; (2) means or methods for the development of procedures for identifying and controlling workplace hazards at the site; (3) means or methods for the development and communication to employees of the various plans, work rules, standard operating procedures and practices that pertain to individual employees and supervisors; (4) means for the training of supervisors and employees to develop the needed skills and knowledge to perform their work in a safe and healthful manner; (5) means to anticipate and prepare for emergency situations; and (6) means for obtaining information feedback to aid in evaluating the program and for improving the effectiveness of the program. The management and employees should be trying continually to improve the effectiveness of the program thereby enhancing the protection being afforded those working on the site.

Accidents on the site or workplace should be investigated to provide information on how such occurrences can be avoided in the future. When injuries or illnesses occur on the site or workplace, they will need to be investigated to determine what needs to be done to prevent this incident from occurring again. Such information will need to be used as feedback on the effectiveness of the program and the information turned into positive steps to prevent any reoccurrence. Receipt of employee suggestions or complaints relating to safety and health issues involved with site or workplace activities is also a feedback mechanism that can be used effectively to improve the program and may serve in part as an evaluative tool(s).

For the development and implementation of the program to be the most effective, professional safety and health personnel should be used. Certified Safety Professionals, Board Certified Industrial Hygienists or Registered Professional Safety Engineers are good examples of professional stature for safety and health managers who will administer the employer's program.

2. *Training.* The training programs for employees subject to the requirements of paragraph (e) of this standard should address: the safety and health hazards employees should expect to find on hazardous waste clean-up sites; what control measures or techniques are effective for those hazards; what monitoring procedures are effective in characterizing exposure levels; what makes an effective employer's safety and health program; what a site safety and health plan should include; hands on training with personal protective equipment and clothing they may be expected to use; the contents of the OSHA standard relevant to the employee's duties and function; and, employee's responsibilities under OSHA and other regulations. Supervisors will need training in their responsibilities under the safety and health program and its subject areas such as the spill containment program, the personal protective equipment program, the medical surveillance program, the emergency response plan and other areas.

The training programs for employees subject to the requirements of paragraph (p) of this standard should address: the employers safety and health program elements impacting employees; the hazard communication program; the medical surveillance program; the hazards and the controls for such hazards that employees need to know for their job duties and functions. All require annual refresher training.

The training programs for employees covered by the requirements of paragraph (q) of this standard should address those competencies required for the various levels of response such as: the hazards associated with hazardous substances; hazard identification and awareness; notification of appropriate persons; the need for and use of personal protective equipment including respirators; the decontamination procedures to be used; preplanning activities for hazardous substance incidents including the emergency reponse plan; company standard operating procedures for hazardous substance emergency responses; the use of the incident command system and other subjects. Hands-on training should be stressed whenever possible. Critiques done after an incident which include an evaluation of what worked and what did not and how could the incident be better handled the next time may be counted as training time.

For hazardous materials specialists (usually members of hazardous materials teams), the training should address the care, use and/or testing of chemical protective clothing including totally encapsulating suits, the medical surveillance program, the standard operating procedures for the hazardous materials team including the use of plugging and patching equipment and other subject areas.

Officers and leaders who may be expected to be in charge at an incident should be fully knowledgeable of their company's incident command system. They should know where and how to obtain additional assistance and be familiar with the local district's emergency response plan and the state emergency response plan.

Specialist employees such as technical experts, medical experts or environmental experts that work with hazardous materials in their regular jobs, who may be sent to the incident scene by the shipper, manufacturer or governmental agency to advise and assist the person in charge of the incident should have training on an annual basis. Their training should include the care and use of personal protective equipment including respirators; knowledge of the incident command system and how they are to relate to it; and those areas needed to keep them current in their respective field as it relates to safety and health involving specific hazardous substances.

Those skilled support personnel, such as employees who work for public works departments or equipment operators who operate bulldozers, sand trucks, backhoes, etc., who may be called to the incident scene to provide emergency support assistance, should have at least a safety and health briefing before entering the area of potential or actual exposure. These skilled support personnel, who have not been a part of the emergency response plan and do not meet the training requirements, should be made aware of the hazards they face and should be provided all necessary protective clothing and equipment required for their tasks.

There are two National Fire Protection Association standards, NFPA 472—"Standard for Professional Competence of Responders to Hazardous Material Incidents" and NFPA 471—"Recommended Practice for Responding to Hazardous Material Incidents", which are excellent resource documents to aid fire departments and other emergency response organizations in developing their training program materials. NFPA 472 provides guidance on the skills and knowledge needed for first responder awareness level, first responder operations level, hazmat technicians, and hazmat specialist. It also offers guidance for the officer corp who will be in charge of hazardous substance incidents.

3. *Decontamination.* Decontamination procedures should be tailored to the specific hazards of the site, and may vary in complexity and number of steps, depending on the level of hazard and the employee's exposure to the hazard. Decontamination procedures and PPE decontamination methods

170

will vary depending upon the specific substance, since one procedure or method may not work for all substances. Evaluation of decontamination methods and procedures should be performed, as necessary, to assure that employees are not exposed to hazards by re-using PPE. References in appendix D may be used for guidance in establishing an effective decontamination program. In addition, the U.S. Coast Guard's Manual, "Policy Guidance for Response to Hazardous Chemical Releases," U.S. Department of Transportation, Washington, DC (COMDTINST M16465.30) is a good reference for establishing an effective decontamination program.

4. *Emergency response plans.* States, along with designated districts within the states, will be developing or have developed local emergency response plans. These state and district plans should be utilized in the emergency response plans called for in the standard. Each employer should assure that its emergency response plan is compatible with the local plan. The major reference being used to aid in developing the state and local district plans is the *Hazardous Materials Emergency Planning Guide*, NRT–1. The current Emergency Response Guidebook from the U.S. Department of Transportation, CMA's CHEMTREC and the Fire Service Emergency Management Handbook may also be used as resources.

Employers involved with treatment, storage, and disposal facilities for hazardous waste, which have the required contingency plan called for by their permit, would not need to duplicate the same planning elements. Those items of the emergency response plan that are properly addressed in the contingency plan may be substituted into the emergency response plan required in 1926.65 or otherwise kept together for employer and employee use.

5. *Personal protective equipment programs.* The purpose of personal protective clothing and equipment (PPE) is to shield or isolate individuals from the chemical, physical, and biologic hazards that may be encountered at a hazardous substance site.

As discussed in appendix B, no single combination of protective equipment and clothing is capable of protecting against all hazards. Thus PPE should be used in conjunction with other protective methods and its effectiveness evaluated periodically.

The use of PPE can itself create significant worker hazards, such as heat stress, physical and psychological stress, and impaired vision, mobility, and communication. For any given situation, equipment and clothing should be selected that provide an adequate level of protection. However, over-protection, as well as under-protection, can be hazardous and should be avoided where possible.

Two basic objectives of any PPE program should be to protect the wearer from safety and health hazards, and to prevent injury to the wearer from incorrect use and/or malfunction of the PPE. To accomplish these goals, a comprehensive PPE program should include hazard identification, medical monitoring, environmental surveillance, selection, use, maintenance, and decontamination of PPE and its associated training.

The written PPE program should include policy statements, procedures, and guidelines. Copies should be made available to all employees, and a reference copy should be made available at the worksite. Technical data on equipment, maintenance manuals, relevant regulations, and other essential information should also be collected and maintained.

6. *Incident command system (ICS).* Paragraph 1926.65(q)(3)(ii) requires the implementation of an ICS. The ICS is an organized approach to effectively control and *manage* operations at an emergency incident. The individual in charge of the ICS is the senior official responding to the incident. The ICS is not much different than the "command post" approach used for many years by the fire service. During large complex fires involving several companies and many pieces of apparatus, a command post would be established. This enabled *one* individual to be in charge of managing the incident, rather than having several officers from different companies making separate, and sometimes conflicting, decisions. The individual in charge of the command post would delegate responsibility for performing various tasks to subordinate officers. Additionally, all communications were routed through the command post to reduce the number of radio transmissions and eliminate confusion. However, strategy, tactics, and all decisions were made by one individual.

The ICS is a very similar system, except it is implemented for emergency response to all incidents, both large and small, that involve hazardous substances.

For a small incident, the individual in charge of the ICS may perform many tasks of the ICS. There may not be any, or little, delegation of tasks to subordinates. For example, in response to a small incident, the individual in charge of the ICS, in addition to normal command activities, may become the safety officer and may designate only one employee (with proper equipment) as a back-up to provide assistance if needed. OSHA does recommend, however, that at least two employees be designated as back-up personnel since the assistance needed may include rescue.

To illustrate the operation of the ICS, the following scenario might develop during a small incident, such as an overturned tank truck with a small leak of flammable liquid.

The first responding senior officer would implement and take command of the ICS. That person would size-up the incident and determine if additional personnel and apparatus were necessary; would determine what actions to take to control the leak; and, determine the proper level of personal protective equipment. If additional assistance is not needed, the individual in charge of the ICS would implement actions to stop and control the leak using the fewest number of personnel that can effectively accomplish the tasks. The individual in charge of the ICS then would designate himself as the safety officer and two other employees as a back-up in case rescue may become necessary. In this scenario, decontamination procedures would not be necessary.

A large complex incident may require many employees and difficult, time-consuming efforts to control. In these situations, the individual in charge of the ICS will want to delegate different tasks to subordinates in order to maintain a span of control that will keep the number of subordinates, that are reporting, to a manageable level.

Delegation of task at large incidents may be by location, where the incident scene is divided into sectors, and subordinate officers coordinate activities within the sector that they have been assigned.

Delegation of tasks can also be by function. Some of the functions that the individual in charge of the ICS may want to delegate at a large incident are: medical services; evacuation; water supply; resources (equipment, apparatus); media relations; safety; and, site control (integrate activities with police for crowd and traffic control). Also for a large incident, the individual in charge of the ICS will designate several employees as back-up personnel; and a number of safety officers to monitor conditions and recommend safety precautions.

Therefore, no matter what size or complexity an incident may be, by implementing an ICS there will be *one individual in charge* who makes the decisions and gives directions; and, all actions, and communications are coordinated through one central point of command. Such a system should reduce confusion, improve safety, organize and coordinate actions, and should facilitate effective management of the incident.

7. *Site Safety and Control Plans.* The safety and security of response personnel and others in the area of an emergeny response incident site should be of primary concern to the incident commander. The use of a site safety and control plan could greatly assist those in charge of assuring the safety and health of employees on the site.

A comprehensive site safety and control plan should include the following: summary analysis of hazards on the site and a risk analysis of those hazards; site map or sketch; site work zones (clean zone, transition or decontamination zone, work or hot zone); use of the buddy system; site communications; command post or command cen-

ter; standard operating procedures and safe work practices; medical assistance and triage area; hazard monitoring plan (air contaminate monitoring, etc.); decontamination procedures and area; and other relevant areas. This plan should be a part of the employer's emergency response plan or an extension of it to the specific site.

8. *Medical surveillance programs.* Workers handling hazardous substances may be exposed to toxic chemicals, safety hazards, biologic hazards, and radiation. Therefore, a medical surveillance program is essential to assess and monitor workers' health and fitness for employment in hazardous waste operations and during the course of work; to provide emergency and other treatment as needed; and to keep accurate records for future reference.

The *Occupational Safety and Health Guidance Manual for Hazardous Waste Site Activities* developed by the National Institute for Occupational Safety and Health (NIOSH), the Occupational Safety and Health Administration (OSHA), the U.S. Coast Guard (USCG), and the Environmental Protection Agency (EPA); October 1985 provides an excellent example of the types of medical testing that should be done as part of a medical surveillance program.

9. *New Technology and Spill Containment Programs.* Where hazardous substances may be released by spilling from a container that will expose employees to the hazards of the materials, the employer will need to implement a program to contain and control the spilled material. Diking and ditching, as well as use of absorbents like diatomaceous earth, are traditional techniques which have proven to be effective over the years. However, in recent years new products have come into the marketplace, the use of which complement and increase the effectiveness of these traditional methods. These new products also provide emergency responders and others with additional tools or agents to use to reduce the hazards of spilled materials.

These agents can be rapidly applied over a large area and can be uniformly applied or otherwise can be used to build a small dam, thus improving the workers' ability to control spilled material. These application techniques enhance the intimate contact between the agent and the spilled material allowing for the quickest effect by the agent or quickest control of the spilled material. Agents are available to solidify liquid spilled materials, to suppress vapor generation from spilled materials, and to do both. Some special agents, which when applied as recommended by the manufacturer, will react in a controlled manner with the spilled material to neutralize acids or caustics, or greatly reduce the level of hazard of the spilled material.

There are several modern methods and devices for use by emergency response personnel or others involved with spill control efforts to safely apply spill control agents to control spilled material hazards. These include portable pressurized applicators similar to hand-held portable fire extinguishing devices, and nozzle and hose systems similar to portable fire fighting foam systems which allow the operator to apply the agent without having to come into contact with the spilled material. The operator is able to apply the agent to the spilled material from a remote position.

The solidification of liquids provides for rapid containment and isolation of hazardous substance spills. By directing the agent at run-off points or at the edges of the spill, the reactant solid will automatically create a barrier to slow or stop the spread of the material. Clean-up of hazardous substances is greatly improved when solidifying agents, acid or caustic neutralizers, or activated carbon adsorbents are used. Properly applied, these agents can totally solidify liquid hazardous substances or neutralize or absorb them, which results in materials which are less hazardous and easier to handle, transport, and dispose of. The concept of spill treatment, to create less hazardous substances, will improve the safety and level of protection of employees working at spill clean-up operations or emergency response operations to spills of hazardous substances.

The use of vapor suppression agents for volatile hazardous substances, such as flammable liquids and those substances which present an inhalation hazard, is important for protecting workers. The rapid and uniform distribution of the agent over the surface of the spilled material can provide quick vapor knockdown. There are temporary and long-term foam-type agents which are effective on vapors and dusts, and activated carbon adsorption agents which are effective for vapor control and soaking-up of the liquid. The proper use of hose lines or hand-held portable pressurized applicators provides good mobility and permits the worker to deliver the agent from a safe distance without having to step into the untreated spilled material. Some of these systems can be recharged in the field to provide coverage of larger spill areas than the design limits of a single charged applicator unit. Some of the more effective agents can solidify the liquid flammable hazardous substances and at the same time elevate the flashpoint above 140 °F so the resulting substance may be handled as a nonhazardous waste material if it meets the U.S. Environmental Protection Agency's 40 CFR part 261 requirements (See particularly § 261.21).

All workers performing hazardous substance spill control work are expected to wear the proper protective clothing and equipment for the materials present and to follow the employer's established standard operating procedures for spill control. All involved workers need to be trained in the established operating procedures; in the use and care of spill control equipment; and in the associated hazards and control of such hazards of spill containment work.

These new tools and agents are the things that employers will want to evaluate as part of their new technology program. The treatment of spills of hazardous substances or wastes at an emergency incident as part of the immediate spill containment and control efforts is sometimes acceptable to EPA and a permit exception is described in 40 CFR 264.1(g)(8) and 265.1(c)(11).

APPENDIX D TO § 1926.65—REFERENCES

The following references may be consulted for further information on the subject of this standard:

1. OSHA Instruction DFO CPL 2.70—January 29, 1986, *Special Emphasis Program: Hazardous Waste Sites.*

2. OSHA Instruction DFO CPL 2–2.37A—January 29, 1986, *Technical Assistance and Guidelines for Superfund and Other Hazardous Waste Site Activities.*

3. OSHA Instruction DTS CPL 2.74—January 29, 1986, *Hazardous Waste Activity Form, OSHA 175.*

4. *Hazardous Waste Inspections Reference Manual,* U.S. Department of Labor, Occupational Safety and Health Administration, 1986.

5. Memorandum of Understanding Among the National Institute for Occupational Safety and Health, the Occupational Safety and Health Administration, the United States Coast Guard, and the United States Environmental Protection Agency, *Guidance for Worker Protection During Hazardous Waste Site Investigations and Clean-up and Hazardous Substance Emergencies.* December 18, 1980.

6. *National Priorities List,* 1st Edition, October 1984; U.S. Environmental Protection Agency, Revised periodically.

7. *The Decontamination of Response Personnel,* Field Standard Operating Procedures (F.S.O.P.) 7; U.S. Environmental Protection Agency, Office of Emergency and Remedial Response, Hazardous Response Support Division, December 1984.

8. *Preparation of a Site Safety Plan,* Field Standard Operating Procedures (F.S.O.P.) 9; U.S. Environmental Protection Agency, Office of Emergency and Remedial Response, Hazardous Response Support Division, April 1985.

9. *Standard Operating Safety Guidelines;* U.S. Environmental Protection Agency, Office of Emergency and Remedial Response, Hazardous Response Support Division, Environmental Response Team; November 1984.

10. *Occupational Safety and Health Guidance Manual for Hazardous Waste Site Activities,* National Institute for Occupational Safety

and Health (NIOSH), Occupational Safety and Health Administration (OSHA), U.S. Coast Guard (USCG), and Environmental Protection Agency (EPA); October 1985.

11. *Protecting Health and Safety at Hazardous Waste Sites: An Overview*, U.S. Environmental Protection Agency, EPA/625/9–85/006; September 1985.

12. *Hazardous Waste Sites and Hazardous Substance Emergencies*, NIOSH Worker Bulletin, U.S. Department of Health and Human Services, Public Health Service, Centers for Disease Control, National Institute for Occupational Safety and Health; December 1982.

13. *Personal Protective Equipment for Hazardous Materials Incidents: A Selection Guide;* U.S. Department of Health and Human Services, Public Health Service, Centers for Disease Control, National Institute for Occupational Safety and Health; October 1984.

14. *Fire Service Emergency Management Handbook*, International Association of Fire Chiefs Foundation, 101 East Holly Avenue, Unit 10B, Sterling, VA 22170, January 1985.

15. *Emergency Response Guidebook*, U.S Department of Transportation, Washington, DC, 1987.

16. *Report to the Congress on Hazardous Materials Training, Planning and Preparedness*, Federal Emergency Management Agency, Washington, DC, July 1986.

17. *Workbook for Fire Command*, Alan V. Brunacini and J. David Beageron, National Fire Protection Association, Batterymarch Park, Quincy, MA 02269, 1985.

18. *Fire Command*, Alan V. Brunacini, National Fire Protection Association, Batterymarch Park,, Quincy, MA 02269, 1985.

19. *Incident Command System*, Fire Protection Publications, Oklahoma State University, Stillwater, OK 74078, 1983.

20. *Site Emergency Response Planning*, Chemical Manufacturers Association, Washington, DC 20037, 1986.

21. *Hazardous Materials Emergency Planning Guide*, NRT–1, Environmental Protection Agency, Washington, DC, March 1987.

22. *Community Teamwork: Working Together to Promote Hazardous Materials Transportation Safety*. U.S. Department of Transportation, Washington, DC, May 1983.

23. *Disaster Planning Guide for Business and Industry*, Federal Emergency Management Agency, Publication No. FEMA 141, August 1987.

APPENDIX E TO § 1926.65—TRAINING
CURRICULUM GUIDELINES

The following non-mandatory general criteria may be used for assistance in developing site-specific training curriculum used to meet the training requirements of 29 CFR 1926.65(e); 29 CFR 1926.65(p)(7), (p)(8)(iii); and 29 CFR 1926.65(q)(6), (q)(7), and (q)(8). These are generic guidelines and they are not presented as a complete training curriculum for any specific employer. Site-specific training

programs must be developed on the basis of a needs assessment of the hazardous waste site, RCRA/TSDF, or emergency response operation in accordance with 29 CFR 1926.65.

It is noted that the legal requirements are set forth in the regulatory text of § 1926.65. The guidance set forth here presents a highly effective program that in the areas covered would meet or exceed the regulatory requirements. In addition, other approaches could meet the regulatory requirements.

Suggested General Criteria
Definitions:

Competent means possessing the skills, knowledge, experience, and judgment to perform assigned tasks or activities satisfactorily as determined by the employer.

Demonstration means the showing by actual use of equipment or procedures.

Hands-on training means training in a simulated work environment that permits each student to have experience performing tasks, making decisions, or using equipment appropriate to the job assignment for which the training is being conducted.

Initial training means training required prior to beginning work.

Lecture means an interactive discourse with a class lead by an instructor.

Proficient means meeting a stated level of achievement.

Site-specific means individual training directed to the operations of a specific job site.

Training hours means the number of hours devoted to lecture, learning activities, small group work sessions, demonstration, evaluations, or hands-on experience.

Suggested Core Criteria:

1. *Training facility*. The training facility should have available sufficient resources, equipment, and site locations to perform didactic and hands-on training when appropriate. Training facilities should have sufficient organization, support staff, and services to conduct training in each of the courses offered.

2. *Training Director*. Each training program should be under the direction of a training director who is responsible for the program. The Training Director should have a minimum of two years of employee education experience.

3. *Instructors*. Instructors should be deem competent on the basis of previous documented experience in their area of instruction, successful completion of a "train-the-trainer" program specific to the topics they will teach, and an evaluation of instructional competence by the Training Director.

Instructors should be required to maintain professional competency by participating in continuing education or professional development programs or by completing successfully an annual refresher course and having an annual review by the Training Director.

The annual review by the Training Director should include observation of an instructor's delivery, a review of those observations with the trainer, and an analysis of any instructor or class evaluations completed by the students during the previous year.

4. *Course materials.* The Training Director should approve all course materials to be used by the training provider. Course materials should be reviewed and updated at least annually. Materials and equipment should be in good working order and maintained properly.

All written and audio-visual materials in training curricula should be peer reviewed by technically competent outside reviewers or by a standing advisory committee.

Reviews should possess expertise in the following disciplines were applicable: occupational health, industrial hygiene and safety, chemical/environmental engineering, employee education, or emergency response. One or more of the peer reviewers should be a employee experienced in the work activities to which the training is directed.

5. *Students.* The program for accepting students should include:

a. Assurance that the student is or will be involved in work where chemical exposures are likely and that the student possesses the skills necessary to perform the work.

b. A policy on the necessary medical clearance.

6. *Ratios.* Student-instructor ratios should not exceed 30 students per instructor. Hands-on activity requiring the use of personal protective equipment should have the following student-instructor ratios. For Level C or Level D personal protective equipment the ratio should be 10 students per instructor. For Level A or Level B personal protective equipment the ratio should be 5 students per instructor.

7. *Proficiency assessment.* Proficiency should be evaluated and documented by the use of a written assessment and a skill demonstration selected and developed by the Training Director and training staff. The assessment and demonstration should evaluate the knowledge and individual skills developed in the course of training. The level of minimum achievement necessary for proficiency shall be specified in writing by the Training Director.

If a written test is used, there should be a minimum of 50 questions. If a written test is used in combination with a skills demonstration, a minimum of 25 questions should be used. If a skills demonstration is used, the tasks chosen and the means to rate successful completion should be fully documented by the Training Director.

The content of the written test or of the skill demonstration shall be relevant to the objectives of the course. The written test and skill demonstration should be updated as necessary to reflect changes in the curriculum and any update should be approved by the Training Director.

The proficiency assessment methods, regardless of the approach or combination of approaches used, should be justified, document and approved by the Training Director.

The proficiency of those taking the additional courses for supervisors should be evaluated and document by using proficiency assessment methods acceptable to the Training Director. These proficiency assessment methods must reflect the additional responsibilities borne by supervisory personnel in hazardous waste operations or emergency response.

8. *Course certificate.* Written documentation should be provided to each student who satisfactorily completes the training course. The documentation should include:

a. Student's name.

b. Course title.

c. Course date.

d. Statement that the student has successfully completed the course.

e. Name and address of the training provider.

f. An individual identification number for the certificate.

g. List of the levels of personal protective equipment used by the student to complete the course.

This documentation may include a certificate and an appropriate wallet-sized laminated card with a photograph of the student and the above information. When such course certificate cards are used, the individual identification number for the training certificate should be shown on the card.

9. *Recordkeeping.* Training providers should maintain records listing the dates courses were presented, the names of the individual course attenders, the names of those students successfully completing each course, and the number of training certificates issued to each successful student. These records should be maintained for a minimum of five years after the date an individual participated in a training program offered by the training provider. These records should be available and provided upon the student's request or as mandated by law.

10. *Program quality control.* The Training Director should conduct or direct an annual written audit of the training program. Program modifications to address deficiencies, if any, should be documented, approved, and implemented by the training provider. The audit and the program modification documents should be maintained at the training facility.

Suggested Program Quality Control Criteria

Factors listed here are suggested criteria for determining the quality and appropriateness of employee health and safety training for hazardous waste operations and emergency response.

A. *Training Plan.*

Adequacy and appropriateness of the training program's curriculum development, instructor training, distribution of course materials, and direct student training should be considered, including

1. The duration of training, course content, and course schedules/agendas;

2. The different training requirements of the various target populations, as specified in the appropriate generic training curriculum;

3. The process for the development of curriculum, which includes appropriate technical input, outside review, evaluation, program pretesting.

4. The adequate and appropriate inclusion of hands-on, demonstration, and instruction methods;

5. Adequate monitoring of student safety, progress, and performance during the training.

B. *Program management, Training Director, staff, and consultants.*

Adequacy and appropriateness of staff performance and delivering an effective training program should be considered, including

1. Demonstration of the training director's leadership in assuring quality of health and safety training.

2. Demonstration of the competency of the staff to meet the demands of delivering high quality hazardous waste employee health and safety training.

3. Organization charts establishing clear lines of authority.

4. Clearly defined staff duties including the relationship of the training staff to the overall program.

5. Evidence that the training organizational structure suits the needs of the training program.

6. Appropriateness and adequacy of the training methods used by the instructors.

7. Sufficiency of the time committed by the training director and staff to the training program.

8. Adequacy of the ratio of training staff to students.

9. Availability and commitment of the training program of adequate human and equipment resources in the areas of

a. Health effects,

b. Safety,

c. Personal protective equipment (PPE),

d. Operational procedures,

e. Employee protection practices/procedures.

10. Appropriateness of management controls.

11. Adequacy of the organization and appropriate resources assigned to assure appropriate training.

12. In the case of multiple-site training programs, adequacy of satellite centers management.

C. *Training facilities and resources.*

Adequacy and appropriateness of the facilities and resources for supporting the training program should be considered, including,

1. Space and equipment to conduct the training.

2. Facilities for representative hands-on training.

3. In the case of multiple-site programs, equipment and facilities at the satellite centers.

4. Adequacy and appropriateness of the quality control and evaluations program to account for instructor performance.

5. Adequacy and appropriateness of the quality control and evaluation program to ensure appropriate course evaluation, feedback, updating, and corrective action.

6. Adequacy and appropriateness of disciplines and expertise being used within the quality control and evaluation program.

7. Adequacy and appropriateness of the role of student evaluations to provide feedback for training program improvement.

D. *Quality control and evaluation.*

Adequacy and appropriateness of quality control and evaluation plans for training programs should be considered, including:

1. A balanced advisory committee and/or competent outside reviewers to give overall policy guidance;

2. Clear and adequate definition of the composition and active programmatic role of the advisory committee or outside reviewers.

3. Adequacy of the minutes or reports of the advisory committee or outside reviewers' meetings or written communication.

4. Adequacy and appropriateness of the quality control and evaluations program to account for instructor performance.

5. Adequacy and appropriateness of the quality control and evaluation program to ensure appropriate course evaluation, feedback, updating, and corrective action.

6. Adequacy and appropriateness of disciplines and expertise being used within the quality control and evaluation program.

7. Adequacy and appropriateness of the role of student evaluations to provide feedback for training program improvement.

E. *Students*

Adequacy and appropriateness of the program for accepting students should be considered, including

1. Assurance that the student already possess the necessary skills for their job, including necessary documentation.

2. Appropriateness of methods the program uses to ensure that recruits are capable of satisfactorily completing training.

3. Review and compliance with any medical clearance policy.

F. *Institutional Environment and Administrative Support.* The adequacy and appropriateness of the institutional environment and administrative support system for the training program should be considered, including

1. Adequacy of the institutional commitment to the employee training program.

2. Adequacy and appropriateness of the administrative structure and administrative support.

G. Summary of Evaluation Questions Key questions for evaluating the quality and appropriateness of an overall training program should include the following:

1. Are the program objectives clearly stated?

2. Is the program accomplishing its objectives?

3. Are appropriate facilities and staff available?

4. Is there an appropriate mix of classroom, demonstration, and hands-on training?

5. Is the program providing quality employee health and safety training that fully meets the intent of regulatory requirements?

6. What are the program's main strengths?

7. What are the program's main weaknesses?

8. What is recommended to improve the program?

9. Are instructors instructing according to their training outlines?

10. Is the evaluation tool current and appropriate for the program content?

11. Is the course material current and relevant to the target group?

Suggested Training Curriculum Guidelines

The following training curriculum guidelines are for those operations specifically identified in 29 CFR 1926.65 as requiring training. Issues such as qualifications of instructors, training certification, and similar criteria appropriate to all categories of operations addressed in 1926.65 have been covered in the preceding section and are not re-addressed in each of the generic guidelines. Basic core requirements for training programs that are addressed include

1. General Hazardous Waste Operations

2. RCRA operations—Treatment, storage, and disposal facilities.

3. Emergency Response.

A. General Hazardous Waste Operations and Site-specific Training 1. *Off-site training.*

Minimum training course content for hazardous waste operations, required by 29 CFR 1926.65(e), should include the following topics or procedures:

a. *Regulatory knowledge.*

(1) A review of 29 CFR 1926.65 and the core elements of an occupational safety and health program.

(2) The content of a medical surveillance program as outlined in 29 CFR 1926.65(f).

(3) The content of an effective site safety and health plan consistent with the requirements of 29 CFR 1926.65(b)(4)(ii).

(4) Emergency response plan and procedures as outlined in 29 CFR 1910.38 and 29 CFR 1926.65(l).

(5) Adequate illumination.

(6) Sanitation recommendation and equipment.

(7) Review and explanation of OSHA's hazard-communication standard (29 CFR 1910.1200) and lock-out-tag-out standard (29 CFR 1910.147).

(8) Review of other applicable standards including but not limited to the construction standards (29 CFR part 1926).

(9) Rights and responsibilities of employers and employees under applicable OSHA and EPA laws.

b. *Technical knowledge.* (1) Type of potential exposures to chemical, biological, and radiological hazards; types of human responses to these hazards and recognition of those responses; principles of toxicology and information about acute and chronic hazards; health and safety considerations of new technology.

(2) Fundamentals of chemical hazards including but not limited to vapor pressure, boiling points, flash points, ph, other physical and chemical properties.

(3) Fire and explosion hazards of chemicals.

(4) General safety hazards such as but not limited to electrical hazards, powered equipment hazards, motor vehicle hazards, walking-working surface hazards, excavation hazards, and hazards associated with working in hot and cold temperature extremes.

(5) Review and knowledge of confined space entry procedures in 29 CFR 1910.146.

(6) Work practices to minimize employee risk from site hazards.

(7) Safe use of engineering controls, equipment, and any new relevant safety technology or safety procedures.

(8) Review and demonstration of competency with air sampling and monitoring equipment that may be used in a site monitoring program.

(9) Container sampling procedures and safeguarding; general drum and container handling procedures including special requirement for laboratory waste packs, shock-sensitive wastes, and radioactive wastes.

(10) The elements of a spill control program.

(11) Proper use and limitations of material handling equipment.

(12) Procedures for safe and healthful preparation of containers for shipping and transport.

(13) Methods of communication including those used while wearing respiratory protection.

c. *Technical skills.* (1) Selection, use maintenance, and limitations of personal protective equipment including the components and procedures for carrying out a respirator program to comply with 29 CFR 1910.134.

(2) Instruction in decontamination programs including personnel, equipment, and hardware; hands-on training including level

177

A, B, and C ensembles and appropriate decontamination lines; field activities including the donning and doffing of protective equipment to a level commensurate with the employee's anticipated job function and responsibility and to the degree required by potential hazards.

(3) Sources for additional hazard information; exercises using relevant manuals and hazard coding systems.

d. *Additional suggested items.* (1) A laminated, dated card or certificate with photo, denoting limitations and level of protection for which the employee is trained should be issued to those students successfully completing a course.

(2) Attendance should be required at all training modules, with successful completion of exercises and a final written or oral examination with at least 50 questions.

(3) A minimum of one-third of the program should be devoted to hands-on exercises.

(4) A curriculum should be established for the 8-hour refresher training required by 29 CFR 1926.65(e)(8), with delivery of such courses directed toward those areas of previous training that need improvement or reemphasis.

(5) A curriculum should be established for the required 8-hour training for supervisors. Demonstrated competency in the skills and knowledge provided in a 40-hour course should be a prerequisite for supervisor training.

2. *Refresher training.* The 8-hour annual refresher training required in 29 CFR 1926.65(e)(8) should be conducted by qualified training providers. Refresher training should include at a minimum the following topics and procedures:

(a) Review of and retraining on relevant topics covered in the 40-hour program, as appropriate, using reports by the students on their work experiences.

(b) Update on developments with respect to material covered in the 40-hour course.

(c) Review of changes to pertinent provisions of EPA or OSHA standards or laws.

(d) Introduction of additional subject areas as appropriate.

(e) Hands-on review of new or altered PPE or decontamination equipment or procedures. Review of new developments in personal protective equipment.

(f) Review of newly developed air and contaminant monitoring equipment.

3. *On-site training.* a. The employer should provide employees engaged in hazardous waste site activities with information and training prior to initial assignment into their work area, as follows:

(1) The requirements of the hazard communication program including the location and availability of the written program, required lists of hazardous chemicals, and safety data sheets.

(2) Activities and locations in their work area where hazardous substance may be present.

(3) Methods and observations that may be used to detect the present or release of a hazardous chemical in the work area (such as monitoring conducted by the employer, continuous monitoring devices, visual appearances, or other evidence (sight, sound or smell) of hazardous chemicals being released, and applicable alarms from monitoring devices that record chemical releases.

(4) The physical and health hazards of substances known or potentially present in the work area.

(5) The measures employees can take to help protect themselves from work-site hazards, including specific procedures the employer has implemented.

(6) An explanation of the labeling system and safety data sheets and how employees can obtain and use appropriate hazard information.

(7) The elements of the confined space program including special PPE, permits, monitoring requirements, communication procedures, emergency response, and applicable lock-out procedures.

b. The employer should provide hazardous waste employees information and training and should provide a review and access to the site safety and plan as follows:

(1) Names of personnel and alternate responsible for site safety and health.

(2) Safety and health hazards present on the site.

(3) Selection, use, maintenance, and limitations of personal protective equipment specific to the site.

(4) Work practices by which the employee can minimize risks from hazards.

(5) Safe use of engineering controls and equipment available on site.

(6) Safe decontamination procedures established to minimize employee contact with hazardous substances, including:

(A) Employee decontamination,

(B) Clothing decontamination, and

(C) Equipment decontamination.

(7) Elements of the site emergency response plan, including:

(A) Pre-emergency planning.

(B) Personnel roles and lines of authority and communication.

(C) Emergency recognition and prevention.

(D) Safe distances and places of refuge.

(E) Site security and control.

(F) Evacuation routes and procedures.

(G) Decontamination procedures not covered by the site safety and health plan.

(H) Emergency medical treatment and first aid.

(I) Emergency equipment and procedures for handling emergency incidents.

c. The employer should provide hazardous waste employees information and training on personal protective equipment used at the site, such as the following:

(1) PPE to be used based upon known or anticipated site hazards.

(2) PPE limitations of materials and construction; limitations during temperature extremes, heat stress, and other appropriate medical considerations; use and limitations of respirator equipment as well as documentation procedures as outlined in 29 CFR 1910.134.

(3) PPE inspection procedures prior to, during, and after use.

(4) PPE donning and doffing procedures.

(5) PPE decontamination and disposal procedures.

(6) PPE maintenance and storage.

(7) Task duration as related to PPE limitations.

d. The employer should instruct the employee about the site medical surveillance program relative to the particular site, including

(1) Specific medical surveillance programs that have been adapted for the site.

(2) Specific signs and symptoms related to exposure to hazardous materials on the site.

(3) The frequency and extent of periodic medical examinations that will be used on the site.

(4) Maintenance and availability of records.

(5) Personnel to be contacted and procedures to be followed when signs and symptoms of exposures are recognized.

e. The employees will review and discuss the site safety plan as part of the training program. The location of the site safety plan and all written programs should be discussed with employees including a discussion of the mechanisms for access, review, and references described.

B. RCRA Operations Training for Treatment, Storage and Disposal Facilities.

1. As a minimum, the training course required in 29 CFR 1926.65 (p) should include the following topics:

(a) Review of the applicable paragraphs of 29 CFR 1926.65 and the elements of the employer's occupational safety and health plan.

(b) Review of relevant hazards such as, but not limited to, chemical, biological, and radiological exposures; fire and explosion hazards; thermal extremes; and physical hazards.

(c) General safety hazards including those associated with electrical hazards, powered equipment hazards, lock-out-tag-out procedures, motor vehicle hazards and walking-working surface hazards.

(d) Confined-space hazards and procedures.

(e) Work practices to minimize employee risk from workplace hazards.

(f) Emergency response plan and procedures including first aid meeting the requirements of paragraph (p)(8).

(g) A review of procedures to minimize exposure to hazardous waste and various type of waste streams, including the materials handling program and spill containment program.

(h) A review of hazard communication programs meeting the requirements of 29 CFR 1910.1200.

(i) A review of medical surveillance programs meeting the requirements of 29 CFR 1926.65(p)(3) including the recognition of signs and symptoms of overexposure to hazardous substance including known synergistic interactions.

(j) A review of decontamination programs and procedures meeting the requirements of 29 CFR 1926.65(p)(4).

(k) A review of an employer's requirements to implement a training program and its elements.

(l) A review of the criteria and programs for proper selection and use of personal protective equipment, including respirators.

(m) A review of the applicable appendices to 29 CFR 1926.65.

(n) Principles of toxicology and biological monitoring as they pertain to occupational health.

(o) Rights and responsibilities of employees and employers under applicable OSHA and EPA laws.

(p) Hands-on exercises and demonstrations of competency with equipment to illustrate the basic equipment principles that may be used during the performance of work duties, including the donning and doffing of PPE.

(q) Sources of reference, efficient use of relevant manuals, and knowledge of hazard coding systems to include information contained in hazardous waste manifests.

(r) At least 8 hours of hands-on training.

(s) Training in the job skills required for an employee's job function and responsibility before they are permitted to participate in or supervise field activities.

2. The individual employer should provide hazardous waste employees with information and training prior to an employee's initial assignment into a work area. The training and information should cover the following topics:

(a) The Emergency response plan and procedures including first aid.

(b) A review of the employer's hazardous waste handling procedures including the materials handling program and elements of the spill containment program, location of spill response kits or equipment, and the names of those trained to respond to releases.

(c) The hazardous communication program meeting the requirements of 29 CFR 1910.1200.

(d) A review of the employer's medical surveillance program including the recognition of signs and symptoms of exposure to relevant hazardous substance including known synergistic interactions.

(e) A review of the employer's decontamination program and procedures.

(f) An review of the employer's training program and the parties responsible for that program.

(g) A review of the employer's personal protective equipment program including the proper selection and use of PPE based upon specific site hazards.

(h) All relevant site-specific procedures addressing potential safety and health hazards. This may include, as appropriate, biological and radiological exposures, fire and explosion hazards, thermal hazards, and physical hazards such as electrical hazards, powered equipment hazards, lock-out-tag-out hazards, motor vehicle hazards, and walking-working surface hazards.

(i) Safe use engineering controls and equipment on site.

(j) Names of personnel and alternates responsible for safety and health.

C. Emergency response training.

Federal OSHA standards in 29 CFR 1926.65(q) are directed toward private sector emergency responders. Therefore, the guidelines provided in this portion of the appendix are directed toward that employee population. However, they also impact indirectly through State OSHA or USEPA regulations some public sector emergency responders. Therefore, the guidelines provided in this portion of the appendix may be applied to both employee populations.

States with OSHA state plans must cover their employees with regulations at least as effective as the Federal OSHA standards. Public employees in states without approved state OSHA programs covering hazardous waste operations and emergency response are covered by the U.S. EPA under 40 CFR 311, a regulation virtually identical to § 1926.65.

Since this is a non-mandatory appendix and therefore not an enforceable standard, OSHA recommends that those employers, employees or volunteers in public sector emergency response organizations outside Federal OSHA jurisdiction consider the following criteria in developing their own training programs. A unified approach to training at the community level between emergency response organizations covered by Federal OSHA and those not covered directly by Federal OSHA can help ensure an effective community response to the release or potential release of hazardous substances in the community.

a. General considerations.

Emergency response organizations are required to consider the topics listed in § 1926.65(q)(6). Emergency response organizations may use some or all of the following topics to supplement those mandatory topics when developing their response training programs. Many of the topics would require an interaction between the response provider and the individuals responsible for the site where the response would be expected.

(1) Hazard recognition, including:

(A) Nature of hazardous substances present,

(B) Practical applications of hazard recognition, including presentations on biology, chemistry, and physics.

(2) Principles of toxicology, biological monitoring, and risk assessment.

(3) Safe work practices and general site safety.

(4) Engineering controls and hazardous waste operations.

(5) Site safety plans and standard operating procedures.

(6) Decontamination procedures and practices.

(7) Emergency procedures, first aid, and self-rescue.

(8) Safe use of field equipment.

(9) Storage, handling, use and transportation of hazardous substances.

(10) Use, care, and limitations of personal protective equipment.

(11) Safe sampling techniques.

(12) Rights and responsibilities of employees under OSHA and other related laws concerning right-to-know, safety and health, compensations and liability.

(13) Medical monitoring requirements.

(14) Community relations.

b. Suggested criteria for specific courses.

(1) *First responder awareness level.*

(A) Review of and demonstration of competency in performing the applicable skills of 29 CFR 1926.65(q).

(B) Hands-on experience with the U.S. Department of Transportation's *Emergency Response Guidebook* (ERG) and familiarization with OSHA standard 29 CFR 1926.60.

(C) Review of the principles and practices for analyzing an incident to determine both the hazardous substances present and the basic hazard and response information for each hazardous substance present.

(D) Review of procedures for implementing actions consistent with the local emergency response plan, the organization's standard operating procedures, and the current edition of DOT's ERG including emergency notification procedures and follow-up communications.

(E) Review of the expected hazards including fire and explosions hazards, confined space hazards, electrical hazards, powered equipment hazards, motor vehicle hazards, and walking-working surface hazards.

(F) Awareness and knowledge of the competencies for the First Responder at the Awareness Level covered in the National Fire Protection Association's Standard No. 472, *Professional Competence of Responders to Hazardous Materials Incidents.*

(2) *First responder operations level.*

(A) Review of and demonstration of competency in performing the applicable skills of 29 CFR 1926.65(q).

(B) Hands-on experience with the U.S. Department of Transportation's *Emergency Response Guidebook* (ERG), manufacturer safety data sheets, CHEMTREC/CANUTEC, shipper or manufacturer contacts and other relevant sources of information addressing hazardous substance releases. Familiarization with OSHA standard 29 CFR 1926.60.

(C) Review of the principles and practices for analyzing an incident to determine the hazardous substances present, the likely behavior of the hazardous substance and its container, the types of hazardous substance transportation containers and vehicles, the types and selection of the appropriate defensive strategy for containing the release.

(D) Review of procedures for implementing continuing response actions consistent with the local emergency response plan, the organization's standard operating procedures, and the current edition of DOT's ERG including extended emergency notification procedures and follow-up communications.

(E) Review of the principles and practice for proper selection and use of personal protective equipment.

(F) Review of the principles and practice of personnel and equipment decontamination.

(G) Review of the expected hazards including fire and explosions hazards, confined space hazards, electrical hazards, powered equipment hazards, motor vehicle hazards, and walking-working surface hazards.

(H) Awareness and knowledge of the competencies for the First Responder at the Operations Level covered in the National Fire Protection Association's Standard No. 472, *Professional Competence of Responders to Hazardous Materials Incidents.*

(3) *Hazardous materials technician.*

(A) Review of and demonstration of competency in performing the applicable skills of 29 CFR 1926.65(q).

(B) Hands-on experience with written and electronic information relative to response decision making including but not limited to the U.S. Department of Transportation's *Emergency Response Guidebook* (ERG), manufacturer safety data sheets, CHEMTREC/CANUTEC, shipper or manufacturer contacts, computer data bases and response models, and other relevant sources of information addressing hazardous substance releases. Familiarization with 29 CFR 1926.60.

(C) Review of the principles and practices for analyzing an incident to determine the hazardous substances present, their physical and chemical properties, the likely behavior of the hazardous substance and its container, the types of hazardous substance transportation containers and vehicles involved in the release, the appropriate strategy for approaching release sites and containing the release.

(D) Review of procedures for implementing continuing response actions consistent with the local emergency response plan, the organization's standard operating procedures, and the current edition of DOT's ERG including extended emergency notification procedures and follow-up communications.

(E) Review of the principles and practice for proper selection and use of personal protective equipment.

(F) Review of the principles and practices of establishing exposure zones, proper decontamination and medical surveillance stations and procedures.

(G) Review of the expected hazards including fire and explosions hazards, confined space hazards, electrical hazards, powered equipment hazards, motor vehicle hazards, and walking-working surface hazards.

(H) Awareness and knowledge of the competencies for the Hazardous Materials Technician covered in the National Fire Protection Association's Standard No. 472, *Professional Competence of Responders to Hazardous Materials Incidents.*

(4) *Hazardous materials specialist.*

(A) Review of and demonstration of competency in performing the applicable skills of 29 CFR 1926.65(q).

(B) Hands-on experience with retrieval and use of written and electronic information relative to response decision making including but not limited to the U.S. Department of Transportation's *Emergency Response Guidebook* (ERG), manufacturer safety data sheets, CHEMTREC/CANUTEC, shipper or manufacturer contacts, computer data bases and response models, and other relevant sources of information addressing hazardous substance releases. Familiarization with 29 CFR 1926.60.

(C) Review of the principles and practices for analyzing an incident to determine the hazardous substances present, their physical and chemical properties, and the likely behavior of the hazardous substance and its container, vessel, or vehicle.

(D) Review of the principles and practices for identification of the types of hazardous substance transportation containers, vessels and vehicles involved in the release; selecting and using the various types of equipment available for plugging or patching transportation containers, vessels or vehicles; organizing and directing the use of multiple teams of hazardous material technicians and selecting the appropriate strategy for approaching release sites and containing or stopping the release.

(E) Review of procedures for implementing continuing response actions consistent with the local emergency response plan, the organization's standard operating procedures, including knowledge of the available public and private response resources, establishment of an incident command post, direction of hazardous material technician teams, and

181

extended emergency notification procedures and follow-up communications.

(F) Review of the principles and practice for proper selection and use of personal protective equipment.

(G) Review of the principles and practices of establishing exposure zones and proper decontamination, monitoring and medical surveillance stations and procedures.

(H) Review of the expected hazards including fire and explosions hazards, confined space hazards, electrical hazards, powered equipment hazards, motor vehicle hazards, and walking-working surface hazards.

(I) Awareness and knowledge of the competencies for the Off-site Specialist Employee covered in the National Fire Protection Association's Standard No. 472, *Professional Competence of Responders to Hazardous Materials Incidents.*

(5) *Incident commander.* The incident commander is the individual who, at any one time, is responsible for and in control of the response effort. This individual is the person responsible for the direction and coordination of the response effort. An incident commander's position should be occupied by the most senior, appropriately trained individual present at the response site. Yet, as necessary and appropriate by the level of response provided, the position may be occupied by many individuals during a particular response as the need for greater authority, responsibility, or training increases. It is possible for the first responder at the awareness level to assume the duties of incident commander until a more senior and appropriately trained individual arrives at the response site.

Therefore, any emergency responder expected to perform as an incident commander should be trained to fulfill the obligations of the position at the level of response they will be providing including the following:

(A) Ability to analyze a hazardous substance incident to determine the magnitude of the response problem.

(B) Ability to plan and implement an appropriate response plan within the capabilities of available personnel and equipment.

(C) Ability to implement a response to favorably change the outcome of the incident in a manner consistent with the local emergency response plan and the organization's standard operating procedures.

(D) Ability to evaluate the progress of the emergency response to ensure that the response objectives are being met safely, effectively, and efficiently.

(E) Ability to adjust the response plan to the conditions of the response and to notify

higher levels of response when required by the changes to the response plan.

[58 FR 35129, June 30, 1993, as amended at 59 FR 43275, Aug. 22, 1994; 61 FR 5510, Feb. 13, 1996; 77 FR 17890, Mar. 26, 2012; 78 FR 9315, Feb. 8, 2013]

§ 1926.66 Criteria for design and construction of spray booths.

(a) *Definitions applicable to this section*—(1) *Aerated solid powders.* Aerated powders shall mean any powdered material used as a coating material which shall be fluidized within a container by passing air uniformly from below. It is common practice to fluidize such materials to form a fluidized powder bed and then dip the part to be coated into the bed in a manner similar to that used in liquid dipping. Such beds are also used as sources for powder spray operations.

(2) *Spraying area.* Any area in which dangerous quantities of flammable vapors or mists, or combustible residues, dusts, or deposits are present due to the operation of spraying processes.

(3) *Spray booth.* A power-ventilated structure provided to enclose or accommodate a spraying operation to confine and limit the escape of spray, vapor, and residue, and to safely conduct or direct them to an exhaust system.

(4) *Waterwash spray booth.* A spray booth equipped with a water washing system designed to minimize dusts or residues entering exhaust ducts and to permit the recovery of overspray finishing material.

(5) *Dry spray booth.* A spray booth not equipped with a water washing system as described in paragraph (a)(4) of this section. A dry spray booth may be equipped with

(i) Distribution or baffle plates to promote an even flow of air through the booth or cause the deposit of overspray before it enters the exhaust duct; or

(ii) Overspray dry filters to minimize dusts; or

(iii) Overspray dry filters to minimize dusts or residues entering exhaust ducts; or

(iv) Overspray dry filter rolls designed to minimize dusts or residues entering exhaust ducts; or

(v) Where dry powders are being sprayed, with powder collection systems so arranged in the exhaust to capture oversprayed material.

(6) *Fluidized bed.* A container holding powder coating material which is aerated from below so as to form an air-supported expanded cloud of such material through which the preheated object to be coated is immersed and transported.

(7) *Electrostatic fluidized bed.* A container holding powder coating material which is aerated from below so as to form an air-supported expanded cloud of such material which is electrically charged with a charge opposite to the charge of the object to be coated; such object is transported, through the container immediately above the charged and aerated materials in order to be coated.

(8) *Approved.* Shall mean approved and listed by a nationally recognized testing laboratory.

(9) *Listed.* See "approved" in paragraph (a)(8) of this section.

(b) *Spray booths—(1) Construction.* Spray booths shall be substantially constructed of steel, securely and rigidly supported, or of concrete or masonry except that aluminum or other substantial noncombustible material may be used for intermittent or low volume spraying. Spray booths shall be designed to sweep air currents toward the exhaust outlet.

(2) *Interiors.* The interior surfaces of spray booths shall be smooth and continuous without edges and otherwise designed to prevent pocketing of residues and facilitate cleaning and washing without injury.

(3) *Floors.* The floor surface of a spray booth and operator's working area, if combustible, shall be covered with noncombustible material of such character as to facilitate the safe cleaning and removal of residues.

(4) *Distribution or baffle plates.* Distribution or baffle plates, if installed to promote an even flow of air through the booth or cause the deposit of overspray before it enters the exhaust duct, shall be of noncombustible material and readily removable or accessible on both sides for cleaning. Such plates shall not be located in exhaust ducts.

(5) *Dry type overspray collectors—(exhaust air filters).* In conventional dry type spray booths, overspray dry filters or filter rolls, if installed, shall conform to the following:

(i) The spraying operations except electrostatic spraying operations shall be so designed, installed and maintained that the average air velocity over the open face of the booth (or booth cross section during spraying operations) shall be not less than 100 linear feet per minute. Electrostatic spraying operations may be conducted with an air velocity over the open face of the booth of not less than 60 linear feet per minute, or more, depending on the volume of the finishing material being applied and its flammability and explosion characteristics. Visible gauges or audible alarm or pressure activated devices shall be installed to indicate or insure that the required air velocity is maintained. Filter rolls shall be inspected to insure proper replacement of filter media.

(ii) All discarded filter pads and filter rolls shall be immediately removed to a safe, well-detached location or placed in a water-filled metal container and disposed of at the close of the day's operation unless maintained completely in water.

(iii) The location of filters in a spray booth shall be so as to not reduce the effective booth enclosure of the articles being sprayed.

(iv) Space within the spray booth on the downstream and upstream sides of filters shall be protected with approved automatic sprinklers.

(v) Filters or filter rolls shall not be used when applying a spray material known to be highly susceptible to spontaneous heating and ignition.

(vi) Clean filters or filter rolls shall be noncombustible or of a type having a combustibility not in excess of class 2 filters as listed by Underwriters' Laboratories, Inc. Filters and filter rolls shall not be alternately used for different types of coating materials, where the combination of materials may be conducive to spontaneous ignition.

(6) *Frontal area.* Each spray booth having a frontal area larger than 9 square feet shall have a metal deflector or curtain not less than 2½ inches (5.35 cm) deep installed at the upper outer edge of the booth over the opening.

(7) *Conveyors.* Where conveyors are arranged to carry work into or out of spray booths, the openings therefor shall be as small as practical.

(8) *Separation of operations.* Each spray booth shall be separated from other operations by not less than 3 feet (0.912 m), or by a greater distance, or by such partition or wall as to reduce the danger from juxtaposition of hazardous operations. See also paragraph (c)(1) of this section.

(9) *Cleaning.* Spray booths shall be so installed that all portions are readily accessible for cleaning. A clear space of not less than 3 feet (0.912 m) on all sides shall be kept free from storage or combustible construction.

(10) *Illumination.* When spraying areas are illuminated through glass panels or other transparent materials, only fixed lighting units shall be used as a source of illumination. Panels shall effectively isolate the spraying area from the area in which the lighting unit is located, and shall be of a noncombustible material of such a nature or so protected that breakage will be unlikely. Panels shall be so arranged that normal accumulations of residue on the exposed surface of the panel will not be raised to a dangerous temperature by radiation or conduction from the source of illumination.

(c) *Electrical and other sources of ignition*—(1) *Conformance.* All electrical equipment, open flames and other sources of ignition shall conform to the requirements of this paragraph, except as follows:

(i) Electrostatic apparatus shall conform to the requirements of paragraphs (e) and (f) of this section;

(ii) Drying, curing, and fusion apparatus shall conform to the requirements of paragraph (g) of this section;

(iii) [Reserved]

(iv) Powder coating equipment shall conform to the requirements of paragraph (c)(1) of this section.

(2) *Minimum separation.* There shall be no open flame or spark producing equipment in any spraying area nor within 20 feet (6.08 m) thereof, unless separated by a partition.

(3) *Hot surfaces.* Space-heating appliances, steampipes, or hot surfaces shall not be located in a spraying area where deposits of combustible residues may readily accumulate.

(4) *Wiring conformance.* Electrical wiring and equipment shall conform to the provisions of this paragraph and shall otherwise be in accordance with subpart S of this part.

(5) *Combustible residues, areas.* Unless specifically approved for locations containing both deposits of readily ignitable residue and explosive vapors, there shall be no electrical equipment in any spraying area, whereon deposits of combustible residues may readily accumulate, except wiring in rigid conduit or in boxes or fittings containing no taps, splices, or terminal connections.

(6) *Wiring type approved.* Electrical wiring and equipment not subject to deposits of combustible residues but located in a spraying area as herein defined shall be of explosion-proof type approved for Class I, group D locations and shall otherwise conform to the provisions of subpart S of this part, for Class I, Division 1, Hazardous Locations. Electrical wiring, motors, and other equipment outside of but within 20 feet (6.08 m) of any spraying area, and not separated therefrom by partitions, shall not produce sparks under normal operating conditions and shall otherwise conform to the provisions of subpart S of this part for Class I, Division 2 Hazardous Locations.

(7) *Lamps.* Electric lamps outside of, but within 20 feet (6.08 m) of any spraying area, and not separated therefrom by a partition, shall be totally enclosed to prevent the falling of hot particles and shall be protected from mechanical injury by suitable guards or by location.

(8) *Portable lamps.* Portable electric lamps shall not be used in any spraying area during spraying operations. Portable electric lamps, if used during cleaning or repairing operations, shall be of the type approved for hazardous Class I locations.

(9) *Grounding.* (i) All metal parts of spray booths, exhaust ducts, and piping systems conveying flammable or combustible liquids or aerated solids shall be properly electrically grounded in an effective and permanent manner.

(d) *Ventilation*—(1) *Conformance.* Ventilating and exhaust systems shall be in accordance with the Standard for

Blower and Exhaust Systems for Vapor Removal, NFPA No. 91–1961, where applicable and shall also conform to the provisions of this section.

(2) *General.* All spraying areas shall be provided with mechanical ventilation adequate to remove flammable vapors, mists, or powders to a safe location and to confine and control combustible residues so that life is not endangered. Mechanical ventilation shall be kept in operation at all times while spraying operations are being conducted and for a sufficient time thereafter to allow vapors from drying coated articles and drying finishing material residue to be exhausted.

(3) *Independent exhaust.* Each spray booth shall have an independent exhaust duct system discharging to the exterior of the building, except that multiple cabinet spray booths in which identical spray finishing material is used with a combined frontal area of not more than 18 square feet may have a common exhaust. If more than one fan serves one booth, all fans shall be so interconnected that one fan cannot operate without all fans being operated.

(4) *Fan-rotating element.* The fan-rotating element shall be nonferrous or nonsparking or the casing shall consist of or be lined with such material. There shall be ample clearance between the fan-rotating element and the fan casing to avoid a fire by friction, necessary allowance being made for ordinary expansion and loading to prevent contact between moving parts and the duct or fan housing. Fan blades shall be mounted on a shaft sufficiently heavy to maintain perfect alignment even when the blades of the fan are heavily loaded, the shaft preferably to have bearings outside the duct and booth. All bearings shall be of the self-lubricating type, or lubricated from the outside duct.

(5) *Electric motors.* Electric motors driving exhaust fans shall not be placed inside booths or ducts. See also paragraph (c) of this section.

(6) *Belts.* Belts shall not enter the duct or booth unless the belt and pulley within the duct or booth are thoroughly enclosed.

(7) *Exhaust ducts.* Exhaust ducts shall be constructed of steel and shall be substantially supported. Exhaust ducts without dampers are preferred; however, if dampers are installed, they shall be maintained so that they will be in a full open position at all times the ventilating system is in operation.

(i) Exhaust ducts shall be protected against mechanical damage and have a clearance from unprotected combustible construction or other combustible material of not less than 18 inches (45.72 cm).

(ii) If combustible construction is provided with the following protection applied to all surfaces within 18 inches (45.72 cm), clearances may be reduced to the distances indicated:

(a) 28-gage sheet metal on 1/4-inch asbestos mill board. — 12 inches (30.48 cm).

(b) 28-gage sheet metal on 1/8-inch asbestos mill board spaced out 1 inch (2.54 cm) on noncombustible spacers. — 9 inches (22.86 cm).

(c) 22-gage sheet metal on 1-inch rockwool batts reinforced with wire mesh or the equivalent. — 3 inches (7.62 cm).

(d) Where ducts are protected with an approved automatic sprinkler system, properly maintained, the clearance required in paragraph (d)(7)(i) of this section may be reduced to 6 inches (15.24 cm).

(8) *Discharge clearance.* Unless the spray booth exhaust duct terminal is from a water-wash spray booth, the terminal discharge point shall be not less than 6 feet from any combustible exterior wall or roof nor discharge in the direction of any combustible construction or unprotected opening in any noncombustible exterior wall within 25 feet (7.6 m).

(9) *Air exhaust.* Air exhaust from spray operations shall not be directed so that it will contaminate makeup air being introduced into the spraying area or other ventilating intakes, nor directed so as to create a nuisance. Air exhausted from spray operations shall not be recirculated.

(10) *Access doors.* When necessary to facilitate cleaning, exhaust ducts shall be provided with an ample number of access doors.

(11) *Room intakes.* Air intake openings to rooms containing spray finishing operations shall be adequate for the efficient operation of exhaust fans and shall be so located as to minimize the creation of dead air pockets.

(12) *Drying spaces.* Freshly sprayed articles shall be dried only in spaces provided with adequate ventilation to

prevent the formation of explosive vapors. In the event adequate and reliable ventilation is not provided such drying spaces shall be considered a spraying area.

(e) *Fixed electrostatic apparatus*—(1) *Conformance.* Where installation and use of electrostatic spraying equipment is used, such installation and use shall conform to all other paragraphs of this section, and shall also conform to the requirements of this paragraph.

(2) *Type approval.* Electrostatic apparatus and devices used in connection with coating operations shall be of approved types.

(3) *Location.* Transformers, power packs, control apparatus, and all other electrical portions of the equipment, with the exception of high-voltage grids, electrodes, and electrostatic atomizing heads and their connections, shall be located outside of the spraying area, or shall otherwise conform to the requirements of paragraph (c) of this section.

(4) *Support.* Electrodes and electrostatic atomizing heads shall be adequately supported in permanent locations and shall be effectively insulated from the ground. Electrodes and electrostatic atomizing heads which are permanently attached to their bases, supports, or reciprocators, shall be deemed to comply with this section. Insulators shall be nonporous and noncombustible.

(5) *Insulators, grounding.* High-voltage leads to electrodes shall be properly insulated and protected from mechanical injury or exposure to destructive chemicals. Electrostatic atomizing heads shall be effectively and permanently supported on suitable insulators and shall be effectively guarded against accidental contact or grounding. An automatic means shall be provided for grounding the electrode system when it is electrically deenergized for any reason. All insulators shall be kept clean and dry.

(6) *Safe distance.* A safe distance shall be maintained between goods being painted and electrodes or electrostatic atomizing heads or conductors of at least twice the sparking distance. A suitable sign indicating this safe distance shall be conspicuously posted near the assembly.

(7) *Conveyors required.* Goods being painted using this process are to be supported on conveyors. The conveyors shall be so arranged as to maintain safe distances between the goods and the electrodes or electrostatic atomizing heads at all times. Any irregularly shaped or other goods subject to possible swinging or movement shall be rigidly supported to prevent such swinging or movement which would reduce the clearance to less than that specified in paragraph (e)(6) of this section.

(8) *Prohibition.* This process is not acceptable where goods being coated are manipulated by hand. When finishing materials are applied by electrostatic equipment which is manipulated by hand, see paragraph (f) of this section for applicable requirements.

(9) *Fail-safe controls.* Electrostatic apparatus shall be equipped with automatic controls which will operate without time delay to disconnect the power supply to the high voltage transformer and to signal the operator under any of the following conditions:

(i) Stoppage of ventilating fans or failure of ventilating equipment from any cause.

(ii) Stoppage of the conveyor carrying goods through the high voltage field.

(iii) Occurrence of a ground or of an imminent ground at any point on the high voltage system.

(iv) Reduction of clearance below that specified in paragraph (e)(6) of this section.

(10) *Guarding.* Adequate booths, fencing, railings, or guards shall be so placed about the equipment that they, either by their location or character or both, assure that a safe isolation of the process is maintained from plant storage or personnel. Such railings, fencing, and guards shall be of conducting material, adequately grounded.

(11) *Ventilation.* Where electrostatic atomization is used the spraying area shall be so ventilated as to insure safe conditions from a fire and health standpoint.

(12) *Fire protection.* All areas used for spraying, including the interior of the booth, shall be protected by automatic sprinklers where this protection is available. Where this protection is not

available, other approved automatic extinguishing equipment shall be provided.

(f) *Electrostatic hand spraying equipment*—(1) *Application.* This paragraph shall apply to any equipment using electrostatically charged elements for the atomization and/or, precipitation of materials for coatings on articles, or for other similar purposes in which the atomizing device is hand held and manipulated during the spraying operation.

(2) *Conformance.* Electrostatic hand spraying equipment shall conform with the other provisions of this section.

(3) *Equipment approval and specifications.* Electrostatic hand spray apparatus and devices used in connection with coating operations shall be of approved types. The high voltage circuits shall be designed so as to not produce a spark of sufficient intensity to ignite any vapor-air mixtures nor result in appreciable shock hazard upon coming in contact with a grounded object under all normal operating conditions. The electrostatically charged exposed elements of the handgun shall be capable of being energized only by a switch which also controls the coating material supply.

(4) *Electrical support equipment.* Transformers, powerpacks, control apparatus, and all other electrical portions of the equipment, with the exception of the handgun itself and its connections to the power supply shall be located outside of the spraying area or shall otherwise conform to the requirements of paragraph (c) of this section.

(5) *Spray gun ground.* The handle of the spraying gun shall be electrically connected to ground by a metallic connection and to be so constructed that the operator in normal operating position is in intimate electrical contact with the grounded handle.

(6) *Grounding-general.* All electrically conductive objects in the spraying area shall be adequately grounded. This requirement shall apply to paint containers, wash cans, and any other objects or devices in the area. The equipment shall carry a prominent permanently installed warning regarding the necessity for this grounding feature.

(7) *Maintenance of grounds.* Objects being painted or coated shall be maintained in metallic contact with the conveyor or other grounded support. Hooks shall be regularly cleaned to insure this contact and areas of contact shall be sharp points or knife edges where possible. Points of support of the object shall be concealed from random spray where feasible and where the objects being sprayed are supported from a conveyor, the point of attachment to the conveyor shall be so located as to not collect spray material during normal operation.

(8) *Interlocks.* The electrical equipment shall be so interlocked with the ventilation of the spraying area that the equipment cannot be operated unless the ventilation fans are in operation.

(9) *Ventilation.* The spraying operation shall take place within a spray area which is adequately ventilated to remove solvent vapors released from the operation.

(g) *Drying, curing, or fusion apparatus*—(1) *Conformance.* Drying, curing, or fusion apparatus in connection with spray application of flammable and combustible finishes shall conform to the Standard for Ovens and Furnaces, NFPA 86A–1969, where applicable and shall also conform with the following requirements of this paragraph.

(2) *Alternate use prohibited.* Spray booths, rooms, or other enclosures used for spraying operations shall not alternately be used for the purpose of drying by any arrangement which will cause a material increase in the surface temperature of the spray booth, room, or enclosure.

(3) *Adjacent system interlocked.* Except as specifically provided in paragraph (g)(4) of this section, drying, curing, or fusion units utilizing a heating system having open flames or which may produce sparks shall not be installed in a spraying area, but may be installed adjacent thereto when equipped with an interlocked ventilating system arranged to:

(i) Thoroughly ventilate the drying space before the heating system can be started;

(ii) Maintain a safe atmosphere at any source of ignition;

(iii) Automatically shut down the heating system in the event of failure of the ventilating system.

187

(4) *Alternate use permitted.* Automobile refinishing spray booths or enclosures, otherwise installed and maintained in full conformity with this section, may alternately be used for drying with portable electrical infrared drying apparatus when conforming with the following:

(i) Interior (especially floors) of spray enclosures shall be kept free of overspray deposits.

(ii) During spray operations, the drying apparatus and electrical connections and wiring thereto shall not be located within spray enclosure nor in any other location where spray residues may be deposited thereon.

(iii) The spraying apparatus, the drying apparatus, and the ventilating system of the spray enclosure shall be equipped with suitable interlocks so arranged that:

(*a*) The spraying apparatus cannot be operated while the drying apparatus is inside the spray enclosure.

(*b*) The spray enclosure will be purged of spray vapors for a period of not less than 3 minutes before the drying apparatus can be energized.

(*c*) The ventilating system will maintain a safe atmosphere within the enclosure during the drying process and the drying apparatus will automatically shut off in the event of failure of the ventilating system.

(iv) All electrical wiring and equipment of the drying apparatus shall conform with the applicable sections of subpart S of this part. Only equipment of a type approved for Class I, Division 2 hazardous locations shall be located within 18 inches (45.72 cm) of floor level. All metallic parts of the drying apparatus shall be properly electrically bonded and grounded.

(v) The drying apparatus shall contain a prominently located, permanently attached warning sign indicating that ventilation should be maintained during the drying period and that spraying should not be conducted in the vicinity that spray will deposit on apparatus.

[58 FR 35149, June 30, 1993]

Subpart E—Personal Protective and Life Saving Equipment

AUTHORITY: 40 U.S.C. 3701 *et seq.*; 29 U.S.C. 653, 655, 657; Secretary of Labor's Order No. 12–71 (36 FR 8754), 8–76 (41 FR 25059), 9–83 (48 FR 35736), 1–90 (55 FR 9033), 6–96 (62 FR 111), 5–2002 (67 FR 65008), 5–2007 (72 FR 31160), or 1–2012 (77 FR 3912), as applicable; and 29 CFR Part 1911.

§ 1926.95 Criteria for personal protective equipment.

(a) *Application.* Protective equipment, including personal protective equipment for eyes, face, head, and extremities, protective clothing, respiratory devices, and protective shields and barriers, shall be provided, used, and maintained in a sanitary and reliable condition wherever it is necessary by reason of hazards of processes or environment, chemical hazards, radiological hazards, or mechanical irritants encountered in a manner capable of causing injury or impairment in the function of any part of the body through absorption, inhalation or physical contact.

(b) *Employee-owned equipment.* Where employees provide their own protective equipment, the employer shall be responsible to assure its adequacy, including proper maintenance, and sanitation of such equipment.

(c) *Design.* All personal protective equipment shall be of safe design and construction for the work to be performed.

(d) *Payment for protective equipment.* (1) Except as provided by paragraphs (d)(2) through (d)(6) of this section, the protective equipment, including personal protective equipment (PPE), used to comply with this part, shall be provided by the employer at no cost to employees.

(2) The employer is not required to pay for non-specialty safety-toe protective footwear (including steel-toe shoes or steel-toe boots) and non-specialty prescription safety eyewear, provided that the employer permits such items to be worn off the job-site.

(3) When the employer provides metatarsal guards and allows the employee, at his or her request, to use shoes or boots with built-in metatarsal

protection, the employer is not required to reimburse the employee for the shoes or boots.

(4) The employer is not required to pay for:

(i) Everyday clothing, such as long-sleeve shirts, long pants, street shoes, and normal work boots; or

(ii) Ordinary clothing, skin creams, or other items, used solely for protection from weather, such as winter coats, jackets, gloves, parkas, rubber boots, hats, raincoats, ordinary sunglasses, and sunscreen.

(5) The employer must pay for replacement PPE, except when the employee has lost or intentionally damaged the PPE.

(6) Where an employee provides adequate protective equipment he or she owns pursuant to paragraph (b) of this section, the employer may allow the employee to use it and is not required to reimburse the employee for that equipment. The employer shall not require an employee to provide or pay for his or her own PPE, unless the PPE is excepted by paragraphs (d)(2) through (d)(5) of this section.

(7) This section shall become effective on February 13, 2008. Employers must implement the PPE payment requirements no later than May 15, 2008.

NOTE TO § 1926.95(d): When the provisions of another OSHA standard specify whether or not the employer must pay for specific equipment, the payment provisions of that standard shall prevail.

[58 FR 35152, June 30, 1993, as amended at 72 FR 64429, Nov. 15, 2007]

§ 1926.96 Occupational foot protection.

Safety-toe footwear for employees shall meet the requirements and specifications in American National Standard for Men's Safety-Toe Footwear, Z41.1–1967.

[58 FR 35152, June 30, 1993]

§ 1926.97 Electrical protective equipment.

(a) *Design requirements for specific types of electrical protective equipment.* Rubber insulating blankets, rubber insulating matting, rubber insulating covers, rubber insulating line hose, rubber insulating gloves, and rubber insulating sleeves shall meet the following requirements:

(1) *Manufacture and marking of rubber insulating equipment.* (i) Blankets, gloves, and sleeves shall be produced by a seamless process.

(ii) Each item shall be clearly marked as follows:

(A) Class 00 equipment shall be marked Class 00.

(B) Class 0 equipment shall be marked Class 0.

(C) Class 1 equipment shall be marked Class 1.

(D) Class 2 equipment shall be marked Class 2.

(E) Class 3 equipment shall be marked Class 3.

(F) Class 4 equipment shall be marked Class 4.

(G) Nonozone-resistant equipment shall be marked Type I.

(H) Ozone-resistant equipment shall be marked Type II.

(I) Other relevant markings, such as the manufacturer's identification and the size of the equipment, may also be provided.

(iii) Markings shall be nonconducting and shall be applied in such a manner as not to impair the insulating qualities of the equipment.

(iv) Markings on gloves shall be confined to the cuff portion of the glove.

(2) *Electrical requirements.* (i) Equipment shall be capable of withstanding the ac proof-test voltage specified in Table E–1 or the dc proof-test voltage specified in Table E–2.

(A) The proof test shall reliably indicate that the equipment can withstand the voltage involved.

(B) The test voltage shall be applied continuously for 3 minutes for equipment other than matting and shall be applied continuously for 1 minute for matting.

(C) Gloves shall also be capable of separately withstanding the ac proof-test voltage specified in Table E–1 after a 16-hour water soak. (See the note following paragraph (a)(3)(ii)(B) of this section.)

(ii) When the ac proof test is used on gloves, the 60-hertz proof-test current may not exceed the values specified in Table E–1 at any time during the test period.

(A) If the ac proof test is made at a frequency other than 60 hertz, the permissible proof-test current shall be computed from the direct ratio of the frequencies.

(B) For the test, gloves (right side out) shall be filled with tap water and immersed in water to a depth that is in accordance with Table E–3. Water shall be added to or removed from the glove, as necessary, so that the water level is the same inside and outside the glove.

(C) After the 16-hour water soak specified in paragraph (a)(2)(i)(C) of this section, the 60-hertz proof-test current may not exceed the values given in Table E–1 by more than 2 milliamperes.

(iii) Equipment that has been subjected to a minimum breakdown voltage test may not be used for electrical protection. (See the note following paragraph (a)(3)(ii)(B) of this section.)

(iv) Material used for Type II insulating equipment shall be capable of withstanding an ozone test, with no visible effects. The ozone test shall reliably indicate that the material will resist ozone exposure in actual use. Any visible signs of ozone deterioration of the material, such as checking, cracking, breaks, or pitting, is evidence of failure to meet the requirements for ozone-resistant material. (See the note following paragraph (a)(3)(ii)(B) of this section.)

(3) *Workmanship and finish.* (i) Equipment shall be free of physical irregularities that can adversely affect the insulating properties of the equipment and that can be detected by the tests or inspections required under this section.

(ii) Surface irregularities that may be present on all rubber goods (because of imperfections on forms or molds or because of inherent difficulties in the manufacturing process) and that may appear as indentations, protuberances, or imbedded foreign material are acceptable under the following conditions:

(A) The indentation or protuberance blends into a smooth slope when the material is stretched.

(B) Foreign material remains in place when the insulating material is folded and stretches with the insulating material surrounding it.

NOTE TO PARAGRAPH (a): Rubber insulating equipment meeting the following national consensus standards is deemed to be in compliance with the performance requirements of paragraph (a) of this section:

American Society for Testing and Materials (ASTM) D120–09, *Standard Specification for Rubber Insulating Gloves.*

ASTM D178–01 (2010), *Standard Specification for Rubber Insulating Matting.*

ASTM D1048–12, *Standard Specification for Rubber Insulating Blankets.*

ASTM D1049–98 (2010), *Standard Specification for Rubber Insulating Covers.*

ASTM D1050–05 (2011), *Standard Specification for Rubber Insulating Line Hose.*

ASTM D1051–08, *Standard Specification for Rubber Insulating Sleeves.*

The preceding standards also contain specifications for conducting the various tests required in paragraph (a) of this section. For example, the ac and dc proof tests, the breakdown test, the water-soak procedure, and the ozone test mentioned in this paragraph are described in detail in these ASTM standards.

ASTM F1236–96 (2012), *Standard Guide for Visual Inspection of Electrical Protective Rubber Products,* presents methods and techniques for the visual inspection of electrical protective equipment made of rubber. This guide also contains descriptions and photographs of irregularities that can be found in this equipment.

ASTM F819–10, *Standard Terminology Relating to Electrical Protective Equipment for Workers,* includes definitions of terms relating to the electrical protective equipment covered under this section.

(b) *Design requirements for other types of electrical protective equipment.* The following requirements apply to the design and manufacture of electrical protective equipment that is not covered by paragraph (a) of this section:

(1) *Voltage withstand.* Insulating equipment used for the protection of employees shall be capable of withstanding, without failure, the voltages that may be imposed upon it.

NOTE TO PARAGRAPH (b)(1): These voltages include transient overvoltages, such as switching surges, as well as nominal line voltage. See appendix B to subpart V of this part for a discussion of transient overvoltages on electric power transmission and distribution systems. See IEEE Std 516–2009, *IEEE Guide for Maintenance Methods on Energized Power Lines,* for methods of determining the magnitude of transient overvoltages on an electrical system and for a discussion comparing the ability of insulation equipment to withstand a transient overvoltage based on its ability to withstand ac voltage testing.

(2) *Equipment current.* (i) Protective equipment used for the primary insulation of employees from energized circuit parts shall be capable of passing a current test when subjected to the highest nominal voltage on which the equipment is to be used.

(ii) When insulating equipment is tested in accordance with paragraph (b)(2)(i) of this section, the equipment current may not exceed 1 microampere per kilovolt of phase-to-phase applied voltage.

NOTE 1 TO PARAGRAPH (b)(2): This paragraph applies to equipment that provides primary insulation of employees from energized parts. It does not apply to equipment used for secondary insulation or equipment used for brush contact only.

NOTE 2 TO PARAGRAPH (b)(2): For ac excitation, this current consists of three components: Capacitive current because of the dielectric properties of the insulating material itself, conduction current through the volume of the insulating equipment, and leakage current along the surface of the tool or equipment. The conduction current is normally negligible. For clean, dry insulating equipment, the leakage current is small, and the capacitive current predominates.

NOTE TO PARAGRAPH (b): Plastic guard equipment is deemed to conform to the performance requirements of paragraph (b) of this section if it meets, and is used in accordance with, ASTM F712–06 (2011), *Standard Test Methods and Specifications for Electrically Insulating Plastic Guard Equipment for Protection of Workers.*

(c) *In-service care and use of electrical protective equipment*—(1) *General.* Electrical protective equipment shall be maintained in a safe, reliable condition.

(2) *Specific requirements.* The following specific requirements apply to rubber insulating blankets, rubber insulating covers, rubber insulating line hose, rubber insulating gloves, and rubber insulating sleeves:

(i) Maximum use voltages shall conform to those listed in Table E–4.

(ii) Insulating equipment shall be inspected for damage before each day's use and immediately following any incident that can reasonably be suspected of causing damage. Insulating gloves shall be given an air test, along with the inspection.

NOTE TO PARAGRAPH (c)(2)(ii): ASTM F1236–96 (2012), *Standard Guide for Visual Inspection of Electrical Protective Rubber Products*, presents methods and techniques for the visual inspection of electrical protective equipment made of rubber. This guide also contains descriptions and photographs of irregularities that can be found in this equipment.

(iii) Insulating equipment with any of the following defects may not be used:

(A) A hole, tear, puncture, or cut;

(B) Ozone cutting or ozone checking (that is, a series of interlacing cracks produced by ozone on rubber under mechanical stress);

(C) An embedded foreign object;

(D) Any of the following texture changes: Swelling, softening, hardening, or becoming sticky or inelastic.

(E) Any other defect that damages the insulating properties.

(iv) Insulating equipment found to have other defects that might affect its insulating properties shall be removed from service and returned for testing under paragraphs (c)(2)(viii) and (c)(2)(ix) of this section.

(v) Insulating equipment shall be cleaned as needed to remove foreign substances.

(vi) Insulating equipment shall be stored in such a location and in such a manner as to protect it from light, temperature extremes, excessive humidity, ozone, and other damaging substances and conditions.

(vii) Protector gloves shall be worn over insulating gloves, except as follows:

(A) Protector gloves need not be used with Class 0 gloves, under limited-use conditions, when small equipment and parts manipulation necessitate unusually high finger dexterity.

NOTE TO PARAGRAPH (c)(2)(vii)(A): Persons inspecting rubber insulating gloves used under these conditions need to take extra care in visually examining them. Employees using rubber insulating gloves under these conditions need to take extra care to avoid handling sharp objects.

(B) If the voltage does not exceed 250 volts, ac, or 375 volts, dc, protector gloves need not be used with Class 00 gloves, under limited-use conditions, when small equipment and parts manipulation necessitate unusually high finger dexterity.

NOTE TO PARAGRAPH (c)(2)(vii)(B): Persons inspecting rubber insulating gloves used under these conditions need to take extra care in visually examining them. Employees using rubber insulating gloves under these conditions need to take extra care to avoid handling sharp objects.

(C) Any other class of glove may be used without protector gloves, under limited-use conditions, when small equipment and parts manipulation necessitate unusually high finger dexterity but only if the employer can demonstrate that the possibility of physical damage to the gloves is small and if the class of glove is one class higher than that required for the voltage involved.

(D) Insulating gloves that have been used without protector gloves may not be reused until they have been tested under the provisions of paragraphs (c)(2)(viii) and (c)(2)(ix) of this section.

(viii) Electrical protective equipment shall be subjected to periodic electrical tests. Test voltages and the maximum intervals between tests shall be in accordance with Table E–4 and Table E–5.

(ix) The test method used under paragraphs (c)(2)(viii) and (c)(2)(xi) of this section shall reliably indicate whether the insulating equipment can withstand the voltages involved.

NOTE TO PARAGRAPH (c)(2)(ix): Standard electrical test methods considered as meeting this paragraph are given in the following national consensus standards:

ASTM D120–09, *Standard Specification for Rubber Insulating Gloves.*

ASTM D178–01 (2010), *Standard Specification for Rubber Insulating Matting.*

ASTM D1048–12, *Standard Specification for Rubber Insulating Blankets.*

ASTM D1049–98 (2010), *Standard Specification for Rubber Insulating Covers.*

ASTM D1050–05 (2011), *Standard Specification for Rubber Insulating Line Hose.*

ASTM D1051–08, *Standard Specification for Rubber Insulating Sleeves.*

ASTM F478–09, *Standard Specification for In-Service Care of Insulating Line Hose and Covers.*

ASTM F479–06 (2011), *Standard Specification for In-Service Care of Insulating Blankets.*

ASTM F496–08, *Standard Specification for In-Service Care of Insulating Gloves and Sleeves.*

(x) Insulating equipment failing to pass inspections or electrical tests may not be used by employees, except as follows:

(A) Rubber insulating line hose may be used in shorter lengths with the defective portion cut off.

(B) Rubber insulating blankets may be salvaged by severing the defective area from the undamaged portion of the blanket. The resulting undamaged area may not be smaller than 560 millimeters by 560 millimeters (22 inches by 22 inches) for Class 1, 2, 3, and 4 blankets.

(C) Rubber insulating blankets may be repaired using a compatible patch that results in physical and electrical properties equal to those of the blanket.

(D) Rubber insulating gloves and sleeves with minor physical defects, such as small cuts, tears, or punctures, may be repaired by the application of a compatible patch. Also, rubber insulating gloves and sleeves with minor surface blemishes may be repaired with a compatible liquid compound. The repaired area shall have electrical and physical properties equal to those of the surrounding material. Repairs to gloves are permitted only in the area between the wrist and the reinforced edge of the opening.

(xi) Repaired insulating equipment shall be retested before it may be used by employees.

(xii) The employer shall certify that equipment has been tested in accordance with the requirements of paragraphs (c)(2)(iv), (c)(2)(vii)(D), (c)(2)(viii), (c)(2)(ix), and (c)(2)(xi) of this section. The certification shall identify the equipment that passed the test and the date it was tested and shall be made available upon request to the Assistant Secretary for Occupational Safety and Health and to employees or their authorized representatives.

NOTE TO PARAGRAPH (c)(2)(xii): Marking equipment with, and entering onto logs, the results of the tests and the dates of testing are two acceptable means of meeting the certification requirement.

TABLE E–1—AC PROOF-TEST REQUIREMENTS

Class of equipment	Proof-test voltage rms V	Maximum proof-test current, mA (gloves only)			
		280-mm (11-in) glove	360-mm (14-in) glove	410-mm (16-in) glove	460-mm (18-in) glove
00	2,500	8	12	....	....
0	5,000	8	12	14	16
1	10,000	....	14	16	18
2	20,000	....	16	18	20
3	30,000	....	18	20	22
4	40,000	....	....	22	24

TABLE E–2—DC PROOF-TEST REQUIREMENTS

Class of equipment	Proof-test voltage
00	10,000
0	20,000
1	40,000
2	50,000
3	60,000
4	70,000

Note: The dc voltages listed in this table are not appropriate for proof testing rubber insulating line hose or covers. For this equipment, dc proof tests shall use a voltage high enough to indicate that the equipment can be safely used at the voltages listed in Table E–4. See ASTM D1050–05 (2011) and ASTM D1049–98 (2010) for further information on proof tests for rubber insulating line hose and covers, respectively.

TABLE E–3—GLOVE TESTS—WATER LEVEL [1] [2]

Class of glove	AC proof test		DC proof test	
	mm	in	mm	in
00	38	1.5	38	1.5
0	38	1.5	38	1.5
1	38	1.5	51	2.0
2	64	2.5	76	3.0
3	89	3.5	102	4.0
4	127	5.0	153	6.0

[1] The water level is given as the clearance from the reinforced edge of the glove to the water line, with a tolerance of ±13 mm. (±0.5 in.).
[2] If atmospheric conditions make the specified clearances impractical, the clearances may be increased by a maximum of 25 mm. (1 in.).

TABLE E–4—RUBBER INSULATING EQUIPMENT, VOLTAGE REQUIREMENTS

Class of equipment	Maximum use voltage [1] AC rms	Retest voltage [2] AC rms	Retest voltage [2] DC avg
00	500	2,500	10,000
0	1,000	5,000	20,000
1	7,500	10,000	40,000
2	17,000	20,000	50,000
3	26,500	30,000	60,000
4	36,000	40,000	70,000

[1] The maximum use voltage is the ac voltage (rms) classification of the protective equipment that designates the maximum nominal design voltage of the energized system that may be safely worked. The nominal design voltage is equal to the phase-to-phase voltage on multiphase circuits. However, the phase-to-ground potential is considered to be the nominal design voltage if:
  (1) There is no multiphase exposure in a system area and the voltage exposure is limited to the phase-to-ground potential, or
  (2) The electric equipment and devices are insulated or isolated or both so that the multiphase exposure on a grounded wye circuit is removed.
[2] The proof-test voltage shall be applied continuously for at least 1 minute, but no more than 3 minutes.

TABLE E–5—RUBBER INSULATING EQUIPMENT, TEST INTERVALS

Type of equipment	When to test
Rubber insulating line hose	Upon indication that insulating value is suspect and after repair.
Rubber insulating covers	Upon indication that insulating value is suspect and after repair.
Rubber insulating blankets	Before first issue and every 12 months thereafter;[1] upon indication that insulating value is suspect; and after repair.

193

TABLE E–5—RUBBER INSULATING EQUIPMENT, TEST INTERVALS—Continued

Type of equipment	When to test
Rubber insulating gloves	Before first issue and every 6 months thereafter;[1] upon indication that insulating value is suspect; after repair; and after use without protectors.
Rubber insulating sleeves	Before first issue and every 12 months thereafter;[1] upon indication that insulating value is suspect; and after repair.

[1] If the insulating equipment has been electrically tested but not issued for service, the insulating equipment may not be placed into service unless it has been electrically tested within the previous 12 months.

[79 FR 20693, Apr. 11, 2014]

§ 1926.98 [Reserved]

§ 1926.100 Head protection.

(a) Employees working in areas where there is a possible danger of head injury from impact, or from falling or flying objects, or from electrical shock and burns, shall be protected by protective helmets.

(b) *Criteria for head protection.* (1) The employer must provide each employee with head protection that meets the specifications contained in any of the following consensus standards:

(i) American National Standards Institute (ANSI) Z89.1–2009, "American National Standard for Industrial Head Protection," incorporated by reference in § 1926.6;

(ii) American National Standards Institute (ANSI) Z89.1–2003, "American National Standard for Industrial Head Protection," incorporated by reference in § 1926.6; or

(iii) American National Standards Institute (ANSI) Z89.1–1997, "American National Standard for Personnel Protection—Protective Headwear for Industrial Workers—Requirements," incorporated by reference in § 1926.6.

(2) The employer must ensure that the head protection provided for each employee exposed to high-voltage electric shock and burns also meets the specifications contained in Section 9.7 ("Electrical Insulation") of any of the consensus standards identified in paragraph (b)(1) of this section.

(3) OSHA will deem any head protection device that the employer demonstrates is at least as effective as a head protection device constructed in accordance with one of the consensus standards identified in paragraph (b)(1)

of this section to be in compliance with the requirements of this section.

[44 FR 8577, Feb. 9, 1979, as amended at 77 FR 37600, June 22, 2012; 77 FR 42988, July 23, 2012]

§ 1926.101 Hearing protection.

(a) Wherever it is not feasible to reduce the noise levels or duration of exposures to those specified in Table D–2, Permissible Noise Exposures, in § 1926.52, ear protective devices shall be provided and used.

(b) Ear protective devices inserted in the ear shall be fitted or determined individually by competent persons.

(c) Plain cotton is not an acceptable protective device.

§ 1926.102 Eye and face protection.

(a) *General.* (1) Employees shall be provided with eye and face protection equipment when machines or operations present potential eye or face injury from physical, chemical, or radiation agents.

(2) Eye and face protection equipment required by this part shall meet the requirements specified in American National Standards Institute, Z87.1–1968, Practice for Occupational and Educational Eye and Face Protection.

(3) Employees whose vision requires the use of corrective lenses in spectacles, when required by this regulation to wear eye protection, shall be protected by goggles or spectacles of one of the following types:

(i) Spectacles whose protective lenses provide optical correction;

(ii) Goggles that can be worn over corrective spectacles without disturbing the adjustment of the spectacles;

(iii) Goggles that incorporate corrective lenses mounted behind the protective lenses.

(4) Face and eye protection equipment shall be kept clean and in good repair. The use of this type equipment with structural or optical defects shall be prohibited.

(5) Table E–1 shall be used as a guide in the selection of face and eye protection for the hazards and operations noted.

TABLE E–1—EYE AND FACE PROTECTOR SELECTION GUIDE

1. GOGGLES, Flexible Fitting, Regular Ventilation
2. GOGGLES, Flexible Fitting, Hooded Ventilation
3. GOGGLES, Cushioned Fitting, Rigid Body
*4. SPECTACLES, Metal Frame, with Sideshields
*5. SPECTACLES, Plastic Frame, with Sideshields
*6. SPECTACLES, Metal-Plastic Frame, with Sideshields

** 7. WELDING GOGGLES, Eyecup Type, Tinted Lenses (Illustrated)
7A. CHIPPING GOGGLES, Eyecup Type, Clear Safety Lenses (Not Illustrated)
** 8. WELDING GOGGLES, Coverspec Type Tinted Lenses (Illustrated)
8A. CHIPPING GOGGLES, Coverspec Type, Clear Safety Lenses (Not Illustrated)
** 9. WELDING GOGGLES, Coverspec Type, Tinted Plate Lens
10. FACE SHIELD (Available with Plastic or Mesh Window)
**11. WELDING HELMETS

*Non-side shield spectacles are available for limited hazard use requiring only frontal protection.

**See Table E–2, in paragraph (b) of this section, Filter Lens Shade Numbers for Protection Against Radiant Energy.

APPLICATIONS

Operation	Hazards	Recommended protectors: Bold type numbers signify preferred protection
Acetylene—Burning, Acetylene—Cutting, Acetylene—Welding.	Sparks, harmful rays, molten metal, flying particles.	7, 8, 9.
Chemical Handling	Splash, acid burns, fumes	2, 10 (For severe exposure add 10 over 2).
Chipping	Flying particles	1, 3, 4, 5, 6, 7A, 8A.
Electric (arc) welding	Sparks, intense rays, molten metal.	9, 11, (11 in combination with 4, 5, 6, in tinted lenses, advisable).
Furnace operations	Glare, heat, molten metal	7, 8, 9 (For severe exposure add 10).
Grinding—Light	Flying particles	1, 3, 4, 5, 6, 10.
Grinding—Heavy	Flying particles	1 , 3, 7A, 8A (For severe exposure add 10).
Laboratory	Chemical splash, glass breakage.	2 (10 when in combination with 4, 5, 6).
Machining	Flying particles	1, 3, 4, 5, 6, 10.
Molten metals	Heat, glare, sparks, splash	7, 8, (10 in combination with 4, 5, 6, in tinted lenses).
Spot welding	Flying particles, sparks	1, 3, 4, 5, 6, 10.

(6) Protectors shall meet the following minimum requirements:

(i) They shall provide adequate protection against the particular hazards for which they are designed.

(ii) They shall be reasonably comfortable when worn under the designated conditions.

(iii) They shall fit snugly and shall not unduly interfere with the movements of the wearer.

(iv) They shall be durable.

(v) They shall be capable of being disinfected.

(vi) They shall be easily cleanable.

(7) Every protector shall be distinctly marked to facilitate identification only of the manufacturer.

(8) When limitations or precautions are indicated by the manufacturer, they shall be transmitted to the user and care taken to see that such limitations and precautions are strictly observed.

(b) *Protection against radiant energy*—(1) *Selection of shade numbers for welding filter.* Table E-2 shall be used as a guide for the selection of the proper shade numbers of filter lenses or plates used in welding. Shades more dense than those listed may be used to suit the individual's needs.

TABLE E-2—FILTER LENS SHADE NUMBERS FOR PROTECTION AGAINST RADIANT ENERGY

Welding operation	Shade number
Shielded metal-arc welding 1/16-, 3/32-, 1/8-, 5/32-inch diameter electrodes	10
Gas-shielded arc welding (nonferrous) 1/16-, 3/32-, 1/8-, 5/32-inch diameter electrodes	11
Gas-shielded arc welding (ferrous) 1/16-, 3/32-, 1/8-, 5/32-inch diameter electrodes	12
Shielded metal-arc welding 3/16-, 7/32-, 1/4-inch diameter electrodes	12
5/16-, 3/8-inch diameter electrodes	14
Atomic hydrogen welding	10–14
Carbon-arc welding	14
Soldering	2
Torch brazing	3 or 4
Light cutting, up to 1 inch	3 or 4
Medium cutting, 1 inch to 6 inches	4 or 5
Heavy cutting, over 6 inches	5 or 6
Gas welding (light), up to 1/8-inch	4 or 5
Gas welding (medium), 1/8-inch to 1/2-inch	5 or 6
Gas welding (heavy), over 1/2-inch	6 or 8

(2) *Laser protection.* (i) Employees whose occupation or assignment requires exposure to laser beams shall be furnished suitable laser safety goggles which will protect for the specific wavelength of the laser and be of opti-

cal density (O.D.) adequate for the energy involved. Table E-3 lists the maximum power or energy density for which adequate protection is afforded by glasses of optical densities from 5 through 8.

TABLE E-3—SELECTING LASER SAFETY GLASS

Intensity, CW maximum power density (watts/cm²)	Attenuation	
	Optical density (O.D.)	Attenuation factor
10^{-2}	5	10^5
10^{-1}	6	10^6
1.0	7	10^7
10.0	8	10^8

Output levels falling between lines in this table shall require the higher optical density.

(ii) All protective goggles shall bear a label identifying the following data:

(*a*) The laser wavelengths for which use is intended;

(*b*) The optical density of those wavelengths;

(*c*) The visible light transmission.

[44 FR 8577, Feb. 9, 1979; 44 FR 20940, Apr. 6, 1979, as amended at 58 FR 35160, June 30, 1993]

§ 1926.103   **Respiratory protection.**

NOTE: The requirements applicable to construction work under this section are identical to those set forth at 29 CFR 1910.134 of this chapter.

[63 FR 1297; Jan. 8, 1998]

§ 1926.104   **Safety belts, lifelines, and lanyards.**

(a) Lifelines, safety belts, and lanyards shall be used only for employee safeguarding. Any lifeline, safety belt, or lanyard actually subjected to in-service loading, as distinguished from static load testing, shall be immediately removed from service and shall not be used again for employee safeguarding.

(b) Lifelines shall be secured above the point of operation to an anchorage or structural member capable of supporting a minimum dead weight of 5,400 pounds.

(c) Lifelines used on rock-scaling operations, or in areas where the lifeline may be subjected to cutting or abrasion, shall be a minimum of 7/8-inch wire core manila rope. For all other lifeline applications, a minimum of 3/4-

inch manila or equivalent, with a minimum breaking strength of 5,400 pounds, shall be used.

(d) Safety belt lanyard shall be a minimum of ½-inch nylon, or equivalent, with a maximum length to provide for a fall of no greater than 6 feet. The rope shall have a nominal breaking strength of 5,400 pounds.

(e) All safety belt and lanyard hardware shall be drop forged or pressed steel, cadmium plated in accordance with type 1, Class B plating specified in Federal Specification QQ-P-416. Surface shall be smooth and free of sharp edges.

(f) All safety belt and lanyard hardware, except rivets, shall be capable of withstanding a tensile loading of 4,000 pounds without cracking, breaking, or taking a permanent deformation.

§ 1926.105 Safety nets.

(a) Safety nets shall be provided when workplaces are more than 25 feet above the ground or water surface, or other surfaces where the use of ladders, scaffolds, catch platforms, temporary floors, safety lines, or safety belts is impractical.

(b) Where safety net protection is required by this part, operations shall not be undertaken until the net is in place and has been tested.

(c)(1) Nets shall extend 8 feet beyond the edge of the work surface where employees are exposed and shall be installed as close under the work surface as practical but in no case more than 25 feet below such work surface. Nets shall be hung with sufficient clearance to prevent user's contact with the surfaces or structures below. Such clearances shall be determined by impact load testing.

(2) It is intended that only one level of nets be required for bridge construction.

(d) The mesh size of nets shall not exceed 6 inches by 6 inches. All new nets shall meet accepted performance standards of 17,500 foot-pounds minimum impact resistance as determined and certified by the manufacturers, and shall bear a label of proof test. Edge ropes shall provide a minimum breaking strength of 5,000 pounds.

(e) Forged steel safety hooks or shackles shall be used to fasten the net to its supports.

(f) Connections between net panels shall develop the full strength of the net.

§ 1926.106 Working over or near water.

(a) Employees working over or near water, where the danger of drowning exists, shall be provided with U.S. Coast Guard-approved life jacket or buoyant work vests.

(b) Prior to and after each use, the buoyant work vests or life preservers shall be inspected for defects which would alter their strength or buoyancy. Defective units shall not be used.

(c) Ring buoys with at least 90 feet of line shall be provided and readily available for emergency rescue operations. Distance between ring buoys shall not exceed 200 feet.

(d) At least one lifesaving skiff shall be immediately available at locations where employees are working over or adjacent to water.

§ 1926.107 Definitions applicable to this subpart.

(a) *Contaminant* means any material which by reason of its action upon, within, or to a person is likely to cause physical harm.

(b) *Lanyard* means a rope, suitable for supporting one person. One end is fastened to a safety belt or harness and the other end is secured to a substantial object or a safety line.

(c) *Lifeline* means a rope, suitable for supporting one person, to which a lanyard or safety belt (or harness) is attached.

(d) *O.D.* means optical density and refers to the light refractive characteristics of a lens.

(e) *Radiant energy* means energy that travels outward in all directions from its sources.

(f) *Safety belt* means a device, usually worn around the waist which, by reason of its attachment to a lanyard and lifeline or a structure, will prevent a worker from falling.

[44 FR 8577, Feb. 9, 1979]

Subpart F—Fire Protection and Prevention

AUTHORITY: Section 107 of the Contract Work Hours and Safety Standards Act (40 U.S.C. 3704); Sections 4, 6, and 8 of the Occupational Safety and Health Act of 1970 (29 U.S.C. 653, 655, 657); Secretary of Labor's Order No. 12–71 (36 FR 8754), 8–76 (41 FR 25059), 9–83 (48 FR 35736),1–90 (55 FR 9033), 6–96 (62 FR 111), 3–2000 (62 FR 50017), 5–2002 (67 FR 650008), 5–2007 (72 FR 31159), 4–2010 (75 FR 55355), or 1–2012 (77 FR 3912), as applicable; and 29 CFR part 1911.

§ 1926.150 Fire protection.

(a) *General requirements.* (1) The employer shall be responsible for the development of a fire protection program to be followed throughout all phases of the construction and demolition work, and he shall provide for the firefighting equipment as specified in this subpart. As fire hazards occur, there shall be no delay in providing the necessary equipment.

(2) Access to all available firefighting equipment shall be maintained at all times.

(3) All firefighting equipment, provided by the employer, shall be conspicuously located.

(4) All firefighting equipment shall be periodically inspected and maintained in operating condition. Defective equipment shall be immediately replaced.

(5) As warranted by the project, the employer shall provide a trained and equipped firefighting organization (Fire Brigade) to assure adequate protection to life.

(b) *Water supply.* (1) A temporary or permanent water supply, of sufficient volume, duration, and pressure, required to properly operate the firefighting equipment shall be made available as soon as combustible materials accumulate.

(2) Where underground water mains are to be provided, they shall be installed, completed, and made available for use as soon as practicable.

(c) *Portable firefighting equipment*—(1) *Fire extinguishers and small hose lines.* (i) A fire extinguisher, rated not less than 2A, shall be provided for each 3,000 square feet of the protected building area, or major fraction thereof. Travel distance from any point of the protected area to the nearest fire extinguisher shall not exceed 100 feet.

(ii) One 55-gallon open drum of water with two fire pails may be substituted for a fire extinguisher having a 2A rating.

(iii) A ½-inch diameter garden-type hose line, not to exceed 100 feet in length and equipped with a nozzle, may be substituted for a 2A-rated fire extinguisher, providing it is capable of discharging a minimum of 5 gallons per minute with a minimum hose stream range of 30 feet horizontally. The garden-type hose lines shall be mounted on conventional racks or reels. The number and location of hose racks or reels shall be such that at least one hose stream can be applied to all points in the area.

(iv) One or more fire extinguishers, rated not less than 2A, shall be provided on each floor. In multistory buildings, at least one fire extinguisher shall be located adjacent to stairway.

(v) Extinguishers and water drums, subject to freezing, shall be protected from freezing.

(vi) A fire extinguisher, rated not less than 10B, shall be provided within 50 feet of wherever more than 5 gallons of flammable or combustible liquids or 5 pounds of flammable gas are being used on the jobsite. This requirement does not apply to the integral fuel tanks of motor vehicles.

(vii) Carbon tetrachloride and other toxic vaporizing liquid fire extinguishers are prohibited.

(viii) Portable fire extinguishers shall be inspected periodically and maintained in accordance with Maintenance and Use of Portable Fire Extinguishers, NFPA No. 10A–1970.

(ix) Fire extinguishers which have been listed or approved by a nationally recognized testing laboratory, shall be used to meet the requirements of this subpart.

(x) Table F–1 may be used as a guide for selecting the appropriate portable fire extinguishers.

Table F-1 FIRE EXTINGUISHERS DATA

| | WATER TYPE | | | | FOAM | CARBON DIOXIDE | DRY CHEMICAL | | | |
| | | | | | | | SODIUM OR POTASSIUM BICARBONATE | | MULTI-PURPOSE ABC | |
	STORED PRESSURE	CARTRIDGE OPERATED	WATER PUMP TANK	SODA ACID	FOAM	CO2	CARTRIDGE OPERATED	STORED PRESSURE	STORED PRESSURE	CARTRIDGE OPERATED
CLASS A FIRES — WOOD, PAPER, TRASH HAVING GLOWING EMBERS	YES	YES	YES	YES	Y.ES	NO (BUT WILL CONTROL SMALL SURFACE FIRES)	NO (BUT WILL CONTROL SMALL SURFACE FIRES)	NO (BUT WILL CONTROL SMALL SURFACE FIRES)	YES	YES
CLASS B FIRES — FLAMMABLE LIQUIDS, GASOLINE, OIL, PAINTS, GREASE, ETC.	NO	NO	NO	NO	YES	YES	YES	YES	YES	YES
CLASS C FIRES — ELECTRICAL EQUIPMENT	NO	NO	NO	NO	NO	YES	YES	YES	YES	YES
CLASS D FIRES — COMBUSTIBLE METALS	SPECIAL EXTINGUISHING AGENTS APPROVED BY RECOGNIZED TESTING LABORATORIES									
METHOD OF OPERATION	PULL PIN— SQUEEZE HANDLES	TURN UPSIDE DOWN	PUMP HANDLE	TURN UPSIDE DOWN	TURN UPSIDE DOWN	PULL PIN— SQUEEZE LEVER	RUPTURE CARTRIDGE— SQUEEZE LEVER	PULL PIN— SQUEEZE HANDLE	PULL PIN— SQUEEZE HANDLE	RUPTURE CARTRIDGE— SQUEEZE LEVER
RANGE	30'- 40'	30'- 40'	30'- 40'	30'- 40'	30'- 40'	3'- 8'	5'- 20'	5'- 20'	5'- 20'	5'- 20'
MAINTENANCE	CHECK AIR PRESSURE GAUGE MONTHLY	WEIGH GAS CARTRIDGE- ADD WATER IF REQUIRED ANNUALLY	DISCHARGE AND FILL WITH WATER ANNUALLY	DISCHARGE ANNUALLY RECHARGE	DISCHARGE ANNUALLY RECHARGE	WEIGH SEMI ANNUALLY	WEIGH GAS CARTRIDGE- CHECK CONDITION OF DRY CHEMICAL ANNUALLY	CHECK PRESSURE GAUGE AND CONDITION OF DRY CHEMICAL ANNUALLY	CHECK PRESSURE GAUGE AND CONDITION OF DRY CHEMICAL ANNUALLY	WEIGH GAS CARTRIDGE- CHECK CONDITION OF DRY CHEMICAL ANNUALLY

(2) *Fire hose and connections.* (i) One hundred feet, or less, of 1½-inch hose, with a nozzle capable of discharging water at 25 gallons or more per minute, may be substituted for a fire extinguisher rated not more than 2A in the designated area provided that the hose line can reach all points in the area.

(ii) If fire hose connections are not compatible with local firefighting equipment, the contractor shall provide adapters, or equivalent, to permit connections.

(iii) During demolition involving combustible materials, charged hose lines, supplied by hydrants, water tank trucks with pumps, or equivalent, shall be made available.

(d) *Fixed firefighting equipment—*(1) *Sprinkler protection.* (i) If the facility being constructed includes the installation of automatic sprinkler protection, the installation shall closely follow the construction and be placed in service as soon as applicable laws permit following completion of each story.

(ii) During demolition or alterations, existing automatic sprinkler installations shall be retained in service as long as reasonable. The operation of sprinkler control valves shall be permitted only by properly authorized persons. Modification of sprinkler systems to permit alterations or additional demolition should be expedited so that the automatic protection may be returned to service as quickly as possible. Sprinkler control valves shall be checked daily at close of work to ascertain that the protection is in service.

(2) *Standpipes.* In all structures in which standpipes are required, or where standpipes exist in structures being altered, they shall be brought up as soon as applicable laws permit, and shall be maintained as construction progresses in such a manner that they are always ready for fire protection use. The standpipes shall be provided with Siamese fire department connections on the outside of the structure, at the street level, which shall be conspicuously marked. There shall be at least one standard hose outlet at each floor.

(e) *Fire alarm devices.* (1) An alarm system, e.g., telephone system, siren, etc., shall be established by the employer whereby employees on the site and the local fire department can be alerted for an emergency.

199

(2) The alarm code and reporting instructions shall be conspicuously posted at phones and at employee entrances.

(f) *Fire cutoffs.* (1) Fire walls and exit stairways, required for the completed buildings, shall be given construction priority. Fire doors, with automatic closing devices, shall be hung on openings as soon as practicable.

(2) Fire cutoffs shall be retained in buildings undergoing alterations or demolition until operations necessitate their removal.

[44 FR 8577, Feb. 9, 1979; 44 FR 20940, Apr. 6, 1979, as amended at 58 FR 35162, June 30, 1993; 61 FR 31432, June 20, 1996]

§ 1926.151   Fire prevention.

(a) *Ignition hazards.* (1) Electrical wiring and equipment for light, heat, or power purposes shall be installed in compliance with the requirements of subpart K of this part.

(2) Internal combustion engine powered equipment shall be so located that the exhausts are well away from combustible materials. When the exhausts are piped to outside the building under construction, a clearance of at least 6 inches shall be maintained between such piping and combustible material.

(3) Smoking shall be prohibited at or in the vicinity of operations which constitute a fire hazard, and shall be conspicuously posted: "No Smoking or Open Flame."

(4) Portable battery powered lighting equipment, used in connection with the storage, handling, or use of flammable gases or liquids, shall be of the type approved for the hazardous locations.

(5) The nozzle of air, inert gas, and steam lines or hoses, when used in the cleaning or ventilation of tanks and vessels that contain hazardous concentrations of flammable gases or vapors, shall be bonded to the tank or vessel shell. Bonding devices shall not be attached or detached in hazardous concentrations of flammable gases or vapors.

(b) *Temporary buildings.* (1) No temporary building shall be erected where it will adversely affect any means of exit.

(2) Temporary buildings, when located within another building or structure, shall be of either noncombustible construction or of combustible construction having a fire resistance of not less than 1 hour.

(3) Temporary buildings, located other than inside another building and not used for the storage, handling, or use of flammable or combustible liquids, flammable gases, explosives, or blasting agents, or similar hazardous occupancies, shall be located at a distance of not less than 10 feet from another building or structure. Groups of temporary buildings, not exceeding 2,000 square feet in aggregate, shall, for the purposes of this part, be considered a single temporary building.

(c) *Open yard storage.* (1) Combustible materials shall be piled with due regard to the stability of piles and in no case higher than 20 feet.

(2) Driveways between and around combustible storage piles shall be at least 15 feet wide and maintained free from accumulation of rubbish, equipment, or other articles or materials. Driveways shall be so spaced that a maximum grid system unit of 50 feet by 150 feet is produced.

(3) The entire storage site shall be kept free from accumulation of unnecessary combustible materials. Weeds and grass shall be kept down and a regular procedure provided for the periodic cleanup of the entire area.

(4) When there is a danger of an underground fire, that land shall not be used for combustible or flammable storage.

(5) Method of piling shall be solid wherever possible and in orderly and regular piles. No combustible material shall be stored outdoors within 10 feet of a building or structure.

(6) Portable fire extinguishing equipment, suitable for the fire hazard involved, shall be provided at convenient, conspicuously accessible locations in the yard area. Portable fire extinguishers, rated not less than 2A, shall be placed so that maximum travel distance to the nearest unit shall not exceed 100 feet.

(d) *Indoor storage.* (1) Storage shall not obstruct, or adversely affect, means of exit.

(2) All materials shall be stored, handled, and piled with due regard to their fire characteristics.

(3) Noncompatible materials, which may create a fire hazard, shall be segregated by a barrier having a fire resistance of at least 1 hour.

(4) Material shall be piled to minimize the spread of fire internally and to permit convenient access for firefighting. Stable piling shall be maintained at all times. Aisle space shall be maintained to safely accommodate the widest vehicle that may be used within the building for firefighting purposes.

(5) Clearance of at least 36 inches shall be maintained between the top level of the stored material and the sprinkler deflectors.

(6) Clearance shall be maintained around lights and heating units to prevent ignition of combustible materials.

(7) A clearance of 24 inches shall be maintained around the path of travel of fire doors unless a barricade is provided, in which case no clearance is needed. Material shall not be stored within 36 inches of a fire door opening.

[44 FR 8577, Feb. 9, 1979; 44 FR 20940, Apr. 6, 1979, as amended at 51 FR 25318, July 11, 1986]

§1926.152 Flammable liquids.

(a) *General requirements.* (1) Only approved containers and portable tanks shall be used for storage and handling of flammable liquids. Approved safety cans or Department of Transportation approved containers shall be used for the handling and use of flammable liquids in quantities of 5 gallons or less, except that this shall not apply to those flammable liquid materials which are highly viscid (extremely hard to pour), which may be used and handled in original shipping containers. For quantities of one gallon or less, the original container may be used, for storage, use and handling of flammable liquids.

(2) Flammable liquids shall not be stored in areas used for exits, stairways, or normally used for the safe passage of people.

(b) *Indoor storage of flammable liquids.* (1) No more than 25 gallons of flammable liquids shall be stored in a room outside of an approved storage cabinet. For storage of liquefied petroleum gas, see §1926.153.

(2) Quantities of flammable liquid in excess of 25 gallons shall be stored in an acceptable or approved cabinet meeting the following requirements:

(i) Acceptable wooden storage cabinets shall be constructed in the following manner, or equivalent: The bottom, sides, and top shall be constructed of an exterior grade of plywood at least 1 inch in thickness, which shall not break down or delaminate under standard fire test conditions. All joints shall be rabbeted and shall be fastened in two directions with flathead wood screws. When more than one door is used, there shall be a rabbeted overlap of not less than 1 inch. Steel hinges shall be mounted in such a manner as to not lose their holding capacity due to loosening or burning out of the screws when subjected to fire. Such cabinets shall be painted inside and out with fire retardant paint.

(ii) Approved metal storage cabinets will be acceptable.

(iii) Cabinets shall be labeled in conspicuous lettering, "Flammable-Keep Away from Open Flames."

(3) Not more than 60 gallons of Category 1, 2 and/or 3 flammable liquids or 120 gallons of Category 4 flammable liquids shall be stored in any one storage cabinet. Not more than three such cabinets may be located in a single storage area. Quantities in excess of this shall be stored in an inside storage room.

(4)(i) Inside storage rooms shall be constructed to meet the required fire-resistive rating for their use. Such construction shall comply with the test specifications set forth in Standard Methods of Fire Test of Building Construction and Material, NFPA 251-1969.

(ii) Where an automatic extinguishing system is provided, the system shall be designed and installed in an approved manner. Openings to other rooms or buildings shall be provided with noncombustible liquid-tight raised sills or ramps at least 4 inches in height, or the floor in the storage area shall be at least 4 inches below the surrounding floor. Openings shall be provided with approved self-closing fire doors. The room shall be liquid-tight where the walls join the floor. A permissible alternate to the sill or ramp is an open-grated trench, inside of the room, which drains to a safe location. Where other portions of the building or other buildings are exposed, windows shall be protected as set forth in the Standard for Fire Doors and Windows, NFPA No. 80–1970, for Class E or F openings. Wood of at least 1-inch nominal thickness may be used for shelving, racks, dunnage, scuffboards, floor overlay, and similar installations.

(iii) Materials which will react with water and create a fire hazard shall not be stored in the same room with flammable liquids.

(iv) Storage in inside storage rooms shall comply with Table F–2 following:

TABLE F–2

Fire protection provided	Fire resistance	Maximum size	Total allowable quantities gals./sq. ft./floor area
Yes	2 hrs	500 sq. ft	10
No	2 hrs	500 sq. ft	4
Yes	1 hr	150 sq. ft	5
No	1 hr	150 sq. ft	2

NOTE: Fire protection system shall be sprinkler, water spray, carbon dioxide or other system approved by a nationally recognized testing laboratory for this purpose.

(v) Electrical wiring and equipment located in inside storage rooms shall be approved for Class I, Division 1, Hazardous Locations. For definition of Class I, Division 1, Hazardous Locations, see § 1926.449.

(vi) Every inside storage room shall be provided with either a gravity or a mechanical exhausting system. Such system shall commence not more than 12 inches above the floor and be designed to provide for a complete change of air within the room at least 6 times per hour. If a mechanical exhausting system is used, it shall be controlled by a switch located outside of the door. The ventilating equipment and any lighting fixtures shall be operated by the same switch. An electric pilot light shall be installed adjacent to the switch if Category 1, 2, or 3 flammable liquids are dispensed within the room. Where gravity ventilation is provided, the fresh air intake, as well as the exhausting outlet from the room, shall be on the exterior of the building in which the room is located.

(vii) In every inside storage room there shall be maintained one clear aisle at least 3 feet wide. Containers over 30 gallons capacity shall not be stacked one upon the other.

(viii) Flammable liquids in excess of that permitted in inside storage rooms shall be stored outside of buildings in accordance with paragraph (c) of this section.

(5) *Quantity.* The quantity of flammable liquids kept in the vicinity of spraying operations shall be the minimum required for operations and should ordinarily not exceed a supply for 1 day or one shift. Bulk storage of portable containers of flammable liquids shall be in a separate, constructed building detached from other important buildings or cut off in a standard manner.

(c) *Storage outside buildings.* (1) Storage of containers (not more than 60 gallons each) shall not exceed 1,100 gallons in any one pile or area. Piles or groups of containers shall be separated by a 5-foot clearance. Piles or groups of containers shall not be nearer than 20 feet to a building.

(2) Within 200 feet of each pile of containers, there shall be a 12-foot-wide access way to permit approach of fire control apparatus.

(3) The storage area shall be graded in a manner to divert possible spills away from buildings or other exposures, or shall be surrounded by a curb or earth dike at least 12 inches high. When curbs or dikes are used, provisions shall be made for draining off accumulations of ground or rain water, or spills of flammable liquids. Drains shall terminate at a safe location and shall be accessible to operation under fire conditions.

(4) Outdoor portable tank storage: (i) Portable tanks shall not be nearer than 20 feet from any building. Two or more portable tanks, grouped together, having a combined capacity in excess of 2,200 gallons, shall be separated by a 5-foot-clear area. Individual portable tanks exceeding 1,100 gallons shall be separated by a 5-foot-clear area.

(ii) Within 200 feet of each portable tank, there shall be a 12-foot-wide access way to permit approach of fire control apparatus.

(5) Storage areas shall be kept free of weeds, debris, and other combustible material not necessary to the storage.

(6) Portable tanks, not exceeding 660 gallons, shall be provided with emergency venting and other devices, as required by chapters III and IV of NFPA 30–1969, The Flammable and Combustible Liquids Code.

(7) Portable tanks, in excess of 660 gallons, shall have emergency venting and other devices, as required by chapters II and III of The Flammable and Combustible Liquids Code, NFPA 30–1969.

(d) *Fire control for flammable liquid storage.* (1) At least one portable fire extinguisher, having a rating of not less than 20–B units, shall be located outside of, but not more than 10 feet from, the door opening into any room used for storage of more than 60 gallons of flammable liquids.

(2) At least one portable fire extinguisher having a rating of not less than 20–B units shall be located not less than 25 feet, nor more than 75 feet, from any flammable liquid storage area located outside.

(3) When sprinklers are provided, they shall be installed in accordance with the Standard for the Installation of Sprinkler Systems, NFPA 13–1969.

(4) At least one portable fire extinguisher having a rating of not less than 20–B:C units shall be provided on all tank trucks or other vehicles used for transporting and/or dispensing flammable liquids.

(e) *Dispensing liquids.* (1) Areas in which flammable liquids are transferred at one time, in quantities greater than 5 gallons from one tank or container to another tank or container, shall be separated from other operations by 25-feet distance or by construction having a fire resistance of at least 1 hour. Drainage or other means shall be provided to control spills. Adequate natural or mechanical ventilation shall be provided to maintain the concentration of flammable vapor at or below 10 percent of the lower flammable limit.

(2) Transfer of Category 1, 2, or 3 flammable liquids from one container to another shall be done only when containers are electrically interconnected (bonded).

(3) Flammable liquids shall be drawn from or transferred into vessels, containers, or tanks within a building or outside only through a closed piping system, from safety cans, by means of a device drawing through the top, or from a container, or portable tanks, by gravity or pump, through an approved self-closing valve. Transferring by means of air pressure on the container or portable tanks is prohibited.

(4) The dispensing units shall be protected against collision damage.

(5) Dispensing devices and nozzles for Category 1, 2, or 3 flammable liquids shall be of an approved type.

(f) *Handling liquids at point of final use.* (1) Category 1, 2, or 3 flammable liquids shall be kept in closed containers when not actually in use.

(2) Leakage or spillage of flammable liquids shall be disposed of promptly and safely.

(3) Category 1, 2, or 3 flammable liquids may be used only where there are no open flames or other sources of ignition within 50 feet of the operation, unless conditions warrant greater clearance.

(g) *Service and refueling areas.* (1) Flammable liquids shall be stored in approved closed containers, in tanks located underground, or in aboveground portable tanks.

(2) The tank trucks shall comply with the requirements covered in the Standard for Tank Vehicles for Flammable and Combustible Liquids, NFPA No. 385–1966.

(3) The dispensing hose shall be an approved type.

(4) The dispensing nozzle shall be an approved automatic-closing type without a latch-open device.

(5) Underground tanks shall not be abandoned.

(6) Clearly identified and easily accessible switch(es) shall be provided at a location remote from dispensing devices to shut off the power to all dispensing devices in the event of an emergency.

(7)(i) Heating equipment of an approved type may be installed in the lubrication or service area where there is no dispensing or transferring of Category 1, 2, or 3 flammable liquids, provided the bottom of the heating unit is at least 18 inches above the floor and is protected from physical damage.

(ii) Heating equipment installed in lubrication or service areas, where Category 1, 2, or 3 flammable liquids are dispensed, shall be of an approved type for garages, and shall be installed at least 8 feet above the floor.

(8) There shall be no smoking or open flames in the areas used for fueling, servicing fuel systems for internal combustion engines, receiving or dispensing of flammable liquids.

(9) Conspicuous and legible signs prohibiting smoking shall be posted.

(10) The motors of all equipment being fueled shall be shut off during the fueling operation.

(11) Each service or fueling area shall be provided with at least one fire extinguisher having a rating of not less than 20-B:C located so that an extinguisher will be within 75 feet of each pump, dispenser, underground fill pipe opening, and lubrication or service area.

(h) *Scope.* This section applies to the handling, storage, and use of flammable liquids with a flashpoint at or below 199.4 °F (93 °C). This section does not apply to:

(1) Bulk transportation of flammable liquids; and

(2) Storage, handling, and use of fuel oil tanks and containers connected with oil burning equipment.

(i) *Tank storage*—(1) *Design and construction of tanks*—(i) *Materials.* (A) Tanks shall be built of steel except as provided in paragraphs (i)(1)(i) (B) through (E) of this section.

(B) Tanks may be built of materials other than steel for installation underground or if required by the properties of the liquid stored. Tanks located above ground or inside buildings shall be of noncombustible construction.

(C) Tanks built of materials other than steel shall be designed to specifications embodying principles recognized as good engineering design for the material used.

(D) Unlined concrete tanks may be used for storing flammable liquids having a gravity of 40° API or heavier. Concrete tanks with special lining may be used for other services provided the design is in accordance with sound engineering practice.

(E) [Reserved]

(F) Special engineering consideration shall be required if the specific gravity of the liquid to be stored exceeds that of water or if the tanks are designed to contain flammable liquids at a liquid temperature below 0 °F.

(ii) *Fabrication.* (A) [Reserved]

(B) Metal tanks shall be welded, riveted, and caulked, brazed, or bolted, or constructed by use of a combination of these methods. Filler metal used in brazing shall be nonferrous metal or an alloy having a melting point above 1000 °F. and below that of the metal joined.

(iii) *Atmospheric tanks.* (A) Atmospheric tanks shall be built in accordance with acceptable good standards of design. Atmospheric tanks may be built in accordance with:

(1) Underwriters' Laboratories, Inc., Subjects No. 142, Standard for Steel Aboveground Tanks for Flammable and Combustible Liquids, 1968; No. 58, Standard for Steel Underground Tanks for Flammable and Combustible Liquids, Fifth Edition, December 1961; or No. 80, Standard for Steel Inside Tanks for Oil-Burner Fuel, September 1963.

(2) American Petroleum Institute Standards No. 12A, Specification for Oil Storage Tanks with Riveted Shells, Seventh Edition, September 1951, or No. 650, Welded Steel Tanks for Oil Storage, Third Edition, 1966.

(3) American Petroleum Institute Standards No. 12B, Specification for Bolted Production Tanks, Eleventh Edition, May 1958, and Supplement 1, March 1962; No. 12D, Specification for Large Welded Production Tanks, Seventh Edition, August 1957; or No. 12F, Specification for Small Welded Production Tanks, Fifth Edition, March 1961. Tanks built in accordance with these standards shall be used only as production tanks for storage of crude petroleum in oil-producing areas.

(B) Tanks designed for underground service not exceeding 2,500 gallons (9,462.5 L) capacity may be used aboveground.

(C) Low-pressure tanks and pressure vessels may be used as atmospheric tanks.

(D) Atmospheric tanks shall not be used for the storage of a flammable liquid at a temperature at or above its boiling point.

(iv) *Low pressure tanks.* (A) The normal operating pressure of the tank shall not exceed the design pressure of the tank.

(B) Low-pressure tanks shall be built in accordance with acceptable standards of design. Low-pressure tanks may be built in accordance with:

(1) American Petroleum Institute Standard No. 620. Recommended Rules for the Design and Construction of Large, Welded, Low-Pressure Storage Tanks, Third Edition, 1966.

(2) The principles of the Code for Unfired Pressure Vessels, Section VIII of the ASME Boiler and Pressure Vessels Code, 1968.

(C) Atmospheric tanks built according to Underwriters' Laboratories, Inc., requirements in paragraph (i)(1)(iii)(A) of this section and shall be limited to 2.5 p.s.i.g. under emergency venting conditions.

This paragraph may be used for operating pressures not exceeding 1 p.s.i.g.

(D) Pressure vessels may be used as low-pressure tanks.

(v) *Pressure vessels.* (A) The normal operating pressure of the vessel shall not exceed the design pressure of the vessel.

(B) Pressure vessels shall be built in accordance with the Code for Unfired Pressure Vessels, Section VIII of the ASME Boiler and Pressure Vessel Code 1968.

(vi) *Provisions for internal corrosion.* When tanks are not designed in accordance with the American Petroleum Institute, American Society of Mechanical Engineers, or the Underwriters' Laboratories, Inc.'s, standards, or if corrosion is anticipated beyond that provided for in the design formulas used, additional metal thickness or suitable protective coatings or linings shall be provided to compensate for the corrosion loss expected during the design life of the tank.

(2) *Installation of outside aboveground tanks.* (i) [Reserved]

(ii) *Spacing (shell-to-shell) between aboveground tanks.* (A) The distance between any two flammable liquid storage tanks shall not be less than 3 feet (0.912 m).

(B) Except as provided in paragraph (i)(2)(ii)(C) of this section, the distance between any two adjacent tanks shall not be less than one-sixth the sum of their diameters. When the diameter of one tank is less than one-half the diameter of the adjacent tank, the distance between the two tanks shall not be less than one-half the diameter of the smaller tank.

(C) Where crude petroleum in conjunction with production facilities are located in noncongested areas and have capacities not exceeding 126,000 gallons (3,000 barrels), the distance between such tanks shall not be less than 3 feet (0.912 m).

(D) Where unstable flammable liquids are stored, the distance between such tanks shall not be less than one-half the sum of their diameters.

(E) When tanks are compacted in three or more rows or in an irregular pattern, greater spacing or other means shall be provided so that inside tanks are accessible for firefighting purposes.

(F) The minimum separation between a liquefied petroleum gas container and a flammable liquid storage tank shall be 20 feet (6.08 m), except in the case of flammable liquid tanks operating at pressures exceeding 2.5 p.s.i.g. or equipped with emergency venting which will permit pressures to exceed 2.5 p.s.i.g. in which case the provisions of paragraphs (i)(2)(ii) (A) and (B) of this section shall apply. Suitable means shall be taken to prevent the accumulation of flammable liquids under adjacent liquefied petroleum gas containers such as by diversion curbs or grading. When flammable liquid storage tanks are within a diked area, the liquefied petroleum gas containers shall be outside the diked area and at least 10 feet (3.04 m) away from the centerline of the wall of the diked area. The foregoing provisions shall not apply when liquefied petroleum gas containers of 125 gallons (473.125 L) or less capacity are installed adjacent to fuel oil supply tanks of 550 gallons (2,081.75 L) or less capacity.

(iii) [Reserved]

(iv) *Normal venting for aboveground tanks.* (A) Atmospheric storage tanks shall be adequately vented to prevent the development of vacuum or pressure sufficient to distort the roof of a cone roof tank or exceeding the design pressure in the case of other atmospheric tanks, as a result of filling or emptying, and atmospheric temperature changes.

(B) Normal vents shall be sized either in accordance with: (*1*) The American Petroleum Institute Standard 2000 (1968), Venting Atmospheric and Low-Pressure Storage Tanks; or (*2*) other accepted standard; or (*3*) shall be at least as large as the filling or withdrawal connection, whichever is larger but in no case less than 1¼ inch (3.175 cm) nominal inside diameter.

(C) Low-pressure tanks and pressure vessels shall be adequately vented to prevent development of pressure or vacuum, as a result of filling or emptying and atmospheric temperature changes, from exceeding the design pressure of the tank or vessel. Protection shall also be provided to prevent overpressure from any pump discharging into the tank or vessel when the pump discharge pressure can exceed the design pressure of the tank or vessel.

(D) If any tank or pressure vessel has more than one fill or withdrawal connection and simultaneous filling or withdrawal can be made, the vent size shall be based on the maximum anticipated simultaneous flow.

(E) Unless the vent is designed to limit the internal pressure 2.5 p.s.i. or less, the outlet of vents and vent drains shall be arranged to discharge in such a manner as to prevent localized overheating of any part of the tank in the event vapors from such vents are ignited.

(F) Tanks and pressure vessels storing Category 1 flammable liquids shall be equipped with venting devices that shall be normally closed except when venting to pressure or vacuum conditions. Tanks and pressure vessels storing Category 2 flammable liquids, or Category 3 flammable liquids with a flashpoint below 100 °F (37.8 °C), shall be equipped with venting devices that shall be normally closed except when venting under pressure or vacuum conditions, or with approved flame arresters.

Exemption: Tanks of 3,000 bbls (barrels) (84 m(3)) capacity or less containing crude petroleum in crude-producing areas; and, outside aboveground

atmospheric tanks under 1,000 gallons (3,785 L) capacity containing other than Category 1 flammable liquids may have open vents. (*See* paragraph (i)(2)(vi)(B) of this section.)

(G) Flame arresters or venting devices required in paragraph (i)(2)(iv)(F) of this section may be omitted for Category 2 flammable liquids or Category 3 flammable liquids with a flashpoint below 100 °F (37.8 °C) where conditions are such that their use may, in case of obstruction, result in tank damage.

(v) *Emergency relief venting for fire exposure for aboveground tanks.* (A) Every aboveground storage tank shall have some form of construction or device that will relieve excessive internal pressure caused by exposure fires.

(B) In a vertical tank the construction referred to in paragraph (i)(2)(v)(A) of this section may take the form of a floating roof, lifter roof, a weak roof-to-shell seam, or other approved pressure relieving construction. The weak roof-to-shell seam shall be constructed to fail preferential to any other seam.

(C) Where entire dependence for emergency relief is placed upon pressure relieving devices, the total venting capacity of both normal and emergency vents shall be enough to prevent rupture of the shell or bottom of the tank if vertical, or of the shell or heads if horizontal. If unstable liquids are stored, the effects of heat or gas resulting from polymerization, decomposition, condensation, or self-reactivity shall be taken into account. The total capacity of both normal and emergency venting devices shall be not less than that derived from Table F–10 except as provided in paragraph (i)(2)(v) (E) or (F) of this section. Such device may be a self-closing manhole cover, or one using long bolts that permit the cover to lift under internal pressure, or an additional or larger relief valve or valves. The wetted area of the tank shall be calculated on the basis of 55 percent of the total exposed area of a sphere or spheroid, 75 percent of the total exposed area of a horizontal tank and the first 30 feet (9.12 m) above grade of the exposed shell area of a vertical tank.

TABLE F–10—WETTED AREA VERSUS CUBIC FEET (METERS) FREE AIR PER HOUR

[14.7 psia and 60 °F. (15.55 °C)]

Square feet (m²)	CFH (m³H)	Square feet (m²)	CFH (m³H)	Square feet (m²)	CFH (m³H)
20 (1.84)	21,100 (590.8)	200 (18.4)	211,000 (5,908)	1,000 (90.2)	524,000 (14,672)
30 (2.76)	31,600 (884.8)	250 (23)	239,000 (6,692)	1,200 (110.4)	557,000 (15,596)
40 (3.68)	42,100 (1,178.8)	300 (27.6)	265,000 (7,420)	1,400 (128.8)	587,000 (16,436)
50 (4.6)	52,700 (1,475.6)	350 (32.2)	288,000 (8,064)	1,600 (147.2)	614,000 (17,192)
60 (5.52)	63,200 (1,769.6)	400 (36.8)	312,000 (8,736)	1,800 (165.6)	639,000 (17,892)
70 (6.44)	73,700 (2,063.6)	500 (46)	354,000 (9,912)	2,000 (180.4)	662,000 (18,536)
80 (7.36)	84,200 (2,357.6)	600 (55.2)	392,000 (10,976)	2,400 (220.8)	704,000 (19,712)
90 (8.28)	94,800 (2,654.4)	700 (64.4)	428,000 (11,984)	2,800 (257.6)	742,000 (20,776)
100 (9.2)	105,000 (2,940)	800 (73.6)	462,000 (12,936)	and	
120 (11.04)	126,000 (3,528)	900 (82.8)	493,000 (13,804)	over	
140 (12.88)	147,000 (4,116)	1,000 (90.2)	524,000 (14,672)		
160 (14.72)	168,000 (4,704)				
180 (16.56)	190,000 (5,320)				
200 (18.4)	211,000 (5,908)				

(D) For tanks and storage vessels designed for pressure over 1 p.s.i.g., the total rate of venting shall be determined in accordance with Table F–10, except that when the exposed wetted area of the surface is greater than 2,800 square feet (257.6 m²), the total rate of venting shall be calculated by the following formula:

$$CFH = 1,107 A^{0.82}$$

Where:

CFH = Venting requirement, in cubic feet (meters) of free air per hour.
A = Exposed wetted surface, in square feet (m²).

NOTE: The foregoing formula is based on $Q=21,000 A^{0.82}$.

(E) The total emergency relief venting capacity for any specific stable liquid may be determined by the following formula:

$$V = 1337 \div L^{\surd} \ M$$

V = Cubic feet (meters) of free air per hour from Table F–10.
L = Latent heat of vaporization of specific liquid in B.t.u. per pound.
M = Molecular weight of specific liquids.

(F) The required airflow rate of paragraph (i)(2)(v) (C) or (E) of this section may be multiplied by the appropriate factor listed in the following schedule when protection is provided as indicated. Only one factor may be used for any one tank.

0.5 for drainage in accordance with paragraph (i)(2)(vii)(B) of this section for tanks over 200 square feet (18.4 m²) of wetted area.
0.3 for approved water spray.
0.3 for approved insulation.

0.15 for approved water spray with approved insulation.

(G) The outlet of all vents and vent drains on tanks equipped with emergency venting to permit pressures exceeding 2.5 p.s.i.g. shall be arranged to discharge in such a way as to prevent localized overheating of any part of the tank, in the event vapors from such vents are ignited.

(H) Each commercial tank venting device shall have stamped on it the opening pressure, the pressure at which the valve reaches the full open position, and the flow capacity at the latter pressure, expressed in cubic feet (meters) per hour of air at 60 °F. (15.55 °C) and at a pressure of 14.7 p.s.i.a.

(I) The flow capacity of tank venting devices 12 inches (30.48 cm) and smaller in nominal pipe size shall be determined by actual test of each type and size of vent. These flow tests may be conducted by the manufacturer if certified by a qualified impartial observer, or may be conducted by an outside agency. The flow capacity of tank venting devices larger than 12 inches (30.48 cm) nominal pipe size, including manhole covers with long bolts or equivalent, may be calculated provided that the opening pressure is actually measured, the rating pressure and corresponding free orifice area are stated, the word "calculated" appears on the nameplate, and the computation is based on a flow coefficient of 0.5 applied to the rated orifice area.

(vi) *Vent piping for aboveground tanks.*
(A) Vent piping shall be constructed in

207

accordance with paragraph (c) of this section.

(B) Where vent pipe outlets for tanks storing Category 1 or 2 flammable liquids, or Category 3 flammable liquids with a flashpoint below 100 °F (37.8 °C), are adjacent to buildings or public ways, they shall be located so that the vapors are released at a safe point outside of buildings and not less than 12 feet (3.658 m) above the adjacent ground level. In order to aid their dispersion, vapors shall be discharged upward or horizontally away from closely adjacent walls. Vent outlets shall be located so that flammable vapors will not be trapped by eaves or other obstructions and shall be at least 5 feet (1.52 m) from building openings.

(C) When tank vent piping is manifolded, pipe sizes shall be such as to discharge, within the pressure limitations of the system, the vapors they may be required to handle when manifolded tanks are subject to the same fire exposure.

(vii) *Drainage, dikes, and walls for aboveground tanks*—(A) *Drainage and diked areas.* The area surrounding a tank or a group of tanks shall be provided with drainage as in paragraph (i)(2)(vii)(B) of this section, or shall be diked as provided in (i)(2)(vii)(C) of this section, to prevent accidental discharge of liquid from endangering adjoining property or reaching waterways.

(B) *Drainage.* Where protection of adjoining property or waterways is by means of a natural or manmade drainage system, such systems shall comply with the following:

(1) [Reserved]

(2) The drainage system shall terminate in vacant land or other area or in an impounding basin having a capacity not smaller than that of the largest tank served. This termination area and the route of the drainage system shall be so located that, if the flammable liquids in the drainage system are ignited, the fire will not seriously expose tanks or adjoining property.

(C) *Diked areas.* Where protection of adjoining property or waterways is accomplished by retaining the liquid around the tank by means of a dike, the volume of the diked area shall comply with the following requirements:

(1) Except as provided in paragraph (i)(2)(vii)(C)(2) of this section, the volumetric capacity of the diked area shall not be less than the greatest amount of liquid that can be released from the largest tank within the diked area, assuming a full tank. The capacity of the diked area enclosing more than one tank shall be calculated by deducting the volume of the tanks other than the largest tank below the height of the dike.

(2) For a tank or group of tanks with fixed roofs containing crude petroleum with boilover characteristics, the volumetric capacity of the diked area shall be not less than the capacity of the largest tank served by the enclosure, assuming a full tank. The capacity of the diked enclosure shall be calculated by deducting the volume below the height of the dike of all tanks within the enclosure.

(3) Walls of the diked area shall be of earth, steel, concrete or solid masonry designed to be liquidtight and to withstand a full hydrostatic head. Earthen walls 3 feet (0.912 m) or more in height shall have a flat section at the top not less than 2 feet (0.608 m) wide. The slope of an earthen wall shall be consistent with the angle of repose of the material of which the wall is constructed.

(4) The walls of the diked area shall be restricted to an average height of 6 feet (1.824 m) above interior grade.

(5) [Reserved]

(6) No loose combustible material, empty or full drum or barrel, shall be permitted within the diked area.

(viii) *Tank openings other than vents for aboveground tanks.*

(A)–(C) [Reserved]

(D) Openings for gaging shall be provided with a vaportight cap or cover.

(E) For Category 2 flammable liquids or Category 3 flammable liquids with a flashpoint below 100 °F (37.8 °C), other than crude oils, gasolines, and asphalts, the fill pipe shall be so designed and installed as to minimize the possibility of generating static electricity. A fill pipe entering the top of a tank shall terminate within 6 inches (15.24 cm) of the bottom of the tank and shall

208

be installed to avoid excessive vibration.

(F) Filling and emptying connections which are made and broken shall be located outside of buildings at a location free from any source of ignition and not less than 5 feet (1.52 m) away from any building opening. Such connection shall be closed and liquidtight when not in use. The connection shall be properly identified.

(3) *Installation of underground tanks*— (i) *Location*. Evacuation for underground storage tanks shall be made with due care to avoid undermining of foundations of existing structures. Underground tanks or tanks under buildings shall be so located with respect to existing building foundations and supports that the loads carried by the latter cannot be transmitted to the tank. The distance from any part of a tank storing Category 1 or 2 flammable liquids, or Category 3 flammable liquids with a flashpoint below 100 °F (37.8 °C), to the nearest wall of any basement or pit shall be not less than 1 foot (0.304 m), and to any property line that may be built upon, not less than 3 feet (0.912 m). The distance from any part of a tank storing Category 3 flammable liquids with a flashpoint at or above 100 °F (37.8 °C) or Category 4 flammable liquids to the nearest wall of any basement, pit or property line shall be not less than 1 foot (0.304 m).

(ii) *Depth and cover*. Underground tanks shall be set on firm foundations and surrounded with at least 6 inches (15.24 cm) of noncorrosive, inert materials such as clean sand, earth, or gravel well tamped in place. The tank shall be placed in the hole with care since dropping or rolling the tank into the hole can break a weld, puncture or damage the tank, or scrape off the protective coating of coated tanks. Tanks shall be covered with a minimum of 2 feet (0.608 m) of earth, or shall be covered with not less than 1 foot (0.304 m) of earth, on top of which shall be placed a slab of reinforced concrete not less than 4 inches (10.16 cm) thick. When underground tanks are, or are likely to be, subject to traffic, they shall be protected against damage from vehicles passing over them by at least

3 feet (0.912 m) of earth cover, or 18 inches (45.72 cm) of well-tamped earth, plus 6 inches (15.24 cm) of reinforced concrete or 8 inches (20.32 cm) of asphaltic concrete. When asphaltic or reinforced concrete paving is used as part of the protection, it shall extend at least 1 foot (0.304 m) horizontally beyond the outline of the tank in all directions.

(iii) *Corrosion protection*. Corrosion protection for the tank and its piping shall be provided by one or more of the following methods:

(A) Use of protective coatings or wrappings;

(B) Cathodic protection; or,

(C) Corrosion resistant materials of construction.

(iv) *Vents*. (A) Location and arrangement of vents for Category 1 or 2 flammable liquids, or Category 3 flammable liquids with a flashpoint below 100 °F (37.8 °C). Vent pipes from tanks storing Category 1 or 2 flammable liquids, or Category 3 flammable liquids with a flashpoint below 100 °F (37.8 °C), shall be so located that the discharge point is outside of buildings, higher than the fill pipe opening, and not less than 12 feet (3.658 m) above the adjacent ground level. Vent pipes shall discharge only upward in order to disperse vapors. Vent pipes 2 inches (5.08 cm) or less in nominal inside diameter shall not be obstructed by devices that will cause excessive back pressure. Vent pipe outlets shall be so located that flammable vapors will not enter building openings, or be trapped under eaves or other obstructions. If the vent pipe is less than 10 feet (3.04 m) in length, or greater than 2 inches (5.08 cm) in nominal inside diameter, the outlet shall be provided with a vacuum and pressure relief device or there shall be an approved flame arrester located in the vent line at the outlet or within the approved distance from the outlet.

(B) Size of vents. Each tank shall be vented through piping adequate in size to prevent blow-back of vapor or liquid at the fill opening while the tank is being filled. Vent pipes shall be not less than 1¼ inch (3.175 cm) nominal inside diameter.

TABLE F-11—VENT LINE DIAMETERS

Maximum flow GPM (L)	Pipe length [1]		
	50 feet (15.2 m)	100 feet (30.4 m)	200 feet (60.8 m)
	Inches　(cm)	Inches　(cm)	Inches　(cm)
100 (378.5)	1¼　(3.175)	1¼　(3.175)	1¼　(3.175)
200 (757)	1¼　(3.175)	1¼　(3.175)	1¼　(3.175)
300 (1,135.5)	1¼　(3.175)	1¼　(3.175)	1½　(3.81)
400 (1,514)	1¼　(3.175)	1½　(3.81)	2　(5.08)
500 (1,892.5)	1½　(3.81)	1½　(3.81)	2　(5.08)
600 (2,271)	1½　(3.81)	2 (5.08)	2 (5.08)
700 (2,649.5)	2 (5.08)	2 (5.08)	2 (5.08)
800 (3,028)	2 (5.08)	2 (5.08)	3 (7.62)
900 (3,406.5)	2 (5.08)	2 (5.08)	3 (7.62)
1,000 (3,785)	2 (5.08)	2 (5.08)	3 (7.62)

[1] Vent lines of 50 ft. (15.2 m), 100 ft. (30.4 m), and 200 ft. (60.8 m) of pipe plus 7 ells.

(C) Location and arrangement of vents for Category 3 flammable liquids with a flashpoint at or above 100 °F (37.8 °C) or Category 4 flammable liquids. Vent pipes from tanks storing Category 3 flammable liquids with a flashpoint at or above 100 °F (37.8 °C) or Category 4 flammable liquids shall terminate outside of the building and higher than the fill pipe opening. Vent outlets shall be above normal snow level. They may be fitted with return bends, coarse screens or other devices to minimize ingress of foreign material.

(D) Vent piping shall be constructed in accordance with paragraph (3)(iv)(C) of this section. Vent pipes shall be so laid as to drain toward the tank without sags or traps in which liquid can collect. They shall be located so that they will not be subjected to physical damage. The tank end of the vent pipe shall enter the tank through the top.

(E) When tank vent piping is manifolded, pipe sizes shall be such as to discharge, within the pressure limitations of the system, the vapors they may be required to handle when manifolded tanks are filled simultaneously.

(v) *Tank openings other than vents.* (A) Connections for all tank openings shall be vapor or liquid tight.

(B) Openings for manual gaging, if independent of the fill pipe, shall be provided with a liquid-tight cap or cover. If inside a building, each such opening shall be protected against liquid overflow and possible vapor release by means of a spring loaded check valve or other approved device.

(C) Fill and discharge lines shall enter tanks only through the top. Fill lines shall be sloped toward the tank.

(D) For Category 2 flammable liquids, or Category 3 flammable liquids with a flashpoint below 100 °F (37.8 °C), other than crude oils, gasolines, and asphalts, the fill pipe shall be so designed and installed as to minimize the possibility of generating static electricity by terminating within 6 inches (15.24 cm) of the bottom of the tank.

(E) Filling and emptying connections which are made and broken shall be located outside of buildings at a location free from any source of ignition and not less than 5 feet (1.52 m) away from any building opening. Such connection shall be closed and liquidtight when not in use. The connection shall be properly identified.

(4) *Installation of tanks inside of buildings*—(i) *Location.* Tanks shall not be permitted inside of buildings except as provided in paragraphs (e), (g), (h), or (i) of this section.

(ii) *Vents.* Vents for tanks inside of buildings shall be as provided in paragraphs (i)(2) (iv), (v), (vi)(B), and (3)(iv) of this section, except that emergency venting by the use of weak roof seams on tanks shall not be permitted. Vents shall discharge vapors outside the buildings.

(iii) *Vent piping.* Vent piping shall be constructed in accordance with paragraph (c) of this section.

(iv) *Tank openings other than vents.* (A) Connections for all tank openings shall be vapor or liquidtight. Vents are covered in paragraph (i)(4)(ii) of this section.

(B) Each connection to a tank inside of buildings through which liquid can normally flow shall be provided with an internal or an external valve located as close as practical to the shell of the tank. Such valves, when external, and their connections to the tank shall be of steel except when the chemical characteristics of the liquid stored are incompatible with steel. When materials other than steel are necessary, they shall be suitable for the pressures, structural stresses, and temperatures involved, including fire exposures.

(C) Flammable liquid tanks located inside of buildings, except in one-story buildings designed and protected for flammable liquid storage, shall be provided with an automatic-closing heat-actuated valve on each withdrawal connection below the liquid level, except for connections used for emergency disposal, to prevent continued flow in the event of fire in the vicinity of the tank. This function may be incorporated in the valve required in paragraph (i)(4)(iv)(B) of this section, and if a separate valve, shall be located adjacent to the valve required in paragraph (i)(4)(iv)(B) of this section.

(D) Openings for manual gaging, if independent of the fill pipe (see paragraph (i)(4)(iv)(F) of this section), shall be provided with a vaportight cap or cover. Each such opening shall be protected against liquid overflow and possible vapor release by means of a spring loaded check valve or other approved device.

(E) For Category 2 flammable liquids, or Category 3 flammable liquids with a flashpoint below 100 °F (37.8 °C), other than crude oils, gasolines, and asphalts, the fill pipe shall be so designed and installed as to minimize the possibility of generating static electricity by terminating within 6 inches (15.24 cm) of the bottom of the tank.

(F) The fill pipe inside of the tank shall be installed to avoid excessive vibration of the pipe.

(G) The inlet of the fill pipe shall be located outside of buildings at a location free from any source of ignition and not less than 5 feet (1.52 m) away from any building opening. The inlet of the fill pipe shall be closed and liquidtight when not in use. The fill connection shall be properly identified.

(H) Tanks inside buildings shall be equipped with a device, or other means shall be provided, to prevent overflow into the building.

(5) *Supports, foundations, and anchorage for all tank locations*—(i) *General.* Tank supports shall be installed on firm foundations. Tank supports shall be of concrete, masonry, or protected steel. Single wood timber supports (not cribbing) laid horizontally may be used for outside aboveground tanks if not more than 12 inches (30.48 cm) high at their lowest point.

(ii) *Fire resistance.* Steel supports or exposed piling shall be protected by materials having a fire resistance rating of not less than 2 hours, except that steel saddles need not be protected if less than 12 inches (30.48 cm) high at their lowest point. Water spray protection or its equivalent may be used in lieu of fire-resistive materials to protect supports.

(iii) *Spheres.* The design of the supporting structure for tanks such as spheres shall receive special engineering consideration.

(iv) *Load distribution.* Every tank shall be so supported as to prevent the excessive concentration of loads on the supporting portion of the shell.

(v) *Foundations.* Tanks shall rest on the ground or on foundations made of concrete, masonry, piling, or steel. Tank foundations shall be designed to minimize the possibility of uneven settling of the tank and to minimize corrosion in any part of the tank resting on the foundation.

(vi) *Flood areas.* Where a tank is located in an area that may be subjected to flooding, the applicable precautions outlined in this subdivision shall be observed.

(A) No aboveground vertical storage tank containing a flammable liquid shall be located so that the allowable liquid level within the tank is below the established maximum flood stage, unless the tank is provided with a guiding structure such as described in paragraphs (i)(5)(vi) (M), (N), and (O) of this section.

(B) Independent water supply facilities shall be provided at locations where there is no ample and dependable public water supply available for loading partially empty tanks with water.

211

(C) In addition to the preceding requirements, each tank so located that more than 70 percent, but less than 100 percent, of its allowable liquid storage capacity will be submerged at the established maximum flood stage, shall be safeguarded by one of the following methods: Tank shall be raised, or its height shall be increased, until its top extends above the maximum flood stage a distance equivalent to 30 percent or more of its allowable liquid storage capacity: *Provided, however,* That the submerged part of the tank shall not exceed two and one-half times the diameter. Or, as an alternative to the foregoing, adequate noncombustible structural guides, designed to permit the tank to float vertically without loss of product, shall be provided.

(D) Each horizontal tank so located that more than 70 percent of its storage capacity will be submerged at the established flood stage, shall be anchored, attached to a foundation of concrete or of steel and concrete, of sufficient weight to provide adequate load for the tank when filled with flammable liquid and submerged by flood waters to the established flood stage, or adequately secured by other means.

(E) [Reserved]

(F) At locations where there is no ample and dependable water supply, or where filling of underground tanks with liquids is impracticable because of the character of their contents, their use, or for other reasons, each tank shall be safeguarded against movement when empty and submerged by high ground water or flood waters by anchoring, weighting with concrete or other approved solid loading material, or securing by other means. Each such tank shall be so constructed and installed that it will safely resist external pressures due to high ground water or flood waters.

(G) At locations where there is an ample and dependable water supply available, underground tanks containing flammable liquids, so installed that more than 70 percent of their storage capacity will be submerged at the maximum flood stage, shall be so anchored, weighted, or secured by other means, as to prevent movement of such tanks when filled with flammable liq-

uids, and submerged by flood waters to the established flood stage.

(H) Pipe connections below the allowable liquid level in a tank shall be provided with valves or cocks located as closely as practicable to the tank shell. Such valves and their connections to tanks shall be of steel or other material suitable for use with the liquid being stored. Cast iron shall not be permitted.

(I) At locations where an independent water supply is required, it shall be entirely independent of public power and water supply. Independent source of water shall be available when flood waters reach a level not less than 10 feet (3.04 m) below the bottom of the lowest tank on a property.

(J) The self-contained power and pumping unit shall be so located or so designed that pumping into tanks may be carried on continuously throughout the rise in flood waters from a level 10 feet (3.04 m) below the lowest tank to the level of the potential flood stage.

(K) Capacity of the pumping unit shall be such that the rate of rise of water in all tanks shall be equivalent to the established potential average rate of rise of flood waters at any stage.

(L) Each independent pumping unit shall be tested periodically to insure that it is in satisfactory operating condition.

(M) Structural guides for holding floating tanks above their foundations shall be so designed that there will be no resistance to the free rise of a tank, and shall be constructed of noncombustible material.

(N) The strength of the structure shall be adequate to resist lateral movement of a tank subject to a horizontal force in any direction equivalent to not less than 25 pounds per square foot (1.05 kg m²) acting on the projected vertical cross-sectional area of the tank.

(O) Where tanks are situated on exposed points or bends in a shoreline where swift currents in flood waters will be present, the structures shall be designed to withstand a unit force of not less than 50 pounds per square foot (2.1 kg m²).

(P) The filling of a tank to be protected by water loading shall be started as soon as flood waters reach a dangerous flood stage. The rate of filling shall be at least equal to the rate of rise of the floodwaters (or the established average potential rate of rise).

(Q) Sufficient fuel to operate the water pumps shall be available at all times to insure adequate power to fill all tankage with water.

(R) All valves on connecting pipelines shall be closed and locked in closed position when water loading has been completed.

(S) Where structural guides are provided for the protection of floating tanks, all rigid connections between tanks and pipelines shall be disconnected and blanked off or blinded before the floodwaters reach the bottom of the tank, unless control valves and their connections to the tank are of a type designed to prevent breakage between the valve and the tank shell.

(T) All valves attached to tanks other than those used in connection with water loading operations shall be closed and locked.

(U) If a tank is equipped with a swing line, the swing pipe shall be raised to and secured at its highest position.

(V) Inspections. The Assistant Secretary or his designated representative shall make periodic inspections of all plants where the storage of flammable liquids is such as to require compliance with the foregoing requirements, in order to assure the following:

(1) That all flammable liquid storage tanks are in compliance with these requirements and so maintained.

(2) That detailed printed instructions of what to do in flood emergencies are properly posted.

(3) That station operators and other employees depended upon to carry out such instructions are thoroughly informed as to the location and operation of such valves and other equipment necessary to effect these requirements.

(vii) *Earthquake areas.* In areas subject to earthquakes, the tank supports and connections shall be designed to resist damage as a result of such shocks.

(6) *Sources of ignition.* In locations where flammable vapors may be present, precautions shall be taken to prevent ignition by eliminating or controlling sources of ignition. Sources of ignition may include open flames, lightning, smoking, cutting and welding, hot surfaces, frictional heat, sparks (static, electrical, and mechanical), spontaneous ignition, chemical and physical-chemical reactions, and radiant heat.

(7) *Testing*—(i) *General.* All tanks, whether shop built or field erected, shall be strength tested before they are placed in service in accordance with the applicable paragraphs of the code under which they were built. The American Society of Mechanical Engineers (ASME) code stamp, American Petroleum Institute (API) monogram, or the label of the Underwriters' Laboratories, Inc., on a tank shall be evidence of compliance with this strength test. Tanks not marked in accordance with the above codes shall be strength tested before they are placed in service in accordance with good engineering principles and reference shall be made to the sections on testing in the codes listed in paragraphs (i)(1) (iii)(A), (iv)(B), or (v)(B) of this section.

(ii) *Strength.* When the vertical length of the fill and vent pipes is such that when filled with liquid the static head imposed upon the bottom of the tank exceeds 10 pounds per square inch (68.94 kPa), the tank and related piping shall be tested hydrostatically to a pressure equal to the static head thus imposed.

(iii) *Tightness.* In addition to the strength test called for in paragraphs (i)(7) (i) and (ii) of this section, all tanks and connections shall be tested for tightness. Except for underground tanks, this tightness test shall be made at operating pressure with air, inert gas, or water prior to placing the tank in service. In the case of field-erected tanks the strength test may be considered to be the test for tank tightness. Underground tanks and piping, before being covered, enclosed, or placed in use, shall be tested for tightness hydrostatically, or with air pressure at not less than 3 pounds per square inch (20.68 kPa) and not more than 5 pounds per square inch (34.47 kPa).

(iv) *Repairs.* All leaks or deformations shall be corrected in an acceptable manner before the tank is placed in service. Mechanical caulking is not permitted for correcting leaks in welded tanks except pinhole leaks in the roof.

(v) *Derated operations.* Tanks to be operated at pressures below their design pressure may be tested by the applicable provisions of paragraphs (i)(7) (i) or (ii) of this section, based upon the pressure developed under full emergency venting of the tank.

(j) *Piping, valves, and fittings*—(1) *General*—(i) *Design.* The design (including selection of materials) fabrication, assembly, test, and inspection of piping systems containing flammable liquids shall be suitable for the expected working pressures and structural stresses. Conformity with the applicable provisions of Pressure Piping, ANSI B31 series and the provisions of this paragraph, shall be considered prima facie evidence of compliance with the foregoing provisions.

(ii) *Exceptions.* This paragraph does not apply to any of the following:

(A) Tubing or casing on any oil or gas wells and any piping connected directly thereto.

(B) Motor vehicle, aircraft, boat, or portable or stationary engines.

(C) Piping within the scope of any applicable boiler and pressures vessel code.

(iii) *Definitions.* As used in this paragraph, piping systems consist of pipe, tubing, flanges, bolting, gaskets, valves, fittings, the pressure containing parts of other components such as expansion joints and strainers, and devices which serve such purposes as mixing, separating, snubbing, distributing, metering, or controlling flow.

(2) *Materials for piping, valves, and fittings*—(i) *Required materials.* Materials for piping, valves, or fittings shall be steel, nodular iron, or malleable iron, except as provided in paragraphs (j)(2) (ii), (iii) and (iv) of this section.

(ii) *Exceptions.* Materials other than steel, nodular iron, or malleable iron may be used underground, or if required by the properties of the flammable liquid handled. Material other than steel, nodular iron, or malleable iron shall be designed to specifications embodying principles recognized as good engineering practices for the material used.

(iii) *Linings.* Piping, valves, and fittings may have combustible or noncombustible linings.

(iv) *Low-melting materials.* When low-melting point materials such as aluminum and brass or materials that soften on fire exposure such as plastics, or non-ductile materials such as cast iron, are necessary, special consideration shall be given to their behavior on fire exposure. If such materials are used in above ground piping systems or inside buildings, they shall be suitably protected against fire exposure or so located that any spill resulting from the failure of these materials could not unduly expose persons, important buildings or structures or can be readily controlled by remote valves.

(3) *Pipe joints.* Joints shall be made liquid tight. Welded or screwed joints or approved connectors shall be used. Threaded joints and connections shall be made up tight with a suitable lubricant or piping compound. Pipe joints dependent upon the friction characteristics of combustible materials for mechanical continuity of piping shall not be used inside buildings. They may be used outside of buildings above or below ground. If used above ground, the piping shall either be secured to prevent disengagement at the fitting or the piping system shall be so designed that any spill resulting from such disengagement could not unduly expose persons, important buildings or structures, and could be readily controlled by remote valves.

(4) *Supports.* Piping systems shall be substantially supported and protected against physical damage and excessive stresses arising from settlement, vibration, expansion, or contraction.

(5) *Protection against corrosion.* All piping for flammable liquids, both aboveground and underground, where subject to external corrosion, shall be painted or otherwise protected.

(6) *Valves.* Piping systems shall contain a sufficient number of valves to operate the system properly and to protect the plant. Piping systems in connection with pumps shall contain a sufficient number of valves to control properly the flow of liquid in normal operation and in the event of physical damage. Each connection to pipelines, by which equipments such as tankcars

or tank vehicles discharge liquids by means of pumps into storage tanks, shall be provided with a check valve for automatic protection against backflow if the piping arrangement is such that backflow from the system is possible.

(7) *Testing.* All piping before being covered, enclosed, or placed in use shall be hydrostatically tested to 150 percent of the maximum anticipated pressure of the system, or pneumatically tested to 110 percent of the maximum anticipated pressure of the system, but not less than 5 pounds per square inch gage at the highest point of the system. This test shall be maintained for a sufficient time to complete visual inspection of all joints and connections, but for at least 10 minutes.

(k) *Marine service stations*—(1) *Dispensing.* (i) The dispensing area shall be located away from other structures so as to provide room for safe ingress and egress of craft to be fueled. Dispensing units shall in all cases be at least 20 feet (6.08 m) from any activity involving fixed sources of ignition.

(ii) Dispensing shall be by approved dispensing units with or without integral pumps and may be located on open piers, wharves, or floating docks or on shore or on piers of the solid fill type.

(iii) Dispensing nozzles shall be automatic-closing without a hold-open latch.

(2) *Tanks and pumps.* (i) Tanks, and pumps not integral with the dispensing unit, shall be on shore or on a pier of the solid fill type, except as provided in paragraphs (k)(2) (ii) and (iii) of this section.

(ii) Where shore location would require excessively long supply lines to dispensers, tanks may be installed on a pier provided that applicable portions of paragraph (b) of this section relative to spacing, diking, and piping are complied with and the quantity so stored does not exceed 1,100 gallons (4,163.5 L) aggregate capacity.

(iii) Shore tanks supplying marine service stations may be located above ground, where rock ledges or high water table make underground tanks impractical.

(iv) Where tanks are at an elevation which would produce gravity head on the dispensing unit, the tank outlet shall be equipped with a pressure control valve positioned adjacent to and outside the tank block valve specified in § 1926.152(c)(8) of this section, so adjusted that liquid cannot flow by gravity from the tank in case of piping or hose failure.

(3) *Piping.* (i) Piping between shore tanks and dispensing units shall be as described in paragraph (k)(2)(iii) of this section, except that, where dispensing is from a floating structure, suitable lengths of oil-resistant flexible hose may be employed between the shore piping and the piping on the floating structure as made necessary by change in water level or shoreline.

TABLE F-19 - ELECTRICAL EQUIPMENT HAZARDOUS AREAS - SERVICE STATIONS

Location	Class I Group D division	Extent of classified area
Underground tank:		
Fill opening	1	Any pit, box or space below grade level, any part of which is within the Division 1 or 2 classified area.
	2	Up to 18 inches (45.72 cm) above grade level within a horizontal radius of 10 feet (3.04 m) from a loose fill connection and within a horizontal radius of 5 feet (1.52 m) from a tight fill connection.
Vent - Discharging upward...	1	Within 3 feet (0.912 m) of open end of vent, extending in all directions.
	2	Area between 3 feet (0.912 m) and 5 feet (1.52 m) of open end of vent, extending in all directions.
Dispenser:		
Pits......................	1	Any pit, box or space below grade level, any part of which is within the Division 1 or 2 classified area.
Dispenser enclosure........	1	The area 4 feet (1.216 m) vertically above base within the enclosure and 18 inches (45.72 cm) horizontally in all directions.
Outdoor...................	2	Up to 18 inches (45.72 cm) above grade level within 20 feet (6.08 m) horizontally of any edge of enclosure.
Indoor:		
With mechanical ventilation.	2	Up to 18 inches (45.72 cm) above grade level within 20 feet (6.08 m) horizontally of any edge of enclosure.
With gravity ventilation....	2	Up to 18 inches (45.72 cm) above grade or floor level within 25 feet (7.6 m) horizontally of any edge of enclosure.
Remote pump - Outdoor.......	1	Any pit, box or space below grade level if any part is within a horizontal distance of 10 feet (3.04 m) from any edge of pump.
	2	Within 3 feet (0.912 m) of any edge of pump, extending

216

		in all directions. Also up to 18 inches (45.72 cm) above grade level within 10 feet (3.04 m) horizontally from any edge of pump.
Remote pump - Indoor........	1	Entire area within any pit.
	2	Within 5 feet (1.52 m) of any edge of pump, extending in all directions. Also up to 3 feet (3.04 m) above floor or grade level within 25 feet (6.08 m) horizontally from any edge of pump.
Lubrication or service room.	1	Entire area within any pit.
	2	Area up to 18 inches (45.72 cm) above floor or grade level within entire lubrication room.
Dispenser for Category 1 or 2 flammable liquids, or Category 3 flammable liquids with a flashpoint below 100 ° F (37.8 ° C)	2	Within 3 feet (0.912 m) of any fill or dispensing point, extending in all directions.
Special enclosure inside building per 1910.106(f)(1)(ii).	1	Entire enclosure.
Sales, storage and rest rooms...............	(1)	If there is any opening to these rooms within the extent of a Division 1 area, the entire room shall be classified as Division 1.

(1) Ordinary.

*   *   *   *   *

(ii) A readily accessible valve to shut off the supply from shore shall be provided in each pipeline at or near the approach to the pier and at the shore end of each pipeline adjacent to the point where flexible hose is attached.

(iii) Piping shall be located so as to be protected from physical damage.

(iv) Piping handling Category 1 or 2 flammable liquids, or Category 3 flammable liquids with a flashpoint below 100 °F (37.8 °C), shall be grounded to control stray currents.

(4) *Definition; as used in this section:* Marine service station shall mean that portion of a property where flammable liquids used as fuels are stored and dispensed from fixed equipment on shore, piers, wharves, or floating docks into the fuel tanks of self-propelled craft, and shall include all facilities used in connection therewith.

[44 FR 8577, Feb. 9, 1979; 44 FR 20940, Apr. 6, 1979, as amended at 51 FR 25318, July 11, 1986; 58 FR 35162, June 30, 1993; 63 FR 33469, June 18, 1998; 77 FR 17891, Mar. 26, 2012]

§ 1926.153 Liquefied petroleum gas (LP-Gas).

(a) *Approval of equipment and systems.* (1) Each system shall have containers, valves, connectors, manifold valve assemblies, and regulators of an approved type.

(2) All cylinders shall meet the Department of Transportation specification identification requirements published in 49 CFR part 178, Shipping Container Specifications.

(3) *Definition.* As used in this section, *Containers*—All vessels, such as tanks, cylinders, or drums, used for transportation or storing liquefied petroleum gases.

(b) *Welding on LP-Gas containers.* Welding is prohibited on containers.

(c) *Container valves and container accessories.* (1) Valves, fittings, and accessories connected directly to the container, including primary shut off valves, shall have a rated working pressure of at least 250 p.s.i.g. and shall be of material and design suitable for LP-Gas service.

(2) Connections to containers, except safety relief connections, liquid level gauging devices, and plugged openings, shall have shutoff valves located as close to the container as practicable.

(d) *Safety devices.* (1) Every container and every vaporizer shall be provided with one or more approved safety relief valves or devices. These valves shall be arranged to afford free vent to the outer air with discharge not less than 5 feet horizontally away from any opening into a building which is below such discharge.

(2) Shutoff valves shall not be installed between the safety relief device and the container, or the equipment or piping to which the safety relief device is connected, except that a shutoff valve may be used where the arrangement of this valve is such that full required capacity flow through the safety relief device is always afforded.

(3) Container safety relief devices and regulator relief vents shall be located not less than 5 feet in any direction from air openings into sealed combustion system appliances or mechanical ventilation air intakes.

(e) *Dispensing.* (1) Filling of fuel containers for trucks or motor vehicles from bulk storage containers shall be performed not less than 10 feet from the nearest masonry-walled building, or not less than 25 feet from the nearest building or other construction and, in any event, not less than 25 feet from any building opening.

(2) Filling of portable containers or containers mounted on skids from storage containers shall be performed not less than 50 feet from the nearest building.

(f) *Requirements for appliances.* (1) LP-Gas consuming appliances shall be approved types.

(2) Any appliance that was originally manufactured for operation with a gaseous fuel other than LP-Gas, and is in good condition, may be used with LP-Gas only after it is properly converted, adapted, and tested for performance with LP-Gas before the appliance is placed in use.

(g) *Containers and regulating equipment installed outside of buildings or structures.* Containers shall be upright upon firm foundations or otherwise firmly secured. The possible effect on the outlet piping of settling shall be guarded against by a flexible connection or special fitting.

(h) *Containers and equipment used inside of buildings or structures.* (1) When operational requirements make portable use of containers necessary, and their location outside of buildings or structures is impracticable, containers and equipment shall be permitted to be used inside of buildings or structures in accordance with paragraphs (h)(2) through (11) of this section.

(2) *Containers in use* means connected for use.

(3) Systems utilizing containers having a water capacity greater than 2½ pounds (nominal 1 pound LP-Gas capacity) shall be equipped with excess flow valves. Such excess flow valves shall be either integral with the container valves or in the connections to the container valve outlets.

(4) Regulators shall be either directly connected to the container valves or to manifolds connected to the container valves. The regulator shall be suitable for use with LP-Gas. Manifolds and fittings connecting containers to pressure regulator inlets shall be designed for at least 250 p.s.i.g. service pressure.

(5) Valves on containers having water capacity greater than 50 pounds (nominal 20 pounds LP-Gas capacity) shall be protected from damage while in use or storage.

(6) Aluminum piping or tubing shall not be used.

(7) Hose shall be designed for a working pressure of at least 250 p.s.i.g. Design, construction, and performance of hose, and hose connections shall have their suitability determined by listing

by a nationally recognized testing agency. The hose length shall be as short as practicable. Hoses shall be long enough to permit compliance with spacing provisions of paragraphs (h)(1) through (13) of this section, without kinking or straining, or causing hose to be so close to a burner as to be damaged by heat.

(8) Portable heaters, including salamanders, shall be equipped with an approved automatic device to shut off the flow of gas to the main burner, and pilot if used, in the event of flame failure. Such heaters, having inputs above 50,000 B.t.u. per hour, shall be equipped with either a pilot, which must be lighted and proved before the main burner can be turned on, or an electrical ignition system.

NOTE: The provisions of this subparagraph do not apply to portable heaters under 7,500 B.t.u. per hour input when used with containers having a maximum water capacity of 2½ pounds.

(9) Container valves, connectors, regulators, manifolds, piping, and tubing shall not be used as structural supports for heaters.

(10) Containers, regulating equipment, manifolds, pipe, tubing, and hose shall be located to minimize exposure to high temperatures or physical damage.

(11) Containers having a water capacity greater than 2½ pounds (nominal 1 pound LP-Gas capacity) connected for use shall stand on a firm and substantially level surface and, when necessary, shall be secured in an upright position.

(12) The maximum water capacity of individual containers shall be 245 pounds (nominal 100 pounds LP-Gas capacity).

(13) For temporary heating, heaters (other than integral heater-container units) shall be located at least 6 feet from any LP-Gas container. This shall not prohibit the use of heaters specifically designed for attachment to the container or to a supporting standard, provided they are designed and installed so as to prevent direct or radiant heat application from the heater onto the containers. Blower and radiant type heaters shall not be directed toward any LP-Gas container within 20 feet.

(14) If two or more heater-container units, of either the integral or non-integral type, are located in an unpartitioned area on the same floor, the container or containers of each unit shall be separated from the container or containers of any other unit by at least 20 feet.

(15) When heaters are connected to containers for use in an unpartitioned area on the same floor, the total water capacity of containers, manifolded together for connection to a heater or heaters, shall not be greater than 735 pounds (nominal 300 pounds LP-Gas capacity). Such manifolds shall be separated by at least 20 feet.

(16) Storage of containers awaiting use shall be in accordance with paragraphs (j) and (k) of this section.

(i) *Multiple container systems.* (1) Valves in the assembly of multiple container systems shall be arranged so that replacement of containers can be made without shutting off the flow of gas in the system. This provision is not to be construed as requiring an automatic changeover device.

(2) Heaters shall be equipped with an approved regulator in the supply line between the fuel cylinder and the heater unit. Cylinder connectors shall be provided with an excess flow valve to minimize the flow of gas in the event the fuel line becomes ruptured.

(3) Regulators and low-pressure relief devices shall be rigidly attached to the cylinder valves, clyinders, supporting standards, the building walls, or otherwise rigidly secured, and shall be so installed or protected from the elements.

(j) *Storage of LPG containers.* Storage of LPG within buildings is prohibited.

(k) *Storage outside of buildings.* (1) Storage outside of buildings, for containers awaiting use, shall be located from the nearest building or group of buildings, in accordance with the following:

TABLE F–3

Quantity of LP-Gas stored	Distance (feet)
500 lbs. or less	0
501 to 6,000 lbs	10
6,001 to 10,000 lbs	20
Over 10,000 lbs	25

(2) Containers shall be in a suitable ventilated enclosure or otherwise protected against tampering.

(l) *Fire protection.* Storage locations shall be provided with at least one approved portable fire extinguisher having a rating of not less than 20–B:C.

(m) *Systems utilizing containers other than DOT containers*—(1) *Application.* This paragraph applies specifically to systems utilizing storage containers other than those constructed in accordance with DOT specifications. Paragraph (b) of this section applies to this paragraph unless otherwise noted in paragraph (b) of this section.

(2) *Design pressure and classification of storage containers.* Storage containers shall be designed and classified in accordance with Table F–31.

TABLE F–31

Container type	For gases with vapor press. Not to exceed lb. per sq. in. gage at 100 °F. (37.8 °C.)	Minimum design pressure of container, lb. per sq. in. gage	
		1949 and earlier editions of ASME Code (Par. U–68, U–69)	1949 edition of ASME Code (Par. U–200, U–201); 1950, 1952, 1956, 1959, 1962, 1965, and 1968 (Division 1) editions of ASME Code; All editions of API-ASME Code [3]
[1]80	[1]80	[1]80	[1]100
100	100	100	125
125	125	125	156
150	150	150	187
175	175	175	219
[2]200	215	200	250

[1] New storage containers of the 80 type have not been authorized since Dec. 31, 1947.

[2] Container type may be increased by increments of 25. The minimum design pressure of containers shall be 100% of the container type designation when constructed under 1949 or earlier editions of the ASME Code (Par. U–68 and U–69). The minimum design pressure of containers shall be 125% of the container type designation when constructed under: (1) the 1949 ASME Code (Par. U–200 and U–201), (2) 1950, 1952, 1956, 1959, 1962, 1965, and 1968 (Division 1) editions of the ASME Code, and (3) all editions of the API-ASME Code.

[3] Construction of containers under the API-ASME Code is not authorized after July 1, 1961.

(3) Containers with foundations attached (portable or semiportable b containers with suitable steel "runners" or "skids" and popularly known in the industry as "skid tanks") shall be designed, installed, and used in accordance with these rules subject to the following provisions:

(i) If they are to be used at a given general location for a temporary period not to exceed 6 months they need not have fire-resisting foundations or saddles but shall have adequate ferrous metal supports.

(ii) They shall not be located with the outside bottom of the container shell more than 5 feet (1.52 m) above the surface of the ground unless fire-resisting supports are provided.

(iii) The bottom of the skids shall not be less than 2 inches (5.08 cm) or more than 12 inches (30.48 cm) below the outside bottom of the container shell.

(iv) Flanges, nozzles, valves, fittings, and the like, having communication with the interior of the container, shall be protected against physical damage.

(v) When not permanently located on fire-resisting foundations, piping connections shall be sufficiently flexible to minimize the possibility of breakage or leakage of connections if the container settles, moves, or is otherwise displaced.

(vi) Skids, or lugs for attachment of skids, shall be secured to the container in accordance with the code or rules under which the container is designed and built (with a minimum factor of safety of four) to withstand loading in any direction equal to four times the weight of the container and attachments when filled to the maximum permissible loaded weight.

(4) Field welding where necessary shall be made only on saddle plates or brackets which were applied by the manufacturer of the tank.

(n) When LP-Gas and one or more other gases are stored or used in the same area, the containers shall be marked to identify their content. Marking shall be in compliance with American National Standard Z48.1–1954, "Method of Marking Portable Compressed Gas Containers To Identify the Material Contained."

(o) *Damage from vehicles.* When damage to LP-Gas systems from vehicular traffic is a possibility, precautions against such damage shall be taken.

[44 FR 8577, Feb. 9, 1979; 44 FR 20940, Apr. 6, 1979, as amended at 58 FR 35170, June 30, 1993]

§ 1926.154 Temporary heating devices.

(a) *Ventilation.* (1) Fresh air shall be supplied in sufficient quantities to maintain the health and safety of workmen. Where natural means of fresh air supply is inadequate, mechanical ventilation shall be provided.

(2) When heaters are used in confined spaces, special care shall be taken to provide sufficient ventilation in order to ensure proper combustion, maintain the health and safety of workmen, and limit temperature rise in the area.

(b) *Clearance and mounting.* (1) Temporary heating devices shall be installed to provide clearance to combustible material not less than the amount shown in Table F–4.

(2) Temporary heating devices, which are listed for installation with lesser clearances than specified in Table F–4, may be installed in accordance with their approval.

TABLE F–4

Heating appliances	Minimum clearance, (inches)		
	Sides	Rear	Chimney connector
Room heater, circulating type	12	12	18
Room heater, radiant type ..	36	36	18

(3) Heaters not suitable for use on wood floors shall not be set directly upon them or other combustible materials. When such heaters are used, they shall rest on suitable heat insulating material or at least 1-inch concrete, or equivalent. The insulating material shall extend beyond the heater 2 feet or more in all directions.

(4) Heaters used in the vicinity of combustible tarpaulins, canvas, or similar coverings shall be located at least 10 feet from the coverings. The coverings shall be securely fastened to prevent ignition or upsetting of the heater due to wind action on the covering or other material.

(c) *Stability.* Heaters, when in use, shall be set horizontally level, unless otherwise permitted by the manufacturer's markings.

(d) *Solid fuel salamanders.* Solid fuel salamanders are prohibited in buildings and on scaffolds.

(e) *Oil-fired heaters.* (1) Flammable liquid-fired heaters shall be equipped with a primary safety control to stop the flow of fuel in the event of flame failure. Barometric or gravity oil feed shall not be considered a primary safety control.

(2) Heaters designed for barometric or gravity oil feed shall be used only with the integral tanks.

(3) [Reserved]

(4) Heaters specifically designed and approved for use with separate supply tanks may be directly connected for gravity feed, or an automatic pump, from a supply tank.

§ 1926.155 Definitions applicable to this subpart.

(a) *Approved,* for the purpose of this subpart, means equipment that has been listed or approved by a nationally recognized testing laboratory such as Factory Mutual Engineering Corp., or Underwriters' Laboratories, Inc., or Federal agencies such as Bureau of Mines, or U.S. Coast Guard, which issue approvals for such equipment.

(b) *Closed container* means a container so sealed by means of a lid or other device that neither liquid nor vapor will escape from it at ordinary temperatures.

(c) [Reserved]

(d) *Combustion* means any chemical process that involves oxidation sufficient to produce light or heat.

(e) *Fire brigade* means an organized group of employees that are knowledgeable, trained, and skilled in the safe evacuation of employees during emergency situations and in assisting in fire fighting operations.

(f) *Fire resistance* means so resistant to fire that, for specified time and under conditions of a standard heat intensity, it will not fail structurally and will not permit the side away from the fire to become hotter than a specified temperature. For purposes of this part, fire resistance shall be determined by the Standard Methods of Fire Tests of Building Construction and Materials, NFPA 251–1969.

(g) *Flammable* means capable of being easily ignited, burning intensely, or having a rapid rate of flame spread.

(h) *Flammable liquid* means any liquid having a vapor pressure not exceeding 40 pounds per square inch (absolute) at 100 °F (37.8 °C) and having a flashpoint at or below 199.4 °F (93 °C). Flammable liquids are divided into four categories as follows:

(1) Category 1 shall include liquids having flashpoints below 73.4 °F (23 °C)

and having a boiling point at or below
95 °F (35 °C).

(2) Category 2 shall include liquids
having flashpoints below 73.4 °F (23 °C)
and having a boiling point above 95 °F
(35 °C).

(3) Category 3 shall include liquids
having flashpoints at or above 73.4 °F
(23 °C) and at or below 140 °F (60 °C).

(4) Category 4 shall include liquids
having flashpoints above 140 °F (60 °C)
and at or below 199.4 °F (93 °C).

(i) *Flash point* of the liquid means the
temperature at which it gives off vapor
sufficient to form an ignitable mixture
with the air near the surface of the liquid or within the vessel used as determined by appropriate test procedure
and apparatus as specified below.

(1) The flashpoint of liquids having a
viscosity less than 45 Saybolt Universal Second(s) at 100 °F (37.8 °C) and
a flashpoint below 175 °F (79.4 °C) shall
be determined in accordance with the
Standard Method of Test for Flash
Point by the Tag Closed Tester, ASTM
D–56–69 (incorporated by reference; *See*
§ 1926.6), or an equivalent method as defined by § 1910.1200 appendix B.

(2) The flashpoints of liquids having a
viscosity of 45 Saybolt Universal Sec-
ond(s) or more at 175 °F (79.4 °C) or
higher shall be determined in accordance with the Standard Method of Test
for Flash Point by the Pensky Martens
Closed Tester, ASTM D–93–69 (incorporated by reference; *See* § 1926.6), or an
equivalent method as defined by
§ 1910.1200 appendix B.

(j) *Liquefied petroleum gases, LPG* and
LP Gas mean and include any material
which is composed predominantly of
any of the following hydrocarbons, or
mixtures of them, such as propane, pro-
pylene, butane (normal butane or iso-
butane), and butylenes.

(k) *Portable tank* means a closed container having a liquid capacity more
than 60 U.S. gallons, and not intended
for fixed installation.

(l) *Safety can* means an approved
closed container, of not more than 5
gallons capacity, having a flash-arrest-
ing screen, spring-closing lid and spout
cover and so designed that it will safely relieve internal pressure when subjected to fire exposure.

(m) *Vapor pressure* means the pressure, measured in pounds per square

inch (absolute), exerted by a volatile
liquid as determined by the "Standard
Method of Test for Vapor Pressure of
Petroleum Products (Reid Method)."
(ASTM D–323–58).

[44 FR 8577, Feb. 9, 1979; 44 FR 20940, Apr. 6,
1979, as amended at 77 FR 17894, Mar. 26, 2012]

Subpart G—Signs, Signals, and Barricades

AUTHORITY: 40 U.S.C. 333; 29 U.S.C. 653, 655,
657; Secretary of Labor's Order No. 12–71 (36
FR 8754), 8–76 (41 FR 25059), 9–83 (48 FR 35736),
3–2000 (65 FR 50017), 5–2002 (67 FR 65008), 5–
2007 (72 FR 31159), 4–2010 (75 FR 55355), or 1–
2012 (77 FR 3912), as applicable; and 29 CFR
part 1911.

§ 1926.200 Accident prevention signs and tags.

(a) *General.* Signs and symbols required by this subpart shall be visible
at all times when work is being performed, and shall be removed or covered promptly when the hazards no
longer exist.

(b) *Danger signs.* (1) Danger signs
shall be used only where an immediate
hazard exists, and shall follow the specifications illustrated in Figure 1 of
ANSI Z35.1–1968 or in Figures 1 to 13 of
ANSI Z535.2–2011, incorporated by reference in § 1926.6.

(2) Danger signs shall have red as the
predominating color for the upper
panel; black outline on the borders;
and a white lower panel for additional
sign wording.

(c) *Caution signs.* (1) Caution signs
shall be used only to warn against potential hazards or to caution against
unsafe practices, and shall follow the
specifications illustrated in Figure 4 of
ANSI Z35.1–1968 or in Figures 1 to 13 of
ANSI Z535.2–2011, incorporated by reference in § 1926.6.

(2) Caution signs shall have yellow as
the predominating color; black upper
panel and borders: yellow lettering of
"caution" on the black panel; and the
lower yellow panel for additional sign
wording. Black lettering shall be used
for additional wording.

Figure G-1

Figure G-2

(3) The standard color of the background shall be yellow; and the panel, black with yellow letters. Any letters used against the yellow background shall be black. The colors shall be those of opaque glossy samples as specified in Table 1 of ANSI Z53.1–1967 or in Table 1 of ANSI Z535.1–2006(R2011), incorporated by reference in § 1926.6.

(d) *Exit signs.* Exit signs, when required, shall be lettered in legible red letters, not less than 6 inches high, on a white field and the principal stroke of the letters shall be at least three-fourths inch in width.

(e) *Safety instruction signs.* Safety instruction signs, when used, shall be white with green upper panel with white letters to convey the principal message. Any additional wording on the sign shall be black letters on the white background.

(f) *Directional signs.* Directional signs, other than automotive traffic signs specified in paragraph (g) of this section, shall be white with a black panel and a white directional symbol. Any additional wording on the sign shall be black letters on the white background.

(g) *Traffic signs.* (1) Construction areas shall be posted with legible traffic signs at points of hazard.

(2) All traffic control signs or devices used for protection of construction workers shall conform to Part VI of the MUTCD, 1988 Edition, Revision 3, or Part VI of the MUTCD, Millennium Edition, incorporated by reference in § 1926.6.

(h) *Accident prevention tags.* (1) Accident prevention tags shall be used as a temporary means of warning employees of an existing hazard, such as defective tools, equipment, etc. They shall not be used in place of, or as a substitute for, accident prevention signs.

(2) For accident prevention tags, employers shall follow specifications that are similar to those in Figures 1 to 4 of ANSI Z35.2–1968 or Figures 1 to 8 of ANSI Z535.5–2011, incorporated by reference in § 1926.6.

(i) *Additional rules.* ANSI Z35.1–1968, ANSI Z535.2–2011, ANSI Z35.2–1968, and ANSI Z535.5–2011, incorporated by reference in § 1926.6, contain rules in addition to those specifically prescribed in this subpart. The employer shall comply with ANSI Z35.1–1968 or ANSI Z535.2–2011, and ANSI Z35.2–1968 or Z535.5–2011, with respect to such additional rules.

[44 FR 8577, Feb. 9, 1979; 44 FR 20940, Apr. 6, 1979, as amended at 58 FR 35173, June 30, 1993; 67 FR 57736, Sept. 12, 2002; 69 FR 18803, Apr. 9, 2004; 78 FR 35567, June 13, 2013; 78 FR 66642, Nov. 6, 2013]

§ 1926.201 Signaling.

(a) *Flaggers.* Signaling by flaggers and the use of flaggers, including warning garments worn by flaggers, shall conform to Part VI of the Manual on Uniform Traffic Control Devices (1988 Edition, Revision 3, or the Millennium Edition), incorporated by reference in § 1926.6.

(b) *Crane and hoist signals.* Regulations for crane and hoist signaling will be found in applicable American National Standards Institute standards.

[44 FR 8577, Feb. 9, 1979; 44 FR 20940, Apr. 6, 1979, as amended at 67 FR 57736, Sept. 12, 2002; 78 FR 35567, June 13, 2013]

§ 1926.202 Barricades.

Barricades for protection of employees shall conform to Part VI of the Manual on Uniform Traffic Control Devices (1988 Edition, Revision 3, or the Millennium Edition), incorporated by reference in § 1926.6.

[78 FR 35567, June 13, 2013]

§ 1926.203 Definitions applicable to this subpart.

(a) *Barricade* means an obstruction to deter the passage of persons or vehicles.

(b) *Signs* are the warnings of hazard, temporarily or permanently affixed or placed, at locations where hazards exist.

(c) *Signals* are moving signs, provided by workers, such as flaggers, or by devices, such as flashing lights, to warn of possible or existing hazards.

(d) *Tags* are temporary signs, usually attached to a piece of equipment or part of a structure, to warn of existing or immediate hazards.

[44 FR 8577, Feb. 9, 1979; 44 FR 20940, Apr. 6, 1979, as amended at 67 FR 57736, Sept. 12, 2002]

Subpart H—Materials Handling, Storage, Use, and Disposal

AUTHORITY: 40 U.S.C. 3701; 29 U.S.C. 653, 655, 657; and Secretary of Labor's Order No. 12–71 (36 FR 8754), 8–76 (41 FR 25059), 9–83 (48 FR 35736), 1–90 (55 FR 9033), 4–2010 (75 FR 55355), or 1–2012 (77 FR 3912), as applicable. Section 1926.250 also issued under 29 CFR part 1911.

§ 1926.250 General requirements for storage.

(a) *General.* (1) All materials stored in tiers shall be stacked, racked, blocked, interlocked, or otherwise secured to prevent sliding, falling or collapse.

(2) Maximum safe load limits of floors within buildings and structures, in pounds per square foot, shall be conspicuously posted in all storage areas, except for floor or slab on grade. Maximum safe loads shall not be exceeded.

(3) Aisles and passageways shall be kept clear to provide for the free and safe movement of material handling equipment or employees. Such areas shall be kept in good repair.

(4) When a difference in road or working levels exist, means such as ramps, blocking, or grading shall be used to ensure the safe movement of vehicles between the two levels.

(b) *Material storage.* (1) Material stored inside buildings under construction shall not be placed within 6 feet of any hoistway or inside floor openings, nor within 10 feet of an exterior wall which does not extend above the top of the material stored.

(2) Each employee required to work on stored material in silos, hoppers, tanks, and similar storage areas shall be equipped with personal fall arrest equipment meeting the requirements of subpart M of this part.

(3) Noncompatible materials shall be segregated in storage.

(4) Bagged materials shall be stacked by stepping back the layers and cross-keying the bags at least every 10 bags high.

(5) Materials shall not be stored on scaffolds or runways in excess of supplies needed for immediate operations.

(6) Brick stacks shall not be more than 7 feet in height. When a loose brick stack reaches a height of 4 feet, it shall be tapered back 2 inches in every foot of height above the 4-foot level.

(7) When masonry blocks are stacked higher than 6 feet, the stack shall be tapered back one-half block per tier above the 6-foot level.

(8) Lumber:

(i) Used lumber shall have all nails withdrawn before stacking.

(ii) Lumber shall be stacked on level and solidly supported sills.

(iii) Lumber shall be so stacked as to be stable and self-supporting.

(iv) Lumber piles shall not exceed 20 feet in height provided that lumber to be handled manually shall not be stacked more than 16 feet high.

(9) Structural steel, poles, pipe, bar stock, and other cylindrical materials, unless racked, shall be stacked and blocked so as to prevent spreading or tilting.

(c) *Housekeeping.* Storage areas shall be kept free from accumulation of materials that constitute hazards from tripping, fire, explosion, or pest harborage. Vegetation control will be exercised when necessary.

(d) *Dockboards (bridge plates).* (1) Portable and powered dockboards shall be strong enough to carry the load imposed on them.

(2) Portable dockboards shall be secured in position, either by being anchored or equipped with devices which will prevent their slipping.

(3) Handholds, or other effective means, shall be provided on portable dockboards to permit safe handling.

(4) Positive protection shall be provided to prevent railroad cars from

being moved while dockboards or bridge plates are in position.

[44 FR 8577, Feb. 9, 1979; 44 FR 20940, Apr. 6, 1979, as amended at 49 FR 18295, Apr. 30, 1984; 54 FR 24334, June 7, 1989; 58 FR 35173, June 30, 1993; 59 FR 40729, Aug. 9, 1994; 61 FR 5510, Feb. 13, 1996]

§1926.251 Rigging equipment for material handling.

(a) *General.* (1) Rigging equipment for material handling shall be inspected prior to use on each shift and as necessary during its use to ensure that it is safe. Defective rigging equipment shall be removed from service.

(2) Employers must ensure that rigging equipment:

(i) Has permanently affixed and legible identification markings as prescribed by the manufacturer that indicate the recommended safe working load;

(ii) Not be loaded in excess of its recommended safe working load as prescribed on the identification markings by the manufacturer; and

(iii) Not be used without affixed, legible identification markings, required by paragraph (a)(2)(i) of this section.

(3) Rigging equipment, when not in use, shall be removed from the immediate work area so as not to present a hazard to employees.

(4) Special custom design grabs, hooks, clamps, or other lifting accessories, for such units as modular panels, prefabricated structures and similar materials, shall be marked to indicate the safe working loads and shall be proof-tested prior to use to 125 percent of their rated load.

(5) *Scope.* This section applies to slings used in conjunction with other material handling equipment for the movement of material by hoisting, in employments covered by this part. The types of slings covered are those made from alloy steel chain, wire rope, metal mesh, natural or synthetic fiber rope (conventional three strand construction), and synthetic web (nylon, polyester, and polypropylene).

(6) *Inspections.* Each day before being used, the sling and all fastenings and attachments shall be inspected for damage or defects by a competent person designated by the employer. Additional inspections shall be performed during sling use, where service conditions warrant. Damaged or defective slings shall be immediately removed from service.

(b) *Alloy steel chains.* (1) Welded alloy steel chain slings shall have permanently affixed durable identification stating size, grade, rated capacity, and sling manufacturer.

(2) Hooks, rings, oblong links, pear-shaped links, welded or mechanical coupling links, or other attachments, when used with alloy steel chains, shall have a rated capacity at least equal to that of the chain.

(3) Job or shop hooks and links, or makeshift fasteners, formed from bolts, rods, etc., or other such attachments, shall not be used.

(4) Employers must not use alloy steel-chain slings with loads in excess of the rated capacities (i.e., working load limits) indicated on the sling by permanently affixed and legible identification markings prescribed by the manufacturer.

(5) Whenever wear at any point of any chain link exceeds that shown in Table H–1, the assembly shall be removed from service.

(6) *Inspections.* (i) In addition to the inspection required by other paragraphs of this section, a thorough periodic inspection of alloy steel chain slings in use shall be made on a regular basis, to be determined on the basis of (A) frequency of sling use; (B) severity of service conditions; (C) nature of lifts being made; and (D) experience gained on the service life of slings used in similar circumstances. Such inspections shall in no event be at intervals greater than once every 12 months.

(ii) The employer shall make and maintain a record of the most recent month in which each alloy steel chain sling was thoroughly inspected, and shall make such record available for examination.

(c) *Wire rope.* (1) Employers must not use improved plow-steel wire rope and wire-rope slings with loads in excess of the rated capacities (i.e., working load limits) indicated on the sling by permanently affixed and legible identification markings prescribed by the manufacturer.

(2) Protruding ends of strands in splices on slings and bridles shall be covered or blunted.

(3) Wire rope shall not be secured by knots, except on haul back lines on scrapers.

(4) The following limitations shall apply to the use of wire rope:

(i) An eye splice made in any wire rope shall have not less than three full tucks. However, this requirement shall not operate to preclude the use of another form of splice or connection which can be shown to be as efficient and which is not otherwise prohibited.

(ii) Except for eye splices in the ends of wires and for endless rope slings, each wire rope used in hoisting or lowering, or in pulling loads, shall consist of one continuous piece without knot or splice.

(iii) Eyes in wire rope bridles, slings, or bull wires shall not be formed by wire rope clips or knots.

(iv) Wire rope shall not be used if, in any length of eight diameters, the total number of visible broken wires exceeds 10 percent of the total number of wires, or if the rope shows other signs of excessive wear, corrosion, or defect.

(5) When U-bolt wire rope clips are used to form eyes, Table H–2 shall be used to determine the number and spacing of clips.

(i) When used for eye splices, the U-bolt shall be applied so that the "U" section is in contact with the dead end of the rope.

(11) [Reserved]

(6) Slings shall not be shortened with knots or bolts or other makeshift devices.

(7) Sling legs shall not be kinked.

(8) Slings used in a basket hitch shall have the loads balanced to prevent slippage.

(9) Slings shall be padded or protected from the sharp edges of their loads.

(10) Hands or fingers shall not be placed between the sling and its load while the sling is being tightened around the load.

(11) Shock loading is prohibited.

(12) A sling shall not be pulled from under a load when the load is resting on the sling.

(13) *Minimum sling lengths.* (i) Cable laid and 6 × 19 and 6 × 37 slings shall have a minimum clear length of wire rope 10 times the component rope diameter between splices, sleeves or end fittings.

(ii) Braided slings shall have a minimum clear length of wire rope 40 times the component rope diameter between the loops or end fittings.

(iii) Cable laid grommets, strand laid grommets and endless slings shall have a minimum circumferential length of 96 times their body diameter.

(14) *Safe operating temperatures.* Fiber core wire rope slings of all grades shall be permanently removed from service if they are exposed to temperatures in excess of 200 °F (93.33 °C). When nonfiber core wire rope slings of any grade are used at temperatures above 400 °F (204.44 °C) or below minus 60 °F (15.55 °C), recommendations of the sling manufacturer regarding use at that temperature shall be followed.

(15) *End attachments.* (i) Welding of end attachments, except covers to thimbles, shall be performed prior to the assembly of the sling.

(ii) All welded end attachments shall not be used unless proof tested by the manufacturer or equivalent entity at twice their rated capacity prior to initial use. The employer shall retain a certificate of the proof test, and make it available for examination.

(16) Wire rope slings shall have permanently affixed, legible identification markings stating size, rated capacity for the type(s) of hitch(es) used and the angle upon which it is based, and the number of legs if more than one.

(d) *Natural rope, and synthetic fiber.* (1) Employers must not use natural- and synthetic-fiber rope slings with loads in excess of the rated capacities (i.e., working load limits) indicated on the sling by permanently affixed and legible identification markings prescribed by the manufacturer.

(2) All splices in rope slings provided by the employer shall be made in accordance with fiber rope manufacturers recommendations.

(i) In manila rope, eye splices shall contain at least three full tucks, and short splices shall contain at least six full tucks (three on each side of the centerline of the splice).

(ii) In layed synthetic fiber rope, eye splices shall contain at least four full tucks, and short splices shall contain at least eight full tucks (four on each side of the centerline of the splice).

(iii) Strand end tails shall not be trimmed short (flush with the surface of the rope) immediately adjacent to the full tucks. This precaution applies to both eye and short splices and all types of fiber rope. For fiber ropes under 1-inch diameter, the tails shall project at least six rope diameters beyond the last full tuck. For fiber ropes 1-inch diameter and larger, the tails shall project at least 6 inches beyond the last full tuck. In applications where the projecting tails may be objectionable, the tails shall be tapered and spliced into the body of the rope using at least two additional tucks (which will require a tail length of approximately six rope diameters beyond the last full tuck).

(iv) For all eye splices, the eye shall be sufficiently large to provide an included angle of not greater than 60° at the splice when the eye is placed over the load or support.

(v) Knots shall not be used in lieu of splices.

(3) *Safe operating temperatures.* Natural and synthetic fiber rope slings, except for wet frozen slings, may be used in a temperature range from minus 20 °F (−28.88 °C) to plus 180 °F (82.2 °C) without decreasing the working load limit. For operations outside this temperature range and for wet frozen slings, the sling manufacturer's recommendations shall be followed.

(4) *Splicing.* Spliced fiber rope slings shall not be used unless they have been spliced in accordance with the following minimum requirements and in accordance with any additional recommendations of the manufacturer:

(i) In manila rope, eye splices shall consist of at least three full tucks, and short splices shall consist of at least six full tucks, three on each side of the splice center line.

(ii) In synthetic fiber rope, eye splices shall consist of at least four full tucks, and short splices shall consist of at least eight full tucks, four on each side of the center line.

(iii) Strand end tails shall not be trimmed flush with the surface of the

rope immediately adjacent to the full tucks. This applies to all types of fiber rope and both eye and short splices. For fiber rope under 1 inch (2.54 cm) in diameter, the tail shall project at least six rope diameters beyond the last full tuck. For fiber rope 1 inch (2.54 cm) in diameter and larger, the tail shall project at least 6 inches (15.24 cm) beyond the last full tuck. Where a projecting tail interferes with the use of the sling, the tail shall be tapered and spliced into the body of the rope using at least two additional tucks (which will require a tail length of approximately six rope diameters beyond the last full tuck).

(iv) Fiber rope slings shall have a minimum clear length of rope between eye splices equal to 10 times the rope diameter.

(v) Knots shall not be used in lieu of splices.

(vi) Clamps not designed specifically for fiber ropes shall not be used for splicing.

(vii) For all eye splices, the eye shall be of such size to provide an included angle of not greater than 60 degrees at the splice when the eye is placed over the load or support.

(5) *End attachments.* Fiber rope slings shall not be used if end attachments in contact with the rope have sharp edges or projections.

(6) *Removal from service.* Natural and synthetic fiber rope slings shall be immediately removed from service if any of the following conditions are present:

(i) Abnormal wear.

(ii) Powdered fiber between strands.

(iii) Broken or cut fibers.

(iv) Variations in the size or roundness of strands.

(v) Discoloration or rotting.

(vi) Distortion of hardware in the sling.

(7) Employers must use natural- and synthetic-fiber rope slings that have permanently affixed and legible identification markings that state the rated capacity for the type(s) of hitch(es) used and the angle upon which it is based, type of fiber material, and the number of legs if more than one.

(e) *Synthetic webbing (nylon, polyester, and polypropylene).* (1) The employer shall have each synthetic web sling marked or coded to show:

(i) Name or trademark of manufacturer.

(ii) Rated capacities for the type of hitch.

(iii) Type of material.

(2) Rated capacity shall not be exceeded.

(3) *Webbing.* Synthetic webbing shall be of uniform thickness and width and selvage edges shall not be split from the webbing's width.

(4) *Fittings.* Fittings shall be:

(i) Of a minimum breaking strength equal to that of the sling; and

(ii) Free of all sharp edges that could in any way damage the webbing.

(5) *Attachment of end fittings to webbing and formation of eyes.* Stitching shall be the only method used to attach end fittings to webbing and to form eyes. The thread shall be in an even pattern and contain a sufficient number of stitches to develop the full breaking strength of the sling.

(6) *Environmental conditions.* When synthetic web slings are used, the following precautions shall be taken:

(i) Nylon web slings shall not be used where fumes, vapors, sprays, mists or liquids of acids or phenolics are present.

(ii) Polyester and polypropylene web slings shall not be used where fumes, vapors, sprays, mists or liquids of caustics are present.

(iii) Web slings with aluminum fittings shall not be used where fumes, vapors, sprays, mists or liquids of caustics are present.

(7) *Safe operating temperatures.* Synthetic web slings of polyester and nylon shall not be used at temperatures in excess of 180 °F (82.2 °C). Polypropylene web slings shall not be used at temperatures in excess of 200 °F (93.33 °C).

(8) *Removal from service.* Synthetic web slings shall be immediately removed from service if any of the following conditions are present:

(i) Acid or caustic burns;

(ii) Melting or charring of any part of the sling surface;

(iii) Snags, punctures, tears or cuts;

(iv) Broken or worn stitches; or

(v) Distortion of fittings.

(f) *Shackles and hooks.* (1) Employers must not use shackles with loads in excess of the rated capacities (i.e., working load limits) indicated on the shackle by permanently affixed and legible identification markings prescribed by the manufacturer.

(2) The manufacturer's recommendations shall be followed in determining the safe working loads of the various sizes and types of specific and identifiable hooks. All hooks for which no applicable manufacturer's recommendations are available shall be tested to twice the intended safe working load before they are initially put into use. The employer shall maintain a record of the dates and results of such tests.

TABLE H–1—MAXIMUM ALLOWABLE WEAR AT ANY POINT OF LINK

Chain size (inches)	Maximum allowable wear (inch)
1/4	3/64
3/8	5/64
1/2	7/64
5/8	9/64
3/4	5/32
7/8	11/64
1	3/16
1 1/8	7/32
1 1/4	1/4
1 3/8	9/32
1 1/2	5/16
1 3/4	11/32

TABLE H–2—NUMBER AND SPACING OF U-BOLT WIRE ROPE CLIPS

Improved plow steel, rope diameter (inches)	Number of clips		Minimum spacing (inches)
	Drop forged	Other material	
1/2	3	4	3
5/8	3	4	3 3/4
3/4	4	5	4 1/2
7/8	4	5	5 1/4
1	5	6	6
1 1/8	6	6	6 3/4
1 1/4	6	7	7 1/2
1 3/8	7	7	8 1/4
1 1/2	7	8	9

[44 FR 8577, Feb. 9, 1979; 44 FR 20940, Apr. 6, 1979, as amended at 58 FR 35173, June 30, 1993; 76 FR 33611, June 8, 2011; 77 FR 23118, Apr. 18, 2012]

§ 1926.252 Disposal of waste materials.

(a) Whenever materials are dropped more than 20 feet to any point lying outside the exterior walls of the building, an enclosed chute of wood, or equivalent material, shall be used. For the purpose of this paragraph, an enclosed chute is a slide, closed in on all sides, through which material is moved from a high place to a lower one.

(b) When debris is dropped through holes in the floor without the use of chutes, the area onto which the material is dropped shall be completely enclosed with barricades not less than 42 inches high and not less than 6 feet back from the projected edge of the opening above. Signs warning of the hazard of falling materials shall be posted at each level. Removal shall not be permitted in this lower area until debris handling ceases above.

(c) All scrap lumber, waste material, and rubbish shall be removed from the immediate work area as the work progresses.

(d) Disposal of waste material or debris by burning shall comply with local fire regulations.

(e) All solvent waste, oily rags, and flammable liquids shall be kept in fire resistant covered containers until removed from worksite.

Subpart I—Tools—Hand and Power

AUTHORITY: Sections 4, 6, and 8 of the Occupational Safety and Health Act of 1970 (29 U.S.C. 653, 655, 657); Secretary of Labor's Order No. 12–71 (36 FR 8754), 8–76 (41 FR 25059), 9–83 (48 FR 35736), 1–90 (55 FR 9033), or 5–2002 (67 FR 65008), as applicable; and 29 CFR part 1911. Section 1926.307 also issued under 5 U.S.C. 553.

§1926.300   General requirements.

(a) *Condition of tools.* All hand and power tools and similar equipment, whether furnished by the employer or the employee, shall be maintained in a safe condition.

(b) *Guarding.* (1) When power operated tools are designed to accommodate guards, they shall be equipped with such guards when in use.

(2) Belts, gears, shafts, pulleys, sprockets, spindles, drums, fly wheels, chains, or other reciprocating, rotating or moving parts of equipment shall be guarded if such parts are exposed to contact by employees or otherwise create a hazard. Guarding shall meet the requirements as set forth in American National Standards Institute, B15.1–1953 (R1958), Safety Code for Mechanical Power-Transmission Apparatus.

(3) *Types of guarding.* One or more methods of machine guarding shall be provided to protect the operator and other employees in the machine area from hazards such as those created by point of operation, ingoing nip points, rotating parts, flying chips and sparks. Examples of guarding methods are—barrier guards, two-hand tripping devices, electronic safety devices, etc.

(4) *Point of operation guarding.* (i) Point of operation is the area on a machine where work is actually performed upon the material being processed.

(ii) The point of operation of machines whose operation exposes an employee to injury, shall be guarded. The guarding device shall be in conformity with any appropriate standards therefor, or, in the absence of applicable specific standards, shall be so designed and constructed as to prevent the operator from having any part of his body in the danger zone during the operating cycle.

(iii) Special handtools for placing and removing material shall be such as to permit easy handling of material without the operator placing a hand in the danger zone. Such tools shall not be in lieu of other guarding required by this section, but can only be used to supplement protection provided.

(iv) The following are some of the machines which usually require point of operation guarding:

(*a*) Guillotine cutters.

(*b*) Shears.

(*c*) Alligator shears.

(*d*) Power presses.

(*e*) Milling machines.

(*f*) Power saws.

(*g*) Jointers.

(*h*) Portable power tools.

(*i*) Forming rolls and calenders.

(5) *Exposure of blades.* When the periphery of the blades of a fan is less than 7 feet (2.128 m) above the floor or working level, the blades shall be guarded. The guard shall have openings no larger than ½ inch (1.27 cm).

(6) *Anchoring fixed machinery.* Machines designed for a fixed location shall be securely anchored to prevent walking or moving.

(7) *Guarding of abrasive wheel machinery—exposure adjustment.* Safety guards of the types described in paragraphs (b)

(8) and (9) of this section, where the operator stands in front of the opening, shall be constructed so that the peripheral protecting member can be adjusted to the constantly decreasing diameter of the wheel. The maximum angular exposure above the horizontal plane of the wheel spindle as specified in paragraphs (b) (8) and (9) of this section shall never be exceeded, and the distance between the wheel periphery and the adjustable tongue or the end of the peripheral member at the top shall never exceed ¼ inch (0.635 cm). (See Figures I–1 through I–6.)

Figure I–1   Figure I–2
Correct

Showing adjustable tongue giving required angle protection for all sizes of wheel used.

Figure I–3   Figure I–4
Correct

Showing movable guard with opening small enough to give required protection for the smallest size wheel used.

Figure I–5   Figure I–6
Incorrect

Showing movable guard with size of opening correct for full size wheel but too large for smaller wheel.

(8) *Bench and floor stands.* The angular exposure of the grinding wheel periphery and sides for safety guards used on machines known as bench and floor stands should not exceed 90° or one-fourth of the periphery. This exposure shall begin at a point not more than 65° above the horizontal plane of the wheel spindle. (See Figures I–7 and I–8 and paragraph (b)(7) of this section.)

Figure I–7   Figure I–8

Wherever the nature of the work requires contact with the wheel below the horizontal plane of the spindle, the exposure shall not exceed 125° (See Figures I–9 and I–10.)

Figure I–9   Figure I–10

(9) *Cylindrical grinders.* The maximum angular exposure of the grinding wheel periphery and sides for safety guards used on cylindrical grinding machines shall not exceed 180°. This exposure shall begin at a point not more than 65° above the horizontal plane of the wheel spindle. (See Figures I–11 and I–12 and paragraph (b)(7) of this section.)

Figure I–11   Figure I–12

(c) *Personal protective equipment.* Employees using hand and power tools and exposed to the hazard of falling, flying, abrasive, and splashing objects, or exposed to harmful dusts, fumes, mists, vapors, or gases shall be provided with the particular personal protective equipment necessary to protect them from the hazard. All personal protective equipment shall meet the requirements and be maintained according to subparts D and E of this part.

(d) *Switches*. (1) All hand-held powered platen sanders, grinders with wheels 2-inch diameter or less, routers, planers, laminate trimmers, nibblers, shears, scroll saws, and jigsaws with blade shanks one-fourth of an inch wide or less may be equipped with only a positive "on-off" control.

(2) All hand-held powered drills, tappers, fastener drivers, horizontal, vertical, and angle grinders with wheels greater than 2 inches in diameter, disc sanders, belt sanders, reciprocating saws, saber saws, and other similar operating powered tools shall be equipped with a momentary contact "on-off" control and may have a lock-on control provided that turnoff can be accomplished by a single motion of the same finger or fingers that turn it on.

(3) All other hand-held powered tools, such as circular saws, chain saws, and percussion tools without positive accessory holding means, shall be equipped with a constant pressure switch that will shut off the power when the pressure is released.

(4) The requirements of this paragraph shall become effective on July 15, 1972.

(5) Exception: This paragraph does not apply to concrete vibrators, concrete breakers, powered tampers, jack hammers, rock drills, and similar hand operated power tools.

[44 FR 8577, Feb. 9, 1979; 44 FR 20940, Apr. 6, 1979, as amended at 58 FR 35175, June 30, 1993; 61 FR 9250, Mar. 7, 1996]

§1926.301 Hand tools.

(a) Employers shall not issue or permit the use of unsafe hand tools.

(b) Wrenches, including adjustable, pipe, end, and socket wrenches shall not be used when jaws are sprung to the point that slippage occurs.

(c) Impact tools, such as drift pins, wedges, and chisels, shall be kept free of mushroomed heads.

(d) The wooden handles of tools shall be kept free of splinters or cracks and shall be kept tight in the tool.

§1926.302 Power-operated hand tools.

(a) *Electric power-operated tools*. (1) Electric power operated tools shall either be of the approved double-insulated type or grounded in accordance with subpart K of this part.

(2) The use of electric cords for hoisting or lowering tools shall not be permitted.

(b) *Pneumatic power tools*. (1) Pneumatic power tools shall be secured to the hose or whip by some positive means to prevent the tool from becoming accidentally disconnected.

(2) Safety clips or retainers shall be securely installed and maintained on pneumatic impact (percussion) tools to prevent attachments from being accidentally expelled.

(3) All pneumatically driven nailers, staplers, and other similar equipment provided with automatic fastener feed, which operate at more than 100 p.s.i. pressure at the tool shall have a safety device on the muzzle to prevent the tool from ejecting fasteners, unless the muzzle is in contact with the work surface.

(4) Compressed air shall not be used for cleaning purposes except where reduced to less than 30 p.s.i. and then only with effective chip guarding and personal protective equipment which meets the requirements of subpart E of this part. The 30 p.s.i. requirement does not apply for concrete form, mill scale and similar cleaning purposes.

(5) The manufacturer's safe operating pressure for hoses, pipes, valves, filters, and other fittings shall not be exceeded,

(6) The use of hoses for hoisting or lowering tools shall not be permitted.

(7) All hoses exceeding ½-inch inside diameter shall have a safety device at the source of supply or branch line to reduce pressure in case of hose failure.

(8) Airless spray guns of the type which atomize paints and fluids at high pressures (1,000 pounds or more per square inch) shall be equipped with automatic or visible manual safety devices which will prevent pulling of the trigger to prevent release of the paint or fluid until the safety device is manually released.

(9) In lieu of the above, a diffuser nut which will prevent high pressure, high velocity release, while the nozzle tip is removed, plus a nozzle tip guard which will prevent the tip from coming into contact with the operator, or other equivalent protection, shall be provided.

(10) *Abrasive blast cleaning nozzles.* The blast cleaning nozzles shall be equipped with an operating valve which must be held open manually. A support shall be provided on which the nozzle may be mounted when it is not in use.

(c) *Fuel powered tools.* (1) All fuel powered tools shall be stopped while being refueled, serviced, or maintained, and fuel shall be transported, handled, and stored in accordance with subpart F of this part.

(2) When fuel powered tools are used in enclosed spaces, the applicable requirements for concentrations of toxic gases and use of personal protective equipment, as outlined in subparts D and E of this part, shall apply.

(d) *Hydraulic power tools.* (1) The fluid used in hydraulic powered tools shall be fire-resistant fluids approved under Schedule 30 of the U.S. Bureau of Mines, Department of the Interior, and shall retain its operating characteristics at the most extreme temperatures to which it will be exposed.

(2) The manufacturer's safe operating pressures for hoses, valves, pipes, filters, and other fittings shall not be exceeded.

(e) *Powder-actuated tools.* (1) Only employees who have been trained in the operation of the particular tool in use shall be allowed to operate a powder-actuated tool.

(2) The tool shall be tested each day before loading to see that safety devices are in proper working condition. The method of testing shall be in accordance with the manufacturer's recommended procedure.

(3) Any tool found not in proper working order, or that develops a defect during use, shall be immediately removed from service and not used until properly repaired.

(4) Personal protective equipment shall be in accordance with subpart E of this part.

(5) Tools shall not be loaded until just prior to the intended firing time. Neither loaded nor empty tools are to be pointed at any employees. Hands shall be kept clear of the open barrel end.

(6) Loaded tools shall not be left unattended.

(7) Fasteners shall not be driven into very hard or brittle materials including, but not limited to, cast iron, glazed tile, surface-hardened steel, glass block, live rock, face brick, or hollow tile.

(8) Driving into materials easily penetrated shall be avoided unless such materials are backed by a substance that will prevent the pin or fastener from passing completely through and creating a flying missile hazard on the other side.

(9) No fastener shall be driven into a spalled area caused by an unsatisfactory fastening.

(10) Tools shall not be used in an explosive or flammable atmosphere.

(11) All tools shall be used with the correct shield, guard, or attachment recommended by the manufacturer.

(12) Powder-actuated tools used by employees shall meet all other applicable requirements of American National Standards Institute, A10.3–1970, Safety Requirements for Explosive-Actuated Fastening Tools.

[44 FR 8577, Feb. 9, 1979; 44 FR 20940, Apr. 6, 1979, as amended at 58 FR 35175, June 30, 1993]

§ 1926.303 Abrasive wheels and tools.

(a) *Power.* All grinding machines shall be supplied with sufficient power to maintain the spindle speed at safe levels under all conditions of normal operation.

(b) *Guarding.* (1) Grinding machines shall be equipped with safety guards in conformance with the requirements of American National Standards Institute, B7.1–1970, Safety Code for the Use, Care and Protection of Abrasive Wheels, and paragraph (d) of this section.

(2) *Guard design.* The safety guard shall cover the spindle end, nut, and flange projections. The safety guard shall be mounted so as to maintain proper alignment with the wheel, and the strength of the fastenings shall exceed the strength of the guard, except:

(i) Safety guards on all operations where the work provides a suitable measure of protection to the operator, may be so constructed that the spindle end, nut, and outer flange are exposed; and where the nature of the work is such as to entirely cover the side of the wheel, the side covers of the guard may be omitted; and

(ii) The spindle end, nut, and outer flange may be exposed on machines designed as portable saws.

(c) *Use of abrasive wheels.* (1) Floor stand and bench mounted abrasive wheels, used for external grinding, shall be provided with safety guards (protection hoods). The maximum angular exposure of the grinding wheel periphery and sides shall be not more than 90°, except that when work requires contact with the wheel below the horizontal plane of the spindle, the angular exposure shall not exceed 125°. In either case, the exposure shall begin not more than 65° above the horizontal plane of the spindle. Safety guards shall be strong enough to withstand the effect of a bursting wheel.

(2) Floor and bench-mounted grinders shall be provided with work rests which are rigidly supported and readily adjustable. Such work rests shall be kept at a distance not to exceed one-eighth inch from the surface of the wheel.

(3) Cup type wheels used for external grinding shall be protected by either a revolving cup guard or a band type guard in accordance with the provisions of the American National Standards Institute, B7.1–1970 Safety Code for the Use, Care, and Protection of Abrasive Wheels. All other portable abrasive wheels used for external grinding, shall be provided with safety guards (protection hoods) meeting the requirements of paragraph (c)(5) of this section, except as follows:

(i) When the work location makes it impossible, a wheel equipped with safety flanges, as described in paragraph (c)(5) of this section, shall be used;

(ii) When wheels 2 inches or less in diameter which are securely mounted on the end of a steel mandrel are used.

(4) Portable abrasive wheels used for internal grinding shall be provided with safety flanges (protection flanges) meeting the requirements of paragraph (c)(6) of this section, except as follows:

(i) When wheels 2 inches or less in diameter which are securely mounted on the end of a steel mandrel are used;

(ii) If the wheel is entirely within the work being ground while in use.

(5) When safety guards are required, they shall be so mounted as to maintain proper alignment with the wheel, and the guard and its fastenings shall be of sufficient strength to retain fragments of the wheel in case of accidental breakage. The maximum angular exposure of the grinding wheel periphery and sides shall not exceed 180°.

(6) When safety flanges are required, they shall be used only with wheels designed to fit the flanges. Only safety flanges, of a type and design and properly assembled so as to ensure that the pieces of the wheel will be retained in case of accidental breakage, shall be used.

(7) All abrasive wheels shall be closely inspected and ring-tested before mounting to ensure that they are free from cracks or defects.

(8) Grinding wheels shall fit freely on the spindle and shall not be forced on. The spindle nut shall be tightened only enough to hold the wheel in place.

(9) All employees using abrasive wheels shall be protected by eye protection equipment in accordance with the requirements of subpart E of this part, except when adequate eye protection is afforded by eye shields which are permanently attached to the bench or floor stand.

(d) *Other requirements.* All abrasive wheels and tools used by employees shall meet other applicable requirements of American National Standards Institute, B7.1–1970, Safety Code for the Use, Care and Protection of Abrasive Wheels.

(e) *Work rests.* On offhand grinding machines, work rests shall be used to support the work. They shall be of rigid construction and designed to be adjustable to compensate for wheel wear. Work rests shall be kept adjusted closely to the wheel with a maximum opening of ⅛ inch (0.3175 cm) to prevent the work from being jammed between the wheel and the rest, which may cause wheel breakage. The work rest shall be securely clamped after each adjustment. The adjustment shall not be made with the wheel in motion.

[44 FR 8577, Feb. 9, 1979; 44 FR 20940, Apr. 6, 1979, as amended at 58 FR 35175, June 30, 1993]

§1926.304 Woodworking tools.

(a) *Disconnect switches.* All fixed power driven woodworking tools shall be provided with a disconnect switch

233

that can either be locked or tagged in the off position.

(b) *Speeds.* The operating speed shall be etched or otherwise permanently marked on all circular saws over 20 inches in diameter or operating at over 10,000 peripheral feet per minute. Any saw so marked shall not be operated at a speed other than that marked on the blade. When a marked saw is retensioned for a different speed, the marking shall be corrected to show the new speed.

(c) *Self-feed.* Automatic feeding devices shall be installed on machines whenever the nature of the work will permit. Feeder attachments shall have the feed rolls or other moving parts covered or guarded so as to protect the operator from hazardous points.

(d) *Guarding.* All portable, power-driven circular saws shall be equipped with guards above and below the base plate or shoe. The upper guard shall cover the saw to the depth of the teeth, except for the minimum arc required to permit the base to be tilted for bevel cuts. The lower guard shall cover the saw to the depth of the teeth, except for the minimum arc required to allow proper retraction and contact with the work. When the tool is withdrawn from the work, the lower guard shall automatically and instantly return to the covering position.

(e) *Personal protective equipment.* All personal protective equipment provided for use shall conform to subpart E of this part.

(f) *Other requirements.* All woodworking tools and machinery shall meet other applicable requirements of American National Standards Institute, 01.1–1961, Safety Code for Woodworking Machinery.

(g) *Radial saws.* (1) The upper hood shall completely enclose the upper portion of the blade down to a point that will include the end of the saw arbor. The upper hood shall be constructed in such a manner and of such material that it will protect the operator from flying splinters, broken saw teeth, etc., and will deflect sawdust away from the operator. The sides of the lower exposed portion of the blade shall be guarded to the full diameter of the blade by a device that will automatically adjust itself to the thickness of the stock and remain in contact with stock being cut to give maximum protection possible for the operation being performed.

(h) *Hand-fed crosscut table saws.* (1) Each circular crosscut table saw shall be guarded by a hood which shall meet all the requirements of paragraph (i)(1) of this section for hoods for circular ripsaws.

(i) *Hand-fed ripsaws.* (1) Each circular hand-fed ripsaw shall be guarded by a hood which shall completely enclose that portion of the saw above the table and that portion of the saw above the material being cut. The hood and mounting shall be arranged so that the hood will automatically adjust itself to the thickness of and remain in contact with the material being cut but it shall not offer any considerable resistance to insertion of material to saw or to passage of the material being sawed. The hood shall be made of adequate strength to resist blows and strains incidental to reasonable operation, adjusting, and handling, and shall be so designed as to protect the operator from flying splinters and broken saw teeth. It shall be made of material that is soft enough so that it will be unlikely to cause tooth breakage. The hood shall be so mounted as to insure that its operation will be positive, reliable, and in true alignment with the saw; and the mounting shall be adequate in strength to resist any reasonable side thrust or other force tending to throw it out of line.

[44 FR 8577, Feb. 9, 1979; 44 FR 20940, Apr. 6, 1979, as amended at 58 FR 35175, June 30, 1993; 61 FR 9251, Mar. 7, 1996]

§ **1926.305 Jacks—lever and ratchet, screw, and hydraulic.**

(a) *General requirements.* (1) The manufacturer's rated capacity shall be legibly marked on all jacks and shall not be exceeded.

(2) All jacks shall have a positive stop to prevent overtravel.

(b) [Reserved]

(c) *Blocking.* When it is necessary to provide a firm foundation, the base of the jack shall be blocked or cribbed. Where there is a possibility of slippage of the metal cap of the jack, a wood block shall be placed between the cap and the load.

(d)(1) *Operation and maintenance.* (i) After the load has been raised, it shall be cribbed, blocked, or otherwise secured at once.

(ii) Hydraulic jacks exposed to freezing temperatures shall be supplied with an adequate antifreeze liquid.

(iii) All jacks shall be properly lubricated at regular intervals.

(iv) Each jack shall be thoroughly inspected at times which depend upon the service conditions. Inspections shall be not less frequent than the following:

(*a*) For constant or intermittent use at one locality, once every 6 months,

(*b*) For jacks sent out of shop for special work, when sent out and when returned,

(*c*) For a jack subjected to abnormal load or shock, immediately before and immediately thereafter.

(v) Repair or replacement parts shall be examined for possible defects.

(vi) Jacks which are out of order shall be tagged accordingly, and shall not be used until repairs are made.

[44 FR 8577, Feb. 9, 1979; 44 FR 20940, Apr. 6, 1979, as amended at 55 FR 42328, Oct. 18, 1990; 58 FR 35176, June 30, 1993]

§ 1926.306 Air receivers.

(a) *General requirements*—(1) *Application.* This section applies to compressed air receivers, and other equipment used in providing and utilizing compressed air for performing operations such as cleaning, drilling, hoisting, and chipping. On the other hand, however, this section does not deal with the special problems created by using compressed air to convey materials nor the problems created when men work in compressed air as in tunnels and caissons. This section is not intended to apply to compressed air machinery and equipment used on transportation vehicles such as steam railroad cars, electric railway cars, and automotive equipment.

(2) *New and existing equipment.* (i) All new air receivers installed after the effective date of these regulations shall be constructed in accordance with the 1968 edition of the A.S.M.E. Boiler and Pressure Vessel Code Section VIII.

(ii) All safety valves used shall be constructed, installed, and maintained in accordance with the A.S.M.E. Boiler

and Pressure Vessel Code, Section VIII Edition 1968.

(b) *Installation and equipment requirements*—(1) *Installation.* Air receivers shall be so installed that all drains, handholes, and manholes therein are easily accessible. Under no circumstances shall an air receiver be buried underground or located in an inaccessible place.

(2) *Drains and traps.* A drain pipe and valve shall be installed at the lowest point of every air receiver to provide for the removal of accumulated oil and water. Adequate automatic traps may be installed in addition to drain valves. The drain valve on the air receiver shall be opened and the receiver completely drained frequently and at such intervals as to prevent the accumulation of excessive amounts of liquid in the receiver.

(3) *Gages and valves.* (i) Every air receiver shall be equipped with an indicating pressure gage (so located as to be readily visible) and with one or more spring-loaded safety valves. The total relieving capacity of such safety valves shall be such as to prevent pressure in the receiver from exceeding the maximum allowable working pressure of the receiver by more than 10 percent.

(ii) No valve of any type shall be placed between the air receiver and its safety valve or valves.

(iii) Safety appliances, such as safety valves, indicating devices and controlling devices, shall be constructed, located, and installed so that they cannot be readily rendered inoperative by any means, including the elements.

(iv) All safety valves shall be tested frequently and at regular intervals to determine whether they are in good operating condition.

[58 FR 35176, June 30, 1993]

§ 1926.307 Mechanical   power-transmission apparatus.

(a) *General requirements.* (1) This section covers all types and shapes of power-transmission belts, except the following when operating at two hundred and fifty (250) feet per minute or less: (i) Flat belts 1 inch (2.54 cm) or less in width, (ii) flat belts 2 inches (5.08 cm) or less in width which are free from metal lacings or fasteners, (iii) round belts ½ inch (1.27 cm) or less in diameter; and (iv) single strand V-belts, the width of which is thirteen thirty-seconds (¹³⁄₃₂) inch or less.

(2) Vertical and inclined belts (paragraphs (e) (3) and (4) of this section) if not more than 2½ inches (6.35 cm) wide and running at a speed of less than one thousand (1,000) feet per minute, and if free from metal lacings or fastenings may be guarded with a nip-point belt and pulley guard.

(3) For the Textile Industry, because of the presence of excessive deposits of lint, which constitute a serious fire hazard, the sides and face sections only of nip-point belt and pulley guards are required, provided the guard shall extend at least 6 inches (15.24 cm) beyond the rim of the pulley on the in-running and off-running sides of the belt and at least 2 inches (5.08 cm) away from the rim and face of the pulley in all other directions.

(4) This section covers the principal features with which power transmission safeguards shall comply.

(b) *Prime-mover guards*—(1) *Flywheels.* Flywheels located so that any part is 7 feet (2.128 m) or less above floor or platform shall be guarded in accordance with the requirements of this subparagraph:

(i) With an enclosure of sheet, perforated, or expanded metal, or woven wire;

(ii) With guard rails placed not less than 15 inches (38.1 cm) nor more than 20 inches (50.8 cm) from rim. When flywheel extends into pit or is within 12 inches (30.48 cm) of floor, a standard toeboard shall also be provided;

(iii) When the upper rim of flywheel protrudes through a working floor, it shall be entirely enclosed or surrounded by a guardrail and toeboard.

(iv) For flywheels with smooth rims 5 feet (1.52 m) or less in diameter, where the preceding methods cannot be applied, the following may be used: A disk attached to the flywheel in such manner as to cover the spokes of the wheel on the exposed side and present a smooth surface and edge, at the same time providing means for periodic inspection. An open space, not exceeding 4 inches (10.16 cm) in width, may be left between the outside edge of the disk and the rim of the wheel if desired, to facilitate turning the wheel over. Where a disk is used, the keys or other dangerous projections not covered by disk shall be cut off or covered. This subdivision does not apply to flywheels with solid web centers.

(v) Adjustable guard to be used for starting engine or for running adjustment may be provided at the flywheel of gas or oil engines. A slot opening for jack bar will be permitted.

(vi) Wherever flywheels are above working areas, guards shall be installed having sufficient strength to hold the weight of the flywheel in the event of a shaft or wheel mounting failure.

(2) *Cranks and connecting rods.* Cranks and connecting rods, when exposed to contact, shall be guarded in accordance with paragraphs (m) and (n) of this section, or by a guardrail as described in paragraph (o)(5) of this section.

(3) *Tail rods or extension piston rods.* Tail rods or extension piston rods shall be guarded in accordance with paragraphs (m) and (o) of this section, or by a guardrail on sides and end, with a clearance of not less than 15 (38.1 cm) nor more than 20 inches (50.8 cm) when rod is fully extended.

(c) *Shafting*—(1) *Installation.* (i) Each continuous line of shafting shall be secured in position against excessive endwise movement.

(ii) Inclined and vertical shafts, particularly inclined idler shafts, shall be securely held in position against endwise thrust.

(2) *Guarding horizontal shafting.* (i) All exposed parts of horizontal shafting 7 feet (2.128 m) or less from floor or working platform, excepting runways used exclusively for oiling, or running adjustments, shall be protected by a stationary casing enclosing shafting completely or by a trough enclosing sides and top or sides and bottom of shafting as location requires.

(ii) Shafting under bench machines shall be enclosed by a stationary casing, or by a trough at sides and top or sides and bottom, as location requires. The sides of the trough shall come within at least 6 inches (15.24 cm) of the underside of table, or if shafting is located near floor within 6 inches (15.24 cm) of floor. In every case the sides of trough shall extend at least 2 inches

(5.08 cm) beyond the shafting or protuberance.

(3) *Guarding vertical and inclined shafting.* Vertical and inclined shafting 7 feet (2.128 m) or less from floor or working platform, excepting maintenance runways, shall be enclosed with a stationary casing in accordance with requirements of paragraphs (m) and (o) of this section.

(4) *Projecting shaft ends.* (i) Projecting shaft ends shall present a smooth edge and end and shall not project more than one-half the diameter of the shaft unless guarded by nonrotating caps or safety sleeves.

(ii) Unused keyways shall be filled up or covered.

(5) *Power-transmission apparatus located in basements.* All mechanical power transmission apparatus located in basements, towers, and rooms used exclusively for power transmission equipment shall be guarded in accordance with this section, except that the requirements for safeguarding belts, pulleys, and shafting need not be complied with when the following requirements are met:

(i) The basement, tower, or room occupied by transmission equipment is locked against unauthorized entrance.

(ii) The vertical clearance in passageways between the floor and power transmission beams, ceiling, or any other objects, is not less than 5 ft. 6 in. (1.672 m).

(iii) The intensity of illumination conforms to the requirements of ANSI A11.1–1965 (R–1970).

(iv) [Reserved]

(v) The route followed by the oiler is protected in such manner as to prevent accident.

(d) *Pulleys*—(1) *Guarding.* Pulleys, any parts of which are 7 feet (2.128 m) or less from the floor or working platform, shall be guarded in accordance with the standards specified in paragraphs (m) and (o) of this section. Pulleys serving as balance wheels (*e.g.*, punch presses) on which the point of contact between belt and pulley is more than 6 ft. 6 in. (1.976 m) from the floor or platform may be guarded with a disk covering the spokes.

(2) *Location of pulleys.* (i) Unless the distance to the nearest fixed pulley, clutch, or hanger exceeds the width of the belt used, a guide shall be provided to prevent the belt from leaving the pulley on the side where insufficient clearance exists.

(ii) [Reserved]

(3) *Broken pulleys.* Pulleys with cracks, or pieces broken out of rims, shall not be used.

(4) *Pulley speeds.* Pulleys intended to operate at rim speed in excess of manufacturers normal recommendations shall be specially designed and carefully balanced for the speed at which they are to operate.

(e) *Belt, rope, and chain drives*—(1) *Horizontal belts and ropes.* (i) Where both runs of horizontal belts are 7 feet (2.128 m) or less from the floor level, the guard shall extend to at least 15 inches (38.1 cm) above the belt or to a standard height except that where both runs of a horizontal belt are 42 inches (106.68 cm) or less from the floor, the belt shall be fully enclosed.

(ii) In powerplants or power-development rooms, a guardrail may be used in lieu of the guard required by paragraph (e)(1)(i) of this section.

(2) *Overhead horizontal belts.* (i) Overhead horizontal belts, with lower parts 7 feet (2.128 m) or less from the floor or platform, shall be guarded on sides and bottom in accordance with paragraph (o)(3) of this section.

(ii) Horizontal overhead belts more than 7 feet (2.128 m) above floor or platform shall be guarded for their entire length under the following conditions:

(*a*) If located over passageways or work places and traveling 1,800 feet or more per minute.

(*b*) If center to center distance between pulleys is 10 feet (3.04 m) or more.

(*c*) If belt is 8 inches (20.32 cm) or more in width.

(iii) Where the upper and lower runs of horizontal belts are so located that passage of persons between them would be possible, the passage shall be either:

(*a*) Completely barred by a guardrail or other barrier in accordance with paragraphs (m) and (o) of this section; or

(*b*) Where passage is regarded as necessary, there shall be a platform over the lower run guarded on either side by a railing completely filled in with wire

237

mesh or other filler, or by a solid barrier. The upper run shall be so guarded as to prevent contact therewith either by the worker or by objects carried by him. In powerplants only the lower run of the belt need be guarded.

(iv) Overhead chain and link belt drives are governed by the same rules as overhead horizontal belts and shall be guarded in the same manner as belts.

(3) *Vertical and inclined belts.* (i) Vertical and inclined belts shall be enclosed by a guard conforming to standards in paragraphs (m) and (o) of this section.

(ii) All guards for inclined belts shall be arranged in such a manner that a minimum clearance of 7 feet (2.128 m) is maintained between belt and floor at any point outside of guard.

(4) *Vertical belts.* Vertical belts running over a lower pulley more than 7 feet (2.128 m) above floor or platform shall be guarded at the bottom in the same manner as horizontal overhead belts, if conditions are as stated in paragraphs (e)(2)(ii) (*a*) and (*c*) of this section.

(5) *Cone-pulley belts.* (i) The cone belt and pulley shall be equipped with a belt shifter so constructed as to adequately guard the nip point of the belt and pulley. If the frame of the belt shifter does not adequately guard the nip point of the belt and pulley, the nip point shall be further protected by means of a vertical guard placed in front of the pulley and extending at least to the top of the largest step of the cone.

(ii) If the belt is of the endless type or laced with rawhide laces, and a belt shifter is not desired, the belt will be considered guarded if the nip point of the belt and pulley is protected by a nip point guard located in front of the cone extending at least to the top of the largest step of the cone, and formed to show the contour of the cone in order to give the nip point of the belt and pulley the maximum protection.

(iii) If the cone is located less than 3 feet (0.912 m) from the floor or working platform, the cone pulley and belt shall be guarded to a height of 3 feet (0.912 m) regardless of whether the belt is endless or laced with rawhide.

(6) *Belt tighteners.* (i) Suspended counterbalanced tighteners and all parts thereof shall be of substantial construction and securely fastened; the bearings shall be securely capped. Means must be provided to prevent tightener from falling, in case the belt breaks.

(ii) Where suspended counterweights are used and not guarded by location, they shall be so encased as to prevent accident.

(f) *Gears, sprockets, and chains*—(1) *Gears.* Gears shall be guarded in accordance with one of the following methods:

(i) By a complete enclosure; or

(ii) By a standard guard as described in paragraph (o) of this section, at least 7 feet (2.128 m) high extending 6 inches (15.24 cm) above the mesh point of the gears; or

(iii) By a band guard covering the face of gear and having flanges extended inward beyond the root of the teeth on the exposed side or sides. Where any portion of the train of gears guarded by a band guard is less than 6 feet (1.824 m) from the floor a disk guard or a complete enclosure to the height of 6 feet (1.824 m) shall be required.

(2) *Hand-operated gears.* Paragraph (f)(1) of this section does not apply to hand-operated gears used only to adjust machine parts and which do not continue to move after hand power is removed. However, the guarding of these gears is highly recommended.

(3) *Sprockets and chains.* All sprocket wheels and chains shall be enclosed unless they are more than 7 feet (2.128 m) above the floor or platform. Where the drive extends over other machine or working areas, protection against falling shall be provided. This subparagraph does not apply to manually operated sprockets.

(4) *Openings for oiling.* When frequent oiling must be done, openings with hinged or sliding self-closing covers shall be provided. All points not readily accessible shall have oil feed tubes if lubricant is to be added while machinery is in motion.

(g) *Guarding friction drives.* The driving point of all friction drives when exposed to contact shall be guarded, all arm or spoke friction drives and all web friction drives with holes in the web shall be entirely enclosed, and all projecting belts on friction drives where exposed to contact shall be guarded.

(h) *Keys, setscrews, and other projections.* (1) All projecting keys, setscrews, and other projections in revolving parts shall be removed or made flush or guarded by metal cover. This subparagraph does not apply to keys or setscrews within gear or sprocket casings or other enclosures, nor to keys, setscrews, or oilcups in hubs of pulleys less than 20 inches (50.8 cm) in diameter where they are within the plane of the rim of the pulley.

(2) It is recommended, however, that no projecting setscrews or oilcups be used in any revolving pulley or part of machinery.

(i) *Collars and couplings*—(1) *Collars.* All revolving collars, including split collars, shall be cylindrical, and screws or bolts used in collars shall not project beyond the largest periphery of the collar.

(2) *Couplings.* Shaft couplings shall be so constructed as to present no hazard from bolts, nuts, setscrews, or revolving surfaces. Bolts, nuts, and setscrews will, however, be permitted where they are covered with safety sleeves or where they are used parallel with the shafting and are countersunk or else do not extend beyond the flange of the coupling.

(j) *Bearings and facilities for oiling.* All drip cups and pans shall be securely fastened.

(k) *Guarding of clutches, cutoff couplings, and clutch pulleys*—(1) *Guards.* Clutches, cutoff couplings, or clutch pulleys having projecting parts, where such clutches are located 7 feet (2.128 m) or less above the floor or working platform, shall be enclosed by a stationary guard constructed in accordance with this section. A "U" type guard is permissible.

(2) *Engine rooms.* In engine rooms a guardrail, preferably with toeboard, may be used instead of the guard required by paragraph (k)(1) of this section, provided such a room is occupied only by engine room attendants.

(1) *Belt shifters, clutches, shippers, poles, perches, and fasteners*—(1) *Belt shifters.* (i) Tight and loose pulleys on all new installations made on or after August 31, 1971, shall be equipped with a permanent belt shifter provided with mechanical means to prevent belt from creeping from loose to tight pulley. It is recommended that old installations be changed to conform to this rule.

(ii) Belt shifter and clutch handles shall be rounded and be located as far as possible from danger of accidental contact, but within easy reach of the operator. Where belt shifters are not directly located over a machine or bench, the handles shall be cut off 6 ft. 6 in. (1.976 m) above floor level.

(2) *Belt shippers and shipper poles.* The use of belt poles as substitutes for mechanical shifters is not recommended.

(3) *Belt perches.* Where loose pulleys or idlers are not practicable, belt perches in form of brackets, rollers, etc., shall be used to keep idle belts away from the shafts.

(4) *Belt fasteners.* Belts which of necessity must be shifted by hand and belts within 7 feet (2.128 m) of the floor or working platform which are not guarded in accordance with this section shall not be fastened with metal in any case, nor with any other fastening which by construction or wear will constitute an accident hazard.

(m) *Standard guards—general requirements*—(1) *Materials.* (i) Standard conditions shall be secured by the use of the following materials. Expanded metal, perforated or solid sheet metal, wire mesh on a frame of angle iron, or iron pipe securely fastened to floor or to frame of machine.

(ii) All metal should be free from burrs and sharp edges.

(2) *Methods of manufacture.* (i) Expanded metal, sheet or perforated metal, and wire mesh shall be securely fastened to frame.

(n) [Reserved]

(o) *Approved materials*—(1) *Minimum requirements.* The materials and dimensions specified in this paragraph shall apply to all guards, except horizontal overhead belts, rope, cable, or chain guards more than 7 feet (2.128 m) above floor, or platform.

(i) [Reserved]

(a) All guards shall be rigidly braced every 3 feet (0.912 m) or fractional part of their height to some fixed part of machinery or building structure. Where guard is exposed to contact with

239

moving equipment additional strength may be necessary.

(2) *Wood guards.* (i) Wood guards may be used in the woodworking and chemical industries, in industries where the presence of fumes or where manufacturing conditions would cause the rapid deterioration of metal guards; also in construction work and in locations outdoors where extreme cold or extreme heat make metal guards and railings undesirable. In all other industries, wood guards shall not be used.

(3) *Guards for horizontal overhead belts.* (i) Guards for horizontal overhead belts shall run the entire length of the belt and follow the line of the pulley to the ceiling or be carried to the nearest wall, thus enclosing the belt effectively. Where belts are so located as to make it impracticable to carry the guard to wall or ceiling, construction of guard shall be such as to enclose completely the top and bottom runs of belt and the face of pulleys.

(ii) [Reserved]

(iii) Suitable reinforcement shall be provided for the ceiling rafters or overhead floor beams, where such is necessary, to sustain safely the weight and stress likely to be imposed by the guard. The interior surface of all guards, by which is meant the surface of the guard with which a belt will come in contact, shall be smooth and free from all projections of any character, except where construction demands it; protruding shallow roundhead rivets may be used. Overhead belt guards shall be at least one-quarter wider than belt which they protect, except that this clearance need not in any case exceed 6 inches (15.24 cm) on each side. Overhead rope drive and block and roller-chain-drive guards shall be not less than 6 inches (15.24 cm) wider than the drive on each side. In overhead silent chain-drive guards where the chain is held from lateral displacement on the sprockets, the side clearances required on drives of 20 inch (50.8 cm) centers or under shall be not less than ¼ inch (0.635 cm) from the nearest moving chain part, and on drives of over 20 inch (50.8 cm) centers a minimum of ½ inch (1.27 cm) from the nearest moving chain part.

(4) *Guards for horizontal overhead rope and chain drives.* Overhead-rope and

chain-drive guard construction shall conform to the rules for overhead-belt guard.

(5) *Guardrails and toeboards.* (i) Guardrail shall be 42 inches (106.68 cm) in height, with midrail between top rail and floor.

(ii) Posts shall be not more than 8 feet (2.432 m) apart; they are to be permanent and substantial, smooth, and free from protruding nails, bolts, and splinters. If made of pipe, the post shall be 1¼ inches (3.175 cm) inside diameter, or larger. If made of metal shapes or bars, their section shall be equal in strength to that of 1½ (3.81 cm) by 1½ (3.81 cm) by ³⁄₁₆ inch angle iron. If made of wood, the posts shall be two by four (2 × 4) inches or larger. The upper rail shall be two by four (2 × 4) inches, or two one by four (1 × 4) strips, one at the top and one at the side of posts. The midrail may be one by four (1 × 4) inches or more. Where panels are fitted with expanded metal or wire mesh the middle rails may be omitted. Where guard is exposed to contact with moving equipment, additional strength may be necessary.

(iii) Toeboards shall be 4 inches (10.16 cm) or more in height, of wood, metal, or of metal grill not exceeding 1 inch (2.54 cm) mesh.

(p) *Care of equipment*—(1) *General.* All power-transmission equipment shall be inspected at intervals not exceeding 60 days and be kept in good working condition at all times.

(2) *Shafting.* (i) Shafting shall be kept in alignment, free from rust and excess oil or grease.

(ii) Where explosives, explosive dusts, flammable vapors or flammable liquids exist, the hazard of static sparks from shafting shall be carefully considered.

(3) *Bearings.* Bearings shall be kept in alignment and properly adjusted.

(4) *Hangers.* Hangers shall be inspected to make certain that all supporting bolts and screws are tight and that supports of hanger boxes are adjusted properly.

(5) *Pulleys.* (i) Pulleys shall be kept in proper alignment to prevent belts from running off.

(6) *Care of belts.*

(i) [Reserved]

(ii) Inspection shall be made of belts, lacings, and fasteners and such equipment kept in good repair.

(7) *Lubrication.* The regular oilers shall wear tight-fitting clothing. Machinery shall be oiled when not in motion, wherever possible.

[58 FR 35176, June 30, 1993, as amended at 69 FR 31882, June 8, 2004]

Subpart J—Welding and Cutting

AUTHORITY: Sec. 107, Contract Work Hours and Safety Standards Act (Construction Safety Act) (40 U.S.C. 333); secs. 4, 6, 8, Occupational Safety and Health Act of 1970 (29 U.S.C. 653, 655, 657); Secretary of Labor's Order No. 12–71 (36 FR 8754), 8–76 (41 FR 25059), or 9–83 (48 FR 35736), as applicable.

§ 1926.350 Gas welding and cutting.

(a) *Transporting, moving, and storing compressed gas cylinders.* (1) Valve protection caps shall be in place and secured.

(2) When cylinders are hoisted, they shall be secured on a cradle, slingboard, or pallet. They shall not be hoisted or transported by means of magnets or choker slings.

(3) Cylinders shall be moved by tilting and rolling them on their bottom edges. They shall not be intentionally dropped, struck, or permitted to strike each other violently.

(4) When cylinders are transported by powered vehicles, they shall be secured in a vertical position.

(5) Valve protection caps shall not be used for lifting cylinders from one vertical position to another. Bars shall not be used under valves or valve protection caps to pry cylinders loose when frozen. Warm, not boiling, water shall be used to thaw cylinders loose.

(6) Unless cylinders are firmly secured on a special carrier intended for this purpose, regulators shall be removed and valve protection caps put in place before cylinders are moved.

(7) A suitable cylinder truck, chain, or other steadying device shall be used to keep cylinders from being knocked over while in use.

(8) When work is finished, when cylinders are empty, or when cylinders are moved at any time, the cylinder valve shall be closed.

(9) Compressed gas cylinders shall be secured in an upright position at all times except, if necessary, for short periods of time while cylinders are actually being hoisted or carried.

(10) Oxygen cylinders in storage shall be separated from fuel-gas cylinders or combustible materials (especially oil or grease), a minimum distance of 20 feet (6.1 m) or by a noncombustible barrier at least 5 feet (1.5 m) high having a fire-resistance rating of at least one-half hour.

(11) Inside of buildings, cylinders shall be stored in a well-protected, well-ventilated, dry location, at least 20 feet (6.1 m) from highly combustible materials such as oil or excelsior. Cylinders should be stored in definitely assigned places away from elevators, stairs, or gangways. Assigned storage places shall be located where cylinders will not be knocked over or damaged by passing or falling objects, or subject to tampering by unauthorized persons. Cylinders shall not be kept in unventilated enclosures such as lockers and cupboards.

(12) The in-plant handling, storage, and utilization of all compressed gases in cylinders, portable tanks, rail tankcars, or motor vehicle cargo tanks shall be in accordance with Compressed Gas Association Pamphlet P–1–1965.

(b) *Placing cylinders.* (1) Cylinders shall be kept far enough away from the actual welding or cutting operation so that sparks, hot slag, or flame will not reach them. When this is impractical, fire resistant shields shall be provided.

(2) Cylinders shall be placed where they cannot become part of an electrical circuit. Electrodes shall not be struck against a cylinder to strike an arc.

(3) Fuel gas cylinders shall be placed with valve end up whenever they are in use. They shall not be placed in a location where they would be subject to open flame, hot metal, or other sources of artificial heat.

(4) Cylinders containing oxygen or acetylene or other fuel gas shall not be taken into confined spaces.

(c) *Treatment of cylinders.* (1) Cylinders, whether full or empty, shall not be used as rollers or supports.

(2) No person other than the gas supplier shall attempt to mix gases in a

cylinder. No one except the owner of the cylinder or person authorized by him, shall refill a cylinder. No one shall use a cylinder's contents for purposes other than those intended by the supplier. All cylinders used shall meet the Department of Transportation requirements published in 49 CFR part 178, subpart C, Specification for Cylinders.

(3) No damaged or defective cylinder shall be used.

(d) *Use of fuel gas.* The employer shall thoroughly instruct employees in the safe use of fuel gas, as follows:

(1) Before a regulator to a cylinder valve is connected, the valve shall be opened slightly and closed immediately. (This action is generally termed "cracking" and is intended to clear the valve of dust or dirt that might otherwise enter the regulator.) The person cracking the valve shall stand to one side of the outlet, not in front of it. The valve of a fuel gas cylinder shall not be cracked where the gas would reach welding work, sparks, flame, or other possible sources of ignition.

(2) The cylinder valve shall always be opened slowly to prevent damage to the regulator. For quick closing, valves on fuel gas cylinders shall not be opened more than 1½ turns. When a special wrench is required, it shall be left in position on the stem of the valve while the cylinder is in use so that the fuel gas flow can be shut off quickly in case of an emergency. In the case of manifolded or coupled cylinders, at least one such wrench shall always be available for immediate use. Nothing shall be placed on top of a fuel gas cylinder, when in use, which may damage the safety device or interfere with the quick closing of the valve.

(3) Fuel gas shall not be used from cylinders through torches or other devices which are equipped with shutoff valves without reducing the pressure through a suitable regulator attached to the cylinder valve or manifold.

(4) Before a regulator is removed from a cylinder valve, the cylinder valve shall always be closed and the gas released from the regulator.

(5) If, when the valve on a fuel gas cylinder is opened, there is found to be a leak around the valve stem, the valve shall be closed and the gland nut tightened. If this action does not stop the leak, the use of the cylinder shall be discontinued, and it shall be properly tagged and removed from the work area. In the event that fuel gas should leak from the cylinder valve, rather than from the valve stem, and the gas cannot be shut off, the cylinder shall be properly tagged and removed from the work area. If a regulator attached to a cylinder valve will effectively stop a leak through the valve seat, the cylinder need not be removed from the work area.

(6) If a leak should develop at a fuse plug or other safety device, the cylinder shall be removed from the work area.

(e) *Fuel gas and oxygen manifolds.* (1) Fuel gas and oxygen manifolds shall bear the name of the substance they contain in letters at least 1-inch high which shall be either painted on the manifold or on a sign permanently attached to it.

(2) Fuel gas and oxygen manifolds shall be placed in safe, well ventilated, and accessible locations. They shall not be located within enclosed spaces.

(3) Manifold hose connections, including both ends of the supply hose that lead to the manifold, shall be such that the hose cannot be interchanged between fuel gas and oxygen manifolds and supply header connections. Adapters shall not be used to permit the interchange of hose. Hose connections shall be kept free of grease and oil.

(4) When not in use, manifold and header hose connections shall be capped.

(5) Nothing shall be placed on top of a manifold, when in use, which will damage the manifold or interfere with the quick closing of the valves.

(f) *Hose.* (1) Fuel gas hose and oxygen hose shall be easily distinguishable from each other. The contrast may be made by different colors or by surface characteristics readily distinguishable by the sense of touch. Oxygen and fuel gas hoses shall not be interchangeable. A single hose having more than one gas passage shall not be used.

(2) When parallel sections of oxygen and fuel gas hose are taped together, not more than 4 inches out of 12 inches shall be covered by tape.

(3) All hose in use, carrying acetylene, oxygen, natural or manufactured fuel gas, or any gas or substance which may ignite or enter into combustion, or be in any way harmful to employees, shall be inspected at the beginning of each working shift. Defective hose shall be removed from service.

(4) Hose which has been subject to flashback, or which shows evidence of severe wear or damage, shall be tested to twice the normal pressure to which it is subject, but in no case less than 300 p.s.i. Defective hose, or hose in doubtful condition, shall not be used.

(5) Hose couplings shall be of the type that cannot be unlocked or disconnected by means of a straight pull without rotary motion.

(6) Boxes used for the storage of gas hose shall be ventilated.

(7) Hoses, cables, and other equipment shall be kept clear of passageways, ladders and stairs.

(g) *Torches.* (1) Clogged torch tip openings shall be cleaned with suitable cleaning wires, drills, or other devices designed for such purpose.

(2) Torches in use shall be inspected at the beginning of each working shift for leaking shutoff valves, hose couplings, and tip connections. Defective torches shall not be used.

(3) Torches shall be lighted by friction lighters or other approved devices, and not by matches or from hot work.

(h) *Regulators and gauges.* Oxygen and fuel gas pressure regulators, including their related gauges, shall be in proper working order while in use.

(i) *Oil and grease hazards.* Oxygen cylinders and fittings shall be kept away from oil or grease. Cylinders, cylinder caps and valves, couplings, regulators, hose, and apparatus shall be kept free from oil or greasy substances and shall not be handled with oily hands or gloves. Oxygen shall not be directed at oily surfaces, greasy clothes, or within a fuel oil or other storage tank or vessel.

(j) *Additional rules.* For additional details not covered in this subpart, applicable technical portions of American National Standards Institute, Z49.1–

1967, Safety in Welding and Cutting, shall apply.

[44 FR 8577, Feb. 9, 1979; 44 FR 20940, Apr. 6, 1979, as amended at 55 FR 42328, Oct. 18, 1990; 58 FR 35179, June 30, 1993]

§1926.351 Arc welding and cutting.

(a) *Manual electrode holders.* (1) Only manual electrode holders which are specifically designed for arc welding and cutting, and are of a capacity capable of safely handling the maximum rated current required by the electrodes, shall be used.

(2) Any current-carrying parts passing through the portion of the holder which the arc welder or cutter grips in his hand, and the outer surfaces of the jaws of the holder, shall be fully insulated against the maximum voltage encountered to ground.

(b) *Welding cables and connectors.* (1) All arc welding and cutting cables shall be of the completely insulated, flexible type, capable of handling the maximum current requirements of the work in progress, taking into account the duty cycle under which the arc welder or cutter is working.

(2) Only cable free from repair or splices for a minimum distance of 10 feet from the cable end to which the electrode holder is connected shall be used, except that cables with standard insulated connectors or with splices whose insulating quality is equal to that of the cable are permitted.

(3) When it becomes necessary to connect or splice lengths of cable one to another, substantial insulated connectors of a capacity at least equivalent to that of the cable shall be used. If connections are effected by means of cable lugs, they shall be securely fastened together to give good electrical contact, and the exposed metal parts of the lugs shall be completely insulated.

(4) Cables in need of repair shall not be used. When a cable, other than the cable lead referred to in paragraph (b)(2) of this section, becomes worn to the extent of exposing bare conductors, the portion thus exposed shall be protected by means of rubber and friction tape or other equivalent insulation.

(c) *Ground returns and machine grounding.* (1) A ground return cable

243

shall have a safe current carrying capacity equal to or exceeding the specified maximum output capacity of the arc welding or cutting unit which it services. When a single ground return cable services more than one unit, its safe current-carrying capacity shall equal or exceed the total specified maximum output capacities of all the units which it services.

(2) Pipelines containing gases or flammable liquids, or conduits containing electrical circuits, shall not be used as a ground return. For welding on natural gas pipelines, the technical portions of regulations issued by the Department of Transportation, Office of Pipeline Safety, 49 CFR part 192, Minimum Federal Safety Standards for Gas Pipelines, shall apply.

(3) When a structure or pipeline is employed as a ground return circuit, it shall be determined that the required electrical contact exists at all joints. The generation of an arc, sparks, or heat at any point shall cause rejection of the structures as a ground circuit.

(4) When a structure or pipeline is continuously employed as a ground return circuit, all joints shall be bonded, and periodic inspections shall be conducted to ensure that no condition of electrolysis or fire hazard exists by virtue of such use.

(5) The frames of all arc welding and cutting machines shall be grounded either through a third wire in the cable containing the circuit conductor or through a separate wire which is grounded at the source of the current. Grounding circuits, other than by means of the structure, shall be checked to ensure that the circuit between the ground and the grounded power conductor has resistance low enough to permit sufficient current to flow to cause the fuse or circuit breaker to interrupt the current.

(6) All ground connections shall be inspected to ensure that they are mechanically strong and electrically adequate for the required current.

(d) *Operating instructions.* Employers shall instruct employees in the safe means of arc welding and cutting as follows:

(1) When electrode holders are to be left unattended, the electrodes shall be removed and the holders shall be so placed or protected that they cannot make electrical contact with employees or conducting objects.

(2) Hot electrode holders shall not be dipped in water; to do so may expose the arc welder or cutter to electric shock.

(3) When the arc welder or cutter has occasion to leave his work or to stop work for any appreciable length of time, or when the arc welding or cutting machine is to be moved, the power supply switch to the equipment shall be opened.

(4) Any faulty or defective equipment shall be reported to the supervisor.

(5) See § 1926.406(c) for additional requirements.

(e) *Shielding.* Whenever practicable, all arc welding and cutting operations shall be shielded by noncombustible or flameproof screens which will protect employees and other persons working in the vicinity from the direct rays of the arc.

[44 FR 8577, Feb. 9, 1979; 44 FR 20940, Apr. 6, 1979, as amended at 51 FR 25318, July 11, 1986]

§ 1926.352 **Fire prevention.**

(a) When practical, objects to be welded, cut, or heated shall be moved to a designated safe location or, if the objects to be welded, cut, or heated cannot be readily moved, all movable fire hazards in the vicinity shall be taken to a safe place, or otherwise protected.

(b) If the object to be welded, cut, or heated cannot be moved and if all the fire hazards cannot be removed, positive means shall be taken to confine the heat, sparks, and slag, and to protect the immovable fire hazards from them.

(c) No welding, cutting, or heating shall be done where the application of flammable paints, or the presence of other flammable compounds, or heavy dust concentrations creates a hazard.

(d) Suitable fire extinguishing equipment shall be immediately available in the work area and shall be maintained in a state of readiness for instant use.

(e) When the welding, cutting, or heating operation is such that normal fire prevention precautions are not sufficient, additional personnel shall be assigned to guard against fire while the actual welding, cutting, or heating operation is being performed, and for a sufficient period of time after completion of the work to ensure that no possibility of fire exists. Such personnel shall be instructed as to the specific anticipated fire hazards and how the firefighting equipment provided is to be used.

(f) When welding, cutting, or heating is performed on walls, floors, and ceilings, since direct penetration of sparks or heat transfer may introduce a fire hazard to an adjacent area, the same precautions shall be taken on the opposite side as are taken on the side on which the welding is being performed.

(g) For the elimination of possible fire in enclosed spaces as a result of gas escaping through leaking or improperly closed torch valves, the gas supply to the torch shall be positively shut off at some point outside the enclosed space whenever the torch is not to be used or whenever the torch is left unattended for a substantial period of time, such as during the lunch period. Overnight and at the change of shifts, the torch and hose shall be removed from the confined space. Open end fuel gas and oxygen hoses shall be immediately removed from enclosed spaces when they are disconnected from the torch or other gas-consuming device.

(h) Except when the contents are being removed or transferred, drums, pails, and other containers which contain or have contained flammable liquids shall be kept closed. Empty containers shall be removed to a safe area apart from hot work operations or open flames.

(i) Drums containers, or hollow structures which have contained toxic or flammable substances shall, before welding, cutting, or heating is undertaken on them, either be filled with water or thoroughly cleaned of such substances and ventilated and tested. For welding, cutting and heating on steel pipelines containing natural gas, the pertinent portions of regulations issued by the Department of Transportation, Office of Pipeline Safety, 49 CFR part 192, Minimum Federal Safety Standards for Gas Pipelines, shall apply.

(j) Before heat is applied to a drum, container, or hollow structure, a vent or opening shall be provided for the release of any built-up pressure during the application of heat.

§ 1926.353 Ventilation and protection in welding, cutting, and heating.

(a) *Mechanical ventilation*. For purposes of this section, mechanical ventilation shall meet the following requirements:

(1) Mechanical ventilation shall consist of either general mechanical ventilation systems or local exhaust systems.

(2) General mechanical ventilation shall be of sufficient capacity and so arranged as to produce the number of air changes necessary to maintain welding fumes and smoke within safe limits, as defined in subpart D of this part.

(3) Local exhaust ventilation shall consist of freely movable hoods intended to be placed by the welder or burner as close as practicable to the work. This system shall be of sufficient capacity and so arranged as to remove fumes and smoke at the source and keep the concentration of them in the breathing zone within safe limits as defined in subpart D of this part.

(4) Contaminated air exhausted from a working space shall be discharged into the open air or otherwise clear of the source of intake air.

(5) All air replacing that withdrawn shall be clean and respirable.

(6) Oxygen shall not be used for ventilation purposes, comfort cooling, blowing dust from clothing, or for cleaning the work area.

(b) *Welding, cutting, and heating in confined spaces*. (1) Except as provided in paragraph (b)(2) of this section, and paragraph (c)(2) of this section, either general mechanical or local exhaust ventilation meeting the requirements of paragraph (a) of this section shall be provided whenever welding, cutting, or heating is performed in a confined space.

(2) When sufficient ventilation cannot be obtained without blocking the means of access, employees in the confined space shall be protected by air line respirators in accordance with the requirements of subpart E of this part, and an employee on the outside of such a confined space shall be assigned to

maintain communication with those working within it and to aid them in an emergency.

(3) *Lifelines.* Where a welder must enter a confined space through a manhole or other small opening, means shall be provided for quickly removing him in case of emergency. When safety belts and lifelines are used for this purpose they shall be so attached to the welder's body that his body cannot be jammed in a small exit opening. An attendant with a pre-planned rescue procedure shall be stationed outside to observe the welder at all times and be capable of putting rescue operations into effect.

(c) *Welding, cutting, or heating of metals of toxic significance.* (1) Welding, cutting, or heating in any enclosed spaces involving the metals specified in this subparagraph shall be performed with either general mechanical or local exhaust ventilation meeting the requirements of paragraph (a) of this section:

(i) Zinc-bearing base or filler metals or metals coated with zinc-bearing materials;

(ii) Lead base metals;

(iii) Cadmium-bearing filler materials;

(iv) Chromium-bearing metals or metals coated with chromium-bearing materials.

(2) Welding, cutting, or heating in any enclosed spaces involving the metals specified in this subparagraph shall be performed with local exhaust ventilation in accordance with the requirements of paragraph (a) of this section, or employees shall be protected by air line respirators in accordance with the requirements of subpart E of this part:

(i) Metals containing lead, other than as an impurity, or metals coated with lead-bearing materials;

(ii) Cadmium-bearing or cadmium-coated base metals;

(iii) Metals coated with mercury-bearing metals;

(iv) Beryllium-containing base or filler metals. Because of its high toxicity, work involving beryllium shall be done with both local exhaust ventilation and air line respirators.

(3) Employees performing such operations in the open air shall be protected by filter-type respirators in accordance with the requirements of subpart E of this part, except that employees performing such operations on beryllium-containing base or filler metals shall be protected by air line respirators in accordance with the requirements of subpart E of this part.

(4) Other employees exposed to the same atmosphere as the welders or burners shall be protected in the same manner as the welder or burner.

(d) *Inert-gas metal-arc welding.* (1) Since the inert-gas metal-arc welding process involves the production of ultra-violet radiation of intensities of 5 to 30 times that produced during shielded metal-arc welding, the decomposition of chlorinated solvents by ultraviolet rays, and the liberation of toxic fumes and gases, employees shall not be permitted to engage in, or be exposed to the process until the following special precautions have been taken:

(i) The use of chlorinated solvents shall be kept at least 200 feet, unless shielded, from the exposed arc, and surfaces prepared with chlorinated solvents shall be thoroughly dry before welding is permitted on such surfaces.

(ii) Employees in the area not protected from the arc by screening shall be protected by filter lenses meeting the requirements of subpart E of this part. When two or more welders are exposed to each other's arc, filter lens goggles of a suitable type, meeting the requirements of subpart E of this part, shall be worn under welding helmets. Hand shields to protect the welder against flashes and radiant energy shall be used when either the helmet is lifted or the shield is removed.

(iii) Welders and other employees who are exposed to radiation shall be suitably protected so that the skin is covered completely to prevent burns and other damage by ultraviolet rays. Welding helmets and hand shields shall be free of leaks and openings, and free of highly reflective surfaces.

(iv) When inert-gas metal-arc welding is being performed on stainless steel, the requirements of paragraph (c)(2) of this section shall be met to protect against dangerous concentrations of nitrogen dioxide.

(e) *General welding, cutting, and heating.* (1) Welding, cutting, and heating, not involving conditions or materials described in paragraph (b), (c), or (d) of this section, may normally be done without mechanical ventilation or respiratory protective equipment, but where, because of unusual physical or atmospheric conditions, an unsafe accumulation of contaminants exists, suitable mechanical ventilation or respiratory protective equipment shall be provided.

(2) Employees performing any type of welding, cutting, or heating shall be protected by suitable eye protective equipment in accordance with the requirements of subpart E of this part.

[44 FR 8577, Feb. 9, 1979; 44 FR 20940, Apr. 6, 1979, as amended at 55 FR 42328, Oct. 18, 1990; 58 FR 35179, June 30, 1993]

§1926.354 Welding, cutting, and heating in way of preservative coatings.

(a) Before welding, cutting, or heating is commenced on any surface covered by a preservative coating whose flammability is not known, a test shall be made by a competent person to determine its flammability. Preservative coatings shall be considered to be highly flammable when scrapings burn with extreme rapidity.

(b) Precautions shall be taken to prevent ignition of highly flammable hardened preservative coatings. When coatings are determined to be highly flammable, they shall be stripped from the area to be heated to prevent ignition.

(c) Protection against toxic preservative coatings: (1) In enclosed spaces, all surfaces covered with toxic preservatives shall be stripped of all toxic coatings for a distance of at least 4 inches from the area of heat application, or the employees shall be protected by air line respirators, meeting the requirements of subpart E of this part.

(2) In the open air, employees shall be protected by a respirator, in accordance with requirements of subpart E of this part.

(d) The preservative coatings shall be removed a sufficient distance from the area to be heated to ensure that the temperature of the unstripped metal will not be appreciably raised. Artificial cooling of the metal surrounding the heating area may be used to limit the size of the area required to be cleaned.

Subpart K—Electrical

AUTHORITY: Sections 6 and 8 of the Occupational Safety and Health Act of 1970 (29 U.S.C. 655 and 657); sec. 107, Contract Work Hours and Safety Standards Act (40 U.S.C. 333); Secretary of Labor's Order No. 9–83 (48 FR 35736) or 1–90 (55 FR 9033), as applicable; 29 CFR part 1911.

SOURCE: 51 FR 25318, July 11, 1986, unless otherwise noted.

GENERAL

§1926.400 Introduction.

This subpart addresses electrical safety requirements that are necessary for the practical safeguarding of employees involved in construction work and is divided into four major divisions and applicable definitions as follows:

(a) *Installation safety requirements.* Installation safety requirements are contained in §§1926.402 through 1926.408. Included in this category are electric equipment and installations used to provide electric power and light on jobsites.

(b) *Safety-related work practices.* Safety-related work practices are contained in §§1926.416 and 1926.417. In addition to covering the hazards arising from the use of electricity at jobsites, these regulations also cover the hazards arising from the accidental contact, direct or indirect, by employees with all energized lines, above or below ground, passing through or near the jobsite.

(c) *Safety-related maintenance and environmental considerations.* Safety-related maintenance and environmental considerations are contained in §§1926.431 and 1926.432.

(d) *Safety requirements for special equipment.* Safety requirements for special equipment are contained in §1926.441.

(e) *Definitions.* Definitions applicable to this subpart are contained in §1926.449.

§1926.401 [Reserved]

INSTALLATION SAFETY REQUIREMENTS

§1926.402 Applicability.

(a) *Covered.* Sections 1926.402 through 1926.408 contain installation safety requirements for electrical equipment and installations used to provide electric power and light at the jobsite. These sections apply to installations, both temporary and permanent, used on the jobsite; but these sections do not apply to existing permanent installations that were in place before the construction activity commenced.

NOTE: If the electrical installation is made in accordance with the National Electrical Code ANSI/NFPA 70–1984, exclusive of Formal Interpretations and Tentative Interim Amendments, it will be deemed to be in compliance with §§ 1926.403 through 1926.408, except for §§ 1926.404(b)(1) and 1926.405(a)(2)(ii) (E), (F), (G), and (J).

(b) *Not covered.* Sections 1926.402 through 1926.408 do not cover installations used for the generation, transmission, and distribution of electric energy, including related communication, metering, control, and transformation installations. (However, these regulations do cover portable and vehicle-mounted generators used to provide power for equipment used at the jobsite.) See subpart V of this part for the construction of power distribution and transmission lines.

§ 1926.403 General requirements.

(a) *Approval.* All electrical conductors and equipment shall be approved.

(b) *Examination, installation, and use of equipment*—(1) *Examination.* The employer shall ensure that electrical equipment is free from recognized hazards that are likely to cause death or serious physical harm to employees. Safety of equipment shall be determined on the basis of the following considerations:

(i) Suitability for installation and use in conformity with the provisions of this subpart. Suitability of equipment for an identified purpose may be evidenced by listing, labeling, or certification for that identified purpose.

(ii) Mechanical strength and durability, including, for parts designed to enclose and protect other equipment, the adequacy of the protection thus provided.

(iii) Electrical insulation.

(iv) Heating effects under conditions of use.

(v) Arcing effects.

(vi) Classification by type, size, voltage, current capacity, specific use.

(vii) Other factors which contribute to the practical safeguarding of employees using or likely to come in contact with the equipment.

(2) *Installation and use.* Listed, labeled, or certified equipment shall be installed and used in accordance with instructions included in the listing, labeling, or certification.

(c) *Interrupting rating.* Equipment intended to break current shall have an interrupting rating at system voltage sufficient for the current that must be interrupted.

(d) *Mounting and cooling of equipment*—(1) *Mounting.* Electric equipment shall be firmly secured to the surface on which it is mounted. Wooden plugs driven into holes in masonry, concrete, plaster, or similar materials shall not be used.

(2) *Cooling.* Electrical equipment which depends upon the natural circulation of air and convection principles for cooling of exposed surfaces shall be installed so that room air flow over such surfaces is not prevented by walls or by adjacent installed equipment. For equipment designed for floor mounting, clearance between top surfaces and adjacent surfaces shall be provided to dissipate rising warm air. Electrical equipment provided with ventilating openings shall be installed so that walls or other obstructions do not prevent the free circulation of air through the equipment.

(e) *Splices.* Conductors shall be spliced or joined with splicing devices designed for the use or by brazing, welding, or soldering with a fusible metal or alloy. Soldered splices shall first be so spliced or joined as to be mechanically and electrically secure without solder and then soldered. All splices and joints and the free ends of conductors shall be covered with an insulation equivalent to that of the conductors or with an insulating device designed for the purpose.

(f) *Arcing parts.* Parts of electric equipment which in ordinary operation produce arcs, sparks, flames, or molten metal shall be enclosed or separated and isolated from all combustible material.

(g) *Marking.* Electrical equipment shall not be used unless the manufacturer's name, trademark, or other descriptive marking by which the organization responsible for the product may be identified is placed on the equipment and unless other markings are provided giving voltage, current, wattage, or other ratings as necessary. The marking shall be of sufficient durability to withstand the environment involved.

(h) *Identification of disconnecting means and circuits.* Each disconnecting means required by this subpart for motors and appliances shall be legibly marked to indicate its purpose, unless located and arranged so the purpose is evident. Each service, feeder, and branch circuit, at its disconnecting means or overcurrent device, shall be legibly marked to indicate its purpose, unless located and arranged so the purpose is evident. These markings shall be of sufficient durability to withstand the environment involved.

(i) *600 Volts, nominal, or less.* This paragraph applies to equipment operating at 600 volts, nominal, or less.

(1) *Working space about electric equipment.* Sufficient access and working space shall be provided and maintained about all electric equipment to permit ready and safe operation and maintenance of such equipment.

(i) *Working clearances.* Except as required or permitted elsewhere in this subpart, the dimension of the working space in the direction of access to live parts operating at 600 volts or less and likely to require examination, adjustment, servicing, or maintenance while alive shall not be less than indicated in Table K–1. In addition to the dimensions shown in Table K–1, workspace shall not be less than 30 inches (762 mm) wide in front of the electric equipment. Distances shall be measured from the live parts if they are exposed, or from the enclosure front or opening if the live parts are enclosed. Walls constructed of concrete, brick, or tile are considered to be grounded. Working space is not required in back of assemblies such as dead-front switchboards or motor control centers where there are no renewable or adjustable parts such as fuses or switches on the back and where all connections are accessible from locations other than the back.

TABLE K–1—WORKING CLEARANCES

Nominal voltage to ground	Minimum clear distance for conditions [1]		
	(a)	(b)	(c)
	Feet [2]	Feet [2]	Feet [2]
0–150	3	3	3
151–600	3	3½	4

[1] Conditions (a), (b), and (c) are as follows: (a) Exposed live parts on one side and no live or grounded parts on the other side of the working space, or exposed live parts on both sides effectively guarded by insulating material. Insulated wire or insulated busbars operating at not over 300 volts are not considered live parts. (b) Exposed live parts on one side and grounded parts on the other side. (c) Exposed live parts on both sides of the workspace [not guarded as provided in Condition (a)] with the operator between.

[2] Note: For International System of Units (SI): one foot=0.3048m.

(ii) *Clear spaces.* Working space required by this subpart shall not be used for storage. When normally enclosed live parts are exposed for inspection or servicing, the working space, if in a passageway or general open space, shall be guarded.

(iii) *Access and entrance to working space.* At least one entrance shall be provided to give access to the working space about electric equipment.

(iv) *Front working space.* Where there are live parts normally exposed on the front of switchboards or motor control centers, the working space in front of such equipment shall not be less than 3 feet (914 mm).

(v) *Headroom.* The minimum headroom of working spaces about service equipment, switchboards, panelboards, or motor control centers shall be 6 feet 3 inches (1.91 m).

(2) *Guarding of live parts.* (i) Except as required or permitted elsewhere in this subpart, live parts of electric equipment operating at 50 volts or more shall be guarded against accidental contact by cabinets or other forms of enclosures, or by any of the following means:

(A) By location in a room, vault, or similar enclosure that is accessible only to qualified persons.

(B) By partitions or screens so arranged that only qualified persons will have access to the space within reach of the live parts. Any openings in such partitions or screens shall be so sized and located that persons are not likely to come into accidental contact with the live parts or to bring conducting objects into contact with them.

(C) By location on a balcony, gallery, or platform so elevated and arranged as to exclude unqualified persons.

(D) By elevation of 8 feet (2.44 m) or more above the floor or other working surface and so installed as to exclude unqualified persons.

(ii) In locations where electric equipment would be exposed to physical damage, enclosures or guards shall be so arranged and of such strength as to prevent such damage.

(iii) Entrances to rooms and other guarded locations containing exposed live parts shall be marked with conspicuous warning signs forbidding unqualified persons to enter.

(j) *Over 600 volts, nominal*—(1) *General.* Conductors and equipment used on circuits exceeding 600 volts, nominal, shall comply with all applicable provisions of paragraphs (a) through (g) of this section and with the following provisions which supplement or modify those requirements. The provisions of paragraphs (j)(2), (j)(3), and (j)(4) of this section do not apply to equipment on the supply side of the service conductors.

(2) *Enclosure for electrical installations.* Electrical installations in a vault, room, closet or in an area surrounded by a wall, screen, or fence, access to which is controlled by lock and key or other equivalent means, are considered to be accessible to qualified persons only. A wall, screen, or fence less than 8 feet (2.44 m) in height is not considered adequate to prevent access unless it has other features that provide a degree of isolation equivalent to an 8-foot (2.44-m) fence. The entrances to all buildings, rooms or enclosures containing exposed live parts or exposed conductors operating at over 600 volts, nominal, shall be kept locked or shall be under the observation of a qualified person at all times.

(i) *Installations accessible to qualified persons only.* Electrical installations having exposed live parts shall be accessible to qualified persons only and shall comply with the applicable provisions of paragraph (j)(3) of this section.

(ii) *Installations accessible to unqualified persons.* Electrical installations that are open to unqualified persons shall be made with metal-enclosed equipment or shall be enclosed in a vault or in an area, access to which is controlled by a lock. Metal-enclosed switchgear, unit substations, transformers, pull boxes, connection boxes, and other similar associated equipment shall be marked with appropriate caution signs. If equipment is exposed to physical damage from vehicular traffic, guards shall be provided to prevent such damage. Ventilating or similar openings in metal-enclosed equipment shall be designed so that foreign objects inserted through these openings will be deflected from energized parts.

(3) *Workspace about equipment.* Sufficient space shall be provided and maintained about electric equipment to permit ready and safe operation and maintenance of such equipment. Where energized parts are exposed, the minimum clear workspace shall not be less than 6 feet 6 inches (1.98 m) high (measured vertically from the floor or platform), or less than 3 feet (914 mm) wide (measured parallel to the equipment). The depth shall be as required in Table K–2. The workspace shall be adequate to permit at least a 90-degree opening of doors or hinged panels.

(i) *Working space.* The minimum clear working space in front of electric equipment such as switchboards, control panels, switches, circuit breakers, motor controllers, relays, and similar equipment shall not be less than specified in Table K–2 unless otherwise specified in this subpart. Distances shall be measured from the live parts if they are exposed, or from the enclosure front or opening if the live parts are enclosed. However, working space is not required in back of equipment such as deadfront switchboards or control assemblies where there are no renewable or adjustable parts (such as fuses or switches) on the back and where all connections are accessible from locations other than the back. Where rear access is required to work on de-energized parts on the back of enclosed equipment, a minimum working space of 30 inches (762 mm) horizontally shall be provided.

TABLE K–2—MINIMUM DEPTH OF CLEAR WORKING SPACE IN FRONT OF ELECTRIC EQUIPMENT

Nominal voltage to ground	Conditions[1]		
	(a)	(b)	(c)
	Feet[2]	Feet[2]	Feet[2]
601 to 2,500	3	4	5
2,501 to 9,000	4	5	6
9,001 to 25,000	5	6	9
25,001 to 75 kV	6	8	10
Above 75kV	8	10	12

[1]Conditions (a), (b), and (c) are as follows: (a) Exposed live parts on one side and no live or grounded parts on the other side of the working space, or exposed live parts on both sides effectively guarded by insulating materials. Insulated wire or insulated busbars operating at not over 300 volts are not considered live parts. (b) Exposed live parts on one side and grounded parts on the other side. Walls constructed of concrete, brick, or tile are considered to be grounded surfaces. (c) Exposed live parts on both sides of the workspace [not guarded as provided in Condition (a)] with the operator between.

[2]NOTE: For SI units: one foot=0.3048 m.

(ii) *Lighting outlets and points of control.* The lighting outlets shall be so arranged that persons changing lamps or making repairs on the lighting system will not be endangered by live parts or other equipment. The points of control shall be so located that persons are not likely to come in contact with any live part or moving part of the equipment while turning on the lights.

(iii) *Elevation of unguarded live parts.* Unguarded live parts above working space shall be maintained at elevations not less than specified in Table K–3.

TABLE K–3—ELEVATION OF UNGUARDED ENERGIZED PARTS ABOVE WORKING SPACE

Nominal voltage between phases	Minimum elevation
601–7,500	8 feet 6 inches.[1]
7,501–35,000	9 feet.
Over 35kV	9 feet+0.37 inches per kV above 35kV.

[1]NOTE: For SI units: one inch=25.4 mm; one foot=0.3048 m.

(4) *Entrance and access to workspace.* At least one entrance not less than 24 inches (610 mm) wide and 6 feet 6 inches (1.98 m) high shall be provided to give access to the working space about electric equipment. On switchboard and control panels exceeding 48 inches (1.22 m) in width, there shall be one entrance at each end of such board where practicable. Where bare energized parts at any voltage or insulated energized parts above 600 volts are located adja-

cent to such entrance, they shall be guarded.

[51 FR 25318, July 11, 1986, as amended at 61 FR 5510, Feb. 13, 1996]

§1926.404 Wiring design and protection.

(a) *Use and identification of grounded and grounding conductors*—(1) *Identification of conductors.* A conductor used as a grounded conductor shall be identifiable and distinguishable from all other conductors. A conductor used as an equipment grounding conductor shall be identifiable and distinguishable from all other conductors.

(2) *Polarity of connections.* No grounded conductor shall be attached to any terminal or lead so as to reverse designated polarity.

(3) *Use of grounding terminals and devices.* A grounding terminal or grounding-type device on a receptacle, cord connector, or attachment plug shall not be used for purposes other than grounding.

(b) *Branch circuits*—(1) *Ground-fault protection*—(i) *General.* The employer shall use either ground fault circuit interrupters as specified in paragraph (b)(1)(ii) of this section or an assured equipment grounding conductor program as specified in paragraph (b)(1)(iii) of this section to protect employees on construction sites. These requirements are in addition to any other requirements for equipment grounding conductors.

(ii) *Ground-fault circuit interrupters.* All 120-volt, single-phase, 15- and 20-ampere receptacle outlets on construction sites, which are not a part of the permanent wiring of the building or structure and which are in use by employees, shall have approved ground-fault circuit interrupters for personnel protection. Receptacles on a two-wire, single-phase portable or vehicle-mounted generator rated not more than 5kW, where the circuit conductors of the generator are insulated from the generator frame and all other grounded surfaces, need not be protected with ground-fault circuit interrupters.

(iii) *Assured equipment grounding conductor program.* The employer shall establish and implement an assured equipment grounding conductor program on construction sites covering all

251

cord sets, receptacles which are not a part of the building or structure, and equipment connected by cord and plug which are available for use or used by employees. This program shall comply with the following minimum requirements:

(A) A written description of the program, including the specific procedures adopted by the employer, shall be available at the jobsite for inspection and copying by the Assistant Secretary and any affected employee.

(B) The employer shall designate one or more competent persons (as defined in § 1926.32(f)) to implement the program.

(C) Each cord set, attachment cap, plug and receptacle of cord sets, and any equipment connected by cord and plug, except cord sets and receptacles which are fixed and not exposed to damage, shall be visually inspected before each day's use for external defects, such as deformed or missing pins or insulation damage, and for indications of possible internal damage. Equipment found damaged or defective shall not be used until repaired.

(D) The following tests shall be performed on all cord sets, receptacles which are not a part of the permanent wiring of the building or structure, and cord- and plug-connected equipment required to be grounded:

(1) All equipment grounding conductors shall be tested for continuity and shall be electrically continuous.

(2) Each receptacle and attachment cap or plug shall be tested for correct attachment of the equipment grounding conductor. The equipment grounding conductor shall be connected to its proper terminal.

(E) All required tests shall be performed:

(1) Before first use;

(2) Before equipment is returned to service following any repairs;

(3) Before equipment is used after any incident which can be reasonably suspected to have caused damage (for example, when a cord set is run over); and

(4) At intervals not to exceed 3 months, except that cord sets and receptacles which are fixed and not exposed to damage shall be tested at intervals not exceeding 6 months.

(F) The employer shall not make available or permit the use by employees of any equipment which has not met the requirements of this paragraph (b)(1)(iii) of this section.

(G) Tests performed as required in this paragraph shall be recorded. This test record shall identify each receptacle, cord set, and cord- and plug-connected equipment that passed the test and shall indicate the last date it was tested or the interval for which it was tested. This record shall be kept by means of logs, color coding, or other effective means and shall be maintained until replaced by a more current record. The record shall be made available on the jobsite for inspection by the Assistant Secretary and any affected employee.

(2) *Outlet devices.* Outlet devices shall have an ampere rating not less than the load to be served and shall comply with the following:

(i) *Single receptacles.* A single receptacle installed on an individual branch circuit shall have an ampere rating of not less than that of the branch circuit.

(ii) *Two or more receptacles.* Where connected to a branch circuit supplying two or more receptacles or outlets, receptacle ratings shall conform to the values listed in Table K–4.

(iii) *Receptacles used for the connection of motors.* The rating of an attachment plug or receptacle used for cord- and plug-connection of a motor to a branch circuit shall not exceed 15 amperes at 125 volts or 10 amperes at 250 volts if individual overload protection is omitted.

TABLE K–4—RECEPTACLE RATINGS FOR VARIOUS SIZE CIRCUITS

Circuit rating amperes	Receptacle rating amperes
15	Not over 15.
20	15 or 20.
30	30.
40	40 or 50.
50	50.

(c) *Outside conductors and lamps*—(1) *600 volts, nominal, or less.* Paragraphs (c)(1)(i) through (c)(1)(iv) of this section apply to branch circuit, feeder, and service conductors rated 600 volts, nominal, or less and run outdoors as open conductors.

(i) *Conductors on poles.* Conductors supported on poles shall provide a horizontal climbing space not less than the following:

(A) Power conductors below communication conductors—30 inches (762 mm).

(B) Power conductors alone or above communication conductors: 300 volts or less—24 inches (610 mm); more than 300 volts—30 inches (762 mm).

(C) Communication conductors below power conductors: with power conductors 300 volts or less—24 inches (610 mm); more than 300 volts—30 inches (762 mm).

(ii) *Clearance from ground.* Open conductors shall conform to the following minimum clearances:

(A) 10 feet (3.05 m)—above finished grade, sidewalks, or from any platform or projection from which they might be reached.

(B) 12 feet (3.66 m)—over areas subject to vehicular traffic other than truck traffic.

(C) 15 feet (4.57 m)—over areas other than those specified in paragraph (c)(1)(ii)(D) of this section that are subject to truck traffic.

(D) 18 feet (5.49 m)—over public streets, alleys, roads, and driveways.

(iii) *Clearance from building openings.* Conductors shall have a clearance of at least 3 feet (914 mm) from windows, doors, fire escapes, or similar locations. Conductors run above the top level of a window are considered to be out of reach from that window and, therefore, do not have to be 3 feet (914 mm) away.

(iv) *Clearance over roofs.* Conductors above roof space accessible to employees on foot shall have a clearance from the highest point of the roof surface of not less than 8 feet (2.44 m) vertical clearance for insulated conductors, not less than 10 feet (3.05 m) vertical or diagonal clearance for covered conductors, and not less than 15 feet (4.57 m) for bare conductors, except that:

(A) Where the roof space is also accessible to vehicular traffic, the vertical clearance shall not be less than 18 feet (5.49 m), or

(B) Where the roof space is not normally accessible to employees on foot, fully insulated conductors shall have a vertical or diagonal clearance of not less than 3 feet (914 mm), or

(C) Where the voltage between conductors is 300 volts or less and the roof has a slope of not less than 4 inches (102 mm) in 12 inches (305 mm), the clearance from roofs shall be at least 3 feet (914 mm), or

(D) Where the voltage between conductors is 300 volts or less and the conductors do not pass over more than 4 feet (1.22 m) of the overhang portion of the roof and they are terminated at a through-the-roof raceway or support, the clearance from roofs shall be at least 18 inches (457 mm).

(2) *Location of outdoor lamps.* Lamps for outdoor lighting shall be located below all live conductors, transformers, or other electric equipment, unless such equipment is controlled by a disconnecting means that can be locked in the open position or unless adequate clearances or other safeguards are provided for relamping operations.

(d) *Services*—(1) *Disconnecting means*—(i) *General.* Means shall be provided to disconnect all conductors in a building or other structure from the service-entrance conductors. The disconnecting means shall plainly indicate whether it is in the open or closed position and shall be installed at a readily accessible location nearest the point of entrance of the service-entrance conductors.

(ii) *Simultaneous opening of poles.* Each service disconnecting means shall simultaneously disconnect all ungrounded conductors.

(2) *Services over 600 volts, nominal.* The following additional requirements apply to services over 600 volts, nominal.

(i) *Guarding.* Service-entrance conductors installed as open wires shall be guarded to make them accessible only to qualified persons.

(ii) *Warning signs.* Signs warning of high voltage shall be posted where unauthorized employees might come in contact with live parts.

(e) *Overcurrent protection*—(1) *600 volts, nominal, or less.* The following requirements apply to overcurrent protection of circuits rated 600 volts, nominal, or less.

253

(i) *Protection of conductors and equipment.* Conductors and equipment shall be protected from overcurrent in accordance with their ability to safely conduct current. Conductors shall have sufficient ampacity to carry the load.

(ii) *Grounded conductors.* Except for motor-running overload protection, overcurrent devices shall not interrupt the continuity of the grounded conductor unless all conductors of the circuit are opened simultaneously.

(iii) *Disconnection of fuses and thermal cutouts.* Except for devices provided for current-limiting on the supply side of the service disconnecting means, all cartridge fuses which are accessible to other than qualified persons and all fuses and thermal cutouts on circuits over 150 volts to ground shall be provided with disconnecting means. This disconnecting means shall be installed so that the fuse or thermal cutout can be disconnected from its supply without disrupting service to equipment and circuits unrelated to those protected by the overcurrent device.

(iv) *Location in or on premises.* Overcurrent devices shall be readily accessible. Overcurrent devices shall not be located where they could create an employee safety hazard by being exposed to physical damage or located in the vicinity of easily ignitible material.

(v) *Arcing or suddenly moving parts.* Fuses and circuit breakers shall be so located or shielded that employees will not be burned or otherwise injured by their operation.

(vi) *Circuit breakers*—(A) Circuit breakers shall clearly indicate whether they are in the open (off) or closed (on) position.

(B) Where circuit breaker handles on switchboards are operated vertically rather than horizontally or rotationally, the up position of the handle shall be the closed (on) position.

(C) If used as switches in 120-volt, fluorescent lighting circuits, circuit breakers shall be marked "SWD."

(2) *Over 600 volts, nominal.* Feeders and branch circuits over 600 volts, nominal, shall have short-circuit protection.

(f) *Grounding.* Paragraphs (f)(1) through (f)(11) of this section contain grounding requirements for systems, circuits, and equipment.

(1) *Systems to be grounded.* The following systems which supply premises wiring shall be grounded:

(i) *Three-wire DC systems.* All 3-wire DC systems shall have their neutral conductor grounded.

(ii) *Two-wire DC systems.* Two-wire DC systems operating at over 50 volts through 300 volts between conductors shall be grounded unless they are rectifier-derived from an AC system complying with paragraphs (f)(1)(iii), (f)(1)(iv), and (f)(1)(v) of this section.

(iii) *AC circuits, less than 50 volts.* AC circuits of less than 50 volts shall be grounded if they are installed as overhead conductors outside of buildings or if they are supplied by transformers and the transformer primary supply system is ungrounded or exceeds 150 volts to ground.

(iv) *AC systems, 50 volts to 1000 volts.* AC systems of 50 volts to 1000 volts shall be grounded under any of the following conditions, unless exempted by paragraph (f)(1)(v) of this section:

(A) If the system can be so grounded that the maximum voltage to ground on the ungrounded conductors does not exceed 150 volts;

(B) If the system is nominally rated 480Y/277 volt, 3-phase, 4-wire in which the neutral is used as a circuit conductor;

(C) If the system is nominally rated 240/120 volt, 3-phase, 4-wire in which the midpoint of one phase is used as a circuit conductor; or

(D) If a service conductor is uninsulated.

(v) *Exceptions.* AC systems of 50 volts to 1000 volts are not required to be grounded if the system is separately derived and is supplied by a transformer that has a primary voltage rating less than 1000 volts, provided all of the following conditions are met:

(A) The system is used exclusively for control circuits,

(B) The conditions of maintenance and supervision assure that only qualified persons will service the installation,

(C) Continuity of control power is required, and

(D) Ground detectors are installed on the control system.

(2) *Separately derived systems.* Where paragraph (f)(1) of this section requires

grounding of wiring systems whose power is derived from generator, transformer, or converter windings and has no direct electrical connection, including a solidly connected grounded circuit conductor, to supply conductors originating in another system, paragraph (f)(5) of this section shall also apply.

(3) *Portable and vehicle-mounted generators*—(i) *Portable generators.* Under the following conditions, the frame of a portable generator need not be grounded and may serve as the grounding electrode for a system supplied by the generator:

(A) The generator supplies only equipment mounted on the generator and/or cord- and plug-connected equipment through receptacles mounted on the generator, and

(B) The noncurrent-carrying metal parts of equipment and the equipment grounding conductor terminals of the receptacles are bonded to the generator frame.

(ii) *Vehicle-mounted generators.* Under the following conditions the frame of a vehicle may serve as the grounding electrode for a system supplied by a generator located on the vehicle:

(A) The frame of the generator is bonded to the vehicle frame, and

(B) The generator supplies only equipment located on the vehicle and/or cord- and plug-connected equipment through receptacles mounted on the vehicle or on the generator, and

(C) The noncurrent-carrying metal parts of equipment and the equipment grounding conductor terminals of the receptacles are bonded to the generator frame, and

(D) The system complies with all other provisions of this section.

(iii) *Neutral conductor bonding.* A neutral conductor shall be bonded to the generator frame if the generator is a component of a separately derived system. No other conductor need be bonded to the generator frame.

(4) *Conductors to be grounded.* For AC premises wiring systems the identified conductor shall be grounded.

(5) *Grounding connections*—(i) *Grounded system.* For a grounded system, a grounding electrode conductor shall be used to connect both the equipment grounding conductor and the grounded

circuit conductor to the grounding electrode. Both the equipment grounding conductor and the grounding electrode conductor shall be connected to the grounded circuit conductor on the supply side of the service disconnecting means, or on the supply side of the system disconnecting means or overcurrent devices if the system is separately derived.

(ii) *Ungrounded systems.* For an ungrounded service-supplied system, the equipment grounding conductor shall be connected to the grounding electrode conductor at the service equipment. For an ungrounded separately derived system, the equipment grounding conductor shall be connected to the grounding electrode conductor at, or ahead of, the system disconnecting means or overcurrent devices.

(6) *Grounding path.* The path to ground from circuits, equipment, and enclosures shall be permanent and continuous.

(7) *Supports, enclosures, and equipment to be grounded*—(i) *Supports and enclosures for conductors.* Metal cable trays, metal raceways, and metal enclosures for conductors shall be grounded, except that:

(A) Metal enclosures such as sleeves that are used to protect cable assemblies from physical damage need not be grounded; and

(B) Metal enclosures for conductors added to existing installations of open wire, knob-and-tube wiring, and nonmetallic-sheathed cable need not be grounded if all of the following conditions are met:

(*1*) Runs are less than 25 feet (7.62 m);

(*2*) Enclosures are free from probable contact with ground, grounded metal, metal laths, or other conductive materials; and

(*3*) Enclosures are guarded against employee contact.

(ii) *Service equipment enclosures.* Metal enclosures for service equipment shall be grounded.

(iii) *Fixed equipment.* Exposed noncurrent-carrying metal parts of fixed equipment which may become energized shall be grounded under any of the following conditions:

(A) If within 8 feet (2.44 m) vertically or 5 feet (1.52 m) horizontally of ground or grounded metal objects and subject to employee contact.

(B) If located in a wet or damp location and subject to employee contact.

(C) If in electrical contact with metal.

(D) If in a hazardous (classified) location.

(E) If supplied by a metal-clad, metal-sheathed, or grounded metal raceway wiring method.

(F) If equipment operates with any terminal at over 150 volts to ground; however, the following need not be grounded:

(1) Enclosures for switches or circuit breakers used for other than service equipment and accessible to qualified persons only;

(2) Metal frames of electrically heated appliances which are permanently and effectively insulated from ground; and

(3) The cases of distribution apparatus such as transformers and capacitors mounted on wooden poles at a height exceeding 8 feet (2.44 m) above ground or grade level.

(iv) *Equipment connected by cord and plug.* Under any of the conditions described in paragraphs (f)(7)(iv)(A) through (f)(7)(iv)(C) of this section, exposed noncurrent-carrying metal parts of cord- and plug-connected equipment which may become energized shall be grounded:

(A) If in a hazardous (classified) location (see § 1926.407).

(B) If operated at over 150 volts to ground, except for guarded motors and metal frames of electrically heated appliances if the appliance frames are permanently and effectively insulated from ground.

(C) If the equipment is one of the types listed in paragraphs (f)(7)(iv)(C)(1) through (f)(7)(iv)(C)(5) of this section. However, even though the equipment may be one of these types, it need not be grounded if it is exempted by paragraph (f)(7)(iv)(C)(6).

(1) Hand held motor-operated tools;

(2) Cord- and plug-connected equipment used in damp or wet locations or by employees standing on the ground or on metal floors or working inside of metal tanks or boilers;

(3) Portable and mobile X-ray and associated equipment;

(4) Tools likely to be used in wet and/or conductive locations; and

(5) Portable hand lamps.

(6) Tools likely to be used in wet and/or conductive locations need not be grounded if supplied through an isolating transformer with an ungrounded secondary of not over 50 volts. Listed or labeled portable tools and appliances protected by a system of double insulation, or its equivalent, need not be grounded. If such a system is employed, the equipment shall be distinctively marked to indicate that the tool or appliance utilizes a system of double insulation.

(v) *Nonelectrical equipment.* The metal parts of the following nonelectrical equipment shall be grounded: Frames and tracks of electrically operated cranes; frames of nonelectrically driven elevator cars to which electric conductors are attached; hand-operated metal shifting ropes or cables of electric elevators, and metal partitions, grill work, and similar metal enclosures around equipment of over IkV between conductors.

(8) *Methods of grounding equipment—* (i) *With circuit conductors.* Noncurrent-carrying metal parts of fixed equipment, if required to be grounded by this subpart, shall be grounded by an equipment grounding conductor which is contained within the same raceway, cable, or cord, or runs with or encloses the circuit conductors. For DC circuits only, the equipment grounding conductor may be run separately from the circuit conductors.

(ii) *Grounding conductor.* A conductor used for grounding fixed or movable equipment shall have capacity to conduct safely any fault current which may be imposed on it.

(iii) *Equipment considered effectively grounded.* Electric equipment is considered to be effectively grounded if it is secured to, and in electrical contact with, a metal rack or structure that is provided for its support and the metal rack or structure is grounded by the method specified for the noncurrent-carrying metal parts of fixed equipment in paragraph (f)(8)(i) of this section. Metal car frames supported by metal hoisting cables attached to or running over metal sheaves or drums of grounded elevator machines are also considered to be effectively grounded.

(9) *Bonding.* If bonding conductors are used to assure electrical continuity, they shall have the capacity to conduct any fault current which may be imposed.

(10) *Made electrodes.* If made electrodes are used, they shall be free from nonconductive coatings, such as paint or enamel; and, if practicable, they shall be embedded below permanent moisture level. A single electrode consisting of a rod, pipe or plate which has a resistance to ground greater than 25 ohms shall be augmented by one additional electrode installed no closer than 6 feet (1.83 m) to the first electrode.

(11) *Grounding of systems and circuits of 1000 volts and over (high voltage)—(i) General.* If high voltage systems are grounded, they shall comply with all applicable provisions of paragraphs (f)(1) through (f)(10) of this section as supplemented and modified by this paragraph (f)(11).

(ii) *Grounding of systems supplying portable or mobile equipment.* Systems supplying portable or mobile high voltage equipment, other than substations installed on a temporary basis, shall comply with the following:

(A) Portable and mobile high voltage equipment shall be supplied from a system having its neutral grounded through an impedance. If a delta-connected high voltage system is used to supply the equipment, a system neutral shall be derived.

(B) Exposed noncurrent-carrying metal parts of portable and mobile equipment shall be connected by an equipment grounding conductor to the point at which the system neutral impedance is grounded.

(C) Ground-fault detection and relaying shall be provided to automatically de-energize any high voltage system component which has developed a ground fault. The continuity of the equipment grounding conductor shall be continuously monitored so as to de-energize automatically the high voltage feeder to the portable equipment upon loss of continuity of the equipment grounding conductor.

(D) The grounding electrode to which the portable or mobile equipment system neutral impedance is connected shall be isolated from and separated in the ground by at least 20 feet (6.1 m) from any other system or equipment grounding electrode, and there shall be no direct connection between the grounding electrodes, such as buried pipe, fence or like objects.

(iii) *Grounding of equipment.* All non-current-carrying metal parts of portable equipment and fixed equipment including their associated fences, housings, enclosures, and supporting structures shall be grounded. However, equipment which is guarded by location and isolated from ground need not be grounded. Additionally, pole-mounted distribution apparatus at a height exceeding 8 feet (2.44 m) above ground or grade level need not be grounded.

[51 FR 25318, July 11, 1986, as amended at 54 FR 24334, June 7, 1989; 61 FR 5510, Feb. 13, 1996]

§1926.405 **Wiring methods, components, and equipment for general use.**

(a) *Wiring methods.* The provisions of this paragraph do not apply to conductors which form an integral part of equipment such as motors, controllers, motor control centers and like equipment.

(1) *General requirements—(i) Electrical continuity of metal raceways and enclosures.* Metal raceways, cable armor, and other metal enclosures for conductors shall be metallically joined together into a continuous electric conductor and shall be so connected to all boxes, fittings, and cabinets as to provide effective electrical continuity.

(ii) *Wiring in ducts.* No wiring systems of any type shall be installed in ducts used to transport dust, loose stock or flammable vapors. No wiring system of any type shall be installed in any duct used for vapor removal or in any shaft containing only such ducts.

(2) *Temporary wiring—(i) Scope.* The provisions of paragraph (a)(2) of this section apply to temporary electrical power and lighting wiring methods which may be of a class less than would be required for a permanent installation. Except as specifically modified in paragraph (a)(2) of this section, all other requirements of this subpart for

permanent wiring shall apply to temporary wiring installations. Temporary wiring shall be removed immediately upon completion of construction or the purpose for which the wiring was installed.

(ii) *General requirements for temporary wiring*—(A) Feeders shall originate in a distribution center. The conductors shall be run as multiconductor cord or cable assemblies or within raceways; or, where not subject to physical damage, they may be run as open conductors on insulators not more than 10 feet (3.05 m) apart.

(B) Branch circuits shall originate in a power outlet or panelboard. Conductors shall be run as multiconductor cord or cable assemblies or open conductors, or shall be run in raceways. All conductors shall be protected by overcurrent devices at their ampacity. Runs of open conductors shall be located where the conductors will not be subject to physical damage, and the conductors shall be fastened at intervals not exceeding 10 feet (3.05 m). No branch-circuit conductors shall be laid on the floor. Each branch circuit that supplies receptacles or fixed equipment shall contain a separate equipment grounding conductor if the branch circuit is run as open conductors.

(C) Receptacles shall be of the grounding type. Unless installed in a complete metallic raceway, each branch circuit shall contain a separate equipment grounding conductor, and all receptacles shall be electrically connected to the grounding conductor. Receptacles for uses other than temporary lighting shall not be installed on branch circuits which supply temporary lighting. Receptacles shall not be connected to the same ungrounded conductor of multiwire circuits which supply temporary lighting.

(D) Disconnecting switches or plug connectors shall be installed to permit the disconnection of all ungrounded conductors of each temporary circuit.

(E) All lamps for general illumination shall be protected from accidental contact or breakage. Metal-case sockets shall be grounded.

(F) Temporary lights shall not be suspended by their electric cords unless cords and lights are designed for this means of suspension.

(G) Portable electric lighting used in wet and/or other conductive locations, as for example, drums, tanks, and vessels, shall be operated at 12 volts or less. However, 120-volt lights may be used if protected by a ground-fault circuit interrupter.

(H) A box shall be used wherever a change is made to a raceway system or a cable system which is metal clad or metal sheathed.

(I) Flexible cords and cables shall be protected from damage. Sharp corners and projections shall be avoided. Flexible cords and cables may pass through doorways or other pinch points, if protection is provided to avoid damage.

(J) Extension cord sets used with portable electric tools and appliances shall be of three-wire type and shall be designed for hard or extra-hard usage. Flexible cords used with temporary and portable lights shall be designed for hard or extra-hard usage.

NOTE: The National Electrical Code, ANSI/NFPA 70, in Article 400, Table 400–4, lists various types of flexible cords, some of which are noted as being designed for hard or extra-hard usage. Examples of these types of flexible cords include hard service cord (types S, ST, SO, STO) and junior hard service cord (types SJ, SJO, SJT, SJTO).

(iii) *Guarding.* For temporary wiring over 600 volts, nominal, fencing, barriers, or other effective means shall be provided to prevent access of other than authorized and qualified personnel.

(b) *Cabinets, boxes, and fittings*—(1) *Conductors entering boxes, cabinets, or fittings.* Conductors entering boxes, cabinets, or fittings shall be protected from abrasion, and openings through which conductors enter shall be effectively closed. Unused openings in cabinets, boxes, and fittings shall also be effectively closed.

(2) *Covers and canopies.* All pull boxes, junction boxes, and fittings shall be provided with covers. If metal covers are used, they shall be grounded. In energized installations each outlet box shall have a cover, faceplate, or fixture canopy. Covers of outlet boxes having holes through which flexible cord pendants pass shall be provided with bushings designed for the purpose or shall have smooth, well-rounded surfaces on which the cords may bear.

(3) *Pull and junction boxes for systems over 600 volts, nominal.* In addition to other requirements in this section for pull and junction boxes, the following shall apply to these boxes for systems over 600 volts, nominal:

(i) *Complete enclosure.* Boxes shall provide a complete enclosure for the contained conductors or cables.

(ii) *Covers.* Boxes shall be closed by covers securely fastened in place. Underground box covers that weigh over 100 pounds (43.6 kg) meet this requirement. Covers for boxes shall be permanently marked "HIGH VOLTAGE." The marking shall be on the outside of the box cover and shall be readily visible and legible.

(c) *Knife switches.* Single-throw knife switches shall be so connected that the blades are dead when the switch is in the open position. Single-throw knife switches shall be so placed that gravity will not tend to close them. Single-throw knife switches approved for use in the inverted position shall be provided with a locking device that will ensure that the blades remain in the open position when so set. Double-throw knife switches may be mounted so that the throw will be either vertical or horizontal. However, if the throw is vertical, a locking device shall be provided to ensure that the blades remain in the open position when so set.

(d) *Switchboards and panelboards.* Switchboards that have any exposed live parts shall be located in permanently dry locations and accessible only to qualified persons. Panelboards shall be mounted in cabinets, cutout boxes, or enclosures designed for the purpose and shall be dead front. However, panelboards other than the dead front externally-operable type are permitted where accessible only to qualified persons. Exposed blades of knife switches shall be dead when open.

(e) *Enclosures for damp or wet locations*—(1) *Cabinets, fittings, and boxes.* Cabinets, cutout boxes, fittings, boxes, and panelboard enclosures in damp or wet locations shall be installed so as to prevent moisture or water from entering and accumulating within the enclosures. In wet locations the enclosures shall be weatherproof.

(2) *Switches and circuit breakers.* Switches, circuit breakers, and switchboards installed in wet locations shall be enclosed in weatherproof enclosures.

(f) *Conductors for general wiring.* All conductors used for general wiring shall be insulated unless otherwise permitted in this subpart. The conductor insulation shall be of a type that is suitable for the voltage, operating temperature, and location of use. Insulated conductors shall be distinguishable by appropriate color or other means as being grounded conductors, ungrounded conductors, or equipment grounding conductors.

(g) *Flexible cords and cables*—(1) *Use of flexible cords and cables*—(i) *Permitted uses.* Flexible cords and cables shall be suitable for conditions of use and location. Flexible cords and cables shall be used only for:

(A) Pendants;

(B) Wiring of fixtures;

(C) Connection of portable lamps or appliances;

(D) Elevator cables;

(E) Wiring of cranes and hoists;

(F) Connection of stationary equipment to facilitate their frequent interchange;

(G) Prevention of the transmission of noise or vibration; or

(H) Appliances where the fastening means and mechanical connections are designed to permit removal for maintenance and repair.

(ii) *Attachment plugs for cords.* If used as permitted in paragraphs (g)(1)(i)(C), (g)(1)(i)(F), or (g)(1)(i)(H) of this section, the flexible cord shall be equipped with an attachment plug and shall be energized from a receptacle outlet.

(iii) *Prohibited uses.* Unless necessary for a use permitted in paragraph (g)(1)(i) of this section, flexible cords and cables shall not be used:

(A) As a substitute for the fixed wiring of a structure;

(B) Where run through holes in walls, ceilings, or floors;

(C) Where run through doorways, windows, or similar openings, except as permitted in paragraph (a)(2)(ii)(1) of this section;

(D) Where attached to building surfaces; or

(E) Where concealed behind building walls, ceilings, or floors.

(2) *Identification, splices, and terminations*—(i) *Identification.* A conductor of a flexible cord or cable that is used as a grounded conductor or an equipment grounding conductor shall be distinguishable from other conductors.

(ii) *Marking.* Type SJ, SJO, SJT, SJTO, S, SO, ST, and STO cords shall not be used unless durably marked on the surface with the type designation, size, and number of conductors.

(iii) *Splices.* Flexible cords shall be used only in continuous lengths without splice or tap. Hard service flexible cords No. 12 or larger may be repaired if spliced so that the splice retains the insulation, outer sheath properties, and usage characteristics of the cord being spliced.

(iv) *Strain relief.* Flexible cords shall be connected to devices and fittings so that strain relief is provided which will prevent pull from being directly transmitted to joints or terminal screws.

(v) *Cords passing through holes.* Flexible cords and cables shall be protected by bushings or fittings where passing through holes in covers, outlet boxes, or similar enclosures.

(h) *Portable cables over 600 volts, nominal.* Multiconductor portable cable for use in supplying power to portable or mobile equipment at over 600 volts, nominal, shall consist of No. 8 or larger conductors employing flexible stranding. Cables operated at over 2000 volts shall be shielded for the purpose of confining the voltage stresses to the insulation. Grounding conductors shall be provided. Connectors for these cables shall be of a locking type with provisions to prevent their opening or closing while energized. Strain relief shall be provided at connections and terminations. Portable cables shall not be operated with splices unless the splices are of the permanent molded, vulcanized, or other equivalent type. Termination enclosures shall be marked with a high voltage hazard warning, and terminations shall be accessible only to authorized and qualified personnel.

(i) *Fixture wires*—(1) *General.* Fixture wires shall be suitable for the voltage, temperature, and location of use. A fixture wire which is used as a grounded conductor shall be identified.

(2) *Uses permitted.* Fixture wires may be used:

(i) For installation in lighting, fixtures and in similar equipment where enclosed or protected and not subject to bending or twisting in use; or

(ii) For connecting lighting fixtures to the branch-circuit conductors supplying the fixtures.

(3) *Uses not permitted.* Fixture wires shall not be used as branch-circuit conductors except as permitted for Class 1 power-limited circuits.

(j) *Equipment for general use*—(1) *Lighting fixtures, lampholders, lamps, and receptacles*—(i) *Live parts.* Fixtures, lampholders, lamps, rosettes, and receptacles shall have no live parts normally exposed to employee contact. However, rosettes and cleat-type lampholders and receptacles located at least 8 feet (2.44 m) above the floor may have exposed parts.

(ii) *Support.* Fixtures, lampholders, rosettes, and receptacles shall be securely supported. A fixture that weighs more than 6 pounds (2.72 kg) or exceeds 16 inches (406 mm) in any dimension shall not be supported by the screw shell of a lampholder.

(iii) *Portable lamps.* Portable lamps shall be wired with flexible cord and an attachment plug of the polarized or grounding type. If the portable lamp uses an Edison-based lampholder, the grounded conductor shall be identified and attached to the screw shell and the identified blade of the attachment plug. In addition, portable handlamps shall comply with the following:

(A) Metal shell, paperlined lampholders shall not be used;

(B) Handlamps shall be equipped with a handle of molded composition or other insulating material;

(C) Handlamps shall be equipped with a substantial guard attached to the lampholder or handle;

(D) Metallic guards shall be grounded by the means of an equipment grounding conductor run within the power supply cord.

(iv) *Lampholders.* Lampholders of the screw-shell type shall be installed for use as lampholders only. Lampholders installed in wet or damp locations shall be of the weatherproof type.

(v) *Fixtures.* Fixtures installed in wet or damp locations shall be identified for the purpose and shall be installed so that water cannot enter or accumulate in wireways, lampholders, or other electrical parts.

(2) *Receptacles, cord connectors, and attachment plugs (caps)*—(i) *Configuration.* Receptacles, cord connectors, and attachment plugs shall be constructed so that no receptacle or cord connector will accept an attachment plug with a different voltage or current rating than that for which the device is intended. However, a 20-ampere T-slot receptacle or cord connector may accept a 15-ampere attachment plug of the same voltage rating. Receptacles connected to circuits having different voltages, frequencies, or types of current (ac or dc) on the same premises shall be of such design that the attachment plugs used on these circuits are not interchangeable.

(ii) *Damp and wet locations.* A receptacle installed in a wet or damp location shall be designed for the location.

(3) *Appliances*—(i) *Live parts.* Appliances, other than those in which the current-carrying parts at high temperatures are necessarily exposed, shall have no live parts normally exposed to employee contact.

(ii) *Disconnecting means.* A means shall be provided to disconnect each appliance.

(iii) *Rating.* Each appliance shall be marked with its rating in volts and amperes or volts and watts.

(4) *Motors.* This paragraph applies to motors, motor circuits, and controllers.

(i) *In sight from.* If specified that one piece of equipment shall be "in sight from" another piece of equipment, one shall be visible and not more than 50 feet (15.2 m) from the other.

(ii) *Disconnecting means*—(A) A disconnecting means shall be located in sight from the controller location. The controller disconnecting means for motor branch circuits over 600 volts, nominal, may be out of sight of the controller, if the controller is marked with a warning label giving the location and identification of the disconnecting means which is to be locked in the open position.

(B) The disconnecting means shall disconnect the motor and the controller from all ungrounded supply conductors and shall be so designed that no pole can be operated independently.

(C) If a motor and the driven machinery are not in sight from the controller location, the installation shall comply with one of the following conditions:

(1) The controller disconnecting means shall be capable of being locked in the open position.

(2) A manually operable switch that will disconnect the motor from its source of supply shall be placed in sight from the motor location.

(D) The disconnecting means shall plainly indicate whether it is in the open (off) or closed (on) position.

(E) The disconnecting means shall be readily accessible. If more than one disconnect is provided for the same equipment, only one need be readily accessible.

(F) An individual disconnecting means shall be provided for each motor, but a single disconnecting means may be used for a group of motors under any one of the following conditions:

(1) If a number of motors drive special parts of a single machine or piece of apparatus, such as a metal or woodworking machine, crane, or hoist;

(2) If a group of motors is under the protection of one set of branch-circuit protective devices; or

(3) If a group of motors is in a single room in sight from the location of the disconnecting means.

(iii) *Motor overload, short-circuit, and ground-fault protection.* Motors, motor-control apparatus, and motor branch-circuit conductors shall be protected against overheating due to motor overloads or failure to start, and against short-circuits or ground faults. These provisions do not require overload protection that will stop a motor where a shutdown is likely to introduce additional or increased hazards, as in the case of fire pumps, or where continued operation of a motor is necessary for a safe shutdown of equipment or process and motor overload sensing devices are connected to a supervised alarm.

(iv) *Protection of live parts—all voltages*—(A) Stationary motors having commutators, collectors, and brush rigging located inside of motor end brackets and not conductively connected to supply circuits operating at

261

more than 150 volts to ground need not have such parts guarded. Exposed live parts of motors and controllers operating at 50 volts or more between terminals shall be guarded against accidental contact by any of the following:

(1) By installation in a room or enclosure that is accessible only to qualified persons;

(2) By installation on a balcony, gallery, or platform, so elevated and arranged as to exclude unqualified persons; or

(3) By elevation 8 feet (2.44 m) or more above the floor.

(B) Where live parts of motors or controllers operating at over 150 volts to ground are guarded against accidental contact only by location, and where adjustment or other attendance may be necessary during the operation of the apparatus, insulating mats or platforms shall be provided so that the attendant cannot readily touch live parts unless standing on the mats or platforms.

(5) *Transformers*—(i) *Application.* The following paragraphs cover the installation of all transformers, except:

(A) Current transformers;

(B) Dry-type transformers installed as a component part of other apparatus;

(C) Transformers which are an integral part of an X-ray, high frequency, or electrostatic-coating apparatus;

(D) Transformers used with Class 2 and Class 3 circuits, sign and outline lighting, electric discharge lighting, and power-limited fire-protective signaling circuits.

(ii) *Operating voltage.* The operating voltage of exposed live parts of transformer installations shall be indicated by warning signs or visible markings on the equipment or structure.

(iii) *Transformers over 35 kV.* Dry-type, high fire point liquid-insulated, and askarel-insulated transformers installed indoors and rated over 35 kV shall be in a vault.

(iv) *Oil-insulated transformers.* If they present a fire hazard to employees, oil-insulated transformers installed indoors shall be in a vault.

(v) *Fire protection.* Combustible material, combustible buildings and parts of buildings, fire escapes, and door and window openings shall be safeguarded from fires which may originate in oil-insulated transformers attached to or adjacent to a building or combustible material.

(vi) *Transformer vaults.* Transformer vaults shall be constructed so as to contain fire and combustible liquids within the vault and to prevent unauthorized access. Locks and latches shall be so arranged that a vault door can be readily opened from the inside.

(vii) *Pipes and ducts.* Any pipe or duct system foreign to the vault installation shall not enter or pass through a transformer vault.

(viii) *Material storage.* Materials shall not be stored in transformer vaults.

(6) *Capacitors*—(i) *Drainage of stored charge.* All capacitors, except surge capacitors or capacitors included as a component part of other apparatus, shall be provided with an automatic means of draining the stored charge and maintaining the discharged state after the capacitor is disconnected from its source of supply.

(ii) *Over 600 volts.* Capacitors rated over 600 volts, nominal, shall comply with the following additional requirements:

(A) Isolating or disconnecting switches (with no interrupting rating) shall be interlocked with the load interrupting device or shall be provided with prominently displayed caution signs to prevent switching load current.

(B) For series capacitors the proper switching shall be assured by use of at least one of the following:

(1) Mechanically sequenced isolating and bypass switches,

(2) Interlocks, or

(3) Switching procedure prominently displayed at the switching location.

[51 FR 25318, July 11, 1986, as amended at 61 FR 5510, Feb. 13, 1996]

§ 1926.406 Specific purpose equipment and installations.

(a) *Cranes and hoists.* This paragraph applies to the installation of electric equipment and wiring used in connection with cranes, monorail hoists, hoists, and all runways.

(1) *Disconnecting means*—(i) *Runway conductor disconnecting means.* A readily accessible disconnecting means shall

be provided between the runway contact conductors and the power supply.

(ii) *Disconnecting means for cranes and monorail hoists.* A disconnecting means, capable of being locked in the open position, shall be provided in the leads from the runway contact conductors or other power supply on any crane or monorail hoist.

(A) If this additional disconnecting means is not readily accessible from the crane or monorail hoist operating station, means shall be provided at the operating station to open the power circuit to all motors of the crane or monorail hoist.

(B) The additional disconnect may be omitted if a monorail hoist or hand-propelled crane bridge installation meets all of the following:

(1) The unit is floor controlled;

(2) The unit is within view of the power supply disconnecting means; and

(3) No fixed work platform has been provided for servicing the unit.

(2) *Control.* A limit switch or other device shall be provided to prevent the load block from passing the safe upper limit of travel of any hoisting mechanism.

(3) *Clearance.* The dimension of the working space in the direction of access to live parts which may require examination, adjustment, servicing, or maintenance while alive shall be a minimum of 2 feet 6 inches (762 mm). Where controls are enclosed in cabinets, the door(s) shall open at least 90 degrees or be removable, or the installation shall provide equivalent access.

(4) *Grounding.* All exposed metal parts of cranes, monorail hoists, hoists and accessories including pendant controls shall be metallically joined together into a continuous electrical conductor so that the entire crane or hoist will be grounded in accordance with § 1926.404(f). Moving parts, other than removable accessories or attachments, having metal-to-metal bearing surfaces shall be considered to be electrically connected to each other through the bearing surfaces for grounding purposes. The trolley frame and bridge frame shall be considered as electrically grounded through the bridge and trolley wheels and its respective tracks unless conditions such as paint or other insulating materials prevent

reliable metal-to-metal contact. In this case a separate bonding conductor shall be provided.

(b) *Elevators, escalators, and moving walks*—(1) *Disconnecting means.* Elevators, escalators, and moving walks shall have a single means for disconnecting all ungrounded main power supply conductors for each unit.

(2) *Control panels.* If control panels are not located in the same space as the drive machine, they shall be located in cabinets with doors or panels capable of being locked closed.

(c) *Electric welders—disconnecting means*—(1) *Motor-generator, AC transformer, and DC rectifier arc welders.* A disconnecting means shall be provided in the supply circuit for each motor-generator arc welder, and for each AC transformer and DC rectifier arc welder which is not equipped with a disconnect mounted as an integral part of the welder.

(2) *Resistance welders.* A switch or circuit breaker shall be provided by which each resistance welder and its control equipment can be isolated from the supply circuit. The ampere rating of this disconnecting means shall not be less than the supply conductor ampacity.

(d) *X-Ray equipment*—(1) *Disconnecting means*—(i) *General.* A disconnecting means shall be provided in the supply circuit. The disconnecting means shall be operable from a location readily accessible from the X-ray control. For equipment connected to a 120-volt branch circuit of 30 amperes or less, a grounding-type attachment plug cap and receptacle of proper rating may serve as a disconnecting means.

(ii) *More than one piece of equipment.* If more than one piece of equipment is operated from the same high-voltage circuit, each piece or each group of equipment as a unit shall be provided with a high-voltage switch or equivalent disconnecting means. This disconnecting means shall be constructed, enclosed, or located so as to avoid contact by employees with its live parts.

(2) *Control—Radiographic and fluoroscopic types.* Radiographic and fluoroscopic-type equipment shall be effectively enclosed or shall have interlocks that deenergize the equipment

automatically to prevent ready access to live current-carrying parts.

§ 1926.407 Hazardous (classified) locations.

(a) *Scope.* This section sets forth requirements for electric equipment and wiring in locations which are classified depending on the properties of the flammable vapors, liquids or gases, or combustible dusts or fibers which may be present therein and the likelihood that a flammable or combustible concentration or quantity is present. Each room, section or area shall be considered individually in determining its classification. These hazardous (classified) locations are assigned six designations as follows:

Class I, Division 1
Class I, Division 2
Class II, Division 1
Class II, Division 2
Class III, Division 1
Class III, Division 2

For definitions of these locations see § 1926.449. All applicable requirements in this subpart apply to all hazardous (classified) locations, unless modified by provisions of this section.

(b) *Electrical installations.* Equipment, wiring methods, and installations of equipment in hazardous (classified) locations shall be approved as intrinsically safe or approved for the hazardous (classified) location or safe for the hazardous (classified) location. Requirements for each of these options are as follows:

(1) *Intrinsically safe.* Equipment and associated wiring approved as intrinsically safe is permitted in any hazardous (classified) location included in its listing or labeling.

(2) *Approved for the hazardous (classified) location*—(i) *General.* Equipment shall be approved not only for the class of location but also for the ignitible or combustible properties of the specific gas, vapor, dust, or fiber that will be present.

NOTE: NFPA 70, the National Electrical Code, lists or defines hazardous gases, vapors, and dusts by "Groups" characterized by their ignitible or combustible properties.

(ii) *Marking.* Equipment shall not be used unless it is marked to show the class, group, and operating tempera-

ture or temperature range, based on operation in a 40-degree C ambient, for which it is approved. The temperature marking shall not exceed the ignition temperature of the specific gas, vapor, or dust to be encountered. However, the following provisions modify this marking requirement for specific equipment:

(A) Equipment of the non-heat-producing type (such as junction boxes, conduit, and fitting) and equipment of the heat-producing type having a maximum temperature of not more than 100 degrees C (212 degrees F) need not have a marked operating temperature or temperature range.

(B) Fixed lighting fixtures marked for use only in Class I, Division 2 locations need not be marked to indicate the group.

(C) Fixed general-purpose equipment in Class I locations, other than lighting fixtures, which is acceptable for use in Class I, Division 2 locations need not be marked with the class, group, division, or operating temperature.

(D) Fixed dust-tight equipment, other than lighting fixtures, which is acceptable for use in Class II, Division 2 and Class III locations need not be marked with the class, group, division, or operating temperature.

(3) *Safe for the hazardous (classified) location.* Equipment which is safe for the location shall be of a type and design which the employer demonstrates will provide protection from the hazards arising from the combustibility and flammability of vapors, liquids, gases, dusts, or fibers.

NOTE: The National Electrical Code, NFPA 70, contains guidelines for determining the type and design of equipment and installations which will meet this requirement. The guidelines of this document address electric wiring, equipment, and systems installed in hazardous (classified) locations and contain specific provisions for the following: wiring methods, wiring connections, conductor insulation, flexible cords, sealing and drainage, transformers, capacitors, switches, circuit breakers, fuses, motor controllers, receptacles, attachment plugs, meters, relays, instruments, resistors, generators, motors, lighting fixtures, storage battery charging equipment, electric cranes, electric hoists and similar equipment, utilization equipment, signaling systems, alarm systems, remote control systems, local loud speaker and communication systems, ventilation piping, live parts, lightning surge protection, and grounding. Compliance with these guidelines will constitute one means, but not the only means, of compliance with this paragraph.

(c) *Conduits*. All conduits shall be threaded and shall be made wrench-tight. Where it is impractical to make a threaded joint tight, a bonding jumper shall be utilized.

[51 FR 25318, July 11, 1986, as amended at 61 FR 5510, Feb. 13, 1996]

§1926.408 Special systems.

(a) *Systems over 600 volts, nominal.* Paragraphs (a)(1) through (a)(4) of this section contain general requirements for all circuits and equipment operated at over 600 volts.

(1) *Wiring methods for fixed installations—(i) Above ground.* Above-ground conductors shall be installed in rigid metal conduit, in intermediate metal conduit, in cable trays, in cablebus, in other suitable raceways, or as open runs of metal-clad cable designed for the use and purpose. However, open runs of non-metallic-sheathed cable or of bare conductors or busbars may be installed in locations which are accessible only to qualified persons. Metallic shielding components, such as tapes, wires, or braids for conductors, shall be grounded. Open runs of insulated wires and cables having a bare lead sheath or a braided outer covering shall be supported in a manner designed to prevent physical damage to the braid or sheath.

(ii) *Installations emerging from the ground.* Conductors emerging from the ground shall be enclosed in raceways. Raceways installed on poles shall be of rigid metal conduit, intermediate metal conduit, PVC schedule 80 or equivalent extending from the ground line up to a point 8 feet (2.44 m) above finished grade. Conductors entering a building shall be protected by an enclosure from the ground line to the point of entrance. Metallic enclosures shall be grounded.

(2) *Interrupting and isolating devices—* (i) *Circuit breakers.* Circuit breakers located indoors shall consist of metal-enclosed or fire-resistant, cell-mounted units. In locations accessible only to qualified personnel, open mounting of circuit breakers is permitted. A means of indicating the open and closed position of circuit breakers shall be provided.

(ii) *Fused cutouts.* Fused cutouts installed in buildings or transformer vaults shall be of a type identified for the purpose. They shall be readily accessible for fuse replacement.

(iii) *Equipment isolating means.* A means shall be provided to completely isolate equipment for inspection and repairs. Isolating means which are not designed to interrupt the load current of the circuit shall be either interlocked with a circuit interrupter or provided with a sign warning against opening them under load.

(3) *Mobile and portable equipment—*(i) *Power cable connections to mobile machines.* A metallic enclosure shall be provided on the mobile machine for enclosing the terminals of the power cable. The enclosure shall include provisions for a solid connection for the ground wire(s) terminal to ground effectively the machine frame. The method of cable termination used shall prevent any strain or pull on the cable from stressing the electrical connections. The enclosure shall have provision for locking so only authorized qualified persons may open it and shall be marked with a sign warning of the presence of energized parts.

(ii) *Guarding live parts.* All energized switching and control parts shall be enclosed in effectively grounded metal cabinets or enclosures. Circuit breakers and protective equipment shall have the operating means projecting through the metal cabinet or enclosure so these units can be reset without locked doors being opened. Enclosures and metal cabinets shall be locked so that only authorized qualified persons have access and shall be marked with a sign warning of the presence of energized parts. Collector ring assemblies on revolving-type machines (shovels, draglines, etc.) shall be guarded.

(4) *Tunnel installations—*(i) *Application.* The provisions of this paragraph apply to installation and use of high-voltage power distribution and utilization equipment which is associated with tunnels and which is portable and/ or mobile, such as substations, trailers, cars, mobile shovels, draglines, hoists, drills, dredges, compressors, pumps,

265

conveyors, and underground excavators.

(ii) *Conductors.* Conductors in tunnels shall be installed in one or more of the following:

(A) Metal conduit or other metal raceway,

(B) Type MC cable, or

(C) Other suitable multiconductor cable.

Conductors shall also be so located or guarded as to protect them from physical damage. Multiconductor portable cable may supply mobile equipment. An equipment grounding conductor shall be run with circuit conductors inside the metal raceway or inside the multiconductor cable jacket. The equipment grounding conductor may be insulated or bare.

(iii) *Guarding live parts.* Bare terminals of transformers, switches, motor controllers, and other equipment shall be enclosed to prevent accidental contact with energized parts. Enclosures for use in tunnels shall be drip-proof, weatherproof, or submersible as required by the environmental conditions.

(iv) *Disconnecting means.* A disconnecting means that simultaneously opens all ungrounded conductors shall be installed at each transformer or motor location.

(v) *Grounding and bonding.* All non-energized metal parts of electric equipment and metal raceways and cable sheaths shall be grounded and bonded to all metal pipes and rails at the portal and at intervals not exceeding 1000 feet (305 m) throughout the tunnel.

(b) *Class 1, Class 2, and Class 3 remote control, signaling, and power-limited circuits*—(1) *Classification.* Class 1, Class 2, or Class 3 remote control, signaling, or power-limited circuits are characterized by their usage and electrical power limitation which differentiates them from light and power circuits. These circuits are classified in accordance with their respective voltage and power limitations as summarized in paragraphs (b)(1)(i) through (b)(1)(iii) of this section.

(i) *Class 1 circuits*—(A) A Class 1 power-limited circuit is supplied from a source having a rated output of not more than 30 volts and 1000 volt-amperes.

(B) A Class 1 remote control circuit or a Class 1 signaling circuit has a voltage which does not exceed 600 volts; however, the power output of the source need not be limited.

(ii) *Class 2 and Class 3 circuits*—(A) Power for Class 2 and Class 3 circuits is limited either inherently (in which no overcurrent protection is required) or by a combination of a power source and overcurrent protection.

(B) The maximum circuit voltage is 150 volts AC or DC for a Class 2 inherently limited power source, and 100 volts AC or DC for a Class 3 inherently limited power source.

(C) The maximum circuit voltage is 30 volts AC and 60 volts DC for a Class 2 power source limited by overcurrent protection, and 150 volts AC or DC for a Class 3 power source limited by overcurrent protection.

(iii) *Application.* The maximum circuit voltages in paragraphs (b)(1)(i) and (b)(1)(ii) of this section apply to sinusoidal AC or continuous DC power sources, and where wet contact occurrence is not likely.

(2) *Marking.* A Class 2 or Class 3 power supply unit shall not be used unless it is durably marked where plainly visible to indicate the class of supply and its electrical rating.

(c) *Communications systems*—(1) *Scope.* These provisions for communication systems apply to such systems as central-station-connected and non-central-station-connected telephone circuits, radio receiving and transmitting equipment, and outside wiring for fire and burglar alarm, and similar central station systems. These installations need not comply with the provisions of §§ 1926.403 through 1926.408(b), except § 1926.404(c)(1)(ii) and § 1926.407.

(2) *Protective devices*—(i) *Circuits exposed to power conductors.* Communication circuits so located as to be exposed to accidental contact with light or power conductors operating at over 300 volts shall have each circuit so exposed provided with an approved protector.

(ii) *Antenna lead-ins.* Each conductor of a lead-in from an outdoor antenna shall be provided with an antenna discharge unit or other means that will drain static charges from the antenna system.

(3) *Conductor location*—(i) *Outside of buildings*—(A) Receiving distribution lead-in or aerial-drop cables attached to buildings and lead-in conductors to radio transmitters shall be so installed as to avoid the possibility of accidental contact with electric light or power conductors.

(B) The clearance between lead-in conductors and any lightning protection conductors shall not be less than 6 feet (1.83 m).

(ii) *On poles*. Where practicable, communication conductors on poles shall be located below the light or power conductors. Communications conductors shall not be attached to a cross-arm that carries light or power conductors.

(iii) *Inside of buildings*. Indoor antennas, lead-ins, and other communication conductors attached as open conductors to the inside of buildings shall be located at least 2 inches (50.8 mm) from conductors of any light or power or Class 1 circuits unless a special and equally protective method of conductor separation is employed.

(4) *Equipment location*. Outdoor metal structures supporting antennas, as well as self-supporting antennas such as vertical rods or dipole structures, shall be located as far away from overhead conductors of electric light and power circuits of over 150 volts to ground as necessary to avoid the possibility of the antenna or structure falling into or making accidental contact with such circuits.

(5) *Grounding*—(i) *Lead-in conductors*. If exposed to contact with electric light or power conductors, the metal sheath of aerial cables entering buildings shall be grounded or shall be interrupted close to the entrance to the building by an insulating joint or equivalent device. Where protective devices are used, they shall be grounded.

(ii) *Antenna structures*. Masts and metal structures supporting antennas shall be permanently and effectively grounded without splice or connection in the grounding conductor.

(iii) *Equipment enclosures*. Transmitters shall be enclosed in a metal frame or grill or separated from the operating space by a barrier, all metallic parts of which are effectively connected to ground. All external metal handles and controls accessible to the operating personnel shall be effectively grounded. Unpowered equipment and enclosures shall be considered grounded where connected to an attached coaxial cable with an effectively grounded metallic shield.

[51 FR 25318, July 11, 1986, as amended at 61 FR 5510, Feb. 13, 1996]

§§ 1926.409–1926.415   [Reserved]

SAFETY-RELATED WORK PRACTICES

§ 1926.416   General requirements.

(a) *Protection of employees*—(1) No employer shall permit an employee to work in such proximity to any part of an electric power circuit that the employee could contact the electric power circuit in the course of work, unless the employee is protected against electric shock by deenergizing the circuit and grounding it or by guarding it effectively by insulation or other means.

(2) In work areas where the exact location of underground electric powerlines is unknown, employees using jack-hammers, bars, or other hand tools which may contact a line shall be provided with insulated protective gloves.

(3) Before work is begun the employer shall ascertain by inquiry or direct observation, or by instruments, whether any part of an energized electric power circuit, exposed or concealed, is so located that the performance of the work may bring any person, tool, or machine into physical or electrical contact with the electric power circuit. The employer shall post and maintain proper warning signs where such a circuit exists. The employer shall advise employees of the location of such lines, the hazards involved, and the protective measures to be taken.

(b) *Passageways and open spaces*—(1) Barriers or other means of guarding shall be provided to ensure that workspace for electrical equipment will not be used as a passageway during periods when energized parts of electrical equipment are exposed.

(2) Working spaces, walkways, and similar locations shall be kept clear of cords so as not to create a hazard to employees.

267

(c) *Load ratings.* In existing installations, no changes in circuit protection shall be made to increase the load in excess of the load rating of the circuit wiring.

(d) *Fuses.* When fuses are installed or removed with one or both terminals energized, special tools insulated for the voltage shall be used.

(e) *Cords and cables.* (1) Worn or frayed electric cords or cables shall not be used.

(2) Extension cords shall not be fastened with staples, hung from nails, or suspended by wire.

[44 FR 8577, Feb. 9, 1979; 44 FR 20940, Apr. 6, 1979, as amended at 55 FR 42328, Oct. 18, 1990; 58 FR 35179, June 30, 1993; 61 FR 9251, Mar. 7, 1996; 61 FR 41738, Aug. 12, 1996]

§ 1926.417 Lockout and tagging of circuits.

(a) *Controls.* Controls that are to be deactivated during the course of work on energized or deenergized equipment or circuits shall be tagged.

(b) *Equipment and circuits.* Equipment or circuits that are deenergized shall be rendered inoperative and shall have tags attached at all points where such equipment or circuits can be energized.

(c) *Tags.* Tags shall be placed to identify plainly the equipment or circuits being worked on.

[44 FR 8577, Feb. 9, 1979; 44 FR 20940, Apr. 6, 1979, as amended at 55 FR 42328, Oct. 18, 1990; 58 FR 35181, June 30, 1993; 61 FR 9251, Mar. 7, 1996; 61 FR 41739, Aug. 12, 1996]]

§§ 1926.418–1926.430 [Reserved]

SAFETY-RELATED MAINTENANCE AND ENVIRONMENTAL CONSIDERATIONS

§ 1926.431 Maintenance of equipment.

The employer shall ensure that all wiring components and utilization equipment in hazardous locations are maintained in a dust-tight, dust-ignition-proof, or explosion-proof condition, as appropriate. There shall be no loose or missing screws, gaskets, threaded connections, seals, or other impairments to a tight condition.

§ 1926.432 Environmental deterioration of equipment.

(a) *Deteriorating agents*—(1) Unless identified for use in the operating environment, no conductors or equipment shall be located:

(i) In damp or wet locations;

(ii) Where exposed to gases, fumes, vapors, liquids, or other agents having a deteriorating effect on the conductors or equipment; or

(iii) Where exposed to excessive temperatures.

(2) Control equipment, utilization equipment, and busways approved for use in dry locations only shall be protected against damage from the weather during building construction.

(b) *Protection against corrosion.* Metal raceways, cable armor, boxes, cable sheathing, cabinets, elbows, couplings, fittings, supports, and support hardware shall be of materials appropriate for the environment in which they are to be installed.

§§ 1926.433–1926.440 [Reserved]

SAFETY REQUIREMENTS FOR SPECIAL EQUIPMENT

§ 1926.441 Batteries and battery charging.

(a) *General requirements*—(1) Batteries of the unsealed type shall be located in enclosures with outside vents or in well ventilated rooms and shall be arranged so as to prevent the escape of fumes, gases, or electrolyte spray into other areas.

(2) Ventilation shall be provided to ensure diffusion of the gases from the battery and to prevent the accumulation of an explosive mixture.

(3) Racks and trays shall be substantial and shall be treated to make them resistant to the electrolyte.

(4) Floors shall be of acid resistant construction unless protected from acid accumulations.

(5) Face shields, aprons, and rubber gloves shall be provided for workers handling acids or batteries.

(6) Facilities for quick drenching of the eyes and body shall be provided within 25 feet (7.62 m) of battery handling areas.

(7) Facilities shall be provided for flushing and neutralizing spilled electrolyte and for fire protection.

(b) *Charging*—(1) Battery charging installations shall be located in areas designated for that purpose.

(2) Charging apparatus shall be protected from damage by trucks.

(3) When batteries are being charged, the vent caps shall be kept in place to avoid electrolyte spray. Vent caps shall be maintained in functioning condition.

§§1926.442–1926.448 [Reserved]

DEFINITIONS

§1926.449 Definitions applicable to this subpart.

The definitions given in this section apply to the terms used in subpart K. The definitions given here for "approved" and "qualified person" apply, instead of the definitions given in §1926.32, to the use of these terms in subpart K.

Acceptable. An installation or equipment is acceptable to the Assistant Secretary of Labor, and approved within the meaning of this subpart K:

(a) If it is accepted, or certified, or listed, or labeled, or otherwise determined to be safe by a qualified testing laboratory capable of determining the suitability of materials and equipment for installation and use in accordance with this standard; or

(b) With respect to an installation or equipment of a kind which no qualified testing laboratory accepts, certifies, lists, labels, or determines to be safe, if it is inspected or tested by another Federal agency, or by a State, municipal, or other local authority responsible for enforcing occupational safety provisions of the National Electrical Code, and found in compliance with those provisions; or

(c) With respect to custom-made equipment or related installations which are designed, fabricated for, and intended for use by a particular customer, if it is determined to be safe for its intended use by its manufacturer on the basis of test data which the employer keeps and makes available for inspection to the Assistant Secretary and his authorized representatives.

Accepted. An installation is "accepted" if it has been inspected and found to be safe by a qualified testing laboratory.

Accessible. (As applied to wiring methods.) Capable of being removed or exposed without damaging the building structure or finish, or not permanently closed in by the structure or finish of the building. (See *"concealed"* and *"exposed."*)

Accessible. (As applied to equipment.) Admitting close approach; not guarded by locked doors, elevation, or other effective means. (See*"Readily accessible."*)

Ampacity. The current in amperes a conductor can carry continuously under the conditions of use without exceeding its temperature rating.

Appliances. Utilization equipment, generally other than industrial, normally built in standardized sizes or types, which is installed or conneceted as a unit to perform one or more functions.

Approved. Acceptable to the authority enforcing this subpart. The authority enforcing this subpart is the Assistant Secretary of Labor for Occupational Safety and Health. The definition of "acceptable" indicates what is acceptable to the Assistant Secretary of Labor, and therefore approved within the meaning of this subpart.

Askarel. A generic term for a group of nonflammable synthetic chlorinated hydrocarbons used as electrical insulating media. Askarels of various compositional types are used. Under arcing conditions the gases produced, while consisting predominantly of noncombustible hydrogen chloride, can include varying amounts of combustible gases depending upon the askarel type.

Attachment plug (Plug cap)(Cap). A device which, by insertion in a receptacle, establishes connection between the conductors of the attached flexible cord and the conductors connected permanently to the receptacle.

Automatic. Self-acting, operating by its own mechanism when actuated by some impersonal influence, as for example, a change in current strength, pressure, temperature, or mechanical configuration.

Bare conductor. See *"Conductor."*

Bonding. The permanent joining of metallic parts to form an electrically conductive path which will assure electrical continuity and the capacity to conduct safely any current likely to be imposed.

Bonding jumper. A reliable conductor to assure the required electrical conductivity between metal parts required to be electrically connected.

Branch circuit. The circuit conductors between the final overcurrent device protecting the circuit and the outlet(s).

Building. A structure which stands alone or which is cut off from adjoining structures by fire walls with all openings therein protected by approved fire doors.

Cabinet. An enclosure designed either for surface or flush mounting, and provided with a frame, mat, or trim in which a swinging door or doors are or may be hung.

Certified. Equipment is "certified" if it:

(a) Has been tested and found by a qualified testing laboratory to meet applicable test standards or to be safe for use in a specified manner, and

(b) Is of a kind whose production is periodically inspected by a qualified testing laboratory. Certified equipment must bear a label, tag, or other record of certification.

Circuit breaker—(a) (600 volts nominal, or less.) A device designed to open and close a circuit by nonautomatic means and to open the circuit automatically on a predetermined overcurrent without injury to itself when properly applied within its rating.

(b) (Over 600 volts, nominal.) A switching device capable of making, carrying, and breaking currents under normal circuit conditions, and also making, carrying for a specified time, and breaking currents under specified abnormal circuit conditions, such as those of short circuit.

Class I locations. Class I locations are those in which flammable gases or vapors are or may be present in the air in quantities sufficient to produce explosive or ignitible mixtures. Class I locations include the following:

(a) *Class I, Division 1.* A Class I, Division 1 location is a location:

(1) In which ignitible concentrations of flammable gases or vapors may exist under normal operating conditions; or

(2) In which ignitible concentrations of such gases or vapors may exist frequently because of repair or maintenance operations or because of leakage; or

(3) In which breakdown or faulty operation of equipment or processes might release ignitible concentrations of flammable gases or vapors, and might also cause simultaneous failure of electric equipment.

NOTE: This classification usually includes locations where volatile flammable liquids or liquefied flammable gases are transferred from one container to another; interiors of spray booths and areas in the vicinity of spraying and painting operations where volatile flammable solvents are used; locations containing open tanks or vats of volatile flammable liquids; drying rooms or compartments for the evaporation of flammable solvents; inadequately ventilated pump rooms for flammable gas or for volatile flammable liquids; and all other locations where ignitible concentrations of flammable vapors or gases are likely to occur in the course of normal operations.

(b) *Class I, Division 2.* A Class I, Division 2 location is a location:

(1) In which volatile flammable liquids or flammable gases are handled, processed, or used, but in which the hazardous liquids, vapors, or gases will normally be confined within closed containers or closed systems from which they can escape only in case of accidental rupture or breakdown of such containers or systems, or in case of abnormal operation of equipment; or

(2) In which ignitible concentrations of gases or vapors are normally prevented by positive mechanical ventilation, and which might become hazardous through failure or abnormal operations of the ventilating equipment; or

(3) That is adjacent to a Class I, Division 1 location, and to which ignitible concentrations of gases or vapors might occasionally be communicated unless such communication is prevented by adequate positive-pressure ventilation from a source of clean air, and effective safeguards against ventilation failure are provided.

NOTE: This classification usually includes locations where volatile flammable liquids or flammable gases or vapors are used, but which would become hazardous only in case of an accident or of some unusual operating condition. The quantity of flammable material that might escape in case of accident, the adequacy of ventilating equipment, the total area involved, and the record of the industry or business with respect to explosions or fires are all factors that merit consideration in determining the classification and extent of each location.

Piping without valves, checks, meters, and similar devices would not ordinarily introduce a hazardous condition even though used for flammable liquids or gases. Locations used for the storage of flammable liquids or of liquefied or compressed gases in sealed containers would not normally be considered hazardous unless also subject to other hazardous conditions.

Electrical conduits and their associated enclosures separated from process fluids by a single seal or barrier are classed as a Division 2 location if the outside of the conduit and enclosures is a nonhazardous location.

Class II locations. Class II locations are those that are hazardous because of the presence of combustible dust. Class II locations include the following:

(a) *Class II, Division 1.* A Class II, Division 1 location is a location:

(1) In which combustible dust is or may be in suspension in the air under normal operating conditions, in quantities sufficient to produce explosive or ignitible mixtures; or

(2) Where mechanical failure or abnormal operation of machinery or equipment might cause such explosive or ignitible mixtures to be produced, and might also provide a source of ignition through simultaneous failure of electric equipment, operation of protection devices, or from other causes, or

(3) In which combustible dusts of an electrically conductive nature may be present.

NOTE: Combustible dusts which are electrically nonconductive include dusts produced in the handling and processing of grain and grain products, pulverized sugar and cocoa, dried egg and milk powders, pulverized spices, starch and pastes, potato and woodflour, oil meal from beans and seed, dried hay, and other organic materials which may produce combustible dusts when processed or handled. Dusts containing magnesium or aluminum are particularly hazardous and the use of extreme caution is necessary to avoid ignition and explosion.

(b) *Class II, Division 2.* A Class II, Division 2 location is a location in which:

(1) Combustible dust will not normally be in suspension in the air in quantities sufficient to produce explosive or ignitible mixtures, and dust accumulations are normally insufficient to interfere with the normal operation of electrical equipment or other apparatus; or

(2) Dust may be in suspension in the air as a result of infrequent malfunctioning of handling or processing equipment, and dust accumulations resulting therefrom may be ignitible by abnormal operation or failure of electrical equipment or other apparatus.

NOTE: This classification includes locations where dangerous concentrations of suspended dust would not be likely but where dust accumulations might form on or in the vicinity of electric equipment. These areas may contain equipment from which appreciable quantities of dust would escape under abnormal operating conditions or be adjacent to a Class II Division 1 location, as described above, into which an explosive or ignitible concentration of dust may be put into suspension under abnormal operating conditions.

Class III locations. Class III locations are those that are hazardous because of the presence of easily ignitible fibers or flyings but in which such fibers or flyings are not likely to be in suspension in the air in quantities sufficient to produce ignitible mixtures. Class 111 locations include the following:

(a) *Class III, Division 1.* A Class III, Division 1 location is a location in which easily ignitible fibers or materials producing combustible flyings are handled, manufactured, or used.

NOTE: Easily ignitible fibers and flyings include rayon, cotton (including cotton linters and cotton waste), sisal or henequen, istle, jute, hemp, tow, cocoa fiber, oakum, baled waste kapok, Spanish moss, excelsior, sawdust, woodchips, and other material of similar nature.

(b) *Class III, Division 2.* A Class III, Division 2 location is a location in which easily ignitible fibers are stored or handled, except in process of manufacture.

Collector ring. A collector ring is an assembly of slip rings for transferring electrical energy from a stationary to a rotating member.

Concealed. Rendered inaccessible by the structure or finish of the building. Wires in concealed raceways are considered concealed, even though they may become accessible by withdrawing them. [See "*Accessible.* (As applied to wiring methods.)"]

271

Conductor—(a) *Bare*. A conductor having no covering or electrical insulation whatsoever.

(b) *Covered*. A conductor encased within material of composition or thickness that is not recognized as electrical insulation.

(c) *Insulated*. A conductor encased within material of composition and thickness that is recognized as electrical insulation.

Controller. A device or group of devices that serves to govern, in some predetermined manner, the electric power delivered to the apparatus to which it is connected.

Covered conductor. See *"Conductor."*

Cutout. (Over 600 volts, nominal.) An assembly of a fuse support with either a fuseholder, fuse carrier, or disconnecting blade. The fuseholder or fuse carrier may include a conducting element (fuse link), or may act as the disconnecting blade by the inclusion of a nonfusible member.

Cutout box. An enclosure designed for surface mounting and having swinging doors or covers secured directly to and telescoping with the walls of the box proper. (See *"Cabinet."*)

Damp location. See *"Location."*

Dead front. Without live parts exposed to a person on the operating side of the equipment.

Device. A unit of an electrical system which is intended to carry but not utilize electric energy.

Disconnecting means. A device, or group of devices, or other means by which the conductors of a circuit can be disconnected from their source of supply.

Disconnecting (or Isolating) switch. (Over 600 volts, nominal.) A mechanical switching device used for isolating a circuit or equipment from a source of power.

Dry location. See *"Location."*

Enclosed. Surrounded by a case, housing, fence or walls which will prevent persons from accidentally contacting energized parts.

Enclosure. The case or housing of apparatus, or the fence or walls surrounding an installation to prevent personnel from accidentally contacting energized parts, or to protect the equipment from physical damage.

Equipment. A general term including material, fittings, devices, appliances, fixtures, apparatus, and the like, used as a part of, or in connection with, an electrical installation.

Equipment grounding conductor. See *"Grounding conductor, equipment."*

Explosion-proof apparatus. Apparatus enclosed in a case that is capable of withstanding an explosion of a specified gas or vapor which may occur within it and of preventing the ignition of a specified gas or vapor surrounding the enclosure by sparks, flashes, or explosion of the gas or vapor within, and which operates at such an external temperature that it will not ignite a surrounding flammable atmosphere.

Exposed. (As applied to live parts.) Capable of being inadvertently touched or approached nearer than a safe distance by a person. It is applied to parts not suitably guarded, isolated, or insulated. (See *"Accessible* and *"Concealed."*)

Exposed. (As applied to wiring methods.) On or attached to the surface or behind panels designed to allow access. [See *"Accessible.* (As applied to wiring methods.)"]

Exposed. (For the purposes of § 1926.408(d), Communications systems.) Where the circuit is in such a position that in case of failure of supports or insulation, contact with another circuit may result.

Externally operable. Capable of being operated without exposing the operator to contact with live parts.

Feeder. All circuit conductors between the service equipment, or the generator switchboard of an isolated plant, and the final branch-circuit overcurrent device.

Festoon lighting. A string of outdoor lights suspended between two points more than 15 feet (4.57 m) apart.

Fitting. An accessory such as a locknut, bushing, or other part of a wiring system that is intended primarily to perform a mechanical rather than an electrical function.

Fuse. (Over 600 volts, nominal.) An overcurrent protective device with a circuit opening fusible part that is heated and severed by the passage of overcurrent through it. A fuse comprises all the parts that form a unit capable of performing the prescribed functions. It may or may not be the complete device necessary to connect it into an electrical circuit.

Ground. A conducting connection, whether intentional or accidental, between an electrical circuit or equipment and the earth, or to some conducting body that serves in place of the earth.

Grounded. Connected to earth or to some conducting body that serves in place of the earth.

Grounded, effectively (Over 600 volts, nominal.) Permanently connected to earth through a ground connection of sufficiently low impedance and having sufficient ampacity that ground fault current which may occur cannot build up to voltages dangerous to personnel.

Grounded conductor. A system or circuit conductor that is intentionally grounded.

Grounding conductor. A conductor used to connect equipment or the grounded circuit of a wiring system to a grounding electrode or electrodes.

Grounding conductor, equipment. The conductor used to connect the noncurrent-carrying metal parts of equipment, raceways, and other enclosures to the system grounded conductor and/ or the grounding electrode conductor at the service equipment or at the source of a separately derived system.

Grounding electrode conductor. The conductor used to connect the grounding electrode to the equipment grounding conductor and/or to the grounded conductor of the circuit at the service equipment or at the source of a separately derived system.

Ground-fault circuit interrupter. A device for the protection of personnel that functions to deenergize a circuit or portion thereof within an established period of time when a current to ground exceeds some predetermined value that is less than that required to operate the overcurrent protective device of the supply circuit.

Guarded. Covered, shielded, fenced, enclosed, or otherwise protected by means of suitable covers, casings, barriers, rails, screens, mats, or platforms to remove the likelihood of approach to a point of danger or contact by persons or objects.

Hoistway. Any shaftway, hatchway, well hole, or other vertical opening or space in which an elevator or dumbwaiter is designed to operate.

Identified (conductors or terminals). Identified, as used in reference to a conductor or its terminal, means that such conductor or terminal can be recognized as grounded.

Identified (for the use). Recognized as suitable for the specific purpose, function, use, environment, application, etc. where described as a requirement in this standard. Suitability of equipment for a specific purpose, environment, or application is determined by a qualified testing laboratory where such identification includes labeling or listing.

Insulated conductor. See "Conductor."

Interrupter switch. (Over 600 volts, nominal.) A switch capable of making, carrying, and interrupting specified currents.

Intrinsically safe equipment and associated wiring. Equipment and associated wiring in which any spark or thermal effect, produced either normally or in specified fault conditions, is incapable, under certain prescribed test conditions, of causing ignition of a mixture of flammable or combustible material in air in its most easily ignitible concentration.

Isolated. Not readily accessible to persons unless special means for access are used.

Isolated power system. A system comprising an isolating transformer or its equivalent, a line isolation monitor, and its ungrounded circuit conductors.

Labeled. Equipment or materials to which has been attached a label, symbol or other identifying mark of a qualified testing laboratory which indicates compliance with appropriate standards or performance in a specified manner.

Lighting outlet. An outlet intended for the direct connection of a lampholder, a lighting fixture, or a pendant cord terminating in a lampholder.

Listed. Equipment or materials included in a list published by a qualified testing laboratory whose listing states either that the equipment or material meets appropriate standards or has been tested and found suitable for use in a specified manner.

Location—(a) Damp location. Partially protected locations under canopies, marquees, roofed open porches, and like locations, and interior locations subject to moderate degrees of moisture, such as some basements.

(b) *Dry location.* A location not normally subject to dampness or wetness. A location classified as dry may be temporarily subject to dampness or wetness, as in the case of a building under construction.

(c) *Wet location.* Installations underground or in concrete slabs or masonry in direct contact with the earth, and locations subject to saturation with water or other liquids, such as locations exposed to weather and unprotected.

Mobile X-ray. X-ray equipment mounted on a permanent base with wheels and/or casters for moving while completely assembled.

Motor control center. An assembly of one or more enclosed sections having a common power bus and principally containing motor control units.

Outlet. A point on the wiring system at which current is taken to supply utilization equipment.

Overcurrent. Any current in excess of the rated current of equipment or the ampacity of a conductor. It may result from overload (see definition), short circuit, or ground fault. A current in excess of rating may be accommodated by certain equipment and conductors for a given set of conditions. Hence the rules for overcurrent protection are specific for particular situations.

Overload. Operation of equipment in excess of normal, full load rating, or of a conductor in excess of rated ampacity which, when it persists for a sufficient length of time, would cause damage or dangerous overheating. A fault, such as a short circuit or ground fault, is not an overload. (See *"Overcurrent."*)

Panelboard. A single panel or group of panel units designed for assembly in the form of a single panel; including buses, automatic overcurrent devices, and with or without switches for the control of light, heat, or power circuits; designed to be placed in a cabinet or cutout box placed in or against a wall or partition and accessible only from the front. (See *"Switchboard."*)

Portable X-ray. X-ray equipment designed to be hand-carried.

Power fuse. (Over 600 volts, nominal.) See *"Fuse."*

Power outlet. An enclosed assembly which may include receptacles, circuit breakers, fuseholders, fused switches, buses and watt-hour meter mounting means; intended to serve as a means for distributing power required to operate mobile or temporarily installed equipment.

Premises wiring system. That interior and exterior wiring, including power, lighting, control, and signal circuit wiring together with all of its associated hardware, fittings, and wiring devices, both permanently and temporarily installed, which extends from the load end of the service drop, or load end of the service lateral conductors to the outlet(s). Such wiring does not include wiring internal to appliances, fixtures, motors, controllers, motor control centers, and similar equipment.

Qualified person. One familiar with the construction and operation of the equipment and the hazards involved.

Qualified testing laboratory. A properly equipped and staffed testing laboratory which has capabilities for and which provides the following services:

(a) Experimental testing for safety of specified items of equipment and materials referred to in this standard to determine compliance with appropriate test standards or performance in a specified manner;

(b) Inspecting the run of such items of equipment and materials at factories for product evaluation to assure compliance with the test standards;

(c) Service-value determinations through field inspections to monitor the proper use of labels on products and with authority for recall of the label in the event a hazardous product is installed;

(d) Employing a controlled procedure for identifying the listed and/or labeled equipment or materials tested; and

(e) Rendering creditable reports or findings that are objective and without bias of the tests and test methods employed.

Raceway. A channel designed expressly for holding wires, cables, or busbars, with additional functions as permitted in this subpart. Raceways may be of metal or insulating material, and the term includes rigid metal conduit, rigid nonmetallic conduit, intermediate metal conduit, liquidtight flexible metal conduit, flexible metallic tubing, flexible metal conduit, electrical metallic tubing, underfloor raceways, cellular concrete floor raceways, cellular metal floor raceways, surface raceways, wireways, and busways.

Readily accessible. Capable of being reached quickly for operation, renewal, or inspections, without requiring those to whom ready access is requisite to climb over or remove obstacles or to resort to portable ladders, chairs, etc. (See *"Accessible."*)

Receptacle. A receptacle is a contact device installed at the outlet for the connection of a single attachment plug. A single receptacle is a single contact device with no other contact device on the same yoke. A multiple receptacle is a single device containing two or more receptacles.

Receptacle outlet. An outlet where one or more receptacles are installed.

Remote-control circuit. Any electric circuit that controls any other circuit through a relay or an equivalent device.

Sealable equipment. Equipment enclosed in a case or cabinet that is provided with a means of sealing or locking so that live parts cannot be made accessible without opening the enclosure. The equipment may or may not be operable without opening the enclosure.

Separately derived system. A premises wiring system whose power is derived from generator, transformer, or converter windings and has no direct electrical connection, including a solidly connected grounded circuit conductor, to supply conductors originating in another system.

Service. The conductors and equipment for delivering energy from the electricity supply system to the wiring system of the premises served.

Service conductors. The supply conductors that extend from the street main or from transformers to the service equipment of the premises supplied.

Service drop. The overhead service conductors from the last pole or other aerial support to and including the splices, if any, connecting to the service-entrance conductors at the building or other structure.

Service-entrance conductors, overhead system. The service conductors between the terminals of the service equipment and a point usually outside the building, clear of building walls, where joined by tap or splice to the service drop.

Service-entrance conductors, underground system. The service conductors between the terminals of the service equipment and the point of connection to the service lateral. Where service equipment is located outside the building walls, there may be no service-entrance conductors, or they may be entirely outside the building.

Service equipment. The necessary equipment, usually consisting of a circuit breaker or switch and fuses, and their accessories, located near the point of entrance of supply conductors to a building or other structure, or an otherwise defined area, and intended to constitute the main control and means of cutoff of the supply.

Service raceway. The raceway that encloses the service-entrance conductors.

Signaling circuit. Any electric circuit that energizes signaling equipment.

Switchboard. A large single panel, frame, or assembly of panels which have switches, buses, instruments, overcurrent and other protective devices mounted on the face or back or both. Switchboards are generally accessible from the rear as well as from the front and are not intended to be installed in cabinets. (See *"Panelboard."*)

Switches—(a) *General-use switch.* A switch intended for use in general distribution and branch circuits. It is rated in amperes, and it is capable of interrupting its rated current at its rated voltage.

(b) *General-use snap switch.* A form of general-use switch so constructed that it can be installed in flush device boxes or on outlet box covers, or otherwise used in conjunction with wiring systems recognized by this subpart.

(c) *Isolating switch.* A switch intended for isolating an electric circuit from the source of power. It has no interrupting rating, and it is intended to be operated only after the circuit has been opened by some other means.

(d) *Motor-circuit switch.* A switch, rated in horsepower, capable of interrupting the maximum operating overload current of a motor of the same horsepower rating as the switch at the rated voltage.

Switching devices. (Over 600 volts, nominal.) Devices designed to close and/or open one or more electric circuits. Included in this category are circuit breakers, cutouts, disconnecting (or isolating) switches, disconnecting means, and interrupter switches.

Transportable X-ray. X-ray equipment installed in a vehicle or that may readily be disassembled for transport in a vehicle.

Utilization equipment. Utilization equipment means equipment which utilizes electric energy for mechanical, chemical, heating, lighting, or similar useful purpose.

Utilization system. A utilization system is a system which provides electric power and light for employee workplaces, and includes the premises wiring system and utilization equipment.

Ventilated. Provided with a means to permit circulation of air sufficient to remove an excess of heat, fumes, or vapors.

Volatile flammable liquid. A flammable liquid having a flash point below 38 degrees C (100 degrees F) or whose temperature is above its flash point, or a Class II combustible liquid having a vapor pressure not exceeding 40 psia (276 kPa) at 38 °C (100 °F) whose temperature is above its flash point.

Voltage. (Of a circuit.) The greatest root-mean-square (effective) difference of potential between any two conductors of the circuit concerned.

Voltage, nominal. A nominal value assigned to a circuit or system for the purpose of conveniently designating its voltage class (as 120/240, 480Y/277, 600, etc.). The actual voltage at which a circuit operates can vary from the nominal within a range that permits satisfactory operation of equipment.

Voltage to ground. For grounded circuits, the voltage between the given conductor and that point or conductor of the circuit that is grounded; for ungrounded circuits, the greatest voltage between the given conductor and any other conductor of the circuit.

Watertight. So constructed that moisture will not enter the enclosure.

Weatherproof. So constructed or protected that exposure to the weather will not interfere with successful operation. Rainproof, raintight, or watertight equipment can fulfill the requirements for weatherproof where varying weather conditions other than wetness, such as snow, ice, dust, or temperature extremes, are not a factor.

Wet location. See "*Location.*"

Subpart L—Scaffolds

AUTHORITY: 40 U.S.C. 333; 29 U.S.C. 653, 655, 657; Secretary of Labor's Order Nos. 1–90 (55 FR 9033), 5–2007 (72 FR 31159), or 1–2012 (77 FR 3912); and 29 CFR part 1911.

SOURCE: 61 FR 46104, Aug. 30, 1996, unless otherwise noted.

§ 1926.450 Scope, application and definitions applicable to this subpart.

(a) *Scope and application.* This subpart applies to all scaffolds used in workplaces covered by this part. It does not apply to crane or derrick suspended personnel platforms. The criteria for aerial lifts are set out exclusively in § 1926.453.

(b) *Definitions. Adjustable suspension scaffold* means a suspension scaffold equipped with a hoist(s) that can be operated by an employee(s) on the scaffold.

Bearer (putlog) means a horizontal transverse scaffold member (which may be supported by ledgers or runners) upon which the scaffold platform rests and which joins scaffold uprights, posts, poles, and similar members.

Boatswains' chair means a single-point adjustable suspension scaffold consisting of a seat or sling designed to support one employee in a sitting position.

Body belt (safety belt) means a strap with means both for securing it about the waist and for attaching it to a lanyard, lifeline, or deceleration device.

Body harness means a design of straps which may be secured about the employee in a manner to distribute the fall arrest forces over at least the thighs, pelvis, waist, chest and shoulders, with means for attaching it to other components of a personal fall arrest system.

Brace means a rigid connection that holds one scaffold member in a fixed position with respect to another member, or to a building or structure.

Bricklayers' square scaffold means a supported scaffold composed of framed squares which support a platform.

Carpenters' bracket scaffold means a supported scaffold consisting of a platform supported by brackets attached to building or structural walls.

Catenary scaffold means a suspension scaffold consisting of a platform supported by two essentially horizontal and parallel ropes attached to structural members of a building or other structure. Additional support may be provided by vertical pickups.

Chimney hoist means a multi-point adjustable suspension scaffold used to provide access to work inside chimneys. (See "Multi-point adjustable suspension scaffold".)

Cleat means a structural block used at the end of a platform to prevent the platform from slipping off its supports. Cleats are also used to provide footing on sloped surfaces such as crawling boards.

Competent person means one who is capable of identifying existing and predictable hazards in the surroundings or working conditions which are unsanitary, hazardous, or dangerous to employees, and who has authorization to take prompt corrective measures to eliminate them.

Continuous run scaffold (Run scaffold) means a two- point or multi-point adjustable suspension scaffold constructed using a series of interconnected braced scaffold members or supporting structures erected to form a continuous scaffold.

Coupler means a device for locking together the tubes of a tube and coupler scaffold.

Crawling board (chicken ladder) means a supported scaffold consisting of a plank with cleats spaced and secured to provide footing, for use on sloped surfaces such as roofs.

Deceleration device means any mechanism, such as a rope grab, rip-stitch lanyard, specially-woven lanyard, tearing or deforming lanyard, or automatic self-retracting lifeline lanyard, which dissipates a substantial amount of energy during a fall arrest or limits the energy imposed on an employee during fall arrest.

Double pole (independent pole) scaffold means a supported scaffold consisting of a platform(s) resting on cross beams (bearers) supported by ledgers and a double row of uprights independent of support (except ties, guys, braces) from any structure.

Equivalent means alternative designs, materials or methods to protect against a hazard which the employer can demonstrate will provide an equal or greater degree of safety for employees than the methods, materials or designs specified in the standard.

Exposed power lines means electrical power lines which are accessible to employees and which are not shielded from contact. Such lines do not include extension cords or power tool cords.

Eye or *Eye splice* means a loop with or without a thimble at the end of a wire rope.

Fabricated decking and planking means manufactured platforms made of wood (including laminated wood, and solid sawn wood planks), metal or other materials.

Fabricated frame scaffold (tubular welded frame scaffold) means a scaffold consisting of a platform(s) supported on fabricated end frames with integral posts, horizontal bearers, and intermediate members.

Failure means load refusal, breakage, or separation of component parts. Load refusal is the point where the ultimate strength is exceeded.

Float (ship) scaffold means a suspension scaffold consisting of a braced platform resting on two parallel bearers and hung from overhead supports by ropes of fixed length.

Form scaffold means a supported scaffold consisting of a platform supported by brackets attached to formwork.

Guardrail system means a vertical barrier, consisting of, but not limited to, toprails, midrails, and posts, erected to prevent employees from falling off a scaffold platform or walkway to lower levels.

Hoist means a manual or power-operated mechanical device to raise or lower a suspended scaffold.

Horse scaffold means a supported scaffold consisting of a platform supported by construction horses (saw horses).

277

Horse scaffolds constructed of metal are sometimes known as trestle scaffolds.

Independent pole scaffold (see "Double pole scaffold").

Interior hung scaffold means a suspension scaffold consisting of a platform suspended from the ceiling or roof structure by fixed length supports.

Ladder jack scaffold means a supported scaffold consisting of a platform resting on brackets attached to ladders.

Ladder stand means a mobile, fixed-size, self-supporting ladder consisting of a wide flat tread ladder in the form of stairs.

Landing means a platform at the end of a flight of stairs.

Large area scaffold means a pole scaffold, tube and coupler scaffold, systems scaffold, or fabricated frame scaffold erected over substantially the entire work area. For example: a scaffold erected over the entire floor area of a room.

Lean-to scaffold means a supported scaffold which is kept erect by tilting it toward and resting it against a building or structure.

Lifeline means a component consisting of a flexible line that connects to an anchorage at one end to hang vertically (vertical lifeline), or that connects to anchorages at both ends to stretch horizontally (horizontal lifeline), and which serves as a means for connecting other components of a personal fall arrest system to the anchorage.

Lower levels means areas below the level where the employee is located and to which an employee can fall. Such areas include, but are not limited to, ground levels, floors, roofs, ramps, runways, excavations, pits, tanks, materials, water, and equipment.

Masons' adjustable supported scaffold (see "Self-contained adjustable scaffold").

Masons' multi-point adjustable suspension scaffold means a continuous run suspension scaffold designed and used for masonry operations.

Maximum intended load means the total load of all persons, equipment, tools, materials, transmitted loads, and other loads reasonably anticipated to be applied to a scaffold or scaffold component at any one time.

Mobile scaffold means a powered or unpowered, portable, caster or wheel-mounted supported scaffold.

Multi-level suspended scaffold means a two-point or multi-point adjustable suspension scaffold with a series of platforms at various levels resting on common stirrups.

Multi-point adjustable suspension scaffold means a suspension scaffold consisting of a platform(s) which is suspended by more than two ropes from overhead supports and equipped with means to raise and lower the platform to desired work levels. Such scaffolds include chimney hoists.

Needle beam scaffold means a platform suspended from needle beams.

Open sides and ends means the edges of a platform that are more than 14 inches (36 cm) away horizontally from a sturdy, continuous, vertical surface (such as a building wall) or a sturdy, continuous horizontal surface (such as a floor), or a point of access. Exception: For plastering and lathing operations the horizontal threshold distance is 18 inches (46 cm).

Outrigger means the structural member of a supported scaffold used to increase the base width of a scaffold in order to provide support for and increased stability of the scaffold.

Outrigger beam (Thrustout) means the structural member of a suspension scaffold or outrigger scaffold which provides support for the scaffold by extending the scaffold point of attachment to a point out and away from the structure or building.

Outrigger scaffold means a supported scaffold consisting of a platform resting on outrigger beams (thrustouts) projecting beyond the wall or face of the building or structure, the inboard ends of which are secured inside the building or structure.

Overhand bricklaying means the process of laying bricks and masonry units such that the surface of the wall to be jointed is on the opposite side of the wall from the mason, requiring the mason to lean over the wall to complete the work. It includes mason tending and electrical installation incorporated into the brick wall during the overhand bricklaying process.

Personal fall arrest system means a system used to arrest an employee's fall. It consists of an anchorage, connectors, a body belt or body harness and may include a lanyard, deceleration device, lifeline, or combinations of these.

Platform means a work surface elevated above lower levels. Platforms can be constructed using individual wood planks, fabricated planks, fabricated decks, and fabricated platforms.

Pole scaffold (see definitions for "Single-pole scaffold" and "Double (independent) pole scaffold").

Power operated hoist means a hoist which is powered by other than human energy.

Pump jack scaffold means a supported scaffold consisting of a platform supported by vertical poles and movable support brackets.

Qualified means one who, by possession of a recognized degree, certificate, or professional standing, or who by extensive knowledge, training, and experience, has successfully demonstrated his/her ability to solve or resolve problems related to the subject matter, the work, or the project.

Rated load means the manufacturer's specified maximum load to be lifted by a hoist or to be applied to a scaffold or scaffold component.

Repair bracket scaffold means a supported scaffold consisting of a platform supported by brackets which are secured in place around the circumference or perimeter of a chimney, stack, tank or other supporting structure by one or more wire ropes placed around the supporting structure.

Roof bracket scaffold means a rooftop supported scaffold consisting of a platform resting on angular-shaped supports.

Runner (ledger or ribbon) means the lengthwise horizontal spacing or bracing member which may support the bearers.

Scaffold means any temporary elevated platform (supported or suspended) and its supporting structure (including points of anchorage), used for supporting employees or materials or both.

Self-contained adjustable scaffold means a combination supported and suspension scaffold consisting of an adjustable platform(s) mounted on an independent supporting frame(s) not a part of the object being worked on, and which is equipped with a means to permit the raising and lowering of the platform(s). Such systems include rolling roof rigs, rolling outrigger systems, and some masons' adjustable supported scaffolds.

Shore scaffold means a supported scaffold which is placed against a building or structure and held in place with props.

Single-point adjustable suspension scaffold means a suspension scaffold consisting of a platform suspended by one rope from an overhead support and equipped with means to permit the movement of the platform to desired work levels.

Single-pole scaffold means a supported scaffold consisting of a platform(s) resting on bearers, the outside ends of which are supported on runners secured to a single row of posts or uprights, and the inner ends of which are supported on or in a structure or building wall.

Stair tower (Scaffold stairway/tower) means a tower comprised of scaffold components and which contains internal stairway units and rest platforms. These towers are used to provide access to scaffold platforms and other elevated points such as floors and roofs.

Stall load means the load at which the prime-mover of a power-operated hoist stalls or the power to the prime-mover is automatically disconnected.

Step, platform, and trestle ladder scaffold means a platform resting directly on the rungs of step ladders or trestle ladders.

Stilts means a pair of poles or similar supports with raised footrests, used to permit walking above the ground or working surface.

Stonesetters' multi-point adjustable suspension scaffold means a continuous run suspension scaffold designed and used for stonesetters' operations.

Supported scaffold means one or more platforms supported by outrigger beams, brackets, poles, legs, uprights, posts, frames, or similar rigid support.

Suspension scaffold means one or more platforms suspended by ropes or other non-rigid means from an overhead structure(s).

System scaffold means a scaffold consisting of posts with fixed connection points that accept runners, bearers, and diagonals that can be interconnected at predetermined levels.

Tank builders' scaffold means a supported scaffold consisting of a platform resting on brackets that are either directly attached to a cylindrical tank or attached to devices that are attached to such a tank.

Top plate bracket scaffold means a scaffold supported by brackets that hook over or are attached to the top of a wall. This type of scaffold is similar to carpenters' bracket scaffolds and form scaffolds and is used in residential construction for setting trusses.

Tube and coupler scaffold means a supported or suspended scaffold consisting of a platform(s) supported by tubing, erected with coupling devices connecting uprights, braces, bearers, and runners.

Tubular welded frame scaffold (see "Fabricated frame scaffold").

Two-point suspension scaffold (swing stage) means a suspension scaffold consisting of a platform supported by hangers (stirrups) suspended by two ropes from overhead supports and equipped with means to permit the raising and lowering of the platform to desired work levels.

Unstable objects means items whose strength, configuration, or lack of stability may allow them to become dislocated and shift and therefore may not properly support the loads imposed on them. Unstable objects do not constitute a safe base support for scaffolds, platforms, or employees. Examples include, but are not limited to, barrels, boxes, loose brick, and concrete blocks.

Vertical pickup means a rope used to support the horizontal rope in catenary scaffolds.

Walkway means a portion of a scaffold platform used only for access and not as a work level.

Window jack scaffold means a platform resting on a bracket or jack which projects through a window opening.

[61 FR 46104, Aug. 30, 1996, as amended at 75 FR 48133, Aug. 9, 2010]

§ 1926.451　General requirements.

This section does not apply to aerial lifts, the criteria for which are set out exclusively in § 1926.453.

(a) *Capacity.* (1) Except as provided in paragraphs (a)(2), (a)(3), (a)(4), (a)(5) and (g) of this section, each scaffold and scaffold component shall be capable of supporting, without failure, its own weight and at least 4 times the maximum intended load applied or transmitted to it.

(2) Direct connections to roofs and floors, and counterweights used to balance adjustable suspension scaffolds, shall be capable of resisting at least 4 times the tipping moment imposed by the scaffold operating at the rated load of the hoist, or 1.5 (minimum) times the tipping moment imposed by the scaffold operating at the stall load of the hoist, whichever is greater.

(3) Each suspension rope, including connecting hardware, used on non-adjustable suspension scaffolds shall be capable of supporting, without failure, at least 6 times the maximum intended load applied or transmitted to that rope.

(4) Each suspension rope, including connecting hardware, used on adjustable suspension scaffolds shall be capable of supporting, without failure, at least 6 times the maximum intended load applied or transmitted to that rope with the scaffold operating at either the rated load of the hoist, or 2 (minimum) times the stall load of the hoist, whichever is greater.

(5) The stall load of any scaffold hoist shall not exceed 3 times its rated load.

(6) Scaffolds shall be designed by a qualified person and shall be constructed and loaded in accordance with that design. Non-mandatory appendix A to this subpart contains examples of criteria that will enable an employer to comply with paragraph (a) of this section.

(b) *Scaffold platform construction.* (1) Each platform on all working levels of scaffolds shall be fully planked or decked between the front uprights and the guardrail supports as follows:

(i) Each platform unit (e.g., scaffold plank, fabricated plank, fabricated deck, or fabricated platform) shall be installed so that the space between adjacent units and the space between the platform and the uprights is no more than 1 inch (2.5 cm) wide, except where the employer can demonstrate that a wider space is necessary (for example, to fit around uprights when side brackets are used to extend the width of the platform).

(ii) Where the employer makes the demonstration provided for in paragraph (b)(1)(i) of this section, the platform shall be planked or decked as fully as possible and the remaining open space between the platform and the uprights shall not exceed 9½ inches (24.1 cm).

Exception to paragraph (b)(1): The requirement in paragraph (b)(1) to provide full planking or decking does not apply to platforms used solely as walkways or solely by employees performing scaffold erection or dismantling. In these situations, only the planking that the employer establishes is necessary to provide safe working conditions is required.

(2) Except as provided in paragraphs (b)(2)(i) and (b)(2)(ii) of this section, each scaffold platform and walkway shall be at least 18 inches (46 cm) wide.

(i) Each ladder jack scaffold, top plate bracket scaffold, roof bracket scaffold, and pump jack scaffold shall be at least 12 inches (30 cm) wide. There is no minimum width requirement for boatswains' chairs.

NOTE TO PARAGRAPH (b)(2)(i): Pursuant to an administrative stay effective November 29, 1996 and published in the FEDERAL REGISTER on November 25, 1996, the requirement in paragraph (b)(2)(i) that roof bracket scaffolds be at least 12 inches wide is stayed until November 25, 1997 or until rulemaking regarding the minimum width of roof bracket scaffolds has been completed, whichever is later.

(ii) Where scaffolds must be used in areas that the employer can demonstrate are so narrow that platforms and walkways cannot be at least 18 inches (46 cm) wide, such platforms and walkways shall be as wide as feasible, and employees on those platforms and walkways shall be protected from fall hazards by the use of guardrails and/or personal fall arrest systems.

(3) Except as provided in paragraphs (b)(3) (i) and (ii) of this section, the front edge of all platforms shall not be more than 14 inches (36 cm) from the face of the work, unless guardrail systems are erected along the front edge and/or personal fall arrest systems are used in accordance with paragraph (g) of this section to protect employees from falling.

(i) The maximum distance from the face for outrigger scaffolds shall be 3 inches (8 cm);

(ii) The maximum distance from the face for plastering and lathing operations shall be 18 inches (46 cm).

(4) Each end of a platform, unless cleated or otherwise restrained by hooks or equivalent means, shall extend over the centerline of its support at least 6 inches (15 cm).

(5)(i) Each end of a platform 10 feet or less in length shall not extend over its support more than 12 inches (30 cm) unless the platform is designed and installed so that the cantilevered portion of the platform is able to support employees and/or materials without tipping, or has guardrails which block employee access to the cantilevered end.

(ii) Each platform greater than 10 feet in length shall not extend over its support more than 18 inches (46 cm), unless it is designed and installed so that the cantilevered portion of the platform is able to support employees without tipping, or has guardrails which block employee access to the cantilevered end.

(6) On scaffolds where scaffold planks are abutted to create a long platform, each abutted end shall rest on a separate support surface. This provision does not preclude the use of common support members, such as "T" sections, to support abutting planks, or hook on platforms designed to rest on common supports.

(7) On scaffolds where platforms are overlapped to create a long platform, the overlap shall occur only over supports, and shall not be less than 12 inches (30 cm) unless the platforms are nailed together or otherwise restrained to prevent movement.

(8) At all points of a scaffold where the platform changes direction, such as turning a corner, any platform that rests on a bearer at an angle other than a right angle shall be laid first, and platforms which rest at right angles over the same bearer shall be laid second, on top of the first platform.

(9) Wood platforms shall not be covered with opaque finishes, except that platform edges may be covered or marked for identification. Platforms may be coated periodically with wood preservatives, fire-retardant finishes, and slip-resistant finishes; however, the coating may not obscure the top or bottom wood surfaces.

(10) Scaffold components manufactured by different manufacturers shall not be intermixed unless the components fit together without force and the scaffold's structural integrity is maintained by the user. Scaffold components manufactured by different manufacturers shall not be modified in order to intermix them unless a competent person determines the resulting scaffold is structurally sound.

(11) Scaffold components made of dissimilar metals shall not be used together unless a competent person has determined that galvanic action will not reduce the strength of any component to a level below that required by paragraph (a)(1) of this section.

(c) *Criteria for supported scaffolds.* (1) Supported scaffolds with a height to base width (including outrigger supports, if used) ratio of more than four to one (4:1) shall be restrained from tipping by guying, tying, bracing, or equivalent means, as follows:

(i) Guys, ties, and braces shall be installed at locations where horizontal members support both inner and outer legs.

(ii) Guys, ties, and braces shall be installed according to the scaffold manufacturer's recommendations or at the closest horizontal member to the 4:1 height and be repeated vertically at locations of horizontal members every 20 feet (6.1 m) or less thereafter for scaffolds 3 feet (0.91 m) wide or less, and every 26 feet (7.9 m) or less thereafter for scaffolds greater than 3 feet (0.91 m) wide. The top guy, tie or brace of completed scaffolds shall be placed no further than the 4:1 height from the top. Such guys, ties and braces shall be installed at each end of the scaffold and at horizontal intervals not to exceed 30 feet (9.1 m) (measured from one end [not both] towards the other).

(iii) Ties, guys, braces, or outriggers shall be used to prevent the tipping of supported scaffolds in all circumstances where an eccentric load, such as a cantilevered work platform, is applied or is transmitted to the scaffold.

(2) Supported scaffold poles, legs, posts, frames, and uprights shall bear on base plates and mud sills or other adequate firm foundation.

(i) Footings shall be level, sound, rigid, and capable of supporting the loaded scaffold without settling or displacement.

(ii) Unstable objects shall not be used to support scaffolds or platform units.

(iii) Unstable objects shall not be used as working platforms.

(iv) Front-end loaders and similar pieces of equipment shall not be used to support scaffold platforms unless they have been specifically designed by the manufacturer for such use.

(v) Fork-lifts shall not be used to support scaffold platforms unless the entire platform is attached to the fork and the fork-lift is not moved horizontally while the platform is occupied.

(3) Supported scaffold poles, legs, posts, frames, and uprights shall be plumb and braced to prevent swaying and displacement.

(d) *Criteria for suspension scaffolds.* (1) All suspension scaffold support devices, such as outrigger beams, cornice hooks, parapet clamps, and similar devices, shall rest on surfaces capable of supporting at least 4 times the load imposed on them by the scaffold operating at the rated load of the hoist (or at least 1.5 times the load imposed on them by the scaffold at the stall capacity of the hoist, whichever is greater).

(2) Suspension scaffold outrigger beams, when used, shall be made of structural metal or equivalent strength material, and shall be restrained to prevent movement.

(3) The inboard ends of suspension scaffold outrigger beams shall be stabilized by bolts or other direct connections to the floor or roof deck, or they shall have their inboard ends stabilized by counterweights, except masons' multi-point adjustable suspension scaffold outrigger beams shall not be stabilized by counterweights.

(i) Before the scaffold is used, direct connections shall be evaluated by a competent person who shall confirm, based on the evaluation, that the supporting surfaces are capable of supporting the loads to be imposed. In addition, masons' multi-point adjustable suspension scaffold connections shall be designed by an engineer experienced in such scaffold design.

(ii) Counterweights shall be made of non-flowable material. Sand, gravel and similar materials that can be easily dislocated shall not be used as counterweights.

(iii) Only those items specifically designed as counterweights shall be used to counterweight scaffold systems. Construction materials such as, but not limited to, masonry units and rolls of roofing felt, shall not be used as counterweights.

(iv) Counterweights shall be secured by mechanical means to the outrigger beams to prevent accidental displacement.

(v) Counterweights shall not be removed from an outrigger beam until the scaffold is disassembled.

(vi) Outrigger beams which are not stabilized by bolts or other direct connections to the floor or roof deck shall be secured by tiebacks.

(vii) Tiebacks shall be equivalent in strength to the suspension ropes.

(viii) Outrigger beams shall be placed perpendicular to its bearing support (usually the face of the building or structure). However, where the employer can demonstrate that it is not possible to place an outrigger beam perpendicular to the face of the building or structure because of obstructions that cannot be moved, the outrigger beam may be placed at some other angle, provided opposing angle tiebacks are used.

(ix) Tiebacks shall be secured to a structurally sound anchorage on the building or structure. Sound anchorages include structural members, but do not include standpipes, vents, other piping systems, or electrical conduit.

(x) Tiebacks shall be installed perpendicular to the face of the building or structure, or opposing angle tiebacks shall be installed. Single tiebacks installed at an angle are prohibited.

(4) Suspension scaffold outrigger beams shall be:

(i) Provided with stop bolts or shackles at both ends;

(ii) Securely fastened together with the flanges turned out when channel iron beams are used in place of I-beams;

(iii) Installed with all bearing supports perpendicular to the beam center line;

(iv) Set and maintained with the web in a vertical position; and

(v) When an outrigger beam is used, the shackle or clevis with which the rope is attached to the outrigger beam shall be placed directly over the center line of the stirrup.

(5) Suspension scaffold support devices such as cornice hooks, roof hooks, roof irons, parapet clamps, or similar devices shall be:

(i) Made of steel, wrought iron, or materials of equivalent strength;

(ii) Supported by bearing blocks; and

(iii) Secured against movement by tiebacks installed at right angles to the face of the building or structure, or opposing angle tiebacks shall be installed and secured to a structurally sound point of anchorage on the building or structure. Sound points of anchorage include structural members, but do not include standpipes, vents, other piping systems, or electrical conduit.

(iv) Tiebacks shall be equivalent in strength to the hoisting rope.

(6) When winding drum hoists are used on a suspension scaffold, they shall contain not less than four wraps of the suspension rope at the lowest point of scaffold travel. When other types of hoists are used, the suspension ropes shall be long enough to allow the scaffold to be lowered to the level below without the rope end passing through the hoist, or the rope end shall be configured or provided with means to prevent the end from passing through the hoist.

(7) The use of repaired wire rope as suspension rope is prohibited.

(8) Wire suspension ropes shall not be joined together except through the use of eye splice thimbles connected with shackles or coverplates and bolts.

(9) The load end of wire suspension ropes shall be equipped with proper size thimbles and secured by eyesplicing or equivalent means.

(10) Ropes shall be inspected for defects by a competent person prior to each workshift and after every occurrence which could affect a rope's integrity. Ropes shall be replaced if any of the following conditions exist:

(i) Any physical damage which impairs the function and strength of the rope.

(ii) Kinks that might impair the tracking or wrapping of rope around the drum(s) or sheave(s).

(iii) Six randomly distributed broken wires in one rope lay or three broken wires in one strand in one rope lay.

(iv) Abrasion, corrosion, scrubbing, flattening or peening causing loss of more than one-third of the original diameter of the outside wires.

(v) Heat damage caused by a torch or any damage caused by contact with electrical wires.

(vi) Evidence that the secondary brake has been activated during an overspeed condition and has engaged the suspension rope.

(11) Swaged attachments or spliced eyes on wire suspension ropes shall not be used unless they are made by the wire rope manufacturer or a qualified person.

(12) When wire rope clips are used on suspension scaffolds:

(i) There shall be a minimum of 3 wire rope clips installed, with the clips a minimum of 6 rope diameters apart;

(ii) Clips shall be installed according to the manufacturer's recommendations;

(iii) Clips shall be retightened to the manufacturer's recommendations after the initial loading;

(iv) Clips shall be inspected and retightened to the manufacturer's recommendations at the start of each workshift thereafter;

(v) U-bolt clips shall not be used at the point of suspension for any scaffold hoist;

(vi) When U-bolt clips are used, the U-bolt shall be placed over the dead end of the rope, and the saddle shall be placed over the live end of the rope.

(13) Suspension scaffold power-operated hoists and manual hoists shall be tested by a qualified testing laboratory.

(14) Gasoline-powered equipment and hoists shall not be used on suspension scaffolds.

(15) Gears and brakes of power-operated hoists used on suspension scaffolds shall be enclosed.

(16) In addition to the normal operating brake, suspension scaffold power-operated hoists and manually operated hoists shall have a braking device or locking pawl which engages automatically when a hoist makes either of the following uncontrolled movements: an instantaneous change in momentum or an accelerated overspeed.

(17) Manually operated hoists shall require a positive crank force to descend.

(18) Two-point and multi-point suspension scaffolds shall be tied or otherwise secured to prevent them from swaying, as determined to be necessary based on an evaluation by a competent person. Window cleaners' anchors shall not be used for this purpose.

(19) Devices whose sole function is to provide emergency escape and rescue shall not be used as working platforms. This provision does not preclude the use of systems which are designed to function both as suspension scaffolds and emergency systems.

(e) *Access.* This paragraph applies to scaffold access for all employees. Access requirements for employees erecting or dismantling supported scaffolds are specifically addressed in paragraph (e)(9) of this section.

(1) When scaffold platforms are more than 2 feet (0.6 m) above or below a point of access, portable ladders, hook-on ladders, attachable ladders, stair towers (scaffold stairways/towers), stairway-type ladders (such as ladder stands), ramps, walkways, integral prefabricated scaffold access, or direct access from another scaffold, structure, personnel hoist, or similar surface shall be used. Crossbraces shall not be used as a means of access.

(2) Portable, hook-on, and attachable ladders (Additional requirements for the proper construction and use of portable ladders are contained in subpart X of this part—Stairways and Ladders):

(i) Portable, hook-on, and attachable ladders shall be positioned so as not to tip the scaffold;

(ii) Hook-on and attachable ladders shall be positioned so that their bottom rung is not more than 24 inches (61 cm) above the scaffold supporting level;

(iii) When hook-on and attachable ladders are used on a supported scaffold more than 35 feet (10.7 m) high, they shall have rest platforms at 35-foot (10.7 m) maximum vertical intervals.

(iv) Hook-on and attachable ladders shall be specifically designed for use with the type of scaffold used;

(v) Hook-on and attachable ladders shall have a minimum rung length of 11½ inches (29 cm); and

(vi) Hook-on and attachable ladders shall have uniformly spaced rungs with a maximum spacing between rungs of 16¾ inches.

(3) Stairway-type ladders shall:

(i) Be positioned such that their bottom step is not more than 24 inches (61 cm) above the scaffold supporting level;

(ii) Be provided with rest platforms at 12 foot (3.7 m) maximum vertical intervals;

(iii) Have a minimum step width of 16 inches (41 cm), except that mobile scaffold stairway-type ladders shall have a minimum step width of 11½ inches (30 cm); and

(iv) Have slip-resistant treads on all steps and landings.

(4) Stairtowers (scaffold stairway/towers) shall be positioned such that their bottom step is not more than 24 inches (61 cm.) above the scaffold supporting level.

(i) A stairrail consisting of a toprail and a midrail shall be provided on each side of each scaffold stairway.

(ii) The toprail of each stairrail system shall also be capable of serving as a handrail, unless a separate handrail is provided.

(iii) Handrails, and toprails that serve as handrails, shall provide an adequate handhold for employees grasping them to avoid falling.

(iv) Stairrail systems and handrails shall be surfaced to prevent injury to employees from punctures or lacerations, and to prevent snagging of clothing.

(v) The ends of stairrail systems and handrails shall be constructed so that they do not constitute a projection hazard.

(vi) Handrails, and toprails that are used as handrails, shall be at least 3 inches (7.6 cm) from other objects.

(vii) Stairrails shall be not less than 28 inches (71 cm) nor more than 37 inches (94 cm) from the upper surface of the stairrail to the surface of the tread, in line with the face of the riser at the forward edge of the tread.

(viii) A landing platform at least 18 inches (45.7 cm) wide by at least 18 inches (45.7 cm) long shall be provided at each level.

(ix) Each scaffold stairway shall be at least 18 inches (45.7 cm) wide between stairrails.

(x) Treads and landings shall have slip-resistant surfaces.

(xi) Stairways shall be installed between 40 degrees and 60 degrees from the horizontal.

(xii) Guardrails meeting the requirements of paragraph (g)(4) of this section shall be provided on the open sides and ends of each landing.

(xiii) Riser height shall be uniform, within ¼ inch, (0.6 cm) for each flight of stairs. Greater variations in riser height are allowed for the top and bottom steps of the entire system, not for each flight of stairs.

(xiv) Tread depth shall be uniform, within ¼ inch, for each flight of stairs.

(5) Ramps and walkways. (i) Ramps and walkways 6 feet (1.8 m) or more above lower levels shall have guardrail systems which comply with subpart M of this part—Fall Protection;

(ii) No ramp or walkway shall be inclined more than a slope of one (1) vertical to three (3) horizontal (20 degrees above the horizontal).

(iii) If the slope of a ramp or a walkway is steeper than one (1) vertical in eight (8) horizontal, the ramp or walkway shall have cleats not more than fourteen (14) inches (35 cm) apart which are securely fastened to the planks to provide footing.

(6) Integral prefabricated scaffold access frames shall:

(i) Be specifically designed and constructed for use as ladder rungs;

(ii) Have a rung length of at least 8 inches (20 cm);

(iii) Not be used as work platforms when rungs are less than 11½ inches in length, unless each affected employee uses fall protection, or a positioning device, which complies with § 1926.502;

(iv) Be uniformly spaced within each frame section;

(v) Be provided with rest platforms at 35-foot (10.7 m) maximum vertical intervals on all supported scaffolds more than 35 feet (10.7 m) high; and

(vi) Have a maximum spacing between rungs of 16¾ inches (43 cm). Nonuniform rung spacing caused by joining end frames together is allowed, provided the resulting spacing does not exceed 16¾ inches (43 cm).

(7) Steps and rungs of ladder and stairway type access shall line up vertically with each other between rest platforms.

(8) Direct access to or from another surface shall be used only when the scaffold is not more than 14 inches (36 cm) horizontally and not more than 24 inches (61 cm) vertically from the other surface.

(9) Effective September 2, 1997, access for employees erecting or dismantling supported scaffolds shall be in accordance with the following:

(i) The employer shall provide safe means of access for each employee erecting or dismantling a scaffold where the provision of safe access is feasible and does not create a greater hazard. The employer shall have a competent person determine whether it is feasible or would pose a greater hazard to provide, and have employees use a safe means of access. This determination shall be based on site conditions and the type of scaffold being erected or dismantled.

(ii) Hook-on or attachable ladders shall be installed as soon as scaffold erection has progressed to a point that permits safe installation and use.

(iii) When erecting or dismantling tubular welded frame scaffolds, (end) frames, with horizontal members that are parallel, level and are not more than 22 inches apart vertically may be used as climbing devices for access, provided they are erected in a manner that creates a usable ladder and provides good hand hold and foot space.

(iv) Cross braces on tubular welded frame scaffolds shall not be used as a means of access or egress.

(f) *Use.* (1) Scaffolds and scaffold components shall not be loaded in excess of their maximum intended loads or rated capacities, whichever is less.

(2) The use of shore or lean-to scaffolds is prohibited.

(3) Scaffolds and scaffold components shall be inspected for visible defects by a competent person before each work shift, and after any occurrence which could affect a scaffold's structural integrity.

(4) Any part of a scaffold damaged or weakened such that its strength is less than that required by paragraph (a) of this section shall be immediately repaired or replaced, braced to meet those provisions, or removed from service until repaired.

(5) Scaffolds shall not be moved horizontally while employees are on them, unless they have been designed by a registered professional engineer specifically for such movement or, for mobile scaffolds, where the provisions of § 1926.452(w) are followed.

(6) The clearance between scaffolds and power lines shall be as follows: Scaffolds shall not be erected, used, dismantled, altered, or moved such that they or any conductive material handled on them might come closer to exposed and energized power lines than as follows:

Insulated lines voltage	Minimum distance	Alternatives
Less than 300 volts	3 feet (0.9 m).	
300 volts to 50 kv	10 feet (3.1m).	
More than 50 kv	10 feet (3.1 m) plus 0.4 inches (1.0 cm) for each 1 kv over 50 kv.	2 times the length of the line insulator, but never less than 10 feet (3.1 m).

Uninsulated lines voltage	Minimum distance	Alternatives
Less than 50 kv	10 feet (3.1 m).	
More than 50 kv	10 feet (3.1 m) plus 0.4 inches (1.0 cm) for each 1 kv over 50 kv.	2 times the length of the line insulator, but never less than 10 feet (3.1 m).

EXCEPTION TO PARAGRAPH (f)(6): Scaffolds and materials may be closer to power lines than specified above where such clearance is necessary for performance of work, and only after the utility company, or electrical system operator, has been notified of the need to work closer and the utility company, or electrical system operator, has deenergized the lines, relocated the lines, or installed protective coverings to prevent accidental contact with the lines.

(7) Scaffolds shall be erected, moved, dismantled, or altered only under the supervision and direction of a competent person qualified in scaffold erection, moving, dismantling or alteration. Such activities shall be performed only by experienced and trained employees selected for such work by the competent person.

(8) Employees shall be prohibited from working on scaffolds covered with snow, ice, or other slippery material except as necessary for removal of such materials.

(9) Where swinging loads are being hoisted onto or near scaffolds such that the loads might contact the scaffold, tag lines or equivalent measures to control the loads shall be used.

(10) Suspension ropes supporting adjustable suspension scaffolds shall be of a diameter large enough to provide sufficient surface area for the functioning of brake and hoist mechanisms.

(11) Suspension ropes shall be shielded from heat-producing processes. When acids or other corrosive substances are used on a scaffold, the ropes shall be shielded, treated to protect against the corrosive substances, or shall be of a material that will not be damaged by the substance being used.

(12) Work on or from scaffolds is prohibited during storms or high winds unless a competent person has determined that it is safe for employees to be on the scaffold and those employees are protected by a personal fall arrest system or wind screens. Wind screens shall not be used unless the scaffold is secured against the anticipated wind forces imposed.

(13) Debris shall not be allowed to accumulate on platforms.

(14) Makeshift devices, such as but not limited to boxes and barrels, shall not be used on top of scaffold platforms to increase the working level height of employees.

(15) Ladders shall not be used on scaffolds to increase the working level height of employees, except on large area scaffolds where employers have satisfied the following criteria:

(i) When the ladder is placed against a structure which is not a part of the scaffold, the scaffold shall be secured against the sideways thrust exerted by the ladder;

(ii) The platform units shall be secured to the scaffold to prevent their movement;

(iii) The ladder legs shall be on the same platform or other means shall be provided to stabilize the ladder against unequal platform deflection, and

(iv) The ladder legs shall be secured to prevent them from slipping or being pushed off the platform.

(16) Platforms shall not deflect more than 1/60 of the span when loaded.

(17) To reduce the possibility of welding current arcing through the suspension wire rope when performing welding from suspended scaffolds, the following precautions shall be taken, as applicable:

(i) An insulated thimble shall be used to attach each suspension wire rope to its hanging support (such as cornice hook or outrigger). Excess suspension wire rope and any additional independent lines from grounding shall be insulated;

(ii) The suspension wire rope shall be covered with insulating material extending at least 4 feet (1.2 m) above the hoist. If there is a tail line below the hoist, it shall be insulated to prevent contact with the platform. The portion of the tail line that hangs free below the scaffold shall be guided or retained, or both, so that it does not become grounded;

(iii) Each hoist shall be covered with insulated protective covers;

(iv) In addition to a work lead attachment required by the welding process, a grounding conductor shall be connected from the scaffold to the structure. The size of this conductor shall be at least the size of the welding process work lead, and this conductor shall not be in series with the welding process or the work piece;

(v) If the scaffold grounding lead is disconnected at any time, the welding machine shall be shut off; and

(vi) An active welding rod or uninsulated welding lead shall not be allowed to contact the scaffold or its suspension system.

(g) *Fall protection.* (1) Each employee on a scaffold more than 10 feet (3.1 m) above a lower level shall be protected from falling to that lower level. Paragraphs (g)(1) (i) through (vii) of this section establish the types of fall protection to be provided to the employees on each type of scaffold. Paragraph (g)(2) of this section addresses fall protection for scaffold erectors and dismantlers.

NOTE TO PARAGRAPH (g)(1): The fall protection requirements for employees installing suspension scaffold support systems on floors, roofs, and other elevated surfaces are set forth in subpart M of this part.

(i) Each employee on a boatswains' chair, catenary scaffold, float scaffold, needle beam scaffold, or ladder jack scaffold shall be protected by a personal fall arrest system;

(ii) Each employee on a single-point or two-point adjustable suspension scaffold shall be protected by both a personal fall arrest system and guardrail system;

(iii) Each employee on a crawling board (chicken ladder) shall be protected by a personal fall arrest system, a guardrail system (with minimum 200 pound toprail capacity), or by a three-fourth inch (1.9 cm) diameter grabline or equivalent handhold securely fastened beside each crawling board;

(iv) Each employee on a self-contained adjustable scaffold shall be protected by a guardrail system (with minimum 200 pound toprail capacity) when the platform is supported by the frame structure, and by both a personal fall arrest system and a guardrail system (with minimum 200 pound toprail capacity) when the platform is supported by ropes;

(v) Each employee on a walkway located within a scaffold shall be protected by a guardrail system (with minimum 200 pound toprail capacity) installed within 9½ inches (24.1 cm) of and along at least one side of the walkway.

(vi) Each employee performing overhand bricklaying operations from a supported scaffold shall be protected from falling from all open sides and ends of the scaffold (except at the side next to the wall being laid) by the use of a personal fall arrest system or guardrail system (with minimum 200 pound toprail capacity).

(vii) For all scaffolds not otherwise specified in paragraphs (g)(1)(i) through (g)(1)(vi) of this section, each employee shall be protected by the use of personal fall arrest systems or guardrail systems meeting the requirements of paragraph (g)(4) of this section.

(2) Effective September 2, 1997, the employer shall have a competent person determine the feasibility and safety of providing fall protection for employees erecting or dismantling supported scaffolds. Employers are required to provide fall protection for employees erecting or dismantling supported scaffolds where the installation and use of such protection is feasible and does not create a greater hazard.

(3) In addition to meeting the requirements of § 1926.502(d), personal fall arrest systems used on scaffolds shall be attached by lanyard to a vertical lifeline, horizontal lifeline, or scaffold structural member. Vertical lifelines shall not be used when overhead components, such as overhead protection or additional platform levels, are part of a single-point or two-point adjustable suspension scaffold.

(i) When vertical lifelines are used, they shall be fastened to a fixed safe point of anchorage, shall be independent of the scaffold, and shall be protected from sharp edges and abrasion. Safe points of anchorage include structural members of buildings, but do not include standpipes, vents, other piping systems, electrical conduit, outrigger beams, or counterweights.

(ii) When horizontal lifelines are used, they shall be secured to two or more structural members of the scaffold, or they may be looped around both suspension and independent suspension lines (on scaffolds so equipped) above the hoist and brake attached to the end of the scaffold. Horizontal lifelines shall not be attached only to the suspension ropes.

(iii) When lanyards are connected to horizontal lifelines or structural members on a single-point or two-point adjustable suspension scaffold, the scaffold shall be equipped with additional independent support lines and automatic locking devices capable of stopping the fall of the scaffold in the event one or both of the suspension ropes fail. The independent support lines shall be equal in number and strength to the suspension ropes.

(iv) Vertical lifelines, independent support lines, and suspension ropes shall not be attached to each other, nor shall they be attached to or use the same point of anchorage, nor shall they be attached to the same point on the scaffold or personal fall arrest system.

(4) Guardrail systems installed to meet the requirements of this section shall comply with the following provisions (guardrail systems built in accordance with appendix A to this subpart will be deemed to meet the requirements of paragraphs (g)(4) (vii), (viii), and (ix) of this section):

(i) Guardrail systems shall be installed along all open sides and ends of platforms. Guardrail systems shall be installed before the scaffold is released for use by employees other than erection/dismantling crews.

(ii) The top edge height of toprails or equivalent member on supported scaffolds manufactured or placed in service after January 1, 2000 shall be installed between 38 inches (0.97 m) and 45 inches (1.2 m) above the platform surface. The top edge height on supported scaffolds manufactured and placed in service before January 1, 2000, and on all suspended scaffolds where both a guardrail and a personal fall arrest system are required shall be between 36 inches (0.9 m) and 45 inches (1.2 m). When conditions warrant, the height of the top edge may exceed the 45-inch height, provided the guardrail system meets all other criteria of paragraph (g)(4).

(iii) When midrails, screens, mesh, intermediate vertical members, solid panels, or equivalent structural members are used, they shall be installed between the top edge of the guardrail system and the scaffold platform.

(iv) When midrails are used, they shall be installed at a height approximately midway between the top edge of the guardrail system and the platform surface.

(v) When screens and mesh are used, they shall extend from the top edge of the guardrail system to the scaffold platform, and along the entire opening between the supports.

(vi) When intermediate members (such as balusters or additional rails) are used, they shall not be more than 19 inches (48 cm) apart.

(vii) Each toprail or equivalent member of a guardrail system shall be capable of withstanding, without failure, a force applied in any downward or horizontal direction at any point along its top edge of at least 100 pounds (445 n) for guardrail systems installed on single-point adjustable suspension scaffolds or two-point adjustable suspension scaffolds, and at least 200 pounds (890 n) for guardrail systems installed on all other scaffolds.

(viii) When the loads specified in paragraph (g)(4)(vii) of this section are applied in a downward direction, the top edge shall not drop below the height above the platform surface that is prescribed in paragraph (g)(4)(ii) of this section.

(ix) Midrails, screens, mesh, intermediate vertical members, solid panels, and equivalent structural members of a guardrail system shall be capable of withstanding, without failure, a force applied in any downward or horizontal direction at any point along the midrail or other member of at least 75 pounds (333 n) for guardrail systems with a minimum 100 pound toprail capacity, and at least 150 pounds (666 n) for guardrail systems with a minimum 200 pound toprail capacity.

(x) Suspension scaffold hoists and non-walk-through stirrups may be used as end guardrails, if the space between the hoist or stirrup and the side guardrail or structure does not allow passage of an employee to the end of the scaffold.

(xi) Guardrails shall be surfaced to prevent injury to an employee from punctures or lacerations, and to prevent snagging of clothing.

(xii) The ends of all rails shall not overhang the terminal posts except when such overhang does not constitute a projection hazard to employees.

289

(xiii) Steel or plastic banding shall not be used as a toprail or midrail.

(xiv) Manila or plastic (or other synthetic) rope being used for toprails or midrails shall be inspected by a competent person as frequently as necessary to ensure that it continues to meet the strength requirements of paragraph (g) of this section.

(xv) Crossbracing is acceptable in place of a midrail when the crossing point of two braces is between 20 inches (0.5 m) and 30 inches (0.8 m) above the work platform or as a toprail when the crossing point of two braces is between 38 inches (0.97 m) and 48 inches (1.3 m) above the work platform. The end points at each upright shall be no more than 48 inches (1.3 m) apart.

(h) *Falling object protection.* (1) In addition to wearing hardhats each employee on a scaffold shall be provided with additional protection from falling hand tools, debris, and other small objects through the installation of toeboards, screens, or guardrail systems, or through the erection of debris nets, catch platforms, or canopy structures that contain or deflect the falling objects. When the falling objects are too large, heavy or massive to be contained or deflected by any of the above-listed measures, the employer shall place such potential falling objects away from the edge of the surface from which they could fall and shall secure those materials as necessary to prevent their falling.

(2) Where there is a danger of tools, materials, or equipment falling from a scaffold and striking employees below, the following provisions apply:

(i) The area below the scaffold to which objects can fall shall be barricaded, and employees shall not be permitted to enter the hazard area; or

(ii) A toeboard shall be erected along the edge of platforms more than 10 feet (3.1 m) above lower levels for a distance sufficient to protect employees below, except on float (ship) scaffolds where an edging of ¾ × 1½ inch (2 × 4 cm) wood or equivalent may be used in lieu of toeboards;

(iii) Where tools, materials, or equipment are piled to a height higher than the top edge of the toeboard, paneling or screening extending from the toeboard or platform to the top of the guardrail shall be erected for a distance sufficient to protect employees below; or

(iv) A guardrail system shall be installed with openings small enough to prevent passage of potential falling objects; or

(v) A canopy structure, debris net, or catch platform strong enough to withstand the impact forces of the potential falling objects shall be erected over the employees below.

(3) Canopies, when used for falling object protection, shall comply with the following criteria:

(i) Canopies shall be installed between the falling object hazard and the employees.

(ii) When canopies are used on suspension scaffolds for falling object protection, the scaffold shall be equipped with additional independent support lines equal in number to the number of points supported, and equivalent in strength to the strength of the suspension ropes.

(iii) Independent support lines and suspension ropes shall not be attached to the same points of anchorage.

(4) Where used, toeboards shall be:

(i) Capable of withstanding, without failure, a force of at least 50 pounds (222 n) applied in any downward or horizontal direction at any point along the toeboard (toeboards built in accordance with appendix A to this subpart will be deemed to meet this requirement); and

(ii) At least three and one-half inches (9 cm) high from the top edge of the toeboard to the level of the walking/working surface. Toeboards shall be securely fastened in place at the outermost edge of the platform and have not more than ¼ inch (0.7 cm) clearance above the walking/working surface. Toeboards shall be solid or with openings not over one inch (2.5 cm) in the greatest dimension.

[61 FR 46107, Aug. 30, 1996, as corrected and amended at 61 FR 59831, 59832, Nov. 25, 1996]

EFFECTIVE DATE NOTE: At 61 FR 59832, Nov. 25, 1996, § 1926.451(b)(2)(i) was amended and certain requirements stayed until Nov. 25, 1997, or until further rulemaking has been completed, whichever is later.

§ 1926.452 Additional requirements applicable to specific types of scaffolds.

In addition to the applicable requirements of § 1926.451, the following requirements apply to the specific types of scaffolds indicated. Scaffolds not specifically addressed by § 1926.452, such as but not limited to systems scaffolds, must meet the requirements of § 1926.451.

(a) *Pole scaffolds.* (1) When platforms are being moved to the next level, the existing platform shall be left undisturbed until the new bearers have been set in place and braced, prior to receiving the new platforms.

(2) Crossbracing shall be installed between the inner and outer sets of poles on double pole scaffolds.

(3) Diagonal bracing in both directions shall be installed across the entire inside face of double-pole scaffolds used to support loads equivalent to a uniformly distributed load of 50 pounds (222 kg) or more per square foot (929 square cm).

(4) Diagonal bracing in both directions shall be installed across the entire outside face of all double- and single-pole scaffolds.

(5) Runners and bearers shall be installed on edge.

(6) Bearers shall extend a minimum of 3 inches (7.6 cm) over the outside edges of runners.

(7) Runners shall extend over a minimum of two poles, and shall be supported by bearing blocks securely attached to the poles.

(8) Braces, bearers, and runners shall not be spliced between poles.

(9) Where wooden poles are spliced, the ends shall be squared and the upper section shall rest squarely on the lower section. Wood splice plates shall be provided on at least two adjacent sides, and shall extend at least 2 feet (0.6 m) on either side of the splice, overlap the abutted ends equally, and have at least the same cross-sectional areas as the pole. Splice plates of other materials of equivalent strength may be used.

(10) Pole scaffolds over 60 feet in height shall be designed by a registered professional engineer, and shall be constructed and loaded in accordance with that design. Non-mandatory appendix A to this subpart contains examples of criteria that will enable an employer to comply with design and loading requirements for pole scaffolds under 60 feet in height.

(b) *Tube and coupler scaffolds.* (1) When platforms are being moved to the next level, the existing platform shall be left undisturbed until the new bearers have been set in place and braced prior to receiving the new platforms.

(2) Transverse bracing forming an "X" across the width of the scaffold shall be installed at the scaffold ends and at least at every third set of posts horizontally (measured from only one end) and every fourth runner vertically. Bracing shall extend diagonally from the inner or outer posts or runners upward to the next outer or inner posts or runners. Building ties shall be installed at the bearer levels between the transverse bracing and shall conform to the requirements of § 1926.451(c)(1).

(3) On straight run scaffolds, longitudinal bracing across the inner and outer rows of posts shall be installed diagonally in both directions, and shall extend from the base of the end posts upward to the top of the scaffold at approximately a 45 degree angle. On scaffolds whose length is greater than their height, such bracing shall be repeated beginning at least at every fifth post. On scaffolds whose length is less than their height, such bracing shall be installed from the base of the end posts upward to the opposite end posts, and then in alternating directions until reaching the top of the scaffold. Bracing shall be installed as close as possible to the intersection of the bearer and post or runner and post.

(4) Where conditions preclude the attachment of bracing to posts, bracing shall be attached to the runners as close to the post as possible.

(5) Bearers shall be installed transversely between posts, and when coupled to the posts, shall have the inboard coupler bear directly on the runner coupler. When the bearers are coupled to the runners, the couplers shall be as close to the posts as possible.

(6) Bearers shall extend beyond the posts and runners, and shall provide full contact with the coupler.

(7) Runners shall be installed along the length of the scaffold, located on

both the inside and outside posts at level heights (when tube and coupler guardrails and midrails are used on outside posts, they may be used in lieu of outside runners).

(8) Runners shall be interlocked on straight runs to form continuous lengths, and shall be coupled to each post. The bottom runners and bearers shall be located as close to the base as possible.

(9) Couplers shall be of a structural metal, such as drop-forged steel, malleable iron, or structural grade aluminum. The use of gray cast iron is prohibited.

(10) Tube and coupler scaffolds over 125 feet in height shall be designed by a registered professional engineer, and shall be constructed and loaded in accordance with such design. Non-mandatory appendix A to this subpart contains examples of criteria that will enable an employer to comply with design and loading requirements for tube and coupler scaffolds under 125 feet in height.

(c) *Fabricated frame scaffolds* (tubular welded frame scaffolds). (1) When moving platforms to the next level, the existing platform shall be left undisturbed until the new end frames have been set in place and braced prior to receiving the new platforms.

(2) Frames and panels shall be braced by cross, horizontal, or diagonal braces, or combination thereof, which secure vertical members together laterally. The cross braces shall be of such length as will automatically square and align vertical members so that the erected scaffold is always plumb, level, and square. All brace connections shall be secured.

(3) Frames and panels shall be joined together vertically by coupling or stacking pins or equivalent means.

(4) Where uplift can occur which would displace scaffold end frames or panels, the frames or panels shall be locked together vertically by pins or equivalent means.

(5) Brackets used to support cantilevered loads shall:

(i) Be seated with side-brackets parallel to the frames and end-brackets at 90 degrees to the frames;

(ii) Not be bent or twisted from these positions; and

(iii) Be used only to support personnel, unless the scaffold has been designed for other loads by a qualified engineer and built to withstand the tipping forces caused by those other loads being placed on the bracket-supported section of the scaffold.

(6) Scaffolds over 125 feet (38.0 m) in height above their base plates shall be designed by a registered professional engineer, and shall be constructed and loaded in accordance with such design.

(d) *Plasterers', decorators', and large area scaffolds.* Scaffolds shall be constructed in accordance with paragraphs (a), (b), or (c) of this section, as appropriate.

(e) *Bricklayers' square scaffolds (squares).* (1) Scaffolds made of wood shall be reinforced with gussets on both sides of each corner.

(2) Diagonal braces shall be installed on all sides of each square.

(3) Diagonal braces shall be installed between squares on the rear and front sides of the scaffold, and shall extend from the bottom of each square to the top of the next square.

(4) Scaffolds shall not exceed three tiers in height, and shall be so constructed and arranged that one square rests directly above the other. The upper tiers shall stand on a continuous row of planks laid across the next lower tier, and shall be nailed down or otherwise secured to prevent displacement.

(f) *Horse scaffolds.* (1) Scaffolds shall not be constructed or arranged more than two tiers or 10 feet (3.0 m) in height, whichever is less.

(2) When horses are arranged in tiers, each horse shall be placed directly over the horse in the tier below.

(3) When horses are arranged in tiers, the legs of each horse shall be nailed down or otherwise secured to prevent displacement.

(4) When horses are arranged in tiers, each tier shall be crossbraced.

(g) *Form scaffolds and carpenters' bracket scaffolds.* (1) Each bracket, except those for wooden bracket-form scaffolds, shall be attached to the supporting formwork or structure by means of one or more of the following: nails; a metal stud attachment device; welding; hooking over a secured structural supporting member, with the form wales either bolted to the form or secured by snap ties or tie bolts extending through the form and securely anchored; or, for carpenters' bracket scaffolds only, by a bolt extending through to the opposite side of the structure's wall.

(2) Wooden bracket-form scaffolds shall be an integral part of the form panel.

(3) Folding type metal brackets, when extended for use, shall be either bolted or secured with a locking-type pin.

(h) *Roof bracket scaffolds.* (1) Scaffold brackets shall be constructed to fit the pitch of the roof and shall provide a level support for the platform.

(2) Brackets (including those provided with pointed metal projections) shall be anchored in place by nails unless it is impractical to use nails. When nails are not used, brackets shall be secured in place with first-grade manila rope of at least three-fourth inch (1.9 cm) diameter, or equivalent.

(i) *Outrigger scaffolds.* (1) The inboard end of outrigger beams, measured from the fulcrum point to the extreme point of anchorage, shall be not less than one and one-half times the outboard end in length.

(2) Outrigger beams fabricated in the shape of an I-beam or channel shall be placed so that the web section is vertical.

(3) The fulcrum point of outrigger beams shall rest on secure bearings at least 6 inches (15.2 cm) in each horizontal dimension.

(4) Outrigger beams shall be secured in place against movement, and shall be securely braced at the fulcrum point against tipping.

(5) The inboard ends of outrigger beams shall be securely anchored either by means of braced struts bearing against sills in contact with the overhead beams or ceiling, or by means of tension members secured to the floor joists underfoot, or by both.

(6) The entire supporting structure shall be securely braced to prevent any horizontal movement.

(7) To prevent their displacement, platform units shall be nailed, bolted, or otherwise secured to outriggers.

(8) Scaffolds and scaffold components shall be designed by a registered professional engineer and shall be constructed and loaded in accordance with such design.

(j) *Pump jack scaffolds.* (1) Pump jack brackets, braces, and accessories shall be fabricated from metal plates and angles. Each pump jack bracket shall have two positive gripping mechanisms to prevent any failure or slippage.

(2) Poles shall be secured to the structure by rigid triangular bracing or equivalent at the bottom, top, and other points as necessary. When the pump jack has to pass bracing already installed, an additional brace shall be installed approximately 4 feet (1.2 m) above the brace to be passed, and shall be left in place until the pump jack has been moved and the original brace reinstalled.

(3) When guardrails are used for fall protection, a workbench may be used as the toprail only if it meets all the requirements in paragraphs (g)(4) (ii), (vii), (viii), and (xiii) of §1926.451.

(4) Work benches shall not be used as scaffold platforms.

(5) When poles are made of wood, the pole lumber shall be straight-grained, free of shakes, large loose or dead knots, and other defects which might impair strength.

(6) When wood poles are constructed of two continuous lengths, they shall be joined together with the seam parallel to the bracket.

(7) When two by fours are spliced to make a pole, mending plates shall be installed at all splices to develop the full strength of the member.

(k) *Ladder jack scaffolds.* (1) Platforms shall not exceed a height of 20 feet (6.1 m).

(2) All ladders used to support ladder jack scaffolds shall meet the requirements of subpart X of this part—Stairways and Ladders, except that job-made ladders shall not be used to support ladder jack scaffolds.

(3) The ladder jack shall be so designed and constructed that it will bear on the side rails and ladder rungs or on the ladder rungs alone. If bearing on rungs only, the bearing area shall include a length of at least 10 inches (25.4 cm) on each rung.

(4) Ladders used to support ladder jacks shall be placed, fastened, or

equipped with devices to prevent slipping.

(5) Scaffold platforms shall not be bridged one to another.

(l) *Window jack scaffolds.* (1) Scaffolds shall be securely attached to the window opening.

(2) Scaffolds shall be used only for the purpose of working at the window opening through which the jack is placed.

(3) Window jacks shall not be used to support planks placed between one window jack and another, or for other elements of scaffolding.

(m) *Crawling boards (chicken ladders).* (1) Crawling boards shall extend from the roof peak to the eaves when used in connection with roof construction, repair, or maintenance.

(2) Crawling boards shall be secured to the roof by ridge hooks or by means that meet equivalent criteria (e.g., strength and durability).

(n) *Step, platform, and trestle ladder scaffolds.* (1) Scaffold platforms shall not be placed any higher than the second highest rung or step of the ladder supporting the platform.

(2) All ladders used in conjunction with step, platform and trestle ladder scaffolds shall meet the pertinent requirements of subpart X of this part—Stairways and Ladders, except that job-made ladders shall not be used to support such scaffolds.

(3) Ladders used to support step, platform, and trestle ladder scaffolds shall be placed, fastened, or equipped with devices to prevent slipping.

(4) Scaffolds shall not be bridged one to another.

(o) *Single-point adjustable suspension scaffolds.* (1) When two single-point adjustable suspension scaffolds are combined to form a two-point adjustable suspension scaffold, the resulting two-point scaffold shall comply with the requirements for two-point adjustable suspension scaffolds in paragraph (p) of this section.

(2) The supporting rope between the scaffold and the suspension device shall be kept vertical unless all of the following conditions are met:

(i) The rigging has been designed by a qualified person, and

(ii) The scaffold is accessible to rescuers, and

(iii) The supporting rope is protected to ensure that it will not chafe at any point where a change in direction occurs, and

(iv) The scaffold is positioned so that swinging cannot bring the scaffold into contact with another surface.

(3) Boatswains' chair tackle shall consist of correct size ball bearings or bushed blocks containing safety hooks and properly "eye-spliced" minimum five-eighth (⅝) inch (1.6 cm) diameter first-grade manila rope, or other rope which will satisfy the criteria (e.g., strength and durability) of manila rope.

(4) Boatswains' chair seat slings shall be reeved through four corner holes in the seat; shall cross each other on the underside of the seat; and shall be rigged so as to prevent slippage which could cause an out-of-level condition.

(5) Boatswains' chair seat slings shall be a minimum of five-eight (⅝) inch (1.6 cm) diameter fiber, synthetic, or other rope which will satisfy the criteria (e.g., strength, slip resistance, durability, etc.) of first grade manila rope.

(6) When a heat-producing process such as gas or arc welding is being conducted, boatswains' chair seat slings shall be a minimum of three-eight (⅜) inch (1.0 cm) wire rope.

(7) Non-cross-laminated wood boatswains' chairs shall be reinforced on their underside by cleats securely fastened to prevent the board from splitting.

(p) *Two-point adjustable suspension scaffolds (swing stages).* The following requirements do not apply to two-point adjustable suspension scaffolds used as masons' or stonesetters' scaffolds. Such scaffolds are covered by paragraph (q) of this section.

(1) Platforms shall not be more than 36 inches (0.9 m) wide unless designed by a qualified person to prevent unstable conditions.

(2) The platform shall be securely fastened to hangers (stirrups) by U-bolts or by other means which satisfy the requirements of § 1926.451(a).

(3) The blocks for fiber or synthetic ropes shall consist of at least one double and one single block. The sheaves of all blocks shall fit the size of the rope used.

(4) Platforms shall be of the ladder-type, plank-type, beam-type, or light-metal type. Light metal-type platforms having a rated capacity of 750 pounds or less and platforms 40 feet (12.2 m) or less in length shall be tested and listed by a nationally recognized testing laboratory.

(5) Two-point scaffolds shall not be bridged or otherwise connected one to another during raising and lowering operations unless the bridge connections are articulated (attached), and the hoists properly sized.

(6) Passage may be made from one platform to another only when the platforms are at the same height, are abutting, and walk-through stirrups specifically designed for this purpose are used.

(q) *Multi-point adjustable suspension scaffolds, stonesetters' multi-point adjustable suspension scaffolds, and masons' multi-point adjustable suspension scaffolds.* (1) When two or more scaffolds are used they shall not be bridged one to another unless they are designed to be bridged, the bridge connections are articulated, and the hoists are properly sized.

(2) If bridges are not used, passage may be made from one platform to another only when the platforms are at the same height and are abutting.

(3) Scaffolds shall be suspended from metal outriggers, brackets, wire rope slings, hooks, or means that meet equivalent criteria (e.g., strength, durability).

(r) *Catenary scaffolds.* (1) No more than one platform shall be placed between consecutive vertical pickups, and no more than two platforms shall be used on a catenary scaffold.

(2) Platforms supported by wire ropes shall have hook-shaped stops on each end of the platforms to prevent them from slipping off the wire ropes. These hooks shall be so placed that they will prevent the platform from falling if one of the horizontal wire ropes breaks.

(3) Wire ropes shall not be tightened to the extent that the application of a scaffold load will overstress them.

(4) Wire ropes shall be continuous and without splices between anchors.

(s) *Float (ship) scaffolds.* (1) The platform shall be supported by a minimum of two bearers, each of which shall

project a minimum of 6 inches (15.2 cm) beyond the platform on both sides. Each bearer shall be securely fastened to the platform.

(2) Rope connections shall be such that the platform cannot shift or slip.

(3) When only two ropes are used with each float:

(i) They shall be arranged so as to provide four ends which are securely fastened to overhead supports.

(ii) Each supporting rope shall be hitched around one end of the bearer and pass under the platform to the other end of the bearer where it is hitched again, leaving sufficient rope at each end for the supporting ties.

(t) *Interior hung scaffolds.* (1) Scaffolds shall be suspended only from the roof structure or other structural member such as ceiling beams.

(2) Overhead supporting members (roof structure, ceiling beams, or other structural members) shall be inspected and checked for strength before the scaffold is erected.

(3) Suspension ropes and cables shall be connected to the overhead supporting members by shackles, clips, thimbles, or other means that meet equivalent criteria (e.g., strength, durability).

(u) *Needle beam scaffolds.* (1) Scaffold support beams shall be installed on edge.

(2) Ropes or hangers shall be used for supports, except that one end of a needle beam scaffold may be supported by a permanent structural member.

(3) The ropes shall be securely attached to the needle beams.

(4) The support connection shall be arranged so as to prevent the needle beam from rolling or becoming displaced.

(5) Platform units shall be securely attached to the needle beams by bolts or equivalent means. Cleats and overhang are not considered to be adequate means of attachment.

(v) *Multi-level suspended scaffolds.* (1) Scaffolds shall be equipped with additional independent support lines, equal in number to the number of points supported, and of equivalent strength to the suspension ropes, and rigged to support the scaffold in the event the suspension rope(s) fail.

(2) Independent support lines and suspension ropes shall not be attached to the same points of anchorage.

(3) Supports for platforms shall be attached directly to the support stirrup and not to any other platform.

(w) *Mobile scaffolds.* (1) Scaffolds shall be braced by cross, horizontal, or diagonal braces, or combination thereof, to prevent racking or collapse of the scaffold and to secure vertical members together laterally so as to automatically square and align the vertical members. Scaffolds shall be plumb, level, and squared. All brace connections shall be secured.

(i) Scaffolds constructed of tube and coupler components shall also comply with the requirements of paragraph (b) of this section;

(ii) Scaffolds constructed of fabricated frame components shall also comply with the requirements of paragraph (c) of this section.

(2) Scaffold casters and wheels shall be locked with positive wheel and/or wheel and swivel locks, or equivalent means, to prevent movement of the scaffold while the scaffold is used in a stationary manner.

(3) Manual force used to move the scaffold shall be applied as close to the base as practicable, but not more than 5 feet (1.5 m) above the supporting surface.

(4) Power systems used to propel mobile scaffolds shall be designed for such use. Forklifts, trucks, similar motor vehicles or add-on motors shall not be used to propel scaffolds unless the scaffold is designed for such propulsion systems.

(5) Scaffolds shall be stabilized to prevent tipping during movement.

(6) Employees shall not be allowed to ride on scaffolds unless the following conditions exist:

(i) The surface on which the scaffold is being moved is within 3 degrees of level, and free of pits, holes, and obstructions;

(ii) The height to base width ratio of the scaffold during movement is two to one or less, unless the scaffold is designed and constructed to meet or exceed nationally recognized stability test requirements such as those listed in paragraph (x) of appendix A to this subpart (ANSI/SIA A92.5 and A92.6);

(iii) Outrigger frames, when used, are installed on both sides of the scaffold;

(iv) When power systems are used, the propelling force is applied directly to the wheels, and does not produce a speed in excess of 1 foot per second (.3 mps); and

(v) No employee is on any part of the scaffold which extends outward beyond the wheels, casters, or other supports.

(7) Platforms shall not extend outward beyond the base supports of the scaffold unless outrigger frames or equivalent devices are used to ensure stability.

(8) Where leveling of the scaffold is necessary, screw jacks or equivalent means shall be used.

(9) Caster stems and wheel stems shall be pinned or otherwise secured in scaffold legs or adjustment screws.

(10) Before a scaffold is moved, each employee on the scaffold shall be made aware of the move.

(x) *Repair bracket scaffolds.* (1) Brackets shall be secured in place by at least one wire rope at least ½ inch (1.27 cm) in diameter.

(2) Each bracket shall be attached to the securing wire rope (or ropes) by a positive locking device capable of preventing the unintentional detachment of the bracket from the rope, or by equivalent means.

(3) Each bracket, at the contact point between the supporting structure and the bottom of the bracket, shall be provided with a shoe (heel block or foot) capable of preventing the lateral movement of the bracket.

(4) Platforms shall be secured to the brackets in a manner that will prevent the separation of the platforms from the brackets and the movement of the platforms or the brackets on a completed scaffold.

(5) When a wire rope is placed around the structure in order to provide a safe anchorage for personal fall arrest systems used by employees erecting or dismantling scaffolds, the wire rope shall meet the requirements of subpart M of this part, but shall be at least ⁵⁄₁₆ inch (0.8 cm) in diameter.

(6) Each wire rope used for securing brackets in place or as an anchorage for personal fall arrest systems shall be protected from damage due to contact with edges, corners, protrusions, or

other discontinuities of the supporting structure or scaffold components.

(7) Tensioning of each wire rope used for securing brackets in place or as an anchorage for personal fall arrest systems shall be by means of a turnbuckle at least 1 inch (2.54 cm) in diameter, or by equivalent means.

(8) Each turnbuckle shall be connected to the other end of its rope by use of an eyesplice thimble of a size appropriate to the turnbuckle to which it is attached.

(9) U-bolt wire rope clips shall not be used on any wire rope used to secure brackets or to serve as an anchor for personal fall arrest systems.

(10) The employer shall ensure that materials shall not be dropped to the outside of the supporting structure.

(11) Scaffold erection shall progress in only one direction around any structure.

(y) *Stilts.* Stilts, when used, shall be used in accordance with the following requirements:

(1) An employee may wear stilts on a scaffold only if it is a large area scaffold.

(2) When an employee is using stilts on a large area scaffold where a guardrail system is used to provide fall protection, the guardrail system shall be increased in height by an amount equal to the height of the stilts being used by the employee.

(3) Surfaces on which stilts are used shall be flat and free of pits, holes and obstructions, such as debris, as well as other tripping and falling hazards.

(4) Stilts shall be properly maintained. Any alteration of the original equipment shall be approved by the manufacturer.

§ 1926.453 Aerial lifts.

(a) *General requirements.* (1) Unless otherwise provided in this section, aerial lifts acquired for use on or after January 22, 1973 shall be designed and constructed in conformance with the applicable requirements of the American National Standards for "Vehicle Mounted Elevating and Rotating Work Platforms," ANSI A92.2–1969, including appendix. Aerial lifts acquired before January 22, 1973 which do not meet the requirements of ANSI A92.2–1969, may not be used after January 1, 1976, un-less they shall have been modified so as to conform with the applicable design and construction requirements of ANSI A92.2–1969. Aerial lifts include the following types of vehicle-mounted aerial devices used to elevate personnel to job-sites above ground:

(i) Extensible boom platforms;

(ii) Aerial ladders;

(iii) Articulating boom platforms;

(iv) Vertical towers; and

(v) A combination of any such devices. Aerial equipment may be made of metal, wood, fiberglass reinforced plastic (FRP), or other material; may be powered or manually operated; and are deemed to be aerial lifts whether or not they are capable of rotating about a substantially vertical axis.

(2) Aerial lifts may be "field modified" for uses other than those intended by the manufacturer provided the modification has been certified in writing by the manufacturer or by any other equivalent entity, such as a nationally recognized testing laboratory, to be in conformity with all applicable provisions of ANSI A92.2–1969 and this section and to be at least as safe as the equipment was before modification.

(b) *Specific requirements—*(1) *Ladder trucks and tower trucks.* Aerial ladders shall be secured in the lower traveling position by the locking device on top of the truck cab, and the manually operated device at the base of the ladder before the truck is moved for highway travel.

(2) *Extensible and articulating boom platforms.* (i) Lift controls shall be tested each day prior to use to determine that such controls are in safe working condition.

(ii) Only authorized persons shall operate an aerial lift.

(iii) Belting off to an adjacent pole, structure, or equipment while working from an aerial lift shall not be permitted.

(iv) Employees shall always stand firmly on the floor of the basket, and shall not sit or climb on the edge of the basket or use planks, ladders, or other devices for a work position.

(v) A body belt shall be worn and a lanyard attached to the boom or basket when working from an aerial lift.

NOTE TO PARAGRAPH (b)(2)(v): As of January 1, 1998, subpart M of this part

(§ 1926.502(d)) provides that body belts are not acceptable as part of a personal fall arrest system. The use of a body belt in a tethering system or in a restraint system is acceptable and is regulated under § 1926.502(e).

(vi) Boom and basket load limits specified by the manufacturer shall not be exceeded.

(vii) The brakes shall be set and when outriggers are used, they shall be positioned on pads or a solid surface. Wheel chocks shall be installed before using an aerial lift on an incline, provided they can be safely installed.

(viii) An aerial lift truck shall not be moved when the boom is elevated in a working position with men in the basket, except for equipment which is specifically designed for this type of operation in accordance with the provisions of paragraphs (a) (1) and (2) of this section.

(ix) Articulating boom and extensible boom platforms, primarily designed as personnel carriers, shall have both platform (upper) and lower controls. Upper controls shall be in or beside the platform within easy reach of the operator. Lower controls shall provide for overriding the upper controls. Controls shall be plainly marked as to their function. Lower level controls shall not be operated unless permission has been obtained from the employee in the lift, except in case of emergency.

(x) Climbers shall not be worn while performing work from an aerial lift.

(xi) The insulated portion of an aerial lift shall not be altered in any manner that might reduce its insulating value.

(xii) Before moving an aerial lift for travel, the boom(s) shall be inspected to see that it is properly cradled and outriggers are in stowed position except as provided in paragraph (b)(2)(viii) of this section.

(3) *Electrical tests.* All electrical tests shall conform to the requirements of ANSI A92.2–1969 section 5. However equivalent d.c.; voltage tests may be used in lieu of the a.c. voltage specified in A92.2–1969; d.c. voltage tests which are approved by the equipment manufacturer or equivalent entity shall be considered an equivalent test for the purpose of this paragraph (b)(3).

(4) *Bursting safety factor.* The provisions of the American National Standards Institute standard ANSI A92.2–

1969, section 4.9 Bursting Safety Factor shall apply to all critical hydraulic and pneumatic components. Critical components are those in which a failure would result in a free fall or free rotation of the boom. All noncritical components shall have a bursting safety factor of at least 2 to 1.

(5) *Welding standards.* All welding shall conform to the following standards as applicable:

(i) Standard Qualification Procedure, AWS B3.0–41.

(ii) Recommended Practices for Automotive Welding Design, AWS D8.4–61.

(iii) Standard Qualification of Welding Procedures and Welders for Piping and Tubing, AWS D10.9–69.

(iv) Specifications for Welding Highway and Railway Bridges, AWS D2.0–69.

NOTE TO § 1926.453: Non-mandatory appendix C to this subpart lists examples of national consensus standards that are considered to provide employee protection equivalent to that provided through the application of ANSI A92.2–1969, where appropriate. This incorporation by reference was approved by the Director of the Federal Register in accordance with 5 U.S.C. 552(a) and 1 CFR part 51. Copies may be obtained from the American National Standards Institute. Copies may be inspected at the Docket Office, Occupational Safety and Health Administration, U.S. Department of Labor, 200 Constitution Avenue, NW., room N2634, Washington, DC or at the National Archives and Records Administration (NARA). For information on the availability of this material at NARA, call 202–741–6030, or go to: *http://www.archives.gov/ federal_register/ code_of_federal_regulations/ ibr_locations.html.*

[61 FR 46116, Aug. 30, 1996; 61 FR 59832, Nov. 25, 1996, as amended at 69 FR 18803, Apr. 9, 2004]

§ 1926.454 Training requirements.

This section supplements and clarifies the requirements of § 1926.21(b)(2) as these relate to the hazards of work on scaffolds.

(a) The employer shall have each employee who performs work while on a scaffold trained by a person qualified in the subject matter to recognize the hazards associated with the type of scaffold being used and to understand the procedures to control or minimize those hazards. The training shall include the following areas, as applicable:

(1) The nature of any electrical hazards, fall hazards and falling object hazards in the work area;

(2) The correct procedures for dealing with electrical hazards and for erecting, maintaining, and disassembling the fall protection systems and falling object protection systems being used;

(3) The proper use of the scaffold, and the proper handling of materials on the scaffold;

(4) The maximum intended load and the load-carrying capacities of the scaffolds used; and

(5) Any other pertinent requirements of this subpart.

(b) The employer shall have each employee who is involved in erecting, disassembling, moving, operating, repairing, maintaining, or inspecting a scaffold trained by a competent person to recognize any hazards associated with the work in question. The training shall include the following topics, as applicable:

(1) The nature of scaffold hazards;

(2) The correct procedures for erecting, disassembling, moving, operating, repairing, inspecting, and maintaining the type of scaffold in question;

(3) The design criteria, maximum intended load-carrying capacity and intended use of the scaffold;

(4) Any other pertinent requirements of this subpart.

(c) When the employer has reason to believe that an employee lacks the skill or understanding needed for safe work involving the erection, use or dismantling of scaffolds, the employer shall retrain each such employee so that the requisite proficiency is regained. Retraining is required in at least the following situations:

(1) Where changes at the worksite present a hazard about which an employee has not been previously trained; or

(2) Where changes in the types of scaffolds, fall protection, falling object protection, or other equipment present a hazard about which an employee has not been previously trained; or

(3) Where inadequacies in an affected employee's work involving scaffolds indicate that the employee has not retained the requisite proficiency.

(NON-MANDATORY) APPENDIX A TO SUBPART L OF PART 1926—SCAFFOLD SPECIFICATIONS

This appendix provides non-mandatory guidelines to assist employers in complying with the requirements of subpart L of this part. An employer may use these guidelines and tables as a starting point for designing scaffold systems. However, the guidelines do not provide all the information necessary to build a complete system, and the employer is still responsible for designing and assembling these components in such a way that the completed system will meet the requirements of §1926.451(a). Scaffold components which are not selected and loaded in accordance with this Appendix, and components for which no specific guidelines or tables are given in this appendix (e.g., joints, ties, components for wood pole scaffolds more than 60 feet in height, components for heavy-duty horse scaffolds, components made with other materials, and components with other dimensions, etc.) must be designed and constructed in accordance with the capacity requirements of §1926.451(a), and loaded in accordance with §1926.451(d)(1).

Index to appendix A for Subpart L

(t) Interior hung scaffolds.
(u) Needle beam scaffolds.
(v) Multi-level suspension scaffolds.
(w) Mobile scaffolds.
(x) Repair bracket scaffolds.
(y) Stilts.
(z) Tank builders' scaffolds.

1. GENERAL GUIDELINES AND TABLES

(a) The following tables, and the tables in part 2—Specific guidelines and tables, assume that all load-carrying timber members (except planks) of the scaffold are a minimum of 1,500 lb-f/in^2 (stress grade) construction grade lumber. All dimensions are nominal sizes as provided in the American Softwood Lumber Standards, dated January 1970, except that, where rough sizes are noted, only rough or undressed lumber of the size specified will satisfy minimum requirements.

(b) Solid sawn wood used as scaffold planks shall be selected for such use following the grading rules established by a recognized lumber grading association or by an independent lumber grading inspection agency. Such planks shall be identified by the grade stamp of such association or agency. The association or agency and the grading rules under which the wood is graded shall be certified by the Board of Review, American Lumber Standard Committee, as set forth in the American Softwood Lumber Standard of the U.S. Department of Commerce.

(i) Allowable spans shall be determined in compliance with the National Design Specification for Wood Construction published by the National Forest Products Association; paragraph 5 of ANSI A10.8–1988 Scaffolding-Safety Requirements published by the American National Standards Institute; or for 2×10 inch (nominal) or 2×9 inch (rough) solid sawn wood planks, as shown in the following table:

Maximum intended nominal load (lb/ft^2)	Maximum permissible span using full thickness undressed lumber (ft)	Maximum permissible span using nominal thickness lumber (ft)
25	10	8
50	8	6
75	6	

(ii) The maximum permissible span for 1¼ × 9-inch or wider wood plank of full thickness with a maximum intended load of 50 lb/ft.^{2} shall be 4 feet.

(c) Fabricated planks and platforms may be used in lieu of solid sawn wood planks. Maximum spans for such units shall be as recommended by the manufacturer based on the maximum intended load being calculated as follows:

Rated load capacity	Intended load
Light-duty	• 25 pounds per square foot applied uniformly over the entire span area.
Medium-duty	• 50 pounds per square foot applied uniformly over the entire span area.
Heavy-duty	• 75 pounds per square foot applied uniformly over the entire span area.
One-person	• 250 pounds placed at the center of the span (total 250 pounds).
Two-person	• 250 pounds placed 18 inches to the left and right of the center of the span (total 500 pounds).
Three-person	• 250 pounds placed at the center of the span and 250 pounds placed 18 inches to the left and right of the center of the span (total 750 pounds).

NOTE: Platform units used to make scaffold platforms intended for light-duty use shall be capable of supporting at least 25 pounds per square foot applied uniformly over the entire unit-span area, or a 250-pound point load placed on the unit at the center of the span, whichever load produces the greater shear force.

(d) Guardrails shall be as follows:
(i) Toprails shall be equivalent in strength to 2 inch by 4 inch lumber; or
1¼ inch × ⅛ inch structural angle iron; or
1 inch × .070 inch wall steel tubing; or 1.990 inch × .058 inch wall aluminum tubing.
(ii) Midrails shall be equivalent in strength to 1 inch by 6 inch lumber; or
1¼ inch × 1¼ inch × ⅛ inch structural angle iron; or
1 inch × .070 inch wall steel tubing; or
1.990 inch × .058 inch wall aluminum tubing.

(iii) Toeboards shall be equivalent in strength to 1 inch by 4 inch lumber; or
1¼ inch × 1¼ inch structural angle iron; or
1 inch × .070 inch wall steel tubing; or
1.990 inch × .058 inch wall aluminum tubing.
(iv) Posts shall be equivalent in strength to 2 inch by 4 inch lumber; or
1¼ inch × 1¼ inch × ⅛ structural angle iron; or
1 inch × .070 inch wall steel tubing; or
1.990 inch × .058 inch wall aluminum tubing.
(v) Distance between posts shall not exceed 8 feet.
(e) Overhead protection shall consist of 2 inch nominal planking laid tight, or ¾-inch plywood.
(f) Screen installed between toeboards and midrails or toprails shall consist of No. 18 gauge U.S. Standard wire one inch mesh.

2. SPECIFIC GUIDELINES AND TABLES.

(a) Pole Scaffolds.

SINGLE POLE WOOD POLE SCAFFOLDS

	Light duty up to 20 feet high	Light duty up to 60 feet high	Medium duty up to 60 feet high	Heavy duty up to 60 feet high
Maximum intended load (lbs/ft^2)	25	25	50	75
Poles or uprights	2×4 in	4×4 in	4×4 in	4×6 in.
Maximum pole spacing (longitudinal)	6 feet	10 feet	8 feet	6 feet
Maximum pole spacing (transverse)	5 feet	5 feet	5 feet	5 feet
Runners	1×4 in	1¼×9 in	2×10 in	2×10 in.
Bearers and maximum spacing of bearers:				
3 feet	2×4 in	2×4 in	2×10 in. or 3×4 in	2×10 in. or 3×5 in.
5 feet	2×6 in. or 3×4 in ..	2×6 in. or 3×4 in. (rough).	2×10 in. or 3×4 in	2×10 in. or 3×5 in.
6 feet			2×10 in. or 3×4 in	2×10 in. or 3×5 in.
8 feet			2×10 in. or 3×4 in	
Planking	1¼×9 in	2×10 in	2×10 in	2×10 in.
Maximum vertical spacing of horizontal members.	7 feet	9 feet	7 feet	6 ft. 6 in.
Bracing horizontal	1×4 in	1×4 in	1×6 in. or 1¼×4 in	2×4 in.
Bracing diagonal	1×4 in	1×4 in	1×4 in	2×4 in.
Tie-ins	1×4 in	1×4 in	1×4 in	1×4 in.

NOTE: All members except planking are used on edge. All wood bearers shall be reinforced with ³⁄₁₆×2 inch steel strip, or the equivalent, secured to the lower edges for the entire length of the bearer.

INDEPENDENT WOOD POLE SCAFFOLDS

	Light duty up to 20 feet high	Light duty up to 60 feet high	Medium duty up to 60 feet high	Heavy duty up to 60 feet high
Maximum intended load	25 lbs/ft^2	25 lbs/ft^2	50 lbs/ft^2	75 lbs/ft^2.
Poles or uprights	2×4 in	4×4 in	4×4 in	4×4 in.
Maximum pole spacing (longitudinal)	6 feet	10 feet	8 feet	6 feet.
Maximum (transverse)	6 feet	10 feet	8 feet	8 feet.
Runners	1¼×4 in	1¼×9 in	2×10 in	2×10 in.
Bearers and maximum spacing of bearers:				
3 feet	2×4 in	2×4 in	2×10 in	2×10 in. (rough).
6 feet	2×6 in. or 3×4 in ..	2×10 in. (rough) or 3×8 in.	2×10 in	2×10 in. (rough).
8 feet	2×6 in. or 3×4 in ..	2×10 in. (rough) or 3×8 in.	2×10 in	
10 feet	2×6 in. or 3×4 in ..	2×10 in. (rough) or 3×3 in.		
Planking	1¼×9 in	2×10 in	2×10 in	2×10 in.
Maximum vertical spacing of horizontal members.	7 feet	7 feet	6 feet	6 feet.
Bracing horizontal	1×4 in	1×4 in	1×6 in. or 1¼×4 in	2×4 in.
Bracing diagonal	1×4 in	1×4 in	1×4 in	2×4 in.
Tie-ins	1×4 in	1×4 in	1×4 in	1×4 in.

NOTE: All members except planking are used on edge. All wood bearers shall be reinforced with ³⁄₁₆×2 inch steel strip, or the equivalent, secured to the lower edges for the entire length of the bearer.

(b) Tube and coupler scaffolds.

MINIMUM SIZE OF MEMBERS

	Light duty	Medium duty	Heavy duty
Maximum intended load	25 lbs/ft^2	50 lbs/ft^2	75 lbs/ft^2.
Posts, runners and braces	Nominal 2 in. (1.90 inches) OD steel tube or pipe.	Nominal 2 in. (1.90 inches) OD steel tube or pipe.	Nominal 2 in. (1.90 inches) OD steel tube or pipe.
Bearers	Nominal 2 in. (1.90 inches) OD steel tube or pipe and a maximum post spacing of 4 ft.×10 ft..	Nominal 2 in. (1.90 inches) OD steel tube or pipe and a maximum post spacing of 4 ft.×7 ft. or. Nominal 2½ in. (2.375 in.). OD steel tube or pipe and a maximum post spacing of 6 ft.×8 ft.*.	Nominal 2½ in. (2.375 in.). OD steel tube or pipe and a maximum post spacing of 6 ft.×6 ft.

MINIMUM SIZE OF MEMBERS—Continued

	Light duty	Medium duty	Heavy duty
Maximum runner spacing vertically.	6 ft. 6 in	6 ft. 6 in	6 ft. 6 in.

*Bearers shall be installed in the direction of the shorter dimension.
NOTE: Longitudinal diagonal bracing shall be installed at an angle of 45° (±5°).

MAXIMUM NUMBER OF PLANKED LEVELS

	Maximum number of additional planked levels			Maximum height of scaffold (in feet)
	Light duty	Me-dium duty	Heavy duty	
Number of Working Levels:				
1	16	11	6	125
2	11	1	0	125
3	6	0	0	125
4	1	0	0	125

(c) *Fabricated frame scaffolds.* Because of their prefabricated nature, no additional guidelines or tables for these scaffolds are being adopted in this Appendix.

(d) *Plasterers', decorators', and large area scaffolds.* The guidelines for pole scaffolds or tube and coupler scaffolds (Appendix A (a) and (b)) may be applied.

(e) *Bricklayers' square scaffolds.*
Maximum intended load: 50 lb/ft.^{2}*
Maximum width: 5 ft.
Maximum height: 5 ft.
Gussets: 1×6 in.
Braces: 1×8 in.
Legs: 2×6 in.
Bearers (horizontal members): 2×6 in.

(f) Horse scaffolds.
Maximum intended load (light duty): 25 lb/ft.^{2}**
Maximum intended load (medium duty): 50 lb/ft.^{2}**
Horizontal members or bearers:
Light duty: 2×4 in.
Medium duty: 3×4 in.
Legs: 2×4 in.
Longitudinal brace between legs: 1×6 in.
Gusset brace at top of legs: 1×8 in.
Half diagonal braces: 2×4 in.

(g) *Form scaffolds and carpenters' bracket scaffolds.* (1) Brackets shall consist of a triangular-shaped frame made of wood with a cross-section not less than 2 inches by 3 inches, or of 1¼ inch × 1¼ inch × ⅛ inch structural angle iron.

*The squares shall be set not more than 8 feet apart for light duty scaffolds and not more than 5 feet apart for medium duty scaffolds.
**Horses shall be spaced not more than 8 feet apart for light duty loads, and not more than 5 feet apart for medium duty loads.

(2) Bolts used to attach brackets to structures shall not be less than ⅝ inches in diameter.

(3) Maximum bracket spacing shall be 8 feet on centers.

(4) No more than two employees shall occupy any given 8 feet of a bracket or form scaffold at any one time. Tools and materials shall not exceed 75 pounds in addition to the occupancy.

(5) Wooden figure-four scaffolds:
Maximum intended load: 25 lb/ft.^{2}
Uprights: 2×4 in. or 2×6 in.
Bearers (two): 1×6 in.
Braces: 1×6 in.
Maximum length of bearers (unsupported): 3 ft. 6 in.

(i) Outrigger bearers shall consist of two pieces of 1×6 inch lumber nailed on opposite sides of the vertical support.

(ii) Bearers for wood figure-four brackets shall project not more than 3 feet 6 inches from the outside of the form support, and shall be braced and secured to prevent tipping or turning. The knee or angle brace shall intersect the bearer at least 3 feet from the form at an angle of approximately 45 degrees, and the lower end shall be nailed to a vertical support.

(6) Metal bracket scaffolds:
Maximum intended load: 25 lb/ft.^{2}
Uprights: 2×4 inch
Bearers: As designed.
Braces: As designed.

(7) Wood bracket scaffolds:
Maximum intended load: 25 lb/ft.^{2}
Uprights: 2×4 in or 2×6 in
Bearers: 2×6 in
Maximum scaffold width: 3 ft 6 in
Braces: 1×6 in

(h) *Roof bracket scaffolds.* No specific guidelines or tables are given.

302

(i) *Outrigger scaffolds (single level)*. No specific guidelines or tables are given.

(j) *Pump jack scaffolds*. Wood poles shall not exceed 30 feet in height. Maximum intended load—500 lbs between poles; applied at the center of the span. Not more than two employees shall be on a pump jack scaffold at one time between any two supports. When 2 × 4's are spliced together to make a 4 × 4 inch wood pole, they shall be spliced with "10 penny" common nails no more than 12 inches center to center, staggered uniformly from the opposite outside edges.

(k) *Ladder jack scaffolds*. Maximum intended load—25 lb/ft². However, not more than two employees shall occupy any platform at any one time. Maximum span between supports shall be 8 feet.

(l) *Window jack scaffolds*. Not more than one employee shall occupy a window jack scaffold at any one time.

(m) *Crawling boards (chicken ladders)*. Crawling boards shall be not less than 10 inches wide and 1 inch thick, with cleats having a minimum 1 × 1½ inch cross-sectional area. The cleats shall be equal in length to the width of the board and spaced at equal intervals not to exceed 24 inches.

(n) *Step, platform, and trestle ladder scaffolds*. No additional guidelines or tables are given.

(o) *Single-point adjustable suspension scaffolds*. Maximum intended load—250 lbs. Wood seats for boatswains' chairs shall be not less than 1 inch thick if made of non-laminated wood, or ⅝ inches thick if made of marine quality plywood.

(p) *Two-point adjustable suspension scaffolds*. (1) In addition to direct connections to buildings (except window cleaners' anchors) acceptable ways to prevent scaffold sway include angulated roping and static lines. Angulated roping is a system of platform suspension in which the upper wire rope sheaves or suspension points are closer to the plane of the building face than the corresponding attachment points on the platform, thus causing the platform to press against the face of the building. Static lines are separate ropes secured at their top and bottom ends closer to the plane of the building face than the outermost edge of the platform. By drawing the static line taut, the platform is drawn against the face of the building.

(2) On suspension scaffolds designed for a working load of 500 pounds, no more than two employees shall be permitted on the scaffold at one time. On suspension scaffolds with a working load of 750 pounds, no more than three employees shall be permitted on the scaffold at one time.

(3) Ladder-type platforms. The side stringer shall be of clear straight-grained spruce. The rungs shall be of straight-grained oak, ash, or hickory, at least 1⅛ inches in diameter, with ⅞ inch tenons mortised into the side stringers at least ⅞ inch. The stringers shall be tied together with tie rods not less than ¼ inch in diameter, passing through the stringers and riveted up tight against washers on both ends. The flooring strips shall be spaced not more than ⅝ inch apart, except at the side rails where the space may be 1 inch. Ladder-type platforms shall be constructed in accordance with the following table:

SCHEDULE FOR LADDER-TYPE PLATFORMS

Length of Platform	12 feet	14 & 16 feet	18 & 20 feet.
Side stringers, minimum cross section (finished sizes):			
At ends	1¾ × 2¾ in	1¾ × 2¾ in	1¾ × 3 in.
At middle	1¾ × 3¾ in	1¾ × 3¾ in	1¾ × 4 in.
Reinforcing strip (minimum)	A⅛ × ⅞ inch steel reinforcing strip shall be attached to the side or underside, full length.		
Rungs	Rungs shall be 1⅛ inch minimum diameter with at least ⅞ inch in diameter tenons, and the maximum spacing shall be 12 inches to center.		
Tie rods:			
Number (minimum)	3	4	4
Diameter (minimum)	¼ inch	¼ inch	¼ inch
Flooring, minimum finished size	½ × 2¾ in	½ × 2¾ in	½ × 2¾ in.

SCHEDULE FOR LADDER-TYPE PLATFORMS

Length of Platform	22 & 24 ft	28 & 30 ft.
Side stringers, minimum cross section (finished sizes):		
At ends	1¾×3 in	1¾ × 3½ in.
At middle	1¾ × 4¼ in	1¾ × 5 in.

SCHEDULE FOR LADDER-TYPE PLATFORMS—Continued

Reinforcing strip (minimum)	A⅛ × ⅞-inch steel reinforcing strip shall be attached to the side or underside, full length.	
Rungs	Rungs shall be 1⅛ inch minimum diameter with at least ⅞ inch in diameter tenons, and the maximum spacing shall be 12 inches to center. Tie rods.	
Number (minimum)	5	6.
Diameter (minimum)	¼ in	¼ in.
Flooring, minimum finished size	½ × 2¾ in	½ × 2¾ in.

(4) *Plank-Type Platforms.* Plank-type platforms shall be composed of not less than nominal 2 × 8 inch unspliced planks, connected together on the underside with cleats at intervals not exceeding 4 feet, starting 6 inches from each end. A bar or other effective means shall be securely fastened to the platform at each end to prevent the platform from slipping off the hanger. The span between hangers for plank-type platforms shall not exceed 10 feet.

(5) *Beam-Type Platforms.* Beam platforms shall have side stringers of lumber not less than 2 × 6 inches set on edge. The span between hangers shall not exceed 12 feet when beam platforms are used. The flooring shall be supported on 2 × 6 inch cross beams, laid flat and set into the upper edge of the stringers with a snug fit, at intervals of not more than 4 feet, securely nailed to the cross beams. Floor-boards shall not be spaced more than ½ inch apart.

(q)(1) *Multi-point adjustable suspension scaffolds and stonesetters' multi-point adjustable suspension scaffolds.* No specific guidelines or tables are given for these scaffolds.

(2) *Masons' multi-point adjustable suspension scaffolds.* Maximum intended load—50 lb/ft². Each outrigger beam shall be at least a standard 7 inch, 15.3 pound steel I-beam, at least 15 feet long. Such beams shall not project more than 6 feet 6 inches beyond the bearing point. Where the overhang exceeds 6 feet 6 inches, outrigger beams shall be composed of stronger beams or multiple beams.

(r) *Catenary scaffolds.* (1) Maximum intended load—500 lbs.

(2) Not more than two employees shall be permitted on the scaffold at one time.

(3) Maximum capacity of come-along shall be 2,000 lbs.

(4) Vertical pickups shall be spaced not more than 50 feet apart.

(5) Ropes shall be equivalent in strength to at least ½ inch (1.3 cm) diameter improved plow steel wire rope.

(s) *Float (ship) scaffolds.* (1) Maximum intended load—750 lbs.

(2) Platforms shall be made of ¾ inch plywood, equivalent in rating to American Plywood Association Grade B-B, Group I, Exterior.

(3) Bearers shall be made from 2×4 inch, or 1×10 inch rough lumber. They shall be free of knots and other flaws.

(4) Ropes shall be equivalent in strength to at least 1 inch (2.5 cm) diameter first grade manila rope.

(t) *Interior hung scaffolds.*

Bearers (use on edge): 2×10 in.
Maximum intended load: Maximum span
25 lb/ft.²: 10 ft.
50 lb/ft.²: 10 ft.
75 lb/ft.²: 7 ft.

(u) *Needle beam scaffolds.*

Maximum intended load: 25 lb/ft.²
Beams: 4×6 in.
Maximum platform span: 8 ft.
Maximum beam span: 10 ft.

(1) Ropes shall be attached to the needle beams by a scaffold hitch or an eye splice. The loose end of the rope shall be tied by a bowline knot or by a round turn and a half hitch.

(2) Ropes shall be equivalent in strength to at least 1 inch (2.5 cm) diameter first grade manila rope.

(v) *Multi-level suspension scaffolds.* No additional guidelines or tables are being given for these scaffolds.

(w) *Mobile Scaffolds.* Stability test as described in the ANSI A92 series documents, as appropriate for the type of scaffold, can be used to establish stability for the purpose of §1926.452(w)(6).

(x) *Repair bracket scaffolds.* No additional guidelines or tables are being given for these scaffolds.

(y) *Stilts.* No specific guidelines or tables are given.

(z) *Tank builder's scaffold.* (1) The maximum distance between brackets to which scaffolding and guardrail supports are attached shall be no more than 10 feet 6 inches.

(2) Not more than three employees shall occupy a 10 feet 6 inch span of scaffold planking at any time.

(3) A taut wire or synthetic rope supported on the scaffold brackets shall be installed at the scaffold plank level between the innermost edge of the scaffold platform and the curved plate structure of the tank shell to serve as a safety line in lieu of an inner guardrail assembly where the space between the scaffold platform and the tank exceeds 12 inches (30.48 cm). In the event the open space on either side of the rope exceeds 12 inches (30.48 cm), a second wire or synthetic rope appropriately placed, or guardrails in accordance with §1926.451(g)(4), shall be installed in order to reduce that open space to less than 12 inches (30.48 cm).

(4) Scaffold planks of rough full-dimensioned 2-inch (5.1 cm)×12-inch (30.5 cm) Douglas Fir or Southern Yellow Pine of Select Structural Grade shall be used. Douglas Fir planks shall have a fiber stress of at least 1900 lb/in² (130,929 n/cm²) and a modulus of elasticity of at least 1,900,000 lb/in² (130,929,000 n/cm²), while Yellow Pine planks shall have a fiber stress of at least 2500 lb/in² (172,275 n/cm²) and a modulus of elasticity of at least 2,000,000 lb/in² (137,820,000 n/cm²).

(5) Guardrails shall be constructed of a taut wire or synthetic rope, and shall be supported by angle irons attached to brackets welded to the steel plates. These guardrails shall comply with §1926.451(g)(4). Guardrail supports shall be located at no greater than 10 feet 6 inch intervals.

[44 FR 8577, Feb. 9, 1979, as amended at 77 FR 46950, Aug. 7, 2012]

(NON-MANDATORY) APPENDIX B TO SUBPART L OF PART 1926—CRITERIA FOR DETERMINING THE FEASIBILITY OF PROVIDING SAFE ACCESS AND FALL PROTECTION FOR SCAFFOLD ERECTORS AND DISMANTLERS [RESERVED]

(NON-MANDATORY) APPENDIX C TO SUBPART L OF PART 1926—LIST OF NATIONAL CONSENSUS STANDARDS

ANSI/SIA A92.2–1990 *Vehicle-Mounted Elevating and Rotating Aerial Devices*
ANSI/SIA A92.3–1990 *Manually Propelled Elevating Aerial Platforms*
ANSI/SIA A92.5–1990 *Boom Supported Elevating Work Platforms*
ANSI/SIA A92.6–1990 *Self-Propelled Elevating Work Platforms*
ANSI/SIA A92.7–1990 *Airline Ground Support Vehicle-Mounted Vertical Lift Devices*
ANSI/SIA A92.8–1993 *Vehicle-Mounted Bridge Inspection and Maintenance Devices*
ANSI/SIA A92.9–1993 *Mast-Climbing Work Platforms*

(NON-MANDATORY) APPENDIX D TO SUBPART L OF PART 1926—LIST OF TRAINING TOPICS FOR SCAFFOLD ERECTORS AND DISMANTLERS

This appendix D is provided to serve as a guide to assist employers when evaluating the training needs of employees erecting or dismantling supported scaffolds.

The Agency believes that employees erecting or dismantling scaffolds should be trained in the following topics:
- *General Overview of Scaffolding*
  - regulations and standards
  - erection/dismantling planning
  - PPE and proper procedures
  - fall protection
  - materials handling
  - access
  - working platforms
  - foundations
  - guys, ties and braces
- *Tubular Welded Frame Scaffolds*
  - specific regulations and standards
  - components
  - parts inspection
  - erection/dismantling planning
  - guys, ties and braces
  - fall protection
  - general safety
  - access and platforms
  - erection/dismantling procedures
  - rolling scaffold assembly
  - putlogs
- *Tube and Clamp Scaffolds*
  - specific regulations and standards
  - components
  - parts inspection
  - erection/dismantling planning
  - guys, ties and braces
  - fall protection
  - general safety
  - access and platforms
  - erection/dismantling procedures
  - buttresses, cantilevers, & bridges
- *System Scaffolds*
  - specific regulations and standards
  - components
  - parts inspection
  - erection/dismantling planning
  - guys, ties and braces
  - fall protection
  - general safety
  - access and platforms
  - erection/dismantling procedures
  - buttresses, cantilevers, & bridges

Scaffold erectors and dismantlers should all receive the general overview, and, in addition, specific training for the type of supported scaffold being erected or dismantled.

(NON-MANDATORY) APPENDIX E TO SUBPART L OF PART 1926—DRAWINGS AND ILLUSTRATIONS

This appendix provides drawings of particular types of scaffolds and scaffold components, and graphic illustrations of bracing patterns and tie spacing patterns.

This appendix is intended to provide visual guidance to assist the user in complying with the requirements of subpart L, part 1926.

BRACING – TUBE & COUPLER SCAFFOLDS

SUSPENDED SCAFFOLD PLATFORM WELDING PRECAUTIONS

HOISTS MUST BE ELECTRONICALLY ISOLATED FROM SCAFFOLD

MAXIMUM VERTICAL TIE SPACING
WIDER THAN 3'-0" BASES

TIE

TIE

TOP OF SCAFFOLD PLATFORM AND
UPPER MOST TIE NOT TO
EXCEED 4 TO 1 RATIO

26'-0" MAX. BETWEEN
INTERMEDIATE TIES

4 TIMES MINIMUM BASE
TIE AT CLOSEST FRAME
HEADER OR BEARER

FIRST TIE CLOSEST FRAME HEADER OR BEARER
ABOVE 4 TIMES THE MINIMUM BASE DIMENSION

WIDER THAN 3'-0"
MINIMUM BASE DIMENSION

MAXIMUM VERTICAL TIE SPACING
3'- 0" AND NARROWER BASES

TOP OF SCAFFOLD PLATFORM
UPPERMOST TIE NOT TO
EXCEED 4 TO 1 RATIO

TIE

20'-0" MAX. BETWEEN
INTERMEDIATE TIES

TIE

4 TIMES MINIMUM BASE
TIE AT CLOSEST FRAME
HEADER OR BEARER

FIRST TIE AT CLOSEST FRAME HEADER OR BEARER
ABOVE 4 TIMES THE MINIMUM BASE DIMENSION

3' -0" AND NARROWER
MINIMUM BASE DIMENSION

SYSTEM SCAFFOLD

JOINT CONNECTIONS
VARY ACCORDING
TO MANUFACTURER

GUARD RAIL SYSTEM

TOEBOARD

WORKING
LEVEL

POSTS

RUNNERS

STAIR
TOWER

BEARERS

SCREW
JACK

SILLS

DIAGONAL BRACES

Grade stamp courtesy of West Coast Lumber Inspection Bureau

Grade stamp courtesy of Southern Pine Inspection Bureau

TUBE and COUPLER SCAFFOLD

RIGID CLAMP

SWIVEL CLAMP

PLANKING

GUARD RAIL SYSTEM WITH TOE BOARDS

RUNNER

BEARER

POST

SILL

DIAGONAL BRACE

CROSS BRACING

TYPICAL JOINT CONNECTION

BASE PLATE

NOTE: ALL TIES SHOULD BE LOCATED AT CLAMP LOCATIONS.

SCAFFOLDING WORK SURFACES

LAMINATED VENIER LUMBER (LVL)

SOLID SAWN LUMBER

SCAFFOLD PLANKS

FABRICATED SCAFFOLD DECK

FABRICATED SCAFFOLD PLANK

DECORATOR PLANK

STAGE PLATFORM

WOOD SCAFFOLD PLATFORM

METAL SCAFFOLD PLATFORM

OUTRIGGER SCAFFOLD

THIS END RIGIDLY SECURED

OUTRIGGER BEAM BLOCKED FOR LATERAL SUPPORT

[61 FR 46122, Aug. 30, 1996; 61 FR 59832, Nov. 25, 1996]

Subpart M—Fall Protection

AUTHORITY: 40 U.S.C. 3701 *et seq.;* 29 U.S.C. 653, 655, 657; Secretary of Labor's Order No. 1–90 (55 FR 9033), 6–96 (62 FR 111), 3–2000 (65 FR 50017), 5–2007 (72 FR 31159), or 1–2012 (77 FR 3912), as applicable; and 29 CFR Part 1911.

SOURCE: 59 FR 40730, Aug. 9, 1994, unless otherwise noted.

§ 1926.500 Scope, application, and definitions applicable to this subpart.

(a) *Scope and application.* (1) This subpart sets forth requirements and criteria for fall protection in construction workplaces covered under 29 CFR part 1926. Exception: The provisions of this subpart do not apply when employees are making an inspection, investigation, or assessment of workplace conditions prior to the actual start of construction work or after all construction work has been completed.

(2) Section 1926.501 sets forth those workplaces, conditions, operations, and circumstances for which fall protection shall be provided except as follows:

(i) Requirements relating to fall protection for employees working on scaffolds are provided in subpart L of this part.

(ii) Requirements relating to fall protection for employees working on cranes and derricks are provided in subpart CC of this part.

(iii) Fall protection requirements for employees performing steel erection work (except for towers and tanks) are provided in subpart R of this part.

(iv) Requirements relating to fall protection for employees working on certain types of equipment used in tunneling operations are provided in subpart S of this part.

(v) Requirements relating to fall protection for employees engaged in the erection of tanks and communication and broadcast towers are provided in §1926.105.

(vi) Subpart V of this part provides requirements relating to fall protection for employees working from aerial lifts or on poles, towers, or similar structures while engaged in the construction of electric transmission or distribution lines or equipment.

(vii) Requirements relating to fall protection for employees working on stairways and ladders are provided in subpart X of this part.

(3) Section 1926.502 sets forth the requirements for the installation, construction, and proper use of fall protection required by part 1926, except as follows:

(i) Performance requirements for guardrail systems used on scaffolds and performance requirements for falling object protection used on scaffolds are provided in subpart L of this part.

(ii) Performance requirements for stairways, stairrail systems, and handrails are provided in subpart X of this part.

(iii) Additional performance requirements for fall arrest and work-positioning equipment are provided in subpart V of this part.

(iv) Section 1926.502 does not apply to the erection of tanks and communication and broadcast towers. (Note: Section 1926.104 sets the criteria for body belts, lanyards and lifelines used for fall protection during tank and communication and broadcast tower erection. Paragraphs (b),(c) and (f) of §1926.107 provide definitions for the pertinent terms.)

(v) Criteria for steps, handholds, ladders, and grabrails/guardrails/railings required by subpart CC are provided in subpart CC. Sections 1926.502(a), (c) through (e), and (i) apply to activities covered under subpart CC unless otherwise stated in subpart CC. No other paragraphs of §1926.502 apply to subpart CC.

(4) Section 1926.503 sets forth requirements for training in the installation and use of fall protection systems, except in relation to steel erection activities and the use of equipment covered by subpart CC.

(b) *Definitions.*

Anchorage means a secure point of attachment for lifelines, lanyards or deceleration devices.

Body belt (safety belt) means a strap with means both for securing it about the waist and for attaching it to a lanyard, lifeline, or deceleration device.

Body harness means straps which may be secured about the employee in a manner that will distribute the fall arrest forces over at least the thighs, pelvis, waist, chest and shoulders with means for attaching it to other components of a personal fall arrest system.

Buckle means any device for holding the body belt or body harness closed around the employee's body.

Connector means a device which is used to couple (connect) parts of the personal fall arrest system and positioning device systems together. It may be an independent component of the system, such as a carabiner, or it may be an integral component of part of the system (such as a buckle or dee-ring sewn into a body belt or body harness, or a snap-hook spliced or sewn to a lanyard or self-retracting lanyard).

Controlled access zone (CAZ) means an area in which certain work (e.g., overhand bricklaying) may take place without the use of guardrail systems, personal fall arrest systems, or safety net systems and access to the zone is controlled.

Dangerous equipment means equipment (such as pickling or galvanizing tanks, degreasing units, machinery, electrical equipment, and other units) which, as a result of form or function, may be hazardous to employees who fall onto or into such equipment.

Deceleration device means any mechanism, such as a rope grab, rip-stitch lanyard, specially-woven lanyard, tearing or deforming lanyards, automatic self-retracting lifelines/lanyards, etc., which serves to dissipate a substantial amount of energy during a fall arrest, or otherwise limit the energy imposed on an employee during fall arrest.

Deceleration distance means the additional vertical distance a falling employee travels, excluding lifeline elongation and free fall distance, before stopping, from the point at which the deceleration device begins to operate. It is measured as the distance between the location of an employee's body belt or body harness attachment point at the moment of activation (at the onset of fall arrest forces) of the deceleration device during a fall, and the location of that attachment point after the employee comes to a full stop.

Equivalent means alternative designs, materials, or methods to protect against a hazard which the employer can demonstrate will provide an equal or greater degree of safety for employees than the methods, materials or designs specified in the standard.

Failure means load refusal, breakage, or separation of component parts. Load refusal is the point where the ultimate strength is exceeded.

Free fall means the act of falling before a personal fall arrest system begins to apply force to arrest the fall.

Free fall distance means the vertical displacement of the fall arrest attachment point on the employee's body belt or body harness between onset of the fall and just before the system begins to apply force to arrest the fall. This distance excludes deceleration distance, and lifeline/lanyard elongation, but includes any deceleration device slide distance or self-retracting lifeline/lanyard extension before they operate and fall arrest forces occur.

Guardrail system means a barrier erected to prevent employees from falling to lower levels.

Hole means a gap or void 2 inches (5.1 cm) or more in its least dimension, in a floor, roof, or other walking/working surface.

Infeasible means that it is impossible to perform the construction work using a conventional fall protection system (i.e., guardrail system, safety net system, or personal fall arrest system) or that it is technologically impossible to use any one of these systems to provide fall protection.

Lanyard means a flexible line of rope, wire rope, or strap which generally has a connector at each end for connecting the body belt or body harness to a deceleration device, lifeline, or anchorage.

Leading edge means the edge of a floor, roof, or formwork for a floor or other walking/working surface (such as the deck) which changes location as additional floor, roof, decking, or formwork sections are placed, formed, or constructed. A leading edge is considered to be an "unprotected side and edge" during periods when it is not actively and continuously under construction.

Lifeline means a component consisting of a flexible line for connection to an anchorage at one end to hang vertically (vertical lifeline), or for connection to anchorages at both ends to stretch horizontally (horizontal lifeline), and which serves as a means for connecting other components of a personal fall arrest system to the anchorage.

Low-slope roof means a roof having a slope less than or equal to 4 in 12 (vertical to horizontal).

Lower levels means those areas or surfaces to which an employee can fall. Such areas or surfaces include, but are not limited to, ground levels, floors, platforms, ramps, runways, excavations, pits, tanks, material, water, equipment, structures, or portions thereof.

Mechanical equipment means all motor or human propelled wheeled equipment used for roofing work, except wheelbarrows and mopcarts.

Opening means a gap or void 30 inches (76 cm) or more high and 18 inches (48 cm) or more wide, in a wall or partition, through which employees can fall to a lower level.

Overhand bricklaying and related work means the process of laying bricks and masonry units such that the surface of the wall to be jointed is on the opposite side of the wall from the mason, requiring the mason to lean over the wall to complete the work. Related work includes mason tending and electrical installation incorporated into the brick wall during the overhand bricklaying process.

Personal fall arrest system means a system used to arrest an employee in a fall from a working level. It consists of an anchorage, connectors, a body belt or body harness and may include a lanyard, deceleration device, lifeline, or suitable combinations of these. As of January 1, 1998, the use of a body belt for fall arrest is prohibited.

Positioning device system means a body belt or body harness system rigged to allow an employee to be supported on an elevated vertical surface, such as a wall, and work with both hands free while leaning.

Rope grab means a deceleration device which travels on a lifeline and automatically, by friction, engages the lifeline and locks so as to arrest the fall of an employee. A rope grab usually employs the principle of inertial locking, cam/level locking, or both.

Roof means the exterior surface on the top of a building. This does not include floors or formwork which, because a building has not been completed, temporarily become the top surface of a building.

Roofing work means the hoisting, storage, application, and removal of roofing materials and equipment, including related insulation, sheet metal, and vapor barrier work, but not including the construction of the roof deck.

Safety-monitoring system means a safety system in which a competent person is responsible for recognizing and warning employees of fall hazards.

Self-retracting lifeline/lanyard means a deceleration device containing a drum-wound line which can be slowly extracted from, or retracted onto, the drum under slight tension during normal employee movement, and which, after onset of a fall, automatically locks the drum and arrests the fall.

Snaphook means a connector comprised of a hook-shaped member with a normally closed keeper, or similar arrangement, which may be opened to permit the hook to receive an object and, when released, automatically closes to retain the object. Snaphooks are generally one of two types:

(1) The locking type with a self-closing, self-locking keeper which remains closed and locked until unlocked and pressed open for connection or disconnection; or

(2) The non-locking type with a self-closing keeper which remains closed until pressed open for connection or disconnection. As of January 1, 1998, the use of a non-locking snaphook as part of personal fall arrest systems and positioning device systems is prohibited.

Steep roof means a roof having a slope greater than 4 in 12 (vertical to horizontal).

Toeboard means a low protective barrier that will prevent the fall of materials and equipment to lower levels and provide protection from falls for personnel.

Unprotected sides and edges means any side or edge (except at entrances to points of access) of a walking/working surface, e.g., floor, roof, ramp, or runway where there is no wall or guardrail system at least 39 inches (1.0 m) high.

Walking/working surface means any surface, whether horizontal or vertical on which an employee walks or works, including, but not limited to, floors, roofs, ramps, bridges, runways, formwork and concrete reinforcing steel but not including ladders, vehicles, or trailers, on which employees must be located in order to perform their job duties.

Warning line system means a barrier erected on a roof to warn employees that they are approaching an unprotected roof side or edge, and which designates an area in which roofing work may take place without the use of guardrail, body belt, or safety net systems to protect employees in the area.

Work area means that portion of a walking/working surface where job duties are being performed.

[59 FR 40730, Aug. 9, 1994, as amended at 60 FR 39255, Aug. 2, 1995; 66 FR 5265, Jan. 18, 2001; 75 FR 48133, Aug. 9, 2010; 79 FR 20696, Apr. 11, 2014]

§ 1926.501 Duty to have fall protection.

(a) *General.* (1) This section sets forth requirements for employers to provide fall protection systems. All fall protection required by this section shall conform to the criteria set forth in § 1926.502 of this subpart.

(2) The employer shall determine if the walking/working surfaces on which its employees are to work have the strength and structural integrity to support employees safely. Employees shall be allowed to work on those surfaces only when the surfaces have the requisite strength and structural integrity.

(b)(1) *Unprotected sides and edges.* Each employee on a walking/working surface (horizontal and vertical surface) with an unprotected side or edge which is 6 feet (1.8 m) or more above a lower level shall be protected from falling by the use of guardrail systems, safety net systems, or personal fall arrest systems.

(2) *Leading edges.* (i) Each employee who is constructing a leading edge 6 feet (1.8 m) or more above lower levels shall be protected from falling by guardrail systems, safety net systems, or personal fall arrest systems. Exception: When the employer can demonstrate that it is infeasible or creates a greater hazard to use these systems, the employer shall develop and implement a fall protection plan which meets the requirements of paragraph (k) of § 1926.502.

NOTE: There is a presumption that it is feasible and will not create a greater hazard to implement at least one of the above-listed fall protection systems. Accordingly, the employer has the burden of establishing that it is appropriate to implement a fall protection plan which complies with § 1926.502(k) for a particular workplace situation, in lieu of implementing any of those systems.

(ii) Each employee on a walking/working surface 6 feet (1.8 m) or more above a lower level where leading edges are under construction, but who is not engaged in the leading edge work, shall be protected from falling by a guardrail system, safety net system, or personal fall arrest system. If a guardrail system is chosen to provide the fall protection, and a controlled access zone has already been established for leading edge work, the control line may be used in lieu of a guardrail along the edge that parallels the leading edge.

(3) *Hoist areas.* Each employee in a hoist area shall be protected from falling 6 feet (1.8 m) or more to lower levels by guardrail systems or personal fall arrest systems. If guardrail systems, [or chain, gate, or guardrail] or portions thereof, are removed to facilitate the hoisting operation (e.g., during landing of materials), and an employee must lean through the access opening or out over the edge of the access opening (to receive or guide equipment and materials, for example), that employee shall be protected from fall hazards by a personal fall arrest system.

(4) *Holes.* (i) Each employee on walking/working surfaces shall be protected from falling through holes (including skylights) more than 6 feet (1.8 m) above lower levels, by personal fall arrest systems, covers, or guardrail systems erected around such holes.

(ii) Each employee on a walking/working surface shall be protected from tripping in or stepping into or through holes (including skylights) by covers.

(iii) Each employee on a walking/working surface shall be protected from objects falling through holes (including skylights) by covers.

(5) *Formwork and reinforcing steel.* Each employee on the face of formwork or reinforcing steel shall be protected from falling 6 feet (1.8 m) or more to lower levels by personal fall arrest systems, safety net systems, or positioning device systems.

(6) *Ramps, runways, and other walkways.* Each employee on ramps, runways, and other walkways shall be protected from falling 6 feet (1.8 m) or more to lower levels by guardrail systems.

(7) *Excavations.* (i) Each employee at the edge of an excavation 6 feet (1.8 m) or more in depth shall be protected from falling by guardrail systems, fences, or barricades when the excavations are not readily seen because of plant growth or other visual barrier;

(ii) Each employee at the edge of a well, pit, shaft, and similar excavation 6 feet (1.8 m) or more in depth shall be protected from falling by guardrail systems, fences, barricades, or covers.

(8) *Dangerous equipment.* (i) Each employee less than 6 feet (1.8 m) above dangerous equipment shall be protected from falling into or onto the dangerous equipment by guardrail systems or by equipment guards.

(ii) Each employee 6 feet (1.8 m) or more above dangerous equipment shall be protected from fall hazards by guardrail systems, personal fall arrest systems, or safety net systems.

(9) *Overhand bricklaying and related work.* (i) Except as otherwise provided in paragraph (b) of this section, each employee performing overhand bricklaying and related work 6 feet (1.8 m) or more above lower levels, shall be protected from falling by guardrail systems, safety net systems, personal fall arrest systems, or shall work in a controlled access zone.

(ii) Each employee reaching more than 10 inches (25 cm) below the level of the walking/working surface on which they are working, shall be protected from falling by a guardrail system, safety net system, or personal fall arrest system.

NOTE: Bricklaying operations performed on scaffolds are regulated by subpart L—Scaffolds of this part.

(10) *Roofing work on Low-slope roofs.* Except as otherwise provided in paragraph (b) of this section, each employee engaged in roofing activities on low-slope roofs, with unprotected sides and edges 6 feet (1.8 m) or more above lower levels shall be protected from falling by guardrail systems, safety net systems, personal fall arrest systems, or a combination of warning line system and guardrail system, warning line system and safety net system, or warning line system and personal fall arrest system, or warning line system and safety monitoring system. Or, on roofs 50-feet (15.25 m) or less in width (see appendix A to subpart M of this part), the use of a safety monitoring system alone [i.e. without the warning line system] is permitted.

(11) *Steep roofs.* Each employee on a steep roof with unprotected sides and edges 6 feet (1.8 m) or more above lower levels shall be protected from falling by guardrail systems with toeboards, safety net systems, or personal fall arrest systems.

(12) *Precast concrete erection.* Each employee engaged in the erection of precast concrete members (including, but not limited to the erection of wall panels, columns, beams, and floor and roof "tees") and related operations such as grouting of precast concrete members, who is 6 feet (1.8 m) or more above lower levels shall be protected from falling by guardrail systems, safety net systems, or personal fall arrest systems, unless another provision in paragraph (b) of this section provides for an alternative fall protection measure. Exception: When the employer can demonstrate that it is infeasible or creates a greater hazard to use these systems, the employer shall develop and implement a fall protection plan which meets the requirements of paragraph (k) of §1926.502.

NOTE: There is a presumption that it is feasible and will not create a greater hazard to implement at least one of the above-listed fall protection systems. Accordingly, the employer has the burden of establishing that it is appropriate to implement a fall protection plan which complies with §1926.502(k) for a particular workplace situation, in lieu of implementing any of those systems.

(13) *Residential construction.* Each employee engaged in residential construction activities 6 feet (1.8 m) or more above lower levels shall be protected by guardrail systems, safety net system, or personal fall arrest system unless another provision in paragraph (b) of this section provides for an alternative fall protection measure. Exception: When the employer can demonstrate that it is infeasible or creates a greater hazard to use these systems, the employer shall develop and implement a fall protection plan which meets the requirements of paragraph (k) of §1926.502.

NOTE: There is a presumption that it is feasible and will not create a greater hazard to implement at least one of the above-listed fall protection systems. Accordingly, the employer has the burden of establishing that it is appropriate to implement a fall protection plan which complies with §1926.502(k) for a particular workplace situation, in lieu of implementing any of those systems.

(14) *Wall openings.* Each employee working on, at, above, or near wall openings (including those with chutes attached) where the outside bottom edge of the wall opening is 6 feet (1.8 m)

or more above lower levels and the inside bottom edge of the wall opening is less than 39 inches (1.0 m) above the walking/working surface, shall be protected from falling by the use of a guardrail system, a safety net system, or a personal fall arrest system.

(15) *Walking/working surfaces not otherwise addressed.* Except as provided in § 1926.500(a)(2) or in § 1926.501 (b)(1) through (b)(14), each employee on a walking/working surface 6 feet (1.8 m) or more above lower levels shall be protected from falling by a guardrail system, safety net system, or personal fall arrest system.

(c) *Protection from falling objects.* When an employee is exposed to falling objects, the employer shall have each employee wear a hard hat and shall implement one of the following measures:

(1) Erect toeboards, screens, or guardrail systems to prevent objects from falling from higher levels; or,

(2) Erect a canopy structure and keep potential fall objects far enough from the edge of the higher level so that those objects would not go over the edge if they were accidentally displaced; or,

(3) Barricade the area to which objects could fall, prohibit employees from entering the barricaded area, and keep objects that may fall far enough away from the edge of a higher level so that those objects would not go over the edge if they were accidentally displaced.

§ 1926.502 Fall protection systems criteria and practices.

(a) *General.* (1) Fall protection systems required by this part shall comply with the applicable provisions of this section.

(2) Employers shall provide and install all fall protection systems required by this subpart for an employee, and shall comply with all other pertinent requirements of this subpart before that employee begins the work that necessitates the fall protection.

(b) *Guardrail systems.* Guardrail systems and their use shall comply with the following provisions:

(1) Top edge height of top rails, or equivalent guardrail system members, shall be 42 inches (1.1 m) plus or minus 3 inches (8 cm) above the walking/

working level. When conditions warrant, the height of the top edge may exceed the 45-inch height, provided the guardrail system meets all other criteria of this paragraph.

NOTE: When employees are using stilts, the top edge height of the top rail, or equivalent member, shall be increased an amount equal to the height of the stilts.

(2) Midrails, screens, mesh, intermediate vertical members, or equivalent intermediate structural members shall be installed between the top edge of the guardrail system and the walking/working surface when there is no wall or parapet wall at least 21 inches (53 cm) high.

(i) Midrails, when used, shall be installed at a height midway between the top edge of the guardrail system and the walking/working level.

(ii) Screens and mesh, when used, shall extend from the top rail to the walking/working level and along the entire opening between top rail supports.

(iii) Intermediate members (such as balusters), when used between posts, shall be not more than 19 inches (48 cm) apart.

(iv) Other structural members (such as additional midrails and architectural panels) shall be installed such that there are no openings in the guardrail system that are more than 19 inches (.5 m) wide.

(3) Guardrail systems shall be capable of withstanding, without failure, a force of at least 200 pounds (890 N) applied within 2 inches (5.1 cm) of the top edge, in any outward or downward direction, at any point along the top edge.

(4) When the 200 pound (890 N) test load specified in paragraph (b)(3) of this section is applied in a downward direction, the top edge of the guardrail shall not deflect to a height less than 39 inches (1.0 m) above the walking/working level. Guardrail system components selected and constructed in accordance with the appendix B to subpart M of this part will be deemed to meet this requirement.

(5) Midrails, screens, mesh, intermediate vertical members, solid panels, and equivalent structural members shall be capable of withstanding, without failure, a force of at least 150 pounds (666 N) applied in any downward

or outward direction at any point along the midrail or other member.

(6) Guardrail systems shall be so surfaced as to prevent injury to an employee from punctures or lacerations, and to prevent snagging of clothing.

(7) The ends of all top rails and midrails shall not overhang the terminal posts, except where such overhang does not constitute a projection hazard.

(8) Steel banding and plastic banding shall not be used as top rails or midrails.

(9) Top rails and midrails shall be at least one-quarter inch (0.6 cm) nominal diameter or thickness to prevent cuts and lacerations. If wire rope is used for top rails, it shall be flagged at not more than 6-foot (1.8 m) intervals with high-visibility material.

(10) When guardrail systems are used at hoisting areas, a chain, gate or removable guardrail section shall be placed across the access opening between guardrail sections when hoisting operations are not taking place.

(11) When guardrail systems are used at holes, they shall be erected on all unprotected sides or edges of the hole.

(12) When guardrail systems are used around holes used for the passage of materials, the hole shall have not more than two sides provided with removable guardrail sections to allow the passage of materials. When the hole is not in use, it shall be closed over with a cover, or a guardrail system shall be provided along all unprotected sides or edges.

(13) When guardrail systems are used around holes which are used as points of access (such as ladderways), they shall be provided with a gate, or be so offset that a person cannot walk directly into the hole.

(14) Guardrail systems used on ramps and runways shall be erected along each unprotected side or edge.

(15) Manila, plastic or synthetic rope being used for top rails or midrails shall be inspected as frequently as necessary to ensure that it continues to meet the strength requirements of paragraph (b)(3) of this section.

(c) *Safety net systems.* Safety net systems and their use shall comply with the following provisions:

(1) Safety nets shall be installed as close as practicable under the walking/working surface on which employees are working, but in no case more than 30 feet (9.1 m) below such level. When nets are used on bridges, the potential fall area from the walking/working surface to the net shall be unobstructed.

(2) Safety nets shall extend outward from the outermost projection of the work surface as follows:

Vertical distance from working level to horizontal plane of net	Minimum required horizontal distance of outer edge of net from the edge of the working surface
Up to 5 feet	8 feet.
More than 5 feet up to 10 feet	10 feet.
More than 10 feet	13 feet.

(3) Safety nets shall be installed with sufficient clearance under them to prevent contact with the surface or structures below when subjected to an impact force equal to the drop test specified in paragraph (c)(4) of this section.

(4) Safety nets and their installations shall be capable of absorbing an impact force equal to that produced by the drop test specified in paragraph (c)(4)(i) of this section.

(i) Except as provided in paragraph (c)(4)(ii) of this section, safety nets and safety net installations shall be drop-tested at the jobsite after initial installation and before being used as a fall protection system, whenever relocated, after major repair, and at 6-month intervals if left in one place. The drop-test shall consist of a 400 pound (180 kg) bag of sand 30 ±2 inches (76 ±5 cm) in diameter dropped into the net from the highest walking/working surface at which employees are exposed to fall hazards, but not from less than 42 inches (1.1 m) above that level.

(ii) When the employer can demonstrate that it is unreasonable to perform the drop-test required by paragraph (c)(4)(i) of this section, the employer (or a designated competent person) shall certify that the net and net installation is in compliance with the provisions of paragraphs (c)(3) and (c)(4)(i) of this section by preparing a certification record prior to the net being used as a fall protection system. The certification record must include an identification of the net and net installation for which the certification record is being prepared; the date that it was determined that the identified net and net installation were in compliance with paragraph (c)(3) of this section and the signature of the person making the determination and certification. The most recent certification record for each net and net installation shall be available at the jobsite for inspection.

(5) Defective nets shall not be used. Safety nets shall be inspected at least once a week for wear, damage, and other deterioration. Defective components shall be removed from service. Safety nets shall also be inspected after any occurrence which could affect the integrity of the safety net system.

(6) Materials, scrap pieces, equipment, and tools which have fallen into the safety net shall be removed as soon as possible from the net and at least before the next work shift.

(7) The maximum size of each safety net mesh opening shall not exceed 36 square inches (230 cm^2) nor be longer than 6 inches (15 cm) on any side, and the opening, measured center-to-center of mesh ropes or webbing, shall not be longer than 6 inches (15 cm). All mesh crossings shall be secured to prevent enlargement of the mesh opening.

(8) Each safety net (or section of it) shall have a border rope for webbing with a minimum breaking strength of 5,000 pounds (22.2 kN).

(9) Connections between safety net panels shall be as strong as integral net components and shall be spaced not more than 6 inches (15 cm) apart.

(d) *Personal fall arrest systems.* Personal fall arrest systems and their use shall comply with the provisions set forth below. Effective January 1, 1998, body belts are not acceptable as part of a personal fall arrest system. Note: The use of a body belt in a positioning device system is acceptable and is regulated under paragraph (e) of this section.

(1) Connectors shall be drop forged, pressed or formed steel, or made of equivalent materials.

(2) Connectors shall have a corrosion-resistant finish, and all surfaces and edges shall be smooth to prevent damage to interfacing parts of the system.

(3) Dee-rings and snaphooks shall have a minimum tensile strength of 5,000 pounds (22.2 kN).

(4) Dee-rings and snaphooks shall be proof-tested to a minimum tensile load of 3,600 pounds (16 kN) without cracking, breaking, or taking permanent deformation.

(5) Snaphooks shall be sized to be compatible with the member to which they are connected to prevent unintentional disengagement of the snaphook by depression of the snaphook keeper by the connected member, or shall be a locking type snaphook designed and used to prevent disengagement of the snaphook by the contact of the snaphook keeper by the connected member. Effective January 1, 1998, only locking type snaphooks shall be used.

(6) Unless the snaphook is a locking type and designed for the following connections, snaphooks shall not be engaged:

(i) directly to webbing, rope or wire rope;

(ii) to each other;

(iii) to a Dee-ring to which another snaphook or other connector is attached;

(iv) to a horizontal lifeline; or

(v) to any object which is incompatibly shaped or dimensioned in relation to the snaphook such that unintentional disengagement could occur by the connected object being able to depress the snaphook keeper and release itself.

(7) On suspended scaffolds or similar work platforms with horizontal lifelines which may become vertical lifelines, the devices used to connect to a horizontal lifeline shall be capable of locking in both directions on the lifeline.

(8) Horizontal lifelines shall be designed, installed, and used, under the supervision of a qualified person, as part of a complete personal fall arrest system, which maintains a safety factor of at least two.

(9) Lanyards and vertical lifelines shall have a minimum breaking strength of 5,000 pounds (22.2 kN).

(10) (i) Except as provided in paragraph (d)(10)(ii) of this section, when vertical lifelines are used, each employee shall be attached to a separate lifeline.

(ii) During the construction of elevator shafts, two employees may be attached to the same lifeline in the hoistway, provided both employees are working atop a false car that is equipped with guardrails; the strength of the lifeline is 10,000 pounds [5,000 pounds per employee attached] (44.4 kN); and all other criteria specified in this paragraph for lifelines have been met.

(11) Lifelines shall be protected against being cut or abraded.

(12) Self-retracting lifelines and lanyards which automatically limit free fall distance to 2 feet (0.61 m) or less shall be capable of sustaining a minimum tensile load of 3,000 pounds (13.3 kN) applied to the device with the lifeline or lanyard in the fully extended position.

(13) Self-retracting lifelines and lanyards which do not limit free fall distance to 2 feet (0.61 m) or less, ripstitch lanyards, and tearing and deforming lanyards shall be capable of sustaining a minimum tensile load of 5,000 pounds (22.2 kN) applied to the device with the lifeline or lanyard in the fully extended position.

(14) Ropes and straps (webbing) used in lanyards, lifelines, and strength components of body belts and body harnesses shall be made from synthetic fibers.

(15) Anchorages used for attachment of personal fall arrest equipment shall be independent of any anchorage being used to support or suspend platforms and capable of supporting at least 5,000 pounds (22.2 kN) per employee attached, or shall be designed, installed, and used as follows:

(i) as part of a complete personal fall arrest system which maintains a safety factor of at least two; and

(ii) under the supervision of a qualified person.

(16) Personal fall arrest systems, when stopping a fall, shall:

(i) limit maximum arresting force on an employee to 900 pounds (4 kN) when used with a body belt;

(ii) limit maximum arresting force on an employee to 1,800 pounds (8 kN) when used with a body harness;

(iii) be rigged such that an employee can neither free fall more than 6 feet (1.8 m), nor contact any lower level;

(iv) bring an employee to a complete stop and limit maximum deceleration distance an employee travels to 3.5 feet (1.07 m); and,

(v) have sufficient strength to withstand twice the potential impact energy of an employee free falling a distance of 6 feet (1.8 m), or the free fall distance permitted by the system, whichever is less.

NOTE: If the personal fall arrest system meets the criteria and protocols contained in appendix C to subpart M, and if the system is being used by an employee having a combined person and tool weight of less than 310 pounds (140 kg), the system will be considered to be in compliance with the provisions of paragraph (d)(16) of this section. If the system is used by an employee having a combined tool and body weight of 310 pounds (140 kg) or more, then the employer must appropriately modify the criteria and protocols of the appendix to provide proper protection for such heavier weights, or the system will not be deemed to be in compliance with the requirements of paragraph (d)(16) of this section.

(17) The attachment point of the body belt shall be located in the center of the wearer's back. The attachment point of the body harness shall be located in the center of the wearer's back near shoulder level, or above the wearer's head.

(18) Body belts, harnesses, and components shall be used only for employee protection (as part of a personal fall arrest system or positioning device system) and not to hoist materials.

(19) Personal fall arrest systems and components subjected to impact loading shall be immediately removed from service and shall not be used again for employee protection until inspected and determined by a competent person to be undamaged and suitable for reuse.

(20) The employer shall provide for prompt rescue of employees in the event of a fall or shall assure that employees are able to rescue themselves.

(21) Personal fall arrest systems shall be inspected prior to each use for wear, damage and other deterioration, and defective components shall be removed from service.

(22) Body belts shall be at least one and five-eighths (1⅝) inches (4.1 cm) wide.

(23) Personal fall arrest systems shall not be attached to guardrail systems,

nor shall they be attached to hoists except as specified in other subparts of this part.

(24) When a personal fall arrest system is used at hoist areas, it shall be rigged to allow the movement of the employee only as far as the edge of the walking/working surface.

(e) *Positioning device systems.* Positioning device systems and their use shall conform to the following provisions:

(1) Positioning devices shall be rigged such that an employee cannot free fall more than 2 feet (.6 m).

(2) Positioning devices shall be secured to an anchorage capable of supporting at least twice the potential impact load of an employee's fall or 3,000 pounds (13.3 kN), whichever is greater.

(3) Connectors shall be drop forged, pressed or formed steel, or made of equivalent materials.

(4) Connectors shall have a corrosion-resistant finish, and all surfaces and edges shall be smooth to prevent damage to interfacing parts of this system.

(5) Connecting assemblies shall have a minimum tensile strength of 5,000 pounds (22.2 kN)

(6) Dee-rings and snaphooks shall be proof-tested to a minimum tensile load of 3,600 pounds (16 kN) without cracking, breaking, or taking permanent deformation.

(7) Snaphooks shall be sized to be compatible with the member to which they are connected to prevent unintentional disengagement of the snaphook by depression of the snaphook keeper by the connected member, or shall be a locking type snaphook designed and used to prevent disengagement of the snaphook by the contact of the snaphook keeper by the connected member. As of January 1, 1998, only locking type snaphooks shall be used.

(8) Unless the snaphook is a locking type and designed for the following connections, snaphooks shall not be engaged:

(i) directly to webbing, rope or wire rope;

(ii) to each other;

(iii) to a Dee-ring to which another snaphook or other connector is attached;

(iv) to a horizontal lifeline; or

(v) to any object which is incompatibly shaped or dimensioned in relation to the snaphook such that unintentional disengagement could occur by the connected object being able to depress the snaphook keeper and release itself.

(9) Positioning device systems shall be inspected prior to each use for wear, damage, and other deterioration, and defective components shall be removed from service.

(10) Body belts, harnesses, and components shall be used only for employee protection (as part of a personal fall arrest system or positioning device system) and not to hoist materials.

(f) *Warning line systems.* Warning line systems [See § 1926.501(b)(10)] and their use shall comply with the following provisions:

(1) The warning line shall be erected around all sides of the roof work area.

(i) When mechanical equipment is not being used, the warning line shall be erected not less than 6 feet (1.8 m) from the roof edge.

(ii) When mechanical equipment is being used, the warning line shall be erected not less than 6 feet (1.8 m) from the roof edge which is parallel to the direction of mechanical equipment operation, and not less than 10 feet (3.1 m) from the roof edge which is perpendicular to the direction of mechanical equipment operation.

(iii) Points of access, materials handling areas, storage areas, and hoisting areas shall be connected to the work area by an access path formed by two warning lines.

(iv) When the path to a point of access is not in use, a rope, wire, chain, or other barricade, equivalent in strength and height to the warning line, shall be placed across the path at the point where the path intersects the warning line erected around the work area, or the path shall be offset such that a person cannot walk directly into the work area.

(2) Warning lines shall consist of ropes, wires, or chains, and supporting stanchions erected as follows:

(i) The rope, wire, or chain shall be flagged at not more than 6-foot (1.8 m) intervals with high-visibility material;

(ii) The rope, wire, or chain shall be rigged and supported in such a way that its lowest point (including sag) is no less than 34 inches (.9 m) from the walking/working surface and its highest point is no more than 39 inches (1.0 m) from the walking/working surface;

(iii) After being erected, with the rope, wire, or chain attached, stanchions shall be capable of resisting, without tipping over, a force of at least 16 pounds (71 N) applied horizontally against the stanchion, 30 inches (.8 m) above the walking/working surface, perpendicular to the warning line, and in the direction of the floor, roof, or platform edge;

(iv) The rope, wire, or chain shall have a minimum tensile strength of 500 pounds (2.22 kN), and after being attached to the stanchions, shall be capable of supporting, without breaking, the loads applied to the stanchions as prescribed in paragraph (f)(2)(iii) of this section; and

(v) The line shall be attached at each stanchion in such a way that pulling on one section of the line between stanchions will not result in slack being taken up in adjacent sections before the stanchion tips over.

(3) No employee shall be allowed in the area between a roof edge and a warning line unless the employee is performing roofing work in that area.

(4) Mechanical equipment on roofs shall be used or stored only in areas where employees are protected by a warning line system, guardrail system, or personal fall arrest system.

(g) *Controlled access zones.* Controlled access zones [See §1926.501(b)(9) and §1926.502(k)] and their use shall conform to the following provisions.

(1) When used to control access to areas where leading edge and other operations are taking place the controlled access zone shall be defined by a control line or by any other means that restricts access.

(i) When control lines are used, they shall be erected not less than 6 feet (1.8 m) nor more than 25 feet (7.7 m) from the unprotected or leading edge, except when erecting precast concrete members.

(ii) When erecting precast concrete members, the control line shall be erected not less than 6 feet (1.8 m) nor more than 60 feet (18 m) or half the length of the member being erected, whichever is less, from the leading edge.

(iii) The control line shall extend along the entire length of the unprotected or leading edge and shall be approximately parallel to the unprotected or leading edge.

(iv) The control line shall be connected on each side to a guardrail system or wall.

(2) When used to control access to areas where overhand bricklaying and related work are taking place:

(i) The controlled access zone shall be defined by a control line erected not less than 10 feet (3.1 m) nor more than 15 feet (4.5 m) from the working edge.

(ii) The control line shall extend for a distance sufficient for the controlled access zone to enclose all employees performing overhand bricklaying and related work at the working edge and shall be approximately parallel to the working edge.

(iii) Additional control lines shall be erected at each end to enclose the controlled access zone.

(iv) Only employees engaged in overhand bricklaying or related work shall be permitted in the controlled access zone.

(3) Control lines shall consist of ropes, wires, tapes, or equivalent materials, and supporting stanchions as follows:

(i) Each line shall be flagged or otherwise clearly marked at not more than 6-foot (1.8 m) intervals with high-visibility material.

(ii) Each line shall be rigged and supported in such a way that its lowest point (including sag) is not less than 39 inches (1 m) from the walking/working surface and its highest point is not more than 45 inches (1.3 m) [50 inches (1.3 m) when overhand bricklaying operations are being performed] from the walking/working surface.

(iii) Each line shall have a minimum breaking strength of 200 pounds (.88 kN).

(4) On floors and roofs where guardrail systems are not in place prior to the beginning of overhand bricklaying operations, controlled access zones shall be enlarged, as necessary, to enclose all points of access, material handling areas, and storage areas.

(5) On floors and roofs where guardrail systems are in place, but need to be removed to allow overhand bricklaying work or leading edge work to take place, only that portion of the guardrail necessary to accomplish that day's work shall be removed.

(h) *Safety monitoring systems.* Safety monitoring systems [See §§ 1926.501(b)(10) and 1926.502(k)] and their use shall comply with the following provisions:

(1) The employer shall designate a competent person to monitor the safety of other employees and the employer shall ensure that the safety monitor complies with the following requirements:

(i) The safety monitor shall be competent to recognize fall hazards;

(ii) The safety monitor shall warn the employee when it appears that the employee is unaware of a fall hazard or is acting in an unsafe manner;

(iii) The safety monitor shall be on the same walking/working surface and within visual sighting distance of the employee being monitored;

(iv) The safety monitor shall be close enough to communicate orally with the employee; and

(v) The safety monitor shall not have other responsibilities which could take the monitor's attention from the monitoring function.

(2) Mechanical equipment shall not be used or stored in areas where safety monitoring systems are being used to monitor employees engaged in roofing operations on low-slope roofs.

(3) No employee, other than an employee engaged in roofing work [on low-sloped roofs] or an employee covered by a fall protection plan, shall be allowed in an area where an employee is being protected by a safety monitoring system.

(4) Each employee working in a controlled access zone shall be directed to comply promptly with fall hazard warnings from safety monitors.

(i) *Covers.* Covers for holes in floors, roofs, and other walking/working surfaces shall meet the following requirements:

(1) Covers located in roadways and vehicular aisles shall be capable of supporting, without failure, at least twice the maximum axle load of the largest vehicle expected to cross over the cover.

(2) All other covers shall be capable of supporting, without failure, at least twice the weight of employees, equipment, and materials that may be imposed on the cover at any one time.

(3) All covers shall be secured when installed so as to prevent accidental displacement by the wind, equipment, or employees.

(4) All covers shall be color coded or they shall be marked with the word "HOLE" or "COVER" to provide warning of the hazard.

NOTE: This provision does not apply to cast iron manhole covers or steel grates used on streets or roadways.

(j) *Protection from falling objects.* Falling object protection shall comply with the following provisions:

(1) Toeboards, when used as falling object protection, shall be erected along the edge of the overhead walking/working surface for a distance sufficient to protect employees below.

(2) Toeboards shall be capable of withstanding, without failure, a force of at least 50 pounds (222 N) applied in any downward or outward direction at any point along the toeboard.

(3) Toeboards shall be a minimum of 3½ inches (9 cm) in vertical height from their top edge to the level of the walking/working surface. They shall have not more than ¼ inch (0.6 cm) clearance above the walking/working surface. They shall be solid or have openings not over 1 inch (2.5 cm) in greatest dimension.

(4) Where tools, equipment, or materials are piled higher than the top edge of a toeboard, paneling or screening shall be erected from the walking/working surface or toeboard to the top of a guardrail system's top rail or midrail, for a distance sufficient to protect employees below.

(5) Guardrail systems, when used as falling object protection, shall have all openings small enough to prevent passage of potential falling objects.

(6) During the performance of overhand bricklaying and related work:

(i) No materials or equipment except masonry and mortar shall be stored within 4 feet (1.2 m) of the working edge.

(ii) Excess mortar, broken or scattered masonry units, and all other materials and debris shall be kept clear from the work area by removal at regular intervals.

(7) During the performance of roofing work:

(i) Materials and equipment shall not be stored within 6 feet (1.8 m) of a roof edge unless guardrails are erected at the edge.

(ii) Materials which are piled, grouped, or stacked near a roof edge shall be stable and self-supporting.

(8) Canopies, when used as falling object protection, shall be strong enough to prevent collapse and to prevent penetration by any objects which may fall onto the canopy.

(k) *Fall protection plan.* This option is available only to employees engaged in leading edge work, precast concrete erection work, or residential construction work (See §1926.501(b)(2), (b)(12), and (b)(13)) who can demonstrate that it is infeasible or it creates a greater hazard to use conventional fall protection equipment. The fall protection plan must conform to the following provisions.

(1) The fall protection plan shall be prepared by a qualified person and developed specifically for the site where the leading edge work, precast concrete work, or residential construction work is being performed and the plan must be maintained up to date.

(2) Any changes to the fall protection plan shall be approved by a qualified person.

(3) A copy of the fall protection plan with all approved changes shall be maintained at the job site.

(4) The implementation of the fall protection plan shall be under the supervision of a competent person.

(5) The fall protection plan shall document the reasons why the use of conventional fall protection systems (guardrail systems, personal fall arrest systems, or safety nets systems) are infeasible or why their use would create a greater hazard.

(6) The fall protection plan shall include a written discussion of other measures that will be taken to reduce or eliminate the fall hazard for workers who cannot be provided with protection from the conventional fall protec-

tion systems. For example, the employer shall discuss the extent to which scaffolds, ladders, or vehicle mounted work platforms can be used to provide a safer working surface and thereby reduce the hazard of falling.

(7) The fall protection plan shall identify each location where conventional fall protection methods cannot be used. These locations shall then be classified as controlled access zones and the employer must comply with the criteria in paragraph (g) of this section.

(8) Where no other alternative measure has been implemented, the employer shall implement a safety monitoring system in conformance with §1926.502(h).

(9) The fall protection plan must include a statement which provides the name or other method of identification for each employee who is designated to work in controlled access zones. No other employees may enter controlled access zones.

(10) In the event an employee falls, or some other related, serious incident occurs, (e.g., a near miss) the employer shall investigate the circumstances of the fall or other incident to determine if the fall protection plan needs to be changed (e.g. new practices, procedures, or training) and shall implement those changes to prevent similar types of falls or incidents.

§1926.503 Training requirements.

The following training provisions supplement and clarify the requirements of §1926.21 regarding the hazards addressed in subpart M of this part.

(a) *Training Program.* (1) The employer shall provide a training program for each employee who might be exposed to fall hazards. The program shall enable each employee to recognize the hazards of falling and shall train each employee in the procedures to be followed in order to minimize these hazards.

(2) The employer shall assure that each employee has been trained, as necessary, by a competent person qualified in the following areas:

(i) The nature of fall hazards in the work area;

(ii) The correct procedures for erecting, maintaining, disassembling, and inspecting the fall protection systems to be used;

(iii) The use and operation of guardrail systems, personal fall arrest systems, safety net systems, warning line systems, safety monitoring systems, controlled access zones, and other protection to be used;

(iv) The role of each employee in the safety monitoring system when this system is used;

(v) The limitations on the use of mechanical equipment during the performance of roofing work on low-sloped roofs;

(vi) The correct procedures for the handling and storage of equipment and materials and the erection of overhead protection; and

(vii) The role of employees in fall protection plans;

(viii) The standards contained in this subpart.

(b) *Certification of training.* (1) The employer shall verify compliance with paragraph (a) of this section by preparing a written certification record. The written certification record shall contain the name or other identity of the employee trained, the date(s) of the training, and the signature of the person who conducted the training or the signature of the employer. If the employer relies on training conducted by another employer or completed prior to the effective date of this section, the certification record shall indicate the date the employer determined the prior training was adequate rather than the date of actual training.

(2) The latest training certification shall be maintained.

(c) *Retraining.* When the employer has reason to believe that any affected employee who has already been trained does not have the understanding and skill required by paragraph (a) of this section, the employer shall retrain each such employee. Circumstances where retraining is required include, but are not limited to, situations where:

(1) Changes in the workplace render previous training obsolete; or

(2) Changes in the types of fall protection systems or equipment to be used render previous training obsolete; or

(3) Inadequacies in an affected employee's knowledge or use of fall protection systems or equipment indicate that the employee has not retained the requisite understanding or skill.

NOTE: The following appendices to subpart M of this part serve as non-mandatory guidelines to assist employers in complying with the appropriate requirements of subpart M of this part.

APPENDIX A TO SUBPART M OF PART 1926—DETERMINING ROOF WIDTHS

Non-mandatory Guidelines for Complying With § 1926.501(b)(10)

(1) This appendix serves as a guideline to assist employers complying with the requirements of § 1926.501(b)(10). Section 1910.501(b)(10) allows the use of a safety monitoring system alone as a means of providing fall protection during the performance of roofing operations on low-sloped roofs 50 feet (15.25 m) or less in width. Each example in the appendix shows a roof plan or plans and indicates where each roof or roof area is to be measured to determine its width. Section views or elevation views are shown where appropriate. Some examples show "correct" and "incorrect" subdivisions of irregularly shaped roofs divided into smaller, regularly shaped areas. In all examples, the dimension selected to be the width of an area is the lesser of the two primary dimensions of the area, as viewed from above. Example A shows that on a simple rectangular roof, width is the lesser of the two primary overall dimensions. This is also the case with roofs which are sloped toward or away from the roof center, as shown in Example B.

(2) Many roofs are not simple rectangles. Such roofs may be broken down into subareas as shown in Example C. The process of dividing a roof area can produce many different configurations. Example C gives the general rule of using dividing lines of minimum length to minimize the size and number of the areas which are potentially less than 50 feet (15.25 m) wide. The intent is to minimize the number of roof areas where safety monitoring systems alone are sufficient protection.

(3) Roofs which are comprised of several separate, non-contiguous roof areas, as in Example D, may be considered as a series of individual roofs. Some roofs have penthouses, additional floors, courtyard openings, or similar architectural features; Example E shows how the rule for dividing roofs into subareas is applied to such configurations. Irregular, non-rectangular roofs must be considered on an individual basis, as shown in Example F.

EXAMPLE A: RECTANGULAR SHAPED ROOFS

EXAMPLE B: SLOPED RECTANGULAR SHAPED ROOFS

EXAMPLE C: IRREGULARLY SHAPED ROOFS WITH RECTANGULAR SHAPED SECTIONS

Such roofs are to be divided into sub-areas by using dividing lines of minimum length to minimize the size and number of the areas which are potentially less than or equal to 50 feet (15.25 meters) in width, in order to limit the size of roof areas where the safety monitoring system alone can be used [1926.502(b)(10)]. Dotted lines are used in the examples to show the location of dividing lines. W denotes incorrect measurements of width.

329

Correct

Incorrect

Correct

Incorrect

Correct

Incorrect

EXAMPLE D: SEPARATE, NON-CONTIGUOUS ROOF AREAS

1.

PLAN

SECTION A-A

FIREWALL PARAPET

2.

PLAN

ELEVATION

EXAMPLE E: ROOFS WITH PENTHOUSES, OPEN COURTYARDS, ADDITIONAL FLOORS, ETC.

Such roofs are to be divided into sub-areas by using dividing lines of minimum length to minimize the size and number of the areas which are potentially less than or equal to 50 feet (15.25 meters) in width, in order to limit the size of roof areas where the safety monitoring system alone can be used [1926.502(b)(10)]. Dotted lines are used in the examples to show the location of dividing

331

lines. W denotes incorrect measurements of width.

Correct

Incorrect

EXAMPLE F: IRREGULAR, NON-RECTANGULAR SHAPED ROOFS

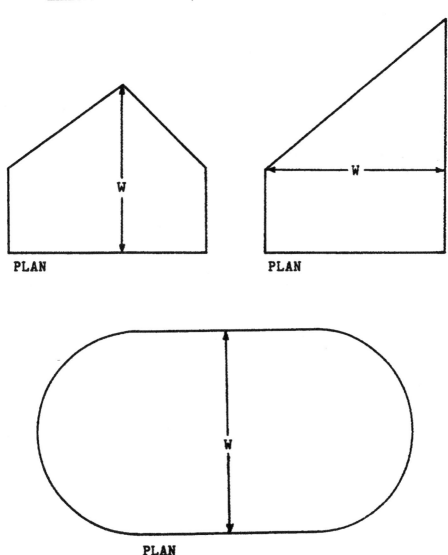

APPENDIX B TO SUBPART M OF PART
1926—GUARDRAIL SYSTEMS

*Non-Mandatory Guidelines for Complying with
§ 1926.502(b)*

The standard requires guardrail systems and components to be designed and built to meet the requirements of § 1926.502 (b) (3), (4), and (5). This appendix serves as a non-mandatory guideline to assist employers in complying with these requirements. An employer may use these guidelines as a starting point for designing guardrail systems. However, the guidelines do not provide all the information necessary to build a complete system, and the employer is still responsible for designing and assembling these components in such a way that the completed system will meet the requirements of § 1926.502(b) (3), (4), and (5). Components for which no specific

333

guidelines are given in this appendix (e.g., joints, base connections, components made with other materials, and components with other dimensions) must also be designed and constructed in such a way that the completed system meets the requirements of §1926.502.

(1) For wood railings: Wood components shall be minimum 1500 lb-ft/in² fiber (stress grade) construction grade lumber; the posts shall be at least 2-inch by 4-inch (5 cm×10 cm) lumber spaced not more than 8 feet (2.4 m) apart on centers; the top rail shall be at least 2-inch by 4-inch (5 cm×10 cm) lumber, the intermediate rail shall be at least 1-inch by 6-inch (2.5 cm×15 cm) lumber. All lumber dimensions are nominal sizes as provided by the American Softwood Lumber Standards, dated January 1970.

(2) For pipe railings: posts, top rails, and intermediate railings shall be at least one and one-half inches nominal diameter (schedule 40 pipe) with posts spaced not more than 8 feet (2.4 m) apart on centers.

(3) For structural steel railings: posts, top rails, and intermediate rails shall be at least 2-inch by 2-inch (5 cm×10 cm) by ⅜-inch (1.1 cm) angles, with posts spaced not more than 8 feet (2.4 m) apart on centers.

APPENDIX C TO SUBPART M OF PART 1926—PERSONAL FALL ARREST SYSTEMS

Non-Mandatory Guidelines for Complying With §1926.502(d)

I. *Test methods for personal fall arrest systems and positioning device systems*—(a) *General.* This appendix serves as a non-mandatory guideline to assist employers comply with the requirements in §1926.502(d). Paragraphs (b), (c), (d) and (e) of this appendix describe test procedures which may be used to determine compliance with the requirements in §1926.502 (d)(16). As noted in appendix D of this subpart, the test methods listed here in appendix C can also be used to assist employers comply with the requirements in §1926.502(e) (3) and (4) for positioning device systems.

(b) *General conditions for all tests in the appendix to §1926.502(d).* (1) Lifelines, lanyards and deceleration devices should be attached to an anchorage and connected to the body-belt or body harness in the same manner as they would be when used to protect employees.

(2) The anchorage should be rigid, and should not have a deflection greater than 0.04 inches (1 mm) when a force of 2,250 pounds (10 kN) is applied.

(3) The frequency response of the load measuring instrumentation should be 500 Hz.

(4) The test weight used in the strength and force tests should be a rigid, metal, cylindrical or torso-shaped object with a girth of 38 inches plus or minus 4 inches (96 cm plus or minus 10 cm).

(5) The lanyard or lifeline used to create the free fall distance should be supplied with the system, or in its absence, the least elastic lanyard or lifeline available to be used with the system.

(6) The test weight for each test should be hoisted to the required level and should be quickly released without having any appreciable motion imparted to it.

(7) The system's performance should be evaluated taking into account the range of environmental conditions for which it is designed to be used.

(8) Following the test, the system need not be capable of further operation.

(c) *Strength test.* (1) During the testing of all systems, a test weight of 300 pounds plus or minus 5 pounds (135 kg plus or minus 2.5 kg) should be used. (See paragraph (b)(4) of this section.)

(2) The test consists of dropping the test weight once. A new unused system should be used for each test.

(3) For lanyard systems, the lanyard length should be 6 feet plus or minus 2 inches (1.83 m plus or minus 5 cm) as measured from the fixed anchorage to the attachment on the body belt or body harness.

(4) For rope-grab-type deceleration systems, the length of the lifeline above the centerline of the grabbing mechanism to the lifeline's anchorage point should not exceed 2 feet (0.61 m).

(5) For lanyard systems, for systems with deceleration devices which do not automatically limit free fall distance to 2 feet (0.61 m) or less, and for systems with deceleration devices which have a connection distance in excess of 1 foot (0.3 m) (measured between the centerline of the lifeline and the attachment point to the body belt or harness), the test weight should be rigged to free fall a distance of 7.5 feet (2.3 m) from a point that is 1.5 feet (.46 m) above the anchorage point, to its hanging location (6 feet below the anchorage). The test weight should fall without interference, obstruction, or hitting the floor or ground during the test. In some cases a non-elastic wire lanyard of sufficient length may need to be added to the system (for test purposes) to create the necessary free fall distance.

(6) For deceleration device systems with integral lifelines or lanyards which automatically limit free fall distance to 2 feet (0.61 m) or less, the test weight should be rigged to free fall a distance of 4 feet (1.22 m).

(7) Any weight which detaches from the belt or harness has failed the strength test.

(d) *Force test*—(1) *General.* The test consists of dropping the respective test weight once as specified in paragraph (d)(2)(i) or (d)(3)(i) of this section. A new, unused system should be used for each test.

(2) *For lanyard systems.* (i) A test weight of 220 pounds plus or minus 3 pounds (100 kg plus or minus 1.6 kg) should be used. (See paragraph (b)(4) of this appendix).

(ii) Lanyard length should be 6 feet plus or minus two inches (1.83 m plus or minus 5 cm) as measured from the fixed anchorage to the attachment on the body belt or body harness.

(iii) The test weight should fall free from the anchorage level to its hanging location (a total of 6 feet (1.83 m) free fall distance) without interference, obstruction, or hitting the floor or ground during the test.

(3) *For all other systems.* (i) A test weight of 220 pounds plus or minus 3 pounds (100 kg plus or minus 1.6 kg) should be used. (See paragraph (b)(4) of this appendix)

(ii) The free fall distance to be used in the test should be the maximum fall distance physically permitted by the system during normal use conditions, up to a maximum free fall distance for the test weight of 6 feet (1.83 m), except as follows:

(A) For deceleration systems which have a connection link or lanyard, the test weight should free fall a distance equal to the connection distance (measured between the centerline of the lifeline and the attachment point to the body belt or harness).

(B) For deceleration device systems with integral lifelines or lanyards which automatically limit free fall distance to 2 feet (0.61 m) or less, the test weight should free fall a distance equal to that permitted by the system in normal use. (For example, to test a system with a self-retracting lifeline or lanyard, the test weight should be supported and the system allowed to retract the lifeline or lanyard as it would in normal use. The test weight would then be released and the force and deceleration distance measured).

(4) A system fails the force test if the recorded maximum arresting force exceeds 1,260 pounds (5.6 kN) when using a body belt, and/or exceeds 2,520 pounds (11.2 kN) when using a body harness.

(5) The maximum elongation and deceleration distance should be recorded during the force test.

(e) *Deceleration device tests—*(1) *General.* The device should be evaluated or tested under the environmental conditions, (such as rain, ice, grease, dirt, type of lifeline, etc.), for which the device is designed.

(2) *Rope-grab-type deceleration devices.* (i) Devices should be moved on a lifeline 1,000 times over the same length of line a distance of not less than 1 foot (30.5 cm), and the mechanism should lock each time.

(ii) Unless the device is permanently marked to indicate the type(s) of lifeline which must be used, several types (different diameters and different materials), of lifelines should be used to test the device.

(3) *Other self-activating-type deceleration devices.* The locking mechanisms of other self-activating-type deceleration devices designed for more than one arrest should lock each of 1,000 times as they would in normal service.

II. *Additional non-mandatory guidelines for personal fall arrest systems.* The following information constitutes additional guidelines for use in complying with requirements for a personal fall arrest system.

(a) *Selection and use considerations.* (1) The kind of personal fall arrest system selected should match the particular work situation, and any possible free fall distance should be kept to a minimum. Consideration should be given to the particular work environment. For example, the presence of acids, dirt, moisture, oil, grease, etc., and their effect on the system, should be evaluated. Hot or cold environments may also have an adverse effect on the system. Wire rope should not be used where an electrical hazard is anticipated. As required by the standard, the employer must plan to have means available to promptly rescue an employee should a fall occur, since the suspended employee may not be able to reach a work level independently.

(2) Where lanyards, connectors, and lifelines are subject to damage by work operations such as welding, chemical cleaning, and sandblasting, the component should be protected, or other securing systems should be used. The employer should fully evaluate the work conditions and environment (including seasonal weather changes) before selecting the appropriate personal fall protection system. Once in use, the system's effectiveness should be monitored. In some cases, a program for cleaning and maintenance of the system may be necessary.

(b) *Testing considerations.* Before purchasing or putting into use a personal fall arrest system, an employer should obtain from the supplier information about the system based on its performance during testing so that the employer can know if the system meets this standard. Testing should be done using recognized test methods. This appendix contains test methods recognized for evaluating the performance of fall arrest systems. Not all systems may need to be individually tested; the performance of some systems may be based on data and calculations derived from testing of similar systems, provided that enough information is available to demonstrate similarity of function and design.

(c) *Component compatibility considerations.* Ideally, a personal fall arrest system is designed, tested, and supplied as a complete system. However, it is common practice for lanyards, connectors, lifelines, deceleration devices, body belts and body harnesses to be interchanged since some components wear

335

out before others. The employer and employee should realize that not all components are interchangeable. For instance, a lanyard should not be connected between a body belt (or harness) and a deceleration device of the self-retracting type since this can result in additional free fall for which the system was not designed. Any substitution or change to a personal fall arrest system should be fully evaluated or tested by a competent person to determine that it meets the standard, before the modified system is put in use.

(d) *Employee training considerations.* Thorough employee training in the selection and use of personal fall arrest systems is imperative. Employees must be trained in the safe use of the system. This should include the following: application limits; proper anchoring and tie-off techniques; estimation of free fall distance, including determination of deceleration distance, and total fall distance to prevent striking a lower level; methods of use; and inspection and storage of the system. Careless or improper use of the equipment can result in serious injury or death. Employers and employees should become familiar with the material in this Appendix, as well as manufacturer's recommendations, before a system is used. Of uppermost importance is the reduction in strength caused by certain tie-offs (such as using knots, tying around sharp edges, etc.) and maximum permitted free fall distance. Also, to be stressed are the importance of inspections prior to use, the limitations of the equipment, and unique conditions at the worksite which may be important in determining the type of system to use.

(e) *Instruction considerations.* Employers should obtain comprehensive instructions from the supplier as to the system's proper use and application, including, where applicable:

(1) The force measured during the sample force test;

(2) The maximum elongation measured for lanyards during the force test;

(3) The deceleration distance measured for deceleration devices during the force test;

(4) Caution statements on critical use limitations;

(5) Application limits;

(6) Proper hook-up, anchoring and tie-off techniques, including the proper dee-ring or other attachment point to use on the body belt and harness for fall arrest;

(7) Proper climbing techniques;

(8) Methods of inspection, use, cleaning, and storage; and

(9) Specific lifelines which may be used. This information should be provided to employees during training.

(f) *Rescue considerations.* As required by §1926.502(d)(20), when personal fall arrest systems are used, the employer must assure that employees can be promptly rescued or can rescue themselves should a fall occur. The availability of rescue personnel, ladders or other rescue equipment should be evaluated. In some situations, equipment which allows employees to rescue themselves after the fall has been arrested may be desirable, such as devices which have descent capability.

(g) *Inspection considerations.* As required by §1926.502(d)(21), personal fall arrest systems must be regularly inspected. Any component with any significant defect, such as cuts, tears, abrasions, mold, or undue stretching; alterations or additions which might affect its efficiency; damage due to deterioration; contact with fire, acids, or other corrosives; distorted hooks or faulty hook springs; tongues unfitted to the shoulder of buckles; loose or damaged mountings; non-functioning parts; or wearing or internal deterioration in the ropes must be withdrawn from service immediately, and should be tagged or marked as unusable, or destroyed.

(h) *Tie-off considerations.* (1) One of the most important aspects of personal fall protection systems is fully planning the system *before* it is put into use. Probably the most overlooked component is planning for suitable anchorage points. Such planning should ideally be done before the structure or building is constructed so that anchorage points can be incorporated during construction for use later for window cleaning or other building maintenance. If properly planned, these anchorage points may be used *during* construction, as well as afterwards.

(i) Properly planned anchorages should be used if they are available. In some cases, anchorages must be installed immediately prior to use. In such cases, a registered professional engineer with experience in designing fall protection systems, or another qualified person with appropriate education and experience should design an anchor point to be installed.

(ii) In other cases, the Agency recognizes that there will be a need to devise an anchor point from existing structures. Examples of what might be appropriate anchor points are steel members or I-beams if an acceptable strap is available for the connection (do not use a lanyard with a snaphook clipped onto itself); large eye-bolts made of an appropriate grade steel; guardrails or railings if they have been designed for use as an anchor point; or masonry or wood members only if the attachment point is substantial and precautions have been taken to assure that bolts or other connectors will not pull through. A qualified person should be used to evaluate the suitable of these "make shift" anchorages with a focus on proper strength.

(2) Employers and employees should at all times be aware that the strength of a personal fall arrest system is based on its being attached to an anchoring system which does not reduce the strength of the system (such

as a properly dimensioned eye-bolt/snap-hook anchorage). Therefore, if a means of attachment is used that will reduce the strength of the system, that component should be replaced by a stronger one, but one that will also maintain the appropriate maximum arrest force characteristics.

(3) Tie-off using a knot in a rope lanyard or lifeline (at any location) can reduce the lifeline or lanyard strength by 50 percent or more. Therefore, a stronger lanyard or lifeline should be used to compensate for the weakening effect of the knot, or the lanyard length should be reduced (or the tie-off location raised) to minimize free fall distance, or the lanyard or lifeline should be replaced by one which has an appropriately incorporated connector to eliminate the need for a knot.

(4) Tie-off of a rope lanyard or lifeline around an "H" or "I" beam or similar support can reduce its strength as much as 70 percent due to the cutting action of the beam edges. Therefore, use should be made of a webbing lanyard or wire core lifeline around the beam; or the lanyard or lifeline should be protected from the edge; or free fall distance should be greatly minimized.

(5) Tie-off where the line passes over or around rough or sharp surfaces reduces strength drastically. Such a tie-off should be avoided or an alternative tie-off rigging should be used. Such alternatives may include use of a snap-hook/dee ring connection, wire rope tie-off, an effective padding of the surfaces, or an abrasion-resistance strap around or over the problem surface.

(6) Horizontal lifelines may, depending on their geometry and angle of sag, be subjected to greater loads than the impact load imposed by an attached component. When the angle of horizontal lifeline sag is less than 30 degrees, the impact force imparted to the lifeline by an attached lanyard is greatly amplified. For example, with a sag angle of 15 degrees, the force amplification is about 2:1 and at 5 degrees sag, it is about 6:1. Depending on the angle of sag, and the line's elasticity, the strength of the horizontal lifeline and the anchorages to which it is attached should be increased a number of times over that of the lanyard. Extreme care should be taken in considering a horizontal lifeline for multiple tie-offs. The reason for this is that in multiple tie-offs to a horizontal lifeline, if one employee falls, the movement of the falling employee and the horizontal lifeline during arrest of the fall may cause other employees to fall also. Horizontal lifeline and anchorage strength should be increased for each additional employee to be tied off. For these and other reasons, the design of systems using horizontal lifelines must only be done by qualified persons. Testing of installed lifelines and anchors prior to use is recommended.

(7) The strength of an eye-bolt is rated along the axis of the bolt and its strength is greatly reduced if the force is applied at an angle to this axis (in the direction of shear). Also, care should be exercised in selecting the proper diameter of the eye to avoid accidental disengagement of snap-hooks not designed to be compatible for the connection.

(8) Due to the significant reduction in the strength of the lifeline/lanyard (in some cases, as much as a 70 percent reduction), the sliding hitch knot (prusik) should not be used for lifeline/lanyard connections except in emergency situations where no other available system is practical. The "one-and-one" sliding hitch knot should never be used because it is unreliable in stopping a fall. The "two-and-two," or "three-and-three" knot (preferable) may be used in emergency situations; however, care should be taken to limit free fall distance to a minimum because of reduced lifeline/lanyard strength.

(i) *Vertical lifeline considerations.* As required by the standard, each employee must have a separate lifeline [except employees engaged in constructing elevator shafts who are permitted to have two employees on one lifeline] when the lifeline is vertical. The reason for this is that in multiple tie-offs to a single lifeline, if one employee falls, the movement of the lifeline during the arrest of the fall may pull other employees' lanyards, causing them to fall as well.

(j) *Snap-hook considerations.* (1) Although not required by this standard for all connections until January 1, 1998, locking snaphooks designed for connection to suitable objects (of sufficient strength) are highly recommended in lieu of the nonlocking type. Locking snaphooks incorporate a positive locking mechanism in addition to the spring loaded keeper, which will not allow the keeper to open under moderate pressure without someone first releasing the mechanism. Such a feature, properly designed, effectively prevents roll-out from occurring.

(2) As required by § 1926.502(d)(6), the following connections must be avoided (unless properly designed locking snaphooks are used) because they are conditions which can result in roll-out when a nonlocking snaphook is used:

(i) Direct connection of a snaphook to a horizontal lifeline.

(ii) Two (or more) snaphooks connected to one dee-ring.

(iii) Two snaphooks connected to each other.

(iv) A snaphook connected back on its integral lanyard.

(v) A snaphook connected to a webbing loop or webbing lanyard.

(vi) Improper dimensions of the dee-ring, rebar, or other connection point in relation to the snaphook dimensions which would allow the snaphook keeper to be depressed by a turning motion of the snaphook.

(k) *Free fall considerations.* The employer and employee should at all times be aware that a system's maximum arresting force is evaluated under normal use conditions established by the manufacturer, and in no case using a free fall distance in excess of 6 feet (1.8 m). A few extra feet of free fall can significantly increase the arresting force on the employee, possibly to the point of causing injury. Because of this, the free fall distance should be kept at a minimum, and, as required by the standard, in no case greater than 6 feet (1.8 m). To help assure this, the tie-off attachment point to the lifeline or anchor should be located at or above the connection point of the fall arrest equipment to belt or harness. (Since otherwise additional free fall distance is added to the length of the connecting means (i.e. lanyard)). Attaching to the working surface will often result in a free fall greater than 6 feet (1.8 m). For instance, if a 6 foot (1.8 m) lanyard is used, the total free fall distance will be the distance from the working level to the body belt (or harness) attachment point plus the 6 feet (1.8 m) of lanyard length. Another important consideration is that the arresting force which the fall system must withstand also goes up with greater distances of free fall, possibly exceeding the strength of the system.

(1) *Elongation and deceleration distance considerations.* Other factors involved in a proper tie-off are elongation and deceleration distance. During the arresting of a fall, a lanyard will experience a length of stretching or elongation, whereas activation of a deceleration device will result in a certain stopping distance. These distances should be available with the lanyard or device's instructions and must be added to the free fall distance to arrive at the total fall distance before an employee is fully stopped. The additional stopping distance may be very significant if the lanyard or deceleration device is attached near or at the end of a long lifeline, which may itself add considerable distance due to its own elongation. As required by the standard, sufficient distance to allow for all of these factors must also be maintained between the employee and obstructions below, to prevent an injury due to impact before the system fully arrests the fall. In addition, a minimum of 12 feet (3.7 m) of lifeline should be allowed below the securing point of a rope grab type deceleration device, and the end terminated to prevent the device from sliding off the lifeline. Alternatively, the lifeline should extend to the ground or the next working level below. These measures are suggested to prevent the worker from inadvertently moving past the end of the lifeline and having the rope grab become disengaged from the lifeline.

(m) *Obstruction considerations.* The location of the tie-off should also consider the hazard of obstructions in the potential fall path of the employee. Tie-offs which minimize the possibilities of exaggerated swinging should be considered. In addition, when a body belt is used, the employee's body will go through a horizontal position to a jack-knifed position during the arrest of all falls. Thus, obstructions which might interfere with this motion should be avoided or a severe injury could occur.

(n) *Other considerations.* Because of the design of some personal fall arrest systems, additional considerations may be required for proper tie-off. For example, heavy deceleration devices of the self-retracting type should be secured overhead in order to avoid the weight of the device having to be supported by the employee. Also, if self-retracting equipment is connected to a horizontal lifeline, the sag in the lifeline should be minimized to prevent the device from sliding down the lifeline to a position which creates a swing hazard during fall arrest. In all cases, manufacturer's instructions should be followed.

APPENDIX D TO SUBPART M OF PART 1926—POSITIONING DEVICE SYSTEMS

Non-Mandatory Guidelines for Complying With § 1926.502(e)

I. *Testing Methods For Positioning Device Systems.* This appendix serves as a non-mandatory guideline to assist employers comply with the requirements for positioning device systems in § 1926.502(e). Paragraphs (b), (c), (d) and (e) of appendix C of subpart M relating to § 1926.502(d)—Personal Fall Arrest Systems—set forth test procedures which may be used, along with the procedures listed below, to determine compliance with the requirements for positioning device systems in § 1926.502(e) (3) and (4) of subpart M.

(a) *General.* (1) Single strap positioning devices shall have one end attached to a fixed anchorage and the other end connected to a body belt or harness in the same manner as they would be used to protect employees. Double strap positioning devices, similar to window cleaner's belts, shall have one end of the strap attached to a fixed anchorage and the other end shall hang free. The body belt or harness shall be attached to the strap in the same manner as it would be used to protect employees. The two strap ends shall be adjusted to their maximum span.

(2) The fixed anchorage shall be rigid, and shall not have a deflection greater than .04 inches (1 mm) when a force of 2,250 pounds (10 kN) is applied.

(3) During the testing of all systems, a test weight of 250 pounds plus or minus 3 pounds (113 kg plus or minus 1.6 kg) shall be used. The weight shall be a rigid object with a girth of 38 inches plus or minus 4 inches (96 cm plus or minus 10 cm).

(4) Each test shall consist of dropping the specified weight one time without failure of

the system being tested. A new system shall be used for each test.

(5) The test weight for each test shall be hoisted exactly 4 feet (1.2 m above its "at rest" position), and shall be dropped so as to permit a vertical free fall of 4 feet (1.2 m).

(6) The test is failed whenever any breakage or slippage occurs which permits the weight to fall free of the system.

(7) Following the test, the system need not be capable of further operation; however, all such incapacities shall be readily apparent.

II. *Inspection Considerations.* As required in § 1926.502 (e)(5), positioning device systems must be regularly inspected. Any component with any significant defect, such as cuts, tears, abrasions, mold, or undue stretching; alterations or additions which might affect its efficiency; damage due to deterioration; contact with fire, acids, or other corrosives; distorted hooks or faulty hook springs; tongues unfitted to the shoulder of buckles; loose or damaged mountings; non-functioning parts; or wearing or internal deterioration in the ropes must be withdrawn from service immediately, and should be tagged or marked as unusable, or destroyed.

Appendix E to Subpart M of Part 1926—Sample Fall Protection Plan

Non-Mandatory Guidelines for Complying With § 1926.502(k)

Employers engaged in leading edge work, precast concrete construction work and residential construction work who can demonstrate that it is infeasible or creates a greater hazard to use conventional fall protection systems must develop and follow a fall protection plan. Below are sample fall protection plans developed for precast concrete construction and residential work that could be tailored to be site specific for other precast concrete or residential jobsite. This sample plan can be modified to be used for other work involving leading edge work. The sample plan outlines the elements that must be addressed in any fall protection plan. The reasons outlined in this sample fall protection plan are for illustrative purposes only and are not necessarily a valid, acceptable rationale (unless the conditions at the job site are the same as those covered by these sample plans) for not using conventional fall protection systems for a particular precast concrete or residential construction worksite. However, the sample plans provide guidance to employers on the type of information that is required to be discussed in fall protection plans.

SAMPLE FALL PROTECTION PLANS

Fall Protection Plan For Precast/Prestress Concrete Structures

This Fall Protection Plan is specific for the following project:

Location of Job _____
Erecting Company _____
Date Plan Prepared or Modified _____
Plan Prepared By _____
Plan Approved By _____
Plan Supervised By _____

The following Fall Protection Plan is a sample program prepared for the prevention of injuries associated with falls. A Fall Protection Plan must be developed and evaluated on a site by site basis. It is recommended that erectors discuss the written Fall Protection Plan with their OSHA Area Office prior to going on a jobsite.

I. Statement of Company Policy

(Company Name) is dedicated to the protection of its employees from on-the-job injuries. All employees of (Company Name) have the responsibility to work safely on the job. The purpose of this plan is: (a) To supplement our standard safety policy by providing safety standards specifically designed to cover fall protection on this job and; (b) to ensure that each employee is trained and made aware of the safety provisions which are to be implemented by this plan prior to the start of erection.

This Fall Protection Plan addresses the use of other than conventional fall protection at a number of areas on the project, as well as identifying specific activities that require non-conventional means of fall protection. These areas include:

a. Connecting activity (point of erection).

b. Leading edge work.

c. Unprotected sides or edge.

d. Grouting.

This plan is designed to enable employers and employees to recognize the fall hazards on this job and to establish the procedures that are to be followed in order to prevent falls to lower levels or through holes and openings in walking/working surfaces. Each employee will be trained in these procedures and strictly adhere to them except when doing so would expose the employee to a greater hazard. If, in the employee's opinion, this is the case, the employee is to notify the foreman of the concern and the concern addressed before proceeding.

Safety policy and procedure on any one project cannot be administered, implemented, monitored and enforced by any one individual. The total objective of a safe, accident free work environment can only be accomplished by a dedicated, concerted effort by every individual involved with the project from management down to the last employee. Each employee must understand

339

their value to the company; the costs of accidents, both monetary, physical, and emotional; the objective of the safety policy and procedures; the safety rules that apply to the safety policy and procedures; and what their individual role is in administering, implementing, monitoring, and compliance of their safety policy and procedures. This allows for a more personal approach to compliance through planning, training, understanding and cooperative effort, rather than by strict enforcement. If for any reason an unsafe act persists, strict enforcement will be implemented.

It is the responsibility of (name of competent person) to implement this Fall Protection Plan. (Name of Competent Person) is responsible for continual observational safety checks of their work operations and to enforce the safety policy and procedures. The foreman also is responsible to correct any unsafe acts or conditions immediately. It is the responsibility of the employee to understand and adhere to the procedures of this plan and to follow the instructions of the foreman. It is also the responsibility of the employee to bring to management's attention any unsafe or hazardous conditions or acts that may cause injury to either themselves or any other employees. Any changes to this Fall Protection Plan must be approved by (name of Qualified Person).

II. FALL PROTECTION SYSTEMS TO BE USED ON THIS PROJECT

Where conventional fall protection is infeasible or creates a greater hazard at the leading edge and during initial connecting activity, we plan to do this work using a safety monitoring system and expose only a minimum number of employees for the time necessary to actually accomplish the job. The maximum number of workers to be monitored by one safety monitor is six (6). We are designating the following trained employees as designated erectors and they are permitted to enter the controlled access zones and work without the use of conventional fall protection.

Safety monitor:
Designated erector:
Designated erector:
Designated erector:
Designated erector:
Designated erector:
Designated erector:

The safety monitor shall be identified by wearing an orange hard hat. The designated erectors will be identified by one of the following methods:

1. They will wear a blue colored arm band, or
2. They will wear a blue colored hard hat, or
3. They will wear a blue colored vest.

Only individuals with the appropriate experience, skills, and training will be authorized as designated erectors. All employees that will be working as designated erectors under the safety monitoring system shall have been trained and instructed in the following areas:

1. Recognition of the fall hazards in the work area (at the leading edge and when making initial connections—point of erection).

2. Avoidance of fall hazards using established work practices which have been made known to the employees.

3. Recognition of unsafe practices or working conditions that could lead to a fall, such as windy conditions.

4. The function, use, and operation of safety monitoring systems, guardrail systems, body belt/harness systems, control zones and other protection to be used.

5. The correct procedure for erecting, maintaining, disassembling and inspecting the system(s) to be used.

6. Knowledge of construction sequence or the erection plan.

A conference will take place prior to starting work involving all members of the erection crew, crane crew and supervisors of any other concerned contractors. This conference will be conducted by the precast concrete erection supervisor in charge of the project. During the pre-work conference, erection procedures and sequences pertinent to this job will be thoroughly discussed and safety practices to be used throughout the project will be specified. Further, all personnel will be informed that the controlled access zones are off limits to all personnel other than those designated erectors specifically trained to work in that area.

Safety Monitoring System

A safety monitoring system means a fall protection system in which a competent person is responsible for recognizing and warning employees of fall hazards. The duties of the safety monitor are to:

1. Warn by voice when approaching the open edge in an unsafe manner.

2. Warn by voice if there is a dangerous situation developing which cannot be seen by another person involved with product placement, such as a member getting out of control.

3. Make the designated erectors aware they are in a dangerous area.

4. Be competent in recognizing fall hazards.

5. Warn employees when they appear to be unaware of a fall hazard or are acting in an unsafe manner.

6. Be on the same walking/working surface as the monitored employees and within visual sighting distance of the monitored employees.

340

7. Be close enough to communicate orally with the employees.

8. Not allow other responsibilities to encumber monitoring. If the safety monitor becomes too encumbered with other responsibilities, the monitor shall (1) stop the erection process; and (2) turn over other responsibilities to a designated erector; or (3) turn over the safety monitoring function to another designated, competent person. The safety monitoring system shall not be used when the wind is strong enough to cause loads with large surface areas to swing out of radius, or result in loss of control of the load, or when weather conditions cause the walking-working surfaces to become icy or slippery.

Control Zone System

A controlled access zone means an area designated and clearly marked, in which leading edge work may take place without the use of guardrail, safety net or personal fall arrest systems to protect the employees in the area. Control zone systems shall comply with the following provisions:

1. When used to control access to areas where leading edge and other operations are taking place the controlled access zone shall be defined by a control line or by any other means that restricts access.

When control lines are used, they shall be erected not less than 6 feet (1.8 m) nor more than 60 feet (18 m) or half the length of the member being erected, whichever is less, from the leading edge.

2. The control line shall extend along the entire length of the unprotected or leading edge and shall be approximately parallel to the unprotected or leading edge.

3. The control line shall be connected on each side to a guardrail system or wall.

4. Control lines shall consist of ropes, wires, tapes, or equivalent materials, and supporting stanchions as follows:

5. Each line shall be flagged or otherwise clearly marked at not more than 6-foot (1.8 m) intervals with high- visibility material.

6. Each line shall be rigged and supported in such a way that its lowest point (including sag) is not less than 39 inches (1 m) from the walking/working surface and its highest point is not more than 45 inches (1.3 m) from the walking/working surface.

7. Each line shall have a minimum breaking strength of 200 pounds (.88 kN).

Holes

All openings greater than 12 in.×12 in. will have perimeter guarding or covering. All predetermined holes will have the plywood covers made in the precasters' yard and shipped with the member to the jobsite. Prior to cutting holes on the job, proper protection for the hole must be provided to protect the workers. Perimeter guarding or covers will not be removed without the approval of the erection foreman.

Precast concrete column erection through the existing deck requires that many holes be provided through this deck. These are to be covered and protected. Except for the opening being currently used to erect a column, all opening protection is to be left undisturbed. The opening being uncovered to erect a column will become part of the point of erection and will be addressed as part of this Fall Protection Plan. This uncovering is to be done at the erection foreman's direction and will only occur immediately prior to "feeding" the column through the opening. Once the end of the column is through the slab opening, there will no longer exist a fall hazard at this location.

III. IMPLEMENTATION OF FALL PROTECTION PLAN

The structure being erected is a multistory total precast concrete building consisting of columns, beams, wall panels and hollow core slabs and double tee floor and roof members. The following is a list of the products and erection situations on this job:

Columns

For columns 10 ft to 36 ft long, employees disconnecting crane hooks from columns will work from a ladder and wear a body belt/harness with lanyard and be tied off when both hands are needed to disconnect. For tying off, a vertical lifeline will be connected to the lifting eye at the top of the column, prior to lifting, to be used with a manually operated or mobile rope grab. For columns too high for the use of a ladder, 36 ft and higher, an added cable will be used to reduce the height of the disconnecting point so that a ladder can be used. This cable will be left in place until a point in erection that it can be removed safely. In some cases, columns will be unhooked from the crane by using an erection tube or shackle with a pull pin which is released from the ground after the column is stabilized.

The column will be adequately connected and/or braced to safely support the weight of a ladder with an employee on it.

Inverted Tee Beams

Employees erecting inverted tee beams, at a height of 6 to 40 ft, will erect the beam, make initial connections, and final alignment from a ladder. If the employee needs to reach over the side of the beam to bar or make an adjustment to the alignment of the beam, they will mount the beam and be tied off to the lifting device in the beam after ensuring the load has been stabilized on its bearing. To disconnect the crane from the beam an employee will stand a ladder against the beam. Because the use of ladders is not practical at heights above 40 ft, beams

341

will be initially placed with the use of tag lines and their final alignment made by a person on a manlift or similar employee positioning systems.

Spandrel Beams

Spandrel beams at the exterior of the building will be aligned as closely as possible with the use of tag lines with the final placement of the spandrel beam made from a ladder at the open end of the structure. A ladder will be used to make the initial connections and a ladder will be used to disconnect the crane. The other end of the beam will be placed by the designated erector from the double tee deck under the observation of the safety monitor.

The beams will be adequately connected and/or braced to safely support the weight of a ladder with an employee on it.

Floor and Roof Members

During installation of the precast concrete floor and/or roof members, the work deck continuously increases in area as more and more units are being erected and positioned. Thus, the unprotected floor/roof perimeter is constantly modified with the leading edge changing location as each member is installed. The fall protection for workers at the leading edge shall be assured by properly constructed and maintained control zone lines not more than 60 ft away from the leading edge supplemented by a safety monitoring system to ensure the safety of all designated erectors working within the area defined by the control zone lines.

The hollow core slabs erected on the masonry portion of the building will be erected and grouted using the safety monitoring system. Grout will be placed in the space between the end of the slab and face shell of the concrete masonry by dumping from a wheelbarrow. The grout in the keyways between the slabs will be dumped from a wheelbarrow and then spread with long handled tools, allowing the worker to stand erect facing toward the unprotected edge and back from any work deck edge.

Whenever possible, the designated erectors will approach the incoming member at the leading edge only after it is below waist height so that the member itself provides protection against falls.

Except for the situations described below, when the arriving floor or roof member is within 2 to 3 inches of its final position, the designated erectors can then proceed to their position of erection at each end of the member under the control of the safety monitor. Crane hooks will be unhooked from double tee members by designated erectors under the direction and supervision of the safety monitor.

Designated erectors, while waiting for the next floor or roof member, will be constantly under the control of the safety monitor for fall protection and are directed to stay a minimum of six (6) ft from the edge. In the event a designated erector must move from one end of a member, which has just been placed at the leading edge, they must first move away from the leading edge a minimum of six (6) ft and then progress to the other end while maintaining the minimum distance of six (6) ft at all times.

Erection of double tees, where conditions require bearing of one end into a closed pocket and the other end on a beam ledge, restricting the tee legs from going directly into the pockets, require special considerations. The tee legs that are to bear in the closed pocket must hang lower than those at the beam bearing. The double tee will be "two-lined" in order to elevate one end higher than the other to allow for the low end to be ducked into the closed pocket using the following procedure.

The double tee will be rigged with a standard four-way spreader off of the main load line. An additional choker will be attached to the married point of the two-legged spreader at the end of the tee that is to be elevated. The double tee will be hoisted with the main load line and swung into a position as close as possible to the tee's final bearing elevation. When the tee is in this position and stabilized, the whip line load block will be lowered to just above the tee deck. At this time, two erectors will walk out on the suspended tee deck at midspan of the tee member and pull the load block to the end of the tee to be elevated and attach the additional choker to the load block. The possibility of entanglement with the crane lines and other obstacles during this two lining process while raising and lowering the crane block on that second line could be hazardous to an encumbered employee. Therefore, the designated erectors will not tie off during any part of this process. While the designated erectors are on the double tee, the safety monitoring system will be used. After attaching the choker, the two erectors then step back on the previously erected tee deck and signal the crane operator to hoist the load with the whip line to the elevation that will allow for enough clearance to let the low end tee legs slide into the pockets when the main load line is lowered. The erector, who is handling the lowered end of the tee at the closed pocket bearing, will step out on the suspended tee. An erection bar will then be placed between the end of the tee leg and the inside face of the pocketed spandrel member. The tee is barred away from the pocketed member to reduce the friction and lateral force against the pocketed member. As the tee is being lowered, the other erector remains on the tee which was previously erected to handle the other end. At this point the tee is slowly lowered by the crane to a point where the tee legs can freely slide into the pockets. The erector working the lowered end of the tee must keep pressure on the bar between the tee and the face of the pocketed spandrel member to very gradually let the tee legs slide into the pocket to its proper bearing dimension. The tee is then slowly lowered into its final erected position.

The designated erector should be allowed onto the suspended double tee, otherwise there is no control over the horizontal movement of the double tee and this movement could knock the spandrel off of its bearing or the column out of plumb. The control necessary to prevent hitting the spandrel can only be done safely from the top of the double tee being erected.

Loadbearing Wall Panels: The erection of the loadbearing wall panels on the elevated decks requires the use of a safety monitor and a controlled access zone that is a minimum of 25 ft and a maximum of ½ the length of the wall panels away from the unprotected edge, so that designated erectors can move freely and unencumbered when receiving the panels. Bracing, if required for stability, will be installed by ladder. After the braces are secured, the crane will be disconnected from the wall by using a ladder. The wall to wall connections will also be performed from a ladder.

Non-Loadbearing Panels (Cladding): The locating of survey lines, panel layout and other installation prerequisites (prewelding, etc.) for non-loadbearing panels (cladding) will not commence until floor perimeter and floor openings have been protected. In some areas, it is necessary because of panel configuration to remove the perimeter protection as the cladding is being installed. Removal of perimeter protection will be performed on a bay to bay basis, just ahead of cladding erection to minimize temporarily unprotected floor edges. Those workers within 6 ft of the edge, receiving and positioning the cladding when the perimeter protection is removed shall be tied off.

Detailing

Employees exposed to falls of six (6) feet or more to lower levels, who are not actively engaged in leading edge work or connecting activity, such as welding, bolting, cutting, bracing, guying, patching, painting or other operations, and who are working less than six (6) ft from an unprotected edge will be tied off at all times or guardrails will be installed. Employees engaged in these activities but who are more than six (6) ft from an unprotected edge as defined by the control zone lines, do not require fall protection but a warning line or control lines must be erected to remind employees they are approaching an area where fall protection is required.

IV. CONVENTIONAL FALL PROTECTION CONSIDERED FOR THE POINT OF ERECTION OR LEADING EDGE ERECTION OPERATIONS

A. Personal Fall Arrest Systems

In this particular erection sequence and procedure, personal fall arrest systems requiring body belt/harness systems, lifelines and lanyards will not reduce possible hazards to workers and will create offsetting hazards during their usage at the leading edge of precast/prestressed concrete construction.

Leading edge erection and initial connections are conducted by employees who are specifically trained to do this type of work and are trained to recognize the fall hazards. The nature of such work normally exposes the employee to the fall hazard for a short period of time and installation of fall protection systems for a short duration is not feasible because it exposes the installers of the system to the same fall hazard, but for a longer period of time.

1. It is necessary that the employee be able to move freely without encumbrance in order to guide the sections of precast concrete into their final position without having lifelines attached which will restrict the employee's ability to move about at the point of erection.

2. A typical procedure requires 2 or more workers to maneuver around each other as a concrete member is positioned to fit into the structure. If they are each attached to a lifeline, part of their attention must be diverted from their main task of positioning a member weighing several tons to the task of avoiding entanglements of their lifelines or avoiding tripping over lanyards. Therefore, if these workers are attached to lanyards, more fall potential would result than from not using such a device.

In this specific erection sequence and procedure, retractable lifelines do not solve the problem of two workers becoming tangled. In fact, such a tangle could prevent the lifeline from retracting as the worker moved, thus potentially exposing the worker to a fall greater than 6 ft. Also, a worker crossing over the lifeline of another worker can create a hazard because the movement of one person can unbalance the other. In the event of a fall by one person there is a likelihood that the other person will be caused to fall as well. In addition, if contamination such as grout (during hollow core grouting) enters the retractable housing it can cause excessive wear and damage to the device and could clog the retracting mechanism as the lanyard is dragged across the deck. Obstructing the cable orifice can defeat the device's shock absorbing function, produce cable slack and damage, and adversely affect cable extraction and retraction.

3. Employees tied to a lifeline can be trapped and crushed by moving structural members if the employee becomes restrained

343

by the lanyard or retractable lifeline and cannot get out of the path of the moving load.

The sudden movement of a precast concrete member being raised by a crane can be caused by a number of factors. When this happens, a connector may immediately have to move a considerable distance to avoid injury. If a tied off body belt/harness is being used, the connector could be trapped. Therefore, there is a greater risk of injury if the connector is tied to the structure for this specific erection sequence and procedure.

When necessary to move away from a retractable device, the worker cannot move at a rate greater than the device locking speed typically 3.5 to 4.5 ft/sec. When moving toward the device it is necessary to move at a rate which does not permit cable slack to build up. This slack may cause cable retraction acceleration and cause a worker to lose their balance by applying a higher than normal jerking force on the body when the cable suddenly becomes taut after building up momentum. This slack can also cause damage to the internal spring-loaded drum, uneven coiling of cable on the drum, and possible cable damage.

The factors causing sudden movements for this location include:

(a) Cranes

(1) Operator error.
(2) Site conditions (soft or unstable ground).
(3) Mechanical failure.
(4) Structural failure.
(5) Rigging failure.
(6) Crane signal/radio communication failure.

(b) Weather Conditions

(1) Wind (strong wind/sudden gusting)—particularly a problem with the large surface areas of precast concrete members.
(2) Snow/rain (visibility).
(3) Fog (visibility).
(4) Cold—causing slowed reactions or mechanical problems.
(c) Structure/Product Conditions.
(1) Lifting Eye failure.
(2) Bearing failure or slippage.
(3) Structure shifting.
(4) Bracing failure.
(5) Product failure.
(d) Human Error.
(1) Incorrect tag line procedure.
(2) Tag line hang-up.
(3) Incorrect or misunderstood crane signals.
(4) Misjudged elevation of member.
(5) Misjudged speed of member.
(6) Misjudged angle of member.
4. Anchorages or special attachment points could be cast into the precast concrete members if sufficient preplanning and consider-ation of erectors' position is done before the members are cast. Any hole or other attachment must be approved by the engineer who designed the member. It is possible that some design restrictions will not allow a member to be weakened by an additional hole; however, it is anticipated that such situations would be the exception, not the rule. Attachment points, other than on the deck surface, will require removal and/or patching. In order to remove and/or patch these points, requires the employee to be exposed to an additional fall hazard at an unprotected perimeter. The fact that attachment points could be available anywhere on the structure does not eliminate the hazards of using these points for tying off as discussed above. A logical point for tying off on double tees would be using the lifting loops, except that they must be cut off to eliminate a tripping hazard at an appropriate time.

5. Providing attachment at a point above the walking/working surface would also create fall exposures for employees installing their devices. Final positioning of a precast concrete member requires it to be moved in such a way that it must pass through the area that would be occupied by the lifeline and the lanyards attached to the point above. Resulting entanglements of lifelines and lanyards on a moving member could pull employees from the work surface. Also, the structure is being created and, in most cases, there is no structure above the members being placed.

(a) Temporary structural supports, installed to provide attaching points for lifelines limit the space which is essential for orderly positioning, alignment and placement of the precast concrete members. To keep the lanyards a reasonable and manageable length, lifeline supports would necessarily need to be in proximity to the positioning process. A sudden shift of the precast concrete member being positioned because of wind pressure or crane movement could make it strike the temporary supporting structure, moving it suddenly and causing tied off employees to fall.

(b) The time in manhours which would be expended in placing and maintaining temporary structural supports for lifeline attaching points could exceed the expended manhours involved in placing the precast concrete members. No protection could be provided for the employees erecting the temporary structural supports and these supports would have to be moved for each successive step in the construction process, thus greatly increasing the employee's exposure to the fall hazard.

(c) The use of a cable strung horizontally between two columns to provide tie off lines for erecting or walking a beam for connecting work is not feasible and creates a greater hazard on this multi-story building for the following reasons:

(1) If a connector is to use such a line, it must be installed between the two columns. To perform this installation requires an erector to have more fall exposure time attaching the cable to the columns than would be spent to make the beam to column connection itself.

(2) If such a line is to be installed so that an erector can walk along a beam, it must be overhead or below him. For example, if a connector must walk along a 24 in. wide beam, the presence of a line next to the connector at waist level, attached directly to the columns, would prevent the connector from centering their weight over the beam and balancing themselves. Installing the line above the connector might be possible on the first level of a two-story column; however, the column may extend only a few feet above the floor level at the second level or be flush with the floor level. Attaching the line to the side of the beam could be a solution; however, it would require the connector to attach the lanyard below foot level which would most likely extend a fall farther than 6 ft.

(3) When lines are strung over every beam, it becomes more and more difficult for the crane operator to lower a precast concrete member into position without the member becoming fouled. Should the member become entangled, it could easily dislodge the line from a column. If a worker is tied to it at the time, a fall could be caused.

6. The ANSI A10.14–1991 American National Standard for Construction and Demolition Operations—Requirements for Safety Belts, Harnesses, Lanyards and Lifelines for Construction and Demolition Use, states that the anchor point of a lanyard or deceleration device should, if possible, be located above the wearer's belt or harness attachment. ANSI A10.14 also states that a suitable anchorage point is one which is located as high as possible to prevent contact with an obstruction below should the worker fall. Most manufacturers also warn in the user's handbook that the safety block/retractable lifeline must be positioned above the D-ring (above the work space of the intended user) and OSHA recommends that fall arrest and restraint equipment be used in accordance with the manufacturer's instructions.

Attachment of a retractable device to a horizontal cable near floor level or using the inserts in the floor or roof members may result in increased free fall due to the dorsal D-ring of the full-body harness riding higher than the attachment point of the snaphook to the cable or insert (e.g., 6 foot tall worker with a dorsal D-ring at 5 feet above the floor or surface, reduces the working length to only one foot, by placing the anchorage five feet away from the fall hazard). In addition, impact loads may exceed maximum fall arrest forces (MAF) because the fall arrest D-ring would be 4 to 5 feet higher than the safe-

ty block/retractable lifeline anchored to the walking-working surface; and the potential for swing hazards is increased.

Manufacturers also require that workers not work at a level where the point of snaphook attachment to the body harness is above the device because this will increase the free fall distance and the deceleration distance and will cause higher forces on the body in the event of an accidental fall.

Manufacturers recommend an anchorage for the retractable lifeline which is immovably fixed in space and is independent of the user's support systems. A moveable anchorage is one which can be moved around (such as equipment or wheeled vehicles) or which can deflect substantially under shock loading (such as a horizontal cable or very flexible beam). In the case of a very flexible anchorage, a shock load applied to the anchorage during fall arrest can cause oscillation of the flexible anchorage such that the retractable brake mechanism may undergo one or more cycles of locking/unlocking/locking (ratchet effect) until the anchorage deflection is dampened. Therefore, use of a moveable anchorage involves critical engineering and safety factors and should only be considered after fixed anchorage has been determined to be not feasible.

Horizontal cables used as an anchorage present an additional hazard due to amplification of the horizontal component of maximum arrest force (of a fall) transmitted to the points where the horizontal cable is attached to the structure. This amplification is due to the angle of sag of a horizontal cable and is most severe for small angles of sag. For a cable sag angle of 2 degrees the horizontal force on the points of cable attachment can be amplified by a factor of 15.

It is also necessary to install the retractable device vertically overhead to minimize swing falls. If an object is in the worker's swing path (or that of the cable) hazardous situations exist: (1) due to the swing, horizontal speed of the user may be high enough to cause injury when an obstacle in the swing fall path is struck by either the user or the cable; (2) the total vertical fall distance of the user may be much greater than if the user had fallen only vertically without a swing fall path.

With retractable lines, overconfidence may cause the worker to engage in inappropriate behavior, such as approaching the perimeter of a floor or roof at a distance appreciably greater than the shortest distance between the anchorage point and the leading edge. Though the retractable lifeline may arrest a worker's fall before he or she has fallen a few feet, the lifeline may drag along the edge of the floor or beam and swing the worker like a pendulum until the line has moved to a position where the distance between the anchorage point and floor edge is the shortest distance between those two points. Accompanying this pendulum swing is a lowering of the worker, with the attendant danger that he or she may violently impact the floor or some obstruction below.

The risk of a cable breaking is increased if a lifeline is dragged sideways across the rough surface or edge of a concrete member at the same moment that the lifeline is being subjected to a maximum impact loading during a fall. The typical ¾₁₆ in. cable in a retractable lifeline has a breaking strength of from 3000 to 3700 lbs.

7. The competent person, who can take into account the specialized operations being performed on this project, should determine when and where a designated erector cannot use a personal fall arrest system.

B. Safety Net Systems

The nature of this particular precast concrete erection worksite precludes the safe use of safety nets where point of erection or leading edge work must take place.

1. To install safety nets in the interior high bay of the single story portion of the building poses rigging attachment problems. Structural members do not exist to which supporting devices for nets can be attached in the area where protection is required. As the erection operation advances, the location of point of erection or leading edge work changes constantly as each member is attached to the structure. Due to this constant change it is not feasible to set net sections and build separate structures to support the nets.

2. The nature of the erection process for the precast concrete members is such that an installed net would protect workers as they position and secure only one structural member. After each member is stabilized the net would have to be moved to a new location (this could mean a move of 8 to 10 ft or the possibility of a move to a different level or area of the structure) to protect workers placing the next piece in the construction sequence. The result would be the installation and dismantling of safety nets repeatedly throughout the normal work day. As the time necessary to install a net, test, and remove it is significantly greater than the time necessary to position and secure a precast concrete member, the exposure time for the worker installing the safety net would be far longer than for the workers whom the net is intended to protect. The time exposure repeats itself each time the nets and supporting hardware must be moved laterally or upward to provide protection at the point of erection or leading edge.

3. Strict interpretation of § 1926.502(c) requires that operations shall not be undertaken until the net is in place and has been tested. With the point of erection constantly changing, the time necessary to install and test a safety net significantly exceeds the time necessary to position and secure the concrete member.

4. Use of safety nets on exposed perimeter wall openings and opensided floors, causes attachment points to be left in architectural concrete which must be patched and filled with matching material after the net supporting hardware is removed. In order to patch these openings, additional numbers of employees must be suspended by swing stages, boatswain chairs or other devices, thereby increasing the amount of fall exposure time to employees.

5. Installed safety nets pose an additional hazard at the perimeter of the erected structure where limited space is available in which members can be turned after being lifted from the ground by the crane. There would be a high probability that the member being lifted could become entangled in net hardware, cables, etc.

6. The use of safety nets where structural wall panels are being erected would prevent movement of panels to point of installation. To be effective, nets would necessarily have to provide protection across the area where structural supporting wall panels would be set and plumbed before roof units could be placed.

7. Use of a tower crane for the erection of the high rise portion of the structure poses a particular hazard in that the crane operator cannot see or judge the proximity of the load in relation to the structure or nets. If the signaler is looking through nets and supporting structural devices while giving instructions to the crane operator, it is not possible to judge precise relationships between the load and the structure itself or to nets and supporting structural devices. This could cause the load to become entangled in the net or hit the structure causing potential damage.

C. Guardrail Systems

On this particular worksite, guardrails, barricades, ropes, cables or other perimeter guarding devices or methods on the erection floor will pose problems to safe erection procedures. Typically, a floor or roof is erected by placing 4 to 10 ft wide structural members next to one another and welding or grouting them together. The perimeter of a floor and roof changes each time a new member is placed into position. It is unreasonable and virtually impossible to erect guardrails and toe boards at the ever changing leading edge of a floor or roof.

1. To position a member safely it is necessary to remove all obstructions extending above the floor level near the point of erection. Such a procedure allows workers to swing a new member across the erected surface as necessary to position it properly without worrying about knocking material off of this surface.

Hollow core slab erection on the masonry wall requires installation of the perimeter protection where the masonry wall has to be constructed. This means the guardrail is installed then subsequently removed to continue the masonry construction. The erector will be exposed to a fall hazard for a longer period of time while installing and removing perimeter protection than while erecting the slabs.

In hollow core work, as in other precast concrete erection, others are not typically on the work deck until the precast concrete erection is complete. The deck is not complete until the leveling, aligning, and grouting of the joints is done. It is normal practice to keep others off the deck until at least the next day after the installation is complete to allow the grout to harden.

2. There is no permanent boundary until all structural members have been placed in the floor or roof. At the leading edge, workers are operating at the temporary edge of the structure as they work to position the next member in the sequence. Compliance with the standard would require a guardrail and toe board be installed along this edge. However, the presence of such a device would prevent a new member from being swung over the erected surface low enough to allow workers to control it safely during the positioning process. Further, these employees would have to work through the guardrail to align the new member and connect it to the structure. The guardrail would not protect an employee who must lean through it to do the necessary work, rather it would hinder the employee to such a degree that a greater hazard is created than if the guardrail were absent.

3. Guardrail requirements pose a hazard at the leading edge of installed floor or roof sections by creating the possibility of employees being caught between guardrails and suspended loads. The lack of a clear work area in which to guide the suspended load into position for placement and welding of members into the existing structure creates still further hazards.

4. Where erection processes require precast concrete stairways or openings to be installed as an integral part of the overall erection process, it must also be recognized that guardrails or handrails must not project above the surface of the erection floor. Such guardrails should be terminated at the level of the erection floor to avoid placing hazardous obstacles in the path of a member being positioned.

V. OTHER FALL PROTECTION MEASURES CONSIDERED FOR THIS JOB

The following is a list and explanation of other fall protection measures available and an explanation of limitations for use on this particular jobsite. If during the course of erecting the building the employee sees an area that could be erected more safely by the use of these fall protection measures, the foreman should be notified.

A. Scaffolds are not used because:

1. The leading edge of the building is constantly changing and the scaffolding would have to be moved at very frequent intervals. Employees erecting and dismantling the scaffolding would be exposed to fall hazards for a greater length of time than they would by merely erecting the precast concrete member.

2. A scaffold tower could interfere with the safe swinging of a load by the crane.

3. Power lines, terrain and site do not allow for the safe use of scaffolding.

B. Vehicle mounted platforms are not used because:

1. A vehicle mounted platform will not reach areas on the deck that are erected over other levels.

2. The leading edge of the building is usually over a lower level of the building and this lower level will not support the weight of a vehicle mounted platform.

3. A vehicle mounted platform could interfere with the safe swinging of a load by the crane, either by the crane swinging the load over or into the equipment.

4. Power lines and surrounding site work do not allow for the safe use of a vehicle mounted platform.

C. Crane suspended personnel platforms are not used because:

1. A second crane close enough to suspend any employee in the working and erecting area could interfere with the safe swinging of a load by the crane hoisting the product to be erected.

2. Power lines and surrounding site work do not allow for the safe use of a second crane on the job.

VI. ENFORCEMENT

Constant awareness of and respect for fall hazards, and compliance with all safety rules are considered conditions of employment. The jobsite Superintendent, as well as individuals in the Safety and Personnel Department, reserve the right to issue disciplinary warnings to employees, up to and including termination, for failure to follow the guidelines of this program.

VII. ACCIDENT INVESTIGATIONS

All accidents that result in injury to workers, regardless of their nature, shall be investigated and reported. It is an integral part of any safety program that documentation take place as soon as possible so that the cause and means of prevention can be identified to prevent a reoccurrence.

In the event that an employee falls or there is some other related, serious incident occurring, this plan shall be reviewed to determine if additional practices, procedures, or training need to be implemented to prevent similar types of falls or incidents from occurring.

VIII. CHANGES TO PLAN

Any changes to the plan will be approved by (name of the qualified person). This plan shall be reviewed by a qualified person as the job progresses to determine if additional practices, procedures or training needs to be implemented by the competent person to improve or provide additional fall protection. Workers shall be notified and trained, if necessary, in the new procedures. A copy of this plan and all approved changes shall be maintained at the jobsite.

Sample Fall Protection Plan for Residential Construction

(INSERT COMPANY NAME)

This Fall Protection Plan Is Specific For The Following Project:

Location of Job _____
Date Plan Prepared or Modified _____
Plan Prepared By _____
Plan Approved By _____
Plan Supervised By _____

The following Fall Protection Plan is a sample program prepared for the prevention of injuries associated with falls. A Fall Protection Plan must be developed and evaluated on a site by site basis. It is recommended that builders discuss the written Fall Protection Plan with their OSHA Area Office prior to going on a jobsite.

I. STATEMENT OF COMPANY POLICY

(Your company name here) is dedicated to the protection of its employees from on-the-job injuries. All employees of (Your company name here) have the responsibility to work safely on the job. The purpose of the plan is to supplement our existing safety and health program and to ensure that every employee who works for (Your company name here) recognizes workplace fall hazards and takes the appropriate measures to address those hazards.

This Fall Protection Plan addresses the use of conventional fall protection at a number of areas on the project, as well as identifies specific activities that require non-conventional means of fall protection. During the construction of residential buildings under 48 feet in height, it is sometimes infeasible or it creates a greater hazard to use conventional fall protection systems at specific areas or for specific tasks. The areas or tasks may include, but are not limited to:

a. Setting and bracing of roof trusses and rafters;

b. Installation of floor sheathing and joists;

c. Roof sheathing operations; and

d. Erecting exterior walls.

In these cases, conventional fall protection systems may not be the safest choice for builders. This plan is designed to enable employers and employees to recognize the fall hazards associated with this job and to establish the safest procedures that are to be followed in order to prevent falls to lower levels or through holes and openings in walking/working surfaces.

Each employee will be trained in these procedures and will strictly adhere to them except when doing so would expose the employee to a greater hazard. If, in the employee's opinion, this is the case, the employee is to notify the competent person of their concern and have the concern addressed before proceeding.

It is the responsibility of (name of competent person) to implement this Fall Protection Plan. Continual observational safety checks of work operations and the enforcement of the safety policy and procedures shall be regularly enforced. The crew supervisor or foreman (insert name) is responsible for correcting any unsafe practices or conditions immediately.

It is the responsibility of the employer to ensure that all employees understand and adhere to the procedures of this plan and to follow the instructions of the crew supervisor. It is also the responsibility of the employee to bring to management's attention any unsafe or hazardous conditions or practices that may cause injury to either themselves or any other employees. Any changes to the Fall Protection Plan must be approved by (name of qualified person).

II. FALL PROTECTION SYSTEMS TO BE USED ON THIS JOB

Installation of roof trusses/rafters, exterior wall erection, roof sheathing, floor sheathing and joist/truss activities will be conducted by employees who are specifically trained to do this type of work and are trained to recognize the fall hazards. The nature of such work normally exposes the employee to the fall hazard for a short period of time. This Plan details how (Your company name here) will minimize these hazards.

Controlled Access Zones

When using the Plan to implement the fall protection options available, workers must be protected through limited access to high hazard locations. Before any non-conventional fall protection systems are used as part of the work plan, a controlled access zone (CAZ) shall be clearly defined by the competent person as an area where a recognized hazard exists. The demarcation of the CAZ shall be communicated by the competent person in a recognized manner, either through signs, wires, tapes, ropes or chains.

(Your company name here) shall take the following steps to ensure that the CAZ is clearly marked or controlled by the competent person:

• All access to the CAZ must be restricted to authorized entrants;

• All workers who are permitted in the CAZ shall be listed in the appropriate sections of the Plan (or be visibly identifiable by the competent person) prior to implementation;

• The competent person shall ensure that all protective elements of the CAZ be implemented prior to the beginning of work.

Installation Procedures for Roof Truss and Rafter Erection

During the erection and bracing of roof trusses/rafters, conventional fall protection may present a greater hazard to workers. On this job, safety nets, guardrails and personal fall arrest systems will not provide adequate fall protection because the nets will cause the walls to collapse, while there are no suitable attachment or anchorage points for guardrails or personal fall arrest systems.

On this job, requiring workers to use a ladder for the entire installation process will cause a greater hazard because the worker must stand on the ladder with his back or side to the front of the ladder. While erecting the truss or rafter the worker will need both hands to maneuver the truss and therefore cannot hold onto the ladder. In addition, ladders cannot be adequately protected from movement while trusses are being maneuvered into place. Many workers may experience additional fatigue because of the increase in overhead work with heavy materials, which can also lead to a greater hazard.

Exterior scaffolds cannot be utilized on this job because the ground, after recent backfilling, cannot support the scaffolding. In most cases, the erection and dismantling of the scaffold would expose workers to a greater fall hazard than erection of the trusses/rafters.

On all walls eight feet or less, workers will install interior scaffolds along the interior wall below the location where the trusses/rafters will be erected. "Sawhorse" scaffolds constructed of 46 inch sawhorses and 2×10 planks will often allow workers to be elevated high enough to allow for the erection of trusses and rafters without working on the top plate of the wall.

In structures that have walls higher than eight feet and where the use of scaffolds and ladders would create a greater hazard, safe working procedures will be utilized when working on the top plate and will be monitored by the crew supervisor. During all stages of truss/rafter erection the stability of the trusses/rafters will be ensured at all times.

(Your company name here) shall take the following steps to protect workers who are exposed to fall hazards while working from the top plate installing trusses/rafters:

• Only the following trained workers will be allowed to work on the top plate during roof truss or rafter installation:

_____

_____

• Workers shall have no other duties to perform during truss/rafter erection procedures;

• All trusses/rafters will be adequately braced before any worker can use the truss/rafter as a support;

• Workers will remain on the top plate using the previously stabilized truss/rafter as a support while other trusses/rafters are being erected;

• Workers will leave the area of the secured trusses only when it is necessary to secure another truss/rafter;

• The first two trusses/rafters will be set from ladders leaning on side walls at points where the walls can support the weight of the ladder; and

• A worker will climb onto the interior top plate via a ladder to secure the peaks of the first two trusses/rafters being set.

The workers responsible for detaching trusses from cranes and/or securing trusses at the peaks traditionally are positioned at the peak of the trusses/rafters. There are also situations where workers securing rafters to ridge beams will be positioned on top of the ridge beam.

(Your company name here) shall take the following steps to protect workers who are exposed to fall hazards while securing trusses/rafters at the peak of the trusses/ridge beam:

• Only the following trained workers will be allowed to work at the peak during roof truss or rafter installation:

_____

_____

• Once truss or rafter installation begins, workers not involved in that activity shall not stand or walk below or adjacent to the roof opening or exterior walls in any area where they could be struck by falling objects;

• Workers shall have no other duties than securing/bracing the trusses/ridge beam;

• Workers positioned at the peaks or in the webs of trusses or on top of the ridge beam shall work from a stable position, either by sitting on a "ridge seat" or other equivalent surface that provides additional stability or by positioning themselves in previously stabilized trusses/rafters and leaning into and reaching through the trusses/rafters;

• Workers shall not remain on or in the peak/ridge any longer than necessary to safely complete the task.

Roof Sheathing Operations

Workers typically install roof sheathing after all trusses/rafters and any permanent truss bracing is in place. Roof structures are unstable until some sheathing is installed, so workers installing roof sheathing cannot be protected from fall hazards by conventional fall protection systems until it is determined that the roofing system can be used as an anchorage point. At that point, employees shall be protected by a personal fall arrest system.

Trusses/rafters are subject to collapse if a worker falls while attached to a single truss with a belt/harness. Nets could also cause collapse, and there is no place to attach guardrails.

All workers will ensure that they have secure footing before they attempt to walk on the sheathing, including cleaning shoes/boots of mud or other slip hazards.

To minimize the time workers must be exposed to a fall hazard, materials will be staged to allow for the quickest installation of sheathing.

(Your company name here) shall take the following steps to protect workers who are exposed to fall hazards while installing roof sheathing:

• Once roof sheathing installation begins, workers not involved in that activity shall not stand or walk below or adjacent to the roof opening or exterior walls in any area where they could be struck by falling objects;

• The competent person shall determine the limits of this area, which shall be clearly communicated to workers prior to placement of the first piece of roof sheathing;

• The competent person may order work on the roof to be suspended for brief periods as necessary to allow other workers to pass through such areas when this would not create a greater hazard;

• Only qualified workers shall install roof sheathing;

• The bottom row of roof sheathing may be installed by workers standing in truss webs;

• After the bottom row of roof sheathing is installed, a slide guard extending the width of the roof shall be securely attached to the roof. Slide guards are to be constructed of no less than nominal 4" height capable of limiting the uncontrolled slide of workers. Workers should install the slide guard while standing in truss webs and leaning over the sheathing;

• Additional rows of roof sheathing may be installed by workers positioned on previously installed rows of sheathing. A slide guard can be used to assist workers in retaining their footing during successive sheathing operations; and

• Additional slide guards shall be securely attached to the roof at intervals not to exceed 13 feet as successive rows of sheathing

are installed. For roofs with pitches in excess of 9-in-12, slide guards will be installed at four-foot intervals.

• When wet weather (rain, snow, or sleet) are present, roof sheathing operations shall be suspended unless safe footing can be assured for those workers installing sheathing.

• When strong winds (above 40 miles per hour) are present, roof sheathing operations are to be suspended unless wind breakers are erected.

Installation of Floor Joists and Sheathing

During the installation of floor sheathing/joists (leading edge construction), the following steps shall be taken to protect workers:

• Only the following trained workers will be allowed to install floor joists or sheathing:

_____

_____

• Materials for the operations shall be conveniently staged to allow for easy access to workers;

• The first floor joists or trusses will be rolled into position and secured either from the ground, ladders or sawhorse scaffolds;

• Each successive floor joist or truss will be rolled into place and secured from a platform created from a sheet of plywood laid over the previously secured floor joists or trusses;

• Except for the first row of sheathing which will be installed from ladders or the ground, workers shall work from the established deck; and

• Any workers not assisting in the leading edge construction while leading edges still exist (e.g. cutting the decking for the installers) shall not be permitted within six feet of the leading edge under construction.

Erection of Exterior Walls

During the construction and erection of exterior walls, employers shall take the following steps to protect workers:

• Only the following trained workers will be allowed to erect exterior walls:

_____

_____

• A painted line six feet from the perimeter will be clearly marked prior to any wall erection activities to warn of the approaching unprotected edge;

• Materials for operations shall be conveniently staged to minimize fall hazards; and

• Workers constructing exterior walls shall complete as much cutting of materials and other preparation as possible away from the edge of the deck.

III. ENFORCEMENT

Constant awareness of and respect for fall hazards, and compliance with all safety rules are considered conditions of employment. The crew supervisor or foreman, as well as individuals in the Safety and Personnel Department, reserve the right to issue disciplinary warnings to employees, up to and including termination, for failure to follow the guidelines of this program.

IV. ACCIDENT INVESTIGATIONS

All accidents that result in injury to workers, regardless of their nature, shall be investigated and reported. It is an integral part of any safety program that documentation take place as soon as possible so that the cause and means of prevention can be identified to prevent a reoccurrence.

In the event that an employee falls or there is some other related, serious incident occurring, this plan shall be reviewed to determine if additional practices, procedures, or training need to be implemented to prevent similar types of falls or incidents from occurring.

V. CHANGES TO PLAN

Any changes to the plan will be approved by (name of the qualified person). This plan shall be reviewed by a qualified person as the job progresses to determine if additional practices, procedures or training needs to be implemented by the competent person to improve or provide additional fall protection. Workers shall be notified and trained, if necessary, in the new procedures. A copy of this plan and all approved changes shall be maintained at the jobsite.

[59 FR 40730, Aug. 9, 1994]

Subpart N—Helicopters, Hoists, Elevators, and Conveyors

AUTHORITY: Section 3704 of the Contract Work Hours and Safety Standards Act (40 U.S.C. 3701); Sections 4, 6, and 8 of the Occupational Safety and Health Act of 1970 (29 U.S.C. 653, 655, 657); Secretary of Labor's Order Nos. 12–71 (36 FR 8754), 8–76 (41 FR 25059), or 9–83 (49 FR 35736), and 5–2007 (72 FR 31159).

§1926.550 [Reserved]

§1926.551 Helicopters.

(a) *Helicopter regulations.* Helicopter cranes shall be expected to comply with any applicable regulations of the Federal Aviation Administration.

(b) *Briefing.* Prior to each day's operation a briefing shall be conducted. This briefing shall set forth the plan of operation for the pilot and ground personnel.

(c) *Slings and tag lines.* Load shall be properly slung. Tag lines shall be of a length that will not permit their being drawn up into rotors. Pressed sleeve, swedged eyes, or equivalent means shall be used for all freely suspended loads to prevent hand splices from spinning open or cable clamps from loosening.

(d) *Cargo hooks.* All electrically operated cargo hooks shall have the electrical activating device so designed and installed as to prevent inadvertent operation. In addition, these cargo hooks shall be equipped with an emergency mechanical control for releasing the load. The hooks shall be tested prior to each day's operation to determine that the release functions properly, both electrically and mechanically.

(e) *Personal protective equipment.* (1) Personal protective equipment for employees receiving the load shall consist of complete eye protection and hard hats secured by chinstraps.

(2) Loose-fitting clothing likely to flap in the downwash, and thus be snagged on hoist line, shall not be worn.

(f) *Loose gear and objects.* Every practical precaution shall be taken to provide for the protection of the employees from flying objects in the rotor downwash. All loose gear within 100 feet of the place of lifting the load, depositing the load, and all other areas susceptible to rotor downwash shall be secured or removed.

(g) *Housekeeping.* Good housekeeping shall be maintained in all helicopter loading and unloading areas.

(h) *Operator responsibility.* The helicopter operator shall be responsible for size, weight, and manner in which loads are connected to the helicopter. If, for any reason, the helicopter operator believes the lift cannot be made safely, the lift shall not be made.

(i) *Hooking and unhooking loads.* When employees are required to perform work under hovering craft, a safe means of access shall be provided for employees to reach the hoist line hook and engage or disengage cargo slings. Employees shall not perform work under hovering craft except when necessary to hook or unhook loads.

(j) *Static charge.* Static charge on the suspended load shall be dissipated with a grounding device before ground personnel touch the suspended load, or protective rubber gloves shall be worn by all ground personnel touching the suspended load.

(k) *Weight limitation.* The weight of an external load shall not exceed the manufacturer's rating.

(l) *Ground lines.* Hoist wires or other gear, except for pulling lines or conductors that are allowed to "pay out" from a container or roll off a reel, shall not be attached to any fixed ground structure, or allowed to foul on any fixed structure.

(m) *Visibility.* When visibility is reduced by dust or other conditions, ground personnel shall exercise special caution to keep clear of main and stabilizing rotors. Precautions shall also be taken by the employer to eliminate as far as practical reduced visibility.

(n) *Signal systems.* Signal systems between aircrew and ground personnel shall be understood and checked in advance of hoisting the load. This applies to either radio or hand signal systems. Hand signals shall be as shown in Figure N–1.

FIGURE N-1 HELICOPTER HAND SIGNAL

(o) *Approach distance.* No unauthorized person shall be allowed to approach within 50 feet of the helicopter when the rotor blades are turning.

(p) *Approaching helicopter.* Whenever approaching or leaving a helicopter with blades rotating, all employees shall remain in full view of the pilot and keep in a crouched position. Employees shall avoid the area from the cockpit or cabin rearward unless authorized by the helicopter operator to work there.

(q) *Personnel.* Sufficient ground personnel shall be provided when required for safe helicopter loading and unloading operations.

(r) *Communications.* There shall be constant reliable communication between the pilot, and a designated employee of the ground crew who acts as a signalman during the period of loading and unloading. This signalman shall be distinctly recognizable from other ground personnel.

(s) *Fires.* Open fires shall not be permitted in an area that could result in such fires being spread by the rotor downwash.

§ 1926.552 Material hoists, personnel hoists, and elevators.

(a) *General requirements.* (1) The employer shall comply with the manufacturer's specifications and limitations applicable to the operation of all hoists and elevators. Where manufacturer's specifications are not available, the limitations assigned to the equipment shall be based on the determinations of a professional engineer competent in the field.

(2) Rated load capacities, recommended operating speeds, and special hazard warnings or instructions shall be posted on cars and platforms.

(3) Wire rope shall be removed from service when any of the following conditions exists:

(i) In hoisting ropes, six randomly distributed broken wires in one rope lay or three broken wires in one strand in one rope lay;

(ii) Abrasion, scrubbing, flattening, or peening, causing loss of more than one-third of the original diameter of the outside wires;

(iii) Evidence of any heat damage resulting from a torch or any damage caused by contact with electrical wires;

(iv) Reduction from nominal diameter of more than three sixty-fourths inch for diameters up to and including three-fourths inch; one-sixteenth inch for diameters seven-eights to 1⅛

inches; and three thirty-seconds inch for diameters 1¼ to 1½ inches.

(4) Hoisting ropes shall be installed in accordance with the wire rope manufacturers' recommendations.

(5) The installation of live booms on hoists is prohibited.

(6) The use of endless belt-type manlifts on construction shall be prohibited.

(b) *Material hoists.* (1)(i) Operating rules shall be established and posted at the operator's station of the hoist. Such rules shall include signal system and allowable line speed for various loads. Rules and notices shall be posted on the car frame or crosshead in a conspicuous location, including the statement "No Riders Allowed."

(ii) No person shall be allowed to ride on material hoists except for the purposes of inspection and maintenance.

(2) All entrances of the hoistways shall be protected by substantial gates or bars which shall guard the full width of the landing entrance. All hoistway entrance bars and gates shall be painted with diagonal contrasting colors, such as black and yellow stripes.

(i) Bars shall be not less than 2- by 4-inch wooden bars or the equivalent, located 2 feet from the hoistway line. Bars shall be located not less than 36 inches nor more than 42 inches above the floor.

(ii) Gates or bars protecting the entrances to hoistways shall be equipped with a latching device.

(3) Overhead protective covering of 2-inch planking, ¾-inch plywood, or other solid material of equivalent strength, shall be provided on the top of every material hoist cage or platform.

(4) The operator's station of a hoisting machine shall be provided with overhead protection equivalent to tight planking not less than 2 inches thick. The support for the overhead protection shall be of equal strength.

(5) Hoist towers may be used with or without an enclosure on all sides. However, whichever alternative is chosen, the following applicable conditions shall be met:

(i) When a hoist tower is enclosed, it shall be enclosed on all sides for its entire height with a screen enclosure of

½-inch mesh, No. 18 U.S. gauge wire or equivalent, except for landing access.

(ii) When a hoist tower is not enclosed, the hoist platform or car shall be totally enclosed (caged) on all sides for the full height between the floor and the overhead protective covering with ½-inch mesh of No. 14 U.S. gauge wire or equivalent. The hoist platform enclosure shall include the required gates for loading and unloading. A 6-foot high enclosure shall be provided on the unused sides of the hoist tower at ground level.

(6) Car arresting devices shall be installed to function in case of rope failure.

(7) All material hoist towers shall be designed by a licensed professional engineer.

(8) All material hoists shall conform to the requirements of ANSI A10.5–1969, Safety Requirements for Material Hoists.

(c) *Personnel hoists.* (1) Hoist towers outside the structure shall be enclosed for the full height on the side or sides used for entrance and exit to the structure. At the lowest landing, the enclosure on the sides not used for exit or entrance to the structure shall be enclosed to a height of at least 10 feet. Other sides of the tower adjacent to floors or scaffold platforms shall be enclosed to a height of 10 feet above the level of such floors or scaffolds.

(2) Towers inside of structures shall be enclosed on all four sides throughout the full height.

(3) Towers shall be anchored to the structure at intervals not exceeding 25 feet. In addition to tie-ins, a series of guys shall be installed. Where tie-ins are not practical the tower shall be anchored by means of guys made of wire rope at least one-half inch in diameter, securely fastened to anchorage to ensure stability.

(4) Hoistway doors or gates shall be not less than 6 feet 6 inches high and shall be provided with mechanical locks which cannot be operated from the landing side, and shall be accessible only to persons on the car.

(5) Cars shall be permanently enclosed on all sides and the top, except sides used for entrance and exit which have car gates or doors.

(6) A door or gate shall be provided at each entrance to the car which shall protect the full width and height of the car entrance opening.

(7) Overhead protective covering of 2-inch planking, ¾-inch plywood or other solid material or equivalent strength shall be provided on the top of every personnel hoist.

(8) Doors or gates shall be provided with electric contacts which do not allow movement of the hoist when door or gate is open.

(9) Safeties shall be capable of stopping and holding the car and rated load when traveling at governor tripping speed.

(10) Cars shall be provided with a capacity and data plate secured in a conspicuous place on the car or crosshead.

(11) Internal combustion engines shall not be permitted for direct drive.

(12) Normal and final terminal stopping devices shall be provided.

(13) An emergency stop switch shall be provided in the car and marked "Stop."

(14) Ropes: (i) The minimum number of hoisting ropes used shall be three for traction hoists and two for drum-type hoists.

(ii) The minimum diameter of hoisting and counterweight wire ropes shall be ½-inch.

(iii) Safety factors:

MINIMUM FACTORS OF SAFETY FOR SUSPENSION WIRE ROPES

Rope speed in feet per minute	Minimum factor of safety
50	7.60
75	7.75
100	7.95
125	8.10
150	8.25
175	8.40
200	8.60
225	8.75
250	8.90
300	9.20
350	9.50
400	9.75
450	10.00
500	10.25
550	10.45
600	10.70

(15) Following assembly and erection of hoists, and before being put in service, an inspection and test of all functions and safety devices shall be made under the supervision of a competent

person. A similar inspection and test is required following major alteration of an existing installation. All hoists shall be inspected and tested at not more than 3-month intervals. The employer shall prepare a certification record which includes the date the inspection and test of all functions and safety devices was performed; the signature of the person who performed the inspection and test; and a serial number, or other identifier, for the hoist that was inspected and tested. The most recent certification record shall be maintained on file.

(16) All personnel hoists used by employees shall be constructed of materials and components which meet the specifications for materials, construction, safety devices, assembly, and structural integrity as stated in the American National Standard A10.4–1963, Safety Requirements for Workmen's Hoists. The requirements of this paragraph (c)(16) do not apply to cantilever type personnel hoists.

(17) (i) Personnel hoists used in bridge tower construction shall be approved by a registered professional engineer and erected under the supervision of a qualified engineer competent in this field.

(ii) When a hoist tower is not enclosed, the hoist platform or car shall be totally enclosed (caged) on all sides for the full height between the floor and the overhead protective covering with ¾-inch mesh of No. 14 U.S. gauge wire or equivalent. The hoist platform enclosure shall include the required gates for loading and unloading.

(iii) These hoists shall be inspected and maintained on a weekly basis. Whenever the hoisting equipment is exposed to winds exceeding 35 miles per hour it shall be inspected and put in operable condition before reuse.

(iv) Wire rope shall be taken out of service when any of the following conditions exist:

(a) In running ropes, six randomly distributed broken wires in one lay or three broken wires in one strand in one lay;

(b) Wear of one-third the original diameter of outside individual wires. Kinking, crushing, bird caging, or any other damage resulting in distortion of the rope structure;

(c) Evidence of any heat damage from any cause;

(d) Reductions from nominal diameter of more than three-sixty-fourths inch for diameters to and including three-fourths inch, one-sixteenth inch for diameters seven-eights inch to 1⅛ inches inclusive, three-thirty-seconds inch for diameters 1¼ to 1½ inches inclusive;

(e) In standing ropes, more than two broken wires in one lay in sections beyond end connections or more than one broken wire at an end connection.

(d) Permanent elevators under the care and custody of the employer and used by employees for work covered by this Act shall comply with the requirements of American National Standards Institute A17.1–1965 with addenda A17.1a–1967, A17.1b–1968, A17.1c–1969, A17.1d–1970, and inspected in accordance with A17.2–1960 with addenda A17.2a–1965, A17.2b–1967.

[44 FR 8577, Feb. 9, 1979; 44 FR 20940, Apr. 6, 1979, as amended at 52 FR 36382, Sept. 28, 1987]

§ 1926.553 Base-mounted drum hoists.

(a) *General requirements.* (1) Exposed moving parts such as gears, projecting screws, setscrews, chain, cables, chain sprockets, and reciprocating or rotating parts, which constitute a hazard, shall be guarded.

(2) All controls used during the normal operation cycle shall be located within easy reach of the operator's station.

(3) Electric motor operated hoists shall be provided with:

(i) A device to disconnect all motors from the line upon power failure and not permit any motor to be restarted until the controller handle is brought to the "off" position;

(ii) Where applicable, an overspeed preventive device;

(iii) A means whereby remotely operated hoists stop when any control is ineffective.

(4) All base-mounted drum hoists in use shall meet the applicable requirements for design, construction, installation, testing, inspection, maintenance, and operations, as prescribed by the manufacturer.

(b) *Specific requirements.* [Reserved]

(c) This section does not apply to base-mounted drum hoists used in conjunction with derricks. Base-mounted drum hoists used in conjunction with derricks must conform to §1926.1436(e).

[44 FR 8577, Feb. 9, 1979 as amended at 75 FR 48134, Aug. 9, 2010]

§1926.554 Overhead hoists.

(a) *General requirements.* (1) The safe working load of the overhead hoist, as determined by the manufacturer, shall be indicated on the hoist, and this safe working load shall not be exceeded.

(2) The supporting structure to which the hoist is attached shall have a safe working load equal to that of the hoist.

(3) The support shall be arranged so as to provide for free movement of the hoist and shall not restrict the hoist from lining itself up with the load.

(4) The hoist shall be installed only in locations that will permit the operator to stand clear of the load at all times.

(5) Air hoists shall be connected to an air supply of sufficient capacity and pressure to safely operate the hoist. All air hoses supplying air shall be positively connected to prevent their becoming disconnected during use.

(6) All overhead hoists in use shall meet the applicable requirements for construction, design, installation, testing, inspection, maintenance, and operation, as prescribed by the manufacturer.

(b) *Specific requirements.* [Reserved]

§1926.555 Conveyors.

(a) *General requirements.* (1) Means for stopping the motor or engine shall be provided at the operator's station. Conveyor systems shall be equipped with an audible warning signal to be sounded immediately before starting up the conveyor.

(2) If the operator's station is at a remote point, similar provisions for stopping the motor or engine shall be provided at the motor or engine location.

(3) Emergency stop switches shall be arranged so that the conveyor cannot be started again until the actuating stop switch has been reset to running or "on" position.

(4) Screw conveyors shall be guarded to prevent employee contact with turning flights.

(5) Where a conveyor passes over work areas, aisles, or thoroughfares, suitable guards shall be provided to protect employees required to work below the conveyors.

(6) All crossovers, aisles, and passageways shall be conspicuously marked by suitable signs, as required by subpart G of this part.

(7) Conveyors shall be locked out or otherwise rendered inoperable, and tagged out with a "Do Not Operate" tag during repairs and when operation is hazardous to employees performing maintenance work.

(8) All conveyors in use shall meet the applicable requirements for design, construction, inspection, testing, maintenance, and operation, as prescribed in the ANSI B20.1–1957, Safety Code for Conveyors, Cableways, and Related Equipment.

Subpart O—Motor Vehicles, Mechanized Equipment, and Marine Operations

AUTHORITY: Section 107, Construction Work Hours and Safety Standards Act (Construction Safety Act) (40 U.S.C. 333); Secs. 4, 6, 8, Occupational Safety and Health Act of 1970 (29 U.S.C. 653, 655, 657); Secretary of Labor's Order No. 12–71 (36 FR 8754), 8–76 (41 FR 25059), 9–83 (48 FR 35736), 1–90 (55 FR 9033), 6–96 (62 FR 111), or 5–2007 (72 FR 31159), as applicable. Section 1926.602 also issued under 29 CFR part 1911.

§1926.600 Equipment.

(a) *General requirements.* (1) All equipment left unattended at night, adjacent to a highway in normal use, or adjacent to construction areas where work is in progress, shall have appropriate lights or reflectors, or barricades equipped with appropriate lights or reflectors, to identify the location of the equipment.

(2) A safety tire rack, cage, or equivalent protection shall be provided and used when inflating, mounting, or dismounting tires installed on split rims, or rims equipped with locking rings or similar devices.

(3) (i) Heavy machinery, equipment, or parts thereof, which are suspended or held aloft by use of slings, hoists, or jacks shall be substantially blocked or cribbed to prevent falling or shifting

before employees are permitted to work under or between them. Bulldozer and scraper blades, end-loader buckets, dump bodies, and similar equipment, shall be either fully lowered or blocked when being repaired or when not in use. All controls shall be in a neutral position, with the motors stopped and brakes set, unless work being performed requires otherwise.

(ii) Whenever the equipment is parked, the parking brake shall be set. Equipment parked on inclines shall have the wheels chocked and the parking brake set.

(4) The use, care and charging of all batteries shall conform to the requirements of subpart K of this part.

(5) All cab glass shall be safety glass, or equivalent, that introduces no visible distortion affecting the safe operation of any machine covered by this subpart.

(6) All equipment covered by this subpart shall comply with the following requirements when working or being moved in the vicinity of power lines or energized transmitters, except where electrical distribution and transmission lines have been deenergized and visibly grounded at point of work or where insulating barriers, not a part of or an attachment to the equipment or machinery, have been erected to prevent physical contact with the lines:

(i) For lines rated 50 kV or below, minimum clearance between the lines and any part of the crane or load shall be 10 feet;

(ii) For lines rated over 50 kV, minimum clearance between the lines and any part of the crane or load shall be 10 feet plus 0.4 inch for each 1 kV over 50 kV, or twice the length of the line insulator, but never less than 10 feet;

(iii) In transit with no load and boom lowered, the equipment clearance shall be a minimum of 4 feet for voltages less than 50 kV, and 10 feet for voltages over 50 kV, up to and including 345 kV, and 16 feet for voltages up to and including 750 kV;

(iv) A person shall be designated to observe clearance of the equipment and give timely warning for all operations where it is difficult for the operator to maintain the desired clearance by visual means;

(v) Cage-type boom guards, insulating links, or proximity warning devices may be used on cranes, but the use of such devices shall not alter the requirements of any other regulation of this part even if such device is required by law or regulation;

(vi) Any overhead wire shall be considered to be an energized line unless and until the person owning such line or the electrical utility authorities indicate that it is not an energized line and it has been visibly grounded;

(vii) Prior to work near transmitter towers where an electrical charge can be induced in the equipment or materials being handled, the transmitter shall be de-energized or tests shall be made to determine if electrical charge is induced on the crane. The following precautions shall be taken when necessary to dissipate induced voltages:

(A) The equipment shall be provided with an electrical ground directly to the upper rotating structure supporting the boom; and

(B) Ground jumper cables shall be attached to materials being handled by boom equipment when electrical charge is induced while working near energized transmitters. Crews shall be provided with nonconductive poles having large alligator clips or other similar protection to attach the ground cable to the load.

(C) Combustible and flammable materials shall be removed from the immediate area prior to operations.

(7) *Rolling railroad cars.* Derail and/or bumper blocks shall be provided on spur railroad tracks where a rolling car could contact other cars being worked, enter a building, work or traffic area.

(b) *Specific requirements.* [Reserved]

[44 FR 8577, Feb. 9, 1979; 44 FR 20940, Apr. 6, 1979, as amended at 58 FR 35183, June 30, 1993; 75 FR 48134, Aug. 9, 2010]

§ 1926.601   Motor vehicles.

(a) *Coverage.* Motor vehicles as covered by this part are those vehicles that operate within an off-highway jobsite, not open to public traffic. The requirements of this section do not apply to equipment for which rules are prescribed in § 1926.602.

(b) *General requirements.* (1) All vehicles shall have a service brake system, an emergency brake system, and a parking brake system. These systems may use common components, and shall be maintained in operable condition.

(2)(i) Whenever visibility conditions warrant additional light, all vehicles, or combinations of vehicles, in use shall be equipped with at least two headlights and two taillights in operable condition.

(ii) All vehicles, or combination of vehicles, shall have brake lights in operable condition regardless of light conditions.

(3) All vehicles shall be equipped with an adequate audible warning device at the operator's station and in an operable condition.

(4) No employer shall use any motor vehicle equipment having an obstructed view to the rear unless:

(i) The vehicle has a reverse signal alarm audible above the surrounding noise level or:

(ii) The vehicle is backed up only when an observer signals that it is safe to do so.

(5) All vehicles with cabs shall be equipped with windshields and powered wipers. Cracked and broken glass shall be replaced. Vehicles operating in areas or under conditions that cause fogging or frosting of the windshields shall be equipped with operable defogging or defrosting devices.

(6) All haulage vehicles, whose pay load is loaded by means of cranes, power shovels, loaders, or similar equipment, shall have a cab shield and/or canopy adequate to protect the operator from shifting or falling materials.

(7) Tools and material shall be secured to prevent movement when transported in the same compartment with employees.

(8) Vehicles used to transport employees shall have seats firmly secured and adequate for the number of employees to be carried.

(9) Seat belts and anchorages meeting the requirements of 49 CFR part 571 (Department of Transportation, Federal Motor Vehicle Safety Standards) shall be installed in all motor vehicles.

(10) Trucks with dump bodies shall be equipped with positive means of support, permanently attached, and capable of being locked in position to prevent accidental lowering of the body while maintenance or inspection work is being done.

(11) Operating levers controlling hoisting or dumping devices on haulage bodies shall be equipped with a latch or other device which will prevent accidental starting or tripping of the mechanism.

(12) Trip handles for tailgates of dump trucks shall be so arranged that, in dumping, the operator will be in the clear.

(13) (i) All rubber-tired motor vehicle equipment manufactured on or after May 1, 1972, shall be equipped with fenders. All rubber-tired motor vehicle equipment manufactured before May 1, 1972, shall be equipped with fenders not later than May 1, 1973.

(ii) Mud flaps may be used in lieu of fenders whenever motor vehicle equipment is not designed for fenders.

(14) All vehicles in use shall be checked at the beginning of each shift to assure that the following parts, equipment, and accessories are in safe operating condition and free of apparent damage that could cause failure while in use: service brakes, including trailer brake connections; parking system (hand brake); emergency stopping system (brakes); tires; horn; steering mechanism; coupling devices; seat belts; operating controls; and safety devices. All defects shall be corrected before the vehicle is placed in service. These requirements also apply to equipment such as lights, reflectors, windshield wipers, defrosters, fire extinguishers, etc., where such equipment is necessary.

§1926.602 Material handling equipment.

(a) *Earthmoving equipment; General.* (1) These rules apply to the following types of earthmoving equipment: scrapers, loaders, crawler or wheel tractors, bulldozers, off-highway trucks, graders, agricultural and industrial tractors, and similar equipment. The promulgation of specific rules for compactors and rubber-tired "skid-steer" equipment is reserved pending consideration of standards currently being developed.

(2) *Seat belts.* (i) Seat belts shall be provided on all equipment covered by

359

this section and shall meet the requirements of the Society of Automotive Engineers, J386–1969, Seat Belts for Construction Equipment. Seat belts for agricultural and light industrial tractors shall meet the seat belt requirements of Society of Automotive Engineers J333a–1970, Operator Protection for Agricultural and Light Industrial Tractors.

(ii) Seat belts need not be provided for equipment which is designed only for standup operation.

(iii) Seat belts need not be provided for equipment which does not have roll-over protective structure (ROPS) or adequate canopy protection.

(3) *Access roadways and grades.* (i) No employer shall move or cause to be moved construction equipment or vehicles upon any access roadway or grade unless the access roadway or grade is constructed and maintained to accommodate safely the movement of the equipment and vehicles involved.

(ii) Every emergency access ramp and berm used by an employer shall be constructed to restrain and control runaway vehicles.

(4) *Brakes.* All earthmoving equipment mentioned in this § 1926.602(a) shall have a service braking system capable of stopping and holding the equipment fully loaded, as specified in Society of Automotive Engineers SAE–J237, Loader Dozer–1971, J236, Graders–1971, and J319b, Scrapers–1971. Brake systems for self-propelled rubber-tired off-highway equipment manufactured after January 1, 1972 shall meet the applicable minimum performance criteria set forth in the following Society of Automotive Engineers Recommended Practices:

Self-Propelled Scrapers	SAE J319b–1971.
Self-Propelled Graders	SAE J236–1971.
Trucks and Wagons	SAE J166–1971.
Front End Loaders and Dozers	SAE J237–1971.

(5) *Fenders.* Pneumatic-tired earthmoving haulage equipment (trucks, scrapers, tractors, and trailing units) whose maximum speed exceeds 15 miles per hour, shall be equipped with fenders on all wheels to meet the requirements of Society of Automotive Engineers SAE J321a–1970, Fenders for Pneumatic-Tired Earthmoving Haulage Equipment. An employer may, of course, at any time seek to show under § 1926.2, that the uncovered wheels

present no hazard to personnel from flying materials.

(6) *Rollover protective structures (ROPS).* See subpart W of this part for requirements for rollover protective structures and overhead protection.

(7) *Rollover protective structures for off-highway trucks.* The promulgation of standards for rollover protective structures for off-highway trucks is reserved pending further study and development.

(8) *Specific effective dates—brakes and fenders.* (i) Equipment mentioned in paragraph (a)(4) and (5) of this section, and manufactured after January 1, 1972, which is used by any employer after that date, shall comply with the applicable rules prescribed therein concerning brakes and fenders. Equipment mentioned in paragraphs (a) (4) and (5) of this section, and manufactured before January 1, 1972, which is used by any employer after that date, shall meet the applicable rules prescribed herein not later than June 30, 1973. It should be noted that, as permitted under § 1926.2, employers may request variations from the applicable brakes and fender standards required by this subpart. Employers wishing to seek variations from the applicable brakes and fenders rules may submit any requests for variations after the publication of this document in the FEDERAL REGISTER. Any statements intending to meet the requirements of § 1926.2(b)(4), should specify how the variation would protect the safety of the employees by providing for any compensating restrictions on the operation of equipment.

(ii) Notwithstanding the provisions of paragraphs (a)(5) and (a)(8)(i) of this section, the requirement that fenders be installed on pneumatic-tired earthmoving haulage equipment, is suspended pending reconsideration of the requirement.

(9) *Audible alarms.* (i) All bidirectional machines, such as rollers, compacters, front-end loaders, bulldozers, and similar equipment, shall be equipped with a horn, distinguishable from the surrounding noise level, which shall be operated as needed when the machine is moving in either direction. The horn shall be maintained in an operative condition.

(ii) No employer shall permit earthmoving or compacting equipment which has an obstructed view to the rear to be used in reverse gear unless the equipment has in operation a reverse signal alarm distinguishable from the surrounding noise level or an employee signals that it is safe to do so.

(10) *Scissor points.* Scissor points on all front-end loaders, which constitute a hazard to the operator during normal operation, shall be guarded.

(b) *Excavating and other equipment.* (1) Tractors covered in paragraph (a) of this section shall have seat belts as required for the operators when seated in the normal seating arrangement for tractor operation, even though backhoes, breakers, or other similar attachments are used on these machines for excavating or other work.

(2) For the purposes of this subpart and of subpart N of this part, the nomenclatures and descriptions for measurement of dimensions of machinery and attachments shall be as described in Society of Automotive Engineers 1970 Handbook, pages 1088 through 1103.

(3) The safety requirements, ratios, or limitations applicable to machines or attachment usage covered in Power Crane and Shovel Associations Standards No. 1 and No. 2 of 1968, and No. 3 of 1969, shall be complied with, and shall apply to cranes, machines, and attachments under this part.

(c) *Lifting and hauling equipment (other than equipment covered under subpart N of this part).* (1) Industrial trucks shall meet the requirements of § 1926.600 and the following:

(i) Lift trucks, stackers, etc., shall have the rated capacity clearly posted on the vehicle so as to be clearly visible to the operator. When auxiliary removable counterweights are provided by the manufacturer, corresponding alternate rated capacities also shall be clearly shown on the vehicle. These ratings shall not be exceeded.

(ii) No modifications or additions which affect the capacity or safe operation of the equipment shall be made without the manufacturer's written approval. If such modifications or changes are made, the capacity, operation, and maintenance instruction plates, tags, or decals shall be changed accordingly. In no case shall the original safety factor of the equipment be reduced.

(iii) If a load is lifted by two or more trucks working in unison, the proportion of the total load carried by any one truck shall not exceed its capacity.

(iv) Steering or spinner knobs shall not be attached to the steering wheel unless the steering mechanism is of a type that prevents road reactions from causing the steering handwheel to spin. The steering knob shall be mounted within the periphery of the wheel.

(v) All high lift rider industrial trucks shall be equipped with overhead guards which meet the configuration and structural requirements as defined in paragraph 421 of American National Standards Institute B56.1-1969, Safety Standards for Powered Industrial Trucks.

(vi) All industrial trucks in use shall meet the applicable requirements of design, construction, stability, inspection, testing, maintenance, and operation, as defined in American National Standards Institute B56.1-1969, Safety Standards for Powered Industrial Trucks.

(vii) Unauthorized personnel shall not be permitted to ride on powered industrial trucks. A safe place to ride shall be provided where riding of trucks is authorized.

(viii) Whenever a truck is equipped with vertical only, or vertical and horizontal controls elevatable with the lifting carriage or forks for lifting personnel, the following additional precautions shall be taken for the protection of personnel being elevated.

(A) Use of a safety platform firmly secured to the lifting carriage and/or forks.

(B) Means shall be provided whereby personnel on the platform can shut off power to the truck.

(C) Such protection from falling objects as indicated necessary by the operating conditions shall be provided.

(d) *Powered industrial truck operator training.*

NOTE: The requirements applicable to construction work under this paragraph are

361

identical to those set forth at § 1910.178(l) of this chapter.

[44 FR 8577, Feb. 9, 1979; 44 FR 20940, Apr. 6, 1979, as amended at 58 FR 35183, June 30, 1993; 63 FR 66274, Dec. 1, 1998]

§ 1926.603 Pile driving equipment.

(a) *General requirements.* (1) Boilers and piping systems which are a part of, or used with, pile driving equipment shall meet the applicable requirements of the American Society of Mechanical Engineers, Power Boilers (section I).

(2) All pressure vessels which are a part of, or used with, pile driving equipment shall meet the applicable requirements of the American Society of Mechanical Engineers, Pressure Vessels (section VIII).

(3) Overhead protection, which will not obscure the vision of the operator and which meets the requirements of subpart N of this part, shall be provided. Protection shall be the equivalent of 2-inch planking or other solid material of equivalent strength.

(4) Stop blocks shall be provided for the leads to prevent the hammer from being raised against the head block.

(5) A blocking device, capable of safely supporting the weight of the hammer, shall be provided for placement in the leads under the hammer at all times while employees are working under the hammer.

(6) Guards shall be provided across the top of the head block to prevent the cable from jumping out of the sheaves.

(7) When the leads must be inclined in the driving of batter piles, provisions shall be made to stabilize the leads.

(8) Fixed leads shall be provided with ladder, and adequate rings, or similar attachment points, so that the loft worker may engage his safety belt lanyard to the leads. If the leads are provided with loft platforms(s), such platform(s) shall be protected by standard guardrails.

(9) Steam hose leading to a steam hammer or jet pipe shall be securely attached to the hammer with an adequate length of at least ¼-inch diameter chain or cable to prevent whipping in the event the joint at the hammer is broken. Air hammer hoses shall be provided with the same protection as required for steam lines.

(10) Safety chains, or equivalent means, shall be provided for each hose connection to prevent the line from thrashing around in case the coupling becomes disconnected.

(11) Steam line controls shall consist of two shutoff valves, one of which shall be a quick-acting lever type within easy reach of the hammer operator.

(12) Guys, outriggers, thrustouts, or counterbalances shall be provided as necessary to maintain stability of pile driver rigs.

(b) *Pile driving from barges and floats.* Barges or floats supporting pile driving operations shall meet the applicable requirements of § 1926.605.

(c) *Pile driving equipment.* (1) Engineers and winchmen shall accept signals only from the designated signalmen.

(2) All employees shall be kept clear when piling is being hoisted into the leads.

(3) When piles are being driven in an excavated pit, the walls of the pit shall be sloped to the angle of repose or sheet-piled and braced.

(4) When steel tube piles are being "blown out", employees shall be kept well beyond the range of falling materials.

(5) When it is necessary to cut off the tops of driven piles, pile driving operations shall be suspended except where the cutting operations are located at least twice the length of the longest pile from the driver.

(6) When driving jacked piles, all access pits shall be provided with ladders and bulkheaded curbs to prevent material from falling into the pit.

§ 1926.604 Site clearing.

(a) *General requirements.* (1) Employees engaged in site clearing shall be protected from hazards of irritant and toxic plants and suitably instructed in the first aid treatment available.

(2) All equipment used in site clearing operations shall be equipped with rollover guards meeting the requirements of this subpart. In addition, rider-operated equipment shall be equipped with an overhead and rear canopy guard meeting the following requirements:

(i) The overhead covering on this canopy structure shall be of not less than ⅛-inch steel plate or ¼-inch woven wire mesh with openings no greater than 1 inch, or equivalent.

(ii) The opening in the rear of the canopy structure shall be covered with not less than ¼-inch woven wire mesh with openings no greater than 1 inch.

(b) *Specific requirements.* [Reserved]

§1926.605 Marine operations and equipment.

(a) *Material handling operations.* (1) Operations fitting the definition of "material handling" shall be performed in conformance with applicable requirements of part 1918, "Safety and Health Regulations for Longshoring" of this chapter. The term "longshoring operations" means the loading, unloading, moving, or handling of construction materials, equipment and supplies, etc. into, in, on, or out of any vessel from a fixed structure or shore-to-vessel, vessel-to-shore or fixed structure or vessel-to-vessel.

(b) *Access to barges.* (1) Ramps for access of vehicles to or between barges shall be of adequate strength, provided with side boards, well maintained, and properly secured.

(2) Unless employees can step safely to or from the wharf, float, barge, or river towboat, either a ramp, meeting the requirements of paragraph (b)(1) of this section, or a safe walkway, shall be provided.

(3) Jacob's ladders shall be of the double rung or flat tread type. They shall be well maintained and properly secured.

(4) A Jacob's ladder shall either hang without slack from its lashings or be pulled up entirely.

(5) When the upper end of the means of access rests on or is flush with the top of the bulwark, substantial steps properly secured and equipped with at least one substantial hand rail approximately 33 inches in height, shall be provided between the top of the bulwark and the deck.

(6) Obstructions shall not be laid on or across the gangway.

(7) The means of access shall be adequately illuminated for its full length.

(8) Unless the structure makes it impossible, the means of access shall be

so located that the load will not pass over employees.

(c) *Working surfaces of barges.* (1) Employees shall not be permitted to walk along the sides of covered lighters or barges with coamings more than 5 feet high, unless there is a 3-foot clear walkway, or a grab rail, or a taut handline is provided.

(2) Decks and other working surfaces shall be maintained in a safe condition.

(3) Employees shall not be permitted to pass fore and aft, over, or around deckloads, unless there is a safe passage.

(4) Employees shall not be permitted to walk over deckloads from rail to coaming unless there is a safe passage. If it is necessary to stand at the outboard or inboard edge of the deckload where less than 24 inches of bulwark, rail, coaming, or other protection exists, all employees shall be provided with a suitable means of protection against falling from the deckload.

(d) *First-aid and lifesaving equipment.* (1) Provisions for rendering first aid and medical assistance shall be in accordance with subpart D of this part.

(2) The employer shall ensure that there is in the vicinity of each barge in use at least one U.S. Coast Guard-approved 30-inch lifering with not less than 90 feet of line attached, and at least one portable or permanent ladder which will reach the top of the apron to the surface of the water. If the above equipment is not available at the pier, the employer shall furnish it during the time that he is working the barge.

(3) Employees walking or working on the unguarded decks of barges shall be protected with U.S. Coast Guard-approved work vests or buoyant vests.

(e) *Commercial diving operations.* Commercial diving operations shall be subject to subpart T of part 1910, §§1910.401–1910.441, of this chapter.

[39 FR 22801, June 24, 1974, as amended at 42 FR 37674, July 22, 1977]

§1926.606 Definitions applicable to this subpart.

(a) *Apron*—The area along the waterfront edge of the pier or wharf.

(b) *Bulwark*—The side of a ship above the upper deck.

(c) *Coaming*—The raised frame, as around a hatchway in the deck, to keep out water.

(d) *Jacob's ladder*—A marine ladder of rope or chain with wooden or metal rungs.

(e) *Rail,* for the purpose of § 1926.605, means a light structure serving as a guard at the outer edge of a ship's deck.

Subpart P—Excavations

AUTHORITY: Sec. 107, Contract Worker Hours and Safety Standards Act (Construction Safety Act) (40 U.S.C. 333); Secs. 4, 6, 8, Occupational Safety and Health Act of 1970 (29 U.S.C. 653, 655, 657); Secretary of Labor's Order No. 12-71 (36 FR 8754), 8-76 (41 FR 25059), or 9-83 (48 FR 35736), as applicable, and 29 CFR part 1911.

SOURCE: 54 FR 45959, Oct. 31, 1989, unless otherwise noted.

§ 1926.650 Scope, application, and definitions applicable to this subpart.

(a) *Scope and application.* This subpart applies to all open excavations made in the earth's surface. Excavations are defined to include trenches.

(b) *Definitions applicable to this subpart.*

Accepted engineering practices means those requirements which are compatible with standards of practice required by a registered professional engineer.

Aluminum Hydraulic Shoring means a pre-engineered shoring system comprised of aluminum hydraulic cylinders (crossbraces) used in conjunction with vertical rails (uprights) or horizontal rails (walers). Such system is designed, specifically to support the sidewalls of an excavation and prevent cave-ins.

Bell-bottom pier hole means a type of shaft or footing excavation, the bottom of which is made larger than the cross section above to form a belled shape.

Benching (Benching system) means a method of protecting employees from cave-ins by excavating the sides of an excavation to form one or a series of horizontal levels or steps, usually with vertical or near-vertical surfaces between levels.

Cave-in means the separation of a mass of soil or rock material from the side of an excavation, or the loss of soil from under a trench shield or support system, and its sudden movement into the excavation, either by falling or sliding, in sufficient quantity so that it could entrap, bury, or otherwise injure and immobilize a person.

Competent person means one who is capable of identifying existing and predictable hazards in the surroundings, or working conditions which are unsanitary, hazardous, or dangerous to employees, and who has authorization to take prompt corrective measures to eliminate them.

Cross braces mean the horizontal members of a shoring system installed perpendicular to the sides of the excavation, the ends of which bear against either uprights or wales.

Excavation means any man-made cut, cavity, trench, or depression in an earth surface, formed by earth removal.

Faces or *sides* means the vertical or inclined earth surfaces formed as a result of excavation work.

Failure means the breakage, displacement, or permanent deformation of a structural member or connection so as to reduce its structural integrity and its supportive capabilities.

Hazardous atmosphere means an atmosphere which by reason of being explosive, flammable, poisonous, corrosive, oxidizing, irritating, oxygen deficient, toxic, or otherwise harmful, may cause death, illness, or injury.

Kickout means the accidental release or failure of a cross brace.

Protective system means a method of protecting employees from cave-ins, from material that could fall or roll from an excavation face or into an excavation, or from the collapse of adjacent structures. Protective systems include support systems, sloping and benching systems, shield systems, and other systems that provide the necessary protection.

Ramp means an inclined walking or working surface that is used to gain access to one point from another, and is constructed from earth or from structural materials such as steel or wood.

Registered Professional Engineer means a person who is registered as a professional engineer in the state where the work is to be performed. However, a professional engineer, registered in any state is deemed to be a "registered professional engineer" within the meaning of this standard when approving designs for "manufactured protective systems" or "tabulated data" to be used in interstate commerce.

Sheeting means the members of a shoring system that retain the earth in position and in turn are supported by other members of the shoring system.

Shield (Shield system) means a structure that is able to withstand the forces imposed on it by a cave-in and thereby protect employees within the structure. Shields can be permanent structures or can be designed to be portable and moved along as work progresses. Additionally, shields can be either premanufactured or job-built in accordance with §1926.652 (c)(3) or (c)(4). Shields used in trenches are usually referred to as "trench boxes" or "trench shields."

Shoring (Shoring system) means a structure such as a metal hydraulic, mechanical or timber shoring system that supports the sides of an excavation and which is designed to prevent cave-ins.

Sides. See "Faces."

Sloping (Sloping system) means a method of protecting employees from cave-ins by excavating to form sides of an excavation that are inclined away from the excavation so as to prevent cave-ins. The angle of incline required to prevent a cave-in varies with differences in such factors as the soil type, environmental conditions of exposure, and application of surcharge loads.

Stable rock means natural solid mineral material that can be excavated with vertical sides and will remain intact while exposed. Unstable rock is considered to be stable when the rock material on the side or sides of the excavation is secured against caving-in or movement by rock bolts or by another protective system that has been designed by a registered professional engineer.

Structural ramp means a ramp built of steel or wood, usually used for vehicle access. Ramps made of soil or rock are not considered structural ramps.

Support system means a structure such as underpinning, bracing, or shoring, which provides support to an adja-

cent structure, underground installation, or the sides of an excavation.

Tabulated data means tables and charts approved by a registered professional engineer and used to design and construct a protective system.

Trench (Trench excavation) means a narrow excavation (in relation to its length) made below the surface of the ground. In general, the depth is greater than the width, but the width of a trench (measured at the bottom) is not greater than 15 feet (4.6 m). If forms or other structures are installed or constructed in an excavation so as to reduce the dimension measured from the forms or structure to the side of the excavation to 15 feet (4.6 m) or less (measured at the bottom of the excavation), the excavation is also considered to be a trench.

Trench box. See "Shield."

Trench shield. See "Shield."

Uprights means the vertical members of a trench shoring system placed in contact with the earth and usually positioned so that individual members do not contact each other. Uprights placed so that individual members are closely spaced, in contact with or interconnected to each other, are often called "sheeting."

Wales means horizontal members of a shoring system placed parallel to the excavation face whose sides bear against the vertical members of the shoring system or earth.

§1926.651 Specific excavation requirements.

(a) *Surface encumbrances.* All surface encumbrances that are located so as to create a hazard to employees shall be removed or supported, as necessary, to safeguard employees.

(b) *Underground installations.* (1) The estimated location of utility installations, such as sewer, telephone, fuel, electric, water lines, or any other underground installations that reasonably may be expected to be encountered during excavation work, shall be determined prior to opening an excavation.

(2) Utility companies or owners shall be contacted within established or customary local response times, advised of

the proposed work, and asked to establish the location of the utility underground installations prior to the start of actual excavation. When utility companies or owners cannot respond to a request to locate underground utility installations within 24 hours (unless a longer period is required by state or local law), or cannot establish the exact location of these installations, the employer may proceed, provided the employer does so with caution, and provided detection equipment or other acceptable means to locate utility installations are used.

(3) When excavation operations approach the estimated location of underground installations, the exact location of the installations shall be determined by safe and acceptable means.

(4) While the excavation is open, underground installations shall be protected, supported or removed as necessary to safeguard employees.

(c) *Access and egress*—(1) *Structural ramps.* (i) Structural ramps that are used solely by employees as a means of access or egress from excavations shall be designed by a competent person. Structural ramps used for access or egress of equipment shall be designed by a competent person qualified in structural design, and shall be constructed in accordance with the design.

(ii) Ramps and runways constructed of two or more structural members shall have the structural members connected together to prevent displacement.

(iii) Structural members used for ramps and runways shall be of uniform thickness.

(iv) Cleats or other appropriate means used to connect runway structural members shall be attached to the bottom of the runway or shall be attached in a manner to prevent tripping.

(v) Structural ramps used in lieu of steps shall be provided with cleats or other surface treatments on the top surface to prevent slipping.

(2) *Means of egress from trench excavations.* A stairway, ladder, ramp or other safe means of egress shall be located in trench excavations that are 4 feet (1.22 m) or more in depth so as to require no more than 25 feet (7.62 m) of lateral travel for employees.

(d) *Exposure to vehicular traffic.* Employees exposed to public vehicular traffic shall be provided with, and shall wear, warning vests or other suitable garments marked with or made of reflectorized or high-visibility material.

(e) *Exposure to falling loads.* No employee shall be permitted underneath loads handled by lifting or digging equipment. Employees shall be required to stand away from any vehicle being loaded or unloaded to avoid being struck by any spillage or falling materials. Operators may remain in the cabs of vehicles being loaded or unloaded when the vehicles are equipped, in accordance with § 1926.601(b)(6), to provide adequate protection for the operator during loading and unloading operations.

(f) *Warning system for mobile equipment.* When mobile equipment is operated adjacent to an excavation, or when such equipment is required to approach the edge of an excavation, and the operator does not have a clear and direct view of the edge of the excavation, a warning system shall be utilized such as barricades, hand or mechanical signals, or stop logs. If possible, the grade should be away from the excavation.

(g) *Hazardous atmospheres*—(1) *Testing and controls.* In addition to the requirements set forth in subparts D and E of this part (29 CFR 1926.50–1926.107) to prevent exposure to harmful levels of atmospheric contaminants and to assure acceptable atmospheric conditions, the following requirements shall apply:

(i) Where oxygen deficiency (atmospheres containing less than 19.5 percent oxygen) or a hazardous atmosphere exists or could reasonably be expected to exist, such as in excavations in landfill areas or excavations in areas where hazardous substances are stored nearby, the atmospheres in the excavation shall be tested before employees enter excavations greater than 4 feet (1.22 m) in depth.

(ii) Adequate precautions shall be taken to prevent employee exposure to atmospheres containing less than 19.5 percent oxygen and other hazardous atmospheres. These precautions include providing proper respiratory protection or ventilation in accordance with subparts D and E of this part respectively.

(iii) Adequate precaution shall be taken such as providing ventilation, to prevent employee exposure to an atmosphere containing a concentration of a flammable gas in excess of 20 percent of the lower flammable limit of the gas.

(iv) When controls are used that are intended to reduce the level of atmospheric contaminants to acceptable levels, testing shall be conducted as often as necessary to ensure that the atmosphere remains safe.

(2) *Emergency rescue equipment.* (i) Emergency rescue equipment, such as breathing apparatus, a safety harness and line, or a basket stretcher, shall be readily available where hazardous atmospheric conditions exist or may reasonably be expected to develop during work in an excavation. This equipment shall be attended when in use.

(ii) Employees entering bell-bottom pier holes, or other similar deep and confined footing excavations, shall wear a harness with a life-line securely attached to it. The lifeline shall be separate from any line used to handle materials, and shall be individually attended at all times while the employee wearing the lifeline is in the excavation.

(h) *Protection from hazards associated with water accumulation.* (1) Employees shall not work in excavations in which there is accumulated water, or in excavations in which water is accumulating, unless adequate precautions have been taken to protect employees against the hazards posed by water accumulation. The precautions necessary to protect employees adequately vary with each situation, but could include special support or shield systems to protect from cave-ins, water removal to control the level of accumulating water, or use of a safety harness and lifeline.

(2) If water is controlled or prevented from accumulating by the use of water removal equipment, the water removal equipment and operations shall be monitored by a competent person to ensure proper operation.

(3) If excavation work interrupts the natural drainage of surface water (such as streams), diversion ditches, dikes, or other suitable means shall be used to prevent surface water from entering the excavation and to provide adequate drainage of the area adjacent to the excavation. Excavations subject to runoff from heavy rains will require an inspection by a competent person and compliance with paragraphs (h)(1) and (h)(2) of this section.

(i) *Stability of adjacent structures.* (1) Where the stability of adjoining buildings, walls, or other structures is endangered by excavation operations, support systems such as shoring, bracing, or underpinning shall be provided to ensure the stability of such structures for the protection of employees.

(2) Excavation below the level of the base or footing of any foundation or retaining wall that could be reasonably expected to pose a hazard to employees shall not be permitted except when:

(i) A support system, such as underpinning, is provided to ensure the safety of employees and the stability of the structure; or

(ii) The excavation is in stable rock; or

(iii) A registered professional engineer has approved the determination that the structure is sufficently removed from the excavation so as to be unaffected by the excavation activity; or

(iv) A registered professional engineer has approved the determination that such excavation work will not pose a hazard to employees.

(3) Sidewalks, pavements, and appurtenant structure shall not be undermined unless a support system or another method of protection is provided to protect employees from the possible collapse of such structures.

(j) *Protection of employees from loose rock or soil.* (1) Adequate protection shall be provided to protect employees from loose rock or soil that could pose a hazard by falling or rolling from an excavation face. Such protection shall consist of scaling to remove loose material; installation of protective barricades at intervals as necessary on the face to stop and contain falling material; or other means that provide equivalent protection.

(2) Employees shall be protected from excavated or other materials or equipment that could pose a hazard by falling or rolling into excavations. Protection shall be provided by placing and keeping such materials or equipment at least 2 feet (.61 m) from the edge of excavations, or by the use of retaining devices that are sufficient to prevent materials or equipment from falling or rolling into excavations, or by a combination of both if necessary.

(k) *Inspections.* (1) Daily inspections of excavations, the adjacent areas, and protective systems shall be made by a competent person for evidence of a situation that could result in possible cave-ins, indications of failure of protective systems, hazardous atmospheres, or other hazardous conditions. An inspection shall be conducted by the competent person prior to the start of work and as needed throughout the shift. Inspections shall also be made after every rainstorm or other hazard increasing occurrence. These inspections are only required when employee exposure can be reasonably anticipated.

(2) Where the competent person finds evidence of a situation that could result in a possible cave-in, indications of failure of protective systems, hazardous atmospheres, or other hazardous conditions, exposed employees shall be removed from the hazardous area until the necessary precautions have been taken to ensure their safety.

(l) Walkways shall be provided where employees or equipment are required or permitted to cross over excavations. Guardrails which comply with §1926.502(b) shall be provided where walkways are 6 feet (1.8 m) or more above lower levels.

[54 FR 45959, Oct. 31, 1989, as amended at 59 FR 40730, Aug. 9, 1994]

§ 1926.652 Requirements for protective systems.

(a) *Protection of employees in excavations.* (1) Each employee in an excavation shall be protected from cave-ins by an adequate protective system designed in accordance with paragraph (b) or (c) of this section except when:

(i) Excavations are made entirely in stable rock; or

(ii) Excavations are less than 5 feet (1.52m) in depth and examination of the ground by a competent person provides no indication of a potential cave-in.

(2) Protective systems shall have the capacity to resist without failure all loads that are intended or could reasonably be expected to be applied or transmitted to the system.

(b) *Design of sloping and benching systems.* The slopes and configurations of sloping and benching systems shall be selected and constructed by the employer or his designee and shall be in accordance with the requirements of paragraph (b)(1); or, in the alternative, paragraph (b)(2); or, in the alternative, paragraph (b)(3), or, in the alternative, paragraph (b)(4), as follows:

(1) *Option (1)—Allowable configurations and slopes.* (i) Excavations shall be sloped at an angle not steeper than one and one-half horizontal to one vertical (34 degrees measured from the horizontal), unless the employer uses one of the other options listed below.

(ii) Slopes specified in paragraph (b)(1)(i) of this section, shall be excavated to form configurations that are in accordance with the slopes shown for Type C soil in appendix B to this subpart.

(2) *Option (2)—Determination of slopes and configurations using Appendices A and B.* Maximum allowable slopes, and allowable configurations for sloping and benching systems, shall be determined in accordance with the conditions and requirements set forth in appendices A and B to this subpart.

(3) *Option (3)—Designs using other tabulated data.* (i) Designs of sloping or benching systems shall be selected from and be in accordance with tabulated data, such as tables and charts.

(ii) The tabulated data shall be in written form and shall include all of the following:

(A) Identification of the parameters that affect the selection of a sloping or benching system drawn from such data;

(B) Identification of the limits of use of the data, to include the magnitude and configuration of slopes determined to be safe;

(C) Explanatory information as may be necessary to aid the user in making a correct selection of a protective system from the data.

(iii) At least one copy of the tabulated data which identifies the registered professional engineer who approved the data, shall be maintained at the jobsite during construction of the protective system. After that time the data may be stored off the jobsite, but a copy of the data shall be made available to the Secretary upon request.

(4) *Option (4)—Design by a registered professional engineer.* (i) Sloping and benching systems not utilizing Option (1) or Option (2) or Option (3) under paragraph (b) of this section shall be approved by a registered professional engineer.

(ii) Designs shall be in written form and shall include at least the following:

(A) The magnitude of the slopes that were determined to be safe for the particular project;

(B) The configurations that were determined to be safe for the particular project; and

(C) The identity of the registered professional engineer approving the design.

(iii) At least one copy of the design shall be maintained at the jobsite while the slope is being constructed. After that time the design need not be at the jobsite, but a copy shall be made available to the Secretary upon request.

(c) *Design of support systems, shield systems, and other protective systems.* Designs of support systems shield systems, and other protective systems shall be selected and constructed by the employer or his designee and shall be in accordance with the requirements of paragraph (c)(1); or, in the alternative, paragraph (c)(2); or, in the alternative, paragraph (c)(3); or, in the alternative paragraph (c)(4) as follows:

(1) *Option (1)—Designs using appendices A, C and D.* Designs for timber shoring in trenches shall be determined in accordance with the conditions and requirements set forth in appendices A and C to this subpart. Designs for aluminum hydraulic shoring shall be in accordance with paragraph (c)(2) of this section, but if manufacturer's tabulated data cannot be utilized, designs shall be in accordance with appendix D.

(2) *Option (2)—Designs Using Manufacturer's Tabulated Data.* (i) Design of support systems, shield systems, or other protective systems that are drawn from manufacturer's tabulated data shall be in accordance with all specifications, recommendations, and limitations issued or made by the manufacturer.

(ii) Deviation from the specifications, recommendations, and limitations issued or made by the manufacturer shall only be allowed after the manufacturer issues specific written approval.

(iii) Manufacturer's specifications, recommendations, and limitations, and manufacturer's approval to deviate from the specifications, recommendations, and limitations shall be in written form at the jobsite during construction of the protective system. After that time this data may be stored off the jobsite, but a copy shall be made available to the Secretary upon request.

(3) *Option (3)—Designs using other tabulated data.* (i) Designs of support systems, shield systems, or other protective systems shall be selected from and be in accordance with tabulated data, such as tables and charts.

(ii) The tabulated data shall be in written form and include all of the following:

(A) Identification of the parameters that affect the selection of a protective system drawn from such data;

(B) Identification of the limits of use of the data;

(C) Explanatory information as may be necessary to aid the user in making a correct selection of a protective system from the data.

(iii) At least one copy of the tabulated data, which identifies the registered professional engineer who approved the data, shall be maintained at the jobsite during construction of the protective system. After that time the data may be stored off the jobsite, but a copy of the data shall be made available to the Secretary upon request.

(4) *Option (4)—Design by a registered professional engineer.* (i) Support systems, shield systems, and other protective systems not utilizing Option 1, Option 2 or Option 3, above, shall be approved by a registered professional engineer.

(ii) Designs shall be in written form and shall include the following:

369

(A) A plan indicating the sizes, types, and configurations of the materials to be used in the protective system; and

(B) The identity of the registered professional engineer approving the design.

(iii) At least one copy of the design shall be maintained at the jobsite during construction of the protective system. After that time, the design may be stored off the jobsite, but a copy of the design shall be made available to the Secretary upon request.

(d) *Materials and equipment.* (1) Materials and equipment used for protective systems shall be free from damage or defects that might impair their proper function.

(2) Manufactured materials and equipment used for protective systems shall be used and maintained in a manner that is consistent with the recommendations of the manufacturer, and in a manner that will prevent employee exposure to hazards.

(3) When material or equipment that is used for protective systems is damaged, a competent person shall examine the material or equipment and evaluate its suitability for continued use. If the competent person cannot assure the material or equipment is able to support the intended loads or is otherwise suitable for safe use, then such material or equipment shall be removed from service, and shall be evaluated and approved by a registered professional engineer before being returned to service.

(e) *Installation and removal of support*—(1) *General.* (i) Members of support systems shall be securely connected together to prevent sliding, falling, kickouts, or other predictable failure.

(ii) Support systems shall be installed and removed in a manner that protects employees from cave-ins, structural collapses, or from being struck by members of the support system.

(iii) Individual members of support systems shall not be subjected to loads exceeding those which those members were designed to withstand.

(iv) Before temporary removal of individual members begins, additional precautions shall be taken to ensure the safety of employees, such as installing other structural members to carry the loads imposed on the support system.

(v) Removal shall begin at, and progress from, the bottom of the excavation. Members shall be released slowly so as to note any indication of possible failure of the remaining members of the structure or possible cave-in of the sides of the excavation.

(vi) Backfilling shall progress together with the removal of support systems from excavations.

(2) *Additional requirements for support systems for trench excavations.* (i) Excavation of material to a level no greater than 2 feet (.61 m) below the bottom of the members of a support system shall be permitted, but only if the system is designed to resist the forces calculated for the full depth of the trench, and there are no indications while the trench is open of a possible loss of soil from behind or below the bottom of the support system.

(ii) Installation of a support system shall be closely coordinated with the excavation of trenches.

(f) *Sloping and benching systems.* Employees shall not be permitted to work on the faces of sloped or benched excavations at levels above other employees except when employees at the lower levels are adequately protected from the hazard of falling, rolling, or sliding material or equipment.

(g) *Shield systems*—(1) *General.* (i) Shield systems shall not be subjected to loads exceeding those which the system was designed to withstand.

(ii) Shields shall be installed in a manner to restrict lateral or other hazardous movement of the shield in the event of the application of sudden lateral loads.

(iii) Employees shall be protected from the hazard of cave-ins when entering or exiting the areas protected by shields.

(iv) Employees shall not be allowed in shields when shields are being installed, removed, or moved vertically.

(2) *Additional requirement for shield systems used in trench excavations.* Excavations of earth material to a level not greater than 2 feet (.61 m) below the bottom of a shield shall be permitted, but only if the shield is designed to resist the forces calculated for the full

depth of the trench, and there are no indications while the trench is open of a possible loss of soil from behind or below the bottom of the shield.

Appendix A to Subpart P of Part 1926—Soil Classification

(a) *Scope and application*—(1) *Scope.* This appendix describes a method of classifying soil and rock deposits based on site and environmental conditions, and on the structure and composition of the earth deposits. The appendix contains definitions, sets forth requirements, and describes acceptable visual and manual tests for use in classifying soils.

(2) *Application.* This appendix applies when a sloping or benching system is designed in accordance with the requirements set forth in § 1926.652(b)(2) as a method of protection for employees from cave-ins. This appendix also applies when timber shoring for excavations is designed as a method of protection from cave-ins in accordance with appendix C to subpart P of part 1926, and when aluminum hydraulic shoring is designed in accordance with appendix D. This appendix also applies if other protective systems are designed and selected for use from data prepared in accordance with the requirements set forth in § 1926.652(c), and the use of the data is predicated on the use of the soil classification system set forth in this appendix.

(b) *Definitions.* The definitions and examples given below are based on, in whole or in part, the following: American Society for Testing Materials (ASTM) Standards D653–85 and D2488; The Unified Soils Classification System, The U.S. Department of Agriculture (USDA) Textural Classification Scheme; and The National Bureau of Standards Report BSS–121.

Cemented soil means a soil in which the particles are held together by a chemical agent, such as calcium carbonate, such that a hand-size sample cannot be crushed into powder or individual soil particles by finger pressure.

Cohesive soil means clay (fine grained soil), or soil with a high clay content, which has cohesive strength. Cohesive soil does not crumble, can be excavated with vertical sideslopes, and is plastic when moist. Cohesive soil is hard to break up when dry, and exhibits significant cohesion when submerged. Cohesive soils include clayey silt, sandy clay, silty clay, clay and organic clay.

Dry soil means soil that does not exhibit visible signs of moisture content.

Fissured means a soil material that has a tendency to break along definite planes of fracture with little resistance, or a material that exhibits open cracks, such as tension cracks, in an exposed surface.

Granular soil means gravel, sand, or silt, (coarse grained soil) with little or no clay content. Granular soil has no cohesive

strength. Some moist granular soils exhibit apparent cohesion. Granular soil cannot be molded when moist and crumbles easily when dry.

Layered system means two or more distinctly different soil or rock types arranged in layers. Micaceous seams or weakened planes in rock or shale are considered layered.

Moist soil means a condition in which a soil looks and feels damp. Moist cohesive soil can easily be shaped into a ball and rolled into small diameter threads before crumbling. Moist granular soil that contains some cohesive material will exhibit signs of cohesion between particles.

Plastic means a property of a soil which allows the soil to be deformed or molded without cracking, or appreciable volume change.

Saturated soil means a soil in which the voids are filled with water. Saturation does not require flow. Saturation, or near saturation, is necessary for the proper use of instruments such as a pocket penetrometer or sheer vane.

Soil classification system means, for the purpose of this subpart, a method of categorizing soil and rock deposits in a hierarchy of Stable Rock, Type A, Type B, and Type C, in decreasing order of stability. The categories are determined based on an analysis of the properties and performance characteristics of the deposits and the environmental conditions of exposure.

Stable rock means natural solid mineral matter that can be excavated with vertical sides and remain intact while exposed.

Submerged soil means soil which is underwater or is free seeping.

Type A means cohesive soils with an unconfined compressive strength of 1.5 ton per square foot (tsf) (144 kPa) or greater. Examples of cohesive soils are: clay, silty clay, sandy clay, clay loam and, in some cases, silty clay loam and sandy clay loam. Cemented soils such as caliche and hardpan are also considered Type A. However, no soil is Type A if:

(i) The soil is fissured; or

(ii) The soil is subject to vibration from heavy traffic, pile driving, or similar effects; or

(iii) The soil has been previously disturbed; or

(iv) The soil is part of a sloped, layered system where the layers dip into the excavation on a slope of four horizontal to one vertical (4H:1V) or greater; or

(v) The material is subject to other factors that would require it to be classified as a less stable material.

Type B means:

(i) Cohesive soil with an unconfined compressive strength greater than 0.5 tsf (48 kPa) but less than 1.5 tsf (144 kPa); or

(ii) Granular cohesionless soils including: angular gravel (similar to crushed rock), silt, silt loam, sandy loam and, in some cases, silty clay loam and sandy clay loam.

(iii) Previously disturbed soils except those which would otherwise be classed as Type C soil.

(iv) Soil that meets the unconfined compressive strength or cementation requirements for Type A, but is fissured or subject to vibration; or

(v) Dry rock that is not stable; or

(vi) Material that is part of a sloped, layered system where the layers dip into the excavation on a slope less steep than four horizontal to one vertical (4H:1V), but only if the material would otherwise be classified as Type B.

Type C means:

(i) Cohesive soil with an unconfined compressive strength of 0.5 tsf (48 kPa) or less; or

(ii) Granular soils including gravel, sand, and loamy sand; or

(iii) Submerged soil or soil from which water is freely seeping; or

(iv) Submerged rock that is not stable, or

(v) Material in a sloped, layered system where the layers dip into the excavation or a slope of four horizontal to one vertical (4H:1V) or steeper.

Unconfined compressive strength means the load per unit area at which a soil will fail in compression. It can be determined by laboratory testing, or estimated in the field using a pocket penetrometer, by thumb penetration tests, and other methods.

Wet soil means soil that contains significantly more moisture than moist soil, but in such a range of values that cohesive material will slump or begin to flow when vibrated. Granular material that would exhibit cohesive properties when moist will lose those cohesive properties when wet.

(c) *Requirements*—(1) *Classification of soil and rock deposits.* Each soil and rock deposit shall be classified by a competent person as Stable Rock, Type A, Type B, or Type C in accordance with the definitions set forth in paragraph (b) of this appendix.

(2) *Basis of classification.* The classification of the deposits shall be made based on the results of at least one visual and at least one manual analysis. Such analyses shall be conducted by a competent person using tests described in paragraph (d) below, or in other recognized methods of soil classification and testing such as those adopted by the America Society for Testing Materials, or the U.S. Department of Agriculture textural classification system.

(3) *Visual and manual analyses.* The visual and manual analyses, such as those noted as being acceptable in paragraph (d) of this appendix, shall be designed and conducted to provide sufficient quantitative and qualitative information as may be necessary to identify properly the properties, factors, and conditions affecting the classification of the deposits.

(4) *Layered systems.* In a layered system, the system shall be classified in accordance with its weakest layer. However, each layer may be classified individually where a more stable layer lies under a less stable layer.

(5) *Reclassification.* If, after classifying a deposit, the properties, factors, or conditions affecting its classification change in any way, the changes shall be evaluated by a competent person. The deposit shall be reclassified as necessary to reflect the changed circumstances.

(d) *Acceptable visual and manual tests*—(1) *Visual tests.* Visual analysis is conducted to determine qualitative information regarding the excavation site in general, the soil adjacent to the excavation, the soil forming the sides of the open excavation, and the soil taken as samples from excavated material.

(i) Observe samples of soil that are excavated and soil in the sides of the excavation. Estimate the range of particle sizes and the relative amounts of the particle sizes. Soil that is primarily composed of fine-grained material is cohesive material. Soil composed primarily of coarse-grained sand or gravel is granular material.

(ii) Observe soil as it is excavated. Soil that remains in clumps when excavated is cohesive. Soil that breaks up easily and does not stay in clumps is granular.

(iii) Observe the side of the opened excavation and the surface area adjacent to the excavation. Crack-like openings such as tension cracks could indicate fissured material. If chunks of soil spall off a vertical side, the soil could be fissured. Small spalls are evidence of moving ground and are indications of potentially hazardous situations.

(iv) Observe the area adjacent to the excavation and the excavation itself for evidence of existing utility and other underground structures, and to identify previously disturbed soil.

(v) Observe the opened side of the excavation to identify layered systems. Examine layered systems to identify if the layers slope toward the excavation. Estimate the degree of slope of the layers.

(vi) Observe the area adjacent to the excavation and the sides of the opened excavation for evidence of surface water, water seeping from the sides of the excavation, or the location of the level of the water table.

(vii) Observe the area adjacent to the excavation and the area within the excavation for sources of vibration that may affect the stability of the excavation face.

(2) *Manual tests.* Manual analysis of soil samples is conducted to determine quantitative as well as qualitative properties of soil and to provide more information in order to classify soil properly.

(i) *Plasticity.* Mold a moist or wet sample of soil into a ball and attempt to roll it into threads as thin as ⅛-inch in diameter. Cohesive material can be successfully rolled into threads without crumbling. For example, if at least a two inch (50 mm) length of ⅛-inch thread can be held on one end without tearing, the soil is cohesive.

(ii) *Dry strength.* If the soil is dry and crumbles on its own or with moderate pressure into individual grains or fine powder, it is granular (any combination of gravel, sand, or silt). If the soil is dry and falls into clumps which break up into smaller clumps, but the smaller clumps can only be broken up with difficulty, it may be clay in any combination with gravel, sand or silt. If the dry soil breaks into clumps which do not break up into small clumps and which can only be broken with difficulty, and there is no visual indication the soil is fissured, the soil may be considered unfissured.

(iii) *Thumb penetration.* The thumb penetration test can be used to estimate the unconfined compressive strength of cohesive soils. (This test is based on the thumb penetration test described in American Society for Testing and Materials (ASTM) Standard designation D2488—"Standard Recommended Practice for Description of Soils (Visual—Manual Procedure).") Type A soils with an unconfined compressive strength of 1.5 tsf can be readily indented by the thumb; however, they can be penetrated by the thumb only with very great effort. Type C soils with an unconfined compressive strength of 0.5 tsf can be easily penetrated several inches by the thumb, and can be molded by light finger pressure. This test should be conducted on an undisturbed soil sample, such as a large clump of spoil, as soon as practicable after excavation to keep to a mimimum the effects of exposure to drying influences. If the excavation is later exposed to wetting influences (rain, flooding), the classification of the soil must be changed accordingly.

(iv) *Other strength tests.* Estimates of unconfined compressive strength of soils can also be obtained by use of a pocket penetrometer or by using a hand-operated shearvane.

(v) *Drying test.* The basic purpose of the drying test is to differentiate between cohesive material with fissures, unfissured cohesive material, and granular material. The procedure for the drying test involves drying a sample of soil that is approximately one inch thick (2.54 cm) and six inches (15.24 cm) in diameter until it is thoroughly dry:

(A) If the sample develops cracks as it dries, significant fissures are indicated.

(B) Samples that dry without cracking are to be broken by hand. If considerable force is necessary to break a sample, the soil has significant cohesive material content. The soil can be classified as a unfissured cohesive material and the unconfined compressive strength should be determined.

(C) If a sample breaks easily by hand, it is either a fissured cohesive material or a granular material. To distinguish between the two, pulverize the dried clumps of the sample by hand or by stepping on them. If the clumps do not pulverize easily, the material is cohesive with fissures. If they pulverize easily into very small fragments, the material is granular.

APPENDIX B TO SUBPART P OF PART 1926—SLOPING AND BENCHING

(a) *Scope and application.* This appendix contains specifications for sloping and benching when used as methods of protecting employees working in excavations from cave-ins. The requirements of this appendix apply when the design of sloping and benching protective systems is to be performed in accordance with the requirements set forth in § 1926.652(b)(2).

(b) *Definitions.*

Actual slope means the slope to which an excavation face is excavated.

Distress means that the soil is in a condition where a cave-in is imminent or is likely to occur. Distress is evidenced by such phenomena as the development of fissures in the face of or adjacent to an open excavation; the subsidence of the edge of an excavation; the slumping of material from the face or the bulging or heaving of material from the bottom of an excavation; the spalling of material from the face of an excavation; and ravelling, i.e., small amounts of material such as pebbles or little clumps of material suddenly separating from the face of an excavation and trickling or rolling down into the excavation.

Maximum allowable slope means the steepest incline of an excavation face that is acceptable for the most favorable site conditions as protection against cave-ins, and is expressed as the ratio of horizontal distance to vertical rise (H:V).

Short term exposure means a period of time less than or equal to 24 hours that an excavation is open.

(c) *Requirements—*(1) *Soil classification.* Soil and rock deposits shall be classified in accordance with appendix A to subpart P of part 1926.

(2) *Maximum allowable slope.* The maximum allowable slope for a soil or rock deposit shall be determined from Table B–1 of this appendix.

(3) *Actual slope.* (i) The actual slope shall not be steeper than the maximum allowable slope.

(ii) The actual slope shall be less steep than the maximum allowable slope, when there are signs of distress. If that situation occurs, the slope shall be cut back to an actual slope which is at least ½ horizontal to one vertical (½H:1V) less steep than the maximum allowable slope.

(iii) When surcharge loads from stored material or equipment, operating equipment, or traffic are present, a competent person shall determine the degree to which the actual slope must be reduced below the maximum allowable slope, and shall assure that such reduction is achieved. Surcharge loads from adjacent structures shall be evaluated in accordance with §1926.651(i).

(4) *Configurations.* Configurations of sloping and benching systems shall be in accordance with Figure B-1.

TABLE B-1

MAXIMUM ALLOWABLE SLOPES

SOIL OR ROCK TYPE	MAXIMUM ALLOWABLE SLOPES (H:V)[1] FOR EXCAVATIONS LESS THAN 20 FEET DEEP [3]
STABLE ROCK TYPE A [2] TYPE B TYPE C	VERTICAL (90°) 3/4 : 1 (53°) 1:1 (45°) 1½: 1 (34°)

NOTES:

1. Numbers shown in parentheses next to maximum allowable slopes are angles expressed in degrees from the horizontal. Angles have been rounded off.

2. A short-term maximum allowable slope of 1/2H:1V (63°) is allowed in excavations in Type A soil that are 12 feet (3.67 m) or less in depth. Short-term maximum allowable slopes for excavations greater than 12 feet (3.67 m) in depth shall be 3/4H:1V (53°).

3. Sloping or benching for excavations greater than 20 feet deep shall be designed by a registered professional engineer.

Figure B-1

Slope Configurations

(All slopes stated below are in the horizontal to vertical ratio)

B-1.1 Excavations made in Type A soil.

1. All simple slope excavation 20 feet or less in depth shall have a maximum allowable slope of ¾:1.

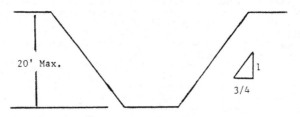

SIMPLE SLOPE—GENERAL

Exception: Simple slope excavations which are open 24 hours or less (short term) and which are 12 feet or less in depth shall have a maximum allowable slope of ½:1.

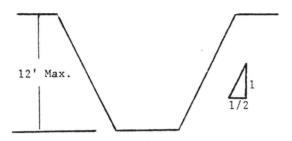

SIMPLE SLOPE—SHORT TERM

2. All benched excavations 20 feet or less in depth shall have a maximum allowable slope of ¾ to 1 and maximum bench dimensions as follows:

SIMPLE BENCH

MULTIPLE BENCH

3. All excavations 8 feet or less in depth which have unsupported vertically sided lower portions shall have a maximum vertical side of 3½ feet.

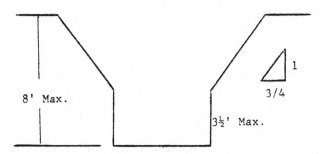

UNSUPPORTED VERTICALLY SIDED LOWER PORTION—MAXIMUM 8 FEET IN DEPTH

All excavations more than 8 feet but not more than 12 feet in depth which unsupported vertically sided lower portions shall have a maximum allowable slope of 1:1 and a maximum vertical side of 3½ feet.

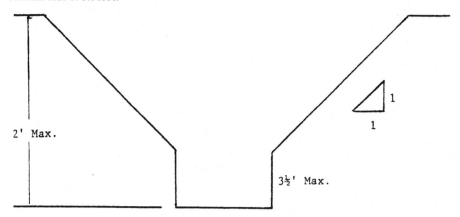

UNSUPPORTED VERTICALLY SIDED LOWER PORTION—MAXIMUM 12 FEET IN DEPTH

All excavations 20 feet or less in depth which have vertically sided lower portions that are supported or shielded shall have a maximum allowable slope of ¾:1. The support or shield system must extend at least 18 inches above the top of the vertical side.

SUPPORTED OR SHIELDED VERTICALLY SIDED LOWER PORTION

4. All other simple slope, compound slope, and vertically sided lower portion excavations shall be in accordance with the other options permitted under § 1926.652(b).

B–1.2 Excavations Made in Type B Soil

1. All simple slope excavations 20 feet or less in depth shall have a maximum allowable slope of 1:1.

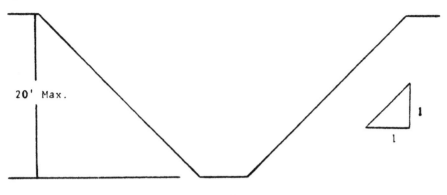

SIMPLE SLOPE

2. All benched excavations 20 feet or less in depth shall have a maximum allowable slope of 1:1 and maximum bench dimensions as follows:

SINGLE BENCH

MULTIPLE BENCH

3. All excavations 20 feet or less in depth which have vertically sided lower portions shall be shielded or supported to a height at least 18 inches above the top of the vertical side. All such excavations shall have a maximum allowable slope of 1:1.

377

VERTICALLY SIDED LOWER PORTION

4. All other sloped excavations shall be in accordance with the other options permitted in § 1926.652(b).

B–1.3 Excavations Made in Type C Soil

1. All simple slope excavations 20 feet or less in depth shall have a maximum allowable slope of 1½:1.

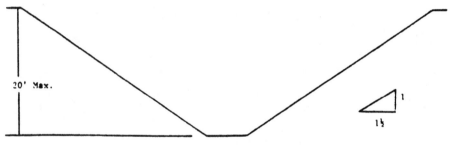

SIMPLE SLOPE

2. All excavations 20 feet or less in depth which have vertically sided lower portions shall be shielded or supported to a height at least 18 inches above the top of the vertical side. All such excavations shall have a maximum allowable slope of 1½:1.

VERTICAL SIDED LOWER PORTION

3. All other sloped excavations shall be in accordance with the other options permitted in § 1926.652(b).

B–1.4 Excavations Made in Layered Soils

1. All excavations 20 feet or less in depth made in layered soils shall have a maximum allowable slope for each layer as set forth below.

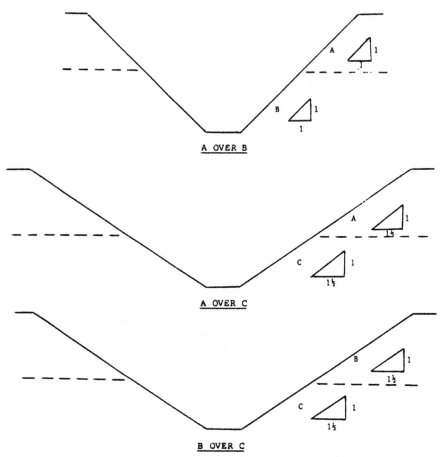

2. All other sloped excavations shall be in accordance with the other options permitted in §1926.652(b).

APPENDIX C TO SUBPART P OF PART 1926—TIMBER SHORING FOR TRENCHES

(a) *Scope.* This appendix contains information that can be used timber shoring is provided as a method of protection from cave-ins in trenches that do not exceed 20 feet (6.1 m) in depth. This appendix must be used when design of timber shoring protective systems is to be performed in accordance with §1926.652(c)(1). Other timber shoring configurations; other systems of support such as hydraulic and pneumatic systems; and other protective systems such as sloping, benching, shielding, and freezing systems must be designed in accordance with the requirements set forth in §1926.652(b) and §1926.652(c).

(b) *Soil Classification.* In order to use the data presented in this appendix, the soil type or types in which the excavation is made must first be determined using the soil classification method set forth in appendix A of subpart P of this part.

(c) *Presentation of Information.* Information is presented in several forms as follows:

(1) Information is presented in tabular form in Tables C–1.1, C–1.2, and C–1.3, and Tables C–2.1, C–2.2 and C–2.3 following paragraph (g) of the appendix. Each table presents the minimum sizes of timber members to use in a shoring system, and each table contains data only for the particular soil type in which the excavation or portion of

380

the excavation is made. The data are arranged to allow the user the flexibility to select from among several acceptable configurations of members based on varying the horizontal spacing of the crossbraces. Stable rock is exempt from shoring requirements and therefore, no data are presented for this condition.

(2) Information concerning the basis of the tabular data and the limitations of the data is presented in paragraph (d) of this appendix, and on the tables themselves.

(3) Information explaining the use of the tabular data is presented in paragraph (e) of this appendix.

(4) Information illustrating the use of the tabular data is presented in paragraph (f) of this appendix.

(5) Miscellaneous notations regarding Tables C–1.1 through C–1.3 and Tables C–2.1 through C–2.3 are presented in paragraph (g) of this Appendix.

(d) *Basis and limitations of the data*—(1) *Dimensions of timber members.* (i) The sizes of the timber members listed in Tables C–1.1 through C–1.3 are taken from the National Bureau of Standards (NBS) report, "Recommended Technical Provisions for Construction Practice in Shoring and Sloping of Trenches and Excavations." In addition, where NBS did not recommend specific sizes of members, member sizes are based on an analysis of the sizes required for use by existing codes and on empirical practice.

(ii) The required dimensions of the members listed in Tables C–1.1 through C–1.3 refer to actual dimensions and not nominal dimensions of the timber. Employers wanting to use nominal size shoring are directed to Tables C–2.1 through C–2.3, or have this choice under § 1926.652(c)(3), and are referred to The Corps of Engineers, The Bureau of Reclamation or data from other acceptable sources.

(2) *Limitation of application.* (i) It is not intended that the timber shoring specification apply to every situation that may be experienced in the field. These data were developed to apply to the situations that are most commonly experienced in current trenching practice. Shoring systems for use in situations that are not covered by the data in this appendix must be designed as specified in § 1926.652(c).

(ii) When any of the following conditions are present, the members specified in the tables are not considered adequate. Either an alternate timber shoring system must be designed or another type of protective system designed in accordance with § 1926.652.

(A) When loads imposed by structures or by stored material adjacent to the trench weigh in excess of the load imposed by a two-foot soil surcharge. The term "adjacent" as used here means the area within a horizontal distance from the edge of the trench equal to the depth of the trench.

(B) When vertical loads imposed on cross braces exceed a 240-pound gravity load distributed on a one-foot section of the center of the crossbrace.

(C) When surcharge loads are present from equipment weighing in excess of 20,000 pounds.

(D) When only the lower portion of a trench is shored and the remaining portion of the trench is sloped or benched unless: The sloped portion is sloped at an angle less steep than three horizontal to one vertical; or the members are selected from the tables for use at a depth which is determined from the top of the overall trench, and not from the toe of the sloped portion.

(e) *Use of Tables.* The members of the shoring system that are to be selected using this information are the cross braces, the uprights, and the wales, where wales are required. Minimum sizes of members are specified for use in different types of soil. There are six tables of information, two for each soil type. The soil type must first be determined in accordance with the soil classification system described in appendix A to subpart P of part 1926. Using the appropriate table, the selection of the size and spacing of the members is then made. The selection is based on the depth and width of the trench where the members are to be installed and, in most instances, the selection is also based on the horizontal spacing of the crossbraces. Instances where a choice of horizontal spacing of crossbracing is available, the horizontal spacing of the crossbraces must be chosen by the user before the size of any member can be determined. When the soil type, the width and depth of the trench, and the horizontal spacing of the crossbraces are known, the size and vertical spacing of the crossbraces, the size and vertical spacing of the wales, and the size and horizontal spacing of the uprights can be read from the appropriate table.

(f) *Examples to Illustrate the Use of Tables C–1.1 through C–1.3.*

(1) *Example 1.*

A trench dug in Type A soil is 13 feet deep and five feet wide.

From *Table C–1.1,* for acceptable arrangements of timber can be used.

Arrangement #B1

Space 4×4 crossbraces at six feet horizontally and four feet vertically.

Wales are not required.

Space 3×8 uprights at six feet horizontally. This arrangement is commonly called "skip shoring."

Arrangement #B2

Space 4×6 crossbraces at eight feet horizontally and four feet vertically.

Space 8×8 wales at four feet vertically.

Space 2×6 uprights at four feet horizontally.

Arrangement #B3

Space 6×6 crossbraces at 10 feet horizontally and four feet vertically.
Space 8×10 wales at four feet vertically.
Space 2×6 uprights at five feet horizontally.

Arrangement #B4

Space 6×6 crossbraces at 12 feet horizontally and four feet vertically.
Space 10×10 wales at four feet vertically.
Spaces 3×8 uprights at six feet horizontally.

(2) *Example 2.*

A trench dug in Type B soil in 13 feet deep and five feet wide. From Table C–1.2 three acceptable arrangements of members are listed.

Arrangement #B1

Space 6×6 crossbraces at six feet horizontally and five feet vertically.
Space 8×8 wales at five feet vertically.
Space 2×6 uprights at two feet horizontally.

Arrangement #B2

Space 6×8 crossbraces at eight feet horizontally and five feet vertically.
Space 10×10 wales at five feet vertically.
Space 2×6 uprights at two feet horizontally.

Arrangement #B3

Space 8×8 crossbraces at 10 feet horizontally and five feet vertically.
Space 10×12 wales at five feet vertically.
Space 2×6 uprights at two feet vertically.

(3) *Example 3.*

A trench dug in Type C soil is 13 feet deep and five feet wide.
From Table C–1.3 two acceptable arrangements of members can be used.

Arrangement #B1

Space 8×8 crossbraces at six feet horizontally and five feet vertically.
Space 10×12 wales at five feet vertically.
Position 2×6 uprights as closely together as possible.
If water must be retained use special tongue and groove uprights to form tight sheeting.

Arrangement #B2

Space 8×10 crossbraces at eight feet horizontally and five feet vertically.

Space 12×12 wales at five feet vertically.
Position 2×6 uprights in a close sheeting configuration unless water pressure must be resisted. Tight sheeting must be used where water must be retained.

(4) *Example 4.*

A trench dug in Type C soil is 20 feet deep and 11 feet wide. The size and spacing of members for the section of trench that is over 15 feet in depth is determined using Table C–1.3. Only one arrangement of members is provided.

Space 8×10 crossbraces at six feet horizontally and five feet vertically.
Space 12×12 wales at five feet vertically.
Use 3×6 tight sheeting.
Use of Tables C–2.1 through C–2.3 would follow the same procedures.

(g) *Notes for all Tables.*

1. Member sizes at spacings other than indicated are to be determined as specified in §1926.652(c), "Design of Protective Systems."

2. When conditions are saturated or submerged use Tight Sheeting. Tight Sheeting refers to the use of specially-edged timber planks (e.g., tongue and groove) at least three inches thick, steel sheet piling, or similar construction that when driven or placed in position provide a tight wall to resist the lateral pressure of water and to prevent the loss of backfill material. Close Sheeting refers to the placement of planks side-by-side allowing as little space as possible between them.

3. All spacing indicated is measured center to center.

4. Wales to be installed with greater dimension horizontal.

5. If the vertical distance from the center of the lowest crossbrace to the bottom of the trench exceeds two and one-half feet, uprights shall be firmly embedded or a mudsill shall be used. Where uprights are embedded, the vertical distance from the center of the lowest crossbrace to the bottom of the trench shall not exceed 36 inches. When mudsills are used, the vertical distance shall not exceed 42 inches. Mudsills are wales that are installed at the toe of the trench side.

6. Trench jacks may be used in lieu of or in combination with timber crossbraces.

7. Placement of crossbraces. When the vertical spacing of crossbraces is four feet, place the top crossbrace no more than two feet below the top of the trench. When the vertical spacing of crossbraces is five feet, place the top crossbrace no more than 2.5 feet below the top of the trench.

TABLE C-1.1

TIMBER TRENCH SHORING -- MINIMUM TIMBER REQUIREMENTS *

SOIL TYPE A P_a = 25 X H + 72 psf (2 ft Surcharge)

SIZE (ACTUAL) AND SPACING OF MEMBERS **

DEPTH OF TRENCH (FEET)	HORIZ. SPACING (FEET)	CROSS BRACES — WIDTH OF TRENCH (FEET) UP TO 4	UP TO 6	UP TO 9	UP TO 12	UP TO 15	VERT. SPACING (FEET)	WALES SIZE (IN)	WALES VERT. SPACING (FEET)	UPRIGHTS — MAXIMUM ALLOWABLE HORIZONTAL SPACING (FEET) CLOSE	4	5	6	8
5 TO 10	UP TO 6	4X4	4X4	4X6	6X6	6X6	4	Not Req'd	---				2X6	
	UP TO 8	4X4	4X4	4X6	6X6	6X6	4	Not Req'd	---					2X8
	UP TO 10	4X6	4X6	4X6	6X6	6X6	4	8X8	4			2X6		
	UP TO 12	4X6	4X6	6X6	6X6	6X6	4	8X8	4				2X6	
10 TO 15	UP TO 6	4X4	4X4	4X6	6X6	6X6	4	Not Req'd	---				3X8	
	UP TO 8	4X6	4X6	6X6	6X6	6X6	4	8X8	4		2X6			
	UP TO 10	6X6	6X5	6X6	6X8	6X8	4	8X10	4			2X6		
	UP TO 12	6X6	6X6	6X6	6X8	6X8	4	10X10	4				3X8	
15 TO 20	UP TO 6	6X6	6X6	6X6	6X8	6X8	4	6X8	4	3X6				
	UP TO 8	6X6	6X6	6X6	6X8	6X8	4	8X8	4	3X6				
	UP TO 10	8X8	8X8	8X8	8X8	8X10	4	8X10	4	3X6				
	UP TO 12	8X8	8X8	8X8	8X8	8X10	4	10X10	4	3X6				
OVER 20	SEE NOTE 1													

* Mixed oak or equivalent with a bending strength not less than 850 psi.
** Manufactured members of equivalent strength may by substituted for wood.

383

TABLE C-1.2

TIMBER TRENCH SHORING -- MINIMUM TIMBER REQUIREMENTS *

SOIL TYPE B P_a = 45 X H + 72 psf (2 ft. Surcharge)

DEPTH OF TRENCH (FEET)	HORIZ. SPACING (FEET)	CROSS BRACES WIDTH OF TRENCH (FEET)						WALES		UPRIGHTS MAXIMUM ALLOWABLE HORIZONTAL SPACING (FEET)		
		UP TO 4	UP TO 6	UP TO 9	UP TO 12	UP TO 15	VERT. SPACING (FEET)	SIZE (IN)	VERT. SPACING (FEET)	CLOSE	2	3
5 TO 10	UP TO 6	4X6	4X6	6X6	6X6	6X6	5	6X8	5			2X6
	UP TO 8	6X6	6X6	6X6	6X8	6X8	5	8X10	5			2X6
	UP TO 10	6X6	6X6	6X6	6X8	6X8	5	10X10	5			2X6
	See Note 1											
10 TO 15	UP TO 6	6X6	6X6	6X6	6X8	6X8	5	8X8	5		2X6	
	UP TO 8	6X8	6X8	6X8	8X8	8X8	5	10X10	5		2X6	
	UP TO 10	8X8	8X8	8X8	8X8	8X10	5	10X12	5		2X6	
	See Note 1											
15 TO 20	UP TO 6	6X8	6X8	6X8	8X8	8X8	5	8X10	5	3X6		
	UP TO 8	8X8	8X8	8X8	8X8	8X10	5	10X12	5	3X6		
	UP TO 10	8X10	8X10	8X10	8X10	10X10	5	12X12	5	3X6		
	See Note 1											
OVER 20	SEE NOTE 1											

* Mixed oak or equivalent with a bending strength not less than 850 psi.
** Manufactured members of equivalent strength may by substituted for wood.

TABLE C-1.3

TIMBER TRENCH SHORING -- MINIMUM TIMBER REQUIREMENTS *

SOIL TYPE C P_a = 80 X H + 72 psf (2 ft. Surcharge)

DEPTH OF TRENCH (FEET)	HORIZ. SPACING (FEET)	CROSS BRACES						SIZE (ACTUAL) AND SPACING OF MEMBERS**		UPRIGHTS
		WIDTH OF TRENCH (FEET)					VERT. SPACING (FEET)	SIZE (IN.)	VERT. SPACING (FEET)	MAXIMUM ALLOWABLE HORIZONTAL SPACING (FEET) (See Note 2)
		UP TO 4	UP TO 6	UP TO 9	UP TO 12	UP TO 15				CLOSE
5 TO 10	UP TO 6	6X8	6X8	6X8	8X8	8X8	5	8X10	5	2X6
	UP TO 8	8X8	8X8	8X8	8X8	8X8	5	10X12	5	2X6
	UP TO 10	8X10	8X10	8X10	8X10	10X10	5	12X12	5	2X6
	See Note 1									
10 TO 15	UP TO 6	8X8	8X8	8X8	8X8	8X8	5	10X12	5	2X6
	UP TO 8	8X10	8X10	8X10	8X10	10X10	5	12X12	5	2X6
	See Note 1									
	See Note 1									
15 TO 20	UP TO 6	8X10	8X10	8X10	8X10	10X10	5	12X12	5	3X6
	See Note 1									
	See Note 1									
	See Note 1									
OVER 20	SEE NOTE 1									

* Mixed Oak or equivalent with a bending strength not less than 850 psi.
** Manufactured members of equivalent strength may be substituted for wood.

TABLE C-2.1

TIMBER TRENCH SHORING -- MINIMUM TIMBER REQUIREMENTS *

SOIL TYPE A P_a = 25 X H + 72 psf (2 ft. Surcharge)

SIZE (S4S) AND SPACING OF MEMBERS **

DEPTH OF TRENCH (FEET)	HORIZ. SPACING (FEET)	CROSS BRACES — WIDTH OF TRENCH (FEET)					VERT. SPACING (FEET)	WALES SIZE (IN)	WALES VERT. SPACING (FEET)	UPRIGHTS — MAXIMUM ALLOWABLE HORIZONTAL SPACING (FEET)				
		UP TO 4	UP TO 6	UP TO 9	UP TO 12	UP TO 15				CLOSE	4	5	6	8
5 TO 10	UP TO 6	4X4	4X4	4X4	4X4	4X6	4	Not Req'd	Not Req'd				4X6	
	UP TO 8	4X4	4X4	4X4	4X4	4X6	4	Not Req'd	Not Req'd					4X8
	UP TO 10	4X6	4X6	4X6	6X6	6X6	4	8X8	4			4X6		
	UP TO 12	4X6	4X6	4X6	6X6	6X6	4	8X8	4		4X6			
10 TO 15	UP TO 6	4X4	4X4	4X4	4X6	6X6	4	Not Req'd	Not Req'd				4X6	
	UP TO 8	6X6	6X6	6X6	6X6	6X6	4	6X8	4				4X10	
	UP TO 10	6X6	6X6	6X6	6X6	6X6	4	8X8	4		4X6	4X8		
	UP TO 12	6X6	6X6	6X6	6X6	6X6	4	8X10	4				4X10	
15 TO 20	UP TO 6	6X6	6X6	6X6	6X6	6X6	4	6X8	4	3X6			4X10	
	UP TO 8	6X6	6X6	6X6	6X6	6X6	4	8X8	4	3X6	4X6	4X8		
	UP TO 10	6X6	6X6	6X6	6X6	6X8	4	8X10	4	3X6	4X12			
	UP TO 12	6X8	6X8	6X8	6X8	6X8	4	8X12	4	3X6	4X12			
OVER 20	SEE NOTE 1													

* Douglas fir or equivalent with a bending strength not less than 1500 psi.

** Manufactured members of equivalent strength may be substituted for wood.

TABLE C-2.2

TIMBER TRENCH SHORING -- MINIMUM TIMBER REQUIREMENTS *

SOIL TYPE B P_a = 45 X H + 72 psf (2 ft. Surcharge)

SIZE (S4S) AND SPACING OF MEMBERS **

DEPTH OF TRENCH (FEET)	HORIZ. SPACING (FEET)	CROSS BRACES — WIDTH OF TRENCH (FEET)						WALES		UPRIGHTS — MAXIMUM ALLOWABLE HORIZONTAL SPACING (FEET)				
		UP TO 4	UP TO 6	UP TO 9	UP TO 12	UP TO 15	VERT. SPACING (FEET)	SIZE (IN)	VERT. SPACING (FEET)	CLOSE	2	3	4	6
5 TO 10	UP TO 6	4X6	4X6	4X6	6X6	6X6	5	6X8	5			3X12 4X8		4X12
	UP TO 8	4X6	4X6	6X6	6X6	6X6	5	8X8	5		3X8		4X8	
	UP TO 10	4X6	4X6	6X6	6X6	6X8	5	8X10	5			4X8		
	See Note 1													
10 TO 15	UP TO 6	6X6	6X6	6X6	6X8	6X8	5	8X8	5	3X6	4X10			
	UP TO 8	6X8	6X8	6X8	8X8	8X8	5	10X10	5	3X6	4X10			
	UP TO 10	6X8	6X8	8X8	8X8	8X8	5	10X12	5	3X6	4X10			
	See Note 1													
15 TO 20	UP TO 6	6X8	6X8	6X8	6X8	6X8	5	8X10	5	4X6				
	UP TO 8	6X8	6X8	6X8	8X8	8X8	5	10X12	5	4X6				
	UP TO 10	8X8	8X8	8X8	8X8	8X8	5	12X12	5	4X6				
	See Note 1													
OVER 20	SEE NOTE 1													

* Douglas fir or equivalent with a bending strength not less than 1500 psi.

** Manufactured members of equivalent strength may be substituted for wood.

387

TABLE C-2.3

TIMBER TRENCH SHORING -- MINIMUM TIMBER REQUIREMENTS *

SOIL TYPE C P_a = 80 X H + 72 psf (2 ft. Surcharge)

DEPTH OF TRENCH (FEET)	CROSS BRACES SIZE (S4S) AND SPACING OF MEMBERS **							WALES		UPRIGHTS MAXIMUM ALLOWABLE HORIZONTAL SPACING (FEET)
	HORIZ. SPACING (FEET)	WIDTH OF TRENCH (FEET)					VERT. SPACING (FEET)	SIZE (IN)	VERT. SPACING (FEET)	CLOSE
		UP TO 4	UP TO 6	UP TO 9	UP TO 12	UP TO 15				
5 TO 10	UP TO 6	6X6	6X6	6X6	6X6	6X6	5	8X8	5	3X6
	UP TO 8	6X6	6X6	6X6	6X6	6X6	5	10X10	5	3X6
	UP TO 10	6X6	6X6	8X8	8X8	8X8	5	10X12	5	3X6
	See Note 1									
10 TO 15	UP TO 6	6X8	6X8	6X8	8X8	8X8	5	10X10	5	4X6
	UP TO 8	8X8	8X8	8X8	8X8	8X8	5	12X12	5	4X6
	See Note 1									
	See Note 1									
15 TO 20	UP TO 6	8X8	8X8	8X8	8X10	8X10	5	10X12	5	4X6
	See Note 1									
	See Note 1									
	See Note 1									
OVER 20	SEE NOTE 1									

* Douglas fir or equivalent with a bending strength not less than 1500 psi.
** Manufactured members of equivalent strength may be substituted for wood.

APPENDIX D TO SUBPART P OF PART 1926—ALUMINUM HYDRAULIC SHORING FOR TRENCHES

(a) *Scope.* This appendix contains information that can be used when aluminum hydraulic shoring is provided as a method of protection against cave-ins in trenches that do not exceed 20 feet (6.1m) in depth. This appendix must be used when design of the aluminum hydraulic protective system cannot be performed in accordance with § 1926.652(c)(2).

(b) *Soil Classification.* In order to use data presented in this appendix, the soil type or types in which the excavation is made must first be determined using the soil classification method set forth in appendix A of subpart P of part 1926.

(c) *Presentation of Information.* Information is presented in several forms as follows:

(1) Information is presented in tabular form in Tables D–1.1, D–1.2, D–1.3 and E–1.4. Each table presents the maximum vertical and horizontal spacings that may be used with various aluminum member sizes and various hydraulic cylinder sizes. Each table contains data only for the particular soil type in which the excavation or portion of the excavation is made. Tables D–1.1 and D–1.2 are for vertical shores in Types A and B soil. Tables D–1.3 and D1.4 are for horizontal waler systems in Types B and C soil.

(2) Information concerning the basis of the tabular data and the limitations of the data is presented in paragraph (d) of this appendix.

(3) Information explaining the use of the tabular data is presented in paragraph (e) of this appendix.

(4) Information illustrating the use of the tabular data is presented in paragraph (f) of this appendix.

(5) Miscellaneous notations (footnotes) regarding Table D–1.1 through D–1.4 are presented in paragraph (g) of this appendix.

(6) Figures, illustrating typical installations of hydraulic shoring, are included just prior to the Tables. The illustrations page is entitled "Aluminum Hydraulic Shoring; Typical Installations."

(d) *Basis and limitations of the data.* (1) Vertical shore rails and horizontal wales are those that meet the Section Modulus requirements in the D–1 Tables. Aluminum material is 6061–T6 or material of equivalent strength and properties.

(2) Hydraulic cylinders specifications. (i) 2-inch cylinders shall be a minimum 2-inch inside diameter with a minimum safe working capacity of no less than 18,000 pounds axial compressive load at maximum extension. Maximum extension is to include full range of cylinder extensions as recommended by product manufaturer.

(ii) 3-inch cylinders shall be a minimum 3-inch inside diameter with a safe working capacity of not less than 30,000 pounds axial compressive load at extensions as recommended by product manufaturer.

(3) Limitation of application.

(i) It is not intended that the aluminum hydraulic specification apply to every situation that may be experienced in the field. These data were developed to apply to the situations that are most commonly experienced in current trenching practice. Shoring systems for use in situations that are not covered by the data in this appendix must be otherwise designed as specified in §1926.652(c).

(ii) When any of the following conditions are present, the members specified in the Ta-

bles are not considered adequate. In this case, an alternative aluminum hydraulic shoring system or other type of protective system must be designed in accordance with §1926.652.

(A) When vertical loads imposed on cross braces exceed a 100 Pound gravity load distributed on a one foot section of the center of the hydraulic cylinder.

(B) When surcharge loads are present from equipment weighing in excess of 20,000 pounds.

(C) When only the lower portion or a trench is shored and the remaining portion of the trench is sloped or benched unless: The sloped portion is sloped at an angle less steep than three horizontal to one vertical; or the members are selected from the tables for use at a depth which is determined from the top of the overall trench, and not from the toe of the sloped portion.

(e) *Use of Tables D–1.1, D–1.2, D–1.3 and D–1.4.* The members of the shoring system that are to be selected using this information are the hydraulic cylinders, and either the vertical shores or the horizontal wales. When a waler system is used the vertical timber sheeting to be used is also selected from these tables. The Tables D–1.1 and D–1.2 for vertical shores are used in Type A and B soils that do not require sheeting. Type B soils that may require sheeting, and Type C soils that always require sheeting are found in the horizontal wale Tables D–1.3 and D–1.4. The soil type must first be determined in accordance with the soil classification system described in appendix A to subpart P of part 1926. Using the appropriate table, the selection of the size and spacing of the members is made. The selection is based on the depth and width of the trench where the members are to be installed. In these tables the vertical spacing is held constant at four feet on center. The tables show the maximum horizontal spacing of cylinders allowed for each size of wale in the waler system tables, and in the vertical shore tables, the hydraulic cylinder horizontal spacing is the same as the vertical shore spacing.

(f) *Example to Illustrate the Use of the Tables:*

(1) Example 1:

A trench dug in Type A soil is 6 feet deep and 3 feet wide. From Table D–1.1: Find vertical shores and 2 inch diameter cylinders spaced 8 feet on center (o.c.) horizontally and 4 feet on center (o.c.) vertically. (See Figures 1 & 3 for typical installations.)

(2) Example 2:

A trench is dug in Type B soil that does not require sheeting, 13 feet deep and 5 feet wide. From Table D–1.2: Find vertical shores and 2 inch diameter cylinders spaced 6.5 feet o.c. horizontally and 4 feet o.c. vertically. (See Figures 1 & 3 for typical installations.)

(3) A trench is dug in Type B soil that does not require sheeting, but does experience some minor raveling of the trench face. The

389

trench is 16 feet deep and 9 feet wide. From Table D–1.2: Find vertical shores and 2 inch diameter cylinder (with special oversleeves as designated by footnote #B2) spaced 5.5 feet o.c. horizontally and 4 feet o.c. vertically, plywood (per footnote (g)(7) to the D–1 Table) should be used behind the shores. (See Figures 2 & 3 for typical installations.)

(4) Example 4: A trench is dug in previously disturbed Type B soil, with characteristics of a Type C soil, and will require sheeting. The trench is 18 feet deep and 12 feet wide. 8 foot horizontal spacing between cylinders is desired for working space. From Table D–1.3: Find horizontal wale with a section modulus of 14.0 spaced at 4 feet o.c. vertically and 3 inch diameter cylinder spaced at 9 feet maximum o.c. horizontally. 3×12 timber sheeting is required at close spacing vertically. (See Figure 4 for typical installation.)

(5) Example 5: A trench is dug in Type C soil, 9 feet deep and 4 feet wide. Horizontal cylinder spacing in excess of 6 feet is desired for working space. From Table D–1.4: Find horizontal wale with a section modulus of 7.0 and 2 inch diameter cylinders spaced at 6.5 feet o.c. horizontally. Or, find horizontal wale with a 14.0 section modulus and 3 inch diameter cylinder spaced at 10 feet o.c. horizontally. Both wales are spaced 4 feet o.c. vertically. 3×12 timber sheeting is required at close spacing vertically. (See Figure 4 for typical installation.)

(g) *Footnotes, and general notes, for Tables D–1.1, D–1.2, D–1.3, and D–1.4.*

(1) For applications other than those listed in the tables, refer to § 1926.652(c)(2) for use of manufacturer's tabulated data. For trench depths in excess of 20 feet, refer to § 1926.652(c)(2) and § 1926.652(c)(3).

(2) 2 inch diameter cylinders, at this width, shall have structural steel tube (3.5×3.5×0.1875) oversleeves, or structural oversleeves of manufacturer's specification, extending the full, collapsed length.

(3) Hydraulic cylinders capacities. (i) 2 inch cylinders shall be a minimum 2-inch inside diameter with a safe working capacity of not less than 18,000 pounds axial compressive load at maximum extension. Maximum extension is to include full range of cylinder extensions as recommended by product manufacturer.

(ii) 3-inch cylinders shall be a minimum 3-inch inside diameter with a safe work capacity of not less than 30,000 pounds axial compressive load at maximum extension. Maximum extension is to include full range of cylinder extensions as recommended by product manufacturer.

(4) All spacing indicated is measured center to center.

(5) Vertical shoring rails shall have a minimum section modulus of 0.40 inch.

(6) When vertical shores are used, there must be a minimum of three shores spaced equally, horizontally, in a group.

(7) Plywood shall be 1.125 in. thick softwood or 0.75 inch. thick, 14 ply, arctic white birch (Finland form). Please note that plywood is not intended as a structural member, but only for prevention of local raveling (sloughing of the trench face) between shores.

(8) See appendix C for timber specifications.

(9) Wales are calculated for simple span conditions.

(10) See appendix D, item (d), for basis and limitations of the data.

ALUMINUM HYDRAULIC SHORING
TYPICAL INSTALLATIONS

TABLE D - 1.1
ALUMINUM HYDRAULIC SHORING
VERTICAL SHORES
FOR SOIL TYPE A

DEPTH OF TRENCH (FEET)	HYDRAULIC CYLINDERS		WIDTH OF TRENCH (FEET)		
	MAXIMUM HORIZONTAL SPACING (FEET)	MAXIMUM VERTICAL SPACING (FEET)	UP TO 8	OVER 8 UP TO 12	OVER 12 UP TO 15
OVER 5 UP TO 10	8	4	2 INCH DIAMETER	2 INCH DIAMETER NOTE (2)	3 INCH DIAMETER
OVER 10 UP TO 15	8				
OVER 15 UP TO 20	7				
OVER 20	NOTE (1)				

Footnotes to tables, and general notes on hydraulic shoring, are found in Appendix D, Item (g)
Note (1): See Appendix D, Item (g) (1)
Note (2): See Appendix D, Item (g) (2)

TABLE D - 1.2
ALUMINUM HYDRAULIC SHORING
VERTICAL SHORES
FOR SOIL TYPE B

DEPTH OF TRENCH	HYDRAULIC CYLINDERS		WIDTH OF TRENCH (FEET)		
	MAXIMUM HORIZONTAL SPACING	MAXIMUM VERTICAL SPACING	UP TO 8	OVER 8 UP TO 12	OVER 12 UP TO 15
(FEET)	(FEET)	(FEET)			
OVER 5 UP TO 10	8	4	2 INCH DIAMETER	2 INCH DIAMETER NOTE (2)	3 INCH DIAMETER
OVER 10 UP TO 15	6.5				
OVER 15 UP TO 20	5.5				
OVER 20	NOTE (1)				

Footnotes to tables, and general notes on hydraulic shoring, are found in Appendix D, Item (g)

Note (1): See Appendix D, Item (g) (1)

Note (2): See Appendix D, Item (g) (2)

393

TABLE D - 1.3
ALUMINUM HYDRAULIC SHORING
WALER SYSTEMS
FOR SOIL TYPE B

DEPTH OF TRENCH (FEET)	WALES		HYDRAULIC CYLINDERS WIDTH OF TRENCH (FEET)						TIMBER UPRIGHTS MAX.HORIZ.SPACING (ON CENTER)		
	VERTICAL SPACING (FEET)	SECTION MODULUS* (IN³)	UP TO 8		OVER 8 UP TO 12		OVER 12 UP TO 15		SOLID SHEET	2 FT.	3 FT.
			HORIZ. SPACING	CYLINDER DIAMETER	HORIZ. SPACING	CYLINDER DIAMETER	HORIZ. SPACING	CYLINDER DIAMETER			
OVER 5 UP TO 10	4	3.5	8.0	2 IN	8.0	2 IN NOTE(2)	8.0	3 IN			3x12
		7.0	9.0	2 IN	9.0	2 IN NOTE(2)	9.0	3 IN	—	—	
		14.0	12.0	3 IN	12.0	3 IN	12.0	3 IN			
OVER 10 UP TO 15	4	3.5	6.0	2 IN	6.0	2 IN NOTE(2)	6.0	3 IN		3x12	
		7.0	8.0	3 IN	8.0	3 IN	8.0	3 IN	—		—
		14.0	10.0	3 IN	10.0	3 IN	10.0	3 IN			
OVER 15 UP TO 20	4	3.5	5.5	2 IN	5.5	2 IN NOTE(2)	5.5	3 IN	3x12		
		7.0	6.0	3 IN	6.0	3 IN	6.0	3 IN		—	—
		14.0	9.0	3 IN	9.0	3 IN	9.0	3 IN			
OVER 20	NOTE (1)										

Footnotes to tables, and general notes on hydraulic shoring, are found in Appendix D, Item (g)

Notes (1): See Appendix D, item (g) (1)

Notes (2): See Appendix D, Item (g) (2)

* Consult product manufacturer and/or qualified engineer for Section Modulus of available wales.

TABLE D - 1.4
ALUMINUM HYDRAULIC SHORING
WALER SYSTEMS
FOR SOIL TYPE C

DEPTH OF TRENCH (FEET)	WALES VERTICAL SPACING (FEET)	SECTION MODULUS * (IN³)	HYDRAULIC CYLINDERS — WIDTH OF TRENCH (FEET)						TIMBER UPRIGHTS — MAX. HORIZ SPACING (ON CENTER)		
			UP TO 8 HORIZ. SPACING	CYLINDER DIAMETER	OVER 8 UP TO 12 HORIZ. SPACING	CYLINDER DIAMETER	OVER 12 UP TO 15 HORIZ. SPACING	CYLINDER DIAMETER	SOLID SHEET	2 FT.	3 FT.
OVER 5 UP TO 10	4	3.5	6.0	2 IN	6.0	2 IN NOTE(2)	6.0	3 IN	3x12	—	—
		7.0	6.5	2 IN	6.5	2 IN NOTE(2)	6.5	3 IN			
		14.0	10.0	3 IN	10.0	3 IN	10.0	3 IN			
OVER 10 UP TO 15	4	3.5	4.0	2 IN	4.0	2 IN NOTE(2)	4.0	3 IN	3x12	—	—
		7.0	5.5	3 IN	5.5	3 IN	5.5	3 IN			
		14.0	8.0	3 IN	8.0	3 IN	8.0	3 IN			
OVER 15 UP TO 20	4	3.5	3.5	2 IN	3.5	2 IN NOTE(2)	3.5	3 IN	3x12	—	—
		7.0	5.0	3 IN	5.0	3 IN	5.0	3 IN			
		14.0	6.0	3 IN	6.0	3 IN	6.0	3 IN			
OVER 20					NOTE (1)						

Footnotes to tables, and general notes on hydraulic shoring, are found in Appendix D, Item (g)

Notes (1): See Appendix D, item (g) (1)

Notes (2): See Appendix D, Item (g) (2)

* Consult product manufacturer and/or qualified engineer for Section Modulus of available wales.

APPENDIX E TO SUBPART P OF PART 1926—ALTERNATIVES TO TIMBER SHORING

Figure 1. Aluminum Hydraulic Shoring

Figure 2. Pneumatic/hydraulic Shoring

Figure 3.　Trench Jacks (Screw Jacks)

Figure 4.　Trench Shields

APPENDIX F TO SUBPART P OF PART 1926—SELECTION OF PROTECTIVE SYSTEMS

The following figures are a graphic summary of the requirements contained in sub-part P for excavations 20 feet or less in depth. Protective systems for use in excavations more than 20 feet in depth must be designed by a registered professional engineer in accordance with § 1926.652 (b) and (c).

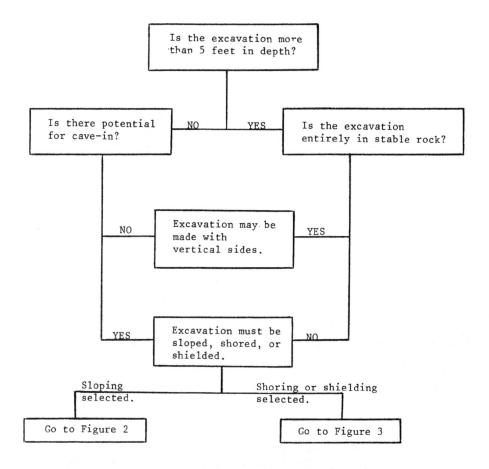

FIGURE 1 - PRELIMINARY DECISIONS

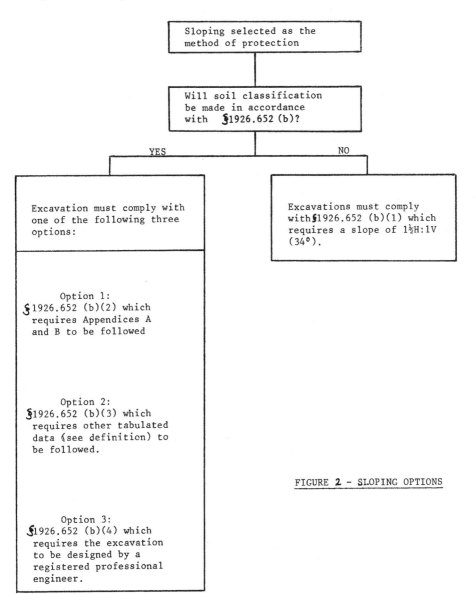

FIGURE **2** – SLOPING OPTIONS

Shoring or shielding selected
as the method of protection.

Soil classification is required
when shoring or shielding is
used. The excavation must comply
with one of the following four
options:

Option 1
§1926.652 (c)(1) which requires
Appendices A and C to be followed
(e.g. timber shoring).

Option 2
§1926.652 (c)(2) which requires
manufacturers data to be followed
(e.g. hydraulic shoring,trench
jacks, air shores, shields).

Option 3
§1926.652 (c)(3) which requires
tabulated data (see definition)
to be followed (e.g. any system
as per the tabulated data).

Option 4
§1926.652 (c)(4) which requires
the excavation to be designed
by a registered professional
engineer (e.g. any designed
system).

FIGURE 3 - SHORING AND SHIELDING OPTIONS

Subpart Q—Concrete and Masonry Construction

AUTHORITY: Sec. 107, Contract Work Hours and Safety Standards Act (Construction Safety Act) (40 U.S.C. 333); Secs. 4, 6 and 8 Occupational Safety and Health Act of 1970 (29 U.S.C. 653, 655, and 657); Secretary of Labor's Order No. 12–71 (36 FR 8754), 8–76 (41 FR 25059), 9–83 (48 FR 35736), or 1–90 (55 FR 9033), as applicable; and 29 CFR part 1911.

SOURCE: 53 FR 22643, June 16, 1988, unless otherwise noted.

§1926.700 Scope, application, and definitions applicable to this subpart.

(a) *Scope and application.* This subpart sets forth requirements to protect all construction employees from the hazards associated with concrete and masonry construction operations performed in workplaces covered under 29 CFR part 1926. In addition to the requirements in subpart Q, other relevant provisions in parts 1910 and 1926 apply to concrete and masonry construction operations.

(b) *Definitions applicable to this subpart.* In addition to the definitions set forth in §1926.32, the following definitions apply to this subpart.

(1) *Bull float* means a tool used to spread out and smooth concrete.

(2) *Formwork* means the total system of support for freshly placed or partially cured concrete, including the mold or sheeting (form) that is in contact with the concrete as well as all supporting members including shores, reshores, hardware, braces, and related hardware.

(3) *Lift slab* means a method of concrete construction in which floor, and roof slabs are cast on or at ground level and, using jacks, lifted into position.

(4) *Limited access zone* means an area alongside a masonry wall, which is under construction, and which is clearly demarcated to limit access by employees.

(5) *Precast concrete* means concrete members (such as walls, panels, slabs, columns, and beams) which have been formed, cast, and cured prior to final placement in a structure.

(6) *Reshoring* means the construction operation in which shoring equipment (also called reshores or reshoring equipment) is placed, as the original forms and shores are removed, in order to support partially cured concrete and construction loads.

(7) *Shore* means a supporting member that resists a compressive force imposed by a load.

(8) *Vertical slip forms* means forms which are jacked vertically during the placement of concrete.

(9) *Jacking operation* means the task of lifting a slab (or group of slabs) vertically from one location to another (e.g., from the casting location to a temporary (parked) location, or from a temporary location to another temporary location, or to its final location in the structure), during the construction of a building/structure where the lift-slab process is being used.

[53 FR 22643, June 16, 1988, as amended at 55 FR 42328, Oct. 18, 1990]

§1926.701 General requirements.

(a) *Construction loads.* No construction loads shall be placed on a concrete structure or portion of a concrete structure unless the employer determines, based on information received from a person who is qualified in structural design, that the structure or portion of the structure is capable of supporting the loads.

(b) *Reinforcing steel.* All protruding reinforcing steel, onto and into which employees could fall, shall be guarded to eliminate the hazard of impalement.

(c) *Post-tensioning operations.* (1) No employee (except those essential to the post-tensioning operations) shall be permitted to be behind the jack during tensioning operations.

(2) Signs and barriers shall be erected to limit employee access to the post-tensioning area during tensioning operations.

(d) *Riding concrete buckets.* No employee shall be permitted to ride concrete buckets.

(e) *Working under loads.* (1) No employee shall be permitted to work under concrete buckets while buckets are being elevated or lowered into position.

(2) To the extent practical, elevated concrete buckets shall be routed so that no employee, or the fewest number of employees, are exposed to the hazards associated with falling concrete buckets.

(f) *Personal protective equipment.* No employee shall be permitted to apply a cement, sand, and water mixture through a pneumatic hose unless the employee is wearing protective head and face equipment.

[53 FR 22643, June 16, 1988, as amended at 59 FR 40730, Aug. 9, 1994]

§ 1926.702 Requirements for equipment and tools.

(a) *Bulk cement storage.* (1) Bulk storage bins, containers, and silos shall be equipped with the following:

(i) Conical or tapered bottoms; and

(ii) Mechanical or pneumatic means of starting the flow of material.

(2) No employee shall be permitted to enter storage facilities unless the ejection system has been shut down, locked out, and tagged to indicate that the ejection system is not to be operated.

(b) *Concrete mixers.* Concrete mixers with one cubic yard (.8 m³) or larger loading skips shall be equipped with the following:

(1) A mechanical device to clear the skip of materials; and

(2) Guardrails installed on each side of the skip.

(c) *Power concrete trowels.* Powered and rotating type concrete troweling machines that are manually guided shall be equipped with a control switch that will automatically shut off the power whenever the hands of the operator are removed from the equipment handles.

(d) *Concrete buggies.* Concrete buggy handles shall not extend beyond the wheels on either side of the buggy.

(e) *Concrete pumping systems.* (1) Concrete pumping systems using discharge pipes shall be provided with pipe supports designed for 100 percent overload.

(2) Compressed air hoses used on concrete pumping system shall be provided with positive fail-safe joint connectors to prevent separation of sections when pressurized.

(f) *Concrete buckets.* (1) Concrete buckets equipped with hydraulic or pneumatic gates shall have positive safety latches or similar safety devices installed to prevent premature or accidental dumping.

(2) Concrete buckets shall be designed to prevent concrete from hanging up on top and the sides.

(g) *Tremies.* Sections of tremies and similar concrete conveyances shall be secured with wire rope (or equivalent materials) in addition to the regular couplings or connections.

(h) *Bull floats.* Bull float handles, used where they might contact energized electrical conductors, shall be constructed of nonconductive material or insulated with a nonconductive sheath whose electrical and mechanical characteristics provide the equivalent protection of a handle constructed of nonconductive material.

(i) *Masonry saws.* (1) Masonry saws shall be guarded with a semicircular enclosure over the blade.

(2) A method for retaining blade fragments shall be incorporated in the design of the semicircular enclosure.

(j) *Lockout/Tagout Procedures.* (1) No employee shall be permitted to perform maintenance or repair activity on equipment (such as compressors, mixers, screens or pumps used for concrete and masonry construction activities) where the inadvertent operation of the equipment could occur and cause injury, unless all potentially hazardous energy sources have been locked out and tagged.

(2) Tags shall read *Do Not Start* or similar language to indicate that the equipment is not to be operated.

§ 1926.703 Requirements for cast-in-place concrete.

(a) *General requirements for formwork.* (1) Formwork shall be designed, fabricated, erected, supported, braced and maintained so that it will be capable of supporting without failure all vertical and lateral loads that may reasonably be anticipated to be applied to the formwork. Formwork which is designed, fabricated, erected, supported, braced and maintained in conformance with the appendix to this section will be deemed to meet the requirements of this paragraph.

(2) Drawings or plans, including all revisions, for the jack layout, formwork (including shoring equipment), working decks, and scaffolds, shall be available at the jobsite.

(b) *Shoring and reshoring.* (1) All shoring equipment (including equipment used in reshoring operations) shall be inspected prior to erection to determine that the equipment meets the requirements specified in the formwork drawings.

(2) Shoring equipment found to be damaged such that its strength is reduced to less than that required by §1926.703(a)(1) shall not be used for shoring.

(3) Erected shoring equipment shall be inspected immediately prior to, during, and immediately after concrete placement.

(4) Shoring equipment that is found to be damaged or weakened after erection, such that its strength is reduced to less than that required by §1926.703(a)(1), shall be immediately reinforced.

(5) The sills for shoring shall be sound, rigid, and capable of carrying the maximum intended load.

(6) All base plates, shore heads, extension devices, and adjustment screws shall be in firm contact, and secured when necessary, with the foundation and the form.

(7) Eccentric loads on shore heads and similar members shall be prohibited unless these members have been designed for such loading.

(8) Whenever single post shores are used one on top of another (tiered), the employer shall comply with the following specific requirements in addition to the general requirements for formwork:

(i) The design of the shoring shall be prepared by a qualified designer and the erected shoring shall be inspected by an engineer qualified in structural design.

(ii) The single post shores shall be vertically aligned.

(iii) The single post shores shall be spliced to prevent misalignment.

(iv) The single post shores shall be adequately braced in two mutually perpendicular directions at the splice level. Each tier shall also be diagonally braced in the same two directions.

(9) Adjustment of single post shores to raise formwork shall not be made after the placement of concrete.

(10) Reshoring shall be erected, as the original forms and shores are removed, whenever the concrete is required to support loads in excess of its capacity.

(c) *Vertical slip forms.* (1) The steel rods or pipes on which jacks climb or by which the forms are lifted shall be—

(i) Specifically designed for that purpose; and

(ii) Adequately braced where not encased in concrete.

(2) Forms shall be designed to prevent excessive distortion of the structure during the jacking operation.

(3) All vertical slip forms shall be provided with scaffolds or work platforms where employees are required to work or pass.

(4) Jacks and vertical supports shall be positioned in such a manner that the loads do not exceed the rated capacity of the jacks.

(5) The jacks or other lifting devices shall be provided with mechanical dogs or other automatic holding devices to support the slip forms whenever failure of the power supply or lifting mechanism occurs.

(6) The form structure shall be maintained within all design tolerances specified for plumbness during the jacking operation.

(7) The predetermined safe rate of lift shall not be exceeded.

(d) *Reinforcing steel.* (1) Reinforcing steel for walls, piers, columns, and similar vertical structures shall be adequately supported to prevent overturning and to prevent collapse.

(2) Employers shall take measures to prevent unrolled wire mesh from recoiling. Such measures may include, but are not limited to, securing each end of the roll or turning over the roll.

(e) *Removal of formwork.* (1) Forms and shores (except those used for slabs on grade and slip forms) shall not be removed until the employer determines that the concrete has gained sufficient strength to support its weight and superimposed loads. Such determination shall be based on compliance with one of the following:

(i) The plans and specifications stipulate conditions for removal of forms and shores, and such conditions have been followed, or

(ii) The concrete has been properly tested with an appropriate ASTM standard test method designed to indicate the concrete compressive strength, and the test results indicate that the concrete has gained sufficient strength to support its weight and superimposed loads.

(2) Reshoring shall not be removed until the concrete being supported has attained adequate strength to support its weight and all loads in place upon it.

APPENDIX TO § 1926.703(a)(1)

GENERAL REQUIREMENTS FOR FORMWORK

(This appendix is non-mandatory.)

This appendix serves as a non-mandatory guideline to assist employers in complying with the formwork requirements in § 1926.703(a)(1). Formwork which has been designed, fabricated, erected, braced, supported and maintained in accordance with Sections 6 and 7 of the American National Standard for Construction and Demolition Operations—Concrete and Masonry Work, ANSI A10.9–1983, shall be deemed to be in compliance with the provision of § 1926.703(a)(1).

[53 FR 22643, June 16, 1988, as amended at 61 FR 5510, Feb. 13, 1996]

§ 1926.704 Requirements for precast concrete.

(a) Precast concrete wall units, structural framing, and tilt-up wall panels shall be adequately supported to prevent overturning and to prevent collapse until permanent connections are completed.

(b) Lifting inserts which are embedded or otherwise attached to tilt-up precast concrete members shall be capable of supporting at least two times the maximum intended load applied or transmitted to them.

(c) Lifting inserts which are embedded or otherwise attached to precast concrete members, other than the tilt-up members, shall be capable of supporting at least four times the maximum intended load applied or transmitted to them.

(d) Lifting hardware shall be capable of supporting at least five times the maximum intended load applied or transmitted to the lifting hardware.

(e) No employee shall be permitted under precast concrete members being lifted or tilted into position except those employees required for the erection of those members.

[53 FR 22643, June 16, 1988, as amended at 54 FR 41088, Oct. 5, 1989]

§ 1926.705 Requirements for lift-slab construction operations.

(a) Lift-slab operations shall be designed and planned by a registered professional engineer who has experience in lift-slab construction. Such plans and designs shall be implemented by the employer and shall include detailed instructions and sketches indicating the prescribed method of erection. These plans and designs shall also include provisions for ensuring lateral stability of the building/structure during construction.

(b) Jacks/lifting units shall be marked to indicate their rated capacity as established by the manufacturer.

(c) Jacks/lifting units shall not be loaded beyond their rated capacity as established by the manufacturer.

(d) Jacking equipment shall be capable of supporting at least two and one-half times the load being lifted during jacking operations and the equipment shall not be overloaded. For the purpose of this provision, jacking equipment includes any load bearing component which is used to carry out the lifting operation(s). Such equipment includes, but is not limited, to the following: threaded rods, lifting attachments, lifting nuts, hook-up collars, T-caps, shearheads, columns, and footings.

(e) Jacks/lifting units shall be designed and installed so that they will neither lift nor continue to lift when they are loaded in excess of their rated capacity.

(f) Jacks/lifting units shall have a safety device installed which will cause the jacks/lifting units to support the load in any position in the event any jack/lifting unit malfunctions or loses its lifting ability.

(g) Jacking operations shall be synchronized in such a manner to ensure even and uniform lifting of the slab. During lifting, all points at which the slab is supported shall be kept within $\frac{1}{2}$ inch of that needed to maintain the slab in a level position.

(h) If leveling is automatically controlled, a device shall be installed that will stop the operation when the $\frac{1}{2}$ inch tolerance set forth in paragraph (g) of this section is exceeded or where there is a malfunction in the jacking (lifting) system.

(i) If leveling is maintained by manual controls, such controls shall be located in a central location and attended by a competent person while lifting is in progress. In addition to meeting the definition in § 1926.32(f), the competent person must be experienced in the lifting operation and with the lifting equipment being used.

(j) The maximum number of manually controlled jacks/lifting units on one slab shall be limited to a number that will permit the operator to maintain the slab level within specified tolerances of paragraph (g) of this section, but in no case shall that number exceed 14.

(k)(1) No employee, except those essential to the jacking operation, shall be permitted in the building/structure while any jacking operation is taking place unless the building/structure has been reinforced sufficiently to ensure its integrity during erection. The phrase "reinforced sufficiently to ensure its integrity" used in this paragraph means that a registered professional engineer, independent of the engineer who designed and planned the lifting operation, has determined from the plans that if there is a loss of support at any jack location, that loss will be confined to that location and the structure as a whole will remain stable.

(2) Under no circumstances, shall any employee who is not essential to the jacking operation be permitted immediately beneath a slab while it is being lifted.

(3) For the purpose of paragraph (k) of this section, a jacking operation begins when a slab or group of slabs is lifted and ends when such slabs are secured (with either temporary connections or permanent connections).

(4) Employers who comply with appendix A to § 1926.705 shall be considered to be in compliance with the provisions of paragraphs (k)(1) through (k)(3) of this section.

(l) When making temporary connections to support slabs, wedges shall be secured by tack welding, or an equivalent method of securing the wedges to prevent them from falling out of position. Lifting rods may not be released

until the wedges at that column have been secured.

(m) All welding on temporary and permanent connections shall be performed by a certified welder, familiar with the welding requirements specified in the plans and specifications for the lift-slab operation.

(n) Load transfer from jacks/lifting units to building columns shall not be executed until the welds on the column shear plates (weld blocks) are cooled to air temperature.

(o) Jacks/lifting units shall be positively secured to building columns so that they do not become dislodged or dislocated.

(p) Equipment shall be designed and installed so that the lifting rods cannot slip out of position or the employer shall institute other measures, such as the use of locking or blocking devices, which will provide positive connection between the lifting rods and attachments and will prevent components from disengaging during lifting operations.

APPENDIX TO § 1926.705—LIFT-SLAB
OPERATIONS

(This appendix is non-mandatory.)

In paragraph 1926.705(k), OSHA requires employees to be removed from the building/structure during jacking operations unless an independent registered professional engineer, other than the engineer who designed and planned the lifting operation, has determined that the building/structure has been sufficiently reinforced to insure the integrity of the building/structure. One method to comply with this provision is for the employer to ensure that continuous bottom steel is provided in every slab and in both directions through every wall or column head area. (Column head area means the distance between lines that are one and one half times the thickness of the slab or drop panel. These lines are located outside opposite faces of the outer edges of the shearhead sections—See Figure 1). The amount of bottom steel shall be established by assuming loss of support at a given lifting jack and then determining the steel necessary to carry, by catenary action over the span between surrounding supports, the slab service dead load *plus* any service dead and live loads likely to be acting on the slab during jacking. In addition, the surrounding supports must be capable of resisting any additional load transferred to them as a result of the loss of support at the lifting jack considered.

x = the slab or drop
    panel thickness

Figure 1--Column Head Area

[55 FR 42328, Oct. 18, 1990]

§ 1926.706 Requirements for masonry construction.

(a) A limited access zone shall be established whenever a masonry wall is being constructed. The limited access zone shall conform to the following.

(1) The limited access zone shall be established prior to the start of construction of the wall.

(2) The limited access zone shall be equal to the height of the wall to be constructed plus four feet, and shall run the entire length of the wall.

(3) The limited access zone shall be established on the side of the wall which will be unscaffolded.

(4) The limited access zone shall be restricted to entry by employees actively engaged in constructing the wall. No other employees shall be permitted to enter the zone.

(5) The limited access zone shall remain in place until the wall is adequately supported to prevent overturning and to prevent collapse unless the height of wall is over eight feet, in which case, the limited access zone shall remain in place until the requirements of paragraph (b) of this section have been met.

(b) All masonry walls over eight feet in height shall be adequately braced to prevent overturning and to prevent collapse unless the wall is adequately supported so that it will not overturn or collapse. The bracing shall remain in place until permanent supporting elements of the structure are in place.

APPENDIX A TO SUBPART Q OF PART 1926—REFERENCES TO SUBPART Q OF PART 1926

(This appendix is non-mandatory.)

The following non-mandatory references provide information which can be helpful in understanding and complying with the requirements contained in subpart Q.

• Accident Prevention Manual for Industrial Operations; Eighth Edition; National Safety Council.
• Building Code Requirements for Reinforced Concrete (ACI 318–83).
• Formwork for Concrete (ACI SP–4).
• Recommended Practice for Concrete Formwork (ACI 347–78).
• Safety Requirements for Concrete and Masonry Work (ANSI A10.9–1983).
• Standard Test Method for Compressive Strength of Cylindrical Concrete Specimens (ASTM C39–86).
• Standard Test Method for Making and Curing Concrete Test Specimens in the Field (ASTM C31–85).
• Standard Test Method for Penetration Resistance of Hardened Concrete (ASTM C803–82).
• Standard Test Method for Compressive Strength of Concrete Cylinders Cast In-Place in Cylindrical Molds (ASTM C873–85).
• Standard Method for Developing Early Age Compressive Test Values and Projecting Later Age Strengths (ASTM C918–80).
• Recommended Practice for Inspection and Testing Agencies for Concrete, Steel and Bituminous Materials as Used in Construction (ASTM E329–77).
• Method of Making and Curing Concrete Test Specimens in the Laboratory (ASTM C192–88).
• Methods of Obtaining and Testing Drilled Cores and Sawed Beams of Concrete (ASTM C42–87).
• Methods of Securing, Preparing and Testing Specimens from Hardened Lightweight Insulating Concrete for Compressive Strength (ASTM C513–86).
• Test Method for Comprehensive Strength of Lightweight Insulating Concrete (ASTM C495–86).
• Method of Making, Accelerating Curing, and Testing of Concrete Compression Test Specimens (ASTM C684–81).
• Test Method for Compressive Strength of Concrete Using Portions of Beams Broken in Flexure (ASTM C116–68 (1980)).

Subpart R—Steel Erection

AUTHORITY: Section 3704 of the Contract Work Hours and Safety Standards Act (40 U.S.C. 3701); Sections 4, 6, and 8 of the Occupational Safety and Health Act of 1970 (29 U.S.C. 653, 655, 657); Secretary of Labor's Order Nos. 3–2000 (65 FR 50017), 5–2002 (67 FR 65008), and 5–2007 (72 FR 31159); and 29 CFR part 1911.

SOURCE: 66 FR 5265, Jan. 18, 2001, unless otherwise noted.

§ 1926.750 Scope.

(a) This subpart sets forth requirements to protect employees from the hazards associated with steel erection activities involved in the construction, alteration, and/or repair of single and multi-story buildings, bridges, and other structures where steel erection occurs. The requirements of this subpart apply to employers engaged in steel erection unless otherwise specified. This subpart does not cover electrical transmission towers, communication and broadcast towers, or tanks.

NOTE TO PARAGRAPH (a): Examples of structures where steel erection may occur include but are not limited to the following: Single and multi-story buildings; systems-engineered metal buildings; lift slab/tilt-up structures; energy exploration structures; energy production, transfer and storage structures and facilities; auditoriums; malls; amphitheaters; stadiums; power plants; mills; chemical process structures; bridges; trestles; overpasses; underpasses; viaducts; aqueducts; aerospace facilities and structures; radar and communication structures; light towers; signage; billboards; scoreboards; conveyor systems; conveyor supports and related framing; stairways; stair towers; fire escapes; draft curtains; fire containment structures; monorails; aerialways; catwalks; curtain walls; window walls; store fronts; elevator fronts; entrances; skylights; metal roofs; industrial structures; hi-bay structures; rail, marine and other transportation structures; sound barriers; water process and water containment structures; air and cable supported structures; space frames; geodesic domes; canopies; racks and rack support structures and frames; platforms; walkways; balconies; atriums; penthouses; car dumpers; stackers/reclaimers; cranes and craneways; bins; hoppers; ovens; furnaces; stacks; amusement park structures and rides; and artistic and monumental structures.

(b)(1) Steel erection activities include hoisting, laying out, placing, connecting, welding, burning, guying, bracing, bolting, plumbing and rigging structural steel, steel joists and metal buildings; installing metal decking, curtain walls, window walls, siding systems, miscellaneous metals, ornamental iron and similar materials; and moving point-to-point while performing these activities.

(2) The following activities are covered by this subpart when they occur during and are a part of steel erection activities: rigging, hoisting, laying out, placing, connecting, guying, bracing, dismantling, burning, welding, bolting, grinding, sealing, caulking, and all related activities for construction, alteration and/or repair of materials and assemblies such as structural steel; ferrous metals and alloys; non-ferrous metals and alloys; glass; plastics and synthetic composite materials; structural metal framing and related bracing and assemblies; anchoring devices; structural cabling; cable stays; permanent and temporary bents and towers; falsework for temporary supports of permanent steel members; stone and other non-precast concrete architectural materials mounted on steel frames; safety systems for steel erection; steel and metal joists; metal decking and raceway systems and accessories; metal roofing and accessories; metal siding; bridge flooring; cold formed steel framing; elevator beams; grillage; shelf racks; multi-purpose supports; crane rails and accessories; miscellaneous, architectural and ornamental metals and metal work; ladders; railings; handrails; fences and gates; gratings; trench covers; floor plates; castings; sheet metal fabrications; metal panels and panel wall systems; louvers; column covers; enclosures and pockets; stairs; perforated metals; ornamental iron work, expansion control including bridge ex-

pansion joint assemblies; slide bearings; hydraulic structures; fascias; soffit panels; penthouse enclosures; skylights; joint fillers; gaskets; sealants and seals; doors; windows; hardware; detention/security equipment and doors, windows and hardware; conveying systems; building specialties; building equipment; machinery and plant equipment, furnishings and special construction.

(c) The duties of controlling contractors under this subpart include, but are not limited to, the duties specified in §§ 1926.752 (a) and (c), 1926.755(b)(2), 1926.759(b), and 1926.760(e).

§ 1926.751 Definitions.

Anchored bridging means that the steel joist bridging is connected to a bridging terminus point.

Bolted diagonal bridging means diagonal bridging that is bolted to a steel joist or joists.

Bridging clip means a device that is attached to the steel joist to allow the bolting of the bridging to the steel joist.

Bridging terminus point means a wall, a beam, tandem joists (with all bridging installed and a horizontal truss in the plane of the top chord) or other element at an end or intermediate point(s) of a line of bridging that provides an anchor point for the steel joist bridging.

Choker means a wire rope or synthetic fiber rigging assembly that is used to attach a load to a hoisting device.

Cold forming means the process of using press brakes, rolls, or other methods to shape steel into desired cross sections at room temperature.

Column means a load-carrying vertical member that is part of the primary skeletal framing system. Columns do not include posts.

Competent person (also defined in § 1926.32) means one who is capable of identifying existing and predictable hazards in the surroundings or working conditions which are unsanitary, hazardous, or dangerous to employees, and who has authorization to take prompt corrective measures to eliminate them.

Connector means an employee who, working with hoisting equipment, is placing and connecting structural members and/or components.

Constructibility means the ability to erect structural steel members in accordance with subpart R without having to alter the over-all structural design.

Construction load (for joist erection) means any load other than the weight of the employee(s), the joists and the bridging bundle.

Controlled Decking Zone (CDZ) means an area in which certain work (for example, initial installation and placement of metal decking) may take place without the use of guardrail systems, personal fall arrest systems, fall restraint systems, or safety net systems and where access to the zone is controlled.

Controlled load lowering means lowering a load by means of a mechanical hoist drum device that allows a hoisted load to be lowered with maximum control using the gear train or hydraulic components of the hoist mechanism. Controlled load lowering requires the use of the hoist drive motor, rather than the load hoist brake, to lower the load.

Controlling contractor means a prime contractor, general contractor, construction manager or any other legal entity which has the overall responsibility for the construction of the project—its planning, quality and completion.

Critical lift means a lift that (1) exceeds 75 percent of the rated capacity of the crane or derrick, or (2) requires the use of more than one crane or derrick.

Decking hole means a gap or void more than 2 inches (5.1 cm) in its least dimension and less than 12 inches (30.5 cm) in its greatest dimension in a floor, roof or other walking/working surface. Pre-engineered holes in cellular decking (for wires, cables, etc.) are not included in this definition.

Derrick floor means an elevated floor of a building or structure that has been designated to receive hoisted pieces of steel prior to final placement.

Double connection means an attachment method where the connection point is intended for two pieces of steel which share common bolts on either side of a central piece.

Double connection seat means a structural attachment that, during the installation of a double connection, supports the first member while the second member is connected.

Erection bridging means the bolted diagonal bridging that is required to be installed prior to releasing the hoisting cables from the steel joists.

Fall restraint system means a fall protection system that prevents the user from falling any distance. The system is comprised of either a body belt or body harness, along with an anchorage, connectors and other necessary equipment. The other components typically include a lanyard, and may also include a lifeline and other devices.

Final interior perimeter means the perimeter of a large permanent open space within a building such as an atrium or courtyard. This does not include openings for stairways, elevator shafts, etc.

Girt (in systems-engineered metal buildings) means a "Z" or "C" shaped member formed from sheet steel spanning between primary framing and supporting wall material.

Headache ball means a weighted hook that is used to attach loads to the hoist load line of the crane.

Hoisting equipment means commercially manufactured lifting equipment designed to lift and position a load of known weight to a location at some known elevation and horizontal distance from the equipment's center of rotation. "Hoisting equipment" includes but is not limited to cranes, derricks, tower cranes, barge-mounted derricks or cranes, gin poles and gantry hoist systems. A "come-a-long" (a mechanical device, usually consisting of a chain or cable attached at each end, that is used to facilitate movement of materials through leverage) is not considered "hoisting equipment."

Leading edge means the unprotected side and edge of a floor, roof, or formwork for a floor or other walking/working surface (such as deck) which changes location as additional floor, roof, decking or formwork sections are placed, formed or constructed.

Metal decking means a commercially manufactured, structural grade, cold rolled metal panel formed into a series of parallel ribs; for this subpart, this includes metal floor and roof decks, standing seam metal roofs, other metal roof systems and other products such as bar gratings, checker plate, expanded metal panels, and similar products. After installation and proper fastening, these decking materials serve a combination of functions including, but not limited to: a structural element designed in combination with the structure to resist, distribute and transfer loads, stiffen the structure and provide a diaphragm action; a walking/working surface; a form for concrete slabs; a support for roofing systems; and a finished floor or roof.

Multiple lift rigging means a rigging assembly manufactured by wire rope rigging suppliers that facilitates the attachment of up to five independent loads to the hoist rigging of a crane.

Opening means a gap or void 12 inches (30.5 cm) or more in its least dimension in a floor, roof or other walking/working surface. For the purposes of this subpart, skylights and smoke domes that do not meet the strength requirements of § 1926.754(e)(3) shall be regarded as openings.

Permanent floor means a structurally completed floor at any level or elevation (including slab on grade).

Personal fall arrest system means a system used to arrest an employee in a fall from a working level. A personal fall arrest system consists of an anchorage, connectors, a body harness and may include a lanyard, deceleration device, lifeline, or suitable combination of these. The use of a body belt for fall arrest is prohibited.

Positioning device system means a body belt or body harness rigged to allow an employee to be supported on an elevated, vertical surface, such as a wall or column and work with both hands free while leaning.

Post means a structural member with a longitudinal axis that is essentially vertical, that: (1) weighs 300 pounds or less and is axially loaded (a load presses down on the top end), or (2) is not axially loaded, but is laterally restrained by the above member. Posts typically support stair landings, wall framing, mezzanines and other substructures.

Project structural engineer of record means the registered, licensed professional responsible for the design of structural steel framing and whose seal appears on the structural contract documents.

Purlin (in systems-engineered metal buildings) means a "Z" or "C" shaped member formed from sheet steel spanning between primary framing and supporting roof material.

Qualified person (also defined in § 1926.32) means one who, by possession of a recognized degree, certificate, or professional standing, or who by extensive knowledge, training, and experience, has successfully demonstrated the ability to solve or resolve problems relating to the subject matter, the work, or the project.

Safety deck attachment means an initial attachment that is used to secure an initially placed sheet of decking to keep proper alignment and bearing with structural support members.

Shear connector means headed steel studs, steel bars, steel lugs, and similar devices which are attached to a structural member for the purpose of achieving composite action with concrete.

Steel erection means the construction, alteration or repair of steel buildings, bridges and other structures, including the installation of metal decking and all planking used during the process of erection.

Steel joist means an open web, secondary load-carrying member of 144 feet (43.9 m) or less, designed by the manufacturer, used for the support of floors and roofs. This does not include structural steel trusses or cold-formed joists.

Steel joist girder means an open web, primary load-carrying member, designed by the manufacturer, used for the support of floors and roofs. This does not include structural steel trusses.

Steel truss means an open web member designed of structural steel components by the project structural engineer of record. For the purposes of this subpart, a steel truss is considered equivalent to a solid web structural member.

Structural steel means a steel member, or a member made of a substitute material (such as, but not limited to, fiberglass, aluminum or composite members). These members include, but are not limited to, steel joists, joist girders, purlins, columns, beams, trusses, splices, seats, metal decking, girts, and all bridging, and cold formed metal framing which is integrated with the structural steel framing of a building.

Systems-engineered metal building means a metal, field-assembled building system consisting of framing, roof and wall coverings. Typically, many of these components are cold-formed shapes. These individual parts are fabricated in one or more manufacturing facilities and shipped to the job site for assembly into the final structure. The engineering design of the system is normally the responsibility of the systems-engineered metal building manufacturer.

Tank means a container for holding gases, liquids or solids.

Unprotected sides and edges means any side or edge (except at entrances to points of access) of a walking/working surface, for example a, floor, roof, ramp or runway, where there is no wall or guardrail system at least 39 inches (1.0 m) high.

§1926.752 Site layout, site-specific erection plan and construction sequence.

(a) *Approval to begin steel erection.* Before authorizing the commencement of steel erection, the controlling contractor shall ensure that the steel erector is provided with the following written notifications:

(1) The concrete in the footings, piers and walls and the mortar in the masonry piers and walls has attained, on the basis of an appropriate ASTM standard test method of field-cured samples, either 75 percent of the intended minimum compressive design strength or sufficient strength to support the loads imposed during steel erection.

(2) Any repairs, replacements and modifications to the anchor bolts were conducted in accordance with §1926.755(b).

(b) *Commencement of steel erection.* A steel erection contractor shall not erect steel unless it has received written notification that the concrete in the footings, piers and walls or the mortar in the masonry piers and walls has attained, on the basis of an appropriate ASTM standard test method of field-cured samples, either 75 percent of the intended minimum compressive design strength or sufficient strength to support the loads imposed during steel erection.

(c) *Site layout.* The controlling contractor shall ensure that the following is provided and maintained:

(1) Adequate access roads into and through the site for the safe delivery and movement of derricks, cranes, trucks, other necessary equipment, and the material to be erected and means and methods for pedestrian and vehicular control. Exception: this requirement does not apply to roads outside of the construction site.

(2) A firm, properly graded, drained area, readily accessible to the work with adequate space for the safe storage of materials and the safe operation of the erector's equipment.

(d) *Pre-planning of overhead hoisting operations.* All hoisting operations in steel erection shall be pre-planned to ensure that the requirements of §1926.753(d) are met.

(e) *Site-specific erection plan.* Where employers elect, due to conditions specific to the site, to develop alternate means and methods that provide employee protection in accordance with §1926.753(c)(5), §1926.757(a)(4) or §1926.757(e)(4), a site-specific erection plan shall be developed by a qualified person and be available at the work site. Guidelines for establishing a site-specific erection plan are contained in appendix A to this subpart.

§1926.753 Hoisting and rigging.

(a) All the provisions of subpart CC apply to hoisting and rigging with the exception of §1926.1431(a).

(b) In addition, paragraphs (c) through (e) of this section apply regarding the hazards associated with hoisting and rigging.

(c) *General.* (1) Pre-shift visual inspection of cranes.

(i) Cranes being used in steel erection activities shall be visually inspected prior to each shift by a competent person; the inspection shall include observation for deficiencies during operation. At a minimum this inspection shall include the following:

(A) All control mechanisms for maladjustments;

(B) Control and drive mechanism for excessive wear of components and contamination by lubricants, water or other foreign matter;

(C) Safety devices, including but not limited to boom angle indicators, boom stops, boom kick out devices, anti-two block devices, and load moment indicators where required;

(D) Air, hydraulic, and other pressurized lines for deterioration or leakage, particularly those which flex in normal operation;

(E) Hooks and latches for deformation, chemical damage, cracks, or wear;

(F) Wire rope reeving for compliance with hoisting equipment manufacturer's specifications;

(G) Electrical apparatus for malfunctioning, signs of excessive deterioration, dirt, or moisture accumulation;

(H) Hydraulic system for proper fluid level;

(I) Tires for proper inflation and condition;

(J) Ground conditions around the hoisting equipment for proper support, including ground settling under and around outriggers, ground water accumulation, or similar conditions;

(K) The hoisting equipment for level position; and

(L) The hoisting equipment for level position after each move and setup.

(ii) If any deficiency is identified, an immediate determination shall be made by the competent person as to whether the deficiency constitutes a hazard.

(iii) If the deficiency is determined to constitute a hazard, the hoisting equipment shall be removed from service until the deficiency has been corrected.

(iv) The operator shall be responsible for those operations under the operator's direct control. Whenever there is any doubt as to safety, the operator shall have the authority to stop and refuse to handle loads until safety has been assured.

(2) A qualified rigger (a rigger who is also a qualified person) shall inspect the rigging prior to each shift in accordance with § 1926.251.

(3) The headache ball, hook or load shall not be used to transport personnel except as provided in paragraph (c)(4) of this section.

(4) Cranes or derricks may be used to hoist employees on a personnel platform when work under this subpart is being conducted, provided that all provisions of § 1926.1431 (except for § 1926.1431(a)) are met.

(5) Safety latches on hooks shall not be deactivated or made inoperable except:

(i) When a qualified rigger has determined that the hoisting and placing of purlins and single joists can be performed more safely by doing so; or

(ii) When equivalent protection is provided in a site-specific erection plan.

(d) *Working under loads.* (1) Routes for suspended loads shall be pre-planned to ensure that no employee is required to work directly below a suspended load except for:

(i) Employees engaged in the initial connection of the steel; or

(ii) Employees necessary for the hooking or unhooking of the load.

(2) When working under suspended loads, the following criteria shall be met:

(i) Materials being hoisted shall be rigged to prevent unintentional displacement;

(ii) Hooks with self-closing safety latches or their equivalent shall be used to prevent components from slipping out of the hook; and

(iii) All loads shall be rigged by a qualified rigger

(e) *Multiple lift rigging procedure.* (1) A multiple lift shall only be performed if the following criteria are met:

(i) A multiple lift rigging assembly is used;

(ii) A maximum of five members are hoisted per lift;

(iii) Only beams and similar structural members are lifted; and

(iv) All employees engaged in the multiple lift have been trained in these procedures in accordance with § 1926.761(c)(1).

(v) No crane is permitted to be used for a multiple lift where such use is contrary to the manufacturer's specifications and limitations.

(2) Components of the multiple lift rigging assembly shall be specifically designed and assembled with a maximum capacity for total assembly and for each individual attachment point. This capacity, certified by the manufacturer or a qualified rigger, shall be based on the manufacturer's specifications with a 5 to 1 safety factor for all components.

(3) The total load shall not exceed:

(i) The rated capacity of the hoisting equipment specified in the hoisting equipment load charts;

(ii) The rigging capacity specified in the rigging rating chart.

(4) The multiple lift rigging assembly shall be rigged with members:

(i) Attached at their center of gravity and maintained reasonably level;

(ii) Rigged from top down; and

(iii) Rigged at least 7 feet (2.1 m) apart.

(5) The members on the multiple lift rigging assembly shall be set from the bottom up.

(6) Controlled load lowering shall be used whenever the load is over the connectors.

[66 FR 5265, Jan. 18, 2001, as amended at 75 FR 48134, Aug. 9, 2010]

§1926.754 Structural steel assembly.

(a) Structural stability shall be maintained at all times during the erection process.

NOTE TO PARAGRAPH (a): Federal Highway Administration (FHWA) regulations incorporate by reference a number of standards, policies, and standard specifications published by the American Association of State Highway and Transportation Officials (AASHTO) and other organizations. (*See* 23 CFR 625.4). Many of these incorporated provisions may be relevant to maintaining structural stability during the erection process. For instance, as of May 17, 2010, in many cases FHWA requires a Registered Engineer to prepare and seal working drawings for falsework used in highway bridge construction. (*See* AASHTO Specifications for Highway Bridges, Div. II, §3.2.1, 15th edition, 1992, which FHWA incorporates by reference in 23 CFR 625.4). FHWA also encourages compliance with AASHTO Specifications that the FHWA regulations do not currently incorporate by reference. (*See* http://www.fhwa.dot.gov/bridge/lrfd/index.htm.)

(b) The following additional requirements shall apply for multi-story structures:

(1) The permanent floors shall be installed as the erection of structural members progresses, and there shall be not more than eight stories between the erection floor and the upper-most permanent floor, except where the structural integrity is maintained as a result of the design.

(2) At no time shall there be more than four floors or 48 feet (14.6 m), whichever is less, of unfinished bolting or welding above the foundation or uppermost permanently secured floor, except where the structural integrity is maintained as a result of the design.

(3) A fully planked or decked floor or nets shall be maintained within two stories or 30 feet (9.1 m), whichever is less, directly under any erection work being performed.

(c) *Walking/working surfaces—shear connectors and other similar devices—(1) Tripping hazards.* Shear connectors (such as headed steel studs, steel bars or steel lugs), reinforcing bars, deformed anchors or threaded studs shall not be attached to the top flanges of beams, joists or beam attachments so that they project vertically from or horizontally across the top flange of the member until after the metal decking, or other walking/working surface, has been installed.

(2) *Installation of shear connectors on composite floors, roofs and bridge decks.* When shear connectors are used in construction of composite floors, roofs and bridge decks, employees shall lay out and install the shear connectors after the metal decking has been installed, using the metal decking as a working platform. Shear connectors shall not be installed from within a controlled decking zone (CDZ), as specified in §1926.760(c)(8).

(d) *Plumbing-up.* (1) When deemed necessary by a competent person, plumbing-up equipment shall be installed in conjunction with the steel erection process to ensure the stability of the structure.

(2) When used, plumbing-up equipment shall be in place and properly installed before the structure is loaded

with construction material such as loads of joists, bundles of decking or bundles of bridging.

(3) Plumbing-up equipment shall be removed only with the approval of a competent person.

(e) *Metal decking*—(1) *Hoisting, landing and placing of metal decking bundles.* (i) Bundle packaging and strapping shall not be used for hoisting unless specifically designed for that purpose.

(ii) If loose items such as dunnage, flashing, or other materials are placed on the top of metal decking bundles to be hoisted, such items shall be secured to the bundles.

(iii) Bundles of metal decking on joists shall be landed in accordance with § 1926.757(e)(4).

(iv) Metal decking bundles shall be landed on framing members so that enough support is provided to allow the bundles to be unbanded without dislodging the bundles from the supports.

(v) At the end of the shift or when environmental or jobsite conditions require, metal decking shall be secured against displacement.

(2) *Roof and floor holes and openings.* Metal decking at roof and floor holes and openings shall be installed as follows:

(i) Framed metal deck openings shall have structural members turned down to allow continuous deck installation except where not allowed by structural design constraints or constructibility.

(ii) Roof and floor holes and openings shall be decked over. Where large size, configuration or other structural design does not allow openings to be decked over (such as elevator shafts, stair wells, etc.) employees shall be protected in accordance with § 1926.760(a)(1).

(iii) Metal decking holes and openings shall not be cut until immediately prior to being permanently filled with the equipment or structure needed or intended to fulfill its specific use and which meets the strength requirements of paragraph (e)(3) of this section, or shall be immediately covered.

(3) *Covering roof and floor openings.* (i) Covers for roof and floor openings shall be capable of supporting, without failure, twice the weight of the employees, equipment and materials that may be imposed on the cover at any one time.

(ii) All covers shall be secured when installed to prevent accidental displacement by the wind, equipment or employees.

(iii) All covers shall be painted with high-visibility paint or shall be marked with the word "HOLE" or "COVER" to provide warning of the hazard.

(iv) Smoke dome or skylight fixtures that have been installed, are not considered covers for the purpose of this section unless they meet the strength requirements of paragraph (e)(3)(i) of this section.

(4) *Decking gaps around columns.* Wire mesh, exterior plywood, or equivalent, shall be installed around columns where planks or metal decking do not fit tightly. The materials used must be of sufficient strength to provide fall protection for personnel and prevent objects from falling through.

(5) *Installation of metal decking.* (i) Except as provided in § 1926.760(c), metal decking shall be laid tightly and immediately secured upon placement to prevent accidental movement or displacement.

(ii) During initial placement, metal decking panels shall be placed to ensure full support by structural members.

(6) Derrick floors. (i) A derrick floor shall be fully decked and/or planked and the steel member connections completed to support the intended floor loading.

(ii) Temporary loads placed on a derrick floor shall be distributed over the underlying support members so as to prevent local overloading of the deck material.

[66 FR 5265, Jan. 18, 2001, as amended at 71 FR 2885, Jan. 18, 2006; 71 FR 16674, Apr. 3, 2006; 75 FR 27429, May 17, 2010]

§ 1926.755 Column anchorage.

(a) *General requirements for erection stability.* (1) All columns shall be anchored by a minimum of 4 anchor rods (anchor bolts).

(2) Each column anchor rod (anchor bolt) assembly, including the column-to-base plate weld and the column foundation, shall be designed to resist a minimum eccentric gravity load of 300 pounds (136.2 kg) located 18 inches (.46m) from the extreme outer face of

the column in each direction at the top of the column shaft.

(3) Columns shall be set on level finished floors, pre-grouted leveling plates, leveling nuts, or shim packs which are adequate to transfer the construction loads.

(4) All columns shall be evaluated by a competent person to determine whether guying or bracing is needed; if guying or bracing is needed, it shall be installed.

(b) *Repair, replacement or field modification of anchor rods (anchor bolts).* (1) Anchor rods (anchor bolts) shall not be repaired, replaced or field-modified without the approval of the project structural engineer of record.

(2) Prior to the erection of a column, the controlling contractor shall provide written notification to the steel erector if there has been any repair, replacement or modification of the anchor rods (anchor bolts) of that column.

§1926.756 Beams and columns.

(a) *General.* (1) During the final placing of solid web structural members, the load shall not be released from the hoisting line until the members are secured with at least two bolts per connection, of the same size and strength as shown in the erection drawings, drawn up wrench-tight or the equivalent as specified by the project structural engineer of record, except as specified in paragraph (b) of this section.

(2) A competent person shall determine if more than two bolts are necessary to ensure the stability of cantilevered members; if additional bolts are needed, they shall be installed.

(b) *Diagonal bracing.* Solid web structural members used as diagonal bracing shall be secured by at least one bolt per connection drawn up wrench-tight or the equivalent as specified by the project structural engineer of record.

(c) (1) *Double connections at columns and/or at beam webs over a column.* When two structural members on opposite sides of a column web, or a beam web over a column, are connected sharing common connection holes, at least one bolt with its wrench-tight nut shall remain connected to the first member unless a shop-attached or field-attached seat or equivalent connection device is supplied with the member to secure the first member and prevent the column from being displaced (See appendix H to this subpart for examples of equivalent connection devices).

(2) If a seat or equivalent device is used, the seat (or device) shall be designed to support the load during the double connection process. It shall be adequately bolted or welded to both a supporting member and the first member before the nuts on the shared bolts are removed to make the double connection.

(d) *Column splices.* Each column splice shall be designed to resist a minimum eccentric gravity load of 300 pounds (136.2 kg) located 18 inches (.46 m) from the extreme outer face of the column in each direction at the top of the column shaft.

(e) *Perimeter columns.* Perimeter columns shall not be erected unless:

(1) The perimeter columns extend a minimum of 48 inches (1.2 m) above the finished floor to permit installation of perimeter safety cables prior to erection of the next tier, except where constructibility does not allow (see appendix F to this subpart);

(2) The perimeter columns have holes or other devices in or attached to perimeter columns at 42–45 inches (107–114 cm) above the finished floor and the midpoint between the finished floor and the top cable to permit installation of perimeter safety cables required by §1926.760(a)(2), except where constructibility does not allow. (See appendix F to this subpart).

§1926.757 Open web steel joists.

(a) *General.* (1) Except as provided in paragraph (a)(2) of this section, where steel joists are used and columns are not framed in at least two directions with solid web structural steel members, a steel joist shall be field-bolted at the column to provide lateral stability to the column during erection. For the installation of this joist:

(i) A vertical stabilizer plate shall be provided on each column for steel joists. The plate shall be a minimum of 6 inch by 6 inch (152 mm by 152 mm) and shall extend at least 3 inches (76 mm) below the bottom chord of the joist with a $^{13}\!/_{16}$ inch (21 mm) hole to

415

provide an attachment point for guying or plumbing cables.

(ii) The bottom chords of steel joists at columns shall be stabilized to prevent rotation during erection.

(iii) Hoisting cables shall not be released until the seat at each end of the steel joist is field-bolted, and each end of the bottom chord is restrained by the column stabilizer plate.

(2) Where constructibility does not allow a steel joist to be installed at the column:

(i) an alternate means of stabilizing joists shall be installed on both sides near the column and shall:

(A) provide stability equivalent to paragraph (a)(1) of this section;

(B) be designed by a qualified person;

(C) be shop installed; and

(D) be included in the erection drawings.

(ii) hoisting cables shall not be released until the seat at each end of the steel joist is field-bolted and the joist is stabilized.

(3) Where steel joists at or near columns span 60 feet (18.3 m) or less, the joist shall be designed with sufficient strength to allow one employee to release the hoisting cable without the need for erection bridging.

(4) Where steel joists at or near columns span more than 60 feet (18.3 m), the joists shall be set in tandem with all bridging installed unless an alternative method of erection, which provides equivalent stability to the steel joist, is designed by a qualified person and is included in the site-specific erection plan.

(5) A steel joist or steel joist girder shall not be placed on any support structure unless such structure is stabilized.

(6) When steel joist(s) are landed on a structure, they shall be secured to prevent unintentional displacement prior to installation.

(7) No modification that affects the strength of a steel joist or steel joist girder shall be made without the approval of the project structural engineer of record.

(8) *Field-bolted joists.* (i) Except for steel joists that have been pre-assembled into panels, connections of individual steel joists to steel structures in bays of 40 feet (12.2 m) or more shall be fabricated to allow for field bolting during erection.

(ii) These connections shall be field-bolted unless constructibility does not allow.

(9) Steel joists and steel joist girders shall not be used as anchorage points for a fall arrest system unless written approval to do so is obtained from a qualified person.

(10) A bridging terminus point shall be established before bridging is installed. (See appendix C to this subpart.)

(b) *Attachment of steel joists and steel joist girders.* (1) Each end of "K" series steel joists shall be attached to the support structure with a minimum of two ⅛-inch (3 mm) fillet welds 1 inch (25 mm) long or with two ½-inch (13 mm) bolts, or the equivalent.

(2) Each end of "LH" and "DLH" series steel joists and steel joist girders shall be attached to the support structure with a minimum of two ¼-inch (6 mm) fillet welds 2 inches (51 mm) long, or with two ¾-inch (19 mm) bolts, or the equivalent.

(3) Except as provided in paragraph (b)(4) of this section, each steel joist shall be attached to the support structure, at least at one end on both sides of the seat, immediately upon placement in the final erection position and before additional joists are placed.

(4) Panels that have been pre-assembled from steel joists with bridging shall be attached to the structure at each corner before the hoisting cables are released.

(c) *Erection of steel joists.* (1) Both sides of the seat of one end of each steel joist that requires bridging under Tables A and B shall be attached to the support structure before hoisting cables are released.

(2) For joists over 60 feet, both ends of the joist shall be attached as specified in paragraph (b) of this section and the provisions of paragraph (d) of this section met before the hoisting cables are released.

(3) On steel joists that do not require erection bridging under Tables A and B, only one employee shall be allowed on the joist until all bridging is installed and anchored.

TABLE A—ERECTION BRIDGING FOR SHORT
SPAN JOISTS

Joist	Span
8L1	NM
10K1	NM
12K1	23–0
12K3	NM
12K5	NM
14K1	27–0
14K3	NM
14K4	NM
14K6	NM
16K2	29–0
16K3	30–0
16K4	32–0
16K5	32–0
16K6	NM
16K7	NM
16K9	NM
18K3	31–0
18K4	32–0
18K5	33–0
18K6	35–0
18K7	NM
18K9	NM
18K10	NM
20K3	32–0
20K4	34–0
20K5	34–0
20K6	36–0
20K7	39–0
20K9	39–0
20K10	NM
22K4	34–0
22K5	35–0
22K6	36–0
22K7	40–0
22K9	40–0
22K10	40–0
22K11	40–0
24K4	36–0
24K5	38–0
24K6	39–0
24K7	43–0
24K8	43–0
24K9	44–0
24K10	NM
24K12	NM
26K5	38–0
26K6	39–0
26K7	43–0
26K8	44–0
26K9	45–0
26K10	49–0
26K12	NM
28K6	40–0
28K7	43–0
28K8	44–0
28K9	45–0
28K10	49–0
28K12	53–0
30K7	44–0
30K8	45–0
30K9	45–0
30K10	50–0
30K11	52–0
30K12	54–0
10KCS1	NM
10KCS2	NM
10KCS3	NM
12KCS1	NM
12KCS2	NM
12KCS3	NM
14KCS1	NM

TABLE A—ERECTION BRIDGING FOR SHORT
SPAN JOISTS—Continued

Joist	Span
14KCS2	NM
14KCS3	NM
16KCS2	NM
16KCS3	NM
16KCS4	NM
16KCS5	NM
18KCS2	35–0
18KCS3	NM
18KCS4	NM
18KCS5	NM
20KCS2	36–0
20KCS3	39–0
20KCS4	NM
20KCS5	NM
22KCS2	36–0
22KCS3	40–0
22KCS4	NM
22KCS5	NM
24KCS2	39–0
24KCS3	44–0
24KCS4	NM
24KCS5	NM
26KCS2	39–0
26KCS3	44–0
26KCS4	NM
26KCS5	NM
28KCS2	40–0
28KCS3	45–0
28KCS4	53–0
28KCS5	53–0
30KC53	45–0
30KCS4	54–0
30KCS5	54–0

NM=diagonal bolted bridging not mandatory for joists under 40 feet.

TABLE B—ERECTION BRIDGING FOR LONG SPAN
JOISTS

Joist	Span
18LH02	33–0.
18LH03	NM.
18LH04	NM.
18LH05	NM.
18LH06	NM.
18LH07	NM.
18LH08	NM.
18LH09	NM.
20LH02	33–0.
20LH03	38–0.
20LH04	NM.
20LH05	NM.
20LH06	NM.
20LH07	NM.
20LH08	NM.
20LH09	NM.
20LH10	NM.
24LH03	35–0.
24LH04	39–0.
24LH05	40–0.
24LH06	45–0.
24LH07	NM.
24LH08	NM.
24LH09	NM.
24LH10	NM.
24LH11	NM.
28LH05	42–0.
28LH06	42–0.
28LH07	NM.

417

Joist	Span
28LH08	NM.
28LH09	NM.
28LH10	NM.
28LH11	NM.
28LH12	NM.
28LH13	NM.
32LH06	47–0 through 60–0.
32LH07	47–0 through 60–0.
32LH08	55–0 through 60–0.
32LH09	NM through 60–0.
32LH10	NM through 60–0.
32LH11	NM through 60–0.
32LH12	NM through 60–0.
32LH13	NM through 60–0.
32LH14	NM through 60–0.
32LH15	NM through 60–0.
36LH07	47–0 through 60–0.
36LH08	47–0 through 60–0.
36LH09	57–0 through 60–0.
36LH10	NM through 60–0.
36LH11	NM through 60–0.
36LH12	NM through 60–0.
36LH13	NM through 60–0.
36LH14	NM through 60–0.
36LH15	NM through 60–0.

NM = diagonal bolted bridging not mandatory for joists under 40 feet.

(4) Employees shall not be allowed on steel joists where the span of the steel joist is equal to or greater than the span shown in Tables A and B except in accordance with § 1926.757(d).

(5) When permanent bridging terminus points cannot be used during erection, additional temporary bridging terminus points are required to provide stability. (See appendix C of this subpart.)

(d) *Erection bridging.* (1) Where the span of the steel joist is equal to or greater than the span shown in Tables A and B, the following shall apply:

(i) A row of bolted diagonal erection bridging shall be installed near the midspan of the steel joist;

(ii) Hoisting cables shall not be released until this bolted diagonal erection bridging is installed and anchored; and

(iii) No more than one employee shall be allowed on these spans until all other bridging is installed and anchored.

(2) Where the span of the steel joist is over 60 feet (18.3 m) through 100 feet (30.5 m), the following shall apply:

(i) All rows of bridging shall be bolted diagonal bridging;

(ii) Two rows of bolted diagonal erection bridging shall be installed near the third points of the steel joist;

(iii) Hoisting cables shall not be released until this bolted diagonal erection bridging is installed and anchored; and

(iv) No more than two employees shall be allowed on these spans until all other bridging is installed and anchored.

(3) Where the span of the steel joist is over 100 feet (30.5 m) through 144 feet (43.9 m), the following shall apply:

(i) All rows of bridging shall be bolted diagonal bridging;

(ii) Hoisting cables shall not be released until all bridging is installed and anchored; and

(iii) No more than two employees shall be allowed on these spans until all bridging is installed and anchored.

(4) For steel members spanning over 144 feet (43.9 m), the erection methods used shall be in accordance with § 1926.756.

(5) Where any steel joist specified in paragraphs (c)(2) and (d)(1), (d)(2), and (d)(3) of this section is a bottom chord bearing joist, a row of bolted diagonal bridging shall be provided near the support(s). This bridging shall be installed and anchored before the hoisting cable(s) is released.

(6) When bolted diagonal erection bridging is required by this section, the following shall apply:

(i) The bridging shall be indicated on the erection drawing;

(ii) The erection drawing shall be the exclusive indicator of the proper placement of this bridging;

(iii) Shop-installed bridging clips, or functional equivalents, shall be used where the bridging bolts to the steel joists;

(iv) When two pieces of bridging are attached to the steel joist by a common bolt, the nut that secures the first piece of bridging shall not be removed from the bolt for the attachment of the second; and

(v) Bridging attachments shall not protrude above the top chord of the steel joist.

(e) *Landing and placing loads.* (1) During the construction period, the employer placing a load on steel joists shall ensure that the load is distributed so as not to exceed the carrying capacity of any steel joist.

(2) Except for paragraph (e)(4) of this section, no construction loads are allowed on the steel joists until all bridging is installed and anchored and all joist-bearing ends are attached.

(3) The weight of a bundle of joist bridging shall not exceed a total of 1,000 pounds (454 kg). A bundle of joist bridging shall be placed on a minimum of three steel joists that are secured at one end. The edge of the bridging bundle shall be positioned within 1 foot (.30 m) of the secured end.

(4) No bundle of decking may be placed on steel joists until all bridging has been installed and anchored and all joist bearing ends attached, unless all of the following conditions are met:

(i) The employer has first determined from a qualified person and documented in a site-specific erection plan that the structure or portion of the structure is capable of supporting the load;

(ii) The bundle of decking is placed on a minimum of three steel joists;

(iii) The joists supporting the bundle of decking are attached at both ends;

(iv) At least one row of bridging is installed and anchored;

(v) The total weight of the bundle of decking does not exceed 4,000 pounds (1816 kg); and

(vi) Placement of the bundle of decking shall be in accordance with paragraph (e)(5) of this section.

(5) The edge of the construction load shall be placed within 1 foot (.30 m) of the bearing surface of the joist end.

§ 1926.758 Systems-engineered metal buildings.

(a) All of the requirements of this subpart apply to the erection of systems-engineered metal buildings except §§ 1926.755 (column anchorage) and 1926.757 (open web steel joists).

(b) Each structural column shall be anchored by a minimum of four anchor rods (anchor bolts).

(c) Rigid frames shall have 50 percent of their bolts or the number of bolts specified by the manufacturer (whichever is greater) installed and tightened on both sides of the web adjacent to

each flange before the hoisting equipment is released.

(d) Construction loads shall not be placed on any structural steel framework unless such framework is safely bolted, welded or otherwise adequately secured.

(e) In girt and eave strut-to-frame connections, when girts or eave struts share common connection holes, at least one bolt with its wrench-tight nut shall remain connected to the first member unless a manufacturer-supplied, field-attached seat or similar connection device is present to secure the first member so that the girt or eave strut is always secured against displacement.

(f) Both ends of all steel joists or cold-formed joists shall be fully bolted and/or welded to the support structure before:

(1) Releasing the hoisting cables;

(2) Allowing an employee on the joists; or

(3) Allowing any construction loads on the joists.

(g) Purlins and girts shall not be used as an anchorage point for a fall arrest system unless written approval is obtained from a qualified person.

(h) Purlins may only be used as a walking/working surface when installing safety systems, after all permanent bridging has been installed and fall protection is provided.

(i) Construction loads may be placed only within a zone that is within 8 feet (2.5 m) of the center-line of the primary support member.

§ 1926.759 Falling object protection.

(a) *Securing loose items aloft.* All materials, equipment, and tools, which are not in use while aloft, shall be secured against accidental displacement.

(b) *Protection from falling objects other than materials being hoisted.* The controlling contractor shall bar other construction processes below steel erection unless overhead protection for the employees below is provided.

§ 1926.760 Fall protection.

(a) *General requirements.* (1) Except as provided by paragraph (a)(3) of this section, each employee engaged in a steel erection activity who is on a walking/working surface with an unprotected side or edge more than 15 feet (4.6 m) above a lower level shall be protected from fall hazards by guardrail systems, safety net systems, personal fall arrest systems, positioning device systems or fall restraint systems.

(2) *Perimeter safety cables.* On multi-story structures, perimeter safety cables shall be installed at the final interior and exterior perimeters of the floors as soon as the metal decking has been installed.

(3) Connectors and employees working in controlled decking zones shall be protected from fall hazards as provided in paragraphs (b) and (c) of this section, respectively.

(b) *Connectors.* Each connector shall:

(1) Be protected in accordance with paragraph (a)(1) of this section from fall hazards of more than two stories or 30 feet (9.1 m) above a lower level, whichever is less;

(2) Have completed connector training in accordance with § 1926.761; and

(3) Be provided, at heights over 15 and up to 30 feet above a lower level, with a personal fall arrest system, positioning device system or fall restraint system and wear the equipment necessary to be able to be tied off; or be provided with other means of protection from fall hazards in accordance with paragraph (a)(1) of this section.

(c) *Controlled Decking Zone (CDZ).* A controlled decking zone may be established in that area of the structure over 15 and up to 30 feet above a lower level where metal decking is initially being installed and forms the leading edge of a work area. In each CDZ, the following shall apply:

(1) Each employee working at the leading edge in a CDZ shall be protected from fall hazards of more than two stories or 30 feet (9.1 m), whichever is less.

(2) Access to a CDZ shall be limited to only those employees engaged in leading edge work.

(3) The boundaries of a CDZ shall be designated and clearly marked. The CDZ shall not be more than 90 feet (27.4 m) wide and 90 (27.4 m) feet deep from any leading edge. The CDZ shall be marked by the use of control lines or the equivalent. Examples of acceptable procedures for demarcating CDZ's can be found in appendix D to this subpart.

(4) Each employee working in a CDZ shall have completed CDZ training in accordance with § 1926.761.

(5) Unsecured decking in a CDZ shall not exceed 3,000 square feet (914.4 m²).

(6) Safety deck attachments shall be performed in the CDZ from the leading edge back to the control line and shall have at least two attachments for each metal decking panel.

(7) Final deck attachments and installation of shear connectors shall not be performed in the CDZ.

(d) *Criteria for fall protection equipment.* (1) Guardrail systems, safety net systems, personal fall arrest systems, positioning device systems and their components shall conform to the criteria in § 1926.502 (see appendix G to this subpart).

(2) Fall arrest system components shall be used in fall restraint systems and shall conform to the criteria in § 1926.502 (see appendix G). Either body belts or body harnesses shall be used in fall restraint systems.

(3) Perimeter safety cables shall meet the criteria for guardrail systems in § 1926.502 (see appendix G).

(e) *Custody of fall protection.* Fall protection provided by the steel erector shall remain in the area where steel erection activity has been completed, to be used by other trades, only if the controlling contractor or its authorized representative:

(1) Has directed the steel erector to leave the fall protection in place; and

(2) Has inspected and accepted control and responsibility of the fall protection prior to authorizing persons other than steel erectors to work in the area.

§ 1926.761 Training.

The following provisions supplement the requirements of § 1926.21 regarding the hazards addressed in this subpart.

(a) *Training personnel.* Training required by this section shall be provided by a qualified person(s).

(b) *Fall hazard training.* The employer shall train each employee exposed to a fall hazard in accordance with the requirements of this section. The employer shall institute a training program and ensure employee participation in the program.

(c) *Special training programs.* In addition to the training required in paragraphs (a) and (b) of this section, the employer shall provide special training to employees engaged in the following activities.

(1) *Multiple lift rigging procedure.* The employer shall ensure that each employee who performs multiple lift rigging has been provided training in the following areas:

(i) The nature of the hazards associated with multiple lifts; and

(ii) The proper procedures and equipment to perform multiple lifts required by § 1926.753(e).

(2) *Connector procedures.* The employer shall ensure that each connector has been provided training in the following areas:

(i) The nature of the hazards associated with connecting; and

(ii) The establishment, access, proper connecting techniques and work practices required by § 1926.756(c) and § 1926.760(b).

(3) *Controlled Decking Zone Procedures.* Where CDZs are being used, the employer shall assure that each employee has been provided training in the following areas:

(i) The nature of the hazards associated with work within a controlled decking zone; and

(ii) The establishment, access, proper installation techniques and work practices required by § 1926.760(c) and § 1926.754(e).

[66 FR 5265, Jan. 18, 2001, as amended at 73 FR 75589, Dec. 12, 2008]

APPENDIX A TO SUBPART R OF PART 1926—GUIDELINES FOR ESTABLISHING THE COMPONENTS OF A SITE-SPECIFIC ERECTION PLAN: NON-MANDATORY GUIDELINES FOR COMPLYING WITH § 1926.752(e)

(a) *General.* This appendix serves as a guideline to assist employers who elect to develop a site-specific erection plan in accordance with § 1926.752(e) with alternate means and methods to provide employee protection in accordance with § 1926.752(e), § 1926.753(c)(5), § 1926.757(a)(4) and § 1926.757(e)(4).

(b) *Development of a site-specific erection plan.* Pre-construction conference(s) and site inspection(s) are held between the erector and the controlling contractor, and others such as the project engineer and fabricator before the start of steel erection. The purpose of such conference(s) is to develop and review the site-specific erection plan that will meet the requirements of this section.

(c) *Components of a site-specific erection plan.* In developing a site-specific erection plan, a steel erector considers the following elements:

(1) The sequence of erection activity, developed in coordination with the controlling contractor, that includes the following:

(i) Material deliveries;

(ii) Material staging and storage; and

(iii) Coordination with other trades and construction activities.

(2) A description of the crane and derrick selection and placement procedures, including the following:

(i) Site preparation;

(ii) Path for overhead loads; and

(iii) Critical lifts, including rigging supplies and equipment.

(3) A description of steel erection activities and procedures, including the following:

(i) Stability considerations requiring temporary bracing and guying;

(ii) Erection bridging terminus point;

(iii) Anchor rod (anchor bolt) notifications regarding repair, replacement and modifications;

(iv) Columns and beams (including joists and purlins);

(v) Connections;

(vi) Decking; and

(vii) Ornamental and miscellaneous iron.

(4) A description of the fall protection procedures that will be used to comply with § 1926.760.

(5) A description of the procedures that will be used to comply with § 1926.759.

(6) A description of the special procedures required for hazardous non-routine tasks.

(7) A certification for each employee who has received training for performing steel erection operations as required by § 1926.761.

(8) A list of the qualified and competent persons.

(9) A description of the procedures that will be utilized in the event of rescue or emergency response.

(d) *Other plan information.* The plan:

(1) Includes the identification of the site and project; and

(2) Is signed and dated by the qualified person(s) responsible for its preparation and modification.

APPENDIX B TO SUBPART R OF PART 1926
[RESERVED]

APPENDIX C TO SUBPART R OF PART 1926—ILLUSTRATIONS OF BRIDGING TERMINUS POINTS: NON-MANDATORY GUIDELINES FOR COMPLYING WITH §§ 1926.757(a)(10) AND § 1926.757(c)(5)

Appendix C to Subpart R — Illustrations of Bridging Terminus Points: Non-mandatory

Guidelines for Complying with §§1926.757(a)(10) and 1926.757(c)(5).

HORIZONTAL BRIDGING
TERMINUS AT WALL

HORIZONTAL BRIDGING
TERMINUS AT WALL

HORIZONTAL BRIDGING
TERMINUS AT PANEL WALL

HORIZONTAL BRIDGING
TERMINUS AT
STRUCTURAL SHAPE

HORIZONTAL BRIDGING
TERMINUS AT STRUCTURAL
SHAPE WITH OPTIONAL
"X-BRIDGING"

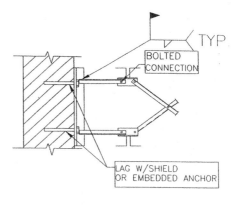

BOLTED DIAGONAL BRIDGING
TERMINUS AT WALL

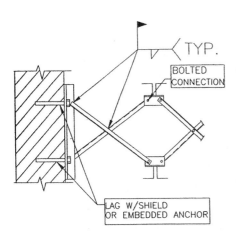

BOLTED DIAGONAL BRIDGING
TERMINUS AT WALL

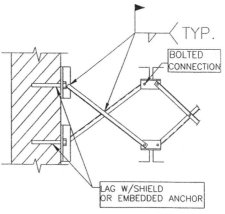

BOLTED DIAGONAL BRIDGING
TERMINUS AT WALL

JOISTS PAIR BRIDGING
TERMINUS POINT

JOISTS PAIR BRIDGING
TERMINUS POINT
W/HORIZ. TRUSS

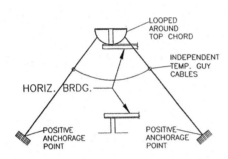

HORIZONTAL BRIDGING
TERMINUS POINT
SECURED BY TEMP.
GUY CABLES

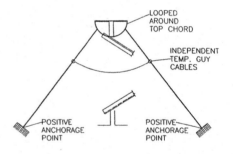

DIAGONAL BRIDGING
TERMINUS POINT
SECURED BY TEMP.
GUY CABLES

APPENDIX D TO SUBPART R OF PART 1926—ILLUSTRATION OF THE USE OF CONTROL LINES TO DEMARCATE CONTROLLED DECKING ZONES (CDZS): NON-MANDATORY GUIDELINES FOR COMPLYING WITH § 1926.760(c)(3)

(1) When used to control access to areas where leading edge and initial securement of metal deck and other operations connected with leading edge work are taking place, the controlled decking zone (CDZ) is defined by a control line or by any other means that restricts access.

(i) A control line for a CDZ is erected not less than 6 feet (1.8 m) nor more than 90 feet (27.4 m) from the leading edge.

(ii) Control lines extend along the entire length of the unprotected or leading edge

424

and are approximately parallel to the unprotected or leading edge.

(iii) Control lines are connected on each side to a guardrail system, wall, stanchion or other suitable anchorage.

(2) Control lines consist of ropes, wires, tapes, or equivalent materials, and supporting stanchions as follows:

(i) Each line is rigged and supported in such a way that its lowest point (including sag) is not less than 39 inches (1.0 m) from the walking/working surface and its highest point is not more than 45 inches (1.3 m) from the walking/working surface.

(ii) Each line has a minimum breaking strength of 200 pounds (90.8 kg).

APPENDIX E TO SUBPART R OF PART 1926—TRAINING: NON-MANDATORY GUIDELINES FOR COMPLYING WITH § 1926.761

The training requirements of § 1926.761 will be deemed to have been met if employees have completed a training course on steel erection, including instruction in the provisions of this standard, that has been approved by the U.S. Department of Labor Bureau of Apprenticeship.

APPENDIX F TO SUBPART R OF PART 1926—PERIMETER COLUMNS: NON-MANDATORY GUIDELINES FOR COMPLYING WITH § 1926.756(e) TO PROTECT THE UNPROTECTED SIDE OR EDGE OF A WALKING/WORKING SURFACE

In multi-story structures, when holes in the column web are used for perimeter safety cables, the column splice must be placed sufficiently high so as not to interfere with any attachments to the column necessary for the column splice. Column splices are recommended to be placed at every other or fourth levels as design allows. Column splices at third levels are detrimental to the erection process and should be avoided if possible.

APPENDIX G TO SUBPART R OF PART 1926—§ 1926.502 (b)–(e) FALL PROTECTION SYSTEMS CRITERIA AND PRACTICES

(b) "Guardrail systems." Guardrail systems and their use shall comply with the following provisions:

(1) Top edge height of top rails, or equivalent guardrail system members, shall be 42 inches (1.1 m) plus or minus 3 inches (8 cm) above the walking/working level. When conditions warrant, the height of the top edge may exceed the 45-inch height, provided the guardrail system meets all other criteria of this paragraph (§ 1926.502(b)).

NOTE: When employees are using stilts, the top edge height of the top rail, or equivalent member, shall be increased an amount equal to the height of the stilts.

(2) Midrails, screens, mesh, intermediate vertical members, or equivalent intermediate structural members shall be installed between the top edge of the guardrail system and the walking/working surface when there is no wall or parapet wall at least 21 inches (53 cm) high.

(i) Midrails, when used, shall be installed at a height midway between the top edge of the guardrail system and the walking/working level.

(ii) Screens and mesh, when used, shall extend from the top rail to the walking/working level and along the entire opening between top rail supports.

(iii) Intermediate members (such as balusters), when used between posts, shall be not more than 19 inches (48 cm) apart.

(iv) Other structural members (such as additional midrails and architectural panels) shall be installed such that there are no openings in the guardrail system that are more than 19 inches (.5 m) wide.

(3) Guardrail systems shall be capable of withstanding, without failure, a force of at least 200 pounds (890 N) applied within 2 inches (5.1 cm) of the top edge, in any outward or downward direction, at any point along the top edge.

(4) When the 200 pound (890 N) test load specified in paragraph (b)(3) of this section (§ 1926.502) is applied in a downward direction, the top edge of the guardrail shall not deflect to a height less than 39 inches (1.0 m) above the walking/working level. Guardrail system components selected and constructed in accordance with the appendix B to subpart M of this part will be deemed to meet this requirement.

(5) Midrails, screens, mesh, intermediate vertical members, solid panels, and equivalent structural members shall be capable of withstanding, without failure, a force of at least 150 pounds (666 N) applied in any downward or outward direction at any point along the midrail or other member.

(6) Guardrail systems shall be so surfaced as to prevent injury to an employee from punctures or lacerations, and to prevent snagging of clothing.

(7) The ends of all top rails and midrails shall not overhang the terminal posts, except where such overhang does not constitute a projection hazard.

(8) Steel banding and plastic banding shall not be used as top rails or midrails.

(9) Top rails and midrails shall be at least one-quarter inch (0.6 cm) nominal diameter or thickness to prevent cuts and lacerations. If wire rope is used for top rails, it shall be flagged at not more than 6-foot intervals with high-visibility material.

(10) When guardrail systems are used at hoisting areas, a chain, gate or removable guardrail section shall be placed across the access opening between guardrail sections when hoisting operations are not taking place.

(11) When guardrail systems are used at holes, they shall be erected on all unprotected sides or edges of the hole.

(12) When guardrail systems are used around holes used for the passage of materials, the hole shall have not more than two sides provided with removable guardrail sections to allow the passage of materials. When the hole is not in use, it shall be closed over with a cover, or a guardrail system shall be provided along all unprotected sides or edges.

(13) When guardrail systems are used around holes which are used as points of access (such as ladderways), they shall be provided with a gate, or be so offset that a person cannot walk directly into the hole.

(14) Guardrail systems used on ramps and runways shall be erected along each unprotected side or edge.

(15) Manila, plastic or synthetic rope being used for top rails or midrails shall be inspected as frequently as necessary to ensure that it continues to meet the strength requirements of paragraph (b)(3) of this section (§ 1926.502).

(c) *Safety net systems.* Safety net systems and their use shall comply with the following provisions:

(1) Safety nets shall be installed as close as practicable under the walking/working surface on which employees are working, but in no case more than 30 feet (9.1 m) below such level. When nets are used on bridges, the potential fall area from the walking/working surface to the net shall be unobstructed.

(2) Safety nets shall extend outward from the outermost projection of the work surface as follows:

Vertical distance from working level to horizontal plane of net	Minimum required horizontal distance of outer edge of net from the edge of the working surface
Up to 5 feet	8 feet
More than 5 feet up to 10 feet	10 feet
More than 10 feet	13 feet

(3) Safety nets shall be installed with sufficient clearance under them to prevent contact with the surface or structures below when subjected to an impact force equal to the drop test specified in paragraph (4) of this section [§ 1926.502].

(4) Safety nets and their installations shall be capable of absorbing an impact force equal to that produced by the drop test specified in paragraph (c)(4)(i) of this section [§ 1926.502].

(i) Except as provided in paragraph (c)(4)(ii) of this section (§ 1926.502), safety nets and safety net installations shall be drop-tested at the jobsite after initial installation and before being used as a fall protection system, whenever relocated, after major repair, and at 6-month intervals if left in one place. The drop-test shall consist of a 400 pound (180 kg) bag of sand 30+ or −2 inches (76+ or −5 cm) in diameter dropped into the net from the highest walking/working surface at which employees are exposed to fall hazards, but not from less than 42 inches (1.1 m) above that level.

(ii) When the employer can demonstrate that it is unreasonable to perform the drop-test required by paragraph (c)(4)(i) of this section (§ 1926.502), the employer (or a designated competent person) shall certify that the net and net installation is in compliance with the provisions of paragraphs (c)(3) and (c)(4)(i) of this section (§ 1926.502) by preparing a certification record prior to the net being used as a fall protection system. The certification record must include an identification of the net and net installation for which the certification record is being prepared; the date that it was determined that the identified net and net installation were in compliance with paragraph (c)(3) of this section (§ 1926.502) and the signature of the person making the determination and certification. The most recent certification record for each net and net installation shall be available at the jobsite for inspection.

(5) Defective nets shall not be used. Safety nets shall be inspected at least once a week for wear, damage, and other deterioration. Defective components shall be removed from service. Safety nets shall also be inspected after any occurrence which could affect the integrity of the safety net system.

(6) Materials, scrap pieces, equipment, and tools which have fallen into the safety net shall be removed as soon as possible from the net and at least before the next work shift.

(7) The maximum size of each safety net mesh opening shall not exceed 36 square inches (230 cm) nor be longer than 6 inches (15 cm) on any side, and the opening, measured center-to-center of mesh ropes or webbing, shall not be longer than 6 inches (15 cm). All mesh crossings shall be secured to prevent enlargement of the mesh opening.

(8) Each safety net (or section of it) shall have a border rope for webbing with a minimum breaking strength of 5,000 pounds (22.2 kN).

(9) Connections between safety net panels shall be as strong as integral net components and shall be spaced not more than 6 inches (15 cm) apart.

(d) "Personal fall arrest systems." Personal fall arrest systems and their use shall comply with the provisions set forth below. Effective January 1, 1998, body belts are not acceptable as part of a personal fall arrest system.

NOTE: The use of a body belt in a positioning device system is acceptable and is regulated under paragraph (e) of this section (§ 1926.502).

(1) Connectors shall be drop forged, pressed or formed steel, or made of equivalent materials.

(2) Connectors shall have a corrosion-resistant finish, and all surfaces and edges shall be smooth to prevent damage to interfacing parts of the system.

(3) Dee-rings and snaphooks shall have a minimum tensile strength of 5,000 pounds (22.2 kN).

(4) Dee-rings and snaphooks shall be proof-tested to a minimum tensile load of 3,600 pounds (16 kN) without cracking, breaking, or taking permanent deformation.

(5) Snaphooks shall be sized to be compatible with the member to which they are connected to prevent unintentional disengagement of the snaphook by depression of the snaphook keeper by the connected member, or shall be a locking type snaphook designed and used to prevent disengagement of the snaphook by the contact of the snaphook keeper by the connected member. Effective January 1, 1998, only locking type snaphooks shall be used.

(6) Unless the snaphook is a locking type and designed for the following connections, snaphooks shall not be engaged:

(i) directly to webbing, rope or wire rope;

(ii) to each other;

(iii) to a dee-ring to which another snaphook or other connector is attached;

(iv) to a horizontal lifeline; or

(v) to any object which is incompatibly shaped or dimensioned in relation to the snaphook such that unintentional disengagement could occur by the connected object being able to depress the snaphook keeper and release itself.

(7) On suspended scaffolds or similar work platforms with horizontal lifelines which may become vertical lifelines, the devices used to connect to a horizontal lifeline shall be capable of locking in both directions on the lifeline.

(8) Horizontal lifelines shall be designed, installed, and used, under the supervision of a qualified person, as part of a complete personal fall arrest system, which maintains a safety factor of at least two.

(9) Lanyards and vertical lifelines shall have a minimum breaking strength of 5,000 pounds (22.2 kN).

(10)(i) Except as provided in paragraph (d)(10)(ii) of this section [§ 1926.502], when vertical lifelines are used, each employee shall be attached to a separate lifeline.

(ii) During the construction of elevator shafts, two employees may be attached to the same lifeline in the hoistway, provided both employees are working atop a false car that is equipped with guardrails; the strength of the lifeline is 10,000 pounds [5,000 pounds per employee attached] (44.4 kN); and all other criteria specified in this paragraph for lifelines have been met.

(11) Lifelines shall be protected against being cut or abraded.

(12) Self-retracting lifelines and lanyards which automatically limit free fall distance to 2 feet (0.61 m) or less shall be capable of sustaining a minimum tensile load of 3,000 pounds (13.3 kN) applied to the device with the lifeline or lanyard in the fully extended position.

(13) Self-retracting lifelines and lanyards which do not limit free fall distance to 2 feet (0.61 m) or less, ripstitch lanyards, and tearing and deforming lanyards shall be capable of sustaining a minimum tensile load of 5,000 pounds (22.2 kN) applied to the device with the lifeline or lanyard in the fully extended position.

(14) Ropes and straps (webbing) used in lanyards, lifelines, and strength components of body belts and body harnesses shall be made from synthetic fibers.

(15) Anchorages used for attachment of personal fall arrest equipment shall be independent of any anchorage being used to support or suspend platforms and capable of supporting at least 5,000 pounds (22.2 kN) per employee attached, or shall be designed, installed, and used as follows:

(i) as part of a complete personal fall arrest system which maintains a safety factor of at least two; and

(ii) under the supervision of a qualified person.

(16) Personal fall arrest systems, when stopping a fall, shall:

(i) limit maximum arresting force on an employee to 900 pounds (4 kN) when used with a body belt;

(ii) limit maximum arresting force on an employee to 1,800 pounds (8 kN) when used with a body harness;

(iii) be rigged such that an employee can neither free fall more than 6 feet (1.8 m), nor contact any lower level;

(iv) bring an employee to a complete stop and limit maximum deceleration distance an employee travels to 3.5 feet (1.07 m); and,

(v) have sufficient strength to withstand twice the potential impact energy of an employee free falling a distance of 6 feet (1.8 m), or the free fall distance permitted by the system, whichever is less.

NOTE: If the personal fall arrest system meets the criteria and protocols contained in appendix C to subpart M, and if the system is being used by an employee having a combined person and tool weight of less than 310 pounds (140 kg), the system will be considered to be in compliance with the provisions of paragraph (d)(16) of this section [§ 1926.502]. If the system is used by an employee having a combined tool and body weight of 310 pounds (140 kg) or more, then the employer must appropriately modify the criteria and protocols of the appendix to provide proper protection for such heavier weights, or the system will not be deemed to be in compliance with the requirements of paragraph (d)(16) of this section (§ 1926.502).

(17) The attachment point of the body belt shall be located in the center of the wearer's back. The attachment point of the body harness shall be located in the center of the wearer's back near shoulder level, or above the wearer's head.

(18) Body belts, harnesses, and components shall be used only for employee protection (as part of a personal fall arrest system or positioning device system) and not to hoist materials.

(19) Personal fall arrest systems and components subjected to impact loading shall be immediately removed from service and shall not be used again for employee protection until inspected and determined by a competent person to be undamaged and suitable for reuse.

(20) The employer shall provide for prompt rescue of employees in the event of a fall or shall assure that employees are able to rescue themselves.

(21) Personal fall arrest systems shall be inspected prior to each use for wear, damage and other deterioration, and defective components shall be removed from service.

(22) Body belts shall be at least one and five-eighths (1⅝) inches (4.1 cm) wide.

(23) Personal fall arrest systems shall not be attached to guardrail systems, nor shall they be attached to hoists except as specified in other subparts of this Part.

(24) When a personal fall arrest system is used at hoist areas, it shall be rigged to allow the movement of the employee only as far as the edge of the walking/working surface.

(e) *Positioning device systems.* Positioning device systems and their use shall conform to the following provisions:

(1) Positioning devices shall be rigged such that an employee cannot free fall more than 2 feet (.9 m).

(2) Positioning devices shall be secured to an anchorage capable of supporting at least twice the potential impact load of an employee's fall or 3,000 pounds (13.3 kN), whichever is greater.

(3) Connectors shall be drop forged, pressed or formed steel, or made of equivalent materials.

(4) Connectors shall have a corrosion-resistant finish, and all surfaces and edges shall be smooth to prevent damage to interfacing parts of this system.

(5) Connecting assemblies shall have a minimum tensile strength of 5,000 pounds (22.2 kN)

(6) Dee-rings and snaphooks shall be proof-tested to a minimum tensile load of 3,600 pounds (16 kN) without cracking, breaking, or taking permanent deformation.

(7) Snaphooks shall be sized to be compatible with the member to which they are connected to prevent unintentional disengagement of the snaphook by depression of the snaphook keeper by the connected member, or shall be a locking type snaphook designed and used to prevent disengagement of the snaphook by the contact of the snaphook keeper by the connected member. As of January 1, 1998, only locking type snaphooks shall be used.

(8) Unless the snaphook is a locking type and designed for the following connections, snaphooks shall not be engaged:

(i) directly to webbing, rope or wire rope;

(ii) to each other;

(iii) to a dee-ring to which another snaphook or other connector is attached;

(iv) to a horizontal lifeline; or to depress the snaphook keeper and release itself.

(v) to any object which is incompatibly shaped or dimensioned in relation to the snaphook such that unintentional disengagement could occur by the connected object being able to depress the snaphook keeper and release itself.

(9) Positioning device systems shall be inspected prior to each use for wear, damage, and other deterioration, and defective components shall be removed from service.

(10) Body belts, harnesses, and components shall be used only for employee protection (as part of a personal fall arrest system or positioning device system) and not to hoist materials.

APPENDIX H TO SUBPART R OF PART 1926—DOUBLE CONNECTIONS: ILLUSTRATION OF A CLIPPED END CONNECTION AND A STAGGERED CONNECTION: NON-MANDATORY GUIDELINES FOR COMPLYING WITH § 1926.756(c)(1)

Clipped end connections are connection material on the end of a structural member which has a notch at the bottom and/or top to allow the bolt(s) of the first member placed on the opposite side of the central member to remain in place. The notch(es) fits around the nut or bolt head of the opposing member to allow the second member to be bolted up without removing the bolt(s) holding the first member.

Staggered connections are connection material on a structural member in which all of the bolt holes in the common member web are not shared by the two incoming members in the final connection. The extra hole in the column web allows the erector to maintain at least a one bolt connection at all times while making the double connection.

Subpart S—Underground Construction, Caissons, Cofferdams and Compressed Air

AUTHORITY: 40 U.S.C. 3701; 29 U.S.C. 653, 655, 657; and Secretary of Labor's Orders 12–71 (36 FR 8754), 8–76 (41 FR 25059), 9–83 (48 FR 35736), 1–90 (55 FR 9033), 6–96 (62 FR 111), 5–2007 (72

FR 31159), or 1–2012 (77 FR 3912), as applicable.

§ 1926.800 Underground construction.

(a) *Scope and application.* (1) This section applies to the construction of underground tunnels, shafts, chambers, and passageways. This section also applies to cut-and-cover excavations which are both physically connected to ongoing underground construction operations within the scope of this section, and covered in such a manner as to create conditions characteristic of underground construction.

(2) This section does not apply to the following:

(i) Excavation and trenching operations covered by subpart P of this part, such as foundation operations for above-ground structures that are not physically connected to underground construction operations, and surface excavation; nor

(ii) Underground electrical transmission and distribution lines, as addressed in subpart V of this part.

(b) *Access and egress.* (1) The employer shall provide and maintain safe means of access and egress to all work stations.

(2) The employer shall provide access and egress in such a manner that employees are protected from being struck by excavators, haulage machines, trains and other mobile equipment.

(3) The employer shall control access to all openings to prevent unauthorized entry underground. Unused chutes, manways, or other openings shall be tightly covered, bulkheaded, or fenced off, and shall be posted with warning signs indicating "Keep Out" or similar language. Completed or unused sections of the underground facility shall be barricaded.

(c) *Check-in/check-out.* The employer shall maintain a check-in/check-out procedure that will ensure that aboveground personnel can determine an accurate count of the number of persons underground in the event of an emergency. However, this procedure is not required when the construction of underground facilities designed for human occupancy has been sufficiently completed so that the permanent environmental controls are effective, and when the remaining construction activity will not cause any environmental hazard or structural failure within the facilities.

(d) *Safety instruction.* All employees shall be instructed in the recognition and avoidance of hazards associated with underground construction activities including, where appropriate, the following subjects:

(1) Air monitoring;

(2) Ventilation;

(3) Illumination;

(4) Communications;

(5) Flood control;

(6) Mechanical equipment;

(7) Personal protective equipment;

(8) Explosives;

(9) Fire prevention and protection; and

(10) Emergency procedures, including evacuation plans and check-in/check-out systems.

(e) *Notification.* (1) Oncoming shifts shall be informed of any hazardous occurrences or conditions that have affected or might affect employee safety, including liberation of gas, equipment failures, earth or rock slides, cave-ins, floodings, fires or explosions.

(2) The employer shall establish and maintain direct communications for coordination of activities with other employers whose operations at the jobsite affect or may affect the safety of employees underground.

(f) *Communications.* (1) When natural unassisted voice communication is ineffective, a power-assisted means of voice communication shall be used to provide communication between the work face, the bottom of the shaft, and the surface.

(2) Two effective means of communication, at least one of which shall be voice communication, shall be provided in all shafts which are being developed or used either for personnel access or for hoisting. Additional requirements for hoist operator communication are contained in paragraph (t)(3)(xiv) of this section.

(3) Powered communication systems shall operate on an independent power supply, and shall be installed so that the use of or disruption of any one phone or signal location will not disrupt the operation of the system from any other location.

(4) Communication systems shall be tested upon initial entry of each shift to the underground, and as often as necessary at later times, to ensure that they are in working order.

(5) Any employee working alone underground in a hazardous location, who is both out of the range of natural unassisted voice communication and not under observation by other persons, shall be provided with an effective means of obtaining assistance in an emergency.

(g) *Emergency provisions*—(1) *Hoisting capability.* When a shaft is used as a means of egress, the employer shall make advance arrangements for power-assisted hoisting capability to be readily available in an emergency, unless the regular hoisting means can continue to function in the event of an electrical power failure at the jobsite. Such hoisting means shall be designed so that the load hoist drum is powered in both directions of rotation and so that the brake is automatically applied upon power release or failure.

(2) *Self-rescuers.* The employer must provide self-rescuers approved by the National Institute for Occupational Safety and Health under 42 CFR part 84. The respirators must be immediately available to all employees at work stations in underground areas where employees might be trapped by smoke or gas. The selection, issuance, use, and care of respirators must be in accordance with 29 CFR 1926.103.

(3) *Designated person.* At least one designated person shall be on duty above ground whenever any employee is working underground. This designated person shall be responsible for securing immediate aid and keeping an accurate count of employees underground in case of emergency. The designated person must not be so busy with other responsibilities that the counting function is encumbered.

(4) *Emergency lighting.* Each employee underground shall have an acceptable portable hand lamp or cap lamp in his or her work area for emergency use, unless natural light or an emergency lighting system provides adequate illumination for escape.

(5) *Rescue teams.* (i) On jobsites where 25 or more employees work underground at one time, the employer shall provide (or make arrangements in advance with locally available rescue services to provide) at least two 5-person rescue teams, one on the jobsite or within one-half hour travel time from the entry point, and the other within 2 hours travel time.

(ii) On jobsites where less than 25 employees work underground at one time, the employer shall provide (or make arrangements in advance with locally available rescue services to provide) at least one 5-person rescue team to be either on the jobsite or within one-half hour travel time from the entry point.

(iii) Rescue team members shall be qualified in rescue procedures, the use and limitations of breathing apparatus, and the use of firefighting equipment. Qualifications shall be reviewed not less than annually.

(iv) On jobsites where flammable or noxious gases are encountered or anticipated in hazardous quantities, rescue team members shall practice donning and using self-contained breathing apparatus monthly.

(v) The employer shall ensure that rescue teams are familiar with conditions at the jobsite.

(h) *Hazardous classifications*—(1) *Potentially gassy operations.* Underground construction operations shall be classified as potentially gassy if either:

(i) Air monitoring discloses 10 percent or more of the lower explosive limit for methane or other flammable gases measured at 12 inches (304.8 mm) ±0.25 inch (6.35 mm) from the roof, face, floor or walls in any underground work area for more than a 24-hour period; or

(ii) The history of the geographical area or geological formation indicates that 10 percent or more of the lower explosive limit for methane or other flammable gases is likely to be encountered in such underground operations.

(2) *Gassy operations.* Underground construction operations shall be classified as gassy if:

(i) Air monitoring discloses 10 percent or more of the lower explosive limit for methane or other flammable gases measured at 12 inches (304.8 mm) ±0.25 inch (6.35 mm) from the roof, face, floor or walls in any underground work area for three consecutive days; or

(ii) There has been an ignition of methane or of other flammable gases emanating from the strata that indicates the presence of such gases; or

(iii) The underground construction operation is both connected to an underground work area which is currently classified as gassy and is also subject to a continuous course of air containing the flammable gas concentration.

(3) *Declassification to potentially gassy operations.* Underground construction gassy operations may be declassified to Potentially Gassy when air monitoring results remain under 10 percent of the lower explosive limit for methane or other flammable gases for three consecutive days.

(i) *Gassy operations-additional requirements.* (1) Only acceptable equipment, maintained in suitable condition, shall be used in gassy operations.

(2) Mobile diesel-powered equipment used in gassy operations shall be either approved in accordance with the requirements of 30 CFR part 36 (formerly Schedule 31) by MSHA, or shall be demonstrated by the employer to be fully equivalent to such MSHA-approved equipment, and shall be operated in accordance with that part.

(3) Each entrance to a gassy operation shall be prominently posted with signs notifying all entrants of the gassy classification.

(4) Smoking shall be prohibited in all gassy operations and the employer shall be responsible for collecting all personal sources of ignition, such as matches and lighters, from all persons entering a gassy operation.

(5) A fire watch as described in § 1926.352(e) shall be maintained when hot work is performed.

(6) Once an operation has met the criteria in paragraph (h)(2) warranting classification as gassy, all operations in the affected area, except the following, shall be discontinued until the operation either is in compliance with all of the gassy operation requirements or has been declassified in accordance with paragraph (h)(3) of this section:

(i) Operations related to the control of the gas concentration;

(ii) Installation of new equipment, or conversion of existing equipment, to comply with this paragraph (i); and

(iii) Installation of above-ground controls for reversing the air flow.

(j) *Air quality and monitoring*—(1) *General.* Air quality limits and control requirements for construction are found in § 1926.55, except as modified by this section.

(i)(A) The employer shall assign a competent person who shall perform all air monitoring required by this section.

(B) Where this paragraph requires monitoring of airborne contaminants "as often as necessary," the competent person shall make a reasonable determination as to which substances to monitor and how frequently to monitor, considering at least the following factors:

(1) Location of jobsite: Proximity to fuel tanks, sewers, gas lines, old landfills, coal deposits, and swamps;

(2) Geology: Geological studies of the jobsite, particularly involving the soil type and its permeability;

(3) History: Presence of air contaminants in nearby jobsites, changes in levels of substances monitored on the prior shift; and

(4) Work practices and jobsite conditions: The use of diesel engines, use of explosives, use of fuel gas, volume and flow of ventilation, visible atmospheric conditions, decompression of the atmosphere, welding, cutting and hot work, and employees' physical reactions to working underground.

(ii)(A) The atmosphere in all underground work areas shall be tested as often as necessary to assure that the atmosphere at normal atmospheric pressure contains at least 19.5 percent oxygen and no more than 22 percent oxygen.

(B) Tests for oxygen content shall be made before tests for air contaminants.

(iii)(A) The atmosphere in all underground work areas shall be tested quantitatively for carbon monoxide, nitrogen dioxide, hydrogen sulfide, and other toxic gases, dusts, vapors, mists, and fumes as often as necessary to ensure that the permissible exposure limits prescribed in § 1926.55 are not exceeded.

(B) The atmosphere in all underground work areas shall be tested quantitatively for methane and other flammable gases as often as necessary to determine:

(1) Whether action is to be taken under paragraphs (j)(1)(vii), (viii), and (ix), of this section; and

(2) Whether an operation is to be classified potentially gassy or gassy under paragraph (h) of this section.

(C) If diesel-engine or gasoline-engine driven ventilating fans or compressors are used, an initial test shall be made of the inlet air of the fan or compressor, with the engines operating, to ensure that the air supply is not contaminated by engine exhaust.

(D) Testing shall be performed as often as necessary to ensure that the ventilation requirements of paragraph (k) of this section are met.

(iv) When rapid excavation machines are used, a continuous flammable gas monitor shall be operated at the face with the sensor(s) placed as high and close to the front of the machine's cutter head as practicable.

(v)(A) Whenever air monitoring indicates the presence of 5 ppm or more of hydrogen sulfide, a test shall be conducted in the affected underground work area(s), at least at the beginning and midpoint of each shift, until the concentration of hydrogen sulfide has been less than 5 ppm for 3 consecutive days.

(B) Whenever hydrogen sulfide is detected in an amount exceeding 10 ppm, a continuous sampling and indicating hydrogen sulfide monitor shall be used to monitor the affected work area.

(C) Employees shall be informed when a concentration of 10 ppm hydrogen sulfide is exceeded.

(D) The continuous sampling and indicating hydrogen sulfide monitor shall be designed, installed, and maintained to provide a visual and aural alarm when the hydrogen sulfide concentration reaches 20 ppm to signal that additional measures, such as respirator use, increased ventilation, or evacuation, might be necessary to maintain hydrogen sulfide exposure below the permissible exposure limit.

(vi) When the competent person determines, on the basis of air monitoring results or other information, that air contaminants may be present in sufficient quantity to be dangerous to life, the employer shall:

(A) Prominently post a notice at all entrances to the underground jobsite to inform all entrants of the hazardous condition; and

(B) Ensure that the necessary precautions are taken.

(vii) Whenever five percent or more of the lower explosive limit for methane or other flammable gases is detected in any underground work area(s) or in the air return, steps shall be taken to increase ventilation air volume or otherwise control the gas concentration, unless the employer is operating in accordance with the potentially gassy or gassy operation requirements. Such additional ventilation controls may be discontinued when gas concentrations are reduced below five percent of the lower explosive limit, but shall be reinstituted whenever the five percent level is exceeded.

(viii) Whenever 10 percent or more of the lower explosive limit for methane or other flammable gases is detected in the vicinity of welding, cutting, or other hot work, such work shall be suspended until the concentration of such flammable gas is reduced to less than 10 percent of the lower explosive limit.

(ix) Whenever 20 percent or more of the lower explosive limit for methane or other flammable gases is detected in any underground work area(s) or in the air return:

(A) All employees, except those necessary to eliminate the hazard, shall be immediately withdrawn to a safe location above ground; and

(B) Electrical power, except for acceptable pumping and ventilation equipment, shall be cut off to the area endangered by the flammable gas until the concentration of such gas is reduced to less than 20 percent of the lower explosive limit.

(2) *Additional monitoring for potentially gassy and gassy operations.* Operations which meet the criteria for potentially gassy and gassy operations set forth in paragraph (h) of this section shall be subject to the additional monitoring requirements of this paragraph.

(i) A test for oxygen content shall be conducted in the affected underground work areas and work areas immediately adjacent to such areas at least at the beginning and midpoint of each shift.

433

(ii) When using rapid excavation machines, continuous automatic flammable gas monitoring equipment shall be used to monitor the air at the heading, on the rib, and in the return air duct. The continuous monitor shall signal the heading, and shut down electric power in the affected underground work area, except for acceptable pumping and ventilation equipment, when 20 percent or more of the lower explosive limit for methane or other flammable gases is encountered.

(iii) A manual flammable gas monitor shall be used as needed, but at least at the beginning and midpoint of each shift, to ensure that the limits prescribed in paragraphs (h) and (j) are not exceeded. In addition, a manual electrical shut down control shall be provided near the heading.

(iv) Local gas tests shall be made prior to and continuously during any welding, cutting, or other hot work.

(v) In underground operations driven by drill-and-blast methods, the air in the affected area shall be tested for flammable gas prior to re-entry after blasting, and continuously when employees are working underground.

(3) *Recordkeeping.* A record of all air quality tests shall be maintained above ground at the worksite and be made available to the Secretary of Labor upon request. The record shall include the location, date, time, substance and amount monitored. Records of exposures to toxic substances shall be retained in accordance with § 1910.33 of this chapter. All other air quality test records shall be retained until completion of the project.

(k) *Ventilation.* (1)(i) Fresh air shall be supplied to all underground work areas in sufficient quantities to prevent dangerous or harmful accumulation of dusts, fumes, mists, vapors or gases.

(ii) Mechanical ventilation shall be provided in all underground work areas except when the employer can demonstrate that natural ventilation provides the necessary air quality through sufficient air volume and air flow.

(2) A minimum of 200 cubic feet (5.7 m^3) of fresh air per minute shall be supplied for each employee underground.

(3) The linear velocity of air flow in the tunnel bore, in shafts, and in all other underground work areas shall be at least 30 feet (9.15 m) per minute where blasting or rock drilling is conducted, or where other conditions likely to produce dust, fumes, mists, vapors, or gases in harmful or explosive quantities are present.

(4) The direction of mechanical air flow shall be reversible.

(5) Following blasting, ventilation systems shall exhaust smoke and fumes to the outside atmosphere before work is resumed in affected areas.

(6) Ventilation doors shall be designed and installed so that they remain closed when in use, regardless of the direction of the air flow.

(7) When ventilation has been reduced to the extent that hazardous levels of methane or flammable gas may have accumulated, a competent person shall test all affected areas after ventilation has been restored and shall determine whether the atmosphere is within flammable limits before any power, other than for acceptable equipment, is restored or work is resumed.

(8) Whenever the ventilation system has been shut down with all employees out of the underground area, only competent persons authorized to test for air contaminants shall be allowed underground until the ventilation has been restored and all affected areas have been tested for air contaminants and declared safe.

(9) When drilling rock or concrete, appropriate dust control measures shall be taken to maintain dust levels within limits set in § 1926.55. Such measures may include, but are not limited to, wet drilling, the use of vacuum collectors, and water mix spray systems.

(10)(i) Internal combustion engines, except diesel-powered engines on mobile equipment, are prohibited underground.

(ii) Mobile diesel-powered equipment used underground in atmospheres other than gassy operations shall be either approved by MSHA in accordance with the provisions of 30 CFR part 32 (formerly Schedule 24), or shall be demonstrated by the employer to be fully equivalent to such MSHA-approved equipment, and shall be operated in accordance with that part. (Each brake horsepower of a diesel engine requires at least 100 cubic feet (28.32 m³) of air per minute for suitable operation in addition to the air requirements for personnel. Some engines may require a greater amount of air to ensure that the allowable levels of carbon monoxide, nitric oxide, and nitrogen dioxide are not exceeded.)

(11) Potentially gassy or gassy operations shall have ventilation systems installed which shall:

(i) Be constructed of fire-resistant materials; and

(ii) Have acceptable electrical systems, including fan motors.

(12) Gassy operations shall be provided with controls located above ground for reversing the air flow of ventilation systems.

(13) In potentially gassy or gassy operations, wherever mine-type ventilation systems using an offset main fan installed on the surface are used, they shall be equipped with explosion-doors or a weak-wall having an area at least equivalent to the cross-sectional area of the airway.

(l) *Illumination.* (1) Illumination requirements applicable to underground construction operations are found in *Table D–3* of § 1926.56 of this part.

(2) Only acceptable portable lighting equipment shall be used within 50 feet (15.24 m) of any underground heading during explosives handling.

(m) *Fire prevention and control.* Fire prevention and protection requirements applicable to underground construction operations are found in subpart F of this part, except as modified by the following additional standards.

(1) Open flames and fires are prohibited in all underground construction operations except as permitted for welding, cutting and other hot work operations in paragraph (n) of this section.

(2) (i) Smoking may be allowed only in areas free of fire and explosion hazards.

(ii) Readily visible signs prohibiting smoking and open flames shall be posted in areas having fire or explosion hazards.

(3) The employer may store underground no more than a 24-hour supply of diesel fuel for the underground equipment used at the worksite.

(4) The piping of diesel fuel from the surface to an underground location is permitted only if:

(i) Diesel fuel is contained at the surface in a tank whose maximum capacity is no more than the amount of fuel required to supply for a 24-hour period the equipment serviced by the underground fueling station; and

(ii) The surface tank is connected to the underground fueling station by an acceptable pipe or hose system that is controlled at the surface by a valve, and at the shaft bottom by a hose nozzle; and

(iii) The pipe is empty at all times except when transferring diesel fuel from the surface tank to a piece of equipment in use underground; and

(iv) Hoisting operations in the shaft are suspended during refueling operations if the supply piping in the shaft is not protected from damage.

(5)(i) Gasoline shall not be carried, stored, or used underground.

(ii) Acetylene, liquefied petroleum gas, and Methylacetylene Propadiene Stabilized gas may be used underground only for welding, cutting and other hot work, and only in accordance with subpart J of this part, and paragraphs (j), (k), (m), and (n) of this section.

(6) Oil, grease, and diesel fuel stored underground shall be kept in tightly sealed containers in fire-resistant areas at least 300 feet (91.44 m) from underground explosive magazines, and at least 100 feet (30.48 m) from shaft stations and steeply inclined passageways. Storage areas shall be positioned or diked so that the contents of ruptured or overturned containers will not flow from the storage area.

(7) Flammable or combustible materials shall not be stored above ground within 100 feet (30.48 m) of any access opening to any underground operation. Where this is not feasible because of space limitations at the jobsite, such materials may be located within the 100-foot limit, provided that:

(i) They are located as far as practicable from the opening; and

(ii) Either a fire-resistant barrier of not less than one-hour rating is placed between the stored material and the opening, or additional precautions are taken which will protect the materials from ignition sources.

(8) Fire-resistant hydraulic fluids shall be used in hydraulically-actuated underground machinery and equipment unless such equipment is protected by a fire suppression system or by multi-purpose fire extinguisher(s) rated at of sufficient capacity for the type and size of hydraulic equipment involved, but rated at least 4A:40B:C.

(9)(i) Electrical installations in underground areas where oil, grease, or diesel fuel are stored shall be used only for lighting fixtures.

(ii) Lighting fixtures in storage areas, or within 25 feet (7.62 m) of underground areas where oil, grease, or diesel fuel are stored, shall be approved for Class I, Division 2 locations, in accordance with subpart K of this part.

(10) Leaks and spills of flammable or combustible fluids shall be cleaned up immediately.

(11) A fire extinguisher of at least 4A:40B:C rating or other equivalent extinguishing means shall be provided at the head pulley and at the tail pulley of underground belt conveyors.

(12) Any structure located underground or within 100 feet (30.48 m) of an opening to the underground shall be constructed of material having a fire-resistance rating of at least one hour.

(n) *Welding, cutting, and other hot work.* In addition to the requirements of subpart J of this part, the following requirements shall apply to underground welding, cutting, and other hot work.

(1) No more than the amount of fuel gas and oxygen cylinders necessary to perform welding, cutting, or other hot work during the next 24-hour period shall be permitted underground.

(2) Noncombustible barriers shall be installed below welding, cutting, or other hot work being done in or over a shaft or raise.

(o) *Ground support*—(1) *Portal areas.* Portal openings and access areas shall be guarded by shoring, fencing, head walls, shotcreting or other equivalent protection to ensure safe access of employees and equipment. Adjacent areas shall be scaled or otherwise secured to prevent loose soil, rock, or fractured materials from endangering the portal and access area.

(2) *Subsidence areas.* The employer shall ensure ground stability in hazardous subsidence areas by shoring, by filling in, or by erecting barricades and posting warning signs to prevent entry.

(3) *Underground areas.* (i)(A) A competent person shall inspect the roof, face, and walls of the work area at the start of each shift and as often as necessary to determine ground stability.

(B) Competent persons conducting such inspections shall be protected from loose ground by location, ground support or equivalent means.

(ii) Ground conditions along haulageways and travelways shall be inspected as frequently as necessary to ensure safe passage.

(iii) Loose ground that might be hazardous to employees shall be taken down, scaled or supported.

(iv) (A) Torque wrenches shall be used wherever bolts that depend on torsionally applied force are used for ground support.

(B) A competent person shall determine whether rock bolts meet the necessary torque, and shall determine the testing frequency in light of the bolt system, ground conditions and the distance from vibration sources.

(v) Suitable protection shall be provided for employees exposed to the hazard of loose ground while installing ground support systems.

(vi) Support sets shall be installed so that the bottoms have sufficient anchorage to prevent ground pressures from dislodging the support base of the sets. Lateral bracing (collar bracing, tie rods, or spreaders) shall be provided between immediately adjacent sets to ensure added stability.

(vii) Damaged or dislodged ground supports that create a hazardous condition shall be promptly repaired or replaced. When replacing supports, the new supports shall be installed before the damaged supports are removed.

(viii) A shield or other type of support shall be used to maintain a safe travelway for employees working in dead-end areas ahead of any support replacement operation.

(4) *Shafts.* (i) Shafts and wells over 5 feet (1.53 m) in depth that employees must enter shall be supported by a steel casing, concrete pipe, timber, solid rock or other suitable material.

(ii) (A) The full depth of the shaft shall be supported by casing or bracing except where the shaft penetrates into solid rock having characteristics that will not change as a result of exposure. Where the shaft passes through earth into solid rock, or through solid rock into earth, and where there is potential for shear, the casing or bracing shall extend at least 5 feet (1.53 m) into the solid rock. When the shaft terminates in solid rock, the casing or bracing shall extend to the end of the shaft or 5 feet (1.53 m) into the solid rock, whichever is less.

(B) The casing or bracing shall extend 42 inches (1.07 m) plus or minus 3 inches (8 cm) above ground level, except that the minimum casing height may be reduced to 12 inches (0.3 m), provided that a standard railing is installed; that the ground adjacent to the top of the shaft is sloped away from the shaft collar to prevent entry of liquids; and that effective barriers are used to prevent mobile equipment operating near the shaft from jumping over the 12 inch (0.3 m) barrier.

(iii) After blasting operations in shafts, a competent person shall determine if the walls, ladders, timbers, blocking, or wedges have loosened. If so, necessary repairs shall be made before employees other than those assigned to make the repairs are allowed in or below the affected areas.

(p) *Blasting.* This paragraph applies in addition to the requirements for blasting and explosives operations, including handling of misfires, which are found in subpart U of this part.

(1) Blasting wires shall be kept clear of electrical lines, pipes, rails, and other conductive material, excluding earth, to prevent explosives initiation or employee exposure to electric current.

(2) Following blasting, an employee shall not enter a work area until the air quality meets the requirements of paragraph (j) of this section.

(q) *Drilling.* (1) A competent person shall inspect all drilling and associated equipment prior to each use. Equipment defects affecting safety shall be corrected before the equipment is used.

(2) The drilling area shall be inspected for hazards before the drilling operation is started.

(3) Employees shall not be allowed on a drill mast while the drill bit is in operation or the drill machine is being moved.

(4) When a drill machine is being moved from one drilling area to another, drill steel, tools, and other equipment shall be secured and the mast shall be placed in a safe position.

(5) Receptacles or racks shall be provided for storing drill steel located on jumbos.

(6) Employees working below jumbo decks shall be warned whenever drilling is about to begin.

(7) Drills on columns shall be anchored firmly before starting drilling, and shall be retightened as necessary thereafter.

(8) (i) The employer shall provide mechanical means on the top deck of a jumbo for lifing unwieldy or heavy material.

(ii) When jumbo decks are over 10 feet (3.05 m) in height, the employer shall install stairs wide enough for two persons.

(iii) Jumbo decks more than 10 feet (3.05 m) in height shall be equipped with guardrails on all open sides, excluding access openings of platforms, unless an adjacent surface provides equivalent fall protection.

(iv) (A) Only employees assisting the operator shall be allowed to ride on jumbos, unless the jumbo meets the requirements of paragraph (r)(6)(ii) of this section.

(B) Jumbos shall be chocked to prevent movement while employees are working on them.

(v) (A) Walking and working surfaces of jumbos shall be maintained to prevent the hazards of slipping, tripping and falling.

(B) Jumbo decks and stair treads shall be designed to be slip-resistant and secured to prevent accidental displacement.

(9) Scaling bars shall be available at scaling operations and shall be maintained in good condition at all times. Blunted or severely worn bars shall not be used.

(10) (i) Blasting holes shall not be drilled through blasted rock (muck) or water.

(ii) Employees in a shaft shall be protected either by location or by suitable

437

barrier(s) if powered mechanical loading equipment is used to remove muck containing unfired explosives.

(11) A caution sign reading "Buried Line," or similar wording shall be posted where air lines are buried or otherwise hidden by water or debris.

(r) *Haulage.* (1)(i) A competent person shall inspect haulage equipment before each shift.

(ii) Equipment defects affecting safety and health shall be corrected before the equipment is used.

(2) Powered mobile haulage equipment shall have suitable means of stopping.

(3)(i) Power mobile haulage equipment, including trains, shall have audible warning devices to warn employees to stay clear. The operator shall sound the warning device before moving the equipment and whenever necessary during travel.

(ii) The operator shall assure that lights which are visible to employees at both ends of any mobile equipment, including a train, are turned on whenever the equipment is operating.

(4) In those cabs where glazing is used, the glass shall be safety glass, or its equivalent, and shall be maintained and cleaned so that vision is not obstructed.

(5) Anti-roll back devices or brakes shall be installed on inclined conveyor drive units to prevent conveyors from inadvertently running in reverse.

(6)(i) (A) Employees shall not be permitted to ride a power-driven chain, belt, or bucket conveyor unless the conveyor is specifically designed for the transportation of persons.

(B) Endless belt-type manlifts are prohibited in underground construction.

(C) General requirements also applicable to underground construction for use of conveyors in construction are found in § 1926.555 of this part.

(ii) No employee shall ride haulage equipment unless it is equipped with seating for each passenger and protects passengers from being struck, crushed, or caught between other equipment or surfaces. Members of train crews may ride on a locomotive if it is equipped with handholds and nonslip steps or footboards. Requirements applicable to Underground Construction for motor vehicle transportation of employees are found in § 1926.601 of this part.

(7) Powered mobile haulage equipment, including trains, shall not be left unattended unless the master switch or motor is turned off; operating controls are in neutral or park position; and the brakes are set, or equivalent precautions are taken to prevent rolling.

(8) Whenever rails serve as a return for a trolley circuit, both rails shall be bonded at every joint and crossbonded every 200 feet (60.96 m).

(9) When dumping cars by hand, the car dumps shall have tiedown chains, bumper blocks, or other locking or holding devices to prevent the cars from overturning.

(10) Rocker-bottom or bottom-dump cars shall be equipped with positive locking devices to prevent unintended dumping.

(11) Equipment to be hauled shall be loaded and secured to prevent sliding or dislodgement.

(12)(i) Mobile equipment, including rail-mounted equipment, shall be stopped for manual connecting or service work.

(ii) Employees shall not reach between moving cars during coupling operations.

(iii) Couplings shall not be aligned, shifted or cleaned on moving cars or locomotives.

(13)(i) Safety chains or other connections shall be used in addition to couplers to connect man cars or powder cars whenever the locomotive is uphill of the cars.

(ii) When the grade exceeds one percent and there is a potential for runaway cars, safety chains or other connections shall be used in addition to couplers to connect haulage cars or, as an alternative, the locomotive must be downhill of the train.

(iii) Such safety chains or other connections shall be capable of maintaining connection between cars in the event of either coupler disconnect, failure or breakage.

(14) Parked rail equipment shall be chocked, blocked, or have brakes set to prevent inadvertent movement.

(15) Berms, bumper blocks, safety hooks, or equivalent means shall be provided to prevent overtravel and

overturning of haulage equipment at dumping locations.

(16) Bumper blocks or equivalent stopping devices shall be provided at all track dead ends.

(17)(i) Only small handtools, lunch pails or similar small items may be transported with employees in man-cars, or on top of a locomotive.

(ii) When small hand tools or other small items are carried on top of a locomotive, the top shall be designed or modified to retain them while traveling.

(18)(i) Where switching facilities are available, occupied personnel-cars shall be pulled, not pushed. If personnel-cars must be pushed and visibility of the track ahead is hampered, then a qualified person shall be stationed in the lead car to give signals to the locomotive operator.

(ii) Crew trips shall consist of personnel-loads only.

(s) *Electrical safety.* This paragraph applies in addition to the general requirements for electrical safety which are found in subpart K of this part.

(1) Electric power lines shall be insulated or located away from water lines, telephone lines, air lines, or other conductive materials so that a damaged circuit will not energize the other systems.

(2) Lighting circuits shall be located so that movement of personnel or equipment will not damage the circuits or disrupt service.

(3) Oil-filled transformers shall not be used underground unless they are located in a fire-resistant enclosure suitably vented to the outside and surrounded by a dike to retain the contents of the transformers in the event of rupture.

(t) *Hoisting unique to underground construction.* Except as modified by this paragraph (t), employers must: Comply with the requirements of subpart CC of this part, except that the limitation in §1926.1431(a) does not apply to the routine access of employees to an underground worksite via a shaft; ensure that material hoists comply with §1926.552(a) and (b) of this part; and ensure that personnel hoists comply with the personnel-hoists requirements of §1926.552(a) and (c) of this part and the

elevator requirements of §1926.552(a) and (d) of this part.

(1) *General requirements for cranes and hoists.* (i) Materials, tools, and supplies being raised or lowered, whether within a cage or otherwise, shall be secured or stacked in a manner to prevent the load from shifting, snagging or falling into the shaft.

(ii) A warning light suitably located to warn employees at the shaft bottom and subsurface shaft entrances shall flash whenever a load is above the shaft bottom or subsurface entrances, or the load is being moved in the shaft. This paragraph does not apply to fully enclosed hoistways.

(iii) Whenever a hoistway is not fully enclosed and employees are at the shaft bottom, conveyances or equipment shall be stopped at least 15 feet (4.57 m) above the bottom of the shaft and held there until the signalman at the bottom of the shaft directs the operator to continue lowering the load, except that the load may be lowered without stopping if the load or conveyance is within full view of a bottom signalman who is in constant voice communication with the operator.

(iv)(A) Before maintenance, repairs, or other work is commenced in the shaft served by a cage, skip, or bucket, the operator and other employees in the area shall be informed and given suitable instructions.

(B) A sign warning that work is being done in the shaft shall be installed at the shaft collar, at the operator's station, and at each underground landing.

(v) Any connection between the hoisting rope and the cage or skip shall be compatible with the type of wire rope used for hoisting.

(vi) Spin-type connections, where used, shall be maintained in a clean condition and protected from foreign matter that could affect their operation.

(vii) Cage, skip, and load connections to the hoist rope shall be made so that the force of the hoist pull, vibration, misalignment, release of lift force, or impact will not disengage the connection. Moused or latched openthroat hooks do not meet this requirement.

(viii) When using wire rope wedge sockets, means shall be provided to

439

prevent wedge escapement and to ensure that the wedge is properly seated.

(2) *Additional requirements for cranes.* Cranes shall be equipped with a limit switch to prevent overtravel at the boom tip. Limit switches are to be used only to limit travel of loads when operational controls malfunction and shall not be used as a substitute for other operational controls.

(3) *Additional requirements for hoists.* (i) Hoists shall be designed so that the load hoist drum is powered in both directions of rotation, and so that brakes are automatically applied upon power release or failure.

(ii) Control levers shall be of the "deadman type" which return automatically to their center (neutral) position upon release.

(iii) When a hoist is used for both personnel hoisting and material hoisting, load and speed ratings for personnel and for materials shall be assigned to the equipment.

(iv) Material hoisting may be performed at speeds higher than the rated speed for personnel hoisting if the hoist and components have been designed for such higher speeds and if shaft conditions permit.

(v) Employees shall not ride on top of any cage, skip or bucket except when necessary to perform inspection or maintenance of the hoisting system, in which case they shall be protected by a body belt/harness system to prevent falling.

(vi) Personnel and materials (other than small tools and supplies secured in a manner that will not create a hazard to employees) shall not be hoisted together in the same conveyance. However, if the operator is protected from the shifting of materials, then the operator may ride with materials in cages or skips which are designed to be controlled by an operator within the cage or skip.

(vii) Line speed shall not exceed the design limitations of the systems.

(viii) Hoists shall be equipped with landing level indicators at the operator's station. Marking the hoist rope does not satisfy this requirement.

(ix) Whenever glazing is used in the hoist house, it shall be safety glass, or its equivalent, and be free of distortions and obstructions.

(x) A fire extinguisher that is rated at least 2A:10B:C (multi-purpose, dry chemical) shall be mounted in each hoist house.

(xi) Hoist controls shall be arranged so that the operator can perform all operating cycle functions and reach the emergency power cutoff without having to reach beyond the operator's normal operating position.

(xii) Hoists shall be equipped with limit switches to prevent overtravel at the top and bottom of the hoistway.

(xiii) Limit switches are to be used only to limit travel of loads when operational controls malfunction and shall not be used as a substitute for other operational controls.

(xiv) Hoist operators shall be provided with a closed-circuit voice communication system to each landing station, with speaker microphones so located that the operator can communicate with individual landing stations during hoist use.

(xv) When sinking shafts 75 feet (22.86 m) or less in depth, cages, skips, and buckets that may swing, bump, or snag against shaft sides or other structural protrusions shall be guided by fenders, rails, ropes, or a combination of those means.

(xvi) When sinking shafts more than 75 feet (22.86 m) in depth, all cages, skips, and buckets shall be rope or rail guided to within a rail length from the sinking operation.

(xvii) Cages, skips, and buckets in all completed shafts, or in all shafts being used as completed shafts, shall be rope or rail-guided for the full length of their travel.

(xviii) Wire rope used in load lines of material hoists shall be capable of supporting, without failure, at least five times the maximum intended load or the factor recommended by the rope manufacturer, whichever is greater. Refer to § 1926.552(c)(14)(iii) of this part for design factors for wire rope used in personnel hoists. The design factor shall be calculated by dividing the breaking strength of wire rope, as reported in the manufacturer's rating tables, by the total static load, including the weight of the wire rope in the shaft when fully extended.

(xix) A competent person shall visually check all hoisting machinery, equipment, anchorages, and hoisting rope at the beginning of each shift and during hoist use, as necessary.

(xx) Each safety device shall be checked by a competent person at least weekly during hoist use to ensure suitable operation and safe condition.

(xxi) In order to ensure suitable operation and safe condition of all functions and safety devices, each hoist assembly shall be inspected and load-tested to 100 percent of its rated capacity: at the time of installation; after any repairs or alterations affecting its structural integrity; after the operation of any safety device; and annually when in use. The employer shall prepare a certification record which includes the date each inspection and load-test was performed; the signature of the person who performed the inspection and test; and a serial number or other identifier for the hoist that was inspected and tested. The most recent certification record shall be maintained on file until completion of the project.

(xxii) Before hoisting personnel or material, the operator shall perform a test run of any cage or skip whenever it has been out of service for one complete shift, and whenever the assembly or components have been repaired or adjusted.

(xxiii) Unsafe conditions shall be corrected before using the equipment.

(4) *Additional requirements for personnel hoists.* (i) Hoist drum systems shall be equipped with at least two means of stopping the load, each of which shall be capable of stopping and holding 150 percent of the hoist's rated line pull. A broken-rope safety, safety catch, or arrestment device is not a permissible means of stopping under this paragraph (t).

(ii) The operator shall remain within sight and sound of the signals at the operator's station.

(iii) All sides of personnel cages shall be enclosed by one-half inch (12.70 mm) wire mesh (not less than No. 14 gauge or equivalent) to a height of not less than 6 feet (1.83 m). However, when the cage or skip is being used as a work platform, its sides may be reduced in height to 42 inches (1.07 m) when the conveyance is not in motion.

(iv) All personnel cages shall be provided with a positive locking door that does not open outward.

(v) All personnel cages shall be provided with a protective canopy. The canopy shall be made of steel plate, at least 3/16-inch (4.763 mm) in thickness, or material of equivalent strength and impact resistance. The canopy shall be sloped to the outside, and so designed that a section may be readily pushed upward to afford emergency egress. The canopy shall cover the top in such a manner as to protect those inside from objects falling in the shaft.

(vi) Personnel platforms operating on guide rails or guide ropes shall be equipped with broken-rope safety devices, safety catches or arrestment devices that will stop and hold 150 percent of the weight of the personnel platform and its maximum rated load.

(vii) During sinking operations in shafts where guides and safeties are not yet used, the travel speed of the personnel platform shall not exceed 200 feet (60.96 m) per minute. Governor controls set for 200 feet (60.96 m) per minute shall be installed in the control system and shall be used during personnel hoisting.

(viii) The personnel platform may travel over the controlled length of the hoistway at rated speeds up to 600 feet (182.88 m) per minute during sinking operations in shafts where guides and safeties are used.

(ix) The personnel platform may travel at rated speeds greater than 600 feet (182.88 m) per minute in completed shafts.

(u) *Definitions.* "Accept"—Any device, equipment, or appliance that is either approved by MSHA and maintained in permissible condition, or is listed or labeled for the class and location under subpart K of this part.

"Rapid Excavation Machine"—Tunnel boring machines, shields, roadheaders, or any other similar excavation machine.

[54 FR 23850, June 2, 1989; 58 FR 35311, June 30, 1993, as amended at 61 FR 5510, Feb. 13, 1996; 63 FR 1297, Jan. 8, 1998; 71 FR 16674, Apr. 3, 2006; 75 FR 48135, Aug. 9, 2010; 77 FR 49728, Aug. 17, 2012; 78 FR 23841, Apr. 24, 2013]

§ 1926.801 Caissons.

(a) Wherever, in caisson work in which compressed air is used, and the working chamber is less than 11 feet in length, and when such caissons are at any time suspended or hung while work is in progress so that the bottom of the excavation is more than 9 feet below the deck of the working chamber, a shield shall be erected therein for the protection of the employees.

(b) Shafts shall be subjected to a hydrostatic or air-pressure test, at which pressure they shall be tight. The shaft shall be stamped on the outside shell about 12 inches from each flange to show the pressure to which they have been subjected.

(c) Whenever a shaft is used, it shall be provided, where space permits, with a safe, proper, and suitable staircase for its entire length, including landing platforms, not more than 20 feet apart. Where this is impracticable, suitable ladders shall be installed with landing platforms located about 20 feet apart to break the climb.

(d) All caissons having a diameter or side greater than 10 feet shall be provided with a man lock and shaft for the exclusive use of employees.

(e) In addition to the gauge in the locks, an accurate gauge shall be maintained on the outer and inner side of each bulkhead. These gauges shall be accessible at all times and kept in accurate working order.

(f) In caisson operations where employees are exposed to compressed air working environments, the requirements contained in § 1926.803 shall be complied with.

§ 1926.802 Cofferdams.

(a) If overtopping of the cofferdam by high waters is possible, means shall be provided for controlled flooding of the work area.

(b) Warning signals for evacuation of employees in case of emergency shall be developed and posted.

(c) Cofferdam walkways, bridges, or ramps with at least two means of rapid exit shall be provided with guardrails as specified in subpart M of this part.

(d) Cofferdams located close to navigable shipping channels shall be protected from vessels in transit, where possible.

§ 1926.803 Compressed air.

(a) *General provisions.* (1) There shall be present, at all times, at least one competent person designated by and representing the employer, who shall be familiar with this subpart in all respects, and responsible for full compliance with these and other applicable subparts.

(2) Every employee shall be instructed in the rules and regulations which concern his safety or the safety of others.

(b) *Medical attendance, examination, and regulations.* (1) There shall be retained one or more licensed physicians familiar with and experienced in the physical requirements and the medical aspects of compressed air work and the treatment of decompression illness. He shall be available at all times while work is in progress in order to provide medical supervision of employees employed in compressed air work. He shall himself be physically qualified and be willing to enter a pressurized environment.

(2) No employee shall be permitted to enter a compressed air environment until he has been examined by the physician and reported by him to be physically qualified to engage in such work.

(3) In the event an employee is absent from work for 10 days, or is absent due to sickness or injury, he shall not resume work until he is reexamined by the physician, and his physical condition reported, as provided in this paragraph, to be such as to permit him to work in compressed air.

(4) After an employee has been employed continuously in compressed air for a period designated by the physician, but not to exceed 1 year, he shall be reexamined by the physician to determine if he is still physically qualified to engage in compressed air work.

(5) Such physician shall at all times keep a complete and full record of examinations made by him. The physician shall also keep an accurate record of any decompression illness or other illness or injury incapacitating any employee for work, and of all loss of life that occurs in the operation of a tunnel, caisson, or other compartment in which compressed air is used.

(6) Records shall be available for the inspection of the Secretary or his representatives, and a copy thereof shall be forwarded to OSHA within 48 hours following the occurrence of the accident, death, injury, or decompression illness. It shall state as fully as possible the cause of said death or decompression illness, and the place where the injured or sick employee was taken, and such other relative information as may be required by the Secretary.

(7) A fully equipped first aid station shall be provided at each tunnel project regardless of the number of persons employed. An ambulance or transportation suitable for a litter case shall be at each project.

(8) Where tunnels are being excavated from portals more than 5 road miles apart, a first aid station and transportation facilities shall be provided at each portal.

(9) A medical lock shall be established and maintained in immediate working order whenever air pressure in the working chamber is increased above the normal atmosphere.

(10) The medical lock shall:

(i) Have at least 6 feet of clear headroom at the center, and be subdivided into not less than two compartments;

(ii) Be readily accessible to employees working under compressed air;

(iii) Be kept ready for immediate use for at least 5 hours subsequent to the emergence of any employee from the working chamber;

(iv) Be properly heated, lighted and ventilated;

(v) Be maintained in a sanitary condition;

(vi) Have a nonshatterable port through which the occupant(s) may be kept under constant observation;

(vii) Be designed for a working pressure of 75 p.s.i.g.;

(viii) Be equipped with internal controls which may be overridden by external controls;

(ix) Be provided with air pressure gauges to show the air pressure within each compartment to observers inside and outside the medical lock.

(x) Be equipped with a manual type sprinkler system that can be activated inside the lock or by the outside lock tender.

(xi) Be provided with oxygen lines and fittings leading into external tanks. The lines shall be fitted with check valves to prevent reverse flow. The oxygen system inside the chamber shall be of a closed circuit design and be so designed as to automatically shut off the oxygen supply whenever the fire system is activated.

(xii) Be in constant charge of an attendant under the direct control of the retained physician. The attendant shall be trained in the use of the lock and suitably instructed regarding steps to be taken in the treatment of employee exhibiting symptoms compatible with a diagnosis of decompression illness;

(xiii) Be adjacent to an adequate emergency medical facility;

(xiv) The medical facility shall be equipped with demand-type oxygen inhalation equipment approved by the U.S. Bureau of Mines;

(xv) Be capable of being maintained at a temperature, in use, not to exceed 90 °F. nor be less than 70 °F.; and

(xvi) Be provided with sources of air, free of oil and carbon monoxide, for normal and emergency use, which are capable of raising the air pressure in the lock from 0 to 75 p.s.i.g. in 5 minutes.

(11) Identification badges shall be furnished to all employees, indicating that the wearer is a compressed air worker. A permanent record shall be kept of all identification badges issued. The badge shall give the employee's name, address of the medical lock, the telephone number of the licensed physician for the compressed air project, and contain instructions that in case of emergency of unknown or doubtful cause or illness, the wearer shall be rushed to the medical lock. The badge shall be worn at all times—off the job, as well as on the job.

(c) *Telephone and signal communication.* (1) Effective and reliable means of communication, such as bells, whistles, or telephones, shall be maintained, at all times between all the following locations:

(i) The working chamber face;

(ii) The working chamber side of the man lock near the door;

(iii) The interior of the man lock;

(iv) Lock attendant's station;

(v) The compressor plant;

443

(vi) The first-aid station;

(vii) The emergency lock (if one is required); and

(viii) The special decompression chamber (if one is required).

(d) *Signs and records.* (1) The time of decompression shall be posted in each man lock as follows:

TIME OF DECOMPRESSION FOR THIS LOCK

___ pounds to ___ pounds in ___ minutes.
___ pounds to ___ pounds in ___ minutes.
(Signed by) _____ (Superintendent)

This form shall be posted in the Man Lock at all times.

(2) Any code of signals used shall be conspicuously posted near workplace entrances and such other locations as may be necessary to bring them to the attention of all employees concerned.

(3) For each 8-hour shift, a record of employees employed under air pressure shall be kept by an employee who shall remain outside the lock near the entrance. This record shall show the period each employee spends in the air chamber and the time taken from decompression. A copy shall be submitted to the appointed physician after each shift.

(e) *Compression.* (1) Every employee going under air pressure for the first time shall be instructed on how to avoid excessive discomfort.

(2) During the compression of employees, the pressure shall not be increased to more than 3 p.s.i.g. within the first minute. The pressure shall be held at 3 p.s.i.g. and again at 7 p.s.i.g. sufficiently long to determine if any employees are experiencing discomfort.

(3) After the first minute the pressure shall be raised uniformly and at a rate not to exceed 10 p.s.i. per minute.

(4) If any employee complains of discomfort, the pressure shall be held to determine if the symptoms are relieved. If, after 5 minutes the discomfort does not disappear, the lock attendant shall gradually reduce the pressure until the employee signals that the discomfort has ceased. If he does not indicate that the discomfort has disappeared, the lock attendant shall reduce the pressure to atmospheric and the employee shall be released from the lock.

(5) No employee shall be subjected to pressure exceeding 50 pounds per square inch except in emergency.

(f) *Decompression.* (1) Decompression to normal condition shall be in accordance with the Decompression Tables in appendix A of this subpart.

(2) In the event it is necessary for an employee to be in compressed air more than once in a 24-hour period, the appointed physician shall be responsible for the establishment of methods and procedures of decompression applicable to repetitive exposures.

(3) If decanting is necessary, the appointed physician shall establish procedures before any employee is permitted to be decompressed by decanting methods. The period of time that the employees spend at atmospheric pressure between the decompression following the shift and recompression shall not exceed 5 minutes.

(g) *Man locks and special decompression chambers*—(1) *Man locks.* (i) Except in emergency, no employees employed in compressed air shall be permitted to pass from the working chamber to atmospheric pressure until after decompression, in accordance with the procedures in this subpart.

(ii) The lock attendant in charge of a man lock shall be under the direct supervision of the appointed physician. He shall be stationed at the lock controls on the free air side during the period of compression and decompression and shall remain at the lock control station whenever there are men in the working chamber or in the man lock.

(iii) Except where air pressure in the working chamber is below 12 p.s.i.g., each man lock shall be equipped with automatic controls which, through taped programs, cams, or similar apparatus, shall automatically regulate decompressions. It shall also be equipped with manual controls to permit the lock attendant to override the automatic mechanism in the event of an emergency, as provided in paragraph (g)(1)(viii) of this section.

(iv) A manual control, which can be used in the event of an emergency, shall be placed inside the man lock.

(v) A clock, thermometer, and continuous recording pressure gauge with a 4-hour graph shall be installed outside of each man lock and shall be changed prior to each shift's decompression. The chart shall be of sufficient size to register a legible record of variations in pressure within the man lock and shall be visible to the lock attendant. A copy of each graph shall be submitted to the appointed physician after each shift. In addition, a pressure gauge, clock, and thermometer shall also be installed in each man lock. Additional fittings shall be provided so that test gauges may be attached whenever necessary.

(vi) Except where air pressure is below 12 p.s.i.g. and there is no danger of rapid flooding, all caissons having a working area greater than 150 square feet, and each bulkhead in tunnels of 14 feet or more in diameter, or equivalent area, shall have at least two locks in perfect working condition, one of which shall be used exclusively as a man lock, the other, as a materials lock.

(vii) Where only a combination man-and-materials lock is required, this single lock shall be of sufficient capacity to hold the employees constituting two successive shifts.

(viii) Emergency locks shall be large enough to hold an entire heading shift and a limit maintained of 12 p.s.i.g. There shall be a chamber available for oxygen decompression therapy to 28 p.s.i.g.

(ix) The man lock shall be large enough so that those using it are not compelled to be in a cramped position, and shall not have less than 5 feet clear head room at the center and a minimum of 30 cubic feet of air space per occupant.

(x) Locks on caissons shall be so located that the bottom door shall be not less than 3 feet above the water level surrounding the caisson on the outside. (The water level, where it is affected by tides, is construed to mean high tide.)

(xi) In addition to the pressure gauge in the locks, an accurate pressure gauge shall be maintained on the outer and inner side of each bulkhead. These gauges shall be accessible at all times and shall be kept in accurate working order.

(xii) Man locks shall have an observation port at least 4 inches in diameter located in such a position that all occupants of the man lock may be observed from the working chamber and from the free air side of the lock.

(xiii) Adequate ventilation in the lock shall be provided.

(xiv) Man locks shall be maintained at a minimum temperature of 70 °F.

(xv) When locks are not in use and employees are in the working chamber, lock doors shall be kept open to the working chamber, where practicable.

(xvi) Provision shall be made to allow for rescue parties to enter the tunnel if the working force is disabled.

(xvii) A special decompression chamber of sufficient size to accommodate the entire force of employees being decompressed at the end of a shift shall be provided whenever the regularly established working period requires a total time of decompression exceeding 75 minutes.

(2) *Special decompression chamber.* (i) The headroom in the special decompression chamber shall be not less than a minimum 7 feet and the cubical content shall provide at least 50 cubic feet of airspace for each employee. For each occupant, there shall be provided 4 square feet of free walking area and 3 square feet of seating space, exclusive of area required for lavatory and toilet facilities. The rated capacity shall be based on the stated minimum space per employee and shall be posted at the chamber entrance. The posted capacity shall not be exceeded, except in case of emergency.

(ii) Each special decompression chamber shall be equipped with the following:

(*a*) A clock or clocks suitably placed so that the attendant and the chamber occupants can readily ascertain the time;

(*b*) Pressure gauges which will indicate to the attendants and to the chamber occupants the pressure in the chamber;

(*c*) Valves to enable the attendant to control the supply and discharge of compressed air into and from the chamber;

(*d*) Valves and pipes, in connection with the air supply and exhaust, arranged so that the chamber pressure can be controlled from within and without;

(*e*) Effective means of oral intercommunication between the attendant, occupants of the chamber, and the air compressor plant; and

(f) An observation port at the entrance to permit observation of the chamber occupants.

(iii) Seating facilities in special decompression chambers shall be so arranged as to permit a normal sitting posture without cramping. Seating space, not less than 18 inches by 24 inches wide, shall be provided per occupant.

(iv) Adequate toilet and washing facilities, in a screened or enclosed recess, shall be provided. Toilet bowls shall have a built-in protector on the rim so that an air space is created when the seat lid is closed.

(v) Fresh and pure drinking water shall be available. This may be accomplished by either piping water into the special decompression chamber and providing drinking fountains, or by providing individual canteens, or by some other sanitary means. Community drinking vessels are prohibited.

(vi) No refuse or discarded material of any kind shall be permitted to accumulate, and the chamber shall be kept clean.

(vii) Unless the special decompression chamber is serving as the man lock to atmospheric pressure, the special decompression chamber shall be situated, where practicable, adjacent to the man lock on the atmospheric pressure side of the bulkhead. A passageway shall be provided, connecting the special chamber with the man lock, to permit employees in the process of decompression to move from the man lock to the special chamber without a reduction in the ambient pressure from that designated for the next stage of decompression. The passageway shall be so arranged as to not interfere with the normal operation of the man lock, nor with the release of the occupants of the special chamber to atmospheric pressure upon the completion of the decompression procedure.

(h) *Compressor plant and air supply.* (1) At all times there shall be a thoroughly experienced, competent, and reliable person on duty at the air control valves as a gauge tender who shall regulate the pressure in the working areas. During tunneling operations, one gauge tender may regulate the

pressure in not more than two headings: *Provided*, That the gauge and controls are all in one location. In caisson work, there shall be a gauge tender for each caisson.

(2) The low air compressor plant shall be of sufficient capacity to not only permit the work to be done safely, but shall also provide a margin to meet emergencies and repairs.

(3) Low air compressor units shall have at least two independent and separate sources of power supply and each shall be capable of operating the entire low air plant and its accessory systems.

(4) The capacity, arrangement, and number of compressors shall be sufficient to maintain the necessary pressure without overloading the equipment and to assure maintenance of such pressure in the working chamber during periods of breakdown, repair, or emergency.

(5) Switching from one independent source of power supply to the other shall be done periodically to ensure the workability of the apparatus in an emergency.

(6) Duplicate low-pressure air feedlines and regulating valves shall be provided between the source of air supply and a point beyond the locks with one of the lines extending to within 100 feet of the working face.

(7) All high- and low-pressure air supply lines shall be equipped with check valves.

(8) Low-pressure air shall be regulated automatically. In addition, manually operated valves shall be provided for emergency conditions.

(9) The air intakes for all air compressors shall be located at a place where fumes, exhaust, gases, and other air contaminants will be at a minimum.

(10) Gauges indicating the pressure in the working chamber shall be installed in the compressor building, the lock attendant's station, and at the employer's field office.

(i) *Ventilation and air quality.* (1) Exhaust valves and exhaust pipes shall be provided and operated so that the working chamber shall be well ventilated, and there shall be no pockets of dead air. Outlets may be required at intermediate points along the main low-pressure air supply line to the heading to eliminate such pockets of dead air. Ventilating air shall be not less than 30 cubic feet per minute.

(2) The air in the workplace shall be analyzed by the employer not less than once each shift, and records of such tests shall be kept on file at the place where the work is in progress. The test results shall be within the threshold limit values specified in subpart D of this part, for hazardous gases, and within 10 percent of the lower explosive limit of flammable gases. If these limits are not met, immediate action to correct the situation shall be taken by the employer.

(3) The temperature of all working chambers which are subjected to air pressure shall, by means of after-coolers or other suitable devices, be maintained at a temperature not to exceed 85 °F.

(4) Forced ventilation shall be provided during decompression. During the entire decompression period, forced ventilation through chemical or mechanical air purifying devices that will ensure a source of fresh air shall be provided.

(5) Whenever heat-producing machines (moles, shields) are used in compressed air tunnel operations, a positive means of removing the heat build-up at the heading shall be provided.

(j) *Electricity.* (1) All lighting in compressed-air chambers shall be by electricity exclusively, and two independent electric-lighting systems with independent sources of supply shall be used. The emergency source shall be arranged to become automatically operative in the event of failure of the regularly used source.

(2) The minimum intensity of light on any walkway, ladder, stairway, or working level shall be not less than 10 foot-candles, and in all workplaces the lighting shall at all times be such as to enable employees to see clearly.

(3) All electrical equipment and wiring for light and power circuits shall comply with the requirements of subpart K of this part for use in damp, hazardous, high temperature, and compressed air environments.

(4) External parts of lighting fixtures and all other electrical equipment, when within 8 feet of the floor, shall be

constructed of noncombustible, nonabsorptive, insulating materials, except that metal may be used if it is effectively grounded.

(5) Portable lamps shall be equipped with noncombustible, nonabsorptive, insulating sockets, approved handles, basket guards, and approved cords.

(6) The use of worn or defective portable and pendant conductors is prohibited.

(k) *Sanitation.* (1) Sanitary, heated, lighted, and ventilated dressing rooms and drying rooms shall be provided for all employees engaged in compressed air work. Such rooms shall contain suitable benches and lockers. Bathing accommodations (showers at the ratio of one to 10 employees per shift), equipped with running hot and cold water, and suitable and adequate toilet accommodations, shall be provided. One toilet for each 15 employees, or fractional part thereof, shall be provided.

(2) When the toilet bowl is shut by a cover, there should be an air space so that the bowl or bucket does not implode when pressure is increased.

(3) All parts of caissons and other working compartments shall be kept in a sanitary condition.

(l) *Fire prevention and protection.* (1) Firefighting equipment shall be available at all times and shall be maintained in working condition.

(2) While welding or flame-cutting is being done in compressed air, a firewatch with a fire hose or approved extinguisher shall stand by until such operation is completed.

(3) Shafts and caissons containing flammable material of any kind, either above or below ground, shall be provided with a waterline and a fire hose connected thereto, so arranged that all points of the shaft or caisson are within reach of the hose stream.

(4) Fire hose shall be at least 1½ inches in nominal diameter; the water pressure shall at all times be adequate for efficient operation of the type of nozzle used; and the water supply shall be such as to ensure an uninterrupted flow. Fire hose, when not in use, shall be located or guarded to prevent injury thereto.

(5) The power house, compressor house, and all buildings housing ventilating equipment, shall be provided with at least one hose connection in the water line, with a fire hose connected thereto. A fire hose shall be maintained within reach of structures of wood over or near shafts.

(6) Tunnels shall be provided with a 2-inch minimum diameter water line extending into the working chamber and to within 100 feet of the working face. Such line shall have hose outlets with 100 feet of fire hose attached and maintained as follows: One at the working face; one immediately inside of the bulkhead of the working chamber; and one immediately outside such bulkhead. In addition, hose outlets shall be provided at 200-foot intervals throughout the length of the tunnel, and 100 feet of fire hose shall be attached to the outlet nearest to any location where flammable material is being kept or stored or where any flame is being used.

(7) In addition to fire hose protection required by this subpart, on every floor of every building not under compressed air, but used in connection with the compressed air work, there shall be provided at least one approved fire extinguisher of the proper type for the hazard involved. At least two approved fire extinguishers shall be provided in the working chamber as follows: One at the working face and one immediately inside the bulkhead (pressure side). Extinguishers in the working chamber shall use water as the primary extinguishing agent and shall not use any extinguishing agent which could be harmful to the employees in the working chamber. The fire extinguisher shall be protected from damage.

(8) Highly combustible materials shall not be used or stored in the working chamber. Wood, paper, and similar combustible material shall not be used in the working chamber in quantities which could cause a fire hazard. The compressor building shall be constructed of non-combustible material.

(9) Man locks shall be equipped with a manual type fire extinguisher system that can be activated inside the man lock and also by the outside lock attendant. In addition, a fire hose and portable fire extinguisher shall be provided inside and outside the man lock. The portable fire extinguisher shall be the dry chemical type.

(10) Equipment, fixtures, and furniture in man locks and special decompression chambers shall be constructed of noncombustible materials. Bedding, etc., shall be chemically treated so as to be fire resistant.

(11) Head frames shall be constructed of structural steel or open frame-work fireproofed timber. Head houses and other temporary surface buildings or structures within 100 feet of the shaft, caisson, or tunnel opening shall be built of fire-resistant materials.

(12) No oil, gasoline, or other combustible material shall be stored within 100 feet of any shaft, caisson, or tunnel opening, except that oils may be stored in suitable tanks in isolated fireproof buildings, provided such buildings are not less than 50 feet from any shaft, caisson, or tunnel opening, or any building directly connected thereto.

(13) Positive means shall be taken to prevent leaking flammable liquids from flowing into the areas specifically mentioned in the preceding paragraph.

(14) All explosives used in connection with compressed air work shall be selected, stored, transported, and used as specified in subpart U of this part.

(m) *Bulkheads and safety screens.* (1) Intermediate bulkheads with locks, or intermediate safety screens or both, are required where there is the danger of rapid flooding.

(2) In tunnels 16 feet or more in diameter, hanging walkways shall be provided from the face to the man lock as high in the tunnel as practicable, with at least 6 feet of head room. Walkways shall be constructed of noncombustible material. Standard railings shall be securely installed throughout the length of all walkways on open sides in accordance with subpart M of this part. Where walkways are ramped under safety screens, the walkway surface shall be skidproofed by cleats or by equivalent means.

(3) Bulkheads used to contain compressed air shall be tested, where practicable, to prove their ability to resist

448

the highest air pressure which may be expected to be used.

[44 FR 8577, Feb. 9, 1979; 44 FR 20940, Apr. 6, 1979, as amended at 47 FR 14696, 14706, Apr. 6, 1982; 51 FR 25318, July 11, 1986; 61 FR 5510, Feb. 13, 1996]

§ 1926.804 Definitions applicable to this subpart.

(a) *Bulkhead*—An airtight structure separating the working chamber from free air or from another chamber under a lesser pressure than the working pressure.

(b) *Caisson*—A wood, steel, concrete or reinforced concrete, air- and water-tight chamber in which it is possible for men to work under air pressure greater than atmospheric pressure to excavate material below water level.

(c) *Decanting*—A method used for decompressing under emergency circumstances. In this procedure, the employees are brought to atmospheric pressure with a very high gas tension in the tissues and then immediately recompressed in a second and separate chamber or lock.

(d) *Emergency locks*—A lock designed to hold and permit the quick passage of an entire shift of employees.

(e) *High air*—Air pressure used to supply power to pneumatic tools and devices.

(f) *Low air*—Air supplied to pressurize working chambers and locks.

(g) *Man lock*—A chamber through which men pass from one air pressure environment into another.

(h) *Materials lock*—A chamber through which materials and equipment pass from one air pressure environment into another.

(i) *Medical lock*—A special chamber in which employees are treated for decompression illness. It may also be used in preemployment physical examinations to determine the adaptability of the prospective employee to changes in pressure.

(j) *Normal condition*—One during which exposure to compressed air is limited to a single continuous working period followed by a single decompression in any given 24-hour period; the total time of exposure to compressed air during the single continuous working period is not interrupted by exposure to normal atmospheric pressure, and a second exposure to compressed air does not occur until at least 12 consecutive hours of exposure to normal atmospheric pressure has elapsed since the employee has been under pressure.

(k) *Pressure*—A force acting on a unit area. Usually shown as pounds per square inch. (p.s.i.)

(l) *Absolute pressure* (p.s.i.a.)—The sum of the atmospheric pressure and gauge pressure (p.s.i.g.).

(m) *Atmospheric pressure*—The pressure of air at sea level, usually 14.7 p.s.i.a. (1 atmosphere), or 0 p.s.i.g.

(n) *Gauge pressure* (p.s.i.g.)—Pressure measured by a gauge and indicating the pressure exceeding atmospheric.

(o) *Safety screen*—An air- and watertight diaphragm placed across the upper part of a compressed air tunnel between the face and bulkhead, in order to prevent flooding the crown of the tunnel between the safety screen and the bulkhead, thus providing a safe means of refuge and exit from a flooding or flooded tunnel.

(p) *Special decompression chamber*—A chamber to provide greater comfort of employees when the total decompression time exceeds 75 minutes.

(q) *Working chamber*—The space or compartment under air pressure in which the work is being done.

APPENDIX A TO SUBPART S OF PART 1926—DECOMPRESSION TABLES

1. *Explanation.* The decompression tables are computed for working chamber pressures from 0 to 14 pounds, and from 14 to 50 pounds per square inch gauge inclusive by 2-pound increments and for exposure times for each pressure extending from one-half to over 8 hours inclusive. Decompressions will be conducted by two or more stages with a maximum of four stages, the latter for a working chamber pressure of 40 pounds per square inch gauge or over.

Stage 1 consists of a reduction in ambient pressure ranging from 10 to a maximum of 16 pounds per square inch, but in no instance will the pressure be reduced below 4 pounds at the end of stage 1. This reduction in pressure in stage 1 will always take place at a rate not greater than 5 pounds per minute.

Further reduction in pressure will take place during stage 2 and subsequent stages as required at a slower rate, but in no event at a rate greater than 1 pound per minute.

Decompression Table No. 1 indicates in the body of the table the total decompression time in minutes for various combinations of

449

working chamber pressure and exposure time.

Decompression Table No. 2 indicates for the same various combinations of working chamber pressure and exposure time the following:

a. The number of stages required;

b. The reduction in pressure and the terminal pressure for each required stage;

c. The time in minutes through which the reduction in pressure is accomplished for each required stage;

d. The pressure reduction rate in minutes per pound for each required stage;

IMPORTANT NOTE: The Pressure Reduction in Each Stage is Accomplished at a Uniform Rate. Do Not Interpolate Between Values Shown on the Tables. Use the Next Higher Value of Working Chamber Pressure or Exposure Time Should the Actual Working Chamber Pressure or the Actual Exposure Time, Respectively, Fall Between Those for Which Calculated Values Are Shown in the Body of the Tables.

Examples	Minutes
Example No. 1: 4 hours working period at 20 pounds gauge.	
Decompression Table No. 1: 20 pounds for 4 hours, total decompression time	43
Decompression Table No. 2:	
Stage 1: Reduce pressure from 20 pounds to 4 pounds at the uniform rate of 5 pounds per minute.	
Elapsed time stage 1: 16/5	3

Examples	Minutes
Stage 2 (final stage): Reduce pressure at a uniform rate from 4 pounds to 0-pound gage over a period of 40 minutes.	
Rate—0.10 pound per minute or 10 minutes per pound.	
Stage 2 (final) elapsed time	40
Total time	43
Example No. 2: 5-hour working period at 24 pounds gage.	
Decompression Table No. 1: 24 pounds for 5 hours, total decompression time	117
Decompression Table No. 2:	
Stage 1: Reduce pressure from 24 pounds to 8 pounds at the uniform rate of 5 pounds per minute.	
Elapsed time stage 1: 16/5	3
Stage 2: Reduce pressure at a uniform rate from 8 pounds to 4 pounds over a period of 4 minutes. Rate, 1 pound per minute elapsed time, stage 2	4
Transfer men to special decompression chamber maintaining the 4-pound pressure during the transfer operation.	
Stage 3 (final stage): In the special decompression chamber, reduce the pressure at a uniform rate from 4 pounds to 0-pound gage over a period of 110 minutes. Rate, 0.037 pound per minute or 27.5 minutes per pound. Stage 3 (final) elapsed time ...	110
Total time	117

DECOMPRESSION TABLE NO. 1—TOTAL DECOMPRESSION TIME

Work pressure p.s.i.g.	Working period hours										
	½	1	1½	2	3	4	5	6	7	8	Over 8
9 to 12	3	3	3	3	3	3	3	3	3	3	3
14	6	6	6	6	6	6	6	6	16	16	33
16	7	7	7	7	7	7	17	33	48	48	62
18	7	7	7	8	11	17	48	63	63	73	87
20	7	7	8	15	15	43	63	73	83	103	113
22	9	9	16	24	38	68	93	103	113	128	133
24	11	12	23	27	52	92	117	122	127	137	151
26	13	14	29	34	69	104	126	141	142	142	163
28	15	23	31	41	98	127	143	153	153	165	183
30	17	28	38	62	105	143	165	168	178	188	204
32	19	35	43	85	126	163	178	193	203	213	226
34	21	39	58	98	151	178	195	218	223	233	248
36	24	44	63	113	170	198	223	233	243	253	273
38	28	49	73	128	178	203	223	238	253	263	278
40	31	49	84	143	183	213	233	248	258	278	288
42	37	56	102	144	189	215	245	260	263	268	293
44	43	64	118	154	199	234	254	264	269	269	293
46	44	74	139	171	214	244	269	274	289	299	318
48	51	89	144	189	229	269	299	309	319	319	....
50	58	94	164	209	249	279	309	329	....	....	....

DECOMPRESSION TABLE NO. 2

[Do not interpolate, use next higher value for conditions not computed]

Working chamber pressure p.s.i.g.	Working period hours	Decompression data					
		Stage No.	Pressure reduc. p.s.i.g.		Time in stage minutes	Pressure reduc. rate Min/pound	Total time decompress minutes
			From	To			
14	½	1	14	4	2	0.20	6
		2	4	0	4	1.00	6
	1	1	14	4	2	0.20	6
		2	4	0	4	1.00	6
	1½	1	14	4	2	0.20	6
		2	4	0	4	1.00	6
	2	1	14	4	2	0.20	6
		2	4	0	4	1.00	6
	3	1	14	4	2	0.20	6
		2	4	0	4	1.00	6
	4	1	14	0	2	0.20	6
		2	4	0	4	1.00	6
	5	1	14	4	2	0.20	6
		2	4	0	4	1.00	6
	6	1	14	4	2	0.20	....
		2	4	0	4	1.00	6
	7	1	14	4	2	0.20	....
		2	4	0	14	3.50	16
	8	1	14	4	2	0.20	....
		2	4	0	14	3.50	16
	Over 8	1	14	4	2	0.20	....
		2	4	0	30	7.50	32
16	½	1	16	4	3	0.20	....
		2	4	0	4	1.00	7
	1	1	16	4	3	0.20	7
		2	4	0	4	1.00	7
	1½	1	16	4	3	0.20	....
		2	4	0	4	1.00	7
	2	1	16	4	3	0.20	....
		2	4	0	4	1.00	7
	3	1	16	4	3	0.20	....
		2	4	0	4	1.00	7
	4	1	14	4	3	0.20	....
		2	4	0	4	1.00	7
	5	1	14	4	3	0.20	7
		2	4	0	4	3.50	17
	6	1	14	4	3	0.20	....
		2	4	0	30	7.50	33
	7	1	14	4	3	0.20	....
		2	4	0	45	11.25	48
	8	1	14	4	3	0.20	....
		2	4	0	45	11.25	48
	Over 8	1	14	4	3	0.20	....
		2	4	0	60	15.00	63
18	½	1	18	4	3	0.20	....
		2	4	0	4	1.00	7
	1	1	18	4	3	0.20	....
		2	4	0	4	1.00	7
	1½	1	18	4	3	0.20	....
		2	4	0	4	1.00	7
	2	1	18	4	3	0.20	....
		2	4	0	5	1.25	8
	3	1	18	4	3	0.20	....
		2	4	0	8	2.00	11
	4	1	18	4	3	0.20	....
		2	4	0	14	3.50	17
	5	1	18	4	3	0.20	....
		2	4	0	45	11.25	48
	6	1	18	4	3	0.20	....
		2	4	0	60	15.00	63
	7	1	18	4	3	0.20	....
		2	4	0	60	15.00	63
	8	1	18	4	3	0.20	....
		2	4	0	70	17.50	73
	Over 8	1	18	4	3	0.20	....
		2	4	0	84	21.00	87

451

DECOMPRESSION TABLE NO. 2—Continued

[Do not interpolate, use next higher value for conditions not computed]

Working chamber pressure p.s.i.g.	Working period hours	Decompression data					
		Stage No.	Pressure reduc. p.s.i.g.		Time in stage minutes	Pressure reduc. rate Min/pound	Total time decompress minutes
			From	To			
20	½	1	20	4	3	0.20	....
		2	4	0	4	1.00	7
	1	1	20	4	3	0.20	....
		2	4	0	4	1.00	7
	1½	1	20	4	3	0.20	....
		2	4	0	5	1.25	8
	2	1	20	4	3	0.20	....
		2	4	0	12	3.00	15
	3	1	20	4	3	0.20	....
		2	4	0	12	3.00	15
	4	1	20	4	3	0.20	....
		2	4	0	40	10.00	43
	5	1	20	4	3	0.20	....
		2	4	0	60	15.00	63
	6	1	20	4	3	0.20	....
		2	4	0	70	17.50	73
	7	1	20	4	3	0.20	....
		2	4	0	80	20.00	83
	8	1	20	4	3	0.20	....
		2	4	0	100	25.00	103
	Over 8	1	20	4	3	0.20	....
		2	4	0	110	27.50	113
22	½	1	22	6	3	0.20	....
		2	6	0	6	1.00	9
	1	1	22	6	3	0.20	....
		2	6	0	6	1.00	9
	1½	1	22	6	3	0.20	....
		2	6	0	13	2.20	16
	2	1	22	6	3	0.20	....
		2	6	0	21	3.50	24
	3	1	22	6	3	0.20	....
		2	6	0	35	5.85	38
	4	1	22	6	3	0.20	....
		2	6	0	65	10.83	68
	5	1	22	6	3	0.20	....
		2	6	0	90	15.00	93
	6	1	22	6	3	0.20	....
		2	4	0	100	16.67	103
	7	1	22	6	3	0.20	....
		2	6	0	110	18.35	113
	8	1	22	6	3	0.20	....
		2	6	0	125	20.80	128
	Over 8	1	22	6	3	0.20	....
		2	6	0	130	21.70	133
24	½	1	24	8	3	0.20	....
		2	8	4	4	1.00	....
		3	4	0	4	1.00	11
	1	1	24	8	3	0.20	....
		2	8	4	4	1.00	....
		3	4	0	5	1.25	12
	1½	1	24	8	3	0.20	....
		2	8	4	4	1.00	....
		3	4	0	16	4.00	23
	2	1	24	8	3	0.20	....
		2	8	4	4	1.00	....
		3	4	0	20	5.00	27
	3	1	24	8	3	0.20	....
		2	8	4	4	1.00	....
		3	4	0	45	11.25	52
	4	1	24	8	3	0.20	....
		2	8	4	4	1.00	....
		3	4	0	85	21.25	92
	5	1	24	8	3	0.20	....
		2	8	4	4	1.00	....
		3	4	0	110	27.50	117
	6	1	24	8	3	0.20	....

DECOMPRESSION TABLE NO. 2—Continued

[Do not interpolate, use next higher value for conditions not computed]

Working chamber pressure p.s.i.g.	Working period hours	Stage No.	Pressure reduc. p.s.i.g.		Time in stage minutes	Pressure reduc. rate Min/pound	Total time decompress minutes
			From	To			
		2	8	4	4	1.00	....
		3	4	0	115	28.80	122
	7	1	24	8	3	0.20	....
		2	8	4	4	1.00	....
		3	4	0	120	30.00	127
	8	1	24	8	3	0.20	....
		2	8	4	4	1.00	....
		3	4	0	130	32.50	137
	Over 8	1	24	8	3	0.20	....
		2	8	4	8	2.00	....
		3	4	0	140	35.00	151
26	½	1	26	10	3	0.20	....
		2	10	4	6	1.00	....
		3	4	0	4	1.00	13
	1	1	26	10	3	0.20	....
		2	10	4	6	1.00	....
		3	4	0	5	1.25	14
	1½	1	26	10	3	0.20	....
		2	10	4	6	1.00	....
		3	4	0	20	5.00	29
	2	1	26	10	3	0.20	....
		2	10	4	6	1.00	....
		3	4	0	25	6.25	34
	3	1	26	10	3	0.20	....
		2	10	4	6	1.00	....
		3	4	0	60	15.00	69
	4	1	26	10	3	0.20	....
		2	10	4	6	1.00	....
		3	4	0	95	23.75	104
	5	1	26	10	3	0.20	....
		2	10	4	8	1.33	....
		3	4	0	115	28.80	126
	6	1	26	10	3	0.20	....
		2	10	4	8	1.33	....
		3	4	0	130	32.50	141
	7	1	26	10	3	2.20	....
		2	10	4	9	1.50	....
		3	4	0	130	32.50	142
	8	1	26	10	3	0.20	....
		2	10	4	9	1.50	....
		3	4	0	130	32.50	142
	Over 8	1	26	10	3	0.20	....
		2	10	4	30	5.00	....
		3	4	0	30	32.50	163
28	½	1	28	12	3	0.20	....
		2	12	4	8	1.00	....
		3	4	0	4	1.00	15
	1	1	28	12	3	0.20	....
		2	12	4	8	1.00	....
		3	4	0	12	3.00	23
	1½	1	28	12	3	0.20	....
		2	12	4	8	1.00	....
		3	4	0	20	5.00	31
	2	1	28	12	3	0.20	....
		2	12	4	8	1.00	....
		3	4	0	30	7.50	41
	3	1	28	12	3	0.20	....
		2	12	4	10	1.25	....
		3	4	0	85	21.20	98
	4	1	28	12	3	0.20	....
		2	12	4	14	1.75	....
		3	4	0	110	27.50	127
	5	1	28	12	3	0.20	....
		2	12	4	20	2.50	....
		3	4	0	120	30.00	143
	6	1	28	12	3	0.20	....

DECOMPRESSION TABLE NO. 2—Continued

[Do not interpolate, use next higher value for conditions not computed]

Working chamber pressure p.s.i.g.	Working period hours	Decompression data				
		Stage No.	Pressure reduc. p.s.i.g.		Time in stage minutes	Pressure reduc. rate Min/pound	Total time decompress minutes
			From	To			
		2	12	4	20	2.50	....
		3	4	0	130	32.50	153
	7	1	28	12	3	0.20	
		2	12	4	20	2.50	....
		3	4	0	120	32.50	153
	8	1	28	12	3	0.20	
		2	12	4	32	4.00	....
		3	4	0	130	32.50	165
	Over 8	1	28	12	3	0.20	
		2	12	4	50	6.25	....
		3	4	0	130	32.50	183
30	½	1	30	14	3	0.20	
		2	14	4	10	1.00	
		3	4	0	4	1.00	17
	1	1	30	14	3	0.20	
		2	14	4	10	1.00	
		3	4	0	15	3.75	28
	1½	1	30	14	3	0.20	
		2	14	4	10	1.00	
		3	4	0	25	6.25	38
	2	1	30	14	3	0.20	
		2	14	4	14	1.40	
		3	4	0	45	11.25	62
	3	1	30	14	3	0.20	
		2	14	4	17	1.70	....
		3	4	0	85	21.20	105
	4	1	30	14	3	0.20	
		2	14	4	30	3.00	....
		3	4	0	110	27.50	143
	5	1	30	14	3	0.20	
		2	14	4	35	3.50	....
		3	4	0	130	32.50	165
	6	1	30	14	3	0.20	
		2	14	4	35	3.50	....
		3	4	0	130	32.50	168
	7	1	30	14	3	0.20	
		2	14	4	45	4.50	....
		3	4	0	130	32.50	178
	8	1	30	14	3	0.20	
		2	14	4	55	5.50	....
		3	4	0	130	32.50	188
	Over 8	1	30	14	3	0.20	
		2	14	4	71	7.10	....
		3	4	0	130	32.50	204
32	½	1	32	16	3	0.20	
		2	16	4	12	1.00	....
		3	4	0	4	1.00	19
	1	1	32	16	3	0.20	
		2	16	4	12	1.00	
		3	4	0	20	5.00	35
	1½	1	32	16	3	0.20	
		2	16	4	15	1.25	....
		3	4	0	25	6.25	43
	2	1	32	16	3	0.20	
		2	16	4	22	1.83	....
		3	4	0	60	15.00	85
	3	1	32	16	3	0.20	
		2	16	4	28	2.33	....
		3	4	0	95	23.75	126
	4	1	32	16	3	0.20	
		2	16	4	40	3.33	....
		3	4	0	120	30.00	163
	5	1	32	16	3	0.20	
		2	16	4	45	3.75	....
		3	4	0	130	32.50	178
	6	1	32	16	3	0.20	

DECOMPRESSION TABLE NO. 2—Continued

[Do not interpolate, use next higher value for conditions not computed]

Working chamber pressure p.s.i.g.	Working period hours	Stage No.	Pressure reduc. p.s.i.g.		Time in stage minutes	Pressure reduc. rate Min/pound	Total time decompress minutes
			From	To			
		2	16	4	60	5.00	....
		3	4	0	130	32.50	193
	7	1	32	16	3	0.20	....
		2	16	4	70	5.83	....
		3	4	0	130	32.50	203
	8	1	32	16	3	0.20	....
		2	16	4	80	6.67	....
		3	4	0	130	32.50	213
	Over 8	1	32	16	3	0.20	....
		2	16	4	93	7.75	....
		3	4	0	130	32.50	226
34	½	1	34	18	3	0.20	....
		2	18	4	14	1.00	....
		3	4	0	4	1.00	21
	1	1	34	18	3	0.20	....
		2	18	4	14	1.00	....
		3	4	0	22	5.50	39
	1½	1	34	18	3	0.20	....
		2	18	4	25	1.80	....
		3	4	0	30	7.50	58
	2	1	34	18	3	0.20	....
		2	18	4	35	2.50	....
		3	4	0	60	15.00	98
	3	1	34	18	3	0.20	....
		2	18	4	43	3.10	....
		3	4	0	105	26.25	151
	4	1	34	18	3	0.20	....
		2	18	4	55	3.93	....
		3	4	0	120	30.00	178
	5	1	34	18	3	0.20	....
		2	18	4	62	4.43	....
		3	4	0	130	32.50	195
	6	1	34	18	3	0.20	....
		2	18	4	85	6.07	....
		3	4	0	130	32.50	218
	7	1	34	18	3	0.20	....
		2	18	4	90	6.43	....
		3	4	0	130	32.50	223
	8	1	34	18	3	0.20	....
		2	18	4	100	7.15	....
		3	4	0	130	32.50	233
	Over 8	1	34	18	3	0.20	....
		2	18	4	115	8.23	....
		3	4	0	130	32.50	248
36	½	1	36	20	3	0.20	....
		2	20	4	16	1.00	....
		3	4	0	5	1.25	24
	1	1	36	20	3	0.20	....
		2	20	4	16	1.00	....
		3	4	0	25	6.25	44
	1½	1	36	20	3	0.20	....
		2	20	4	30	1.88	....
		3	4	0	30	7.50	63
	2	1	36	20	3	0.20	....
		2	20	4	40	2.50	....
		3	4	0	70	17.50	113
	3	1	36	20	3	0.20	....
		2	20	4	52	3.25	....
		3	4	0	115	28.75	170
	4	1	36	20	3	0.20	....
		2	20	4	65	4.06	....
		3	4	0	130	32.50	198
	5	1	36	20	3	0.20	....
		2	20	4	90	5.63	....
		3	4	0	130	32.50	223
	6	1	36	20	3	0.20	....

DECOMPRESSION TABLE No. 2—Continued

[Do not interpolate, use next higher value for conditions not computed]

Working chamber pressure p.s.i.g.	Working period hours	Stage No.	Pressure reduc. p.s.i.g.		Time in stage minutes	Pressure reduc. rate Min/pound	Total time decompress minutes
			From	To			
		2	20	4	100	6.25	....
		3	4	0	130	32.50	233
	7	1	36	20	3	0.20	
		2	20	4	110	6.88	....
		3	4	0	130	32.50	243
	8	1	36	20	3	0.20	
		2	20	4	120	7.50	....
		3	4	0	130	32.50	253
	Over 8	1	36	20	3	0.20	
		2	20	4	140	8.75	....
38		3	4	0	130	32.50	273
	½	1	38	22	3	0.20	
		2	22	6	16	1.00	....
		3	6	0	9	1.50	28
	1	1	38	22	3	0.20	
		2	22	6	16	1.00	....
		3	6	0	30	5.00	49
	1½	1	38	22	3	0.20	
		2	22	6	20	1.25	....
		3	6	0	50	8.34	73
	2	1	38	22	3	0.20	
		2	22	6	30	1.88	....
		3	6	0	95	15.83	128
	3	1	38	22	3	0.20	
		2	22	6	35	2.19	....
		3	6	0	140	23.35	178
	4	1	38	22	3	0.20	
		2	22	6	50	3.12	....
		3	6	0	150	25.00	203
	5	1	38	22	3	0.20	
		2	22	6	55	3.44	....
		3	6	0	165	27.50	223
	6	1	38	22	3	0.20	
		2	22	6	70	4.38	....
		3	6	0	165	27.50	238
	7	1	38	22	3	0.20	
		2	22	6	85	5.32	....
		3	6	0	165	27.50	253
	8	1	38	22	3	0.20	
		2	22	6	95	5.93	....
		3	6	0	165	27.50	263
	Over 8	1	38	22	3	0.20	
		2	22	6	110	6.88	....
		3	6	0	165	27.50	278
40	½	1	40	24	3	0.20	
		2	24	8	16	1.00	....
		3	8	4	4	1.00	....
		4	4	0	8	2.00	31
	1	1	40	24	3	0.20	
		2	24	8	16	1.00	....
		3	8	4	5	1.25	....
		4	4	0	25	6.25	49
	1½	1	40	24	3	0.20	
		2	24	8	16	1.00	....
		3	8	4	20	5.00	....
		4	4	0	45	11.25	84
	2	2	40	24	3	0.20	
		1	24	8	25	1.56	....
		3	8	4	20	5.00	....
		4	4	0	95	23.75	143
	3	1	40	24	3	0.20	
		2	24	8	30	1.88	....
		3	8	4	30	7.50	....
		4	4	0	120	30.00	183
	4	1	40	24	3	0.20	
		2	24	8	45	2.81	....

DECOMPRESSION TABLE NO. 2—Continued

[Do not interpolate, use next higher value for conditions not computed]

Working chamber pressure p.s.i.g.	Working period hours	Stage No.	Pressure reduc. p.s.i.g. From	To	Time in stage minutes	Pressure reduc. rate Min/pound	Total time decompress minutes
		3	8	4	35	8.75	....
		4	4	0	130	32.50	213
	5	1	40	24	3	0.20	....
		2	24	8	47	2.94	....
		3	8	4	53	13.25	....
		4	4	0	130	32.50	233
	6	1	40	24	3	0.20	....
		2	24	8	55	3.44	....
		3	8	4	60	15.00	....
		4	4	0	130	32.50	248
	7	1	40	24	3	0.20	....
		2	24	8	65	4.06	....
		3	8	4	60	15.00	....
		4	4	0	130	32.50	258
	8	1	40	24	3	0.20	....
		2	24	8	75	4.70	....
		3	8	4	60	15.00	....
		4	4	0	130	32.50	268
	Over 8	1	40	24	3	0.20	....
		2	24	8	95	5.93	....
		3	8	4	60	15.00	....
		4	4	0	130	32.50	288
42	½	1	42	26	3	0.20	....
		2	26	10	16	1.00	....
		3	10	4	6	1.00	....
		4	4	0	12	3.00	37
	1	1	42	26	3	0.20	....
		2	26	10	16	1.00	....
		3	10	4	12	2.00	....
		4	4	0	25	6.25	56
	1½	1	42	26	3	0.20	....
		2	26	10	16	1.00	....
		3	10	4	23	3.83	....
		4	4	0	60	15.00	102
	2	1	42	26	3	0.20	....
		2	26	10	16	1.00	....
		3	10	4	30	5.00	....
		4	4	0	95	23.75	144
	3	1	42	26	3	0.20	....
		2	26	10	16	1.00	....
		3	10	4	50	8.34	....
		4	4	0	120	30.00	189
	4	1	42	26	3	0.20	....
		2	26	10	17	1.06	....
		3	10	4	65	10.83	....
		4	4	0	130	32.50	215
	5	1	42	26	3	0.20	....
		2	26	10	27	1.69	....
		3	10	4	85	14.18	....
		4	4	0	130	32.50	245
	6	1	42	26	3	0.20	....
		2	26	10	27	1.69	....
		3	10	4	100	16.67	....
		4	4	0	130	32.50	260
	7	1	42	26	3	0.20	....
		2	26	10	30	1.88	....
		3	10	4	100	16.67	....
		4	4	0	130	32.50	263
	8	1	42	26	3	0.20	....
		2	26	10	35	2.19	....
		3	10	4	100	16.67	....
		4	4	0	130	32.50	268
	Over 8	1	42	26	3	0.20	....
		2	26	10	60	3.75	....
		3	10	4	100	16.67	....
		4	4	0	130	32.50	293

DECOMPRESSION TABLE NO. 2—Continued

[Do not interpolate, use next higher value for conditions not computed]

Working chamber pressure p.s.i.g.	Working period hours	Decompression data				
		Stage No.	Pressure reduc. p.s.i.g.		Time in stage minutes	Pressure reduc. rate Min/pound	Total time decompress minutes
			From	To			
44	½	1	44	28	3	0.20	....
		2	28	12	16	1.00	....
		3	12	4	8	1.00	....
		4	4	0	16	4.00	43
	1	1	44	28	3	0.20	....
		2	28	12	16	1.00	....
		3	12	4	20	2.50	....
		4	4	0	25	6.25	64
	1½	1	44	28	3	0.20	....
		2	28	12	16	1.00	....
		3	12	4	27	3.38	....
		4	4	0	72	18.00	118
	2	1	44	28	3	0.20	....
		2	28	12	16	1.00	....
		3	12	4	40	5.00	....
		4	4	0	95	23.75	154
	3	1	44	28	3	0.20	....
		2	28	12	16	1.00	....
		3	12	4	60	7.50	....
		4	4	0	120	30.00	199
	4	1	44	28	3	0.20	....
		2	28	12	16	1.00	....
		3	12	4	85	10.62	....
		4	4	0	130	32.50	234
	5	1	44	28	3	0.20	....
		2	28	12	16	1.00	....
		3	12	4	105	13.13	....
		4	4	0	130	32.50	254
	6	1	44	28	3	0.20	....
		2	28	12	16	1.00	....
		3	12	4	115	14.38	....
		4	4	0	130	32.50	264
	7	1	44	28	3	0.20	....
		2	28	12	16	1.00	....
		3	12	4	120	15.00	....
		4	4	0	130	32.50	269
	8	1	44	28	3	0.20	....
		2	28	12	16	1.00	....
		3	12	4	120	15.00	....
		4	4	0	130	32.50	269
	Over 8	1	44	28	3	0.20	....
		2	28	12	40	2.50	....
		3	12	4	120	15.00	....
		4	4	0	130	32.50	293
46	½	1	46	30	3	0.20	....
		2	30	14	16	1.00	....
		3	14	4	10	1.00	....
		4	4	0	15	3.75	44
	1	1	46	30	3	0.20	....
		2	30	14	16	1.00	....
		3	14	4	25	2.50	....
		4	4	0	30	7.50	74
	1½	1	46	30	3	0.20	....
		2	30	14	16	1.00	....
		3	14	4	35	3.50	....
		4	4	0	85	21.20	139
	2	1	46	30	3	0.20	....
		2	30	14	16	1.00	....
		3	14	4	47	4.70	....
		4	4	0	105	26.25	171
	3	1	46	30	3	0.20	....
		2	30	14	16	1.00	....
		3	14	4	65	6.50	....
		4	4	0	130	32.50	214
	4	1	46	30	3	0.20	....
		2	30	14	16	1.00	....

DECOMPRESSION TABLE NO. 2—Continued

[Do not interpolate, use next higher value for conditions not computed]

Working chamber pressure p.s.i.g.	Working period hours		Decompression data				
		Stage No.	Pressure reduc. p.s.i.g.		Time in stage minutes	Pressure reduc. rate Min/pound	Total time decompress minutes
			From	To			
		3	14	4	95	9.50	....
		4	4	0	130	32.50	244
	5	1	46	30	3	0.20	....
		2	30	14	16	1.00	....
		3	14	4	120	12.00	....
		4	4	0	130	32.50	269
	6	1	46	30	3	0.20	....
		2	30	14	16	1.00	....
		3	14	4	125	12.50	....
		4	4	0	130	32.50	274
	7	1	46	30	3	0.20	....
		2	34	14	16	1.00	....
		3	10	4	140	14.00	....
		4	4	0	130	32.50	289
	8	1	46	30	3	0.20	....
		2	30	14	16	1.00	....
		3	14	4	150	15.00	....
		4	4	0	130	32.50	299
	Over 8	1	46	30	3	0.20	....
		2	30	14	25	1.56	....
		3	14	4	160	16.00	....
		4	4	0	130	32.50	318
48	½	1	48	32	3	0.20	....
		2	32	16	16	1.00	....
		3	16	4	12	1.00	....
		4	4	0	20	5.00	51
	1	1	48	32	3	0.20	....
		2	32	16	16	1.00	....
		3	16	4	35	2.92	....
		4	4	0	35	8.75	89
	1½	1	48	32	3	0.20	....
		2	32	16	16	1.00	....
		3	16	4	45	3.75	....
		4	4	0	80	20.00	144
	2	1	48	32	3	0.20	....
		2	32	16	16	1.00	....
		3	16	4	60	5.00	....
		4	4	0	110	27.50	189
	3	1	48	32	3	0.20	....
		2	32	16	16	1.00	....
		3	16	4	90	7.50	....
		4	4	0	120	30.00	229
	4	1	48	32	3	0.20	....
		2	32	16	16	1.00	....
		3	16	4	120	10.00	....
		4	4	0	130	32.50	269
	5	1	48	32	3	0.20	....
		2	32	16	16	1.00	....
		3	16	4	140	11.67	....
		4	4	0	130	32.50	209
	6	1	48	32	3	0.20	....
		2	32	16	16	1.00	....
		3	16	4	160	13.33	....
		4	4	0	130	32.50	309
	7	1	48	32	3	0.20	....
		2	32	16	16	1.00	....
		3	16	4	170	14.17	....
		4	4	0	130	32.50	
	8	1	48	32	3	0.20	....
		2	32	16	16	1.00	....
		3	16	4	170	14.17	....
		4	4	0	130	32.50	....
50	½	1	50	34	3	0.20	....
		2	34	18	16	1.00	....
		3	18	4	14	1.00	....
		4	4	0	25	6.25	58

459

DECOMPRESSION TABLE NO. 2—Continued

[Do not interpolate, use next higher value for conditions not computed]

Working chamber pressure p.s.i.g.	Working period hours	Decompression data					
		Stage No.	Pressure reduc. p.s.i.g.		Time in stage minutes	Pressure reduc. rate Min/pound	Total time decompress minutes
			From	To			
	1	1	50	34	3	0.20	....
		2	34	18	16	1.00	....
		3	18	4	40	2.86	....
		4	4	0	35	8.75	94
	1½	1	50	34	3	0.20	....
		2	34	18	16	1.00	....
		3	18	4	55	3.93	....
		4	4	0	90	22.50	164
	2	1	50	34	3	0.20	....
		2	34	18	16	1.00	....
		3	18	4	70	5.00	....
		4	4	0	120	30.00	209
	3	1	50	34	3	0.20	....
		2	34	18	16	1.00	....
		3	18	4	100	7.15	....
		4	4	0	130	32.50	249
	4	1	50	34	3	0.20	....
		2	34	18	16	1.00	....
		3	18	4	130	8.58	....
		4	4	0	130	32.50	279
	5	1	50	34	3	0.20	....
		2	34	18	16	1.00	....
		3	18	4	160	11.42	....

DECOMPRESSION TABLE NO. 2—CONTINUED

[Do not interpolate, use next higher value for conditions not computed]

Working chamber pressure p.s.i.g.	Working period hours	Decompression data					
		Stage No.	Pressure reduc. p.s.i.g.		Time in stage minutes	Pressure reduc. rate Min/pound	Total time decompress minutes
			From	To			
		4	4	0	130	32.50	309
	6	1	50	34	3	0.20	....
		2	34	18	16	1.00	....
		3	18	4	180	12.85	....
		4	4	0	130	32.50	329

[44 FR 8577, Feb. 9, 1979; 44 FR 20940, Apr. 6. 1979; as amended at 58 FR 35311, June 30, 1993]

Subpart T—Demolition

AUTHORITY: 40 U.S.C. 3701; 29 U.S.C. 653, 655, 657; and Secretary of Labor's Orders 12–71 (36 FR 8754), 8–76 (41 FR 25059), 9–83 (48 FR 35736), 1–90 (55 FR 9033), 6–96 (62 FR 111), 5–2007 (72 FR 31159), or 1–2012 (77 FR 3912), as applicable.

§ 1926.850 Preparatory operations.

(a) Prior to permitting employees to start demolition operations, an engineering survey shall be made, by a competent person, of the structure to determine the condition of the framing, floors, and walls, and possibility of unplanned collapse of any portion of the structure. Any adjacent structure where employees may be exposed shall also be similarly checked. The employer shall have in writing evidence that such a survey has been performed.

(b) When employees are required to work within a structure to be demolished which has been damaged by fire, flood, explosion, or other cause, the walls or floor shall be shored or braced.

(c) All electric, gas, water, steam, sewer, and other service lines shall be shut off, capped, or otherwise controlled, outside the building line before demolition work is started. In each case, any utility company which is involved shall be notified in advance.

(d) If it is necessary to maintain any power, water or other utilities during demolition, such lines shall be temporarily relocated, as necessary, and protected.

(e) It shall also be determined if any type of hazardous chemicals, gases, explosives, flammable materials, or similarly dangerous substances have been used in any pipes, tanks, or other equipment on the property. When the presence of any such substances is apparent or suspected, testing and purging shall be performed and the hazard eliminated before demolition is started.

(f) Where a hazard exists from fragmentation of glass, such hazards shall be removed.

(g) Where a hazard exists to employees falling through wall openings, the opening shall be protected to a height of approximately 42 inches.

(h) When debris is dropped through holes in the floor without the use of chutes, the area onto which the material is dropped shall be completely enclosed with barricades not less than 42 inches high and not less than 6 feet back from the projected edge of the opening above. Signs, warning of the hazard of falling materials, shall be posted at each level. Removal shall not be permitted in this lower area until debris handling ceases above.

(i) All floor openings, not used as material drops, shall be covered over with material substantial enough to support the weight of any load which may be imposed. Such material shall be properly secured to prevent its accidental movement.

(j) Except for the cutting of holes in floors for chutes, holes through which to drop materials, preparation of storage space, and similar necessary preparatory work, the demolition of exterior walls and floor construction shall begin at the top of the structure and proceed downward. Each story of exterior wall and floor construction shall be removed and dropped into the storage space before commencing the removal of exterior walls and floors in the story next below.

(k) Employee entrances to multistory structures being demolished shall be completely protected by sidewalk sheds or canopies, or both, providing protection from the face of the building for a minimum of 8 feet. All such canopies shall be at least 2 feet wider than the building entrances or openings (1 foot wider on each side thereof), and shall be capable of sustaining a load of 150 pounds per square foot.

§1926.851 Stairs, passageways, and ladders.

(a) Only those stairways, passageways, and ladders, designated as means of access to the structure of a building, shall be used. Other access ways shall be entirely closed at all times.

(b) All stairs, passageways, ladders and incidental equipment thereto, which are covered by this section, shall be periodically inspected and maintained in a clean safe condition.

(c) In a multistory building, when a stairwell is being used, it shall be properly illuminated by either natural or artificial means, and completely and substantially covered over at a point not less than two floors below the floor on which work is being performed, and access to the floor where the work is in progress shall be through a properly lighted, protected, and separate passageway.

§1926.852 Chutes.

(a) No material shall be dropped to any point lying outside the exterior walls of the structure unless the area is effectively protected.

(b) All materials chutes, or sections thereof, at an angle of more than 45° from the horizontal, shall be entirely enclosed, except for openings equipped with closures at or about floor level for the insertion of materials. The openings shall not exceed 48 inches in height measured along the wall of the chute. At all stories below the top floor, such openings shall be kept closed when not in use.

(c) A substantial gate shall be installed in each chute at or near the discharge end. A competent employee shall be assigned to control the operation of the gate, and the backing and loading of trucks.

(d) When operations are not in progress, the area surrounding the discharge end of a chute shall be securely closed off.

(e) Any chute opening, into which workmen dump debris, shall be protected by a substantial guardrail approximately 42 inches above the floor or other surface on which the men stand to dump the material. Any space between the chute and the edge of openings in the floors through which it passes shall be solidly covered over.

(f) Where the material is dumped from mechanical equipment or wheelbarrows, a securely attached toeboard or bumper, not less than 4 inches thick and 6 inches high, shall be provided at each chute opening.

(g) Chutes shall be designed and constructed of such strength as to eliminate failure due to impact of materials or debris loaded therein.

§ 1926.853 Removal of materials through floor openings.

Any openings cut in a floor for the disposal of materials shall be no larger in size than 25 percent of the aggregate of the total floor area, unless the lateral supports of the removed flooring remain in place. Floors weakened or otherwise made unsafe by demolition operations shall be shored to carry safely the intended imposed load from demolition operations.

§ 1926.854 Removal of walls, masonry sections, and chimneys.

(a) Masonry walls, or other sections of masonry, shall not be permitted to fall upon the floors of the building in such masses as to exceed the safe carrying capacities of the floors.

(b) No wall section, which is more than one story in height, shall be permitted to stand alone without lateral bracing, unless such wall was originally designed and constructed to stand without such lateral support, and is in a condition safe enough to be self-supporting. All walls shall be left in a stable condition at the end of each shift.

(c) Employees shall not be permitted to work on the top of a wall when weather conditions constitute a hazard.

(d) Structural or load-supporting members on any floor shall not be cut or removed until all stories above such a floor have been demolished and removed. This provision shall not pro-

hibit the cutting of floor beams for the disposal of materials or for the installation of equipment, provided that the requirements of §§ 1926.853 and 1926.855 are met.

(e) Floor openings within 10 feet of any wall being demolished shall be planked solid, except when employees are kept out of the area below.

(f) In buildings of "skeleton-steel" construction, the steel framing may be left in place during the demolition of masonry. Where this is done, all steel beams, girders, and similar structural supports shall be cleared of all loose material as the masonry demolition progresses downward.

(g) Walkways or ladders shall be provided to enable employees to safely reach or leave any scaffold or wall.

(h) Walls, which serve as retaining walls to support earth or adjoining structures, shall not be demolished until such earth has been properly braced or adjoining structures have been properly underpinned.

(i) Walls, which are to serve as retaining walls against which debris will be piled, shall not be so used unless capable of safely supporting the imposed load.

§ 1926.855 Manual removal of floors.

(a) Openings cut in a floor shall extend the full span of the arch between supports.

(b) Before demolishing any floor arch, debris and other material shall be removed from such arch and other adjacent floor area. Planks not less than 2 inches by 10 inches in cross section, full size undressed, shall be provided for, and shall be used by employees to stand on while breaking down floor arches between beams. Such planks shall be so located as to provide a safe support for the workmen should the arch between the beams collapse. The open space between planks shall not exceed 16 inches.

(c) Safe walkways, not less than 18 inches wide, formed of planks not less than 2 inches thick if wood, or of equivalent strength if metal, shall be provided and used by workmen when necessary to enable them to reach any point without walking upon exposed beams.

(d) Stringers of ample strength shall be installed to support the flooring planks, and the ends of such stringers shall be supported by floor beams or girders, and not by floor arches alone.

(e) Planks shall be laid together over solid bearings with the ends overlapping at least 1 foot.

(f) When floor arches are being removed, employees shall not be allowed in the area directly underneath, and such an area shall be barricaded to prevent access to it.

(g) Demolition of floor arches shall not be started until they, and the surrounding floor area for a distance of 20 feet, have been cleared of debris and any other unnecessary materials.

§1926.856 **Removal of walls, floors, and material with equipment.**

(a) Mechanical equipment shall not be used on floors or working surfaces unless such floors or surfaces are of sufficient strength to support the imposed load.

(b) Floor openings shall have curbs or stop-logs to prevent equipment from running over the edge.

(c) *Cranes, derricks, and other mechanical equipment.* Employers must meet the requirements specified in subparts N, O, and CC of this part.

[44 FR 8577, Feb. 9, 1979 , 75 FR 48135, Aug. 9, 2010; 77 FR 49730, Aug. 17, 2012; 78 FR 23843, Apr. 23, 2013]

§1926.857 **Storage.**

(a) The storage of waste material and debris on any floor shall not exceed the allowable floor loads.

(b) In buildings having wooden floor construction, the flooring boards may be removed from not more than one floor above grade to provide storage space for debris, provided falling material is not permitted to endanger the stability of the structure.

(c) When wood floor beams serve to brace interior walls or free-standing exterior walls, such beams shall be left in place until other equivalent support can be installed to replace them.

(d) Floor arches, to an elevation of not more than 25 feet above grade, may be removed to provide storage area for debris: *Provided,* That such removal does not endanger the stability of the structure.

(e) Storage space into which material is dumped shall be blocked off, except for openings necessary for the removal of material. Such openings shall be kept closed at all times when material is not being removed.

§1926.858 **Removal of steel construction.**

(a) When floor arches have been removed, planking in accordance with §1926.855(b) shall be provided for the workers engaged in razing the steel framing.

(b) *Cranes, derricks, and other hoisting equipment.* Employers must meet the requirements specified in subparts N and CC of this part.

(c) Steel construction shall be dismantled column length by column length, and tier by tier (columns may be in two-story lengths).

(d) Any structural member being dismembered shall not be overstressed.

[44 FR 8577, Feb. 9, 1979 , 75 FR 48135, Aug. 9, 2010; 77 FR 49730, Aug. 17, 2012; 78 FR 23843, Apr. 23, 2013]

§1926.859 **Mechanical demolition.**

(a) No workers shall be permitted in any area, which can be adversely affected by demolition operations, when balling or clamming is being performed. Only those workers necessary for the performance of the operations shall be permitted in this area at any other time.

(b) The weight of the demolition ball shall not exceed 50 percent of the crane's rated load, based on the length of the boom and the maximum angle of operation at which the demolition ball will be used, or it shall not exceed 25 percent of the nominal breaking strength of the line by which it is suspended, whichever results in a lesser value.

(c) The crane boom and loadline shall be as short as possible.

(d) The ball shall be attached to the loadline with a swivel-type connection to prevent twisting of the loadline, and shall be attached by positive means in such manner that the weight cannot become accidentally disconnected.

(e) When pulling over walls or portions thereof, all steel members affected shall have been previously cut free.

(f) All roof cornices or other such ornamental stonework shall be removed prior to pulling walls over.

(g) During demoliton, continuing inspections by a competent person shall be made as the work progresses to detect hazards resulting from weakened or deteriorated floors, or walls, or loosened material. No employee shall be permitted to work where such hazards exist until they are corrected by shoring, bracing, or other effective means.

§ 1926.860 Selective demolition by explosives.

Selective demolition by explosives shall be conducted in accordance with the applicable sections of subpart U of this part.

Subpart U—Blasting and the Use of Explosives

Authority: Sec. 107, Contract Work Hours and Safety Standards Act (40 U.S.C. 333); secs. 4, 6, 8, Occupational Safety and Health Act of 1970 (29 U.S.C. 653, 655, 657); Secretary of Labor's Order No. 12–71 (36 FR 8754), 8–76 (41 FR 25059), 9–83 (48 FR 35736), or 6–96 (62 FR 111), as applicable; and 29 CFR part 1911.

§ 1926.900 General provisions.

(a) The employer shall permit only authorized and qualified persons to handle and use explosives.

(b) Smoking, firearms, matches, open flame lamps, and other fires, flame or heat producing devices and sparks shall be prohibited in or near explosive magazines or while explosives are being handled, transported or used.

(c) No person shall be allowed to handle or use explosives while under the influence of intoxicating liquors, narcotics, or other dangerous drugs.

(d) All explosives shall be accounted for at all times. Explosives not being used shall be kept in a locked magazine, unavailable to persons not authorized to handle them. The employer shall maintain an inventory and use record of all explosives. Appropriate authorities shall be notified of any loss, theft, or unauthorized entry into a magazine.

(e) No explosives or blasting agents shall be abandoned.

(f) No fire shall be fought where the fire is in imminent danger of contact with explosives. All employees shall be removed to a safe area and the fire area guarded against intruders.

(g) Original containers, or Class II magazines, shall be used for taking detonators and other explosives from storage magazines to the blasting area.

(h) When blasting is done in congested areas or in proximity to a structure, railway, or highway, or any other installation that may be damaged, the blaster shall take special precautions in the loading, delaying, initiation, and confinement of each blast with mats or other methods so as to control the throw of fragments, and thus prevent bodily injury to employees.

(i) Employees authorized to prepare explosive charges or conduct blasting operations shall use every reasonable precaution including, but not limited to, visual and audible warning signals, flags, or barricades, to ensure employee safety.

(j) Insofar as possible, blasting operations above ground shall be conducted between sunup and sundown.

(k) Due precautions shall be taken to prevent accidental discharge of electric blasting caps from current induced by radar, radio transmitters, lightning, adjacent powerlines, dust storms, or other sources of extraneous electricity. These precautions shall include:

(1) Detonators shall be short-circuited in holes which have been primed and shunted until wired into the blasting circuit.

(2) The suspension of all blasting operations and removal of persons from the blasting area during the approach and progress of an electric storm;

(3) (i) The prominent display of adequate signs, warning against the use of mobile radio transmitters, on all roads within 1,000 feet of blasting operations. Whenever adherence to the 1,000-foot distance would create an operational handicap, a competent person shall be consulted to evaluate the particular situation, and alternative provisions may be made which are adequately designed to prevent any premature firing of electric blasting caps. A description of any such alternatives shall be reduced to writing and shall be certified

as meeting the purposes of this subdivision by the competent person consulted. The description shall be maintained at the construction site during the duration of the work, and shall be available for inspection by representatives of the Secretary of Labor.

(ii) Specimens of signs which would meet the requirements of paragraph (k)(3) of this section are the following:

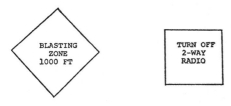

About 48" x 48"   About 42" x 36"

(4) Ensuring that mobile radio transmitters which are less than 100 feet away from electric blasting caps, in other than original containers, shall be deenergized and effectively locked;

(5) Compliance with the recommendations of The Institute of the Makers of Explosives with regard to blasting in the vicinity of radio transmitters as stipulated in Radio Frequency Energy—A Potential Hazard in the Use of Electric Blasting Caps, IME Publication No. 20, March 1971.

(l) Empty boxes and paper and fiber packing materials, which have previously contained high explosives, shall not be used again for any purpose, but shall be destroyed by burning at an approved location.

(m) Explosives, blasting agents, and blasting supplies that are obviously deteriorated or damaged shall not be used.

(n) Delivery and issue of explosives shall only be made by and to authorized persons and into authorized magazines or approved temporary storage or handling areas.

(o) Blasting operations in the proximity of overhead power lines, communication lines, utility services, or other services and structures shall not be carried on until the operators and/or owners have been notified and measures for safe control have been taken.

(p) The use of black powder shall be prohibited.

(q) All loading and firing shall be directed and supervised by competent persons thoroughly experienced in this field.

(r) All blasts shall be fired electrically with an electric blasting machine or properly designed electric power source, except as provided in § 1926.906 (a) and (r).

(s) Buildings used for the mixing of blasting agents shall conform to the requirements of this section.

(1) Buildings shall be of noncombustible construction or sheet metal on wood studs.

(2) Floors in a mixing plant shall be of concrete or of other nonabsorbent materials.

(3) All fuel oil storage facilities shall be separated from the mixing plant and located in such a manner that in case of tank rupture, the oil will drain away from the mixing plant building.

(4) The building shall be well ventilated.

(5) Heating units which do not depend on combustion processes, when properly designed and located, may be used in the building. All direct sources of heat shall be provided exclusively from units located outside the mixing building.

(6) All internal-combustion engines used for electric power generation shall be located outside the mixing plant building, or shall be properly ventilated and isolated by a firewall. The exhaust systems on all such engines shall be located so any spark emission cannot be a hazard to any materials in or adjacent to the plant.

(t) Buildings used for the mixing of water gels shall conform to the requirements of this subdivision.

(1) Buildings shall be of noncombustible construction or sheet metal on wood studs.

(2) Floors in a mixing plant shall be of concrete or of other nonabsorbent materials.

(3) Where fuel oil is used all fuel oil storage facilities shall be separated from the mixing plant and located in such a manner that in case of tank rupture, the oil will drain away from the mixing plant building.

(4) The building shall be well ventilated.

465

(5) Heating units that do not depend on combustion processes, when properly designed and located, may be used in the building. All direct sources of heat shall be provided exclusively from units located outside of the mixing building.

(6) All internal-combustion engines used for electric power generation shall be located outside the mixing plant building, or shall be properly ventilated and isolated by a firewall. The exhaust systems on all such engines shall be located so any spark emission cannot be a hazard to any materials in or adjacent to the plant.

[44 FR 8577, Feb. 9, 1979; 44 FR 20940, Apr. 6, 1979, as amended at 58 FR 35183, June 30, 1993]

§ 1926.901 Blaster qualifications.

(a) A blaster shall be able to understand and give written and oral orders.

(b) A blaster shall be in good physical condition and not be addicted to narcotics, intoxicants, or similar types of drugs.

(c) A blaster shall be qualified, by reason of training, knowledge, or experience, in the field of transporting, storing, handling, and use of explosives, and have a working knowledge of State and local laws and regulations which pertain to explosives.

(d) Blasters shall be required to furnish satisfactory evidence of competency in handling explosives and performing in a safe manner the type of blasting that will be required.

(e) The blaster shall be knowledgeable and competent in the use of each type of blasting method used.

§ 1926.902 Surface transportation of explosives.

(a) Transportation of explosives shall meet the provisions of Department of Transportation regulations contained in 46 CFR parts 146–149, Water Carriers; 49 CFR parts 171–179, Highways and Railways; 49 CFR part 195, Pipelines; and 49 CFR parts 390–397, Motor Carriers.

(b) Motor vehicles or conveyances transporting explosives shall only be driven by, and be in the charge of, a licensed driver who is physically fit. He shall be familiar with the local, State, and Federal regulation governing the transportation of explosives.

(c) No person shall smoke, or carry matches or any other flame-producing device, nor shall firearms or loaded cartridges be carried while in or near a motor vehicle or conveyance transporting explosives.

(d) Explosives, blasting agents, and blasting supplies shall not be transported with other materials or cargoes. Blasting caps (including electric) shall not be transported in the same vehicle with other explosives.

(e) Vehicles used for transporting explosives shall be strong enough to carry the load without difficulty, and shall be in good mechanical condition.

(f) When explosives are transported by a vehicle with an open body, a Class II magazine or original manufacturer's container shall be securely mounted on the bed to contain the cargo.

(g) All vehicles used for the transportation of explosives shall have tight floors and any exposed spark-producing metal on the inside of the body shall be covered with wood, or other non-sparking material, to prevent contact with containers of explosives.

(h) Every motor vehicle or conveyance used for transporting explosives shall be marked or placarded on both sides, the front, and the rear with the word "Explosives" in red letters, not less than 4 inches in height, on white background. In addition to such marking or placarding, the motor vehicle or conveyance may display, in such a manner that it will be readily visible from all directions, a red flag 18 inches by 30 inches, with the word "Explosives" painted, stamped, or sewed thereon, in white letters, at least 6 inches in height.

(i) Each vehicle used for transportation of explosives shall be equipped with a fully charged fire extinguisher, in good condition. An Underwriters Laboratory-approved extinguisher of not less than 10-ABC rating will meet the minimum requirement. The driver shall be trained in the use of the extinguisher on his vehicle.

(j) Motor vehicles or conveyances carrying explosives, blasting agents, or blasting supplies, shall not be taken inside a garage or shop for repairs or servicing.

(k) No motor vehicle transporting explosives shall be left unattended.

[44 FR 8577, Feb. 9, 1979; 44 FR 20940, Apr. 6, 1979, as amended at 58 FR 35311, June 30, 1993]

§1926.903 Underground transportation of explosives.

(a) All explosives or blasting agents in transit underground shall be taken to the place of use or storage without delay.

(b) The quantity of explosives or blasting agents taken to an underground loading area shall not exceed the amount estimated to be necessary for the blast.

(c) Explosives in transit shall not be left unattended.

(d) The hoist operator shall be notified before explosives or blasting agents are transported in a shaft conveyance.

(e) Trucks used for the transportation of explosives underground shall have the electrical system checked weekly to detect any failures which may constitute an electrical hazard. A certification record which includes the date of the inspection; the signature of the person who performed the inspection; and a serial number, or other identifier, of the truck inspected shall be prepared and the most recent certification record shall be maintained on file.

(f) The installation of auxiliary lights on truck beds, which are powered by the truck's electrical system, shall be prohibited.

(g) Explosives and blasting agents shall be hoisted, lowered, or conveyed in a powder car. No other materials, supplies, or equipment shall be transported in the same conveyance at the same time.

(h) No one, except the operator, his helper, and the powderman, shall be permitted to ride on a conveyance transporting explosives and blasting agents.

(i) No person shall ride in any shaft conveyance transporting explosives and blasting agents.

(j) No explosives or blasting agents shall be transported on any locomotive. At least two car lengths shall separate the locomotive from the powder car.

(k) No explosives or blasting agents shall be transported on a man haul trip.

(l) The car or conveyance containing explosives or blasting agents shall be pulled, not pushed, whenever possible.

(m) The powder car or conveyance especially built for the purpose of transporting explosives or blasting agents shall bear a reflectorized sign on each side with the word "Explosives" in letters, not less than 4 inches in height; upon a background of sharply contrasting color.

(n) Compartments for transporting detonators and explosives in the same car or conveyance shall be physically separated by a distance of 24 inches or by a solid partition at least 6 inches thick.

(o) Detonators and other explosives shall not be transported at the same time in any shaft conveyance.

(p) Explosives, blasting agents, or blasting supplies shall not be transported with other materials.

(q) Explosives or blasting agents, not in original containers, shall be placed in a suitable container when transported manually.

(r) Detonators, primers, and other explosives shall be carried in separate containers when transported manually.

[44 FR 8577, Feb. 9, 1979; 44 FR 20940, Apr. 6, 1979, as amended at 52 FR 36382, Sept. 28, 1987]

§1926.904 Storage of explosives and blasting agents.

(a) Explosives and related materials shall be stored in approved facilities required under the applicable provisions of the Bureau of Alcohol, Tobacco and Firearms regulations contained in 27 CFR part 55, Commerce in Explosives.

(b) Blasting caps, electric blasting caps, detonating primers, and primed cartridges shall not be stored in the same magazine with other explosives or blasting agents.

(c) Smoking and open flames shall not be permitted within 50 feet of explosives and detonator storage magazine.

(d) No explosives or blasting agents shall be permanently stored in any underground operation until the operation has been developed to the point

467

where at least two modes of exit have been provided.

(e) Permanent underground storage magazines shall be at least 300 feet from any shaft, adit, or active underground working area.

(f) Permanent underground magazines containing detonators shall not be located closer than 50 feet to any magazine containing other explosives or blasting agents.

[44 FR 8577, Feb. 9, 1979; 44 FR 20940, Apr. 6, 1979, as amended at 58 FR 35311, June 30, 1993]

§ 1926.905 Loading of explosives or blasting agents.

(a) Procedures that permit safe and efficient loading shall be established before loading is started.

(b) All drill holes shall be sufficiently large to admit freely the insertion of the cartridges of explosives.

(c) Tamping shall be done only with wood rods or plastic tamping poles without exposed metal parts, but nonsparking metal connectors may be used for jointed poles. Violent tamping shall be avoided. The primer shall never be tamped.

(d) No holes shall be loaded except those to be fired in the next round of blasting. After loading, all remaining explosives and detonators shall be immediately returned to an authorized magazine.

(e) Drilling shall not be started until all remaining butts of old holes are examined for unexploded charges, and if any are found, they shall be refired before work proceeds.

(f) No person shall be allowed to deepen drill holes which have contained explosives or blasting agents.

(g) No explosives or blasting agents shall be left unattended at the blast site.

(h) Machines and all tools not used for loading explosives into bore holes shall be removed from the immediate location of holes before explosives are delivered. Equipment shall not be operated within 50 feet of loaded holes.

(i) No activity of any nature other than that which is required for loading holes with explosives shall be permitted in a blast area.

(j) Powerlines and portable electric cables for equipment being used shall be kept a safe distance from explosives or blasting agents being loaded into drill holes. Cables in the proximity of the blast area shall be deenergized and locked out by the blaster.

(k) Holes shall be checked prior to loading to determine depth and conditions. Where a hole has been loaded with explosives but the explosives have failed to detonate, there shall be no drilling within 50 feet of the hole.

(l) When loading a long line of holes with more than one loading crew, the crews shall be separated by practical distance consistent with efficient operation and supervision of crews.

(m) No explosive shall be loaded or used underground in the presence of combustible gases or combustible dusts.

(n) No explosives other than those in Fume Class 1, as set forth by the Institute of Makers of Explosives, shall be used; however, explosives complying with the requirements of Fume Class 2 and Fume Class 3 may be used if adequate ventilation has been provided.

(o) All blast holes in open work shall be stemmed to the collar or to a point which will confine the charge.

(p) Warning signs, indicating a blast area, shall be maintained at all approaches to the blast area. The warning sign lettering shall not be less than 4 inches in height on a contrasting background.

(q) A bore hole shall never be sprung when it is adjacent to or near a hole that is loaded. Flashlight batteries shall not be used for springing holes.

(r) Drill holes which have been sprung or chambered, and which are not water-filled, shall be allowed to cool before explosives are loaded.

(s) No loaded holes shall be left unattended or unprotected.

(t) The blaster shall keep an accurate, up-to-date record of explosives, blasting agents, and blasting supplies used in a blast and shall keep an accurate running inventory of all explosives and blasting agents stored on the operation.

(u) When loading blasting agents pneumatically over electric blasting caps, semiconductive delivery hose shall be used and the equipment shall be bonded and grounded.

[44 FR 8577, Feb. 9, 1979; 44 FR 20940, Apr. 6, 1979, as amended at 58 FR 35184, June 30, 1993]

§1926.906 Initiation of explosive charges—electric blasting.

(a) Electric blasting caps shall not be used where sources of extraneous electricity make the use of electric blasting caps dangerous. Blasting cap leg wires shall be kept short-circuited (shunted) until they are connected into the circuit for firing.

(b) Before adopting any system of electrical firing, the blaster shall conduct a thorough survey for extraneous currents, and all dangerous currents shall be eliminated before any holes are loaded.

(c) In any single blast using electric blasting caps, all caps shall be of the same style or function, and of the same manufacture.

(d) Electric blasting shall be carried out by using blasting circuits or power circuits in accordance with the electric blasting cap manufacturer's recommendations, or an approved contractor or his designated representative.

(e) When firing a circuit of electric blasting caps, care must be exercised to ensure that an adequate quantity of delivered current is available, in accordance with the manufacturer's recommendations.

(f) Connecting wires and lead wires shall be insulated single solid wires of sufficient current-carrying capacity.

(g) Bus wires shall be solid single wires of sufficient current-carrying capacity.

(h) When firing electrically, the insulation on all firing lines shall be adequate and in good condition.

(i) A power circuit used for firing electric blasting caps shall not be grounded.

(j) In underground operations when firing from a power circuit, a safety switch shall be placed in the permanent firing line at intervals. This switch shall be made so it can be locked only in the "Off" position and shall be provided with a short-circuiting arrangement of the firing lines to the cap circuit.

(k) In underground operations there shall be a "lightning" gap of at least 5 feet in the firing system ahead of the main firing switch; that is, between this switch and the source of power.

This gap shall be bridged by a flexible jumper cord just before firing the blast.

(l) When firing from a power circuit, the firing switch shall be locked in the open or "Off" position at all times, except when firing. It shall be so designed that the firing lines to the cap circuit are automatically short-circuited when the switch is in the "Off" position. Keys to this switch shall be entrusted only to the blaster.

(m) Blasting machines shall be in good condition and the efficiency of the machine shall be tested periodically to make certain that it can deliver power at its rated capacity.

(n) When firing with blasting machines, the connections shall be made as recommended by the manufacturer of the electric blasting caps used.

(o) The number of electric blasting caps connected to a blasting machine shall not be in excess of its rated capacity. Furthermore, in primary blasting, a series circuit shall contain no more caps than the limits recommended by the manufacturer of the electric blasting caps in use.

(p) The blaster shall be in charge of the blasting machines, and no other person shall connect the leading wires to the machine.

(q) Blasters, when testing circuits to charged holes, shall use only blasting galvanometers or other instruments that are specifically designed for this purpose.

(r) Whenever the possibility exists that a leading line or blasting wire might be thrown over a live powerline by the force of an explosion, care shall be taken to see that the total length of wires are kept too short to hit the lines, or that the wires are securely anchored to the ground. If neither of these requirements can be satisfied, a nonelectric system shall be used.

(s) In electrical firing, only the man making leading wire connections shall fire the shot. All connections shall be made from the bore hole back to the source of firing current, and the leading wires shall remain shorted and not be connected to the blasting machine or other source of current until the charge is to be fired.

(t) After firing an electric blast from a blasting machine, the leading wires shall be immediately disconnected from the machine and short-circuited.

[44 FR 8577, Feb. 9, 1979; 44 FR 20940, Apr. 6, 1979, as amended at 63 FR 33469, June 18, 1998]

§ 1926.907   Use of safety fuse.

(a) Safety fuse shall only be used where sources of extraneous electricity make the use of electric blasting caps dangerous. The use of a fuse that has been hammered or injured in any way shall be forbidden.

(b) The hanging of a fuse on nails or other projections which will cause a sharp bend to be formed in the fuse is prohibited.

(c) Before capping safety fuse, a short length shall be cut from the end of the supply reel so as to assure a fresh cut end in each blasting cap.

(d) Only a cap crimper of approved design shall be used for attaching blasting caps to safety fuse. Crimpers shall be kept in good repair and accessible for use.

(e) No unused cap or short capped fuse shall be placed in any hole to be blasted; such unused detonators shall be removed from the working place and destroyed.

(f) No fuse shall be capped, or primers made up, in any magazine or near any possible source of ignition.

(g) No one shall be permitted to carry detonators or primers of any kind on his person.

(h) The minimum length of safety fuse to be used in blasting shall be as required by State law, but shall not be less than 30 inches.

(i) At least two men shall be present when multiple cap and fuse blasting is done by hand lighting methods.

(j) Not more than 12 fuses shall be lighted by each blaster when hand lighting devices are used. However, when two or more safety fuses in a group are lighted as one by means of igniter cord, or other similar fuse-lighting devices, they may be considered as one fuse.

(k) The so-called "drop fuse" method of dropping or pushing a primer or any explosive with a lighted fuse attached is forbidden.

(l) Cap and fuse shall not be used for firing mudcap charges unless charges are separated sufficiently to prevent one charge from dislodging other shots in the blast.

(m) When blasting with safety fuses, consideration shall be given to the length and burning rate of the fuse. Sufficient time, with a margin of safety, shall always be provided for the blaster to reach a place of safety.

§ 1926.908   Use of detonating cord.

(a) Care shall be taken to select a detonating cord consistent with the type and physical condition of the bore hole and stemming and the type of explosives used.

(b) Detonating cord shall be handled and used with the same respect and care given other explosives.

(c) The line of detonating cord extending out of a bore hole or from a charge shall be cut from the supply spool before loading the remainder of the bore hole or placing additional charges.

(d) Detonating cord shall be handled and used with care to avoid damaging or severing the cord during and after loading and hooking-up.

(e) Detonating cord connections shall be competent and positive in accordance with approved and recommended methods. Knot-type or other cord-to-cord connections shall be made only with detonating cord in which the explosive core is dry.

(f) All detonating cord trunklines and branchlines shall be free of loops, sharp kinks, or angles that direct the cord back toward the oncoming line of detonation.

(g) All detonating cord connections shall be inspected before firing the blast.

(h) When detonating cord millisecond-delay connectors or short-interval-delay electric blasting caps are used with detonating cord, the practice shall conform strictly to the manufacturer's recommendations.

(i) When connecting a blasting cap or an electric blasting cap to detonating cord, the cap shall be taped or otherwise attached securely along the side or the end of the detonating cord, with the end of the cap containing the explosive charge pointed in the direction in which the detonation is to proceed.

(j) Detonators for firing the trunkline shall not be brought to the loading area nor attached to the detonating cord until everything else is in readiness for the blast.

§1926.909 Firing the blast.

(a) A code of blasting signals equivalent to Table U–1, shall be posted on one or more conspicuous places at the operation, and all employees shall be required to familiarize themselves with the code and conform to it. Danger signs shall be placed at suitable locations.

(b) Before a blast is fired, a loud warning signal shall be given by the blaster in charge, who has made certain that all surplus explosives are in a safe place and all employees, vehicles, and equipment are at a safe distance, or under sufficient cover.

(c) Flagmen shall be safely stationed on highways which pass through the danger zone so as to stop traffic during blasting operations.

(d) It shall be the duty of the blaster to fix the time of blasting.

(e) Before firing an underground blast, warning shall be given, and all possible entries into the blasting area, and any entrances to any working place where a drift, raise, or other opening is about to hole through, shall be carefully guarded. The blaster shall make sure that all employees are out of the blast area before firing a blast.

TABLE U–1

WARNING SIGNAL—A 1-minute series of long blasts 5 minutes prior to blast signal.
BLAST SIGNAL—A series of short blasts 1 minute prior to the shot.
ALL CLEAR SIGNAL—A prolonged blast following the inspection of blast area.

§1926.910 Inspection after blasting.

(a) Immediately after the blast has been fired, the firing line shall be disconnected from the blasting machine, or where power switches are used, they shall be locked open or in the off position.

(b) Sufficient time shall be allowed, not less than 15 minutes in tunnels, for the smoke and fumes to leave the blasted area before returning to the shot. An inspection of the area and the surrounding rubble shall be made by the blaster to determine if all charges have been exploded before employees are allowed to return to the operation,

and in tunnels, after the muck pile has been wetted down.

§1926.911 Misfires.

(a) If a misfire is found, the blaster shall provide proper safeguards for excluding all employees from the danger zone.

(b) No other work shall be done except that necessary to remove the hazard of the misfire and only those employees necessary to do the work shall remain in the danger zone.

(c) No attempt shall be made to extract explosives from any charged or misfired hole; a new primer shall be put in and the hole reblasted. If refiring of the misfired hole presents a hazard, the explosives may be removed by washing out with water or, where the misfire is under water, blown out with air.

(d) If there are any misfires while using cap and fuse, all employees shall remain away from the charge for at least 1 hour. Misfires shall be handled under the direction of the person in charge of the blasting. All wires shall be carefully traced and a search made for unexploded charges.

(e) No drilling, digging, or picking shall be permitted until all missed holes have been detonated or the authorized representative has approved that work can proceed.

§1926.912 Underwater blasting.

(a) A blaster shall conduct all blasting operations, and no shot shall be fired without his approval.

(b) Loading tubes and casings of dissimilar metals shall not be used because of possible electric transient currents from galvanic action of the metals and water.

(c) Only water-resistant blasting caps and detonating cords shall be used for all marine blasting. Loading shall be done through a nonsparking metal loading tube when tube is necessary.

(d) No blast shall be fired while any vessel under way is closer than 1,500 feet to the blasting area. Those on board vessels or craft moored or anchored within 1,500 feet shall be notified before a blast is fired.

(e) No blast shall be fired while any swimming or diving operations are in progress in the vicinity of the blasting

471

area. If such operations are in progress, signals and arrangements shall be agreed upon to assure that no blast shall be fired while any person is in the water.

(f) Blasting flags shall be displayed.

(g) The storage and handling of explosives aboard vessels used in underwater blasting operations shall be according to provisions outlined herein on handling and storing explosives.

(h) When more than one charge is placed under water, a float device shall be attached to an element of each charge in such manner that it will be released by the firing. Misfires shall be handled in accordance with the requirements of § 1926.911.

§ 1926.913 Blasting in excavation work under compressed air.

(a) Detonators and explosives shall not be stored or kept in tunnels, shafts, or caissons. Detonators and explosives for each round shall be taken directly from the magazines to the blasting zone and immediately loaded. Detonators and explosives left over after loading a round shall be removed from the working chamber before the connecting wires are connected up.

(b) When detonators or explosives are brought into an air lock, no employee except the powderman, blaster, lock tender and the employees necessary for carrying, shall be permitted to enter the air lock. No other material, supplies, or equipment shall be locked through with the explosives.

(c) Detonators and explosives shall be taken separately into pressure working chambers.

(d) The blaster or powderman shall be responsible for the receipt, unloading, storage, and on-site transportation of explosives and detonators.

(e) All metal pipes, rails, air locks, and steel tunnel lining shall be electrically bonded together and grounded at or near the portal or shaft, and such pipes and rails shall be cross-bonded together at not less than 1,000-foot intervals throughout the length of the tunnel. In addition, each low air supply pipe shall be grounded at its delivery end.

(f) The explosives suitable for use in wet holes shall be water-resistant and shall be Fume Class 1.

(g) When tunnel excavation in rock face is approaching mixed face, and when tunnel excavation is in mixed face, blasting shall be performed with light charges and with light burden on each hole. Advance drilling shall be performed as tunnel excavation in rock face approaches mixed face, to determine the general nature and extent of rock cover and the remaining distance ahead to soft ground as excavation advances.

§ 1926.914 Definitions applicable to this subpart.

(a) *American Table of Distances* (also known as Quantity Distance Tables) means American Table of Distances for Storage of Explosives as revised and approved by the Institute of the Makers of Explosives, June 5, 1964.

(b) *Approved storage facility*—A facility for the storage of explosive materials conforming to the requirements of this part and covered by a license or permit issued under authority of the Bureau of Alcohol, Tobacco and Firearms. (See 27 CFR part 55)

(c) *Blast area*—The area in which explosives loading and blasting operations are being conducted.

(d) *Blaster*—The person or persons authorized to use explosives for blasting purposes and meeting the qualifications contained in § 1926.901.

(e) *Blasting agent*—A blasting agent is any material or mixture consisting of a fuel and oxidizer used for blasting, but not classified an explosive and in which none of the ingredients is classified as an explosive provided the furnished (mixed) product cannot be detonated with a No. 8 test blasting cap when confined. A common blasting agent presently in use is a mixture of ammonium nitrate (NH_4 NO_3) and carbonaceous combustibles, such as fuel oil or coal, and may either be procured, premixed and packaged from explosives companies or mixed in the field.

(f) *Blasting cap*—A metallic tube closed at one end, containing a charge of one or more detonating compounds, and designed for and capable of detonation from the sparks or flame from a safety fuse inserted and crimped into the open end.

(g) *Block holing*—The breaking of boulders by firing a charge of explosives that has been loaded in a drill hole.

(h) *Conveyance*—Any unit for transporting explosives or blasting agents, including but not limited to trucks, trailers, rail cars, barges, and vessels.

(i) *Detonating cord*—A flexible cord containing a center core of high explosives which when detonated, will have sufficient strength to detonate other cap-sensitive explosives with which it is in contact.

(j) *Detonator*—Blasting caps, electric blasting caps, delay electric blasting caps, and nonelectric delay blasting caps.

(k) *Electric blasting cap*—A blasting cap designed for and capable of detonation by means of an electric current.

(l) *Electric blasting circuitry*—

(1) Bus wire. An expendable wire, used in parallel or series, in parallel circuits, to which are connected the leg wires of electric blasting caps.

(2) Connecting wire. An insulated expendable wire used between electric blasting caps and the leading wires or between the bus wire and the leading wires.

(3) Leading wire. An insulated wire used between the electric power source and the electric blasting cap circuit.

(4) Permanent blasting wire. A permanently mounted insulated wire used between the electric power source and the electric blasting cap circuit.

(m) *Electric delay blasting caps*—Caps designed to detonate at a predetermined period of time after energy is applied to the ignition system.

(n) *Explosives*—(1) Any chemical compound, mixture, or device, the primary or common purpose of which is to function by explosion; that is, with substantially instantaneous release of gas and heat, unless such compound, mixture or device is otherwise specifically classified by the U.S. Department of Transportation.

(2) All material which is classified as Class A, Class B, and Class C Explosives by the U.S. Department of Transportation.

(3) Classification of explosives by the U.S. Department of Transportation is as follows:

Class A Explosives. Possessing detonating hazard, such as dynamite, nitroglycerin, picric acid, lead azide, fulminate of mercury, black powder, blasting caps, and detonating primers.

Class B Explosives. Possessing flammable hazard, such as propellant explosives, including some smokeless propellants.

Class C Explosives. Include certain types of manufactured articles which contain Class A or Class B explosives, or both, as components, but in restricted quantities.

(o) *Fuse lighters*—Special devices for the purpose of igniting safety fuse.

(p) *Magazine*—Any building or structure, other than an explosives manufacturing building, used for the storage of explosives.

(q) *Misfire*—An explosive charge which failed to detonate.

(r) *Mud-capping* (sometimes known as bulldozing, adobe blasting, or dobying). The blasting of boulders by placing a quantity of explosives against a rock, boulder, or other object without confining the explosives in a drill hole.

(s) *Nonelectric delay blasting cap*—A blasting cap with an integral delay element in conjunction with and capable of being detonated by a detonation impulse or signal from miniaturized detonating cord.

(t) *Primary blasting*—The blasting operation by which the original rock formation is dislodged from its natural location.

(u) *Primer*—A cartridge or container of explosives into which a detonator or detonating cord is inserted or attached.

(v) *Safety fuse*—A flexible cord containing an internal burning medium by which fire is conveyed at a continuous and uniform rate for the purpose of firing blasting caps.

(w) *Secondary blasting*—The reduction of oversize material by the use of explosives to the dimension required for handling, including mudcapping and blockholing.

(x) *Stemming*—A suitable inert incombustible material or device used to confine or separate explosives in a drill hole, or to cover explosives in mud-capping.

(y) *Springing*—The creation of a pocket in the bottom of a drill hole by the use of a moderate quantity of explosives in order that larger quantities or explosives may be inserted therein.

(z) *Water gels, or slurry explosives*—A wide variety of materials used for blasting. They all contain substantial proportions of water and high proportions of ammonium nitrate, some of which is in solution in the water. Two broad classes of water gels are: (1) Those which are sensitized by a material classed as an explosive, such as TNT or smokeless powder, and (2) those which contain no ingredient classified as an explosive; these are sensitized with metals such as aluminum or with other fuels. Water gels may be premixed at an explosives plant or mixed at the site immediately before delivery into the bore hole.

(aa) *Semiconductive hose.* Semiconductive hose—a hose with an electrical resistance high enough to limit flow of stray electric currents to safe levels, yet not so high as to prevent drainage of static electric charges to ground; hose of not more than 2 megohms resistance over its entire length and of not less than 5,000 ohms per foot meets the requirement.

[44 FR 8577, Feb. 9, 1979; 44 FR 20940, Apr. 6, 1979, as amended at 58 FR 35184 and 35311, June 30, 1993]

Subpart V—Electric Power Transmission and Distribution

SOURCE: 79 FR 20696, Apr. 11, 2014, unless otherwise noted.

AUTHORITY: 40 U.S.C. 3701 *et seq.*; 29 U.S.C. 653, 655, 657; Secretary of Labor's Order No. 1-2012 (77 FR 3912); and 29 CFR Part 1911.

§ 1926.950 General.

(a) *Application*—(1) *Scope.* (i) This subpart, except for paragraph (a)(3) of this section, covers the construction of electric power transmission and distribution lines and equipment. As used in this subpart, the term "construction" includes the erection of new electric transmission and distribution lines and equipment, and the alteration, conversion, and improvement of existing electric transmission and distribution lines and equipment.

NOTE TO PARAGRAPH (a)(1)(i): An employer that complies with § 1910.269 of this chapter will be considered in compliance with requirements in this subpart that do not reference other subparts of this part. Compli-

ance with § 1910.269 of this chapter will not excuse an employer from compliance obligations under other subparts of this part.

(ii) Notwithstanding paragraph (a)(1)(i) of this section, this subpart does not apply to electrical safety-related work practices for unqualified employees.

(2) *Other part 1926 standards.* This subpart applies in addition to all other applicable standards contained in this part 1926. Employers covered under this subpart are not exempt from complying with other applicable provisions in part 1926 by the operation of § 1910.5(c) of this chapter. Specific references in this subpart to other sections of part 1926 are provided for emphasis only.

(3) *Applicable part 1910 requirements.* Line-clearance tree-trimming operations and work involving electric power generation installations shall comply with § 1910.269 of this chapter.

(b) *Training*—(1) *All employees.* (i) Each employee shall be trained in, and familiar with, the safety-related work practices, safety procedures, and other safety requirements in this subpart that pertain to his or her job assignments.

(ii) Each employee shall also be trained in and familiar with any other safety practices, including applicable emergency procedures (such as pole-top and manhole rescue), that are not specifically addressed by this subpart but that are related to his or her work and are necessary for his or her safety.

(iii) The degree of training shall be determined by the risk to the employee for the hazard involved.

(2) *Qualified employees.* Each qualified employee shall also be trained and competent in:

(i) The skills and techniques necessary to distinguish exposed live parts from other parts of electric equipment,

(ii) The skills and techniques necessary to determine the nominal voltage of exposed live parts,

(iii) The minimum approach distances specified in this subpart corresponding to the voltages to which the qualified employee will be exposed and the skills and techniques necessary to maintain those distances,

(iv) The proper use of the special precautionary techniques, personal protective equipment, insulating and shielding materials, and insulated tools for working on or near exposed energized parts of electric equipment, and

(v) The recognition of electrical hazards to which the employee may be exposed and the skills and techniques necessary to control or avoid these hazards.

NOTE TO PARAGRAPH (b)(2): For the purposes of this subpart, a person must have the training required by paragraph (b)(2) of this section to be considered a qualified person.

(3) *Supervision and annual inspection.* The employer shall determine, through regular supervision and through inspections conducted on at least an annual basis, that each employee is complying with the safety-related work practices required by this subpart.

(4) *Additional training.* An employee shall receive additional training (or retraining) under any of the following conditions:

(i) If the supervision or annual inspections required by paragraph (b)(3) of this section indicate that the employee is not complying with the safety-related work practices required by this subpart, or

(ii) If new technology, new types of equipment, or changes in procedures necessitate the use of safety-related work practices that are different from those which the employee would normally use, or

(iii) If he or she must employ safety-related work practices that are not normally used during his or her regular job duties.

NOTE TO PARAGRAPH (b)(4)(iii): The Occupational Safety and Health Administration considers tasks that are performed less often than once per year to necessitate retraining before the performance of the work practices involved.

(5) *Type of training.* The training required by paragraph (b) of this section shall be of the classroom or on-the-job type.

(6) *Training goals.* The training shall establish employee proficiency in the work practices required by this subpart and shall introduce the procedures necessary for compliance with this subpart.

(7) *Demonstration of proficiency.* The employer shall ensure that each employee has demonstrated proficiency in the work practices involved before that employee is considered as having completed the training required by paragraph (b) of this section.

NOTE 1 TO PARAGRAPH (b)(7): Though they are not required by this paragraph, employment records that indicate that an employee has successfully completed the required training are one way of keeping track of when an employee has demonstrated proficiency.

NOTE 2 TO PARAGRAPH (b)(7): For an employee with previous training, an employer may determine that that employee has demonstrated the proficiency required by this paragraph using the following process: (1) Confirm that the employee has the training required by paragraph (b) of this section, (2) use an examination or interview to make an initial determination that the employee understands the relevant safety-related work practices before he or she performs any work covered by this subpart, and (3) supervise the employee closely until that employee has demonstrated proficiency as required by this paragraph.

(c) *Information transfer—*(1) *Host employer responsibilities.* Before work begins, the host employer shall inform contract employers of:

(i) The characteristics of the host employer's installation that are related to the safety of the work to be performed and are listed in paragraphs (d)(1) through (d)(5) of this section;

NOTE TO PARAGRAPH (c)(1)(i): This paragraph requires the host employer to obtain information listed in paragraphs (d)(1) through (d)(5) of this section if it does not have this information in existing records.

(ii) Conditions that are related to the safety of the work to be performed, that are listed in paragraphs (d)(6) through (d)(8) of this section, and that are known to the host employer;

NOTE TO PARAGRAPH (c)(1)(ii): For the purposes of this paragraph, the host employer need only provide information to contract employers that the host employer can obtain from its existing records through the exercise of reasonable diligence. This paragraph does not require the host employer to make inspections of worksite conditions to obtain this information.

(iii) Information about the design and operation of the host employer's installation that the contract employer needs to make the assessments required by this subpart; and

NOTE TO PARAGRAPH (c)(1)(iii): This paragraph requires the host employer to obtain information about the design and operation of its installation that contract employers need to make required assessments if it does not have this information in existing records.

(iv) Any other information about the design and operation of the host employer's installation that is known by the host employer, that the contract employer requests, and that is related to the protection of the contract employer's employees.

NOTE TO PARAGRAPH (c)(1)(iv): For the purposes of this paragraph, the host employer need only provide information to contract employers that the host employer can obtain from its existing records through the exercise of reasonable diligence. This paragraph does not require the host employer to make inspections of worksite conditions to obtain this information.

(2) *Contract employer responsibilities.* (i) The contract employer shall ensure that each of its employees is instructed in the hazardous conditions relevant to the employee's work that the contract employer is aware of as a result of information communicated to the contract employer by the host employer under paragraph (c)(1) of this section.

(ii) Before work begins, the contract employer shall advise the host employer of any unique hazardous conditions presented by the contract employer's work.

(iii) The contract employer shall advise the host employer of any unanticipated hazardous conditions found during the contract employer's work that the host employer did not mention under paragraph (c)(1) of this section. The contract employer shall provide this information to the host employer within 2 working days after discovering the hazardous condition.

(3) *Joint host- and contract-employer responsibilities.* The contract employer and the host employer shall coordinate their work rules and procedures so that each employee of the contract employer and the host employer is protected as required by this subpart.

(d) *Existing characteristics and conditions.* Existing characteristics and conditions of electric lines and equipment that are related to the safety of the work to be performed shall be determined before work on or near the lines or equipment is started. Such characteristics and conditions include, but are not limited to:

(1) The nominal voltages of lines and equipment,

(2) The maximum switching-transient voltages,

(3) The presence of hazardous induced voltages,

(4) The presence of protective grounds and equipment grounding conductors,

(5) The locations of circuits and equipment, including electric supply lines, communication lines, and fire-protective signaling circuits,

(6) The condition of protective grounds and equipment grounding conductors,

(7) The condition of poles, and

(8) Environmental conditions relating to safety.

§ 1926.951   Medical services and first aid.

(a) *General.* The employer shall provide medical services and first aid as required in § 1926.50.

(b) *First-aid training.* In addition to the requirements of § 1926.50, when employees are performing work on, or associated with, exposed lines or equipment energized at 50 volts or more, persons with first-aid training shall be available as follows:

(1) *Field work.* For field work involving two or more employees at a work location, at least two trained persons shall be available.

(2) *Fixed work locations.* For fixed work locations such as substations, the number of trained persons available shall be sufficient to ensure that each employee exposed to electric shock can be reached within 4 minutes by a trained person. However, where the existing number of employees is insufficient to meet this requirement (at a remote substation, for example), each employee at the work location shall be a trained employee.

§ 1926.952   Job briefing.

(a) *Before each job—(1) Information provided by the employer.* In assigning an employee or a group of employees to perform a job, the employer shall provide the employee in charge of the job with all available information that relates to the determination of existing characteristics and conditions required by § 1926.950(d).

(2) *Briefing by the employee in charge.* The employer shall ensure that the employee in charge conducts a job briefing that meets paragraphs (b), (c), and (d) of this section with the employees involved before they start each job.

(b) *Subjects to be covered.* The briefing shall cover at least the following subjects: Hazards associated with the job, work procedures involved, special precautions, energy-source controls, and personal protective equipment requirements.

(c) *Number of briefings*—(1) *At least one before each day or shift.* If the work or operations to be performed during the work day or shift are repetitive and similar, at least one job briefing shall be conducted before the start of the first job of each day or shift.

(2) *Additional briefings.* Additional job briefings shall be held if significant changes, which might affect the safety of the employees, occur during the course of the work.

(d) *Extent of briefing*—(1) *Short discussion.* A brief discussion is satisfactory if the work involved is routine and if the employees, by virtue of training and experience, can reasonably be expected to recognize and avoid the hazards involved in the job.

(2) *Detailed discussion.* A more extensive discussion shall be conducted:

(i) If the work is complicated or particularly hazardous, or

(ii) If the employee cannot be expected to recognize and avoid the hazards involved in the job.

NOTE TO PARAGRAPH (d): The briefing must address all the subjects listed in paragraph (b) of this section.

(e) *Working alone.* An employee working alone need not conduct a job briefing. However, the employer shall ensure that the tasks to be performed are planned as if a briefing were required.

§ 1926.953 Enclosed spaces.

(a) *General.* This section covers enclosed spaces that may be entered by employees. It does not apply to vented vaults if the employer makes a determination that the ventilation system is operating to protect employees before they enter the space. This section applies to routine entry into enclosed spaces. If, after the employer takes the precautions given in this section and in § 1926.965, the hazards remaining in the enclosed space endanger the life of an entrant or could interfere with an entrant's escape from the space, then entry into the enclosed space shall meet the permit-space entry requirements of paragraphs (d) through (k) of § 1910.146 of this chapter.

(b) *Safe work practices.* The employer shall ensure the use of safe work practices for entry into, and work in, enclosed spaces and for rescue of employees from such spaces.

(c) *Training.* Each employee who enters an enclosed space or who serves as an attendant shall be trained in the hazards of enclosed-space entry, in enclosed-space entry procedures, and in enclosed-space rescue procedures.

(d) *Rescue equipment.* Employers shall provide equipment to ensure the prompt and safe rescue of employees from the enclosed space.

(e) *Evaluating potential hazards.* Before any entrance cover to an enclosed space is removed, the employer shall determine whether it is safe to do so by checking for the presence of any atmospheric pressure or temperature differences and by evaluating whether there might be a hazardous atmosphere in the space. Any conditions making it unsafe to remove the cover shall be eliminated before the cover is removed.

NOTE TO PARAGRAPH (e): The determination called for in this paragraph may consist of a check of the conditions that might foreseeably be in the enclosed space. For example, the cover could be checked to see if it is hot and, if it is fastened in place, could be loosened gradually to release any residual pressure. An evaluation also needs to be made of whether conditions at the site could cause a hazardous atmosphere, such as an oxygen-deficient or flammable atmosphere, to develop within the space.

(f) *Removing covers.* When covers are removed from enclosed spaces, the opening shall be promptly guarded by a railing, temporary cover, or other barrier designed to prevent an accidental fall through the opening and to protect employees working in the space from objects entering the space.

(g) *Hazardous atmosphere.* Employees may not enter any enclosed space while it contains a hazardous atmosphere, unless the entry conforms to the permit-required confined spaces standard in § 1910.146 of this chapter.

(h) *Attendants.* While work is being performed in the enclosed space, an attendant with first-aid training shall be immediately available outside the enclosed space to provide assistance if a hazard exists because of traffic patterns in the area of the opening used for entry. The attendant is not precluded from performing other duties outside the enclosed space if these duties do not distract the attendant from: Monitoring employees within the space or ensuring that it is safe for employees to enter and exit the space.

NOTE TO PARAGRAPH (h): See § 1926.965 for additional requirements on attendants for work in manholes and vaults.

(i) *Calibration of test instruments.* Test instruments used to monitor atmospheres in enclosed spaces shall be kept in calibration and shall have a minimum accuracy of ±10 percent.

(j) *Testing for oxygen deficiency.* Before an employee enters an enclosed space, the atmosphere in the enclosed space shall be tested for oxygen deficiency with a direct-reading meter or similar instrument, capable of collection and immediate analysis of data samples without the need for off-site evaluation. If continuous forced-air ventilation is provided, testing is not required provided that the procedures used ensure that employees are not exposed to the hazards posed by oxygen deficiency.

(k) *Testing for flammable gases and vapors.* Before an employee enters an enclosed space, the internal atmosphere shall be tested for flammable gases and vapors with a direct-reading meter or similar instrument capable of collection and immediate analysis of data samples without the need for off-site evaluation. This test shall be performed after the oxygen testing and ventilation required by paragraph (j) of this section demonstrate that there is sufficient oxygen to ensure the accuracy of the test for flammability.

(l) *Ventilation, and monitoring for flammable gases or vapors.* If flammable gases or vapors are detected or if an oxygen deficiency is found, forced-air ventilation shall be used to maintain oxygen at a safe level and to prevent a hazardous concentration of flammable gases and vapors from accumulating. A continuous monitoring program to ensure that no increase in flammable gas or vapor concentration above safe levels occurs may be followed in lieu of ventilation if flammable gases or vapors are initially detected at safe levels.

NOTE TO PARAGRAPH (l): See the definition of "hazardous atmosphere" for guidance in determining whether a specific concentration of a substance is hazardous.

(m) *Specific ventilation requirements.* If continuous forced-air ventilation is used, it shall begin before entry is made and shall be maintained long enough for the employer to be able to demonstrate that a safe atmosphere exists before employees are allowed to enter the work area. The forced-air ventilation shall be so directed as to ventilate the immediate area where employees are present within the enclosed space and shall continue until all employees leave the enclosed space.

(n) *Air supply.* The air supply for the continuous forced-air ventilation shall be from a clean source and may not increase the hazards in the enclosed space.

(o) *Open flames.* If open flames are used in enclosed spaces, a test for flammable gases and vapors shall be made immediately before the open flame device is used and at least once per hour while the device is used in the space. Testing shall be conducted more frequently if conditions present in the enclosed space indicate that once per hour is insufficient to detect hazardous accumulations of flammable gases or vapors.

NOTE TO PARAGRAPH (o): See the definition of "hazardous atmosphere" for guidance in determining whether a specific concentration of a substance is hazardous.

NOTE TO § 1926.953: Entries into enclosed spaces conducted in accordance with the permit-space entry requirements of paragraphs (d) through (k) of § 1910.146 of this chapter are considered as complying with this section.

EFFECTIVE DATE NOTE: At 80 FR 25518, May 4, 2015, §1926.953 was amended by revising paragraphs (a) and (g) and the note at the end of the section, effective Aug. 3, 2015. For the convenience of the user, the revised text is set forth as follows:

§1926.953 Enclosed spaces.

(a) *General.* This section covers enclosed spaces that may be entered by employees. It does not apply to vented vaults if the employer makes a determination that the ventilation system is operating to protect employees before they enter the space. This section applies to routine entry into enclosed spaces. If, after the employer takes the precautions given in this section and in §1926.965, the hazards remaining in the enclosed space endanger the life of an entrant or could interfere with an entrant's escape from the space, then entry into the enclosed space must meet the permit space entry requirements of subpart AA of this part. For routine entries where the hazards remaining in the enclosed space do not endanger the life of an entrant or interfere with an entrant's escape from the space, this section applies in lieu of the permit-space entry requirements contained in §§1926.1204 through 926.1211.

*   *   *   *   *

(g) *Hazardous atmosphere.* Employees may not enter any enclosed space while it contains a hazardous atmosphere, unless the entry conforms to the confined spaces in construction standard in subpart AA of this part.

*   *   *   *   *

NOTE TO §1926.953.: Entries into enclosed spaces conducted in accordance with the permit space entry requirements of subpart AA of this part are considered as complying with this section.

§1926.954 Personal protective equipment.

(a) *General.* Personal protective equipment shall meet the requirements of subpart E of this part.

NOTE TO PARAGRAPH (a): Paragraph (d) of §1926.95 sets employer payment obligations for the personal protective equipment required by this subpart, including, but not limited to, the fall protection equipment required by paragraph (b) of this section, the electrical protective equipment required by §1926.960(c), and the flame-resistant and arc-rated clothing and other protective equipment required by §1926.960(g).

(b) *Fall protection*—(1) *Personal fall arrest systems.* (i) Personal fall arrest systems shall meet the requirements of subpart M of this part.

(ii) Personal fall arrest equipment used by employees who are exposed to hazards from flames or electric arcs, as determined by the employer under §1926.960(g)(1), shall be capable of passing a drop test equivalent to that required by paragraph (b)(2)(xii) of this section after exposure to an electric arc with a heat energy of 40±5 cal/cm².

(2) *Work-positioning equipment.* Body belts and positioning straps for work-positioning equipment shall meet the following requirements:

(i) Hardware for body belts and positioning straps shall meet the following requirements:

(A) Hardware shall be made of drop-forged steel, pressed steel, formed steel, or equivalent material.

(B) Hardware shall have a corrosion-resistant finish.

(C) Hardware surfaces shall be smooth and free of sharp edges.

(ii) Buckles shall be capable of withstanding an 8.9-kilonewton (2,000-pound-force) tension test with a maximum permanent deformation no greater than 0.4 millimeters (0.0156 inches).

(iii) D rings shall be capable of withstanding a 22-kilonewton (5,000-pound-force) tensile test without cracking or breaking.

(iv) Snaphooks shall be capable of withstanding a 22-kilonewton (5,000-pound-force) tension test without failure.

NOTE TO PARAGRAPH (b)(2)(iv): Distortion of the snaphook sufficient to release the keeper is considered to be tensile failure of a snaphook.

(v) Top grain leather or leather substitute may be used in the manufacture of body belts and positioning straps; however, leather and leather substitutes may not be used alone as a load-bearing component of the assembly.

(vi) Plied fabric used in positioning straps and in load-bearing parts of body belts shall be constructed in such a way that no raw edges are exposed and the plies do not separate.

(vii) Positioning straps shall be capable of withstanding the following tests:

(A) A dielectric test of 819.7 volts, AC, per centimeter (25,000 volts per foot) for 3 minutes without visible deterioration;

(B) A leakage test of 98.4 volts, AC, per centimeter (3,000 volts per foot) with a leakage current of no more than 1 mA;

NOTE TO PARAGRAPHS (b)(2)(vii)(A) AND (b)(2)(vii)(B): Positioning straps that pass direct-current tests at equivalent voltages are considered as meeting this requirement.

(C) Tension tests of 20 kilonewtons (4,500 pounds-force) for sections free of buckle holes and of 15 kilonewtons (3,500 pounds-force) for sections with buckle holes;

(D) A buckle-tear test with a load of 4.4 kilonewtons (1,000 pounds-force); and

(E) A flammability test in accordance with Table V-1.

TABLE V-1—FLAMMABILITY TEST

Test method	Criteria for passing the test
Vertically suspend a 500-mm (19.7-inch) length of strapping supporting a 100-kg (220.5-lb) weight.	Any flames on the positioning strap shall self extinguish.
Use a butane or propane burner with a 76-mm (3-inch) flame.	The positioning strap shall continue to support the 100-kg (220.5-lb) mass.
Direct the flame to an edge of the strapping at a distance of 25 mm (1 inch). Remove the flame after 5 seconds.	
Wait for any flames on the positioning strap to stop burning.	

(viii) The cushion part of the body belt shall contain no exposed rivets on the inside and shall be at least 76 millimeters (3 inches) in width.

(ix) Tool loops shall be situated on the body of a body belt so that the 100 millimeters (4 inches) of the body belt that is in the center of the back, measuring from D ring to D ring, is free of tool loops and any other attachments.

(x) Copper, steel, or equivalent liners shall be used around the bars of D rings to prevent wear between these members and the leather or fabric enclosing them.

(xi) Snaphooks shall be of the locking type meeting the following requirements:

(A) The locking mechanism shall first be released, or a destructive force

shall be placed on the keeper, before the keeper will open.

(B) A force in the range of 6.7 N (1.5 lbf) to 17.8 N (4 lbf) shall be required to release the locking mechanism.

(C) With the locking mechanism released and with a force applied on the keeper against the face of the nose, the keeper may not begin to open with a force of 11.2 N (2.5 lbf) or less and shall begin to open with a maximum force of 17.8 N (4 lbf).

(xii) Body belts and positioning straps shall be capable of withstanding a drop test as follows:

(A) The test mass shall be rigidly constructed of steel or equivalent material with a mass of 100 kg (220.5 lbm). For work-positioning equipment used by employees weighing more than 140 kg (310 lbm) fully equipped, the test mass shall be increased proportionately (that is, the test mass must equal the mass of the equipped worker divided by 1.4).

(B) For body belts, the body belt shall be fitted snugly around the test mass and shall be attached to the test-structure anchorage point by means of a wire rope.

(C) For positioning straps, the strap shall be adjusted to its shortest length possible to accommodate the test and connected to the test-structure anchorage point at one end and to the test mass on the other end.

(D) The test mass shall be dropped an unobstructed distance of 1 meter (39.4 inches) from a supporting structure that will sustain minimal deflection during the test.

(E) Body belts shall successfully arrest the fall of the test mass and shall be capable of supporting the mass after the test.

(F) Positioning straps shall successfully arrest the fall of the test mass without breaking, and the arrest force may not exceed 17.8 kilonewtons (4,000 pounds-force). Additionally, snaphooks on positioning straps may not distort to such an extent that the keeper would release.

NOTE TO PARAGRAPH (b)(2): When used by employees weighing no more than 140 kg (310 lbm) fully equipped, body belts and positioning straps that conform to American Society of Testing and Materials *Standard Specifications for Personal Climbing Equipment,*

ASTM F887–12e1, are deemed to be in compliance with paragraph (b)(2) of this section.

(3) *Care and use of personal fall protection equipment.* (i) Work-positioning equipment shall be inspected before use each day to determine that the equipment is in safe working condition. Work-positioning equipment that is not in safe working condition may not be used.

NOTE TO PARAGRAPH (b)(3)(i): Appendix F to this subpart contains guidelines for inspecting work-positioning equipment.

(ii) Personal fall arrest systems shall be used in accordance with § 1926.502(d).

NOTE TO PARAGRAPH (b)(3)(ii): Fall protection equipment rigged to arrest falls is considered a fall arrest system and must meet the applicable requirements for the design and use of those systems. Fall protection equipment rigged for work positioning is considered work-positioning equipment and must meet the applicable requirements for the design and use of that equipment.

(iii) The employer shall ensure that employees use fall protection systems as follows:

(A) Each employee working from an aerial lift shall use a fall restraint system or a personal fall arrest system. Paragraph (b)(2)(v) of § 1926.453 does not apply.

(B) Except as provided in paragraph (b)(3)(iii)(C) of this section, each employee in elevated locations more than 1.2 meters (4 feet) above the ground on poles, towers, or similar structures shall use a personal fall arrest system, work-positioning equipment, or fall restraint system, as appropriate, if the employer has not provided other fall protection meeting subpart M of this part.

(C) Until March 31, 2015, a qualified employee climbing or changing location on poles, towers, or similar structures need not use fall protection equipment, unless conditions, such as, but not limited to, ice, high winds, the design of the structure (for example, no provision for holding on with hands), or the presence of contaminants on the structure, could cause the employee to lose his or her grip or footing. On and after April 1, 2015, each qualified employee climbing or changing location on poles, towers, or similar structures must use fall protection equipment un-

less the employer can demonstrate that climbing or changing location with fall protection is infeasible or creates a greater hazard than climbing or changing location without it.

NOTE 1 TO PARAGRAPHS (b)(3)(iii)(B) AND (b)(3)(iii)(C): These paragraphs apply to structures that support overhead electric power transmission and distribution lines and equipment. They do not apply to portions of buildings, such as loading docks, or to electric equipment, such as transformers and capacitors. Subpart M of this part contains the duty to provide fall protection associated with walking and working surfaces.

NOTE 2 TO PARAGRAPHS (b)(3)(iii)(B) AND (b)(3)(iii)(C): Until the employer ensures that employees are proficient in climbing and the use of fall protection under § 1926.950(b)(7), the employees are not considered "qualified employees" for the purposes of paragraphs (b)(3)(iii)(B) and (b)(3)(iii)(C) of this section. These paragraphs require unqualified employees (including trainees) to use fall protection any time they are more than 1.2 meters (4 feet) above the ground.

(iv) On and after April 1, 2015, work-positioning systems shall be rigged so that an employee can free fall no more than 0.6 meters (2 feet).

(v) Anchorages for work-positioning equipment shall be capable of supporting at least twice the potential impact load of an employee's fall, or 13.3 kilonewtons (3,000 pounds-force), whichever is greater.

NOTE TO PARAGRAPH (b)(3)(v): Wood-pole fall-restriction devices meeting American Society of Testing and Materials *Standard Specifications for Personal Climbing Equipment,* ASTM F887–12e1, are deemed to meet the anchorage-strength requirement when they are used in accordance with manufacturers' instructions.

(vi) Unless the snaphook is a locking type and designed specifically for the following connections, snaphooks on work-positioning equipment may not be engaged:

(A) Directly to webbing, rope, or wire rope;

(B) To each other;

(C) To a D ring to which another snaphook or other connector is attached;

(D) To a horizontal lifeline; or

(E) To any object that is incompatibly shaped or dimensioned in relation to the snaphook such that accidental disengagement could occur should the connected object sufficiently depress the snaphook keeper to allow release of the object.

§ 1926.955 Portable ladders and platforms.

(a) *General.* Requirements for portable ladders contained in subpart X of this part apply in addition to the requirements of this section, except as specifically noted in paragraph (b) of this section.

(b) *Special ladders and platforms.* Portable ladders used on structures or conductors in conjunction with overhead line work need not meet § 1926.1053(b)(5)(i) and (b)(12). Portable ladders and platforms used on structures or conductors in conjunction with overhead line work shall meet the following requirements:

(1) *Design load.* In the configurations in which they are used, portable platforms shall be capable of supporting without failure at least 2.5 times the maximum intended load.

(2) *Maximum load.* Portable ladders and platforms may not be loaded in excess of the working loads for which they are designed.

(3) *Securing in place.* Portable ladders and platforms shall be secured to prevent them from becoming dislodged.

(4) *Intended use.* Portable ladders and platforms may be used only in applications for which they are designed.

(c) *Conductive ladders.* Portable metal ladders and other portable conductive ladders may not be used near exposed energized lines or equipment. However, in specialized high-voltage work, conductive ladders shall be used when the employer demonstrates that nonconductive ladders would present a greater hazard to employees than conductive ladders.

§ 1926.956 Hand and portable power equipment.

(a) *General.* Paragraph (b) of this section applies to electric equipment connected by cord and plug. Paragraph (c) of this section applies to portable and vehicle-mounted generators used to supply cord- and plug-connected equipment. Paragraph (d) of this section applies to hydraulic and pneumatic tools.

(b) *Cord- and plug-connected equipment.* Cord- and plug-connected equip-

ment not covered by subpart K of this part shall comply with one of the following instead of § 1926.302(a)(1):

(1) The equipment shall be equipped with a cord containing an equipment grounding conductor connected to the equipment frame and to a means for grounding the other end of the conductor (however, this option may not be used where the introduction of the ground into the work environment increases the hazard to an employee); or

(2) The equipment shall be of the double-insulated type conforming to subpart K of this part; or

(3) The equipment shall be connected to the power supply through an isolating transformer with an ungrounded secondary of not more than 50 volts.

(c) *Portable and vehicle-mounted generators.* Portable and vehicle-mounted generators used to supply cord- and plug-connected equipment covered by paragraph (b) of this section shall meet the following requirements:

(1) *Equipment to be supplied.* The generator may only supply equipment located on the generator or the vehicle and cord- and plug-connected equipment through receptacles mounted on the generator or the vehicle.

(2) *Equipment grounding.* The non-current-carrying metal parts of equipment and the equipment grounding conductor terminals of the receptacles shall be bonded to the generator frame.

(3) *Bonding the frame.* For vehicle-mounted generators, the frame of the generator shall be bonded to the vehicle frame.

(4) *Bonding the neutral conductor.* Any neutral conductor shall be bonded to the generator frame.

(d) *Hydraulic and pneumatic tools*—(1) *Hydraulic fluid in insulating tools.* Paragraph (d)(1) of § 1926.302 does not apply to hydraulic fluid used in insulating sections of hydraulic tools.

(2) *Operating pressure.* Safe operating pressures for hydraulic and pneumatic tools, hoses, valves, pipes, filters, and fittings may not be exceeded.

NOTE TO PARAGRAPH (d)(2): If any hazardous defects are present, no operating pressure is safe, and the hydraulic or pneumatic equipment involved may not be used. In the absence of defects, the maximum rated operating pressure is the maximum safe pressure.

(3) *Work near energized parts.* A hydraulic or pneumatic tool used where it may contact exposed energized parts shall be designed and maintained for such use.

(4) *Protection against vacuum formation.* The hydraulic system supplying a hydraulic tool used where it may contact exposed live parts shall provide protection against loss of insulating value, for the voltage involved, due to the formation of a partial vacuum in the hydraulic line.

NOTE TO PARAGRAPH (d)(4): Use of hydraulic lines that do not have check valves and that have a separation of more than 10.7 meters (35 feet) between the oil reservoir and the upper end of the hydraulic system promotes the formation of a partial vacuum.

(5) *Protection against the accumulation of moisture.* A pneumatic tool used on energized electric lines or equipment, or used where it may contact exposed live parts, shall provide protection against the accumulation of moisture in the air supply.

(6) *Breaking connections.* Pressure shall be released before connections are broken, unless quick-acting, self-closing connectors are used.

(7) *Leaks.* Employers must ensure that employees do not use any part of their bodies to locate, or attempt to stop, a hydraulic leak.

(8) *Hoses.* Hoses may not be kinked.

§ 1926.957 Live-line tools.

(a) *Design of tools.* Live-line tool rods, tubes, and poles shall be designed and constructed to withstand the following minimum tests:

(1) *Fiberglass-reinforced plastic.* If the tool is made of fiberglass-reinforced plastic (FRP), it shall withstand 328,100 volts per meter (100,000 volts per foot) of length for 5 minutes, or

NOTE TO PARAGRAPH (a)(1): Live-line tools using rod and tube that meet ASTM F711–02 (2007), *Standard Specification for Fiberglass-Reinforced Plastic (FRP) Rod and Tube Used in Live Line Tools,* are deemed to comply with paragraph (a)(1) of this section.

(2) *Wood.* If the tool is made of wood, it shall withstand 246,100 volts per meter (75,000 volts per foot) of length for 3 minutes, or

(3) *Equivalent tests.* The tool shall withstand other tests that the employer can demonstrate are equivalent.

(b) *Condition of tools*—(1) *Daily inspection.* Each live-line tool shall be wiped clean and visually inspected for defects before use each day.

(2) *Defects.* If any defect or contamination that could adversely affect the insulating qualities or mechanical integrity of the live-line tool is present after wiping, the tool shall be removed from service and examined and tested according to paragraph (b)(3) of this section before being returned to service.

(3) *Biennial inspection and testing.* Live-line tools used for primary employee protection shall be removed from service every 2 years, and whenever required under paragraph (b)(2) of this section, for examination, cleaning, repair, and testing as follows:

(i) Each tool shall be thoroughly examined for defects.

(ii) If a defect or contamination that could adversely affect the insulating qualities or mechanical integrity of the live-line tool is found, the tool shall be repaired and refinished or shall be permanently removed from service. If no such defect or contamination is found, the tool shall be cleaned and waxed.

(iii) The tool shall be tested in accordance with paragraphs (b)(3)(iv) and (b)(3)(v) of this section under the following conditions:

(A) After the tool has been repaired or refinished; and

(B) After the examination if repair or refinishing is not performed, unless the tool is made of FRP rod or foam-filled FRP tube and the employer can demonstrate that the tool has no defects that could cause it to fail during use.

(iv) The test method used shall be designed to verify the tool's integrity along its entire working length and, if the tool is made of fiberglass-reinforced plastic, its integrity under wet conditions.

(v) The voltage applied during the tests shall be as follows:

(A) 246,100 volts per meter (75,000 volts per foot) of length for 1 minute if the tool is made of fiberglass, or

483

(B) 164,000 volts per meter (50,000 volts per foot) of length for 1 minute if the tool is made of wood, or

(C) Other tests that the employer can demonstrate are equivalent.

NOTE TO PARAGRAPH (b): Guidelines for the examination, cleaning, repairing, and in-service testing of live-line tools are specified in the Institute of Electrical and Electronics Engineers' *IEEE Guide for Maintenance Methods on Energized Power Lines*, IEEE Std 516-2009.

§ 1926.958 Materials handling and storage.

(a) *General.* Materials handling and storage shall comply with applicable material-handling and material-storage requirements in this part, including those in subparts N and CC of this part.

(b) *Materials storage near energized lines or equipment*—(1) *Unrestricted areas.* In areas to which access is not restricted to qualified persons only, materials or equipment may not be stored closer to energized lines or exposed energized parts of equipment than the following distances, plus a distance that provides for the maximum sag and side swing of all conductors and for the height and movement of material-handling equipment:

(i) For lines and equipment energized at 50 kilovolts or less, the distance is 3.05 meters (10 feet).

(ii) For lines and equipment energized at more than 50 kilovolts, the distance is 3.05 meters (10 feet) plus 0.10 meter (4 inches) for every 10 kilovolts over 50 kilovolts.

(2) *Restricted areas.* In areas restricted to qualified employees, materials may not be stored within the working space about energized lines or equipment.

NOTE TO PARAGRAPH (b)(2): Paragraph (b) of § 1926.966 specifies the size of the working space.

§ 1926.959 Mechanical equipment.

(a) *General requirements*—(1) *Other applicable requirements.* Mechanical equipment shall be operated in accordance with applicable requirements in this part, including subparts N, O, and CC of this part, except that § 1926.600(a)(6) does not apply to operations performed by qualified employees.

(2) *Inspection before use.* The critical safety components of mechanical elevating and rotating equipment shall receive a thorough visual inspection before use on each shift.

NOTE TO PARAGRAPH (a)(2): Critical safety components of mechanical elevating and rotating equipment are components for which failure would result in free fall or free rotation of the boom.

(3) *Operator.* The operator of an electric line truck may not leave his or her position at the controls while a load is suspended, unless the employer can demonstrate that no employee (including the operator) is endangered.

(b) *Outriggers*—(1) *Extend outriggers.* Mobile equipment, if provided with outriggers, shall be operated with the outriggers extended and firmly set, except as provided in paragraph (b)(3) of this section.

(2) *Clear view.* Outriggers may not be extended or retracted outside of the clear view of the operator unless all employees are outside the range of possible equipment motion.

(3) *Operation without outriggers.* If the work area or the terrain precludes the use of outriggers, the equipment may be operated only within its maximum load ratings specified by the equipment manufacturer for the particular configuration of the equipment without outriggers.

(c) *Applied loads.* Mechanical equipment used to lift or move lines or other material shall be used within its maximum load rating and other design limitations for the conditions under which the mechanical equipment is being used.

(d) *Operations near energized lines or equipment*—(1) *Minimum approach distance.* Mechanical equipment shall be operated so that the minimum approach distances, established by the employer under § 1926.960(c)(1)(i), are maintained from exposed energized lines and equipment. However, the insulated portion of an aerial lift operated by a qualified employee in the lift is exempt from this requirement if the applicable minimum approach distance is maintained between the uninsulated portions of the aerial lift and exposed objects having a different electrical potential.

(2) *Observer.* A designated employee other than the equipment operator shall observe the approach distance to exposed lines and equipment and provide timely warnings before the minimum approach distance required by paragraph (d)(1) of this section is reached, unless the employer can demonstrate that the operator can accurately determine that the minimum approach distance is being maintained.

(3) *Extra precautions.* If, during operation of the mechanical equipment, that equipment could become energized, the operation also shall comply with at least one of paragraphs (d)(3)(i) through (d)(3)(iii) of this section.

(i) The energized lines or equipment exposed to contact shall be covered with insulating protective material that will withstand the type of contact that could be made during the operation.

(ii) The mechanical equipment shall be insulated for the voltage involved. The mechanical equipment shall be positioned so that its uninsulated portions cannot approach the energized lines or equipment any closer than the minimum approach distances, established by the employer under § 1926.960(c)(1)(i).

(iii) Each employee shall be protected from hazards that could arise from mechanical equipment contact with energized lines or equipment. The measures used shall ensure that employees will not be exposed to hazardous differences in electric potential. Unless the employer can demonstrate that the methods in use protect each employee from the hazards that could arise if the mechanical equipment contacts the energized line or equipment, the measures used shall include all of the following techniques:

(A) Using the best available ground to minimize the time the lines or electric equipment remain energized,

(B) Bonding mechanical equipment together to minimize potential differences,

(C) Providing ground mats to extend areas of equipotential, and

(D) Employing insulating protective equipment or barricades to guard against any remaining hazardous electrical potential differences.

NOTE TO PARAGRAPH (d)(3)(iii): Appendix C to this subpart contains information on hazardous step and touch potentials and on methods of protecting employees from hazards resulting from such potentials.

§ 1926.960 Working on or near exposed energized parts.

(a) *Application.* This section applies to work on exposed live parts, or near enough to them to expose the employee to any hazard they present.

(b) *General*—(1) *Qualified employees only.* (i) Only qualified employees may work on or with exposed energized lines or parts of equipment.

(ii) Only qualified employees may work in areas containing unguarded, uninsulated energized lines or parts of equipment operating at 50 volts or more.

(2) *Treat as energized.* Electric lines and equipment shall be considered and treated as energized unless they have been deenergized in accordance with § 1926.961.

(3) *At least two employees.* (i) Except as provided in paragraph (b)(3)(ii) of this section, at least two employees shall be present while any employees perform the following types of work:

(A) Installation, removal, or repair of lines energized at more than 600 volts,

(B) Installation, removal, or repair of deenergized lines if an employee is exposed to contact with other parts energized at more than 600 volts,

(C) Installation, removal, or repair of equipment, such as transformers, capacitors, and regulators, if an employee is exposed to contact with parts energized at more than 600 volts,

(D) Work involving the use of mechanical equipment, other than insulated aerial lifts, near parts energized at more than 600 volts, and

(E) Other work that exposes an employee to electrical hazards greater than, or equal to, the electrical hazards posed by operations listed specifically in paragraphs (b)(3)(i)(A) through (b)(3)(i)(D) of this section.

(ii) Paragraph (b)(3)(i) of this section does not apply to the following operations:

(A) Routine circuit switching, when the employer can demonstrate that conditions at the site allow safe performance of this work,

485

(B) Work performed with live-line tools when the position of the employee is such that he or she is neither within reach of, nor otherwise exposed to contact with, energized parts, and

(C) Emergency repairs to the extent necessary to safeguard the general public.

(c) *Live work*—(1) *Minimum approach distances.* (i) The employer shall establish minimum approach distances no less than the distances computed by Table V–2 for ac systems or Table V–7 for dc systems.

(ii) No later than April 1, 2015, for voltages over 72.5 kilovolts, the employer shall determine the maximum anticipated per-unit transient overvoltage, phase-to-ground, through an engineering analysis or assume a maximum anticipated per-unit transient overvoltage, phase-to-ground, in accordance with Table V–8. When the employer uses portable protective gaps to control the maximum transient overvoltage, the value of the maximum anticipated per-unit transient overvoltage, phase-to-ground, must provide for five standard deviations between the statistical sparkover voltage of the gap and the statistical withstand voltage corresponding to the electrical component of the minimum approach distance. The employer shall make any engineering analysis conducted to determine maximum anticipated per-unit transient overvoltage available upon request to employees and to the Assistant Secretary or designee for examination and copying.

NOTE TO PARAGRAPH (c)(1)(ii): See appendix B to this subpart for information on how to calculate the maximum anticipated per-unit transient overvoltage, phase-to-ground, when the employer uses portable protective gaps to reduce maximum transient overvoltages.

(iii) The employer shall ensure that no employee approaches or takes any conductive object closer to exposed energized parts than the employer's established minimum approach distance, unless:

(A) The employee is insulated from the energized part (rubber insulating gloves or rubber insulating gloves and sleeves worn in accordance with paragraph (c)(2) of this section constitutes insulation of the employee from the energized part upon which the employee is working provided that the employee has control of the part in a manner sufficient to prevent exposure to uninsulated portions of the employee's body), or

(B) The energized part is insulated from the employee and from any other conductive object at a different potential, or

(C) The employee is insulated from any other exposed conductive object in accordance with the requirements for live-line barehand work in § 1926.964(c).

(2) *Type of insulation.* (i) When an employee uses rubber insulating gloves as insulation from energized parts (under paragraph (c)(1)(iii)(A) of this section), the employer shall ensure that the employee also uses rubber insulating sleeves. However, an employee need not use rubber insulating sleeves if:

(A) Exposed energized parts on which the employee is not working are insulated from the employee; and

(B) When installing insulation for purposes of paragraph (c)(2)(i)(A) of this section, the employee installs the insulation from a position that does not expose his or her upper arm to contact with other energized parts.

(ii) When an employee uses rubber insulating gloves or rubber insulating gloves and sleeves as insulation from energized parts (under paragraph (c)(1)(iii)(A) of this section), the employer shall ensure that the employee:

(A) Puts on the rubber insulating gloves and sleeves in a position where he or she cannot reach into the minimum approach distance, established by the employer under paragraph (c)(1) of this section; and

(B) Does not remove the rubber insulating gloves and sleeves until he or she is in a position where he or she cannot reach into the minimum approach distance, established by the employer under paragraph (c)(1) of this section.

(d) *Working position*—(1) *Working from below.* The employer shall ensure that each employee, to the extent that other safety-related conditions at the worksite permit, works in a position from which a slip or shock will not bring the employee's body into contact with exposed, uninsulated parts energized at a potential different from the employee's.

(2) *Requirements for working without electrical protective equipment.* When an employee performs work near exposed parts energized at more than 600 volts, but not more than 72.5 kilovolts, and is not wearing rubber insulating gloves, being protected by insulating equipment covering the energized parts, performing work using live-line tools, or performing live-line barehand work under §1926.964(c), the employee shall work from a position where he or she cannot reach into the minimum approach distance, established by the employer under paragraph (c)(1) of this section.

(e) *Making connections.* The employer shall ensure that employees make connections as follows:

(1) *Connecting.* In connecting deenergized equipment or lines to an energized circuit by means of a conducting wire or device, an employee shall first attach the wire to the deenergized part;

(2) *Disconnecting.* When disconnecting equipment or lines from an energized circuit by means of a conducting wire or device, an employee shall remove the source end first; and

(3) *Loose conductors.* When lines or equipment are connected to or disconnected from energized circuits, an employee shall keep loose conductors away from exposed energized parts.

(f) *Conductive articles.* When an employee performs work within reaching distance of exposed energized parts of equipment, the employer shall ensure that the employee removes or renders nonconductive all exposed conductive articles, such as keychains or watch chains, rings, or wrist watches or bands, unless such articles do not increase the hazards associated with contact with the energized parts.

(g) *Protection from flames and electric arcs*—(1) *Hazard assessment.* The employer shall assess the workplace to identify employees exposed to hazards from flames or from electric arcs.

(2) *Estimate of available heat energy.* For each employee exposed to hazards from electric arcs, the employer shall make a reasonable estimate of the incident heat energy to which the employee would be exposed.

NOTE 1 TO PARAGRAPH (g)(2): Appendix E to this subpart provides guidance on estimating available heat energy. The Occupational Safety and Health Administration will deem employers following the guidance in appendix E to this subpart to be in compliance with paragraph (g)(2) of this section. An employer may choose a method of calculating incident heat energy not included in appendix E to this subpart if the chosen method reasonably predicts the incident energy to which the employee would be exposed.

NOTE 2 TO PARAGRAPH (g)(2): This paragraph does not require the employer to estimate the incident heat energy exposure for every job task performed by each employee. The employer may make broad estimates that cover multiple system areas provided the employer uses reasonable assumptions about the energy-exposure distribution throughout the system and provided the estimates represent the maximum employee exposure for those areas. For example, the employer could estimate the heat energy just outside a substation feeding a radial distribution system and use that estimate for all jobs performed on that radial system.

(3) *Prohibited clothing.* The employer shall ensure that each employee who is exposed to hazards from flames or electric arcs does not wear clothing that could melt onto his or her skin or that could ignite and continue to burn when exposed to flames or the heat energy estimated under paragraph (g)(2) of this section.

NOTE TO PARAGRAPH (g)(3): This paragraph prohibits clothing made from acetate, nylon, polyester, rayon and polypropylene, either alone or in blends, unless the employer demonstrates that the fabric has been treated to withstand the conditions that may be encountered by the employee or that the employee wears the clothing in such a manner as to eliminate the hazard involved.

(4) *Flame-resistant clothing.* The employer shall ensure that the outer layer of clothing worn by an employee, except for clothing not required to be arc rated under paragraphs (g)(5)(i) through (g)(5)(v) of this section, is flame resistant under any of the following conditions:

(i) The employee is exposed to contact with energized circuit parts operating at more than 600 volts,

(ii) An electric arc could ignite flammable material in the work area that,

487

in turn, could ignite the employee's clothing,

(iii) Molten metal or electric arcs from faulted conductors in the work area could ignite the employee's clothing, or

NOTE TO PARAGRAPH (g)(4)(iii): This paragraph does not apply to conductors that are capable of carrying, without failure, the maximum available fault current for the time the circuit protective devices take to interrupt the fault.

(iv) The incident heat energy estimated under paragraph (g)(2) of this section exceeds 2.0 cal/cm².

(5) *Arc rating.* The employer shall ensure that each employee exposed to hazards from electric arcs wears protective clothing and other protective equipment with an arc rating greater than or equal to the heat energy estimated under paragraph (g)(2) of this section whenever that estimate exceeds 2.0 cal/cm². This protective equipment shall cover the employee's entire body, except as follows:

(i) Arc-rated protection is not necessary for the employee's hands when the employee is wearing rubber insulating gloves with protectors or, if the estimated incident energy is no more than 14 cal/cm², heavy-duty leather work gloves with a weight of at least 407 gm/m² (12 oz/yd²),

(ii) Arc-rated protection is not necessary for the employee's feet when the employee is wearing heavy-duty work shoes or boots,

(iii) Arc-rated protection is not necessary for the employee's head when the employee is wearing head protection meeting § 1926.100(b)(2) if the estimated incident energy is less than 9 cal/cm² for exposures involving single-phase arcs in open air or 5 cal/cm² for other exposures,

(iv) The protection for the employee's head may consist of head protection meeting § 1926.100(b)(2) and a faceshield with a minimum arc rating of 8 cal/cm² if the estimated incident-energy exposure is less than 13 cal/cm² for exposures involving single-phase arcs in open air or 9 cal/cm² for other exposures, and

(v) For exposures involving single-phase arcs in open air, the arc rating for the employee's head and face protection may be 4 cal/cm² less than the estimated incident energy.

NOTE TO PARAGRAPH (g): See appendix E to this subpart for further information on the selection of appropriate protection.

(6) *Dates.* (i) The obligation in paragraph (g)(2) of this section for the employer to make reasonable estimates of incident energy commences January 1, 2015.

(ii) The obligation in paragraph (g)(4)(iv) of this section for the employer to ensure that the outer layer of clothing worn by an employee is flame-resistant when the estimated incident heat energy exceeds 2.0 cal/cm² commences April 1, 2015.

(iii) The obligation in paragraph (g)(5) of this section for the employer to ensure that each employee exposed to hazards from electric arcs wears the required arc-rated protective equipment commences April 1, 2015.

(h) *Fuse handling.* When an employee must install or remove fuses with one or both terminals energized at more than 300 volts, or with exposed parts energized at more than 50 volts, the employer shall ensure that the employee uses tools or gloves rated for the voltage. When an employee installs or removes expulsion-type fuses with one or both terminals energized at more than 300 volts, the employer shall ensure that the employee wears eye protection meeting the requirements of subpart E of this part, uses a tool rated for the voltage, and is clear of the exhaust path of the fuse barrel.

(i) *Covered (noninsulated) conductors.* The requirements of this section that pertain to the hazards of exposed live parts also apply when an employee performs work in proximity to covered (noninsulated) wires.

(j) *Non-current-carrying metal parts.* Non-current-carrying metal parts of equipment or devices, such as transformer cases and circuit-breaker housings, shall be treated as energized at the highest voltage to which these parts are exposed, unless the employer inspects the installation and determines that these parts are grounded before employees begin performing the work.

(k) *Opening and closing circuits under load.* (1) The employer shall ensure that devices used by employees to open circuits under load conditions are designed to interrupt the current involved.

(2) The employer shall ensure that devices used by employees to close circuits under load conditions are designed to safely carry the current involved.

Table V-2—AC Live-Line Work Minimum Approach Distance

The minimum approach distance (MAD; in meters) shall conform to the following equations.

For phase-to-phase system voltages of 50 V to 300 V:[1]	
MAD = avoid contact	
For phase-to-phase system voltages of 301 V to 5 kV:[1]	
$MAD = M + D$, where	
$D =$ 0.02 m	the electrical component of the minimum approach distance
$M =$ 0.31 m for voltages up to 750 V and 0.61 m otherwise	the inadvertent movement factor
For phase-to-phase system voltages of 5.1 kV to 72.5 kV:[14]	
$MAD = M + AD$, where	
$M =$ 0.61 m	the inadvertent movement factor
$A =$ the applicable value from Table V-4	the altitude correction factor
$D =$ the value from Table V-3 corresponding to the voltage and exposure or the value of the electrical component of the minimum approach distance calculated using the method provided in Appendix B to this subpart.	the electrical component of the minimum approach distance

Table V-2 (Continued)

For phase-to-phase system voltages of more than 72.5 kV, nominal:[2][4]

$$MAD = 0.3048(C + a)V_{L-G}TA + M, \text{ where}$$

C = 0.01 for phase-to-ground exposures that the employer can demonstrate consist only of air across the approach distance (gap),
0.01 for phase-to-phase exposures if the employer can demonstrate that no insulated tool spans the gap and that no large conductive object is in the gap, or
0.011 otherwise

V_{L-G} = phase-to-ground rms voltage, in kV

T = maximum anticipated per-unit transient overvoltage; for phase-to-ground exposures, T equals T_{L-G}, the maximum per-unit transient overvoltage, phase-to-ground, determined by the employer under paragraph (c)(1)(ii) of this section; for phase-to-phase exposures, T equals $1.35T_{L-G} + 0.45$

A = altitude correction factor from Table V-4
M = 0.31 m, the inadvertent movement factor
a = saturation factor, as follows:

Phase-to-Ground Exposures

$V_{Peak} = T_{L-G}V_{L-G}\sqrt{2}$	635 kV or less	635.1 to 915 kV	915.1 to 1,050 kV	More than 1,050 kV
a	0	$(V_{Peak} - 635)/140,000$	$(V_{Peak} - 645)/135,000$	$(V_{Peak} - 675)/125,000$

Phase-to-Phase Exposures[3]

$V_{Peak} = (1.35T_{L-G} + 0.45)V_{L-G}\sqrt{2}$	630 kV or less	630.1 to 848 kV	848.1 to 1,131 kV	1,131.1 to 1,485 kV	More than 1,485 kV
a	0	$(V_{Peak}-630)/155,000$	$(V_{Peak}-633.6)/152,207$	$(V_{Peak}-628)/153,846$	$(V_{Peak}-350.5)/203,666$

[1] Employers may use the minimum approach distances in Table V-5. If the worksite is at an elevation of more than 900 meters (3,000 feet), see footnote 1 to Table V-5.

[2] Employers may use the minimum approach distances in Table V-6, except that the employer may not use the minimum approach distances in Table V-6 for phase-to-phase exposures if an insulated tool spans the gap or if any large conductive object is in the gap. If the worksite is at an elevation of more than 900 meters (3,000 feet), see footnote 1 to Table V-6. Employers may use the minimum approach distances in Table 7 through Table 14 in Appendix B to this subpart, which calculated MAD for various values of T, provided the employer follows the notes to those tables.

[3] Use the equations for phase-to-ground exposures (with V_{Peak} for phase-to-phase exposures) unless the employer can demonstrate that no insulated tool spans the gap and that no large conductive object is in the gap.

[4] Until March 31, 2015, employers may use the minimum approach distances in Table 6 in Appendix B to this subpart.

TABLE V–3—ELECTRICAL COMPONENT OF THE MINIMUM APPROACH DISTANCE (D; IN METERS) AT 5.1 TO 72.5 KV

Nominal voltage (kV) phase-to-phase	Phase-to-ground exposure	Phase-to-phase exposure
	D (m)	D (m)
5.1 to 15.0	0.04	0.07
15.1 to 36.0	0.16	0.28
36.1 to 46.0	0.23	0.37
46.1 to 72.5	0.39	0.59

TABLE V–4—ALTITUDE CORRECTION FACTOR

Altitude above sea level (m)	A
0 to 900	1.00
901 to 1,200	1.02
1,201 to 1,500	1.05
1,501 to 1,800	1.08
1,801 to 2,100	1.11
2,101 to 2,400	1.14
2,401 to 2,700	1.17
2,701 to 3,000	1.20

TABLE V–4—ALTITUDE CORRECTION FACTOR—Continued

Altitude above sea level (m)	A
3,001 to 3,600	1.25
3,601 to 4,200	1.30
4,201 to 4,800	1.35
4,801 to 5,400	1.39
5,401 to 6,000	1.44

TABLE V–5—ALTERNATIVE MINIMUM APPROACH DISTANCES FOR VOLTAGES OF 72.5 KV AND LESS [1]

Nominal voltage (kV) phase-to-phase	Distance			
	Phase-to-ground exposure		Phase-to-phase exposure	
	m	ft	m	ft
0.50 0.300 [2]	Avoid contact		Avoid contact	
0.301 to 0.750 [2]	0.33	1.09	0.33	1.09
0.751 to 5.0	0.63	2.07	0.63	2.07
5.1 to 15.0	0.65	2.14	0.68	2.24
15.1 to 36.0	0.77	2.53	0.89	2.92
36.1 to 46.0	0.84	2.76	0.98	3.22
46.1 to 72.5	1.00	3.29	1.20	3.94

[1] Employers may use the minimum approach distances in this table provided the worksite is at an elevation of 900 meters (3,000 feet) or less. If employees will be working at elevations greater than 900 meters (3,000 feet) above mean sea level, the employer shall determine minimum approach distances by multiplying the distances in this table by the correction factor in Table V–4 corresponding to the altitude of the work.

[2] For single-phase systems, use voltage-to-ground.

TABLE V–6—ALTERNATIVE MINIMUM APPROACH DISTANCES FOR VOLTAGES OF MORE THAN 72.5 KV [1] [2] [3]

Voltage range phase to phase (kV)	Phase-to-ground exposure		Phase-to-phase exposure	
	m	ft	m	ft
72.6 to 121.0	1.13	3.71	1.42	4.66
121.1 to 145.0	1.30	4.27	1.64	5.38
145.1 to 169.0	1.46	4.79	1.94	6.36
169.1 to 242.0	2.01	6.59	3.08	10.10
242.1 to 362.0	3.41	11.19	5.52	18.11
362.1 to 420.0	4.25	13.94	6.81	22.34
420.1 to 550.0	5.07	16.63	8.24	27.03
550.1 to 800.0	6.88	22.57	11.38	37.34

[1] Employers may use the minimum approach distances in this table provided the worksite is at an elevation of 900 meters (3,000 feet) or less. If employees will be working at elevations greater than 900 meters (3,000 feet) above mean sea level, the employer shall determine minimum approach distances by multiplying the distances in this table by the correction factor in Table V–4 corresponding to the altitude of the work.

[2] Employers may use the phase-to-phase minimum approach distances in this table provided that no insulated tool spans the gap and no large conductive object is in the gap.

[3] The clear live-line tool distance shall equal or exceed the values for the indicated voltage ranges.

TABLE V–7—DC LIVE-LINE MINIMUM APPROACH DISTANCE (IN METERS) WITH OVERVOLTAGE FACTOR [1]

Maximum anticipated per-unit transient overvoltage	distance (m) maximum line-to-ground voltage (kV)				
	250	400	500	600	750
1.5 or less	1.12	1.60	2.06	2.62	3.61
1.6	1.17	1.69	2.24	2.86	3.98
1.7	1.23	1.82	2.42	3.12	4.37
1.8	1.28	1.95	2.62	3.39	4.79

[1] The distances specified in this table are for air, bare-hand, and live-line tool conditions. If employees will be working at elevations greater than 900 meters (3,000 feet) above mean sea level, the employer shall determine minimum approach distances by multiplying the distances in this table by the correction factor in Table V–4 corresponding to the altitude of the work.

TABLE V–8—ASSUMED MAXIMUM PER-UNIT TRANSIENT OVERVOLTAGE

Voltage range (kV)	Type of current (ac or dc)	Assumed maximum per-unit transient overvoltage
72.6 to 420.0	ac	3.5
420.1 to 550.0	ac	3.0
550.1 to 800.0	ac	2.5
250 to 750	dc	1.8

[79 FR 20696, Apr. 11, 2014, as amended at 79 FR 56962, Sept. 24, 2014]

§ 1926.961 Deenergizing lines and equipment for employee protection.

(a) *Application.* This section applies to the deenergizing of transmission and distribution lines and equipment for the purpose of protecting employees. Conductors and parts of electric equipment that have been deenergized under procedures other than those required by this section shall be treated as energized.

(b) *General*—(1) *System operator.* If a system operator is in charge of the lines or equipment and their means of disconnection, the employer shall designate one employee in the crew to be in charge of the clearance and shall comply with all of the requirements of paragraph (c) of this section in the order specified.

(2) *No system operator.* If no system operator is in charge of the lines or equipment and their means of disconnection, the employer shall designate one employee in the crew to be in charge of the clearance and to perform the functions that the system operator would otherwise perform under this section. All of the requirements of paragraph (c) of this section apply, in the order specified, except as provided in paragraph (b)(3) of this section.

(3) *Single crews working with the means of disconnection under the control of the employee in charge of the clearance.* If only one crew will be working on the lines or equipment and if the means of disconnection is accessible and visible to, and under the sole control of, the employee in charge of the clearance, paragraphs (c)(1), (c)(3), and (c)(5) of this section do not apply. Additionally, the employer does not need to use the tags required by the remaining provisions of paragraph (c) of this section.

(4) *Multiple crews.* If two or more crews will be working on the same lines or equipment, then:

(i) The crews shall coordinate their activities under this section with a single employee in charge of the clearance for all of the crews and follow the requirements of this section as if all of the employees formed a single crew, or

(ii) Each crew shall independently comply with this section and, if there is no system operator in charge of the lines or equipment, shall have separate tags and coordinate deenergizing and reenergizing the lines and equipment with the other crews.

(5) *Disconnecting means accessible to general public.* The employer shall render any disconnecting means that are accessible to individuals outside the employer's control (for example, the general public) inoperable while

the disconnecting means are open for the purpose of protecting employees.

(c) *Deenergizing lines and equipment—* (1) *Request to deenergize.* The employee that the employer designates pursuant to paragraph (b) of this section as being in charge of the clearance shall make a request of the system operator to deenergize the particular section of line or equipment. The designated employee becomes the employee in charge (as this term is used in paragraph (c) of this section) and is responsible for the clearance.

(2) *Open disconnecting means.* The employer shall ensure that all switches, disconnectors, jumpers, taps, and other means through which known sources of electric energy may be supplied to the particular lines and equipment to be deenergized are open. The employer shall render such means inoperable, unless its design does not so permit, and then ensure that such means are tagged to indicate that employees are at work.

(3) *Automatically and remotely controlled switches.* The employer shall ensure that automatically and remotely controlled switches that could cause the opened disconnecting means to close are also tagged at the points of control. The employer shall render the automatic or remote control feature inoperable, unless its design does not so permit.

(4) *Network protectors.* The employer need not use the tags mentioned in paragraphs (c)(2) and (c)(3) of this section on a network protector for work on the primary feeder for the network protector's associated network transformer when the employer can demonstrate all of the following conditions:

(i) Every network protector is maintained so that it will immediately trip open if closed when a primary conductor is deenergized;

(ii) Employees cannot manually place any network protector in a closed position without the use of tools, and any manual override position is blocked, locked, or otherwise disabled; and

(iii) The employer has procedures for manually overriding any network protector that incorporate provisions for determining, before anyone places a

network protector in a closed position, that: The line connected to the network protector is not deenergized for the protection of any employee working on the line; and (if the line connected to the network protector is not deenergized for the protection of any employee working on the line) the primary conductors for the network protector are energized.

(5) *Tags.* Tags shall prohibit operation of the disconnecting means and shall indicate that employees are at work.

(6) *Test for energized condition.* After the applicable requirements in paragraphs (c)(1) through (c)(5) of this section have been followed and the system operator gives a clearance to the employee in charge, the employer shall ensure that the lines and equipment are deenergized by testing the lines and equipment to be worked with a device designed to detect voltage.

(7) *Install grounds.* The employer shall ensure the installation of protective grounds as required by § 1926.962.

(8) *Consider lines and equipment deenergized.* After the applicable requirements of paragraphs (c)(1) through (c)(7) of this section have been followed, the lines and equipment involved may be considered deenergized.

(9) *Transferring clearances.* To transfer the clearance, the employee in charge (or the employee's supervisor if the employee in charge must leave the worksite due to illness or other emergency) shall inform the system operator and employees in the crew; and the new employee in charge shall be responsible for the clearance.

(10) *Releasing clearances.* To release a clearance, the employee in charge shall:

(i) Notify each employee under that clearance of the pending release of the clearance;

(ii) Ensure that all employees under that clearance are clear of the lines and equipment;

(iii) Ensure that all protective grounds protecting employees under that clearance have been removed; and

(iv) Report this information to the system operator and then release the clearance.

(11) *Person releasing clearance.* Only the employee in charge who requested

the clearance may release the clearance, unless the employer transfers responsibility under paragraph (c)(9) of this section.

(12) *Removal of tags.* No one may remove tags without the release of the associated clearance as specified under paragraphs (c)(10) and (c)(11) of this section.

(13) *Reenergizing lines and equipment.* The employer shall ensure that no one initiates action to reenergize the lines or equipment at a point of disconnection until all protective grounds have been removed, all crews working on the lines or equipment release their clearances, all employees are clear of the lines and equipment, and all protective tags are removed from that point of disconnection.

§1926.962 Grounding for the protection of employees.

(a) *Application.* This section applies to grounding of transmission and distribution lines and equipment for the purpose of protecting employees. Paragraph (d) of this section also applies to protective grounding of other equipment as required elsewhere in this Subpart.

NOTE TO PARAGRAPH (a): This section covers grounding of transmission and distribution lines and equipment when this subpart requires protective grounding and whenever the employer chooses to ground such lines and equipment for the protection of employees.

(b) *General.* For any employee to work transmission and distribution lines or equipment as deenergized, the employer shall ensure that the lines or equipment are deenergized under the provisions of §1926.961 and shall ensure proper grounding of the lines or equipment as specified in paragraphs (c) through (h) of this section. However, if the employer can demonstrate that installation of a ground is impracticable or that the conditions resulting from the installation of a ground would present greater hazards to employees than working without grounds, the lines and equipment may be treated as deenergized provided that the employer establishes that all of the following conditions apply:

(1) *Deenergized.* The employer ensures that the lines and equipment are deenergized under the provisions of §1926.961.

(2) *No possibility of contact.* There is no possibility of contact with another energized source.

(3) *No induced voltage.* The hazard of induced voltage is not present.

(c) *Equipotential zone.* Temporary protective grounds shall be placed at such locations and arranged in such a manner that the employer can demonstrate will prevent each employee from being exposed to hazardous differences in electric potential.

NOTE TO PARAGRAPH (c): Appendix C to this subpart contains guidelines for establishing the equipotential zone required by this paragraph. The Occupational Safety and Health Administration will deem grounding practices meeting these guidelines as complying with paragraph (c) of this section.

(d) *Protective grounding equipment*—(1) *Ampacity.* (i) Protective grounding equipment shall be capable of conducting the maximum fault current that could flow at the point of grounding for the time necessary to clear the fault.

(ii) Protective grounding equipment shall have an ampacity greater than or equal to that of No. 2 AWG copper.

(2) *Impedance.* Protective grounds shall have an impedance low enough so that they do not delay the operation of protective devices in case of accidental energizing of the lines or equipment.

NOTE TO PARAGRAPH (d): American Society for Testing and Materials *Standard Specifications for Temporary Protective Grounds to Be Used on De-Energized Electric Power Lines and Equipment,* ASTM F855–09, contains guidelines for protective grounding equipment. The Institute of Electrical Engineers *Guide for Protective Grounding of Power Lines,* IEEE Std 1048–2003, contains guidelines for selecting and installing protective grounding equipment.

(e) *Testing.* The employer shall ensure that, unless a previously installed ground is present, employees test lines and equipment and verify the absence of nominal voltage before employees install any ground on those lines or that equipment.

(f) *Connecting and removing grounds*— (1) *Order of connection.* The employer shall ensure that, when an employee attaches a ground to a line or to equipment, the employee attaches the

495

ground-end connection first and then attaches the other end by means of a live-line tool. For lines or equipment operating at 600 volts or less, the employer may permit the employee to use insulating equipment other than a live-line tool if the employer ensures that the line or equipment is not energized at the time the ground is connected or if the employer can demonstrate that each employee is protected from hazards that may develop if the line or equipment is energized.

(2) *Order of removal.* The employer shall ensure that, when an employee removes a ground, the employee removes the grounding device from the line or equipment using a live-line tool before he or she removes the ground-end connection. For lines or equipment operating at 600 volts or less, the employer may permit the employee to use insulating equipment other than a live-line tool if the employer ensures that the line or equipment is not energized at the time the ground is disconnected or if the employer can demonstrate that each employee is protected from hazards that may develop if the line or equipment is energized.

(g) *Additional precautions.* The employer shall ensure that, when an employee performs work on a cable at a location remote from the cable terminal, the cable is not grounded at the cable terminal if there is a possibility of hazardous transfer of potential should a fault occur.

(h) *Removal of grounds for test.* The employer may permit employees to remove grounds temporarily during tests. During the test procedure, the employer shall ensure that each employee uses insulating equipment, shall isolate each employee from any hazards involved, and shall implement any additional measures necessary to protect each exposed employee in case the previously grounded lines and equipment become energized.

§ 1926.963 Testing and test facilities.

(a) *Application.* This section provides for safe work practices for high-voltage and high-power testing performed in laboratories, shops, and substations, and in the field and on electric transmission and distribution lines and equipment. It applies only to testing involving interim measurements using high voltage, high power, or combinations of high voltage and high power, and not to testing involving continuous measurements as in routine metering, relaying, and normal line work.

NOTE TO PARAGRAPH (a): OSHA considers routine inspection and maintenance measurements made by qualified employees to be routine line work not included in the scope of this section, provided that the hazards related to the use of intrinsic high-voltage or high-power sources require only the normal precautions associated with routine work specified in the other paragraphs of this subpart. Two typical examples of such excluded test work procedures are "phasing-out" testing and testing for a "no-voltage" condition.

(b) *General requirements*—(1) *Safe work practices.* The employer shall establish and enforce work practices for the protection of each worker from the hazards of high-voltage or high-power testing at all test areas, temporary and permanent. Such work practices shall include, as a minimum, test area safeguarding, grounding, the safe use of measuring and control circuits, and a means providing for periodic safety checks of field test areas.

(2) *Training.* The employer shall ensure that each employee, upon initial assignment to the test area, receives training in safe work practices, with retraining provided as required by § 1926.950(b).

(c) *Safeguarding of test areas*—(1) *Safeguarding.* The employer shall provide safeguarding within test areas to control access to test equipment or to apparatus under test that could become energized as part of the testing by either direct or inductive coupling and to prevent accidental employee contact with energized parts.

(2) *Permanent test areas.* The employer shall guard permanent test areas with walls, fences, or other barriers designed to keep employees out of the test areas.

(3) *Temporary test areas.* In field testing, or at a temporary test site not guarded by permanent fences and gates, the employer shall ensure the use of one of the following means to prevent employees without authorization from entering:

(i) Distinctively colored safety tape supported approximately waist high with safety signs attached to it,

496

(ii) A barrier or barricade that limits access to the test area to a degree equivalent, physically and visually, to the barricade specified in paragraph (c)(3)(i) of this section, or

(iii) One or more test observers stationed so that they can monitor the entire area.

(4) *Removal of safeguards.* The employer shall ensure the removal of the safeguards required by paragraph (c)(3) of this section when employees no longer need the protection afforded by the safeguards.

(d) *Grounding practices*—(1) *Establish and implement practices.* The employer shall establish and implement safe grounding practices for the test facility.

(i) The employer shall maintain at ground potential all conductive parts accessible to the test operator while the equipment is operating at high voltage.

(ii) Wherever ungrounded terminals of test equipment or apparatus under test may be present, they shall be treated as energized until tests demonstrate that they are deenergized.

(2) *Installation of grounds.* The employer shall ensure either that visible grounds are applied automatically, or that employees using properly insulated tools manually apply visible grounds, to the high-voltage circuits after they are deenergized and before any employee performs work on the circuit or on the item or apparatus under test. Common ground connections shall be solidly connected to the test equipment and the apparatus under test.

(3) *Isolated ground return.* In high-power testing, the employer shall provide an isolated ground-return conductor system designed to prevent the intentional passage of current, with its attendant voltage rise, from occurring in the ground grid or in the earth. However, the employer need not provide an isolated ground-return conductor if the employer can demonstrate that both of the following conditions exist:

(i) The employer cannot provide an isolated ground-return conductor due to the distance of the test site from the electric energy source, and

(ii) The employer protects employees from any hazardous step and touch po-

tentials that may develop during the test.

NOTE TO PARAGRAPH (d)(3)(ii): See appendix C to this subpart for information on measures that employers can take to protect employees from hazardous step and touch potentials.

(4) *Equipment grounding conductors.* For tests in which using the equipment grounding conductor in the equipment power cord to ground the test equipment would result in greater hazards to test personnel or prevent the taking of satisfactory measurements, the employer may use a ground clearly indicated in the test set-up if the employer can demonstrate that this ground affords protection for employees equivalent to the protection afforded by an equipment grounding conductor in the power supply cord.

(5) *Grounding after tests.* The employer shall ensure that, when any employee enters the test area after equipment is deenergized, a ground is placed on the high-voltage terminal and any other exposed terminals.

(i) Before any employee applies a direct ground, the employer shall discharge high capacitance equipment or apparatus through a resistor rated for the available energy.

(ii) A direct ground shall be applied to the exposed terminals after the stored energy drops to a level at which it is safe to do so.

(6) *Grounding test vehicles.* If the employer uses a test trailer or test vehicle in field testing, its chassis shall be grounded. The employer shall protect each employee against hazardous touch potentials with respect to the vehicle, instrument panels, and other conductive parts accessible to employees with bonding, insulation, or isolation.

(e) *Control and measuring circuits*—(1) *Control wiring.* The employer may not run control wiring, meter connections, test leads, or cables from a test area unless contained in a grounded metallic sheath and terminated in a grounded metallic enclosure or unless the employer takes other precautions that it can demonstrate will provide employees with equivalent safety.

(2) *Instruments.* The employer shall isolate meters and other instruments with accessible terminals or parts from

test personnel to protect against hazards that could arise should such terminals and parts become energized during testing. If the employer provides this isolation by locating test equipment in metal compartments with viewing windows, the employer shall provide interlocks to interrupt the power supply when someone opens the compartment cover.

(3) *Routing temporary wiring.* The employer shall protect temporary wiring and its connections against damage, accidental interruptions, and other hazards. To the maximum extent possible, the employer shall keep signal, control, ground, and power cables separate from each other.

(4) *Test observer.* If any employee will be present in the test area during testing, a test observer shall be present. The test observer shall be capable of implementing the immediate deenergizing of test circuits for safety purposes.

(f) *Safety check*—(1) *Before each test.* Safety practices governing employee work at temporary or field test areas shall provide, at the beginning of each series of tests, for a routine safety check of such test areas.

(2) *Conditions to be checked.* The test operator in charge shall conduct these routine safety checks before each series of tests and shall verify at least the following conditions:

(i) Barriers and safeguards are in workable condition and placed properly to isolate hazardous areas;

(ii) System test status signals, if used, are in operable condition;

(iii) Clearly marked test-power disconnects are readily available in an emergency;

(iv) Ground connections are clearly identifiable;

(v) Personal protective equipment is provided and used as required by subpart E of this part and by this subpart; and

(vi) Proper separation between signal, ground, and power cables.

§ 1926.964   Overhead lines and live-line barehand work.

(a) *General*—(1) *Application.* This section provides additional requirements for work performed on or near overhead lines and equipment and for live-line barehand work.

(2) *Checking structure before climbing.* Before allowing employees to subject elevated structures, such as poles or towers, to such stresses as climbing or the installation or removal of equipment may impose, the employer shall ascertain that the structures are capable of sustaining the additional or unbalanced stresses. If the pole or other structure cannot withstand the expected loads, the employer shall brace or otherwise support the pole or structure so as to prevent failure.

NOTE TO PARAGRAPH (a)(2): Appendix D to this subpart contains test methods that employers can use in ascertaining whether a wood pole is capable of sustaining the forces imposed by an employee climbing the pole. This paragraph also requires the employer to ascertain that the pole can sustain all other forces imposed by the work employees will perform.

(3) *Setting and moving poles.* (i) When a pole is set, moved, or removed near an exposed energized overhead conductor, the pole may not contact the conductor.

(ii) When a pole is set, moved, or removed near an exposed energized overhead conductor, the employer shall ensure that each employee wears electrical protective equipment or uses insulated devices when handling the pole and that no employee contacts the pole with uninsulated parts of his or her body.

(iii) To protect employees from falling into holes used for placing poles, the employer shall physically guard the holes, or ensure that employees attend the holes, whenever anyone is working nearby.

(b) *Installing and removing overhead lines.* The following provisions apply to the installation and removal of overhead conductors or cable (overhead lines).

(1) *Tension stringing method.* When lines that employees are installing or removing can contact energized parts, the employer shall use the tension-stringing method, barriers, or other equivalent measures to minimize the possibility that conductors and cables the employees are installing or removing will contact energized power lines or equipment.

(2) *Conductors, cables, and pulling and tensioning equipment.* For conductors, cables, and pulling and tensioning equipment, the employer shall provide the protective measures required by §1926.959(d)(3) when employees are installing or removing a conductor or cable close enough to energized conductors that any of the following failures could energize the pulling or tensioning equipment or the conductor or cable being installed or removed:

(i) Failure of the pulling or tensioning equipment,

(ii) Failure of the conductor or cable being pulled, or

(iii) Failure of the previously installed lines or equipment.

(3) *Disable automatic-reclosing feature.* If the conductors that employees are installing or removing cross over energized conductors in excess of 600 volts and if the design of the circuit-interrupting devices protecting the lines so permits, the employer shall render inoperable the automatic-reclosing feature of these devices.

(4) *Induced voltage.* (i) Before employees install lines parallel to existing energized lines, the employer shall make a determination of the approximate voltage to be induced in the new lines, or work shall proceed on the assumption that the induced voltage is hazardous.

(ii) Unless the employer can demonstrate that the lines that employees are installing are not subject to the induction of a hazardous voltage or unless the lines are treated as energized, temporary protective grounds shall be placed at such locations and arranged in such a manner that the employer can demonstrate will prevent exposure of each employee to hazardous differences in electric potential.

NOTE TO PARAGRAPH (b)(4)(ii): Appendix C to this subpart contains guidelines for protecting employees from hazardous differences in electric potential as required by this paragraph.

NOTE TO PARAGRAPH (b)(4): If the employer takes no precautions to protect employees from hazards associated with involuntary reactions from electric shock, a hazard exists if the induced voltage is sufficient to pass a current of 1 milliampere through a 500-ohm resistor. If the employer protects employees from injury due to involuntary reactions from electric shock, a hazard exists if the resultant current would be more than 6 milliamperes.

(5) *Safe operating condition.* Reel-handling equipment, including pulling and tensioning devices, shall be in safe operating condition and shall be leveled and aligned.

(6) *Load ratings.* The employer shall ensure that employees do not exceed load ratings of stringing lines, pulling lines, conductor grips, load-bearing hardware and accessories, rigging, and hoists.

(7) *Defective pulling lines.* The employer shall repair or replace defective pulling lines and accessories.

(8) *Conductor grips.* The employer shall ensure that employees do not use conductor grips on wire rope unless the manufacturer specifically designed the grip for this application.

(9) *Communications.* The employer shall ensure that employees maintain reliable communications, through two-way radios or other equivalent means, between the reel tender and the pulling-rig operator.

(10) *Operation of pulling rig.* Employees may operate the pulling rig only when it is safe to do so.

NOTE TO PARAGRAPH (b)(10): Examples of unsafe conditions include: employees in locations prohibited by paragraph (b)(11) of this section, conductor and pulling line hang-ups, and slipping of the conductor grip.

(11) *Working under overhead operations.* While a power-driven device is pulling the conductor or pulling line and the conductor or pulling line is in motion, the employer shall ensure that employees are not directly under overhead operations or on the crossarm, except as necessary for the employees to guide the stringing sock or board over or through the stringing sheave.

(c) *Live-line barehand work.* In addition to other applicable provisions contained in this subpart, the following requirements apply to live-line barehand work:

(1) *Training.* Before an employee uses or supervises the use of the live-line barehand technique on energized circuits, the employer shall ensure that the employee completes training conforming to §1926.950(b) in the technique and in the safety requirements of paragraph (c) of this section.

(2) *Existing conditions.* Before any employee uses the live-line barehand technique on energized high-voltage conductors or parts, the employer shall ascertain the following information in addition to information about other existing conditions required by § 1926.950(d):

(i) The nominal voltage rating of the circuit on which employees will perform the work,

(ii) The clearances to ground of lines and other energized parts on which employees will perform the work, and

(iii) The voltage limitations of equipment employees will use.

(3) *Insulated tools and equipment.* (i) The employer shall ensure that the insulated equipment, insulated tools, and aerial devices and platforms used by employees are designed, tested, and made for live-line barehand work.

(ii) The employer shall ensure that employees keep tools and equipment clean and dry while they are in use.

(4) *Disable automatic-reclosing feature.* The employer shall render inoperable the automatic-reclosing feature of circuit-interrupting devices protecting the lines if the design of the devices permits.

(5) *Adverse weather conditions.* The employer shall ensure that employees do not perform work when adverse weather conditions would make the work hazardous even after the employer implements the work practices required by this subpart. Additionally, employees may not perform work when winds reduce the phase-to-phase or phase-to-ground clearances at the work location below the minimum approach distances specified in paragraph (c)(13) of this section, unless insulating guards cover the grounded objects and other lines and equipment.

NOTE TO PARAGRAPH (c)(5): Thunderstorms in the vicinity, high winds, snow storms, and ice storms are examples of adverse weather conditions that make live-line barehand work too hazardous to perform safely even after the employer implements the work practices required by this subpart.

(6) *Bucket liners and electrostatic shielding.* The employer shall provide and ensure that employees use a conductive bucket liner or other conductive device for bonding the insulated aerial device to the energized line or equipment.

(i) The employee shall be connected to the bucket liner or other conductive device by the use of conductive shoes, leg clips, or other means.

(ii) Where differences in potentials at the worksite pose a hazard to employees, the employer shall provide electrostatic shielding designed for the voltage being worked.

(7) *Bonding the employee to the energized part.* The employer shall ensure that, before the employee contacts the energized part, the employee bonds the conductive bucket liner or other conductive device to the energized conductor by means of a positive connection. This connection shall remain attached to the energized conductor until the employee completes the work on the energized circuit.

(8) *Aerial-lift controls.* Aerial lifts used for live-line barehand work shall have dual controls (lower and upper) as follows:

(i) The upper controls shall be within easy reach of the employee in the bucket. On a two-bucket-type lift, access to the controls shall be within easy reach of both buckets.

(ii) The lower set of controls shall be near the base of the boom and shall be designed so that they can override operation of the equipment at any time.

(9) *Operation of lower controls.* Lower (ground-level) lift controls may not be operated with an employee in the lift except in case of emergency.

(10) *Check controls.* The employer shall ensure that, before employees elevate an aerial lift into the work position, the employees check all controls (ground level and bucket) to determine that they are in proper working condition.

(11) *Body of aerial lift truck.* The employer shall ensure that, before employees elevate the boom of an aerial lift, the employees ground the body of the truck or barricade the body of the truck and treat it as energized.

(12) *Boom-current test.* The employer shall ensure that employees perform a boom-current test before starting work each day, each time during the day when they encounter a higher voltage, and when changed conditions indicate a need for an additional test.

(i) This test shall consist of placing the bucket in contact with an energized source equal to the voltage to be encountered for a minimum of 3 minutes.

(ii) The leakage current may not exceed 1 microampere per kilovolt of nominal phase-to-ground voltage.

(iii) The employer shall immediately suspend work from the aerial lift when there is any indication of a malfunction in the equipment.

(13) *Minimum approach distance.* The employer shall ensure that employees maintain the minimum approach distances, established by the employer under §1926.960(c)(1)(i), from all grounded objects and from lines and equipment at a potential different from that to which the live-line barehand equipment is bonded, unless insulating guards cover such grounded objects and other lines and equipment.

(14) *Approaching, leaving, and bonding to energized part.* The employer shall ensure that, while an employee is approaching, leaving, or bonding to an energized circuit, the employee maintains the minimum approach distances, established by the employer under §1926.960(c)(1)(i), between the employee and any grounded parts, including the lower boom and portions of the truck and between the employee and conductive objects energized at different potentials.

(15) *Positioning bucket near energized bushing or insulator string.* While the bucket is alongside an energized bushing or insulator string, the employer shall ensure that employees maintain the phase-to-ground minimum approach distances, established by the employer under §1926.960(c)(1)(i), between all parts of the bucket and the grounded end of the bushing or insulator string or any other grounded surface.

(16) *Handlines.* The employer shall ensure that employees do not use handlines between the bucket and the boom or between the bucket and the ground. However, employees may use nonconductive-type handlines from conductor to ground if not supported from the bucket. The employer shall ensure that no one uses ropes used for live-line barehand work for other purposes.

(17) *Passing objects to employee.* The employer shall ensure that employees do not pass uninsulated equipment or material between a pole or structure and an aerial lift while an employee working from the bucket is bonded to an energized part.

(18) *Nonconductive measuring device.* A nonconductive measuring device shall be readily accessible to employees performing live-line barehand work to assist them in maintaining the required minimum approach distance.

(d) *Towers and structures.* The following requirements apply to work performed on towers or other structures that support overhead lines.

(1) *Working beneath towers and structures.* The employer shall ensure that no employee is under a tower or structure while work is in progress, except when the employer can demonstrate that such a working position is necessary to assist employees working above.

(2) *Tag lines.* The employer shall ensure that employees use tag lines or other similar devices to maintain control of tower sections being raised or positioned, unless the employer can demonstrate that the use of such devices would create a greater hazard to employees.

(3) *Disconnecting load lines.* The employer shall ensure that employees do not detach the loadline from a member or section until they safely secure the load.

(4) *Adverse weather conditions.* The employer shall ensure that, except during emergency restoration procedures, employees discontinue work when adverse weather conditions would make the work hazardous in spite of the work practices required by this subpart.

NOTE TO PARAGRAPH (d)(4): Thunderstorms in the vicinity, high winds, snow storms, and ice storms are examples of adverse weather conditions that make this work too hazardous to perform even after the employer implements the work practices required by this subpart.

§1926.965 Underground electrical installations.

(a) *Application.* This section provides additional requirements for work on underground electrical installations.

(b) *Access.* The employer shall ensure that employees use a ladder or other climbing device to enter and exit a manhole or subsurface vault exceeding 1.22 meters (4 feet) in depth. No employee may climb into or out of a manhole or vault by stepping on cables or hangers.

(c) *Lowering equipment into manholes—* (1) *Hoisting equipment.* Equipment used to lower materials and tools into manholes or vaults shall be capable of supporting the weight to be lowered and shall be checked for defects before use.

(2) *Clear the area of employees.* Before anyone lowers tools or material into the opening for a manhole or vault, each employee working in the manhole or vault shall be clear of the area directly under the opening.

(d) *Attendants for manholes and vaults—*(1) *When required.* While work is being performed in a manhole or vault containing energized electric equipment, an employee with first-aid training shall be available on the surface in the immediate vicinity of the manhole or vault entrance to render emergency assistance.

(2) *Brief entries allowed.* Occasionally, the employee on the surface may briefly enter a manhole or vault to provide nonemergency assistance.

NOTE 1 TO PARAGRAPH (d)(2): Paragraph (h) of 1926.953 may also require an attendant and does not permit this attendant to enter the manhole or vault.

NOTE 2 TO PARAGRAPH (d)(2): Paragraph (b)(1)(ii) of § 1926.960 requires employees entering manholes or vaults containing unguarded, uninsulated energized lines or parts of electric equipment operating at 50 volts or more to be qualified.

(3) *Entry without attendant.* For the purpose of inspection, housekeeping, taking readings, or similar work, an employee working alone may enter, for brief periods of time, a manhole or vault where energized cables or equipment are in service if the employer can demonstrate that the employee will be protected from all electrical hazards.

(4) *Communications.* The employer shall ensure that employees maintain reliable communications, through two-way radios or other equivalent means, among all employees involved in the job.

(e) *Duct rods.* The employer shall ensure that, if employees use duct rods, the employees install the duct rods in the direction presenting the least hazard to employees. The employer shall station an employee at the far end of the duct line being rodded to ensure that the employees maintain the required minimum approach distances.

(f) *Multiple cables.* When multiple cables are present in a work area, the employer shall identify the cable to be worked by electrical means, unless its identity is obvious by reason of distinctive appearance or location or by other readily apparent means of identification. The employer shall protect cables other than the one being worked from damage.

(g) *Moving cables.* Except when paragraph (h)(2) of this section permits employees to perform work that could cause a fault in an energized cable in a manhole or vault, the employer shall ensure that employees inspect energized cables to be moved for abnormalities.

(h) *Protection against faults—*(1) *Cables with abnormalities.* Where a cable in a manhole or vault has one or more abnormalities that could lead to a fault or be an indication of an impending fault, the employer shall deenergize the cable with the abnormality before any employee may work in the manhole or vault, except when service-load conditions and a lack of feasible alternatives require that the cable remain energized. In that case, employees may enter the manhole or vault provided the employer protects them from the possible effects of a failure using shields or other devices that are capable of containing the adverse effects of a fault. The employer shall treat the following abnormalities as indications of impending faults unless the employer can demonstrate that the conditions could not lead to a fault: Oil or compound leaking from cable or joints, broken cable sheaths or joint sleeves, hot localized surface temperatures of cables or joints, or joints swollen beyond normal tolerance.

(2) *Work-related faults.* If the work employees will perform in a manhole or vault could cause a fault in a cable, the employer shall deenergize that cable before any employee works in the

502

manhole or vault, except when service-load conditions and a lack of feasible alternatives require that the cable remain energized. In that case, employees may enter the manhole or vault provided the employer protects them from the possible effects of a failure using shields or other devices that are capable of containing the adverse effects of a fault.

(i) *Sheath continuity.* When employees perform work on buried cable or on cable in a manhole or vault, the employer shall maintain metallic-sheath continuity, or the cable sheath shall be treated as energized.

§1926.966 Substations.

(a) *Application.* This section provides additional requirements for substations and for work performed in them.

(b) *Access and working space.* The employer shall provide and maintain sufficient access and working space about electric equipment to permit ready and safe operation and maintenance of such equipment by employees.

NOTE TO PARAGRAPH (b): American National Standard *National Electrical Safety Code,* ANSI/IEEE C2–2012 contains guidelines for the dimensions of access and working space about electric equipment in substations. Installations meeting the ANSI provisions comply with paragraph (b) of this section. The Occupational Safety and Health Administration will determine whether an installation that does not conform to this ANSI standard complies with paragraph (b) of this section based on the following criteria:

(1) Whether the installation conforms to the edition of ANSI C2 that was in effect when the installation was made;

(2) Whether the configuration of the installation enables employees to maintain the minimum approach distances, established by the employer under §1926.960(c)(1)(i), while the employees are working on exposed, energized parts; and

(3) Whether the precautions taken when employees perform work on the installation provide protection equivalent to the protection provided by access and working space meeting ANSI/IEEE C2–2012.

(c) *Draw-out-type circuit breakers.* The employer shall ensure that, when employees remove or insert draw-out-type circuit breakers, the breaker is in the open position. The employer shall also render the control circuit inoperable if the design of the equipment permits.

(d) *Substation fences.* Conductive fences around substations shall be grounded. When a substation fence is expanded or a section is removed, fence sections shall be isolated, grounded, or bonded as necessary to protect employees from hazardous differences in electric potential.

NOTE TO PARAGRAPH (d): IEEE Std 80–2000, *IEEE Guide for Safety in AC Substation Grounding,* contains guidelines for protection against hazardous differences in electric potential.

(e) *Guarding of rooms and other spaces containing electric supply equipment*—(1) *When to guard rooms and other spaces.* Rooms and other spaces in which electric supply lines or equipment are installed shall meet the requirements of paragraphs (e)(2) through (e)(5) of this section under the following conditions:

(i) If exposed live parts operating at 50 to 150 volts to ground are within 2.4 meters (8 feet) of the ground or other working surface inside the room or other space,

(ii) If live parts operating at 151 to 600 volts to ground and located within 2.4 meters (8 feet) of the ground or other working surface inside the room or other space are guarded only by location, as permitted under paragraph (f)(1) of this section, or

(iii) If live parts operating at more than 600 volts to ground are within the room or other space, unless:

(A) The live parts are enclosed within grounded, metal-enclosed equipment whose only openings are designed so that foreign objects inserted in these openings will be deflected from energized parts, or

(B) The live parts are installed at a height, above ground and any other working surface, that provides protection at the voltage on the live parts corresponding to the protection provided by a 2.4-meter (8-foot) height at 50 volts.

(2) *Prevent access by unqualified persons.* Fences, screens, partitions, or walls shall enclose the rooms and other spaces so as to minimize the possibility that unqualified persons will enter.

(3) *Restricted entry.* Unqualified persons may not enter the rooms or other

503

spaces while the electric supply lines or equipment are energized.

(4) *Warning signs.* The employer shall display signs at entrances to the rooms and other spaces warning unqualified persons to keep out.

(5) *Entrances to rooms and other.* The employer shall keep each entrance to a room or other space locked, unless the entrance is under the observation of a person who is attending the room or other space for the purpose of preventing unqualified employees from entering.

(f) *Guarding of energized parts*—(1) *Type of guarding.* The employer shall provide guards around all live parts operating at more than 150 volts to ground without an insulating covering unless the location of the live parts gives sufficient clearance (horizontal, vertical, or both) to minimize the possibility of accidental employee contact.

NOTE TO PARAGRAPH (f)(1): American National Standard *National Electrical Safety Code,* ANSI/IEEE C2–2002 contains guidelines for the dimensions of clearance distances about electric equipment in substations. Installations meeting the ANSI provisions comply with paragraph (f)(1) of this section. The Occupational Safety and Health Administration will determine whether an installation that does not conform to this ANSI standard complies with paragraph (f)(1) of this section based on the following criteria:

(1) Whether the installation conforms to the edition of ANSI C2 that was in effect when the installation was made;

(2) Whether each employee is isolated from energized parts at the point of closest approach; and

(3) Whether the precautions taken when employees perform work on the installation provide protection equivalent to the protection provided by horizontal and vertical clearances meeting ANSI/IEEE C2–2002.

(2) *Maintaining guards during operation.* Except for fuse replacement and other necessary access by qualified persons, the employer shall maintain guarding of energized parts within a compartment during operation and maintenance functions to prevent accidental contact with energized parts and to prevent dropped tools or other equipment from contacting energized parts.

(3) *Temporary removal of guards.* Before guards are removed from energized equipment, the employer shall install barriers around the work area to prevent employees who are not working on the equipment, but who are in the area, from contacting the exposed live parts.

(g) *Substation entry*—(1) *Report upon entering.* Upon entering an attended substation, each employee, other than employees regularly working in the station, shall report his or her presence to the employee in charge of substation activities to receive information on special system conditions affecting employee safety.

(2) *Job briefing.* The job briefing required by § 1926.952 shall cover information on special system conditions affecting employee safety, including the location of energized equipment in or adjacent to the work area and the limits of any deenergized work area.

§ 1926.967 Special conditions.

(a) *Capacitors.* The following additional requirements apply to work on capacitors and on lines connected to capacitors.

NOTE TO PARAGRAPH (a): See §§ 1926.961 and 1926.962 for requirements pertaining to the deenergizing and grounding of capacitor installations.

(1) *Disconnect from energized source.* Before employees work on capacitors, the employer shall disconnect the capacitors from energized sources and short circuit the capacitors. The employer shall ensure that the employee short circuiting the capacitors waits at least 5 minutes from the time of disconnection before applying the short circuit,

(2) *Short circuiting units.* Before employees handle the units, the employer shall short circuit each unit in series-parallel capacitor banks between all terminals and the capacitor case or its rack. If the cases of capacitors are on ungrounded substation racks, the employer shall bond the racks to ground.

(3) *Short circuiting connected lines.* The employer shall short circuit any line connected to capacitors before the line is treated as deenergized.

(b) *Current transformer secondaries.* The employer shall ensure that employees do not open the secondary of a current transformer while the transformer is energized. If the employer cannot deenergize the primary of the current transformer before employees perform work on an instrument, a relay, or other section of a current transformer secondary circuit, the employer shall bridge the circuit so that the current transformer secondary does not experience an open-circuit condition.

(c) *Series streetlighting*—(1) *Applicable requirements.* If the open-circuit voltage exceeds 600 volts, the employer shall ensure that employees work on series streetlighting circuits in accordance with § 1926.964 or § 1926.965, as appropriate.

(2) *Opening a series loop.* Before any employee opens a series loop, the employer shall deenergize the streetlighting transformer and isolate it from the source of supply or shall bridge the loop to avoid an open-circuit condition.

(d) *Illumination.* The employer shall provide sufficient illumination to enable the employee to perform the work safely.

NOTE TO PARAGRAPH (d): See § 1926.56, which requires specific levels of illumination.

(e) *Protection against drowning*—(1) *Personal flotation devices.* Whenever an employee may be pulled or pushed, or might fall, into water where the danger of drowning exists, the employer shall provide the employee with, and shall ensure that the employee uses, a personal flotation device meeting § 1926.106.

(2) *Maintaining flotation devices in safe condition.* The employer shall maintain each personal flotation device in safe condition and shall inspect each personal flotation device frequently enough to ensure that it does not have rot, mildew, water saturation, or any other condition that could render the device unsuitable for use.

(3) *Crossing bodies of water.* An employee may cross streams or other bodies of water only if a safe means of passage, such as a bridge, is available.

(f) *Excavations.* Excavation operations shall comply with subpart P of this part.

(g) *Employee protection in public work areas*—(1) *Traffic control devices.* Traffic-control signs and traffic-control devices used for the protection of employees shall meet § 1926.200(g)(2).

(2) *Controlling traffic.* Before employees begin work in the vicinity of vehicular or pedestrian traffic that may endanger them, the employer shall place warning signs or flags and other traffic-control devices in conspicuous locations to alert and channel approaching traffic.

(3) *Barricades.* The employer shall use barricades where additional employee protection is necessary.

(4) *Excavated areas.* The employer shall protect excavated areas with barricades.

(5) *Warning lights.* The employer shall display warning lights prominently at night.

(h) *Backfeed.* When there is a possibility of voltage backfeed from sources of cogeneration or from the secondary system (for example, backfeed from more than one energized phase feeding a common load), the requirements of § 1926.960 apply if employees will work the lines or equipment as energized, and the requirements of §§ 1926.961 and 1926.962 apply if employees will work the lines or equipment as deenergized.

(i) *Lasers.* The employer shall install, adjust, and operate laser equipment in accordance with § 1926.54.

(j) *Hydraulic fluids.* Hydraulic fluids used for the insulated sections of equipment shall provide insulation for the voltage involved.

(k) *Communication facilities*—(1) *Microwave transmission.* (i) The employer shall ensure that no employee looks into an open waveguide or antenna connected to an energized microwave source.

(ii) If the electromagnetic-radiation level within an accessible area associated with microwave communications systems exceeds the radiation-protection guide specified by § 1910.97(a)(2) of this chapter, the employer shall post the area with warning signs containing the warning symbol described in § 1910.97(a)(3) of this chapter. The lower half of the warning symbol shall include the following statements, or ones that the employer can demonstrate are equivalent: "Radiation in this area may exceed hazard limitations and special precautions are required. Obtain specific instruction before entering."

505

(iii) When an employee works in an area where the electromagnetic radiation could exceed the radiation-protection guide, the employer shall institute measures that ensure that the employee's exposure is not greater than that permitted by that guide. Such measures may include administrative and engineering controls and personal protective equipment.

(2) *Power-line carrier.* The employer shall ensure that employees perform power-line carrier work, including work on equipment used for coupling carrier current to power line conductors, in accordance with the requirements of this subpart pertaining to work on energized lines.

§ 1926.968 Definitions.

Attendant. An employee assigned to remain immediately outside the entrance to an enclosed or other space to render assistance as needed to employees inside the space.

Automatic circuit recloser. A self-controlled device for automatically interrupting and reclosing an alternating-current circuit, with a predetermined sequence of opening and reclosing followed by resetting, hold closed, or lockout.

Barricade. A physical obstruction such as tapes, cones, or A-frame type wood or metal structures that provides a warning about, and limits access to, a hazardous area.

Barrier. A physical obstruction that prevents contact with energized lines or equipment or prevents unauthorized access to a work area.

Bond. The electrical interconnection of conductive parts designed to maintain a common electric potential.

Bus. A conductor or a group of conductors that serve as a common connection for two or more circuits.

Bushing. An insulating structure that includes a through conductor or that provides a passageway for such a conductor, and that, when mounted on a barrier, insulates the conductor from the barrier for the purpose of conducting current from one side of the barrier to the other.

Cable. A conductor with insulation, or a stranded conductor with or without insulation and other coverings (single-conductor cable), or a combination of conductors insulated from one another (multiple-conductor cable).

Cable sheath. A conductive protective covering applied to cables.

NOTE TO THE DEFINITION OF "CABLE SHEATH": A cable sheath may consist of multiple layers one or more of which is conductive.

Circuit. A conductor or system of conductors through which an electric current is intended to flow.

Clearance (between objects). The clear distance between two objects measured surface to surface.

Clearance (for work). Authorization to perform specified work or permission to enter a restricted area.

Communication lines. (See *Lines;* (1) *Communication lines.*)

Conductor. A material, usually in the form of a wire, cable, or bus bar, used for carrying an electric current.

Contract employer. An employer, other than a host employer, that performs work covered by subpart V of this part under contract.

Covered conductor. A conductor covered with a dielectric having no rated insulating strength or having a rated insulating strength less than the voltage of the circuit in which the conductor is used.

Current-carrying part. A conducting part intended to be connected in an electric circuit to a source of voltage. Non-current-carrying parts are those not intended to be so connected.

Deenergized. Free from any electrical connection to a source of potential difference and from electric charge; not having a potential that is different from the potential of the earth.

NOTE TO THE DEFINITION OF "DEENERGIZED": The term applies only to current-carrying parts, which are sometimes energized (alive).

Designated employee (designated person). An employee (or person) who is assigned by the employer to perform specific duties under the terms of this subpart and who has sufficient knowledge of the construction and operation of the equipment, and the hazards involved, to perform his or her duties safely.

Electric line truck. A truck used to transport personnel, tools, and material for electric supply line work.

Electric supply equipment. Equipment that produces, modifies, regulates, controls, or safeguards a supply of electric energy.

Electric supply lines. (See "Lines; (2) Electric supply lines.")

Electric utility. An organization responsible for the installation, operation, or maintenance of an electric supply system.

Enclosed space. A working space, such as a manhole, vault, tunnel, or shaft, that has a limited means of egress or entry, that is designed for periodic employee entry under normal operating conditions, and that, under normal conditions, does not contain a hazardous atmosphere, but may contain a hazardous atmosphere under abnormal conditions.

Energized (alive, live). Electrically connected to a source of potential difference, or electrically charged so as to have a potential significantly different from that of earth in the vicinity.

Energy source. Any electrical, mechanical, hydraulic, pneumatic, chemical, nuclear, thermal, or other energy source that could cause injury to employees.

Entry (as used in §1926.953). The action by which a person passes through an opening into an enclosed space. Entry includes ensuing work activities in that space and is considered to have occurred as soon as any part of the entrant's body breaks the plane of an opening into the space.

Equipment (electric). A general term including material, fittings, devices, appliances, fixtures, apparatus, and the like used as part of or in connection with an electrical installation.

Exposed, Exposed to contact (as applied to energized parts). Not isolated or guarded.

Fall restraint system. A fall protection system that prevents the user from falling any distance.

First-aid training. Training in the initial care, including cardiopulmonary resuscitation (which includes chest compressions, rescue breathing, and, as appropriate, other heart and lung resuscitation techniques), performed by a person who is not a medical practitioner, of a sick or injured person until definitive medical treatment can be administered.

Ground. A conducting connection, whether planned or unplanned, between an electric circuit or equipment and the earth, or to some conducting body that serves in place of the earth.

Grounded. Connected to earth or to some conducting body that serves in place of the earth.

Guarded. Covered, fenced, enclosed, or otherwise protected, by means of suitable covers or casings, barrier rails or screens, mats, or platforms, designed to minimize the possibility, under normal conditions, of dangerous approach or inadvertent contact by persons or objects.

NOTE TO THE DEFINITION OF "GUARDED": Wires that are insulated, but not otherwise protected, are not guarded.

Hazardous atmosphere. An atmosphere that may expose employees to the risk of death, incapacitation, impairment of ability to self-rescue (that is, escape unaided from an enclosed space), injury, or acute illness from one or more of the following causes:

(1) Flammable gas, vapor, or mist in excess of 10 percent of its lower flammable limit (LFL);

(2) Airborne combustible dust at a concentration that meets or exceeds its LFL;

NOTE TO THE DEFINITION OF "HAZARDOUS ATMOSPHERE" (2): This concentration may be approximated as a condition in which the dust obscures vision at a distance of 1.52 meters (5 feet) or less.

(3) Atmospheric oxygen concentration below 19.5 percent or above 23.5 percent;

(4) Atmospheric concentration of any substance for which a dose or a permissible exposure limit is published in Subpart D, *Occupational Health and Environmental Controls*, or in Subpart Z, *Toxic and Hazardous Substances*, of this part and which could result in employee exposure in excess of its dose or permissible exposure limit;

NOTE TO THE DEFINITION OF "HAZARDOUS ATMOSPHERE" (4): An atmospheric concentration of any substance that is not capable of causing death, incapacitation, impairment of ability to self-rescue, injury, or acute illness due to its health effects is not covered by this provision.

(5) Any other atmospheric condition that is immediately dangerous to life or health.

NOTE TO THE DEFINITION OF "HAZARDOUS ATMOSPHERE" (5): For air contaminants for which the Occupational Safety and Health Administration has not determined a dose or permissible exposure limit, other sources of information, such as Material Safety Data Sheets that comply with the Hazard Communication Standard, § 1926.59, published information, and internal documents can provide guidance in establishing acceptable atmospheric conditions.

High-power tests. Tests in which the employer uses fault currents, load currents, magnetizing currents, and line-dropping currents to test equipment, either at the equipment's rated voltage or at lower voltages.

High-voltage tests. Tests in which the employer uses voltages of approximately 1,000 volts as a practical minimum and in which the voltage source has sufficient energy to cause injury.

High wind. A wind of such velocity that one or more of the following hazards would be present:

(1) The wind could blow an employee from an elevated location,

(2) The wind could cause an employee or equipment handling material to lose control of the material, or

(3) The wind would expose an employee to other hazards not controlled by the standard involved.

NOTE TO THE DEFINITION OF "HIGH WIND": The Occupational Safety and Health Administration normally considers winds exceeding 64.4 kilometers per hour (40 miles per hour), or 48.3 kilometers per hour (30 miles per hour) if the work involves material handling, as meeting this criteria, unless the employer takes precautions to protect employees from the hazardous effects of the wind.

Host employer. An employer that operates, or that controls the operating procedures for, an electric power generation, transmission, or distribution installation on which a contract employer is performing work covered by subpart V of this part.

NOTE TO THE DEFINITION OF "HOST EMPLOYER": The Occupational Safety and Health Administration will treat the electric utility or the owner of the installation as the host employer if it operates or controls operating procedures for the installation. If the electric utility or installation owner neither operates nor controls operating procedures for the installation, the Occupational Safety and Health Administration will treat the employer that the utility or owner has contracted with to operate or control the operating procedures for the installation as the host employer. In no case will there be more than one host employer.

Immediately dangerous to life or health (IDLH). Any condition that poses an immediate or delayed threat to life or that would cause irreversible adverse health effects or that would interfere with an individual's ability to escape unaided from a permit space.

NOTE TO THE DEFINITION OF "IMMEDIATELY DANGEROUS TO LIFE OR HEALTH": Some materials—hydrogen fluoride gas and cadmium vapor, for example—may produce immediate transient effects that, even if severe, may pass without medical attention, but are followed by sudden, possibly fatal collapse 12–72 hours after exposure. The victim "feels normal" from recovery from transient effects until collapse. Such materials in hazardous quantities are considered to be "immediately" dangerous to life or health.

Insulated. Separated from other conducting surfaces by a dielectric (including air space) offering a high resistance to the passage of current.

NOTE TO THE DEFINITION OF "INSULATED": When any object is said to be insulated, it is understood to be insulated for the conditions to which it normally is subjected. Otherwise, it is, for the purpose of this subpart, uninsulated.

Insulation (cable). Material relied upon to insulate the conductor from other conductors or conducting parts or from ground.

Isolated. Not readily accessible to persons unless special means for access are used.

Line-clearance tree trimming. The pruning, trimming, repairing, maintaining, removing, or clearing of trees, or the cutting of brush, that is within the following distance of electric supply lines and equipment:

(1) For voltages to ground of 50 kilovolts or less—3.05 meters (10 feet);

(2) For voltages to ground of more than 50 kilovolts—3.05 meters (10 feet) plus 0.10 meters (4 inches) for every 10 kilovolts over 50 kilovolts.

Lines—(1) *Communication lines.* The conductors and their supporting or containing structures which are used for public or private signal or communication service, and which operate at potentials not exceeding 400 volts to ground or 750 volts between any two points of the circuit, and the transmitted power of which does not exceed 150 watts. If the lines are operating at less than 150 volts, no limit is placed on the transmitted power of the system. Under certain conditions, communication cables may include communication circuits exceeding these limitations where such circuits are also used to supply power solely to communication equipment.

NOTE TO THE DEFINITION OF "COMMUNICATION LINES": Telephone, telegraph, railroad signal, data, clock, fire, police alarm, cable television, and other systems conforming to this definition are included. Lines used for signaling purposes, but not included under this definition, are considered as electric supply lines of the same voltage.

(2) *Electric supply lines.* Conductors used to transmit electric energy and their necessary supporting or containing structures. Signal lines of more than 400 volts are always supply lines within this subpart, and those of less than 400 volts are considered as supply lines, if so run and operated throughout.

Manhole. A subsurface enclosure that personnel may enter and that is used for installing, operating, and maintaining submersible equipment or cable.

Minimum approach distance. The closest distance an employee may approach an energized or a grounded object.

NOTE TO THE DEFINITION OF "MINIMUM APPROACH DISTANCE": Paragraph (c)(1)(i) of §1926.960 requires employers to establish minimum approach distances.

Personal fall arrest system. A system used to arrest an employee in a fall from a working level.

Qualified employee (qualified person). An employee (person) knowledgeable in the construction and operation of the electric power generation, transmission, and distribution equipment involved, along with the associated hazards.

NOTE 1 TO THE DEFINITION OF "QUALIFIED EMPLOYEE (QUALIFIED PERSON)": An employee must have the training required by §1926.950(b)(2) to be a qualified employee.

NOTE 2 TO THE DEFINITION OF "QUALIFIED EMPLOYEE (QUALIFIED PERSON)": Except under §1926.954(b)(3)(iii), an employee who is under-

going on-the-job training and who has demonstrated, in the course of such training, an ability to perform duties safely at his or her level of training and who is under the direct supervision of a qualified person is a qualified person for the performance of those duties.

Statistical sparkover voltage. A transient overvoltage level that produces a 97.72-percent probability of sparkover (that is, two standard deviations above the voltage at which there is a 50-percent probability of sparkover).

Statistical withstand voltage. A transient overvoltage level that produces a 0.14-percent probability of sparkover (that is, three standard deviations below the voltage at which there is a 50-percent probability of sparkover).

Switch. A device for opening and closing or for changing the connection of a circuit. In this subpart, a switch is manually operable, unless otherwise stated.

System operator. A qualified person designated to operate the system or its parts.

Vault. An enclosure, above or below ground, that personnel may enter and that is used for installing, operating, or maintaining equipment or cable.

Vented vault. A vault that has provision for air changes using exhaust-flue stacks and low-level air intakes operating on pressure and temperature differentials that provide for airflow that precludes a hazardous atmosphere from developing.

Voltage. The effective (root mean square, or rms) potential difference between any two conductors or between a conductor and ground. This subpart expresses voltages in nominal values, unless otherwise indicated. The nominal voltage of a system or circuit is the value assigned to a system or circuit of a given voltage class for the purpose of convenient designation. The operating voltage of the system may vary above or below this value.

Work-positioning equipment. A body belt or body harness system rigged to allow an employee to be supported on an elevated vertical surface, such as a utility pole or tower leg, and work with both hands free while leaning.

[79 FR 20696, Apr. 11, 2014, as amended at 79 FR 56962, Sept. 24, 2014]

EFFECTIVE DATE NOTE: At 80 FR 25518, May 4, 2015, § 1926.968 was amended by adding a note to the definition of "Enclosed spaces", effective Aug. 3, 2015. For the convenience of the user, the added text is set forth as follows:

§ **1926.968   Definitions.**

*   *   *   *   *

Enclosed space. * * *

NOTE TO THE DEFINITION OF "ENCLOSED SPACE". The Occupational Safety and Health Administration does not consider spaces that are enclosed but not designed for employee entry under normal operating conditions to be enclosed spaces for the purposes of this subpart. Similarly, the Occupational Safety and Health Administration does not consider spaces that are enclosed and that are expected to contain a hazardous atmosphere to be enclosed spaces for the purposes of this subpart. Such spaces meet the definition of permit spaces in subpart AA of this part, and entry into them must conform to that standard.

*   *   *   *   *

APPENDIX A TO SUBPART V OF PART 1926 [RESERVED]

APPENDIX B TO SUBPART V OF PART 1926—WORKING ON EXPOSED ENERGIZED PARTS

I. INTRODUCTION

Electric utilities design electric power generation, transmission, and distribution installations to meet National Electrical Safety Code (NESC), ANSI C2, requirements. Electric utilities also design transmission and distribution lines to limit line outages as required by system reliability criteria[1] and to withstand the maximum overvoltages impressed on the system. Conditions such as switching surges, faults, and lightning can cause overvoltages. Electric utilities generally select insulator design and lengths and the clearances to structural parts so as to prevent outages from contaminated line insulation and during storms. Line insulator lengths and structural clearances have, over the years, come closer to the minimum approach distances used by workers. As minimum approach distances and structural clearances converge, it is increasingly important that system designers and system

operating and maintenance personnel understand the concepts underlying minimum approach distances.

The information in this appendix will assist employers in complying with the minimum approach-distance requirements contained in §§ 1926.960(c)(1) and 1926.964(c). Employers must use the technical criteria and methodology presented in this appendix in establishing minimum approach distances in accordance with § 1926.960(c)(1)(i) and Table V–2 and Table V–7. This appendix provides essential background information and technical criteria for the calculation of the required minimum approach distances for live-line work on electric power generation, transmission, and distribution installations.

Unless an employer is using the maximum transient overvoltages specified in Table V–8 for voltages over 72.5 kilovolts, the employer must use persons knowledgeable in the techniques discussed in this appendix, and competent in the field of electric transmission and distribution system design, to determine the maximum transient overvoltage.

II. GENERAL

A. *Definitions.* The following definitions from § 1926.968 relate to work on or near electric power generation, transmission, and distribution lines and equipment and the electrical hazards they present.

Exposed. . . . Not isolated or guarded.

Guarded. Covered, fenced, enclosed, or otherwise protected, by means of suitable covers or casings, barrier rails or screens, mats, or platforms, designed to minimize the possibility, under normal conditions, of dangerous approach or inadvertent contact by persons or objects.

NOTE TO THE DEFINITION OF "GUARDED": Wires that are insulated, but not otherwise protected, are not guarded.

Insulated. Separated from other conducting surfaces by a dielectric (including air space) offering a high resistance to the passage of current.

NOTE TO THE DEFINITION OF "INSULATED": When any object is said to be insulated, it is understood to be insulated for the conditions to which it normally is subjected. Otherwise, it is, for the purpose of this subpart, uninsulated.

Isolated. Not readily accessible to persons unless special means for access are used.

Statistical sparkover voltage. A transient overvoltage level that produces a 97.72-percent probability of sparkover (that is, two standard deviations above the voltage at which there is a 50-percent probability of sparkover).

Statistical withstand voltage. A transient overvoltage level that produces a 0.14-percent probability of sparkover (that is, three

[1] Federal, State, and local regulatory bodies and electric utilities set reliability requirements that limit the number and duration of system outages.

standard deviations below the voltage at which there is a 50-percent probability of sparkover).

B. *Installations energized at 50 to 300 volts.* The hazards posed by installations energized at 50 to 300 volts are the same as those found in many other workplaces. That is not to say that there is no hazard, but the complexity of electrical protection required does not compare to that required for high-voltage systems. The employee must avoid contact with the exposed parts, and the protective equipment used (such as rubber insulating gloves) must provide insulation for the voltages involved.

C. *Exposed energized parts over 300 volts AC.* Paragraph (c)(1)(i) of §1926.960 requires the employer to establish minimum approach distances no less than the distances computed by Table V–2 for ac systems so that employees can work safely without risk of sparkover.[2]

Unless the employee is using electrical protective equipment, air is the insulating medium between the employee and energized parts. The distance between the employee and an energized part must be sufficient for the air to withstand the maximum transient overvoltage that can reach the worksite under the working conditions and practices the employee is using. This distance is the minimum air insulation distance, and it is equal to the electrical component of the minimum approach distance.

Normal system design may provide or include a means (such as lightning arrestors) to control maximum anticipated transient overvoltages, or the employer may use temporary devices (portable protective gaps) or measures (such as preventing automatic circuit breaker reclosing) to achieve the same result. Paragraph (c)(1)(ii) of §1926.960 requires the employer to determine the maximum anticipated per-unit transient overvoltage, phase-to-ground, through an engineering analysis or assume a maximum anticipated per-unit transient overvoltage, phase-to-ground, in accordance with Table V–8, which specifies the following maximums for ac systems:

72.6 to 420.0 kilovolts .... 3.5 per unit.
420.1 to 550.0 kilovolts .... 3.0 per unit.
550.1 to 800.0 kilovolts .... 2.5 per unit.

See paragraph IV.A.2, later in this appendix, for additional discussion of maximum transient overvoltages.

D. *Types of exposures.* Employees working on or near energized electric power generation, transmission, and distribution systems face two kinds of exposures: Phase-to-ground and phase-to-phase. The exposure is phase-

to-ground: (1) With respect to an energized part, when the employee is at ground potential or (2) with respect to ground, when an employee is at the potential of the energized part during live-line barehand work. The exposure is phase-to-phase, with respect to an energized part, when an employee is at the potential of another energized part (at a different potential) during live-line barehand work.

III. DETERMINATION OF MINIMUM APPROACH DISTANCES FOR AC VOLTAGES GREATER THAN 300 VOLTS

A. *Voltages of 301 to 5,000 volts.* Test data generally forms the basis of minimum air insulation distances. The lowest voltage for which sufficient test data exists is 5,000 volts, and these data indicate that the minimum air insulation distance at that voltage is 20 millimeters (1 inch). Because the minimum air insulation distance increases with increasing voltage, and, conversely, decreases with decreasing voltage, an assumed minimum air insulation distance of 20 millimeters will protect against sparkover at voltages of 301 to 5,000 volts. Thus, 20 millimeters is the electrical component of the minimum approach distance for these voltages.

B. *Voltages of 5.1 to 72.5 kilovolts.* For voltages from 5.1 to 72.5 kilovolts, the Occupational Safety and Health Administration bases the methodology for calculating the electrical component of the minimum approach distance on Institute of Electrical and Electronic Engineers (IEEE) Standard 4–1995, *Standard Techniques for High-Voltage Testing.* Table 1 lists the critical sparkover distances from that standard as listed in IEEE Std 516–2009, *IEEE Guide for Maintenance Methods on Energized Power Lines.*

TABLE 1—SPARKOVER DISTANCE FOR ROD-TO-ROD GAP

60 Hz rod-to-rod sparkover (kV peak)	Gap spacing from IEEE Std 4–1995 (cm)
25	2
36	3
46	4
53	5
60	6
70	8
79	10
86	12
95	14
104	16
112	18
120	20
143	25
167	30
192	35
218	40
243	45
270	50

[2] Sparkover is a disruptive electric discharge in which an electric arc forms and electric current passes through air.

511

TABLE 1—SPARKOVER DISTANCE FOR ROD-TO-
ROD GAP—Continued

60 Hz rod-to-rod sparkover (kV peak)	Gap spacing from IEEE Std 4–1995 (cm)
322	60

Source: IEEE Std 516–2009.

To use this table to determine the electrical component of the minimum approach distance, the employer must determine the peak phase-to-ground transient overvoltage and select a gap from the table that corresponds to that voltage as a withstand voltage rather than a critical sparkover voltage. To calculate the electrical component of the minimum approach distance for voltages between 5 and 72.5 kilovolts, use the following procedure:

1. Divide the phase-to-phase voltage by the square root of 3 to convert it to a phase-to-ground voltage.

2. Multiply the phase-to-ground voltage by the square root of 2 to convert the rms value

of the voltage to the peak phase-to-ground voltage.

3. Multiply the peak phase-to-ground voltage by the maximum per-unit transient overvoltage, which, for this voltage range, is 3.0, as discussed later in this appendix. This is the maximum phase-to-ground transient overvoltage, which corresponds to the withstand voltage for the relevant exposure.[3]

4. Divide the maximum phase-to-ground transient overvoltage by 0.85 to determine the corresponding critical sparkover voltage. (The critical sparkover voltage is 3 standard deviations (or 15 percent) greater than the withstand voltage.)

5. Determine the electrical component of the minimum approach distance from Table 1 through interpolation.

Table 2 illustrates how to derive the electrical component of the minimum approach distance for voltages from 5.1 to 72.5 kilovolts, before the application of any altitude correction factor, as explained later.

TABLE 2—CALCULATING THE ELECTRICAL COMPONENT OF MAD—751 V TO 72.5 KV

Step	Maximum system phase-to-phase voltage (kV)			
	15	36	46	72.5
1. Divide by √3	8.7	20.8	26.6	41.9
2. Multiply by √2	12.2	29.4	37.6	59.2
3. Multiply by 3.0	36.7	88.2	112.7	177.6
4. Divide by 0.85	43.2	103.7	132.6	208.9
5. Interpolate from Table 1	3+(7.2/10)*1	14+(8.7/9)*2	20+(12.6/23)*5	35+(16.9/26)*5
Electrical component of MAD (cm)	3.72	15.93	22.74	38.25

C. *Voltages of 72.6 to 800 kilovolts.* For voltages of 72.6 kilovolts to 800 kilovolts, this subpart bases the electrical component of minimum approach distances, before the application of any altitude correction factor, on the following formula:

EQUATION 1—FOR VOLTAGES OF 72.6 KV TO 800 KV

$$D = 0.3048(C + a)V_{L-G}T$$

Where:

D = Electrical component of the minimum approach distance in air in meters;

C = a correction factor associated with the variation of gap sparkover with voltage;

a = A factor relating to the saturation of air at system voltages of 345 kilovolts or higher;[4]

V_{L-G} = Maximum system line-to-ground rms voltage in kilovolts—it should be the "actual" maximum, or the normal highest voltage for the range (for example, 10 percent above the nominal voltage); and

T = Maximum transient overvoltage factor in per unit.

In Equation 1, C is 0.01: (1) For phase-to-ground exposures that the employer can demonstrate consist only of air across the approach distance (gap) and (2) for phase-to-phase exposures if the employer can demonstrate that no insulated tool spans the gap and that no large conductive object is in the gap. Otherwise, C is 0.011.

---

[3] The withstand voltage is the voltage at which sparkover is not likely to occur across a specified distance. It is the voltage taken at the 3σ point below the sparkover voltage, assuming that the sparkover curve follows a normal distribution.

[4] Test data demonstrates that the saturation factor is greater than 0 at peak voltages

of about 630 kilovolts. Systems operating at 345 kilovolts (or maximum system voltages of 362 kilovolts) can have peak maximum transient overvoltages exceeding 630 kilovolts. Table V–2 sets equations for calculating a based on peak voltage.

In Equation 1, the term a varies depending on whether the employee's exposure is phase-to-ground or phase-to-phase and on whether objects are in the gap. The employer must use the equations in Table 3 to calculate a. Sparkover test data with insulation spanning the gap form the basis for the equations for phase-to-ground exposures, and sparkover test data with only air in the gap form the basis for the equations for phase-to-phase exposures. The phase-to-phase equations result in slightly higher values of a, and, consequently, produce larger minimum approach distances, than the phase-to-phase equations for the same value of V_{Peak}.

Table 3—Equations for Calculating the Surge Factor, a

Phase-to-Ground Exposures			
$V_{Peak} = T_{L\text{-}G}V_{L\text{-}G}\sqrt{2}$	635 kV or less	635.1 to 915 kV	915.1 to 1,050 kV
a	0	$(V_{Peak}- 635)/140,000$	$(V_{Peak}-645)/135,000$
$V_{Peak} = T_{L\text{-}G}V_{L\text{-}G}\sqrt{2}$	More than 1,050 kV		
a	$(V_{Peak}-675)/125,000$		
Phase-to-Phase Exposures[1]			
$V_{Peak} = (1.35T_{L\text{-}G} + 0.45)V_{L\text{-}G}\sqrt{2}$	630 kV or less	630.1 to 848 kV	848.1 to 1,131 kV
a	0	$(V_{Peak}-630)/155,000$	$(V_{Peak}-633.6)/152,207$
$V_{Peak} = (1.35T_{L\text{-}G} + 0.45)V_{L\text{-}G}\sqrt{2}$	1,131.1 to 1,485 kV	More than 1,485 kV	
a	$(V_{Peak}-628)/153,846$	$(V_{Peak}-350.5)/203,666$	

[1]Use the equations for phase-to-ground exposures (with V_{Peak} for phase-to-phase exposures) unless the employer can demonstrate that no insulated tool spans the gap and that no large conductive object is in the gap.

In Equation 1, T is the maximum transient overvoltage factor in per unit. As noted earlier, § 1926.960(c)(1)(ii) requires the employer to determine the maximum anticipated per-unit transient overvoltage, phase-to-ground, through an engineering analysis or assume a maximum anticipated per-unit transient overvoltage, phase-to-ground, in accordance with Table V–8. For phase-to-ground exposures, the employer uses this value, called $T_{L\text{-}G}$, as T in Equation 1. IEEE Std 516–2009 provides the following formula to calculate the phase-to-phase maximum transient overvoltage, $T_{L\text{-}L}$, from $T_{L\text{-}G}$:

$$T_{L\text{-}L} = 1.35T_{L\text{-}G} + 0.45.$$

For phase-to-phase exposures, the employer uses this value as T in Equation 1.

D. *Provisions for inadvertent movement.* The minimum approach distance must include an "adder" to compensate for the inadvertent movement of the worker relative to an energized part or the movement of the part relative to the worker. This "adder" must account for this possible inadvertent movement and provide the worker with a comfortable and safe zone in which to work. Employers must add the distance for inadvertent movement (called the "ergonomic component of the minimum approach distance") to the electrical component to determine the total safe minimum approach distances used in live-line work.

The Occupational Safety and Health Administration based the ergonomic component of the minimum approach distance on response time-distance analysis. This technique uses an estimate of the total response time to a hazardous incident and converts that time to the distance traveled. For example, the driver of a car takes a given amount of time to respond to a "stimulus" and stop the vehicle. The elapsed time involved results in the car's traveling some distance before coming to a complete stop. This distance depends on the speed of the car at the time the stimulus appears and the reaction time of the driver.

In the case of live-line work, the employee must first perceive that he or she is approaching the danger zone. Then, the worker responds to the danger and must decelerate and stop all motion toward the energized part. During the time it takes to stop, the employee will travel some distance. This is the distance the employer must add to the electrical component of the minimum approach distance to obtain the total safe minimum approach distance.

At voltages from 751 volts to 72.5 kilovolts,[5] the electrical component of the minimum approach distance is smaller than the ergonomic component. At 72.5 kilovolts, the electrical component is only a little more than 0.3 meters (1 foot). An ergonomic component of the minimum approach distance must provide for all the worker's unanticipated movements. At these voltages, workers generally use rubber insulating gloves; however, these gloves protect only a worker's hands and arms. Therefore, the energized object must be at a safe approach distance to protect the worker's face. In this case, 0.61 meters (2 feet) is a sufficient and practical ergonomic component of the minimum approach distance.

For voltages between 72.6 and 800 kilovolts, employees must use different work practices during energized line work. Generally, employees use live-line tools (hot sticks) to perform work on energized equipment. These tools, by design, keep the energized part at a constant distance from the employee and, thus, maintain the appropriate minimum approach distance automatically.

The location of the worker and the type of work methods the worker is using also influence the length of the ergonomic component of the minimum approach distance. In this higher voltage range, the employees use work methods that more tightly control their movements than when the workers perform work using rubber insulating gloves. The worker, therefore, is farther from the energized line or equipment and must be more precise in his or her movements just to perform the work. For these reasons, this subpart adopts an ergonomic component of the minimum approach distance of 0.31 m (1 foot) for voltages between 72.6 and 800 kilovolts.

Table 4 summarizes the ergonomic component of the minimum approach distance for various voltage ranges.

TABLE 4—ERGONOMIC COMPONENT OF MINIMUM APPROACH DISTANCE

Voltage range (kV)	Distance	
	m	ft
0.301 to 0.750	0.31	1.0
0.751 to 72.5	0.61	2.0
72.6 to 800	0.31	1.0

Note: The employer must add this distance to the electrical component of the minimum approach distance to obtain the full minimum approach distance.

The ergonomic component of the minimum approach distance accounts for errors in maintaining the minimum approach distance (which might occur, for example, if an employee misjudges the length of a conductive object he or she is holding), and for errors in judging the minimum approach distance. The ergonomic component also accounts for inadvertent movements by the employee, such as slipping. In contrast, the working position selected to properly maintain the minimum approach distance must account for all of an employee's reasonably likely movements and still permit the employee to adhere to the applicable minimum approach distance. (See Figure 1.) Reasonably likely movements include an employee's adjustments to tools, equipment, and working positions and all movements needed to perform the work. For example, the employee should be able to perform all of the following actions without straying into the minimum approach distance:

• Adjust his or her hardhat,

• maneuver a tool onto an energized part with a reasonable amount of overreaching or underreaching,

• reach for and handle tools, material, and equipment passed to him or her, and

• adjust tools, and replace components on them, when necessary during the work procedure.

[5] For voltages of 50 to 300 volts, Table V–2 specifies a minimum approach distance of "avoid contact." The minimum approach distance for this voltage range contains neither an electrical component nor an ergonomic component.

The training of qualified employees required under § 1926.950, and the job planning and briefing required under § 1926.952, must address selection of a proper working position.

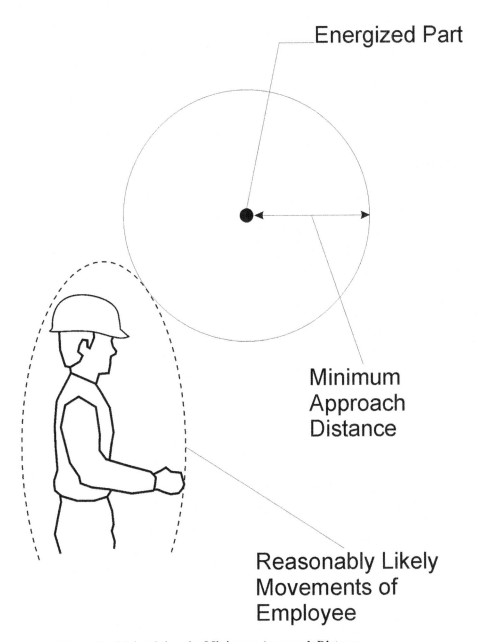

Energized Part

Minimum Approach Distance

Reasonably Likely Movements of Employee

Figure 1—Maintaining the Minimum Approach Distance

E. *Miscellaneous correction factors.* Changes in the air medium that forms the insulation influences the strength of an air gap. A brief discussion of each factor follows.

1. *Dielectric strength of air.* The dielectric strength of air in a uniform electric field at standard atmospheric conditions is approximately 3 kilovolts per millimeter.[6] The pressure, temperature, and humidity of the air, the shape, dimensions, and separation of the electrodes, and the characteristics of the applied voltage (wave shape) affect the disruptive gradient.

2. *Atmospheric effect.* The empirically determined electrical strength of a given gap is normally applicable at standard atmospheric conditions (20 °C, 101.3 kilopascals, 11 grams/ cubic centimeter humidity). An increase in the density (humidity) of the air inhibits sparkover for a given air gap. The combination of temperature and air pressure that results in the lowest gap sparkover voltage is high temperature and low pressure. This combination of conditions is not likely to occur. Low air pressure, generally associated with high humidity, causes increased electrical strength. An average air pressure generally correlates with low humidity. Hot and dry working conditions normally result in reduced electrical strength. The equations for minimum approach distances in Table V–2 assume standard atmospheric conditions.

3. *Altitude.* The reduced air pressure at high altitudes causes a reduction in the electrical strength of an air gap. An employer must increase the minimum approach distance by about 3 percent per 300 meters (1,000 feet) of increased altitude for altitudes above 900 meters (3,000 feet). Table V–4 specifies the altitude correction factor that the employer must use in calculating minimum approach distances.

IV. DETERMINING MINIMUM APPROACH DISTANCES

A. Factors Affecting Voltage Stress at the Worksite

1. *System voltage (nominal).* The nominal system voltage range determines the voltage for purposes of calculating minimum approach distances. The employer selects the range in which the nominal system voltage falls, as given in the relevant table, and uses

---

[6] For the purposes of estimating arc length, Subpart V generally assumes a more conservative dielectric strength of 10 kilovolts per 25.4 millimeters, consistent with assumptions made in consensus standards such as the National Electrical Safety Code (IEEE C2–2012). The more conservative value accounts for variables such as electrode shape, wave shape, and a certain amount of overvoltage.

the highest value within that range in per-unit calculations.

2. *Transient overvoltages.* Operation of switches or circuit breakers, a fault on a line or circuit or on an adjacent circuit, and similar activities may generate transient overvoltages on an electrical system. Each overvoltage has an associated transient voltage wave shape. The wave shape arriving at the site and its magnitude vary considerably.

In developing requirements for minimum approach distances, the Occupational Safety and Health Administration considered the most common wave shapes and the magnitude of transient overvoltages found on electric power generation, transmission, and distribution systems. The equations in Table V–2 for minimum approach distances use per-unit maximum transient overvoltages, which are relative to the nominal maximum voltage of the system. For example, a maximum transient overvoltage value of 3.0 per unit indicates that the highest transient overvoltage is 3.0 times the nominal maximum system voltage.

3. *Typical magnitude of overvoltages.* Table 5 lists the magnitude of typical transient overvoltages.

TABLE 5—MAGNITUDE OF TYPICAL TRANSIENT OVERVOLTAGES

Cause	Magnitude (per unit)
Energized 200-mile line without closing resistors	3.5
Energized 200-mile line with one-step closing resistor	2.1
Energized 200-mile line with multistep resistor	2.5
Reclosing with trapped charge one-step resistor	2.2
Opening surge with single restrike	3.0
Fault initiation unfaulted phase	2.1
Fault initiation adjacent circuit	2.5
Fault clearing	1.7 to 1.9

4. *Standard deviation—air-gap withstand.* For each air gap length under the same atmospheric conditions, there is a statistical variation in the breakdown voltage. The probability of breakdown against voltage has a normal (Gaussian) distribution. The standard deviation of this distribution varies with the wave shape, gap geometry, and atmospheric conditions. The withstand voltage of the air gap is three standard deviations (3σ) below the critical sparkover voltage. (The critical sparkover voltage is the crest value of the impulse wave that, under specified conditions, causes sparkover 50 percent of the time. An impulse wave of three standard deviations below this value, that is, the withstand voltage, has a probability of sparkover of approximately 1 in 1,000.)

5. *Broken Insulators.* Tests show reductions in the insulation strength of insulator strings with broken skirts. Broken units may lose up to 70 percent of their withstand

capacity. Because an employer cannot determine the insulating capability of a broken unit without testing it, the employer must consider damaged units in an insulator to have no insulating value. Additionally, the presence of a live-line tool alongside an insulator string with broken units may further reduce the overall insulating strength. The number of good units that must be present in a string for it to be "insulated" as defined by § 1926.968 depends on the maximum overvoltage possible at the worksite.

B. Minimum Approach Distances Based on Known, Maximum-Anticipated Per-Unit Transient Overvoltages

1. *Determining the minimum approach distance for AC systems.* Under § 1926.960(c)(1)(ii), the employer must determine the maximum anticipated per-unit transient overvoltage, phase-to-ground, through an engineering analysis or must assume a maximum anticipated per-unit transient overvoltage, phase-to-ground, in accordance with Table V–8. When the employer conducts an engineering analysis of the system and determines that the maximum transient overvoltage is lower than specified by Table V–8, the employer must ensure that any conditions assumed in the analysis, for example, that employees block reclosing on a circuit or install portable protective gaps, are present during energized work. To ensure that these conditions are present, the employer may need to institute new live-work procedures reflecting the conditions and limitations set by the engineering analysis.

2. *Calculation of reduced approach distance values.* An employer may take the following steps to reduce minimum approach distances when the maximum transient overvoltage on the system (that is, the maximum transient overvoltage without additional steps to control overvoltages) produces unacceptably large minimum approach distances:

Step 1. Determine the maximum voltage (with respect to a given nominal voltage range) for the energized part.

Step 2. Determine the technique to use to control the maximum transient overvoltage. (See paragraphs IV.C and IV.D of this appendix.) Determine the maximum transient overvoltage that can exist at the worksite with that form of control in place and with a confidence level of 3σ . This voltage is the withstand voltage for the purpose of calculating the appropriate minimum approach distance.

Step 3. Direct employees to implement procedures to ensure that the control technique is in effect during the course of the work.

Step 4. Using the new value of transient overvoltage in per unit, calculate the required minimum approach distance from Table V–2.

C. Methods of Controlling Possible Transient Overvoltage Stress Found on a System

1. *Introduction.* There are several means of controlling overvoltages that occur on transmission systems. For example, the employer can modify the operation of circuit breakers or other switching devices to reduce switching transient overvoltages. Alternatively, the employer can hold the overvoltage to an acceptable level by installing surge arresters or portable protective gaps on the system. In addition, the employer can change the transmission system to minimize the effect of switching operations. Section 4.8 of IEEE Std 516–2009 describes various ways of controlling, and thereby reducing, maximum transient overvoltages.

2. *Operation of circuit breakers.*[7] The maximum transient overvoltage that can reach the worksite is often the result of switching on the line on which employees are working. Disabling automatic reclosing during energized line work, so that the line will not be reenergized after being opened for any reason, limits the maximum switching surge overvoltage to the larger of the opening surge or the greatest possible fault-generated surge, provided that the devices (for example, insertion resistors) are operable and will function to limit the transient overvoltage and that circuit breaker restrikes do not occur. The employer must ensure the proper functioning of insertion resistors and other overvoltage-limiting devices when the employer's engineering analysis assumes their proper operation to limit the overvoltage level. If the employer cannot disable the reclosing feature (because of system operating conditions), other methods of controlling the switching surge level may be necessary.

Transient surges on an adjacent line, particularly for double circuit construction, may cause a significant overvoltage on the line on which employees are working. The employer's engineering analysis must account for coupling to adjacent lines.

3. *Surge arresters.* The use of modern surge arresters allows a reduction in the basic impulse-insulation levels of much transmission system equipment. The primary function of early arresters was to protect the system insulation from the effects of lightning. Modern arresters not only dissipate lightning-caused transients, but may also control many other system transients caused by switching or faults.

---

[7] The detailed design of a circuit interrupter, such as the design of the contacts, resistor insertion, and breaker timing control, are beyond the scope of this appendix. The design of the system generally accounts for these features. This appendix only discusses features that can limit the maximum switching transient overvoltage on a system.

The employer may use properly designed arresters to control transient overvoltages along a transmission line and thereby reduce the requisite length of the insulator string and possibly the maximum transient overvoltage on the line.[8]

4. *Switching Restrictions.* Another form of overvoltage control involves establishing switching restrictions, whereby the employer prohibits the operation of circuit breakers until certain system conditions are present. The employer restricts switching by using a tagging system, similar to that used for a permit, except that the common term used for this activity is a "hold-off" or "restriction." These terms indicate that the restriction does not prevent operation, but only modifies the operation during the live-work activity.

D. Minimum Approach Distance Based on Control of Maximum Transient Overvoltage at the Worksite

When the employer institutes control of maximum transient overvoltage at the worksite by installing portable protective gaps, the employer may calculate the minimum approach distance as follows:

Step 1. Select the appropriate withstand voltage for the protective gap based on system requirements and an acceptable probability of gap sparkover.[9]

Step 2. Determine a gap distance that provides a withstand voltage[10] greater than or equal to the one selected in the first step.[11]

Step 3. Use 110 percent of the gap's critical sparkover voltage to determine the phase-to-ground peak voltage at gap sparkover ($V_{PPG\ Peak}$).

Step 4. Determine the maximum transient overvoltage, phase-to-ground, at the worksite from the following formula:

$$T = \frac{V_{PPG\,Peak}}{V_{L\text{-}G}\sqrt{2}}.$$

Step 5. Use this value of T[12] in the equation in Table V-2 to obtain the minimum approach distance. If the worksite is no more than 900 meters (3,000 feet) above sea level, the employer may use this value of T to determine the minimum approach distance from Table 7 through Table 14.

NOTE: All rounding must be to the next higher value (that is, always round up).

Sample protective gap calculations.

Problem: Employees are to perform work on a 500-kilovolt transmission line at sea level that is subject to transient overvoltages of 2.4 p.u. The maximum operating voltage of the line is 550 kilovolts. Determine the length of the protective gap that will provide the minimum practical safe approach distance. Also, determine what that minimum approach distance is.

Step 1. Calculate the smallest practical maximum transient overvoltage (1.25 times the crest phase-to-ground voltage):[13]

---

[8] Surge arrester application is beyond the scope of this appendix. However, if the employer installs the arrester near the work site, the application would be similar to the protective gaps discussed in paragraph IV.D of this appendix.

[9] The employer should check the withstand voltage to ensure that it results in a probability of gap flashover that is acceptable from a system outage perspective. (In other words, a gap sparkover will produce a system outage. The employer should determine whether such an outage will impact overall system performance to an acceptable degree.) In general, the withstand voltage should be at least 1.25 times the maximum crest operating voltage.

[10] The manufacturer of the gap provides, based on test data, the critical sparkover

voltage for each gap spacing (for example, a critical sparkover voltage of 665 kilovolts for a gap spacing of 1.2 meters). The withstand voltage for the gap is equal to 85 percent of its critical sparkover voltage.

[11] Switch steps 1 and 2 if the length of the protective gap is known.

[12] IEEE Std 516–2009 states that most employers add 0.2 to the calculated value of T as an additional safety factor.

[13] To eliminate sparkovers due to minor system disturbances, the employer should use a withstand voltage no lower than 1.25 p.u. Note that this is a practical, or operational, consideration only. It may be feasible for the employer to use lower values of withstand voltage.

$$550kV \times \frac{\sqrt{2}}{\sqrt{3}} \times 1.25 = 561kV.$$

This value equals the withstand voltage of the protective gap.

Step 2. Using test data for a particular protective gap, select a gap that has a critical sparkover voltage greater than or equal to:

$561kV \div 0.85 = 660kV$

For example, if a protective gap with a 1.22-m (4.0-foot) spacing tested to a critical sparkover voltage of 665 kilovolts (crest), select this gap spacing.

Step 3. The phase-to-ground peak voltage at gap sparkover ($V_{PPG\ Peak}$) is 110 percent of the value from the previous step:

$665kV \times 1.10 = 732kV$

This value corresponds to the withstand voltage of the electrical component of the minimum approach distance.

Step 4. Use this voltage to determine the worksite value of T:

$$T = \frac{732}{564} = 1.7\,p.u.$$

Step 5. Use this value of T in the equation in Table V–2 to obtain the minimum approach distance, or look up the minimum approach distance in Table 7 through Table 14:

$MAD = 2.29m(7.6ft)$

E. *Location of Protective Gaps*

1. *Adjacent structures.* The employer may install the protective gap on a structure adjacent to the worksite, as this practice does not significantly reduce the protection afforded by the gap.

2. *Terminal stations.* Gaps installed at terminal stations of lines or circuits provide a level of protection; however, that level of protection may not extend throughout the length of the line to the worksite. The use of substation terminal gaps raises the possibility that separate surges could enter the line at opposite ends, each with low enough magnitude to pass the terminal gaps without sparkover. When voltage surges occur simultaneously at each end of a line and travel toward each other, the total voltage on the line at the point where they meet is the arithmetic sum of the two surges. A gap installed within 0.8 km (0.5 mile) of the worksite will protect against such intersecting waves. Engineering studies of a particular line or system may indicate that employers can adequately protect employees by installing gaps at even more distant locations. In any event, unless using the default values for T from Table V–8, the employer must determine T at the worksite.

3. *Worksite.* If the employer installs protective gaps at the worksite, the gap setting establishes the worksite impulse insulation strength. Lightning strikes as far as 6 miles from the worksite can cause a voltage surge greater than the gap withstand voltage, and a gap sparkover can occur. In addition, the gap can sparkover from overvoltages on the line that exceed the withstand voltage of the gap. Consequently, the employer must protect employees from hazards resulting from any sparkover that could occur.

F. *Disabling automatic reclosing.* There are two reasons to disable the automatic-reclosing feature of circuit-interrupting devices while employees are performing live-line work:

• To prevent reenergization of a circuit faulted during the work, which could create a hazard or result in more serious injuries or damage than the injuries or damage produced by the original fault;

• To prevent any transient overvoltage caused by the switching surge that would result if the circuit were reenergized.

However, due to system stability considerations, it may not always be feasible to disable the automatic-reclosing feature.

V. Minimum Approach-Distance Tables

A. *Legacy tables.* Employers may use the minimum approach distances in Table 6 until March 31, 2015.

TABLE 6—MINIMUM APPROACH DISTANCES UNTIL MARCH 31, 2015

Voltage range phase to phase (kV)	Phase-to-ground exposure		Phase-to-phase exposure	
	m	ft	m	ft
2.1 to 15.0	0.64	2.1	0.61	2.0
15.1 to 35.0	0.71	2.3	0.71	2.3
35.1 to 46.0	0.76	2.5	0.76	2.5
46.1 to 72.5	0.91	3.0	0.91	3.0
72.6 to 121	1.02	3.3	1.37	4.5
138 to 145	1.07	3.5	1.52	5.0
161 to 169	1.12	3.7	1.68	5.5
230 to 242	1.52	5.0	2.54	8.3
345 to 362*	2.13	7.0	4.06	13.3
500 to 552*	3.35	11.0	6.10	20.0
700 to 765*	4.57	15.0	9.45	31.0

*The minimum approach distance may be the shortest distance between the energized part and the grounded surface.

B. *Alternative minimum approach distances.* Employers may use the minimum approach distances in Table 7 through Table 14 provided that the employer follows the notes to those tables.

TABLE 7—AC MINIMUM APPROACH DISTANCES—72.6 TO 121.0 KV

T (p.u.)	Phase-to-ground exposure		Phase-to-phase exposure	
	m	ft	m	ft
1.5	0.67	2.2	0.84	2.8
1.6	0.69	2.3	0.87	2.9
1.7	0.71	2.3	0.90	3.0
1.8	0.74	2.4	0.93	3.1
1.9	0.76	2.5	0.96	3.1
2.0	0.78	2.6	0.99	3.2
2.1	0.81	2.7	1.01	3.3
2.2	0.83	2.7	1.04	3.4
2.3	0.85	2.8	1.07	3.5
2.4	0.88	2.9	1.10	3.6
2.5	0.90	3.0	1.13	3.7
2.6	0.92	3.0	1.16	3.8
2.7	0.95	3.1	1.19	3.9
2.8	0.97	3.2	1.22	4.0
2.9	0.99	3.2	1.24	4.1
3.0	1.02	3.3	1.27	4.2
3.1	1.04	3.4	1.30	4.3
3.2	1.06	3.5	1.33	4.4
3.3	1.09	3.6	1.36	4.5
3.4	1.11	3.6	1.39	4.6
3.5	1.13	3.7	1.42	4.7

TABLE 8—AC MINIMUM APPROACH DISTANCES—121.1 TO 145.0 KV

T (p.u.)	Phase-to-ground rxposure		Phase-to-phase rxposure	
	m	ft	m	ft
1.5	0.74	2.4	0.95	3.1
1.6	0.76	2.5	0.98	3.2
1.7	0.79	2.6	1.02	3.3
1.8	0.82	2.7	1.05	3.4
1.9	0.85	2.8	1.08	3.5
2.0	0.88	2.9	1.12	3.7
2.1	0.90	3.0	1.15	3.8
2.2	0.93	3.1	1.19	3.9
2.3	0.96	3.1	1.22	4.0
2.4	0.99	3.2	1.26	4.1
2.5	1.02	3.3	1.29	4.2
2.6	1.04	3.4	1.33	4.4
2.7	1.07	3.5	1.36	4.5
2.8	1.10	3.6	1.39	4.6
2.9	1.13	3.7	1.43	4.7
3.0	1.16	3.8	1.46	4.8
3.1	1.19	3.9	1.50	4.9

TABLE 8—AC MINIMUM APPROACH DISTANCES—121.1 TO 145.0 KV—Continued

T (p.u.)	Phase-to-ground rxposure		Phase-to-phase rxposure	
	m	ft	m	ft
3.2	1.21	4.0	1.53	5.0
3.3	1.24	4.1	1.57	5.2
3.4	1.27	4.2	1.60	5.2
3.5	1.30	4.3	1.64	5.4

TABLE 9—AC MINIMUM APPROACH DISTANCES—145.1 TO 169.0 KV

T (p.u.)	Phase-to-ground exposure		Phase-to-phase exposure	
	m	ft	m	ft
1.5	0.81	2.7	1.05	3.4
1.6	0.84	2.8	1.09	3.6
1.7	0.87	2.9	1.13	3.7
1.8	0.90	3.0	1.17	3.8
1.9	0.94	3.1	1.21	4.0
2.0	0.97	3.2	1.25	4.1
2.1	1.00	3.3	1.29	4.2
2.2	1.03	3.4	1.33	4.4
2.3	1.07	3.5	1.37	4.5
2.4	1.10	3.6	1.41	4.6
2.5	1.13	3.7	1.45	4.8
2.6	1.17	3.8	1.49	4.9
2.7	1.20	3.9	1.53	5.0
2.8	1.23	4.0	1.57	5.2
2.9	1.26	4.1	1.61	5.3
3.0	1.30	4.3	1.65	5.4
3.1	1.33	4.4	1.70	5.6
3.2	1.36	4.5	1.76	5.8
3.3	1.39	4.6	1.82	6.0
3.4	1.43	4.7	1.88	6.2
3.5	1.46	4.8	1.94	6.4

TABLE 10—AC MINIMUM APPROACH DISTANCES—169.1 TO 242.0 KV

T (p.u.)	Phase-to-ground exposure		Phase-to-phase exposure	
	m	ft	m	ft
1.5	1.02	3.3	1.37	4.5
1.6	1.06	3.5	1.43	4.7
1.7	1.11	3.6	1.48	4.9
1.8	1.16	3.8	1.54	5.1
1.9	1.21	4.0	1.60	5.2
2.0	1.25	4.1	1.66	5.4
2.1	1.30	4.3	1.73	5.7
2.2	1.35	4.4	1.81	5.9
2.3	1.39	4.6	1.90	6.2
2.4	1.44	4.7	1.99	6.5
2.5	1.49	4.9	2.08	6.8
2.6	1.53	5.0	2.17	7.1
2.7	1.58	5.2	2.26	7.4
2.8	1.63	5.3	2.36	7.7
2.9	1.67	5.5	2.45	8.0
3.0	1.72	5.6	2.55	8.4
3.1	1.77	5.8	2.65	8.7
3.2	1.81	5.9	2.76	9.1
3.3	1.88	6.2	2.86	9.4
3.4	1.95	6.4	2.97	9.7
3.5	2.01	6.6	3.08	10.1

TABLE 11—AC MINIMUM APPROACH DISTANCES—242.1 TO 362.0 KV

T (p.u.)	Phase-to-ground exposure		Phase-to-phase exposure	
	m	ft	m	ft
1.5	1.37	4.5	1.99	6.5
1.6	1.44	4.7	2.13	7.0

TABLE 11—AC MINIMUM APPROACH DISTANCES—242.1 TO 362.0 KV—Continued

T (p.u.)	Phase-to-ground exposure		Phase-to-phase exposure	
	m	ft	m	ft
1.7	1.51	5.0	2.27	7.4
1.8	1.58	5.2	2.41	7.9
1.9	1.65	5.4	2.56	8.4
2.0	1.72	5.6	2.71	8.9
2.1	1.79	5.9	2.87	9.4
2.2	1.87	6.1	3.03	9.9
2.3	1.97	6.5	3.20	10.5
2.4	2.08	6.8	3.37	11.1
2.5	2.19	7.2	3.55	11.6
2.6	2.29	7.5	3.73	12.2
2.7	2.41	7.9	3.91	12.8
2.8	2.52	8.3	4.10	13.5
2.9	2.64	8.7	4.29	14.1
3.0	2.76	9.1	4.49	14.7
3.1	2.88	9.4	4.69	15.4
3.2	3.01	9.9	4.90	16.1
3.3	3.14	10.3	5.11	16.8
3.4	3.27	10.7	5.32	17.5
3.5	3.41	11.2	5.52	18.1

TABLE 12—AC MINIMUM APPROACH DISTANCES—362.1 TO 420.0 KV

T (p.u.)	Phase-to-ground exposure		Phase-to-phase exposure	
	m	ft	m	ft
1.5	1.53	5.0	2.40	7.9
1.6	1.62	5.3	2.58	8.5
1.7	1.70	5.6	2.75	9.0
1.8	1.78	5.8	2.94	9.6
1.9	1.88	6.2	3.13	10.3
2.0	1.99	6.5	3.33	10.9
2.1	2.12	7.0	3.53	11.6
2.2	2.24	7.3	3.74	12.3
2.3	2.37	7.8	3.95	13.0
2.4	2.50	8.2	4.17	13.7
2.5	2.64	8.7	4.40	14.4
2.6	2.78	9.1	4.63	15.2
2.7	2.93	9.6	4.87	16.0
2.8	3.07	10.1	5.11	16.8
2.9	3.23	10.6	5.36	17.6
3.0	3.38	11.1	5.59	18.3
3.1	3.55	11.6	5.82	19.1
3.2	3.72	12.2	6.07	19.9
3.3	3.89	12.8	6.31	20.7
3.4	4.07	13.4	6.56	21.5
3.5	4.25	13.9	6.81	22.3

TABLE 13—AC MINIMUM APPROACH DISTANCES—420.1 TO 550.0 KV

T (p.u.)	Phase-to-ground exposure		Phase-to-phase exposure	
	m	ft	m	ft
1.5	1.95	6.4	3.46	11.4
1.6	2.11	6.9	3.73	12.2
1.7	2.28	7.5	4.02	13.2
1.8	2.45	8.0	4.31	14.1
1.9	2.62	8.6	4.61	15.1
2.0	2.81	9.2	4.92	16.1
2.1	3.00	9.8	5.25	17.2
2.2	3.20	10.5	5.55	18.2
2.3	3.40	11.2	5.86	19.2
2.4	3.62	11.9	6.18	20.3
2.5	3.84	12.6	6.50	21.3
2.6	4.07	13.4	6.83	22.4
2.7	4.31	14.1	7.18	23.6
2.8	4.56	15.0	7.52	24.7
2.9	4.81	15.8	7.88	25.9

TABLE 13—AC MINIMUM APPROACH DISTANCES—420.1 TO 550.0 KV—Continued

T (p.u.)	Phase-to-ground exposure		Phase-to-phase exposure	
	m	ft	m	ft
3.0	5.07	16.6	8.24	27.0

TABLE 14—AC MINIMUM APPROACH DISTANCES—550.1 TO 800.0 KV

T (p.u.)	Phase-to-ground exposure		Phase-to-phase exposure	
	m	ft	m	ft
1.5	3.16	10.4	5.97	19.6
1.6	3.46	11.4	6.43	21.1
1.7	3.78	12.4	6.92	22.7
1.8	4.12	13.5	7.42	24.3
1.9	4.47	14.7	7.93	26.0
2.0	4.83	15.8	8.47	27.8
2.1	5.21	17.1	9.02	29.6
2.2	5.61	18.4	9.58	31.4
2.3	6.02	19.8	10.16	33.3
2.4	6.44	21.1	10.76	35.3
2.5	6.88	22.6	11.38	37.3

Notes to Table 7 through Table 14:
1. The employer must determine the maximum anticipated per-unit transient overvoltage, phase-to-ground, through an engineering analysis, as required by § 1926.960(c)(1)(ii), or assume a maximum anticipated per-unit transient overvoltage, phase-to-ground, in accordance with Table V–8.
2. For phase-to-phase exposures, the employer must demonstrate that no insulated tool spans the gap and that no large conductive object is in the gap.
3. The worksite must be at an elevation of 900 meters (3,000 feet) or less above sea level.

[79 FR 20696, Apr. 11, 2014, as amended at 79 FR 56962, Sept. 24, 2014]

APPENDIX C TO SUBPART V OF PART 1926—PROTECTION FROM HAZARDOUS DIFFERENCES IN ELECTRIC POTENTIAL

I. INTRODUCTION

Current passing through an impedance impresses voltage across that impedance. Even conductors have some, albeit low, value of impedance. Therefore, if a "grounded"[1] object, such as a crane or deenergized and grounded power line, results in a ground fault on a power line, voltage is impressed on that grounded object. The voltage impressed on the grounded object depends largely on the voltage on the line, on the impedance of the faulted conductor, and on the impedance to "true," or "absolute," ground represented by the object. If the impedance of the object causing the fault is relatively large, the voltage impressed on the object is essentially the phase-to-ground system voltage. However, even faults to grounded power lines or to well grounded transmission towers or sub-

station structures (which have relatively low values of impedance to ground) can result in hazardous voltages.[2] In all cases, the degree of the hazard depends on the magnitude of the current through the employee and the time of exposure. This appendix discusses methods of protecting workers against the possibility that grounded objects, such as cranes and other mechanical equipment, will contact energized power lines and that deenergized and grounded power lines will become accidentally energized.

II. VOLTAGE-GRADIENT DISTRIBUTION

A. *Voltage-gradient distribution curve.* Absolute, or true, ground serves as a reference and always has a voltage of 0 volts above ground potential. Because there is an impedance between a grounding electrode and absolute ground, there will be a voltage difference between the grounding electrode and absolute ground under ground-fault conditions. Voltage dissipates from the grounding electrode (or from the grounding point) and creates a ground potential gradient. The voltage decreases rapidly with increasing distance from the grounding electrode. A voltage drop associated with this dissipation

---

[1] This appendix generally uses the term "grounded" only with respect to grounding that the employer intentionally installs, for example, the grounding an employer installs on a deenergized conductor. However, in this case, the term "grounded" means connected to earth, regardless of whether or not that connection is intentional.

[2] Thus, grounding systems for transmission towers and substation structures should be designed to minimize the step and touch potentials involved.

of voltage is a ground potential. Figure 1 is a typical voltage-gradient distribution curve (assuming a uniform soil texture).

Figure 1—Typical Voltage-Gradient Distribution Curve

B. *Step and touch potentials.* Figure 1 also shows that workers are at risk from step and touch potentials. Step potential is the voltage between the feet of a person standing near an energized grounded object (the electrode). In Figure 1, the step potential is equal to the difference in voltage between two points at different distances from the electrode (where the points represent the location of each foot in relation to the electrode). A person could be at risk of injury during a fault simply by standing near the object.

Touch potential is the voltage between the energized grounded object (again, the electrode) and the feet of a person in contact with the object. In Figure 1, the touch potential is equal to the difference in voltage between the electrode (which is at a distance of 0 meters) and a point some distance away from the electrode (where the point represents the location of the feet of the person in contact with the object). The touch potential could be nearly the full voltage across the grounded object if that object is grounded at a point remote from the place where the person is in contact with it. For example, a crane grounded to the system neutral and that contacts an energized line would expose any person in contact with the crane or its uninsulated load line to a touch potential nearly equal to the full fault voltage.

Figure 2 illustrates step and touch potentials.

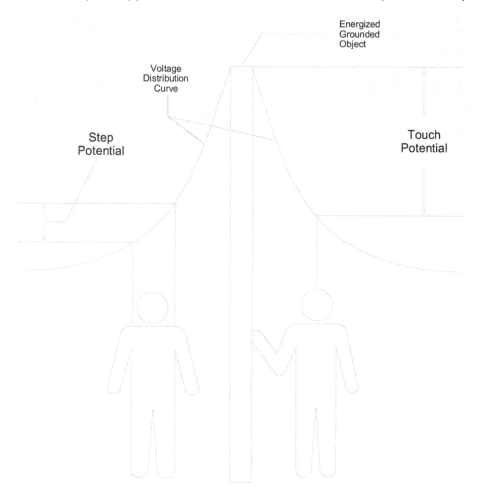

Figure 2—Step and Touch Potentials

III. PROTECTING WORKERS FROM HAZARDOUS DIFFERENCES IN ELECTRICAL POTENTIAL

A. *Definitions.* The following definitions apply to section III of this appendix:

Bond. The electrical interconnection of conductive parts designed to maintain a common electric potential.

Bonding cable (bonding jumper). A cable connected to two conductive parts to bond the parts together.

Cluster bar. A terminal temporarily attached to a structure that provides a means for the attachment and bonding of grounding and bonding cables to the structure.

Ground. A conducting connection between an electric circuit or equipment and the earth, or to some conducting body that serves in place of the earth.

Grounding cable (grounding jumper). A cable connected between a deenergized part and ground. Note that grounding cables carry fault current and bonding cables generally do not. A cable that bonds two conductive parts but carries substantial fault current (for example, a jumper connected between one phase and a grounded phase) is a grounding cable.

Ground mat (grounding grid). A temporarily or permanently installed metallic mat or grating that establishes an equipotential surface and provides connection points for attaching grounds.

B. *Analyzing the hazard.* The employer can use an engineering analysis of the power system under fault conditions to determine whether hazardous step and touch voltages will develop. The analysis should determine the voltage on all conductive objects in the work area and the amount of time the voltage will be present. Based on the this analysis, the employer can select appropriate measures and protective equipment, including the measures and protective equipment outlined in Section III of this appendix, to protect each employee from hazardous differences in electric potential. For example, from the analysis, the employer will know the voltage remaining on conductive objects after employees install bonding and grounding equipment and will be able to select insulating equipment with an appropriate rating, as described in paragraph III.C.2 of this appendix.

C. *Protecting workers on the ground.* The employer may use several methods, including equipotential zones, insulating equipment, and restricted work areas, to protect employees on the ground from hazardous differences in electrical potential.

1. An equipotential zone will protect workers within it from hazardous step and touch potentials. (See Figure 3.) Equipotential zones will not, however, protect employees located either wholly or partially outside the protected area. The employer can establish an equipotential zone for workers on the ground, with respect to a grounded object, through the use of a metal mat connected to the grounded object. The employer can use a grounding grid to equalize the voltage within the grid or bond conductive objects in the immediate work area to minimize the potential between the objects and between each object and ground. (Bonding an object outside the work area can increase the touch potential to that object, however.) Section III.D of this appendix discusses equipotential zones for employees working on deenergized and grounded power lines.

2. Insulating equipment, such as rubber gloves, can protect employees handling grounded equipment and conductors from hazardous touch potentials. The insulating equipment must be rated for the highest voltage that can be impressed on the grounded objects under fault conditions (rather than for the full system voltage).

3. Restricting employees from areas where hazardous step or touch potentials could arise can protect employees not directly involved in performing the operation. The employer must ensure that employees on the ground in the vicinity of transmission structures are at a distance where step voltages would be insufficient to cause injury. Employees must not handle grounded conductors or equipment likely to become energized to hazardous voltages unless the employees are within an equipotential zone or protected by insulating equipment.

527

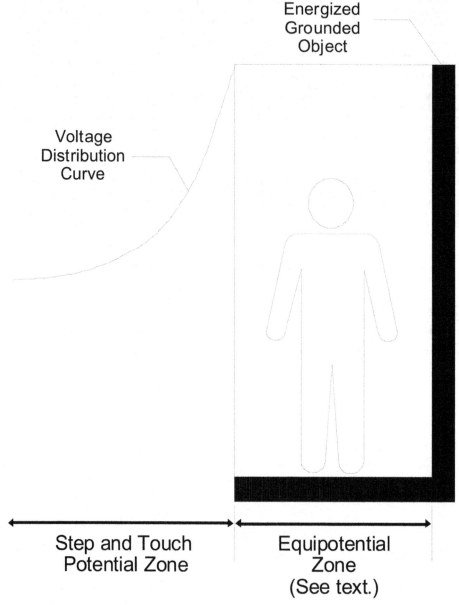

Energized Grounded Object

Voltage Distribution Curve

Step and Touch Potential Zone

Equipotential Zone (See text.)

Figure 3—Protection from Ground-Potential Gradients

D. *Protecting employees working on deenergized and grounded power lines.* This Section III.D of Appendix C establishes guidelines to help employers comply with requirements in §1926.962 for using protective grounding to protect employees working on deenergized power lines. Section 1926.962 applies to grounding of transmission and distribution lines and equipment for the purpose of protecting workers. Paragraph (c) of §1926.962

requires temporary protective grounds to be placed at such locations and arranged in such a manner that the employer can demonstrate will prevent exposure of each employee to hazardous differences in electric potential.[3] Sections III.D.1 and III.D.2 of this appendix provide guidelines that employers can use in making the demonstration required by § 1926.962(c). Section III.D.1 of this appendix provides guidelines on how the employer can determine whether particular grounding practices expose employees to hazardous differences in electric potential. Section III.D.2 of this appendix describes grounding methods that the employer can use in lieu of an engineering analysis to make the demonstration required by § 1926.962(c). The Occupational Safety and Health Administration will consider employers that comply with the criteria in this appendix as meeting § 1926.962(c).

Finally, Section III.D.3 of this appendix discusses other safety considerations that will help the employer comply with other requirements in § 1926.962. Following these guidelines will protect workers from hazards that can occur when a deenergized and grounded line becomes energized.

1. *Determining safe body current limits.* This Section III.D.1 of Appendix C provides guidelines on how an employer can determine whether any differences in electric potential to which workers could be exposed are hazardous as part of the demonstration required by § 1926.962(c).

Institute of Electrical and Electronic Engineers (IEEE) Standard 1048–2003, *IEEE Guide for Protective Grounding of Power Lines,* provides the following equation for determining the threshold of ventricular fibrillation when the duration of the electric shock is limited:

$$I = \frac{116}{\sqrt{t}},$$

where I is the current through the worker's body, and t is the duration of the current in seconds. This equation represents the ventricular fibrillation threshold for 95.5 percent of the adult population with a mass of 50 kilograms (110 pounds) or more. The equation is valid for current durations between 0.0083 to 3.0 seconds.

To use this equation to set safe voltage limits in an equipotential zone around the worker, the employer will need to assume a value for the resistance of the worker's body. IEEE Std 1048–2003 states that "total body resistance is usually taken as 1000 Ω for determining . . . body current limits." However, employers should be aware that the impedance of a worker's body can be substantially less than that value. For instance, IEEE Std 1048–2003 reports a minimum hand-to-hand resistance of 610 ohms and an internal body resistance of 500 ohms. The internal resistance of the body better represents the minimum resistance of a worker's body when the skin resistance drops near zero, which occurs, for example, when there are breaks in the worker's skin, for instance, from cuts or from blisters formed as a result of the current from an electric shock, or when the worker is wet at the points of contact.

Employers may use the IEEE Std 1048–2003 equation to determine safe body current limits only if the employer protects workers from hazards associated with involuntary muscle reactions from electric shock (for example, the hazard to a worker from falling as a result of an electric shock). Moreover, the equation applies only when the duration of the electric shock is limited. If the precautions the employer takes, including those required by applicable standards, do not adequately protect employees from hazards associated with involuntary reactions from electric shock, a hazard exists if the induced voltage is sufficient to pass a current of 1 milliampere through a 500-ohm resistor. (The 500-ohm resistor represents the resistance of an employee. The 1-milliampere current is the threshold of perception.) Finally, if the employer protects employees from injury due to involuntary reactions from electric shock, but the duration of the electric shock is unlimited (that is, when the fault current at the work location will be insufficient to trip the devices protecting the circuit), a hazard exists if the resultant current would

---

[3] The protective grounding required by § 1926.962 limits to safe values the potential differences between accessible objects in each employee's work environment. Ideally, a protective grounding system would create a true equipotential zone in which every point is at the same electric potential. In practice, current passing through the grounding and bonding elements creates potential differences. If these potential differences are hazardous, the employer may not treat the zone as an equipotential zone.

be more than 6 milliamperes (the recognized let-go threshold for workers [4]).

2. *Acceptable methods of grounding for employers that do not perform an engineering determination.* The grounding methods presented in this section of this appendix ensure that differences in electric potential are as low as possible and, therefore, meet §1926.962(c) without an engineering determination of the potential differences. These methods follow two principles: (i) The grounding method must ensure that the circuit opens in the fastest available clearing time, and (ii) the grounding method must ensure that the potential differences between conductive objects in the employee's work area are as low as possible.

Paragraph (c) of §1926.962 does not require grounding methods to meet the criteria embodied in these principles. Instead, the paragraph requires that protective grounds be "placed at such locations and arranged in such a manner that the employer can demonstrate will prevent exposure of each employee to hazardous differences in electric potential." However, when the employer's grounding practices do not follow these two principles, the employer will need to perform an engineering analysis to make the demonstration required by §1926.962(c).

i. *Ensuring that the circuit opens in the fastest available clearing time.* Generally, the higher the fault current, the shorter the clearing times for the same type of fault. Therefore, to ensure the fastest available clearing time, the grounding method must maximize the fault current with a low impedance connection to ground. The employer accomplishes this objective by grounding the circuit conductors to the best ground available at the worksite. Thus, the employer must ground to a grounded system neutral conductor, if one is present. A grounded system neutral has a direct connection to the system ground at the source, resulting in an extremely low impedance to ground. In a substation, the employer may instead ground to the substation grid, which also has an extremely low impedance to the system ground and, typically, is connected to a grounded system neutral when one is present. Remote system grounds, such as pole and tower grounds, have a higher impedance to the system ground than grounded system neutrals and substation grounding grids; however, the employer may use a re-

mote ground when lower impedance grounds are not available. In the absence of a grounded system neutral, substation grid, and remote ground, the employer may use a temporary driven ground at the worksite.

In addition, if employees are working on a three-phase system, the grounding method must short circuit all three phases. Short circuiting all phases will ensure faster clearing and lower the current through the grounding cable connecting the deenergized line to ground, thereby lowering the voltage across that cable. The short circuit need not be at the worksite; however, the employer must treat any conductor that is not grounded at the worksite as energized because the ungrounded conductors will be energized at fault voltage during a fault.

ii. *Ensuring that the potential differences between conductive objects in the employee's work area are as low as possible.* To achieve as low a voltage as possible across any two conductive objects in the work area, the employer must bond all conductive objects in the work area. This section of this appendix discusses how to create a zone that minimizes differences in electric potential between conductive objects in the work area.

The employer must use bonding cables to bond conductive objects, except for metallic objects bonded through metal-to-metal contact. The employer must ensure that metal-to-metal contacts are tight and free of contamination, such as oxidation, that can increase the impedance across the connection. For example, a bolted connection between metal lattice tower members is acceptable if the connection is tight and free of corrosion and other contamination. Figure 4 shows how to create an equipotential zone for metal lattice towers.

Wood poles are conductive objects. The poles can absorb moisture and conduct electricity, particularly at distribution and transmission voltages. Consequently, the employer must either: (1) Provide a conductive platform, bonded to a grounding cable, on which the worker stands or (2) use cluster bars to bond wood poles to the grounding cable. The employer must ensure that employees install the cluster bar below, and close to, the worker's feet. The inner portion of the wood pole is more conductive than the outer shell, so it is important that the cluster bar be in conductive contact with a metal spike or nail that penetrates the wood to a depth greater than or equal to the depth the worker's climbing gaffs will penetrate the wood. For example, the employer could mount the cluster bar on a bare pole ground wire fastened to the pole with nails or staples that penetrate to the required depth. Alternatively, the employer may temporarily nail a conductive strap to the pole and connect the strap to the cluster bar. Figure 5 shows how to create an equipotential zone for wood poles.

---

[4] Electric current passing through the body has varying effects depending on the amount of the current. At the let-go threshold, the current overrides a person's control over his or her muscles. At that level, an employee grasping an object will not be able to let go of the object. The let-go threshold varies from person to person; however, the recognized value for workers is 6 milliamperes.

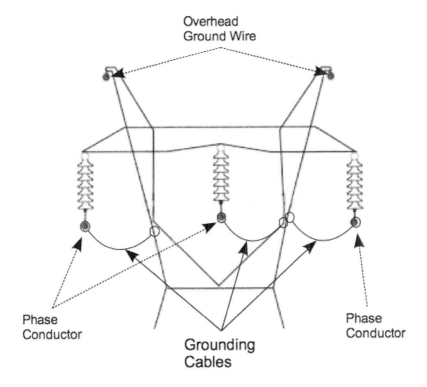

Notes:

1. Employers must ground overhead ground wires that are within reach of the employee.

2. The grounding cable must be as short as practicable; therefore, the attachment points between the grounding cable and the tower may be different from that shown in the figure.

Figure 4—Equipotential Zone for Metal Lattice Tower

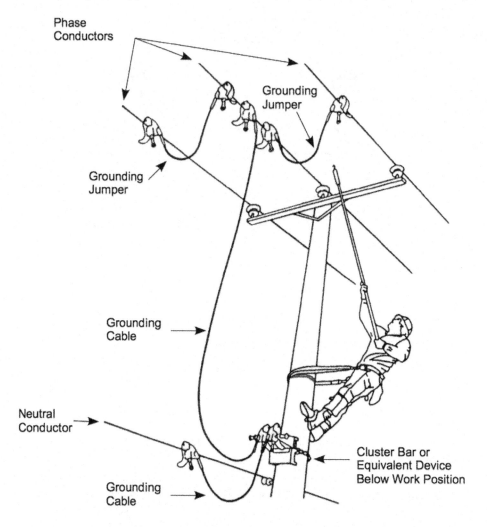

Phase Conductors

Grounding Jumper

Grounding Jumper

Grounding Cable

Neutral Conductor

Grounding Cable

Cluster Bar or Equivalent Device Below Work Position

Figure 5—Equipotential Grounding for Wood Poles

Figure reprinted with permission from Hubbell Power Systems, Inc. (Hubbell).

OSHA revised the figure from Hubbell's original.

For underground systems, employers commonly install grounds at the points of disconnection of the underground cables. These grounding points are typically remote from the manhole or underground vault where employees will be working on the cable. Workers in contact with a cable grounded at a remote location can experience hazardous potential differences if the cable becomes ener- gized or if a fault occurs on a different, but nearby, energized cable. The fault current causes potential gradients in the earth, and a potential difference will exist between the earth where the worker is standing and the earth where the cable is grounded. Consequently, to create an equipotential zone for the worker, the employer must provide a means of connecting the deenergized cable to ground at the worksite by having the worker stand on a conductive mat bonded to the de-energized cable. If the cable is cut, the employer must install a bond across the opening in the cable or install one bond on each side of the opening to ensure that the separate cable ends are at the same potential. The employer must protect the worker from any hazardous differences in potential any time there is no bond between the mat and the cable (for example, before the worker installs the bonds).

3. *Other safety-related considerations.* To ensure that the grounding system is safe and effective, the employer should also consider the following factors: [5]

i. *Maintenance of grounding equipment.* It is essential that the employer properly maintain grounding equipment. Corrosion in the connections between grounding cables and clamps and on the clamp surface can increase the resistance of the cable, thereby increasing potential differences. In addition, the surface to which a clamp attaches, such as a conductor or tower member, must be clean and free of corrosion and oxidation to ensure a low-resistance connection. Cables must be free of damage that could reduce their current-carrying capacity so that they can carry the full fault current without failure. Each clamp must have a tight connection to the cable to ensure a low resistance and to ensure that the clamp does not separate from the cable during a fault.

ii. *Grounding cable length and movement.* The electromagnetic forces on grounding cables during a fault increase with increasing cable length. These forces can cause the cable to move violently during a fault and can be high enough to damage the cable or clamps and cause the cable to fail. In addition, flying cables can injure workers. Consequently, cable lengths should be as short as possible, and grounding cables that might carry high fault current should be in positions where the cables will not injure workers during a fault.

---

[5] This appendix only discusses factors that relate to ensuring an equipotential zone for employees. The employer must consider other factors in selecting a grounding system that is capable of conducting the maximum fault current that could flow at the point of grounding for the time necessary to clear the fault, as required by § 1926.962(d)(1)(i). IEEE Std 1048–2003 contains guidelines for selecting and installing grounding equipment that will meet § 1926.962(d)(1)(i).

APPENDIX D TO SUBPART V OF PART 1926—METHODS OF INSPECTING AND TESTING WOOD POLES

I. INTRODUCTION

When employees are to perform work on a wood pole, it is important to determine the condition of the pole before employees climb it. The weight of the employee, the weight of equipment to be installed, and other working stresses (such as the removal or retensioning of conductors) can lead to the failure of a defective pole or a pole that is not designed to handle the additional stresses.[1] For these reasons, it is essential that, before an employee climbs a wood pole, the employer ascertain that the pole is capable of sustaining the stresses of the work. The determination that the pole is capable of sustaining these stresses includes an inspection of the condition of the pole.

If the employer finds the pole to be unsafe to climb or to work from, the employer must secure the pole so that it does not fail while an employee is on it. The employer can secure the pole by a line truck boom, by ropes or guys, or by lashing a new pole alongside it. If a new one is lashed alongside the defective pole, employees should work from the new one.

II. INSPECTING WOOD POLES

A qualified employee should inspect wood poles for the following conditions:[2]

A. *General condition.* Buckling at the ground line or an unusual angle with respect to the ground may indicate that the pole has rotted or is broken.

B. *Cracks.* Horizontal cracks perpendicular to the grain of the wood may weaken the pole. Vertical cracks, although not normally considered to be a sign of a defective pole, can pose a hazard to the climber, and the employee should keep his or her gaffs away from them while climbing.

C. *Holes.* Hollow spots and woodpecker holes can reduce the strength of a wood pole.

D. *Shell rot and decay.* Rotting and decay are cutout hazards and possible indications of the age and internal condition of the pole.

E. *Knots.* One large knot or several smaller ones at the same height on the pole may be evidence of a weak point on the pole.

F. *Depth of setting.* Evidence of the existence of a former ground line substantially

---

[1] A properly guyed pole in good condition should, at a minimum, be able to handle the weight of an employee climbing it.

[2] The presence of any of these conditions is an indication that the pole may not be safe to climb or to work from. The employee performing the inspection must be qualified to make a determination as to whether it is safe to perform the work without taking additional precautions.

above the existing ground level may be an indication that the pole is no longer buried to a sufficient depth.

G. *Soil conditions.* Soft, wet, or loose soil around the base of the pole may indicate that the pole will not support any change in stress.

H. *Burn marks.* Burning from transformer failures or conductor faults could damage the pole so that it cannot withstand changes in mechanical stress.

III. TESTING WOOD POLES

The following tests, which are from §1910.268(n)(3) of this chapter, are acceptable methods of testing wood poles:

A. *Hammer test.* Rap the pole sharply with a hammer weighing about 1.4 kg (3 pounds), starting near the ground line and continuing upwards circumferentially around the pole to a height of approximately 1.8 meters (6 feet). The hammer will produce a clear sound and rebound sharply when striking sound wood. Decay pockets will be indicated by a dull sound or a less pronounced hammer rebound. Also, prod the pole as near the ground line as possible using a pole prod or a screwdriver with a blade at least 127 millimeters (5 inches) long. If substantial decay is present, the pole is unsafe.

B. *Rocking test.* Apply a horizontal force to the pole and attempt to rock it back and forth in a direction perpendicular to the line. Exercise caution to avoid causing power lines to swing together. Apply the force to the pole either by pushing it with a pike pole or pulling the pole with a rope. If the pole cracks during the test, it is unsafe.

APPENDIX E TO SUBPART V OF PART 1926—PROTECTION FROM FLAMES AND ELECTRIC ARCS

I. INTRODUCTION

Paragraph (g) of §1926.960 addresses protecting employees from flames and electric arcs. This paragraph requires employers to: (1) Assess the workplace for flame and electric-arc hazards (paragraph (g)(1)); (2) estimate the available heat energy from electric arcs to which employees would be exposed (paragraph (g)(2)); (3) ensure that employees wear clothing that will not melt, or ignite and continue to burn, when exposed to flames or the estimated heat energy (paragraph (g)(3)); and (4) ensure that employees wear flame-resistant clothing[1] and protec-

tive clothing and other protective equipment that has an arc rating greater than or equal to the available heat energy under certain conditions (paragraphs (g)(4) and (g)(5)). This appendix contains information to help employers estimate available heat energy as required by §1926.960(g)(2), select protective clothing and other protective equipment with an arc rating suitable for the available heat energy as required by §1926.960(g)(5), and ensure that employees do not wear flammable clothing that could lead to burn injury as addressed by §§1926.960(g)(3) and (g)(4).

II. ASSESSING THE WORKPLACE FOR FLAME AND ELECTRIC-ARC HAZARDS

Paragraph (g)(1) of §1926.960 requires the employer to assess the workplace to identify employees exposed to hazards from flames or from electric arcs. This provision ensures that the employer evaluates employee exposure to flames and electric arcs so that employees who face such exposures receive the required protection. The employer must conduct an assessment for each employee who performs work on or near exposed, energized parts of electric circuits.

A. Assessment Guidelines

Sources electric arcs. Consider possible sources of electric arcs, including:

• Energized circuit parts not guarded or insulated,

• Switching devices that produce electric arcs in normal operation,

• Sliding parts that could fault during operation (for example, rack-mounted circuit breakers), and

• Energized electric equipment that could fail (for example, electric equipment with damaged insulation or with evidence of arcing or overheating).

Exposure to flames. Identify employees exposed to hazards from flames. Factors to consider include:

• The proximity of employees to open flames, and

• For flammable material in the work area, whether there is a reasonable likelihood that an electric arc or an open flame can ignite the material.

Probability that an electric arc will occur. Identify employees exposed to electric-arc hazards. The Occupational Safety and Health Administration will consider an employee exposed to electric-arc hazards if there is a reasonable likelihood that an electric arc will occur in the employee's work area, in other words, if the probability of such an event is higher than it is for the normal operation of enclosed equipment. Factors to consider include:

---

[1] Flame-resistant clothing includes clothing that is inherently flame resistant and clothing chemically treated with a flame retardant. (See ASTM F1506–10a, *Standard Performance Specification for Flame Resistant Textile Materials for Wearing Apparel for Use by Electrical Workers Exposed to Momentary Electric Arc and Related Thermal Hazards,* and

ASTM F1891–12 *Standard Specification for Arc and Flame Resistant Rainwear.*)

• For energized circuit parts not guarded or insulated, whether conductive objects can come too close to or fall onto the energized parts,

• For exposed, energized circuit parts, whether the employee is closer to the part than the minimum approach distance established by the employer (as permitted by § 1926.960(c)(1)(iii)).

• Whether the operation of electric equipment with sliding parts that could fault during operation is part of the normal operation of the equipment or occurs during servicing or maintenance, and

• For energized electric equipment, whether there is evidence of impending failure, such as evidence of arcing or overheating.

B. Examples

Table 1 provides task-based examples of exposure assessments.

TABLE 1—EXAMPLE ASSESSMENTS FOR VARIOUS TASKS

Task		Is employee exposed to flame or electric-arc hazard?
Normal operation of enclosed equipment, such as closing or opening a switch.	The employer properly installs and maintains enclosed equipment, and there is no evidence of impending failure.	No.
	There is evidence of arcing or overheating.	Yes.
	Parts of the equipment are loose or sticking, or the equipment otherwise exhibits signs of lack of maintenance.	Yes.
Servicing electric equipment, such as racking in a circuit breaker or replacing a switch.		Yes.
Inspection of electric equipment with exposed energized parts.	The employee is not holding conductive objects and remains outside the minimum approach distance established by the employer.	No.
	The employee is holding a conductive object, such as a flashlight, that could fall or otherwise contact energized parts (irrespective of whether the employee maintains the minimum approach distance).	Yes.
	The employee is closer than the minimum approach distance established by the employer (for example, when wearing rubber insulating gloves or rubber insulating gloves and sleeves).	Yes.
Using open flames, for example, in wiping cable splice sleeves		Yes.

III. PROTECTION AGAINST BURN INJURY

A. Estimating Available Heat Energy

Calculation methods. Paragraph (g)(2) of § 1926.960 provides that, for each employee exposed to an electric-arc hazard, the employer must make a reasonable estimate of the heat energy to which the employee would be exposed if an arc occurs. Table 2 lists various methods of calculating values of available heat energy from an electric circuit. The Occupational Safety and Health Administration does not endorse any of these specific methods. Each method requires the input of various parameters, such as fault current, the expected length of the electric arc, the distance from the arc to the employee, and the clearing time for the fault (that is, the time the circuit protective devices take to open the circuit and clear the fault). The employer can precisely determine some of these parameters, such as the fault current and the clearing time, for a given system. The employer will need to estimate other parameters, such as the length of the arc and the distance between the arc and the employee, because such parameters vary widely.

535

TABLE 2—METHODS OF CALCULATING INCIDENT HEAT ENERGY FROM AN ELECTRIC ARC

1. *Standard for Electrical Safety Requirements for Employee Workplaces,* NFPA 70E–2012, Annex D, "Sample Calculation of Flash Protection Boundary."
2. Doughty, T.E., Neal, T.E., and Floyd II, H.L., "Predicting Incident Energy to Better Manage the Electric Arc Hazard on 600 V Power Distribution Systems," *Record of Conference Papers IEEE IAS 45th Annual Petroleum and Chemical Industry Conference,* September 28—30, 1998.
3. *Guide for Performing Arc-Flash Hazard Calculations,* IEEE Std 1584–2002, 1584a—2004 (Amendment 1 to IEEE Std 1584–2002), and 1584b–2011 (Amendment 2: Changes to Clause 4 of IEEE Std 1584–2002).*
4. ARCPRO, a commercially available software program developed by Kinectrics, Toronto, ON, CA.
*This appendix refers to IEEE Std 1584–2002 with both amendments as IEEE Std 1584b–2011.

The amount of heat energy calculated by any of the methods is approximately inversely proportional to the square of the distance between the employee and the arc. In other words, if the employee is very close to the arc, the heat energy is very high; but if the employee is just a few more centimeters away, the heat energy drops substantially. Thus, estimating the distance from the arc to the employee is key to protecting employees.

The employer must select a method of estimating incident heat energy that provides a reasonable estimate of incident heat energy for the exposure involved. Table 3 shows which methods provide reasonable estimates for various exposures.

TABLE 3—SELECTING A REASONABLE INCIDENT-ENERGY CALCULATION METHOD [1]

Incident-energy calculation method	600 V and Less[2]			601 V to 15 kV[2]			More than 15 kV		
	1Φ	3Φa	3Φb	1Φ	3Φa	3Φb	1Φ	3Φa	3Φb
NFPA 70E–2012 Annex D (Lee equation)	Y–C	Y	N	Y–C	Y–C	N	N[3]	N[3]	N[3]
Doughty, Neal, and Floyd	Y–C	Y	Y	N	N	N	N	N	N
IEEE Std 1584b–2011	Y	Y	Y	Y	Y	Y	N	N	N
ARCPRO	Y	N	N	Y	N	N	Y	Y[4]	Y[4]

Key:
1Φ: Single-phase arc in open air
3Φa: Three-phase arc in open air
3Φb: Three-phase arc in an enclosure (box)
Y: Acceptable; produces a reasonable estimate of incident heat energy from this type of electric arc
N: Not acceptable; does not produce a reasonable estimate of incident heat energy from this type of electric arc
Y–C: Acceptable; produces a reasonable, but conservative, estimate of incident heat energy from this type of electric arc.
Notes:[1] Although the Occupational Safety and Health Administration will consider these methods reasonable for enforcement purposes when employers use the methods in accordance with this table, employers should be aware that the listed methods do not necessarily result in estimates that will provide full protection from internal faults in transformers and similar equipment or from arcs in underground manholes or vaults.
[2] At these voltages, the presumption is that the arc is three-phase unless the employer can demonstrate that only one phase is present or that the spacing of the phases is sufficient to prevent a multiphase arc from occurring.
[3] Although the Occupational Safety and Health Administration will consider this method acceptable for purposes of assessing whether incident energy exceeds 2.0 cal/cm[2], the results at voltages of more than 15 kilovolts are extremely conservative and unrealistic.
[4] The Occupational Safety and Health Administration will deem the results of this method reasonable when the employer adjusts them using the conversion factors for three-phase arcs in open air or in an enclosure, as indicated in the program's instructions.

Selecting a reasonable distance from the employee to the arc. In estimating available heat energy, the employer must make some reasonable assumptions about how far the employee will be from the electric arc. Table 4 lists reasonable distances from the employee to the electric arc. The distances in Table 4 are consistent with national consensus standards, such as the Institute of Electrical and Electronic Engineers' *National Electrical Safety Code,* ANSI/IEEE C2–2012, and *IEEE Guide for Performing Arc-Flash Hazard Calculations,* IEEE Std 1584b–2011. The employer is free to use other reasonable distances, but must consider equipment enclosure size and the working distance to the employee in selecting a distance from the employee to the arc. The Occupational Safety and Health Administration will consider a distance reasonable when the employer bases it on equipment size and working distance.

TABLE 4—SELECTING A REASONABLE DISTANCE FROM THE EMPLOYEE TO THE ELECTRIC ARC

Class of equipment	Single-phase arc mm (inches)	Three-phase arc mm (inches)
Cable	NA*	455 (18)
Low voltage MCCs and panelboards	NA	455 (18)
Low-voltage switchgear	NA	610 (24)
5-kV switchgear	NA	910 (36)
15-kV switchgear	NA	910 (36)
Single conductors in air (up to 46 kilovolts), work with rubber insulating gloves.	380 (15)	NA
Single conductors in air, work with live-line tools and live-line bare-hand work.	$MAD - (2 \times kV \times 2.54)$ ($MAD - (2 \times kV/10)$)[†]	NA

* NA = not applicable.
[†] The terms in this equation are:
MAD = The applicable minimum approach distance, and
kV = The system voltage in kilovolts.

Selecting a reasonable arc gap. For a single-phase arc in air, the electric arc will almost always occur when an energized conductor approaches too close to ground. Thus, an employer can determine the arc gap, or arc length, for these exposures by the dielectric strength of air and the voltage on the line. The dielectric strength of air is approximately 10 kilovolts for every 25.4 millimeters (1 inch). For example, at 50 kilovolts, the arc gap would be $50 \div 10 \times 25.4$ (or 50×2.54), which equals 127 millimeters (5 inches).

For three-phase arcs in open air and in enclosures, the arc gap will generally be dependent on the spacing between parts energized at different electrical potentials. Documents such as IEEE Std 1584b–2011 provide information on these distances. Employers may select a reasonable arc gap from Table 5, or they may select any other reasonable arc gap based on sparkover distance or on the spacing between (1) live parts at different potentials or (2) live parts and grounded parts (for example, bus or conductor spacings in equipment). In any event, the employer must use an estimate that reasonably resembles the actual exposures faced by the employee.

TABLE 5—SELECTING A REASONABLE ARC GAP

Class of equipment	Single-phase arc mm (inches)	Three-phase arc mm [1] (inches)
Cable	NA [2]	13 (0.5)
Low voltage MCCs and panelboards	NA	25 (1.0)
Low-voltage switchgear	NA	32 (1.25)
5-kV switchgear	NA	104 (4.0)
15-kV switchgear	NA	152 (6.0)
Single conductors in air, 15 kV and less	51 (2.0)	Phase conductor spacings.
Single conductor in air, more than 15 kV	Voltage in kV × 2.54 (Voltage in kV × 0.1), but no less than 51 mm (2 inches)	Phase conductor spacings.

[1] Source: IEEE Std 1584b–2011.
[2] NA = not applicable.

Making estimates over multiple system areas. The employer need not estimate the heat-energy exposure for every job task performed by each employee. Paragraph (g)(2) of §1926.960 permits the employer to make broad estimates that cover multiple system areas provided that: (1) The employer uses reasonable assumptions about the energy-exposure distribution throughout the system, and (2) the estimates represent the maximum exposure for those areas. For example, the employer can use the maximum fault current and clearing time to cover several system areas at once.

Incident heat energy for single-phase-to-ground exposures. Table 6 and Table 7 provide incident heat energy levels for open-air, phase-to-ground electric-arc exposures typical for overhead systems.[2] Table 6 presents estimates of available energy for employees using rubber insulating gloves to perform work on overhead systems operating at 4 to 46 kilovolts. The table assumes that the employee will be 380 millimeters (15 inches) from the electric arc, which is a reasonable

[2] The Occupational Safety and Health Administration used metric values to calculate the clearing times in Table 6 and Table 7. An employer may use English units to calculate clearing times instead even though the results will differ slightly.

estimate for rubber insulating glove work. Table 6 also assumes that the arc length equals the sparkover distance for the maximum transient overvoltage of each voltage range.[3] To use the table, an employer would use the voltage, maximum fault current, and maximum clearing time for a system area and, using the appropriate voltage range and fault-current and clearing-time values corresponding to the next higher values listed in the table, select the appropriate heat energy (4, 5, 8, or 12 cal/cm²) from the table. For example, an employer might have a 12,470-volt power line supplying a system area. The power line can supply a maximum fault current of 8 kiloamperes with a maximum clearing time of 10 cycles. For rubber glove work, this system falls in the 4.0-to-15.0-kilovolt range; the next-higher fault current is 10 kA (the second row in that voltage range); and the clearing time is under 18 cycles (the first column to the right of the fault current column). Thus, the available heat energy for this part of the system will be 4 cal/cm² or less (from the column heading), and the employer could select protection with a 5-cal/cm² rating to meet §1926.960(g)(5). Alternatively, an employer could select a base incident-energy value and ensure that the clearing times for each voltage range and fault current listed in the table do not exceed the corresponding clearing time specified in the table. For example, an employer that provides employees with arc-flash protective equipment rated at 8 cal/cm² can use the table to determine if any system area exceeds 8 cal/cm² by checking the clearing time for the highest fault current for each voltage range and ensuring that the clearing times do not exceed the values specified in the 8-cal/cm² column in the table.

Table 7 presents similar estimates for employees using live-line tools to perform work on overhead systems operating at voltages of 4 to 800 kilovolts. The table assumes that the arc length will be equal to the sparkover distance[4] and that the employee will be a distance from the arc equal to the minimum approach distance minus twice the sparkover distance.

The employer will need to use other methods for estimating available heat energy in situations not addressed by Table 6 or Table 7. The calculation methods listed in Table 2 and the guidance provided in Table 3 will help employers do this. For example, employers can use IEEE Std 1584b–2011 to estimate the available heat energy (and to select appropriate protective equipment) for many specific conditions, including lower-voltage, phase-to-phase arc, and enclosed arc exposures.

TABLE 6—INCIDENT HEAT ENERGY FOR VARIOUS FAULT CURRENTS, CLEARING TIMES, AND VOLTAGES OF 4.0 TO 46.0 KV: RUBBER INSULATING GLOVE EXPOSURES INVOLVING PHASE-TO-GROUND ARCS IN OPEN AIR ONLY[*][†][‡]

Voltage range (kV) **	Fault current (kA)	Maximum clearing time (cycles)			
		4 cal/cm²	5 cal/cm²	8 cal/cm²	12 cal/cm²
4.0 to 15.0	5	46	58	92	138
	10	18	22	36	54
	15	10	12	20	30
	20	6	8	13	19
15.1 to 25.0	5	28	34	55	83
	10	11	14	23	34
	15	7	8	13	20
	20	4	5	9	13
25.1 to 36.0	5	21	26	42	62
	10	9	11	18	26
	15	5	6	10	16
	20	4	4	7	11
36.1 to 46.0	5	16	20	32	48
	10	7	9	14	21
	15	4	5	8	13
	20	3	4	6	9

Notes:
[*] This table is for open-air, phase-to-ground electric-arc exposures. It is not for phase-to-phase arcs or enclosed arcs (arc in a box).
[†] The table assumes that the employee will be 380 mm (15 in.) from the electric arc. The table also assumes the arc length to be the sparkover distance for the maximum transient overvoltage of each voltage range (see Appendix B to this subpart), as follows:

[3] The Occupational Safety and Health Administration based this assumption, which is more conservative than the arc length specified in Table 5, on Table 410–2 of the 2012 NESC.

[4] The dielectric strength of air is about 10 kilovolts for every 25.4 millimeters (1 inch). Thus, the employer can estimate the arc length in millimeters to be the phase-to-ground voltage in kilovolts multiplied by 2.54 (or voltage (in kilovolts) × 2.54).

```
4.0 to 15.0 kV    51 mm (2 in.)
15.1 to 25.0 kV   102 mm (4 in.)
25.1 to 36.0 kV   152 mm (6 in.)
36.1 to 46.0 kV   229 mm (9 in.)
```

‡ The Occupational Safety and Health Administration calculated the values in this table using the ARCPRO method listed in Table 2.
** The voltage range is the phase-to-phase system voltage.

TABLE 7—INCIDENT HEAT ENERGY FOR VARIOUS FAULT CURRENTS, CLEARING TIMES, AND VOLTAGES: LIVE-LINE TOOL EXPOSURES INVOLVING PHASE-TO-GROUND ARCS IN OPEN AIR ONLY *
† ‡ #

Voltage range (kV) **	Fault current (kA)	Maximum clearing time (cycles)			
		4 cal/cm^2	5 cal/cm^2	8 cal/cm^2	12 cal/cm^2
4.0 to 15.0	5	197	246	394	591
	10	73	92	147	220
	15	39	49	78	117
	20	24	31	49	73
15.1 to 25.0	5	197	246	394	591
	10	75	94	150	225
	15	41	51	82	122
	20	26	33	52	78
25.1 to 36.0	5	138	172	275	413
	10	53	66	106	159
	15	30	37	59	89
	20	19	24	38	58
36.1 to 46.0	5	129	161	257	386
	10	51	64	102	154
	15	29	36	58	87
	20	19	24	38	57
46.1 to 72.5	20	18	23	36	55
	30	10	13	20	30
	40	6	8	13	19
	50	4	6	9	13
72.6 to 121.0	20	10	12	20	30
	30	6	7	11	17
	40	4	5	7	11
	50	3	3	5	8
121.1 to 145.0	20	12	15	24	35
	30	7	9	15	22
	40	5	6	10	15
	50	4	5	8	11
145.1 to 169.0	20	12	15	24	36
	30	7	9	15	22
	40	5	7	10	16
	50	4	5	8	12
169.1 to 242.0	20	13	17	27	40
	30	8	10	17	25
	40	6	7	12	17
	50	4	5	9	13
242.1 to 362.0	20	25	32	51	76
	30	16	19	31	47
	40	11	14	22	33
	50	8	10	16	25
362.1 to 420.0	20	12	15	25	37
	30	8	10	15	23
	40	5	7	11	16
	50	4	5	8	12
420.1 to 550.0	20	23	29	47	70
	30	14	18	29	43
	40	10	13	20	30
	50	8	9	15	23
550.1 to 800.0	20	25	31	50	75
	30	15	19	31	46
	40	11	13	21	32
	50	8	10	16	24

Notes:
* This table is for open-air, phase-to-ground electric-arc exposures. It is not for phase-to-phase arcs or enclosed arcs (arc in a box).
† The table assumes the arc length to be the sparkover distance for the maximum phase-to-ground voltage of each voltage range (see Appendix B to this subpart). The table also assumes that the employee will be the minimum approach distance minus twice the arc length from the electric arc.
‡ The Occupational Safety and Health Administration calculated the values in this table using the ARCPRO method listed in Table 2.
# For voltages of more than 72.6 kV, employers may use this table only when the minimum approach distance established under § 1926.960(c)(1) is greater than or equal to the following values:

72.6 to 121.0 kV	1.02 m
121.1 to 145.0 kV	1.16 m
145.1 to 169.0 kV	1.30 m
169.1 to 242.0 kV	1.72 m
242.1 to 362.0 kV	2.76 m
362.1 to 420.0 kV	2.50 m
420.1 to 550.0 kV	3.62 m
550.1 to 800.0 kV	4.83 m

**The voltage range is the phase-to-phase system voltage.

B. Selecting Protective Clothing and Other Protective Equipment

Paragraph (g)(5) of §1926.960 requires employers, in certain situations, to select protective clothing and other protective equipment with an arc rating that is greater than or equal to the incident heat energy estimated under §1926.960(g)(2). Based on laboratory testing required by ASTM F1506–10a, the expectation is that protective clothing with an arc rating equal to the estimated incident heat energy will be capable of preventing second-degree burn injury to an employee exposed to that incident heat energy from an electric arc. Note that actual electric-arc exposures may be more or less severe than the estimated value because of factors such as arc movement, arc length, arcing from reclosing of the system, secondary fires or explosions, and weather conditions. Additionally, for arc rating based on the fabric's arc thermal performance value [5] (ATPV), a worker exposed to incident energy at the arc rating has a 50-percent chance of just barely receiving a second-degree burn. Therefore, it is possible (although not likely) that an employee will sustain a second-degree (or worse) burn wearing clothing conforming to §1926.960(g)(5) under some circumstances. However, reasonable employer estimates and maintaining appropriate minimum approach distances for employees should limit burns to relatively small burns that just barely extend beyond the epidermis (that is, just barely a second-degree burn). Consequently, protective clothing and other protective equipment meeting §1926.960(g)(5) will provide an appropriate degree of protection for an employee exposed to electric-arc hazards.

Paragraph (g)(5) of §1926.960 does not require arc-rated protection for exposures of 2 cal/cm² or less. Untreated cotton clothing will reduce a 2-cal/cm² exposure below the 1.2- to 1.5-cal/cm² level necessary to cause burn injury, and this material should not ignite at such low heat energy levels. Although §1926.960(g)(5) does not require clothing to have an arc rating when exposures are 2 cal/cm² or less, §1926.960(g)(4) requires the outer layer of clothing to be flame resistant under certain conditions, even when the estimated incident heat energy is less than 2 cal/cm², as discussed later in this appendix. Additionally, it is especially important to ensure that employees do not wear undergarments made from fabrics listed in the note to §1926.960(g)(3) even when the outer layer is flame resistant or arc rated. These fabrics can melt or ignite easily when an electric arc occurs. Logos and name tags made from non-flame-resistant material can adversely affect the arc rating or the flame-resistant characteristics of arc-rated or flame-resistant clothing. Such logos and name tags may violate §1926.960(g)(3), (g)(4), or (g)(5).

Paragraph (g)(5) of §1926.960 requires that arc-rated protection cover the employee's entire body, with limited exceptions for the employee's hands, feet, face, and head. Paragraph (g)(5)(i) of §1926.960 provides that arc-rated protection is not necessary for the employee's hands under the following conditions:

For any estimated incident heat energy.	When the employee is wearing rubber insulating gloves with protectors
If the estimated incident heat energy does not exceed 14 cal/cm².	When the employee is wearing heavy-duty leather work gloves with a weight of at least 407 gm/m² (12 oz/yd²)

Paragraph (g)(5)(ii) of §1926.960 provides that arc-rated protection is not necessary for the employee's feet when the employee is wearing heavy-duty work shoes or boots. Finally, §1926.960(g)(5)(iii), (g)(5)(iv), and (g)(5)(v) require arc-rated head and face protection as follows:

---

[5] ASTM F1506–10a defines "arc thermal performance value" as "the incident energy on a material or a multilayer system of materials that results in a 50% probability that sufficient heat transfer through the tested specimen is predicted to cause the onset of a second-degree skin burn injury based on the Stoll [footnote] curve, cal/cm²." The footnote to this definition reads: "Derived from: Stoll, A.M., and Chianta, M.A., 'Method and Rating System for Evaluations of Thermal Protection,' Aerospace Medicine, Vol 40, 1969, pp. 1232–1238 and Stoll A.M., and Chianta, M.A., 'Heat Transfer through Fabrics as Related to Thermal Injury,' Transactions—New York Academy of Sciences, Vol 33(7), Nov. 1971, pp. 649–670.''

Exposure	Minimum head and face protection		
	None*	Arc-rated faceshield with a minimum rating of 8 cal/cm² *	Arc-rated hood or faceshield with balaclava
Single-phase, open air	2–8 cal/cm²	9–12 cal/cm²	13 cal/² or higher.†
Three-phase	2–4 cal/cm²	5–8 cal/cm²	9 cal/cm² or higher.‡

*These ranges assume that employees are wearing hardhats meeting the specifications in §1910.135 or §1926.100(b)(2), as applicable.
† The arc rating must be a minimum of 4 cal/cm² less than the estimated incident energy. Note that §1926.960(g)(5)(v) permits this type of head and face protection, with a minimum arc rating of 4 cal/cm² less than the estimated incident energy, at any incident energy level.
‡ Note that §1926.960(g)(5) permits this type of head and face protection at any incident energy level.

IV. PROTECTION AGAINST IGNITION

Paragraph (g)(3) of §1926.960 prohibits clothing that could melt onto an employee's skin or that could ignite and continue to burn when exposed to flames or to the available heat energy estimated by the employer under §1926.960(g)(2). Meltable fabrics, such as acetate, nylon, polyester, and polypropylene, even in blends, must be avoided. When these fibers melt, they can adhere to the skin, thereby transferring heat rapidly, exacerbating burns, and complicating treatment. These outcomes can result even if the meltable fabric is not directly next to the skin. The remainder of this section focuses on the prevention of ignition.

Paragraph (g)(5) of §1926.960 generally requires protective clothing and other protective equipment with an arc rating greater than or equal to the employer's estimate of available heat energy. As explained earlier in this appendix, untreated cotton is usually acceptable for exposures of 2 cal/cm² or less.[6] If the exposure is greater than that, the employee generally must wear flame-resistant clothing with a suitable arc rating in accordance with §1926.960(g)(4) and (g)(5). However, even if an employee is wearing a layer of flame-resistant clothing, there are circumstances under which flammable layers of clothing would be uncovered, and an electric arc could ignite them. For example, clothing ignition is possible if the employee is wearing flammable clothing under the flame-resistant clothing and the underlayer is uncovered because of an opening in the flame-resistant clothing. Thus, for purposes of §1926.960(g)(3), it is important for the employer to consider the possibility of clothing ignition even when an employee is wearing flame-resistant clothing with a suitable arc rating.

Under §1926.960(g)(3), employees may not wear flammable clothing in conjunction with flame-resistant clothing if the flammable clothing poses an ignition hazard.[7] Although outer flame-resistant layers may not have openings that expose flammable inner layers, when an outer flame-resistant layer would be unable to resist breakopen,[8] the next (inner) layer must be flame-resistant if it could ignite.

Non-flame-resistant clothing can ignite even when the heat energy from an electric arc is insufficient to ignite the clothing. For example, nearby flames can ignite an employee's clothing; and, even in the absence of flames, electric arcs pose ignition hazards beyond the hazard of ignition from incident energy under certain conditions. In addition to requiring flame-resistant clothing when the estimated incident energy exceeds 2.0 cal/cm², §1926.960(g)(4) requires flame-resistant clothing when: The employee is exposed to contact with energized circuit parts operating at more than 600 volts (§1926.960(g)(4)(i)), an electric arc could ignite flammable material in the work area that, in turn, could ignite the employee's clothing (§1926.960(g)(4)(ii)), and molten metal or electric arcs from faulted conductors in the work area could ignite the employee's clothing (§1926.960(g)(4)(iii)). For example, grounding conductors can become a source of heat energy if they cannot carry fault current without failure. The employer must consider these possible sources of electric arcs[9] in determining whether the employee's clothing could ignite under §1926.960(g)(4)(iii).

---

[6] See §1926.960(g)(4)(i), (g)(4)(ii), and (g)(4)(iii) for conditions under which employees must wear flame-resistant clothing as the outer layer of clothing even when the incident heat energy does not exceed 2 cal/cm².

[7] Paragraph (g)(3) of §1926.960 prohibits clothing that could ignite and continue to burn when exposed to the heat energy estimated under paragraph (g)(2) of that section.
[8] Breakopen occurs when a hole, tear, or crack develops in the exposed fabric such that the fabric no longer effectively blocks incident heat energy.
[9] Static wires and pole grounds are examples of grounding conductors that might not be capable of carrying fault current without failure. Grounds that can carry the maximum available fault current are not a concern, and employers need not consider such grounds a possible electric arc source.

APPENDIX F TO SUBPART V OF PART
1926—WORK-POSITIONING EQUIPMENT
INSPECTION GUIDELINES

I. BODY BELTS

Inspect body belts to ensure that:
A. The hardware has no cracks, nicks, distortion, or corrosion;
B. No loose or worn rivets are present;
C. The waist strap has no loose grommets;
D. The fastening straps are not 100-percent leather; and
E. No worn materials that could affect the safety of the user are present.

II. POSITIONING STRAPS

Inspect positioning straps to ensure that:
A. The warning center of the strap material is not exposed;
B. No cuts, burns, extra holes, or fraying of strap material is present;
C. Rivets are properly secured;
D. Straps are not 100-percent leather; and
E. Snaphooks do not have cracks, burns, or corrosion.

III. CLIMBERS

Inspect pole and tree climbers to ensure that:
A. Gaffs are at least as long as the manufacturer's recommended minimums (generally 32 and 51 millimeters (1.25 and 2.0 inches) for pole and tree climbers, respectively, measured on the underside of the gaff);

NOTE: Gauges are available to assist in determining whether gaffs are long enough and shaped to easily penetrate poles or trees.

B. Gaffs and leg irons are not fractured or cracked;
C. Stirrups and leg irons are free of excessive wear;
D. Gaffs are not loose;
E. Gaffs are free of deformation that could adversely affect use;
F. Gaffs are properly sharpened; and
G. There are no broken straps or buckles.

APPENDIX G TO SUBPART V OF PART
1926—REFERENCE DOCUMENTS

The references contained in this appendix provide information that can be helpful in understanding and complying with the requirements contained in Subpart V of this part. The national consensus standards referenced in this appendix contain detailed specifications that employers may follow in complying with the more performance-based requirements of Subpart V of this part. Except as specifically noted in Subpart V of this part, however, the Occupational Safety and Health Administration will not necessarily deem compliance with the national consensus standards to be compliance with the provisions of Subpart V of this part.

ANSI/SIA A92.2–2009, *American National Standard for Vehicle-Mounted Elevating and Rotating Aerial Devices.*

ANSI Z133–2012, *American National Standard Safety Requirements for Arboricultural Operations—Pruning, Trimming, Repairing, Maintaining, and Removing Trees, and Cutting Brush.*

ANSI/IEEE Std 935–1989, *IEEE Guide on Terminology for Tools and Equipment to Be Used in Live Line Working.*

ASME B20.1–2012, *Safety Standard for Conveyors and Related Equipment.*

ASTM D120–09, *Standard Specification for Rubber Insulating Gloves.*

ASTM D149–09 (2013), *Standard Test Method for Dielectric Breakdown Voltage and Dielectric Strength of Solid Electrical Insulating Materials at Commercial Power Frequencies.*

ASTM D178–01 (2010), *Standard Specification for Rubber Insulating Matting.*

ASTM D1048–12, *Standard Specification for Rubber Insulating Blankets.*

ASTM D1049–98 (2010), *Standard Specification for Rubber Insulating Covers.*

ASTM D1050–05 (2011), *Standard Specification for Rubber Insulating Line Hose.*

ASTM D1051–08, *Standard Specification for Rubber Insulating Sleeves.*

ASTM F478–09, *Standard Specification for In-Service Care of Insulating Line Hose and Covers.*

ASTM F479–06 (2011), *Standard Specification for In-Service Care of Insulating Blankets.*

ASTM F496–08, *Standard Specification for In-Service Care of Insulating Gloves and Sleeves.*

ASTM F711–02 (2007), *Standard Specification for Fiberglass-Reinforced Plastic (FRP) Rod and Tube Used in Live Line Tools.*

ASTM F712–06 (2011), *Standard Test Methods and Specifications for Electrically Insulating Plastic Guard Equipment for Protection of Workers.*

ASTM F819–10, *Standard Terminology Relating to Electrical Protective Equipment for Workers.*

ASTM F855–09, *Standard Specifications for Temporary Protective Grounds to Be Used on De-energized Electric Power Lines and Equipment.*

ASTM F887–12e1, *Standard Specifications for Personal Climbing Equipment.*

ASTM F914/F914M–10, *Standard Test Method for Acoustic Emission for Aerial Personnel Devices Without Supplemental Load Handling Attachments.*

ASTM F1116–03 (2008), *Standard Test Method for Determining Dielectric Strength of Dielectric Footwear.*

ASTM F1117–03 (2008), *Standard Specification for Dielectric Footwear.*

ASTM F1236–96 (2012), *Standard Guide for Visual Inspection of Electrical Protective Rubber Products.*

ASTM F1430/F1430M–10, *Standard Test Method for Acoustic Emission Testing of Insulated and Non-Insulated Aerial Personnel Devices with Supplemental Load Handling Attachments.*

ASTM F1505–10, *Standard Specification for Insulated and Insulating Hand Tools.*

ASTM F1506–10a, *Standard Performance Specification for Flame Resistant and Arc Rated Textile Materials for Wearing Apparel for Use by Electrical Workers Exposed to Momentary Electric Arc and Related Thermal Hazards.*

ASTM F1564–13, *Standard Specification for Structure-Mounted Insulating Work Platforms for Electrical Workers.*

ASTM F1701–12, *Standard Specification for Unused Polypropylene Rope with Special Electrical Properties.*

ASTM F1742–03 (2011), *Standard Specification for PVC Insulating Sheeting.*

ASTM F1796–09, *Standard Specification for High Voltage Detectors—Part 1 Capacitive Type to be Used for Voltages Exceeding 600 Volts AC.*

ASTM F1797–09 ᵉ1, *Standard Test Method for Acoustic Emission Testing of Insulated and Non-Insulated Digger Derricks.*

ASTM F1825–03 (2007), *Standard Specification for Clampstick Type Live Line Tools.*

ASTM F1826–00 (2011), *Standard Specification for Live Line and Measuring Telescoping Tools.*

ASTM F1891–12, *Standard Specification for Arc and Flame Resistant Rainwear.*

ASTM F1958/F1958M–12, *Standard Test Method for Determining the Ignitability of Non-flame-Resistant Materials for Clothing by Electric Arc Exposure Method Using Mannequins.*

ASTM F1959/F1959M–12, *Standard Test Method for Determining the Arc Rating of Materials for Clothing.*

IEEE Stds 4–1995, 4a–2001 (Amendment to IEEE Standard Techniques for High-Voltage Testing), *IEEE Standard Techniques for High-Voltage Testing.*

IEEE Std 62–1995, *IEEE Guide for Diagnostic Field Testing of Electric Power Apparatus—Part 1: Oil Filled Power Transformers, Regulators, and Reactors.*

IEEE Std 80–2000, *Guide for Safety in AC Substation Grounding.*

IEEE Std 100–2000, *The Authoritative Dictionary of IEEE Standards Terms Seventh Edition.*

IEEE Std 516–2009, *IEEE Guide for Maintenance Methods on Energized Power Lines.*

IEEE Std 524–2003, *IEEE Guide to the Installation of Overhead Transmission Line Conductors.*

IEEE Std 957–2005, *IEEE Guide for Cleaning Insulators.*

IEEE Std 1048–2003, *IEEE Guide for Protective Grounding of Power Lines.*

IEEE Std 1067–2005, *IEEE Guide for In-Service Use, Care, Maintenance, and Testing of Conductive Clothing for Use on Voltages up to 765 kV AC and ±750 kV DC.*

IEEE Std 1307–2004, *IEEE Standard for Fall Protection for Utility Work.*

IEEE Stds 1584–2002, 1584a–2004 (Amendment 1 to IEEE Std 1584–2002), and 1584b–2011 (Amendment 2: Changes to Clause 4 of IEEE Std 1584–2002), *IEEE Guide for Performing Arc-Flash Hazard Calculations.*

IEEE C2–2012, *National Electrical Safety Code.*

NFPA 70E–2012, *Standard for Electrical Safety in the Workplace.*

Subpart W—Rollover Protective Structures; Overhead Protection

AUTHORITY: Section 3704 of the Contract Work Hours and Safety Standards Act (40 U.S.C. 3701); Sections 4, 6, and 8 of the Occupational Safety and Health Act of 1970 (29 U.S.C. 653, 655, 657); and Secretary of Labor's Order No. 12–71 (36 FR 8754), 8–76 (41 FR 25059), 9–83 (48 FR 35736), 1–90 (55 FR 9033), 6–96 (62 FR 111), 3–2000 (65 FR 50017), or 5–2002 (67 FR 65008), as applicable.

§ 1926.1000 Rollover protective structures (ROPS) for material handling equipment.

(a) *Coverage.* (1) This section applies to the following types of material handling equipment: To all rubber-tired, self-propelled scrapers, rubber-tired front-end loaders, rubber-tired dozers, wheel-type agricultural and industrial tractors, crawler tractors, crawler-type loaders, and motor graders, with or without attachments, that are used in construction work. This requirement does not apply to sideboom pipelaying tractors.

(2) The promulgation of specific standards for rollover protective structures for compactors and rubber-tired skid-steer equipment is reserved pending consideration of standards currently being developed.

(b) *Equipment manufactured on or after September 1, 1972.* Material handling machinery described in paragraph (a) of this section and manufactured on or after September 1, 1972, shall be equipped with rollover protective structures which meet the minimum performance standards prescribed in §§ 1926.1001 and 1926.1002, as applicable.

(c) *Equipment manufactured before September 1, 1972.* (1) All material handling equipment described in paragraph (a) of this section and manufactured or placed in service (owned or operated by the employer) prior to September 1, 1972, shall be fitted with rollover protective structures no later than the dates listed below:

(i) Machines manufactured on or after January 1, 1972, shall be fitted no later than April 1, 1973.

(ii) Machines manufactured between July 1, 1971, and December 31, 1971, shall be fitted no later than July 1, 1973.

(iii) Machines manufactured between July 1, 1970, and June 30, 1971, shall be fitted no later than January 1, 1974.

(iv) Machines manufactured between July 1, 1969, and June 30, 1970, shall be fitted no later than July 1, 1974.

(v) Machines manufactured before July 1, 1969: Reserved pending further study, development, and review.

(2) Rollover protective structures and supporting attachment shall meet the minimum performance criteria detailed in §§ 1926.1001 and 1926.1002, as applicable or shall be designed, fabricated, and installed in a manner which will support, based on the ultimate strength of the metal, at least two times the weight of the prime mover applied at the point of impact.

(i) The design objective shall be to minimize the likelihood of a complete overturn and thereby minimize the possibility of the operator being crushed as a result of a rollover or upset.

(ii) The design shall provide a vertical clearance of at least 52 inches from the work deck to the ROPS at the point of ingress or egress.

(d) *Remounting.* ROPS removed for any reason, shall be remounted with equal quality, or better, bolts or welding as required for the original mounting.

(e) *Labeling.* Each ROPS shall have the following information permanently affixed to the structure:

(1) Manufacturer or fabricator's name and address;

(2) ROPS model number, if any;

(3) Machine make, model, or series number that the structure is designed to fit.

(f) *Machines meeting certain existing governmental requirements.* Any machine in use, equipped with rollover protective structures, shall be deemed in compliance with this section if it meets the rollover protective structure requirements of the State of California, the U.S. Army Corps of Engineers, or the Bureau of Reclamation of the U.S. Department of the Interior in effect on April 5, 1972. The requirements in effect are:

(1) State of California: Construction Safety Orders, issued by the Department of Industrial Relations pursuant to Division 5, Labor Code, § 6312, State of California.

(2) U.S. Army Corps of Engineers: General Safety Requirements, EM–385–1–1 (March 1967).

(3) Bureau of Reclamation, U.S. Department of the Interior: Safety and Health Regulations for Construction. Part II (September 1971).

§ 1926.1001 Minimum performance criteria for rollover protective structures for designated scrapers, loaders, dozers, graders, and crawler tractors.

(a) *General.* This section prescribes minimum performance criteria for rollover protective structures (ROPS) for rubber-tired self-propelled scrapers; rubber-tired front-end loaders and rubber-tired dozers; crawler tractors, and crawler-type loaders, and motor graders. The vehicle and ROPS as a system shall have the structural characteristics prescribed in paragraph (f) of this section for each type of machine described in this paragraph.

(b) The static laboratory test prescribed herein will determine the adequacy of the structures used to protect the operator under the following conditions:

(1) For rubber-tired self-propelled scrapers, rubber-tired front-end loaders, and rubber-tired dozers: Operating between 0 and 10 miles per hour over hard clay where rollover would be limited to a maximum roll angle of 360° down a slope of 30° maximum.

(2) For motor graders: Operating between 0 and 10 miles per hour over hard clay where rollover would be limited to 360° down a slope of 30° maximum.

(3) For crawler tractors and crawler-type loaders: Operating between 0 and 10 miles per hour over hard clay where

rollover would be limited to a maximum roll angle of 360° down a slope of 45°.

(c) *Facilities and apparatus.* (1) The following material is necessary:

(i) Material, equipment, and tiedown means adequate to insure that the ROPS and its vehicle frame absorb the applied energy.

(ii) Equipment necessary to measure and apply loads to the ROPS. Adequate means to measure deflections and lengths should also be provided.

(iii) Recommended, but not mandatory, types of test setups are illustrated in Figure W–1 for all types of equipment to which this section applies; and in Figure W–2 for rubber-tired self-propelled scrapers; Figure W–3 for rubber-tired front-end loaders, rubber-tired dozers, and motor graders; and Figure W–4 for crawler tractors and crawler-type loaders.

(2) Table W–1 contains a listing of the required apparatus for all types of equipment described in paragraph (a) of this section.

TABLE W–1

Means to measure	Accuracy
Deflection of ROPS, inches	±5% of deflection measured.
Vehicle weight, pounds	±5% of the weight measured.
Force applied to frame, pounds ...	±5% of force measured.
Dimensions of critical zone, inches.	±0.5 in.

(d) *Vehicle condition.* The ROPS to be tested must be attached to the vehicle structure in the same manner as it will be attached during vehicle use. A totally assembled vehicle is not required. However, the vehicle structure and frame which support the ROPS must represent the actual vehicle installation. All normally detachable windows, panels, or nonstructural fittings shall be removed so that they do not contribute to the strength of the ROPS.

(e) *Test procedure.* The test procedure shall include the following, in the sequence indicated:

(1) Energy absorbing capabilities of ROPS shall be verified when loaded laterally by incrementally applying a distributed load to the longitudinal outside top member of the ROPS, as shown in Figure W–1, W–2, or W–3, as applicable. The distributed load must be applied so as to result in approximately uniform deflection of the ROPS. The load increments should correspond with approximately 0.5 in. ROPS deflection increment in the direction of the load application, measured at the ROPS top edge. Should the operator's seat be offcenter, the load shall be applied on the offcenter side. For each applied load increment, the total load (lb.) versus corresponding deflection (in.) shall be plotted, and the area under the load -deflection curve shall be calculated. This area is equal to the energy (in.-lb.) absorbed by the ROPS. For a typical load-deflection curve and calculation method, see Figure W–5.

FIGURE W-1—Vertical loading setup for all types of equipment described in § 1518.1001(a).

FIGURE W-2—Test setup for rubber-tired self-propelled scrapers.

FIGURE W-3—Test setup for rubber-tired front-end loaders, rubber-tired dozers, and motor graders.

FIGURE W-4—Side-loading setup for crawler tractors and crawler loaders.

Incremental loading shall be continued until the ROPS has absorbed the amount of energy and the minimum applied load specified under paragraph (f) of this section has been reached or surpassed.

(2) To cover the possibility of the vehicle coming to rest on its top, the support capability shall be verified by applying a distributed vertical load to the top of the ROPS so as to result in approximately uniform deflection (see Figure W-1). The load magnitude is specified in paragraph (f)(2)(iii) of this section.

(3) The low temperature impact strength of the material used in the ROPS shall be verified by suitable material tests or material certification (see paragraph (f)(2)(iv) of this section).

Δ - TOTAL DEFLECTION
F - FORCE APPLIED

$$AREA = \frac{\Delta_1 F_1}{2} + (\Delta_2 - \Delta_1)\frac{F_1 + F_2}{2} + (\Delta_3 - \Delta_2)\frac{F_2 + F_3}{2} +$$

$$\cdots + (\Delta_N - \Delta_{N-1})\frac{F_{N-1} + F_N}{2}$$

FIGURE W-5—Determination of energy area under force deflection curve for all types of ROPS equipment defined in § 1926.1001.

(f) *Performance requirements*—(1) *General performance requirements.* (i) No repairs or straightening of any member shall be carried out between each prescribed test.

(ii) During each test, no part of the ROPS shall enter the critical zone as detailed in SAE J397 (1969). Deformation of the ROPS shall not allow the plane of the ground to enter this zone.

(2) *Specific performance requirements.* (i) The energy requirement for purposes of meeting the requirements of paragraph (e)(1) of this section is to be determined by referring to the plot of the energy versus weight of vehicle (see Figure W-6 for rubber-tired self-propelled scrapers; Figure W-7 for rubber-tired front-end loaders and rubber-tired dozers; Figure W-8 for crawler tractors and crawler-type loaders; and Figure W-9 for motor graders. For purposes of this section, force and weight are measured as pounds (lb.); energy (U) is measured as inch-pounds.

Figure W-6—Energy absorbed versus vehicle weight.

(ii) The applied load must attain at least a value which is determined by multiplying the vehicle weight by the corresponding factor shown in Figure W-10 for rubber-tired self-propelled scrapers; in Figure W-11 for rubber-tired front-end loaders and rubber-tired dozers; in Figure W-12 for crawler tractors and crawler-type loaders; and in Figure W-13 for motor graders.

(iii) The load magnitude for purposes of compliance with paragraph (e)(2) of this section is equal to the vehicle weight. The test of load magnitude shall only be made after the requirements of paragraph (f)(2)(i) of this section are met.

Figure W-7—Energy absorbed versus vehicle weight.

(iv) Material used in the ROPS must have the capability of performing at zero degrees Fahrenheit, or exhibit Charpy V notch impact strength of 8 foot-pounds at minus 20 °Fahrenheit.

This is a standard Charpy specimen as described in American Society of Testing and Materials A 370, Methods and Definitions for Mechanical Testing of Steel Products (available at each Regional Office of the Occupational Safety and Health Administration). The purpose of this requirement is to reduce the tendency of brittle fracture associated with dynamic loading, low temperature operation, and stress raisers which cannot be entirely avoided on welded structures.

weight of the vehicle plus the heaviest attachment.

FIGURE W-8—Energy absorbed versus vehicle weight.

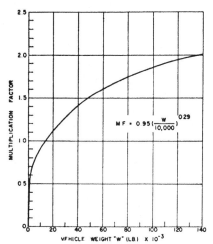

FIGURE W-10—Minimum horizontal load factor for self-propelled scrapers.

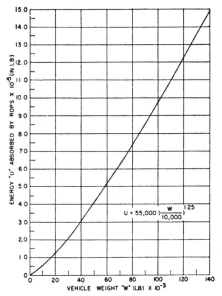

FIGURE W-9—Energy absorbed Versus Vehicle Weight.

FIGURE W-11—Minimum horizontal load factor for rubber-tired loaders and dozers.

(g) *Definitions.* For purposes of this section, "vehicle weight" means the manufacturer's maximum weight of the prime mover for rubber-tired self-propelled scrapers. For other types of equipment to which this section applies, "vehicle weight" means the manufacturer's maximum recommended

FIGURE W-12—Minimum horizontal load factor for crawler tractors and crawler-type loaders.

FIGURE W-13—Minimum horizontal load factor for motor graders.

(h) *Source of standard.* This standard is derived from, and restates, the following Society of Automotive Engineers Recommended Practices: SAE J320a, Minimum Performance Criteria for Roll-Over Protective Structure for Rubber-Tired, Self-Propelled Scrapers; SAE J394, Minimum Performance Criteria for Roll-Over Protective Structure for Rubber-Tired Front End Loaders and Rubber-Tired Dozers; SAE J395, Minimum Performance Criteria for Roll-Over Protective Structure for Crawler Tractors and Crawler-Type Loaders; and SAE J396, Minimum Performance Criteria for Roll-Over Protective Structure for Motor Graders. These recommended practices shall be resorted to in the event that questions

of interpretation arise. The recommended practices appear in the 1971 SAE Handbook, which may be examined in each of the Regional Offices of the Occupational Safety and Health Administration.

§ 1926.1002 Protective frames (roll-over protective structures, known as ROPS) for wheel-type agricultural and industrial tractors used in construction.

(a) *General.* (1) The purpose of this section is to set forth requirements for frames used to protect operators of wheel-type agricultural and industrial tractors that will minimize the possibility of operator injury resulting from accidental upsets during normal operation. With respect to agricultural and industrial tractors, the provisions of 29 CFR 1926.1001 and 1926.1003 for rubber-tired dozers and rubber-tired loaders may be used instead of the requirements of this section.

(2) The protective frame that is the subject of this standard is a structure mounted to the tractor that extends above the operator's seat and conforms generally to Figure W-14.

(3) When an overhead weather shield is attached to the protective frame, it may be in place during testing, provided that it does not contribute to the strength of the protective frame. When such an overhead weather shield is attached, it must meet the requirements of paragraph (i) of this section.

(4) For overhead protection requirements, see 29 CFR 1926.1003.

(5) The following provisions address requirements for protective enclosures.

(i) When protective enclosures are used on wheel-type agricultural and industrial tractors, they shall meet the requirements of Society of Automotive Engineers ("SAE") standard J168–1970 ("Protective enclosures—test procedures and performance requirements"), which is incorporated by reference. The incorporation by reference was approved by the Director of the Federal Register in accordance with 5 U.S.C. 552(a) and 1 CFR part 51.

(ii) SAE standard J168–1970 appears in the 1971 SAE Handbook, or it may be examined at: any OSHA Regional Office; the OSHA Docket Office, U.S. Department of Labor, 200 Constitution

Avenue, NW., Room N–2625, Washington, DC 20210 (telephone: (202) 693–2350 (TTY number: (877) 889–5627)); or the National Archives and Records Administration ("NARA"). (For information on the availability of this material at NARA, telephone (202) 741–6030 or access the NARA Web site at *www.archives.gov/federal_register/ code_of_federal_regulations/ ibr_locations.html.*) Copies may be purchased from the Society of Automotive Engineers, 400 Commonwealth Drive, Warrendale, Pennsylvania 15096–0001.

(b) *Applicability.* The requirements of this section apply to wheel-type agricultural and industrial tractors used in construction work. See paragraph (j) of this section for definitions of agricultural tractors set forth in paragraph (i) of this section.

(c) *Performance requirements.* (1) Either a laboratory test or a field test is required to determine the performance requirements set forth in paragraph (i) of this section.

(2) A laboratory test may be either static or dynamic. The laboratory test must be under conditions of repeatable and controlled loading to permit analysis of the protective frame.

(3) A field-upset test, when used, shall be conducted under reasonably controlled conditions, both rearward and sideways to verify the effectiveness of the protective frame under actual dynamic conditions.

(d) *Test procedures—general.* (1) The tractor used shall be the tractor with the greatest weight on which the protective frame is to be used.

(2) A new protective frame and mounting connections of the same design shall be used for each test procedure.

(3) Instantaneous and permanent frame deformation shall be measured and recorded for each segment of the test.

(4) Dimensions relative to the seat shall be determined with the seat unloaded and adjusted to its highest and most rearward latched position provided for a seated operator.

(5) When the seat is offset, the frame loading shall be on the side with the least space between the centerline of the seat and the upright.

(6) The low-temperature impact strength of the material used in the protective structure shall be verified by suitable material tests or material certifications according to 29 CFR 1926.1001(f)(2)(iv).

(e) *Test procedure for vehicle overturn—* (1) *Vehicle weight.* The weight of the tractor, for purposes of this section, includes the protective frame, all fuels, and other components required for normal use of the tractor. Ballast must be added when necessary to achieve a minimum total weight of 130 lb (59 kg) per maximum power-takeoff horsepower at the rated engine speed. The weight of the front end must be at least 33 lb (15 kg) per maximum power-takeoff horsepower. In case power-takeoff horsepower is unavailable, 95 percent of net engine flywheel horsepower shall be used.

(2) Agricultural tractors shall be tested at the weight set forth in paragraph (e)(1) of this section.

(3) Industrial tractors shall be tested with items of integral or mounted equipment and ballast that are sold as standard equipment or approved by the vehicle manufacturer for use with the vehicle when the protective frame is expected to provide protection for the operator with such equipment installed. The total vehicle weight and front-end weight as tested shall not be less than the weights established in paragraph (e)(1) of this section.

(4) The following provisions address soil bank test conditions.

(i) The test shall be conducted on a dry, firm soil bank as illustrated in Figure W–15. The soil in the impact area shall have an average cone index in the 0-in. to 6-in. (0-mm to 153-mm) layer not less than 150 according to American Society of Agricultural Engineers ("ASAE") recommendation ASAE R313.1–1971 ("Soil cone penetrometer"), as reconfirmed in 1975, which is incorporated by reference. The incorporation by reference was approved by the Director of the Federal Register in accordance with 5 U.S.C. 552(a) and 1 CFR part 51. The path of vehicle travel shall be 12° ±2° to the top edge of the bank.

(ii) ASAE recommendation ASAE R313.1–1971, as reconfirmed in 1975, appears in the 1977 Agricultural Engineers Yearbook, or it may be examined at: any OSHA Regional Office; the OSHA Docket Office, U.S. Department of Labor, 200 Constitution Avenue, NW., Room N–2625, Washington, DC 20210 (telephone: (202) 693–2350 (TTY number: (877) 889–5627)); or the National Archives and Records Administration ("NARA"). (For information on the availability of this material at NARA, telephone (202) 741–6030 or access the NARA Web site at *www.archives.gov/ federal_register/ code_of_federal_regulations/ ibr_locations.html*). Copies may be purchased from the American Society of Agricultural Engineers 2950 Niles Road, St. Joseph, MI 49085.

(5) The upper edge of the bank shall be equipped with an 18-in. (457-mm) high ramp as described in Figure W–15 to assist in tipping the vehicle.

(6) The front and rear wheel-tread settings, when adjustable, shall be at the position nearest to halfway between the minimum and maximum settings obtainable on the vehicle. When only two settings are obtainable, the minimum setting shall be used.

(7) *Vehicle overturn test—sideways and rearward.* (i) The tractor shall be driven under its own power along the specified path of travel at a minimum speed of 10 mph (16 kph), or maximum vehicle speed when under 10 mph (16 kph), up the ramp as described in paragraph (d)(5) of this section to induce sideways overturn.

(ii) Rear upset shall be induced by engine power with the tractor operating in gear to obtain 3 to 5 mph (4.8 to 8 kph) at maximum governed engine rpm, preferably by driving forward directly up a minimum slope of two vertical to one horizontal. The engine clutch may be used to aid in inducing the upset.

(f) *Other test procedures.* When the field-upset test is not used to determine ROPS performance, either the static test or the dynamic test, contained in paragraph (g) or (h) of this section, shall be made.

(g) *Static test—(1) Test conditions.* (i) The laboratory mounting base shall include that part of the tractor chassis to which the protective frame is attached, including the mounting parts.

(ii) The protective frame shall be instrumented with the necessary equipment to obtain the required load-deflection data at the locations and directions specified in Figures W–16, W–17, and W–18.

(iii) The protective frame and mounting connections shall be instrumented with the necessary recording equipment to obtain the required load-deflection data to be used in calculating FSB (see paragraph (j)(3) of this section). The gauges shall be placed on mounting connections before the installation load is applied.

(2) *Test procedure.* (i) The side-load application shall be at the upper extremity of the frame upright at a 90° angle to the centerline of the vehicle. The side load L shall be applied according to Figure W–16. L and D shall be recorded simultaneously. The test shall be stopped when:

(A) The strain energy absorbed by the frame is equal to the required input energy (E_{is});

(B) Deflection of the frame exceeds the allowable deflection; or

(C) The frame load limit occurs before the allowable deflection is reached in the side load.

(ii) The L–D diagram (see Figure W–19 for an example) shall be constructed using the data obtained according to paragraph (g)(2)(i) of this section.

(iii) The modified L_m–D_m diagram shall be constructed according to paragraph (g)(2)(ii) and Figure W–20 of this section. The strain energy absorbed by the frame (E_u) shall then be determined.

(iv) E_{is}, FER, and FSB shall be calculated.

(v) The test procedure shall be repeated on the same frame using L (rear input; see Figure W–18) and E_{ir}. Rear-load application shall be distributed uniformly along a maximum projected dimension of 27 in. (686 mm) and a maximum area of 160 sq. in. (1,032 sq. cm) normal to the direction of load application. The load shall be applied to the upper extremity of the frame at the point that is midway between the centerline of the seat and the inside of the frame upright.

(h) *Dynamic test*—(1) *Test conditions.* (i) The protective frame and tractor shall meet the requirements of paragraphs (e)(2) or (3) of this section, as appropriate.

(ii) The dynamic loading shall be produced by using a 4,410-lb (2,000-kg) weight acting as a pendulum. The impact face of the weight shall be 27 ±1 in. by 27 ±1 in. (686 ±25 mm by 686 ±25 mm), and shall be constructed so that its center of gravity is within 1.0 in. (25.4 mm) of its geometric center. The weight shall be suspended from a pivot point 18 to 22 ft (5.5 to 6.7 m) above the point of impact on the frame, and shall be conveniently and safely adjustable for height (see Figure W–21).

(iii) For each phase of testing, the tractor shall be restrained from moving when the dynamic load is applied. The restraining members shall be 0.50- to 0.63-in. (12.5- to 16.0-mm) steel cable, and points for attaching restraining members shall be located an appropriate distance behind the rear axle and in front of the front axle to provide a 15° to 30° angle between the restraining cable and the horizontal. The restraining cables shall either be in the plane in which the center of gravity of the pendulum will swing, or more than one restraining cable shall give a resultant force in this plane (see Figure W–22).

(iv) The wheel-tread setting shall comply with the requirements of paragraph (e)(6) of this section. The tires shall have no liquid ballast, and shall be inflated to the maximum operating pressure recommended by the tire manufacturer. With the specified tire inflation, the restraining cables shall be tightened to provide tire deflection of 6 to 8 percent of the nominal tire-section width. After the vehicle is restrained properly, a wooden beam that is 6-in. × 6-in. (150 mm × 150 mm) shall be driven tightly against the appropriate wheels and clamped. For the test to the side, an additional wooden beam shall be placed as a prop against the wheel nearest to the operator's station, and shall be secured to the floor so that when it is positioned against the wheel rim, it is at an angle of 25° to 40° to the horizontal. It shall have a length 20 to 25 times its depth, and a width two to three times its depth (see Figures W–22 and W–23).

(v) Means shall be provided for indicating the maximum instantaneous deflection along the line of impact. A simple friction device is illustrated in Figure W–18.

(vi) No repair or adjustments may be carried out during the test.

(vii) When any cables, props, or blocking shift or break during the test, the test shall be repeated.

(2) *Test procedure*—(i) *General.* The frame shall be evaluated by imposing dynamic loading to the rear, followed by a load to the side on the same frame. The pendulum dropped from the height (see the definition of "*H*" in paragraph (j)(3) of this section) imposes the dynamic load. The position of the pendulum shall be so selected that the initial point of impact on the frame shall be in line with the arc of travel of the center of gravity of the pendulum. A quick-release mechanism should be used but, when used, it shall not influence the attitude of the block.

(ii) *Impact at rear.* The tractor shall be restrained properly according to paragraphs (h)(1)(iii) and (h)(1)(iv) of this section. The tractor shall be positioned with respect to the pivot point of the pendulum so that the pendulum is 20° from the vertical prior to impact as shown in Figure W–22. The impact shall be applied to the upper extremity of the frame at the point that is midway between the centerline of the frame and the inside of the frame upright of a new frame.

(iii) *Impact at side.* The blocking and restraining shall conform to paragraphs (h)(1)(iii) and (h)(1)(iv) of this section. The center point of impact shall be that structural member of the protective frame likely to hit the ground first in a sideways accidental upset. The side impact shall be applied to the side opposite that used for rear impact.

(i) *Performance requirements*—(1) *General.* (i) The frame, overhead weather shield, fenders, or other parts in the operator area may be deformed in these tests, but shall not shatter or leave sharp edges exposed to the operator, or violate the dimensions shown in Figures W–16 and W–17, and specified as follows:

553

D = 2 in. (51 mm) inside of the frame upright to the vertical centerline of the seat;

E = 30 in. (762 mm);

F = Not less than 0 in. (0 mm) and not more than 12 in. (305 mm), measured at the centerline of the seat backrest to the crossbar along the line of load application as shown in Figure W–17; and

G = 24 in. (610 mm).

(ii) The material and design combination used in the protective structure must be such that the structure can meet all prescribed performance tests at 0 °F (−18 °C) according to 29 CFR 1926.1001(f)(2)(iv).

(2) *Vehicle overturn performance requirements.* The requirements of this paragraph (i) must be met in both side and rear overturns.

(3) *Static test performance requirements.* Design factors shall be incorporated in each design to withstand an overturn test as specified by this paragraph (i). The structural requirements will be met generally when *FER* is greater than 1.0 and *FSB* is greater than K–1 in both side and rear loadings.

(4) *Dynamic test performance requirements.* Design factors shall be incorporated in each design to withstand the overturn test specified by this paragraph (i). The structural requirements will be met generally when the dimensions in this paragraph (i) are used during both side and rear loads.

(j) *Definitions applicable to this section.* (1) "Agricultural tractor" means a wheel-type vehicle of more than 20 engine horsepower, used in construction work, that is designed to furnish the power to pull, propel, or drive implements. (SAE standard J333a–1970 ("Operator protection for wheel-type agricultural and industrial tractors") defines "agricultural tractor" as a "wheel-type vehicle of more than 20 engine horsepower designed to furnish the power to pull, carry, propel, or drive implements that are designed for agricultural usage." Since this part 1926 applies only to construction work, the SAE definition of "agricultural tractor" is adopted for purposes of this subpart.)

(2) "Industrial tractor" means that class of wheel-type tractors of more than 20 engine horsepower (other than

rubber-tired loaders and dozers described in 29 CFR 1926.1001), used in operations such as landscaping, construction services, loading, digging, grounds keeping, and highway maintenance.

(3) The following symbols, terms, and explanations apply to this section:

E_{is} = Energy input to be absorbed during side loading in ft-lb (E'_{is} in J [joules]);

E_{is} = 723 + 0.4 W ft-lb (E'_{is} = 100 + 0.12 W', J);

E_{ir} = Energy input to be absorbed during rear loading in ft-lb (E'_{ir} in J);

E_{ir} = 0.47 W ft-lb (E'_{ir} = 0.14 W', J);

W = Tractor weight as specified by 29 CFR 1926.1002(e)(1) and (e)(3), in lb (W', kg);

L = Static load, lb (kg);

D = Deflection under L, in. (mm);

L–D = Static load-deflection diagram;

L_m–D_m = Modified static load-deflection diagram (Figure W–20). To account for an increase in strength due to an increase in strain rate, raise L in the plastic range $L \times K$;

K = Increase in yield strength induced by higher rate of loading (1.3 for hot, rolled, low-carbon steel 1010–1030). Low carbon is preferable; however, when higher carbon or other material is used, K must be determined in the laboratory. Refer to Norris, C.H., Hansen, R.J., Holley, M.J., Biggs, J.M., Namyet, S., and Minami, J.V., *Structural Design for Dynamic Loads*, McGraw-Hill, New York, 1959, p. 3;

L_{max} = Maximum observed static load;

Load Limit = Point on a continuous L–D curve at which the observed static load is 0.8 L_{max} (refer to Figure W–19);

E_u = Strain energy absorbed by the frame, ft-lb (J); area under the L_m–D_m curve;

FER = Factor of energy ratio, *FER* = $E_u E_{is}$; also, *FER* = $E_u E_{ir}$;

P_b = Maximum observed force in mounting connection under a static load, L, lb (kg);

P_u = Ultimate force capacity of mounting connection, lb (kg);

FSB = Design margin for a mounting connection ($P_u P_b$) – 1; and

H = Vertical height of lift of 4,410-lb (2,000-kg) weight, in. (H', mm). The weight shall be pulled back so that the height of its center of gravity above the point of impact is defined as follows: $H = 4.92 + 0.00190\ W$ ($H' = 125 + 0.107\ W'$) (see Figure W–24).

(k) *Source of standard.* The standard in this section is derived from, and restates, in part, Society of Automotive Engineers ("SAE") standard J334a-1970 ("Protective frame test procedures and performance requirements"). The SAE standard appears in the 1971 SAE Handbook, which may be examined at any OSHA regional office.

[70 FR 76985, Dec. 29, 2005, as amended at 71 FR 41129, July 20, 2006]

§ 1926.1003 Overhead protection for operators of agricultural and industrial tractors used in construction.

(a) *General*—(1) *Purpose.* When overhead protection is provided on wheel-type agricultural and industrial tractors, the overhead protection shall be designed and installed according to the requirements contained in this section. The provisions of 29 CFR 1926.1001 for rubber-tired dozers and rubber-tired loaders may be used instead of the standards contained in this section. The purpose of this standard is to minimize the possibility of operator injury resulting from overhead hazards such as flying and falling objects, and at the same time to minimize the possibility of operator injury from the cover itself in the event of accidental upset.

(2) *Applicability.* This standard applies to wheel-type agricultural and industrial tractors used in construction work (see 29 CFR 1926.1002(b) and (j)). In the case of machines to which 29 CFR 1926.604 (relating to site clearing) also applies, the overhead protection may be either the type of protection provided in 29 CFR 1926.604, or the type of protection provided by this section.

(b) *Overhead protection.* When overhead protection is installed on wheel-type agricultural or industrial tractors used in construction work, it shall meet the requirements of this paragraph. The overhead protection may be constructed of a solid material. When grid or mesh is used, the largest permissible opening shall be such that the maximum circle that can be inscribed between the elements of the grid or mesh is 1.5 in. (38 mm) in diameter. The overhead protection shall not be in-

stalled in such a way as to become a hazard in the case of upset.

(c) *Test procedures—general.* (1) The requirements of 29 CFR 1926.1002(d), (e), and (f) shall be met.

(2) Static and dynamic rear load application shall be distributed uniformly along a maximum projected dimension of 27 in. (686 mm), and a maximum area of 160 sq. in. (1,032 sq. cm), normal to the direction of load application. The load shall be applied to the upper extremity of the frame at the point that is midway between the centerline of the seat and the inside of the frame upright.

(3) The static and dynamic side load application shall be distributed uniformly along a maximum projected dimension of 27 in. (686 mm), and a maximum area of 160 sq. in. (1,032 sq. cm), normal to the direction of load application. The direction of load application is the same as in 29 CFR 1926.1002 (g) and (h). To simulate the characteristics of the structure during an upset, the center of load application may be located from a point 24 in. (610 mm) (K) forward to 12 in. (305 mm) (L) rearward of the front of the seat backrest, to best use the structural strength (see Figure W–25).

(d) *Drop test procedures.* (1) The same frame shall be subjected to the drop test following either the static or dynamic test.

(2) A solid steel sphere or material of equivalent spherical dimension weighing 100 lb (45.4 kg) shall be dropped once from a height 10 ft (3.08 m) above the overhead cover.

(3) The point of impact shall be on the overhead cover at a point within the zone of protection as shown in Figure W–26, which is furthest removed from major structural members.

(e) *Crush test procedure.* (1) The same frame shall be subjected to the crush test following the drop test and static or dynamic test.

(2) The test load shall be applied as shown in Figure W–27, with the seat positioned as specified in 29 CFR 1926.1002(d)(4). Loading cylinders shall be mounted pivotally at both ends. Loads applied by each cylinder shall be equal within two percent, and the sum of the loads of the two cylinders shall be two times the tractor weight as set

555

forth in 29 CFR 1926.1002(e)(1). The maximum width of the beam illustrated in Figure W-27 shall be 6 in. (152 mm).

(f) *Performance requirements (1)—General.* The performance requirements set forth in 29 CFR 1926.1002(i)(2), (3), and (4) shall be met.

(2) *Drop test performance requirements.* (i) Instantaneous deformation due to impact of the sphere shall not enter the protected zone as illustrated in Figures W-25, W-26, and W-28.

(ii) In addition to the dimensions set forth in 29 CFR 1926.1002(i)(1)(i), the following dimensions apply to Figure W-28:

H = 17.5 in. (444 mm); and
J = 2 in. (50.8 mm), measured from the outer periphery of the steering wheel.

(3) *Crush test performance requirements.* The protected zone as described in Figure W-28 must not be violated.

(g) *Source of standard.* This standard is derived from, and restates, in part, the portions of Society of Automotive Engineers ("SAE") standard J167-1970 ("Protective frame with overhead protection—test procedures and performance requirements"), which pertain to overhead protection requirements. The SAE standard appears in the 1971 SAE Handbook, which may be examined at any OSHA regional office.

[70 FR 76985, Dec. 29, 2005]

APPENDIX A TO SUBPART W OF PART 1926—FIGURES W-14 THROUGH W-28

FIGURE W-14 - TYPICAL FRAME CONFIGURATION.

FIGURE W-15 - SIDE OVERTURN BANK AND RAMP.

FIGURE W-16 - SIDE LOAD APPLICATION.

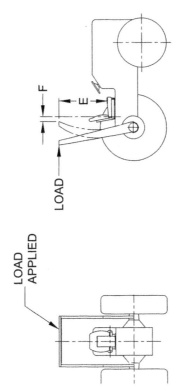

FIGURE W-17 - REAR LOAD APPLICATION.

FIGURE W-18 - METHOD OF MEASURING INSTANTANEOUS DEFLECTION.

FIGURE W-19 - TYPICAL L-D DIAGRAM.

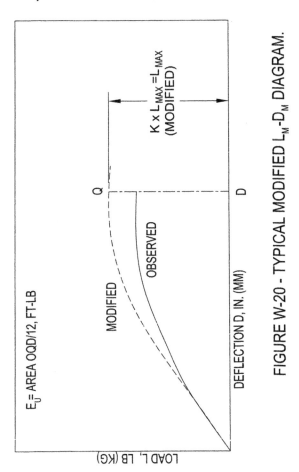

FIGURE W-20 - TYPICAL MODIFIED L_M-D_M DIAGRAM.

FIGURE W-21 - PENDULUM.

RESTRAINING CABLE

15°-30°

BEAM CLAMPED IN FRONT OF BOTH REAR WHEELS AFTER ANCHORING, 6 IN. (15 CM) SQUARE

20°

H

RESTRAINING CABLE

15°-30°

FIGURE W-22 - METHOD OF IMPACT FROM REAR.

RESTRAINING CABLE

BEAM CLAMPED AGAINST SIDES OF FRONT AND REAR WHEELS AND AGAINST PROP

PROP WEDGED AGAINST WHEEL RIM AFTER ANCHORING

25°-40°

H

FIGURE W-23 - METHOD OF IMPACT FROM SIDE.

NOTATION OF FORMULAE
H=4.92+0.00190W or H'=125+0.107W'
W=tractor weight specified by 29 CFR
1926.1002(e)(1) and (e)(3) in lbs (W' in kg).

FIGURE W-24 - IMPACT ENERGY AND CORRESPONDING LIFT HEIGHT OF 4,410 lb (2,000 kg) WEIGHT.

FIGURE W-25 - LOCATION OF SIDE LOAD.

ALL POSSIBLE LATERAL WORKING POSITIONS OF SEAT

6 IN.
152 MM

20 IN.
508 MM R

FIGURE W-26 - ZONE OF PROTECTION FOR DROP TEST.

FIGURE W-27 - METHOD OF LOAD APPLICATION FOR CRUSH TEST.

FIGURE W-28 - PROTECTED ZONE DURING CRUSH AND DROP TEST.

[70 FR 76985, Dec. 29, 2005, as amended at 71 FR 41130, July 20, 2006]

Subpart X—Stairways and Ladders

AUTHORITY: 40 U.S.C. 3701 *et seq.;* 29 U.S.C. 653, 655, 657; Secretary of Labor's Order No. 1–90 (55 FR 9033), 5–2007 (72 FR 31159), or 1–2012 (77 FR 3912), as applicable; and 29 CFR Part 1911.

SOURCE: 55 FR 47687, Nov. 14, 1990, unless otherwise noted.

§ 1926.1050 Scope, application, and definitions applicable to this subpart.

(a) *Scope and application.* This subpart applies to all stairways and ladders used in construction, alteration, repair (including painting and decorating), and demolition workplaces covered under 29 CFR part 1926, and also sets forth, in specified circumstances, when ladders and stairways are required to be provided. Additional requirements for ladders used on or with scaffolds are contained in subpart L—Scaffolds. This subpart does not apply to integral components of equipment covered by subpart CC. Subpart CC exclusively sets forth the circumstances when ladders and stairways must be provided on equipment covered by subpart CC.

(b) *Definitions. Cleat* means a ladder crosspiece of rectangular cross section placed on edge upon which a person may step while ascending or descending a ladder.

Double-cleat ladder means a ladder similar in construction to a single-cleat ladder, but with a center rail to allow simultaneous two-way traffic for employees ascending or descending.

Equivalent means alternative designs, materials, or methods that the employer can demonstrate will provide an equal or greater degree of safety for employees than the method or item specified in the standard.

Extension trestle ladder means a self-supporting portable ladder, adjustable in length, consisting of a trestle ladder base and a vertically adjustable extension section, with a suitable means for locking the ladders together.

Failure means load refusal, breakage, or separation of component parts. Load refusal is the point where the structural members lose their ability to carry the loads.

Fixed ladder means a ladder that cannot be readily moved or carried because it is an integral part of a building or structure. A *side-step fixed ladder* is a fixed ladder that requires a person getting off at the top to step to the side of the ladder side rails to reach the landing. A *through fixed ladder* is a fixed ladder that requires a person getting off at the top to step between the side rails of the ladder to reach the landing.

Handrail means a rail used to provide employees with a handhold for support.

Individual-rung/step ladders means ladders without a side rail or center rail support. Such ladders are made by mounting individual steps or rungs directly to the side or wall of the structure.

Job-made ladder means a ladder that is fabricated by employees, typically at the construction site, and is not commercially manufactured. This definition does not apply to any individual-rung/step ladders.

Ladder stand. A mobile fixed size self-supporting ladder consisting of a wide flat tread ladder in the form of stairs. The assembly may include handrails.

Lower levels means those areas to which an employee can fall from a stairway or ladder. Such areas include ground levels, floors, roofs, ramps, runways, excavations, pits, tanks, material, water, equipment, and similar surfaces. It does not include the surface from which the employee falls.

Maximum intended load means the total load of all employees, equipment, tools, materials, transmitted loads, and other loads anticipated to be applied to a ladder component at any one time.

Nosing means that portion of a tread projecting beyond the face of the riser immediately below.

Point of access means all areas used by employees for work-related passage from one area or level to another. Such open areas include doorways, 1passageways, stairway openings, studded walls, and various other permanent or temporary openings used for such travel.

Portable ladder means a ladder that can be readily moved or carried.

Riser height means the vertical distance from the top of a tread to the top of the next higher tread or platform/landing or the distance from the top of a platform/landing to the top of the next higher tread or platform/landing.

Side-step fixed ladder. See "Fixed ladder."

Single-cleat ladder means a ladder consisting of a pair of side rails, connected together by cleats, rungs, or steps.

Single-rail ladder means a portable ladder with rungs, cleats, or steps mounted on a single rail instead of the normal two rails used on most other ladders.

Spiral stairway means a series of steps attached to a vertical pole and progressing upward in a winding fashion within a cylindrical space.

Stairrail system means a vertical barrier erected along the unprotected sides and edges of a stariway to prevent employees from falling to lower levels. The top surface of a stairrail system may also be a "handrail."

Step stool (ladder type) means a self-supporting, foldable, portable ladder, nonadjustable in length, 32 inches or less in overall size, with flat steps and without a pail shelf, designed to be climbed on the ladder top cap as well as all steps. The side rails may continue above the top cap.

Through fixed ladder. See "Fixed ladder."

Tread depth means the horizontal distance from front to back of a tread (excluding nosing, if any).

Unprotected sides and edges means any side or edge (except at entrances to points of access) of a stairway where there is no stairrail system or wall 36 inches (.9 m) or more in height, and any side or edge (except at entrances to points of access) of a stairway landing, or ladder platform where there is no wall or guardrail system 39 inches (1 m) or more in height.

[55 FR 47687, Nov. 14, 1990; 56 FR 2585, Jan. 23, 1991, as amended at 58 FR 35184, June 30, 1993; 75 FR 48135, Aug. 9, 2010]

§1926.1051 General requirements.

(a) A stairway or ladder shall be provided at all personnel points of access where there is a break in elevation of 19 inches (48 cm) or more, and no ramp, runway, sloped embankment, or personnel hoist is provided.

(1) Employees shall not use any spiral stairways that will not be a permanent part of the structure on which construction work is being performed.

(2) A double-cleated ladder or two or more separate ladders shall be provided when ladders are the only mean of access or exit from a working area for 25 or more employees, or when a ladder is to serve simultaneous two-way traffic.

(3) When a building or structure has only one point of access between levels, that point of access shall be kept clear to permit free passage of employees. When work must be performed or equipment must be used such that free passage at that point of access is restricted, a second point of access shall be provided and used.

(4) When a building or structure has two or more points of access between levels, at least one point of access shall be kept clear to permit free passage of employees.

(b) Employers shall provide and install all stairway and ladder fall protection systems required by this subpart and shall comply with all other pertinent requirements of this subpart before employees begin the work that necessitates the installation and use of stairways, ladders, and their respective fall protection systems.

§1926.1052 Stairways.

(a) *General.* The following requirements apply to all stairways as indicated:

(1) Stairways that will not be a permanent part of the structure on which construction work is being performed shall have landings of not less than 30 inches (76 cm) in the direction of travel and extend at least 22 inches (56 cm) in width at every 12 feet (3.7 m) or less of vertical rise.

(2) Stairs shall be installed between 30° and 50° from horizontal.

(3) Riser height and tread depth shall be uniform within each flight of stairs, including any foundation structure used as one or more treads of the stairs. Variations in riser height or tread depth shall not be over ¼-inch (0.6 cm) in any stairway system.

(4) Where doors or gates open directly on a stairway, a platform shall be provided, and the swing of the door shall not reduce the effective width of the platform to less than 20 inches (51 cm).

(5) Metal pan landings and metal pan treads, when used, shall be secured in place before filling with concrete or other material.

(6) All parts of stairways shall be free of hazardous projections, such as protruding nails.

(7) Slippery conditions on stairways shall be eliminated before the stairways are used to reach other levels.

(b) *Temporary service.* The following requirements apply to all stairways as indicated:

(1) Except during stairway construction, foot traffic is prohibited on stairways with pan stairs where the treads and/or landings are to be filled in with concrete or other material at a later date, unless the stairs are temporarily fitted with wood or other solid material at least to the top edge of each pan. Such temporary treads and landings shall be replaced when worn below the level of the top edge of the pan.

(2) Except during stairway construction, foot traffic is prohibited on skeleton metal stairs where permanent treads and/or landings are to be installed at a later date, unless the stairs are fitted with secured temporary treads and landings long enough to cover the entire tread and/or landing area.

(3) Treads for temporary service shall be made of wood or other solid material, and shall be installed the full width and depth of the stair.

(c) *Stairrails and handrails.* The following requirements apply to all stairways as indicated:

(1) Stairways having four or more risers or rising more than 30 inches (76 cm), whichever is less, shall be equipped with:

(i) At least one handrail; and

571

(ii) One stairrail system along each unprotected side or edge.

NOTE: When the top edge of a stairrail system also serves as a handrail, paragraph (c)(7) of this section applies.

(2) Winding and spiral stairways shall be equipped with a handrail offset sufficiently to prevent walking on those portions of the stairways where the tread width is less than 6 inches (15 cm).

(3) The height of stairrails shall be as follows:

(i) Stairrails installed after March 15, 1991, shall be not less than 36 inches (91.5 cm) from the upper surface of the stairrail system to the surface of the tread, in line with the face of the riser at the forward edge of the tread.

(ii) Stairrails installed before March 15, 1991, shall be not less than 30 inches (76 cm) nor more than 34 inches (86 cm) from the upper surface of the stairrail system to the surface of the tread, in line with the face of the riser at the forward edge of the tread.

(4) Midrails, screens, mesh, intermediate vertical members, or equivalent intermediate structural members, shall be provided between the top rail of the stairrail system and the stairway steps.

(i) Midrails, when used, shall be located at a height midway between the top edge of the stairrail system and the stairway steps.

(ii) Screens or mesh, when used, shall extend from the top rail to the stairway step, and along the entire opening between top rail supports.

(iii) When intermediate vertical members, such as balusters, are used between posts, they shall be not more than 19 inches (48 cm) apart.

(iv) Other structural members, when used, shall be installed such that there are no openings in the stairrail system that are more than 19 inches (48 cm) wide.

(5) Handrails and the top rails of stairrail systems shall be capable of withstanding, without failure, a force of at least 200 pounds (890 n) applied within 2 inches (5 cm) of the top edge, in any downward or outward direction, at any point along the top edge.

(6) The height of handrails shall be not more than 37 inches (94 cm) nor less than 30 inches (76 cm) from the upper surface of the handrail to the surface of the tread, in line with the face of the riser at the forward edge of the tread.

(7) When the top edge of a stairrail system also serves as a handrail, the height of the top edge shall be not more than 37 inches (94 cm) nor less than 36 inches (91.5 cm) from the upper surface of the stairrail system to the surface of the tread, in line with the face of the riser at the forward edge of the tread.

(8) Stairrail systems and handrails shall be so surfaced as to prevent injury to employees from punctures or lacerations, and to prevent snagging of clothing.

(9) Handrails shall provide an adequate handhold for employees grasping them to avoid falling.

(10) The ends of stairrail systems and handrails shall be constructed so as not to constitute a projection hazard.

(11) Handrails that will not be a permanent part of the structure being built shall have a minimum clearance of 3 inches (8 cm) between the handrail and walls, stairrail systems, and other objects.

(12) Unprotected sides and edges of stairway landings shall be provided with guardrail systems. Guardrail system criteria are contained in subpart M of this part.

[55 FR 47687, Nov. 14, 1990; 56 FR 2585, Jan. 23, 1991; 56 FR 5061, Feb. 7, 1991; 56 FR 41794, Aug. 23, 1991]

§ 1926.1053 Ladders.

(a) *General.* The following requirements apply to all ladders as indicated, including job-made ladders.

(1) Ladders shall be capable of supporting the following loads without failure:

(i) Each self-supporting portable ladder: At least four times the maximum intended load, except that each extra-heavy-duty type 1A metal or plastic ladder shall sustain at least 3.3 times the maximum intended load. The ability of a ladder to sustain the loads indicated in this paragraph shall be determined by applying or transmitting the requisite load to the ladder in a downward vertical direction. Ladders built and tested in conformance with the applicable provisions of appendix A of this subpart will be deemed to meet this requirement.

(ii) Each portable ladder that is not self-supporting: At least four times the maximum intended load, except that each extra-heavy-duty type 1A metal or plastic ladders shall sustain at least 3.3 times the maximum intended load. The ability of a ladder to sustain the loads indicated in this paragraph shall be determined by applying or transmitting the requisite load to the ladder in a downward vertical direction when the ladder is placed at an angle of 75½ degrees from the horizontal. Ladders built and tested in conformance with the applicable provisions of appendix A will be deemed to meet this requirement.

(iii) Each fixed ladder: At least two loads of 250 pounds (114 kg) each, concentrated between any two consecutive attachments (the number and position of additional concentrated loads of 250 pounds (114 kg) each, determined from anticipated usage of the ladder, shall also be included), plus anticipated loads caused by ice buildup, winds, rigging, and impact loads resulting from the use of ladder safety devices. Each step or rung shall be capable of supporting a single concentrated load of at least 250 pounds (114 kg) applied in the middle of the step or rung. Ladders built in conformance with the applicable provisions of appendix A will be deemed to meet this requirement.

(2) Ladder rungs, cleats, and steps shall be parallel, level, and uniformly spaced when the ladder is in position for use.

(3)(i) Rungs, cleats, and steps of portable ladders (except as provided below) and fixed ladders (including individual-rung/step ladders) shall be spaced not less than 10 inches (25 cm) apart, nor more than 14 inches (36 cm) apart, as measured between center lines of the rungs, cleats, and steps.

(ii) Rungs, cleats, and steps of step stools shall be not less than 8 inches (20 cm) apart, nor more than 12 inches (31 cm) apart, as measured between center lines of the rungs, cleats, and steps.

(iii) Rungs, cleats, and steps of the base section of extension trestle ladders shall not be less than 8 inches (20 cm) nor more than 18 inches (46 cm) apart, as measured between center lines of the rungs, cleats, and steps. The rung spacing on the extension section of the extension trestle ladder shall be not less than 6 inches (15 cm) nor more than 12 inches (31 cm), as measured between center lines of the rungs, cleats, and steps.

(4)(i) The minimum clear distance between the sides of individual-rung/step ladders and the minimum clear distance between the side rails of other fixed ladders shall be 16 inches (41 cm).

(ii) The minimum clear distance between side rails for all portable ladders shall be 11½ inches (29 cm).

(5) The rungs of individual-rung/step ladders shall be shaped such that employees' feet cannot slide off the end of the rungs.

(6)(i) The rungs and steps of fixed metal ladders manufactured after March 15, 1991, shall be corrugated, knurled, dimpled, coated with skid-resistant material, or otherwise treated to minimize slipping.

(ii) The rungs and steps of portable metal ladders shall be corrugated, knurled, dimpled, coated with skid-resistant material, or otherwise treated to minimize slipping.

(7) Ladders shall not be tied or fastened together to provide longer sections unless they are specifically designed for such use.

(8) A metal spreader or locking device shall be provided on each stepladder to hold the front and back sections in an open position when the ladder is being used.

(9) When splicing is required to obtain a given length of side rail, the resulting side rail must be at least equivalent in strength to a one-piece side rail made of the same material.

(10) Except when portable ladders are used to gain access to fixed ladders (such as those on utility towers, billboards, and other structures where the bottom of the fixed ladder is elevated to limit access), when two or more separate ladders are used to reach an elevated work area, the ladders shall be offset with a platform or landing between the ladders. (The requirements to have guardrail systems with toeboards for falling object and overhead protection on platforms and landings are set forth in subpart M of this part.)

573

(11) Ladder components shall be surfaced so as to prevent injury to an employee from punctures or lacerations, and to prevent snagging of clothing.

(12) Wood ladders shall not be coated with any opaque covering, except for identification or warning labels which may be placed on one face only of a side rail.

(13) The minimum perpendicular clearance between fixed ladder rungs, cleats, and steps, and any obstruction behind the ladder shall be 7 inches (18 cm), except in the case of an elevator pit ladder, for which a minimum perpendicular clearance of 4½ inches (11 cm) is required.

(14) The minimum perpendicular clearance between the center line of fixed ladder rungs, cleats, and steps, and any obstruction on the climbing side of the ladder shall be 30 inches (76 cm), except as provided in paragraph (a)(15) of this section.

(15) When unavoidable obstructions are encountered, the minimum perpendicular clearance between the centerline of fixed ladder rungs, cleats, and steps, and the obstruction on the climbing side of the ladder may be reduced to 24 inches (61 cm), provided that a deflection device is installed to guide employees around the obstruction.

(16) Through fixed ladders at their point of access/egress shall have a step-across distance of not less than 7 inches (18 cm) nor more than 12 inches (30 cm) as measured from the centerline of the steps or rungs to the nearest edge of the landing area. If the normal step-across distance exceeds 12 inches (30 cm), a landing platform shall be provided to reduce the distance to the specified limit.

(17) Fixed ladders without cages or wells shall have a clear width to the nearest permanent object of at least 15 inches (38 cm) on each side of the centerline of the ladder.

(18) Fixed ladders shall be provided with cages, wells, ladder safety devices, or self-retracting lifelines where the length of climb is less than 24 feet (7.3 m) but the top of the ladder is at a distance greater than 24 feet (7.3 m) above lower levels.

(19) Where the total length of a climb equals or exceeds 24 feet (7.3 m), fixed ladders shall be equipped with one of the following:

(i) Ladder safety devices; or

(ii) Self-retracting lifelines, and rest platforms at intervals not to exceed 150 feet (45.7 m); or

(iii) A cage or well, and multiple ladder sections, each ladder section not to exceed 50 feet (15.2 m) in length. Ladder sections shall be offset from adjacent sections, and landing platforms shall be provided at maximum intervals of 50 feet (15.2 m).

(20) Cages for fixed ladders shall conform to all of the following:

(i) Horizontal bands shall be fastened to the side rails of rail ladders, or directly to the structure, building, or equipment for individual-rung ladders;

(ii) Vertical bars shall be on the inside of the horizontal bands and shall be fastened to them;

(iii) Cages shall extend not less than 27 inches (68 cm), or more than 30 inches (76 cm) from the centerline of the step or rung (excluding the flare at the bottom of the cage), and shall not be less than 27 inches (68 cm) in width;

(iv) The inside of the cage shall be clear of projections;

(v) Horizontal bands shall be spaced not more than 4 feet (1.2 m) on center vertically;

(vi) Vertical bars shall be spaced at intervals not more than 9½ inches (24 cm) on center horizontally;

(vii) The bottom of the cage shall be at a level not less than 7 feet (2.1 m) nor more than 8 feet (2.4 m) above the point of access to the bottom of the ladder. The bottom of the cage shall be flared not less than 4 inches (10 cm) all around within the distance between the bottom horizontal band and the next higher band;

(viii) The top of the cage shall be a minimum of 42 inches (1.1 m) above the top of the platform, or the point of access at the top of the ladder, with provision for access to the platform or other point of access.

(21) Wells for fixed ladders shall conform to all of the following:

(i) They shall completely encircle the ladder;

(ii) They shall be free of projections;

(iii) Their inside face on the climbing side of the ladder shall extend not less than 27 inches (68 cm) nor more than 30 inches (76 cm) from the centerline of the step or rung;

(iv) The inside clear width shall be at least 30 inches (76 cm);

(v) The bottom of the wall on the access side shall start at a level not less than 7 feet (2.1 m) nor more than 8 feet (2.4 m) above the point of access to the bottom of the ladder.

(22) Ladder safety devices, and related support systems, for fixed ladders shall conform to all of the following:

(i) They shall be capable of withstanding without failure a drop test consisting of an 18-inch (41 cm) drop of a 500-pound (226 kg) weight;

(ii) They shall permit the employee using the device to ascend or descend without continually having to hold, push or pull any part of the device, leaving both hands free for climbing;

(iii) They shall be activated within 2 feet (.61 m) after a fall occurs, and limit the descending velocity of an employee to 7 feet/sec. (2.1 m/sec.) or less;

(iv) The connection between the carrier or lifeline and the point of attachment to the body belt or harness shall not exceed 9 inches (23 cm) in length.

(23) The mounting of ladder safety devices for fixed ladders shall conform to the following:

(i) Mountings for rigid carriers shall be attached at each end of the carrier, with intermediate mountings, as necessary, spaced along the entire length of the carrier, to provide the strength necessary to stop employees' falls.

(ii) Mountings for flexible carriers shall be attached at each end of the carrier. When the system is exposed to wind, cable guides for flexible carriers shall be installed at a minimum spacing of 25 feet (7.6 m) and maximum spacing of 40 feet (12.2 m) along the entire length of the carrier, to prevent wind damage to the system.

(iii) The design and installation of mountings and cable guides shall not reduce the design strength of the ladder.

(24) The side rails of through or side-step fixed ladders shall extend 42 inches (1.1 m) above the top of the access level or landing platform served by the ladder. For a parapet ladder, the access level shall be the roof if the parapet is cut to permit passage through the parapet; if the parapet is continuous,

the access level shall be the top of the parapet.

(25) For through-fixed-ladder extensions, the steps or rungs shall be omitted from the extension and the extension of the side rails shall be flared to provide not less than 24 inches (61 cm) nor more than 30 inches (76 cm) clearance between side rails. Where ladder safety devices are provided, the maximum clearance between side rails of the extensions shall not exceed 36 inches (91 cm).

(26) For side-step fixed ladders, the side rails and the steps or rungs shall be continuous in the extension.

(27) Individual-rung/step ladders, except those used where their access openings are covered with manhole covers or hatches, shall extend at least 42 inches (1.1 m) above an access level or landing platform either by the continuation of the rung spacings as horizontal grab bars or by providing vertical grab bars that shall have the same lateral spacing as the vertical legs of the rungs.

(b) *Use.* The following requirements apply to the use of all ladders, including job-made ladders, except as otherwise indicated:

(1) When portable ladders are used for access to an upper landing surface, the ladder side rails shall extend at least 3 feet (.9 m) above the upper landing surface to which the ladder is used to gain access; or, when such an extension is not possible because of the ladder's length, then the ladder shall be secured at its top to a rigid support that will not deflect, and a grasping device, such as a grabrail, shall be provided to assist employees in mounting and dismounting the ladder. In no case shall the extension be such that ladder deflection under a load would, by itself, cause the ladder to slip off its support.

(2) Ladders shall be maintained free of oil, grease, and other slipping hazards.

(3) Ladders shall not be loaded beyond the maximum intended load for which they were built, nor beyond their manufacturer's rated capacity.

(4) Ladders shall be used only for the purpose for which they were designed.

(5)(i) Non-self-supporting ladders shall be used at an angle such that the horizontal distance from the top support to the foot of the ladder is approximately one-quarter of the working length of the ladder (the distance along the ladder between the foot and the top support).

(ii) Wood job-made ladders with spliced side rails shall be used at an angle such that the horizontal distance is one-eighth the working length of the ladder.

(iii) Fixed ladders shall be used at a pitch no greater than 90 degrees from the horizontal, as measured to the back side of the ladder.

(6) Ladders shall be used only on stable and level surfaces unless secured to prevent accidental displacement.

(7) Ladders shall not be used on slippery surfaces unless secured or provided with slip-resistant feet to prevent accidental displacement. Slip-resistant feet shall not be used as a substitute for care in placing, lashing, or holding a ladder that is used upon slippery surfaces including, but not limited to, flat metal or concrete surfaces that are constructed so they cannot be prevented from becoming slippery.

(8) Ladders placed in any location where they can be displaced by workplace activities or traffic, such as in passageways, doorways, or driveways, shall be secured to prevent accidental displacement, or a barricade shall be used to keep the activities or traffic away from the ladder.

(9) The area around the top and bottom of ladders shall be kept clear.

(10) The top of a non-self-supporting ladder shall be placed with the two rails supported equally unless it is equipped with a single support attachment.

(11) Ladders shall not be moved, shifted, or extended while occupied.

(12) Ladders shall have nonconductive siderails if they are used where the employee or the ladder could contact exposed energized electrical equipment, except as provided in § 1926.955(b) and (c) of this part.

(13) The top or top step of a stepladder shall not be used as a step.

(14) Cross-bracing on the rear section of stepladders shall not be used for climbing unless the ladders are designed and provided with steps for climbing on both front and rear sections.

(15) Ladders shall be inspected by a competent person for visible defects on a periodic basis and after any occurrence that could affect their safe use.

(16) Portable ladders with structural defects, such as, but not limited to, broken or missing rungs, cleats, or steps, broken or split rails, corroded components, or other faulty or defective components, shall either be immediately marked in a manner that readily identifies them as defective, or be tagged with "Do Not Use" or similar language, and shall be withdrawn from service until repaired.

(17) Fixed ladders with structural defects, such as, but not limited to, broken or missing rungs, cleats, or steps, broken or split rails, or corroded components, shall be withdrawn from service until repaired. The requirement to withdraw a defective ladder from service is satisfied if the ladder is either:

(i) Immediately tagged with "Do Not Use" or similar language,

(ii) Marked in a manner that readily identifies it as defective;

(iii) Or blocked (such as with a plywood attachment that spans several rungs).

(18) Ladder repairs shall restore the ladder to a condition meeting its original design criteria, before the ladder is returned to use.

(19) Single-rail ladders shall not be used.

(20) When ascending or descending a ladder, the user shall face the ladder.

(21) Each employee shall use at least one hand to grasp the ladder when progressing up and/or down the ladder.

(22) An employee shall not carry any object or load that could cause the employee to lose balance and fall.

[55 FR 47687, Nov. 14, 1990; 56 FR 2585, Jan. 23, 1991, as amended at 56 FR 41794, Aug. 23, 1991; 79 FR 20743, Apr. 11, 2014]

§§ 1926.1054–1926.1059 [Reserved]

§ 1926.1060 Training requirements.

The following training provisions clarify the requirements of § 1926.21(b)(2), regarding the hazards addressed in subpart X.

(a) The employer shall provide a training program for each employee using ladders and stairways, as necessary. The program shall enable each employee to recognize hazards related to ladders and stairways, and shall train each employee in the procedures to be followed to minimize these hazards.

(1) The employer shall ensure that each employee has been trained by a competent person in the following areas, as applicable:

(i) The nature of fall hazards in the work area;

(ii) The correct procedures for erecting, maintaining, and disassembling the fall protection systems to be used;

(iii) The proper construction, use, placement, and care in handling of all stairways and ladders;

(iv) The maximum intended load-carrying capacities of ladders used; and

(v) The standards contained in this subpart.

(b) Retraining shall be provided for each employee as necessary so that the employee maintains the understanding and knowledge acquired through compliance with this section.

APPENDIX A TO SUBPART X OF PART 1926—LADDERS

This appendix serves as a non-mandatory guideline to assist employers in complying with the ladder loading and strength requirements of §1926.1053(a)(1). A ladder designed and built in accordance with the applicable national consensus standards, as set forth below, will be considered to meet the requirements of §1926.1053(a)(1):

• Manufactured portable wood ladders: American National Standards Institute (ANSI) A14.1–1982—American National Standard for Ladders-Portable Wood-Safety Requirements.

• Manufactured portable metal ladders: ANSI A14.2–1982—American National Standard for Ladders—Portable Metal-Safety Requirements.

• Manufactured fixed ladders: ANSI A14.3–1984—American National Standard for Ladders-Fixed-Safety Requirements.

• Job-made ladders: ANSI A14.4–1979—Safety Requirements for Job-Made Ladders.

• Plastic ladders: ANSI A14.5–1982—American National Standard for Ladders-Portable Reinforced Plastic-Safety Requirements.

Subpart Y—Diving

AUTHORITY: Sections 4, 6, and 8 of the Occupational Safety and Health Act of 1970 (29

U.S.C. 653, 655, 657); Sec. 107, Contract Work Hours and Safety Standards Act (the Construction Safety Standards Act) (40 U.S.C. 333); Sec. 41, Longshore and Harbor Workers' Compensation Act (33 U.S.C. 941); Secretary of Labor's Order No. 12–71 (36 FR 8754), 8–76 (41 FR 25059), 9–83 (48 FR 35736), 1–90 (55 FR 9033), 3–2000 (65 FR 50017) or 5–2002 (67 FR 65008) as applicable; and 29 CFR part 1911.

SOURCE: 58 FR 35184, June 30, 1993, unless otherwise noted.

GENERAL

§1926.1071 Scope and application.

NOTE: The requirements applicable to construction work under this section are identical to those set forth at §1910.401 of this chapter.

[61 FR 31432, June 20, 1996]

§1926.1072 Definitions.

NOTE: The provisions applicable to construction work under this section are identical to those set forth at §1910.402 of this chapter.

[61 FR 31432, June 20, 1996]

PERSONNEL REQUIREMENTS

§1926.1076 Qualifications of dive team.

NOTE: The requirements applicable to construction work under this section are identical to those set forth at §1910.410 of this chapter.

[61 FR 31432, June 20, 1996]

GENERAL OPERATIONS PROCEDURES

§1926.1080 Safe practices manual.

NOTE: The requirements applicable to construction work under this section are identical to those set forth at §1910.420 of this chapter.

[61 FR 31432, June 20, 1996]

§1926.1081 Pre-dive procedures.

NOTE: The requirements applicable to construction work under this section are identical to those set forth at §1910.421 of this chapter.

[61 FR 31432, June 20, 1996]

§1926.1082 Procedures during dive.

NOTE: The requirements applicable to construction work under this section are identical to those set forth at §1910.422 of this chapter.

[61 FR 31432, June 20, 1996]

§ 1926.1083 Post-dive procedures.

NOTE: The requirements applicable to construction work under this section are identical to those set forth at § 1910.423 of this chapter.

[61 FR 31432, June 20, 1996]

SPECIFIC OPERATIONS PROCEDURES

§ 1926.1084 SCUBA diving.

NOTE: The requirements applicable to construction work under this section are identical to those set forth at § 1910.424 of this chapter.

[61 FR 31432, June 20, 1996]

§ 1926.1085 Surface-supplied air diving.

NOTE: The requirements applicable to construction work under this section are identical to those set forth at § 1910.425 of this chapter.

[61 FR 31432, June 20, 1996]

§ 1926.1086 Mixed-gas diving.

NOTE: The requirements applicable to construction work under this section are identical to those set forth at § 1910.426 of this chapter.

[61 FR 31432, June 20, 1996]

§ 1926.1087 Liveboating.

NOTE: The requirements applicable to construction work under this section are identical to those set forth at § 1910.427 of this chapter.

[61 FR 31432, June 20, 1996]

EQUIPMENT PROCEDURES AND REQUIREMENTS

§ 1926.1090 Equipment.

NOTE: The requirements applicable to construction work under this section are identical to those set forth at § 1910.430 of this chapter.

[61 FR 31432, June 20, 1996]

RECORDKEEPING

§ 1926.1091 Recordkeeping requirements.

NOTE: The requirements applicable to construction work under this section are identical to those set forth at § 1910.440 of this chapter.

[61 FR 31432, June 20, 1996]

APPENDIX A TO SUBPART Y OF PART 1926—EXAMPLES OF CONDITIONS WHICH MAY RESTRICT OR LIMIT EXPOSURE TO HYPERBARIC CONDITIONS

NOTE: The requirements applicable to construction work under this appendix A are identical to those set forth at appendix A to Subpart T of part 1910 of this chapter.

[61 FR 31432, June 20, 1996]

APPENDIX B TO SUBPART Y OF PART 1926—GUIDELINES FOR SCIENTIFIC DIVING

NOTE: The requirements applicable to construction work under this appendix B are identical to those set forth at appendix B to subpart T of part 1910 of this chapter.

[61 FR 31433, June 20, 1996]

Subpart Z—Toxic and Hazardous Substances

AUTHORITY: Section 107 of the Contract Work Hours and Safety Standards Act (40 U.S.C. 3704); Sections 4, 6, and 8 of the Occupational Safety and Health Act of 1970 (29 U.S.C. 653, 655, 657); and Secretary of Labor's Order No. 12–71 (36 FR 8754), 8–76 (41 FR 25059), 9–83 (48 FR 35736), 1–90 (55 FR 9033), 6–96 (62 FR 111), 3–2000 (65 FR 50017), 5–2002 (67 FR 65008), 5–2007 (72 FR 31159), 4–2010 (75 FR 55355), or 1–2012 (77 FR 3912) as applicable; and 29 CFR part 1911.

Section 1926.1102 not issued under 29 U.S.C. 655 or 29 CFR part 1911; also issued under 5 U.S.C. 553.

§ 1926.1100 [Reserved]

§ 1926.1101 Asbestos.

(a) *Scope and application.* This section regulates asbestos exposure in all work as defined in 29 CFR 1910.12(b), including but not limited to the following:

(1) Demolition or salvage of structures where asbestos is present;

(2) Removal or encapsulation of materials containing asbestos;

(3) Construction, alteration, repair, maintenance, or renovation of structures, substrates, or portions thereof, that contain asbestos;

(4) Installation of products containing asbestos;

(5) Asbestos spill/emergency cleanup; and

(6) Transportation, disposal, storage, containment of and housekeeping activities involving asbestos or products

containing asbestos, on the site or location at which construction activities are performed.

(7) Coverage under this standard shall be based on the nature of the work operation involving asbestos exposure.

(8) This section does not apply to asbestos-containing asphalt roof coatings, cements and mastics.

(b) *Definitions.*

Aggressive method means removal or disturbance of building material by sanding, abrading, grinding or other method that breaks, crumbles, or disintegrates intact ACM.

Amended water means water to which surfactant (wetting agent) has been added to increase the ability of the liquid to penetrate ACM.

Asbestos includes chrysotile, amosite, crocidolite, tremolite asbestos, anthophyllite asbestos, actinolite asbestos, and any of these minerals that has been chemically treated and/or altered. For purposes of this standard, "asbestos" includes PACM, as defined below.

Asbestos-containing material (ACM), means any material containing more than one percent asbestos.

Assistant Secretary means the Assistant Secretary of Labor for Occupational Safety and Health, U.S. Department of Labor, or designee.

Authorized person means any person authorized by the employer and required by work duties to be present in regulated areas.

Building/facility owner is the legal entity, including a lessee, which exercises control over management and record keeping functions relating to a building and/or facility in which activities covered by this standard take place.

Certified Industrial Hygienist (CIH) means one certified in the practice of industrial hygiene by the American Board of Industrial Hygiene.

Class I asbestos work means activities involving the removal of TSI and surfacing ACM and PACM.

Class II asbestos work means activities involving the removal of ACM which is not thermal system insulation or surfacing material. This includes, but is not limited to, the removal of asbestos-containing wallboard, floor tile and sheeting, roofing and siding shingles, and construction mastics.

Class III asbestos work means repair and maintenance operations, where "ACM", including TSI and surfacing ACM and PACM, is likely to be disturbed.

Class IV asbestos work means maintenance and custodial activities during which employees contact but do not disturb ACM or PACM and activities to clean up dust, waste and debris resulting from Class I, II, and III activities.

Clean room means an uncontaminated room having facilities for the storage of employees' street clothing and uncontaminated materials and equipment.

Closely resemble means that the major workplace conditions which have contributed to the levels of historic asbestos exposure, are no more protective than conditions of the current workplace.

Competent person means, in addition to the definition in 29 CFR 1926.32 (f), one who is capable of identifying existing asbestos hazards in the workplace and selecting the appropriate control strategy for asbestos exposure, who has the authority to take prompt corrective measures to eliminate them, as specified in 29 CFR 1926.32(f): in addition, for Class I and Class II work who is specially trained in a training course which meets the criteria of EPA's Model Accreditation Plan (40 CFR part 763) for supervisor, or its equivalent and, for Class III and Class IV work, who is trained in a manner consistent with EPA requirements for training of local education agency maintenance and custodial staff as set forth at 40 CFR 763.92 (a)(2).

Critical barrier means one or more layers of plastic sealed over all openings into a work area or any other similarly placed physical barrier sufficient to prevent airborne asbestos in a work area from migrating to an adjacent area.

Decontamination area means an enclosed area adjacent and connected to the regulated area and consisting of an equipment room, shower area, and clean room, which is used for the decontamination of workers, materials, and equipment that are contaminated with asbestos.

Demolition means the wrecking or taking out of any load-supporting structural member and any related razing, removing, or stripping of asbestos products.

Director means the Director, National Institute for Occupational Safety and Health, U.S. Department of Health and Human Services, or designee.

Disturbance means activities that disrupt the matrix of ACM or PACM, crumble or pulverize ACM or PACM, or generate visible debris from ACM or PACM. In no event shall the amount of ACM or PACM so disturbed exceed that which can be contained in one glove bag or waste bag which shall not exceed 60 inches in length and width.

Employee exposure means that exposure to airborne asbestos that would occur if the employee were not using respiratory protective equipment.

Equipment room (change room) means a contaminated room located within the decontamination area that is supplied with impermeable bags or containers for the disposal of contaminated protective clothing and equipment.

Fiber means a particulate form of asbestos, 5 micrometers or longer, with a length-to-diameter ratio of at least 3 to 1.

Glovebag means not more than a 60×60 inch impervious plastic bag-like enclosure affixed around an asbestos-containing material, with glove-like appendages through which material and tools may be handled.

High-efficiency particulate air (HEPA) filter means a filter capable of trapping and retaining at least 99.97 percent of all mono-dispersed particles of 0.3 micrometers in diameter.

Homogeneous area means an area of surfacing material or thermal system insulation that is uniform in color and texture.

Industrial hygienist means a professional qualified by education, training, and experience to anticipate, recognize, evaluate and develop controls for occupational health hazards.

Intact means that the ACM has not crumbled, been pulverized, or otherwise deteriorated so that the asbestos is no longer likely to be bound with its matrix.

Modification for purposes of paragraph (g)(6)(ii), means a changed or altered procedure, material or component of a control system, which replaces a procedure, material or component of a required system. Omitting a procedure or component, or reducing or diminishing the stringency or strength of a material or component of the control system is not a "modification" for purposes of paragraph (g)(6) of this section.

Negative Initial Exposure Assessment means a demonstration by the employer, which complies with the criteria in paragraph (f)(2)(iii) of this section, that employee exposure during an operation is expected to be consistently below the PELs.

PACM means "presumed asbestos containing material".

Presumed Asbestos Containing Material means thermal system insulation and surfacing material found in buildings constructed no later than 1980. The designation of a material as "PACM" may be rebutted pursuant to paragraph (k)(5) of this section.

Project Designer means a person who has successfully completed the training requirements for an abatement project designer established by 40 U.S.C. 763.90(g).

Regulated area means: an area established by the employer to demarcate areas where Class I, II, and III asbestos work is conducted, and any adjoining area where debris and waste from such asbestos work accumulate; and a work area within which airborne concentrations of asbestos, exceed or there is a reasonable possibility they may exceed the permissible exposure limit. Requirements for regulated areas are set out in paragraph (e) of this section.

Removal means all operations where ACM and/or PACM is taken out or stripped from structures or substrates, and includes demolition operations.

Renovation means the modifying of any existing structure, or portion thereof.

Repair means overhauling, rebuilding, reconstructing, or reconditioning of structures or substrates, including encapsulation or other repair of ACM or PACM attached to structures or substrates.

Surfacing material means material that is sprayed, troweled-on or otherwise applied to surfaces (such as acoustical plaster on ceilings and fireproofing materials on structural members, or other materials on surfaces for acoustical, fireproofing, and other purposes).

Surfacing ACM means surfacing material which contains more than 1% asbestos.

Thermal system insulation (TSI) means ACM applied to pipes, fittings, boilers, breeching, tanks, ducts or other structural components to prevent heat loss or gain.

Thermal system insulation ACM is thermal system insulation which contains more than 1% asbestos.

(c) *Permissible exposure limits (PELS)*—(1) *Time-weighted average limit (TWA).* The employer shall ensure that no employee is exposed to an airborne concentration of asbestos in excess of 0.1 fiber per cubic centimeter of air as an eight (8) hour time-weighted average (TWA), as determined by the method prescribed in appendix A to this section, or by an equivalent method.

(2) *Excursion limit.* The employer shall ensure that no employee is exposed to an airborne concentration of asbestos in excess of 1.0 fiber per cubic centimeter of air (1 f/cc) as averaged over a sampling period of thirty (30) minutes, as determined by the method prescribed in appendix A to this section, or by an equivalent method.

(d) *Multi-employer worksites.* (1) On multi-employer worksites, an employer performing work requiring the establishment of a regulated area shall inform other employers on the site of the nature of the employer's work with asbestos and/or PACM, of the existence of and requirements pertaining to regulated areas, and the measures taken to ensure that employees of such other employers are not exposed to asbestos.

(2) Asbestos hazards at a multi-employer work site shall be abated by the contractor who created or controls the source of asbestos contamination. For example, if there is a significant breach of an enclosure containing Class I work, the employer responsible for erecting the enclosure shall repair the breach immediately.

(3) In addition, all employers of employees exposed to asbestos hazards shall comply with applicable protective provisions to protect their employees. For example, if employees working immediately adjacent to a Class I asbestos job are exposed to asbestos due to the inadequate containment of such job, their employer shall either remove the employees from the area until the enclosure breach is repaired; or perform an initial exposure assessment pursuant to (f) of this section.

(4) All employers of employees working adjacent to regulated areas established by another employer on a multi-employer work-site, shall take steps on a daily basis to ascertain the integrity of the enclosure and/or the effectiveness of the control method relied on by the primary asbestos contractor to assure that asbestos fibers do not migrate to such adjacent areas.

(5) All general contractors on a construction project which includes work covered by this standard shall be deemed to exercise general supervisory authority over the work covered by this standard, even though the general contractor is not qualified to serve as the asbestos "competent person" as defined by paragraph (b) of this section. As supervisor of the entire project, the general contractor shall ascertain whether the asbestos contractor is in compliance with this standard, and shall require such contractor to come into compliance with this standard when necessary.

(e) *Regulated areas.* (1) All Class I, II and III asbestos work shall be conducted within regulated areas. All other operations covered by this standard shall be conducted within a regulated area where airborne concentrations of asbestos exceed, or there is a reasonable possibility they may exceed a PEL. Regulated areas shall comply with the requirements of paragraphs (2), (3),(4) and (5) of this section.

(2) *Demarcation.* The regulated area shall be demarcated in any manner that minimizes the number of persons within the area and protects persons outside the area from exposure to airborne asbestos. Where critical barriers or negative pressure enclosures are used, they may demarcate the regulated area. Signs shall be provided and

displayed pursuant to the requirements of paragraph (k)(7) of this section.

(3) *Access.* Access to regulated areas shall be limited to authorized persons and to persons authorized by the Act or regulations issued pursuant thereto.

(4) *Respirators.* All persons entering a regulated area where employees are required pursuant to paragraph (h)(1) of this section to wear respirators shall be supplied with a respirator selected in accordance with paragraph (h)(2) of this section.

(5) *Prohibited activities.* The employer shall ensure that employees do not eat, drink, smoke, chew tobacco or gum, or apply cosmetics in the regulated area.

(6) *Competent Persons.* The employer shall ensure that all asbestos work performed within regulated areas is supervised by a competent person, as defined in paragraph (b) of this section. The duties of the competent person are set out in paragraph (o) of this section.

(f) *Exposure assessments and monitoring*—(1) *General monitoring criteria.* (i) Each employer who has a workplace or work operation where exposure monitoring is required under this section shall perform monitoring to determine accurately the airborne concentrations of asbestos to which employees may be exposed.

(ii) Determinations of employee exposure shall be made from breathing zone air samples that are representative of the 8-hour TWA and 30-minute short-term exposures of each employee.

(iii) Representative 8-hour TWA employee exposure shall be determined on the basis of one or more samples representing full-shift exposure for employees in each work area. Representative 30-minute short-term employee exposures shall be determined on the basis of one or more samples representing 30 minute exposures associated with operations that are most likely to produce exposures above the excursion limit for employees in each work area.

(2) *Initial Exposure Assessment.* (i) Each employer who has a workplace or work operation covered by this standard shall ensure that a "competent person" conducts an exposure assessment immediately before or at the initiation of the operation to ascertain expected exposures during that operation or workplace. The assessment must be completed in time to comply with requirements which are triggered by exposure data or the lack of a "negative exposure assessment," and to provide information necessary to assure that all control systems planned are appropriate for that operation and will work properly.

(ii) Basis of Initial Exposure Assessment: Unless a negative exposure assessment has been made pursuant to paragraph (f)(2)(iii) of this section, the initial exposure assessment shall, if feasible, be based on monitoring conducted pursuant to paragraph (f)(1)(iii) of this section. The assessment shall take into consideration both the monitoring results and all observations, information or calculations which indicate employee exposure to asbestos, including any previous monitoring conducted in the workplace, or of the operations of the employer which indicate the levels of airborne asbestos likely to be encountered on the job. For Class I asbestos work, until the employer conducts exposure monitoring and documents that employees on that job will not be exposed in excess of the PELs, or otherwise makes a negative exposure assessment pursuant to paragraph (f)(2)(iii) of this section, the employer shall presume that employees are exposed in excess of the TWA and excursion limit.

(iii) Negative Exposure Assessment: For any one specific asbestos job which will be performed by employees who have been trained in compliance with the standard, the employer may demonstrate that employee exposures will be below the PELs by data which conform to the following criteria;

(A) Objective data demonstrating that the product or material containing asbestos minerals or the activity involving such product or material cannot release airborne fibers in concentrations exceeding the TWA and excursion limit under those work conditions having the greatest potential for releasing asbestos; or

(B) Where the employer has monitored prior asbestos jobs for the PEL and the excursion limit within 12 months of the current or projected job, the monitoring and analysis were performed in compliance with the asbestos

582

standard in effect; and the data were obtained during work operations conducted under workplace conditions "closely resembling" the processes, type of material, control methods, work practices, and environmental conditions used and which will prevail in the employer's current operations, the operations were conducted by employees whose training and experience are no more extensive than that of employees performing the current job, and these data show that under the conditions prevailing and which will prevail in the current workplace there is a high degree of certainty that employee exposures will not exceed the TWA and excursion limit; or

(C) The results of initial exposure monitoring of the current job made from breathing zone air samples that are representative of the 8-hour TWA and 30-minute short-term exposures of each employee covering operations which are most likely during the performance of the entire asbestos job to result in exposures over the PELs.

(3) *Periodic monitoring*—(i) *Class I and II operations.* The employer shall conduct daily monitoring that is representative of the exposure of each employee who is assigned to work within a regulated area who is performing Class I or II work, unless the employer pursuant to (f)(2)(iii) of this section, has made a negative exposure assessment for the entire operation.

(ii) All operations under the standard other than Class I and II operations. The employer shall conduct periodic monitoring of all work where exposures are expected to exceed a PEL, at intervals sufficient to document the validity of the exposure prediction.

(iii) Exception: When all employees required to be monitored daily are equipped with supplied-air respirators operated in the pressure demand mode, or other positive pressure mode respirator, the employer may dispense with the daily monitoring required by this paragraph. However, employees performing Class I work using a control method which is not listed in paragraph (g)(4) (i), (ii), or (iii) of this section or using a modification of a listed control method, shall continue to be monitored daily even if they are equipped with supplied-air respirators.

(4) *Termination of monitoring.* (i) If the periodic monitoring required by paragraph (f)(3) of this section reveals that employee exposures, as indicated by statistically reliable measurements, are below the permissible exposure limit and excursion limit the employer may discontinue monitoring for those employees whose exposures are represented by such monitoring.

(ii) Additional monitoring. Notwithstanding the provisions of paragraph (f) (2) and (3), and (f)(4) of this section, the employer shall institute the exposure monitoring required under paragraph (f)(3) of this section whenever there has been a change in process, control equipment, personnel or work practices that may result in new or additional exposures above the permissible exposure limit and/or excursion limit or when the employer has any reason to suspect that a change may result in new or additional exposures above the permissible exposure limit and/or excursion limit. Such additional monitoring is required regardless of whether a "negative exposure assessment" was previously produced for a specific job.

(5) *Employee notification of monitoring results.* The employer must, as soon as possible but no later than 5 working days after the receipt of the results of any monitoring performed under this section, notify each affected employee of these results either individually in writing or by posting the results in an appropriate location that is accessible to employees.

(6) *Observation of monitoring.* (i) The employer shall provide affected employees and their designated representatives an opportunity to observe any monitoring of employee exposure to asbestos conducted in accordance with this section.

(ii) When observation of the monitoring of employee exposure to asbestos requires entry into an area where the use of protective clothing or equipment is required, the observer shall be provided with and be required to use such clothing and equipment and shall comply with all other applicable safety and health procedures.

(g) *Methods of compliance.* (1) Engineering controls and work practices for all operations covered by this section. The employer shall use the following engineering controls and work practices in all operations covered by this section, regardless of the levels of exposure:

(i) Vacuum cleaners equipped with HEPA filters to collect all debris and dust containing ACM and PACM, except as provided in paragraph (g)(8)(ii) of this section in the case of roofing material.

(ii) Wet methods, or wetting agents, to control employee exposures during asbestos handling, mixing, removal, cutting, application, and cleanup, except where employers demonstrate that the use of wet methods is infeasible due to for example, the creation of electrical hazards, equipment malfunction, and, in roofing, except as provided in paragraph (g)(8)(ii) of this section; and

(iii) Prompt clean-up and disposal of wastes and debris contaminated with asbestos in leak-tight containers except in roofing operations, where the procedures specified in paragraph (g)(8)(ii) of this section apply.

(2) In addition to the requirements of paragraph (g)(1) of this section, the employer shall use the following control methods to achieve compliance with the TWA permissible exposure limit and excursion limit prescribed by paragraph (c) of this section;

(i) Local exhaust ventilation equipped with HEPA filter dust collection systems;

(ii) Enclosure or isolation of processes producing asbestos dust;

(iii) Ventilation of the regulated area to move contaminated air away from the breathing zone of employees and toward a filtration or collection device equipped with a HEPA filter;

(iv) Use of other work practices and engineering controls that the Assistant Secretary can show to be feasible.

(v) Wherever the feasible engineering and work practice controls described above are not sufficient to reduce employee exposure to or below the permissible exposure limit and/or excursion limit prescribed in paragraph (c) of this section, the employer shall use them to reduce employee exposure to the lowest levels attainable by these controls and shall supplement them by the use of respiratory protection that complies with the requirements of paragraph (h) of this section.

(3) *Prohibitions.* The following work practices and engineering controls shall not be used for work related to asbestos or for work which disturbs ACM or PACM, regardless of measured levels of asbestos exposure or the results of initial exposure assessments:

(i) High-speed abrasive disc saws that are not equipped with point of cut ventilator or enclosures with HEPA filtered exhaust air.

(ii) Compressed air used to remove asbestos, or materials containing asbestos, unless the compressed air is used in conjunction with an enclosed ventilation system designed to capture the dust cloud created by the compressed air.

(iii) Dry sweeping, shoveling or other dry clean-up of dust and debris containing ACM and PACM.

(iv) Employee rotation as a means of reducing employee exposure to asbestos.

(4) *Class I Requirements.* In addition to the provisions of paragraphs (g) (1) and (2) of this section, the following engineering controls and work practices and procedures shall be used.

(i) All Class I work, including the installation and operation of the control system shall be supervised by a competent person as defined in paragraph (b) of this section;

(ii) For all Class I jobs involving the removal of more than 25 linear or 10 square feet of thermal system insulation or surfacing material; for all other Class I jobs, where the employer cannot produce a negative exposure assessment pursuant to paragraph (f)(2)(iii) of this section, or where employees are working in areas adjacent to the regulated area, while the Class I work is being performed, the employer shall use one of the following methods to ensure that airborne asbestos does not migrate from the regulated area:

(A) Critical barriers shall be placed over all the openings to the regulated area, except where activities are performed outdoors; or

(B) The employer shall use another barrier or isolation method which prevents the migration of airborne asbestos from the regulated area, as verified by perimeter area surveillance during each work shift at each boundary of the regulated area, showing no visible asbestos dust; and perimeter area monitoring showing that clearance levels contained in 40 CFR part 763, subpt. E, of the EPA Asbestos in Schools Rule are met, or that perimeter area levels, measured by Phase Contrast Microscopy (PCM) are no more than background levels representing the same area before the asbestos work began. The results of such monitoring shall be made known to the employer no later than 24 hours from the end of the work shift represented by such monitoring. Exception: For work completed outdoors where employees are not working in areas adjacent to the regulated areas, this paragraph (g)(4)(ii) is satisfied when the specific control methods in paragraph (g)(5) of this section are used.

(iii) For all Class I jobs, HVAC systems shall be isolated in the regulated area by sealing with a double layer of 6 mil plastic or the equivalent;

(iv) For all Class I jobs, impermeable dropcloths shall be placed on surfaces beneath all removal activity;

(v) For all Class I jobs, all objects within the regulated area shall be covered with impermeable dropcloths or plastic sheeting which is secured by duct tape or an equivalent.

(vi) For all Class I jobs where the employer cannot produce a negative exposure assessment, or where exposure monitoring shows that a PEL is exceeded, the employer shall ventilate the regulated area to move contaminated air away from the breathing zone of employees toward a HEPA filtration or collection device.

(5) *Specific control methods for Class I work.* In addition, Class I asbestos work shall be performed using one or more of the following control methods pursuant to the limitations stated below:

(i) Negative Pressure Enclosure (NPE) systems: NPE systems may be used where the configuration of the work area does not make the erection of the enclosure infeasible, with the following specifications and work practices.

(A) *Specifications:*

(1) The negative pressure enclosure (NPE) may be of any configuration,

(2) At least 4 air changes per hour shall be maintained in the NPE,

(3) A minimum of −0.02 column inches of water pressure differential, relative to outside pressure, shall be maintained within the NPE as evidenced by manometric measurements,

(4) The NPE shall be kept under negative pressure throughout the period of its use, and

(5) Air movement shall be directed away from employees performing asbestos work within the enclosure, and toward a HEPA filtration or a collection device.

(B) *Work Practices:*

(1) Before beginning work within the enclosure and at the beginning of each shift, the NPE shall be inspected for breaches and smoke-tested for leaks, and any leaks sealed.

(2) Electrical circuits in the enclosure shall be deactivated, unless equipped with ground-fault circuit interrupters.

(ii) Glove bag systems may be used to remove PACM and/or ACM from straight runs of piping and elbows and other connections with the following specifications and work practices:

(A) *Specifications:*

(1) Glovebags shall be made of 6 mil thick plastic and shall be seamless at the bottom.

(2) Glovebags used on elbows and other connections must be designed for that purpose and used without modifications.

(B) *Work Practices:*

(1) Each glovebag shall be installed so that it completely covers the circumference of pipe or other structure where the work is to be done.

(2) Glovebags shall be smoke-tested for leaks and any leaks sealed prior to use.

(3) Glovebags may be used only once and may not be moved.

(4) Glovebags shall not be used on surfaces whose temperature exceeds 150 °F.

(5) Prior to disposal, glovebags shall be collapsed by removing air within them using a HEPA vacuum.

(6) Before beginning the operation, loose and friable material adjacent to the glovebag/box operation shall be wrapped and sealed in two layers of six

mil plastic or otherwise rendered intact,

(7) Where system uses attached waste bag, such bag shall be connected to collection bag using hose or other material which shall withstand pressure of ACM waste and water without losing its integrity:

(8) Sliding valve or other device shall separate waste bag from hose to ensure no exposure when waste bag is disconnected:

(9) At least two persons shall perform Class I glovebag removal operations.

(iii) *Negative Pressure Glove Bag Systems.* Negative pressure glove bag systems may be used to remove ACM or PACM from piping.

(A) *Specifications:* In addition to specifications for glove bag systems above, negative pressure glove bag systems shall attach HEPA vacuum systems or other devices to bag to prevent collapse during removal.

(B) *Work Practices:* (1) The employer shall comply with the work practices for glove bag systems in paragraph (g)(5)(ii)(B)(4) of this section.

(2) The HEPA vacuum cleaner or other device used to prevent collapse of bag during removal shall run continually during the operation until it is completed at which time the bag shall be collapsed prior to removal of the bag from the pipe.

(3) Where a separate waste bag is used along with a collection bag and discarded after one use, the collection bag may be reused if rinsed clean with amended water before reuse.

(iv) Negative Pressure Glove Box Systems: Negative pressure glove boxes may be used to remove ACM or PACM from pipe runs with the following specifications and work practices.

(A) *Specifications:*

(1) Glove boxes shall be constructed with rigid sides and made from metal or other material which can withstand the weight of the ACM and PACM and water used during removal:

(2) A negative pressure generator shall be used to create negative pressure in the system:

(3) An air filtration unit shall be attached to the box:

(4) The box shall be fitted with gloved apertures:

(5) An aperture at the base of the box shall serve as a bagging outlet for waste ACM and water:

(6) A back-up generator shall be present on site:

(7) Waste bags shall consist of 6 mil thick plastic double-bagged before they are filled or plastic thicker than 6 mil.

(B) *Work practices:*

(1) At least two persons shall perform the removal:

(2) The box shall be smoke-tested for leaks and any leaks sealed prior to each use.

(3) Loose or damaged ACM adjacent to the box shall be wrapped and sealed in two layers of 6 mil plastic prior to the job, or otherwise made intact prior to the job.

(4) A HEPA filtration system shall be used to maintain pressure barrier in box.

(v) *Water Spray Process System.* A water spray process system may be used for removal of ACM and PACM from cold line piping if, employees carrying out such process have completed a 40-hour separate training course in its use, in addition to training required for employees performing Class I work. The system shall meet the following specifications and shall be performed by employees using the following work practices.

(A) *Specifications:*

(1) Piping shall be surrounded on 3 sides by rigid framing,

(2) A 360 degree water spray, delivered through nozzles supplied by a high pressure separate water line, shall be formed around the piping.

(3) The spray shall collide to form a fine aerosol which provides a liquid barrier between workers and the ACM and PACM.

(B) *Work Practices:*

(1) The system shall be run for at least 10 minutes before removal begins.

(2) All removal shall take place within the water barrier.

(3) The system shall be operated by at least three persons, one of whom shall not perform removal, but shall check equipment, and ensure proper operation of the system.

(4) After removal, the ACM and PACM shall be bagged while still inside the water barrier.

(vi) A small walk-in enclosure which accommodates no more than two persons (mini-enclosure) may be used if the disturbance or removal can be completely contained by the enclosure with the following specifications and work practices.

(A) *Specifications:*

(*1*) The fabricated or job-made enclosure shall be constructed of 6 mil plastic or equivalent:

(*2*) The enclosure shall be placed under negative pressure by means of a HEPA filtered vacuum or similar ventilation unit:

(B) *Work practices:*

(*1*) Before use, the mini-enclosure shall be inspected for leaks and smoke-tested to detect breaches, and any breaches sealed.

(*2*) Before reuse, the interior shall be completely washed with amended water and HEPA-vacuumed.

(*3*) During use, air movement shall be directed away from the employee's breathing zone within the mini-enclosure.

(6) *Alternative control methods for Class I work.* Class I work may be performed using a control method which is not referenced in paragraph (g)(5) of this section, or which modifies a control method referenced in paragraph (g)(5)of this section, if the following provisions are complied with:

(i) The control method shall enclose, contain or isolate the processes or source of airborne asbestos dust, or otherwise capture or redirect such dust before it enters the breathing zone of employees.

(ii) A certified industrial hygienist or licensed professional engineer who is also qualified as a project designer as defined in paragraph (b) of this section, shall evaluate the work area, the projected work practices and the engineering controls and shall certify in writing that the planned control method is adequate to reduce direct and indirect employee exposure to below the PELs under worst-case conditions of use, and that the planned control method will prevent asbestos contamination outside the regulated area, as measured by clearance sampling which meets the requirements of EPA's Asbestos in Schools rule issued under AHERA, or perimeter monitoring which meets the criteria in paragraph (g)(4)(ii)(B) of this section.

(A) Where the TSI or surfacing material to be removed is 25 linear or 10 square feet or less , the evaluation required in paragraph (g)(6) of this section may be performed by a "competent person", and may omit consideration of perimeter or clearance monitoring otherwise required.

(B) The evaluation of employee exposure required in paragraph (g)(6) of this section, shall include and be based on sampling and analytical data representing employee exposure during the use of such method under worst-case conditions and by employees whose training and experience are equivalent to employees who are to perform the current job.

(7) Work Practices and Engineering Controls for Class II work.

(i) All Class II work shall be supervised by a competent person as defined in paragraph (b) of this section.

(ii) For all indoor Class II jobs, where the employer has not produced a negative exposure assessment pursuant to paragraph (f)(2)(iii) of this section, or where during the job, changed conditions indicate there may be exposure above the PEL or where the employer does not remove the ACM in a substantially intact state, the employer shall use one of the following methods to ensure that airborne asbestos does not migrate from the regulated area;

(A) Critical barriers shall be placed over all openings to the regulated area; or,

(B) The employer shall use another barrier or isolation method which prevents the migration of airborne asbestos from the regulated area, as verified by perimeter area monitoring or clearance monitoring which meets the criteria set out in paragraph (g)(4)(ii)(B) of this section.

(C) Impermeable dropcloths shall be placed on surfaces beneath all removal activity;

(iii) [Reserved]

(iv) All Class II asbestos work shall be performed using the work practices and requirements set out above in paragraph (g)(1) (i) through (g)(1)(iii) of this section.

(8) *Additional Controls for Class II work.* Class II asbestos work shall also

587

be performed by complying with the work practices and controls designated for each type of asbestos work to be performed, set out in this paragraph. Where more than one control method may be used for a type of asbestos work, the employer may choose one or a combination of designated control methods. Class II work also may be performed using a method allowed for Class I work, except that glove bags and glove boxes are allowed if they fully enclose the Class II material to be removed.

(i) For removing vinyl and asphalt flooring materials which contain ACM or for which in buildings constructed no later than 1980, the employer has not verified the absence of ACM pursuant to paragraph (g)(8)(i)(I) of this section. The employer shall ensure that employees comply with the following work practices and that employees are trained in these practices pursuant to paragraph (k)(9):

(A) Flooring or its backing shall not be sanded.

(B) Vacuums equipped with HEPA filter, disposable dust bag, and metal floor tool (no brush) shall be used to clean floors.

(C) Resilient sheeting shall be removed by cutting with wetting of the snip point and wetting during delamination. Rip-up of resilient sheet floor material is prohibited.

(D) All scraping of residual adhesive and/or backing shall be performed using wet methods.

(E) Dry sweeping is prohibited.

(F) Mechanical chipping is prohibited unless performed in a negative pressure enclosure which meets the requirements of paragraph (g)(5)(i) of this section.

(G) Tiles shall be removed intact, unless the employer demonstrates that intact removal is not possible.

(H) When tiles are heated and can be removed intact, wetting may be omitted.

(I) Resilient flooring material including associated mastic and backing shall be assumed to be asbestos-containing unless an industrial hygienist determines that it is asbestos-free using recognized analytical techniques.

(ii) For removing roofing material which contains ACM the employer shall ensure that the following work practices are followed:

(A) Roofing material shall be removed in an intact state to the extent feasible.

(B) Wet methods shall be used to remove roofing materials that are not intact, or that will be rendered not intact during removal, unless such wet methods are not feasible or will create safety hazards.

(C) Cutting machines shall be continuously misted during use, unless a competent person determines that misting substantially decreases worker safety.

(D) When removing built-up roofs with asbestos-containing roofing felts and an aggregate surface using a power roof cutter, all dust resulting from the cutting operation shall be collected by a HEPA dust collector, or shall be HEPA vacuumed by vacuuming along the cut line. When removing built-up roofs with asbestos-containing roofing felts and a smooth surface using a power roof cutter, the dust resulting from the cutting operation shall be collected either by a HEPA dust collector or HEPA vacuuming along the cut line, or by gently sweeping and then carefully and completely wiping up the still-wet dust and debris left along the cut line. The dust and debris shall be immediately bagged or placed in covered containers.

(E) Asbestos-containing material that has been removed from a roof shall not be dropped or thrown to the ground. Unless the material is carried or passed to the ground by hand, it shall be lowered to the ground via covered, dust-tight chute, crane or hoist:

(1) Any ACM that is not intact shall be lowered to the ground as soon as is practicable, but in any event no later than the end of the work shift. While the material remains on the roof it shall either be kept wet, placed in an impermeable waste bag, or wrapped in plastic sheeting.

(2) Intact ACM shall be lowered to the ground as soon as is practicable, but in any event no later than the end of the work shift.

(F) Upon being lowered, unwrapped material shall be transferred to a closed receptacle in such manner so as to preclude the dispersion of dust.

(G) Roof level heating and ventilation air intake sources shall be isolated or the ventilation system shall be shut down.

(H) Notwithstanding any other provision of this section, removal or repair of sections of intact roofing less than 25 square feet in area does not require use of wet methods or HEPA vacuuming as long as manual methods which do not render the material non-intact are used to remove the material and no visible dust is created by the removal method used. In determining whether a job involves less than 25 square feet, the employer shall include all removal and repair work performed on the same roof on the same day.

(iii) When removing cementitious asbestos-containing siding and shingles or transite panels containing ACM on building exteriors (other than roofs, where paragraph (g)(8)(ii) of this section applies) the employer shall ensure that the following work practices are followed:

(A) Cutting, abrading or breaking siding, shingles, or transite panels, shall be prohibited unless the employer can demonstrate that methods less likely to result in asbestos fiber release cannot be used.

(B) Each panel or shingle shall be sprayed with amended water prior to removal.

(C) Unwrapped or unbagged panels or shingles shall be immediately lowered to the ground via covered dust-tight chute, crane or hoist, or placed in an impervious waste bag or wrapped in plastic sheeting and lowered to the ground no later than the end of the work shift.

(D) Nails shall be cut with flat, sharp instruments.

(iv) When removing gaskets containing ACM, the employer shall ensure that the following work practices are followed:

(A) If a gasket is visibly deteriorated and unlikely to be removed intact, removal shall be undertaken within a glovebag as described in paragraph (g)(5)(ii) of this section.

(B) [Reserved]

(C) The gasket shall be immediately placed in a disposal container.

(D) Any scraping to remove residue must be performed wet.

(v) When performing any other Class II removal of asbestos containing material for which specific controls have not been listed in paragraph (g)(8)(iv) (A) through (D) of this section, the employer shall ensure that the following work practices are complied with.

(A) The material shall be thoroughly wetted with amended water prior to and during its removal.

(B) The material shall be removed in an intact state unless the employer demonstrates that intact removal is not possible.

(C) Cutting, abrading or breaking the material shall be prohibited unless the employer can demonstrate that methods less likely to result in asbestos fiber release are not feasible.

(D) Asbestos-containing material removed, shall be immediately bagged or wrapped, or kept wetted until transferred to a closed receptacle, no later than the end of the work shift.

(vi) *Alternative Work Practices and Controls.* Instead of the work practices and controls listed in paragraph (g)(8) (i) through (v) of this section, the employer may use different or modified engineering and work practice controls if the following provisions are complied with.

(A) The employer shall demonstrate by data representing employee exposure during the use of such method under conditions which closely resemble the conditions under which the method is to be used, that employee exposure will not exceed the PELs under any anticipated circumstances.

(B) A competent person shall evaluate the work area, the projected work practices and the engineering controls, and shall certify in writing, that the different or modified controls are adequate to reduce direct and indirect employee exposure to below the PELs under all expected conditions of use and that the method meets the requirements of this standard. The evaluation shall include and be based on data representing employee exposure during the use of such method under conditions which closely resemble the conditions under which the method is to be used for the current job, and by employees whose training and experience are equivalent to employees who are to perform the current job.

589

(9) *Work Practices and Engineering Controls for Class III asbestos work.* Class III asbestos work shall be conducted using engineering and work practice controls which minimize the exposure to employees performing the asbestos work and to bystander employees.

(i) The work shall be performed using wet methods.

(ii) To the extent feasible, the work shall be performed using local exhaust ventilation.

(iii) Where the disturbance involves drilling, cutting, abrading, sanding, chipping, breaking, or sawing of thermal system insulation or surfacing material, the employer shall use impermeable dropcloths, and shall isolate the operation using mini-enclosures or glove bag systems pursuant to paragraph (g)(5) of this section or another isolation method.

(iv) Where the employer does not produce a "negative exposure assessment" for a job, or where monitoring results show the PEL has been exceeded, the employer shall contain the area using impermeable dropcloths and plastic barriers or their equivalent, or shall isolate the operation using a control system listed in and in compliance with paragraph (g)(5) of this section.

(v) Employees performing Class III jobs, which involve the disturbance of thermal system insulation or surfacing material, or where the employer does not produce a "negative exposure assessment" or where monitoring results show a PEL has been exceeded, shall wear respirators which are selected, used and fitted pursuant to provisions of paragraph (h) of this section.

(10) *Class IV asbestos work.* Class IV asbestos jobs shall be conducted by employees trained pursuant to the asbestos awareness training program set out in paragraph (k)(9) of this section. In addition, all Class IV jobs shall be conducted in conformity with the requirements set out in paragraph (g)(1) of this section, mandating wet methods, HEPA vacuums, and prompt clean up of debris containing ACM or PACM.

(i) Employees cleaning up debris and waste in a regulated area where respirators are required shall wear respirators which are selected, used and fitted pursuant to provisions of paragraph (h) of this section.

(ii) Employers of employees who clean up waste and debris in, and employers in control of, areas where friable thermal system insulation or surfacing material is accessible, shall assume that such waste and debris contain asbestos.

(11) *Alternative methods of compliance for installation, removal, repair, and maintenance of certain roofing and pipeline coating materials.* Notwithstanding any other provision of this section, an employer who complies with all provisions of this paragraph (g)(11) when installing, removing, repairing, or maintaining intact pipeline asphaltic wrap, or roof flashings which contain asbestos fibers encapsulated or coated by bituminous or resinous compounds shall be deemed to be in compliance with this section. If an employer does not comply with all provisions of this paragraph (g)(11) or if during the course of the job the material does not remain intact, the provisions of paragraph (g)(8) of this section apply instead of this paragraph (g)(11).

(i) Before work begins and as needed during the job, a competent person who is capable of identifying asbestos hazards in the workplace and selecting the appropriate control strategy for asbestos exposure, and who has the authority to take prompt corrective measures to eliminate such hazards, shall conduct an inspection of the worksite and determine that the roofing material is intact and will likely remain intact.

(ii) All employees performing work covered by this paragraph (g)(11) shall be trained in a training program that meets the requirements of paragraph (k)(9)(viii) of this section.

(iii) The material shall not be sanded, abraded, or ground. Manual methods which do not render the material non-intact shall be used.

(iv) Material that has been removed from a roof shall not be dropped or thrown to the ground. Unless the material is carried or passed to the ground by hand, it shall be lowered to the ground via covered, dust-tight chute, crane or hoist. All such material shall be removed from the roof as soon as is practicable, but in any event no later than the end of the work shift.

(v) Where roofing products which have been labeled as containing asbestos pursuant to paragraph (k)(8) of this section are installed on non-residential roofs during operations covered by this paragraph (g)(11), the employer shall notify the building owner of the presence and location of such materials no later than the end of the job.

(vi) All removal or disturbance of pipeline asphaltic wrap shall be performed using wet methods.

(h) *Respiratory protection*—(1) *General.* For employees who use respirators required by this section, the employer must provide each employee an appropriate respirator that complies with the requirements of this paragraph. Respirators must be used during:

(i) Class I asbestos work.

(ii) Class II asbestos work when ACM is not removed in a substantially intact state.

(iii) Class II and III asbestos work that is not performed using wet methods, except for removal of ACM from sloped roofs when a negative-exposure assessment has been conducted and ACM is removed in an intact state.

(iv) Class II and III asbestos work for which a negative-exposure assessment has not been conducted.

(v) Class III asbestos work when TSI or surfacing ACM or PACM is being disturbed.

(vi) Class IV asbestos work performed within regulated areas where employees who are performing other work are required to use respirators.

(vii) Work operations covered by this section for which employees are exposed above the TWA or excursion limit.

(viii) Emergencies.

(2) *Respirator program.* (i) The employer must implement a respiratory protection program in accordance with §1910.134 (b) through (d) (except (d)(1)(iii)), and (f) through (m), which covers each employee required by this section to use a respirator.

(ii) No employee shall be assigned to asbestos work that requires respirator use if, based on their most recent medical examination, the examining physician determines that the employee will be unable to function normally while using a respirator, or that the safety or health of the employee or other employees will be impaired by the employee's respirator use. Such employees must be assigned to another job or given the opportunity to transfer to a different position that they can perform. If such a transfer position is available, it must be with the same employer, in the same geographical area, and with the same seniority, status, rate of pay, and other job benefits the employee had just prior to such transfer.

(3) *Respirator selection.* (i) Employers must:

(A) Select, and provide to employees, the appropriate respirators specified in paragraph (d)(3)(i)(A) of 29 CFR 1910.134; however, employers must not select or use filtering facepiece respirators for use against asbestos fibers.

(B) Provide HEPA filters for powered and non-powered air-purifying respirators.

(ii) Employers must provide an employee with tight-fitting, powered air-purifying respirator (PAPR) instead of a negative pressure respirator selected according to paragraph (h)(3)(i)(A) of this standard when the employee chooses to use a PAPR and it provides adequate protection to the employee.

(iii) Employers must provide employees with an air-purifying half mask respirator, other than a filtering facepiece respirator, whenever the employees perform:

(A) Class II or Class III asbestos work for which no negative exposure assessment is available.

(B) Class III asbestos work involving disturbance of TSI or surfacing ACM or PACM.

(iv) Employers must provide employees with:

(A) A tight-fitting powered air-purifying respirator or a full facepiece, supplied-air respirator operated in the pressure-demand mode and equipped with either HEPA egress cartridges or an auxiliary positive-pressure, self-contained breathing apparatus (SCBA) whenever the employees are in a regulated area performing Class I asbestos work for which a negative exposure assessment is not available and the exposure assessment indicates that the exposure level will be at or below 1 f/cc as an 8-hour time-weighted average (TWA).

591

(B) A full facepiece supplied-air respirator operated in the pressure-demand mode and equipped with an auxiliary positive-pressure SCBA whenever the employees are in a regulated area performing Class I asbestos work for which a negative exposure assessment is not available and the exposure assessment indicates that the exposure level will be above 1 f/cc as an 8-hour TWA.

(i) *Protective clothing*—(1) *General.* The employer shall provide or require the use of protective clothing, such as coveralls or similar whole-body clothing, head coverings, gloves, and foot coverings for any employee exposed to airborne concentrations of asbestos that exceed the TWA and/or excursion limit prescribed in paragraph (c) of this section, or for which a required negative exposure assessment is not produced, or for any employee performing Class I operations which involve the removal of over 25 linear or 10 square feet of TSI or surfacing ACM and PACM.

(2) *Laundering.* (i) The employer shall ensure that laundering of contaminated clothing is done so as to prevent the release of airborne asbestos in excess of the TWA or excursion limit prescribed in paragraph (c) of this section.

(ii) Any employer who gives contaminated clothing to another person for laundering shall inform such person of the requirement in paragraph (i)(2)(i) of this section to effectively prevent the release of airborne asbestos in excess of the TWA and excursion limit prescribed in paragraph (c) of this section.

(3) *Contaminated clothing.* Contaminated clothing shall be transported in sealed impermeable bags, or other closed, impermeable containers, and be labeled in accordance with paragraph (k) of this section.

(4) *Inspection of protective clothing.* (i) The competent person shall examine worksuits worn by employees at least once per workshift for rips or tears that may occur during performance of work.

(ii) When rips or tears are detected while an employee is working, rips and tears shall be immediately mended, or the worksuit shall be immediately replaced.

(j) *Hygiene facilities and practices for employees.* (1) Requirements for employees performing Class I asbestos jobs involving over 25 linear or 10 square feet of TSI or surfacing ACM and PACM.

(i) *Decontamination areas.* The employer shall establish a decontamination area that is adjacent and connected to the regulated area for the decontamination of such employees. The decontamination area shall consist of an equipment room, shower area, and clean room in series. The employer shall ensure that employees enter and exit the regulated area through the decontamination area.

(A) *Equipment room.* The equipment room shall be supplied with impermeable, labeled bags and containers for the containment and disposal of contaminated protective equipment.

(B) *Shower area.* Shower facilities shall be provided which comply with 29 CFR 1910.141(d)(3), unless the employer can demonstrate that they are not feasible. The showers shall be adjacent both to the equipment room and the clean room, unless the employer can demonstrate that this location is not feasible. Where the employer can demonstrate that it is not feasible to locate the shower between the equipment room and the clean room, or where the work is performed outdoors, the employers shall ensure that employees:

(1) Remove asbestos contamination from their worksuits in the equipment room using a HEPA vacuum before proceeding to a shower that is not adjacent to the work area; or

(2) Remove their contaminated worksuits in the equipment room, then don clean worksuits, and proceed to a shower that is not adjacent to the work area.

(C) *Clean change room.* The clean room shall be equipped with a locker or appropriate storage container for each employee's use. When the employer can demonstrate that it is not feasible to provide a clean change area adjacent to the work area or where the work is performed outdoors, the employer may permit employees engaged in Class I asbestos jobs to clean their protective clothing with a portable HEPA-equipped vacuum before such employees leave the regulated area. Following showering, such employees however must then change into street clothing in clean change areas provided by the employer which otherwise meet the requirements of this section.

(ii) *Decontamination area entry procedures.* The employer shall ensure that employees:

(A) Enter the decontamination area through the clean room;

(B) Remove and deposit street clothing within a locker provided for their use; and

(C) Put on protective clothing and respiratory protection before leaving the clean room.

(D) Before entering the regulated area, the employer shall ensure that employees pass through the equipment room.

(iii) *Decontamination area exit procedures.* The employer shall ensure that:

(A) Before leaving the regulated area, employees shall remove all gross contamination and debris from their protective clothing.

(B) Employees shall remove their protective clothing in the equipment room and deposit the clothing in labeled impermeable bags or containers.

(C) Employees shall not remove their respirators in the equipment room.

(D) Employees shall shower prior to entering the clean room.

(E) After showering, employees shall enter the clean room before changing into street clothes.

(iv) *Lunch Areas.* Whenever food or beverages are consumed at the worksite where employees are performing Class I asbestos work, the employer shall provide lunch areas in which the airborne concentrations of asbestos are below the permissible exposure limit and/or excursion limit.

(2) Requirements for Class I work involving less than 25 linear or 10 square feet of TSI or surfacing ACM and PACM, and for Class II and Class III asbestos work operations where exposures exceed a PEL or where there is no negative exposure assessment produced before the operation.

(i) The employer shall establish an equipment room or area that is adjacent to the regulated area for the decontamination of employees and their equipment which is contaminated with asbestos which shall consist of an area covered by an impermeable drop cloth on the floor or horizontal working surface.

(ii) The area must be of sufficient size as to accommodate cleaning of equipment and removing personal protective equipment without spreading contamination beyond the area (as determined by visible accumulations).

(iii) Work clothing must be cleaned with a HEPA vacuum before it is removed.

(iv) All equipment and surfaces of containers filled with ACM must be cleaned prior to removing them from the equipment room or area.

(v) The employer shall ensure that employees enter and exit the regulated area through the equipment room or area.

(3) *Requirements for Class IV work.* Employers shall ensure that employees performing Class IV work within a regulated area comply with the hygiene practice required of employees performing work which has a higher classification within that regulated area. Otherwise employers of employees cleaning up debris and material which is TSI or surfacing ACM or identified as PACM shall provide decontamination facilities for such employees which are required by paragraph (j)(2) of this section.

(4) *Smoking in work areas.* The employer shall ensure that employees do not smoke in work areas where they are occupationally exposed to asbestos because of activities in that work area.

(k) *Communication of hazards*—(1) *Hazard communication.* (i) This section applies to the communication of information concerning asbestos hazards in construction activities to facilitate compliance with this standard. Most asbestos-related construction activities involve previously installed building materials. Building owners often are the only and/or best sources of information concerning them. Therefore, they, along with employers of potentially exposed employees, are assigned specific information conveying and retention duties under this section. Installed Asbestos Containing Building Material. Employers and building owners shall identify TSI and sprayed or troweled on surfacing materials in buildings as asbestos-containing, unless they determine in compliance with

593

paragraph (k)(5) of this section that the material is not asbestos-containing. Asphalt and vinyl flooring material installed no later than 1980 must also be considered as asbestos containing unless the employer, pursuant to paragraph (g)(8)(i)(I) of this section determines that it is not asbestos-containing. If the employer/building owner has actual knowledge, or should have known through the exercise of due diligence, that other materials are asbestos-containing, they too must be treated as such. When communicating information to employees pursuant to this standard, owners and employers shall identify "PACM" as ACM. Additional requirements relating to communication of asbestos work on multi-employer worksites are set out in paragraph (d) of this section.

(ii) The employer shall include asbestos in the program established to comply with the Hazard Communication Standard (HCS) (§ 1910.1200). The employer shall ensure that each employee has access to labels on containers of asbestos and safety data sheets, and is trained in accordance with the provisions of HCS and paragraphs (k)(9) and (10) of this section. The employer shall provide information on at least the following hazards: Cancer and lung effects.

(2) *Duties of building and facility owners.* (i) Before work subject to this standard is begun, building and facility owners shall determine the presence, location, and quantity of ACM and/or PACM at the work site pursuant to paragraph (k)(1)(i) of this section.

(ii) Building and/or facility owners shall notify the following persons of the presence, location and quantity of ACM or PACM, at the work sites in their buildings and facilities. Notification either shall be in writing, or shall consist of a personal communication between the owner and the person to whom notification must be given or their authorized representatives:

(A) Prospective employers applying or bidding for work whose employees reasonably can be expected to work in or adjacent to areas containing such material;

(B) Employees of the owner who will work in or adjacent to areas containing such material;

(C) On multi-employer worksites, all employers of employees who will be performing work within or adjacent to areas containing such materials;

(D) Tenants who will occupy areas containing such material.

(3) Duties of employers whose employees perform work subject to this standard in or adjacent to areas containing ACM and PACM. Building/facility owners whose employees perform such work shall comply with these provisions to the extent applicable.

(i) Before work in areas containing ACM and PACM is begun; employers shall identify the presence, location, and quantity of ACM, and/or PACM therein pursuant to paragraph (k)(1)(i) of this section.

(ii) Before work under this standard is performed employers of employees who will perform such work shall inform the following persons of the location and quantity of ACM and/or PACM present in the area and the precautions to be taken to insure that airborne asbestos is confined to the area.

(A) Owners of the building/facility;

(B) Employees who will perform such work and employers of employees who work and/or will be working in adjacent areas.

(iii) Within 10 days of the completion of such work, the employer whose employees have performed work subject to this standard, shall inform the building/facility owner and employers of employees who will be working in the area of the current location and quantity of PACM and/or ACM remaining in the area and final monitoring results, if any.

(4) In addition to the above requirements, all employers who discover ACM and/or PACM on a worksite shall convey information concerning the presence, location and quantity of such newly discovered ACM and/or PACM to the owner and to other employers of employees working at the work site, within 24 hours of the discovery.

(5) Criteria to rebut the designation of installed material as PACM. (i) At any time, an employer and/or building owner may demonstrate, for purposes of this standard, that PACM does not contain asbestos. Building owners and/

or employers are not required to communicate information about the presence of building material for which such a demonstration pursuant to the requirements of paragraph (k)(5)(ii) of this section has been made. However, in all such cases, the information, data and analysis supporting the determination that PACM does not contain asbestos, shall be retained pursuant to paragraph (n) of this section.

(ii) An employer or owner may demonstrate that PACM does not contain more than 1% asbestos by the following: (A) Having a completed inspection conducted pursuant to the requirements of AHERA (40 CFR part 763, subpart E) which demonstrates that the material is not ACM; or

(B) Performing tests of the material containing PACM which demonstrate that no ACM is present in the material. Such tests shall include analysis of bulk samples collected in the manner described in 40 CFR 763.86. The tests, evaluation and sample collection shall be conducted by an accredited inspector or by a CIH. Analysis of samples shall be performed by persons or laboratories with proficiency demonstrated by current successful participation in a nationally recognized testing program such as the National Voluntary Laboratory Accreditation Program (NVLAP) or the National Institute for Standards and Technology (NIST) or the Round Robin for bulk samples administered by the American Industrial Hygiene Association (AIHA) or an equivalent nationally-recognized round robin testing program.

(iii) The employer and/or building owner may demonstrate that flooring material including associated mastic and backing does not contain asbestos, by a determination of an industrial hygienist based upon recognized analytical techniques showing that the material is not ACM.

(6) At the entrance to mechanical rooms/areas in which employees reasonably can be expected to enter and which contain ACM and/or PACM, the building owner shall post signs which identify the material which is present, its location, and appropriate work practices which, if followed, will ensure that ACM and/or PACM will not be disturbed. The employer shall ensure, to

the extent feasible, that employees who come in contact with these signs can comprehend them. Means to ensure employee comprehension may include the use of foreign languages, pictographs, graphics, and awareness training.

(7) *Signs.* (i) Warning signs that demarcate the regulated area shall be provided and displayed at each location where a regulated area is required to be established by paragraph (e) of this section. Signs shall be posted at such a distance from such a location that an employee may read the signs and take necessary protective steps before entering the area marked by the signs.

(ii) (A) The warning signs required by paragraph (k)(7) of this section shall bear the following information.

DANGER
ASBESTOS
MAY CAUSE CANCER
CAUSES DAMAGE TO LUNGS
AUTHORIZED PERSONNEL ONLY

(B) In addition, where the use of respirators and protective clothing is required in the regulated area under this section, the warning signs shall include the following:

WEAR RESPIRATORY PROTECTION AND
PROTECTIVE CLOTHING IN THIS AREA

(C) Prior to June 1, 2016, employers may use the following legend in lieu of that specified in paragraph (k)(7)(ii)(A) of this section:

DANGER
ASBESTOS
CANCER AND LUNG DISEASE HAZARD
AUTHORIZED PERSONNEL ONLY

(D) Prior to June 1, 2016, employers may use the following legend in lieu of that specified in paragraph (k)(7)(ii)(B) of this section:

RESPIRATORS AND PROTECTIVE
CLOTHING ARE REQUIRED IN THIS AREA

(iii) The employer shall ensure that employees working in and contiguous to regulated areas comprehend the warning signs required to be posted by paragraph (k)(7)(i) of this section. Means to ensure employee comprehension may include the use of foreign languages, pictographs and graphics.

(8) *Labels.* (i) Labels shall be affixed to all products containing asbestos and

to all containers containing such products, including waste containers. Where feasible, installed asbestos products shall contain a visible label.

(ii) The employer shall ensure that such labels comply with paragraphs (k) of this section.

(iii) The employer shall ensure that labels of bags or containers of protective clothing and equipment, scrap, waste, and debris containing asbestos fibers bear the following information:

DANGER
CONTAINS ASBESTOS FIBERS
MAY CAUSE CANCER
CAUSES DAMAGE TO LUNGS
DO NOT BREATHE DUST
AVOID CREATING DUST

(iv) (A) Prior to June 1, 2015, employers may include the following information on raw materials, mixtures or labels of bags or containers of protective clothing and equipment, scrap, waste, and debris containing asbestos fibers in lieu of the labeling requirements in paragraphs (k)(8)(ii) and (k)(8)(iii) of this section:

DANGER
CONTAINS ASBESTOS FIBERS
AVOID CREATING DUST
CANCER AND LUNG DISEASE HAZARD

(B) Labels shall also contain a warning statement against breathing asbestos fibers.

(v) [Reserved]

(vi) The provisions for labels required by paragraphs (k)(8)(i) through (k)(8)(iii) of this section do not apply where:

(A) Asbestos fibers have been modified by a bonding agent, coating, binder, or other material, provided that the manufacturer can demonstrate that, during any reasonably foreseeable use, handling, storage, disposal, processing, or transportation, no airborne concentrations of asbestos fibers in excess of the permissible exposure limit and/or excursion limit will be released, or

(B) Asbestos is present in a product in concentrations less than 1.0 percent.

(vii) When a building owner or employer identifies previously installed PACM and/or ACM, labels or signs shall be affixed or posted so that employees will be notified of what materials contain PACM and/or ACM. The employer shall attach such labels in areas where they will clearly be noticed by employees who are likely to be exposed, such as at the entrance to mechanical room/areas. Signs required by paragraph (k)(6) of this section may be posted in lieu of labels so long as they contain information required for labelling. The employer shall ensure, to the extent feasible, that employees who come in contact with these signs or labels can comprehend them. Means to ensure employee comprehension may include the use of foreign languages, pictographs, graphics, and awareness training.

(9) *Employee Information and Training.* (i) The employer shall train each employee who is likely to be exposed in excess of a PEL, and each employee who performs Class I through IV asbestos operations, in accordance with the requirements of this section. Such training shall be conducted at no cost to the employee. The employer shall institute a training program and ensure employee participation in the program.

(ii) Training shall be provided prior to or at the time of initial assignment and at least annually thereafter.

(iii) Training for Class I operations and for Class II operations that require the use of critical barriers (or equivalent isolation methods) and/or negative pressure enclosures under this section shall be the equivalent in curriculum, training method and length to the EPA Model Accreditation Plan (MAP) asbestos abatement workers training (40 CFR part 763, subpart E, appendix C).

(iv) Training for other Class II work.

(A) For work with asbestos containing roofing materials, flooring materials, siding materials, ceiling tiles, or transite panels, training shall include at a minimum all the elements included in paragraph (k)(9)(viii) of this section and in addition, the specific work practices and engineering controls set forth in paragraph (g) of this section which specifically relate to that category. Such course shall include "hands-on" training and shall take at least 8 hours.

(B) An employee who works with more than one of the categories of material specified in paragraph (k)(9)(iv)(A) of this section shall receive training in the work practices applicable to each category of material that the employee removes and each removal method that the employee uses.

(C) For Class II operations not involving the categories of material specified in paragraph (k)(9)(iv)(A) of this section, training shall be provided which shall include at a minimum all the elements included in paragraph (k)(9)(viii) of this section and in addition, the specific work practices and engineering controls set forth in paragraph (g) of this section which specifically relate to the category of material being removed, and shall include "hands-on" training in the work practices applicable to each category of material that the employee removes and each removal method that the employee uses.

(v) Training for Class III employees shall be consistent with EPA requirements for training of local education agency maintenance and custodial staff as set forth at 40 CFR 763.92(a)(2). Such a course shall also include "hands-on" training and shall take at least 16 hours. Exception: For Class III operations for which the competent person determines that the EPA curriculum does not adequately cover the training needed to perform that activity, training shall include as a minimum all the elements included in paragraph (k)(9)(viii) of this section and in addition, the specific work practices and engineering controls set forth in paragraph (g) of this section which specifically relate to that activity, and shall include "hands-on" training in the work practices applicable to each category of material that the employee disturbs.

(vi) Training for employees performing Class IV operations shall be consistent with EPA requirements for training of local education agency maintenance and custodial staff as set forth at 40 CFR 763.92(a)(1). Such a course shall include available information concerning the locations of thermal system insulation and surfacing ACM/PACM, and asbestos-containing flooring material, or flooring material where the absence of asbestos has not yet been certified; and instruction in recognition of damage, deterioration, and delamination of asbestos con-

taining building materials. Such course shall take at least 2 hours.

(vii) Training for employees who are likely to be exposed in excess of the PEL and who are not otherwise required to be trained under paragraph (k)(9)(iii) through (vi) of this section, shall meet the requirements of paragraph (k)(9)(viii) of this section.

(viii) The training program shall be conducted in a manner that the employee is able to understand. In addition to the content required by provisions in paragraphs (k)(9)(iii) through (vi) of this section, the employer shall ensure that each such employee is informed of the following:

(A) Methods of recognizing asbestos, including the requirement in paragraph (k)(1) of this section to presume that certain building materials contain asbestos;

(B) The health effects associated with asbestos exposure;

(C) The relationship between smoking and asbestos in producing lung cancer;

(D) The nature of operations that could result in exposure to asbestos, the importance of necessary protective controls to minimize exposure including, as applicable, engineering controls, work practices, respirators, housekeeping procedures, hygiene facilities, protective clothing, decontamination procedures, emergency procedures, and waste disposal procedures, and any necessary instruction in the use of these controls and procedures; where Class III and IV work will be or is performed, the contents of EPA 20T–2003, "Managing Asbestos In-Place" July 1990 or its equivalent in content;

(E) The purpose, proper use, fitting instructions, and limitations of respirators as required by 29 CFR 1910.134;

(F) The appropriate work practices for performing the asbestos job;

(G) Medical surveillance program requirements;

(H) The content of this standard including appendices;

(I) The names, addresses and phone numbers of public health organizations which provide information, materials and/or conduct programs concerning smoking cessation. The employer may distribute the list of such organizations contained in appendix J to this section, to comply with this requirement; and

(J) The requirements for posting signs and affixing labels and the meaning of the required legends for such signs and labels.

(10) Access to training materials. (i) The employer shall make readily available to affected employees without cost, written materials relating to the employee training program, including a copy of this regulation.

(ii) The employer shall provide to the Assistant Secretary and the Director, upon request, all information and training materials relating to the employee information and training program.

(iii) The employer shall inform all employees concerning the availability of self-help smoking cessation program material. Upon employee request, the employer shall distribute such material, consisting of NIH Publication No, 89–1647, or equivalent self-help material, which is approved or published by a public health organization listed in appendix J to this section.

(l) *Housekeeping*—(1) *Vacuuming.* Where vacuuming methods are selected, HEPA filtered vacuuming equipment must be used. The equipment shall be used and emptied in a manner that minimizes the reentry of asbestos into the workplace.

(2) *Waste disposal.* Asbestos waste, scrap, debris, bags, containers, equipment, and contaminated clothing consigned for disposal shall be collected and disposed of in sealed, labeled, impermeable bags or other closed, labeled, impermeable containers except in roofing operations, where the procedures specified in paragraph (g)(8)(ii) of this section apply.

(3) *Care of asbestos-containing flooring material.* (i) All vinyl and asphalt flooring material shall be maintained in accordance with this paragraph unless the building/facility owner demonstrates, pursuant to paragraph (g)(8)(i)(I) of this section that the flooring does not contain asbestos.

(ii) Sanding of flooring material is prohibited.

(iii) Stripping of finishes shall be conducted using low abrasion pads at speeds lower than 300 rpm and wet methods.

(iv) Burnishing or dry buffing may be performed only on flooring which has sufficient finish so that the pad cannot contact the flooring material.

(4) Waste and debris and accompanying dust in an area containing accessible thermal system insulation or surfacing ACM/PACM or visibly deteriorated ACM:

(i) Shall not be dusted or swept dry, or vacuumed without using a HEPA filter;

(ii) Shall be promptly cleaned up and disposed of in leak tight containers.

(m) *Medical surveillance.* (1) General— (i) *Employees covered.* (A) The employer shall institute a medical surveillance program for all employees who for a combined total of 30 or more days per year are engaged in Class I, II and III work or are exposed at or above a permissible exposure limit. For purposes of this paragraph, any day in which a worker engages in Class II or Class III operations or a combination thereof on intact material for one hour or less (taking into account the entire time spent on the removal operation, including cleanup) and, while doing so, adheres fully to the work practices specified in this standard, shall not be counted.

(B) For employees otherwise required by this standard to wear a negative pressure respirator, employers shall ensure employees are physically able to perform the work and use the equipment. This determination shall be made under the supervision of a physician.

(ii) *Examination.* (A) The employer shall ensure that all medical examinations and procedures are performed by or under the supervision of a licensed physician, and are provided at no cost to the employee and at a reasonable time and place.

(B) Persons other than such licensed physicians who administer the pulmonary function testing required by this section shall complete a training course in spirometry sponsored by an appropriate academic or professional institution.

(2) *Medical examinations and consultations*—(i) *Frequency.* The employer shall make available medical examinations and consultations to each employee

covered under paragraph (m)(1)(i) of this section on the following schedules:

(A) Prior to assignment of the employee to an area where negative-pressure respirators are worn;

(B) When the employee is assigned to an area where exposure to asbestos may be at or above the permissible exposure limit for 30 or more days per year, or engage in Class I, II, or III work for a combined total of 30 or more days per year, a medical examination must be given within 10 working days following the thirtieth day of exposure;

(C) And at least annually thereafter.

(D) If the examining physician determines that any of the examinations should be provided more frequently than specified, the employer shall provide such examinations to affected employees at the frequencies specified by the physician.

(E) Exception: No medical examination is required of any employee if adequate records show that the employee has been examined in accordance with this paragraph within the past 1-year period.

(ii) *Content.* Medical examinations made available pursuant to paragraphs (m)(2)(i)(A) through (m)(2)(i)(C) of this section shall include:

(A) A medical and work history with special emphasis directed to the pulmonary, cardiovascular, and gastrointestinal systems.

(B) On initial examination, the standardized questionnaire contained in part 1 of appendix D to this section, and, on annual examination, the abbreviated standardized questionnaire contained in part 2 of appendix D to this section.

(C) A physical examination directed to the pulmonary and gastrointestinal systems, including a chest roentgenogram to be administered at the discretion of the physician, and pulmonary function tests of forced vital capacity (FVC) and forced expiratory volume at one second (FEV(1)). Interpretation and classification of chest shall be conducted in accordance with appendix E to this section.

(D) Any other examinations or tests deemed necessary by the examining physician.

(3) *Information provided to the physician.* The employer shall provide the following information to the examining physician:

(i) A copy of this standard and Appendices D, E, and I to this section;

(ii) A description of the affected employee's duties as they relate to the employee's exposure;

(iii) The employee's representative exposure level or anticipated exposure level;

(iv) A description of any personal protective and respiratory equipment used or to be used; and

(v) Information from previous medical examinations of the affected employee that is not otherwise available to the examining physician.

(4) *Physician's written opinion.* (i) The employer shall obtain a written opinion from the examining physician. This written opinion shall contain the results of the medical examination and shall include:

(A) The physician's opinion as to whether the employee has any detected medical conditions that would place the employee at an increased risk of material health impairment from exposure to asbestos;

(B) Any recommended limitations on the employee or on the use of personal protective equipment such as respirators; and

(C) A statement that the employee has been informed by the physician of the results of the medical examination and of any medical conditions that may result from asbestos exposure.

(D) A statement that the employee has been informed by the physician of the increased risk of lung cancer attributable to the combined effect of smoking and asbestos exposure.

(ii) The employer shall instruct the physician not to reveal in the written opinion given to the employer specific findings or diagnoses unrelated to occupational exposure to asbestos.

(iii) The employer shall provide a copy of the physician's written opinion to the affected employee within 30 days from its receipt.

(n) *Recordkeeping*—(1) *Objective data relied on pursuant to paragraph (f) to this section.* (i) Where the employer has relied on objective data that demonstrates that products made from or containing asbestos or the activity involving such products or material are

599

not capable of releasing fibers of asbestos in concentrations at or above the permissible exposure limit and/or excursion limit under the expected conditions of processing, use, or handling to satisfy the requirements of paragraph (f), the employer shall establish and maintain an accurate record of objective data reasonably relied upon in support of the exemption.

(ii) The record shall include at least the following information:

(A) The product qualifying for exemption;

(B) The source of the objective data;

(C) The testing protocol, results of testing, and/or analysis of the material for the release of asbestos;

(D) A description of the operation exempted and how the data support the exemption; and

(E) Other data relevant to the operations, materials, processing, or employee exposures covered by the exemption.

(iii) The employer shall maintain this record for the duration of the employer's reliance upon such objective data.

(2) *Exposure measurements.* (i) The employer shall keep an accurate record of all measurements taken to monitor employee exposure to asbestos as prescribed in paragraph (f) of this section. NOTE: The employer may utilize the services of competent organizations such as industry trade associations and employee associations to maintain the records required by this section.

(ii) This record shall include at least the following information:

(A) The date of measurement;

(B) The operation involving exposure to asbestos that is being monitored;

(C) Sampling and analytical methods used and evidence of their accuracy;

(D) Number, duration, and results of samples taken;

(E) Type of protective devices worn, if any; and

(F) Name, social security number, and exposure of the employees whose exposures are represented.

(iii) The employer shall maintain this record for at least thirty (30) years, in accordance with 29 CFR 1910.33.

(3) *Medical surveillance.* (i) The employer shall establish and maintain an accurate record for each employee subject to medical surveillance by paragraph (m) of this section, in accordance with 29 CFR 1910.33.

(ii) The record shall include at least the following information:

(A) The name and social security number of the employee;

(B) A copy of the employee's medical examination results, including the medical history, questionnaire responses, results of any tests, and physician's recommendations.

(C) Physician's written opinions;

(D) Any employee medical complaints related to exposure to asbestos; and

(E) A copy of the information provided to the physician as required by paragraph (m) of this section.

(iii) The employer shall ensure that this record is maintained for the duration of employment plus thirty (30) years, in accordance with 29 CFR 1910.33.

(4) *Training records.* The employer shall maintain all employee training records for one (1) year beyond the last date of employment by that employer.

(5) *Data to Rebut PACM.* Where the building owner and employer have relied on data to demonstrate that PACM is not asbestos-containing, such data shall be maintained for as long as they are relied upon to rebut the presumption.

(6) *Records of required notifications.* Where the building owner has communicated and received information concerning the identification, location and quantity of ACM and PACM, written records of such notifications and their content shall be maintained by the building owner for the duration of ownership and shall be transferred to successive owners of such buildings/facilities.

(7) *Availability.* (i) The employer, upon written request, shall make all records required to be maintained by this section available to the Assistant Secretary and the Director for examination and copying.

(ii) The employer must comply with the requirements concerning availability of records set forth in 29 CFR 1910.1020.

(8) *Transfer of records.* The employer must comply with the requirements

concerning transfer of records set forth in 29 CFR 1910.1020(h).

(o) *Competent person*—(1) *General.* On all construction worksites covered by this standard, the employer shall designate a competent person, having the qualifications and authorities for ensuring worker safety and health required by subpart C, General Safety and Health Provisions for Construction (29 CFR 1926.20 through 1926.32).

(2) *Required inspections by the competent person.* Section 1926.20(b)(2) which requires health and safety prevention programs to provide for frequent and regular inspections of the job sites, materials, and equipment to be made by competent persons, is incorporated.

(3) *Additional inspections.* In addition, the competent person shall make frequent and regular inspections of the job sites, in order to perform the duties set out below in paragraph (o)(3)(i) of this section. For Class I jobs, on-site inspections shall be made at least once during each work shift, and at any time at employee request. For Class II, III, and IV jobs, on-site inspections shall be made at intervals sufficient to assess whether conditions have changed, and at any reasonable time at employee request.

(i) On all worksites where employees are engaged in Class I or II asbestos work, the competent person designated in accordance with paragraph (e)(6) of this section shall perform or supervise the following duties, as applicable:

(A) Set up the regulated area, enclosure, or other containment;

(B) Ensure (by on-site inspection) the integrity of the enclosure or containment;

(C) Set up procedures to control entry to and exit from the enclosure and/or area;

(D) Supervise all employee exposure monitoring required by this section and ensure that it is conducted as required by paragraph (f) of this section;

(E) Ensure that employees working within the enclosure and/or using glove bags wear respirators and protective clothing as required by paragraphs (h) and (i) of this section;

(F) Ensure through on-site supervision, that employees set up, use, and remove engineering controls, use work practices and personal protective equipment in compliance with all requirements;

(G) Ensure that employees use the hygiene facilities and observe the decontamination procedures specified in paragraph (j) of this section;

(H) Ensure that through on-site inspection, engineering controls are functioning properly and employees are using proper work practices; and,

(I) Ensure that notification requirement in paragraph (k) of this section are met.

(ii) [Reserved]

(4) *Training for the competent person.* (i) For Class I and II asbestos work the competent person shall be trained in all aspects of asbestos removal and handling, including: abatement, installation, removal and handling; the contents of this standard; the identification of asbestos; removal procedures, where appropriate; and other practices for reducing the hazard. Such training shall be obtained in a comprehensive course for supervisors that meets the criteria of EPA's Model Accreditation Plan (40 CFR part 763, subpart E, appendix C), such as a course conducted by an EPA-approved or state-approved training provider, certified by EPA or a state, or a course equivalent in stringency, content, and length.

(ii) For Class III and IV asbestos work, the competent person shall be trained in aspects of asbestos handling appropriate for the nature of the work, to include procedures for setting up glove bags and mini-enclosures, practices for reducing asbestos exposures, use of wet methods, the contents of this standard, and the identification of asbestos. Such training shall include successful completion of a course that is consistent with EPA requirements for training of local education agency maintenance and custodial staff as set forth at 40 CFR 763.92(a)(2), or its equivalent in stringency, content and length. Competent persons for Class III and IV work, may also be trained pursuant to the requirements of paragraph (o)(4)(i) of this section.

(p) *Appendices.* (1) Appendices A, C, D, and E to this section are incorporated as part of this section and the contents of these appendices are mandatory.

(2) Appendices B, F, H, I, J, and K to this section are informational and are not intended to create any additional obligations not otherwise imposed or to detract from any existing obligations.

APPENDIX A TO § 1926.1101—OSHA REFERENCE METHOD—MANDATORY

This mandatory appendix specifies the procedure for analyzing air samples for asbestos and specifies quality control procedures that must be implemented by laboratories performing the analysis. The sampling and analytical methods described below represent the elements of the available monitoring methods (such as appendix B of this regulation, the most current version of the OSHA method ID–160, or the most current version of the NIOSH Method 7400). All employers who are required to conduct air monitoring under paragraph (f) of the standard are required to utilize analytical laboratories that use this procedure, or an equivalent method, for collecting and analyzing samples.

Sampling and Analytical Procedure

1. The sampling medium for air samples shall be mixed cellulose ester filter membranes. These shall be designated by the manufacturer as suitable for asbestos counting. See below for rejection of blanks.

2. The preferred collection device shall be the 25-mm diameter cassette with an open-faced 50-mm electrically conductive extension cowl. The 37-mm cassette may be used if necessary but only if written justification for the need to use the 37-mm filter cassette accompanies the sample results in the employee's exposure monitoring record. Do not reuse or reload cassettes for asbestos sample collection.

3. An air flow rate between 0.5 liter/min and 2.5 liters/min shall be selected for the 25/mm cassette. If the 37-mm cassette is used, an air flow rate between 1 liter/min and 2.5 liters/min shall be selected.

4. Where possible, a sufficient air volume for each air sample shall be collected to yield between 100 and 1,300 fibers per square millimeter on the membrane filter. If a filter darkens in appearance or if loose dust is seen on the filter, a second sample shall be started.

5. Ship the samples in a rigid container with sufficient packing material to prevent dislodging the collected fibers. Packing material that has a high electrostatic charge on its surface (e.g., expanded polystyrene) cannot be used because such material can cause loss of fibers to the sides of the cassette.

6. Calibrate each personal sampling pump before and after use with a representative filter cassette installed between the pump and the calibration devices.

7. Personal samples shall be taken in the "breathing zone" of the employee (i.e., attached to or near the collar or lapel near the worker's face).

8. Fiber counts shall be made by positive phase contrast using a microscope with an 8 to 10 X eyepiece and a 40 to 45 X objective for a total magnification of approximately 400 X and a numerical aperture of 0.65 to 0.75. The microscope shall also be fitted with a green or blue filter.

9. The microscope shall be fitted with a Walton-Beckett eyepiece graticule calibrated for a field diameter of 100 micrometers (±2 micrometers).

10. The phase-shift detection limit of the microscope shall be about 3 degrees measured using the HSE phase shift test slide as outlined below.

a. Place the test slide on the microscope stage and center it under the phase objective.

b. Bring the blocks of grooved lines into focus.

NOTE: The slide consists of seven sets of grooved lines (ca. 20 grooves to each block) in descending order of visibility from sets 1 to 7, seven being the least visible. The requirements for asbestos counting are that the microscope optics must resolve the grooved lines in set 3 completely, although they may appear somewhat faint, and that the grooved lines in sets 6 and 7 must be invisible. Sets 4 and 5 must be at least partially visible but may vary slightly in visibility between microscopes. A microscope that fails to meet these requirements has either too low or too high a resolution to be used for asbestos counting.

c. If the image deteriorates, clean and adjust the microscope optics. If the problem persists, cosult the microscope manufacturer.

11. Each set of samples taken will include 10% field blanks or a minimum of 2 field blanks. These blanks must come from the same lot as the filters used for sample collection. The field blank results shall be averaged and subtracted from the analytical results before reporting. A set consists of any sample or group of samples for which an evaluation for this standard must be made. Any samples represented by a field blank having a fiber count in excess of the detection limit of the method being used shall be rejected.

12. The samples shall be mounted by the acetone/triacetin method or a method with an equivalent index of refraction and similar clarity.

13. Observe the following counting rules.

a. Count only fibers equal to or longer than 5 micrometers. Measure the length of curved fibers along the curve.

b. In the absence of other information, count all particles as asbestos, that have a length-to-width ratio (aspect ratio) of 3:1 or greater.

c. Fibers lying entirely within the boundary of the Walton-Beckett graticule field shall receive a count of 1. Fibers crossing the boundary once, having one end within the circle, shall receive the count of one half (½). Do not count any fiber that crosses the graticule boundary more than once. Reject and do not count any other fibers even though they may be visible outside the graticule area.

d. Count bundles of fibers as one fiber unless individual fibers can be identified by observing both ends of an individual fiber.

e. Count enough graticule fields to yield 100 fibers. Count a minimum of 20 fields; stop counting at 100 fields regardless of fiber count.

14. Blind recounts shall be conducted at the rate of 10 percent.

Quality Control Procedures

1. Intralaboratory program. Each laboratory and/or each company with more than one microscopist counting slides shall establish a statistically designed quality assurance program involving blind recounts and comparisons between microscopists to monitor the variability of counting by each microscopist and between microscopists. In a company with more than one laboratory, the program shall include all laboratories, and shall also evaluate the laboratory-to-laboratory variability.

2a. Interlaboratory program. Each laboratory analyzing asbestos samples for compliance determination shall implement an interlaboratory quality assurance program that, as a minimum, includes participation of at least two other independent laboratories. Each laboratory shall participate in round robin testing at least once every 6 months with at least all the other laboratories in its interlaboratory quality assurance group. Each laboratory shall submit slides typical of its own workload for use in this program. The round robin shall be designed and results analyzed using appropriate statistical methodology.

b. All laboratories should also participate in a national sample testing scheme such as the Proficiency Analytical Testing Program (PAT), or the Asbestos Registry sponsored by the American Industrial Hygiene Association (AIHA).

3. All individuals performing asbestos analysis must have taken the NIOSH course for sampling and evaluating airborne asbestos dust or an equivalent course.

4. When the use of different microscopes contributes to differences between counters and laboratories, the effect of the different microscope shall be evaluated and the microscope shall be replaced, as necessary.

5. Current results of these quality assurance programs shall be posted in each laboratory to keep the microscopists informed.

APPENDIX B TO § 1926.1101—SAMPLING AND ANALYSIS (NON-MANDATORY)

Matrix Air:
  OSHA Permissible Exposure Limits:
    Time Weighted Average .... 0.1 fiber/cc
    Excursion Level (30 minutes) .... 1.0 fiber/cc
Collection Procedure:
  A known volume of air is drawn through a 25-mm diameter cassette containing a mixed-cellulose ester filter. The cassette must be equipped with an electrically conductive 50-mm extension cowl. The sampling time and rate are chosen to give a fiber density of between 100 to 1,300 fibers/mm2 on the filter.

Recommended Sampling Rate .... 0.5 to 5.0 liters/minute
    (L/min)

Recommended Air Volumes:
  Minimum .... 25 L
  Maximum .... 2,400 L

Analytical Procedure:

A portion of the sample filter is cleared and prepared for asbestos fiber counting by Phase Contrast Microscopy (PCM) at 400X.

Commercial manufacturers and products mentioned in this method are for descriptive use only and do not constitute endorsements by USDOL-OSHA. Similar products from other sources can be substituted.

1. Introduction

This method describes the collection of airborne asbestos fibers using calibrated sampling pumps with mixed-cellulose ester (MCE) filters and analysis by phase contrast microscopy (PCM). Some terms used are unique to this method and are defined below:

Asbestos: A term for naturally occurring fibrous minerals. Asbestos includes chrysotile, crocidolite, amosite (cummingtonite-grunerite asbestos), tremolite asbestos, actinolite asbestos, anthophyllite asbestos, and any of these minerals that have been chemically treated and/or altered. The precise chemical formulation of each species will vary with the location from which it was mined. Nominal compositions are listed:

Chrysotile	$Mg_3 Si_2 O_5(OH)_4$
Crocidolite	$Na_2 Fe_3^{2+} Fe_2^{3+} Si_8$ $O_{22}(OH)_2$
Amosite	$(Mg,Fe)_7 Si_8 O_{22}(OH)_2$
Tremolite-actin- olite	$Ca_2(Mg,Fe)_5 Si_8 O_{22}(OH)_2$
Anthophyllite	$(Mg,Fe)_7 Si_8 O_{22}(OH)_2$

Asbestos Fiber: A fiber of asbestos which meets the criteria specified below for a fiber.

Aspect Ratio: The ratio of the length of a fiber to it's diameter (e.g. 3:1, 5:1 aspect ratios).

Cleavage Fragments: Mineral particles formed by comminution of minerals, especially those characterized by parallel sides and a moderate aspect ratio (usually less than 20:1).

Detection Limit: The number of fibers necessary to be 95% certain that the result is greater than zero.

Differential Counting: The term applied to the practice of excluding certain kinds of fibers from the fiber count because they do not appear to be asbestos.

Fiber: A particle that is 5 μm or longer, with a length-to-width ratio of 3 to 1 or longer.

Field: The area within the graticule circle that is superimposed on the microscope image.

Set: The samples which are taken, submitted to the laboratory, analyzed, and for which, interim or final result reports are generated.

Tremolite, Anthophyllite, and Actinolite: The non-asbestos form of these minerals which meet the definition of a fiber. It includes any of these minerals that have been chemically treated and/or altered.

Walton-Beckett Graticule: An eyepiece graticule specifically designed for asbestos fiber counting. It consists of a circle with a projected diameter of 100 ±2 μm (area of about 0.00785 mm²) with a crosshair having tic-marks at 3-μm intervals in one direction and 5-μm in the orthogonal direction. There are marks around the periphery of the circle to demonstrate the proper sizes and shapes of fibers. This design is reproduced in Figure 1. The disk is placed in one of the microscope eyepieces so that the design is superimposed on the field of view.

1.1. History

Early surveys to determine asbestos exposures were conducted using impinger counts of total dust with the counts expressed as million particles per cubic foot. The British Asbestos Research Council recommended filter membrane counting in 1969. In July 1969, the Bureau of Occupational Safety and Health published a filter membrane method for counting asbestos fibers in the United States. This method was refined by NIOSH and published as P & CAM 239. On May 29, 1971, OSHA specified filter membrane sampling with phase contrast counting for evaluation of asbestos exposures at work sites in the United States. The use of this technique was again required by OSHA in 1986. Phase contrast microscopy has continued to be the method of choice for the measurement of occupational exposure to asbestos.

1.2. Principle

Air is drawn through a MCE filter to capture airborne asbestos fibers. A wedge shaped portion of the filter is removed, placed on a glass microscope slide and made transparent. A measured area (field) is viewed by PCM. All the fibers meeting defined criteria for asbestos are counted and considered a measure of the airborne asbestos concentration.

1.3. Advantages and Disadvantages

There are four main advantages of PCM over other methods:

(1) The technique is specific for fibers. Phase contrast is a fiber counting technique which excludes non-fibrous particles from the analysis.

(2) The technique is inexpensive and does not require specialized knowledge to carry out the analysis for total fiber counts.

(3) The analysis is quick and can be performed on-site for rapid determination of air concentrations of asbestos fibers.

(4) The technique has continuity with historical epidemiological studies so that estimates of expected disease can be inferred from long-term determinations of asbestos exposures.

The main disadvantage of PCM is that it does not positively identify asbestos fibers. Other fibers which are not asbestos may be included in the count unless differential counting is performed. This requires a great deal of experience to adequately differentiate asbestos from non-asbestos fibers. Positive identification of asbestos must be performed by polarized light or electron microscopy techniques. A further disadvantage of PCM is that the smallest visible fibers are about 0.2 μm in diameter while the finest asbestos fibers may be as small as 0.02 μm in diameter. For some exposures, substantially more fibers may be present than are actually counted.

1.4. Workplace Exposure

Asbestos is used by the construction industry in such products as shingles, floor tiles, asbestos cement, roofing felts, insulation and acoustical products. Non-construction uses include brakes, clutch facings, paper, paints, plastics, and fabrics. One of the most significant exposures in the workplace is the removal and encapsulation of asbestos in schools, public buildings, and homes. Many workers have the potential to be exposed to asbestos during these operations.

About 95% of the asbestos in commercial use in the United States is chrysotile. Crocidolite and amosite make up most of the remainder. Anthophyllite and tremolite or actinolite are likely to be encountered as contaminants in various industrial products.

1.5. Physical Properties

Asbestos fiber possesses a high tensile strength along its axis, is chemically inert, non-combustible, and heat resistant. It has a high electrical resistance and good sound absorbing properties. It can be weaved into cables, fabrics or other textiles, and also matted into asbestos papers, felts, or mats.

2. Range and Detection Limit

2.1. The ideal counting range on the filter is 100 to 1,300 fibers/mm². With a Walton-Beckett graticule this range is equivalent to 0.8 to 10 fibers/field. Using NIOSH counting statistics, a count of 0.8 fibers/field would give an approximate coefficient of variation (CV) of 0.13.

2.2. The detection limit for this method is 4.0 fibers per 100 fields or 5.5 fibers/mm². This was determined using an equation to estimate the maximum CV possible at a specific concentration (95% confidence) and a Lower Control Limit of zero. The CV value was then used to determine a corresponding concentration from historical CV vs fiber relationships. As an example:

Lower Control Limit (95% Confidence) =
$AC - 1.645(CV)(AC)$

Where:

AC = Estimate of the airborne fiber concentration (fibers/cc) Setting the Lower Control Limit=0 and solving for CV:

$0 = AC - 1.645(CV)(AC)$
$CV = 0.61$

This value was compared with CV vs. count curves. The count at which CV = 0.61 for Leidel-Busch counting statistics or for an OSHA Salt Lake Technical Center (OSHA-SLTC) CV curve (see appendix A for further information) was 4.4 fibers or 3.9 fibers per 100 fields, respectively. Although a lower detection limit of 4 fibers per 100 fields is supported by the OSHA-SLTC data, both data sets support the 4.5 fibers per 100 fields value.

3. Method Performance—Precision and Accuracy

Precision is dependent upon the total number of fibers counted and the uniformity of the fiber distribution on the filter. A general rule is to count at least 20 and not more than 100 fields. The count is discontinued when 100 fibers are counted, provided that 20 fields have already been counted. Counting more than 100 fibers results in only a small gain in precision. As the total count drops below 10 fibers, an accelerated loss of precision is noted.

At this time, there is no known method to determine the absolute accuracy of the asbestos analysis. Results of samples prepared through the Proficiency Analytical Testing (PAT) Program and analyzed by the OSHA-SLTC showed no significant bias when compared to PAT reference values. The PAT samples were analyzed from 1987 to 1989 (N=36) and the concentration range was from 120 to 1,300 fibers/mm².

4. Interferences

Fibrous substances, if present, may interfere with asbestos analysis.

Some common fibers are:

fiberglass
anhydrite
plant fibers
perlite veins
gypsum
some synthetic fibers
membrane structures
sponge spicules
diatoms
microorganisms
wollastonite

The use of electron microscopy or optical tests such as polarized light, and dispersion staining may be used to differentiate these materials from asbestos when necessary.

5. Sampling

5.1. Equipment

5.1.1. Sample assembly (The assembly is shown in Figure 3). Conductive filter holder consisting of a 25-mm diameter, 3-piece cassette having a 50-mm long electrically conductive extension cowl. Backup pad, 25-mm, cellulose. Membrane filter, mixed-cellulose ester (MCE), 25-mm, plain, white, 0.4 to 1.2-μm pore size.

NOTES:

(a) DO NOT RE-USE CASSETTES.

(b) Fully conductive cassettes are required to reduce fiber loss to the sides of the cassette due to electrostatic attraction.

(c) Purchase filters which have been selected by the manufacturer for asbestos counting or analyze representative filters for fiber background before use. Discard the filter lot if more than 4 fibers/100 fields are found.

(d) To decrease the possibility of contamination, the sampling system (filter-backup pad-cassette) for asbestos is usually preassembled by the manufacturer.

(e) Other cassettes, such as the Bell-mouth, may be used within the limits of their validation.

5.1.2. Gel bands for sealing cassettes.

5.1.3. Sampling pump.

Each pump must be a battery operated, self-contained unit small enough to be placed on the monitored employee and not interfere with the work being performed. The pump must be capable of sampling at the collection rate for the required sampling time.

5.1.4. Flexible tubing, 6-mm bore.

5.1.5. Pump calibration.

Stopwatch and bubble tube/burette or electronic meter.

5.2. Sampling Procedure

5.2.1. Seal the point where the base and cowl of each cassette meet with a gel band or tape.

5.2.2. Charge the pumps completely before beginning.

5.2.3. Connect each pump to a calibration cassette with an appropriate length of 6-mm bore plastic tubing. Do not use luer connectors—the type of cassette specified above has built-in adapters.

5.2.4. Select an appropriate flow rate for the situation being monitored. The sampling flow rate must be between 0.5 and 5.0 L/min for personal sampling and is commonly set between 1 and 2 L/min. Always choose a flow rate that will not produce overloaded filters.

5.2.5. Calibrate each sampling pump before and after sampling with a calibration cassette in-line (Note: This calibration cassette should be from the same lot of cassettes used for sampling). Use a primary standard (e.g. bubble burette) to calibrate each pump. If possible, calibrate at the sampling site.

NOTE: If sampling site calibration is not possible, environmental influences may affect the flow rate. The extent is dependent on the type of pump used. Consult with the pump manufacturer to determine dependence on environmental influences. If the pump is affected by temperature and pressure changes, correct the flow rate using the formula shown in the section "Sampling Pump Flow Rate Corrections" at the end of this appendix.

5.2.6. Connect each pump to the base of each sampling cassette with flexible tubing. Remove the end cap of each cassette and take each air sample open face. Assure that each sample cassette is held open side down in the employee's breathing zone during sampling. The distance from the nose/mouth of the employee to the cassette should be about 10 cm. Secure the cassette on the collar or lapel of the employee using spring clips or other similar devices.

5.2.7. A suggested minimum air volume when sampling to determine TWA compliance is 25 L. For Excursion Limit (30 min sampling time) evaluations, a minimum air volume of 48 L is recommended.

5.2.8. The most significant problem when sampling for asbestos is overloading the filter with non-asbestos dust. Suggested maximum air sample volumes for specific environments are:

Environment	Air Vol. (L)
Asbestos removal operations (visible dust).	100.
Asbestos removal operations (little dust).	240.
Office environments	400 to 2,400.

CAUTION: Do not overload the filter with dust. High levels of non-fibrous dust particles may obscure fibers on the filter and lower the count or make counting impossible. If more than about 25 to 30% of the field area is obscured with dust, the result may be biased low. Smaller air volumes may be necessary when there is excessive non-asbestos dust in the air.

While sampling, observe the filter with a small flashlight. If there is a visible layer of dust on the filter, stop sampling, remove and seal the cassette, and replace with a new sampling assembly. The total dust loading should not exceed 1 mg.

5.2.9. Blank samples are used to determine if any contamination has occurred during sample handling. Prepare two blanks for the first 1 to 20 samples. For sets containing greater than 20 samples, prepare blanks as 10% of the samples. Handle blank samples in the same manner as air samples with one exception: Do not draw any air through the blank samples. Open the blank cassette in the place where the sample cassettes are mounted on the employee. Hold it open for about 30 seconds. Close and seal the cassette appropriately. Store blanks for shipment with the sample cassettes.

5.2.10. Immediately after sampling, close and seal each cassette with the base and plastic plugs. Do not touch or puncture the filter membrane as this will invalidate the analysis.

5.2.11 Attach and secure a sample seal around each sample cassette in such a way as to assure that the end cap and base plugs cannot be removed without destroying the seal. Tape the ends of the seal together since the seal is not long enough to be wrapped end-to-end. Also wrap tape around the cassette at each joint to keep the seal secure.

5.3.1. Send the samples to the laboratory with paperwork requesting asbestos analysis. List any known fibrous interferences present during sampling on the paperwork. Also, note the workplace operation(s) sampled.

5.3.2. Secure and handle the samples in such that they will not rattle during shipment nor be exposed to static electricity. Do not ship samples in expanded polystyrene peanuts, vermiculite, paper shreds, or excelsior. Tape sample cassettes to sheet bubbles and place in a container that will cushion the samples in such a manner that they will not rattle.

5.3.3. To avoid the possibility of sample contamination, always ship bulk samples in separate mailing containers.

6. Analysis

6.1. Safety Precautions

6.1.1. Acetone is extremely flammable and precautions must be taken not to ignite it. Avoid using large containers or quantities of acetone. Transfer the solvent in a ventilated laboratory hood. Do not use acetone near any open flame. For generation of acetone vapor, use a spark free heat source.

6.1.2. Any asbestos spills should be cleaned up immediately to prevent dispersal of fibers. Prudence should be exercised to avoid contamination of laboratory facilities or exposure of personnel to asbestos. Asbestos spills should be cleaned up with wet methods and/or a High Efficiency Particulate-Air (HEPA) filtered vacuum.

CAUTION: Do not use a vacuum without a HEPA filter—It will disperse fine asbestos fibers in the air.

6.2. Equipment

6.2.1. Phase contrast microscope with binocular or trinocular head.

6.2.2. Widefield or Huygenian 10X eyepieces (NOTE: The eyepiece containing the graticule must be a focusing eyepiece. Use a 40X phase objective with a numerical aperture of 0.65 to 0.75).

6.2.3. Kohler illumination (if possible) with green or blue filter.

6.2.4. Walton-Beckett Graticule, type G–22 with 100 ±2 µm projected diameter.

6.2.5. Mechanical stage. A rotating mechanical stage is convenient for use with polarized light.

6.2.6. Phase telescope.

6.2.7. Stage micrometer with 0.01-mm subdivisions.

6.2.8. Phase-shift test slide, mark II (Available from PTR optics Ltd., and also McCrone).

6.2.9. Precleaned glass slides, 25 mm×75 mm. One end can be frosted for convenience in writing sample numbers, etc., or paste-on labels can be used.

6.2.10. Cover glass #1½.

6.2.11. Scalpel (#10, curved blade).

6.2.12. Fine tipped forceps.

6.2.13. Aluminum block for clearing filter (see appendix D and Figure 4).

6.2.14. Automatic adjustable pipette, 100- to 500-µL.

6.2.15. Micropipette, 5 µL.

6.3. Reagents

6.3.1. Acetone (HPLC grade).

6.3.2. Triacetin (glycerol triacetate).

6.3.3. Lacquer or nail polish.

6.4. Standard Preparation

A way to prepare standard asbestos samples of known concentration has not been developed. It is possible to prepare replicate samples of nearly equal concentration. This has been performed through the PAT program. These asbestos samples are distributed by the AIHA to participating laboratories.

Since only about one-fourth of a 25-mm sample membrane is required for an asbestos count, any PAT sample can serve as a "standard" for replicate counting.

6.5. Sample Mounting

NOTE: See Safety Precautions in Section 6.1. before proceeding. The objective is to produce samples with a smooth (non-grainy) background in a medium with a refractive index of approximately 1.46. The technique below collapses the filter for easier focusing and produces permanent mounts which are useful for quality control and interlaboratory comparison.

An aluminum block or similar device is required for sample preparation.

6.5.1. Heat the aluminum block to about 70 °C. The hot block should not be used on any surface that can be damaged by either the heat or from exposure to acetone.

6.5.2. Ensure that the glass slides and cover glasses are free of dust and fibers.

6.5.3. Remove the top plug to prevent a vacuum when the cassette is opened. Clean the outside of the cassette if necessary. Cut the seal and/or tape on the cassette with a razor blade. Very carefully separate the base from the extension cowl, leaving the filter and backup pad in the base.

6.5.4. With a rocking motion cut a triangular wedge from the filter using the scalpel. This wedge should be one-sixth to one-fourth of the filter. Grasp the filter wedge with the forceps on the perimeter of the filter which was clamped between the cassette pieces. DO NOT TOUCH the filter with your finger. Place the filter on the glass slide sample side up. Static electricity will usually keep the filter on the slide until it is cleared.

6.5.5. Place the tip of the micropipette containing about 200 µL acetone into the aluminum block. Insert the glass slide into the receiving slot in the aluminum block. Inject the acetone into the block with slow, steady pressure on the plunger while holding the pipette firmly in place. Wait 3 to 5 seconds for the filter to clear, then remove the pipette and slide from the aluminum block.

6.5.6. Immediately (less than 30 seconds) place 2.5 to 3.5 µL of triacetin on the filter (NOTE: Waiting longer than 30 seconds will result in increased index of refraction and decreased contrast between the fibers and the preparation. This may also lead to separation of the cover slip from the slide).

6.5.7. Lower a cover slip gently onto the filter at a slight angle to reduce the possibility of forming air bubbles. If more than 30 seconds have elapsed between acetone exposure and triacetin application, glue the edges of

607

the cover slip to the slide with lacquer or nail polish.

6.5.8. If clearing is slow, warm the slide for 15 min on a hot plate having a surface temperature of about 50 °C to hasten clearing. The top of the hot block can be used if the slide is not heated too long.

6.5.9. Counting may proceed immediately after clearing and mounting are completed.

6.6. Sample Analysis

Completely align the microscope according to the manufacturer's instructions. Then, align the microscope using the following general alignment routine at the beginning of every counting session and more often if necessary.

6.6.1. Alignment

(1) Clean all optical surfaces. Even a small amount of dirt can significantly degrade the image.

(2) Rough focus the objective on a sample.

(3) Close down the field iris so that it is visible in the field of view. Focus the image of the iris with the condenser focus. Center the image of the iris in the field of view.

(4) Install the phase telescope and focus on the phase rings. Critically center the rings. Misalignment of the rings results in astigmatism which will degrade the image.

(5) Place the phase-shift test slide on the microscope stage and focus on the lines. The analyst must see line set 3 and should see at least parts of 4 and 5 but, not see line set 6 or 6. A microscope/microscopist combination which does not pass this test may not be used.

6.6.2. Counting Fibers

(1) Place the prepared sample slide on the mechanical stage of the microscope. Position the center of the wedge under the objective lens and focus upon the sample.

(2) Start counting from one end of the wedge and progress along a radial line to the other end (count in either direction from perimeter to wedge tip). Select fields randomly, without looking into the eyepieces, by slightly advancing the slide in one direction with the mechanical stage control.

(3) Continually scan over a range of focal planes (generally the upper 10 to 15 μm of the filter surface) with the fine focus control during each field count. Spend at least 5 to 15 seconds per field.

(4) Most samples will contain asbestos fibers with fiber diameters less than 1 μm. Look carefully for faint fiber images. The small diameter fibers will be very hard to see. However, they are an important contribution to the total count.

(5) Count only fibers equal to or longer than 5 μm. Measure the length of curved fibers along the curve.

(6) Count fibers which have a length to width ratio of 3:1 or greater.

(7) Count all the fibers in at least 20 fields. Continue counting until either 100 fibers are counted or 100 fields have been viewed; whichever occurs first. Count all the fibers in the final field.

(8) Fibers lying entirely within the boundary of the Walton-Beckett graticule field shall receive a count of 1. Fibers crossing the boundary once, having one end within the circle shall receive a count of ½. Do not count any fiber that crosses the graticule boundary more than once. Reject and do not count any other fibers even though they may be visible outside the graticule area. If a fiber touches the circle, it is considered to cross the line.

(9) Count bundles of fibers as one fiber unless individual fibers can be clearly identified and each individual fiber is clearly not connected to another counted fiber. See Figure 1 for counting conventions.

(10) Record the number of fibers in each field in a consistent way such that filter non-uniformity can be assessed.

(11) Regularly check phase ring alignment.

(12) When an agglomerate (mass of material) covers more than 25% of the field of view, reject the field and select another. Do not include it in the number of fields counted.

(13) Perform a "blind recount" of 1 in every 10 filter wedges (slides). Re-label the slides using a person other than the original counter.

6.7. Fiber Identification

As previously mentioned in Section 1.3., PCM does not provide positive confirmation of asbestos fibers. Alternate differential counting techniques should be used if discrimination is desirable. Differential counting may include primary discrimination based on morphology, polarized light analysis of fibers, or modification of PCM data by Scanning Electron or Transmission Electron Microscopy.

A great deal of experience is required to routinely and correctly perform differential counting. It is discouraged unless it is legally necessary. Then, only if a fiber is obviously not asbestos should it be excluded from the count. Further discussion of this technique can be found in reference 8.10.

If there is a question whether a fiber is asbestos or not, follow the rule:

"WHEN IN DOUBT, COUNT."

6.8. Analytical Recommendations—Quality Control System

6.8.1. All individuals performing asbestos analysis must have taken the NIOSH course for sampling and evaluating airborne asbestos or an equivalent course.

6.8.2. Each laboratory engaged in asbestos counting shall set up a slide trading arrangement with at least two other laboratories in order to compare performance and eliminate inbreeding of error. The slide exchange occurs at least semiannually. The round robin results shall be posted where all analysts can view individual analyst's results.

6.8.3. Each laboratory engaged in asbestos counting shall participate in the Proficiency Analytical Testing Program, the Asbestos Analyst Registry or equivalent.

6.8.4. Each analyst shall select and count prepared slides from a "slide bank". These are quality assurance counts. The slide bank shall be prepared using uniformly distributed samples taken from the workload. Fiber densities should cover the entire range routinely analyzed by the laboratory. These slides are counted blind by all counters to establish an original standard deviation. This historical distribution is compared with the quality assurance counts. A counter must have 95% of all quality control samples counted within three standard deviations of the historical mean. This count is then integrated into a new historical mean and standard deviation for the slide.

The analyses done by the counters to establish the slide bank may be used for an interim quality control program if the data are treated in a proper statistical fashion.

7. Calculations

7.1. Calculate the estimated airborne asbestos fiber concentration on the filter sample using the following formula:

$$AC = \frac{\left[\left(\dfrac{FB}{FL}\right)-\left(\dfrac{BFB}{BFL}\right)\right] \times ECA}{1000 \times FR \times T \times MFA}$$

where:

AC=Airborne fiber concentration

FB=Total number of fibers greater than 5 μm counted

FL=Total number of fields counted on the filter

BFB=Total number of fibers greater than 5 μm counted in the blank

BFL=Total number of fields counted on the blank

ECA=Effective collecting area of filter (385 mm² nominal for a 25-mm filter.)

FR=Pump flow rate (L/min)

MFA=Microscope count field area (mm²). This is 0.00785 mm² for a Walton-Beckett Graticule.

T=Sample collection time (min)

1,000=Conversion of L to cc

NOTE: The collection area of a filter is seldom equal to 385 mm². It is appropriate for laboratories to routinely monitor the exact diameter using an inside micrometer. The collection area is calculated according to the formula:

Area = †(d/2)²

7.2. Short-Cut Calculation

Since a given analyst always has the same interpupillary distance, the number of fields per filter for a particular analyst will remain constant for a given size filter. The field size for that analyst is constant (i.e. the analyst is using an assigned microscope and is not changing the reticle).

For example, if the exposed area of the filter is always 385 mm² and the size of the field is always 0.00785 mm² the number of fields per filter will always be 49,000. In addition it is necessary to convert liters of air to cc. These three constants can then be combined such that ECA/(1,000×MFA)=49. The previous equation simplifies to:

$$AC = \frac{\left(\dfrac{FB}{FL}\right)-\left(\dfrac{BFB}{BFL}\right) \times 49}{FR \times T}$$

7.3. Recount Calculations

As mentioned in step 13 of Section 6.6.2., a "blind recount" of 10% of the slides is performed. In all cases, differences will be observed between the first and second counts of the same filter wedge. Most of these differences will be due to chance alone, that is, due to the random variability (precision) of the count method. Statistical recount criteria enables one to decide whether observed differences can be explained due to chance alone or are probably due to systematic differences between analysts, microscopes, or other biasing factors.

The following recount criterion is for a pair of counts that estimate AC in fibers/cc. The criterion is given at the type-I error level. That is, there is 5% maximum risk that we will reject a pair of counts for the reason that one might be biased, when the large observed difference is really due to chance.

Reject a pair of counts if:

$$\left|\sqrt{AC_2} - \sqrt{AC_1}\right| > 2.78$$

$$\times \left(\sqrt{AC_{AVG}}\right) \times CV_{FB}$$

Where:

AC₁=lower estimated airborne fiber concentration

AC₂=higher estimated airborne fiber concentration

AC_avg=average of the two concentration estimates

CV_FB=CV for the average of the two concentration estimates

If a pair of counts are rejected by this criterion then, recount the rest of the filters in the submitted set. Apply the test and reject any other pairs failing the test. Rejection shall include a memo to the industrial hygienist stating that the sample failed a statistical test for homogeneity and the true air concentration may be significantly different than the reported value.

7.4. Reporting Results

Report results to the industrial hygienist as fibers/cc. Use two significant figures. If multiple analyses are performed on a sample, an average of the results is to be reported unless any of the results can be rejected for cause.

8. References

8.1. Dreesen, W.C., et al., *U.S. Public Health Service: A Study of Asbestosis in the Asbestos Textile Industry* (Public Health Bulletin No. 241), U.S. Treasury Dept., Washington, DC, 1938.

8.2. *Asbestos Research Council: The Measurement of Airborne Asbestos Dust by the Membrane Filter Method* (Technical Note), Asbestos Research Council, Rockdale, Lancashire, Great Britain, 1969.

8.3. Bayer, S.G., Zumwalde, R.D., Brown, T.A., *Equipment and Procedure for Mounting Millipore Filters and Counting Asbestos Fibers by Phase Contrast Microscopy*, Bureau of Occupational Health, U.S. Dept. of Health, Education and Welfare, Cincinnati, OH, 1969.

8.4. *NIOSH Manual of Analytical Methods*, 2nd ed., Vol. 1 (DHEW/NIOSH Pub. No. 77-157-A). National Institute for Occupational Safety and Health, Cincinnati, OH, 1977. pp. 239-1—239-21.

8.5. *Asbestos*, Code of Federal Regulations 29 CFR 1910.1001. 1971.

8.6. *Occupational Exposure to Asbestos, Tremolite, Anthophyllite, and Actinolite. Final Rule*, FEDERAL REGISTER 51:119 (20 June 1986). pp. 22612-22790.

8.7. *Asbestos, Tremolite, Anthophyllite, and Actinolite*, Code of Federal Regulations 1910.1001. 1988. pp. 711-752.

8.8. *Criteria for a Recommended Standard—Occupational Exposure to Asbestos* (DHEW/NIOSH Pub. No. HSM 72-10267), National Institute for Occupational Safety and Health, NIOSH, Cincinnati, OH, 1972. pp. III-1—III-24.

8.9. Leidel, N.A., Bayer, S.G., Zumwalde, R.D., Busch, K.A., *USPHS/NIOSH Membrane Filter Method for Evaluating Airborne Asbestos Fibers* (DHEW/NIOSH Pub. No. 79-127). National Institute for Occupational Safety and Health, Cincinnati, OH, 1979.

8.10. Dixon, W.C., *Applications of Optical Microscopy in Analysis of Asbestos and Quartz*, Analytical Techniques in Occupational Health Chemistry, edited by D.D. Dollberg and A.W. Verstuyft. Wash. DC: American Chemical Society, (ACS Symposium Series 120) 1980. pp. 13-41.

Quality Control

The OSHA asbestos regulations require each laboratory to establish a quality control program. The following is presented as an example of how the OSHA-SLTC constructed its internal CV curve as part of meeting this requirement. Data is from 395 samples collected during OSHA compliance inspections and analyzed from October 1980 through April 1986.

Each sample was counted by 2 to 5 different counters independently of one another. The standard deviation and the CV statistic was calculated for each sample. This data was then plotted on a graph of CV vs. fibers/mm^2. A least squares regression was performed using the following equation:

$$CV = antilog_{10}[A(log_{10}(x))^2 + B(log_{10}(x)) + C]$$

where:

x = the number of fibers/mm^2

Application of least squares gave:

$A = 0.182205$

$B = 0.973343$

$C = 0.327499$

Using these values, the equation becomes:

$$CV = antilog_{10}[0.182205(log_{10}(x))^2 - 0.973343(log_{10}(x)) + 0.327499]$$

Sampling Pump Flow Rate Corrections

This correction is used if a difference greater than 5% in ambient temperature and/or pressure is noted between calibration and sampling sites and the pump does not compensate for the differences.

$$Q_{act} = Q_{cal} \times \sqrt{\left(\frac{P_{cal}}{P_{act}}\right) \times \left(\frac{T_{act}}{T_{cal}}\right)}$$

Where:

Q_{act} = actual flow rate

Q_{cal} = calibrated flow rate (if a rotameter was used, the rotameter value)

P_{cal} = uncorrected air pressure at calibration

P_{act} = uncorrected air pressure at sampling site

T_{act} = temperature at sampling site (K)

T_{cal} = temperature at calibration (K)

Walton-Beckett Graticule

When ordering the Graticule for asbestos counting, specify the exact disc diameter needed to fit the ocular of the microscope and the diameter (mm) of the circular counting area. Instructions for measuring the dimensions necessary are listed:

(1) Insert any available graticule into the focusing eyepiece and focus so that the graticule lines are sharp and clear.

(2) Align the microscope.

(3) Place a stage micrometer on the microscope object stage and focus the microscope on the graduated lines.

(4) Measure the magnified grid length, PL (μm), using the stage micrometer.

(5) Remove the graticule from the microscope and measure its actual grid length, AL (mm). This can be accomplished by using a mechanical stage fitted with verniers, or a jeweler's loupe with a direct reading scale.

(6) Let D=100 μm. Calculate the circle diameter, d_c (mm), for the Walton-Beckett graticule and specify the diameter when making a purchase:

$$d_c = \frac{AL \times D}{PL}$$

Example: If PL=108 μm, AL=2.93 mm and D=100 μm, then,

$$d_c = \frac{2.93 \times 100}{108} = 2.71mm$$

(7) Each eyepiece-objective-reticle combination on the microscope must be cali-
brated. Should any of the three be changed (by zoom adjustment, disassembly, replacement, etc.), the combination must be recalibrated. Calibration may change if interpupillary distance is changed.

Measure the field diameter, D (acceptable range: 100 ±2 μm) with a stage micrometer upon receipt of the graticule from the manufacturer. Determine the field area (mm²).

Field Area = †(D/2)²

If D = 100 μm=0.1 mm, then

Field Area = †(0.1 mm/2)²=0.00785 mm²

The Graticule is available from: Graticules Ltd., Morley Road, Tonbridge TN9 IRN, Kent, England (Telephone 011–44–732–359061). Also available from PTR Optics Ltd., 145 Newton Street, Waltham, MA 02154 [telephone (617) 891–6000] or McCrone Accessories and Components, 2506 S. Michigan Ave., Chicago, IL 60616 [phone (312)-842–7100]. The graticule is custom made for each microscope.

Figure 1: Walton-Beckett Graticule with some explanatory fibers.

COUNTS FOR THE FIBERS IN THE FIGURE

Structure No.	Count	Explanation
1 to 6	1	Single fibers all contained within the Circle.
7	½	Fiber crosses circle once.
8	0	Fiber too short.
9	2	Two crossing fibers.
10	0	Fiber outside graticule.
11	0	Fiber crosses graticule twice.
12	½	Although split, fiber only crosses once.

APPENDIX C TO § 1926.1101 [RESERVED]

APPENDIX D TO § 1926.1101—MEDICAL
QUESTIONNAIRES; MANDATORY

This mandatory appendix contains the medical questionnaires that must be admin-istered to all employees who are exposed to asbestos above the permissible exposure limit, and who will therefore be included in their employer's medical surveillance pro-gram. part 1 of the appendix contains the Initial Medical Questionnaire, which must be obained for all new hires who will be covered by the medical surveillance requirements. part 2 includes the abbreviated Periodical Medical Questionnaire, which must be ad-ministered to all employees who are pro-vided periodic medical examinations under the medical surveillance provisions of the standard.

Part 1
INITIAL MEDICAL QUESTIONNAIRE

1.   NAME _____

2.   SOCIAL SECURITY #   __ __ __ __ __ __ __ __ __
                          1   2   3   4   5   6   7   8   9

3.   CLOCK NUMBER   __ __ __ __ __ __
                                     10 11 12 13 14 15

4.   PRESENT OCCUPATION _____

5.   PLANT _____

6.   ADDRESS _____

7.   _____
                            (Zip Code)

8.   TELEPHONE NUMBER _____

9.   INTERVIEWER _____

10. DATE _____   __ __ __ __ __ __
                                   16 17 18 19 20 21

11. Date of Birth _____   __ __ __ __ __ __
                   Month Day Year   22 23 24 25 26 27

12. Place of Birth _____

13. Sex   1. Male   ___
                                2. Female   ___

14. What is your marital status?   1. Single   ___   4. Separated/
                                    2. Married ___   Divorced ___
                                    3. Widowed ___

15. Race   1. White ___   4. Hispanic ___
                                2. Black ___   5. Indian   ___
                                3. Asian ___   6. Other   ___

16. What is the highest grade completed in school? _____
     (For example 12 years is completion of high school)

OCCUPATIONAL HISTORY

17A. Have you ever worked full time (30 hours   1. Yes __   2. No __
     per week or more) for 6 months or more?

     IF YES TO 17A:

  B. Have you ever worked for a year or more in   1. Yes __   2. No __
     any dusty job?   3. Does Not Apply __

613

Specify job/industry _____ Total Years Worked ___

Was dust exposure: 1. Mild ___   2. Moderate ___   3. Severe ___

C. Have you even been exposed to gas or   1. Yes ___ 2. No ___
chemical fumes in your work?
Specify job/industry _____ Total Years Worked ___

Was exposure: 1. Mild ___   2. Moderate ___   3. Severe ___

D. What has been your usual occupation or job--the one you have
worked at the longest?

1. Job occupation _____

2. Number of years employed in this occupation _____

3. Position/job title _____

4. Business, field or
industry _____

(Record on lines the years in which you have worked in any of these
industries, e.g. 1960-1969)

Have you ever worked:

		YES	NO
E.	In a mine?................................	[__]	[__]
F.	In a quarry?..............................	[__]	[__]
G.	In a foundry?.............................	[__]	[__]
H.	In a pottery?.............................	[__]	[__]
I.	In a cotton, flax or hemp mill?...........	[__]	[__]
J.	With asbestos?............................	[__]	[__]

18. PAST MEDICAL HISTORY

	YES	NO
A. Do you consider yourself to be in good health?	[__]	[__]

If "NO" state reason _____

B. Have you any defect of vision?............... [__]   [__]

If "YES" state nature of defect _____

C. Have you any hearing defect?.................. [__]   [__]

If "YES" state nature of defect _____

D. Are you suffering from or have you ever suffered from:

a. Epilepsy (or fits, seizures, convulsions)? [__] [__]

b. Rheumatic fever? [__] [__]

c. Kidney disease? [__] [__]

d. Bladder disease? [__] [__]

e. Diabetes? [__] [__]

f. Jaundice? [__] [__]

19. CHEST COLDS AND CHEST ILLNESSES

19A. If you get a cold, does it usually go to your   1. Yes __   2. No __
chest? (Usually means more than 1/2 the time)   3. Don't get colds __

20A. During the past 3 years, have you had any chest   1. Yes __   2. No __
illnesses that have kept you off work, indoors at
home, or in bed?

        IF YES TO 20A:
B. Did you produce phlegm with any of these chest   1. Yes __   2. No __
illnesses?   3. Does Not Apply __

C. In the last 3 years, how many such illnesses   Number of illnesses __
with (increased) phlegm did you have which   No such illnesses __
lasted a week or more?

21. Did you have any lung trouble before the age of   1. Yes __   2. No __
16?

22. Have you ever had any of the following?

    1A. Attacks of bronchitis?   1. Yes __   2. No __

        IF YES TO 1A:
    B. Was it confirmed by a doctor?   1. Yes __   2. No __
       3. Does Not Apply __

    C. At what age was your first attack?   Age in Years __
       Does Not Apply __

    2A. Pneumonia (include bronchopneumonia)?   1. Yes __   2. No __

        IF YES TO 2A:
    B. Was it confirmed by a doctor?   1. Yes __   2. No __
       3. Does Not Apply __

    C. At what age did you first have it?   Age in Years __
       Does Not Apply __

615

3A. Hay Fever?   1. Yes __   2. No __

    IF YES TO 3A:
B. Was it confirmed by a doctor?   1. Yes __   2. No __
                                                  3. Does Not Apply __

C. At what age did it start?   Age in Years   __
                                                  Does Not Apply __

23A. Have you ever had chronic bronchitis?   1. Yes __   2. No __

    IF YES TO 23A:
B. Do you still have it?   1. Yes __   2. No __
                                                  3. Does Not Apply __

C. Was it confirmed by a doctor?   1. Yes __   2. No __
                                                  3. Does Not Apply __

D. At what age did it start?   Age in Years   __
                                                  Does Not Apply __

24A. Have you ever had emphysema?   1. Yes __   2. No __

    IF YES TO 24A:
B. Do you still have it?   1. Yes __   2. No __
                                                  3. Does Not Apply __

C. Was it confirmed by a doctor?   1. Yes __   2. No __
                                                  3. Does Not Apply __

D. At what age did it start?   Age in Years   __
                                                  Does Not Apply __

25A. Have you ever had asthma?   1. Yes __   2. No __

    IF YES TO 25A:
B. Do you still have it?   1. Yes __   2. No __
                                                  3. Does Not Apply __

C. Was it confirmed by a doctor?   1. Yes __   2. No __
                                                  3. Does Not Apply __

D. At what age did it start?   Age in Years   __
                                                  Does Not Apply __

E. If you no longer have it, at what age did it   Age stopped   __
   stop?   Does Not Apply __

26. Have you ever had:

A. Any other chest illness?   1. Yes __   2. No __

    If yes, please specify _____

B. Any chest operations?   1. Yes ___   2. No ___

    If yes, please specify _____

C. Any chest injuries?   1. Yes ___   2. No ___

    If yes, please specify _____

27A. Has a doctor ever told you that you had heart   1. Yes ___   2. No ___
     trouble?

     IF YES TO 27A:
   B. Have you ever had treatment for heart trouble   1. Yes ___   2. No ___
      in the past 10 years?   3. Does Not Apply ___

28A. Has a doctor ever told you that you had high   1. Yes ___   2. No ___
     blood pressure?

     IF YES TO 28A:
   B. Have you had any treatment for high blood   1. Yes ___   2. No ___
      pressure (hypertension) in the past 10 years?   3. Does Not Apply ___

29. When did you last have your chest X-rayed?   (Year) ___ ___ ___ ___
                                                        25   26   27   28

30. Where did you last have your chest X-rayed (if known)? _____

    What was the outcome? _____

FAMILY HISTORY

31. Were either of your natural parents ever told by a doctor that they had a
    chronic lung condition such as:

	FATHER			MOTHER		
	1. Yes	2. No	3. Don't Know	1. Yes	2. No	3. Don't Know
A. Chronic Bronchitis?	___	___	___	___	___	___
B. Emphysema?	___	___	___	___	___	___
C. Asthma?	___	___	___	___	___	___
D. Lung cancer?	___	___	___	___	___	___
E. Other chest conditions	___	___	___	___	___	___
F. Is parent currently alive?	___	___	___	___	___	___

G. Please Specify   ___ Age if Living   ___ Age if Living
                          ___ Age at Death   ___ Age at Death
                          ___ Don't Know   ___ Don't Know

H. Please specify cause of death
_____   _____

COUGH

32A. Do you usually have a cough? (Count   1. Yes __   2. No __
     a cough with first smoke or on first
     going out of doors. Exclude clearing
     of throat.) [If no, skip to question
     32C.]

  B. Do you usually cough as much as 4 to   1. Yes __   2. No __
     6 times a day 4 or more days out of
     the week?

  C. Do you usually cough at all on getting   1. Yes __   2. No __
     up or first thing in the morning?

  D. Do you usually cough at all during the   1. Yes __   2. No __
     rest of the day or at night?

IF YES TO ANY OF ABOVE (32A, B, C, or D), ANSWER THE FOLLOWING.   IF NO
TO ALL, CHECK DOES NOT APPLY AND SKIP TO NEXT PAGE

  E. Do you usually cough like this on most   1. Yes __   2. No __
     days for 3 consecutive months or more   3. Does not apply __
     during the year?

  F. For how many years have you had the cough?   Number of years __
                                                   Does not apply __

33A. Do you usually bring up phlegm from your   1. Yes __   2. No __
     chest?
     (Count phlegm with the first smoke or
     on first going out of doors. Exclude
     phlegm from the nose. Count swallowed
     phlegm.) (If no, skip to 33C)

  B. Do you usually bring up phlegm like this   1. Yes __   2. No __
     as much as twice a day 4 or more days
     out of the week?

  C. Do you usually bring up phlegm at all on   1. Yes __   2. No __
     getting up or first thing in the morning?

  D. Do you usually bring up phlegm at all   1. Yes __   2. No __
     during the rest of the day or at night?

IF YES TO ANY OF THE ABOVE (33A, B, C, or D), ANSWER THE FOLLOWING:
IF NO TO ALL, CHECK DOES NOT APPLY AND SKIP TO 34A.

  E. Do you bring up phlegm like this on most   1. Yes __   2. No __
     days for 3 consecutive months or more   3. Does not apply __
     during the year?

F. For how many years have you had trouble
with phlegm?

Number of years __
Does not apply __

EPISODES OF COUGH AND PHLEGM

34A. Have you had periods or episodes of (increased*) cough and phlegm lasting for 3
weeks or more each year?
*(For persons who usually have cough and/or
phlegm)

1. Yes __   2. No __

If YES TO 34A
B. For how long have you had at least 1 such
episode per year?

Number of years __
Does not apply __

WHEEZING

35A. Does your chest ever sound wheezy or
whistling
1.   When you have a cold?
2.   Occasionally apart from colds?
3.   Most days or nights?

1. Yes __   2. No __
1. Yes __   2. No __
1. Yes __   2. No __

IF YES TO 1, 2, or 3 in 35A
B. For how many years has this been present?

Number of years __
Does not apply __

36A. Have you ever had an attack of wheezing
that has made you feel short of breath?

1. Yes __   2. No __

IF YES TO 36A
B. How old were you when you had your first
such attack?

Age in years   __
Does not apply __

C. Have you had 2 or more such episodes?

1. Yes __   2. No __
3. Does not apply __

D. Have you ever required medicine or
treatment for the(se) attack(s)?

1. Yes __   2. No __
3. Does not apply __

BREATHLESSNESS

37. If disabled from walking by any condition
other than heart or lung disease, please
describe and proceed to question 39A.
Nature of condition(s)_____

38A. Are you troubled by shortness of breath when
hurrying on the level or walking up a
slight hill?

1. Yes __   2. No __

IF YES TO 38A

B. Do you have to walk slower than people of   1. Yes ___   2. No ___
your age on the level because of breath-   3. Does not apply ___
lessness?

C. Do you ever have to stop for breath when   1. Yes ___   2. No ___
walking at your own pace on the level?   3. Does not apply ___

D. Do you ever have to stop for breath   1. Yes ___   2. No ___
after walking about 100 yards (or   3. Does not apply ___
after a few minutes) on the level?

E. Are you too breathless to leave the   1. Yes ___   2. No ___
house or breathless on dressing or   3. Does not apply ___
climbing one flight of stairs?

TOBACCO SMOKING

39A. Have you ever smoked cigarettes? (No   1. Yes ___   2. No ___
means less than 20 packs of cigarettes
or 12 oz. of tobacco in a lifetime or less
than 1 cigarette a day for 1 year.)

IF YES TO 39A

B. Do you now smoke cigarettes (as of   1. Yes ___   2. No ___
one month ago)   3. Does not apply ___

C. How old were you when you first started   Age in years ___
regular cigarette smoking?   Does not apply ___

D. If you have stopped smoking cigarettes   Age stopped ___
completely, how old were you when you   Check if still smoking ___
stopped?   Does not apply ___

E. How many cigarettes do you smoke per   Cigarettes per day ___
day now?   Does not apply ___

F. On the average of the entire time you   Cigarettes per day ___
smoked, how many cigarettes did you   Does not apply ___
smoke per day?

G. Do or did you inhale the cigarette smoke?   1. Does not apply ___
                                                      2. Not at all ___
                                                      3. Slightly ___
                                                      4. Moderately ___
                                                      5. Deeply ___

40A. Have you ever smoked a pipe regularly?   1. Yes ___   2. No ___
(Yes means more than 12 oz. of tobacco
in a lifetime.)

IF YES TO 40A:
FOR PERSONS WHO HAVE EVER SMOKED A PIPE

B. 1. How old were you when you started to
smoke a pipe regularly? Age __

2. If you have stopped smoking a pipe
completely, how old were you when you
stopped?

Age stopped __
Check if still
smoking pipe __
Does not apply __

C. On the average over the entire time you
smoked a pipe, how much pipe tobacco did
you smoke per week?

__ oz. per week (a standard
pouch of tobacco contains
1 1/2 oz.)
__ Does not apply

D. How much pipe tobacco are you smoking now?

oz. per week __
Not currently
smoking a pipe __

E. Do you or did you inhale the pipe smoke?

1. Never smoked __
2. Not at all __
3. Slightly __
4. Moderately __
5. Deeply __

41A. Have you ever smoked cigars regularly?
(Yes means more than 1 cigar a week for a
year)

1. Yes __   2. No

IF YES TO 41A
FOR PERSONS WHO HAVE EVER SMOKED CIGARS

B. 1. How old were you when you started
smoking cigars regularly?

Age __

2. If you have stopped smoking cigars
completely, how old were you when
you stopped.

Age stopped __
Check if still
smoking cigars __
Does not apply __

C. On the average over the entire time you
smoked cigars, how many cigars did you
smoke per week?

Cigars per week __
Does not apply __

D. How many cigars are you smoking per week
now?

Cigars per week __
Check if not
smoking cigars
currently __

E. Do or did you inhale the cigar smoke?

1. Never smoked __
2. Not at all __
3. Slightly __
4. Moderately __
5. Deeply __

Signature _____   Date _____

621

Part 2
PERIODIC MEDICAL QUESTIONNAIRE

1.   NAME _____

2.   SOCIAL SECURITY #   __ __ __ __ __   __ __ __   __   __
                          1   2   3   4   5   6   7 8   9

3.   CLOCK NUMBER   __ __   __ __ __   __   __
                              10 11   12 13 14   15

4.   PRESENT OCCUPATION _____

5.   PLANT _____

6.   ADDRESS _____

7.   _____
                          (Zip Code)

8.   TELEPHONE NUMBER _____

9.   INTERVIEWER _____

10. DATE _____   __ __   __ __ __   __   __
                                    16 17   18 19 20   21

11. What is your marital status?   1. Single ___   4. Separated/
                                       2. Married ___   Divorced ___
                                       3. Widowed ___

12. OCCUPATIONAL HISTORY

12A. In the past year, did you work   1. Yes ___   2. No ___
     full time (30 hours per week
     or more) for 6 months or more?

     IF YES TO 12A:

12B. In the past year, did you work   1. Yes ___   2. No ___
     in a dusty job?   3. Does Not Apply ___

12C. Was dust exposure: 1. Mild ___   2. Moderate ___   3. Severe ___

12D. In the past year, were you   1. Yes ___   2. No ___
     exposed to gas or chemical
     fumes in your work?

12E. Was exposure: 1. Mild ___   2. Moderate ___   3. Severe ___

12F. In the past year,
     what was your: 1. Job/occupation? _____
                            2. Position/job title? _____

622

13. <u>RECENT MEDICAL HISTORY</u>

13A. Do you consider yourself to
be in good health?   Yes ___   No ___

If NO, state reason _____

13B. In the past year, have you
developed: <u>Yes</u>   <u>No</u>
                          Epilepsy?   ___   ___
                          Rheumatic fever?   ___   ___
                          Kidney disease?   ___   ___
                          Bladder disease?   ___   ___
                          Diabetes?   ___   ___
                          Jaundice?   ___   ___
                          Cancer?   ___   ___

14. <u>CHEST COLDS AND CHEST ILLNESSES</u>

14A. If you get a cold, does it <u>usually</u> go to your chest?
(Usually means more than 1/2 the time)
                                          1. Yes ___   2. No ___
                                          3. Don't get colds ___

15A. During the past year, have you had
any chest illnesses that have kept you   1. Yes ___   2. No ___
off work, indoors at home, or in bed?   3. Does Not Apply ___

IF YES TO 15A:

15B. Did you produce phlegm with any   1. Yes ___   2. No ___
of these chest illnesses?   3. Does Not Apply ___

15C. In the past year, how many such   Number of illnesses ___
illnesses with (increased) phlegm   No such illnesses ___
did you have which lasted a week
or more?

16. <u>RESPIRATORY SYSTEM</u>

In the past year have you had:

	<u>Yes or No</u>	<u>Further Comment on Positive Answers</u>
Asthma	_____	
Bronchitis	_____	
Hay Fever	_____	
Other Allergies	_____	

	Yes or No	Further Comment on Positive Answers
Pneumonia	_____	
Tuberculosis	_____	
Chest Surgery	_____	
Other Lung Problems	_____	
Heart Disease	_____	

Do you have:

	Yes or No	Further Comment on Positive Answers
Frequent colds	_____	
Chronic cough	_____	
Shortness of breath when walking or climbing one flight or stairs	_____	

Do you:

Wheeze	_____	
Cough up phlegm	_____	
Smoke cigarettes	_____	Packs per day ____ How many years ____

Date _____   Signature _____

APPENDIX E TO § 1926.1101—INTERPRETATION AND CLASSIFICATION OF CHEST ROENTGENO-GRAMS—MANDATORY

(a) Chest roentgenograms shall be interpreted and classified in accordance with a professionally accepted classification system and recorded on an interpretation form following the format of the CDC/NIOSH (M) 2.8 form. As a minimum, the content within the bold lines of this form (items 1 through 4) shall be included. This form is not to be submitted to NIOSH.

(b) Roentgenograms shall be interpreted and classified only by a B-reader, a board eligible/certified radiologist, or an experienced physician with known s.

(c) All interpreters, whenever interpreting chest roentgenograms made under this section, shall have immediately available for reference a complete set of the ILO-U/C International Classification of Radiographs for Pneumoconioses, 1980.

APPENDIX F TO § 1926.1101—WORK PRACTICES AND ENGINEERING CONTROLS FOR CLASS I ASBESTOS OPERATIONS (NON-MANDATORY)

This is a non-mandatory appendix to the asbestos standards for construction and for shipyards. It describes criteria and procedures for erecting and using negative pressure enclosures for Class I Asbestos Work, when NPEs are used as an allowable control method to comply with paragraph (g)(5)(i) of this section. Many small and variable details are involved in the erection of a negative pressure enclosure. OSHA and most participants in the rulemaking agreed that only the major, more performance oriented criteria should be made mandatory. These criteria are set out in paragraph (g) of this section. In addition, this appendix includes these mandatory specifications and procedures in its guidelines in order to make this appendix coherent and helpful. The mandatory nature of the criteria which appear in the regulatory text is not changed because they are included in this "non-mandatory" appendix.

Similarly, the additional criteria and procedures included as guidelines in the appendix, do not become mandatory because mandatory criteria are also included in these comprehensive guidelines.

In addition, none of the criteria, both mandatory and recommended, are meant to specify or imply the need for use of patented or licensed methods or equipment. Recommended specifications included in this attachment should not discourage the use of creative alternatives which can be shown to reliably achieve the objectives of negative-pressure enclosures.

Requirements included in this appendix, cover general provisions to be followed in all asbestos jobs, provisions which must be followed for all Class I asbestos jobs, and provisions governing the construction and testing of negative pressure enclosures. The first category includes the requirement for use of wet methods, HEPA vacuums, and immediate bagging of waste; Class I work must conform to the following provisions:

• oversight by competent person
• use of critical barriers over all openings to work area
• isolation of HVAC systems
• use of impermeable dropcloths and coverage of all objects within regulated areas

In addition, more specific requirements for NPEs include:

• maintenance of −0.02 inches water gauge within enclosure
• manometric measurements
• air movement away from employees performing removal work
• smoke testing or equivalent for detection of leaks and air direction
• deactivation of electrical circuits, if not provided with ground-fault circuit interrupters.

Planning the Project

The standard requires that an exposure assessment be conducted before the asbestos job is begun [§ 1926.1101 (f)(1)]. Information needed for that assessment, includes data relating to prior similar jobs, as applied to the specific variables of the current job. The information needed to conduct the assessment will be useful in planning the project, and in complying with any reporting requirements under this standard, when significant changes are being made to a control system listed in the standard, [see also those of USEPA (40 CFR 61, subpart M). Thus, although the standard does not explicitly require the preparation of a written asbestos removal plan, the usual constituents of such a plan, i.e., a description of the enclosure, the equipment, and the procedures to be used throughout the project, must be determined before the enclosure can be erected. The following information should be included in the planning of the system:

A physical description of the work area;
A description of the approximate amount of material to be removed;
A schedule for turning off and sealing existing ventilation systems;
Personnel hygiene procedures;
A description of personal protective equipment and clothing to be worn by employees;
A description of the local exhaust ventilation systems to be used and how they are to be tested;
A description of work practices to be observed by employees;
An air monitoring plan;
A description of the method to be used to transport waste material; and
The location of the dump site.

Materials and Equipment Necessary for Asbestos Removal

Although individual asbestos removal projects vary in terms of the equipment required to accomplish the removal of the materials, some equipment and materials are common to most asbestos removal operations.

Plastic sheeting used to protect horizontal surfaces, seal HVAC openings or to seal vertical openings and ceilings should have a minimum thickness of 6 mils. Tape or other adhesive used to attach plastic sheeting should be of sufficient adhesive strength to support the weight of the material plus all stresses encountered during the entire duration of the project without becoming detached from the surface.

Other equipment and materials which should be available at the beginning of each project are:

—HEPA Filtered Vacuum is essential for cleaning the work area after the asbestos has been removed. It should have a long hose capable of reaching out-of-the-way places, such as areas above ceiling tiles, behind pipes, etc.

—Portable air ventilation systems installed to provide the negative air pressure and air removal from the enclosure must be equipped with a HEPA filter. The number and capacity of units required to ventilate an enclosure depend on the size of the area to be ventilated. The filters for these systems should be designed in such a manner that they can be replaced when the air flow volume is reduced by the build-up of dust in the filtration material. Pressure monitoring devices with alarms and strip chart recorders attached to each system to indicate the pressure differential and the loss due to dust buildup on the filter are recommended.

—Water sprayers should be used to keep the asbestos material as saturated as possible during removal; the sprayers will provide a fine mist that minimizes the impact of the spray on the material.

—Water used to saturate the asbestos containing material can be amended by adding at least 15 milliliters (¼ ounce) of wetting agent in 1 liter (1 pint) of water. An example of a wetting agent is a 50/50 mixture of polyoxyethylene ether and polyoxyethylene polyglycol ester.

—Backup power supplies are recommended, especially for ventilation systems.

—Shower and bath water should be with mixed hot and cold water faucets. Water that has been used to clean personnel or equipment should either be filtered or be collected and discarded as asbestos waste. Soap and shampoo should be provided to aid in removing dust from the workers' skin and hair.

—See paragraphs (h) and (i) of this section for appropriate respiratory protection and protective clothing.

—See paragraph (k) of this section for required signs and labels.

Preparing the Work Area

Disabling HVAC Systems: The power to the heating, ventilation, and air conditioning systems that service the restricted area must be deactivated and locked off. All ducts, grills, access ports, windows and vents must be sealed off with two layers of plastic to prevent entrainment of contaminated air.

Operating HVAC Systems in the Restricted Area: If components of a HVAC system located in the restricted area are connected to a system that will service another zone during the project, the portion of the duct in the restricted area must be sealed and pressurized. Necessary precautions include caulking the duct joints, covering all cracks and openings with two layers of sheeting, and pressurizing the duct throughout the duration of the project by restricting the return air flow. The power to the fan supplying the positive pressure should be locked "on" to prevent pressure loss.

Sealing Elevators: If an elevator shaft is located in the restricted area, it should be either shut down or isolated by sealing with two layers of plastic sheeting. The sheeting should provide enough slack to accommodate the pressure changes in the shaft without breaking the air-tight seal.

Removing Mobile Objects: All movable objects should be cleaned and removed from the work area before an enclosure is constructed unless moving the objects creates a hazard. Mobile objects will be assumed to be contaminated and should be either cleaned with amended water and a HEPA vacuum and then removed from the area or wrapped and then disposed of as hazardous waste.

Cleaning and Sealing Surfaces: After cleaning with water and a HEPA vacuum, surfaces of stationary objects should be covered with two layers of plastic sheeting. The

sheeting should be secured with duct tape or an equivalent method to provide a tight seal around the object.

Bagging Waste: In addition to the requirement for immediate bagging of waste for disposal, it is further recommended that the waste material be double-bagged and sealed in plastic bags designed for asbestos disposal. The bags should be stored in a waste storage area that can be controlled by the workers conducting the removal. Filters removed from air handling units and rubbish removed from the area are to be bagged and handled as hazardous waste.

Constructing the Enclosure

The enclosure should be constructed to provide an air-tight seal around ducts and openings into existing ventilation systems and around penetrations for electrical conduits, telephone wires, water lines, drain pipes, etc. Enclosures should be both airtight and watertight except for those openings designed to provide entry and/or air flow control.

Size: An enclosure should be the minimum volume to encompass all of the working surfaces yet allow unencumbered movement by the worker(s), provide unrestricted air flow past the worker(s), and ensure walking surfaces can be kept free of tripping hazards.

Shape: The enclosure may be any shape that optimizes the flow of ventilation air past the worker(s).

Structural Integrity: The walls, ceilings and floors must be supported in such a manner that portions of the enclosure will not fall down during normal use.

Openings: It is not necessary that the structure be airtight; openings may be designed to direct air flow. Such openings should be located at a distance from active removal operations. They should be designed to draw air into the enclosure under all anticipated circumstances. In the event that negative pressure is lost, they should be fitted with either HEPA filters to trap dust or automatic trap doors that prevent dust from escaping the enclosure. Openings for exits should be controlled by an airlock or a vestibule.

Barrier Supports: Frames should be constructed to support all unsupported spans of sheeting.

Sheeting: Walls, barriers, ceilings, and floors should be lined with two layers of plastic sheeting having a thickness of at least 6 mil.

Seams: Seams in the sheeting material should be minimized to reduce the possibilities of accidental rips and tears in the adhesive or connections. All seams in the sheeting should overlap, be staggered and not be located at corners or wall-to-floor joints. Areas Within an Enclosure: Each enclosure consists of a work area, a decontamination area, and waste storage area. The work area where the asbestos removal operations occur should be separated from both the waste storage area and the contamination control area by physical curtains, doors, and/or airflow patterns that force any airborne contamination back into the work area.

See paragraph (j) of this section for requirements for hygiene facilities.

During egress from the work area, each worker should step into the equipment room, clean tools and equipment, and remove gross contamination from clothing by wet cleaning and HEPA vacuuming. Before entering the shower area, foot coverings, head coverings, hand coverings, and coveralls are removed and placed in impervious bags for disposal or cleaning. Airline connections from airline respirators with HEPA disconnects and power cables from powered air-purifying respirators (PAPRs) will be disconnected just prior to entering the shower room.

Establishing Negative Pressure Within the Enclosure

Negative Pressure: Air is to be drawn into the enclosure under all anticipated conditions and exhausted through a HEPA filter for 24 hours a day during the entire duration of the project.

Air Flow Tests: Air flow patterns will be checked before removal operations begin, at least once per operating shift and any time there is a question regarding the integrity of the enclosure. The primary test for air flow is to trace air currents with smoke tubes or other visual methods. Flow checks are made at each opening and at each doorway to demonstrate that air is being drawn into the enclosure and at each worker's position to show that air is being drawn away from the breathing zone.

Monitoring Pressure Within the Enclosure: After the initial air flow patterns have been checked, the static pressure must be monitored within the enclosure. Monitoring may be made using manometers, pressure gauges, or combinations of these devices. It is recommended that they be attached to alarms and strip chart recorders at points identified by the design engineer.

Corrective Actions: If the manometers or pressure gauges demonstrate a reduction in pressure differential below the required level, work should cease and the reason for the change investigated and appropriate changes made. The air flow patterns should be retested before work begins again.

Pressure Differential: The design parameters for static pressure differentials between the inside and outside of enclosures typically range from 0.02 to 0.10 inches of water gauge, depending on conditions. All zones inside the enclosure must have less pressure than the ambient pressure outside of the enclosure (−0.02 inches water gauge differential). Design specifications for the differential vary according to the size, con-

figuration, and shape of the enclosure as well as ambient and mechanical air pressure conditions around the enclosure.

Air Flow Patterns: The flow of air past each worker shall be enhanced by positioning the intakes and exhaust ports to remove contaminated air from the worker's breathing zone, by positioning HEPA vacuum cleaners to draw air from the worker's breathing zone, by forcing relatively uncontaminated air past the worker toward an exhaust port, or by using a combination of methods to reduce the worker's exposure.

Air Handling Unit Exhaust: The exhaust plume from air handling units should be located away from adjacent personnel and intakes for HVAC systems.

Air Flow Volume: The air flow volume (cubic meters per minute) exhausted (removed) from the workplace must exceed the amount of makeup air supplied to the enclosure. The rate of air exhausted from the enclosure should be designed to maintain a negative pressure in the enclosure and air movement past each worker. The volume of air flow removed from the enclosure should replace the volume of the container at every 5 to 15 minutes. Air flow volume will need to be relatively high for large enclosures, enclosures with awkward shapes, enclosures with multiple openings, and operations employing several workers in the enclosure.

Air Flow Velocity: At each opening, the air flow velocity must visibly "drag" air into the enclosure. The velocity of air flow within the enclosure must be adequate to remove airborne contamination from each worker's breathing zone without disturbing the asbestos-containing material on surfaces.

Airlocks: Airlocks are mechanisms on doors and curtains that control the air flow patterns in the doorways. If air flow occurs, the patterns through doorways must be such that the air flows toward the inside of the enclosure. Sometimes vestibules, double doors, or double curtains are used to prevent air movement through the doorways. To use a vestibule, a worker enters a chamber by opening the door or curtain and then closing the entry before opening the exit door or curtain.

Airlocks should be located between the equipment room and shower room, between the shower room and the clean room, and between the waste storage area and the outside of the enclosure. The air flow between adjacent rooms must be checked using smoke tubes or other visual tests to ensure the flow patterns draw air toward the work area without producing eddies.

Monitoring for Airborne Concentrations

In addition to the breathing zone samples taken as outlined in paragraph (f) of this section, samples of air should be taken to demonstrate the integrity of the enclosure, the cleanliness of the clean room and shower area, and the effectiveness of the HEPA filter. If the clean room is shown to be contaminated, the room must be relocated to an uncontaminated area.

Samples taken near the exhaust of portable ventilation systems must be done with care.

General Work Practices

Preventing dust dispersion is the primary means of controlling the spread of asbestos within the enclosure. Whenever practical, the point of removal should be isolated, enclosed, covered, or shielded from the workers in the area. Waste asbestos containing materials must be bagged during or immediately after removal; the material must remain saturated until the waste container is sealed.

Waste material with sharp points or corners must be placed in hard air-tight containers rather than bags.

Whenever possible, large components should be sealed in plastic sheeting and removed intact.

Bags or containers of waste will be moved to the waste holding area, washed, and wrapped in a bag with the appropriate labels.

Cleaning the Work Area

Surfaces within the work area should be kept free of visible dust and debris to the extent feasible. Whenever visible dust appears on surfaces, the surfaces within the enclosure must be cleaned by wiping with a wet sponge, brush, or cloth and then vacuumed with a HEPA vacuum.

All surfaces within the enclosure should be cleaned before the exhaust ventilation system is deactivated and the enclosure is disassembled. An approved encapsulant may be sprayed onto areas after the visible dust has been removed.

APPENDIX G TO § 1926.1101 [RESERVED]

APPENDIX H TO § 1926.1101—SUBSTANCE TECHNICAL INFORMATION FOR ASBESTOS. NON-MANDATORY

I. Substance Identification

A. Substance: "Asbestos" is the name of a class of magnesium-silicate minerals that occur in fibrous form. Minerals that are included in this group are chrysotile, crocidolite, amosite, anthophyllite asbestos, tremolite asbestos, and actinolite asbestos.

B. Asbestos is and was used in the manufacture of heat-resistant clothing, automotive brake and clutch linings, and a variety of building materials including floor tiles, roofing felts, ceiling tiles, asbestos-cement pipe and sheet, and fire-resistant drywall. Asbestos is also present in pipe and boiler insulation materials and in sprayed-on materials located on beams, in crawlspaces, and between walls.

C. The potential for an asbestos-containing product to release breathable fibers depends largely on its degree of friability. Friable means that the material can be crumbled with hand pressure and is therefore likely to emit fibers. The fibrous fluffy sprayed-on materials used for fireproofing, insulation, or sound proofing are considered to be friable, and they readily release airborne fibers if disturbed. Materials such as vinyl-asbestos floor tile or roofing felt are considered non-friable if intact and generally do not emit airborne fibers unless subjected to sanding, sawing and other aggressive operations. Asbestos-cement pipe or sheet can emit airborne fibers if the materials are cut or sawed, or if they are broken.

D. Permissible exposure: Exposure to airborne asbestos fibers may not exceed 0.1 fibers per cubic centimeter of air (0.1 f/cc) averaged over the 8-hour workday, and 1 fiber per cubic centimeter of air (1.0 f/cc) averaged over a 30 minute work period.

II. Health Hazard Data

A. Asbestos can cause disabling respiratory disease and various types of cancers if the fibers are inhaled. Inhaling or ingesting fibers from contaminated clothing or skin can also result in these diseases. The symptoms of these diseases generally do not appear for 20 or more years after initial exposure.

B. Exposure to asbestos has been shown to cause lung cancer, mesothelioma, and cancer of the stomach and colon. Mesothelioma is a rare cancer of the thin membrane lining of the chest and abdomen. Symptoms of mesothelioma include shortness of breath, pain in the walls of the chest, and/or abdominal pain.

III. Respirators and Protective Clothing

A. Respirators: You are required to wear a respirator when performing tasks that result in asbestos exposure that exceeds the permissible exposure limit (PEL) of 0.1 f/cc and when performing certain designated operations. Air-purifying respirators equipped with a high-efficiency particulate air (HEPA) filter can be used where airborne asbestos fiber concentrations do not exceed 1.0 f/cc; otherwise, more protective respirators such as air-supplied, positive-pressure, full facepiece respirators must be used. Disposable respirators or dust masks are not permitted to be used for asbestos work. For effective protection, respirators must fit your face and head snugly. Your employer is required to conduct a fit test when you are first assigned a respirator and every 6 months thereafter. Respirators should not be loosened or removed in work situations where their use is required.

B. Protective Clothing: You are required to wear protective clothing in work areas where asbestos fiber concentrations exceed the permissible exposure limit (PEL) of 0.1 f/cc.

IV. Disposal Procedures and Clean-up

A. Wastes that are generated by processes where asbestos is present include:

1. Empty asbestos shipping containers.

2. Process wastes such as cuttings, trimmings, or reject materials.

3. Housekeeping waste from wet-sweeping or HEPA-vacuuming.

4. Asbestos fireproofing or insulating material that is removed from buildings.

5. Asbestos-containing building products removed during building renovation or demolition.

6. Contaminated disposable protective clothing.

B. Empty shipping bags can be flattened under exhaust hoods and packed into airtight containers for disposal. Empty shipping drums are difficult to clean and should be sealed.

C. Vacuum bags or disposable paper filters should not be cleaned, but should be sprayed with a fine water mist and placed into a labeled waste container.

D. Process waste and housekeeping waste should be wetted with water or a mixture of water and surfactant prior to packaging in disposable containers.

E. Asbestos-containing material that is removed from buildings must be disposed of in leak-tight 6-mil plastic bags, plastic-lined cardboard containers, or plastic-lined metal containers. These wastes, which are removed while wet, should be sealed in containers before they dry out to minimize the release of asbestos fibers during handling.

V. Access to Information

A. Each year, your employer is required to inform you of the information contained in this standard and appendices for asbestos. In addition, your employer must instruct you in the proper work practices for handling asbestos-containing materials, and the correct use of protective equipment.

B. Your employer is required to determine whether you are being exposed to asbestos. Your employer must treat exposure to thermal system insulation and sprayed-on and troweled-on surfacing material as asbestos exposure, unless results of laboratory analysis show that the material does not contain asbestos. You or your representative has the right to observe employee measurements and to record the results obtained. Your employer is required to inform you of your exposure, and, if you are exposed above the permissible exposure limit, he or she is required to inform you of the actions that are being taken to reduce your exposure to within the permissible limit.

C. Your employer is required to keep records of your exposures and medical examinations. These exposure records must be kept for at least thirty (30) years. Medical records must be kept for the period of your employment plus thirty (30) years.

D. Your employer is required to release your exposure and medical records to your physician or designated representative upon your written request.

APPENDIX I TO §1926.1101—MEDICAL SURVEILLANCE GUIDELINES FOR ASBESTOS, NONMANDATORY

I. Route of Entry

Inhalation, ingestion.

II. Toxicology

Clinical evidence of the adverse effects associated with exposure to asbestos is present in the form of several well-conducted epidemiological studies of occupationally exposed workers, family contacts of workers, and persons living near asbestos mines. These studies have shown a definite association between exposure to asbestos and an increased incidence of lung cancer, pleural and peritoneal mesothelioma, gastrointestinal cancer, and asbestosis. The latter is a disabling fibrotic lung disease that is caused only by exposure to asbestos. Exposure to asbestos has also been associated with an increased incidence of esophageal, kidney, laryngeal, pharyngeal, and buccal cavity cancers. As with other known chronic occupational diseases, disease associated with asbestos generally appears about 20 years following the first occurrence of exposure: There are no known acute effects associated with exposure to asbestos.

Epidemiological studies indicate that the risk of lung cancer among exposed workers who smoke cigarettes is greatly increased over the risk of lung cancer among non-exposed smokers or exposed nonsmokers. These studies suggest that cessation of smoking will reduce the risk of lung cancer for a person exposed to asbestos but will not reduce it to the same level of risk as that existing for an exposed worker who has never smoked.

III. Signs and Symptoms of Exposure-Related Disease

The signs and symptoms of lung cancer or gastrointestinal cancer induced by exposure to asbestos are not unique, except that a chest X-ray of an exposed patient with lung cancer may show pleural plaques, pleural calcification, or pleural fibrosis. Symptoms characteristic of mesothelioma include shortness of breath, pain in the walls of the chest, or abdominal pain. Mesothelioma has a much longer latency period compared with lung cancer (40 years versus 15–20 years), and mesothelioma is therefore more likely to be found among workers who were first exposed to asbestos at an early age. Mesothelioma is always fatal.

Asbestosis is pulmonary fibrosis caused by the accumulation of asbestos fibers in the lungs. Symptoms include shortness of breath, coughing, fatigue, and vague feelings of sickness. When the fibrosis worsens, shortness of breath occurs even at rest. The diagnosis of asbestosis is based on a history of exposure to asbestos, the presence of characteristics radiologic changes, end-inspiratory crackles (rales), and other clinical features of fibrosing lung disease. Pleural plaques and thickening are observed on X-rays taken during the early stages of the disease. Asbestosis is often a progressive disease even in the absence of continued exposure, although this appears to be a highly individualized characteristic. In severe cases, death may be caused by respiratory or cardiac failure.

IV. Surveillance and Preventive Considerations

As noted above, exposure to asbestos has been linked to an increased risk of lung cancer, mesothelioma, gastrointestinal cancer, and asbestosis among occupationally exposed workers. Adequate screening tests to determine an employee's potential for developing serious chronic diseases, such as a cancer, from exposure to asbestos do not presently exist. However, some tests, particularly chest X-rays and pulmonary function tests, may indicate that an employee has been overexposed to asbestos increasing his or her risk of developing exposure related chronic diseases. It is important for the physician to become familiar with the operating conditions in which occupational exposure to asbestos is likely to occur. This is particularly important in evaluating medical and work histories and in conducting physical examinations. When an active employee has been identified as having been overexposed to asbestos measures taken by the employer to eliminate or mitigate further exposure should also lower the risk of serious long-term consequences.

The employer is required to institute a medical surveillance program for all employees who are or will be exposed to asbestos at or above the permissible exposure limit (0.1 fiber per cubic centimeter of air). All examinations and procedures must be performed by or under the supervision of a licensed physician, at a reasonable time and place, and at no cost to the employee.

Although broad latitude is given to the physician in prescribing specific tests to be included in the medical surveillance program, OSHA requires inclusion of the following elements in the routine examination:

(i) Medical and work histories with special emphasis directed to symptoms of the respiratory system, cardiovascular system, and digestive tract.

(ii) Completion of the respiratory disease questionnaire contained in appendix D.

(iii) A physical examination including a chest roentgenogram and pulmonary function test that includes measurement of the employee's forced vital capacity (FVC) and forced expiratory volume at one second (FEV_1).

(iv) Any laboratory or other test that the examining physician deems by sound medical practice to be necessary.

The employer is required to make the prescribed tests available at least annually to those employees covered; more often than specified if recommended by the examining physician; and upon termination of employment.

The employer is required to provide the physician with the following information: A copy of this standard and appendices; a description of the employee's duties as they relate to asbestos exposure; the employee's representative level of exposure to asbestos; a description of any personal protective and respiratory equipment used; and information from previous medical examinations of the affected employee that is not otherwise available to the physician. Making this information available to the physician will aid in the evaluation of the employee's health in relation to assigned duties and fitness to wear personal protective equipment, if required.

The employer is required to obtain a written opinion from the examining physician containing the results of the medical examination; the physician's opinion as to whether the employee has any detected medical conditions that would place the employee at an increased risk of exposure-related disease; any recommended limitations on the employee or on the use of personal protective equipment; and a statement that the employee has been informed by the physician of the results of the medical examination and of any medical conditions related to asbestos exposure that require further explanation or treatment. This written opinion must not reveal specific findings or diagnoses unrelated to exposure to asbestos, and a copy of the opinion must be provided to the affected employee.

APPENDIX J TO § 1926.1101—SMOKING CESSATION PROGRAM INFORMATION FOR ASBESTOS—NON-MANDATORY

The following organizations provide smoking cessation information.

1. The National Cancer Institute operates a toll-free Cancer Information Service (CIS) with trained personnel to help you. Call 1-800-4-CANCER* to reach the CIS office serving your area, or write: Office of Cancer Communications, National Cancer Institute, National Institutes of Health, Building 31 Room 10A24, Bethesda, Maryland 20892.

2. American Cancer Society, 3340 Peachtree Road, N.E., Atlanta, Georgia 30026, (404) 320–3333

The American Cancer Society (ACS) is a voluntary organization composed of 58 divisions and 3,100 local units. Through "The Great American Smokeout" in November, the annual Cancer Crusade in April, and numerous educational materials, ACS helps people learn about the health hazards of smoking and become successful ex-smokers.

3. American Heart Association, 7320 Greenville Avenue, Dallas, Texas 75231, (214) 750–5300

The American Heart Association (AHA) is a voluntary organization with 130,000 members (physicians, scientists, and laypersons) in 55 state and regional groups. AHA produces a variety of publications and audiovisual materials about the effects of smoking on the heart. AHA also has developed a guidebook for incorporating a weight-control component into smoking cessation programs.

4. American Lung Association, 1740 Broadway, New York, New York 10019, (212) 245–8000

A voluntary organization of 7,500 members (physicians, nurses, and laypersons), the American Lung Association (ALA) conducts numerous public information programs about the health effects of smoking. ALA has 59 state and 85 local units. The organization actively supports legislation and information campaigns for non-smokers' rights and provides help for smokers who want to quit, for example, through "Freedom From Smoking," a self-help smoking cessation program.

5. Office on Smoking and Health, U.S. Department of Health and Human Services, 5600 Fishers Lane, Park Building, Room 110, Rockville, Maryland 20857

The Office on Smoking and Health (OSH) is the Department of Health and Human Services' lead agency in smoking control. OSH has sponsored distribution of publications on smoking-related topics, such as free flyers on relapse after initial quitting, helping a friend or family member quit smoking, the health hazards of smoking, and the effects of parental smoking on teenagers.

*In Hawaii, on Oahu call 524–1234 (call collect from neighboring islands),

Spanish-speaking staff members are available during daytime hours to callers from the following areas: California, Florida, Georgia, Illinois, New Jersey (area code 201), New York, and Texas. Consult your local telephone directory for listings of local chapters.

APPENDIX K TO § 1926.1101—POLARIZED LIGHT MICROSCOPY OF ASBESTOS (NON-MANDATORY)

Method number:

ID–191

Matrix: Bulk

Collection Procedure:

Collect approximately 1 to 2 grams of each type of material and place into separate 20 mL scintillation vials.

Analytical Procedure:

A portion of each separate phase is analyzed by gross examination, phase-polar examination, and central stop dispersion microscopy.

Commercial manufacturers and products mentioned in this method are for descriptive use only and do not constitute endorsements by USDOL-OSHA. Similar products from other sources may be substituted.

1. Introduction

This method describes the collection and analysis of asbestos bulk materials by light microscopy techniques including phase-polar illumination and central-stop dispersion microscopy. Some terms unique to asbestos analysis are defined below:

Amphibole: A family of minerals whose crystals are formed by long, thin units which have two thin ribbons of double chain silicate with a brucite ribbon in between. The shape of each unit is similar to an "I beam". Minerals important in asbestos analysis include cummingtonite-grunerite, crocidolite, tremolite-actinolite and anthophyllite.

Asbestos: A term for naturally occurring fibrous minerals. Asbestos includes chrysotile, cummingtonite-grunerite asbestos (amosite), anthophyllite asbestos, tremolite asbestos, crocidolite, actinolite asbestos and any of these minerals which have been chemically treated or altered. The precise chemical formulation of each species varies with the location from which it was mined. Nominal compositions are listed:

Chrysotile	$Mg_3 Si_2 O_5(OH)_4$
Crocidolite (Riebeckite asbestos)	$Na_2 Fe_3{}^{2+}+Fe_3{}^{3+}+Si_8 O_{22}(OH)_2$
Cummingtonite-Grunerite asbestos (Amosite)	$(Mg,Fe)_7 Si_8 O_{22}(OH)_2$
Tremolite-Actinolite asbestos	$Ca_2(Mg,Fe)_5 Si_8 O_{22}(OH)_2$
Anthophyllite asbestos	$(Mg,Fe)_7 Si_8 O_{22}(OH)_2$

Asbestos Fiber: A fiber of asbestos meeting the criteria for a fiber. (See section 3.5. of this Appendix)

Aspect Ratio: The ratio of the length of a fiber to its diameter usually defined as "length : width", e.g. 3:1.

Brucite: A sheet mineral with the composition $Mg(OH)_2$.

Central Stop Dispersion Staining (microscope): This is a dark field microscope technique that images particles using only light refracted by the particle, excluding light that travels through the particle unrefracted. This is usually accomplished with a McCrone objective or other arrangement which places a circular stop with apparent aperture equal to the objective aperture in the back focal plane of the microscope.

Cleavage Fragments: Mineral particles formed by the comminution of minerals, especially those characterized by relatively parallel sides and moderate aspect ratio.

Differential Counting: The term applied to the practice of excluding certain kinds of fibers from a phase contrast asbestos count because they are not asbestos.

Fiber: A particle longer than or equal to 5 μm with a length to width ratio greater than or equal to 3:1. This may include cleavage fragments. (see section 3.5 of this appendix).

Phase Contrast: Contrast obtained in the microscope by causing light scattered by small particles to destructively interfere with unscattered light, thereby enhancing the visibility of very small particles and particles with very low intrinsic contrast.

Phase Contrast Microscope: A microscope configured with a phase mask pair to create phase contrast. The technique which uses this is called Phase Contrast Microscopy (PCM).

Phase-Polar Analysis: This is the use of polarized light in a phase contrast microscope. It is used to see the same size fibers that are visible in air filter analysis. Although fibers finer than 1 μm are visible, analysis of these is inferred from analysis of larger bundles that are usually present.

Phase-Polar Microscope: The phase-polar microscope is a phase contrast microscope which has an analyzer, a polarizer, a first order red plate and a rotating phase condenser all in place so that the polarized light image is enhanced by phase contrast.

Sealing Encapsulant: This is a product which can be applied, preferably by spraying, onto an asbestos surface which will seal the surface so that fibers cannot be released.

Serpentine: A mineral family consisting of minerals with the general composition $Mg_3(Si_2\,O_5)(OH)_4$ having the magnesium in brucite layer over a silicate layer. Minerals important in asbestos analysis included in this family are chrysotile, lizardite, antigorite.

1.1. History

Light microscopy has been used for well over 100 years for the determination of mineral species. This analysis is carried out using specialized polarizing microscopes as well as bright field microscopes. The identification of minerals is an on-going process with many new minerals described each year. The first recorded use of asbestos was in Finland about 2500 B.C. where the material was used in the mud wattle for the wooden huts the people lived in as well as strengthening for pottery. Adverse health aspects of the mineral were noted nearly 2000 years ago when Pliny the Younger wrote about the poor health of slaves in the asbestos mines. Although known to be injurious for centuries, the first modern references to its toxicity were by the British Labor Inspectorate when it banned asbestos dust from the workplace in 1898. Asbestosis cases were described in the literature after the turn of the century. Cancer was first suspected in the mid 1930's and a causal link to mesothelioma was made in 1965. Because of the public concern for worker and public safety with the use of this material, several different types of analysis were applied to the determination of asbestos content. Light microscopy requires a great deal of experience and craft. Attempts were made to apply less subjective methods to the analysis. X-ray diffraction was partially successful in determining the mineral types but was unable to separate out the fibrous portions from the non-fibrous portions. Also, the minimum detection limit for asbestos analysis by X-ray diffraction (XRD) is about 1%. Differential Thermal Analysis (DTA) was no more successful. These provide useful corroborating information when the presence of asbestos has been shown by microscopy; however, neither can determine the difference between fibrous and non-fibrous minerals when both habits are present. The same is true of Infrared Absorption (IR).

When electron microscopy was applied to asbestos analysis, hundreds of fibers were discovered present too small to be visible in any light microscope. There are two different types of electron microscope used for asbestos analysis: Scanning Electron Microscope (SEM) and Transmission Electron Microscope (TEM). Scanning Electron Microscopy is useful in identifying minerals. The SEM can provide two of the three pieces of information required to identify fibers by electron microscopy: morphology and chemistry. The third is structure as determined by Selected Area Electron Diffraction—SAED which is performed in the TEM. Although the resolution of the SEM is sufficient for very fine fibers to be seen, accuracy of chemical analysis that can be performed on the fibers varies with fiber diameter in fibers of less than 0.2 μm diameter. The TEM is a powerful tool to identify fibers too small to be resolved by light microscopy and should be used in conjunction with this method when necessary. The TEM can provide all three pieces of information required for fiber identification. Most fibers thicker than 1 μm can adequately be defined in the light microscope. The light microscope remains as the best instrument for the determination of mineral type. This is because the minerals under investigation were first described analytically with the light microscope. It is inexpensive and gives positive identification for most samples analyzed. Further, when optical techniques are inadequate, there is ample indication that alternative techniques should be used for complete identification of the sample.

1.2. Principle

Minerals consist of atoms that may be arranged in random order or in a regular arrangement. Amorphous materials have atoms in random order while crystalline materials have long range order. Many materials are transparent to light, at least for small particles or for thin sections. The properties of these materials can be investigated by the effect that the material has on light passing through it. The six asbestos minerals are all crystalline with particular properties that have been identified and cataloged. These six minerals are anisotropic. They have a regular array of atoms, but the arrangement is not the same in all directions. Each major direction of the crystal presents a different regularity. Light photons travelling in each of these main directions will encounter different electrical neighborhoods, affecting the path and time of travel. The techniques outlined in this method use the fact that light traveling through fibers or crystals in different directions will behave differently, but predictably. The behavior of the light as it travels through a crystal can be measured and compared with known or determined values to identify the mineral species. Usually, Polarized Light Microscopy (PLM) is performed with strain-free objectives on a bright-field microscope platform. This would limit the resolution of the microscope to about 0.4 μm. Because OSHA requires the counting and identification of fibers visible in phase contrast, the phase contrast platform is used to visualize the fibers with the polarizing elements added into the light path. Polarized light methods cannot identify fibers finer than about 1 μm in diameter even though they are visible. The finest fibers are usually identified by inference from the presence of larger, identifiable fiber bundles. When fibers are present, but not identifiable by light microscopy, use either SEM or TEM to determine the fiber identity.

1.3. Advantages and Disadvantages

The advantages of light microcopy are:

(a) Basic identification of the materials was first performed by light microscopy and gross analysis. This provides a large base of published information against which to check analysis and analytical technique.

(b) The analysis is specific to fibers. The minerals present can exist in asbestiform, fibrous, prismatic, or massive varieties all at the same time. Therefore, bulk methods of analysis such as X-ray diffraction, IR analysis, DTA, etc. are inappropriate where the material is not known to be fibrous.

(c) The analysis is quick, requires little preparation time, and can be performed on-site if a suitably equipped microscope is available.

The disadvantages are:

(a) Even using phase-polar illumination, not all the fibers present may be seen. This is a problem for very low asbestos concentrations where agglomerations or large bundles of fibers may not be present to allow identification by inference.

(b) The method requires a great degree of sophistication on the part of the microscopist. An analyst is only as useful as his mental catalog of images. Therefore, a microscopist's accuracy is enhanced by experience. The mineralogical training of the analyst is very important. It is the basis on which subjective decisions are made.

(c) The method uses only a tiny amount of material for analysis. This may lead to sampling bias and false results (high or low). This is especially true if the sample is severely inhomogeneous.

(d) Fibers may be bound in a matrix and not distinguishable as fibers so identification cannot be made.

1.4. Method Performance

1.4.1. This method can be used for determination of asbestos content from 0 to 100% asbestos. The detection limit has not been adequately determined, although for selected samples, the limit is very low, depending on the number of particles examined. For mostly homogeneous, finely divided samples, with no difficult fibrous interferences, the detection limit is below 1%. For inhomogeneous samples (most samples), the detection limit remains undefined. NIST has conducted proficiency testing of laboratories on a national scale. Although each round is reported statistically with an average, control limits, etc., the results indicate a difficulty in establishing precision especially in the low concentration range. It is suspected that there is significant bias in the low range especially near 1%. EPA tried to remedy this by requiring a mandatory point counting scheme for samples less than 10%. The point counting procedure is tedious, and may introduce significant biases of its own. It has not been incorporated into this method.

1.4.2. The precision and accuracy of the quantitation tests performed in this method are unknown. Concentrations are easier to determine in commercial products where asbestos was deliberately added because the amount is usually more than a few percent. An analyst's results can be "calibrated" against the known amounts added by the manufacturer. For geological samples, the degree of homogeneity affects the precision.

1.4.3. The performance of the method is analyst dependent. The analyst must choose carefully and not necessarily randomly the portions for analysis to assure that detection of asbestos occurs when it is present. For this reason, the analyst must have adequate training in sample preparation, and experience in the location and identification of asbestos in samples. This is usually accomplished through substantial on-the-job training as well as formal education in mineralogy and microscopy.

1.5. Interferences

Any material which is long, thin, and small enough to be viewed under the microscope can be considered an interference for asbestos. There are literally hundreds of interferences in workplaces. The techniques described in this method are normally sufficient to eliminate the interferences. An analyst's success in eliminating the interferences depends on proper training.

Asbestos minerals belong to two mineral families: the serpentines and the amphiboles. In the serpentine family, the only common fibrous mineral is chrysotile. Occasionally, the mineral antigorite occurs in a fibril habit with morphology similar to the amphiboles. The amphibole minerals consist of a score of different minerals of which only five are regulated by federal standard: amosite, crocidolite, anthophyllite asbestos, tremolite asbestos and actinolite asbestos. These are the only amphibole minerals that have been commercially exploited for their fibrous properties; however, the rest can and do occur occasionally in asbestiform habit.

In addition to the related mineral interferences, other minerals common in building material may present a problem for some microscopists: gypsum, anhydrite, brucite, quartz fibers, talc fibers or ribbons, wollastonite, perlite, attapulgite, etc. Other fibrous materials commonly present in workplaces are: fiberglass, mineral wool, ceramic wool, refractory ceramic fibers, kevlar, nomex, synthetic fibers, graphite or carbon fibers, cellulose (paper or wood) fibers, metal fibers, etc.

Matrix embedding material can sometimes be a negative interference. The analyst may not be able to easily extract the fibers from the matrix in order to use the method. Where possible, remove the matrix before the analysis, taking careful note of the loss of weight. Some common matrix materials are: vinyl, rubber, tar, paint, plant fiber, cement, and epoxy. A further negative interference is that the asbestos fibers themselves may be either too small to be seen in Phase contrast Microscopy (PCM) or of a very low fibrous quality, having the appearance of plant fibers. The analyst's ability to deal with these materials increases with experience.

1.6. Uses and Occupational Exposure

Asbestos is ubiquitous in the environment. More than 40% of the land area of the United States is composed of minerals which may contain asbestos. Fortunately, the actual formation of great amounts of asbestos is relatively rare. Nonetheless, there are locations in which environmental exposure can be severe such as in the Serpentine Hills of California.

There are thousands of uses for asbestos in industry and the home. Asbestos abatement workers are the most current segment of the population to have occupational exposure to great amounts of asbestos. If the material is undisturbed, there is no exposure. Exposure occurs when the asbestos-containing material is abraded or otherwise disturbed during maintenance operations or some other activity. Approximately 95% of the asbestos in place in the United States is chrysotile.

Amosite and crocidolite make up nearly all the difference. Tremolite and anthophyllite make up a very small percentage. Tremolite is found in extremely small amounts in certain chrysotile deposits. Actinolite exposure is probably greatest from environmental sources, but has been identified in vermiculite containing, sprayed-on insulating materials which may have been certified as asbestos-free.

1.7. Physical and Chemical Properties

The nominal chemical compositions for the asbestos minerals were given in Section 1. Compared to cleavage fragments of the same minerals, asbestiform fibers possess a high tensile strength along the fiber axis. They are chemically inert, non-combustible, and heat resistant. Except for chrysotile, they are insoluble in Hydrochloric acid (HCl). Chrysotile is slightly soluble in HCl. Asbestos has high electrical resistance and good sound absorbing characteristics. It can be woven into cables, fabrics or other textiles, or matted into papers, felts, and mats.

1.8. Toxicology (This section is for Information Only and Should Not Be Taken as OSHA Policy)

Possible physiologic results of respiratory exposure to asbestos are mesothelioma of the pleura or peritoneum, interstitial fibrosis, asbestosis, pneumoconiosis, or respiratory cancer. The possible consequences of asbestos exposure are detailed in the NIOSH Criteria Document or in the OSHA Asbestos Standards 29 CFR 1910.1001 and 29 CFR 1926.1101 and 29 CFR 1915.1001.

2. Sampling Procedure

2.1. Equipment for sampling

(a) Tube or cork borer sampling device
(b) Knife
(c) 20 mL scintillation vial or similar vial

(d) Sealing encapsulant

2.2. Safety Precautions

Asbestos is a known carcinogen. Take care when sampling. While in an asbestos-containing atmosphere, a properly selected and fit-tested respirator should be worn. Take samples in a manner to cause the least amount of dust. Follow these general guidelines:

(a) Do not make unnecessary dust.

(b) Take only a small amount (1 to 2 g).

(c) Tightly close the sample container.

(d) Use encapsulant to seal the spot where the sample was taken, if necessary.

2.3. Sampling Procedure

Samples of any suspect material should be taken from an inconspicuous place. Where the material is to remain, seal the sampling wound with an encapsulant to eliminate the potential for exposure from the sample site. Microscopy requires only a few milligrams of material. The amount that will fill a 20 mL scintillation vial is more than adequate. Be sure to collect samples from all layers and phases of material. If possible, make separate samples of each different phase of the material. This will aid in determining the actual hazard. *DO NOT USE ENVELOPES, PLASTIC OR PAPER BAGS OF ANY KIND TO COLLECT SAMPLES.* The use of plastic bags presents a contamination hazard to laboratory personnel and to other samples. When these containers are opened, a bellows effect blows fibers out of the container onto everything, including the person opening the container.

If a cork-borer type sampler is available, push the tube through the material all the way, so that all layers of material are sampled. Some samplers are intended to be disposable. These should be capped and sent to the laboratory. If a non-disposable cork borer is used, empty the contents into a scintillation vial and send to the laboratory. Vigorously and completely clean the cork borer between samples.

2.4 Shipment

Samples packed in glass vials must not touch or they might break in shipment.

(a) Seal the samples with a sample seal over the end to guard against tampering and to identify the sample.

(b) Package the bulk samples in separate packages from the air samples. They may cross-contaminate each other and will invalidate the results of the air samples.

(c) Include identifying paperwork *with* the samples, but not in contact with the suspected asbestos.

(d) To maintain sample accountability, ship the samples by certified mail, overnight express, or hand carry them to the laboratory.

3. Analysis

The analysis of asbestos samples can be divided into two major parts: sample preparation and microscopy. Because of the different asbestos uses that may be encountered by the analyst, each sample may need different preparation steps. The choices are outlined below. There are several different tests that are performed to identify the asbestos species and determine the percentage. They will be explained below.

3.1. Safety

(a) Do not create unnecessary dust. Handle the samples in HEPA-filter equipped hoods. If samples are received in bags, envelopes or other inappropriate container, open them only in a hood having a face velocity at or greater than 100 fpm. Transfer a small amount to a scintillation vial and only handle the smaller amount.

(b) Open samples in a hood, never in the open lab area.

(c) Index of refraction oils can be toxic. Take care not to get this material on the skin. Wash immediately with soap and water if this happens.

(d) Samples that have been heated in the muffle furnace or the drying oven may be hot. Handle them with tongs until they are cool enough to handle.

(e) Some of the solvents used, such as THF (tetrahydrofuran), are toxic and should only be handled in an appropriate fume hood and according to instructions given in the Material Safety Data Sheet (MSDS).

3.2. Equipment

(a) Phase contrast microscope with 10x, 16x and 40x objectives, 10x wide-field eyepieces, G–22 Walton-Beckett graticule, Whipple disk, polarizer, analyzer and first order red or gypsum plate, 100 Watt illuminator, rotating position condenser with oversize phase rings, central stop dispersion objective, Kohler illumination and a rotating mechanical stage.

(b) Stereo microscope with reflected light illumination, transmitted light illumination, polarizer, analyzer and first order red or gypsum plate, and rotating stage.

(c) Negative pressure hood for the stereo microscope

(d) Muffle furnace capable of 600 °C

(e) Drying oven capable of 50–150 °C

(f) Aluminum specimen pans

(g) Tongs for handling samples in the furnace

(h) High dispersion index of refraction oils (Special for dispersion staining.)

n = 1.550
n = 1.585
n = 1.590
n = 1.605
n = 1.620
n = 1.670

n = 1.680
n = 1.690

(i) A set of index of refraction oils from about n=1.350 to n=2.000 in n=0.005 increments. (Standard for Becke line analysis.)

(j) Glass slides with painted or frosted ends 1x3 inches 1mm (thick, precleaned.

(k) Cover Slips 22×22 mm, #1½

(l) Paper clips or dissection needles

(m) Hand grinder

(n) Scalpel with both #10 and #11 blades

(o) 0.1 molar HCl

(p) Decalcifying solution (Baxter Scientific Products) Ethylenediaminetetraacetic Acid,

Tetrasodium ....0.7 g/l
Sodium Potassium Tartrate ....8.0 mg/liter
Hydrochloric Acid ....99.2 g/liter
Sodium Tartrate.............................0.14 g/liter

(q) Tetrahydrofuran (THF)

(r) Hotplate capable of 60 °C

(s) Balance

(t) Hacksaw blade

(u) Ruby mortar and pestle

3.3. Sample Pre-Preparation

Sample preparation begins with pre-preparation which may include chemical reduction of the matrix, heating the sample to dryness or heating in the muffle furnace. The end result is a sample which has been reduced to a powder that is sufficiently fine to fit under the cover slip. Analyze different phases of samples separately, e.g., tile and the tile mastic should be analyzed separately as the mastic may contain asbestos while the tile may not.

(a) *Wet Samples*

Samples with a high water content will not give the proper dispersion colors and must be dried prior to sample mounting. Remove the lid of the scintillation vial, place the bottle in the drying oven and heat at 100 °C to dryness (usually about 2 h). Samples which are not submitted to the lab in glass must be removed and placed in glass vials or aluminum weighing pans before placing them in the drying oven.

(b) *Samples With Organic Interference—Muffle Furnace*

These may include samples with tar as a matrix, vinyl asbestos tile, or any other organic that can be reduced by heating. Remove the sample from the vial and weigh in a balance to determine the weight of the submitted portion. Place the sample in a muffle furnace at 500 °C for 1 to 2 h or until all obvious organic material has been removed. Retrieve, cool and weigh again to determine the weight loss on ignition. This is necessary to determine the asbestos content of the submitted sample, because the analyst will be looking at a reduced sample.

NOTE: Heating above 600 °C will cause the sample to undergo a structural change which, given sufficient time, will convert the chrysotile to forsterite. Heating even at lower temperatures for 1 to 2 h may have a measurable effect on the optical properties of the minerals. If the analyst is unsure of what to expect, a sample of standard asbestos should be heated to the same temperature for the same length of time so that it can be examined for the proper interpretation.

(c) *Samples With Organic Interference—THF*

Vinyl asbestos tile is the most common material treated with this solvent, although, substances containing tar will sometimes yield to this treatment. Select a portion of the material and then grind it up if possible. Weigh the sample and place it in a test tube. Add sufficient THF to dissolve the organic matrix. This is usually about 4 to 5 mL. *Remember, THF is highly flammable.* Filter the remaining material through a tared silver membrane, dry and weigh to determine how much is left after the solvent extraction. Further process the sample to remove carbonate or mount directly.

(d) *Samples With Carbonate Interference*

Carbonate material is often found on fibers and sometimes must be removed in order to perform dispersion microscopy. Weigh out a portion of the material and place it in a test tube. Add a sufficient amount of 0.1 M HCl or decalcifying solution in the tube to react all the carbonate as evidenced by gas formation; i.e., when the gas bubbles stop, add a little more solution. If no more gas forms, the reaction is complete. Filter the material out through a tared silver membrane, dry and weigh to determine the weight lost.

3.4. Sample Preparation

Samples must be prepared so that accurate determination can be made of the asbestos type and amount present. The following steps are carried out in the low-flow hood (a low-flow hood has less than 50 fpm flow):

(1) If the sample has large lumps, is hard, or cannot be made to lie under a cover slip, the grain size must be reduced. Place a small amount between two slides and grind the material between them or grind a small amount in a clean mortar and pestle. The choice of whether to use an alumina, ruby, or diamond mortar depends on the hardness of the material. Impact damage can alter the asbestos mineral if too much mechanical shock occurs. (Freezer mills can completely destroy the observable crystallinity of asbestos and should not be used). For some samples, a portion of material can be shaved off with a scalpel, ground off with a hand grinder or hack saw blade.

The preparation tools should either be disposable or cleaned thoroughly. Use vigorous scrubbing to loosen the fibers during the washing. Rinse the implements with copious amounts of water and air-dry in a dust-free environment.

(2) If the sample is powder or has been reduced as in (1) above, it is ready to mount. Place a glass slide on a piece of optical tissue and write the identification on the painted or frosted end. Place two drops of index of refraction medium n=1.550 on the slide. (The medium n=1.550 is chosen because it is the matching index for chrysotile. Dip the end of a clean paper-clip or dissecting needle into the droplet of refraction medium *on the slide* to moisten it. Then dip the probe into the powder sample. Transfer what sticks on the probe to the slide. The material on the end of the probe should have a diameter of about 3 mm for a good mount. If the material is very fine, less sample may be appropriate. For non-powder samples such as fiber mats, forceps should be used to transfer a small amount of material to the slide. Stir the material in the medium on the slide, spreading it out and making the preparation as uniform as possible. Place a cover-slip on the preparation by gently lowering onto the slide and allowing it to fall "trapdoor" fashion on the preparation to push out any bubbles. Press gently on the cover slip to even out the distribution of particulate on the slide. If there is insufficient mounting oil on the slide, one or two drops may be placed near the edge of the coverslip on the slide. Capillary action will draw the necessary amount of liquid into the preparation. Remove excess oil with the point of a laboratory wiper.

Treat at least two different areas of each phase in this fashion. Choose representative areas of the sample. It may be useful to select particular areas or fibers for analysis.

This is useful to identify asbestos in severely inhomogeneous samples.

When it is determined that amphiboles may be present, repeat the above process using the appropriate high-dispersion oils until an identification is made or all six asbestos minerals have been ruled out. Note that percent determination must be done in the index medium 1.550 because amphiboles tend to disappear in their matching mediums.

3.5. Analytical procedure

NOTE: This method presumes some knowledge of mineralogy and optical petrography.

The analysis consists of three parts: The determination of whether there is asbestos present, what type is present and the determination of how much is present. The general flow of the analysis is:

(1) Gross examination.

(2) Examination under polarized light on the stereo microscope.

(3) Examination by phase-polar illumination on the compound phase microscope.

(4) Determination of species by dispersion stain. Examination by Becke line analysis may also be used; however, this is usually more cumbersome for asbestos determination.

(5) Difficult samples may need to be analyzed by SEM or TEM, or the results from those techniques combined with light microscopy for a definitive identification.

Identification of a particle as asbestos requires that it be asbestiform. Description of particles should follow the suggestion of Campbell. (Figure 1)

637

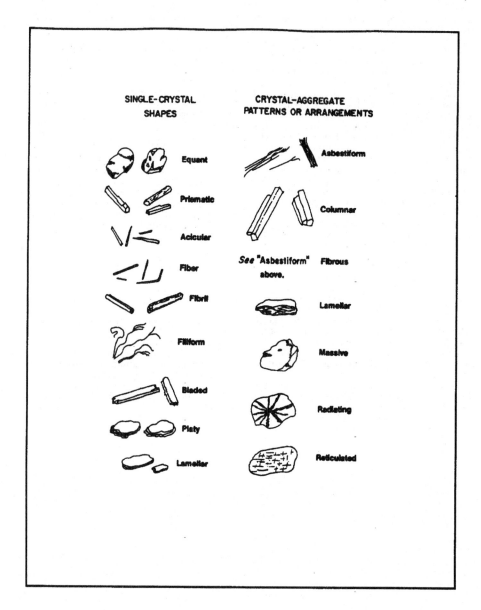

Figure 1.   Particle definitions showing mineral growth habits.
From the U.S. Bureau of Mines

For the purpose of regulation, the mineral must be one of the six minerals covered and must be in the asbestos growth habit. Large specimen samples of asbestos generally have the gross appearance of wood. Fibers are easily parted from it. Asbestos fibers are very long compared with their widths. The fibers have a very high tensile strength as demonstrated by bending without breaking. Asbestos fibers exist in bundles that are easily parted, show longitudinal fine structure and may be tufted at the ends showing "bundle of sticks" morphology. In the microscope some of these properties may not be observable. Amphiboles do not always show striations along their length even when they are asbestos. Neither will they always show tufting. They generally do not show a curved nature except for very long fibers. Asbestos and asbestiform minerals are usually characterized in groups by extremely high aspect ratios (greater than 100:1). While aspect ratio analysis is useful for characterizing populations of fibers, it cannot be used to identify individual fibers of intermediate to short aspect ratio. Observation of many fibers is often necessary to determine whether a sample consists of "cleavage fragments" or of asbestos fibers.

Most cleavage fragments of the asbestos minerals are easily distinguishable from true asbestos fibers. This is because true cleavage fragments usually have larger diameters than 1 µm. Internal structure of particles larger than this usually shows them to have no internal fibrillar structure. In addition, cleavage fragments of the monoclinic amphiboles show inclined extinction under crossed polars with no compensator. Asbestos fibers usually show extinction at zero degrees or ambiguous extinction if any at all. Morphologically, the larger cleavage fragments are obvious by their blunt or stepped ends showing prismatic habit. Also, they tend to be acicular rather than filiform.

Where the particles are less than 1 µm in diameter and have an aspect ratio greater than or equal to 3:1, it is recommended that the sample be analyzed by SEM or TEM if there is any question whether the fibers are cleavage fragments or asbestiform particles.

Care must be taken when analyzing by electron microscopy because the interferences are different from those in light microscopy and may structurally be very similar to asbestos. The classic interference is between anthophyllite and biopyribole or intermediate fiber. Use the same morphological clues for electron microscopy as are used for light microscopy, e.g. fibril splitting, internal longitudinal striation, fraying, curvature, etc.

(1) Gross examination:

Examine the sample, preferably in the glass vial. Determine the presence of any obvious fibrous component. Estimate a percentage based on previous experience and current observation. Determine whether any pre-preparation is necessary. Determine the number of phases present. This step may be carried out or augmented by observation at 6 to 40× under a stereo microscope.

(2) After performing any necessary pre-preparation, prepare slides of each phase as described above. Two preparations of the same phase in the same index medium can be made side-by-side on the same glass for con-

venience. Examine with the polarizing stereo microscope. Estimate the percentage of asbestos based on the amount of birefringent fiber present.

(3) Examine the slides on the phase-polar microscopes at magnifications of 160 and 400×. Note the morphology of the fibers. Long, thin, very straight fibers with little curvature are indicative of fibers from the amphibole family. Curved, wavy fibers are usually indicative of chrysotile. Estimate the percentage of asbestos on the phase-polar microscope under conditions of crossed polars and a gypsum plate. Fibers smaller than 1.0 µm in thickness must be identified by inference to the presence of larger, identifiable fibers and morphology. If no larger fibers are visible, electron microscopy should be performed. At this point, only a tentative identification can be made. Full identification must be made with dispersion microscopy. Details of the tests are included in the appendices.

(4) Once fibers have been determined to be present, they must be identified. Adjust the microscope for dispersion mode and observe the fibers. The microscope has a rotating stage, one polarizing element, and a system for generating dark-field dispersion microscopy (see Section 4.6. of this appendix). Align a fiber with its length parallel to the polarizer and note the color of the Becke lines. Rotate the stage to bring the fiber length perpendicular to the polarizer and note the color. Repeat this process for every fiber or fiber bundle examined. The colors must be consistent with the colors generated for a standard asbestos reference materials for a positive identification. In n=1.550, amphiboles will generally show a yellow to straw-yellow color indicating that the fiber indices of refraction are higher than the liquid. If long, thin fibers are noted and the colors are yellow, prepare further slides as above in the suggested matching liquids listed below:

Type of asbestos	Index of refraction
Chrysotile	n=1.550.
Amosite	n=1.670 or 1.680.
Crocidolite	n=1.690.
Anthophyllite	n=1.605 and 1.620.
Tremolite	n=1.605 and 1.620.
Actinolite	n=1.620.

Where more than one liquid is suggested, the first is preferred; however, in some cases this liquid will not give good dispersion color. Take care to avoid interferences in the other liquid; e.g., wollastonite in n=1.620 will give the same colors as tremolite. In n=1.605 wollastonite will appear yellow in all directions. Wollastonite may be determined under crossed polars as it will change from blue to yellow as it is rotated along its fiber axis by tapping on the cover slip. Asbestos minerals will not change in this way.

639

Determination of the angle of extinction may, when present, aid in the determination of anthophyllite from tremolite. True asbestos fibers usually have 0° extinction or ambiguous extinction, while cleavage fragments have more definite extinction.

Continue analysis until both preparations have been examined and all present species of asbestos are identified. If there are no fibers present, or there is less than 0.1% present, end the analysis with the minimum number of slides (2).

(5) Some fibers have a coating on them which makes dispersion microscopy very difficult or impossible. Becke line analysis or electron microscopy may be performed in those cases. Determine the percentage by light microscopy. TEM analysis tends to overestimate the actual percentage present.

(6) Percentage determination is an estimate of occluded area, tempered by gross observation. Gross observation information is used to make sure that the high magnification microscopy does not greatly over- or under- estimate the amount of fiber present. This part of the analysis requires a great deal of experience. Satisfactory models for asbestos content analysis have not yet been developed, although some models based on metallurgical grain-size determination have found some utility. Estimation is more easily handled in situations where the grain sizes visible at about 160× are about the same and the sample is relatively homogeneous.

View all of the area under the cover slip to make the percentage determination. View the fields while moving the stage, paying attention to the clumps of material. These are not usually the best areas to perform dispersion microscopy because of the interference from other materials. But, they are the areas most likely to represent the accurate percentage in the sample. Small amounts of asbestos require slower scanning and more frequent analysis of individual fields.

Report the area occluded by asbestos as the concentration. This estimate does not generally take into consideration the difference in density of the different species present in the sample. For most samples this is adequate. Simulation studies with similar materials must be carried out to apply microvisual estimation for that purpose and is beyond the scope of this procedure.

(7) Where successive concentrations have been made by chemical or physical means, the amount reported is the percentage of the material in the "as submitted" or original state. The percentage determined by microscopy is multiplied by the fractions remaining after pre-preparation steps to give the percentage in the original sample. For example:

Step 1. 60% remains after heating at 550 °C for 1 h.

Step 2. 30% of the residue of step 1 remains after dissolution of carbonate in 0.1 m HCl.

Step 3. Microvisual estimation determines that 5% of the sample is chrysotile asbestos.

The reported result is:

R = (Microvisual result in percent) × (Fraction remaining after step 2) × (Fraction remaining of original sample after step 1)

R = (5)×(.30)×(.60)=0.9%

(8) Report the percent and type of asbestos present. For samples where asbestos was identified, but is less than 1.0%, report "Asbestos present, less than 1.0%." There must have been at least two observed fibers or fiber bundles in the two preparations to be reported as present. For samples where asbestos was not seen, report as "None Detected."

Auxiliary Information

Because of the subjective nature of asbestos analysis, certain concepts and procedures need to be discussed in more depth. This information will help the analyst understand why some of the procedures are carried out the way they are.

4.1. Light

Light is electromagnetic energy. It travels from its source in packets called quanta. It is instructive to consider light as a plane wave. The light has a direction of travel. Perpendicular to this and mutually perpendicular to each other, are two vector components. One is the magnetic vector and the other is the electric vector. We shall only be concerned with the electric vector. In this description, the interaction of the vector and the mineral will describe all the observable phenomena. From a light source such a microscope illuminator, light travels in all different direction from the filament.

In any given direction away from the filament, the electric vector is perpendicular to the direction of travel of a light ray. While perpendicular, its orientation is random about the travel axis. If the electric vectors from all the light rays were lined up by passing the light through a filter that would only let light rays with electric vectors oriented in one direction pass, the light would then be *POLARIZED*.

Polarized light interacts with matter in the direction of the electric vector. This is the polarization direction. Using this property it is possible to use polarized light to probe different materials and identify them by how they interact with light.

The speed of light in a vacuum is a constant at about 2.99×10^8 m/s. When light travels in different materials such as air, water, minerals or oil, it does not travel at this speed. It travels slower. This slowing is a function of both the material through which the light is traveling and the wavelength or frequency of the light. In general, the more dense the material, the slower the light travels. Also, generally, the higher the frequency, the slower the light will travel. The ratio of the speed of light in a vacuum to that in a material is called the index of refraction (n). It is usually measured at 589 nm (the sodium D line). If white light (light containing all the visible wavelengths) travels through a material, rays of longer wavelengths will travel faster than those of shorter wavelengths, this separation is called dispersion. Dispersion is used as an identifier of materials as described in Section 4.6.

4.2. Material Properties

Materials are either amorphous or crystalline. The difference between these two descriptions depends on the positions of the atoms in them. The atoms in amorphous materials are randomly arranged with no long range order. An example of an amorphous material is glass. The atoms in crystalline materials, on the other hand, are in regular arrays and have long range order. Most of the atoms can be found in highly predictable locations. Examples of crystalline material are salt, gold, and the asbestos minerals.

It is beyond the scope of this method to describe the different types of crystalline materials that can be found, or the full description of the classes into which they can fall. However, some general crystallography is provided below to give a foundation to the procedures described.

With the exception of anthophyllite, all the asbestos minerals belong to the monoclinic crystal type. The unit cell is the basic repeating unit of the crystal and for monoclinic crystals can be described as having three unequal sides, two 90° angles and one angle not equal to 90°. The orthorhombic group, of which anthophyllite is a member has three unequal sides and three 90° angles. The unequal sides are a consequence of the complexity of fitting the different atoms into the unit cell. Although the atoms are in a regular array, that array is not symmetrical in all directions. There is long range order in the three major directions of the crystal. However, the order is different in each of the three directions. This has the effect that the index of refraction is different in each of the three directions. Using polarized light, we can investigate the index of refraction in each of the directions and identify the mineral or material under investigation. The indices α, β, and γ are used to identify the lowest, middle, and highest index of refraction respectively. The x direction, associated with α is called the fast axis. Conversely, the z direction is associated with γ and is the slow direction. Crocidolite has α along the fiber length making it "length-fast". The remainder of the asbestos minerals have the γ axis along the fiber length. They are called "length-slow". This orientation to fiber length is used to aid in the identification of asbestos.

4.3. Polarized Light Technique

Polarized light microscopy as described in this section uses the phase-polar microscope described in Section 3.2. A phase contrast microscope is fitted with two polarizing elements, one below and one above the sample. The polarizers have their polarization directions at right angles to each other. Depending on the tests performed, there may be a compensator between these two polarizing elements. A compensator is a piece of mineral with known properties that "compensates" for some deficiency in the optical train. Light emerging from a polarizing element has its electric vector pointing in the polarization direction of the element. The light will not be subsequently transmitted through a second element set at a right angle to the first element. Unless the light is altered as it passes from one element to the other, there is no transmission of light.

4.4. Angle of Extinction

Crystals which have different crystal regularity in two or three main directions are said to be anisotropic. They have a different index of refraction in each of the main directions. When such a crystal is inserted between the crossed polars, the field of view is no longer dark but shows the crystal in color. The color depends on the properties of the crystal. The light acts as if it travels through the crystal along the optical axes. If a crystal optical axis were lined up along one of the polarizing directions (either the polarizer or the analyzer) the light would appear to travel only in that direction, and it would blink out or go dark. The difference in degrees between the fiber direction and the angle at which it blinks out is called the angle of extinction. When this angle can be measured, it is useful in identifying the mineral. The procedure for measuring the angle of extinction is to first identify the polarization direction in the microscope. A commercial alignment slide can be used to establish the polarization directions or use anthophyllite or another suitable mineral. This mineral has a zero degree angle of extinction and will go dark to extinction as it aligns with the polarization directions. When a fiber of anthophyllite has gone to extinction, align the eyepiece reticle or graticule with the fiber so that there is a visual cue as to the direction of polarization in the field of view. Tape or otherwise secure the eyepiece in this position so it will not shift.

After the polarization direction has been identified in the field of view, move the particle of interest to the center of the field of view and align it with the polarization direction. For fibers, align the fiber along this direction. Note the angular reading of the rotating stage. Looking at the particle, rotate the stage until the fiber goes dark or "blinks out". Again note the reading of the stage. The difference in the first reading and the second is an angle of extinction.

The angle measured may vary as the orientation of the fiber changes about its long axis. Tables of mineralogical data usually report the maximum angle of extinction. Asbestos forming minerals, when they exhibit an angle of extinction, usually do show an angle of extinction close to the reported maximum, or as appropriate depending on the substitution chemistry.

4.5. Crossed Polars with Compensator

When the optical axes of a crystal are not lined up along one of the polarizing directions (either the polarizer or the analyzer) part of the light travels along one axis and part travels along the other visible axis. This is characteristic of birefringent materials.

The color depends on the difference of the two visible indices of refraction and the thickness of the crystal. The maximum difference available is the difference between the α and the γ axes. This maximum difference is usually tabulated as the birefringence of the crystal.

For this test, align the fiber at 45° to the polarization directions in order to maximize the contribution to each of the optical axes. The colors seen are called retardation colors. They arise from the recombination of light which has traveled through the two separate directions of the crystal. One of the rays is retarded behind the other since the light in that direction travels slower. On recombination, some of the colors which make up white light are enhanced by constructive interference and some are suppressed by destructive interference. The result is a color dependent on the difference between the indices and the thickness of the crystal. The proper colors, thicknesses, and retardations are shown on a Michel-Levy chart. The three items, retardation, thickness and birefringence are related by the following relationship:

$R=t(n_\gamma - n_\alpha)$

R=retardation, t=crystal thickness in μm, and

$n_{\alpha,\gamma}$=indices of refraction.

Examination of the equation for asbestos minerals reveals that the visible colors for almost all common asbestos minerals and fiber sizes are shades of gray and black. The eye is relatively poor at discriminating different shades of gray. It is very good at discriminating different colors. In order to compensate for the low retardation, a compensator is added to the light train between the polarization elements. The compensator

used for this test is a gypsum plate of known thickness and birefringence. Such a compensator when oriented at 45° to the polarizer direction, provides a retardation of 530 nm of the 530 nm wavelength color. This enhances the red color and gives the background a characteristic red to red-magenta color. If this "full-wave" compensator is in place when the asbestos preparation is inserted into the light train, the colors seen on the fibers are quite different. Gypsum, like asbestos has a fast axis and a slow axis. When a fiber is aligned with its fast axis in the same direction as the fast axis of the gypsum plate, the ray vibrating in the slow direction is retarded by both the asbestos and the gypsum. This results in a higher retardation than would be present for either of the two minerals. The color seen is a second order blue. When the fiber is rotated 90° using the rotating stage, the slow direction of the fiber is now aligned with the fast direction of the gypsum and the fast direction of the fiber is aligned with the slow direction of the gypsum. Thus, one ray vibrates faster in the fast direction of the gypsum, and slower in the slow direction of the fiber; the other ray will vibrate slower in the slow direction of the gypsum and faster in the fast direction of the fiber. In this case, the effect is subtractive and the color seen is a first order yellow. As long as the fiber thickness does not add appreciably to the color, the same basic colors will be seen for all asbestos types except crocidolite. In crocidolite the colors will be weaker, may be in the opposite directions, and will be altered by the blue absorption color natural to crocidolite. Hundreds of other materials will give the same colors as asbestos, and therefore, this test is not definitive for asbestos. The test is useful in discriminating against fiberglass or other amorphous fibers such as some synthetic fibers. Certain synthetic fibers will show retardation colors different than asbestos; however, there are some forms of polyethylene and aramid which will show morphology and retardation colors similar to asbestos minerals. This test must be supplemented with a positive identification test when birefringent fibers are present which can not be excluded by morphology. This test is relatively ineffective for use on fibers less than 1 μm in diameter. For positive confirmation TEM or SEM should be used if no larger bundles or fibers are visible.

4.6. Dispersion Staining

Dispersion microscopy or dispersion staining is the method of choice for the identification of asbestos in bulk materials. Becke line analysis is used by some laboratories and yields the same results as does dispersion staining for asbestos and can be used in lieu of dispersion staining. Dispersion staining is performed on the same platform as the phase-polar analysis with the analyzer and compensator removed. One polarizing element remains to define the direction of the light so that the different indices of refraction of the fibers may be separately determined. Dispersion microscopy is a dark-field technique when used for asbestos. Particles are imaged with scattered light. Light which is unscattered is blocked from reaching the eye either by the back field image mask in a McCrone objective or a back field image mask in the phase condenser. The most convenient method is to use the rotating phase condenser to move an oversized phase ring into place. The ideal size for this ring is for the central disk to be just larger than the objective entry aperture as viewed in the back focal plane. The larger the disk, the less scattered light reaches the eye. This will have the effect of diminishing the intensity of dispersion color and will shift the actual color seen. The colors seen vary even on microscopes from the same manufacturer. This is due to the different bands of wavelength exclusion by different mask sizes. The mask may either reside in the condenser or in the objective back focal plane. It is imperative that the analyst determine by experimentation with asbestos standards what the appropriate colors should be for each asbestos type. The colors depend also on the temperature of the preparation and the exact chemistry of the asbestos. Therefore, some slight differences from the standards should be allowed. This is not a serious problem for commercial asbestos uses. This technique is used for identification of the indices of refraction for fibers by recognition of color. There is no direct numerical readout of the index of refraction. Correlation of color to actual index of refraction is possible by referral to published conversion tables. This is not necessary for the analysis of asbestos. Recognition of appropriate colors along with the proper morphology are deemed sufficient to identify the commercial asbestos minerals. Other techniques including SEM, TEM, and XRD may be required to provide additional information in order to identify other types of asbestos.

Make a preparation in the suspected matching high dispersion oil, e.g., n=1.550 for chrysotile. Perform the preliminary tests to determine whether the fibers are birefringent or not. Take note of the morphological character. Wavy fibers are indicative of chrysotile while long, straight, thin, frayed fibers are indicative of amphibole asbestos. This can aid in the selection of the appropriate matching oil. The microscope is set up and the polarization direction is noted as in Section 4.4. Align a fiber with the polarization direction. Note the color. This is the color parallel to the polarizer. Then rotate the fiber rotating the stage 90° so that the polarization direction is across the fiber. This is the perpendicular position. Again

note the color. Both colors must be consistent with standard asbestos minerals in the correct direction for a positive identification of asbestos. If only one of the colors is correct while the other is not, the identification is not positive. If the colors in both directions are bluish-white, the analyst has chosen a matching index oil which is higher than the correct matching oil, e.g. the analyst has used n=1.620 where chrysotile is present. The next lower oil (Section 3.5.) should be used to prepare another specimen. If the color in both directions is yellow-white to straw-yellow-white, this indicates that the index of the oil is lower than the index of the fiber, e.g. the preparation is in n=1.550 while anthophyllite is present. Select the next higher oil (Section 3.5.) and prepare another slide. Continue in this fashion until a positive identification of all asbestos species present has been made or all possible asbestos species have been ruled out by negative results in this test. Certain plant fibers can have similar dispersion colors as asbestos. Take care to note and evaluate the morphology of the fibers or remove the plant fibers in pre-preparation. Coating material on the fibers such as carbonate or vinyl may destroy the dispersion color. Usually, there will be some outcropping of fiber which will show the colors sufficient for identification. When this is not the case, treat the sample as described in Section 3.3. and then perform dispersion staining. Some samples will yield to Becke line analysis if they are coated or electron microscopy can be used for identification.

5. References

5.1. Crane, D.T., *Asbestos in Air*, OSHA method ID160, Revised November 1992.

5.2. Ford, W.E., *Dana's Textbook of Mineralogy*; Fourth Ed.; John Wiley and Son, New York, 1950, p. vii.

5.3. Selikoff, I.J., Lee, D.H.K., *Asbestos and Disease*, Academic Press, New York, 1978, pp. 3,20.

5.4. *Women Inspectors of Factories.* Annual Report for 1898, H.M. Statistical Office, London, p. 170 (1898).

5.5. Selikoff,.I.J., Lee, D.H.K., *Asbestos and Disease*, Academic Press, New York, 1978, pp. 26,30.

5.6. Campbell, W.J., et al, *Selected Silicate Minerals and Their Asbestiform Varieties*, United States Department of the Interior, Bureau of Mines, Information Circular 8751, 1977.

5.7. *Asbestos*, Code of Federal Regulations, 29 CFR 1910.1001 and 29 CFR 1926.58.

5.8. *National Emission Standards for Hazardous Air Pollutants; Asbestos NESHAP Revision*, FEDERAL REGISTER, Vol. 55, No. 224, 20 November 1990, p. 48410.

5.9. Ross, M. *The Asbestos Minerals: Definitions, Description, Modes of Formation, Physical and Chemical Properties and Health Risk*

643

to the *Mining Community*, Nation Bureau of Standards Special Publication, Washington, DC, 1977.

5.10. Lilis, R., Fibrous Zeolites and Endemic Mesothelioma in Cappadocia, Turkey, *J. Occ Medicine*, 1981, 23,(8),548–550.

5.11. *Occupational Exposure to Asbestos—1972*, U.S. Department of Health Education and Welfare, Public Health Service, Center for Disease Control, National Institute for Occupational Safety and Health, HSM–72–10267.

5.12. Campbell,W.J., et al, Relationship of Mineral Habit to Size *Characteristics for Tremolite Fragments and Fibers*, United States Department of the Interior, Bureau of Mines, Information Circular 8367, 1979.

5.13. Mefford, D., DCM Laboratory, Denver, private communication, July 1987.

5.14. Deer, W.A., Howie, R.A., Zussman, J., *Rock Forming Minerals*, Longman, Thetford, UK, 1974.

5.15. Kerr, P.F., *Optical Mineralogy*; Third Ed. McGraw-Hill, New York, 1959.

5.16. Veblen, D.R. (Ed.), *Amphiboles and Other Hydrous Pyriboles—Mineralogy, Reviews in Mineralogy*, Vol 9A, Michigan, 1982, pp 1–102.

5.17. Dixon, W.C., *Applications of Optical Microscopy in the Analysis of Asbestos* and Quartz, ACS Symposium Series, No. 120, Analytical Techniques in Occupational Health Chemistry, 1979.

5.18. Polarized Light Microscopy, McCrone Research Institute, Chicago, 1976.

5.19. Asbestos Identification, McCrone Research Institute, G & G printers, Chicago, 1987.

5.20. McCrone, W.C., Calculation of Refractive Indices from Dispersion Staining Data, The Microscope, No 37, Chicago, 1989.

5.21. Levadie, B. (Ed.), *Asbestos and Other Health Related Silicates*, ASTM Technical Publication 834, ASTM, Philadelphia 1982.

5.22. Steel, E. and Wylie, A., Riordan, P.H. (Ed.), Mineralogical Characteristics of Asbestos, *Geology of Asbestos Deposits*, pp. 93–101, SME-AIME, 1981.

5.23. Zussman, J., The Mineralogy of Asbestos, *Asbestos: Properties, Applications and Hazards*, pp. 45–67 Wiley, 1979.

[51 FR 22756, June 20, 1986]

EDITORIAL NOTE: For FEDERAL REGISTER citations affecting § 1926.1101, see the List of CFR Sections Affected, which appears in the Finding Aids section of the printed volume and at *www.fdsys.gov*.

§ 1926.1102 Coal tar pitch volatiles; interpretation of term.

NOTE: The requirements applicable to construction work under this section are identical to those set forth at § 1910.1002 of this chapter.

[61 FR 31433, June 20, 1996]

§ 1926.1103 13 carcinogens (4-Nitrobiphenyl, etc.).

NOTE: The requirements applicable to construction work under this section are identical to those set forth at § 1910.1003 of this chapter.

[61 FR 31433, June 20, 1996]

§ 1926.1104 alpha-Naphthylamine.

NOTE: The requirements applicable to construction work under this section are identical to those set forth at § 1910.1003 of this chapter.

[61 FR 31433, June 20, 1996]

§ 1926.1105 [Reserved]

§ 1926.1106 Methyl chloromethyl ether.

NOTE: The requirements applicable to construction work under this section are identical to those set forth at § 1910.1003 of this chapter.

[61 FR 31433, June 20, 1996]

§ 1926.1107 3,3'-Dichlorobenzidiene (and its salts).

NOTE: The requirements applicable to construction work under this section are identical to those set forth at § 1910.1003 of this chapter.

[61 FR 31433, June 20, 1996]

§ 1926.1108 bis-Chloromethyl ether.

NOTE: The requirements applicable to construction work under this section are identical to those set forth at § 1910.1003 of this chapter.

[61 FR 31433, June 20, 1996]

§ 1926.1109 beta-Naphthylamine.

NOTE: The requirements applicable to construction work under this section are identical to those set forth at § 1910.1003 of this chapter.

[61 FR 31433, June 20, 1996]

§ 1926.1110 Benzidine.

NOTE: The requirements applicable to construction work under this section are identical to those set forth at § 1910.1003 of this chapter.

[61 FR 31433, June 20, 1996]

§ 1926.1111 4-Aminodiphenyl.

NOTE: The requirements applicable to construction work under this section are identical to those set forth at § 1910.1003 of this chapter.

[61 FR 31433, June 20, 1996]

§ 1926.1112 Ethyleneimine.

NOTE: The requirements applicable to construction work under this section are identical to those set forth at § 1910.1003 of this chapter.

[61 FR 31433, June 20, 1996]

§ 1926.1113 beta-Propiolactone.

NOTE: The requirements applicable to construction work under this section are identical to those set forth at § 1910.1003 of this chapter.

[61 FR 31433, June 20, 1996]

§ 1926.1114 2-Acetylaminofluorene.

NOTE: The requirements applicable to construction work under this section are identical to those set forth at § 1910.1003 of this chapter.

[61 FR 31433, June 20, 1996]

§ 1926.1115 4-Dimethylaminoazobenzene.

NOTE: The requirements applicable to construction work under this section are identical to those set forth at § 1910.1003 of this chapter.

[61 FR 31433, June 20, 1996]

§ 1926.1116 N-Nitrosodimethylamine.

NOTE: The requirements applicable to construction work under this section are identical to those set forth at § 1910.1003 of this chapter.

[61 FR 31433, June 20, 1996]

§ 1926.1117 Vinyl chloride.

NOTE: The requirements applicable to construction work under this section are identical to those set forth at § 1910.1017 of this chapter.

[61 FR 31433, June 20, 1996]

§ 1926.1118 Inorganic arsenic.

NOTE: The requirements applicable to construction work under this section are identical to those set forth at § 1910.1018 of this chapter.

[61 FR 31433, June 20, 1996]

§ 1926.1126 Chromium (VI).

(a) *Scope.* (1) This standard applies to occupational exposures to chromium (VI) in all forms and compounds in construction, except:

(2) Exposures that occur in the application of pesticides regulated by the Environmental Protection Agency or another Federal government agency (*e.g.*, the treatment of wood with preservatives);

(3) Exposures to portland cement; or

(4) Where the employer has objective data demonstrating that a material containing chromium or a specific process, operation, or activity involving chromium cannot release dusts, fumes, or mists of chromium (VI) in concentrations at or above 0.5 µgm/m³ as an 8-hour time-weighted average (TWA) under any expected conditions of use.

(b) *Definitions.* For the purposes of this section the following definitions apply:

Action level means a concentration of airborne chromium (VI) of 2.5 micrograms per cubic meter of air (2.5 µgm/m³) calculated as an 8-hour time-weighted average (TWA).

Assistant Secretary means the Assistant Secretary of Labor for Occupational Safety and Health, U.S. Department of Labor, or designee.

Chromium (VI) [hexavalent chromium or Cr(VI)] means chromium with a valence of positive six, in any form and in any compound.

Director means the Director of the National Institute for Occupational Safety and Health (NIOSH), U.S. Department of Health and Human Services, or designee.

Emergency means any occurrence that results, or is likely to result, in an uncontrolled release of chromium (VI). If an incidental release of chromium (VI) can be controlled at the time of release by employees in the immediate release area, or by maintenance personnel, it is not an emergency.

Employee exposure means the exposure to airborne chromium (VI) that would occur if the employee were not using a respirator.

High-efficiency particulate air [HEPA] filter means a filter that is at least 99.97 percent efficient in removing mono-dispersed particles of 0.3 micrometers in diameter or larger.

Historical monitoring data means data from chromium (VI) monitoring conducted prior to May 30, 2006, obtained during work operations conducted under workplace conditions closely resembling the processes, types of material, control methods, work practices, and environmental conditions in the employer's current operations.

Objective data means information such as air monitoring data from industry-wide surveys or calculations based on the composition or chemical and physical properties of a substance demonstrating the employee exposure to chromium (VI) associated with a particular product or material or a specific process, operation, or activity. The data must reflect workplace conditions closely resembling the processes, types of material, control methods, work practices, and environmental conditions in the employer's current operations.

Physician or other licensed health care professional [PLHCP] is an individual whose legally permitted scope of practice (*i.e.*, license, registration, or certification) allows him or her to independently provide or be delegated the responsibility to provide some or all of the particular health care services required by paragraph (i) of this section.

This section means this § 1926.1126 chromium (VI) standard.

(c) *Permissible exposure limit (PEL)*. The employer shall ensure that no employee is exposed to an airborne concentration of chromium (VI) in excess of 5 micrograms per cubic meter of air (5 μgm/m^3), calculated as an 8-hour time-weighted average (TWA).

(d) *Exposure determination*—(1) *General*. Each employer who has a workplace or work operation covered by this section shall determine the 8-hour TWA exposure for each employee exposed to chromium (VI). This determination shall be made in accordance with either paragraph (d)(2) or paragraph (d)(3) of this section.

(2) *Scheduled monitoring option*. (i) The employer shall perform initial monitoring to determine the 8-hour TWA exposure for each employee on the basis of a sufficient number of personal breathing zone air samples to accurately characterize full shift exposure on each shift, for each job classification, in each work area. Where an employer does representative sampling instead of sampling all employees in order to meet this requirement, the employer shall sample the employee(s) expected to have the highest chromium (VI) exposures.

(ii) If initial monitoring indicates that employee exposures are below the action level, the employer may discontinue monitoring for those employees whose exposures are represented by such monitoring.

(iii) If monitoring reveals employee exposures to be at or above the action level, the employer shall perform periodic monitoring at least every six months.

(iv) If monitoring reveals employee exposures to be above the PEL, the employer shall perform periodic monitoring at least every three months.

(v) If periodic monitoring indicates that employee exposures are below the action level, and the result is confirmed by the result of another monitoring taken at least seven days later, the employer may discontinue the monitoring for those employees whose exposures are represented by such monitoring.

(vi) The employer shall perform additional monitoring when there has been any change in the production process, raw materials, equipment, personnel, work practices, or control methods that may result in new or additional exposures to chromium (VI), or when the employer has any reason to believe that new or additional exposures have occurred.

(3) *Performance-oriented option*. The employer shall determine the 8-hour TWA exposure for each employee on the basis of any combination of air monitoring data, historical monitoring data, or objective data sufficient to accurately characterize employee exposure to chromium (VI).

(4) *Employee notification of determination results*. (i) Within 5 work days after making an exposure determination in accordance with paragraph (d)(2) or paragraph (d)(3) of this section, the employer shall individually notify each affected employee in writing of the results of that determination or post the results in an appropriate location accessible to all affected employees.

(ii) Whenever the exposure determination indicates that employee exposure is above the PEL, the employer shall describe in the written notification the corrective action being taken to reduce employee exposure to or below the PEL.

(5) *Accuracy of measurement.* Where air monitoring is performed to comply with the requirements of this section, the employer shall use a method of monitoring and analysis that can measure chromium (VI) to within an accuracy of plus or minus 25 percent (±25%) and can produce accurate measurements to within a statistical confidence level of 95 percent for airborne concentrations at or above the action level.

(6) *Observation of monitoring.* (i) Where air monitoring is performed to comply with the requirements of this section, the employer shall provide affected employees or their designated representatives an opportunity to observe any monitoring of employee exposure to chromium (VI).

(ii) When observation of monitoring requires entry into an area where the use of protective clothing or equipment is required, the employer shall provide the observer with clothing and equipment and shall assure that the observer uses such clothing and equipment and complies with all other applicable safety and health procedures.

(e) *Methods of compliance—*(1) *Engineering and work practice controls.* (i) Except as permitted in paragraph (e)(1)(ii) of this section, the employer shall use engineering and work practice controls to reduce and maintain employee exposure to chromium (VI) to or below the PEL unless the employer can demonstrate that such controls are not feasible. Wherever feasible engineering and work practice controls are not sufficient to reduce employee exposure to or below the PEL, the employer shall use them to reduce employee exposure to the lowest levels achievable, and shall supplement them by the use of respiratory protection that complies with the requirements of paragraph (f) of this section.

(ii) Where the employer can demonstrate that a process or task does not result in any employee exposure to chromium (VI) above the PEL for 30 or more days per year (12 consecutive months), the requirement to implement engineering and work practice controls to achieve the PEL does not apply to that process or task.

(2) *Prohibition of rotation.* The employer shall not rotate employees to different jobs to achieve compliance with the PEL.

(f) *Respiratory protection—*(1) *General.* Where respiratory protection is required by this section, the employer must provide each employee an appropriate respirator that complies with the requirements of this paragraph. Respiratory protection is required during:

(i) Periods necessary to install or implement feasible engineering and work practice controls;

(ii) Work operations, such as maintenance and repair activities, for which engineering and work practice controls are not feasible;

(iii) Work operations for which an employer has implemented all feasible engineering and work practice controls and such controls are not sufficient to reduce exposures to or below the PEL;

(iv) Work operations where employees are exposed above the PEL for fewer than 30 days per year, and the employer has elected not to implement engineering and work practice controls to achieve the PEL; or

(v) Emergencies.

(2) *Respiratory protection program.* Where respirator use is required by this section, the employer shall institute a respiratory protection program in accordance with § 1910.134, which covers each employee required to use a respirator.

(g) *Protective work clothing and equipment—*(1) *Provision and use.* Where a hazard is present or is likely to be present from skin or eye contact with chromium (VI), the employer shall provide appropriate personal protective clothing and equipment at no cost to employees, and shall ensure that employees use such clothing and equipment.

(2) *Removal and storage.* (i) The employer shall ensure that employees remove all protective clothing and equipment contaminated with chromium (VI) at the end of the work shift or at the completion of their tasks involving chromium (VI) exposure, whichever comes first.

(ii) The employer shall ensure that no employee removes chromium (VI)-contaminated protective clothing or equipment from the workplace, except for those employees whose job it is to launder, clean, maintain, or dispose of such clothing or equipment.

(iii) When contaminated protective clothing or equipment is removed for laundering, cleaning, maintenance, or disposal, the employer shall ensure that it is stored and transported in sealed, impermeable bags or other closed, impermeable containers.

(iv) The employer shall ensure that bags or containers of contaminated protective clothing or equipment that are removed from change rooms for laundering, cleaning, maintenance, or disposal shall be labeled in accordance with the requirements of the Hazard Communication Standard, § 1910.1200.

(3) *Cleaning and replacement.* (i) The employer shall clean, launder, repair and replace all protective clothing and equipment required by this section as needed to maintain its effectiveness.

(ii) The employer shall prohibit the removal of chromium (VI) from protective clothing and equipment by blowing, shaking, or any other means that disperses chromium (VI) into the air or onto an employee's body.

(iii) The employer shall inform any person who launders or cleans protective clothing or equipment contaminated with chromium (VI) of the potentially harmful effects of exposure to chromium (VI) and that the clothing and equipment should be laundered or cleaned in a manner that minimizes skin or eye contact with chromium (VI) and effectively prevents the release of airborne chromium (VI) in excess of the PEL.

(h) *Hygiene areas and practices*—(1) *General.* Where protective clothing and equipment is required, the employer shall provide change rooms in conformance with 29 CFR 1926.51 Where skin contact with chromium (VI) occurs, the employer shall provide washing facilities in conformance with 29 CFR 1926.51. Eating and drinking areas provided by the employer shall also be in conformance with § 1926.51.

(2) *Change rooms.* The employer shall assure that change rooms are equipped with separate storage facilities for protective clothing and equipment and for street clothes, and that these facilities prevent cross-contamination.

(3) *Washing facilities.* (i) The employer shall provide readily accessible washing facilities capable of removing chromium (VI) from the skin, and shall ensure that affected employees use these facilities when necessary.

(ii) The employer shall ensure that employees who have skin contact with chromium (VI) wash their hands and faces at the end of the work shift and prior to eating, drinking, smoking, chewing tobacco or gum, applying cosmetics, or using the toilet.

(4) *Eating and drinking areas.* (i) Whenever the employer allows employees to consume food or beverages at a worksite where chromium (VI) is present, the employer shall ensure that eating and drinking areas and surfaces are maintained as free as practicable of chromium (VI).

(ii) The employer shall ensure that employees do not enter eating and drinking areas with protective work clothing or equipment unless surface chromium (VI) has been removed from the clothing and equipment by methods that do not disperse chromium (VI) into the air or onto an employee's body.

(5) *Prohibited activities.* The employer shall ensure that employees do not eat, drink, smoke, chew tobacco or gum, or apply cosmetics in areas where skin or eye contact with chromium (VI) occurs; or carry the products associated with these activities, or store such products in these areas.

(i) *Medical surveillance*—(1) *General.* (i) The employer shall make medical surveillance available at no cost to the employee, and at a reasonable time and place, for all employees:

(A) Who are or may be occupationally exposed to chromium (VI) at or above the action level for 30 or more days a year;

(B) Experiencing signs or symptoms of the adverse health effects associated with chromium (VI) exposure; or

(C) Exposed in an emergency.

(ii) The employer shall assure that all medical examinations and procedures required by this section are performed by or under the supervision of a PLHCP.

(2) *Frequency.* The employer shall provide a medical examination:

(i) Within 30 days after initial assignment, unless the employee has received a chromium (VI) related medical examination that meets the requirements of this paragraph within the last twelve months;

(ii) Annually;

(iii) Within 30 days after a PLHCP's written medical opinion recommends an additional examination;

(iv) Whenever an employee shows signs or symptoms of the adverse health effects associated with chromium (VI) exposure;

(v) Within 30 days after exposure during an emergency which results in an uncontrolled release of chromium (VI); or

(vi) At the termination of employment, unless the last examination that satisfied the requirements of paragraph (i) of this section was less than six months prior to the date of termination.

(3) *Contents of examination.* A medical examination consists of:

(i) A medical and work history, with emphasis on: past, present, and anticipated future exposure to chromium (VI); any history of respiratory system dysfunction; any history of asthma, dermatitis, skin ulceration, or nasal septum perforation; and smoking status and history;

(ii) A physical examination of the skin and respiratory tract; and

(iii) Any additional tests deemed appropriate by the examining PLHCP.

(4) *Information provided to the PLHCP.* The employer shall ensure that the examining PLHCP has a copy of this standard, and shall provide the following information:

(i) A description of the affected employee's former, current, and anticipated duties as they relate to the employee's occupational exposure to chromium (VI);

(ii) The employee's former, current, and anticipated levels of occupational exposure to chromium (VI);

(iii) A description of any personal protective equipment used or to be used by the employee, including when and for how long the employee has used that equipment; and

(iv) Information from records of employment-related medical examinations previously provided to the affected employee, currently within the control of the employer.

(5) *PLHCP's written medical opinion.* (i) The employer shall obtain a written medical opinion from the PLHCP, within 30 days for each medical examination performed on each employee, which contains:

(A) The PLHCP's opinion as to whether the employee has any detected medical condition(s) that would place the employee at increased risk of material impairment to health from further exposure to chromium (VI);

(B) Any recommended limitations upon the employee's exposure to chromium (VI) or upon the use of personal protective equipment such as respirators;

(C) A statement that the PLHCP has explained to the employee the results of the medical examination, including any medical conditions related to chromium (VI) exposure that require further evaluation or treatment, and any special provisions for use of protective clothing or equipment.

(ii) The PLHCP shall not reveal to the employer specific findings or diagnoses unrelated to occupational exposure to chromium (VI).

(iii) The employer shall provide a copy of the PLHCP's written medical opinion to the examined employee within two weeks after receiving it.

(j) *Communication of chromium (VI) hazards to employees*—(1) *Hazard communication.* The employer shall include chromium (VI) in the program established to comply with the Hazard Communication Standard (HCS) (§ 1910.1200). The employer shall ensure that each employee has access to labels on containers of chromium and safety data sheets, and is trained in accordance with the provisions of § 1910.1200 and paragraph (j)(2) of this section. The employer shall provide information on at least the following hazards: Cancer; eye irritation; and skin sensitization.

(2) *Employee information and training.* (i) The employer shall ensure that each employee can demonstrate knowledge of at least the following:

(A) The contents of this section; and

(B) The purpose and a description of the medical surveillance program required by paragraph (i) of this section.

(ii) The employer shall make a copy of this section readily available without cost to all affected employees.

(k) *Recordkeeping*—(1) *Air monitoring data.* (i) The employer shall maintain an accurate record of all air monitoring conducted to comply with the requirements of this section.

(ii) This record shall include at least the following information:

(A) The date of measurement for each sample taken;

(B) The operation involving exposure to chromium (VI) that is being monitored;

(C) Sampling and analytical methods used and evidence of their accuracy;

(D) Number, duration, and the results of samples taken;

(E) Type of personal protective equipment, such as respirators worn; and

(F) Name, social security number, and job classification of all employees represented by the monitoring, indicating which employees were actually monitored.

(iii) The employer shall ensure that exposure records are maintained and made available in accordance with 29 CFR 1910.1020.

(2) *Historical monitoring data.* (i) Where the employer has relied on historical monitoring data to determine exposure to chromium (VI), the employer shall establish and maintain an accurate record of the historical monitoring data relied upon.

(ii) The record shall include information that reflects the following conditions:

(A) The data were collected using methods that meet the accuracy requirements of paragraph (d)(5) of this section;

(B) The processes and work practices that were in use when the historical monitoring data were obtained are essentially the same as those to be used during the job for which exposure is being determined;

(C) The characteristics of the chromium (VI) containing material being handled when the historical monitoring data were obtained are the same as those on the job for which exposure is being determined;

(D) Environmental conditions prevailing when the historical monitoring data were obtained are the same as those on the job for which exposure is being determined; and

(E) Other data relevant to the operations, materials, processing, or employee exposures covered by the exception.

(iii) The employer shall ensure that historical exposure records are maintained and made available in accordance with 29 CFR 1910.1020.

(3) *Objective data.* (i) The employer shall maintain an accurate record of all objective data relied upon to comply with the requirements of this section.

(ii) This record shall include at least the following information:

(A) The chromium containing material in question;

(B) The source of the objective data;

(C) The testing protocol and results of testing, or analysis of the material for the release of chromium (VI);

(D) A description of the process, operation, or activity and how the data support the determination; and

(E) Other data relevant to the process, operation, activity, material, or employee exposures.

(iii) The employer shall ensure that objective data are maintained and made available in accordance with 29 CFR 1910.1020.

(4) *Medical surveillance.* (i) The employer shall establish and maintain an accurate record for each employee covered by medical surveillance under paragraph (i) of this section.

(ii) The record shall include the following information about the employee:

(A) Name and social security number;

(B) A copy of the PLHCP's written opinions;

(C) A copy of the information provided to the PLHCP as required by paragraph (i)(4) of this section.

(iii) The employer shall ensure that medical records are maintained and made available in accordance with 29 CFR 1910.1020.

(l) *Dates.* (1) For employers with 20 or more employees, all obligations of this section, except engineering controls required by paragraph (e) of this section, commence November 27, 2006.

(2) For employers with 19 or fewer employees, all obligations of this section, except engineering controls required by paragraph (e) of this section, commence May 30, 2007.

(3) For all employers, engineering controls required by paragraph (e) of this section shall be implemented no later than May 31, 2010.

[71 FR 10382, Feb. 28, 2006, as amended at 73 FR 75589, Dec. 12, 2008; 75 FR 12686, Mar. 17, 2010; 77 FR 17895, Mar. 26, 2012]

§1926.1127 Cadmium.

(a) *Scope.* This standard applies to all occupational exposures to cadmium and cadmium compounds, in all forms, in all construction work where an employee may potentially be exposed to cadmium. Construction work is defined as work involving construction, alteration and/or repair, including but not limited to the following:

(1) Wrecking, demolition or salvage of structures where cadmium or materials containing cadmium are present;

(2) Use of cadmium containing-paints and cutting, brazing, burning, grinding or welding on surfaces that were painted with cadmium-containing paints;

(3) Construction, alteration, repair, maintenance, or renovation of structures, substrates, or portions thereof, that contain cadmium, or materials containing cadmium;

(4) Cadmium welding; cutting and welding cadmium-plated steel; brazing or welding with cadmium alloys;

(5) Installation of products containing cadmium;

(6) Electrical grounding with cadmium welding, or electrical work using cadmium-coated conduit;

(7) Maintaining or retrofitting cadmium-coated equipment;

(8) Cadmium contamination/emergency cleanup; and

(9) Transportation, disposal, storage, or containment of cadmium or materials containing cadmium on the site or location at which construction activities are performed.

(b) *Definitions.*

Action level (AL) is defined as an airborne concentration of cadmium of 2.5 micrograms per cubic meter of air (2.5 µg/m³), calculated as an 8-hour time-weighted average (TWA).

Assistant Secretary means the Assistant Secretary of Labor for Occupational Safety and Health, U.S. Department of Labor, or designee.

Authorized person means any person authorized by the employer and required by work duties to be present in regulated areas or any person authorized by the OSH Act or regulations issued under it to be in regulated areas.

Competent person, in accordance with 29 CFR 1926.32(f), means a person designated by the employer to act on the employer's behalf who is capable of identifying existing and potential cadmium hazards in the workplace and the proper methods to control them in order to protect workers, and has the authority necessary to take prompt corrective measures to eliminate or control such hazards. The duties of a competent person include at least the following: Determining prior to the performance of work whether cadmium is present in the workplace; establishing, where necessary, regulated areas and assuring that access to and from those areas is limited to authorized employees; assuring the adequacy of any employee exposure monitoring required by this standard; assuring that all employees exposed to air cadmium levels above the PEL wear appropriate personal protective equipment and are trained in the use of appropriate methods of exposure control; assuring that proper hygiene facilities are provided and that workers are trained to use those facilities; and assuring that the engineering controls required by this standard are implemented, maintained in proper operating condition, and functioning properly.

Director means the Director of the National Institute for Occupational Safety and Health (NIOSH), U.S. Department of Health and Human Services, or designee.

Employee exposure and similar language referring to the air cadmium level to which an employee is exposed means the exposure to airborne cadmium that would occur if the employee were not using respiratory protective equipment.

Final medical determination is the written medical opinion of the employee's health status by the examining physician under paragraphs (l)(3)-(12) of this section or, if multiple physician review under paragraph (l)(13) of this section or the alternative physician determination under paragraph (l)(14) of this section is invoked, it is the final, written medical finding, recommendation or determination that emerges from that process.

High-efficiency Particulate Air [HEPA] filter means a filter capable of trapping and retaining at least 99.97 percent of mono-dispersed particles of 0.3 micrometers in diameter.

Regulated area means an area demarcated by the employer where an employee's exposure to airborne concentrations of cadmium exceeds, or can reasonably be expected to exceed the permissible exposure limit (PEL).

This section means this cadmium standard.

(c) *Permissible Exposure Limit (PEL)*. The employer shall assure that no employee is exposed to an airborne concentration of cadmium in excess of five micrograms per cubic meter of air (5 µg/m³), calculated as an eight-hour time-weighted average exposure (TWA).

(d) *Exposure Monitoring—(1) General.* (i) Prior to the performance of any construction work where employees may be potentially exposed to cadmium, the employer shall establish the applicability of this standard by determining whether cadmium is present in the workplace and whether there is the possibility that employee exposures will be at or above the action level. The employer shall designate a competent person who shall make this determination. Investigation and material testing techniques shall be used, as appropriate, in the determination. Investigation shall include a review of relevant plans, past reports, material safety data sheets, and other available records, and consultations with the property owner and discussions with appropriate individuals and agencies.

(ii) Where cadmium has been determined to be present in the workplace, and it has been determined that there is a possibility the employee's exposure will be at or above the action level, the competent person shall identify employees potentially exposed to cadmium at or above the action level.

(iii) Determinations of employee exposure shall be made from breathing-zone air samples that reflect the monitored employee's regular, daily 8-hour TWA exposure to cadmium.

(iv) Eight-hour TWA exposures shall be determined for each employee on the basis of one or more personal breathing-zone air samples reflecting full shift exposure on each shift, for each job classification, in each work area. Where several employees perform the same job tasks, in the same job classification, on the same shift, in the same work area, and the length, duration, and level of cadmium exposures are similar, an employer may sample a representative fraction of the employees instead of all employees in order to meet this requirement. In representative sampling, the employer shall sample the employee(s) expected to have the highest cadmium exposures.

(2) *Specific.* (i) Initial monitoring. Except as provided for in paragraph (d)(2)(iii) of this section, where a determination conducted under paragraph (d)(1)(i) of this section shows the possibility of employee exposure to cadmium at or above the action level, the employer shall conduct exposure monitoring as soon as practicable that is representative of the exposure for each employee in the workplace who is or may be exposed to cadmium at or above the action level.

(ii) In addition, if the employee periodically performs tasks that may expose the employee to a higher concentration of airborne cadmium, the employee shall be monitored while performing those tasks.

(iii) Where the employer has objective data, as defined in paragraph (n)(2) of this section, demonstrating that employee exposure to cadmium will not exceed airborne concentrations at or above the action level under the expected conditions of processing, use, or handling, the employer may rely upon such data instead of implementing initial monitoring.

(iv) Where a determination conducted under paragraphs (d)(1) or (d)(2) of this section is made that a potentially exposed employee is not exposed to airborne concentrations of cadmium at or above the action level, the employer shall make a written record of such determination. The record shall include at least the monitoring data developed under paragraphs (d)(2)(i)–(iii) of this section, where applicable, and shall also include the date of determination, and the name and social security number of each employee.

(3) *Monitoring frequency (periodic monitoring).* (i) If the initial monitoring or periodic monitoring reveals employee exposures to be at or above the action level, the employer shall monitor at a frequency and pattern needed to assure that the monitoring results reflect with reasonable accuracy the employee's typical exposure levels, given the variability in the tasks performed, work practices, and environmental conditions on the job site, and to assure the adequacy of respiratory selection and the effectiveness of engineering and work practice controls.

(ii) If the initial monitoring or the periodic monitoring indicates that employee exposures are below the action level and that result is confirmed by the results of another monitoring taken at least seven days later, the employer may discontinue the monitoring for those employees whose exposures are represented by such monitoring.

(4) *Additional monitoring.* The employer also shall institute the exposure monitoring required under paragraphs (d)(2)(i) and (d)(3) of this section whenever there has been a change in the raw materials, equipment, personnel, work practices, or finished products that may result in additional employees being exposed to cadmium at or above the action level or in employees already exposed to cadmium at or above the action level being exposed above the PEL, or whenever the employer or competent person has any reason to suspect that any other change might result in such further exposure.

(5) *Employee notification of monitoring results.* (i) The employer must, as soon as possible but no later than 5 working days after the receipt of the results of any monitoring performed under this section, notify each affected employee of these results either individually in writing or by posting the results in an appropriate location that is accessible to employees.

(ii) Wherever monitoring results indicate that employee exposure exceeds the PEL, the employer shall include in the written notice a statement that the PEL has been exceeded and a description of the corrective action being taken by the employer to reduce employee exposure to or below the PEL.

(6) *Accuracy of measurement.* The employer shall use a method of monitoring and analysis that has an accuracy of not less than plus or minus 25 percent (±25%), with a confidence level of 95 percent, for airborne concentrations of cadmium at or above the action level and the permissible exposure limit.

(e) *Regulated areas—(1) Establishment.* The employer shall establish a regulated area wherever an employee's exposure to airborne concentrations of cadmium is, or can reasonably be expected to be in excess of the permissible exposure limit (PEL).

(2) *Demarcation.* Regulated areas shall be demarcated from the rest of the workplace in any manner that adequately establishes and alerts employees of the boundaries of the regulated area, including employees who are or may be incidentally in the regulated areas, and that protects persons outside the area from exposure to airborne concentrations of cadmium in excess of the PEL.

(3) *Access.* Access to regulated areas shall be limited to authorized persons.

(4) *Provision of respirators.* Each person entering a regulated area shall be supplied with and required to use a respirator, selected in accordance with paragraph (g)(2) of this section.

(5) *Prohibited activities.* The employer shall assure that employees do not eat, drink, smoke, chew tobacco or gum, or apply cosmetics in regulated areas, or carry the products associated with any of these activities into regulated areas or store such products in those areas.

(f) *Methods of compliance—(1) Compliance hierarchy.* (i) Except as specified in paragraph (f)(1)(ii) of this section, the employer shall implement engineering and work practice controls to reduce and maintain employee exposure to cadmium at or below the PEL, except to the extent that the employer can demonstrate that such controls are not feasible.

(ii) The requirement to implement engineering controls to achieve the PEL does not apply where the employer demonstrates the following:

(A) The employee is only intermittently exposed; and

(B) The employee is not exposed above the PEL on 30 or more days per year (12 consecutive months).

(iii) Wherever engineering and work practice controls are not sufficient to reduce employee exposure to or below the PEL, the employer nonetheless shall implement such controls to reduce exposures to the lowest levels achievable. The employer shall supplement such controls with respiratory protection that complies with the requirements of paragraph (g) of this section and the PEL.

(iv) The employer shall not use employee rotation as a method of compliance.

(2) *Specific operations*—(i) *Abrasive blasting.* Abrasive blasting on cadmium or cadmium-containing materials shall be conducted in a manner that will provide adequate protection.

(ii) *Heating cadmium and cadmium-containing materials.* Welding, cutting, and other forms of heating of cadmium or cadmium-containing materials shall be conducted in accordance with the requirements of 29 CFR 1926.353 and 29 CFR 1926.354, where applicable.

(3) *Prohibitions.* (i) High speed abrasive disc saws and similar abrasive power equipment shall not be used for work on cadmium or cadmium-containing materials unless they are equipped with appropriate engineering controls to minimize emissions, if the exposure levels are above the PEL.

(ii) Materials containing cadmium shall not be applied by spray methods, if exposures are above the PEL, unless employees are protected with supplied-air respirators with full facepiece, hood, helmet, suit, operated in positive pressure mode and measures are instituted to limit overspray and prevent contamination of adjacent areas.

(4) *Mechanical ventilation.* (i) When ventilation is used to control exposure, measurements that demonstrate the effectiveness of the system in controlling exposure, such as capture velocity, duct velocity, or static pressure shall be made as necessary to maintain its effectiveness.

(ii) Measurements of the system's effectiveness in controlling exposure shall be made as necessary within five working days of any change in production, process, or control that might re-

sult in a significant increase in employee exposure to cadmium.

(iii) Recirculation of air. If air from exhaust ventilation is recirculated into the workplace, the system shall have a high efficiency filter and be monitored to assure effectiveness.

(iv) Procedures shall be developed and implemented to minimize employee exposure to cadmium when maintenance of ventilation systems and changing of filters is being conducted.

(5) *Compliance program.* (i) Where employee exposure to cadmium exceeds the PEL and the employer is required under paragraph (f)(1) of this section to implement controls to comply with the PEL, prior to the commencement of the job the employer shall establish and implement a written compliance program to reduce employee exposure to or below the PEL. To the extent that engineering and work practice controls cannot reduce exposures to or below the PEL, the employer shall include in the written compliance program the use of appropriate respiratory protection to achieve compliance with the PEL.

(ii) Written compliance programs shall be reviewed and updated as often and as promptly as necessary to reflect significant changes in the employer's compliance status or significant changes in the lowest air cadmium level that is technologically feasible.

(iii) A competent person shall review the comprehensive compliance program initially and after each change.

(iv) Written compliance programs shall be provided upon request for examination and copying to the Assistant Secretary, the Director, affected employees, and designated employee representatives.

(g) *Respirator protection*—(1) *General.* For employees who use respirators required by this section, the employer must provide each employee an appropriate respirator that complies with the requirements of this paragraph. Respirators must be used during:

(i) Periods necessary to install or implement feasible engineering and work-practice controls when employee exposures exceed the PEL.

(ii) Maintenance and repair activities, and brief or intermittent work operations, for which employee exposures exceed the PEL and engineering and work-practice controls are not feasible or are not required.

(iii) Work operations in the regulated areas specified in paragraph (e) of this section.

(iv) Work operations for which the employer has implemented all feasible engineering and work-practice controls, and such controls are not sufficient to reduce employee exposures to or below the PEL.

(v) Work operations for which an employee, who is exposed to cadmium at or above the action level, requests a respirator.

(vi) Work operations for which engineering controls are not required by paragraph (f)(1)(ii) of this section to reduce employee exposures that exceed the PEL.

(vii) Emergencies.

(2) *Respirator program.* (i) The employer must implement a respiratory protection program in accordance with § 1910.134 (b) through (d) (except (d)(1)(iii)), and (f) through (m), which covers each employee required by this section to use a respirator.

(ii) If an employee exhibits breathing difficulty during fit testing or respirator use, the employer must provide the employee with a medical examination in accordance with paragraph (l)(6)(ii) of this section to determine if the employee can use a respirator while performing the required duties.

(iii) No employee must use a respirator when, based on their most recent medical examination, the examining physician determines that the employee will be unable to continue to function normally while using a respirator. If the physician determines the employee must be limited in, or removed from, their current job because of the employee's inability to use a respirator, the job limitation or removal must be conducted in accordance with paragraphs (l) (11) and (12) of this section.

(3) *Respirator selection.* (i) Employers must:

(A) Select, and provide to employees, the appropriate respirators specified in paragraph (d)(3)(i)(A) of 29 CFR 1910.134.

(B) Provide employees with full facepiece respirators when they experience eye irritation.

(C) Provide HEPA filters for powered and non-powered air-purifying respirators.

(ii) The employer must provide a powered air-purifying respirator instead of a negative-pressure respirator when an employee entitled to a respirator chooses to use this type of respirator and such a respirator will provide adequate protection to the employee.

(h) *Emergency situations.* The employer shall develop and implement a written plan for dealing with emergency situations involving substantial releases of airborne cadmium. The plan shall include provisions for the use of appropriate respirators and personal protective equipment. In addition, employees not essential to correcting the emergency situation shall be restricted from the area and normal operations halted in that area until the emergency is abated.

(i) *Protective work clothing and equipment*—(1) *Provision and use.* If an employee is exposed to airborne cadmium above the PEL or where skin or eye irritation is associated with cadmium exposure at any level, the employer shall provide at no cost to the employee, and assure that the employee uses, appropriate protective work clothing and equipment that prevents contamination of the employee and the employee's garments. Protective work clothing and equipment includes, but is not limited to:

(i) Coveralls or similar full-body work clothing;

(ii) Gloves, head coverings, and boots or foot coverings; and

(iii) Face shields, vented goggles, or other appropriate protective equipment that complies with 29 CFR 1910.133.

(2) *Removal and storage.* (i) The employer shall assure that employees remove all protective clothing and equipment contaminated with cadmium at the completion of the work shift and do so only in change rooms provided in accordance with paragraph (j)(1) of this section.

655

(ii) The employer shall assure that no employee takes cadmium-contaminated protective clothing or equipment from the workplace, except for employees authorized to do so for purposes of laundering, cleaning, maintaining, or disposing of cadmium-contaminated protective clothing and equipment at an appropriate location or facility away from the workplace.

(iii) The employer shall assure that contaminated protective clothing and equipment, when removed for laundering, cleaning, maintenance, or disposal, is placed and stored in sealed, impermeable bags or other closed, impermeable containers that are designed to prevent dispersion of cadmium dust.

(iv) The employer shall ensure that containers of contaminated protective clothing and equipment that are to be taken out of the change rooms or the workplace for laundering, cleaning, maintenance or disposal shall bear labels in accordance with paragraph (m)(3)(ii) of this section.

(3) *Cleaning, replacement, and disposal.* (i) The employer shall provide the protective clothing and equipment required by paragraph (i)(1) of this section in a clean and dry condition as often as necessary to maintain its effectiveness, but in any event at least weekly. The employer is responsible for cleaning and laundering the protective clothing and equipment required by this paragraph to maintain its effectiveness and is also responsible for disposing of such clothing and equipment.

(ii) The employer also is responsible for repairing or replacing required protective clothing and equipment as needed to maintain its effectiveness. When rips or tears are detected while an employee is working they shall be immediately mended, or the worksuit shall be immediately replaced.

(iii) The employer shall prohibit the removal of cadmium from protective clothing and equipment by blowing, shaking, or any other means that disperses cadmium into the air.

(iv) The employer shall assure that any laundering of contaminated clothing or cleaning of contaminated equipment in the workplace is done in a manner that prevents the release of airborne cadmium in excess of the permissible exposure limit prescribed in paragraph (c) of this section.

(v) The employer shall inform any person who launders or cleans protective clothing or equipment contaminated with cadmium of the potentially harmful effects of exposure to cadmium, and that the clothing and equipment should be laundered or cleaned in a manner to effectively prevent the release of airborne cadmium in excess of the PEL.

(j) *Hygiene areas and practices*—(1) *General.* For employees whose airborne exposure to cadmium is above the PEL, the employer shall provide clean change rooms, handwashing facilities, showers, and lunchroom facilities that comply with 29 CFR 1926.51.

(2) *Change rooms.* The employer shall assure that change rooms are equipped with separate storage facilities for street clothes and for protective clothing and equipment, which are designed to prevent dispersion of cadmium and contamination of the employee's street clothes.

(3) *Showers and handwashing facilities.* (i) The employer shall assure that employees whose airborne exposure to cadmium is above the PEL shower during the end of the work shift.

(ii) The employer shall assure that employees who are exposed to cadmium above the PEL wash their hands and faces prior to eating, drinking, smoking, chewing tobacco or gum, or applying cosmetics.

(4) *Lunchroom facilities.* (i) The employer shall assure that the lunchroom facilities are readily accessible to employees, that tables for eating are maintained free of cadmium, and that no employee in a lunchroom facility is exposed at any time to cadmium at or above a concentration of 2.5 $\mu g/m^3$.

(ii) The employer shall assure that employees do not enter lunchroom facilities with protective work clothing or equipment unless surface cadmium has been removed from the clothing and equipment by HEPA vacuuming or some other method that removes cadmium dust without dispersing it.

(k) *Housekeeping.* (1) All surfaces shall be maintained as free as practicable of accumulations of cadmium.

(2) All spills and sudden releases of material containing cadmium shall be cleaned up as soon as possible.

(3) Surfaces contaminated with cadmium shall, wherever possible, be cleaned by vacuuming or other methods that minimize the likelihood of cadmium becoming airborne.

(4) HEPA-filtered vacuuming equipment or equally effective filtration methods shall be used for vacuuming. The equipment shall be used and emptied in a manner that minimizes the reentry of cadmium into the workplace.

(5) Shoveling, dry or wet sweeping, and brushing may be used only where vacuuming or other methods that minimize the likelihood of cadmium becoming airborne have been tried and found not to be effective.

(6) Compressed air shall not be used to remove cadmium from any surface unless the compressed air is used in conjunction with a ventilation system designed to capture the dust cloud created by the compressed air.

(7) Waste, scrap, debris, bags, and containers, personal protective equipment and clothing contaminated with cadmium and consigned for disposal shall be collected and disposed of in sealed impermeable bags or other closed, impermeable containers. These bags and containers shall be labeled in accordance with paragraph (m)(3)(ii) of this section.

(l) *Medical Surveillance*—(1) *General*— (i) *Scope*—(A) *Currently exposed*—The employer shall institute a medical surveillance program for all employees who are or may be exposed at or above the action level and all employees who perform the following tasks, operations or jobs: Electrical grounding with cadmium welding; cutting, brazing, burning, grinding or welding on surfaces that were painted with cadmium-containing paints; electrical work using cadmium-coated conduit; use of cadmium containing paints; cutting and welding cadmium-plated steel; brazing or welding with cadmium alloys; fusing of reinforced steel by cadmium welding; maintaining or retrofitting cadmium-coated equipment; and, wrecking and demolition where cadmium is present. A medical surveillance program will not be required if the em-

ployer demonstrates that the employee:

(*1*) Is not currently exposed by the employer to airborne concentrations of cadmium at or above the action level on 30 or more days per year (twelve consecutive months); and,

(*2*) Is not currently exposed by the employer in those tasks on 30 or more days per year (twelve consecutive months).

(B) *Previously exposed*— The employer shall also institute a medical surveillance program for all employees who might previously have been exposed to cadmium by the employer prior to the effective date of this standard in tasks specified under paragraph (l)(1)(i)(A) of this section, unless the employer demonstrates that the employee did not in the years prior to the effective date of this section work in those tasks for the employer with exposure to cadmium for an aggregated total of more than 12 months.

(ii) To determine an employee's fitness for using a respirator, the employer shall provide the limited medical examination specified in paragraph (l)(6) of this section.

(iii) The employer shall assure that all medical examinations and procedures required by this section are performed by or under the supervision of a licensed physician, who has read and is familiar with the health effects section of appendix A to this section, the regulatory text of this section, the protocol for sample handling and lab selection in appendix F to this section, and the questionnaire of appendix D to this section.

(iv) The employer shall provide the medical surveillance required by this section, including multiple physician review under paragraph (l)(13) of this section without cost to employees, and at a time and place that is reasonable and convenient to employees.

(v) The employer shall assure that the collecting and handling of biological samples of cadmium in urine (CdU), cadmium in blood (CdB), and beta-2 microglobulin in urine (β_2-M) taken from employees under this section is done in a manner that assures their reliability and that analysis of biological samples of cadmium in urine (CdU), cadmium in blood (CdB), and beta-2 microglobulin in urine (β_2-M) taken from employees under this section is performed in laboratories with demonstrated proficiency to perform the particular analysis. (See appendix F to this section.)

(2) *Initial Examination.* (i) For employees covered by medical surveillance under paragraph (l)(1)(i) of this section, the employer shall provide an initial medical examination. The examination shall be provided to those employees within 30 days after initial assignment to a job with exposure to cadmium or no later than 90 days after the effective date of this section, whichever date is later.

(ii) The initial medical examination shall include:

(A) A detailed medical and work history, with emphasis on: Past, present, and anticipated future exposure to cadmium; any history of renal, cardiovascular, respiratory, hematopoietic, reproductive, and/or musculo-skeletal system dysfunction; current usage of medication with potential nephrotoxic side-effects; and smoking history and current status; and

(B) Biological monitoring that includes the following tests:

(1) Cadmium in urine (CdU), standardized to grams of creatinine (g/Cr);

(2) Beta-2 microglobulin in urine (β_2-M), standardized to grams of creatinine (g/Cr), with pH specified, as described in appendix F to this section; and

(3) Cadmium in blood (CdB), standardized to liters of whole blood (lwb).

(iii) Recent Examination: An initial examination is not required to be provided if adequate records show that the employee has been examined in accordance with the requirements of paragraph (l)(2)(ii) of this section within the past 12 months. In that case, such records shall be maintained as part of the employee's medical record and the prior exam shall be treated as if it were an initial examination for the purposes of paragraphs (l)(3) and (4) of this section.

(3) *Actions triggered by initial biological monitoring.* (i) If the results of the biological monitoring tests in the initial examination show the employee's CdU level to be at or below 3 μg/g Cr, β_2-M level to be at or below 300 μg/g Cr and

CdB level to be at or below 5 μg/lwb, then:

(A) For employees who are subject to medical surveillance under paragraphs (l)(1)(i)(A) of this section because of current or anticipated exposure to cadmium, the employer shall provide the minimum level of periodic medical surveillance in accordance with the requirements in paragraph (l)(4)(i) of this section; and

(B) For employees who are subject to medical surveillance under paragraph (l)(1)(i)(B) of this section because of prior but not current exposure, the employer shall provide biological monitoring for CdU, β_2-M, and CdB one year after the initial biological monitoring and then the employer shall comply with the requirements of paragraph (l)(4)(vi) of this section.

(ii) For all employees who are subject to medical surveillance under paragraph (l)(1)(i) of this section, if the results of the initial biological monitoring tests show the level of CdU to exceed 3 μg/g Cr, the level of β_2-M to be in excess of 300 μg/g Cr, or the level of CdB to be in excess of 5 μg/lwb, the employer shall:

(A) Within two weeks after receipt of biological monitoring results, reassess the employee's occupational exposure to cadmium as follows:

(1) Reassess the employee's work practices and personal hygiene;

(2) Reevaluate the employee's respirator use, if any, and the respirator program;

(3) Review the hygiene facilities;

(4) Reevaluate the maintenance and effectiveness of the relevant engineering controls;

(5) Assess the employee's smoking history and status;

(B) Within 30 days after the exposure reassessment, specified in paragraph (l)(3)(ii)(A) of this section, take reasonable steps to correct any deficiencies found in the reassessment that may be responsible for the employee's excess exposure to cadmium; and,

(C) Within 90 days after receipt of biological monitoring results, provide a full medical examination to the employee in accordance with the requirements of paragraph (l)(4)(ii) of this section. After completing the medical examination, the examining physician shall determine in a written medical opinion whether to medically remove the employee. If the physician determines that medical removal is not necessary, then until the employee's CdU level falls to or below 3 µg/g Cr, β_2-M level falls to or below 300 µg/g Cr and CdB level falls to or below 5 µg/lwb, the employer shall:

(1) Provide biological monitoring in accordance with paragraph (l)(2)(ii)(B) of this section on a semiannual basis; and

(2) Provide annual medical examinations in accordance with paragraph (l)(4)(ii) of this section.

(iii) For all employees who are subject to medical surveillance under paragraph (l)(1)(i) of this section, if the results of the initial biological monitoring tests show the level of CdU to be in excess of 15 µg/g Cr, or the level of CdB to be in excess of 15 µg/lwb, or the level of β_2-M to be in excess of 1,500 µg/g Cr, the employer shall comply with the requirements of paragraphs (l)(3)(ii)(A)–(B) of this section. Within 90 days after receipt of biological monitoring results, the employer shall provide a full medical examination to the employee in accordance with the requirements of paragraph (l)(4)(ii) of this section. After completing the medical examination, the examining physician shall determine in a written medical opinion whether to medically remove the employee. However, if the initial biological monitoring results and the biological monitoring results obtained during the medical examination both show that: CdU exceeds 15 µg/g Cr; or CdB exceeds 15 µg/lwb; or β_2-M exceeds 1500 µg/g Cr, and in addition CdU exceeds 3 µg/g Cr or CdB exceeds 5 µg/liter of whole blood, then the physician shall medically remove the employee from exposure to cadmium at or above the action level. If the second set of biological monitoring results obtained during the medical examination does not show that a mandatory removal trigger level has been exceeded, then the employee is not required to be removed by the mandatory provisions of this paragraph. If the employee is not required to be removed by the mandatory provisions of this paragraph or by the physician's determination, then until the employee's CdU level falls to

or below 3 µg/g Cr, β_2-M level falls to or below 300 µg/g Cr and CdB level falls to or below 5 µg/lwb, the employer shall:

(A) Periodically reassess the employee's occupational exposure to cadmium;

(B) Provide biological monitoring in accordance with paragraph (l)(2)(ii)(B) of this section on a quarterly basis; and

(C) Provide semiannual medical examinations in accordance with paragraph (l)(4)(ii) of this section.

(iv) For all employees to whom medical surveillance is provided, beginning on January 1, 1999, and in lieu of paragraph (l)(3)(iii) of this section, whenever the results of initial biological monitoring tests show the employee's CdU level to be in excess of 7 µg/g Cr, or β_2-M level to be in excess of 750 µg/g Cr, or CdB level to be in excess of 10 µg/lwb, the employer shall comply with the requirements of paragraphs (l)(3)(ii)(A)–(B) of this section. Within 90 days after receipt of biological monitoring results, the employer shall provide a full medical examination to the employee in accordance with the requirements of paragraph (l)(4)(ii) of this section. After completing the medical examination, the examining physician shall determine in a written medical opinion whether to medically remove the employee. However, if the initial biological monitoring results and the biological monitoring results obtained during the medical examination both show that: CdU exceeds 7 µg/g Cr; or CdB exceeds 10 µg/lwb; or β_2-M exceeds 750 µg/g Cr, and in addition CdU exceeds 3 µg/g Cr or CdB exceeds 5 µg/liter of whole blood, then the physician shall medically remove the employee from exposure to cadmium at or above the action level. If the second set of biological monitoring results obtained during the medical examination does not show that a mandatory removal trigger level has been exceeded, then the employee is not required to be removed by the mandatory provisions of this paragraph. If the employee is not required to be removed by the mandatory provisions of this paragraph or by the physician's determination, then until the employee's CdU level falls to or below 3 µg/g Cr, β_2-M level falls to or below 300 µg/g Cr and CdB level falls to or below 5 µg/lwb, the employer shall:

(A) Periodically reassess the employee's occupational exposure to cadmium;

(B) Provide biological monitoring in accordance with paragraph (l)(2)(ii)(B) of this section on a quarterly basis; and

(C) Provide semiannual medical examinations in accordance with paragraph (l)(4)(ii) of this section.

(4) *Periodic medical surveillance.* (i) For each employee who is covered by medical surveillance under paragraph (l)(1)(i)(A) of this section because of current or anticipated exposure to cadmium, the employer shall provide at least the minimum level of periodic medical surveillance, which consists of periodic medical examinations and periodic medical biological monitoring. A periodic medical examination shall be provided within one year after the initial examination required by paragraph (l)(2) of this section and thereafter at least biennially. Biological sampling shall be provided at least annually either as part of a periodic medical examination or separately as periodic biological monitoring.

(ii) The periodic medical examination shall include:

(A) A detailed medical and work history, or update thereof, with emphasis on: Past, present and anticipated future exposure to cadmium; smoking history and current status; reproductive history; current use of medications with potential nephrotoxic side-effects; any history of renal, cardiovascular, respiratory, hematopoietic, and/or musculo-skeletal system dysfunction; and as part of the medical and work history, for employees who wear respirators, questions 3–11 and 25–32 in appendix D to this section;

(B) A complete physical examination with emphasis on: blood pressure, the respiratory system, and the urinary system;

(C) A 14 inch by 17 inch, or a reasonably standard sized posterior-anterior chest X-ray (after the initial X-ray, the frequency of chest X-rays is to be determined by the examining physician);

(D) Pulmonary function tests, including forced vital capacity (FVC) and forced expiratory volume at 1 second (FEV1);

(E) Biological monitoring, as required in paragraph (l)(2)(ii)(B) of this section;

(F) Blood analysis, in addition to the analysis required under paragraph (l)(2)(ii)(B) of this section, including blood urea nitrogen, complete blood count, and serum creatinine;

(G) Urinalysis, in addition to the analysis required under paragraph (l)(2)(ii)(B) of this section, including the determination of albumin, glucose, and total and low molecular weight proteins;

(H) For males over 40 years old, prostate palpation, or other at least as effective diagnostic test(s), and;

(I) Any additional tests or procedures deemed appropriate by the examining physician.

(iii) Periodic biological monitoring shall be provided in accordance with paragraph (l)(2)(ii)(B) of this section.

(iv) If the results of periodic biological monitoring or the results of biological monitoring performed as part of the periodic medical examination show the level of the employee's CdU, β_2–M, or CdB to be in excess of the levels specified in paragraphs (l)(3)(ii) or (iii) of this section; or beginning on January 1, 1999, in excess of the levels specified in paragraphs (l)(3)(ii) or (iv), the employer shall take the appropriate actions specified in paragraphs (l)(3)(ii)–(iv) of this section, respectively.

(v) For previously exposed employees under paragraph (l)(1)(i)(B) of this section:

(A) If the employee's levels of CdU did not exceed 3 µg/g Cr, CdB did not exceed 5 µg/lwb, and β_2–M did not exceed 300 µg/g Cr in the initial biological monitoring tests, and if the results of the followup biological monitoring required by paragraph (l)(3)(i)(B) of this section one year after the initial examination confirm the previous results, the employer may discontinue all periodic medical surveillance for that employee.

(B) If the initial biological monitoring results for CdU, CdB, or β_2–M were in excess of the levels specified in paragraph (l)(3)(i) of this section, but subsequent biological monitoring results required by paragraph (l)(3)(ii)–

(iv) of this section show that the employee's CdU levels no longer exceed 3 µg/g Cr, CdB levels no longer exceed 5 µg/lwb, and β_2–M levels no longer exceed 300 µg/g Cr, the employer shall provide biological monitoring for CdU, CdB, and β_2–M one year after these most recent biological monitoring results. If the results of the followup biological monitoring specified in this paragraph, confirm the previous results, the employer may discontinue all periodic medical surveillance for that employee.

(C) However, if the results of the follow-up tests specified in paragraph (l)(4)(v)(A) or (B) of this section indicate that the level of the employee's CdU, β_2–M, or CdB exceeds these same levels, the employer is required to provide annual medical examinations in accordance with the provisions of paragraph (l)(4)(ii) of this section until the results of biological monitoring are consistently below these levels or the examining physician determines in a written medical opinion that further medical surveillance is not required to protect the employee's health.

(vi) A routine, biennial medical examination is not required to be provided in accordance with paragraphs (l)(3)(i) and (l)(4) of this section if adequate medical records show that the employee has been examined in accordance with the requirements of paragraph (l)(4)(ii) of this section within the past 12 months. In that case, such records shall be maintained by the employer as part of the employee's medical record, and the next routine, periodic medical examination shall be made available to the employee within two years of the previous examination.

(5) *Actions triggered by medical examinations.* (i) If the results of a medical examination carried out in accordance with this section indicate any laboratory or clinical finding consistent with cadmium toxicity that does not require employer action under paragraphs (l)(2), (3) or (4) of this section, the employer shall take the following steps and continue to take them until the physician determines that they are no longer necessary.

(A) Periodically reassess: The employee's work practices and personal hygiene; the employee's respirator use, if any; the employee's smoking history and status; the respiratory protection program; the hygiene facilities; the maintenance and effectiveness of the relevant engineering controls; and take all reasonable steps to correct the deficiencies found in the reassessment that may be responsible for the employee's excess exposure to cadmium.

(B) Provide semi-annual medical reexaminations to evaluate the abnormal clinical sign(s) of cadmium toxicity until the results are normal or the employee is medically removed; and

(C) Where the results of tests for total proteins in urine are abnormal, provide a more detailed medical evaluation of the toxic effects of cadmium on the employee's renal system.

(6) *Examination for respirator use.* (i) To determine an employee's fitness for respirator use, the employer shall provide a medical examination that includes the elements specified in paragraph (l)(6)(i)(A)–(D) of this section. This examination shall be provided prior to the employee's being assigned to a job that requires the use of a respirator or no later than 90 days after this section goes into effect, whichever date is later, to any employee without a medical examination within the preceding 12 months that satisfies the requirements of this paragraph.

(A) A detailed medical and work history, or update thereof, with emphasis on: past exposure to cadmium; smoking history and current status; any history of renal, cardiovascular, respiratory, hematopoietic, and/or musculo-skeletal system dysfunction; a description of the job for which the respirator is required; and questions 3–11 and 25–32 in appendix D;

(B) A blood pressure test;

(C) Biological monitoring of the employee's levels of CdU, CdB and β_2–M in accordance with the requirements of paragraph (l)(2)(ii)(B) of this section, unless such results already have been obtained within the twelve months; and

(D) Any other test or precedure that the examining physician deems appropriate.

(ii) After reviewing all the information obtained from the medical examination required in paragraph (l)(6)(i)

661

of this section, the physician shall determine whether the employee is fit to wear a respirator.

(iii) Whenever an employee has exhibited difficulty in breathing during a respirator fit test or during use of a respirator, the employer, as soon as possible, shall provide the employee with a periodic medical examination in accordance with paragraph (l)(4)(ii) of this section to determine the employee's fitness to wear a respirator.

(iv) Where the results of the examination required under paragraphs (l)(6)(i), (ii), or (iii) of this section are abnormal, medical limitation or prohibition of respirator use shall be considered. If the employee is allowed to wear a respirator, the employee's ability to continue to do so shall be periodically evaluated by a physician.

(7) *Emergency Examinations.* (i) In addition to the medical surveillance required in paragraphs (l)(2)–(6) of this section, the employer shall provide a medical examination as soon as possible to any employee who may have been acutely exposed to cadmium because of an emergency.

(ii) The examination shall include the requirements of paragraph (l)(4)(ii), of this section, with emphasis on the respiratory system, other organ systems considered appropriate by the examining physician, and symptoms of acute overexposure, as identified in paragraphs II(B)(1)–(2) and IV of appendix A of this section.

(8) *Termination of employment examination.* (i) At termination of employment, the employer shall provide a medical examination in accordance with paragraph (l)(4)(ii) of this section, including a chest X-ray where necessary, to any employee to whom at any prior time the employer was required to provide medical surveillance under paragraph (l)(1)(i) or (l)(7) of this section. However, if the last examination satisfied the requirements of paragraph (l)(4)(ii) of this section and was less than six months prior to the date of termination, no further examination is required unless otherwise specified in paragraph (l)(3) or (l)(5) of this section;

(ii) In addition, if the employer has discontinued all periodic medical surveillance under paragraph (l)(4)(v) of this section, no termination of employment medical examination is required.

(9) *Information provided to the physician.* The employer shall provide the following information to the examining physician:

(i) A copy of this standard and appendices;

(ii) A description of the affected employee's former, current, and anticipated duties as they relate to the employee's occupational exposure to cadmium;

(iii) The employee's former, current, and anticipated future levels of occupational exposure to cadmium;

(iv) A description of any personal protective equipment, including respirators, used or to be used by the employee, including when and for how long the employee has used that equipment; and

(v) Relevant results of previous biological monitoring and medical examinations.

(10) *Physician's written medical opinion.* (i) The employer shall promptly obtain a written, medical opinion from the examining physician for each medical examination performed on each employee. This written opinion shall contain:

(A) The physician's diagnosis for the employee;

(B) The physician's opinion as to whether the employee has any detected medical condition(s) that would place the employee at increased risk of material impairment to health from further exposure to cadmium, including any indications of potential cadmium toxicity;

(C) The results of any biological or other testing or related evaluations that directly assess the employee's absorption of cadmium;

(D) Any recommended removal from, or limitation on the activities or duties of the employee or on the employee's use of personal protective equipment, such as respirators;

(E) A statement that the physician has clearly and carefully explained to the employee the results of the medical examination, including all biological monitoring results and any medical conditions related to cadmium exposure that require further evaluation or treatment, and any limitation on the employee's diet or use of medications.

(ii) The employer shall promptly obtain a copy of the results of any biological monitoring provided by an employer to an employee independently of a medical examination under paragraphs (l)(2) and (l)(4) of this section, and, in lieu of a written medical opinion, an explanation sheet explaining those results.

(iii) The employer shall instruct the physician not to reveal orally or in the written medical opinion given to the employer specific findings or diagnoses unrelated to occupational exposure to cadmium.

(11) *Medical Removal Protection (MRP)*—(i) *General.* (A) The employer shall temporarily remove an employee from work where there is excess exposure to cadmium on each occasion that medical removal is required under paragraphs (l)(3), (l)(4), or (l)(6) of this section and on each occasion that a physician determines in a written medical opinion that the employee should be removed from such exposure. The physician's determination may be based on biological monitoring results, inability to wear a respirator, evidence of illness, other signs or symptoms of cadmium-related dysfunction or disease, or any other reason deemed medically sufficient by the physician.

(B) The employer shall medically remove an employee in accordance with paragraph (l)(11) of this section regardless of whether at the time of removal a job is available into which the removed employee may be transferred.

(C) Whenever an employee is medically removed under paragraph (l)(11) of this section, the employer shall transfer the removed employee to a job where the exposure to cadmium is within the permissible levels specified in that paragraph as soon as one becomes available.

(D) For any employee who is medically removed under the provisions of paragraph (l)(11)(i) of this section, the employer shall provide follow-up medical examinations semi-annually until, in a written medical opinion, the examining physician determines that either the employee may be returned to his/her former job status or the employee must be permanently removed from excess cadmium exposure.

(E) The employer may not return an employee who has been medically removed for any reason to his/her former job status until a physician determines in a written medical opinion that continued medical removal is no longer necessary to protect the employee's health.

(ii) Where an employee is found unfit to wear a respirator under paragraph (l)(6)(ii) of this section, the employer shall remove the employee from work where exposure to cadmium is above the PEL.

(iii) Where removal is based upon any reason other than the employee's inability to wear a respirator, the employer shall remove the employee from work where exposure to cadmium is at or above the action level.

(iv) Except as specified in paragraph (l)(11)(v) of this section, no employee who was removed because his/her level of CdU, CdB and/or β_2-M exceeded the trigger levels in paragraph (l)(3) or (l)(4) of this section may be returned to work with exposure to cadmium at or above the action level until the employee's levels of CdU fall to or below 3 $\mu g/g$ Cr, CdB fall to or below 5 $\mu g/lwb$, and β_2-M fall to or below 300 $\mu g/g$ Cr.

(v) However, when in the examining physician's opinion continued exposure to cadmium will not pose an increased risk to the employee's health and there are special circumstances that make continued medical removal an inappropriate remedy, the physician shall fully discuss these matters with the employee, and then in a written determination may return a worker to his/her former job status despite what would otherwise be unacceptably high biological monitoring results. Thereafter and until such time as the employee's biological monitoring results have decreased to levels where he/she could have been returned to his/her former job status, the returned employee shall continue medical surveillance as if he/she were still on medical removal. Until such time, the employee is no longer subject to mandatory medical removal. Subsequent questions regarding the employee's medical removal shall be decided solely by a final medical determination.

(vi) Where an employer, although not required by this section to do so, removes an employee from exposure to cadmium or otherwise places limitations on an employee due to the effects of cadmium exposure on the employee's medical condition, the employer shall provide the same medical removal protection benefits to that employee under paragraph (l)(12) of this section as would have been provided had the removal been required under paragraph (l)(11) of this section.

(12) *Medical removal protection benefits.* (i) The employer shall provide medical removal protection benefits to an employee for up to a maximum of 18 months each time, and while the employee is temporarily medically removed under paragraph (l)(11) of this section.

(ii) For purposes of this section, the requirement that the employer provide medical removal protection benefits means that the employer shall maintain the total normal earnings, seniority, and all other employee rights and benefits of the removed employee, including the employee's right to his/her former job status, as if the employee had not been removed from the employee's job or otherwise medically limited.

(iii) Where, after 18 months on medical removal because of elevated biological monitoring results, the employee's monitoring results have not declined to a low enough level to permit the employee to be returned to his/her former job status:

(A) The employer shall make available to the employee a medical examination pursuant to this section in order to obtain a final medical determination as to whether the employee may be returned to his/her former job status or must be permanently removed from excess cadmium exposure; and

(B) The employer shall assure that the final medical determination indicates whether the employee may be returned to his/her former job status and what steps, if any, should be taken to protect the employee's health;

(iv) The employer may condition the provision of medical removal protection benefits upon the employee's participation in medical surveillance provided in accordance with this section.

(13) *Multiple physician review.* (i) If the employer selects the initial physician to conduct any medical examination or consultation provided to an employee under this section, the employee may designate a second physician to:

(A) Review any findings, determinations, or recommendations of the initial physician; and

(B) Conduct such examinations, consultations, and laboratory tests as the second physician deems necessary to facilitate this review.

(ii) The employer shall promptly notify an employee of the right to seek a second medical opinion after each occasion that an initial physician provided by the employer conducts a medical examination or consultation pursuant to this section. The employer may condition its participation in, and payment for, multiple physician review upon the employee doing the following within fifteen (15) days after receipt of this notice, or receipt of the initial physician's written opinion, whichever is later:

(A) Informing the employer that he or she intends to seek a medical opinion; and

(B) Initiating steps to make an appointment with a second physician.

(iii) If the findings, determinations, or recommendations of the second physician differ from those of the initial physician, then the employer and the employee shall assure that efforts are made for the two physicians to resolve any disagreement.

(iv) If the two physicians have been unable to quickly resolve their disagreement, then the employer and the employee, through their respective physicians, shall designate a third physician to:

(A) Review any findings, determinations, or recommendations of the other two physicians; and

(B) Conduct such examinations, consultations, laboratory tests, and discussions with the other two physicians as the third physician deems necessary to resolve the disagreement among them.

(v) The employer shall act consistently with the findings, determinations, and recommendations of the third physician, unless the employer and the employee reach an agreement that is consistent with the recommendations of at least one of the other two physicians.

(14) *Alternate physician determination.* The employer and an employee or designated employee representative may agree upon the use of any alternate form of physician determination in lieu of the multiple physician review provided by paragraph (l)(13) of this section, so long as the alternative is expeditious and at least as protective of the employee.

(15) *Information the employer must provide the employee.* (i) The employer shall provide a copy of the physician's written medical opinion to the examined employee within five working days after receipt thereof.

(ii) The employer shall provide the employee with a copy of the employee's biological monitoring results and an explanation sheet explaining the results within five working days after receipt thereof.

(iii) Within 30 days after a request by an employee, the employer shall provide the employee with the information the employer is required to provide the examining physician under paragraph (l)(9) of this section.

(16) *Reporting.* In addition to other medical events that are required to be reported on the OSHA Form No. 200, the employer shall report any abnormal condition or disorder caused by occupational exposure to cadmium associated with employment as specified in Chapter (V)(E) of the *Reporting Guidelines for Occupational Injuries and Illnesses.*

(m) *Communication of cadmium hazards to employees—*(1) *Hazard communication.* The employer shall include cadmium in the program established to comply with the Hazard Communication Standard (HCS) (§ 1910.1200). The employer shall ensure that each employee has access to labels on containers of cadmium and safety data sheets, and is trained in accordance with the provisions of HCS and paragraph (m)(4) of this section. The employer shall provide information on at least the following hazards: Cancer; lung effects; kidney effects; and acute toxicity effects.

(2) *Warning signs.* (i) Warning signs shall be provided and displayed in regulated areas. In addition, warning signs shall be posted at all approaches to regulated areas so that an employee may read the signs and take necessary protective steps before entering the area.

(ii) Warning signs required by paragraph (m)(2)(i) of this section shall bear the following legend:

DANGER
CADMIUM
MAY CAUSE CANCER
CAUSES DAMAGE TO LUNGS AND KIDNEYS
WEAR RESPIRATORY PROTECTION IN THIS AREA
AUTHORIZED PERSONNEL ONLY

(iii) The employer shall ensure that signs required by this paragraph (m)(2) are illuminated, cleaned, and maintained as necessary so that the legend is readily visible.

(iv) Prior to June 1, 2016, employers may use the following legend in lieu of that specified in paragraph (m)(2)(ii) of this section:

DANGER
CADMIUM
CANCER HAZARD
CAN CAUSE LUNG AND KIDNEY DISEASE
AUTHORIZED PERSONNEL ONLY
RESPIRATORS REQUIRED IN THIS AREA

(3) *Warning labels.* (i) Shipping and storage containers containing cadmium or cadmium compounds shall bear appropriate warning labels, as specified in paragraph (m)(1) of this section.

(ii) The warning labels for containers of cadmium-contaminated protective clothing, equipment, waste, scrap, or debris shall include at least the following information:

DANGER
CONTAINS CADMIUM
MAY CAUSE CANCER
CAUSES DAMAGE TO LUNGS AND KIDNEYS
AVOID CREATING DUST

(iii) Where feasible, installed cadmium products shall have a visible label or other indication that cadmium is present.

(iv) Prior to June 1, 2015, employers may include the following information on shipping and storage containers containing cadmium, cadmium compounds, or cadmium-contaminated clothing, equipment, waste, scrap, or debris in lieu of the labeling requirements specified in paragraphs (m)(3)(i) and (m)(3)(ii) of this section:

DANGER
CONTAINS CADMIUM
CANCER HAZARD
AVOID CREATING DUST
CAN CAUSE LUNG AND KIDNEY DISEASE

(4) *Employee information and training.* (i) The employer shall train each employee who is potentially exposed to cadmium in accordance with the requirements of this section. The employer shall institute a training program, ensure employee participation in the program, and maintain a record of the contents of the training program.

(ii) Training shall be provided prior to or at the time of initial assignment to a job involving potential exposure to cadmium and at least annually thereafter.

(iii) The employer shall make the training program understandable to the employee and shall assure that each employee is informed of the following:

(A) The health hazards associated with cadmium exposure, with special attention to the information incorporated in appendix A to this section;

(B) The quantity, location, manner of use, release, and storage of cadmium in the workplace and the specific nature of operations that could result in exposure to cadmium, especially exposures above the PEL;

(C) The engineering controls and work practices associated with the employee's job assignment;

(D) The measures employees can take to protect themselves from exposure to cadmium, including modification of such habits as smoking and personal hygiene, and specific procedures the employer has implemented to protect employees from exposure to cadmium such as appropriate work practices, emergency procedures, and the provision of personal protective equipment;

(E) The purpose, proper selection, fitting, proper use, and limitations of respirators and protective clothing;

(F) The purpose and a description of the medical surveillance program required by paragraph (l) of this section;

(G) The contents of this section and its appendices, and,

(H) The employee's rights of access to records under § 1926.33(g) (1) and (2).

(iv) Additional access to information and training program and materials.

(A) The employer shall make a copy of this section and its appendices readily available to all affected employees and shall provide a copy without cost if requested.

(B) Upon request, the employer shall provide to the Assistant Secretary or the Director all materials relating to the employee information and the training program.

(5) *Multi-employer workplace.* In a multi-employer workplace, an employer who produces, uses, or stores cadmium in a manner that may expose employees of other employers to cadmium shall notify those employers of the potential hazard in accordance with paragraph (e) of the hazard communication standard for construction, 29 CFR 1926.59.

(n) *Recordkeeping*—(1) *Exposure monitoring.* (i) The employer shall establish and keep an accurate record of all air monitoring for cadmium in the workplace.

(ii) This record shall include at least the following information:

(A) The monitoring date, shift, duration, air volume, and results in terms of an 8-hour TWA of each sample taken, and if cadmium is not detected, the detection level;

(B) The name, social security number, and job classification of all employees monitored and of all other employees whose exposures the monitoring result is intended to represent, including, where applicable, a description of how it was determined that the employee's monitoring result could be taken to represent other employee's exposures;

(C) A description of the sampling and analytical methods used and evidence of their accuracy;

(D) The type of respiratory protective device, if any, worn by the monitored employee and by any other employee whose exposure the monitoring result is intended to represent;

(E) A notation of any other conditions that might have affected the monitoring results.

(F) Any exposure monitoring or objective data that were used and the levels.

(iii) The employer shall maintain this record for at least thirty (30) years, in accordance with § 1926.33 of this part.

(iv) The employer shall also provide a copy of the results of an employee's air monitoring prescribed in paragraph (d) of this section to an industry trade association and to the employee's union, if any, or, if either of such associations or unions do not exist, to another comparable organization that is competent to maintain such records and is reasonably accessible to employers and employees in the industry.

(2) *Objective data for exemption from requirement for initial monitoring.* (i) For purposes of this section, objective data are information demonstrating that a particular product or material containing cadmium or a specific process, operation, or activity involving cadmium cannot release dust or fumes in concentrations at or above the action level even under the worst-case release conditions. Objective data can be obtained from an industry-wide study or from laboratory product test results from manufacturers of cadmium-containing products or materials. The data the employer uses from an industry-wide survey must be obtained under workplace conditions closely resembling the processes, types of material, control methods, work practices and environmental conditions in the employer's current operations.

(ii) The employer shall maintain the record for at least 30 years of the objective data relied upon.

(3) *Medical surveillance.* (i) The employer shall establish and maintain an accurate record for each employee covered by medical surveillance under paragraph (l)(1)(i) of this section.

(ii) The record shall include at least the following information about the employee:

(A) Name, social security number, and description of duties;

(B) A copy of the physician's written opinions and of the explanation sheets for biological monitoring results;

(C) A copy of the medical history, and the results of any physical examination and all test results that are re-

quired to be provided by this section, including biological tests, X-rays, pulmonary function tests, etc., or that have been obtained to further evaluate any condition that might be related to cadmium exposure;

(D) The employee's medical symptoms that might be related to exposure to cadmium; and

(E) A copy of the information provided to the physician as required by paragraph (l)(9) of this section.

(iii) The employer shall assure that this record is maintained for the duration of employment plus thirty (30) years, in accordance with § 1926.33 of this part.

(iv) At the employee's request, the employer shall promptly provide a copy of the employee's medical record, or update as appropriate, to a medical doctor or a union specified by the employee.

(4) *Availability.* (i) Except as otherwise provided for in this section, access to all records required to be maintained by paragraphs (n)(1) through (3) of this section shall be in accordance with the provisions of 29 CFR 1910.1020.

(ii) Within 15 days after a request, the employer shall make an employee's medical records required to be kept by paragraph (n)(3) of this section available for examination and copying to the subject employee, to designated representatives, to anyone having the specific written consent of the subject employee, and after the employee's death or incapacitation, to the employee's family members.

(5) *Transfer of records.* Whenever an employer ceases to do business and there is no successor employer or designated organization to receive and retain records for the prescribed period, the employer shall comply with the requirements concerning transfer of records set forth in § 1926.33 (h) of this part.

(o) *Observation of monitoring—*(1) *Employee observation.* The employer shall provide affected employees or their designated representatives an opportunity to observe any monitoring of employee exposure to cadmium.

(2) *Observation procedures.* When observation of monitoring requires entry into an area where the use of protective clothing or equipment is required,

the employer shall provide the observer with that clothing and equipment and shall assure that the observer uses such clothing and equipment and complies with all other applicable safety and health procedures.

(p) [Reserved]

(q) *Appendices.* Except where portions of appendices A, B, D, E, and F to this section are expressly incorporated in requirements of this section, these appendices are purely informational and are not intended to create any additional obligations not otherwise imposed or to detract from any existing obligations.

APPENDIX A TO § 1926.1127—SUBSTANCE SAFETY DATA SHEET

NOTE: The requirements applicable to construction work under this appendix A are identical to those set forth in appendix A to § 1910.1027 of this chapter.

APPENDIX B TO § 1926.1127—SUBSTANCE TECHNICAL GUIDELINES FOR CADMIUM

NOTE: The requirements applicable to construction work under this appendix B are identical to those set forth in appendix B to § 1910.1027 of this chapter.

APPENDIX C TO § 1926.1127 [RESERVED]

APPENDIX D TO § 1926.1127—OCCUPATIONAL HEALTH HISTORY INTERVIEW WITH REFERENCE TO CADMIUM EXPOSURE

NOTE: The requirements applicable to construction work under this appendix D are identical to those set forth in appendix D to § 1910.1027 of this chapter.

APPENDIX E TO § 1926.1127—CADMIUM IN WORKPLACE ATMOSPHERES

NOTE: The requirements applicable to construction work under this appendix E are identical to those set forth in appendix E to § 1910.1027 of this chapter.

APPENDIX F TO § 1926.1127—NONMANDATORY PROTOCOL FOR BIOLOGICAL MONITORING

NOTE: The requirements applicable to construction work under this appendix F are identical to those set forth in appendix F to § 1910.1027 of this chapter.

[57 FR 42452, Sept. 14, 1992, as amended at 57 FR 49272, Oct. 30, 1992; 58 FR 21787, Apr. 23, 1993. Redesignated and amended at 59 FR 215, Jan. 3, 1994; 61 FR 5510, Feb. 13, 1996; 61 FR 31433, 31434, June 20, 1996; 63 FR 1298, Jan. 8, 1998; 70 FR 1144, Jan. 5, 2005; 71 FR 16675, Apr. 3, 2006; 71 FR 50192, Aug. 24, 2006; 73 FR 75589, Dec. 12, 2008; 76 FR 33612, June 8, 2011; 77 FR 17895, Mar. 26, 2012]

§ 1926.1128 Benzene.

NOTE: The requirements applicable to construction work under this section are identical to those set forth at § 1910.1028 of this chapter.

[61 FR 31434, June 20, 1996]

§ 1926.1129 Coke oven emissions.

NOTE: The requirements applicable to construction work under this section are identical to those set forth at § 1910.1029 of this chapter.

[61 FR 31434, June 20, 1996]

§ 1926.1144 1,2-dibromo-3-chloropropane.

NOTE: The requirements applicable to construction work under this section are identical to those set forth at § 1910.1044 of this chapter.

[61 FR 31434, June 20, 1996]

§ 1926.1145 Acrylonitrile.

NOTE: The requirements applicable to construction work under this section are identical to those set forth at § 1910.1045 of this chapter.

[61 FR 31434, June 20, 1996]

§ 1926.1147 Ethylene oxide.

NOTE: The requirements applicable to construction work under this section are identical to those set forth at § 1910.1047 of this chapter.

[61 FR 31434, June 20, 1996]

§ 1926.1148 Formaldehyde.

NOTE: The requirements applicable to construction work under this section are identical to those set forth at § 1910.1048 of this chapter.

[61 FR 31434, June 20, 1996]

§ 1926.1152 Methylene chloride.

NOTE: The requirements applicable to construction employment under this section are identical to those set forth at 29 CFR 1910.1052.

[62 FR 1619, Jan. 10, 1997]

Subpart AA—Confined Spaces in Construction

AUTHORITY: 40 U.S.C. 3701 *et seq.;* 29 U.S.C. 653, 655, 657; Secretary of Labor's Order No. 1–2012 (77 FR 3912); and 29 CFR part 1911.

SOURCE: 80 FR 25518, May 4, 2015, unless otherwise noted.

EFFECTIVE DATE NOTE: At 80 FR 25518, May 4, 2015, subpart AA was added to part 1926, effective Aug. 3, 2015.

§1926.1200 [Reserved]

§1926.1201 Scope.

(a) This standard sets forth requirements for practices and procedures to protect employees engaged in construction activities at a worksite with one or more confined spaces, subject to the exceptions in paragraph (b) of this section.

NOTE TO PARAGRAPH (a). Examples of locations where confined spaces may occur include, but are not limited to, the following: Bins; boilers; pits (such as elevator, escalator, pump, valve or other equipment); manholes (such as sewer, storm drain, electrical, communication, or other utility); tanks (such as fuel, chemical, water, or other liquid, solid or gas); incinerators; scrubbers; concrete pier columns; sewers; transformer vaults; heating, ventilation, and air-conditioning (HVAC) ducts; storm drains; water mains; precast concrete and other preformed manhole units; drilled shafts; enclosed beams; vessels; digesters; lift stations; cesspools; silos; air receivers; sludge gates; air preheaters; step up transformers; turbines; chillers; bag houses; and/or mixers/reactors.

(b) *Exceptions.* This standard does not apply to:

(1) Construction work regulated by subpart P of this part (Excavations).

(2) Construction work regulated by subpart S of this part (Underground Construction, Caissons, Cofferdams and Compressed Air).

(3) Construction work regulated by subpart Y of this part (Diving).

(c) Where this standard applies and there is a provision that addresses a confined space hazard in another applicable OSHA standard, the employer must comply with both that requirement and the applicable provisions of this standard.

§1926.1202 Definitions.

The following terms are defined for the purposes of this subpart only:

Acceptable entry conditions means the conditions that must exist in a permit space, before an employee may enter that space, to ensure that employees can safely enter into, and safely work within, the space.

Attendant means an individual stationed outside one or more permit spaces who assesses the status of authorized entrants and who must perform the duties specified in §1926.1209.

Authorized entrant means an employee who is authorized by the entry supervisor to enter a permit space.

Barrier means a physical obstruction that blocks or limits access.

Blanking or *blinding* means the absolute closure of a pipe, line, or duct by the fastening of a solid plate (such as a spectacle blind or a skillet blind) that completely covers the bore and that is capable of withstanding the maximum pressure of the pipe, line, or duct with no leakage beyond the plate.

Competent person means one who is capable of identifying existing and predictable hazards in the surroundings or working conditions which are unsanitary, hazardous, or dangerous to employees, and who has the authorization to take prompt corrective measures to eliminate them.

Confined space means a space that:

(1) Is large enough and so configured that an employee can bodily enter it;

(2) Has limited or restricted means for entry and exit; and

(3) Is not designed for continuous employee occupancy.

Control means the action taken to reduce the level of any hazard inside a confined space using engineering methods (for example, by ventilation), and then using these methods to maintain the reduced hazard level. Control also refers to the engineering methods used for this purpose. Personal protective equipment is not a control.

Controlling Contractor is the employer that has overall responsibility for construction at the worksite.

NOTE TO THE DEFINITION OF "CONTROLLING CONTRACTOR". If the controlling contractor owns or manages the property, then it is both a controlling employer and a host employer.

Double block and bleed means the closure of a line, duct, or pipe by closing and locking or tagging two in-line valves and by opening and locking or tagging a drain or vent valve in the line between the two closed valves.

669

Early-warning system means the method used to alert authorized entrants and attendants that an engulfment hazard may be developing. Examples of early-warning systems include, but are not limited to: Alarms activated by remote sensors; and lookouts with equipment for immediately communicating with the authorized entrants and attendants.

Emergency means any occurrence (including any failure of power, hazard control or monitoring equipment) or event, internal or external, to the permit space that could endanger entrants.

Engulfment means the surrounding and effective capture of a person by a liquid or finely divided (flowable) solid substance that can be aspirated to cause death by filling or plugging the respiratory system or that can exert enough force on the body to cause death by strangulation, constriction, crushing, or suffocation.

Entry means the action by which any part of a person passes through an opening into a permit-required confined space. Entry includes ensuing work activities in that space and is considered to have occurred as soon as any part of the entrant's body breaks the plane of an opening into the space, whether or not such action is intentional or any work activities are actually performed in the space.

Entry Employer means any employer who decides that an employee it directs will enter a permit space.

NOTE TO THE DEFINITION OF "ENTRY EM-PLOYER". An employer cannot avoid the duties of the standard merely by refusing to decide whether its employees will enter a permit space, and OSHA will consider the failure to so decide to be an implicit decision to allow employees to enter those spaces if they are working in the proximity of the space.

Entry permit (permit) means the written or printed document that is provided by the employer who designated the space a permit space to allow and control entry into a permit space and that contains the information specified in § 1926.1206.

Entry rescue occurs when a rescue service enters a permit space to rescue one or more employees.

Entry supervisor means the qualified person (such as the employer, foreman,

or crew chief) responsible for determining if acceptable entry conditions are present at a permit space where entry is planned, for authorizing entry and overseeing entry operations, and for terminating entry as required by this standard.

NOTE TO THE DEFINITION OF "ENTRY SUPER-VISOR" An entry supervisor also may serve as an attendant or as an authorized entrant, as long as that person is trained and equipped as required by this standard for each role he or she fills. Also, the duties of entry supervisor may be passed from one individual to another during the course of an entry operation.

Hazard means a physical hazard or hazardous atmosphere. See definitions below.

Hazardous atmosphere means an atmosphere that may expose employees to the risk of death, incapacitation, impairment of ability to self-rescue (that is, escape unaided from a permit space), injury, or acute illness from one or more of the following causes:

(1) Flammable gas, vapor, or mist in excess of 10 percent of its lower flammable limit (LFL);

(2) Airborne combustible dust at a concentration that meets or exceeds its LFL;

NOTE TO PARAGRAPH (2) OF THE DEFINITION OF "HAZARDOUS ATMOSPHERE". This concentration may be approximated as a condition in which the combustible dust obscures vision at a distance of 5 feet (1.52 meters) or less.

(3) Atmospheric oxygen concentration below 19.5 percent or above 23.5 percent;

(4) Atmospheric concentration of any substance for which a dose or a permissible exposure limit is published in subpart D of this part (Occupational Health and Environmental Control), or in subpart Z of this part (Toxic and Hazardous Substances), and which could result in employee exposure in excess of its dose or permissible exposure limit;

NOTE TO PARAGRAPH (4) OF THE DEFINITION OF "HAZARDOUS ATMOSPHERE". An atmospheric concentration of any substance that is not capable of causing death, incapacitation, impairment of ability to self-rescue, injury, or acute illness due to its health effects is not covered by this definition.

(5) Any other atmospheric condition that is immediately dangerous to life or health.

NOTE TO PARAGRAPH (5) OF THE DEFINITION OF "HAZARDOUS ATMOSPHERE". For air contaminants for which OSHA has not determined a dose or permissible exposure limit, other sources of information, such as Safety Data Sheets that comply with the Hazard Communication Standard, § 1926.59, published information, and internal documents can provide guidance in establishing acceptable atmospheric conditions.

Host employer means the employer that owns or manages the property where the construction work is taking place.

NOTE TO THE DEFINITION OF "HOST EM-PLOYER". If the owner of the property on which the construction activity occurs has contracted with an entity for the general management of that property, and has transferred to that entity the information specified in § 1926.1203(h)(1), OSHA will treat the contracted management entity as the host employer for as long as that entity manages the property. Otherwise, OSHA will treat the owner of the property as the host employer. In no case will there be more than one host employer.

Hot work means operations capable of providing a source of ignition (for example, riveting, welding, cutting, burning, and heating).

Immediately dangerous to life or health (IDLH) means any condition that would interfere with an individual's ability to escape unaided from a permit space and that poses a threat to life or that would cause irreversible adverse health effects.

NOTE TO THE DEFINITION OF "IMMEDIATELY DANGEROUS TO LIFE OR HEALTH". Some materials—hydrogen fluoride gas and cadmium vapor, for example—may produce immediate transient effects that, even if severe, may pass without medical attention, but are followed by sudden, possibly fatal collapse 12–72 hours after exposure. The victim "feels normal" after recovery from transient effects until collapse. Such materials in hazardous quantities are considered to be "immediately" dangerous to life or health.

Inerting means displacing the atmosphere in a permit space by a noncombustible gas (such as nitrogen) to such an extent that the resulting atmosphere is noncombustible.

NOTE TO THE DEFINITION OF "INTERING". This procedure produces an IDLH oxygen-deficient atmosphere.

Isolate or isolation means the process by which employees in a confined space are completely protected against the release of energy and material into the space, and contact with a physical hazard, by such means as: Blanking or blinding; misaligning or removing sections of lines, pipes, or ducts; a double block and bleed system; lockout or tagout of all sources of energy; blocking or disconnecting all mechanical linkages; or placement of barriers to eliminate the potential for employee contact with a physical hazard.

Limited or restricted means for entry or exit means a condition that has a potential to impede an employee's movement into or out of a confined space. Such conditions include, but are not limited to, trip hazards, poor illumination, slippery floors, inclining surfaces and ladders.

Line breaking means the intentional opening of a pipe, line, or duct that is or has been carrying flammable, corrosive, or toxic material, an inert gas, or any fluid at a volume, pressure, or temperature capable of causing injury.

Lockout means the placement of a lockout device on an energy isolating device, in accordance with an established procedure, ensuring that the energy isolating device and the equipment being controlled cannot be operated until the lockout device is removed.

Lower flammable limit or lower explosive limit means the minimum concentration of a substance in air needed for an ignition source to cause a flame or explosion.

Monitor or monitoring means the process used to identify and evaluate the hazards after an authorized entrant enters the space. This is a process of checking for changes that is performed in a periodic or continuous manner after the completion of the initial testing or evaluation of that space.

Non-entry rescue occurs when a rescue service, usually the attendant, retrieves employees in a permit space without entering the permit space.

Non-permit confined space means a confined space that meets the definition of a confined space but does not meet the requirements for a permit-required confined space, as defined in this subpart.

Oxygen deficient atmosphere means an atmosphere containing less than 19.5 percent oxygen by volume.

Oxygen enriched atmosphere means an atmosphere containing more than 23.5 percent oxygen by volume.

Permit-required confined space (permit space) means a confined space that has one or more of the following characteristics:

(1) Contains or has a potential to contain a hazardous atmosphere;

(2) Contains a material that has the potential for engulfing an entrant;

(3) Has an internal configuration such that an entrant could be trapped or asphyxiated by inwardly converging walls or by a floor which slopes downward and tapers to a smaller cross-section; or

(4) Contains any other recognized serious safety or health hazard.

Permit-required confined space program (permit space program) means the employer's overall program for controlling, and, where appropriate, for protecting employees from, permit space hazards and for regulating employee entry into permit spaces.

Physical hazard means an existing or potential hazard that can cause death or serious physical damage. Examples include, but are not limited to: Explosives (as defined by paragraph (n) of § 1926.914, definition of "explosive"); mechanical, electrical, hydraulic and pneumatic energy; radiation; temperature extremes; engulfment; noise; and inwardly converging surfaces. Physical hazard also includes chemicals that can cause death or serious physical damage through skin or eye contact (rather than through inhalation).

Prohibited condition means any condition in a permit space that is not allowed by the permit during the period when entry is authorized. A hazardous atmosphere is a prohibited condition unless the employer can demonstrate that personal protective equipment (PPE) will provide effective protection for each employee in the permit space and provides the appropriate PPE to each employee.

Qualified person means one who, by possession of a recognized degree, certificate, or professional standing, or who by extensive knowledge, training, and experience, has successfully demonstrated his ability to solve or resolve problems relating to the subject matter, the work, or the project.

Representative permit space means a mock-up of a confined space that has entrance openings that are similar to, and is of similar size, configuration, and accessibility to, the permit space that authorized entrants enter.

Rescue means retrieving, and providing medical assistance to, one or more employees who are in a permit space.

Rescue service means the personnel designated to rescue employees from permit spaces.

Retrieval system means the equipment (including a retrieval line, chest or full body harness, wristlets or anklets, if appropriate, and a lifting device or anchor) used for non-entry rescue of persons from permit spaces.

Serious physical damage means an impairment or illness in which a body part is made functionally useless or is substantially reduced in efficiency. Such impairment or illness may be permanent or temporary and includes, but is not limited to, loss of consciousness, disorientation, or other immediate and substantial reduction in mental efficiency. Injuries involving such impairment would usually require treatment by a physician or other licensed healthcare professional.

Tagout means:

(1) Placement of a tagout device on a circuit or equipment that has been de-energized, in accordance with an established procedure, to indicate that the circuit or equipment being controlled may not be operated until the tagout device is removed; and

(2) The employer ensures that:

(i) Tagout provides equivalent protection to lockout; or

(ii) That lockout is infeasible and the employer has relieved, disconnected, restrained and otherwise rendered safe stored (residual) energy.

Test or testing means the process by which the hazards that may confront entrants of a permit space are identified and evaluated. Testing includes specifying the tests that are to be performed in the permit space.

NOTE TO THE DEFINITION OF "TEST OR TEST-ING". Testing enables employers both to devise and implement adequate control measures for the protection of authorized entrants and to determine if acceptable entry conditions are present immediately prior to, and during, entry.

Ventilate or *ventilation* means controlling a hazardous atmosphere using continuous forced-air mechanical systems that meet the requirements of §1926.57 (Ventilation).

§1926.1203 General requirements.

(a) Before it begins work at a worksite, each employer must ensure that a competent person identifies all confined spaces in which one or more of the employees it directs may work, and identifies each space that is a permit space, through consideration and evaluation of the elements of that space, including testing as necessary.

(b) If the workplace contains one or more permit spaces, the employer who identifies, or who receives notice of, a permit space must:

(1) Inform exposed employees by posting danger signs or by any other equally effective means, of the existence and location of, and the danger posed by, each permit space; and

NOTE TO PARAGRAPH (b)(1). A sign reading "DANGER—PERMIT-REQUIRED CONFINED SPACE, DO NOT ENTER" or using other similar language would satisfy the requirement for a sign.

(2) Inform, in a timely manner and in a manner other than posting, its employees' authorized representatives and the controlling contractor of the existence and location of, and the danger posed by, each permit space.

(c) Each employer who identifies, or receives notice of, a permit space and has not authorized employees it directs to work in that space must take effective measures to prevent those employees from entering that permit space, in addition to complying with all other applicable requirements of this standard.

(d) If any employer decides that employees it directs will enter a permit space, that employer must have a written permit space program that complies with §1926.1204 implemented at the construction site. The written program must be made available prior to

and during entry operations for inspection by employees and their authorized representatives.

(e) An employer may use the alternate procedures specified in paragraph (e)(2) of this section for entering a permit space only under the conditions set forth in paragraph (e)(1) of this section.

(1) An employer whose employees enter a permit space need not comply with §§1926.1204 through 1206 and §§1926.1208 through 1211, provided that all of the following conditions are met:

(i) The employer can demonstrate that all physical hazards in the space are eliminated or isolated through engineering controls so that the only hazard posed by the permit space is an actual or potential hazardous atmosphere;

(ii) The employer can demonstrate that continuous forced air ventilation alone is sufficient to maintain that permit space safe for entry, and that, in the event the ventilation system stops working, entrants can exit the space safely;

(iii) The employer develops monitoring and inspection data that supports the demonstrations required by paragraphs (e)(1)(i) and (ii) of this section;

(iv) If an initial entry of the permit space is necessary to obtain the data required by paragraph (e)(1)(iii) of this section, the entry is performed in compliance with §§1926.1204 through 1926.1211;

(v) The determinations and supporting data required by paragraphs (e)(1)(i), (ii), and (iii) of this section are documented by the employer and are made available to each employee who enters the permit space under the terms of paragraph (e) of this section or to that employee's authorized representative; and

(vi) Entry into the permit space under the terms of paragraph (e)(1) of this section is performed in accordance with the requirements of paragraph (e)(2) of this section.

NOTE TO PARAGRAPH (e)(1). See paragraph (g) of this section for reclassification of a permit space after all hazards within the space have been eliminated.

(2) The following requirements apply to entry into permit spaces that meet

the conditions set forth in paragraph (e)(1) of this section:

(i) Any conditions making it unsafe to remove an entrance cover must be eliminated before the cover is removed.

(ii) When entrance covers are removed, the opening must be immediately guarded by a railing, temporary cover, or other temporary barrier that will prevent an accidental fall through the opening and that will protect each employee working in the space from foreign objects entering the space.

(iii) Before an employee enters the space, the internal atmosphere must be tested, with a calibrated direct-reading instrument, for oxygen content, for flammable gases and vapors, and for potential toxic air contaminants, in that order. Any employee who enters the space, or that employee's authorized representative, must be provided an opportunity to observe the pre-entry testing required by this paragraph.

(iv) No hazardous atmosphere is permitted within the space whenever any employee is inside the space.

(v) Continuous forced air ventilation must be used, as follows:

(A) An employee must not enter the space until the forced air ventilation has eliminated any hazardous atmosphere;

(B) The forced air ventilation must be so directed as to ventilate the immediate areas where an employee is or will be present within the space and must continue until all employees have left the space;

(C) The air supply for the forced air ventilation must be from a clean source and must not increase the hazards in the space.

(vi) The atmosphere within the space must be continuously monitored unless the entry employer can demonstrate that equipment for continuous monitoring is not commercially available or periodic monitoring is sufficient. If continuous monitoring is used, the employer must ensure that the monitoring equipment has an alarm that will notify all entrants if a specified atmospheric threshold is achieved, or that an employee will check the monitor with sufficient frequency to ensure that entrants have adequate time to escape. If continuous monitoring is not

used, periodic monitoring is required. All monitoring must ensure that the continuous forced air ventilation is preventing the accumulation of a hazardous atmosphere. Any employee who enters the space, or that employee's authorized representative, must be provided with an opportunity to observe the testing required by this paragraph (e)(2)(vi).

(vii) If a hazard is detected during entry:

(A) Each employee must leave the space immediately;

(B) The space must be evaluated to determine how the hazard developed; and

(C) The employer must implement measures to protect employees from the hazard before any subsequent entry takes place.

(viii) The employer must ensure a safe method of entering and exiting the space. If a hoisting system is used, it must be designed and manufactured for personnel hoisting; however, a job-made hoisting system is permissible if it is approved for personnel hoisting by a registered professional engineer, in writing, prior to use.

(ix) The employer must verify that the space is safe for entry and that the pre-entry measures required by paragraph (e)(2) of this section have been taken, through a written certification that contains the date, the location of the space, and the signature of the person providing the certification. The certification must be made before entry and must be made available to each employee entering the space or to that employee's authorized representative.

(f) When there are changes in the use or configuration of a non-permit confined space that might increase the hazards to entrants, or some indication that the initial evaluation of the space may not have been adequate, each entry employer must have a competent person reevaluate that space and, if necessary, reclassify it as a permit-required confined space.

(g) A space classified by an employer as a permit-required confined space may only be reclassified as a non-permit confined space when a competent person determines that all of the applicable requirements in paragraphs (g)(1) through (4) of this section have been met:

(1) If the permit space poses no actual or potential atmospheric hazards and if all hazards within the space are eliminated or isolated without entry into the space (unless the employer can demonstrate that doing so without entry is infeasible), the permit space may be reclassified as a non-permit confined space for as long as the non-atmospheric hazards remain eliminated or isolated;

(2) The entry employer must eliminate or isolate the hazards without entering the space, unless it can demonstrate that this is infeasible. If it is necessary to enter the permit space to eliminate or isolate hazards, such entry must be performed under §§1926.1204 through 1926.1211. If testing and inspection during that entry demonstrate that the hazards within the permit space have been eliminated or isolated, the permit space may be reclassified as a non-permit confined space for as long as the hazards remain eliminated or isolated;

NOTE TO PARAGRAPH (g)(2). Control of atmospheric hazards through forced air ventilation does not constitute elimination or isolation of the hazards. Paragraph (e) of this section covers permit space entry where the employer can demonstrate that forced air ventilation alone will control all hazards in the space.

(3) The entry employer must document the basis for determining that all hazards in a permit space have been eliminated or isolated, through a certification that contains the date, the location of the space, and the signature of the person making the determination. The certification must be made available to each employee entering the space or to that employee's authorized representative; and

(4) If hazards arise within a permit space that has been reclassified as a non-permit space under paragraph (g) of this section, each employee in the space must exit the space. The entry employer must then reevaluate the space and reclassify it as a permit space as appropriate in accordance with all other applicable provisions of this standard.

(h) *Permit space entry communication and coordination.* (1) Before entry oper-

ations begin, the host employer must provide the following information, if it has it, to the controlling contractor:

(i) The location of each known permit space;

(ii) The hazards or potential hazards in each space or the reason it is a permit space; and

(iii) Any precautions that the host employer or any previous controlling contractor or entry employer implemented for the protection of employees in the permit space.

(2) Before entry operations begin, the controlling contractor must:

(i) Obtain the host employer's information about the permit space hazards and previous entry operations; and

(ii) Provide the following information to each entity entering a permit space and any other entity at the worksite whose activities could foreseeably result in a hazard in the permit space:

(A) The information received from the host employer;

(B) Any additional information the controlling contractor has about the subjects listed in paragraph (h)(1) of this section; and

(C) The precautions that the host employer, controlling contractor, or other entry employers implemented for the protection of employees in the permit spaces.

(3) Before entry operations begin, each entry employer must:

(i) Obtain all of the controlling contractor's information regarding permit space hazards and entry operations; and

(ii) Inform the controlling contractor of the permit space program that the entry employer will follow, including any hazards likely to be confronted or created in each permit space.

(4) The controlling contractor and entry employer(s) must coordinate entry operations when:

(i) More than one entity performs permit space entry at the same time; or

(ii) Permit space entry is performed at the same time that any activities that could foreseeably result in a hazard in the permit space are performed.

(5) After entry operations:

(i) The controlling contractor must debrief each entity that entered a permit space regarding the permit space program followed and any hazards confronted or created in the permit space(s) during entry operations;

(ii) The entry employer must inform the controlling contractor in a timely manner of the permit space program followed and of any hazards confronted or created in the permit space(s) during entry operations; and

(iii) The controlling contractor must apprise the host employer of the information exchanged with the entry entities pursuant to this subparagraph.

NOTE TO PARAGRAPH (h). Unless a host employer or controlling contractor has or will have employees in a confined space, it is not required to enter any confined space to collect the information specified in this paragraph (h).

(i) If there is no controlling contractor present at the worksite, the requirements for, and role of, controlling contactors in this section must be fulfilled by the host employer or other employer who arranges to have employees of another employer perform work that involves permit space entry.

§ 1926.1204 Permit-required confined space program.

Each entry employer must:

(a) Implement the measures necessary to prevent unauthorized entry;

(b) Identify and evaluate the hazards of permit spaces before employees enter them;

(c) Develop and implement the means, procedures, and practices necessary for safe permit space entry operations, including, but not limited to, the following:

(1) Specifying acceptable entry conditions;

(2) Providing each authorized entrant or that employee's authorized representative with the opportunity to observe any monitoring or testing of permit spaces;

(3) Isolating the permit space and physical hazard(s) within the space;

(4) Purging, inerting, flushing, or ventilating the permit space as necessary to eliminate or control atmospheric hazards;

NOTE TO PARAGRAPH (c)(4). When an employer is unable to reduce the atmosphere below 10 percent LFL, the employer may only enter if the employer inerts the space so as to render the entire atmosphere in the space non-combustible, and the employees use PPE to address any other atmospheric hazards (such as oxygen deficiency), and the employer eliminates or isolates all physical hazards in the space.

(5) Determining that, in the event the ventilation system stops working, the monitoring procedures will detect an increase in atmospheric hazard levels in sufficient time for the entrants to safely exit the permit space;

(6) Providing pedestrian, vehicle, or other barriers as necessary to protect entrants from external hazards;

(7) Verifying that conditions in the permit space are acceptable for entry throughout the duration of an authorized entry, and ensuring that employees are not allowed to enter into, or remain in, a permit space with a hazardous atmosphere unless the employer can demonstrate that personal protective equipment (PPE) will provide effective protection for each employee in the permit space and provides the appropriate PPE to each employee; and

(8) Eliminating any conditions (for example, high pressure) that could make it unsafe to remove an entrance cover.

(d) Provide the following equipment (specified in paragraphs (d)(1) through (9) of this section) at no cost to each employee, maintain that equipment properly, and ensure that each employee uses that equipment properly:

(1) Testing and monitoring equipment needed to comply with paragraph (e) of this section;

(2) Ventilating equipment needed to obtain acceptable entry conditions;

(3) Communications equipment necessary for compliance with §§ 1926.1208(c) and 1926.1209(e), including any necessary electronic communication equipment for attendants assessing entrants' status in multiple spaces;

(4) Personal protective equipment insofar as feasible engineering and work-practice controls do not adequately protect employees;

NOTE TO PARAGRAPH (d)(4). The requirements of subpart E of this part and other PPE requirements continue to apply to the use of PPE in a permit space. For example, if employees use respirators, then the respirator requirements in §1926.103 (Respiratory protection) must be met.

(5) Lighting equipment that meets the minimum illumination requirements in §1926.56, that is approved for the ignitable or combustible properties of the specific gas, vapor, dust, or fiber that will be present, and that is sufficient to enable employees to see well enough to work safely and to exit the space quickly in an emergency;

(6) Barriers and shields as required by paragraph (c)(4) of this section;

(7) Equipment, such as ladders, needed for safe ingress and egress by authorized entrants;

(8) Rescue and emergency equipment needed to comply with paragraph (i) of this section, except to the extent that the equipment is provided by rescue services; and

(9) Any other equipment necessary for safe entry into, safe exit from, and rescue from, permit spaces.

(e) Evaluate permit space conditions in accordance with the following paragraphs (e)(1) through (6) of this section when entry operations are conducted:

(1) Test conditions in the permit space to determine if acceptable entry conditions exist before changes to the space's natural ventilation are made, and before entry is authorized to begin, except that, if an employer demonstrates that isolation of the space is infeasible because the space is large or is part of a continuous system (such as a sewer), the employer must:

(i) Perform pre-entry testing to the extent feasible before entry is authorized; and,

(ii) If entry is authorized, continuously monitor entry conditions in the areas where authorized entrants are working, except that employers may use periodic monitoring in accordance with paragraph (e)(2) of this section for monitoring an atmospheric hazard if they can demonstrate that equipment for continuously monitoring that hazard is not commercially available;

(iii) Provide an early-warning system that continuously monitors for non-isolated engulfment hazards. The system must alert authorized entrants and attendants in sufficient time for the authorized entrants to safely exit the space.

(2) Continuously monitor atmospheric hazards unless the employer can demonstrate that the equipment for continuously monitoring a hazard is not commercially available or that periodic monitoring is of sufficient frequency to ensure that the atmospheric hazard is being controlled at safe levels. If continuous monitoring is not used, periodic monitoring is required with sufficient frequency to ensure that acceptable entry conditions are being maintained during the course of entry operations;

(3) When testing for atmospheric hazards, test first for oxygen, then for combustible gases and vapors, and then for toxic gases and vapors;

(4) Provide each authorized entrant or that employee's authorized representative an opportunity to observe the pre-entry and any subsequent testing or monitoring of permit spaces;

(5) Reevaluate the permit space in the presence of any authorized entrant or that employee's authorized representative who requests that the employer conduct such reevaluation because there is some indication that the evaluation of that space may not have been adequate; and

(6) Immediately provide each authorized entrant or that employee's authorized representative with the results of any testing conducted in accordance with this section.

(f) Provide at least one attendant outside the permit space into which entry is authorized for the duration of entry operations:

(1) Attendants may be assigned to more than one permit space provided the duties described in §1926.1209 can be effectively performed for each permit space.

(2) Attendants may be stationed at any location outside the permit space as long as the duties described in §1926.1209 can be effectively performed for each permit space to which the attendant is assigned.

(g) If multiple spaces are to be assigned to a single attendant, include in the permit program the means and procedures to enable the attendant to respond to an emergency affecting one or more of those permit spaces without distraction from the attendant's responsibilities under §1926.1209;

677

(h) Designate each person who is to have an active role (as, for example, authorized entrants, attendants, entry supervisors, or persons who test or monitor the atmosphere in a permit space) in entry operations, identify the duties of each such employee, and provide each such employee with the training required by § 1926.1207;

(i) Develop and implement procedures for summoning rescue and emergency services (including procedures for summoning emergency assistance in the event of a failed non-entry rescue), for rescuing entrants from permit spaces, for providing necessary emergency services to rescued employees, and for preventing unauthorized personnel from attempting a rescue;

(j) Develop and implement a system for the preparation, issuance, use, and cancellation of entry permits as required by this standard, including the safe termination of entry operations under both planned and emergency conditions;

(k) Develop and implement procedures to coordinate entry operations, in consultation with the controlling contractor, when employees of more than one employer are working simultaneously in a permit space or elsewhere on the worksite where their activities could, either alone or in conjunction with the activities within a permit space, foreseeably result in a hazard within the confined space, so that employees of one employer do not endanger the employees of any other employer;

(l) Develop and implement procedures (such as closing off a permit space and canceling the permit) necessary for concluding the entry after entry operations have been completed;

(m) Review entry operations when the measures taken under the permit space program may not protect employees and revise the program to correct deficiencies found to exist before subsequent entries are authorized; and

NOTE TO PARAGRAPH (m). Examples of circumstances requiring the review of the permit space program include, but are not limited to: Any unauthorized entry of a permit space, the detection of a permit space hazard not covered by the permit, the detection of a condition prohibited by the permit, the occurrence of an injury or near-miss during entry, a change in the use or configuration

of a permit space, and employee complaints about the effectiveness of the program.

(n) Review the permit space program, using the canceled permits retained under § 1926.1205(f), within 1 year after each entry and revise the program as necessary to ensure that employees participating in entry operations are protected from permit space hazards.

NOTE TO PARAGRAPH (n). Employers may perform a single annual review covering all entries performed during a 12-month period. If no entry is performed during a 12-month period, no review is necessary.

§ 1926.1205 Permitting process.

(a) Before entry is authorized, each entry employer must document the completion of measures required by § 1926.1204(c) by preparing an entry permit.

(b) Before entry begins, the entry supervisor identified on the permit must sign the entry permit to authorize entry.

(c) The completed permit must be made available at the time of entry to all authorized entrants or their authorized representatives, by posting it at the entry portal or by any other equally effective means, so that the entrants can confirm that pre-entry preparations have been completed.

(d) The duration of the permit may not exceed the time required to complete the assigned task or job identified on the permit in accordance with § 1926.1206(b).

(e) The entry supervisor must terminate entry and take the following action when any of the following apply:

(1) Cancel the entry permit when the entry operations covered by the entry permit have been completed; or

(2) Suspend or cancel the entry permit and fully reassess the space before allowing reentry when a condition that is not allowed under the entry permit arises in or near the permit space and that condition is temporary in nature and does not change the configuration of the space or create any new hazards within it; and

(3) Cancel the entry permit when a condition that is not allowed under the entry permit arises in or near the permit space and that condition is not covered by paragraph (e)(2) of this section.

(f) The entry employer must retain each canceled entry permit for at least 1 year to facilitate the review of the permit-required confined space program required by §1926.1204(n). Any problems encountered during an entry operation must be noted on the pertinent permit so that appropriate revisions to the permit space program can be made.

§1926.1206 Entry permit.

The entry permit that documents compliance with this section and authorizes entry to a permit space must identify:

(a) The permit space to be entered;

(b) The purpose of the entry;

(c) The date and the authorized duration of the entry permit;

(d) The authorized entrants within the permit space, by name or by such other means (for example, through the use of rosters or tracking systems) as will enable the attendant to determine quickly and accurately, for the duration of the permit, which authorized entrants are inside the permit space;

NOTE TO PARAGRAPH (d). This requirement may be met by inserting a reference on the entry permit as to the means used, such as a roster or tracking system, to keep track of the authorized entrants within the permit space.

(e) Means of detecting an increase in atmospheric hazard levels in the event the ventilation system stops working;

(f) Each person, by name, currently serving as an attendant;

(g) The individual, by name, currently serving as entry supervisor, and the signature or initials of each entry supervisor who authorizes entry;

(h) The hazards of the permit space to be entered;

(i) The measures used to isolate the permit space and to eliminate or control permit space hazards before entry;

NOTE TO PARAGRAPH (i). Those measures can include, but are not limited to, the lockout or tagging of equipment and procedures for purging, inerting, ventilating, and flushing permit spaces.

(j) The acceptable entry conditions;

(k) The results of tests and monitoring performed under §1926.1204(e), accompanied by the names or initials of the testers and by an indication of when the tests were performed;

(l) The rescue and emergency services that can be summoned and the means (such as the equipment to use and the numbers to call) for summoning those services;

(m) The communication procedures used by authorized entrants and attendants to maintain contact during the entry;

(n) Equipment, such as personal protective equipment, testing equipment, communications equipment, alarm systems, and rescue equipment, to be provided for compliance with this standard;

(o) Any other information necessary, given the circumstances of the particular confined space, to ensure employee safety; and

(p) Any additional permits, such as for hot work, that have been issued to authorize work in the permit space.

§1926.1207 Training.

(a) The employer must provide training to each employee whose work is regulated by this standard, at no cost to the employee, and ensure that the employee possesses the understanding, knowledge, and skills necessary for the safe performance of the duties assigned under this standard. This training must result in an understanding of the hazards in the permit space and the methods used to isolate, control or in other ways protect employees from these hazards, and for those employees not authorized to perform entry rescues, in the dangers of attempting such rescues.

(b) Training required by this section must be provided to each affected employee:

(1) In both a language and vocabulary that the employee can understand;

(2) Before the employee is first assigned duties under this standard;

(3) Before there is a change in assigned duties;

(4) Whenever there is a change in permit space entry operations that presents a hazard about which an employee has not previously been trained; and

(5) Whenever there is any evidence of a deviation from the permit space entry procedures required by

§ 1926.1204(c) or there are inadequacies in the employee's knowledge or use of these procedures.

(c) The training must establish employee proficiency in the duties required by this standard and must introduce new or revised procedures, as necessary, for compliance with this standard.

(d) The employer must maintain training records to show that the training required by paragraphs (a) through (c) of this section has been accomplished. The training records must contain each employee's name, the name of the trainers, and the dates of training. The documentation must be available for inspection by employees and their authorized representatives, for the period of time the employee is employed by that employer.

§ 1926.1208 Duties of authorized entrants.

The entry employer must ensure that all authorized entrants:

(a) Are familiar with and understand the hazards that may be faced during entry, including information on the mode, signs or symptoms, and consequences of the exposure;

(b) Properly use equipment as required by § 1926.1204(d);

(c) Communicate with the attendant as necessary to enable the attendant to assess entrant status and to enable the attendant to alert entrants of the need to evacuate the space as required by § 1926.1209(f);

(d) Alert the attendant whenever:

(1) There is any warning sign or symptom of exposure to a dangerous situation; or

(2) The entrant detects a prohibited condition; and

(e) Exit from the permit space as quickly as possible whenever:

(1) An order to evacuate is given by the attendant or the entry supervisor;

(2) There is any warning sign or symptom of exposure to a dangerous situation;

(3) The entrant detects a prohibited condition; or

(4) An evacuation alarm is activated.

§ 1926.1209 Duties of attendants.

The entry employer must ensure that each attendant:

(a) Is familiar with and understands the hazards that may be faced during entry, including information on the mode, signs or symptoms, and consequences of the exposure;

(b) Is aware of possible behavioral effects of hazard exposure in authorized entrants;

(c) Continuously maintains an accurate count of authorized entrants in the permit space and ensures that the means used to identify authorized entrants under § 1926.1206(d) accurately identifies who is in the permit space;

(d) Remains outside the permit space during entry operations until relieved by another attendant;

NOTE TO PARAGRAPH (d). Once an attendant has been relieved by another attendant, the relieved attendant may enter a permit space to attempt a rescue when the employer's permit space program allows attendant entry for rescue and the attendant has been trained and equipped for rescue operations as required by § 1926.1211(a).

(e) Communicates with authorized entrants as necessary to assess entrant status and to alert entrants of the need to evacuate the space under § 1926.1208(e);

(f) Assesses activities and conditions inside and outside the space to determine if it is safe for entrants to remain in the space and orders the authorized entrants to evacuate the permit space immediately under any of the following conditions:

(1) If there is a prohibited condition;

(2) If the behavioral effects of hazard exposure are apparent in an authorized entrant;

(3) If there is a situation outside the space that could endanger the authorized entrants; or

(4) If the attendant cannot effectively and safely perform all the duties required under this section;

(g) Summons rescue and other emergency services as soon as the attendant determines that authorized entrants may need assistance to escape from permit space hazards;

(h) Takes the following actions when unauthorized persons approach or enter a permit space while entry is underway:

(1) Warns the unauthorized persons that they must stay away from the permit space;

(2) Advises the unauthorized persons that they must exit immediately if they have entered the permit space; and

(3) Informs the authorized entrants and the entry supervisor if unauthorized persons have entered the permit space;

(i) Performs non-entry rescues as specified by the employer's rescue procedure; and

(j) Performs no duties that might interfere with the attendant's primary duty to assess and protect the authorized entrants.

§1926.1210 Duties of entry supervisors.

The entry employer must ensure that each entry supervisor:

(a) Is familiar with and understands the hazards that may be faced during entry, including information on the mode, signs or symptoms, and consequences of the exposure;

(b) Verifies, by checking that the appropriate entries have been made on the permit, that all tests specified by the permit have been conducted and that all procedures and equipment specified by the permit are in place before endorsing the permit and allowing entry to begin;

(c) Terminates the entry and cancels or suspends the permit as required by §1926.1205(e);

(d) Verifies that rescue services are available and that the means for summoning them are operable, and that the employer will be notified as soon as the services become unavailable;

(e) Removes unauthorized individuals who enter or who attempt to enter the permit space during entry operations; and

(f) Determines, whenever responsibility for a permit space entry operation is transferred, and at intervals dictated by the hazards and operations performed within the space, that entry operations remain consistent with terms of the entry permit and that acceptable entry conditions are maintained.

§1926.1211 Rescue and emergency services.

(a) An employer who designates rescue and emergency services, pursuant to §1926.1204(i), must:

(1) Evaluate a prospective rescuer's ability to respond to a rescue summons in a timely manner, considering the hazard(s) identified;

NOTE TO PARAGRAPH (a)(1). What will be considered timely will vary according to the specific hazards involved in each entry. For example, §1926.103 (Respiratory protection) requires that employers provide a standby person or persons capable of immediate action to rescue employee(s) wearing respiratory protection while in work areas defined as IDLH atmospheres.

(2) Evaluate a prospective rescue service's ability, in terms of proficiency with rescue-related tasks and equipment, to function appropriately while rescuing entrants from the particular permit space or types of permit spaces identified;

(3) Select a rescue team or service from those evaluated that:

(i) Has the capability to reach the victim(s) within a time frame that is appropriate for the permit space hazard(s) identified;

(ii) Is equipped for, and proficient in, performing the needed rescue services;

(iii) Agrees to notify the employer immediately in the event that the rescue service becomes unavailable;

(4) Inform each rescue team or service of the hazards they may confront when called on to perform rescue at the site; and

(5) Provide the rescue team or service selected with access to all permit spaces from which rescue may be necessary so that the rescue team or service can develop appropriate rescue plans and practice rescue operations.

(b) An employer whose employees have been designated to provide permit space rescue and/or emergency services must take the following measures and provide all equipment and training at no cost to those employees:

(1) Provide each affected employee with the personal protective equipment (PPE) needed to conduct permit space rescues safely and train each affected employee so the employee is proficient in the use of that PPE;

(2) Train each affected employee to perform assigned rescue duties. The employer must ensure that such employees successfully complete the training required and establish proficiency as authorized entrants, as provided by §§ 1926.1207 and 1926.1208;

(3) Train each affected employee in basic first aid and cardiopulmonary resuscitation (CPR). The employer must ensure that at least one member of the rescue team or service holding a current certification in basic first aid and CPR is available; and

(4) Ensure that affected employees practice making permit space rescues before attempting an actual rescue, and at least once every 12 months, by means of simulated rescue operations in which they remove dummies, manikins, or actual persons from the actual permit spaces or from representative permit spaces, except practice rescue is not required where the affected employees properly performed a rescue operation during the last 12 months in the same permit space the authorized entrant will enter, or in a similar permit space. Representative permit spaces must, with respect to opening size, configuration, and accessibility, simulate the types of permit spaces from which rescue is to be performed.

(c) Non-entry rescue is required unless the retrieval equipment would increase the overall risk of entry or would not contribute to the rescue of the entrant. The employer must designate an entry rescue service whenever non-entry rescue is not selected. Whenever non-entry rescue is selected, the entry employer must ensure that retrieval systems or methods are used whenever an authorized entrant enters a permit space, and must confirm, prior to entry, that emergency assistance would be available in the event that non-entry rescue fails. Retrieval systems must meet the following requirements:

(1) Each authorized entrant must use a chest or full body harness, with a retrieval line attached at the center of the entrant's back near shoulder level, above the entrant's head, or at another point which the employer can establish presents a profile small enough for the successful removal of the entrant. Wristlets or anklets may be used in lieu of the chest or full body harness if the employer can demonstrate that the use of a chest or full body harness is infeasible or creates a greater hazard and that the use of wristlets or anklets is the safest and most effective alternative.

(2) The other end of the retrieval line must be attached to a mechanical device or fixed point outside the permit space in such a manner that rescue can begin as soon as the rescuer becomes aware that rescue is necessary. A mechanical device must be available to retrieve personnel from vertical type permit spaces more than 5 feet (1.52 meters) deep.

(3) Equipment that is unsuitable for retrieval must not be used, including, but not limited to, retrieval lines that have a reasonable probability of becoming entangled with the retrieval lines used by other authorized entrants, or retrieval lines that will not work due to the internal configuration of the permit space.

(d) If an injured entrant is exposed to a substance for which a Safety Data Sheet (SDS) or other similar written information is required to be kept at the worksite, that SDS or written information must be made available to the medical facility treating the exposed entrant.

§ 1926.1212　Employee participation.

(a) Employers must consult with affected employees and their authorized representatives on the development and implementation of all aspects of the permit space program required by § 1926.1203.

(b) Employers must make available to each affected employee and his/her authorized representatives all information required to be developed by this standard.

§ 1926.1213　Provision of documents to Secretary.

For each document required to be retained in this standard, the retaining employer must make the document available on request to the Secretary of Labor or the Secretary's designee.

Subpart BB [Reserved]

Subpart CC—Cranes and Derricks in Construction

AUTHORITY: 40 U.S.C. 3701 *et seq.;* 29 U.S.C. 653, 655, 657; Secretary of Labor's Order No. 5–2007 (72 FR 31159) or 1–2012 (77 FR 3912), as applicable; and 29 CFR Part 1911.

SOURCE: 75 FR 48135, Aug. 9, 2010, unless otherwise noted.

§1926.1400 Scope.

(a) This standard applies to power-operated equipment, when used in construction, that can hoist, lower and horizontally move a suspended load. Such equipment includes, but is not limited to: Articulating cranes (such as knuckle-boom cranes); crawler cranes; floating cranes; cranes on barges; locomotive cranes; mobile cranes (such as wheel-mounted, rough-terrain, all-terrain, commercial truck-mounted, and boom truck cranes); multi-purpose machines when configured to hoist and lower (by means of a winch or hook) and horizontally move a suspended load; industrial cranes (such as carry-deck cranes); dedicated pile drivers; service/mechanic trucks with a hoisting device; a crane on a monorail; tower cranes (such as a fixed jib, *i.e.,* "hammerhead boom"), luffing boom and self-erecting); pedestal cranes; portal cranes; overhead and gantry cranes; straddle cranes; sideboom cranes; derricks; and variations of such equipment. However, items listed in paragraph (c) of this section are excluded from the scope of this standard.

(b) *Attachments.* This standard applies to equipment included in paragraph (a) of this section when used with attachments. Such attachments, whether crane-attached or suspended include, but are not limited to: Hooks, magnets, grapples, clamshell buckets, orange peel buckets, concrete buckets, drag lines, personnel platforms, augers or drills and pile driving equipment.

(c) *Exclusions.* This subpart does not cover:

(1) Machinery included in paragraph (a) of this section while it has been converted or adapted for a non-hoisting/lifting use. Such conversions/adaptations include, but are not limited to, power shovels, excavators and concrete pumps.

(2) Power shovels, excavators, wheel loaders, backhoes, loader backhoes, track loaders. This machinery is also excluded when used with chains, slings or other rigging to lift suspended loads.

(3) Automotive wreckers and tow trucks when used to clear wrecks and haul vehicles.

(4) Digger derricks when used for augering holes for poles carrying electric or telecommunication lines, placing and removing the poles, and for handling associated materials for installation on, or removal from, the poles, or when used for any other work subject to subpart V of this part. To be eligible for this exclusion, digger-derrick use in work subject to subpart V of this part must comply with all of the provisions of that subpart, and digger-derrick use in construction work for telecommunication service (as defined at §1910.268(s)(40)) must comply with all of the provisions of §1910.268.

(5) Machinery originally designed as vehicle-mounted aerial devices (for lifting personnel) and self-propelled elevating work platforms.

(6) Telescopic/hydraulic gantry systems.

(7) Stacker cranes.

(8) Powered industrial trucks (forklifts), except when configured to hoist and lower (by means of a winch or hook) and horizontally move a suspended load.

(9) Mechanic's truck with a hoisting device when used in activities related to equipment maintenance and repair.

(10) Machinery that hoists by using a come-a-long or chainfall.

(11) Dedicated drilling rigs.

(12) Gin poles when used for the erection of communication towers.

(13) Tree trimming and tree removal work.

(14) Anchor handling or dredge-related operations with a vessel or barge using an affixed A-frame.

(15) Roustabouts.

(16) Helicopter cranes.

(17) *Material Delivery*

(i) Articulating/knuckle-boom truck cranes that deliver material to a construction site when used to transfer materials from the truck crane to the ground, without arranging the materials in a particular sequence for hoisting.

(ii) Articulating/knuckle-boom truck cranes that deliver material to a construction site when the crane is used to transfer building supply sheet goods or building supply packaged materials from the truck crane onto a structure, using a fork/cradle at the end of the boom, but only when the truck crane is equipped with a properly functioning automatic overload prevention device. Such sheet goods or packaged materials include, but are not limited to: Sheets of sheet rock, sheets of plywood, bags of cement, sheets or packages of roofing shingles, and rolls of roofing felt.

(iii) This exclusion does not apply when:

(A) The articulating/knuckle-boom crane is used to hold, support or stabilize the material to facilitate a construction activity, such as holding material in place while it is attached to the structure;

(B) The material being handled by the articulating/knuckle-boom crane is a prefabricated component. Such prefabricated components include, but are not limited to: Precast concrete members or panels, roof trusses (wooden, cold-formed metal, steel, or other material), prefabricated building sections such as, but not limited to: Floor panels, wall panels, roof panels, roof structures, or similar items;

(C) The material being handled by the crane is a structural steel member (for example, steel joists, beams, columns, steel decking (bundled or unbundled) or a component of a systems-engineered metal building (as defined in 29 CFR 1926 subpart R).

(D) The activity is not specifically excluded under § 1400(c)(17)(i) and (ii).

(d) All sections of this subpart CC apply to the equipment covered by this standard unless specified otherwise.

(e) The duties of controlling entities under this subpart include, but are not limited to, the duties specified in §§ 1926.1402(c), 1926.1402(e) and 1926.1424(b).

(f) Where provisions of this standard direct an operator, crewmember, or other employee to take certain actions, the employer must establish, effectively communicate to the relevant persons, and enforce, work rules to ensure compliance with such provisions.

(g) For work covered by subpart V of this part, compliance with § 1926.959 is deemed compliance with §§ 1926.1407 through 1926.1411.

(h) Section 1926.1402 does not apply to cranes designed for use on railroad tracks, when used on railroad tracks that are part of the general railroad system of transportation that is regulated pursuant to the Federal Railroad Administration under 49 CFR part 213, and that comply with applicable Federal Railroad Administration requirements. *See* § 1926.1402(f).

[75 FR 48135, Aug. 9, 2010, as amended at 78 FR 32116, May 29, 2013; 79 FR 20743, Apr. 11, 2014]

§ 1926.1401 Definitions.

A/D director (Assembly/Disassembly director) means an individual who meets this subpart's requirements for an A/D director, irrespective of the person's formal job title or whether the person is non-management or management personnel.

Articulating crane means a crane whose boom consists of a series of folding, pin connected structural members, typically manipulated to extend or retract by power from hydraulic cylinders.

Assembly/Disassembly means the assembly and/or disassembly of equipment covered under this standard. With regard to tower cranes, "erecting and climbing" replaces the term "assembly," and "dismantling" replaces the term "disassembly." Regardless of whether the crane is initially erected to its full height or is climbed in stages, the process of increasing the height of the crane is an erection process.

Assist crane means a crane used to assist in assembling or disassembling a crane.

Attachments means any device that expands the range of tasks that can be done by the equipment. Examples include, but are not limited to: An auger, drill, magnet, pile-driver, and boom-attached personnel platform.

Audible signal means a signal made by a distinct sound or series of sounds. Examples include, but are not limited to, sounds made by a bell, horn, or whistle.

Blocking (also referred to as "cribbing") is wood or other material used to support equipment or a component and distribute loads to the ground. It is typically used to support lattice boom sections during assembly/disassembly and under outrigger and stabilizer floats.

Boatswain's chair means a single-point adjustable suspension scaffold consisting of a seat or sling (which may be incorporated into a full body harness) designed to support one employee in a sitting position.

Bogie means "travel bogie," which is defined below.

Boom (equipment other than tower crane) means an inclined spar, strut, or other long structural member which supports the upper hoisting tackle on a crane or derrick. Typically, the length and vertical angle of the boom can be varied to achieve increased height or height and reach when lifting loads. Booms can usually be grouped into general categories of hydraulically extendible, cantilevered type, latticed section, cable supported type or articulating type.

Boom (tower cranes): On tower cranes, if the "boom" (*i.e.*, principal horizontal structure) is fixed, it is referred to as a jib; if it is moveable up and down, it is referred to as a boom.

Boom angle indicator means a device which measures the angle of the boom relative to horizontal.

Boom hoist limiting device includes boom hoist disengaging device, boom hoist shut-off, boom hoist disconnect, boom hoist hydraulic relief, boom hoist kick-outs, automatic boom stop device, or derricking limiter. This type of device disengages boom hoist power when the boom reaches a predetermined operating angle. It also sets brakes or closes valves to prevent the boom from lowering after power is disengaged.

Boom length indicator indicates the length of the permanent part of the boom (such as ruled markings on the boom) or, as in some computerized systems, the length of the boom with extensions/attachments.

Boom stop includes boom stops, (belly straps with struts/standoff), telescoping boom stops, attachment boom stops, and backstops. These devices restrict the boom from moving above a certain maximum angle and toppling over backward.

Boom suspension system means a system of pendants, running ropes, sheaves, and other hardware which supports the boom tip and controls the boom angle.

Builder means the builder/constructor of equipment.

Center of gravity: The center of gravity of any object is the point in the object around which its weight is evenly distributed. If you could put a support under that point, you could balance the object on the support.

Certified welder means a welder who meets nationally recognized certification requirements applicable to the task being performed.

Climbing means the process in which a tower crane is raised to a new working height, either by adding additional tower sections to the top of the crane (top climbing), or by a system in which the entire crane is raised inside the structure (inside climbing).

Come-a-long means a mechanical device typically consisting of a chain or cable attached at each end that is used to facilitate movement of materials through leverage.

Competent person means one who is capable of identifying existing and predictable hazards in the surroundings or working conditions which are unsanitary, hazardous, or dangerous to employees, and who has authorization to take prompt corrective measures to eliminate them.

Controlled load lowering means lowering a load by means of a mechanical hoist drum device that allows a hoisted load to be lowered with maximum control using the gear train or hydraulic components of the hoist mechanism. Controlled load lowering requires the use of the hoist drive motor, rather than the load hoist brake, to lower the load.

Controlling entity means an employer that is a prime contractor, general contractor, construction manager or any other legal entity which has the overall responsibility for the construction of the project—its planning, quality and completion.

Counterweight means a weight used to supplement the weight of equipment in providing stability for lifting loads by counterbalancing those loads.

685

Crane/derrick includes all equipment covered by this subpart.

Crawler crane means equipment that has a type of base mounting which incorporates a continuous belt of sprocket driven track.

Crossover points means locations on a wire rope which is spooled on a drum where one layer of rope climbs up on and crosses over the previous layer. This takes place at each flange of the drum as the rope is spooled onto the drum, reaches the flange, and begins to wrap back in the opposite direction.

Dedicated channel means a line of communication assigned by the employer who controls the communication system to only one signal person and crane/derrick or to a coordinated group of cranes/derricks/signal person(s).

Dedicated pile-driver is a machine that is designed to function exclusively as a pile-driver. These machines typically have the ability to both hoist the material that will be pile-driven and to pile-drive that material.

Dedicated spotter (power lines): To be considered a dedicated spotter, the requirements of § 1926.1428 (Signal person qualifications) must be met and his/her sole responsibility is to watch the separation between the power line and the equipment, load line and load (including rigging and lifting accessories), and ensure through communication with the operator that the applicable minimum approach distance is not breached.

Directly under the load means a part or all of an employee is directly beneath the load.

Dismantling includes partial dismantling (such as dismantling to shorten a boom or substitute a different component).

Drum rotation indicator means a device on a crane or hoist which indicates in which direction and at what relative speed a particular hoist drum is turning.

Electrical contact occurs when a person, object, or equipment makes contact or comes in close proximity with an energized conductor or equipment that allows the passage of current.

Employer-made equipment means floating cranes/derricks designed and built by an employer for the employer's own use.

Encroachment is where any part of the crane, load line or load (including rigging and lifting accessories) breaches a minimum clearance distance that this subpart requires to be maintained from a power line.

Equipment means equipment covered by this subpart.

Equipment criteria means instructions, recommendations, limitations and specifications.

Fall protection equipment means guardrail systems, safety net systems, personal fall arrest systems, positioning device systems or fall restraint systems.

Fall restraint system means a fall protection system that prevents the user from falling any distance. The system is comprised of either a body belt or body harness, along with an anchorage, connectors and other necessary equipment. The other components typically include a lanyard, and may also include a lifeline and other devices.

Fall zone means the area (including but not limited to the area directly beneath the load) in which it is reasonably foreseeable that partially or completely suspended materials could fall in the event of an accident.

Flange points are points of contact between rope and drum flange where the rope changes layers.

Floating cranes/derricks means equipment designed by the manufacturer (or employer) for marine use by permanent attachment to a barge, pontoons, vessel or other means of flotation.

For example means "one example, although there are others."

Free fall (of the load line) means that only the brake is used to regulate the descent of the load line (the drive mechanism is not used to drive the load down faster or retard its lowering).

Free surface effect is the uncontrolled transverse movement of liquids in compartments which reduce a vessel's transverse stability.

Hoist means a mechanical device for lifting and lowering loads by winding a line onto or off a drum.

Hoisting is the act of raising, lowering or otherwise moving a load in the air with equipment covered by this standard. As used in this standard, "hoisting" can be done by means other than wire rope/hoist drum equipment.

Include/including means "including, but not limited to."

Insulating link/device means an insulating device listed, labeled, or accepted by a Nationally Recognized Testing Laboratory in accordance with 29 CFR 1910.7.

Jib stop (also referred to as a jib backstop), is the same type of device as a boom stop but is for a fixed or luffing jib.

Land crane/derrick is equipment not originally designed by the manufacturer for marine use by permanent attachment to barges, pontoons, vessels, or other means of floatation.

List means the angle of inclination about the longitudinal axis of a barge, pontoons, vessel or other means of floatation.

Load refers to the object(s) being hoisted and/or the weight of the object(s); both uses refer to the object(s) and the load-attaching equipment, such as, the load block, ropes, slings, shackles, and any other ancillary attachment.

Load moment (or rated capacity) indicator means a system which aids the equipment operator by sensing (directly or indirectly) the overturning moment on the equipment, *i.e.*, load multiplied by radius. It compares this lifting condition to the equipment's rated capacity, and indicates to the operator the percentage of capacity at which the equipment is working. Lights, bells, or buzzers may be incorporated as a warning of an approaching overload condition.

Load moment (or rated capacity) limiter means a system which aids the equipment operator by sensing (directly or indirectly) the overturning moment on the equipment, *i.e.*, load multiplied by radius. It compares this lifting condition to the equipment's rated capacity, and when the rated capacity is reached, it shuts off power to those equipment functions which can increase the severity of loading on the equipment, *e.g.*, hoisting, telescoping out, or luffing out. Typically, those functions which decrease the severity of loading on the equipment remain operational, *e.g.*, lowering, telescoping in, or luffing in.

Locomotive crane means a crane mounted on a base or car equipped for travel on a railroad track.

Luffing jib limiting device is similar to a boom hoist limiting device, except that it limits the movement of the luffing jib.

Marine hoisted personnel transfer device means a device, such as a "transfer net," that is designed to protect the employees being hoisted during a marine transfer and to facilitate rapid entry into and exit from the device. Such devices do not include boatswain's chairs when hoisted by equipment covered by this standard.

Marine worksite means a construction worksite located in, on or above the water.

Mobile crane means a lifting device incorporating a cable suspended latticed boom or hydraulic telescopic boom designed to be moved between operating locations by transport over the road.

Moving point-to-point means the times during which an employee is in the process of going to or from a work station.

Multi-purpose machine means a machine that is designed to be configured in various ways, at least one of which allows it to hoist (by means of a winch or hook) and horizontally move a suspended load. For example, a machine that can rotate and can be configured with removable forks/tongs (for use as a forklift) or with a winch pack, jib (with a hook at the end) or jib used in conjunction with a winch. When configured with the forks/tongs, it is not covered by this subpart. When configured with a winch pack, jib (with a hook at the end) or jib used in conjunction with a winch, it is covered by this subpart.

Nationally recognized accrediting agency is an organization that, due to its independence and expertise, is widely recognized as competent to accredit testing organizations. Examples of such accrediting agencies include, but are not limited to, the National Commission for Certifying Agencies and the American National Standards Institute.

Nonconductive means that, because of the nature and condition of the materials used, and the conditions of use (including environmental conditions

687

and condition of the material), the object in question has the property of not becoming energized (that is, it has high dielectric properties offering a high resistance to the passage of current under the conditions of use).

Operational aids are devices that assist the operator in the safe operation of the crane by providing information or automatically taking control of a crane function. These include, but are not limited to, the devices listed in § 1926.1416 ("listed operational aids").

Operational controls means levers, switches, pedals and other devices for controlling equipment operation.

Operator means a person who is operating the equipment.

Overhead and gantry cranes includes overhead/bridge cranes, semigantry, cantilever gantry, wall cranes, storage bridge cranes, launching gantry cranes, and similar equipment, irrespective of whether it travels on tracks, wheels, or other means.

Paragraph refers to a paragraph in the same section of this subpart that the word "paragraph" is used, unless otherwise specified.

Pendants includes both wire and bar types. Wire type: A fixed length of wire rope with mechanical fittings at both ends for pinning segments of wire rope together. Bar type: Instead of wire rope, a bar is used. Pendants are typically used in a latticed boom crane system to easily change the length of the boom suspension system without completely changing the rope on the drum when the boom length is increased or decreased.

Personal fall arrest system means a system used to arrest an employee in a fall from a working level. It consists of an anchorage, connectors, a body harness and may include a lanyard, deceleration device, lifeline, or suitable combination of these.

Portal crane is a type of crane consisting of a rotating upperstructure, hoist machinery, and boom mounted on top of a structural gantry which may be fixed in one location or have travel capability. The gantry legs or columns usually have portal openings in between to allow passage of traffic beneath the gantry.

Power lines means electric transmission and distribution lines.

Procedures include, but are not limited to: Instructions, diagrams, recommendations, warnings, specifications, protocols and limitations.

Proximity alarm is a device that provides a warning of proximity to a power line and that has been listed, labeled, or accepted by a Nationally Recognized Testing Laboratory in accordance with 29 CFR 1910.7.

Qualified evaluator (not a third party) means a person employed by the signal person's employer who has demonstrated that he/she is competent in accurately assessing whether individuals meet the Qualification Requirements in this subpart for a signal person.

Qualified evaluator (third party) means an entity that, due to its independence and expertise, has demonstrated that it is competent in accurately assessing whether individuals meet the Qualification Requirements in this subpart for a signal person.

Qualified person means a person who, by possession of a recognized degree, certificate, or professional standing, or who by extensive knowledge, training and experience, successfully demonstrated the ability to solve/resolve problems relating to the subject matter, the work, or the project.

Qualified rigger is a rigger who meets the criteria for a qualified person.

Range control limit device is a device that can be set by an equipment operator to limit movement of the boom or jib tip to a plane or multiple planes.

Range control warning device is a device that can be set by an equipment operator to warn that the boom or jib tip is at a plane or multiple planes.

Rated capacity means the maximum working load permitted by the manufacturer under specified working conditions. Such working conditions typically include a specific combination of factors such as equipment configuration, radii, boom length, and other parameters of use.

Rated capacity indicator: See load moment indicator.

Rated capacity limiter: See load moment limiter.

Repetitive pickup points refer to, when operating on a short cycle operation, the rope being used on a single layer and being spooled repetitively over a short portion of the drum.

Running wire rope means a wire rope that moves over sheaves or drums.

Runway means a firm, level surface designed, prepared and designated as a path of travel for the weight and configuration of the crane being used to lift and travel with the crane suspended platform. An existing surface may be used as long as it meets these criteria.

Section means a section of this subpart, unless otherwise specified.

Sideboom crane means a track-type or wheel-type tractor having a boom mounted on the side of the tractor, used for lifting, lowering or transporting a load suspended on the load hook. The boom or hook can be lifted or lowered in a vertical direction only.

Special hazard warnings means warnings of site-specific hazards (for example, proximity of power lines).

Stability (flotation device) means the tendency of a barge, pontoons, vessel or other means of flotation to return to an upright position after having been inclined by an external force.

Standard Method means the protocol in appendix A of this subpart for hand signals.

Such as means "such as, but not limited to."

Superstructure: See Upperworks.

Tagline means a rope (usually fiber) attached to a lifted load for purposes of controlling load spinning and pendular motions or used to stabilize a bucket or magnet during material handling operations.

Tender means an individual responsible for monitoring and communicating with a diver.

Tilt up or tilt down operation means raising/lowering a load from the horizontal to vertical or vertical to horizontal.

Tower crane is a type of lifting structure which utilizes a vertical mast or tower to support a working boom (jib) in an elevated position. Loads are suspended from the working boom. While the working boom may be of the fixed type (horizontal or angled) or have luffing capability, it can always rotate to swing loads, either by rotating on the top of the tower (top slewing) or by the rotation of the tower (bottom slewing). The tower base may be fixed in one location or ballasted and moveable between locations. Mobile cranes that are configured with luffing jib and/or tower attachments are not considered tower cranes under this section.

Travel bogie (tower cranes) is an assembly of two or more axles arranged to permit vertical wheel displacement and equalize the loading on the wheels.

Trim means angle of inclination about the transverse axis of a barge, pontoons, vessel or other means of floatation.

Two blocking means a condition in which a component that is uppermost on the hoist line such as the load block, hook block, overhaul ball, or similar component, comes in contact with the boom tip, fixed upper block or similar component. This binds the system and continued application of power can cause failure of the hoist rope or other component.

Unavailable procedures means procedures that are no longer available from the manufacturer, or have never been available, from the manufacturer.

Upperstructure: See Upperworks.

Upperworks means the revolving frame of equipment on which the operating machinery (and many cases the engine) are mounted along with the operator's cab. The counterweight is typically supported on the rear of the upperstructure and the boom or other front end attachment is mounted on the front.

Up to means "up to and including."

Wire rope means a flexible rope constructed by laying steel wires into various patterns of multi-wired strands around a core system to produce a helically wound rope.

§1926.1402 Ground conditions.

(a) *Definitions.* (1) "Ground conditions" means the ability of the ground to support the equipment (including slope, compaction, and firmness).

(2) "Supporting materials" means blocking, mats, cribbing, marsh buggies (in marshes/wetlands), or similar supporting materials or devices.

(b) The equipment must not be assembled or used unless ground conditions are firm, drained, and graded to a

689

sufficient extent so that, in conjunction (if necessary) with the use of supporting materials, the equipment manufacturer's specifications for adequate support and degree of level of the equipment are met. The requirement for the ground to be drained does not apply to marshes/wetlands.

(c) The controlling entity must:

(1) Ensure that ground preparations necessary to meet the requirements in paragraph (b) of this section are provided.

(2) Inform the user of the equipment and the operator of the location of hazards beneath the equipment set-up area (such as voids, tanks, utilities) if those hazards are identified in documents (such as site drawings, as-built drawings, and soil analyses) that are in the possession of the controlling entity (whether at the site or off-site) or the hazards are otherwise known to that controlling entity.

(d) If there is no controlling entity for the project, the requirement in paragraph (c)(1) of this section must be met by the employer that has authority at the site to make or arrange for ground preparations needed to meet paragraph (b) of this section.

(e) If the A/D director or the operator determines that ground conditions do not meet the requirements in paragraph (b) of this section, that person's employer must have a discussion with the controlling entity regarding the ground preparations that are needed so that, with the use of suitable supporting materials/devices (if necessary), the requirements in paragraph (b) of this section can be met.

(f) This section does not apply to cranes designed for use on railroad tracks when used on railroad tracks that are part of the general railroad system of transportation that is regulated pursuant to the Federal Railroad Administration under 49 CFR part 213 and that comply with applicable Federal Railroad Administration requirements.

§ 1926.1403 Assembly/Disassembly—selection of manufacturer or employer procedures.

When assembling or disassembling equipment (or attachments), the employer must comply with all applicable manufacturer prohibitions and must comply with either:

(a) Manufacturer procedures applicable to assembly and disassembly, or

(b) Employer procedures for assembly and disassembly. Employer procedures may be used only where the employer can demonstrate that the procedures used meet the requirements in § 1926.1406.

NOTE: The employer must follow manufacturer procedures when an employer uses synthetic slings during assembly or disassembly rigging. (See § 1926.1404(r).)

§ 1926.1404 Assembly/Disassembly—general requirements (applies to all assembly and disassembly operations).

(a) *Supervision—competent-qualified person.* (1) Assembly/disassembly must be directed by a person who meets the criteria for both a competent person and a qualified person, or by a competent person who is assisted by one or more qualified persons ("A/D director").

(2) Where the assembly/disassembly is being performed by only one person, that person must meet the criteria for both a competent person and a qualified person. For purposes of this standard, that person is considered the A/D director.

(b) *Knowledge of procedures.* The A/D director must understand the applicable assembly/disassembly procedures.

(c) *Review of procedures.* The A/D director must review the applicable assembly/disassembly procedures immediately prior to the commencement of assembly/disassembly unless the A/D director understands the procedures and has applied them to the same type and configuration of equipment (including accessories, if any).

(d) *Crew instructions.* (1) Before commencing assembly/disassembly operations, the A/D director must ensure that the crew members understand all of the following:

(i) Their tasks.

(ii) The hazards associated with their tasks.

(iii) The hazardous positions/locations that they need to avoid.

(2) During assembly/disassembly operations, before a crew member takes on a different task, or when adding new

personnel during the operations, the requirements in paragraphs (d)(1)(i) through (d)(1)(iii) of this section must be met.

(e) *Protecting assembly/disassembly crew members out of operator view.* (1) Before a crew member goes to a location that is out of view of the operator and is either in, on, or under the equipment, or near the equipment (or load) where the crew member could be injured by movement of the equipment (or load), the crew member must inform the operator that he/she is going to that location.

(2) Where the operator knows that a crew member went to a location covered by paragraph (e)(1) of this section, the operator must not move any part of the equipment (or load) until the operator is informed in accordance with a pre-arranged system of communication that the crew member is in a safe position.

(f) *Working under the boom, jib or other components.* (1) When pins (or similar devices) are being removed, employees must not be under the boom, jib, or other components, except where the requirements of paragraph (f)(2) of this section are met.

(2) *Exception.* Where the employer demonstrates that site constraints require one or more employees to be under the boom, jib, or other components when pins (or similar devices) are being removed, the A/D director must implement procedures that minimize the risk of unintended dangerous movement and minimize the duration and extent of exposure under the boom. (*See* Non-mandatory appendix B of this subpart for an example.)

(g) *Capacity limits.* During all phases of assembly/disassembly, rated capacity limits for loads imposed on the equipment, equipment components (including rigging), lifting lugs and equipment accessories, must not be exceeded for the equipment being assembled/disassembled.

(h) *Addressing specific hazards.* The A/D director supervising the assembly/disassembly operation must address the hazards associated with the operation, which include:

(1) *Site and ground bearing conditions.* Site and ground conditions must be adequate for safe assembly/disassembly operations and to support the equipment during assembly/disassembly (*see* §1926.1402 for ground condition requirements).

(2) *Blocking material.* The size, amount, condition and method of stacking the blocking must be sufficient to sustain the loads and maintain stability.

(3) *Proper location of blocking.* When used to support lattice booms or components, blocking must be appropriately placed to:

(i) Protect the structural integrity of the equipment, and

(ii) Prevent dangerous movement and collapse.

(4) *Verifying assist crane loads.* When using an assist crane, the loads that will be imposed on the assist crane at each phase of assembly/disassembly must be verified in accordance with §1926.1417(o)(3) before assembly/disassembly begins.

(5) *Boom and jib pick points.* The point(s) of attachment of rigging to a boom (or boom sections or jib or jib sections) must be suitable for preventing structural damage and facilitating safe handling of these components.

(6) *Center of gravity.* (i) The center of gravity of the load must be identified if that is necessary for the method used for maintaining stability.

(ii) Where there is insufficient information to accurately identify the center of gravity, measures designed to prevent unintended dangerous movement resulting from an inaccurate identification of the center of gravity must be used. (*See* Non-mandatory appendix B of this subpart for an example.)

(7) *Stability upon pin removal.* The boom sections, boom suspension systems (such as gantry A-frames and jib struts), and components must be rigged or supported to maintain stability upon the removal of the pins.

(8) *Snagging.* Suspension ropes and pendants must not be allowed to catch on the boom or jib connection pins or cotter pins (including keepers and locking pins).

(9) *Struck by counterweights.* The potential for unintended movement from inadequately supported counterweights and from hoisting counterweights.

(10) *Boom hoist brake failure.* Each time reliance is to be placed on the boom hoist brake to prevent boom movement during assembly/disassembly, the brake must be tested prior to such reliance to determine if it is sufficient to prevent boom movement. If it is not sufficient, a boom hoist pawl, other locking device/backup braking device, or another method of preventing dangerous movement of the boom (such as blocking or using an assist crane) from a boom hoist brake failure must be used.

(11) *Loss of backward stability.* Backward stability before swinging the upperworks, travel, and when attaching or removing equipment components.

(12) *Wind speed and weather.* The effect of wind speed and weather on the equipment.

(i) [Reserved]

(j) *Cantilevered boom sections.* Manufacturer limitations on the maximum amount of boom supported only by cantilevering must not be exceeded. Where these are unavailable, a registered professional engineer familiar with the type of equipment involved must determine in writing this limitation, which must not be exceeded.

(k) *Weight of components.* The weight of each of the components must be readily available.

(l) [Reserved]

(m) *Components and configuration.*

(1) The selection of components, and configuration of the equipment, that affect the capacity or safe operation of the equipment must be in accordance with:

(i) Manufacturer instructions, prohibitions, limitations, and specifications. Where these are unavailable, a registered professional engineer familiar with the type of equipment involved must approve, in writing, the selection and configuration of components; or

(ii) Approved modifications that meet the requirements of § 1926.1434 (Equipment modifications).

(2) *Post-assembly inspection.* Upon completion of assembly, the equipment must be inspected to ensure compliance with paragraph (m)(1) of this section (*see* § 1926.1412(c) for post-assembly inspection requirements).

(n) [Reserved]

(o) *Shipping pins.* Reusable shipping pins, straps, links, and similar equipment must be removed. Once they are removed they must either be stowed or otherwise stored so that they do not present a falling object hazard.

(p) *Pile driving.* Equipment used for pile driving must not have a jib attached during pile driving operations.

(q) *Outriggers and stabilizers.* When the load to be handled and the operating radius require the use of outriggers or stabilizers, or at any time when outriggers or stabilizers are used, all of the following requirements must be met (except as otherwise indicated):

(1) The outriggers or stabilizers must be either fully extended or, if manufacturer procedures permit, deployed as specified in the load chart.

(2) The outriggers must be set to remove the equipment weight from the wheels, except for locomotive cranes (*see* paragraph (q)(6) of this section for use of outriggers on locomotive cranes). This provision does not apply to stabilizers.

(3) When outrigger floats are used, they must be attached to the outriggers. When stabilizer floats are used, they must be attached to the stabilizers.

(4) Each outrigger or stabilizer must be visible to the operator or to a signal person during extension and setting.

(5) Outrigger and stabilizer blocking must:

(i) Meet the requirements in paragraphs (h)(2) and (h)(3) of this section.

(ii) Be placed only under the outrigger or stabilizer float/pad of the jack or, where the outrigger or stabilizer is designed without a jack, under the outer bearing surface of the extended outrigger or stabilizer beam.

(6) For locomotive cranes, when using outriggers or stabilizers to handle loads, the manufacturer's procedures must be followed. When lifting loads without using outriggers or stabilizers, the manufacturer's procedures must be met regarding truck wedges or screws.

(r) *Rigging.* In addition to following the requirements in 29 CFR 1926.251 and other requirements in this and other standards applicable to rigging, when rigging is used for assembly/disassembly, the employer must ensure that:

(1) The rigging work is done by a qualified rigger.

(2) Synthetic slings are protected from: Abrasive, sharp or acute edges, and configurations that could cause a reduction of the sling's rated capacity, such as distortion or localized compression.

NOTE: Requirements for the protection of wire rope slings are contained in 29 CFR 1926.251(c)(9).

(3) When synthetic slings are used, the synthetic sling manufacturer's instructions, limitations, specifications and recommendations must be followed.

§1926.1405 Disassembly—additional requirements for dismantling of booms and jibs (applies to both the use of manufacturer procedures and employer procedures).

Dismantling (including dismantling for changing the length of) booms and jibs.

(a) None of the pins in the pendants are to be removed (partly or completely) when the pendants are in tension.

(b) None of the pins (top or bottom) on boom sections located between the pendant attachment points and the crane/derrick body are to be removed (partly or completely) when the pendants are in tension.

(c) None of the pins (top or bottom) on boom sections located between the uppermost boom section and the crane/derrick body are to be removed (partly or completely) when the boom is being supported by the uppermost boom section resting on the ground (or other support).

(d) None of the top pins on boom sections located on the cantilevered portion of the boom being removed (the portion being removed ahead of the pendant attachment points) are to be removed (partly or completely) until the cantilevered section to be removed is fully supported.

§1926.1406 Assembly/Disassembly— employer procedures—general requirements.

(a) When using employer procedures instead of manufacturer procedures for assembly/disassembly, the employer must ensure that the procedures:

(1) Prevent unintended dangerous movement, and prevent collapse, of any part of the equipment.

(2) Provide adequate support and stability of all parts of the equipment.

(3) Position employees involved in the assembly/disassembly operation so that their exposure to unintended movement or collapse of part or all of the equipment is minimized.

(b) *Qualified person.* Employer procedures must be developed by a qualified person.

§1926.1407 Power line safety (up to 350 kV)—assembly and disassembly.

(a) Before assembling or disassembling equipment, the employer must determine if any part of the equipment, load line, or load (including rigging and lifting accessories) could get, in the direction or area of assembly/disassembly, closer than 20 feet to a power line during the assembly/disassembly process. If so, the employer must meet the requirements in Option (1), Option (2), or Option (3) of this section, as follows:

(1) *Option (1)—Deenergize and ground.* Confirm from the utility owner/operator that the power line has been deenergized and visibly grounded at the worksite.

(2) *Option (2)—20 foot clearance.* Ensure that no part of the equipment, load line or load (including rigging and lifting accessories), gets closer than 20 feet to the power line by implementing the measures specified in paragraph (b) of this section.

(3) *Option (3)—Table A clearance.* (i) Determine the line's voltage and the minimum clearance distance permitted under Table A (*see* §1926.1408).

(ii) Determine if any part of the equipment, load line, or load (including rigging and lifting accessories), could get closer than the minimum clearance distance to the power line permitted under Table A (*see* §1926.1408). If so, then the employer must follow the requirements in paragraph (b) of this section to ensure that no part of the equipment, load line, or load (including rigging and lifting accessories), gets closer to the line than the minimum clearance distance.

(b) *Preventing encroachment/electrocution.* Where encroachment precautions are required under Option (2), or Option (3) of this section, all of the following requirements must be met:

(1) Conduct a planning meeting with the Assembly/Disassembly director (A/D director), operator, assembly/disassembly crew and the other workers who will be in the assembly/disassembly area to review the location of the power line(s) and the steps that will be implemented to prevent encroachment/electrocution.

(2) If tag lines are used, they must be nonconductive.

(3) At least one of the following additional measures must be in place. The measure selected from this list must be effective in preventing encroachment.

The additional measures are:

(i) Use a dedicated spotter who is in continuous contact with the equipment operator. The dedicated spotter must:

(A) Be equipped with a visual aid to assist in identifying the minimum clearance distance. Examples of a visual aid include, but are not limited to: A clearly visible line painted on the ground; a clearly visible line of stanchions; a set of clearly visible line-of-sight landmarks (such as a fence post behind the dedicated spotter and a building corner ahead of the dedicated spotter).

(B) Be positioned to effectively gauge the clearance distance.

(C) Where necessary, use equipment that enables the dedicated spotter to communicate directly with the operator.

(D) Give timely information to the operator so that the required clearance distance can be maintained.

(ii) A proximity alarm set to give the operator sufficient warning to prevent encroachment.

(iii) A device that automatically warns the operator when to stop movement, such as a range control warning device. Such a device must be set to give the operator sufficient warning to prevent encroachment.

(iv) A device that automatically limits range of movement, set to prevent encroachment.

(v) An elevated warning line, barricade, or line of signs, in view of the operator, equipped with flags or similar high-visibility markings.

(c) *Assembly/disassembly below power lines prohibited.* No part of a crane/derrick, load line, or load (including rigging and lifting accessories), whether partially or fully assembled, is allowed below a power line unless the employer has confirmed that the utility owner/operator has deenergized and (at the worksite) visibly grounded the power line.

(d) *Assembly/disassembly inside Table A clearance prohibited.* No part of a crane/derrick, load line, or load (including rigging and lifting accessories), whether partially or fully assembled, is allowed closer than the minimum approach distance under Table A (*see* § 1926.1408) to a power line unless the employer has confirmed that the utility owner/operator has deenergized and (at the worksite) visibly grounded the power line.

(e) *Voltage information.* Where Option (3) of this section is used, the utility owner/operator of the power lines must provide the requested voltage information within two working days of the employer's request.

(f) *Power lines presumed energized.* The employer must assume that all power lines are energized unless the utility owner/operator confirms that the power line has been and continues to be deenergized and visibly grounded at the worksite.

(g) *Posting of electrocution warnings.* There must be at least one electrocution hazard warning conspicuously posted in the cab so that it is in view of the operator and (except for overhead gantry and tower cranes) at least two on the outside of the equipment.

§ 1926.1408 Power line safety (up to 350 kV)—equipment operations.

(a) *Hazard assessments and precautions inside the work zone.* Before beginning equipment operations, the employer must:

(1) *Identify the work zone by either:*

(i) Demarcating boundaries (such as with flags, or a device such as a range limit device or range control warning device) and prohibiting the operator from operating the equipment past those boundaries, or

(ii) Defining the work zone as the area 360 degrees around the equipment, up to the equipment's maximum working radius.

(2) Determine if any part of the equipment, load line or load (including rigging and lifting accessories), if operated up to the equipment's maximum working radius in the work zone, could get closer than 20 feet to a power line. If so, the employer must meet the requirements in Option (1), Option (2), or Option (3) of this section, as follows:

(i) *Option (1)—Deenergize and ground.* Confirm from the utility owner/operator that the power line has been deenergized and visibly grounded at the worksite.

(ii) *Option (2)—20 foot clearance.* Ensure that no part of the equipment, load line, or load (including rigging and lifting accessories), gets closer than 20 feet to the power line by implementing the measures specified in paragraph (b) of this section.

(iii) *Option (3)—Table A clearance.* (A) Determine the line's voltage and the minimum approach distance permitted under Table A (*see* § 1926.1408).

(B) Determine if any part of the equipment, load line or load (including rigging and lifting accessories), while operating up to the equipment's maximum working radius in the work zone, could get closer than the minimum approach distance of the power line permitted under Table A (*see* § 1926.1408). If so, then the employer must follow the requirements in paragraph (b) of this section to ensure that no part of the equipment, load line, or load (including rigging and lifting accessories), gets closer to the line than the minimum approach distance.

(b) *Preventing encroachment/electrocution.* Where encroachment precautions are required under Option (2) or Option (3) of this section, all of the following requirements must be met:

(1) Conduct a planning meeting with the operator and the other workers who will be in the area of the equipment or load to review the location of the power line(s), and the steps that will be implemented to prevent encroachment/electrocution.

(2) If tag lines are used, they must be non-conductive.

(3) Erect and maintain an elevated warning line, barricade, or line of signs, in view of the operator, equipped with flags or similar high-visibility markings, at 20 feet from the power line (if using Option (2) of this section) or at the minimum approach distance under Table A (*see* § 1926.1408) (if using Option (3) of this section). If the operator is unable to see the elevated warning line, a dedicated spotter must be used as described in § 1926.1408(b)(4)(ii) in addition to implementing one of the measures described in §§ 1926.1408(b)(4)(i), (iii), (iv) and (v).

(4) Implement at least one of the following measures:

(i) A proximity alarm set to give the operator sufficient warning to prevent encroachment.

(ii) A dedicated spotter who is in continuous contact with the operator. Where this measure is selected, the dedicated spotter must:

(A) Be equipped with a visual aid to assist in identifying the minimum clearance distance. Examples of a visual aid include, but are not limited to: A clearly visible line painted on the ground; a clearly visible line of stanchions; a set of clearly visible line-of-sight landmarks (such as a fence post behind the dedicated spotter and a building corner ahead of the dedicated spotter).

(B) Be positioned to effectively gauge the clearance distance.

(C) Where necessary, use equipment that enables the dedicated spotter to communicate directly with the operator.

(D) Give timely information to the operator so that the required clearance distance can be maintained.

(iii) A device that automatically warns the operator when to stop movement, such as a range control warning device. Such a device must be set to give the operator sufficient warning to prevent encroachment.

(iv) A device that automatically limits its range of movement, set to prevent encroachment.

(v) An insulating link/device, as defined in § 1926.1401, installed at a point between the end of the load line (or below) and the load.

(5) The requirements of paragraph (b)(4) of this section do not apply to work covered by subpart V of this part.

(c) *Voltage information.* Where Option (3) of this section is used, the utility owner/operator of the power lines must provide the requested voltage information within two working days of the employer's request.

(d) *Operations below power lines.* (1) No part of the equipment, load line, or load (including rigging and lifting accessories) is allowed below a power line unless the employer has confirmed that the utility owner/operator has deenergized and (at the worksite) visibly grounded the power line, except where one of the exceptions in paragraph (d)(2) of this section applies.

(2) *Exceptions.* Paragraph (d)(1) of this section is inapplicable where the employer demonstrates that one of the following applies:

(i) The work is covered by subpart V of this part.

(ii) For equipment with non-extensible booms: The uppermost part of the equipment, with the boom at true vertical, would be more than 20 feet below the plane of the power line or more than the Table A of this section minimum clearance distance below the plane of the power line.

(iii) For equipment with articulating or extensible booms: The uppermost part of the equipment, with the boom in the fully extended position, at true vertical, would be more than 20 feet below the plane of the power line or more than the Table A of this section minimum clearance distance below the plane of the power line.

(iv) The employer demonstrates that compliance with paragraph (d)(1) of this section is infeasible and meets the requirements of § 1926.1410.

(e) *Power lines presumed energized.* The employer must assume that all power lines are energized unless the utility owner/operator confirms that the power line has been and continues to be deenergized and visibly grounded at the worksite.

(f) When working near transmitter/communication towers where the equipment is close enough for an electrical charge to be induced in the equipment or materials being handled, the transmitter must be deenergized or the following precautions must be taken:

(1) The equipment must be provided with an electrical ground.

(2) If tag lines are used, they must be non-conductive.

(g) *Training.*

(1) The employer must train each operator and crew member assigned to work with the equipment on all of the following:

(i) The procedures to be followed in the event of electrical contact with a power line. Such training must include:

(A) Information regarding the danger of electrocution from the operator simultaneously touching the equipment and the ground.

(B) The importance to the operator's safety of remaining inside the cab except where there is an imminent danger of fire, explosion, or other emergency that necessitates leaving the cab.

(C) The safest means of evacuating from equipment that may be energized.

(D) The danger of the potentially energized zone around the equipment (step potential).

(E) The need for crew in the area to avoid approaching or touching the equipment and the load.

(F) Safe clearance distance from power lines.

(ii) Power lines are presumed to be energized unless the utility owner/operator confirms that the power line has been and continues to be deenergized and visibly grounded at the worksite.

(iii) Power lines are presumed to be uninsulated unless the utility owner/operator or a registered engineer who is a qualified person with respect to electrical power transmission and distribution confirms that a line is insulated.

(iv) The limitations of an insulating link/device, proximity alarm, and range control (and similar) device, if used.

(v) The procedures to be followed to properly ground equipment and the limitations of grounding.

(2) Employees working as dedicated spotters must be trained to enable them to effectively perform their task, including training on the applicable requirements of this section.

696

(3) Training under this section must be administered in accordance with §1926.1430(g).

(h) Devices originally designed by the manufacturer for use as: A safety device (*see* §1926.1415), operational aid, or a means to prevent power line contact or electrocution, when used to comply with this section, must meet the manufacturer's procedures for use and conditions of use.

TABLE A—MINIMUM CLEARANCE DISTANCES

Voltage (nominal, kV, alternating current)	Minimum clearance distance (feet)
up to 50	10
over 50 to 200	15
over 200 to 350	20
over 350 to 500	25
over 500 to 750	35
over 750 to 1,000	45
over 1,000	(as established by the utility owner/operator or registered professional engineer who is a qualified person with respect to electrical power transmission and distribution).

Note: The value that follows "to" is up to and includes that value. For example, over 50 to 200 means up to and including 200kV.

§1926.1409 Power line safety (over 350 kV).

The requirements of §1926.1407 and §1926.1408 apply to power lines over 350 kV except:

(a) For power lines at or below 1000 kV, wherever the distance "20 feet" is specified, the distance "50 feet" must be substituted; and

(b) For power lines over 1000 kV, the minimum clearance distance must be established by the utility owner/operator or registered professional engineer who is a qualified person with respect to electrical power transmission and distribution.

§1926.1410 Power line safety (all voltages)—equipment operations closer than the Table A zone.

Equipment operations in which any part of the equipment, load line, or load (including rigging and lifting accessories) is closer than the minimum approach distance under Table A of §1926.1408 to an energized power line is prohibited, except where the employer demonstrates that all of the following requirements are met:

(a) The employer determines that it is infeasible to do the work without breaching the minimum approach distance under Table A of §1926.1408.

(b) The employer determines that, after consultation with the utility owner/operator, it is infeasible to deen-ergize and ground the power line or relocate the power line.

(c) *Minimum clearance distance.* (1) The power line owner/operator or registered professional engineer who is a qualified person with respect to electrical power transmission and distribution determines the minimum clearance distance that must be maintained to prevent electrical contact in light of the on-site conditions. The factors that must be considered in making this determination include, but are not limited to: Conditions affecting atmospheric conductivity; time necessary to bring the equipment, load line, and load (including rigging and lifting accessories) to a complete stop; wind conditions; degree of sway in the power line; lighting conditions, and other conditions affecting the ability to prevent electrical contact.

(2) Paragraph (c)(1) of this section does not apply to work covered by subpart V of this part; instead, for such work, the minimum approach distances established by the employer under sect;1926.960(c)(1)(i) apply.

(d) A planning meeting with the employer and utility owner/operator (or registered professional engineer who is a qualified person with respect to electrical power transmission and distribution) is held to determine the procedures that will be followed to prevent electrical contact and electrocution. At a minimum these procedures must include:

697

(1) If the power line is equipped with a device that automatically reenergizes the circuit in the event of a power line contact, before the work begins, the automatic reclosing feature of the circuit interrupting device must be made inoperative if the design of the device permits.

(2) A dedicated spotter who is in continuous contact with the operator. The dedicated spotter must:

(i) Be equipped with a visual aid to assist in identifying the minimum clearance distance. Examples of a visual aid include, but are not limited to: A line painted on the ground; a clearly visible line of stanchions; a set of clearly visible line-of-sight landmarks (such as a fence post behind the dedicated spotter and a building corner ahead of the dedicated spotter).

(ii) Be positioned to effectively gauge the clearance distance.

(iii) Where necessary, use equipment that enables the dedicated spotter to communicate directly with the operator.

(iv) Give timely information to the operator so that the required clearance distance can be maintained.

(3) An elevated warning line, or barricade (not attached to the crane), in view of the operator (either directly or through video equipment), equipped with flags or similar high-visibility markings, to prevent electrical contact. However, this provision does not apply to work covered by subpart V of this part.

(4) *Insulating link/device.* (i) An insulating link/device installed at a point between the end of the load line (or below) and the load.

(ii) Paragraph (d)(4)(i) of this section does not apply to work covered by subpart V of this part.

(iii) [Reserved]

(iv) Until November 8, 2011, the following procedure may be substituted for the requirement in paragraph (d)(4)(i) of this section: All employees, excluding equipment operators located on the equipment, who may come in contact with the equipment, the load line, or the load must be insulated or guarded from the equipment, the load line, and the load. Insulating gloves rated for the voltage involved are ade-

quate insulation for the purposes of this paragraph.

(v) Until November 8, 2013, the following procedure may be substituted for the requirement in (d)(4)(i) of this section:

(A) The employer must use a link/device manufactured on or before November 8, 2011, that meets the definition of an insulating link/device, except that it has not been approved by a Nationally Recognized Testing Laboratory, and that is maintained and used in accordance with manufacturer requirements and recommendations, and is installed at a point between the end of the load line (or below) and the load; and

(B) All employees, excluding equipment operators located on the equipment, who may come in contact with the equipment, the load line, or the load must be insulated or guarded from the equipment, the load line, and the load through an additional means other than the device described in paragraph (d)(4)(v)(A) of this section. Insulating gloves rated for the voltage involved are adequate additional means of protection for the purposes of this paragraph.

(5) Nonconductive rigging if the rigging may be within the Table A of § 1926.1408 distance during the operation.

(6) If the equipment is equipped with a device that automatically limits range of movement, it must be used and set to prevent any part of the equipment, load line, or load (including rigging and lifting accessories) from breaching the minimum approach distance established under paragraph (c) of this section.

(7) If a tag line is used, it must be of the nonconductive type.

(8) Barricades forming a perimeter at least 10 feet away from the equipment to prevent unauthorized personnel from entering the work area. In areas where obstacles prevent the barricade from being at least 10 feet away, the barricade must be as far from the equipment as feasible.

(9) Workers other than the operator must be prohibited from touching the load line above the insulating link/device and crane. Operators remotely operating the equipment from the ground

must use either wireless controls that isolate the operator from the equipment or insulating mats that insulate the operator from the ground.

(10) Only personnel essential to the operation are permitted to be in the area of the crane and load.

(11) The equipment must be properly grounded.

(12) Insulating line hose or cover-up must be installed by the utility owner/operator except where such devices are unavailable for the line voltages involved.

(e) The procedures developed to comply with paragraph (d) of this section are documented and immediately available on-site.

(f) The equipment user and utility owner/operator (or registered professional engineer) meet with the equipment operator and the other workers who will be in the area of the equipment or load to review the procedures that will be implemented to prevent breaching the minimum approach distance established in paragraph (c) of this section and prevent electrocution.

(g) The procedures developed to comply with paragraph (d) of this section are implemented.

(h) The utility owner/operator (or registered professional engineer) and all employers of employees involved in the work must identify one person who will direct the implementation of the procedures. The person identified in accordance with this paragraph must direct the implementation of the procedures and must have the authority to stop work at any time to ensure safety.

(i) [Reserved]

(j) If a problem occurs implementing the procedures being used to comply with paragraph (d) of this section, or indicating that those procedures are inadequate to prevent electrocution, the employer must safely stop operations and either develop new procedures to comply with paragraph (d) of this section or have the utility owner/operator deenergize and visibly ground or relocate the power line before resuming work.

(k) Devices originally designed by the manufacturer for use as a safety device (*see* §1926.1415), operational aid, or a means to prevent power line contact or electrocution, when used to comply with this section, must comply with the manufacturer's procedures for use and conditions of use.

(l) [Reserved]

(m) The employer must train each operator and crew member assigned to work with the equipment in accordance with §1926.1408(g).

[75 FR 48135, Aug. 9, 2010, as amended at 79 FR 20743, Apr. 11, 2014]

§1926.1411 Power line safety—while traveling under or near power lines with no load.

(a) This section establishes procedures and criteria that must be met for equipment traveling under or near a power line on a construction site with no load. Equipment traveling on a construction site with a load is governed by §§1926.1408, 1926.1409 or 1926.1410, whichever is appropriate, and §1926.1417(u).

(b) The employer must ensure that:

(1) The boom/mast and boom/mast support system are lowered sufficiently to meet the requirements of this paragraph.

(2) The clearances specified in Table T of this section are maintained.

(3) The effects of speed and terrain on equipment movement (including movement of the boom/mast) are considered so that those effects do not cause the minimum clearance distances specified in Table T of this section to be breached.

(4) *Dedicated spotter.* If any part of the equipment while traveling will get closer than 20 feet to the power line, the employer must ensure that a dedicated spotter who is in continuous contact with the driver/operator is used. The dedicated spotter must:

(i) Be positioned to effectively gauge the clearance distance.

(ii) Where necessary, use equipment that enables the dedicated spotter to communicate directly with the operator.

(iii) Give timely information to the operator so that the required clearance distance can be maintained.

(5) *Additional precautions for traveling in poor visibility.* When traveling at night, or in conditions of poor visibility, in addition to the measures specified in paragraphs (b)(1) through

(4) of this section, the employer must ensure that:

(i) The power lines are illuminated or another means of identifying the location of the lines is used.

(ii) A safe path of travel is identified and used.

TABLE T—MINIMUM CLEARANCE DISTANCES WHILE TRAVELING WITH NO LOAD

Voltage (nominal, kV, alternating current)	While traveling—minimum clearance distance (feet)
up to 0.75	4
over .75 to 50	6
over 50 to 345	10
over 345 to 750	16
Over 750 to 1,000	20
Over 1,000	(as established by the utility owner/operator or registered professional engineer who is a qualified person with respect to electrical power transmission and distribution).

§ 1926.1412 Inspections.

(a) *Modified equipment.* (1) Equipment that has had modifications or additions which affect the safe operation of the equipment (such as modifications or additions involving a safety device or operational aid, critical part of a control system, power plant, braking system, load-sustaining structural components, load hook, or in-use operating mechanism) or capacity must be inspected by a qualified person after such modifications/additions have been completed, prior to initial use. The inspection must meet all of the following requirements:

(i) The inspection must assure that the modifications or additions have been done in accordance with the approval obtained pursuant to § 1926.1434 (Equipment modifications).

(ii) The inspection must include functional testing of the equipment.

(2) Equipment must not be used until an inspection under this paragraph demonstrates that the requirements of paragraph (a)(1)(i) of this section have been met.

(b) *Repaired/adjusted equipment.* (1) Equipment that has had a repair or adjustment that relates to safe operation (such as: A repair or adjustment to a safety device or operator aid, or to a critical part of a control system, power plant, braking system, load-sustaining structural components, load hook, or in-use operating mechanism), must be inspected by a qualified person after such a repair or adjustment has been completed, prior to initial use. The in-spection must meet all of the following requirements:

(i) The qualified person must determine if the repair/adjustment meets manufacturer equipment criteria (where applicable and available).

(ii) Where manufacturer equipment criteria are unavailable or inapplicable, the qualified person must:

(A) Determine if a registered professional engineer (RPE) is needed to develop criteria for the repair/adjustment. If an RPE is not needed, the employer must ensure that the criteria are developed by the qualified person. If an RPE is needed, the employer must ensure that they are developed by an RPE.

(B) Determine if the repair/adjustment meets the criteria developed in accordance with paragraph (b)(1)(ii)(A) of this section.

(iii) The inspection must include functional testing of the repaired/adjusted parts and other components that may be affected by the repair/adjustment.

(4) Equipment must not be used until an inspection under this paragraph demonstrates that the repair/adjustment meets the requirements of paragraph (b)(1)(i) of this section (or, where applicable, paragraph (b)(1)(ii) of this section).

(c) *Post-assembly.* (1) Upon completion of assembly, the equipment must be inspected by a qualified person to assure that it is configured in accordance with manufacturer equipment criteria.

(2) Where manufacturer equipment criteria are unavailable, a qualified person must:

(i) Determine if a registered professional engineer (RPE) familiar with the type of equipment involved is needed to develop criteria for the equipment configuration. If an RPE is not needed, the employer must ensure that the criteria are developed by the qualified person. If an RPE is needed, the employer must ensure that they are developed by an RPE.

(ii) Determine if the equipment meets the criteria developed in accordance with paragraph (c)(2)(i) of this section.

(3) Equipment must not be used until an inspection under this paragraph demonstrates that the equipment is configured in accordance with the applicable criteria.

(d) *Each shift.* (1) A competent person must begin a visual inspection prior to each shift the equipment will be used, which must be completed before or during that shift. The inspection must consist of observation for apparent deficiencies. Taking apart equipment components and booming down is not required as part of this inspection unless the results of the visual inspection or trial operation indicate that further investigation necessitating taking apart equipment components or booming down is needed. Determinations made in conducting the inspection must be reassessed in light of observations made during operation. At a minimum the inspection must include all of the following:

(i) Control mechanisms for maladjustments interfering with proper operation.

(ii) Control and drive mechanisms for apparent excessive wear of components and contamination by lubricants, water or other foreign matter.

(iii) Air, hydraulic, and other pressurized lines for deterioration or leakage, particularly those which flex in normal operation.

(iv) Hydraulic system for proper fluid level.

(v) Hooks and latches for deformation, cracks, excessive wear, or damage such as from chemicals or heat.

(vi) Wire rope reeving for compliance with the manufacturer's specifications.

(vii) Wire rope, in accordance with §1926.1413(a).

(viii) Electrical apparatus for malfunctioning, signs of apparent excessive deterioration, dirt or moisture accumulation.

(ix) Tires (when in use) for proper inflation and condition.

(x) Ground conditions around the equipment for proper support, including ground settling under and around outriggers/stabilizers and supporting foundations, ground water accumulation, or similar conditions. This paragraph does not apply to the inspection of ground conditions for railroad tracks and their underlying support when the railroad tracks are part of the general railroad system of transportation that is regulated pursuant to the Federal Railroad Administration under 49 CFR part 213.

(xi) The equipment for level position within the tolerances specified by the equipment manufacturer's recommendations, both before each shift and after each move and setup.

(xii) Operator cab windows for significant cracks, breaks, or other deficiencies that would hamper the operator's view.

(xiii) Rails, rail stops, rail clamps and supporting surfaces when the equipment has rail traveling. This paragraph does not apply to the inspection of rails, rail stops, rail clamps and supporting surfaces when the railroad tracks are part of the general railroad system of transportation that is regulated pursuant to the Federal Railroad Administration under 49 CFR part 213.

(xiv) Safety devices and operational aids for proper operation.

(2) If any deficiency in paragraphs (d)(1)(i) through (xiii) of this section (or in additional inspection items required to be checked for specific types of equipment in accordance with other sections of this standard) is identified, an immediate determination must be made by the competent person as to whether the deficiency constitutes a safety hazard. If the deficiency is determined to constitute a safety hazard, the equipment must be taken out of service until it has been corrected. *See* §1926.1417.

701

(3) If any deficiency in paragraph (d)(1)(xiv) of this section (safety devices/operational aids) is identified, the action specified in § 1926.1415 and § 1926.1416 must be taken prior to using the equipment.

(e) *Monthly.* (1) Each month the equipment is in service it must be inspected in accordance with paragraph (d) of this section (each shift).

(2) Equipment must not be used until an inspection under this paragraph demonstrates that no corrective action under paragraphs (d)(2) and (3) of this section is required.

(3) *Documentation.* (i) The following information must be documented and maintained by the employer that conducts the inspection:

(A) The items checked and the results of the inspection.

(B) The name and signature of the person who conducted the inspection and the date.

(ii) This document must be retained for a minimum of three months.

(f) *Annual/comprehensive.* (1) At least every 12 months the equipment must be inspected by a qualified person in accordance with paragraph (d) of this section (each shift) except that the corrective action set forth in paragraphs (f)(4), (f)(5), and (f)(6) of this section must apply in place of the corrective action required by paragraphs (d)(2) and (d)(3) of this section.

(2) In addition, at least every 12 months, the equipment must be inspected by a qualified person. Disassembly is required, as necessary, to complete the inspection. The equipment must be inspected for all of the following:

(i) Equipment structure (including the boom and, if equipped, the jib):

(A) Structural members: Deformed, cracked, or significantly corroded.

(B) Bolts, rivets and other fasteners: loose, failed or significantly corroded.

(C) Welds for cracks.

(ii) Sheaves and drums for cracks or significant wear.

(iii) Parts such as pins, bearings, shafts, gears, rollers and locking devices for distortion, cracks or significant wear.

(iv) Brake and clutch system parts, linings, pawls and ratchets for excessive wear.

(v) Safety devices and operational aids for proper operation (including significant inaccuracies).

(vi) Gasoline, diesel, electric, or other power plants for safety-related problems (such as leaking exhaust and emergency shut-down feature) and conditions, and proper operation.

(vii) Chains and chain drive sprockets for excessive wear of sprockets and excessive chain stretch.

(viii) Travel steering, brakes, and locking devices, for proper operation.

(ix) Tires for damage or excessive wear.

(x) Hydraulic, pneumatic and other pressurized hoses, fittings and tubing, as follows:

(A) Flexible hose or its junction with the fittings for indications of leaks.

(B) Threaded or clamped joints for leaks.

(C) Outer covering of the hose for blistering, abnormal deformation or other signs of failure/impending failure.

(D) Outer surface of a hose, rigid tube, or fitting for indications of excessive abrasion or scrubbing.

(xi) Hydraulic and pneumatic pumps and motors, as follows:

(A) Performance indicators: Unusual noises or vibration, low operating speed, excessive heating of the fluid, low pressure.

(B) Loose bolts or fasteners.

(C) Shaft seals and joints between pump sections for leaks.

(xii) Hydraulic and pneumatic valves, as follows:

(A) Spools: Sticking, improper return to neutral, and leaks.

(B) Leaks.

(C) Valve housing cracks.

(D) Relief valves: Failure to reach correct pressure (if there is a manufacturer procedure for checking pressure, it must be followed).

(xiii) Hydraulic and pneumatic cylinders, as follows:

(A) Drifting caused by fluid leaking across the piston.

(B) Rod seals and welded joints for leaks.

(C) Cylinder rods for scores, nicks, or dents.

(D) Case (barrel) for significant dents.

(E) Rod eyes and connecting joints: Loose or deformed.

(xiv) Outrigger or stabilizer pads/ floats for excessive wear or cracks.

(xv) Slider pads for excessive wear or cracks.

(xvi) Electrical components and wiring for cracked or split insulation and loose or corroded terminations.

(xvii) Warning labels and decals originally supplied with the equipment by the manufacturer or otherwise required under this standard: Missing or unreadable.

(xviii) Originally equipped operator seat (or equivalent): Missing.

(xix) Operator seat: Unserviceable.

(xx) Originally equipped steps, ladders, handrails, guards: Missing.

(xxi) Steps, ladders, handrails, guards: In unusable/unsafe condition.

(3) This inspection must include functional testing to determine that the equipment as configured in the inspection is functioning properly.

(4) If any deficiency is identified, an immediate determination must be made by the qualified person as to whether the deficiency constitutes a safety hazard or, though not yet a safety hazard, needs to be monitored in the monthly inspections.

(5) If the qualified person determines that a deficiency is a safety hazard, the equipment must be taken out of service until it has been corrected, except when temporary alternative measures are implemented as specified in §1926.1416(d) or §1926.1435(e). *See* §1926.1417.

(6) If the qualified person determines that, though not presently a safety hazard, the deficiency needs to be monitored, the employer must ensure that the deficiency is checked in the monthly inspections.

(7) *Documentation of annual/comprehensive inspection.* The following information must be documented, maintained, and retained for a minimum of 12 months, by the employer that conducts the inspection:

(i) The items checked and the results of the inspection.

(ii) The name and signature of the person who conducted the inspection and the date.

(g) *Severe service.* Where the severity of use/conditions is such that there is a reasonable probability of damage or excessive wear (such as loading that may have exceeded rated capacity, shock loading that may have exceeded rated capacity, prolonged exposure to a corrosive atmosphere), the employer must stop using the equipment and a qualified person must:

(1) Inspect the equipment for structural damage to determine if the equipment can continue to be used safely.

(2) In light of the use/conditions determine whether any items/conditions listed in paragraph (f) of this section need to be inspected; if so, the qualified person must inspect those items/conditions.

(3) If a deficiency is found, the employer must follow the requirements in paragraphs (f)(4) through (6) of this section.

(h) *Equipment not in regular use.* Equipment that has been idle for 3 months or more must be inspected by a qualified person in accordance with the requirements of paragraph (e) (Monthly) of this section before initial use.

(i) [Reserved]

(j) Any part of a manufacturer's procedures regarding inspections that relate to safe operation (such as to a safety device or operational aid, critical part of a control system, power plant, braking system, load-sustaining structural components, load hook, or in-use operating mechanism) that is more comprehensive or has a more frequent schedule of inspection than the requirements of this section must be followed.

(k) All documents produced under this section must be available, during the applicable document retention period, to all persons who conduct inspections under this section.

§1926.1413 Wire rope—inspection.

(a) *Shift inspection.* (1) A competent person must begin a visual inspection prior to each shift the equipment is used, which must be completed before or during that shift. The inspection must consist of observation of wire ropes (running and standing) that are likely to be in use during the shift for apparent deficiencies, including those listed in paragraph (a)(2) of this section. Untwisting (opening) of wire rope

703

or booming down is not required as part of this inspection.

(2) *Apparent deficiencies*—(i) *Category I.* Apparent deficiencies in this category include the following:

(A) Significant distortion of the wire rope structure such as kinking, crushing, unstranding, birdcaging, signs of core failure or steel core protrusion between the outer strands.

(B) Significant corrosion.

(C) Electric arc damage (from a source other than power lines) or heat damage.

(D) Improperly applied end connections.

(E) Significantly corroded, cracked, bent, or worn end connections (such as from severe service).

(ii) *Category II.* Apparent deficiencies in this category are:

(A) Visible broken wires, as follows:

(*1*) In running wire ropes: Six randomly distributed broken wires in one rope lay or three broken wires in one strand in one rope lay, where a rope lay is the length along the rope in which one strand makes a complete revolution around the rope.

(*2*) In rotation resistant ropes: Two randomly distributed broken wires in six rope diameters or four randomly distributed broken wires in 30 rope diameters.

(*3*) In pendants or standing wire ropes: More than two broken wires in one rope lay located in rope beyond end connections and/or more than one broken wire in a rope lay located at an end connection.

(B) A diameter reduction of more than 5% from nominal diameter.

(iii) *Category III.* Apparent deficiencies in this category include the following:

(A) In rotation resistant wire rope, core protrusion or other distortion indicating core failure.

(B) Prior electrical contact with a power line.

(C) A broken strand.

(3) *Critical review items.* The competent person must give particular attention to all of the following:

(i) Rotation resistant wire rope in use.

(ii) Wire rope being used for boom hoists and luffing hoists, particularly at reverse bends.

(iii) Wire rope at flange points, crossover points and repetitive pickup points on drums.

(iv) Wire rope at or near terminal ends.

(v) Wire rope in contact with saddles, equalizer sheaves or other sheaves where rope travel is limited.

(4) *Removal from service.* (i) If a deficiency in Category I (*see* paragraph (a)(2)(i) of this section) is identified, an immediate determination must be made by the competent person as to whether the deficiency constitutes a safety hazard. If the deficiency is determined to constitute a safety hazard, operations involving use of the wire rope in question must be prohibited until:

(A) The wire rope is replaced (*see* § 1926.1417), or

(B) If the deficiency is localized, the problem is corrected by severing the wire rope in two; the undamaged portion may continue to be used. Joining lengths of wire rope by splicing is prohibited. If a rope is shortened under this paragraph, the employer must ensure that the drum will still have two wraps of wire when the load and/or boom is in its lowest position.

(ii) If a deficiency in Category II (*see* paragraph (a)(2)(ii) of this section) is identified, operations involving use of the wire rope in question must be prohibited until:

(A) The employer complies with the wire rope manufacturer's established criterion for removal from service or a different criterion that the wire rope manufacturer has approved in writing for that specific wire rope (*see* § 1926.1417),

(B) The wire rope is replaced (*see* § 1926.1417), or

(C) If the deficiency is localized, the problem is corrected by severing the wire rope in two; the undamaged portion may continue to be used. Joining lengths of wire rope by splicing is prohibited. If a rope is shortened under this paragraph, the employer must ensure that the drum will still have two wraps of wire when the load and/or boom is in its lowest position.

(iii) If a deficiency in Category III is identified, operations involving use of the wire rope in question must be prohibited until:

(A) The wire rope is replaced (*see* §1926.1417), or

(B) If the deficiency (other than power line contact) is localized, the problem is corrected by severing the wire rope in two; the undamaged portion may continue to be used. Joining lengths of wire rope by splicing is prohibited. Repair of wire rope that contacted an energized power line is also prohibited. If a rope is shortened under this paragraph, the employer must ensure that the drum will still have two wraps of wire when the load and/or boom is in its lowest position.

(iv) Where a wire rope is required to be removed from service under this section, either the equipment (as a whole) or the hoist with that wire rope must be tagged-out, in accordance with §1926.1417(f)(1), until the wire rope is repaired or replaced.

(b) *Monthly inspection.* (1) Each month an inspection must be conducted in accordance with paragraph (a) (shift inspection) of this section.

(2) The inspection must include any deficiencies that the qualified person who conducts the annual inspection determines under paragraph (c)(3)(ii) of this section must be monitored.

(3) Wire ropes on equipment must not be used until an inspection under this paragraph demonstrates that no corrective action under paragraph (a)(4) of this section is required.

(4) The inspection must be documented according to §1926.1412(e)(3) (monthly inspection documentation).

(c) *Annual/comprehensive.* (1) At least every 12 months, wire ropes in use on equipment must be inspected by a qualified person in accordance with paragraph (a) of this section (shift inspection).

(2) In addition, at least every 12 months, the wire ropes in use on equipment must be inspected by a qualified person, as follows:

(i) The inspection must be for deficiencies of the types listed in paragraph (a)(2) of this section.

(ii) The inspection must be complete and thorough, covering the surface of the entire length of the wire ropes, with particular attention given to all of the following:

(A) Critical review items listed in paragraph (a)(3) of this section.

(B) Those sections that are normally hidden during shift and monthly inspections.

(C) Wire rope subject to reverse bends.

(D) Wire rope passing over sheaves.

(iii) *Exception:* In the event an inspection under paragraph (c)(2) of this section is not feasible due to existing set-up and configuration of the equipment (such as where an assist crane is needed) or due to site conditions (such as a dense urban setting), such inspections must be conducted as soon as it becomes feasible, but no longer than an additional 6 months for running ropes and, for standing ropes, at the time of disassembly.

(3) If a deficiency is identified, an immediate determination must be made by the qualified person as to whether the deficiency constitutes a safety hazard.

(i) If the deficiency is determined to constitute a safety hazard, operations involving use of the wire rope in question must be prohibited until:

(A) The wire rope is replaced (*see* §1926.1417), or

(B) If the deficiency is localized, the problem is corrected by severing the wire rope in two; the undamaged portion may continue to be used. Joining lengths of wire rope by splicing is prohibited. If a rope is shortened under this paragraph, the employer must ensure that the drum will still have two wraps of wire when the load and/or boom is in its lowest position.

(ii) If the qualified person determines that, though not presently a safety hazard, the deficiency needs to be monitored, the employer must ensure that the deficiency is checked in the monthly inspections.

(4) The inspection must be documented according to §1926.1412(f)(7) (annual/comprehensive inspection documentation).

(d) Rope lubricants that are of the type that hinder inspection must not be used.

(e) All documents produced under this section must be available, during the applicable document retention period, to all persons who conduct inspections under this section.

705

§ 1926.1414 Wire rope—selection and installation criteria.

(a) Original equipment wire rope and replacement wire rope must be selected and installed in accordance with the requirements of this section. Selection of replacement wire rope must be in accordance with the recommendations of the wire rope manufacturer, the equipment manufacturer, or a qualified person.

(b) *Wire rope design criteria:* Wire rope (other than rotation resistant rope) must comply with either Option (1) or Option (2) of this section, as follows:

(1) *Option (1).* Wire rope must comply with section 5–1.7.1 of ASME B30.5–2004 (incorporated by reference, *see* § 1926.6) except that section's paragraph (c) must not apply.

(2) *Option (2).* Wire rope must be designed to have, in relation to the equipment's rated capacity, a sufficient minimum breaking force and design factor so that compliance with the applicable inspection provisions in § 1926.1413 will be an effective means of preventing sudden rope failure.

(c) Wire rope must be compatible with the safe functioning of the equipment.

(d) *Boom hoist reeving.* (1) Fiber core ropes must not be used for boom hoist reeving, except for derricks.

(2) Rotation resistant ropes must be used for boom hoist reeving only where the requirements of paragraph (e)(4)(ii) of this section are met.

(e) *Rotation resistant ropes—*(1) *Definitions—*(i) *Type I rotation resistant wire rope ("Type I").* Type I rotation resistant rope is stranded rope constructed to have little or no tendency to rotate or, if guided, transmits little or no torque. It has at least 15 outer strands and comprises an assembly of at least three layers of strands laid helically over a center in two operations. The direction of lay of the outer strands is opposite to that of the underlying layer.

(ii) *Type II rotation resistant wire rope ("Type II").* Type II rotation resistant rope is stranded rope constructed to have significant resistance to rotation. It has at least 10 outer strands and comprises an assembly of two or more layers of strands laid helically over a center in two or three operations. The direction of lay of the outer strands is opposite to that of the underlying layer.

(iii) *Type III rotation resistant wire rope ("Type III").* Type III rotation resistant rope is stranded rope constructed to have limited resistance to rotation. It has no more than nine outer strands, and comprises an assembly of two layers of strands laid helically over a center in two operations. The direction of lay of the outer strands is opposite to that of the underlying layer.

(2) *Requirements.* (i) Types II and III with an operating design factor of less than 5 must not be used for duty cycle or repetitive lifts.

(ii) Rotation resistant ropes (including Types I, II and III) must have an operating design factor of no less than 3.5.

(iii) Type I must have an operating design factor of no less than 5, except where the wire rope manufacturer and the equipment manufacturer approves the design factor, in writing.

(iv) Types II and III must have an operating design factor of no less than 5, except where the requirements of paragraph (e)(3) of this section are met.

(3) When Types II and III with an operating design factor of less than 5 are used (for non-duty cycle, non-repetitive lifts), the following requirements must be met for each lifting operation:

(i) A qualified person must inspect the rope in accordance with § 1926.1413(a). The rope must be used only if the qualified person determines that there are no deficiencies constituting a hazard. In making this determination, more than one broken wire in any one rope lay must be considered a hazard.

(ii) Operations must be conducted in such a manner and at such speeds as to minimize dynamic effects.

(iii) Each lift made under § 1926.1414(e)(3) must be recorded in the monthly and annual inspection documents. Such prior uses must be considered by the qualified person in determining whether to use the rope again.

(4) *Additional requirements for rotation resistant ropes for boom hoist reeving.* (i) Rotation resistant ropes must not be used for boom hoist reeving, except

where the requirements of paragraph (e)(4)(ii) of this section are met.

(ii) Rotation resistant ropes may be used as boom hoist reeving when load hoists are used as boom hoists for attachments such as luffing attachments or boom and mast attachment systems. Under these conditions, all of the following requirements must be met:

(A) The drum must provide a first layer rope pitch diameter of not less than 18 times the nominal diameter of the rope used.

(B) The requirements in §1926.1426(a) (irrespective of the date of manufacture of the equipment), and §1926.1426(b).

(C) The requirements in ASME B30.5–2004 sections 5–1.3.2(a), (a)(2) through (a)(4), (b) and (d) (incorporated by reference, *see* §1926.6) except that the minimum pitch diameter for sheaves used in multiple rope reeving is 18 times the nominal diameter of the rope used (instead of the value of 16 specified in section 5–1.3.2(d)).

(D) All sheaves used in the boom hoist reeving system must have a rope pitch diameter of not less than 18 times the nominal diameter of the rope used.

(E) The operating design factor for the boom hoist reeving system must be not less than five.

(F) The operating design factor for these ropes must be the total minimum breaking force of all parts of rope in the system divided by the load imposed on the rope system when supporting the static weights of the structure and the load within the equipment's rated capacity.

(G) When provided, a power-controlled lowering system must be capable of handling rated capacities and speeds as specified by the manufacturer.

(f) Wire rope clips used in conjunction with wedge sockets must be attached to the unloaded dead end of the rope only, except that the use of devices specifically designed for dead-ending rope in a wedge socket is permitted.

(g) Socketing must be done in the manner specified by the manufacturer of the wire rope or fitting.

(h) Prior to cutting a wire rope, seizings must be placed on each side of the point to be cut. The length and number of seizings must be in accordance with the wire rope manufacturer's instructions.

§1926.1415 Safety devices.

(a) *Safety devices.* The following safety devices are required on all equipment covered by this subpart, unless otherwise specified:

(1) *Crane level indicator.* (i) The equipment must have a crane level indicator that is either built into the equipment or is available on the equipment.

(ii) If a built-in crane level indicator is not working properly, it must be tagged-out or removed. If a removable crane level indicator is not working properly, it must be removed.

(iii) This requirement does not apply to portal cranes, derricks, floating cranes/derricks and land cranes/derricks on barges, pontoons, vessels or other means of flotation.

(2) Boom stops, except for derricks and hydraulic booms.

(3) Jib stops (if a jib is attached), except for derricks.

(4) Equipment with foot pedal brakes must have locks.

(5) Hydraulic outrigger jacks and hydraulic stabilizer jacks must have an integral holding device/check valve.

(6) Equipment on rails must have rail clamps and rail stops, except for portal cranes.

(7) *Horn.* (i) The equipment must have a horn that is either built into the equipment or is on the equipment and immediately available to the operator.

(ii) If a built-in horn is not working properly, it must be tagged-out or removed. If a removable horn is not working properly, it must be removed.

(b) *Proper operation required.* Operations must not begin unless all of the devices listed in this section are in proper working order. If a device stops working properly during operations, the operator must safely stop operations. If any of the devices listed in this section are not in proper working order, the equipment must be taken out of service and operations must not resume until the device is again working properly. *See* §1926.1417 (Operation). Alternative measures are not permitted to be used.

§ 1926.1416 Operational aids.

(a) The devices listed in this section ("listed operational aids") are required on all equipment covered by this subpart, unless otherwise specified.

(1) The requirements in paragraphs (e)(1), (e)(2), and (e)(3) of this section do not apply to articulating cranes.

(2) The requirements in paragraphs (d)(3), (e)(1), and (e)(4) of this section apply only to those digger derricks manufactured after November 8, 2011.

(b) Operations must not begin unless the listed operational aids are in proper working order, except where an operational aid is being repaired the employer uses the specified temporary alternative measures. The time periods permitted for repairing defective operational aids are specified in paragraphs (d) and (e) of this section. More protective alternative measures specified by the crane/derrick manufacturer, if any, must be followed.

(c) If a listed operational aid stops working properly during operations, the operator must safely stop operations until the temporary alternative measures are implemented or the device is again working properly. If a replacement part is no longer available, the use of a substitute device that performs the same type of function is permitted and is not considered a modification under § 1926.1434.

(d) *Category I operational aids and alternative measures.* Operational aids listed in this paragraph that are not working properly must be repaired no later than 7 calendar days after the deficiency occurs. *Exception:* If the employer documents that it has ordered the necessary parts within 7 calendar days of the occurrence of the deficiency, the repair must be completed within 7 calendar days of receipt of the parts. *See* § 1926.1417(j) for additional requirements.

(1) *Boom hoist limiting device.* (i) For equipment manufactured after December 16, 1969, a boom hoist limiting device is required. *Temporary alternative measures (use at least one).* One or more of the following methods must be used:

(A) Use a boom angle indicator.

(B) Clearly mark the boom hoist cable (so that it can easily be seen by the operator) at a point that will give the operator sufficient time to stop the

hoist to keep the boom within the minimum allowable radius. In addition, install mirrors or remote video cameras and displays if necessary for the operator to see the mark.

(C) Clearly mark the boom hoist cable (so that it can easily be seen by a spotter) at a point that will give the spotter sufficient time to signal the operator and have the operator stop the hoist to keep the boom within the minimum allowable radius.

(ii) If the equipment was manufactured on or before December 16, 1969, and is not equipped with a boom hoist limiting device, at least one of the measures in paragraphs (d)(1)(i)(A) through (C) of this section must be used.

(2) *Luffing jib limiting device.* Equipment with a luffing jib must have a luffing jib limiting device. Temporary alternative measures are the same as in paragraph (d)(1)(i) of this section, except to limit the movement of the luffing jib rather than the boom hoist.

(3) *Anti two-blocking device.* (i) Telescopic boom cranes manufactured after February 28, 1992, must be equipped with a device which automatically prevents damage from contact between the load block, overhaul ball, or similar component, and the boom tip (or fixed upper block or similar component). The device(s) must prevent such damage at all points where two-blocking could occur.

Temporary alternative measures: Clearly mark the cable (so that it can easily be seen by the operator) at a point that will give the operator sufficient time to stop the hoist to prevent two-blocking, and use a spotter when extending the boom.

(ii) *Lattice boom cranes.* (A) Lattice boom cranes manufactured after Feb 28, 1992, must be equipped with a device that either automatically prevents damage and load failure from contact between the load block, overhaul ball, or similar component, and the boom tip (or fixed upper block or similar component), or warns the operator in time for the operator to prevent two-blocking. The device must prevent such damage/failure or provide adequate warning for all points where two-blocking could occur.

(B) Lattice boom cranes and derricks manufactured after November 8, 2011 must be equipped with a device which automatically prevents damage and load failure from contact between the load block, overhaul ball, or similar component, and the boom tip (or fixed upper block or similar component). The device(s) must prevent such damage/failure at all points where two-blocking could occur.

(C) *Exception.* The requirements in paragraphs (d)(3)(ii)(A) and (B) of this section do not apply to such lattice boom equipment when used for drag-line, clamshell (grapple), magnet, drop ball, container handling, concrete bucket, marine operations that do not involve hoisting personnel, and pile driving work.

(D) *Temporary alternative measures.* Clearly mark the cable (so that it can easily be seen by the operator) at a point that will give the operator sufficient time to stop the hoist to prevent two-blocking, or use a spotter.

(iii) Articulating cranes manufactured after December 31, 1999, that are equipped with a load hoist must be equipped with a device that automatically prevents damage from contact between the load block, overhaul ball, or similar component, and the boom tip (or fixed upper block or similar component). The device must prevent such damage at all points where two-blocking could occur. *Temporary alternative measures:* When two-blocking could only occur with movement of the load hoist, clearly mark the cable (so that it can easily be seen by the operator) at a point that will give the operator sufficient time to stop the hoist to prevent two-blocking, or use a spotter. When two-blocking could occur without movement of the load hoist, clearly mark the cable (so that it can easily be seen by the operator) at a point that will give the operator sufficient time to stop the hoist to prevent two-blocking, and use a spotter when extending the boom.

(e) *Category II operational aids and alternative measures.* Operational aids listed in this paragraph that are not working properly must be repaired no later than 30 calendar days after the deficiency occurs. *Exception:* If the employer documents that it has ordered the necessary parts within 7 calendar days of the occurrence of the deficiency, and the part is not received in time to complete the repair in 30 calendar days, the repair must be completed within 7 calendar days of receipt of the parts. *See* §1926.1417(j) for additional requirements.

(1) *Boom angle or radius indicator.* The equipment must have a boom angle or radius indicator readable from the operator's station. *Temporary alternative measures:* Radii or boom angle must be determined by measuring the radii or boom angle with a measuring device.

(2) Jib angle indicator if the equipment has a luffing jib. *Temporary alternative measures:* Radii or jib angle must be determined by ascertaining the main boom angle and then measuring the radii or jib angle with a measuring device.

(3) Boom length indicator if the equipment has a telescopic boom, except where the rated capacity is independent of the boom length. *Temporary alternative measures.* One or more of the following methods must be used:

(i) Mark the boom with measured marks to calculate boom length,

(ii) Calculate boom length from boom angle and radius measurements,

(iii) Measure the boom with a measuring device.

(4) *Load weighing and similar devices.* (i) Equipment (other than derricks and articulating cranes) manufactured after March 29, 2003 with a rated capacity over 6,000 pounds must have at least one of the following: load weighing device, load moment (or rated capacity) indicator, or load moment (or rated capacity) limiter. *Temporary alternative measures:* The weight of the load must be determined from a source recognized by the industry (such as the load's manufacturer) or by a calculation method recognized by the industry (such as calculating a steel beam from measured dimensions and a known per foot weight). This information must be provided to the operator prior to the lift.

(ii) Articulating cranes manufactured after November 8, 2011 must have at least one of the following: automatic overload prevention device, load weighing device, load moment (or rated capacity) indicator, or load moment

709

(rated capacity) limiter. *Temporary alternative measures:* The weight of the load must be determined from a source recognized by the industry (such as the load's manufacturer) or by a calculation method recognized by the industry (such as calculating a steel beam from measured dimensions and a known per foot weight). This information must be provided to the operator prior to the lift.

(5) The following devices are required on equipment manufactured after November 8, 2011:

(i) Outrigger/stabilizer position (horizontal beam extension) sensor/monitor if the equipment has outriggers or stabilizers. *Temporary alternative measures:* The operator must verify that the position of the outriggers or stabilizers is correct (in accordance with manufacturer procedures) before beginning operations requiring outrigger or stabilizer deployment.

(ii) Hoist drum rotation indicator if the equipment has a hoist drum not visible from the operator's station. *Temporary alternative measures:* Mark the drum to indicate the rotation of the drum. In addition, install mirrors or remote video cameras and displays if necessary for the operator to see the mark.

§ 1926.1417 Operation.

(a) The employer must comply with all manufacturer procedures applicable to the operational functions of equipment, including its use with attachments.

(b) *Unavailable operation procedures.* (1) Where the manufacturer procedures are unavailable, the employer must develop and ensure compliance with all procedures necessary for the safe operation of the equipment and attachments.

(2) Procedures for the operational controls must be developed by a qualified person.

(3) Procedures related to the capacity of the equipment must be developed and signed by a registered professional engineer familiar with the equipment.

(c) *Accessibility of procedures.* (1) The procedures applicable to the operation of the equipment, including rated capacities (load charts), recommended operating speeds, special hazard warnings, instructions, and operator's manual, must be readily available in the cab at all times for use by the operator.

(2) Where rated capacities are available in the cab only in electronic form: In the event of a failure which makes the rated capacities inaccessible, the operator must immediately cease operations or follow safe shut-down procedures until the rated capacities (in electronic or other form) are available.

(d) The operator must not engage in any practice or activity that diverts his/her attention while actually engaged in operating the equipment, such as the use of cellular phones (other than when used for signal communications).

(e) *Leaving the equipment unattended.* (1) The operator must not leave the controls while the load is suspended, except where all of the following are met:

(i) The operator remains adjacent to the equipment and is not engaged in any other duties.

(ii) The load is to be held suspended for a period of time exceeding normal lifting operations.

(iii) The competent person determines that it is safe to do so and implements measures necessary to restrain the boom hoist and telescoping, load, swing, and outrigger or stabilizer functions.

(iv) Barricades or caution lines, and notices, are erected to prevent all employees from entering the fall zone. No employees, including those listed in §§ 1926.1425(b)(1) through (3), § 1926.1425(d) or § 1926.1425(e), are permitted in the fall zone.

(2) The provisions in § 1926.1417(e)(1) do not apply to working gear (such as slings, spreader bars, ladders, and welding machines) where the weight of the working gear is negligible relative to the lifting capacity of the equipment as positioned, and the working gear is suspended over an area other than an entrance or exit.

(f) *Tag-out—(1) Tagging out of service equipment/functions.* Where the employer has taken the equipment out of service, a tag must be placed in the cab stating that the equipment is out of service and is not to be used. Where the employer has taken a function(s) out of service, a tag must be placed in a conspicuous position stating that the function is out of service and is not to be used.

(2) *Response to "do not operate"/tag-out signs.* (i) If there is a warning (tag-out or maintenance/do not operate) sign on the equipment or starting control, the operator must not activate the switch or start the equipment until the sign has been removed by a person authorized to remove it, or until the operator has verified that:

(A) No one is servicing, working on, or otherwise in a dangerous position on the machine.

(B) The equipment has been repaired and is working properly.

(ii) If there is a warning (tag-out or maintenance/do not operate) sign on any other switch or control, the operator must not activate that switch or control until the sign has been removed by a person authorized to remove it, or until the operator has verified that the requirements in paragraphs (f)(2)(i)(A) and (B) of this section have been met.

(g) Before starting the engine, the operator must verify that all controls are in the proper starting position and that all personnel are in the clear.

(h) *Storm warning.* When a local storm warning has been issued, the competent person must determine whether it is necessary to implement manufacturer recommendations for securing the equipment.

(i) [Reserved]

(j) If equipment adjustments or repairs are necessary:

(1) The operator must, in writing, promptly inform the person designated by the employer to receive such information and, where there are successive shifts, to the next operator; and

(2) The employer must notify all affected employees, at the beginning of each shift, of the necessary adjustments or repairs and all alternative measures.

(k) Safety devices and operational aids must not be used as a substitute for the exercise of professional judgment by the operator.

(l) [Reserved]

(m) If the competent person determines that there is a slack rope condition requiring re-spooling of the rope, it must be verified (before starting to lift) that the rope is seated on the drum and in the sheaves as the slack is removed.

(n) The competent person must adjust the equipment and/or operations to address the effect of wind, ice, and snow on equipment stability and rated capacity.

(o) *Compliance with rated capacity.* (1) The equipment must not be operated in excess of its rated capacity.

(2) The operator must not be required to operate the equipment in a manner that would violate paragraph (o)(1) of this section.

(3) *Load weight.* The operator must verify that the load is within the rated capacity of the equipment by at least one of the following methods:

(i) The weight of the load must be determined from a source recognized by the industry (such as the load's manufacturer), or by a calculation method recognized by the industry (such as calculating a steel beam from measured dimensions and a known per foot weight), or by other equally reliable means. In addition, when requested by the operator, this information must be provided to the operator prior to the lift; or

(ii) The operator must begin hoisting the load to determine, using a load weighing device, load moment indicator, rated capacity indicator, or rated capacity limiter, if it exceeds 75 percent of the maximum rated capacity at the longest radius that will be used during the lift operation. If it does, the operator must not proceed with the lift until he/she verifies the weight of the load in accordance with paragraph (o)(3)(i) of this section.

(p) The boom or other parts of the equipment must not contact any obstruction.

(q) The equipment must not be used to drag or pull loads sideways.

(r) On wheel-mounted equipment, no loads must be lifted over the front area, except as permitted by the manufacturer.

(s) The operator must test the brakes each time a load that is 90% or more of the maximum line pull is handled by lifting the load a few inches and applying the brakes. In duty cycle and repetitive lifts where each lift is 90% or more of the maximum line pull, this requirement applies to the first lift but not to successive lifts.

(t) Neither the load nor the boom must be lowered below the point where less than two full wraps of rope remain on their respective drums.

(u) *Traveling with a load.* (1) Traveling with a load is prohibited if the practice is prohibited by the manufacturer.

(2) Where traveling with a load, the employer must ensure that:

(i) A competent person supervises the operation, determines if it is necessary to reduce rated capacity, and makes determinations regarding load position, boom location, ground support, travel route, overhead obstructions, and speed of movement necessary to ensure safety.

(ii) The determinations of the competent person required in paragraph (u)(2)(i) of this section are implemented.

(iii) For equipment with tires, tire pressure specified by the manufacturer is maintained.

(v) Rotational speed of the equipment must be such that the load does not swing out beyond the radius at which it can be controlled.

(w) A tag or restraint line must be used if necessary to prevent rotation of the load that would be hazardous.

(x) The brakes must be adjusted in accordance with manufacturer procedures to prevent unintended movement.

(y) The operator must obey a stop (or emergency stop) signal, irrespective of who gives it.

(z) *Swinging locomotive cranes.* A locomotive crane must not be swung into a position where railway cars on an adjacent track could strike it, until it is determined that cars are not being moved on the adjacent track and that proper flag protection has been established.

(aa) *Counterweight/ballast.* (1) The following applies to equipment other than tower cranes:

(i) Equipment must not be operated without the counterweight or ballast in place as specified by the manufacturer.

(ii) The maximum counterweight or ballast specified by the manufacturer

for the equipment must not be exceeded.

(2) Counterweight/ballast requirements for tower cranes are specified in § 1926.1435(b)(8).

§ 1926.1418 Authority to stop operation.

Whenever there is a concern as to safety, the operator must have the authority to stop and refuse to handle loads until a qualified person has determined that safety has been assured.

§ 1926.1419 Signals—general requirements.

(a) A signal person must be provided in each of the following situations:

(1) The point of operation, meaning the load travel or the area near or at load placement, is not in full view of the operator.

(2) When the equipment is traveling, the view in the direction of travel is obstructed.

(3) Due to site specific safety concerns, either the operator or the person handling the load determines that it is necessary.

(b) *Types of signals.* Signals to operators must be by hand, voice, audible, or new signals.

(c) *Hand signals.* (1) When using hand signals, the Standard Method must be used (*see* appendix A of this subpart). *Exception:* Where use of the Standard Method for hand signals is infeasible, or where an operation or use of an attachment is not covered in the Standard Method, non-standard hand signals may be used in accordance with paragraph (c)(2) of this section.

(2) *Non-standard hand signals.* When using non-standard hand signals, the signal person, operator, and lift director (where there is one) must contact each other prior to the operation and agree on the non-standard hand signals that will be used.

(d) *New signals.* Signals other than hand, voice, or audible signals may be used where the employer demonstrates that:

(1) The new signals provide at least equally effective communication as voice, audible, or Standard Method hand signals, or

(2) The new signals comply with a national consensus standard that provides at least equally effective communication as voice, audible, or Standard Method hand signals.

(e) *Suitability.* The signals used (hand, voice, audible, or new), and means of transmitting the signals to the operator (such as direct line of sight, video, radio, *etc.*), must be appropriate for the site conditions.

(f) During operations requiring signals, the ability to transmit signals between the operator and signal person must be maintained. If that ability is interrupted at any time, the operator must safely stop operations requiring signals until it is reestablished and a proper signal is given and understood.

(g) If the operator becomes aware of a safety problem and needs to communicate with the signal person, the operator must safely stop operations. Operations must not resume until the operator and signal person agree that the problem has been resolved.

(h) Only one person may give signals to a crane/derrick at a time, except in circumstances covered by paragraph (j) of this section.

(i) [Reserved]

(j) Anyone who becomes aware of a safety problem must alert the operator or signal person by giving the stop or emergency stop signal. (NOTE: § 1926.1417(y) requires the operator to obey a stop or emergency stop signal).

(k) All directions given to the operator by the signal person must be given from the operator's direction perspective.

(l) [Reserved]

(m) *Communication with multiple cranes/derricks.* Where a signal person(s) is in communication with more than one crane/derrick, a system must be used for identifying the crane/derrick each signal is for, as follows:

(1) for each signal, prior to giving the function/direction, the signal person must identify the crane/derrick the signal is for, or

(2) must use an equally effective method of identifying which crane/derrick the signal is for.

§ 1926.1420 **Signals—radio, telephone or other electronic transmission of signals.**

(a) The device(s) used to transmit signals must be tested on site before beginning operations to ensure that the signal transmission is effective, clear, and reliable.

(b) Signal transmission must be through a dedicated channel, except:

(1) Multiple cranes/derricks and one or more signal persons may share a dedicated channel for the purpose of coordinating operations.

(2) Where a crane is being operated on or adjacent to railroad tracks, and the actions of the crane operator need to be coordinated with the movement of other equipment or trains on the same or adjacent tracks.

(c) The operator's reception of signals must be by a hands-free system.

§ 1926.1421 **Signals—voice signals—additional requirements.**

(a) Prior to beginning operations, the operator, signal person and lift director (if there is one), must contact each other and agree on the voice signals that will be used. Once the voice signals are agreed upon, these workers need not meet again to discuss voice signals unless another worker is added or substituted, there is confusion about the voice signals, or a voice signal is to be changed.

(b) Each voice signal must contain the following three elements, given in the following order: function (such as hoist, boom, *etc.*), direction; distance and/or speed; function, stop command.

(c) The operator, signal person and lift director (if there is one), must be able to effectively communicate in the language used.

§ 1926.1422 **Signals—hand signal chart.**

Hand signal charts must be either posted on the equipment or conspicuously posted in the vicinity of the hoisting operations.

§ 1926.1423 **Fall protection.**

(a) *Application.* (1) Paragraphs (b), (c)(3), (e) and (f) of this section apply to all equipment covered by this subpart except tower cranes.

(2) Paragraphs (c)(1), (c)(2), (d), (g), (j) and (k) of this section apply to all equipment covered by this subpart.

(3) Paragraphs (c)(4) and (h) of this section apply only to tower cranes.

(b) *Boom walkways.* (1) Equipment manufactured after November 8, 2011 with lattice booms must be equipped with walkways on the boom(s) if the vertical profile of the boom (from cord centerline to cord centerline) is 6 or more feet.

(2) *Boom walkway criteria.* (i) The walkways must be at least 12 inches wide.

(ii) Guardrails, railings and other permanent fall protection attachments along walkways are:

(A) Not required.

(B) Prohibited on booms supported by pendant ropes or bars if the guardrails/ railings/attachments could be snagged by the ropes or bars.

(C) Prohibited if of the removable type (designed to be installed and removed each time the boom is assembled/disassembled).

(D) Where not prohibited, guardrails or railings may be of any height up to, but not more than, 45 inches.

(c) *Steps, handholds, ladders, grabrails, guardrails and railings.* (1) Section 1926.502(b) does not apply to equipment covered by this subpart.

(2) The employer must maintain in good condition originally-equipped steps, handholds, ladders and guardrails/railings/grabrails.

(3) Equipment manufactured after November 8, 2011 must be equipped so as to provide safe access and egress between the ground and the operator work station(s), including the forward and rear positions, by the provision of devices such as steps, handholds, ladders, and guardrails/railings/grabrails. These devices must meet the following criteria:

(i) Steps, handholds, ladders and guardrails/railings/grabrails must meet the criteria of SAE J185 (May 2003) (incorporated by reference, *see* § 1926.6) or ISO 11660-2:1994(E) (incorporated by reference, *see* § 1926.6) except where infeasible.

(ii) Walking/stepping surfaces, except for crawler treads, must have slip-resistant features/properties (such as diamond plate metal, strategically placed

grip tape, expanded metal, or slip-resistant paint).

(4) Tower cranes manufactured after November 8, 2011 must be equipped so as to provide safe access and egress between the ground and the cab, machinery platforms, and tower (mast), by the provision of devices such as steps, handholds, ladders, and guardrails/railings/grabrails. These devices must meet the following criteria:

(i) Steps, handholds, ladders, and guardrails/railings/grabrails must meet the criteria of ISO 11660-1:2008(E) (incorporated by reference, *see* § 1926.6) and ISO 11660-3:2008(E) (incorporated by reference, *see* § 1926.6) or SAE J185 (May 2003) (incorporated by reference, *see* § 1926.6) except where infeasible.

(ii) Walking/stepping surfaces must have slip-resistant features/properties (such as diamond plate metal, strategically placed grip tape, expanded metal, or slip-resistant paint).

(d) *Personal fall arrest and fall restraint systems.* Personal fall arrest system components must be used in personal fall arrest and fall restraint systems and must conform to the criteria in § 1926.502(d) except that § 1926.502(d)(15) does not apply to components used in personal fall arrest and fall restraint systems. Either body belts or body harnesses must be used in personal fall arrest and fall restraint systems.

(e) For non-assembly/disassembly work, the employer must provide and ensure the use of fall protection equipment for employees who are on a walking/working surface with an unprotected side or edge more than 6 feet above a lower level as follows:

(1) When moving point-to-point:

(i) On non-lattice booms (whether horizontal or not horizontal).

(ii) On lattice booms that are not horizontal.

(iii) On horizontal lattice booms where the fall distance is 15 feet or more.

(2) While at a work station on any part of the equipment (including the boom, of any type), except when the employee is at or near draw-works (when the equipment is running), in the cab, or on the deck.

(f) For assembly/disassembly work, the employer must provide and ensure the use of fall protection equipment for employees who are on a walking/working surface with an unprotected side or edge more than 15 feet above a lower level, except when the employee is at or near draw-works (when the equipment is running), in the cab, or on the deck.

(g) *Anchorage criteria.* (1) Sections 1926.502(d)(15) and 1926.502(e)(2) apply to equipment covered by this subpart only to the extent delineated in paragraph (g)(2) of this section.

(2) *Anchorages for personal fall arrest and positioning device systems.* (i) Personal fall arrest systems must be anchored to any apparently substantial part of the equipment unless a competent person, from a visual inspection, without an engineering analysis, would conclude that the criteria in §1926.502(d)(15) would not be met.

(ii) Positioning device systems must be anchored to any apparently substantial part of the equipment unless a competent person, from a visual inspection, without an engineering analysis, would conclude that the criteria in §1926.502(e)(2) would not be met.

(iii) Attachable anchor devices (portable anchor devices that are attached to the equipment) must meet the anchorage criteria in §1926.502(d)(15) for personal fall arrest systems and §1926.502(e)(2) for positioning device systems.

(3) *Anchorages for fall restraint systems.* Fall restraint systems must be anchored to any part of the equipment that is capable of withstanding twice the maximum load that an employee may impose on it during reasonably anticipated conditions of use.

(h) *Tower cranes.* (1) For work other than erecting, climbing, and dismantling, the employer must provide and ensure the use of fall protection equipment for employees who are on a walking/working surface with an unprotected side or edge more than 6 feet above a lower level, except when the employee is at or near draw-works (when the equipment is running), in the cab, or on the deck.

(2) For erecting, climbing, and dismantling work, the employer must provide and ensure the use of fall protection equipment for employees who are on a walking/working surface with an

unprotected side or edge more than 15 feet above a lower level.

(i) [Reserved]

(j) *Anchoring to the load line.* A personal fall arrest system is permitted to be anchored to the crane/derrick's hook (or other part of the load line) where all of the following requirements are met:

(1) A qualified person has determined that the set-up and rated capacity of the crane/derrick (including the hook, load line and rigging) meets or exceeds the requirements in §1926.502(d)(15).

(2) The equipment operator must be at the work site and informed that the equipment is being used for this purpose.

(3) No load is suspended from the load line when the personal fall arrest system is anchored to the crane/derrick's hook (or other part of the load line).

(k) *Training.* The employer must train each employee who may be exposed to fall hazards while on, or hoisted by, equipment covered by this subpart on all of the following:

(1) the requirements in this subpart that address fall protection.

(2) the applicable requirements in §§1926.500 and 1926.502.

§1926.1424 Work area control.

(a) *Swing radius hazards.* (1) The requirements in paragraph (a)(2) of this section apply where there are accessible areas in which the equipment's rotating superstructure (whether permanently or temporarily mounted) poses a reasonably foreseeable risk of:

(i) Striking and injuring an employee; or

(ii) Pinching/crushing an employee against another part of the equipment or another object.

(2) To prevent employees from entering these hazard areas, the employer must:

(i) Train each employee assigned to work on or near the equipment ("authorized personnel") in how to recognize struck-by and pinch/crush hazard areas posed by the rotating superstructure.

(ii) Erect and maintain control lines, warning lines, railings or similar barriers to mark the boundaries of the

715

hazard areas. *Exception:* When the employer can demonstrate that it is neither feasible to erect such barriers on the ground nor on the equipment, the hazard areas must be clearly marked by a combination of warning signs (such as "Danger—Swing/Crush Zone") and high visibility markings on the equipment that identify the hazard areas. In addition, the employer must train each employee to understand what these markings signify.

(3) *Protecting employees in the hazard area.* (i) Before an employee goes to a location in the hazard area that is out of view of the operator, the employee (or someone instructed by the employee) must ensure that the operator is informed that he/she is going to that location.

(ii) Where the operator knows that an employee went to a location covered by paragraph (a)(1) of this section, the operator must not rotate the superstructure until the operator is informed in accordance with a pre-arranged system of communication that the employee is in a safe position.

(b) Where any part of a crane/derrick is within the working radius of another crane/derrick, the controlling entity must institute a system to coordinate operations. If there is no controlling entity, the employer (if there is only one employer operating the multiple pieces of equipment), or employers, must institute such a system.

§ 1926.1425 Keeping clear of the load.

(a) Where available, hoisting routes that minimize the exposure of employees to hoisted loads must be used, to the extent consistent with public safety.

(b) While the operator is not moving a suspended load, no employee must be within the fall zone, except for employees:

(1) Engaged in hooking, unhooking or guiding a load;

(2) Engaged in the initial attachment of the load to a component or structure; or

(3) Operating a concrete hopper or concrete bucket.

(c) When employees are engaged in hooking, unhooking, or guiding the load, or in the initial connection of a load to a component or structure and are within the fall zone, all of the following criteria must be met:

(1) The materials being hoisted must be rigged to prevent unintentional displacement.

(2) Hooks with self-closing latches or their equivalent must be used. *Exception:* "J" hooks are permitted to be used for setting wooden trusses.

(3) The materials must be rigged by a qualified rigger.

(d) *Receiving a load.* Only employees needed to receive a load are permitted to be within the fall zone when a load is being landed.

(e) During a tilt-up or tilt-down operation:

(1) No employee must be directly under the load.

(2) Only employees essential to the operation are permitted in the fall zone (but not directly under the load). An employee is essential to the operation if the employee is conducting one of the following operations and the employer can demonstrate it is infeasible for the employee to perform that operation from outside the fall zone: (1) Physically guide the load; (2) closely monitor and give instructions regarding the load's movement; or (3) either detach it from or initially attach it to another component or structure (such as, but not limited to, making an initial connection or installing bracing).

NOTE: Boom free fall is prohibited when an employee is in the fall zone of the boom or load, and load line free fall is prohibited when an employee is directly under the load; *see* § 1926.1426.

§ 1926.1426 Free fall and controlled load lowering.

(a) *Boom free fall prohibitions.* (1) The use of equipment in which the boom is designed to free fall (live boom) is prohibited in each of the following circumstances:

(i) An employee is in the fall zone of the boom or load.

(ii) An employee is being hoisted.

(iii) The load or boom is directly over a power line, or over any part of the area extending the Table A of § 1926.1408 clearance distance to each side of the power line, or any part of the area extending the Table A clearance distance to each side of the power line is within the radius of vertical travel of the boom or the load.

(iv) The load is over a shaft, except where there are no employees in the shaft.

(v) The load is over a cofferdam, except where there are no employees in the fall zone of the boom or the load.

(vi) Lifting operations are taking place in a refinery or tank farm.

(2) The use of equipment in which the boom is designed to free fall (live boom) is permitted only where none of the circumstances listed in paragraph (a)(1) of this section are present and:

(i) The equipment was manufactured prior to October 31, 1984; or

(ii) The equipment is a floating crane/derrick or a land crane/derrick on a vessel/flotation device.

(b) *Preventing boom free fall.* Where the use of equipment with a boom that is designed to free fall (live boom) is prohibited, the boom hoist must have a secondary mechanism or device designed to prevent the boom from falling in the event the primary system used to hold or regulate the boom hoist fails, as follows:

(1) Friction drums must have:

(i) A friction clutch and, in addition, a braking device, to allow for controlled boom lowering.

(ii) A secondary braking or locking device, which is manually or automatically engaged, to back-up the primary brake while the boom is held (such as a secondary friction brake or a ratchet and pawl device).

(2) Hydraulic drums must have an integrally mounted holding device or internal static brake to prevent boom hoist movement in the event of hydraulic failure.

(3) Neither clutches nor hydraulic motors must be considered brake or locking devices for purposes of this subpart.

(4) Hydraulic boom cylinders must have an integrally mounted holding device.

(c) *Preventing uncontrolled retraction.* Hydraulic telescoping booms must have an integrally mounted holding device to prevent the boom from retracting in the event of hydraulic failure.

(d) *Load line free fall.* In each of the following circumstances, controlled load lowering is required and free fall of the load line hoist is prohibited:

(1) An employee is directly under the load.

(2) An employee is being hoisted.

(3) The load is directly over a power line, or over any part of the area extending the Table A of §1926.1408 clearance distance to each side of the power line; or any part of the area extending the Table A of §1926.1408 clearance distance to each side of the power line is within the radius of vertical travel of the load.

(4) The load is over a shaft.

(5) The load is over a cofferdam, except where there are no employees in the fall zone of the load.

§1926.1427 Operator qualification and certification.

(a) The employer must ensure that, prior to operating any equipment covered under subpart CC, the person is operating the equipment during a training period in accordance with paragraph (f) of this section, or the operator is qualified or certified to operate the equipment in accordance with the following:

(1) When a non-military government entity issues operator licenses for equipment covered under subpart CC, and that government licensing program meets the requirements of paragraphs (e)(2) and (j) of this section, the equipment operator must either be:

(i) Licensed by that government entity for operation of equipment within that entity's jurisdiction; or

(ii) qualified in compliance with paragraph (d) of this section.

(2) Where paragraph (a)(1) of this section is not applicable, the certification or qualification must comply with one of the options in paragraphs (b) through (d) of this section.

(3) *Exceptions:* Operator qualification or certification under this section is not required for operators of derricks (*see* §1926.1436), sideboom cranes (*see* §1926.1440), or equipment with a maximum manufacturer-rated hoisting/lifting capacity of 2,000 pounds or less (*see* §1926.1441).

(4) Whenever operator qualification or certification is required under §1926.1427, the employer must provide the qualification or certification at no

717

cost to operators who are employed by the employer on November 8, 2010.

(b) *Option (1): Certification by an accredited crane operator testing organization.* (1) For a testing organization to be considered accredited to certify operators under this subpart, it must:

(i) Be accredited by a nationally recognized accrediting agency based on that agency's determination that industry recognized criteria for written testing materials, practical examinations, test administration, grading, facilities/equipment and personnel have been met.

(ii) Administer written and practical tests that:

(A) Assess the operator applicant regarding, at a minimum, the knowledge and skills listed in paragraphs (j)(1) and (2) of this section.

(B) Provide different levels of certification based on equipment capacity and type.

(iii) Have procedures for operators to re-apply and be re-tested in the event an operator applicant fails a test or is decertified.

(iv) Have testing procedures for re-certification designed to ensure that the operator continues to meet the technical knowledge and skills requirements in paragraphs (j)(1) and (2) of this section.

(v) Have its accreditation reviewed by the nationally recognized accrediting agency at least every three years.

(2) An operator will be deemed qualified to operate a particular piece of equipment if the operator is certified under paragraph (b) of this section for that type and capacity of equipment or for higher-capacity equipment of that type. If no accredited testing agency offers certification examinations for a particular type and/or capacity of equipment, an operator will be deemed qualified to operate that equipment if the operator has been certified for the type/capacity that is most similar to that equipment and for which a certification examination is available. The operator's certificate must state the type/capacity of equipment for which the operator is certified.

(3) A certification issued under this option is portable and meets the requirements of paragraph (a)(2) of this section.

(4) A certification issued under this paragraph is valid for 5 years.

(c) *Option (2): Qualification by an audited employer program.* The employer's qualification of its employee must meet the following requirements:

(1) The written and practical tests must be either:

(i) Developed by an accredited crane operator testing organization (*see* paragraph (b) of this section); or

(ii) Approved by an auditor in accordance with the following requirements:

(A) The auditor is certified to evaluate such tests by an accredited crane operator testing organization (*see* paragraph (b) of this section).

(B) The auditor is not an employee of the employer.

(C) The approval must be based on the auditor's determination that the written and practical tests meet nationally recognized test development criteria and are valid and reliable in assessing the operator applicants regarding, at a minimum, the knowledge and skills listed in paragraphs (j)(1) and (2) of this section.

(D) The audit must be conducted in accordance with nationally recognized auditing standards.

(2) *Administration of tests.* (i) The written and practical tests must be administered under circumstances approved by the auditor as meeting nationally recognized test administration standards.

(ii) The auditor must be certified to evaluate the administration of the written and practical tests by an accredited crane operator testing organization (*see* paragraph (b) of this section).

(iii) The auditor must not be an employee of the employer.

(iv) The audit must be conducted in accordance with nationally recognized auditing standards.

(3) The employer program must be audited within 3 months of the beginning of the program and at least every 3 years thereafter.

(4) The employer program must have testing procedures for re-qualification designed to ensure that the operator continues to meet the technical knowledge and skills requirements in paragraphs (j)(1) and (2) of this section. The

re-qualification procedures must be audited in accordance with paragraphs (c)(1) and (2) of this section.

(5) *Deficiencies.* If the auditor determines that there is a significant deficiency ("deficiency") in the program, the employer must ensure that:

(i) No operator is qualified until the auditor confirms that the deficiency has been corrected.

(ii) The program is audited again within 180 days of the confirmation that the deficiency was corrected.

(iii) The auditor files a documented report of the deficiency to the appropriate Regional Office of the Occupational Safety and Health Administration within 15 days of the auditor's determination that there is a deficiency.

(iv) Records of the audits of the employer's program are maintained by the auditor for three years and are made available by the auditor to the Secretary of Labor or the Secretary's designated representative upon request.

(6) A qualification under this paragraph is:

(i) Not portable. Such a qualification meets the requirements of paragraph (a) of this section only where the operator is employed by (and operating the equipment for) the employer that issued the qualification.

(ii) Valid for 5 years.

(d) *Option (3): Qualification by the U.S. military.* (1) For purposes of this section, an operator who is an employee of the U.S. military is considered qualified if he/she has a current operator qualification issued by the U.S. military for operation of the equipment. An employee of the U.S. military is a Federal employee of the Department of Defense or Armed Forces and does not include employees of private contractors.

(2) A qualification under this paragraph is:

(i) Not portable. Such a qualification meets the requirements of paragraph (a) of this section only where the operator is employed by (and operating the equipment for) the employer that issued the qualification.

(ii) Valid for the period of time stipulated by the issuing entity.

(e) *Option (4): Licensing by a government entity.* (1) For purposes of this section, a government licensing department/office that issues operator licenses for operating equipment covered by this standard is considered a government accredited crane operator testing organization if the criteria in paragraph (e)(2) of this section are met.

(2) *Licensing criteria.* (i) The requirements for obtaining the license include an assessment, by written and practical tests, of the operator applicant regarding, at a minimum, the knowledge and skills listed in paragraphs (j)(1) and (2) of this section.

(ii) The testing meets industry recognized criteria for written testing materials, practical examinations, test administration, grading, facilities/equipment and personnel.

(iii) The government authority that oversees the licensing department/office, has determined that the requirements in paragraphs (e)(2)(i) and (ii) of this section have been met.

(iv) The licensing department/office has testing procedures for re-licensing designed to ensure that the operator continues to meet the technical knowledge and skills requirements in paragraphs (j)(1) and (2) of this section.

(3) A license issued by a government accredited crane operator testing organization that meets the requirements of this option:

(i) Meets the operator qualification requirements of this section for operation of equipment only within the jurisdiction of the government entity.

(ii) Is valid for the period of time stipulated by the licensing department/office, but no longer than 5 years.

(f) *Pre-qualification/certification training period.* An employee who is not qualified or certified under this section is permitted to operate equipment only as an operator-in-training and only where the requirements of this paragraph are met.

(1) The employer must provide each operator-in-training with sufficient training prior to operating the equipment to enable the operator-in-training to operate the equipment safely under limitations established by this section (including continuous monitoring) and any additional limitations established by the employer.

(2) The tasks performed by the operator-in-training while operating the

equipment must be within the operator-in-training's ability.

(3) *Trainer.* While operating the equipment, the operator-in-training must be continuously monitored by an individual ("operator's trainer") who meets all of the following requirements:

(i) The operator's trainer is an employee or agent of the operator-in-training's employer.

(ii) The operator's trainer is either a certified operator under this section, or has passed the written portion of a certification test under one of the options in paragraphs (b) through (e) of this section, and is familiar with the proper use of the equipment's controls.

(iii) While monitoring the operator-in-training, the operator's trainer performs no tasks that detract from the trainer's ability to monitor the operator-in-training.

(iv) For equipment other than tower cranes: The operator's trainer and the operator-in-training must be in direct line of sight of each other. In addition, they must communicate verbally or by hand signals. For tower cranes: The operator's trainer and the operator-in-training must be in direct communication with each other.

(4) *Continuous monitoring.* The operator-in-training must be monitored by the operator's trainer at all times, except for short breaks where all of the following are met:

(i) The break lasts no longer than 15 minutes and there is no more than one break per hour.

(ii) Immediately prior to the break the operator's trainer informs the operator-in-training of the specific tasks that the operator-in-training is to perform and limitations to which he/she must adhere during the operator trainer's break.

(iii) The specific tasks that the operator-in-training will perform during the operator trainer's break are within the operator-in-training's abilities.

(5) The operator-in-training must not operate the equipment in any of the following circumstances unless the exception stated in paragraph (f)(5)(v) of this section is applicable:

(i) If any part of the equipment, load line or load (including rigging and lifting accessories), if operated up to the equipment's maximum working radius in the work zone (*see* § 1926.1408(a)(1)), could get within 20 feet of a power line that is up to 350 kV, or within 50 feet of a power line that is over 350 kV.

(ii) If the equipment is used to hoist personnel.

(iii) In multiple-equipment lifts.

(iv) If the equipment is used over a shaft, cofferdam, or in a tank farm.

(v) In multiple-lift rigging operations, except where the operator's trainer determines that the operator-in-training skills are sufficient for this high-skill work.

(g) Under this section, a testing entity is permitted to provide training as well as testing services as long as the criteria of the applicable accrediting agency (in the option selected) for an organization providing both services are met.

(h) *Language and Literacy Requirements.* (1) Tests under this section may be administered verbally, with answers given verbally, where the operator candidate:

(i) Passes a written demonstration of literacy relevant to the work.

(ii) Demonstrates the ability to use the type of written manufacturer procedures applicable to the class/type of equipment for which the candidate is seeking certification.

(2) Tests under this section may be administered in any language the operator candidate understands, and the operator's certificate must note the language in which the test was given. The operator is qualified under paragraph (b)(2) of this section to operate equipment that is furnished with materials required by this subpart that are written in the language of the certification. The operator may only operate equipment furnished with such materials.

(i) [Reserved]

(j) *Certification criteria.* Qualifications and certifications must be based, at a minimum, on the following:

(1) A determination through a written test that:

(i) The individual knows the information necessary for safe operation of the specific type of equipment the individual will operate, including all of the following:

(A) The controls and operational/performance characteristics.

(B) Use of, and the ability to calculate (manually or with a calculator), load/capacity information on a variety of configurations of the equipment.

(C) Procedures for preventing and responding to power line contact.

(D) Technical knowledge similar to the subject matter criteria listed in appendix C of this subpart applicable to the specific type of equipment the individual will operate. Use of the appendix C criteria meets the requirements of this provision.

(E) Technical knowledge applicable to:

(1) The suitability of the supporting ground and surface to handle expected loads.

(2) Site hazards.

(3) Site access.

(F) This subpart, including applicable incorporated materials.

(ii) The individual is able to read and locate relevant information in the equipment manual and other materials containing information referred to in paragraph (j)(1)(i) of this section.

(2) A determination through a practical test that the individual has the skills necessary for safe operation of the equipment, including the following:

(i) Ability to recognize, from visual and auditory observation, the items listed in §1926.1412(d) (shift inspection).

(ii) Operational and maneuvering skills.

(iii) Application of load chart information.

(iv) Application of safe shut-down and securing procedures.

(k) *Phase-in.* (1) The provisions of this section became applicable on November 8, 2010, except for paragraphs (a)(2) and (f), which are applicable November 10, 2017.

(2) When §1926.1427(a)(1) is not applicable, all of the requirements in paragraphs (k)(2)(i) and (ii) of this section apply until November 10, 2017.

(i) The employer must ensure that operators of equipment covered by this standard are competent to operate the equipment safely.

(ii) When an employee assigned to operate machinery does not have the required knowledge or ability to operate the equipment safely, the employer

must train that employee prior to operating the equipment. The employer must ensure that each operator is evaluated to confirm that he/she understands the information provided in the training.

[75 FR 48135, Aug. 9, 2010, as amended at 79 FR 57798, Sept. 26, 2014]

§1926.1428 Signal person qualifications.

(a) The employer of the signal person must ensure that each signal person meets the Qualification Requirements (paragraph (c) of this section) prior to giving any signals. This requirement must be met by using either Option (1) or Option (2) of this section.

(1) *Option (1)—Third party qualified evaluator.* The signal person has documentation from a third party qualified evaluator (*see* Qualified Evaluator (third party), §1926.1401 for definition) showing that the signal person meets the Qualification Requirements (*see* paragraph (c) of this section).

(2) *Option (2)—Employer's qualified evaluator.* The employer's qualified (*see* Qualified Evaluator (not a third party), §1926.1401 for definition) evaluator assesses the individual and determines that the individual meets the Qualification Requirements (*see* paragraph (c) of this section) and provides documentation of that determination. An assessment by an employer's qualified evaluator under this option is not portable—other employers are not permitted to use it to meet the requirements of this section.

(3) The employer must make the documentation for whichever option is used available at the site while the signal person is employed by the employer. The documentation must specify each type of signaling (*e.g.* hand signals, radio signals, *etc.*) for which the signal person meets the requirements of paragraph (c) of this section.

(b) If subsequent actions by the signal person indicate that the individual does not meet the Qualification Requirements (*see* paragraph (c) of this section), the employer must not allow the individual to continue working as a signal person until re-training is provided and a re-assessment is made in accordance with paragraph (a) of this section that confirms that the individual meets the Qualification Requirements.

(c) *Qualification Requirements.* Each signal person must:

(1) Know and understand the type of signals used. If hand signals are used, the signal person must know and understand the Standard Method for hand signals.

(2) Be competent in the application of the type of signals used.

(3) Have a basic understanding of equipment operation and limitations, including the crane dynamics involved in swinging and stopping loads and boom deflection from hoisting loads.

(4) Know and understand the relevant requirements of §§ 1926.1419 through 1926.1422 and 1926.1428.

(5) Demonstrate that he/she meets the requirements in paragraphs (c)(1) through (4) of this section through an oral or written test, and through a practical test.

§ 1926.1429 Qualifications of maintenance & repair employees.

(a) Maintenance, inspection and repair personnel are permitted to operate the equipment only where all of the following requirements are met:

(1) The operation is limited to those functions necessary to perform maintenance, inspect the equipment, or verify its performance.

(2) The personnel either:

(i) Operate the equipment under the direct supervision of an operator who meets the requirements of § 1926.1427 (Operator qualification and certification); or

(ii) Are familiar with the operation, limitations, characteristics and hazards associated with the type of equipment.

(b) Maintenance and repair personnel must meet the definition of a qualified person with respect to the equipment and maintenance/repair tasks performed.

§ 1926.1430 Training.

The employer must provide training as follows:

(a) *Overhead powerlines.* The employer must train each employee specified in § 1926.1408(g) and § 1926.1410(m) in the topics listed in § 1926.1408(g).

(b) *Signal persons.* The employer must train each employee who will be assigned to work as a signal persons who does not meet the requirements of § 1926.1428(c) in the areas addressed in that paragraph.

(c) *Operators*—(1) *Operators-in-Training for equipment where certification or qualification is required by this subpart.* The employer must train each operator-in-training in the areas addressed in § 1926.1427(j). The employer must provide re-training if the operator-in-training does not pass a qualification or certification test.

(2) *Transitional Period.* During the four-year phase-in period for operator certification or qualification, as provided in § 1926.1427(k), employers must train each operator who has not yet been certified or qualified in the areas addressed in § 1926.1427(j).

(3) *Operators excepted from the requirements of § 1926.1427.* The employer must train each operator excepted under § 1926.1427(a) from the requirements of § 1926.1427 on the safe operation of the equipment the operator will be using.

(4) The employer must train each operator of the equipment covered by this subpart in the following practices:

(i) On friction equipment, whenever moving a boom off a support, first raise the boom a short distance (sufficient to take the load of the boom) to determine if the boom hoist brake needs to be adjusted. On other types of equipment with a boom, the same practice is applicable, except that typically there is no means of adjusting the brake; if the brake does not hold, a repair is necessary. *See* § 1926.1417(f) and (j) for additional requirements.

(ii) Where available, the manufacturer's emergency procedures for halting unintended equipment movement.

(d) *Competent persons and qualified persons.* The employer must train each competent person and each qualified person regarding the requirements of this subpart applicable to their respective roles.

(e) *Crush/pinch points.* The employer must train each employee who works with the equipment to keep clear of holes, and crush/pinch points and the hazards addressed in § 1926.1424 (Work area control).

(f) *Tag-out.* The employer must train each operator and each additional employee authorized to start/energize equipment or operate equipment controls (such as maintenance and repair employees), in the tag-out and start-up procedures in §§ 1926.1417(f) and (g).

(g) *Training administration.* (1) The employer must evaluate each employee required to be trained under this subpart to confirm that the employee understands the information provided in the training.

(2) The employer must provide refresher training in relevant topics for each employee when, based on the conduct of the employee or an evaluation of the employee's knowledge, there is an indication that retraining is necessary.

(3) Whenever training is required under subpart CC, the employer must provide the training at no cost to the employee.

§ 1926.1431 Hoisting personnel.

The requirements of this section are supplemental to the other requirements in this subpart and apply when one or more employees are hoisted.

(a) The use of equipment to hoist employees is prohibited except where the employer demonstrates that the erection, use, and dismantling of conventional means of reaching the work area, such as a personnel hoist, ladder, stairway, aerial lift, elevating work platform, or scaffold, would be more hazardous, or is not possible because of the project's structural design or worksite conditions. This paragraph does not apply to work covered by subpart R (Steel Erection) of this part.

(b) *Use of personnel platform.* (1) When using equipment to hoist employees, the employees must be in a personnel platform that meets the requirements of paragraph (e) of this section.

(2) *Exceptions:* A personnel platform is not required for hoisting employees:

(i) Into and out of drill shafts that are up to and including 8 feet in diameter (*see* paragraph (o) of this section for requirements for hoisting these employees).

(ii) In pile driving operations (*see* paragraph (p) of this section for requirements for hoisting these employees).

(iii) Solely for transfer to or from a marine worksite in a marine-hoisted personnel transfer device (*see* paragraph (r) of this section for requirements for hoisting these employees).

(iv) In storage-tank (steel or concrete), shaft and chimney operations (*see* paragraph (s) of this section for requirements for hoisting these employees).

(c) *Equipment set-up.* (1) The equipment must be uniformly level, within one percent of level grade, and located on footing that a qualified person has determined to be sufficiently firm and stable.

(2) Equipment with outriggers or stabilizers must have them all extended and locked. The amount of extension must be the same for all outriggers and stabilizers and in accordance with manufacturer procedures and load charts.

(d) *Equipment criteria—*(1) *Capacity: Use of suspended personnel platforms.* The total load (with the platform loaded, including the hook, load line and rigging) must not exceed 50 percent of the rated capacity for the radius and configuration of the equipment, except during proof testing.

(2) *Capacity: Use of boom-attached personnel platforms.* The total weight of the loaded personnel platform must not exceed 50 percent of the rated capacity for the radius and configuration of the equipment (except during proof testing).

(3) *Capacity: Hoisting personnel without a personnel platform.* When hoisting personnel without a personnel platform pursuant to paragraph (b)(2) of this section, the total load (including the hook, load line, rigging and any other equipment that imposes a load) must not exceed 50 percent of the rated capacity for the radius and configuration of the equipment, except during proof testing.

(4) When the occupied personnel platform is in a stationary working position, the load and boom hoist brakes, swing brakes, and operator actuated secondary braking and locking features (such as pawls or dogs) or automatic secondary brakes must be engaged.

(5) *Devices.* (i) Equipment (except for derricks and articulating cranes) with

723

a variable angle boom must be equipped with all of the following:

(A) A boom angle indicator, readily visible to the operator, and

(B) A boom hoist limiting device.

(ii) Articulating cranes must be equipped with a properly functioning automatic overload protection device.

(iii) Equipment with a luffing jib must be equipped with:

(A) A jib angle indicator, readily visible to the operator, and.

(B) A jib hoist limiting device.

(iv) Equipment with telescoping booms must be equipped with a device to indicate the boom's extended length clearly to the operator, or must have measuring marks on the boom.

(v) *Anti two-block.* A device which automatically prevents damage and load failure from contact between the load block, overhaul ball, or similar component, and the boom tip (or fixed upper block or similar component) must be used. The device(s) must prevent such damage/failure at all points where two-blocking could occur. *Exception:* This device is not required when hoisting personnel in pile driving operations. Instead, paragraph (p)(2) of this section specifies how to prevent two-blocking during such operations.

(vi) *Controlled load lowering.* The load line hoist drum must have a system, other than the load line hoist brake, which regulates the lowering rate of speed of the hoist mechanism. This system or device must be used when hoisting personnel.

NOTE: Free fall of the load line hoist is prohibited (*see* § 1926.1426(d); the use of equipment in which the boom hoist mechanism can free fall is also prohibited (*see* § 1926.1426(a)(1).

(vii) *Proper operation required.* Personnel hoisting operations must not begin unless the devices listed in this section are in proper working order. If a device stops working properly during such operations, the operator must safely stop operations. Personnel hoisting operations must not resume until the device is again working properly. Alternative measures are not permitted. (*See* § 1926.1417 for tag-out and related requirements.)

(6) Direct attachment of a personnel platform to a luffing jib is prohibited.

(e) *Personnel platform criteria.* (1) A qualified person familiar with structural design must design the personnel platform and attachment/suspension system used for hoisting personnel.

(2) The system used to connect the personnel platform to the equipment must allow the platform to remain within 10 degrees of level, regardless of boom angle.

(3) The suspension system must be designed to minimize tipping of the platform due to movement of employees occupying the platform.

(4) The personnel platform itself (excluding the guardrail system and personal fall arrest system anchorages), must be capable of supporting, without failure, its own weight and at least five times the maximum intended load.

(5) All welding of the personnel platform and its components must be performed by a certified welder familiar with the weld grades, types and material specified in the platform design.

(6) The personnel platform must be equipped with a guardrail system which meets the requirements of subpart M of this part, and must be enclosed at least from the toeboard to mid-rail with either solid construction material or expanded metal having openings no greater than ½ inch (1.27 cm). Points to which personal fall arrest systems are attached must meet the anchorage requirements in subpart M of this part.

(7) A grab rail must be installed inside the entire perimeter of the personnel platform except for access gates/doors.

(8) *Access gates/doors.* If installed, access gates/doors of all types (including swinging, sliding, folding, or other types) must:

(i) Not swing outward. If due to the size of the personnel platform, such as a 1-person platform, it is infeasible for the door to swing inward and allow safe entry for the platform occupant, then the access gate/door may swing outward.

(ii) Be equipped with a device that prevents accidental opening.

(9) Headroom must be sufficient to allow employees to stand upright in the platform.

(10) In addition to the use of hard hats, employees must be protected by

overhead protection on the personnel platform when employees are exposed to falling objects. The platform overhead protection must not obscure the view of the operator or platform occupants (such as wire mesh that has up to ½ inch openings), unless full protection is necessary.

(11) All edges exposed to employee contact must be smooth enough to prevent injury.

(12) The weight of the platform and its rated capacity must be conspicuously posted on the platform with a plate or other permanent marking.

(f) *Personnel platform loading.* (1) The personnel platform must not be loaded in excess of its rated capacity.

(2) *Use.* (i) Personnel platforms must be used only for employees, their tools, and the materials necessary to do their work. Platforms must not be used to hoist materials or tools when not hoisting personnel.

(ii) *Exception:* Materials and tools to be used during the lift, if secured and distributed in accordance with paragraph (f)(3) of this section may be in the platform for trial lifts.

(3) Materials and tools must be:

(i) Secured to prevent displacement.

(ii) Evenly distributed within the confines of the platform while it is suspended.

(4) The number of employees occupying the personnel platform must not exceed the maximum number the platform was designed to hold or the number required to perform the work, whichever is less.

(g) *Attachment and rigging—*(1) *Hooks and other detachable devices.* (i) Hooks used in the connection between the hoist line and the personnel platform (including hooks on overhaul ball assemblies, lower load blocks, bridle legs, or other attachment assemblies or components) must be:

(A) Of a type that can be closed and locked, eliminating the throat opening.

(B) Closed and locked when attached.

(ii) Shackles used in place of hooks must be of the alloy anchor type, with either:

(A) A bolt, nut and retaining pin, in place; or

(B) Of the screw type, with the screw pin secured from accidental removal.

(iii) Where other detachable devices are used, they must be of the type that can be closed and locked to the same extent as the devices addressed in paragraphs (g)(1)(i) and (ii) of this section. Such devices must be closed and locked when attached.

(2) *Rope bridle.* When a rope bridle is used to suspend the personnel platform, each bridle leg must be connected to a master link or shackle (*see* paragraph (g)(1) of this section) in a manner that ensures that the load is evenly divided among the bridle legs.

(3) Rigging hardware (including wire rope, shackles, rings, master links, and other rigging hardware) and hooks must be capable of supporting, without failure, at least five times the maximum intended load applied or transmitted to that component. Where rotation resistant rope is used, the slings must be capable of supporting without failure at least ten times the maximum intended load.

(4) Eyes in wire rope slings must be fabricated with thimbles.

(5) Bridles and associated rigging for suspending the personnel platform must be used only for the platform and the necessary employees, their tools and materials necessary to do their work. The bridles and associated rigging must not have been used for any purpose other than hoisting personnel.

(h) *Trial lift and inspection.* (1) A trial lift with the unoccupied personnel platform loaded at least to the anticipated liftweight must be made from ground level, or any other location where employees will enter the platform, to each location at which the platform is to be hoisted and positioned. Where there is more than one location to be reached from a single set-up position, either individual trial lifts for each location, or a single trial lift, in which the platform is moved sequentially to each location, must be performed; the method selected must be the same as the method that will be used to hoist the personnel.

(2) The trial lift must be performed immediately prior to each shift in which personnel will be hoisted. In addition, the trial lift must be repeated prior to hoisting employees in each of the following circumstances:

(i) The equipment is moved and set up in a new location or returned to a previously used location.

(ii) The lift route is changed, unless the competent person determines that the new route presents no new factors affecting safety.

(3) The competent person must determine that:

(i) Safety devices and operational aids required by this section are activated and functioning properly. Other safety devices and operational aids must meet the requirements of § 1926.1415 and § 1926.1416.

(ii) Nothing interferes with the equipment or the personnel platform in the course of the trial lift.

(iii) The lift will not exceed 50 percent of the equipment's rated capacity at any time during the lift.

(iv) The load radius to be used during the lift has been accurately determined.

(4) Immediately after the trial lift, the competent person must:

(i) Conduct a visual inspection of the equipment, base support or ground, and personnel platform, to determine whether the trial lift has exposed any defect or problem or produced any adverse effect.

(ii) Confirm that, upon the completion of the trial lift process, the test weight has been removed.

(5) Immediately prior to each lift:

(i) The platform must be hoisted a few inches with the personnel and materials/tools on board and inspected by a competent person to ensure that it is secure and properly balanced.

(ii) The following conditions must be determined by a competent person to exist before the lift of personnel proceeds:

(A) Hoist ropes must be free of deficiencies in accordance with § 1926.1413(a).

(B) Multiple part lines must not be twisted around each other.

(C) The primary attachment must be centered over the platform.

(D) If the load rope is slack, the hoisting system must be inspected to ensure that all ropes are properly seated on drums and in sheaves.

(6) Any condition found during the trial lift and subsequent inspection(s) that fails to meet a requirement of this standard or otherwise creates a safety hazard must be corrected before hoisting personnel. (*See* § 1926.1417 for tag-out and related requirements.)

(i) [Reserved]

(j) *Proof testing.* (1) At each jobsite, prior to hoisting employees on the personnel platform, and after any repair or modification, the platform and rigging must be proof tested to 125 percent of the platform's rated capacity. The proof test may be done concurrently with the trial lift.

(2) The platform must be lowered by controlled load lowering, braked, and held in a suspended position for a minimum of five minutes with the test load evenly distributed on the platform.

(3) After proof testing, a competent person must inspect the platform and rigging to determine if the test has been passed. If any deficiencies are found that pose a safety hazard, the platform and rigging must not be used to hoist personnel unless the deficiencies are corrected, the test is repeated, and a competent person determines that the test has been passed. (*See* § 1926.1417 for tag-out and related requirements.)

(4) Personnel hoisting must not be conducted until the competent person determines that the platform and rigging have successfully passed the proof test.

(k) *Work practices.* (1) Hoisting of the personnel platform must be performed in a slow, controlled, cautious manner, with no sudden movements of the equipment or the platform.

(2) Platform occupants must:

(i) Keep all parts of the body inside the platform during raising, lowering, and horizontal movement. This provision does not apply to an occupant of the platform when necessary to position the platform or while performing the duties of a signal person.

(ii) Not stand, sit on, or work from the top or intermediate rail or toeboard, or use any other means/device to raise their working height.

(iii) Not pull the platform out of plumb in relation to the hoisting equipment.

(3) Before employees exit or enter a hoisted personnel platform that is not landed, the platform must be secured

to the structure where the work is to be performed, unless the employer can demonstrate that securing to the structure would create a greater hazard.

(4) If the platform is tied to the structure, the operator must not move the platform until the operator receives confirmation that it is freely suspended.

(5) Tag lines must be used when necessary to control the platform.

(6) *Platforms without controls.* Where the platform is not equipped with controls, the equipment operator must remain at the equipment controls, on site, and in view of the equipment, at all times while the platform is occupied.

(7) *Platforms with controls.* Where the platform is equipped with controls, all of the following must be met at all times while the platform is occupied:

(i) The occupant using the controls in the platform must be a qualified person with respect to their use, including the safe limitations of the equipment and hazards associated with its operation.

(ii) The equipment operator must be at a set of equipment controls that include boom and swing functions of the equipment, and must be on site and in view of the equipment.

(iii) The platform operating manual must be in the platform or on the equipment.

(8) *Environmental conditions—*(i) *Wind.* When wind speed (sustained or gusts) exceeds 20 mph at the personnel platform, a qualified person must determine if, in light of the wind conditions, it is not safe to lift personnel. If it is not, the lifting operation must not begin (or, if already in progress, must be terminated).

(ii) *Other weather and environmental conditions.* A qualified person must determine if, in light of indications of dangerous weather conditions, or other impending or existing danger, it is not safe to lift personnel. If it is not, the lifting operation must not begin (or, if already in progress, must be terminated).

(9) Employees being hoisted must remain in direct communication with the signal person (where used), or the operator.

(10) *Fall protection.* (i) Except over water, employees occupying the personnel platform must be provided and use a personal fall arrest system. The system must be attached to a structural member within the personnel platform. When working over or near water, the requirements of § 1926.106 apply.

(ii) The fall arrest system, including the attachment point (anchorage) used to comply with paragraph (i) of this section, must meet the requirements in § 1926.502.

(11) *Other load lines.* (i) No lifts must be made on any other of the equipment's load lines while personnel are being hoisted, except in pile driving operations.

(ii) *Factory-produced boom-mounted personnel platforms that incorporate a winch as original equipment.* Loads are permitted to be hoisted by such a winch while employees occupy the personnel platform only where the load on the winch line does not exceed 500 pounds and does not exceed the rated capacity of the winch and platform.

(12) *Traveling—equipment other than derricks.* (i) Hoisting of employees while the equipment is traveling is prohibited, except for:

(A) Equipment that travels on fixed rails; or

(B) Where the employer demonstrates that there is no less hazardous way to perform the work.

(C) This exception does not apply to rubber-tired equipment.

(ii) Where employees are hoisted while the equipment is traveling, all of the following criteria must be met:

(A) Equipment travel must be restricted to a fixed track or runway.

(B) Where a runway is used, it must be a firm, level surface designed, prepared and designated as a path of travel for the weight and configuration of the equipment being used to lift and travel with the personnel platform. An existing surface may be used as long as it meets these criteria.

(C) Equipment travel must be limited to boom length.

(D) The boom must be parallel to the direction of travel, except where it is safer to do otherwise.

(E) A complete trial run must be performed to test the route of travel before employees are allowed to occupy the platform. This trial run can be performed at the same time as the trial lift required by paragraph (h) of this section which tests the lift route.

(13) *Traveling—derricks.* Derricks are prohibited from traveling while personnel are hoisted.

(l) [Reserved]

(m) *Pre-lift meeting.* A pre-lift meeting must be:

(1) Held to review the applicable requirements of this section and the procedures that will be followed.

(2) Attended by the equipment operator, signal person (if used for the lift), employees to be hoisted, and the person responsible for the task to be performed.

(3) Held prior to the trial lift at each new work location, and must be repeated for any employees newly assigned to the operation.

(n) *Hoisting personnel near power lines.* Hoisting personnel within 20 feet of a power line that is up to 350 kV, and hoisting personnel within 50 feet of a power line that is over 350 kV, is prohibited, except for work covered by subpart V of this part (Power Transmission and Distribution).

(o) *Hoisting personnel in drill shafts.* When hoisting employees into and out of drill shafts that are up to and including 8 feet in diameter, all of the following requirements must be met:

(1) The employee must be in either a personnel platform or on a boatswain's chair.

(2) If using a personnel platform, paragraphs (a) through (n) of this section apply.

(3) If using a boatswain's chair:

(i) The following paragraphs of this section apply: (a), (c), (d)(1), (d)(3), (d)(4), (e)(1), (e)(2), (e)(3), (f)(1), (f)(2)(i), (f)(3)(i), (g), (h), (k)(1), (k)(6), (k)(8), (k)(9), (k)(11)(i), (m), (n). Where the terms "personnel platform" or "platform" are used in these paragraphs, substitute them with "boatswain's chair."

(ii) A signal person must be stationed at the shaft opening.

(iii) The employee must be hoisted in a slow, controlled descent and ascent.

(iv) The employee must use personal fall protection equipment, including a full body harness, attached independent of the crane/derrick.

(v) The fall protection equipment must meet the applicable requirements in § 1926.502.

(vi) The boatswain's chair itself (excluding the personal fall arrest system anchorages), must be capable of supporting, without failure, its own weight and at least five times the maximum intended load.

(vii) No more than one person must be hoisted at a time.

(p) *Hoisting personnel for pile driving operations.* When hoisting an employee in pile driving operations, the following requirements must be met:

(1) The employee must be in a personnel platform or boatswain's chair.

(2) For lattice boom cranes: Clearly mark the cable (so that it can easily be seen by the operator) at a point that will give the operator sufficient time to stop the hoist to prevent two-blocking, or use a spotter who is in direct communication with the operator to inform the operator when this point is reached. For telescopic boom cranes: Clearly mark the cable (so that it can be easily seen by the operator) at a point that will give the operator sufficient time to stop the hoist to prevent two-blocking, and use a spotter who is in direct communication with the operator to inform the operator when this point is reached.

(3) If using a personnel platform, paragraphs (b) through (n) of this section apply.

(4) If using a boatswain's chair:

(i) The following paragraphs of this section apply: (a), (c), (d)(1), (d)(3), (d)(4), (e)(1), (e)(2), (e)(3), (f)(1), (f)(2)(i), (f)(3)(i), (g), (h), (j), (k)(1), (k)(6), (k)(8), (k)(9), (k)(11)(i), (m), and (n). Where the terms "personnel platform" or "platform" are used in these paragraphs, substitute them with "boatswains chair."

(ii) The employee must be hoisted in a slow, controlled descent and ascent.

(iii) The employee must use personal fall protection equipment, including a full body harness, independently attached to the lower load block or overhaul ball.

(iv) The fall protection equipment must meet the applicable requirements in §1926.502.

(v) The boatswain's chair itself (excluding the personal fall arrest system anchorages), must be capable of supporting, without failure, its own weight and at least five times the maximum intended load.

(vi) No more than one person must be hoisted at a time.

(q) [Reserved]

(r) *Hoisting personnel for marine transfer.* When hoisting employees solely for transfer to or from a marine worksite, the following requirements must be met:

(1) The employee must be in either a personnel platform or a marine-hoisted personnel transfer device.

(2) If using a personnel platform, paragraphs (a) through (n) of this section apply.

(3) If using a marine-hoisted personnel transfer device:

(i) The following paragraphs of this section apply: (a), (c)(2), (d)(1), (d)(3), (d)(4), (e)(1) through (5), (e)(12), (f)(1), (g), (h), (j), (k)(1), (k)(8), (k)(9), (k)(10)(ii), (k)(11)(i), (k)(12), (m), and (n). Where the terms "personnel platform" or "platform" are used in these paragraphs, substitute them with "marine-hoisted personnel transfer device."

(ii) The transfer device must be used only for transferring workers.

(iii) The number of workers occupying the transfer device must not exceed the maximum number it was designed to hold.

(iv) Each employee must wear a U.S. Coast Guard personal flotation device approved for industrial use.

(s) *Hoisting personnel for storage-tank (steel or concrete), shaft and chimney operations.* When hoisting an employee in storage tank (steel or concrete), shaft and chimney operations, the following requirements must be met:

(1) The employee must be in a personnel platform except when the employer can demonstrate that use of a personnel platform is infeasible; in such a case, a boatswain's chair must be used.

(2) If using a personnel platform, paragraphs (a) through (n) of this section apply.

(3) If using a boatswain's chair:

(i) The following paragraphs of this section apply: (a), (c), (d)(1), (d)(3), (d)(4), (e)(1), (e)(2), (e)(3), (f)(1), (f)(2)(i), (f)(3)(i), (g), (h), (k)(1), (k)(6), (k)(8), (k)(9), (k)(11)(i), (m), (n). Where the terms "personnel platform" or "platform" are used in these paragraphs, substitute them with "boatswains chair."

(ii) The employee must be hoisted in a slow, controlled descent and ascent.

(iii) The employee must use personal fall protection equipment, including a full body harness, attached independent of the crane/derrick. When there is no adequate structure for attachment of personal fall arrest equipment as required in §1926.502(d)(15), the attachment must be to the lower load block or overhaul ball.

(iv) The fall protection equipment must meet the applicable requirements in §1926.502.

(v) The boatswain's chair itself (excluding the personal fall arrest system anchorages), must be capable of supporting, without failure, its own weight and at least five times the maximum intended load.

(vi) No more than one person must be hoisted at a time.

§1926.1432 Multiple-crane/derrick lifts—supplemental requirements.

(a) *Plan development.* Before beginning a crane/derrick operation in which more than one crane/derrick will be supporting the load, the operation must be planned. The planning must meet the following requirements:

(1) The plan must be developed by a qualified person.

(2) The plan must be designed to ensure that the requirements of this subpart are met.

(3) Where the qualified person determines that engineering expertise is needed for the planning, the employer must ensure that it is provided.

(b) *Plan implementation.* (1) The multiple-crane/derrick lift must be directed by a person who meets the criteria for both a competent person and a qualified person, or by a competent person who is assisted by one or more qualified persons (lift director).

729

(2) The lift director must review the plan in a meeting with all workers who will be involved with the operation.

§ 1926.1433 Design, construction and testing.

The following requirements apply to equipment that has a manufacturer-rated hoisting/lifting capacity of more than 2,000 pounds.

(a) Crawler, truck and locomotive cranes manufactured prior to November 8, 2010 must meet the applicable requirements for design, construction, and testing as prescribed in ANSI B30.5–1968 (incorporated by reference, *see* § 1926.6), PCSA Std. No. 2 (1968) (incorporated by reference, *see* § 1926.6), the requirements in paragraph (b) of this section, or the applicable DIN standards that were in effect at the time of manufacture.

(b) Mobile (including crawler and truck) and locomotive cranes manufactured on or after November 8, 2010 must meet the following portions of ASME B30.5–2004 (incorporated by reference, *see* § 1926.6) as applicable:

(1) In section 5–1.1.1 ("Load Ratings—Where Stability Governs Lifting Performance"), paragraphs (a)–(d) (including subparagraphs).

(2) In section 5–1.1.2 ("Load Ratings—Where Structural Competence Governs Lifting Performance"), paragraph (b).

(3) Section 5–1.2 ("Stability (Backward and Forward)").

(4) In section 5–1.3.1 ("Boom Hoist Mechanism"), paragraphs (a), (b)(1) and (b)(2), except that when using rotation resistant rope, § 1926.1414(c)(4)(ii)(A) applies.

(5) In section 5–1.3.2 ("Load Hoist Mechanism"), paragraphs (a)(2) through (a)(4) (including subparagraphs), (b) (including subparagraphs), (c) (first sentence only) and (d).

(6) Section 5–1.3.3 ("Telescoping Boom").

(7) Section 5–1.4 ("Swing Mechanism").

(8) In section 5–1.5 ("Crane Travel"), all provisions except 5–1.5.3(d).

(9) In section 5–1.6 ("Controls"), all provisions except 5–1.6.1 (c).

(10) Section 5–1.7.4 ("Sheaves").

(11) Section 5–1.7.5 ("Sheave sizes").

(12) In section 5–1.9.1 ("Booms"), paragraph (f).

(13) Section 5–1.9.3 ("Outriggers").

(14) Section 5–1.9.4 ("Locomotive Crane Equipment").

(15) Section 5–1.9.7 ("Clutch and Brake Protection").

(16) In section 5–1.9.11 ("Miscellaneous equipment"), paragraphs (a), (c), (e), and (f).

(c) Prototype testing: mobile (including crawler and truck) and locomotive cranes manufactured on or after November 8, 2010 must meet the prototype testing requirements in Test Option A or Test Option B of this section. Tower cranes manufactured on or after November 8, 2010 must meet the prototype testing requirements in BS EN 14439:2006 (incorporated by reference, *see* § 1926.6).

NOTE: Prototype testing of crawler, locomotive and truck cranes manufactured prior to November 8, 2010 must conform to paragraph (a) of this section.

(1) *Test Option A.* (i) The following applies to equipment with cantilevered booms (such as hydraulic boom cranes): All the tests listed in SAE J1063 (Nov. 1993) Table 1 (incorporated by reference, *see* § 1926.6) must be performed to load all critical structural elements to their respective limits. All the strength margins listed in SAE J1063 (Nov. 1993) Table 2 (incorporated by reference, *see* § 1926.6) must be met.

(ii) The following applies to equipment with pendant supported lattice booms: All the tests listed in SAE J987 (Jun. 2003) Table 1 (incorporated by reference, *see* § 1926.6) must be performed to load all critical structural elements to their respective limits. All the strength margins listed in SAE J987 (Jun. 2003) Table 2 (incorporated by reference, *see* § 1926.6) must be met.

(2) *Test Option B.* The testing and verification requirements of BS EN 13000:2004 (incorporated by reference, *see* § 1926.6) must be met. In applying BS EN 13000:2004, the following additional requirements must be met:

(i) The following applies to equipment with cantilevered booms (such as hydraulic boom cranes): The analysis methodology (computer modeling) must demonstrate that all load cases listed in SAE J1063 (Nov. 1993) (incorporated by reference, *see* § 1926.6) meet the strength margins listed in SAE J1063 (Nov. 1993) Table 2.

(ii) The following applies to equipment with pendant supported lattice booms: The analysis methodology (computer modeling) must demonstrate that all load cases listed in SAE J987 (Jun. 2003) (incorporated by reference, *see* §1926.6) meet the strength margins listed in SAE J987 (Jun. 2003) Table 2.

(iii) *Analysis verification.* The physical testing requirements under SAE J1063 (Nov. 1993) (incorporated by reference, *see* §1926.6) and SAE J987 (Jun. 2003) (incorporated by reference, *see* §1926.6) must be met unless the reliability of the analysis methodology (computer modeling) has been demonstrated by a documented history of verification through strain gauge measuring or strain gauge measuring in combination with other physical testing.

(d) All equipment covered by this subpart must meet the following requirements:

(1) *Rated capacity and related information.* The information available in the cab (*see* §1926.1417(c)) regarding "rated capacity" and related information must include, at a minimum, the following information:

(i) A complete range of the manufacturer's equipment rated capacities, as follows:

(A) At all manufacturer approved operating radii, boom angles, work areas, boom lengths and configurations, jib lengths and angles (or offset).

(B) Alternate ratings for use and nonuse of option equipment which affects rated capacities, such as outriggers, stabilizers, and extra counterweights.

(ii) A work area chart for which capacities are listed in the load chart. (NOTE: An example of this type of chart is in ASME B30.5–2004, section 5–1.1.3, Figure 11).

(iii) The work area figure and load chart must clearly indicate the areas where no load is to be handled.

(iv) Recommended reeving for the hoist lines must be shown.

(v) Recommended parts of hoist reeving, size, and type of wire rope for various equipment loads.

(vi) Recommended boom hoist reeving diagram, where applicable; size, type and length of wire rope.

(vii) Tire pressure (where applicable).

(viii) Caution or warnings relative to limitations on equipment and operating procedures, including an indication of the least stable direction.

(ix) Position of the gantry and requirements for intermediate boom suspension (where applicable).

(x) Instructions for boom erection and conditions under which the boom, or boom and jib combinations, may be raised or lowered.

(xi) Whether the hoist holding mechanism is automatically or manually controlled, whether free fall is available, or any combination of these.

(xii) The maximum telescopic travel length of each boom telescopic section.

(xiii) Whether sections are telescoped manually or with power.

(xiv) The sequence and procedure for extending and retracting the telescopic boom section.

(xv) Maximum loads permitted during the boom extending operation, and any limiting conditions or cautions.

(xvi) Hydraulic relief valve settings specified by the manufacturer.

(2) Load hooks (including latched and unlatched types), ball assemblies and load blocks must be of sufficient weight to overhaul the line from the highest hook position for boom or boom and jib lengths and the number of parts of the line in use.

(3) Hook and ball assemblies and load blocks must be marked with their rated capacity and weight.

(4) *Latching hooks.* (i) Hooks must be equipped with latches, except where the requirements of paragraph (d)(4)(ii) of this section are met.

(ii) Hooks without latches, or with latches removed or disabled, must not be used unless:

(A) A qualified person has determined that it is safer to hoist and place the load without latches (or with the latches removed/tied-back).

(B) Routes for the loads are preplanned to ensure that no employee is required to work in the fall zone except for employees necessary for the hooking or unhooking of the load.

(iii) The latch must close the throat opening and be designed to retain slings or other lifting devices/accessories in the hook when the rigging apparatus is slack.

(5) *Posted warnings.* Posted warnings required by this subpart as well as those originally supplied with the equipment by the manufacturer must be maintained in legible condition.

(6) An accessible fire extinguisher must be on the equipment.

(7) *Cabs.* Equipment with cabs must meet the following requirements:

(i) Cabs must be designed with a form of adjustable ventilation and method for clearing the windshield for maintaining visibility and air circulation. Examples of means for adjustable ventilation include air conditioner or window that can be opened (for ventilation and air circulation); examples of means for maintaining visibility include heater (for preventing windshield icing), defroster, fan, windshield wiper.

(ii) Cab doors (swinging, sliding) must be designed to prevent inadvertent opening or closing while traveling or operating the machine. Swinging doors adjacent to the operator must open outward. Sliding operator doors must open rearward.

(iii) *Windows.*

(A) The cab must have windows in front and on both sides of the operator. Forward vertical visibility must be sufficient to give the operator a view of the boom point at all times.

(B) Windows may have sections designed to be opened or readily removed. Windows with sections designed to be opened must be designed so that they can be secured to prevent inadvertent closure.

(C) Windows must be of safety glass or material with similar optical and safety properties, that introduce no visible distortion or otherwise obscure visibility that interferes with the safe operation of the equipment.

(iv) A clear passageway must be provided from the operator's station to an exit door on the operator's side.

(v) Areas of the cab roof that serve as a workstation for rigging, maintenance or other equipment-related tasks must be capable of supporting 250 pounds without permanent distortion.

(8) Belts, gears, shafts, pulleys, sprockets, spindles, drums, fly wheels, chains, and other parts or components that reciprocate, rotate or otherwise move must be guarded where contact by employees (except for maintenance

and repair employees) is possible in the performance of normal duties.

(9) All exhaust pipes, turbochargers, and charge air coolers must be insulated or guarded where contact by employees (except for maintenance and repair employees) is possible in the performance of normal duties.

(10) Hydraulic and pneumatic lines must be protected from damage to the extent feasible.

(11) The equipment must be designed so that exhaust fumes are not discharged in the cab and are discharged in a direction away from the operator.

(12) *Friction mechanisms.* Where friction mechanisms (such as brakes and clutches) are used to control the boom hoist or load line hoist, they must be:

(i) Of a size and thermal capacity sufficient to control all rated loads with the minimum recommended reeving.

(ii) Adjustable to permit compensation for lining wear to maintain proper operation.

(13) *Hydraulic load hoists.* Hydraulic drums must have an integrally mounted holding device or internal static brake to prevent load hoist movement in the event of hydraulic failure.

(e) The employer's obligations under paragraphs (a) through (c) and (d)(7) through (13) of this section are met where the equipment has not changed (except in accordance with § 1926.1434 (Equipment modifications)) and it can refer to documentation from the manufacturer showing that the equipment has been designed, constructed and tested in accordance with those paragraphs.

§ 1926.1434 Equipment modifications.

(a) Modifications or additions which affect the capacity or safe operation of the equipment are prohibited except where the requirements of paragraphs (a)(1), (a)(2), (a)(3), (a)(4), or (a)(5) of this section are met.

(1) *Manufacturer review and approval.* (i) The manufacturer approves the modifications/additions in writing.

(ii) The load charts, procedures, instruction manuals and instruction plates/tags/decals are modified as necessary to accord with the modification/addition.

(iii) The original safety factor of the equipment is not reduced.

(2) *Manufacturer refusal to review request.* The manufacturer is provided a detailed description of the proposed modification/addition, is asked to approve the modification/addition, but it declines to review the technical merits of the proposal or fails, within 30 days, to acknowledge the request or initiate the review, and all of the following are met:

(i) A registered professional engineer who is a qualified person with respect to the equipment involved:

(A) Approves the modification/addition and specifies the equipment configurations to which that approval applies, and

(B) Modifies load charts, procedures, instruction manuals and instruction plates/tags/decals as necessary to accord with the modification/addition.

(ii) The original safety factor of the equipment is not reduced.

(3) *Unavailable manufacturer.* The manufacturer is unavailable and the requirements of paragraphs (a)(2)(i) and (ii) of this section are met.

(4) *Manufacturer does not complete the review within 120 days of the request.* The manufacturer is provided a detailed description of the proposed modification/addition, is asked to approve the modification/addition, agrees to review the technical merits of the proposal, but fails to complete the review of the proposal within 120 days of the date it was provided the detailed description of the proposed modification/addition, and the requirements of paragraphs (a)(2)(i) and (ii) of this section are met.

(5) *Multiple manufacturers of equipment designed for use on marine work sites.* The equipment is designed for marine work sites, contains major structural components from more than one manufacturer, and the requirements of paragraphs (a)(2)(i) and (ii) of this section are met.

(b) Modifications or additions which affect the capacity or safe operation of the equipment are prohibited where the manufacturer, after a review of the technical safety merits of the proposed modification/addition, rejects the proposal and explains the reasons for the rejection in a written response. If the manufacturer rejects the proposal but does not explain the reasons for the rejection in writing, the employer may

treat this as a manufacturer refusal to review the request under paragraph (a)(2) of this section.

(c) The provisions in paragraphs (a) and (b) of this section do not apply to modifications made or approved by the U.S. military.

§1926.1435 Tower cranes.

(a) This section contains supplemental requirements for tower cranes; all sections of this subpart apply to tower cranes unless specified otherwise.

(b) *Erecting, climbing and dismantling.* (1) Section 1926.1403 (Assembly/Disassembly—selection of manufacturer or employer procedures), §1926.1404 (Assembly/Disassembly—general requirements (applies to all assembly and disassembly operations)), §1926.1405 (Disassembly—additional requirements for dismantling of booms and jibs (applies to both the use of manufacturer procedures and employer procedures)), and §1926.1406 (Assembly/Disassembly—employer procedures—general requirements), apply to tower cranes (except as otherwise specified), except that the term "assembly/disassembly" is replaced by "erecting, climbing and dismantling," and the term "disassembly" is replaced by "dismantling."

(2) *Dangerous areas (self-erecting tower cranes).* In addition to the requirements in §1926.1404(e), for self-erecting tower cranes, the following applies: Employees must not be in or under the tower, jib, or rotating portion of the crane during erecting, climbing and dismantling operations until the crane is secured in a locked position and the competent person in charge indicates it is safe to enter this area, unless the manufacturer's instructions direct otherwise and only the necessary personnel are permitted in this area.

(3) *Foundations and structural supports.* Tower crane foundations and structural supports (including both the portions of the structure used for support and the means of attachment) must be designed by the manufacturer or a registered professional engineer.

(4) *Addressing specific hazards.* The requirements in §1926.1404(h)(1) through (9) apply. In addition, the A/D director must address the following:

733

(i) *Foundations and structural supports.* The A/D director must determine that tower crane foundations and structural supports are installed in accordance with their design.

(ii) *Loss of backward stability.* Backward stability before swinging self erecting cranes or cranes on traveling or static undercarriages.

(iii) *Wind speed.* Wind must not exceed the speed recommended by the manufacturer or, where manufacturer does not specify this information, the speed determined by a qualified person.

(5) *Plumb tolerance.* Towers must be erected plumb to the manufacturer's tolerance and verified by a qualified person. Where the manufacturer does not specify plumb tolerance, the crane tower must be plumb to a tolerance of at least 1:500 (approximately 1 inch in 40 feet).

(6) *Multiple tower crane jobsites.* On jobsites where more than one fixed jib (hammerhead) tower crane is installed, the cranes must be located such that no crane can come in contact with the structure of another crane. Cranes are permitted to pass over one another.

(7) *Climbing procedures.* Prior to, and during, all climbing procedures (including inside climbing and top climbing), the employer must:

(i) Comply with all manufacturer prohibitions.

(ii) Have a registered professional engineer verify that the host structure is strong enough to sustain the forces imposed through the braces, brace anchorages and supporting floors.

(8) *Counterweight/ballast.* (i) Equipment must not be erected, dismantled or operated without the amount and position of counterweight and/or ballast in place as specified by the manufacturer or a registered professional engineer familiar with the equipment.

(ii) The maximum counterweight and/or ballast specified by the manufacturer or registered professional engineer familiar with the equipment must not be exceeded.

(c) *Signs.* The size and location of signs installed on tower cranes must be in accordance with manufacturer specifications. Where these are unavailable, a registered professional engineer familiar with the type of equipment involved must approve in writing the size and location of any signs.

(d) *Safety devices.* (1) Section 1926.1415 does not apply to tower cranes.

(2) The following safety devices are required on all tower cranes unless otherwise specified:

(i) Boom stops on luffing boom type tower cranes.

(ii) Jib stops on luffing boom type tower cranes if equipped with a jib attachment.

(iii) Travel rail end stops at both ends of travel rail.

(iv) Travel rail clamps on all travel bogies.

(v) Integrally mounted check valves on all load supporting hydraulic cylinders.

(vi) Hydraulic system pressure limiting device.

(vii) The following brakes, which must automatically set in the event of pressure loss or power failure, are required:

(A) A hoist brake on all hoists.

(B) Swing brake.

(C) Trolley brake.

(D) Rail travel brake.

(viii) Deadman control or forced neutral return control (hand) levers.

(ix) Emergency stop switch at the operator's station.

(x) Trolley end stops must be provided at both ends of travel of the trolley.

(3) *Proper operation required.* Operations must not begin unless the devices listed in this section are in proper working order. If a device stops working properly during operations, the operator must safely stop operations. The equipment must be taken out of service, and operations must not resume until the device is again working properly. *See* § 1926.1417(f). Alternative measures are not permitted to be used.

(e) *Operational aids.* (1) Section 1926.1416 does not apply to tower cranes.

(2) The devices listed in this section ("operational aids") are required on all tower cranes covered by this subpart, unless otherwise specified.

(3) Operations must not begin unless the operational aids are in proper working order, except where the employer meets the specified temporary alternative measures. More protective

alternative measures specified by the tower crane manufacturer, if any, must be followed. *See* §1926.1417(j) for additional requirements.

(4) If an operational aid stops working properly during operations, the operator must safely stop operations until the temporary alternative measures are implemented or the device is again working properly. If a replacement part is no longer available, the use of a substitute device that performs the same type of function is permitted and is not considered a modification under §1926.1434.

(5) *Category I operational aids and alternative measures.* Operational aids listed in this paragraph that are not working properly must be repaired no later than 7 calendar days after the deficiency occurs. *Exception:* If the employer documents that it has ordered the necessary parts within 7 calendar days of the occurrence of the deficiency, the repair must be completed within 7 calendar days of receipt of the parts.

(i) *Trolley travel limiting device.* The travel of the trolley must be restricted at both ends of the jib by a trolley travel limiting device to prevent the trolley from running into the trolley end stops. *Temporary alternative measures:*

(A) *Option A.* The trolley rope must be marked (so it can be seen by the operator) at a point that will give the operator sufficient time to stop the trolley prior to the end stops.

(B) *Option B.* A spotter who is in direct communication with the operator must be used when operations are conducted within 10 feet of the outer or inner trolley end stops.

(ii) *Boom hoist limiting device.* The range of the boom must be limited at the minimum and maximum radius. *Temporary alternative measures:* Clearly mark the cable (so it can be seen by the operator) at a point that will give the operator sufficient time to stop the boom hoist within the minimum and maximum boom radius, or use a spotter who is in direct communication with the operator to inform the operator when this point is reached.

(iii) *Anti two-blocking device.* The tower crane must be equipped with a device which automatically prevents damage from contact between the load block, overhaul ball, or similar component, and the boom tip (or fixed upper block or similar component). The device(s) must prevent such damage at all points where two-blocking could occur. *Temporary alternative measures:* Clearly mark the cable (so it can be seen by the operator) at a point that will give the operator sufficient time to stop the hoist to prevent two-blocking, or use a spotter who is in direct communication with the operator to inform the operator when this point is reached.

(iv) *Hoist drum lower limiting device.* Tower cranes manufactured after November 8, 2011 must be equipped with a device that prevents the last 2 wraps of hoist cable from being spooled off the drum. *Temporary alternative measures:* Mark the cable (so it can be seen by the operator) at a point that will give the operator sufficient time to stop the hoist prior to last 2 wraps of hoist cable being spooled off the drum, or use a spotter who is in direct communication with the operator to inform the operator when this point is reached

(v) *Load moment limiting device.* The tower crane must have a device that prevents moment overloading. *Temporary alternative measures:* A radius indicating device must be used (if the tower crane is not equipped with a radius indicating device, the radius must be measured to ensure the load is within the rated capacity of the crane). In addition, the weight of the load must be determined from a source recognized by the industry (such as the load's manufacturer), or by a calculation method recognized by the industry (such as calculating a steel beam from measured dimensions and a known per foot weight), or by other equally reliable means. This information must be provided to the operator prior to the lift.

(vi) *Hoist line pull limiting device.* The capacity of the hoist must be limited to prevent overloading, including each individual gear ratio if equipped with a multiple speed hoist transmission. *Temporary alternative measures:* The operator must ensure that the weight of the load does not exceed the capacity

735

of the hoist (including for each individual gear ratio if equipped with a multiple speed hoist transmission).

(vii) *Rail travel limiting device.* The travel distance in each direction must be limited to prevent the travel bogies from running into the end stops or buffers. *Temporary alternative measures:* A spotter who is in direct communication with the operator must be used when operations are conducted within 10 feet of either end of the travel rail end stops; the spotter must inform the operator of the distance of the travel bogies from the end stops or buffers.

(viii) *Boom hoist drum positive locking device and control.* The boom hoist drum must be equipped with a control that will enable the operator to positively lock the boom hoist drum from the cab. *Temporary alternative measures:* The device must be manually set when required if an electric, hydraulic or automatic control is not functioning.

(6) *Category II operational aids and alternative measures.* Operational aids listed in this paragraph that are not working properly must be repaired no later than 30 calendar days after the deficiency occurs. *Exception:* If the employer documents that it has ordered the necessary parts within 7 calendar days of the occurrence of the deficiency, and the part is not received in time to complete the repair in 30 calendar days, the repair must be completed within 7 calendar days of receipt of the parts.

(i) *Boom angle or hook radius indicator.*

(A) Luffing boom tower cranes must have a boom angle indicator readable from the operator's station.

(B) Hammerhead tower cranes manufactured after November 8, 2011 must have a hook radius indicator readable from the operator's station.

(C) *Temporary alternative measures:* Hook radii or boom angle must be determined by measuring the hook radii or boom angle with a measuring device.

(ii) *Trolley travel deceleration device.* The trolley speed must be automatically reduced prior to the trolley reaching the end limit in both directions. *Temporary alternative measure:* The employer must post a notice in the cab of the crane notifying the operator that the trolley travel deceleration device is malfunctioning and instructing the operator to take special care to reduce the trolley speed when approaching the trolley end limits.

(iii) *Boom hoist deceleration device.* The boom speed must be automatically reduced prior to the boom reaching the minimum or maximum radius limit. *Temporary alternative measure:* The employer must post a notice in the cab of the crane notifying the operator that the boom hoist deceleration device is malfunctioning and instructing the operator to take special care to reduce the boom speed when approaching the minimum or maximum radius limits.

(iv) *Load hoist deceleration device.* The load speed must be automatically reduced prior to the hoist reaching the upper limit. *Temporary alternative measure:* The employer must post a notice in the cab of the crane notifying the operator that the load hoist deceleration device is malfunctioning and instructing the operator to take special care to reduce the load speed when approaching the upper limits.

(v) *Wind speed indicator.* A device must be provided to display the wind speed and must be mounted above the upper rotating structure on tower cranes. On self erecting cranes, it must be mounted at or above the jib level. *Temporary alternative measures:* Use of wind speed information from a properly functioning indicating device on another tower crane on the same site, or a qualified person estimates the wind speed.

(vi) *Load indicating device.* Cranes manufactured after November 8, 2011 must have a device that displays the magnitude of the load on the hook. Displays that are part of load moment limiting devices that display the load on the hook meet this requirement. *Temporary alternative measures:* The weight of the load must be determined from a source recognized by the industry (such as the load's manufacturer), or by a calculation method recognized by the industry (such as calculating a steel beam from measured dimensions and a known per foot weight), or by other equally reliable means. This information must be provided to the operator prior to the lift.

(f) *Inspections.* (1) Section 1926.1412 (Inspections) applies to tower cranes, except that the term "assembly" is replaced by "erection." Section 1926.1413 (Wire rope—inspection) applies to tower cranes.

(2) *Pre-erection inspection.* Before each crane component is erected, it must be inspected by a qualified person for damage or excessive wear.

(i) The qualified person must pay particular attention to components that will be difficult to inspect thoroughly during shift inspections.

(ii) If the qualified person determines that a component is damaged or worn to the extent that it would create a safety hazard if used on the crane, that component must not be erected on the crane unless it is repaired and, upon reinspection by the qualified person, found to no longer create a safety hazard.

(iii) If the qualified person determines that, though not presently a safety hazard, the component needs to be monitored, the employer must ensure that the component is checked in the monthly inspections. Any such determination must be documented, and the documentation must be available to any individual who conducts a monthly inspection.

(3) *Post-erection inspection.* In addition to the requirements in § 1926.1412(c), the following requirements must be met:

(i) A load test using certified weights, or scaled weights using a certified scale with a current certificate of calibration, must be conducted after each erection.

(ii) The load test must be conducted in accordance with the manufacturer's instructions when available. Where these instructions are unavailable, the test must be conducted in accordance with written load test procedures developed by a registered professional engineer familiar with the type of equipment involved.

(4) *Monthly.* The following additional items must be included:

(i) Tower (mast) bolts and other structural bolts (for loose or dislodged condition) from the base of the tower crane up or, if the crane is tied to or braced by the structure, those above the upper-most brace support.

(ii) The upper-most tie-in, braces, floor supports and floor wedges where the tower crane is supported by the structure, for loose or dislodged components.

(5) *Annual.* In addition to the items that must be inspected under § 1926.1412(f), all turntable and tower bolts must be inspected for proper condition and torque.

§ 1926.1436 Derricks.

(a) This section contains supplemental requirements for derricks, whether temporarily or permanently mounted; all sections of this subpart apply to derricks unless specified otherwise. A derrick is powered equipment consisting of a mast or equivalent member that is held at or near the end by guys or braces, with or without a boom, and its hoisting mechanism. The mast/equivalent member and/or the load is moved by the hoisting mechanism (typically base-mounted) and operating ropes. Derricks include: A-frame, basket, breast, Chicago boom, gin pole (except gin poles used for erection of communication towers), guy, shearleg, stiffleg, and variations of such equipment.

(b) *Operation—procedures.* (1) Section 1926.1417 (Operation) applies except for § 1926.1417(c) (Accessibility of procedures).

(2) *Load chart contents.* Load charts must contain at least the following information:

(i) Rated capacity at corresponding ranges of boom angle or operating radii.

(ii) Specific lengths of components to which the rated capacities apply.

(iii) Required parts for hoist reeving.

(iv) Size and construction of rope must be included on the load chart or in the operating manual.

(3) *Load chart location*—(i) *Permanent installations.* For permanently installed derricks with fixed lengths of boom, guy, and mast, a load chart must be posted where it is visible to personnel responsible for the operation of the equipment.

(ii) *Non-permanent installations.* For derricks that are not permanently installed, the load chart must be readily available at the job site to personnel responsible for the operation of the equipment.

(c) *Construction*—(1) *General requirements.* (i) Derricks must be constructed

737

to meet all stresses imposed on members and components when installed and operated in accordance with the manufacturer's/builder's procedures and within its rated capacity.

(ii) Welding of load sustaining members must conform to recommended practices in ANSI/AWS D14.3–94 (incorporated by reference, *see* § 1926.6) or AWS D1.1/D1.1M:2002 (incorporated by reference, *see* § 1926.6).

(2) *Guy derricks.* (i) The minimum number of guys must be 6, with equal spacing, except where a qualified person or derrick manufacturer approves variations from these requirements and revises the rated capacity to compensate for such variations.

(ii) Guy derricks must not be used unless the employer has the following guy information from the manufacturer or a qualified person, when not available from the manufacturer:

(A) The number of guys.

(B) The spacing around the mast.

(C) The size, grade, and construction of rope to be used for each guy.

(iii) For guy derricks manufactured after December 18, 1970, in addition to the information required in paragraph (c)(2)(ii) of this section, the employer must have the following guy information from the manufacturer or a qualified person, when not available from the manufacturer:

(A) The amount of initial sag or tension.

(B) The amount of tension in guy line rope at anchor.

(iv) The mast base must permit the mast to rotate freely with allowance for slight tilting of the mast caused by guy slack.

(v) The mast cap must:

(A) Permit the mast to rotate freely.

(B) Withstand tilting and cramping caused by the guy loads.

(C) Be secured to the mast to prevent disengagement during erection.

(D) Be provided with means for attaching guy ropes.

(3) *Stiffleg derricks.* (i) The mast must be supported in the vertical position by at least two stifflegs; one end of each must be connected to the top of the mast and the other end securely anchored.

(ii) The stifflegs must be capable of withstanding the loads imposed at any point of operation within the load chart range.

(iii) The mast base must:

(A) Permit the mast to rotate freely (when necessary).

(B) Permit deflection of the mast without binding.

(iv) The mast must be prevented from lifting out of its socket when the mast is in tension.

(v) The stiffleg connecting member at the top of the mast must:

(A) Permit the mast to rotate freely (when necessary).

(B) Withstand the loads imposed by the action of the stifflegs.

(C) Be secured so as to oppose separating forces.

(4) *Gin pole derricks.* (i) Guy lines must be sized and spaced so as to make the gin pole stable in both boomed and vertical positions. *Exception:* Where the size and/or spacing of guy lines do not result in the gin pole being stable in both boomed and vertical positions, the employer must ensure that the derrick is not used in an unstable position.

(ii) The base of the gin pole must permit movement of the pole (when necessary).

(iii) The gin pole must be anchored at the base against horizontal forces (when such forces are present).

(5) *Chicago boom derricks.* The fittings for stepping the boom and for attaching the topping lift must be arranged to:

(i) Permit the derrick to swing at all permitted operating radii and mounting heights between fittings.

(ii) Accommodate attachment to the upright member of the host structure.

(iii) Withstand the forces applied when configured and operated in accordance with the manufacturer's/builder's procedures and within its rated capacity.

(iv) Prevent the boom or topping lift from lifting out under tensile forces.

(d) *Anchoring and guying.* (1) Load anchoring data developed by the manufacturer or a qualified person must be used.

(2) *Guy derricks.* (i) The mast base must be anchored.

(ii) The guys must be secured to the ground or other firm anchorage.

(iii) The anchorage and guying must be designed to withstand maximum horizontal and vertical forces encountered when operating within rated capacity with the particular guy slope and spacing specified for the application.

(3) *Stiffleg derricks.* (i) The mast base and stifflegs must be anchored.

(ii) The mast base and stifflegs must be designed to withstand maximum horizontal and vertical forces encountered when operating within rated capacity with the particular stiffleg spacing and slope specified for the application.

(e) *Swingers and hoists.* (1) The boom, swinger mechanisms and hoists must be suitable for the derrick work intended and must be anchored to prevent displacement from the imposed loads.

(2) *Hoists.* (i) Base mounted drum hoists must meet the requirements in the following sections of ASME B30.7–2001 (incorporated by reference, *see* §1926.6):

(A) Sections 7–1.1 ("Load ratings and markings").

(B) Section 7–1.2 ("Construction"), except: 7–1.2.13 ("Operator's cab"); 7–1.2.15 ("Fire extinguishers").

(C) Section 7–1.3 ("Installation").

(D) Applicable terms in section 7–0.2 ("Definitions").

(ii) *Load tests for new hoists.* The employer must ensure that new hoists are load tested to a minimum of 110% of rated capacity, but not more than 125% of rated capacity, unless otherwise recommended by the manufacturer. This requirement is met where the manufacturer has conducted this testing.

(iii) *Repaired or modified hoists.* Hoists that have had repairs, modifications or additions affecting their capacity or safe operation must be evaluated by a qualified person to determine if a load test is necessary. If it is, load testing must be conducted in accordance with paragraphs (e)(2)(ii) and (iv) of this section.

(iv) *Load test procedure.* Load tests required by paragraphs (e)(2)(ii) or (e)(2)(iii) of this section must be conducted as follows:

(A) The test load must be hoisted a vertical distance to assure that the load is supported by the hoist and held by the hoist brake(s).

(B) The test load must be lowered, stopped and held with the brake(s).

(C) The hoist must not be used unless a competent person determines that the test has been passed.

(f) *Operational aids.* (1) Section 1926.1416 (Operational aids) applies, except for §1926.1416(d)(1) (Boom hoist limiting device), §1926.1416(e)(1) (Boom angle or radius indicator), and §1926.1416(e)(4) (Load weighing and similar devices).

(2) *Boom angle aid.* A boom angle indicator is not required but if the derrick is not equipped with a functioning one, the employer must ensure that either:

(i) The boom hoist cable must be marked with caution and stop marks. The stop marks must correspond to maximum and minimum allowable boom angles. The caution and stop marks must be in view of the operator, or a spotter who is in direct communication with the operator; or

(ii) An electronic or other device that signals the operator in time to prevent the boom from moving past its maximum and minimum angles, or automatically prevents such movement, is used.

(3) *Load weight/capacity devices.* (i) Derricks manufactured more than one year after November 8, 2010 with a maximum rated capacity over 6,000 pounds must have at least one of the following: load weighing device, load moment indicator, rated capacity indicator, or rated capacity limiter. *Temporary alternative measures:* The weight of the load must be determined from a source recognized by the industry (such as the load's manufacturer), or by a calculation method recognized by the industry (such as calculating a steel beam from measured dimensions and a known per foot weight), or by other equally reliable means. This information must be provided to the operator prior to the lift. *See* §1926.1417(j) for additional requirements.

(ii) A load weight/capacity device that is not working properly must be repaired no later than 30 days after the deficiency occurs. *Exception:* If the employer documents that it has ordered the necessary parts within 7 days of the occurrence of the deficiency, and the part is not received in time to complete the repair in 30 days, the repair must be completed within 7 days of receipt of the parts.

(g) *Post-assembly approval and testing—new or reinstalled derricks—*(1) *Anchorages.* (i) Anchorages, including the structure to which the derrick is attached (if applicable), must be approved by a qualified person.

(ii) If using a rock or hairpin anchorage, the qualified person must determine if any special testing of the anchorage is needed. If so, it must be tested accordingly.

(2) *Functional test.* Prior to initial use, new or reinstalled derricks must be tested by a competent person with no hook load to verify proper operation. This test must include:

(i) Lifting and lowering the hook(s) through the full range of hook travel.

(ii) Raising and lowering the boom through the full range of boom travel.

(iii) Swinging in each direction through the full range of swing.

(iv) Actuating the anti two-block and boom hoist limit devices (if provided).

(v) Actuating locking, limiting and indicating devices (if provided).

(3) *Load test.* Prior to initial use, new or reinstalled derricks must be load tested by a competent person. The test load must meet the following requirements:

(i) Test loads must be at least 100% and no more than 110% of the rated capacity, unless otherwise recommended by the manufacturer or qualified person, but in no event must the test load be less than the maximum anticipated load.

(ii) The test must consist of:

(A) Hoisting the test load a few inches and holding to verify that the load is supported by the derrick and held by the hoist brake(s).

(B) Swinging the derrick, if applicable, the full range of its swing, at the maximum allowable working radius for the test load.

(C) Booming the derrick up and down within the allowable working radius for the test load.

(D) Lowering, stopping and holding the load with the brake(s).

(iii) The derrick must not be used unless the competent person determines that the test has been passed.

(4) *Documentation.* Tests conducted under this paragraph must be docu-

mented. The document must contain the date, test results and the name of the tester. The document must be retained until the derrick is re-tested or dismantled, whichever occurs first. All such documents must be available, during the applicable document retention period, to all persons who conduct inspections in accordance with § 1926.1412.

(h) *Load testing repaired or modified derricks.* Derricks that have had repairs, modifications or additions affecting the derrick's capacity or safe operation must be evaluated by a qualified person to determine if a load test is necessary. If it is, load testing must be conducted and documented in accordance with paragraph (g) of this section.

(i) [Reserved]

(j) *Power failure procedures.* If power fails during operations, the derrick operator must safely stop operations. This must include:

(1) Setting all brakes or locking devices.

(2) Moving all clutch and other power controls to the off position.

(k) *Use of winch heads.* (1) Ropes must not be handled on a winch head without the knowledge of the operator.

(2) While a winch head is being used, the operator must be within reach of the power unit control lever.

(l) [Reserved]

(m) *Securing the boom.* (1) When the boom is being held in a fixed position, dogs, pawls, or other positive holding mechanisms on the boom hoist must be engaged.

(2) When taken out of service for 30 days or more, the boom must be secured by one of the following methods:

(i) Laid down.

(ii) Secured to a stationary member, as nearly under the head as possible, by attachment of a sling to the load block.

(iii) For guy derricks, lifted to a vertical position and secured to the mast.

(iv) For stiffleg derricks, secured against the stiffleg.

(n) The process of jumping the derrick must be supervised by the A/D director.

(o) Derrick operations must be supervised by a competent person.

(p) *Inspections.* In addition to the requirements in §1926.1412, the following additional items must be included in the inspections:

(1) *Daily:* Guys for proper tension.

(2) *Annual.* (i) Gudgeon pin for cracks, wear, and distortion.

(ii) Foundation supports for continued ability to sustain the imposed loads.

(q) *Qualification and Training.* The employer must train each operator of a derrick on the safe operation of equipment the individual will operate. Section 1926.1427 of this subpart (Operator qualification and certification) does not apply.

§1926.1437 Floating cranes/derricks and land cranes/derricks on barges.

(a) This section contains supplemental requirements for floating cranes/derricks and land cranes/derricks on barges, pontoons, vessels or other means of flotation (*i.e.*, vessel/flotation device). The sections of this subpart apply to floating cranes/derricks and land cranes/derricks on barges, pontoons, vessels or other means of flotation, unless specified otherwise. The requirements of this section do not apply when using jacked barges when the jacks are deployed to the river, lake, or sea bed and the barge is fully supported by the jacks.

(b) *General requirements.* The requirements in paragraphs (c) through (k) of this section apply to both floating cranes/derricks and land cranes/derricks on barges, pontoons, vessels or other means of flotation.

(c) *Work area control.* (1) The requirements of §1926.1424 (Work area control) apply, except for §1926.1424(a)(2)(ii).

(2) The employer must either:

(i) Erect and maintain control lines, warning lines, railings or similar barriers to mark the boundaries of the hazard areas; or

(ii) Clearly mark the hazard areas by a combination of warning signs (such as, "Danger—Swing/Crush Zone") and high visibility markings on the equipment that identify the hazard areas. In addition, the employer must train each employee to understand what these markings signify.

(d) *Keeping clear of the load.* Section 1926.1425 does not apply.

(e) *Additional safety devices.* In addition to the safety devices listed in §1926.1415, the following safety devices are required:

(1) Barge, pontoon, vessel or other means of flotation list and trim device. The safety device must be located in the cab or, when there is no cab, at the operator's station.

(2) Positive equipment house lock.

(3) *Wind speed and direction indicator.* A competent person must determine if wind is a factor that needs to be considered; if wind needs to be considered, a wind speed and direction indicator must be used.

(f) *Operational aids.* (1) An anti two-block device is required only when hoisting personnel or hoisting over an occupied cofferdam or shaft.

(2) Section 1926.1416(e)(4) (Load weighing and similar devices) does not apply to dragline, clamshell (grapple), magnet, drop ball, container handling, concrete bucket, and pile driving work performed under this section.

(g) *Accessibility of procedures applicable to equipment operation.* If the crane/derrick has a cab, the requirements of §1926.1417(c) apply. If the crane/derrick does not have a cab, the employer must ensure that:

(1) Rated capacities (load charts) are posted at the operator's station. If the operator's station is moveable (such as with pendant-controlled equipment), the load charts are posted on the equipment.

(2) Procedures applicable to the operation of the equipment (other than load charts), recommended operating speeds, special hazard warnings, instructions and operators manual, must be readily available on board the vessel/flotation device.

(h) *Inspections.* In addition to meeting the requirements of §1926.1412 for inspecting the crane/derrick, the employer must inspect the barge, pontoons, vessel or other means of flotation used to support a floating crane/derrick or land crane/derrick, and ensure that:

(1) *Shift.* For each shift inspection, the means used to secure/attach the equipment to the vessel/flotation device is in proper condition, including

wear, corrosion, loose or missing fasteners, defective welds, and (when applicable) insufficient tension.

(2) *Monthly.* For each monthly inspection:

(i) The means used to secure/attach the equipment to the vessel/flotation device is in proper condition, including inspection for wear, corrosion, and, when applicable, insufficient tension.

(ii) The vessel/flotation device is not taking on water.

(iii) The deckload is properly secured.

(iv) The vessel/flotation device is watertight based on the condition of the chain lockers, storage, fuel compartments, and hatches.

(v) The firefighting and lifesaving equipment is in place and functional.

(3) The shift and monthly inspections are conducted by a competent person, and:

(i) If any deficiency is identified, an immediate determination is made by a qualified person whether the deficiency constitutes a hazard.

(ii) If the deficiency is determined to constitute a hazard, the vessel/flotation device is removed from service until the deficiency has been corrected.

(4) *Annual: external vessel/flotation device inspection.* For each annual inspection:

(i) The external portion of the barge, pontoons, vessel or other means of flotation used is inspected annually by a qualified person who has expertise with respect to vessels/flotation devices and that the inspection includes the following items:

(A) The items identified in paragraphs (h)(1) (*Shift*) and (h)(2) (*Monthly*) of this section.

(B) Cleats, bitts, chocks, fenders, capstans, ladders, and stanchions, for significant corrosion, wear, deterioration, or deformation that could impair the function of these items.

(C) External evidence of leaks and structural damage; evidence of leaks and damage below the waterline may be determined through internal inspection of the vessel/flotation device.

(D) Four-corner draft readings.

(E) Firefighting equipment for serviceability.

(ii) Rescue skiffs, lifelines, work vests, life preservers and ring buoys are inspected for proper condition.

(iii) If any deficiency is identified, an immediate determination is made by the qualified person whether the deficiency constitutes a hazard or, though not yet a hazard, needs to be monitored in the monthly inspections.

(A) If the qualified person determines that the deficiency constitutes a hazard, the vessel/flotation device is removed from service until it has been corrected. *See* requirements in § 1926.1417(f).

(B) If the qualified person determines that, though not presently a hazard, the deficiency needs to be monitored, the deficiency is checked in the monthly inspections.

(5) *Four-year: internal vessel/flotation device inspection.* For each four-year inspection:

(i) A marine engineer, marine architect, licensed surveyor, or other qualified person who has expertise with respect to vessels/flotation devices surveys the internal portion of the barge, pontoons, vessel, or other means of flotation.

(ii) If the surveyor identifies a deficiency, an immediate determination is made by the surveyor as to whether the deficiency constitutes a hazard or, though not yet a hazard, needs to be monitored in the monthly or annual inspections, as appropriate.

(A) If the surveyor determines that the deficiency constitutes a hazard, the vessel/flotation device is removed from service until it has been corrected.

(B) If the surveyor determines that, though not presently a hazard, the deficiency needs to be monitored, the deficiency is checked in the monthly or annual inspections, as appropriate.

(6) *Documentation.* The monthly and annual inspections required in paragraphs (h)(2) and (h)(4) of this section are documented in accordance with §§ 1926.1412 (e)(3) and 1926.1412(f)(7), respectively, and that the four-year inspection required in paragraph (h)(5) of this section is documented in accordance with § 1926.1412(f)(7), except that the documentation for that inspection must be retained for a minimum of 4 years. All such documents must be made available, during the applicable

document retention period, to all persons who conduct inspections in accordance with § 1926.1412.

(i) [Reserved]

(j) *Working with a diver.* The employer must meet the following additional requirements when working with a diver in the water:

(1) If a crane/derrick is used to get a diver into and out of the water, it must not be used for any other purpose until the diver is back on board. When used for more than one diver, it must not be used for any other purpose until all divers are back on board.

(2) The operator must remain at the controls of the crane/derrick at all times.

(3) In addition to the requirements in §§ 1926.1419 through 1926.1422 (Signals), either:

(i) A clear line of sight must be maintained between the operator and tender; or

(ii) The signals between the operator and tender must be transmitted electronically.

(4) The means used to secure the crane/derrick to the vessel/flotation device (*see* paragraph (n)(5) of this section) must not allow any amount of shifting in any direction.

(k) *Manufacturer's specifications and limitations.* (1) The employer must ensure that the barge, pontoons, vessel, or other means of flotation must be capable of withstanding imposed environmental, operational and in-transit loads when used in accordance with the manufacturer's specifications and limitations.

(2) The employer must ensure that the manufacturer's specifications and limitations with respect to environmental, operational, and in-transit loads for a barge, pontoon, vessel, or other means of flotation are not exceeded or violated.

(3) When the manufacturer's specifications and limitations are unavailable, the employer must ensure that the specifications and limitations established by a qualified person with respect to environmental, operational and in-transit loads for the barge, pontoons, vessel, or other means of flotation are not exceeded or violated.

(1) [Reserved]

(m) *Floating cranes/derricks.* For equipment designed by the manufacturer (or employer) for marine use by permanent attachment to barges, pontoons, vessels or other means of flotation:

(1) *Load charts.* (i) The employer must not exceed the manufacturer load charts applicable to operations on water. When using these charts, the employer must comply with all parameters and limitations (such as dynamic and environmental parameters) applicable to the use of the charts.

(ii) The employer must ensure that load charts take into consideration a minimum wind speed of 40 miles per hour.

(2) The employer must ensure that the requirements for maximum allowable list and maximum allowable trim as specified in Table M1 of this section are met.

TABLE M1

Rated capacity	Maximum allowable list (degrees)	Maximum allowable trim (degrees)
Equipment designed for marine use by permanent attachment (other than derricks):		
25 tons or less	5	5
Over 25 tons	7	7
Derricks designed for marine use by permanent attachment:		
Any rated capacity	10	10

(3) The employer must ensure that the equipment is stable under the conditions specified in Tables M2 and M3 of this section. (NOTE: Freeboard is the vertical distance between the water line and the main deck of the vessel.)

TABLE M2

Operated at	Wind speed (mph)	Minimum freeboard (ft)
Rated capacity	60	2
Rated capacity plus 25%	60	1
High boom, no load	60	2

TABLE M3

Operated at	Wind speed
For backward stability of the boom:	
High boom, no load, full back list (least stable condition).	90 mph.

(4) If the equipment is employer-made, it must not be used unless the employer has documents demonstrating that the load charts and applicable parameters for use meet the requirements of paragraphs (m)(1) through (3) of this section. Such documents must be signed by a registered professional engineer who is a qualified person with respect to the design of this type of equipment (including the means of flotation).

(5) The employer must ensure that the barge, pontoons, vessel or other means of flotation used:

(i) Are structurally sufficient to withstand the static and dynamic loads of the crane/derrick when operating at the crane/derrick's maximum rated capacity with all planned and actual deck loads and ballasted compartments.

(ii) Have a subdivided hull with one or more longitudinal watertight bulkheads for reducing the free-surface effect.

(iii) Have access to void compartments to allow for inspection and pumping.

(n) *Land cranes/derricks.* For land cranes/derricks used on barges, pontoons, vessels or other means of flotation, the employer must ensure that:

(1) The rated capacity of the equipment (including but not limited to modification of load charts) applicable for use on land is reduced to:

(i) Account for increased loading from list, trim, wave action, and wind.

(ii) Be applicable to a specified location(s) on the specific barge, pontoons, vessel or other means of flotation that will be used, under the environmental conditions expected and encountered.

(iii) The conditions required in paragraphs (n)(3) and (n)(4) of this section are met.

(2) The rated capacity modification required in paragraph (n)(1) of this section is performed by the equipment manufacturer, or a qualified person who has expertise with respect to both land crane/derrick capacity and the stability of vessels/flotation devices.

(3) For list and trim.

(i) The maximum allowable list and the maximum allowable trim for the barge, pontoon, vessel or other means of flotation must not exceed the amount necessary to ensure that the conditions in paragraph (n)(4) of this section are met. In addition, the maximum allowable list and the maximum allowable trim does not exceed the least of the following: 5 degrees, the amount specified by the crane/derrick manufacturer, or, when, an amount is not so specified, the amount specified by the qualified person.

(ii) The maximum allowable list and the maximum allowable trim for the land crane/derrick does not exceed the amount specified by the crane/derrick manufacturer, or, when, an amount is not so specified, the amount specified by the qualified person.

(4) For the following conditions:

(i) All deck surfaces of the barge, pontoons, vessel or other means of flotation used are above water.

(ii) The entire bottom area of the barge, pontoons, vessel or other means of flotation used is submerged.

(5) Physical attachment, corralling, rails system and centerline cable system meet the requirements in Option (1), Option (2), Option (3), or Option (4) of this section, and that whichever option is used also meets the requirements of paragraph (n)(5)(v) of this section.

(i) *Option (1)—Physical attachment.* The crane/derrick is physically attached to the barge, pontoons, vessel or other means of flotation. Methods of physical attachment include crossed-cable systems attached to the crane/derrick and vessel/flotation device, bolting or welding the crane/derrick to the vessel/flotation device, strapping the crane/derrick to the vessel/flotation device with chains, or other methods of physical attachment.

(ii) *Option (2)—Corralling.* The crane/derrick is prevented from shifting by installing barricade restraints (*i.e.,* corralling system). Employers must ensure that corralling systems do not allow the equipment to shift by any amount of shifting in any direction.

(iii) *Option (3)—Rails.* The crane/derrick must be prevented from shifting by being mounted on a rail system. Employers must ensure that rail clamps and rail stops are used unless the system is designed to prevent movement during operation by other means.

(iv) *Option (4)—Centerline cable system.* The crane/derrick is prevented from shifting by being mounted to a wire rope system. The employer must ensure that the wire rope system meets the following requirements:

(A) The wire rope and attachments are of sufficient size and strength to support the side load of crane/derrick.

(B) The wire rope is attached physically to the vessel/flotation device.

(C) The wire rope is attached to the crane/derrick by appropriate attachment methods (such as shackles or sheaves) on the undercarriage, and that the method used will allow the crew to secure the crane/derrick from movement during operation and to move the crane/derrick longitudinally along the vessel/flotation device for repositioning.

(D) Means are installed to prevent the crane/derrick from passing the forward or aft end of the wire rope attachments.

(E) The crane/derrick is secured from movement during operation.

(v) The systems/means used to comply with Option (1), Option (2), Option (3), or Option (4) of this section are designed by a marine engineer, registered professional engineer familiar with floating crane/derrick design, or qualified person familiar with floating crane/derrick design.

(6) *Exception.* For mobile auxiliary cranes used on the deck of a floating crane/derrick, the requirement specified by paragraph (n)(5) of this section to use Option (1), Option (2), Option (3), or Option (4) does not apply when the employer demonstrates implementation of a plan and procedures that meet the following requirements:

(i) A marine engineer or registered professional engineer familiar with floating crane/derrick design develops and signs a written plan for the use of the mobile auxiliary crane.

(ii) The plan is designed so that the applicable requirements of this section are met despite the position, travel, operation, and lack of physical attachment (or corralling, use of rails or cable system) of the mobile auxiliary crane.

(iii) The plan specifies the areas of the deck where the mobile auxiliary crane is permitted to be positioned, travel, and operate, and the parameters and limitations of such movements and operation.

(iv) The deck is marked to identify the permitted areas for positioning, travel, and operation.

(v) The plan specifies the dynamic and environmental conditions that must be present for use of the plan.

(vi) If the dynamic and environmental conditions in paragraph (n)(6)(v) of this section are exceeded, the mobile auxiliary crane is attached physically or corralled in accordance with Option (1), Option (2) or Option (4) of paragraph (n)(5) of this section.

(7) The barge, pontoons, vessel or other means of flotation used:

(i) Are structurally sufficient to withstand the static and dynamic loads of the crane/derrick when operating at the crane/derrick's maximum rated capacity with all anticipated deck loads and ballasted compartments.

(ii) Have a subdivided hull with one or more longitudinal watertight bulkheads for reducing the free surface effect.

(iii) Have access to void compartments to allow for inspection and pumping.

§ 1926.1438 Overhead & gantry cranes.

(a) *Permanently installed overhead and gantry cranes.* The requirements of § 1910.179, except for § 1910.179(b)(1), and not the requirements of this subpart CC, apply to the following equipment when used in construction and permanently installed in a facility: overhead and gantry cranes, including semigantry, cantilever gantry, wall cranes, storage bridge cranes, and others having the same fundamental characteristics.

(b) *Overhead and gantry cranes that are not permanently installed in a facility.* (1) This paragraph applies to the following equipment when used in construction and not permanently installed in a facility: Overhead and gantry cranes, overhead/bridge cranes, semigantry, cantilever gantry, wall cranes, storage bridge cranes, launching gantry cranes, and similar equipment having the same fundamental characteristics, irrespective of whether it travels on tracks, wheels, or other means.

(2) The following requirements apply to equipment identified in paragraph (b)(1) of this section:

(i) Sections 1926.1400 through 1926.1414; §§ 1926.1417 through 1926.1425; § 1926.1426(d), §§ 1926.1427 through 1926.1434; § 1926.1437, § 1926.1439, and § 1926.1441.

(ii) The following portions of § 1910.179:

(A) Paragraphs (b)(5),(6),(7); (e)(1),(3),(5),(6); (f)(1),(4); (g); (h)(1),(3); (k); and (n) of § 1910.179.

(B) The definitions in § 1910.179(a) except for "hoist" and "load." For those words, the definitions in § 1926.1401 apply.

(C) Section 1910.179(b)(2), but only where the equipment identified in paragraph (b)(1) of this section (§ 1926.1438) was manufactured before September 19, 2001.

(iii) For equipment manufactured on or after September 19, 2001, the following sections of ASME B30.2–2005 (incorporated by reference, *see* § 1926.6) apply: 2–1.3.1; 2–1.3.2; 2–1.4.1; 2–1.6; 2–1.7.2; 2–1.8.2; 2–1.9.1; 2–1.9.2; 2–1.11; 2–1.12.2; 2–1.13.7; 2–1.14.2; 2–1.14.3; 2–1.14.5; 2–1.15.; 2–2.2.2; 2–3.2.1.1. In addition, 2–3.5 applies, except in 2–3.5.1(b), "29 CFR 1910.147" is substituted for "ANSI Z244.1."

§ 1926.1439 Dedicated pile drivers.

(a) The provisions of subpart CC apply to dedicated pile drivers, except as specified in this section.

(b) Section 1926.1416(d)(3) (Anti two-blocking device) does not apply.

(c) Section 1926.1416(e)(4) (Load weighing and similar devices) applies only to dedicated pile drivers manufactured after November 8, 2011.

(d) In § 1926.1433, only §§ 1926.1433(d) and (e) apply to dedicated pile drivers.

§ 1926.1440 Sideboom cranes.

(a) The provisions of this standard apply, except § 1926.1402 (Ground conditions), § 1926.1415 (Safety devices), § 1926.1416 (Operational aids), and § 1926.1427 (Operator qualification and certification).

(b) Section 1926.1426 (Free fall and controlled load lowering) applies, except § 1926.1426(a)(2)(i). Sideboom cranes in which the boom is designed to free fall (live boom) are permitted only if

manufactured prior to November 8, 2010.

(c) Sideboom cranes mounted on wheel or crawler tractors must meet all of the following requirements of ASME B30.14–2004 (incorporated by reference, *see* § 1926.6):

(1) Section 14–1.1 ("Load Ratings").

(2) Section 14–1.3 ("Side Boom Tractor Travel").

(3) Section 14–1.5 ("Ropes and Reeving Accessories").

(4) Section 14–1.7.1 ("Booms").

(5) Section 14–1.7.2 ("General Requirements—Exhaust Gases").

(6) Section 14–1.7.3 ("General Requirements—Stabilizers (Wheel-Type Side Boom Tractors)").

(7) Section 14–1.7.4 ("General Requirements—Welded Construction").

(8) Section 14–1.7.6 ("General Requirements—Clutch and Brake Protection").

(9) Section 14–2.2.2 ("Testing—Rated Load Test"), except that it applies only to equipment that has been altered or modified.

(10) In section 14–3.1.2 ("Operator Qualifications"), paragraph (a), except the phrase "When required by law."

(11) In section 14–3.1.3 ("Operating Practices"), paragraphs (e), (f)(1)–(f)(4), (f)(6), (f)(7), (h), and (i).

(12) In section 14–3.2.3 ("Moving the Load"), paragraphs (j), (l), and (m).

§ 1926.1441 Equipment with a rated hoisting/lifting capacity of 2,000 pounds or less.

The following paragraphs of this section specify requirements for employers using equipment with a maximum rated hoisting/lifting capacity of 2,000 pounds or less.

(a) The employer using this equipment must comply with the following provisions of this subpart: § 1926.1400 (Scope); § 1926.1401 (Definitions); § 1926.1402 (Ground conditions); § 1926.1403 (Assembly/disassembly—selection of manufacturer or employer procedures); § 1926.1406 (Assembly/disassembly—employer procedures); §§ 1926.1407 through 1926.1411 (Power line safety); § 1926.1412(c) (*Post-assembly*); §§ 1926.1413 through 1926.1414 (Wire rope); § 1926.1418 (Authority to stop operation); §§ 1926.1419 through 1926.1422 (Signals); § 1926.1423 (Fall protection);

§ 1926.1425 (Keeping clear of the load) (except for § 1926.1425(c)(3) (qualified rigger)); § 1926.1426 (Free fall and controlled load lowering); § 1926.1432 (Multiple crane/derrick lifts—supplemental requirements); § 1926.1434 (Equipment modifications); § 1926.1435 (Tower cranes); § 1926.1436 (Derricks); § 1926.1437 (Floating cranes/derricks and land cranes/derricks on barges); § 1926.1438 (Overhead & gantry cranes).

(b) *Assembly/disassembly.* (1) In addition to compliance with §§ 1926.1403 (Assembly/disassembly—selection of manufacturer or employer procedures) and 1926.1406 (Assembly/disassembly—employer procedures), the employer must also comply with § 1926.1441(b)(2)–(3).

(2) *Components and configuration.* The employer must ensure that:

(i) The selection of components, and the configuration of the equipment, that affect the capacity or safe operation of the equipment complies with either the:

(A) Manufacturer instructions, recommendations, limitations, and specifications. When these documents and information are unavailable, a registered professional engineer familiar with the type of equipment involved must approve, in writing, the selection and configuration of components; or

(B) Approved modifications that meet the requirements of § 1926.1434 (Equipment modifications).

(ii) *Post-assembly inspection.* Upon completion of assembly, the equipment is inspected to ensure that it is in compliance with paragraph (b)(2)(i) of this section (*see* § 1926.1412(c) for post-assembly inspection requirements).

(3) *Manufacturer prohibitions.* The employer must comply with applicable manufacturer prohibitions.

(c) *Operation—procedures.* (1) The employer must comply with all manufacturer procedures applicable to the operational functions of the equipment, including its use with attachments.

(2) *Unavailable operation procedures.* The employer must:

(i) When the manufacturer's procedures are unavailable, develop, and ensure compliance with, all procedures necessary for the safe operation of the equipment and attachments.

(ii) Ensure that procedures for the operational controls are developed by a qualified person.

(iii) Ensure that procedures related to the capacity of the equipment are developed and signed by a registered professional engineer familiar with the equipment.

(3) *Accessibility.* The employer must ensure that:

(i) The load chart is available to the operator at the control station;

(ii) Procedures applicable to the operation of the equipment, recommended operating speeds, special hazard warnings, instructions, and operator's manual are readily available for use by the operator.

(iii) When rated capacities are available at the control station only in electronic form and a failure occurs that makes the rated capacities inaccessible, the operator immediately ceases operations or follows safe shut-down procedures until the rated capacities (in electronic or other form) are available.

(d) *Safety devices and operational aids.* (1) The employer must ensure that safety devices and operational aids that are part of the original equipment are maintained in accordance with manufacturer procedures.

(2) *Anti two-blocking.* The employer must ensure that equipment covered by this section manufactured more than one year after November 8, 2010 have either an anti two-block device that meets the requirements of § 1926.1416(d)(3), or is designed so that, in the event of a two-block situation, no damage or load failure will occur (for example, by using a power unit that stalls in response to a two-block situation).

(e) *Operator qualifications.* The employer must train each operator, prior to operating the equipment, on the safe operation of the type of equipment the operator will be using.

(f) *Signal person qualifications.* The employer must train each signal person in the proper use of signals applicable to the use of the equipment.

(g) [Reserved]

(h) *Inspections.* The employer must ensure that equipment is inspected in accordance with manufacturer procedures.

(i) [Reserved]

(j) *Hoisting personnel.* The employer must ensure that equipment covered by this section is not used to hoist personnel.

(k) *Design.* The employer must ensure that the equipment is designed by a qualified engineer.

§ 1926.1442 Severability.

Should a court of competent jurisdiction hold any provision(s) of subpart CC to be invalid, such action shall not affect any other provision of the subpart.

APPENDIX A TO SUBPART CC OF PART 1926—STANDARD HAND SIGNALS

 STOP – With arm extended horizontally to the side, palm down, arm is swung back and forth.	 **EMERGENCY STOP** – With both arms extended horizontally to the side, palms down, arms are swung back and forth.	 **HOIST** – With upper arm extended to the side, forearm and index finger pointing straight up, hand and finger make small circles.
 RAISE BOOM – With arm extended horizontally to the side, thumb points up with other fingers closed.	 **SWING** – With arm extended horizontally, index finger points in direction that boom is to swing.	 **RETRACT TELESCOPING BOOM** – With hands to the front at waist level, thumbs point at each other with other fingers closed.
 RAISE THE BOOM AND LOWER THE LOAD – With arm extended horizontally to the side and thumb pointing up, fingers open and close while load movement is desired.	 **DOG EVERYTHING** – Hands held together at waist level.	 **LOWER** – With arm and index finger pointing down, hand and finger make small circles.
 LOWER BOOM – With arm extended horizontally to the side, thumb points down with other fingers closed.	 **EXTEND TELESCOPING BOOM** – With hands to the front at waist level, thumbs point outward with other fingers closed.	 **TRAVEL/TOWER TRAVEL** – With all fingers pointing up, arm is extended horizontally out and back to make a pushing motion in the direction of travel.

LOWER THE BOOM AND RAISE THE LOAD – With arm extended horizontally to the side and thumb pointing down, fingers open and close while load movement is desired.

MOVE SLOWLY – A hand is placed in front of the hand that is giving the action signal.

USE AUXILIARY HOIST (whipline) – With arm bent at elbow and forearm vertical, elbow is tapped with other hand. Then regular signal is used to indicate desired action.

CRAWLER CRANE TRAVEL, BOTH TRACKS – Rotate fists around each other in front of body; direction of rotation away from body indicates travel forward; rotation towards body indicates travel backward.

USE MAIN HOIST – A hand taps on top of the head. Then regular signal is given to indicate desired action.

CRAWLER CRANE TRAVEL, ONE TRACK – Indicate track to be locked by raising fist on that side. Rotate other fist in front of body in direction that other track is to travel.

TROLLEY TRAVEL – With palm up, fingers closed and thumb pointing in direction of motion, hand is jerked horizontally in direction trolley is to travel.

APPENDIX B TO SUBPART CC OF PART 1926—ASSEMBLY/DISASSEMBLY: SAMPLE PROCEDURES FOR MINIMIZING THE RISK OF UNINTENDED DANGEROUS BOOM MOVEMENT

1. Section 1926.1404(f)(1) provides that when pins (or similar devices) are being removed, employees must not be under the boom, jib, or other components, except where the requirements of § 1926.1404(f)(2) are met. The exception in § 1926.1404(f)(2) applies when the employer demonstrates that site constraints require one or more employees to be under the boom, jib, or other components when pins (or similar devices) are being removed. In such a situation, the A/D director must implement procedures that minimize the risk of unintended dangerous movement and minimize the duration and extent of exposure under the boom.

The following scenario is an example of how the exception applies: A boom cannot be disassembled on the ground because of aboveground piping (as might be found, for example, in an oil refinery) that precludes lowering the boom to the ground. The boom must therefore be disassembled in the air, and the employees who remove the pins must perform that work from an aerial lift whose base is positioned on one side (the near side) of the boom. To gain access to the pins on the far side, the aerial lift basket must move under the boom, since, due to lack of room, the aerial lift cannot be repositioned on the far side. Due to lack of room, the aerial lift cannot be repositioned on the far side, so the aerial basket must move under the boom to gain access to the pins on the far side.

To minimize the risk of unintended dangerous movement while the pins are removed, the A/D director uses an assist crane that is rigged to support the boom section that is being detached, using particular care to ensure that the section end that is near the employee(s) removing the pins is well supported. The duration and extent of exposure is minimized by removing the far side pins first, moving the aerial lift basket as soon as possible to the near side so that the employees are no longer under the boom, and then removing the near side pins.

2. Section 1926.1404(h)(6)(i) provides that, during assembly/disassembly, the center of gravity of the load must be identified if that is necessary for the method used for maintaining stability. Section 1926.1404(h)(6)(ii) states that, where there is insufficient information to accurately identify the center of gravity, measures designed to prevent unintended dangerous movement resulting from an inaccurate identification of the center of gravity must be used.

An example of the application of § 1926.1404(h)(6)(ii) is as follows: The boom is assembled by lowering boom sections sequentially into place using an assist crane. The A/D director's plan is to keep the boom sections stable while they are lowered into place by attaching the assist crane hoist line above the center of gravity of each section. However, in assembling the non-symmetrical top section of the boom, the A/D director is not able to determine where to attach the assist crane hoist line so that it is above the center of gravity. In this situation, before raising the section, all personnel are kept clear of the section and the section is first raised a few inches to determine whether it tips when raised (if it did tip, it would indicate it is not rigged over the center of gravity). If this occurs, the hoist line is repositioned and the procedure repeated (with employees kept clear of the section while it is raised) until the A/D director determines that it is rigged over the center of gravity and can be moved into place without dangerous movement.

APPENDIX C TO SUBPART CC OF PART 1926—OPERATOR CERTIFICATION: WRITTEN EXAMINATION: TECHNICAL KNOWLEDGE CRITERIA

This appendix contains information for employers, accredited testing organizations, auditors and government entities developing criteria for a written examination to test an individual's technical knowledge relating to the operation of cranes.

(a) General technical information.

(1) The functions and limitations of the crane and attachments.

(2) Wire rope:

(i) Background information necessary to understand the inspection and removal from service criteria in § 1926.1413 and § 1926.1414.

(ii) Capacity and when multi-part rope is needed.

(iii) Relationship between line pull and safe working load.

(iv) How to determine the manufacturer's recommended rope for the crane.

(3) Rigging devices and their use, such as:

(i) Slings.

(ii) Spreaders.

(iii) Lifting beams.

(iv) Wire rope fittings, such as clips, shackles and wedge sockets.

(v) Saddles (softeners).

(vi) Clamps (beams).

(4) The technical limitations of protective measures against electrical hazards:

(i) Grounding.

(ii) Proximity warning devices.

(iii) Insulated links.

(iv) Boom cages.

(v) Proximity to electric power lines, radii, and microwave structures.

(5) The effects of load share and load transfer in multi-crane lifts.

(6) Basic crane terms.

(7) The basics of machine power flow systems.

(i) Mechanical.

(ii) Electrical.

(iii) Pneumatic.

(iv) Hydraulic.

(v) Combination.

(8) The significance of the instruments and gauge readings.

(9) The effects of thermal expansion and contraction in hydraulic cylinders.

(10) Background information necessary to understand the requirements of pre-operation and inspection.

(11) How to use the safety devices and operational aids required under § 1926.1415 and § 1926.1416.

(12) The difference between duty-cycle and lifting operations.

(13) How to calculate net capacity for every possible configuration of the equipment using the manufacturer's load chart.

(14) How to use manufacturer-approved attachments and their effect on the equipment.

(15) How to obtain dimensions, weight, and center of gravity of the load.

(16) The effects of dynamic loading from:

(i) Wind.

(ii) Stopping and starting.

(iii) Impact loading.

(iv) Moving with the load.

(17) The effect of side loading.

(18) The principles of backward stability.

(b) Site information.

(1) How to identify the suitability of the supporting ground/surface to support the expected loads of the operation. Elements include:

(i) Weaknesses below the surface (such as voids, tanks, loose fill).

(ii) Weaknesses on the surface (such as retaining walls, slopes, excavations, depressions).

(2) Proper use of mats, blocking/cribbing, outriggers, stabilizers, or crawlers.

(3) Identification of site hazards such as power lines, piping, and traffic.

(4) How to review operation plans with supervisors and other workers (such as the signal person), including how to determine working height, boom length, load radius, and travel clearance.

(5) How to determine if there is adequate room for extension of crawlers or outriggers/stabilizers and counterweights.

(c) Operations.

(1) How to pick, carry, swing and place the load smoothly and safely on rubber tires and on outriggers/stabilizers or crawlers (where applicable).

(2) How to communicate at the site with supervisors, the crew and the signal person.

(3) Proper procedures and methods of reeving wire ropes and methods of reeving multiple-part lines and selecting the proper load block and/or ball.

(4) How to react to changes in conditions that affect the safe operation of the equipment.

(5) How to shut down and secure the equipment properly when leaving it unattended.

(6) Know how to apply the manufacturer's specifications for operating in various weather conditions, and understand how environmental conditions affect the safe operation of the equipment.

(7) How to properly level the equipment.

(8) How to verify the weight of the load and rigging prior to initiating the lift.

(9) How to determine where the load is to be picked up and placed and how to verify the radii.

(10) Know basic rigging procedures.

(11) How to carry out the shift inspection required in this subpart.

(12) Know that the following operations require specific procedures and skill levels:

(i) Multi-crane lifts.

(ii) Hoisting personnel.

(iii) Clamshell/dragline operations.

(iv) Pile driving and extracting.

(v) Concrete operations, including poured-in-place and tilt-up.

(vi) Demolition operations.

(vii) Operations on water.

(viii) Magnet operations.

(ix) Multi-drum operations.

(13) Know the proper procedures for operating safely under the following conditions:

(i) Traveling with suspended loads.

(ii) Approaching a two-block condition.

(iii) Operating near power lines.

(iv) Hoisting personnel.

(v) Using other than full outrigger/crawler or stabilizer extensions.

(vi) Lifting loads from beneath the surface of the water.

(vii) Using various approved counterweight configurations.

(viii) Handling loads out of the operator's vision ("operating in the blind").

(ix) Using electronic communication systems for signal communication.

(14) Know the proper procedures for load control and the use of hand-held tag lines.

(15) Know the emergency response procedure for:

(i) Fires.

(ii) Power line contact.

(iii) Loss of stability.

(iv) Control malfunction.

(v) Two-blocking.

(vi) Overload.

(vii) Carrier or travel malfunction.

(16) Know how to properly use outriggers and stabilizers in accordance with manufacturer specifications.

(d) Use of load charts.

(1) Know the terminology necessary to use load charts.

(2) Know how to ensure that the load chart is the appropriate chart for the equipment in its particular configuration and application.

(3) Know how to use load charts. This includes knowing:

(i) The operational limitations of load charts and footnotes.

(ii) How to relate the chart to the configuration of the crane, crawlers, or outriggers/stabilizers extended or retracted, jib erected or offset, and various counterweight configurations.

(iii) The difference between structural capacity and capacity limited by stability.

(iv) What is included in capacity ratings.

(v) The range diagram and its relationship to the load chart.

(vi) The work area chart and its relationship to the load chart.

(vii) Where to find and how to use the "parts-of-line" information.

(4) Know how to use the load chart together with the load indicators and/or load moment devices.

APPENDIX A TO PART 1926—DESIGNATIONS FOR GENERAL INDUSTRY STANDARDS INCORPORATED INTO BODY OF CONSTRUCTION STANDARDS

New Designations for General Industry Standards Incorporated Into Body of Construction Standards

1926 DESIGNATIONS FOR APPLICABLE 1910 STANDARDS

New § no. and/or para.	Source § no. and/or para.
1926.20 (c)	1910.5 (a)
[Do.] (d)	[Do.] (c)
[Do.] (e)	[Do.] (d)
1926.32(g)	1910.12(b)
1926.33	1910.20
1926.34 (a)	1910.36(b)(4)
[Do.] (b)	1910.37 (q)(1)
[Do.] (c)	[Do.] (k)(2)
1926.35	1910.38(a)
1926.50(g)	1910.151(c)
1926.51(a)(6)	1910.141(a)(2)(v)
[Do.] (d)(2)	[Do.] (h)
[Do.] (f) (2)–(4)	[Do.] (d) (1)–(3)
[Do.] (g)	[Do.] (g)(2)
[Do.] (h)	[Do.] (a)(5)
[Do.] (i)	[Do.] (e)
1926.53 (c)–(r)	1910.96
1926.57 (f)–(i)	1910.94
1926.64	1910.119
1926.65	1910.120
1926.66 (a)	1910.107 (a)
[Do.] (b)	[Do.] (b) (1)–(10)
[Do.] (c)–(d)	[Do.] (c)–(d)
[Do.] (e)–(g)	[Do.] (h)–(j)
1926.95	1910.132
1926.96	1910.136
1926.97 (a)–(e)	1910.156(e)
[Do.] (f)–(h)	[Do.] Subpt. L App. E
1926.98	1910.156(f)
1926.102(a) (6)	1910.133(a) (2)
[Do.] (7)	[Do.] (4)
[Do.] (8)	[Do.] (5)
1926.103 (d)	1910.134 (a)
[Do.] (e)	[Do.] (b)
[Do.] (f)–(i)	[Do.] (d)–(g)
1926.150(c)(1) (xi)	1910.157 (g)(1)
[Do.] (xii)	[Do.] (g)(2)
[Do.] (xiii)	[Do.] (c)(4)
[Do.] (xiv)	[Do.] (e)(3)
1926.152 (b)(5)	1910.107(e)(2)
[Do.] (h)	1910.106(j)
[Do.] (i)	[Do.] (b)
[Do.] (j)	[Do.] (c)
[Do.] (k) (1)–(3)	[Do.] (g)(4)
[Do.] (k)(4)	[Do.] (a)(22)
1926.153(a) (3)	1910.110(a)(4)
[Do.] (m) (1)	[Do.] (d)(1)
[Do.] (2)	[Do.] (d)(2)
[Do.] (3)	[Do.] (d)(7)(vii)
[Do.] (4)	[Do.] (d)(7)(viii)
[Do.] (n)	[Do.] (b)(5)(iii)

1926 DESIGNATIONS FOR APPLICABLE 1910 STANDARDS—Continued

New § no. and/or para.	Source § no. and/or para.
[Do.] (o)	[Do.] (d)(10)
1926.156	1910.160
1926.157	1910.162
1926.158	1910.164
1926.159	1910.165
1926.200(c)(3)	1910.145(d)(4)
1926.250(c)	1910.176(c)
[Do.] (d) (1)–(4)	1910.30(a) (1), (2), (4) and (5)
1926.251(a)(5)	1910.184(a)
[Do.] (a)(6)	[Do.] (d)
[Do.] (b)(6)(i)–(ii)	[Do.] (e)(3)(i)–(ii)
[Do.] (c)(6)–(7)	[Do.] (c) (2)–(3)
[Do.] (c)(8)	[Do.] (c)(5)
[Do.] (c)(9)	[Do.] (c)(7)
[Do.] (c)(10)–(12)	[Do.] (c)(10)–(12)
[Do.] (c)(13)–(15)	[Do.](f) (2)–(4)
[Do.] (d)(3)–(6)	[Do.] (h) (2)–(5)
[Do.] (e)(3)–(5)	[Do.] (i) (2)–(4)
[Do.] (e)(6)–(7)	[Do.] (i) (6)–(7)
[Do.] (e)(8)	[Do.] (i)(9)
1926.300(b) (3)	1910.212(a)(1)
[Do.] (4)	[Do.] (a)(3)
[Do.] (5)	[Do.] (a)(5)
[Do.] (6)	[Do.] (b)
[Do.] (7)	1910.215(b)(9)
[Do.] (8) and (9)	[Do.] (b) (3) and (4)
1926.302(b)(10)	1910.244(b)
1926.303(b)(2)	1910.215(a) (2)
[Do.] (e)	[Do.] (4)
1926.304 (g)	1910.213(h)(1)
[Do.] (h)	[Do.] (d)(1)
[Do.] (i)	[Do.] (c)(1)
1926.305(d)(1)	1910.244(a)(2) (iii)–(viii)
1926.306	1910.169
1926.307	1910.219
1926.350(a) (10)	1910.253(b) (4)(iii)
[Do.] (11)	[Do.] (2)(ii)
[Do.] (12)	1910.101(b)
1926.353(b)(3)	1910.252(b)(4)(iv)
1926.416 (a)(4)	1910.333(c)(2)
[Do.] (f) (1)	[Do.] (c)(10)
[Do.] (2)	1910.334(a)(1)
[Do.] (3)	[Do.] (a)(2)(iii)
[Do.] (4)	[Do.] (a)(5)
[Do.] (5)–(6)	[Do.] (b) (1)–(2)
[Do.] (7)–(9)	[Do.] (c) (1)–(3)
[Do.] (10)	[Do.] (d)
1926.417(d)	1910.333(b)(2)
1926.451(a) (22)	1910.28(a) (15)
[Do.] (23)	[Do.] (18)
[Do.] (24)	[Do.] (20)
1926.453 (a)	1910.29(a)
[Do.] (b)	[Do.] (c)
1926.600(a)(7)	1910.176(f)
1926.602(c)(1) (vii)	1910.178(m) (3)
[Do.] (viii)	[Do.] (12)
1926.900 (s)	1910.109 (g)(2)(ii)
[Do.] (t)	[Do.] (h)(3)(ii)
1926.905(u)	[Do.] (e)(3)(iii)
1926.914(aa)	[Do.] (a)(12)

1926 DESIGNATIONS FOR APPLICABLE 1910 STANDARDS—Continued

New § no. and/or para.	Source § no. and/or para.
1926.1050(b)	1910.21(g)(9)
1926.1071	1910.401
1926.1072	1910.402
1926.1076	1910.410
1926.1080	1910.420
1926.1081	1910.421
1926.1082	1910.422
1926.1083	1910.423
1926.1084	1910.424
1926.1085	1910.425
1926.1086	1910.426
1926.1087	1910.427
1926.1090	1910.430
1926.1091	1910.440
1926.1092	1910.441
1926.1102	1910.1002
1926.1103	1910.1003
1926.1104	1910.1004
1926.1105	1910.1005
1926.1106	1910.1006

1926 DESIGNATIONS FOR APPLICABLE 1910 STANDARDS—Continued

New § no. and/or para.	Source § no. and/or para.
1926.1107	1910.1007
1926.1108	1910.1008
1926.1109	1910.1009
1926.1110	1910.1010
1926.1111	1910.1011
1926.1112	1910.1012
1926.1113	1910.1013
1926.1114	1910.1014
1926.1115	1910.1015
1926.1116	1910.1016
1926.1117	1910.1017
1926.1118	1910.1018
1926.1128	1910.1028
1926.1129	1910.1029
1926.1144	1910.1044
1926.1145	1910.1045
1926.1147	1910.1047
1926.1148	1910.1048

[58 FR 35305, June 30, 1993, as amended at 61 FR 9255, Mar. 7, 1996; 75 FR 48135, Aug. 9, 2010]

FINDING AIDS

A list of CFR titles, subtitles, chapters, subchapters and parts and an alphabetical list of agencies publishing in the CFR are included in the CFR Index and Finding Aids volume to the Code of Federal Regulations which is published separately and revised annually.

Table of CFR Titles and Chapters
(Revised as of July 1, 2015)

Title 1—General Provisions

Title 2—Grants and Agreements

Title 2—Grants and Agreements—Continued

Title 3—The President

Title 4—Accounts

Title 5—Administrative Personnel

Title 5—Administrative Personnel—Continued

Title 5—Administrative Personnel—Continued

Title 6—Domestic Security

Title 7—Agriculture

Title 7—Agriculture—Continued

Title 8—Aliens and Nationality

Title 9—Animals and Animal Products

Title 10—Energy

Title 11—Federal Elections

Title 12—Banks and Banking

Title 24—Housing and Urban Development

Title 25—Indians

766

Title 25—Indians—Continued

Title 26—Internal Revenue

Title 27—Alcohol, Tobacco Products and Firearms

Title 28—Judicial Administration

Title 29—Labor

Title 34—Education—Continued

Title 35 [Reserved]

Title 36—Parks, Forests, and Public Property

Title 37—Patents, Trademarks, and Copyrights

Title 38—Pensions, Bonuses, and Veterans' Relief

Title 39—Postal Service

Title 40—Protection of Environment

Title 41—Public Contracts and Property Management

Title 41—Public Contracts and Property Management—Continued

Chap.

302   Relocation Allowances (Parts 302-1—302-99)

303   Payment of Expenses Connected with the Death of Certain Employees (Part 303-1—303-99)

304   Payment of Travel Expenses from a Non-Federal Source (Parts 304-1—304-99)

Title 42—Public Health

I   Public Health Service, Department of Health and Human Services (Parts 1—199)

IV   Centers for Medicare & Medicaid Services, Department of Health and Human Services (Parts 400—599)

V   Office of Inspector General-Health Care, Department of Health and Human Services (Parts 1000—1999)

Title 43—Public Lands: Interior

SUBTITLE A—OFFICE OF THE SECRETARY OF THE INTERIOR (PARTS 1—199)

SUBTITLE B—REGULATIONS RELATING TO PUBLIC LANDS

I   Bureau of Reclamation, Department of the Interior (Parts 400—999)

II   Bureau of Land Management, Department of the Interior (Parts 1000—9999)

III   Utah Reclamation Mitigation and Conservation Commission (Parts 10000—10099)

Title 44—Emergency Management and Assistance

I   Federal Emergency Management Agency, Department of Homeland Security (Parts 0—399)

IV   Department of Commerce and Department of Transportation (Parts 400—499)

Title 45—Public Welfare

SUBTITLE A—DEPARTMENT OF HEALTH AND HUMAN SERVICES (PARTS 1—199)

SUBTITLE B—REGULATIONS RELATING TO PUBLIC WELFARE

II   Office of Family Assistance (Assistance Programs), Administration for Children and Families, Department of Health and Human Services (Parts 200—299)

III   Office of Child Support Enforcement (Child Support Enforcement Program), Administration for Children and Families, Department of Health and Human Services (Parts 300—399)

IV   Office of Refugee Resettlement, Administration for Children and Families, Department of Health and Human Services (Parts 400—499)

V   Foreign Claims Settlement Commission of the United States, Department of Justice (Parts 500—599)

772

773

Title 49—Transportation

Title 50—Wildlife and Fisheries

CFR Index and Finding Aids

Alphabetical List of Agencies Appearing in the CFR

(Revised as of July 1, 2015)

Agency	CFR Title, Subtitle or Chapter
Administrative Committee of the Federal Register	1, I
Administrative Conference of the United States	1, III
Advisory Council on Historic Preservation	36, VIII
Advocacy and Outreach, Office of	7, XXV
Afghanistan Reconstruction, Special Inspector General for	5, LXXXIII
African Development Foundation	22, XV
Federal Acquisition Regulation	48, 57
Agency for International Development	2, VII; 22, II
Federal Acquisition Regulation	48, 7
Agricultural Marketing Service	7, I, IX, X, XI
Agricultural Research Service	7, V
Agriculture Department	2, IV; 5, LXXIII
Advocacy and Outreach, Office of	7, XXV
Agricultural Marketing Service	7, I, IX, X, XI
Agricultural Research Service	7, V
Animal and Plant Health Inspection Service	7, III; 9, I
Chief Financial Officer, Office of	7, XXX
Commodity Credit Corporation	7, XIV
Economic Research Service	7, XXXVII
Energy Policy and New Uses, Office of	2, IX; 7, XXIX
Environmental Quality, Office of	7, XXXI
Farm Service Agency	7, VII, XVIII
Federal Acquisition Regulation	48, 4
Federal Crop Insurance Corporation	7, IV
Food and Nutrition Service	7, II
Food Safety and Inspection Service	9, III
Foreign Agricultural Service	7, XV
Forest Service	36, II
Grain Inspection, Packers and Stockyards Administration	7, VIII; 9, II
Information Resources Management, Office of	7, XXVII
Inspector General, Office of	7, XXVI
National Agricultural Library	7, XLI
National Agricultural Statistics Service	7, XXXVI
National Institute of Food and Agriculture	7, XXXIV
Natural Resources Conservation Service	7, VI
Operations, Office of	7, XXVIII
Procurement and Property Management, Office of	7, XXXII
Rural Business-Cooperative Service	7, XVIII, XLII, L
Rural Development Administration	7, XLII
Rural Housing Service	7, XVIII, XXXV, L
Rural Telephone Bank	7, XVI
Rural Utilities Service	7, XVII, XVIII, XLII, L
Secretary of Agriculture, Office of	7, Subtitle A
Transportation, Office of	7, XXXIII
World Agricultural Outlook Board	7, XXXVIII
Air Force Department	32, VII
Federal Acquisition Regulation Supplement	48, 53
Air Transportation Stabilization Board	14, VI
Alcohol and Tobacco Tax and Trade Bureau	27, I
Alcohol, Tobacco, Firearms, and Explosives, Bureau of	27, II
AMTRAK	49, VII
American Battle Monuments Commission	36, IV
American Indians, Office of the Special Trustee	25, VII

777

List of CFR Sections Affected

All changes in this volume of the Code of Federal Regulations (CFR) that were made by documents published in the FEDERAL REGISTER since January 1, 2010 are enumerated in the following list. Entries indicate the nature of the changes effected. Page numbers refer to FEDERAL REGISTER pages. The user should consult the entries for chapters, parts and subparts as well as sections for revisions.

For changes to this volume of the CFR prior to this listing, consult the annual edition of the monthly List of CFR Sections Affected (LSA). The LSA is available at *www.fdsys.gov.* For changes to this volume of the CFR prior to 2001, see the "List of CFR Sections Affected, 1949–1963, 1964–1972, 1973–1985, and 1986–2000" published in 11 separate volumes. The "List of CFR Sections Affected 1986–2000" is available at *www.fdsys.gov.*

2015

29 CFR—Continued
80 FR
Page

○

CPSIA information can be obtained
at www.ICGtesting.com
Printed in the USA
LVOW03s1119240416
485087LV00008B/102/P